14.95
W9-ABO-956
LEWIS EGERTON SMOOT MEM'L. LIB.
KING GEORGE, VA. 22485

# SPURGEON ON THE PSALMS

LEWIS EGERTON SMOOT MEM'L. LIB.
KING GEORGE, VA. 22485

# PSALMS

**by**

**Charles Haddon Spurgeon**

One volume edition of THE TREASURY OF DAVID, Spurgeon's great work of a lifetime, condensed by David Otis Fuller, D.D.

LEWIS EGERTON SMOOT MEM'L. LIB
KING GEORGE, VA. 22485

KREGEL PUBLICATIONS
Grand Rapids, MI 49501

PSALMS, formerly published under the title *The Treasury of David* in two volumes, copyright © 1968 by David Otis Fuller, D.D., reprinted by Kregel Publications, a division of Kregel, Inc. Complete and unabridged in one volume by special arrangement with the copyright owner. All rights reserved.

Library of Congress Catalog Card Number 76-12085
ISBN 0-8254-3712-1

First Kregel Publications edition ..................1976
Second Printing ...................................1978
Third Printing.....................................1980

Printed in the United States of America

DEDICATED TO

*Those fearless Christian scholars, formerly of Princeton Seminary,*

J. GRESHAM MACHEN, ROBERT DICK WILSON,
AND OTHERS,

*who exemplified in their daily lives the spirit of true Christianity, who taught us to appreciate and understand more fully "the Faith which was once delivered unto the saints"; and who gave us added courage and inspiration to "fight the good fight of faith".*

# PREFACE

Charles Haddon Spurgeon has long been recognized as "the Prince of Preachers." Not only does his phenomenal work in London testify to this, which still flourishes long years after his death, but the universal demand for his sermons to this day is a silent witness to the amazing grace of God, which was not bestowed upon him in vain.

Few people realize the tremendous amount of labor and effort that Mr. Spurgeon and his collaborators put upon this great work, *The Treasury of David.* Its preparation covered a period of twenty years, and the final result was a seven-volume commentary (three thousand pages, comprising nearly two million words) on all the verses—and more often the phrases and words themselves—of the one hundred and fifty Psalms that comprise the Psalter of the Holy Scriptures.

But let no one mistake this as being a mere commentary on the Psalms. Such a title would not begin to do it justice. Truly it may be termed a theological anthology of the whole realm of Christian truth. All the great doctrines of God's Word—the resurrection, the atonement, the second coming, etc., are dwelt upon at length by the master minds of nearly every age since the first coming of Jesus Christ, the eternal Son of God, by men whose giant intellects were dedicated to the one ruling passion of their lives, that of extolling the glory and majesty of a sovereign God.

The reader will find within these pages some of the greatest and grandest words of comfort and inspiration that have ever been penned. For sheer power of expression and literary style, nothing can ever surpass them. Over four thousand separate quotations (over seventeen hundred from Mr. Spurgeon alone) have been condensed into these two volumes, taken from the writings of seven hundred and twenty different writers whose names to this day shine brighter than ever, their luster and brilliance undimmed by the passing of time. The Early Church Fathers, the reformers, the Puritan divines, all have given us "treasure in earthen vessels" that serves to increase our faith and renew our courage in troublous times.

Some of these great expositors of divine truth whose writings scintillate within these volumes are such men as Augustine, Chrysostom, Athanasius, Calvin, Luther, Bunyan, Matthew Henry, and of course Mr. Spurgeon himself. Even Plato, Socrates, the satirist Juvenal, and Shakespeare have been used to good advantage. Here indeed is a vast Thesaurus of golden truth that endures and will endure though skepticism is rife and infidelity rages.

The so-called imprecatory Psalms have been a source of much perplexity to many devout Christians, but the reader will find complete and satisfactory explanations for these difficult passages, hard to be understood. There is in these condensed volumes a wealth of suggestive material for sermons, sermon illustrations, and outlines. Every page is a tonic and stimulant for spiritual growth.

We can truthfully state that we have never set ourselves to a more enjoyable task. Although it has required hours on end in selecting the best from three thousand pages of fine print and solid reading matter, we have felt amply repaid for all the "digging" we have done in this mine of priceless gems.

Are you looking for light in days of darkness? You will find it here. Are you looking for strength in times of weakness? Faith in place of doubt? Courage for cowardice? Hope for despair? Then pick your favorite Psalm, sit down for an hour or two and drink deeply from the well of eternal truth always accessible to the thirsty soul.

DAVID OTIS FULLER.

Grand Rapids, Mich.

# CONDENSED PREFACE

The delightful study of the Psalms has yielded me boundless profit and ever-growing pleasure; common gratitude constrains me to communicate to others a portion of the benefit, with the prayer that it may induce them to search further for themselves. That I have nothing better of my own to offer upon this peerless book is to me matter of deepest regret; that I have anything whatever to present is subject for devout gratitude to the Lord of grace. I have done my best, but, conscious of many defects, I heartily wish I could have done far better.

One thing the reader will please clearly understand, and I beg him to bear it in mind: *I am far from endorsing all I have quoted.* I am neither responsible for the scholarship or orthodoxy of the writers. The names are given that each author may bear his own burden.

Readers little know how great labor the finding of but one pertinent extract may involve; labor certainly I have not spared. My earnest prayer is that some measure of good may come of it to my brethren in the ministry and to the church at large.

It may be added, that although the comments were the work of my health, the rest of the volume is the product of my sickness. When protracted illness and weakness laid me aside from daily preaching, I resorted to my pen as an available means of doing good. I would have preached had I been able, but as my Master denied me the privilege of thus serving Him, I gladly availed myself of the other method of bearing testimony for His Name. Oh, that He may give me fruit in this field also, and His shall be all the praise.

C. H. S.

Clapham, December, 1869.

# INTRODUCTION

I am sure that many people will have cause for gratitude in the work that Dr. David Otis Fuller, pastor of the *Baptist Temple, Grand Rapids, Michigan,* has done in the condensation of Charles Haddon Spurgeon's "TREASURY OF DAVID." Reading this condensation one has the joy of a diver who "standing naked for the plunge, rejoices when he comes up with hands filled with pearls."

Robert Browning wrote:

*"All the breath and the bloom of the year in*
*the bag of one bee;*
*All the wonder and wealth of the mine in the*
*heart of one gem;*
*In the core of one pearl all the shade and the*
*shine of the sea;*
*Breath and bloom, shade and shine—wonder, wealth,*
*and—how far above them—*
*Truth that's brighter than gem,*
*Truth that's purer than pearl,—*
*Brightest truth, purest trust in the universe—*
*all were for me*
*In the kiss of one girl!"*

But how much more than that, and how far beyond all that, is the wealth of the spiritual riches of God's truth and the wonder of God's gospel found in these condensations of this mighty preacher's thought—thought and truth upon which Dr. Fuller would have us pitch our mental tents and around which he asks us to gather the meditations of our hearts.

As with the microscope we see worlds in water drops, as with the spectograph we learn the constituent elements of remotest astral bodies, as with the telescope we view landscapes millions of miles away, so, in this valued work, the result of much labor on the part of the author, we discover worlds of redemptive revelation—continents of truth compressed into a corner of phraseology, firmaments of wisdom contracted to the compass of a text; so in this condensation of Spurgeon's great work do we find fortunes in a single diamond of language, infinities flung into mere phrases, oceans of truth in teacups of words, volumes in single lines, oratorios in single statements, many organs in one diapason, oceans lifting high tides within the shores.

It is my conviction that all who get this condensation of Spurgeon's great work by Dr. Fuller will feel that they have made a wise investment and will be grateful to the pastor of the *Baptist Temple* for the many hours of work he has done in bringing this to the public. Surely we will be grateful recipients of his vision and high purpose resulting in a service which brings us the assembled sweetness of many fields into one garden of rare and radiant blossoms and fruitage.

Roblrt G. Lee.

*Bellevue Baptist Church,*
*Memphis, Tennessee*

# FOREWORD

Over a quarter of a century ago a friend made me a marriage present of the seven volumes comprising C. H. Spurgeon's "The Treasury of David," and through the years I have counted this set of incomparable expositions on *The Psalms* as the most valuable books in my library.

To my mind this standard work, which Spurgeon considered the masterpiece of his literary compositions, contains more unique sermonic hints than all the rest of the books on *The Psalms* put together. When it is remembered that "the Prince of Preachers," as Spurgeon was known, whose Anglo-Saxon language should have the closest study of every preacher and aspirant for the ministry, spent over twenty years of research and original writing on this monumental treatise, the acclamations of the finest scholars and teachers concerning this priceless treasure are easily understood.

One has felt, however, that some form of condensation of Spurgeon's "treasure-trove" would be of practical value to busy pastors. Here are many, who, with limited means, are not able to afford the seven volumes, but who can now possess all the best of the two million words Spurgeon wrote. When Dr. Fuller discussed with me the possibility of gathering out all the jewels of "The Treasury of David," and placing them in a two-volume commentary, I assured him that his endeavors would meet with instant success.

That Dr. Fuller has admirably succeeded in his great task is evident from the two beautiful volumes before you. The selection, it will be found, in no way detracts from Spurgeon's original work. In fact, Dr. Fuller's labors will result in a widespread desire for Spurgeon's other productions. Spurgeonic in his theology and preaching, Dr. Fuller testifies to the influence Mr. Spurgeon has had over his own life— a fact that gave him much joy in this long and arduous task of his I am happy to commend.

HERBERT LOCKYER.

Everything in the above mentioned 2-volume edition is now contained in this Kregel Publications one volume edition.

## CONTENTS

CONTENTS

# PSALM 1

This Psalm may be regarded as THE PREFACE PSALM, having in it a notification of the contents of the entire Book. It is the Psalmist's desire to teach us the way to blessedness and to warn us of the sure destruction of sinners. This, then, is the matter of the First Psalm, which may be looked upon, in some respects, as the text upon which the whole of the Psalms make up a divine sermon. C. H. S.

The Psalmist saith more to the point about true happiness in this short Psalm than any one of the philosophers, or all of them put together; they did but beat the bush; God hath here put the bird into our hand. JOHN TRAPP

Vs. 1. *Blessed*—See how this Book of Psalms opens with a benediction, even as did the famous Sermon of our Lord upon the Mount! The word translated "blessed" is a very expressive one. The original word is plural, and it is a controverted matter whether it is an adjective or a substantive. Hence we may learn the multiplicity of the blessings which shall rest upon the man whom God hath justified, and the perfection and greatness of the blessedness he shall enjoy. C. H. S.

*Blessed is the man that walketh not in the counsel of the ungodly.* He takes wiser counsel, and walks in the commandments of the Lord, his God. To him the ways of piety are paths of peace and pleasantness. His footsteps are ordered by the Word of God and not by the cunning and wicked devices of carnal man. It is a rich sign of inward grace when the outward walk is changed and when ungodliness is put far from our actions. C. H. S.

The word *haish* is emphatic—*that man;* that one among a thousand who lives for the accomplishment of the end for which God created him. ADAM CLARKE

*Nor standeth in the way of sinners.* The sinner has a particular way of trangressing; one is a drunkard, another dishonest, another unclean. Few are given to every species of vice. There are many covetous men who abhor drunkenness, many drunkards who abhor covetousness; and so of others. Each has his easily besetting sin; therefore, says the prophet, *Let the wicked forsake his way.* Now, blessed is he who stands not in such a man's way. ADAM CLARKE

*Nor sitteth in the seat of the scornful.* Let others make a mock of sin, of eternity, of hell, and heaven, and of the eternal God; this man has learned better philosophy than that of the infidel and has too much sense of God's presence to endure to hear His Name blasphemed.

When men are living in sin, they go from bad to worse. At first they merely *walk* in the counsel of the careless and ungodly, who forget God—the evil is rather practical than habitual—but after that, they become habituated to evil, and they *stand* in the way of open sinners who wilfully violate God's commandments; and if left alone, they go one step farther and become themselves pestilent teachers and tempters of others, and thus they *sit in the seat of the scornful.* They have taken their degree in vice, and as true Doctors of Damnation they are installed, and are looked up to by others as Masters in Belial. But the blessed man, the man to whom all the blessings of God belong, can hold no communion with such characters as these. He keeps himself pure from these lepers; he puts away evil things from him as garments spotted by the flesh; he comes out from among the wicked, and goes without the camp, bearing the reproach of Christ. Oh, for grace to be thus separate from sinners. C. H. S.

Vs. 2. *But his delight is in the law of the Lord.* "The law of the Lord" is the daily bread of the true believer. And yet, in David's day, how small was the volume of inspiration, for they scarcely had anything save the first five books of Moses! How much more, then, should we prize the whole written Word which it is our privilege to have in all our houses! But, alas, what ill-treatment is given to this angel from heaven! We are not all Berean searchers of the Scriptures. How few among us can lay claim to the benediction of the text! C. H. S.

The "will" which is here signified, is that delight of heart, and that certain pleasure, in the law, which does not look at what the law promises, nor at what it threatens, but at this only: that "the law is holy, and just, and good." Hence it is not only a love of the law, but that loving delight in the law which no prosperity, nor adversity, nor the world, nor the prince of it, can either take away or destroy; for it victoriously bursts its way through poverty, evil report, the cross, death, and hell, and in the midst of adversities, shines the brightest. MARTIN LUTHER.

*In His law doth he meditate day and night.* In the plainest text there is a world of holiness and spirituality; and if we in prayer and dependence upon God did sit down and study it, we should behold much more than appears to us. It may be, at once reading or looking, we see little or nothing; as Elijah's servant went once, and saw nothing; therefore he was commanded to look seven times. "What now?" says the prophet, "I see a cloud rising, like a man's hand"; and, by-and-by, the whole surface of the heavens was covered with clouds. So you may look lightly upon a Scripture and see nothing; meditate upon it often; there you shall see a light, like the light of the sun. JOS. CARYL

"The mouth of the righteous shall meditate wisdom." Hence, Augustine has, in his translation, "chatter"; and a beautiful metaphor it is—as chattering is the employment of birds, so a continual conversing in the law of the Lord (for talking is peculiar to man) ought to be the employment of man. MARTIN LUTHER

The godly man will read the Word by *day*, that man, seeing his good works may glorify his Father Who is in heaven; he will do it in the *night* that he may not be seen of men: by *day*, to show that he is not one of those who dread the light; by *night*, to show that he is one who can shine in the shade: by *day*, for that is the time for working—work whilst it is day; by *night*, lest his Master should come as a thief, and find him idle. SIR RICHARD BAKER

I have no rest, but in a nook with *the book*. THOS. à KEMPIS

Vs. 3. *And he shall be like a tree planted;* not a wild tree, but "a tree planted," chosen, considered as property, cultivated, and secured from the last terrible uprooting, for "every plant, which my heavenly Father hath not planted, shall be rooted up."

*By the rivers of water.* So that even if one river should fail, he hath another The rivers of pardon and the rivers of grace, the rivers of the promise and the rivers of communion with Christ, are never-failing sources of supply.

*That bringeth forth his fruit in his season.* The man who delights in God's Word, being taught by it, bringeth forth patience in the time of suffering, faith in the day of trial, and holy joy in the hour of prosperity. Fruitfulness is an essential quality of a gracious man, and that fruitfulness should be seasonable. C. H. S.

The ungodly have their stated days, stated times, certain works, and certain places; to which they stick so closely, that if their neighbors were perishing with hunger, they could not be torn from them. But the blessed man, being free at all times, in all places, for every work, and to every person, will serve you whenever an opportunity is offered him.

*His leaf also shall not wither.* He describes the fruit before he does the leaf, and thus, let him who professes the word of doctrine, first put forth the fruits of life, if he would not have his fruit to wither, for Christ cursed the fig-tree which bore no fruit. MARTIN LUTHER

*And whatsoever he doeth shall prosper.* As there is a curse wrapped up in the wicked man's mercies, so there is a blessing concealed in the righteous man's crosses, losses, and sorrows. The trials of the saint are a divine husbandry, by which he grows and brings forth abundant fruit. C. H. S.

Outward prosperity, if it follow close walking with God, is very sweet; as the cipher, when it follows a figure, adds to the number, though it be nothing in itself. JOHN TRAPP

Vs. 4. *The ungodly are not so.* Mark the use of the term "ungodly," for, as we have seen in the opening of the Psalm, these are the beginners in evil and are the least offensive of sinners. Oh, if such is the sad state of those who quietly continue in their morality, and neglect their God, what must be the condition of open sinners and shameless infidels? C. H. S.

*But are like the chaff.* Here is their character—intrinsically worthless, dead, unserviceable, without substance, and easily carried away. C. H. S.

*Which the wind driveth away.* Here, also, mark their doom—death shall hurry them with its terrible blast into the fire in which they shall be utterly consumed. C. H. S.

Here, by the way, we may let the wicked know they have a thanks to give they little think of; that they may thank the godly for all the good days they live upon the earth, seeing it is for their sakes and not for their own that they enjoy them. For as the chaff while it is united and keeps close to the wheat, enjoys some privileges for the wheat's sake, and is laid up carefully in the barn; but as soon as it is divided, and parted from the wheat, it is cast out and scattered by the wind; so the wicked, whilst the godly are in company and live amongst them, partake for their sake of some blessedness promised to the godly; but if the godly forsake them or be taken from them, then either a deluge of water comes suddenly upon them, as it did upon the old world when Noah left it; or a deluge of fire, as it did upon Sodom, when Lot left it, and went out of the city. SIR RICHARD BAKER

Vs. 5. *Nor sinners in the congregation of the righteous.* Every church hath one devil in it. The tares grow in the same furrows as the wheat. There is no floor which is as yet purged from chaff. Sinners mix with saints, as dross mingles with gold. God's precious diamonds still lie in the same field with pebbles.

Sinners cannot live in heaven. They would be out of their element. Sooner could a fish live upon a tree than the wicked in Paradise. C. H. S.

Vs. 6. *For the Lord knoweth the way of the righteous*, or, as the Hebrew hath it yet more fully, "The Lord is *knowing* the way of the righteous." He is constantly looking on their way, and though it may be often in mist and darkness, yet the Lord knoweth it.

*But the way of the ungodly shall perish.* Not only shall they perish themselves, but their way shall perish, too. The righteous carves his name upon the rock, but the wicked writes his remembrance in the sand. C. H. S.

## PSALM 2

We shall not greatly err in our summary of this sublime Psalm if we call it "The Psalm of Messiah The Prince," for it sets forth, as in a wondrous vision, the tumult of the people against the Lord's anointed, the determinate purpose of God to exalt His own Son, and the ultimate reign of that Son over all His enemies. Let us read it with the eye of faith, beholding, as in a glass, the final triumph of our Lord Jesus Christ over all His enemies.

We have, in the first three verses, a description of the hatred of human nature against the Christ of God. No better comment is needed upon it than the apostolic song in Acts 4:27-28: "For of a truth against thy holy child Jesus, Whom Thou hast anointed, both Herod, and Pontius Pilate, with the Gentiles, and the people of Israel, were gathered together, for to do whatsoever Thy hand and Thy counsel determined before to be done." C. H. S.

Vs. 1. *Why do the heathen rage, and the people imagine a vain thing?* The Psalm begins abruptly with an angry interrogation; and well it may: it is surely but little to be wondered at that the sight of creatures in arms against their God should amaze the Psalmist's mind. C. H. S.

*A vain thing.* In Spain, two monumental pillars were raised on which were written:—I. "Diocletian Jovian Maximian Herculeus Cæsares Augusti, for having extended the Roman Empire in the east and the west, and for having extinguished the name of Christians, who brought the Republic to ruin." II. "Diocletian Jovian Maximian Herculeus Cæsares Augusti, for having adopted Galerius in the east, for having everywhere abolished the superstition of Christ, for having extended the worship of the gods."

"We have here a monument raised by Paganism over the grave of its vanquished foe, but in this, 'the people imagined a vain thing.' Neither in Spain nor elsewhere can be pointed out the burial place of Christianity; 'it is not, for the living have no tomb'."

Vs. 2. *The kings of the earth set themselves.* In determined malice, they arrayed themselves in opposition against God. It was not temporary rage, but deep-seated hate, for they *set themselves* resolutely to withstand the Prince of Peace. C. H. S.

*And the rulers take counsel together, against the Lord, and against His Anointed.* They go about their warfare craftily, not with foolish haste, but deliberately. They use all the skill art can give. Like Pharaoh, they cry, "Let us deal wisely with them." Oh, that men were half as careful in God's service to serve Him wisely as His enemies are to attack His kingdom craftily. Sinners have their wits about them, and yet saints are dull. C. H. S.

Why did they band themselves against the Lord and against His Anointed? What, would they have, His blood? Yea, "they took counsel," saith Matthew, "to put Him to death." They had the devil's mind, which is not satisfied but with death. And how do they contrive it? He saith, "they took counsel about it." HENRY SMITH

Vs. 3. *Let us break their bands asunder.* Let us be free to commit all manner of abominations. Let us be our own gods. Let us rid ourselves of all restraint.

*Let us cast away their cords from us.* There are monarchs who have spoken thus, and there are still rebels upon thrones. However mad the resolution to revolt from God, it is one in which man has persevered ever since his creation, and he continues in it to this very day. The glorious reign of Jesus in the latter day will not be consummated until a terrible struggle has convulsed the nations. To a graceless neck, the yoke of Christ is intolerable, but to the saved sinner it is easy and light. We may judge ourselves by this: Do we love that yoke, or do we wish to cast it from us? C. H. S.

Vs. 4. *He that sitteth in the heavens shall laugh.* According to our capacities, the Prophet describes God, as ourselves would be in a merry disposition, deriding vain attempts. He laughs, but it is in scorn; He scorns, but it is with vengeance. He permitted His temple to be sacked and rifled, the holy vessels to be profaned and caroused in; but did not God's smile make Belshazzar to tremble at the handwriting on the wall? Oh, what are His frowns, if His smiles be so terrible? THOS. ADAMS

*The Lord,* in Hebrew, "Adonai," mystically signifieth "my stays," or "my sustainers—my pillars." Our English word, "Lord," hath much the same force, being contracted of the old Saxon word "Llaford," or "Hlafford," which cometh from "Laef," to sustain, refresh, cherish. HENRY AINSWORTH

*He that sitteth in the heavens shall laugh: the Lord shall have them in derision.* This tautology, or repetition of the same thing, is a sign of the thing being established: according to the authority of the patriarch Joseph (Gen. 41:32), where, having interpreted the dreams of Pharaoh, he said, "And for that the dream was doubled unto Pharaoh twice; it is because the thing is established by God, and God will shortly bring it to pass." And therefore, here also, *"shall laugh,"* and *shall have them in derision,* is a repetition to show that there is not a doubt to be entertained that all these things will most surely come to pass. MARTIN LUTHER

Vs. 5. *Then shall He speak unto them in His wrath.* After He has laughed He shall speak; He needs not smite; the breath of His lips is enough. C. H. S.

*Vex them:* either by horror of conscience or corporal plagues; one way or the other He will have His pennyworths of them, as He always has had of the persecutors of His people. JOHN TRAPP

Vs. 5, 9. It is easy for God to destroy His foes. Of thirty Roman emperors, governors of provinces, and others high in office, who distinguished themselves by their zeal and bitterness in persecuting the early Christians, one became speedily deranged after some atrocious cruelty, one was slain by his own son, one became blind, the eyes of one started out of his head, one was drowned, one was strangled, one died in a miserable captivity, one fell dead in a manner that will not bear recital, one died of so loathsome a disease that several of his physicians were put to death because they could not abide the stench that filled his room, two committed suicide, a third attempted it, but had to call for help to finish the work, five were assassinated by their own people or servants, five others died the most miserable and excruciating deaths, several of them having an untold complication of diseases, and eight were killed in battle, or after being taken prisoners.

Among these was Julian the Apostate. In the days of his prosperity, he is said to have pointed his dagger to heaven, defying the Son of God, whom he commonly called the Galilean. But when he was wounded in battle, he saw that all was over with him, and he gathered up his clotted blood, and threw it into the air, exclaiming, "Thou hast conquered, O Thou Galilean." WM. S. PLUMER

Vs. 6. *Yet have I set My King upon My holy hill of Zion*, despite your malice, despite your tumultuous gatherings, despite the wisdom of your counsels, and despite the craft of your lawgivers. He has already done that which the enemy seeks to prevent. While they are proposing, He has disposed the matter. Jehovah's will is done, and man's will frets and raves in vain. C. H .S.

Christ is a King above all kings. What are all the mighty men, the great, the honorable men of the earth to Jesus Christ? They are but like a little bubble in the water; for if all the nations, in comparison with God, be but as a drop of the bucket, or the dust of the balance, as the prophet speaks in Isa. 40:15, how little then must be the kings of the earth! WM. DYER'S *Christ's Famous Titles*

Vs. 7. *I will declare the decree.* Looking into the angry faces of the rebellious kings, the Anointed One seems to say, "If this sufficeth not to make you silent, *I will declare the decree.* Now, this decree is directly in conflict with the device of man, for its tenor is the establishment of the very dominion against which the nations are raving. C. H. S.

*Thou art My Son.* Here is a noble proof of the glorious divinity of our Immanuel.

*This day have I begotten Thee.* If this refers to the godhead of our Lord, let us not attempt to fathom it, for it is a great truth, a truth reverently to be received, but not irreverently to be scanned. In attempting to define the Trinity, or unveil the essence of divinity, many men have lost themselves: here great ships have floundered. What have we to do in such a sea with our frail skiffs?

The dispute concerning the eternal filiation of our Lord betrays more of presumptuous curiosity than of reverent faith. It is an attempt to explain where it is far better to adore. We could give rival expositions of this verse, but we forbear. The controversy is one of the most unprofitable which ever engaged the pens of theologians. C. H. S.

Vs. 9. *Thou shalt break them with a rod of iron; Thou shalt dash them in pieces like a potter's vessel.* Those who will not bend must break. Potters' vessels are not to be restored if dashed in pieces, and the ruin of sinners will be hopeless if Jesus shall smite them. C. H. S.

Vs. 10. *Be wise.* Oh, how wise, how infinitely wise is obedience to Jesus, and how dreadful is the folly of those who continue to be His enemies! C. H. S.

Vs. 11. *Rejoice with trembling.* Fear, without joy, is torment; and joy, without holy fear, would be presumption. C. H. S.

Vs. 12. *Kiss the Son, lest He be angry.* Judas betrayed his Master by a kiss, and yet God commands this, and expresses love in this; everything that hath, or may be abused, must not therefore be abandoned; the turning of a thing out of the way is not a taking of that thing away, but good things deflected to ill uses by some, may be by others reduced to their first goodness. Then let us consider and magnify the goodness of God, that hath brought us into this distance, that we may *kiss the Son;* that the expressing of this love lies in our hands.

God, Who is love, can be angry; and then, that this God Who is angry here is the Son of God, He that hath done so much for us, and therefore in justice may be angry; He that is our Judge, and therefore in reason we are to fear His anger: and then, in a third branch, we shall see how easily this anger departs—a kiss removes it.

If thou be despised for loving Christ in His gospel, remember that when David was thought base for dancing before the ark, his way was to be more base. "The more thou troublest thyself, or art troubled by others for Christ, the more peace thou hast in Christ." *From Sermons of John Donne.*

To make peace with the Father, kiss the Son. "Let Him kiss me," was the church's prayer (Cant. 1:2). Let us kiss Him—that be our endeavor. Indeed, the Son must first kiss us by His mercy before we can kiss Him by our piety. Lord, grant in these mutual kisses and interchangeable embraces now, that we may come to the plenary wedding supper hereafter; when the choir of heaven, even the voices of angels, shall sing epithalamiums, nuptial songs, at the bridal of the spouse of the Lamb. THOS. ADAMS

*And ye perish from the way, when His wrath is kindled but a little.* It is an awful thing to perish in the midst of sin, in the very way of rebellion; and yet how easily could His wrath destroy us suddenly! It needs not that His anger should be heated seven times hotter; let the fuel kindle but a little, and we are consumed. O sinner! Take heed of the terrors of the Lord; for "our God is a consuming fire." C. H. S.

Unspeakable must the wrath of God be when it is kindled fully, since perdition may come upon the kindling of it but a little. JOHN NEWTON.

In the First Psalm, we saw the wicked driven away like chaff; in the Second Psalm, we see them broken in pieces like a potter's vessel. In the First Psalm, we beheld the righteous like a tree planted by the rivers of water; and here, we contemplate Christ the Covenant Head of the righteous, made better than a tree planted by the rivers of water, for He is made king of all the islands, and all the heathen bow before Him and kiss the dust; while He Himself gives a blessing to all those who put their trust in Him. C. H. S.

# PSALM 3

A Psalm of David, when he fled from Absalom, his son. You will remember the sad story of David's flight from his own palace, when, in the dead of the night, he forded the brook Kedron and went with a few faithful followers to hide himself for a while from the fury of his rebellious son. Remember that David in this was a type of the Lord Jesus Christ. He, too, fled; He, too, passed over the brook Kedron when His own people were in rebellion against Him, and with a feeble band of followers, He went to the Garden of Gethsemane. He, too, drank of the brook by the way, and therefore doth He lift up the head. By very many expositors, this is entitled "The Morning Hymn." May we ever wake with holy confidence in our hearts and a song upon our lips!

This Psalm may be divided into four parts of two verses each. In the first two verses, you have David making a complaint to God concerning his enemies; he then declares his confidence in the Lord (3-4), sings of his safety in sleep (5-6), and strengthens himself for future conflict (7-8). C. H. S.

Vs. 1. *Lord, how are they increased that trouble me!* Troubles always come in flocks. Sorrow hath a numerous family.

*Many are they that rise up against me.* The legions of our sins, the armies of fiends, the crowd of bodily pains, the host of spiritual sorrows, and all the allies of death and hell, set themselves in battle against the Son of man. C. H. S.

How slippery and deceitful are the many! And how little fidelity and constancy is to be found among men! David had had the hearts of his subjects as much as ever any king had, and yet now of a sudden he had lost them! MATTHEW HENRY

Vs. 2. *Many there be which say of my soul, There is no help for him in God.* David complains before his loving God of the worst weapon of his enemies' attacks, and the bitterest drop of his distresses. This was "the unkindest cut of all," when they declared that his God had forsaken him. Yet David knew in his own conscience that he had given them some ground for this exclamation, for he had committed sin against God in the very light of day.

If all the trials which come from heaven, all the temptations which ascend from hell, and all the crosses which arise from earth, could be mixed and pressed together, they would not make a trial so terrible as that which is contained in this verse. It is the most bitter of all afflictions to be led to fear that there is no help for us in God. And yet remember our most blessed Savior had to endure this in the deepest degree when He cried, "My God, My God, why hast Thou forsaken Me?" C. H. S.

When the believer questions the power of God, or His interest in it, his joy gusheth out as blood out of a broken vein. This verse is a sore stab indeed. WM. GURNALL

A child of God startles at the very thought of despairing of help in God; you cannot vex him with anything so much as if you offer to persuade him, "There is no help for him in God." MATTHEW HENRY

*Selah.* The word occurs seventy-three times in the Psalms and three times in the book of Habakkuk. ALBERT BARNES

Vs. 3. Thou art *My glory.* Oh, for grace to see our future glory amid present shame! There is a present glory in our afflictions, if we could but discern it;

for it is no mean thing to have fellowship with Christ in His sufferings. David was honored when he made the ascent of Olivet, weeping, with his head covered; for he was in all this made like unto his Lord. May we learn, in this respect, to glory in tribulations also! C. H. S.

Vs. 4. *I cried unto the Lord with my voice.* When prayer leads the van, in due time deliverance brings up the rear. THOS. WATSON

*He heard me.* I have often heard persons say in prayer, "Thou art a prayer-hearing and a prayer-answering God," but the expression contains a superfluity, since for God to hear is, according to Scripture, the same thing as to answer. C. H. S.

Vs. 5. *I laid me down and slept.* There is a sleep of presumption; God, deliver us from it! There is a sleep of holy confidence; God, help us so to close our eyes! C. H. S.

Truly it must have been a soft pillow indeed that could make David forget his danger, who then had such a disloyal army at his back hunting of him; yea, so transcendent is the influence of this peace, that it can make the creature lie down as cheerfully to sleep in the grave as on the softest bed. You will say that child is willing that calls to be put to bed; some of the saints have desired God to lay them at rest in their beds of dust, and that not in a pet and discontent with their present trouble, as Job did, but from a sweet sense of this peace in their bosoms. "Now let thy servant depart in peace, for mine eyes have seen thy salvation," was the swan-like song of old Simeon. WM. GURNALL

A good conscience can sleep in the mouth of a cannon; grace is a Christian's coat of mail, which fears not the arrow or bullet. THOS. WATSON

*The Lord sustained me.* It would not be unprofitable to consider the sustaining power manifested in us while we lie asleep. In the flowing of the blood, heaving of the lung, etc., in the body, and the continuance of mental faculties while the image of death is upon us. C. H. S.

Christ, by the words of this verse, signifies His death and burial. MARTIN LUTHER

Vs. 6. *I will not be afraid of ten thousands of people, that have set themselves against me round about.* The Psalmist will trust, despite appearances. He will not be afraid though ten thousands of people have set themselves against him round about. Weak believers are now ready to make excuses for us, and we are only too ready to make them for ourselves; instead of rising above the weakness of the flesh, we take refuge under it and use it as an excuse. To trust only when appearances are favorable, is to sail only with the wind and tide, to believe only when we can see. Oh! let us follow the example of the Psalmist and seek that unreservedness of faith which will enable us to trust God, come what will. PHILIP BENNETT POWER'S *'I Wills' of the Psalms*

It makes no matter what our enemies be, though for number, legions; for power, principalities; for subtlety, serpents; for cruelty, dragons; for vantage of place, a prince of the air; for maliciousness, spiritual wickedness; stronger is He that is in us than they who are against us; nothing is able to separate us from the love of God. In Christ Jesus our Lord, we shall be more than conquerors. WM. COWPER

Vs. 8. *Salvation belongeth unto the Lord.* This verse contains the sum and substance of Calvinistic doctrine. Search Scripture through, and you must, if you read it with a candid mind, be persuaded that the doctrine of salvation by grace alone is the great doctrine of the Word of God. This is a point concerning which we are daily fighting. Our opponents say, "Salvation belongeth to the free will of man; if not to man's merit, yet at least to man's will"; but we hold and teach that salvation from first to last, in every iota of it, belongs to the Most high God. It is God that chooses His people. He calls them by His grace; He quickens them by His Spirit, and keeps them by His power. It is not of man, neither by man; "not of him that willeth, nor of him that runneth, but of God that showeth mercy." May we all learn this truth experimentally, for our proud flesh and blood will never permit us to learn it in any other way. C. H. S.

*Thy blessing is upon Thy people.* Those Christians of the first magnitude, of whom the world was not worthy, "Had trials of cruel mockings and scourgings, they were sawn asunder, they were slain with the sword" (Heb. 11:36-37). What! and were all these during the time of their sufferings blessed? A carnal man would think, if this be to be blessed, God deliver him from it. But, however sense would give their vote, our Savior Christ pronounceth the godly man blessed; though a mourner, though a martyr, yet blessed. Job on the dunghill was blessed Job. The saints are blessed when they are cursed. The saints though they are bruised, yet they are blessed. THOS. WATSON

# PSALM 4

If the Third Psalm may be entitled The Morning Psalm, this from its matter is equally deserving of the title of "The Evening Hymn."

In the first verse, David pleads with God for help. In the second, he expostulates with his enemies, and continues to address them to the end of verse 5. Then from verse 6 to the close, he delightfully contrasts his own satisfaction and safety with the disquietude of the ungodly in their best estate. C. H. S.

Vs. 1. *Hear me when I call.* It is not to be imagined that He who has helped us in six troubles will leave us in the seventh. God does nothing by halves, and He will never cease to help us until we cease to need. The manna shall fall every morning until we cross the Jordan. C. H. S.

Faith is a good orator and a noble disputer in a strait; it can reason from God's readiness to hear. DAVID DICKSON

Vs. 2. *How long?* He asks them how long they mean to make His honor a jest and His fame a mockery. A little of such mirth is too much; why need they continue to indulge in it? C. H. S.

*O ye sons of men, how long will ye turn My glory into shame?* etc. We might imagine every syllable of this precious Psalm used by our Master some evening, when about to leave the Temple for the day, and retiring to His wonted rest at Bethany (vs. 8) after another fruitless expostulation with the men of Israel. ANDREW BONAR

*How long will ye love vanity, and seek after leasing?* Chrysostom said once, "that if he were the fittest in the world to preach a sermon to the whole world, gathered together in one congregation, and had some high mountain for his pulpit, from whence he might have a prospect of all the world in his view, and were furnished with a voice of brass, a voice as loud as the trumpets of the archangel, that all the world might hear him, he would choose to preach upon no other text than that in the Psalms, O mortal men, *How long will ye love vanity, and follow after leasing?* THOS. BROOKS

*Selah.* Surely we too may stop awhile and meditate upon the deep-seated folly of the wicked, their continuance in evil, and their sure destruction; and we may learn to admire that grace which has made us to differ, and taught us to love truth, and seek after righteousness. C. H. S.

Vs. 3. *The Lord hath set apart him that is godly for Himself.* David was king by Divine decree, and we are the Lord's people in the same manner; let us tell our enemies to their faces that they fight against God and destiny when they strive to overthrow our souls. C. H. S.

Vs. 4. *Commune with your own heart upon your bed, and be still.* "Tremble and sin not." How many reverse this counsel and sin but tremble not. Oh that men would take the advice of this verse and *commune with their own hearts.* C. H. S.

Self-communion will much help to curb your headstrong, ungodly passions. Serious consideration, like the casting up of earth amongst bees, will allay inordinate affections when they are full of fury, and make such a hideous noise. GEORGE SWINNOCK

Vs. 6. *There be many that say, Who will show us any good?* There were many, even among David's own followers, who wanted to see rather than to believe. Alas, this is the tendency of us all! As for worldlings, this is their unceasing cry—"*Who will show us any good?*" Never satisfied, their gaping mouths are turned in every direction, their empty hearts are ready to drink in any fine delusion which impostors may invent; and when these fail, they soon yield to despair and declare that there is no good thing in either heaven or earth. C. H. S.

Man wants good; he hates evil, because he has pain, suffering, and death through it; and he wishes to find that supreme good which will content his heart and save him from evil. But men mistake this good. They look for a good that is to gratify their passions; they have no notion of any happiness that does not come to them through the medium of their senses. Therefore, they reject spiritual good, and they reject the supreme God, by Whom alone all the powers of the soul of man can be gratified. ADAM CLARKE

Lest riches should be accounted evil in themselves, God sometimes gives them to the righteous; and lest they should be considered as the chief good, He frequently bestows them on the wicked. But they are more generally the portion of His enemies than His friends. Alas, what is it to receive and not to be received, to have none other dews of blessing than such as shall be followed by showers of brimstone?

The world is a floating island, and so sure as we cast anchor upon it, we shall be carried away by it. God, and all that He has made, is not more than God without anything that He has made. He is enough without the creature, but the creature is not anything without Him. It is, therefore, better to enjoy Him without anything else, than to enjoy everything else without Him. WM. SECKER'S *Nonsuch Professor.*

Vs. 7. *Thou hast put gladness in my heart, more than in the time that their corn and their wine increased.* "It is better," said one, "to feel God's favor one hour in our repenting souls than to sit whole ages under the warmest sunshine that this world affordeth." Christ in the heart is better than corn in the barn or wine in the vat. Corn and wine are but fruits of the world, but the light of God's countenance is the ripe fruit of heaven. Let my granary be empty, I am yet full of blessings if Jesus Christ smiles upon me; but if I have all the world, I am poor without him.

This verse is the saying of the righteous man in opposition to the saying of the many. How quickly doth the tongue betray the character! "Speak, that I may see thee!" said Socrates to a fair boy. The metal of a bell is best known by its sound. Birds reveal their nature by their song. C. H. S.

What madness and folly is it that the favorites of heaven should envy the men of the world, who at best do but feed upon the scraps that come from God's table! THOS. BROOKS

Vs. 8. *I will both lay me down in peace, and sleep: for Thou, Lord, only makest me dwell in safety.* A quiet conscience is a good bedfellow. How many of our sleepless hours might be traced to our untrusting and disordered minds! They slumber sweetly whom faith rocks to sleep. No pillow so soft as a promise; no coverlet so warm as an assured interest in Christ. C. H. S.

We have now to retire for a moment from the strife of tongues and the open hostility of foes into the stillness and privacy of the chamber of sleep. And there is something here which should be inexpressibly sweet to the believer, for this shows the minuteness of God's care, the individuality of His love; how it condescends and stoops, and acts, not only in great, but also in little spheres; not only where glory might be procured from great results, but where nought is to be had save the gratitude and love of a poor feeble creature whose life has been protected and preserved in a period of helplessness and sleep. How blessed would it be if we thought of Him as being there in all hours of illness, of weariness, and pain!

There is something inexpressibly touching in this "lying down" of the Psalmist. In thus lying down, he voluntarily gave up any guardianship of himself. Many a believer lies down, but it is not to sleep. Perhaps he feels safe enough so far as his body is concerned, but cares and anxieties invade the privacy of his chamber. There is a trial in stillness; and oftentimes the still chamber makes a larger demand upon loving trust than the battlefield. Oh, that we could trust God more and more with personal things! Oh, that He were the God of our chamber, as well as of our temples and houses!

Ridley's brother offered to remain with him during the night preceding his martyrdom, but the bishop declined, saying that "he meant to go to bed and sleep as quietly as ever he did in his life." PHILIP BENNETT POWER

## PSALM 5

To the devout mind there is here presented a precious view of the Lord Jesus, of Whom it is said that in the days of His flesh, He offered up prayers and supplication with strong crying and tears.

Vs. 1. *Give ear to my words, O Lord, consider my meditation.* Words are not the essence but the garments of prayer. C. H. S.

Meditation is the best beginning of prayer, and prayer is the best conclusion of meditation. George Swinnock

It is certain that the greater part of men, as they babble out vain, languid, and inefficacious prayers, most unworthy the ear of the blessed God, so they seem in some degree to set a just estimate upon them, neither hoping for any success from them, nor indeed seeming to be at all solicitous about it, but committing them to the wind as vain words, which in truth they are. Robert Leighton

Vs. 1-2. Observe the order and force of the words, "my cry," "the voice of my prayer"; and also, "give ear," "consider," "hearken." These expressions all evince the urgency and energy of David's feelings and petitions. First, we have, "Give ear" that is, "Hear me." But it is of little service for the words to be heard unless the "cry," or the roaring, or the meditation, be considered. As if he said, I cannot express myself nor make myself understood as I wish. Do Thou, therefore, understand from my feelings more than I am able to express in words. Martin Luther

Vs. 2. *The voice of my cry.* To a loving father, his children's cries are music, and they have a magic influence which his heart cannot resist.

*My King, and my God.* Observe carefully these little pronouns, "*my* King, and *my* God." They are the pith and marrow of the plea. Here is a grand argument why God should answer prayer—because He is *our* King and *our* God. We are not aliens to Him: He is the King of our country. Kings are expected to hear the appeals of their own people. We are not strangers to Him; we are His worshippers, and He is our God: ours by covenant, by promise, by oath, by blood. C. H. S.

Vs. 3. *My voice shalt Thou hear.* Observe, this is not so much a prayer as a resolution. We can sooner die than live without prayer.

*In the morning.* An hour in the morning is worth two in the evening. While the dew is on the grass, let grace drop upon the soul. Let us give God the mornings of our days and the morning of our lives. Prayer should be the key of the day and the lock of the night. C. H. S.

"In the days of our fathers," says Bishop Burnet, "when a person came early to the door of his neighbor, and desired to speak with the master of the house, it was as common a thing for the servants to tell him with freedom—'My master is at prayer,' as it now is to say, 'My master is not up'."

*I will direct my prayer unto Thee, and will look up.* I will put my prayer upon the bow, I will direct it toward heaven, and then when I have shot up my arrow, I will look up to see where it has gone. But the Hebrew has a still fuller meaning than this—"I will *direct* my prayer." It is the word that is used for the laying in order of the wood and the pieces of the victim upon the altar, and it is used also for the putting of the shewbread upon the table. It means just this: "I will arrange my prayer before Thee"; I will lay it out upon the altar in the morning, just as the priest lays out the morning sacrifice. I will arrange my prayer; or, as old Master Trapp has it, "I will marshall up my prayers," I will put them in order, call up all my powers, and bid them stand in their proper places, that I may pray with all my might, and pray acceptably.

*And will look up*, or, as the Hebrew might better be translated, " 'I will look out,' I will look out for the answer. After I have prayed, I will expect that the blessing shall come." It is the word that is used in another place where we read of those who watched for the morning. So will I watch for Thine answer, O my Lord! I will spread out my prayer like the victim on the altar, and I will look up and expect to receive the answer by fire from heaven to consume the sacrifice. Do we not miss very much of the sweetness and efficacy of prayer by a want of careful meditation before it and of hopeful expectation after it? Prayer without fervency is like hunting with a dead dog, and prayer without preparation is hawking with a blind falcon. God made man, but He used the dust of the earth as a material: the Holy Ghost is the Author of prayer, but He employs the thoughts of a fervent soul as the gold with which to fashion the vessel. Let not our prayers and praises be the flashes of a hot and hasty brain, but the steady burning of a well-kindled fire.

We are like the ostrich, which lays her eggs and looks not for her young. We sow the seed and are too idle to seek a harvest. Let holy preparation link hands with patient expectation, and we shall have far larger answers to our prayers. C. H. S.

David would direct his prayer to God and look up; not down to the world, down to corruption, but up to God what He would speak. WM. GREENHILL

And if you believe, why do you not expect? O Christian, stand to your prayer in a holy expectation of what you have begged upon the credit of promise. WM. GURNALL

Vs. 4. *For Thou art not a God that hath pleasure in wickedness.* "When I pray against my tempters," says David, "I pray against the very things which Thou thyself abhorrest." Thou hatest evil. Let us learn here the solemn truth of the hatred which a righteous God must bear towards sin. C. H. S.

As a man that cutteth with a dull knife is the cause of cutting, but not of the ill-cutting and hacking of the knife—the knife is the cause of that; or if a man strike upon an instrument that is out of tune, he is the cause of the sound, but not of the jarring sound—that is the fault of the untuned strings; or as a man riding upon a lame horse, stirs him—the man is the cause of the motion, but the horse himself of the halting motion: thus God is the author of every action, but not of the evil of that action—this is from man. SPENCER'S *Things New and Old*

*Neither shall evil dwell with Thee.* Oh, how foolish we are if we attempt to entertain two guests so hostile to one another as Christ Jesus and the devil! Rest assured, Christ will not live in the parlor of our hearts if we entertain the devil in the cellar of our thoughts. C. H. S.

Vs. 4-6. Here the Lord's alienation from the wicked is set forth gradually and seems to rise by six steps. First, *He hath no pleasure in them;* second, *they shall not dwell with Him;* third, He casteth them forth, *they shall not stand in His sight;* fourth, His heart turns from them, *Thou hatest all workers of iniquity;* fifth, His hand is turned upon them, *Thou shalt destroy them that speak leasing;* sixth, His Spirit riseth against them, and is alienated from them, *the Lord will abhor the bloody man.*

These words, *the workers of iniquity,* may be considered in two ways; first, as intending (not all degrees of sinners, or sinners of every degree, but) the highest degree of sinners, great and gross sinners, resolved and wilful sinners. Such as sin industriously, and as it were, artificially, with skill and care to get themselves a name, as if they had an ambition to be accounted workmen that need not be ashamed in doing that whereof all ought to be ashamed; these in the strictness of Scripture sense, are *workers of iniquity.* Hence, note, notorious sinners make sin their business, or their trade. Though every sin be a work of iniquity, yet only some sinners are *workrs of iniquity;* and those who are called so make it their calling to sin. We read of some who love and make a lie (Rev. 22:15). JOS. CARYL

Vs. 5. *The foolish shall not stand in Thy sight.* Sinners are fools written large. A little sin is a great folly, and the greatest of all folly is great sin.

*Thou hatest all workers of iniquity.* It is not a little dislike, but a thorough hatred which God bears to workers of iniquity. To be hated of God is an awful thing. Oh, let us be very faithful in warning the wicked around us, for it will be a terrible thing for them to fall into the hands of an angry God. C. H. S.

What an astonishing thing is sin, which maketh the God of love and Father of mercies an enemy to His creatures, and which could only be purged by the blood of the Son of God. THOS. ADAMS' *Private Thoughts*

For what God thinks of sin, see Deut. 7:22; Prov. 6:16; Rev. 2:6, 15. WM. GURNALL

If a man hate a poisonous creature, he hates poison much more. The strength of God's hatred is against sin, and so should we hate sin, and hate it with strength; it is an abomination unto God, let it be so unto us. WM. GREENHILL

The workers of iniquity must perish (Luke 13:27). DAVID CLARKSON

Vs. 6. *Thou shalt destroy them that speak leasing.* Evil speakers must be punished as well as evil workers. All liars shall have their portion in the lake which burneth with fire and brimstone. C. H. S.

Whether in jest or earnest—those that lie in jest will (without repentance) go to hell in earnest. JOHN TRAPP

In the same field wherein Absalom raised battle against his father stood the oak that was his gibbet. The mule whereon he rode was his hangman, for the mule carried him to the tree, and the hair wherein he gloried served for a rope to hang. Little know the wicked how everything which now they have shall be a snare to trap them when God begins to punish them. WM. COWPER

Vs. 7. *But as for me, I will come into Thy house.* A blessed verse this! a blessed saying! The words and the sense itself carry with them a powerful contrast. For there are two things with which this life is exercised, Hope and Fear, which are, as it were, those two springs of Judges 1:15, the one from above, the other from beneath. Fear comes from beholding the threats and fearful judgments of God; but hope comes from beholding the promises and the all-sweet mercies of God. MARTIN LUTHER

*In the multitude of Thy mercy.* I will not come there by my own merits; no, I have a multitude of sins, and therefore, I will come *in the multitude of Thy mercy.* C. H. S.

Vs. 8. *Lead me, O Lord.* It is safe and pleasant walking when God leads the way.

*In Thy righteousness,* not in *my* righteousness, for that is imperfect, but in *Thine,* for Thou art righteousness itself.

*Make Thy way straight before my face;* not my way. When we have learned to give up *our* own way and long to walk in *God's* way, it is a happy sign of grace; and it is no small mercy to see the way of God with clear vision straight before our face. C. H. S.

Vs. 9. This description of depraved man has been copied by the Apostle Paul as being an accurate description of the whole human race, not of David's enemies only, but of all men by nature. C. H. S.

*Their inward part is very wickedness.* If the whole soul be infected with such a desperate disease, what a great and difficult work is it to regenerate, to restore men again to spiritual life and vigor, when every part of them is seized by such a mortal distemper! To heal but the lungs or the liver, if corrupted, is counted a great cure, though performed but upon one part of thee; but all thy inward parts are very rottenness. How great a cure is it then to heal thee! Such as is only in the skill and power of God to do. THOS. GOODWIN

*Their throat is an open sepulcher,* a sepulcher full of loathsomeness, of miasma, of pestilence and death. But, worse than that, it is an *open* sepulcher with all its evil gases issuing forth to spread death and destruction all around. So, with the throat of the wicked, it would be a great mercy if it could always be closed, but "their throat is an open sepulcher," consequently all the wickedness of their heart exhales and comes forth. How dangerous is an open sepulcher; men in their journeys might easily stumble therein and find themselves among the dead. Ah, take heed of the wicked man, for there is nothing that he will not say to ruin you. One sweet thought here, however. At the resurrection there will be a resurrection not only of bodies but characters. C. H. S.

This figure graphically portrays the filthy conversation of the wicked. Nothing can be more abominable to the senses than an open sepulcher, when a dead body beginning to putrefy steams forth its tainted exhalations. ROBERT HALDANE'S *Expositions of the Epistle of Romans*

As a sepulcher, having devoured many corpses is still ready to consume more, being never satisfied, so wicked men, having overthrown many with their words, do proceed in their outrage, seeking whom they may devour. THOS. WILSON

*They flatter with their tongue.* When the wolf licks the lamb, he is preparing to wet his teeth with its blood. C. H. S.

Vs. 10. *Against Thee:* not against me. If they were my enemies I would forgive them, but I cannot forgive Thine. We are to forgive *our* enemies, but God's enemies it is not in our power to forgive. These expressions have often been noticed by men of over-refinement as being harsh and grating on the ear. Let us remember that they might be translated as prophecies, not as wished. We have never heard of a reader of the Bible who, after perusing these passages, was made revengeful by reading them. When we hear a judge condemning a a murderer, however severe his sentence, we do not feel that we should be justified in condemning others for any private injury done to us. C. H. S.

Had Abraham stood beside the angel who destroyed Sodom and seen how Jehovah's Name required the ruin of these impenitent rebels, he would have cried out, "Let the shower descend; let the fire and brimstone come down!" not in any spirit of revenge; not from want of tender love to souls, but from intense earnestness of concern for the glory of his God. THOS. FULLER

Vs. 11. *But let all those that put their trust in Thee rejoice: let them ever shout for joy, because Thou defendest them: let them also that love Thy Name be joyful in Thee.* Joy is the privilege of the believer. When sinners are de-

LEWIS EGERTON SMOOT MEM'L LIB.
KING GEORGE, VA 22485

stroyed, our rejoicing shall be full. They laugh first and weep ever after; we weep now, but shall rejoice eternally. C. H. S.

Vs. 12. *Thou, Lord, wilt bless the righteous.* This is a promise of infinite length, of unbounded breadth, and of unutterable preciousness. C. H. S.

*With favor wilt Thou compass him as with a shield.* The shield is not for the defense of any particular part of the body, as almost all the other pieces are, but it is a piece that is intended for the defense of the whole body. The shield doth not only defend the whole body, but it is a defense to the soldier's armor also. Thus, faith, it is armor upon armor, a grace that preserves all the other graces. WM. GURNALL

# PSALM 6

This Psalm is commonly known as the first of "The Penitential Psalms," and certainly its language well becomes the lip of a penitent, for it expresses at once the sorrow (verses 3, 6-7), the humiliation (verses 2,4), and the hatred of sin (verse 8), which are the unfailing marks of the contrite spirit when it turns to God.

Vs. 1. *O Lord, rebuke me not in Thine anger.* The Psalmist is very conscious that he deserves to be rebuked, and he does not ask that the rebuke may be totally withheld, for he might thus lose a blessing in disguise; but, "Lord, rebuke me not *in Thine anger.*" If Thou remindest me of my sin, it is good; but, oh, remind me not of it as one incensed against me, lest Thy servant's heart should sink in despair. Thus saith Jeremiah, "O Lord, correct me, but with judgment; not in Thine anger, lest Thou bring me to nothing." C. H. S.

Vs. 2. *"Have mercy upon me, O Lord.* To fly and escape the anger of God, David sees no means in heaven or in earth, and therefore retires himself to God, even to Him who wounded him that He might heal him. He flies not with Adam to the bush, nor with Saul to the witch, nor with Jonah to Tarshish; but he appeals from an angry and just God to a merciful God, and from Himself to Himself. The woman who was condemned by King Philip appealed from Philip being drunken to Philip being sober. But David appeals from one virtue, justice, to another, mercy. ARCHIBALD SYMSON

*For I am weak.* Urge not your goodness or your greatness, but plead your sin and your littleness. A sense of sin had so spoiled the Psalmist's pride, so taken away his vaunted strength, that he found himself weak to obey the law, weak through the sorrow that was in him, too weak perhaps, to lay hold on the promise. "I am weak." The original may be read, "I am one who droops," or withered like a blighted plant. C. H. S.

Coming before God, the most forcible argument that ye can use is your necessity, poverty, tears, misery, unworthiness, and confessing them to Him, it shall be an open door to furnish you with all things that He hath. The beggars lay open their sores to the view of the world, that the more they may move men to pity them. So let us deplore our miseries to God, that He, with the pitiful Samaritan, at the sight of our wounds, may help us in due time. ARCHIBALD SYMSON

*O Lord, heal me; for my bones are vexed.* His terror had become so great that his very bones shook; not only did his flesh quiver, but the bones, the solid pillars of the house of manhood, were made to tremble. Ah, when the soul has a sense of sin, it is enough to make the bones shake; it is enough to make a man's hair stand up on end to see the flames of hell beneath him, an angry God above him, and danger and doubt surrounding him. C. H. S.

The term *bones* is sometimes applied literally to our blessed Lord's human body, to the body which hung upon the cross. It has sometimes also a further reference to His mystical body, the church. In some passages it is applied to the soul and not to the body, to the inner man of the individual Christian. Then it implies the strength and fortitude of the soul, the determined courage which faith in God gives to the righteous. This is the sense in which it is used in the second verse of this Psalm. AUGUSTINE, AMBROSE, AND CHRYSOSTOM.

Vs. 3. *My soul is sore vexed.* Soul trouble is the very soul of trouble. C. H. S.

Yoke-fellows in sin are yoke-fellows in pain; the soul is punished for informing, the body for performing, and as both the informer and performer, the cause and the instrument, so shall the stirrer up of sin and the executor of it be punished. JOHN DONNE

*But Thou, O Lord, how long?* This sentence ends abruptly, for words failed and grief drowned the little comfort which dawned upon him.

Calvin's favorite exclamation was, *Domine usuequo*—"O Lord, how long?" And this should be the cry of the saints waiting for the millennial glories, "Why are His chariots so long in coming; Lord, how long?" C. H. S.

Out of this we have three things to observe; first, that there is an appointed time which God hath measured for the crosses of all His children, before which time they shall not be delivered, and for which they must patiently attend, not thinking to prescribe time to God for their delivery or limit the Holy One of Israel. The Israelites remained in Egypt till the complete number of four hundred and thirty years were accomplished. Joseph was three years and more in the prison till the appointed time of his delivery came. The Jews remained seventy years in Babylon. God knoweth the convenient times both of our humiliation and exaltation.

Next see the impatience of our nature in our miseries, our flesh still rebelling against the Spirit, which oftentimes forgetteth itself so far that it will enter into reasoning with God and quarrelling with Him, as we may read of Job, Jonas, etc., and here also of David.

Thirdly, albeit the Lord delay His coming to relieve His saints, yet hath He cause if we could ponder it; for when we were in the heat of our sins, many times He cried by the mouth of His prophets and servants, "O fools, how long will you continue in your folly?" And we would not hear; and therefore when we are in the heat of our pains, thinking long, yea, every day a year till we be delivered, no wonder it is if God will not hear; let us consider with ourselves the just dealing of God with us; that as He cried and we would not hear, so now we cry and He will not hear. A. SYMSON

Vs. 4. *Return, O Lord, deliver my soul.* As the mathematician said that he could make an engine, a screw, that should move the whole frame of the world, if he could have a place assigned him to fix that engine, that screw upon, that so it might work upon the world; so prayer, when one petition hath taken hold upon God, works upon God, moves God, prevails with God, entirely for all. David, then having got this ground, this footing in God, he brings his works closer; he comes from the deprecatory to a postulatory prayer; not only that God would do nothing against him, but that He would do something for him. JOHN DONNE

*For Thy mercies' sake.* If we turn to justice, what plea can we urge? But if we turn to mercy, we may still cry, notwithstanding the greatness of our guilt, "Save me for Thy mercies' sake." C. H. S.

Observe how frequently David here pleads the Name of Jehovah, which is always intended where the word LORD is given in capitals. Five times in four verses we here meet with it. Is not this a proof that the glorious name is full of consolation to the tempted saint? C. H. S.

Vs. 5. *For in death there is no remembrance of Thee: in the grave who shall give Thee thanks?* It is for God's glory that a sinner should be saved. Mercy honors God. C. H. S.

Vs. 6. *I am weary with my groaning.* God's people may groan but they may not grumble. C. H. S.

It may seem a marvelous change in David, being a man of such magnitude of mind, to be thus dejected and cast down. Prevailed he not against Goliath, against the lion and the bear, through fortitude and magnanimity? But now he is sobbing, sighing, and weeping like a child! When men and beasts are his opposites, then he is more than a conqueror; but when he hath to do with God against whom he sinned, then he is less than nothing.

*All the night make I my bed to swim;* or, "I caused my bed to swim." As the woman with the bloody issue that touched the hem of Christ's garment was no less welcome to Christ than Thomas, who put his fingers in the print of the nails, so God looketh not at the quantity, but the sincerity of our repentance.

Vs. 6-7. *I water my couch with my tears. Mine eye is consumed because of grief; it waxeth old because of all mine enemies.* Conviction sometimes has such an effect upon the body that even the outward organs are made to suffer. C. H. S.

*Mine enemies.* If a man have no grace within him, Satan passeth by him as not a convenient prey for him; but being loaded with graces, as the love of God, His fear, and such other spiritual virtues, let him be persuaded that according as he knows what stuff is in him, so will he not fail to rob him of them, if in any case he may. ARCHIBALD SYMSON

Vs. 8. *Depart from me, all ye workers of iniquity.* Repentance is a practical thing. It is not enough to bemoan the desecration of the temple of the heart; we must scourge out the buyers and sellers and overturn the tables of the money-changers. A pardoned sinner will hate the sins which cost the Savior His blood. C. H. S.

May not too much familiarity with profane wretches be justly charged upon church-members? I know man is a sociable creature, but that will not excuse saints as to their carelessness of the choice of their company. LEWIS STUCKLEY'S *Gospel Glass*

The wicked are called "workers of iniquity" because they are free and ready to sin. They have a strong tide and bent of spirit to do evil, and they do it not by halves, but thoroughly; they do not only begin or nibble at the bait a little (as a good man often doth), but greedily swallow it down, hook and all; they are fully in it, and do it fully; they make a work of it, and so are "workers of iniquity." JOS. CARYL

*For the Lord hath heard the voice of my weeping.* Does weeping speak? In what language doth it utter its meaning? Why, in that universal tongue which is known and understood in all the earth, and even in heaven above. Weeping is the eloquence of sorrow. Let us learn to think of tears as liquid prayers and of weeping as a constant dropping of importunate intercession which will wear its way right surely into the very heart of mercy, despite the stony difficulties which obstruct the way. C. H. S.

It is not so much the weeping eye God respects as the broken heart; yet I would be loath to stop their tears who can weep. God stood looking on Hezekiah's tears (Isa. 38:5), "I have seen thy tears." David's tears made music in God's ears. T. WATSON

Weeping hath a voice, and as music upon the water sounds farther and more harmoniously than upon the land, so prayers, joined with tears, cry louder in God's ears, and make sweeter music than when tears are absent. SPENCER'S *Things New and Old*

As God sees the water in the spring in the veins of the earth before it bubble upon the face of the earth, so God sees tears in the heart of a man before they blubber his face. JOHN DONNE

Well might Luther say, "Prayer is the leech of the soul that sucks out the venom and swelling thereof." Bernard saith, "How oft hath prayer found me despairing almost, but left me triumphing and well assured of pardon!" JOHN TRAPP

Vs. 9. *The Lord hath heard my supplication. The Lord will receive my prayer.* Here is a past experience used for future encouragement. *He hath, He will.* C. H. S.

Vs. 10. *Let all mine enemies be ashamed and sore vexed: let them return and be ashamed suddenly.* The Romans were wont to say, "The feet of the avenging Deity are shod with wool." With noiseless footsteps, vengeance nears its victim, and sudden and overwhelming shall be its destroying stroke. If this were an imprecation, we must remember that the language of the old dispensation is not that of the new. We pray for our enemies, not against them. C. H. S.

# PSALM 7

The title—"Shiggaion of David." As far as we can gather from the observations of learned men and from a comparison of this Psalm with the only other "Shiggaion" in the Word of God (Hab. 3), this title seems to mean "variable songs," with which the idea of solace and pleasure is associated.

It appears probable that Cush the Benjamite had accused David to Saul of treasonable conspiracy against his royal authority.

This may be called the "Song of the Slandered Saint." Even this sorest of evils may furnish occasion for a Psalm.

Vs. 1. *O Lord my God, in Thee do I put my trust.* The case is here opened with an avowal of confidence in God. Whatever may be the emergency of our condition, we shall never find it amiss to retain our reliance upon our God. "O Lord, *my* God"—mine by a special covenant, sealed by Jesus' blood, and ratified in my own soul by a sense of union to Thee; *in Thee,* and in Thee only, *do I put my trust,* even now in my sore distress. I shake, but my rock moves not. It is never right to distrust God and never vain to trust Him. C. H. S.

Vs. 2. *Lest he tear my soul like a lion.* There was one among David's foes mightier than the rest. From this foe, he urgently seeks deliverance. Perhaps this was Saul, his royal enemy; but in our case there is one who goes about like a lion, seeking whom he may devour, concerning whom we should cry, "Deliver us from the evil one." C. H. S.

I have read of some barbarous nations, who, when the sun shines hot upon them, they shoot up their arrows against it; so do wicked men at the light and heat of godliness. JEREMIAH BURROUGHS

*Rending it in pieces, while there is none to deliver.* This is a soul-moving portrait of a saint delivered over to the will of Satan. This will make the bowels of Jehovah yearn. A father cannot be silent when a child is in such peril.

It will be well for us here to remember that this is a description of the danger to which the Psalmist was exposed from slanderous tongues. Slander leaves a slur, even if it be wholly disproved. If God was slandered in Eden, we shall surely be maligned in this land of sinners. If we would live without being slandered, we must wait till we get to heaven. C. H. S.

Vs. 3. *O Lord my God, if I have done this; if there be iniquity in my hands.* Josephus tells us of Apollinaris, speaking concerning the Jews and Christians, that they were more foolish than any barbarian. And Paulus Fagius reports a story of an Egyptian, concerning the Christians, who said, "They were a gathering together of a most filthy, lecherous people"; and for the keeping of the Sabbath he says, "They had a disease that was upon them, and they were fain to rest the seventh day because of the disease." JEREMIAH BURROUGHS

The applause of the wicked usually denotes some evil, and their censure imports some good. THOS. WATSON

Vs. 4. *If I have rewarded evil unto him that was at peace with me.* To do evil for good is human corruption; to do good for good is civil retribution; but to do good for evil is Christian perfection. Though this be not the grace of nature, yet it is the nature of grace. WM. SECKER

Vs. 6. *The judgment that Thou hast commanded.* David, in order to pray aright, reposes himself on the Word and promise of God; and the import of his exercise is this: Lord, I am not led by ambition or foolish, headstrong passion, or depraved desire, inconsiderately to ask from Thee whatever is pleasing to my flesh; but it is the clear light of Thy Word which directs me, and upon it I securely depend. JOHN CALVIN

Vs. 8. In the last two verses, he besought Jehovah to arise, and now that He is arisen, he prepares to mingle with "the congregation of the people" who compass the Lord about. C. H. S.

Vs. 9. *Oh let the wickedness of the wicked come to an end; but establish the just.* Is not this the universal longing of the whole company of the elect? C. H. S.

Vs. 10. *My defense is of God, which saveth the upright in heart.* Truth, like oil, is ever above; no power of our enemies can drown it. C. H. S.

Vs. 11. *God is angry with the wicked every day.* We have no insensible and stolid God to deal with; He can be angry, nay, He is angry today and every day with you, ye ungodly and impenitent sinners. The best day that ever dawns on a sinner brings a curse with it. C. H. S.

*God is angry.* The original expression here is very forcible. The true idea of it appears to be to *froth* or *foam at the mouth* with indignation. RICHARD MANT

Vs. 12. *If he turn not, He will whet His sword.* God's sword has been sharpening upon the revolving stone of our daily wickedness, and if we will not repent, it will speedily cut us in pieces. Turn or burn is the sinner's only alternative. C. H. S.

How few do believe what a quarrel God hath with wicked men! If we did we would tremble as much to be among them as to be in a house that is falling; we would endeavor to "save" ourselves "from this untoward generation." C. H. S.

*He hath bent His bow, and made it ready.* And is it safe to be there where the arrows of God are ready to fly about our ears? How was the Apostle afraid to be in the bath with Cerinthus! "Depart," saith God by Moses, "from the tents of Korah, Dathan, and Abiram, lest ye be consumed in all their sins." How have the baskets of good figs suffered with the bad! Is it not prejudicial to the gold to be with the dross? LEWIS STUCKLEY

Vs. 13. *Instruments of death.* Remember, God's arrows never miss the mark, and are every one of them "instruments of death." C. H. S.

*He ordaineth His arrows against the persecutors.* The word "ordain" signifies such as burn in anger and malice against the godly; and the word translated "ordained" signifies God hath wrought His arrows; He doth not shoot them at random, but He works them against the wicked. One Felix, Earl of Wartenberg, one of the captains of the Emperor Charles V, swore in the presence of divers at supper that before he died he would ride up to the spurs in the blood of the Lutherans. Here was one that burned in malice, but behold how God works His arrows against him; that very night the hand of God so struck him that he was strangled and choked in his own blood; so he rode not, but bathed himself, not up to the spurs, but up to the throat, not in the blood of the Lutherans, but in his own blood before he died. JEREMIAH BURROUGHS

Vs. 14. *He travaileth with iniquity.* A woman in travail furnishes the first metaphor. *He travaileth with iniquity.* He is full of it, pained until he can carry it out; he longs to work his will; he is full of pangs until his evil intent is executed. C. H. S.

*And hath conceived mischief.* He was not put upon it or forced into it: it was voluntary. RICHARD SIBBS

All note that conceiving is before travailing but here travailing, as a woman in labor, goeth first; the reason whereof is, that the wicked are so hotly set upon the evil which they maliciously intend that they would be immediately acting of it if they could tell how, even before they have conceived by what means. J. MAYER

*And brought forth falsehood.* "Earth's entertainments are like those of Jael; her left hand brings me milk, her right, a nail." THOS. FULLER

Vs. 15. *He made a pit, and digged it.* He was cunning in his plans and industrious in his labors. He stooped to the dirty work of digging. He did not fear to soil his own hands; he was willing to work in a ditch if others might fall therein. What mean things men will do to wreak revenge on the godly!

Vs. 16. *His mischief shall return upon his own head.* Ashes always fly back in the face of him that throws them. C. H. S.

# PSALM 8

We may style this Psalm "the Song of the Astronomer."

Vs. 1. *O Lord our Lord, how excellent is Thy name in all the earth! Who hast set Thy glory above the heavens.* Unable to express the glory of God, the Psalmist utters a note of exclamation. O Jehovah, our Lord! The solid fabric of the universe leans upon His eternal arm. Universally is He present, and everywhere is His name excellent.

Descend, if you will, into the lowest depths of the ocean, where undisturbed the water sleeps, and the very sand is motionless in unbroken quiet, but the glory of the Lord is there, revealing its excellence in the silent palace of the sea. Borrow the wings of the morning and fly to the uttermost parts of the sea, but God is there. Mount to the highest heaven, or dive into the deepest hell, and God is in both hymned in everlasting song or justified in terrible vengeance. Everywhere and in every place, God dwells and is manifestly at work.

We can scarcely find more fitting words than those of Nehemiah, "Thou, even Thou, art Lord alone; Thou hast made heaven, the heaven of heavens, with all their host, the earth, and all things that are therein, the seas, and all that is therein, and Thou preservest them all; and the host of heaven worshippeth Thee." Returning to the text, we are led to observe that this Psalm is addressed to God, because none but the Lord Himself can fully know His own glory. C. H. S.

Vs. 2. *Out of the mouth of babes and sucklings hast Thou ordained strength because of Thine enemies.* How often will children tell us of a God Whom we have forgotten! Did not the children cry, "Hosannah!" in the Temple, when proud Pharisees were silent and contemptuous? And did not the Savior quote these very words as a justification of their infantile cries?

Fox tells us, in the *Book of Martyrs*, that when Mr. Lawrence was burnt in Colchester, he was carried to the fire in a chair, because, through the cruelty of the Papists, he could not stand upright, several young children came about the fire and cried, as well as they could speak, "Lord, strengthen Thy servant, and keep Thy promise." God answered their prayer, for Mr. Lawrence died as firmly and calmly as anyone could wish to breathe his last.

When one of the popish chaplains told Mr. Wishart, the great Scotch martyr, that he had a devil in him, a child that stood by cried out, "A devil cannot speak such words as yonder man speaketh." One more instance is still nearer to our time. In a postscript to one of his letters, in which he details his persecution when first preaching in Moorfields, Whitefield says, "I cannot help adding that several little boys and girls who were fond of sitting round me on the pulpit while I preached, and handed to me people's notes—though they were often pelted with eggs, dirt, etc., thrown at me—never once gave way; but on the contrary, every time I was struck, turned up their little weeping eyes, and seemed to wish they could receive the blows for me. God make them, in their growing years, great and living martyrs for Him, who, 'out of the mouths of babes and sucklings, perfects praise!'" C. H. S.

Who are these "babes and sucklings"? Man in general, who springeth from so weak and poor a beginning as that of babes and sucklings, yet is at length advanced to such power as to grapple with, and overcome the enemy and the avenger. The Apostles, who to outward appearance were despicable, in a manner children and sucklings in comparison of the great ones of the world; poor, despised creatures, yet principal instruments of God's service and glory. Therefore 'tis notable, that when Christ glorifieth His Father for the wise and free dispensation of His saving grace (Matt. 11:25), He saith, "I thank Thee, O Father, Lord of heaven and earth, because Thou hast hid these things from the wise and prudent, and hast revealed them unto babes."

We are told (Matt. 18:3), "Except ye be converted, and become as little children," etc. As if He had said, you strive for preëminence and worldly greatness in My kingdom; I tell you My kingdom is a kingdom of babes, and containeth none but the humble and such as are little in their own eyes, and are contented to be small and despised in the eyes of others, and so do not seek after great matters in the world. THOS. MANTON

The work that is done in love loses half its tedium and difficulty. It is as with a stone, which in the air and on the dry ground we strain at but cannot stir. Flood the field where it lies, bury the block beneath the rising water; and now, when its head is submerged, bend to the work. Put your strength to it. Ah! it moves, rises from its bed, rolls on before your arm. So, when under the heavenly influences of grace, the tide of love rises, and goes swelling over our duties and difficulties, a child can do a man's work, and a man can do a giant's. THOS. GUTHRIE

Do not all as much and more wonder at God's rare workmanship in the ant, the poorest bug that creeps, as in the biggest elephant? That so many parts and limbs should be united in such a little space; that so poor a creature should provide in the summer-time for her winter food? DANIEL ROGERS

*That Thou mightest still the enemy and the avenger.* This very confusion and revenge upon Satan, who was the cause of man's fall, was aimed at by God at first; therefore is the first promise and preaching of the Gospel to Adam brought in rather in sentencing him than in speaking to Adam, that the seed of the woman should break the serpent's head, it being in God's aim as much to confound him as to save poor man. THOS. GOODWIN

Vs. 3. *When I consider Thy heavens, the work of Thy fingers, the moon and the stars, which Thou hast ordained.* The carnal mind sees God in nothing, not even in spiritual things, His Word and ordinances. The spiritual mind sees Him in everything, even in natural things, in looking on the heavens and the earth and all the creatures. ROBERT LEIGHTON

Could we transport ourselves above the moon, could we reach the highest star above our heads, we should instantly discover new skies, new stars, new suns, new systems, and perhaps more magnificently adorned. But even there, the vast dominions of our great Creator would not terminate; we should then find, to our astonishment, that we had only arrived at the borders of the works of God.

How admirable are those celestial bodies! I am dazzled with their splendor and enchanted with their beauty! But notwithstanding this, however beautiful, and however richly adorned, yet this sky is void of intelligence. It is a stranger to its own beauty, while I, who am mere clay, moulded by a divine hand, am endowed with sense and reason. CHRISTOPHER CHRISTIAN STURM'S *Reflections.*

Vs. 4. *What is man, that Thou art mindful of him? and the son of man, that Thou visitest him?* Perhaps there are no rational beings throughout the universe among whom pride would appear more unseemly or incompatible than in man, considering the situation in which he is placed. He is exposed to numerous degradations and calamities, to the rage of storms and tempests, the devastations of earthquakes and volcanoes, the fury of whirlwinds, and the tempestuous billows of the ocean, to the ravages of the sword, famine, pestilence, and numerous diseases; and at length he must sink into the grave, and his body must become the companion of worms! The most dignified and haughty of the sons of men are liable to these and similar degradations as well as the meanest of the human family. Yet, in such circumstances, man—that puny worm of the dust, whose knowledge is so limited, and whose follies are so numerous and glaring—has the effrontery to strut in all the haughtiness of pride, and to glory in his shame.

Dr. Chalmers, in his *Astronomical Discourses,* very truthfully says, "We gave you but a feeble image of our comparative insignificance, when we said that the glories of an extended forest would suffer no more from the fall of a single leaf, than the glories of this extended universe would suffer though the globe we tread upon, 'and all that it inherits, should dissolve.' " C. H. S.

This is a marvelous thing, that God thinks upon men and remembers them continually. JOHN CALVIN

Shall such a loathsome creature as I find favor in His eyes? In Ezek. 16:1-5, we have a relation of the wonderful condescension of God to man, who is there resembled to a wretched infant cast out in the day of its birth, in his blood and filthiness, no eye pitying it; such loathsome creatures are we before God; and yet when He passed by and saw us polluted in our blood, He said unto us, "Live." JAMES JANEWAY

Ask the prophet Isaiah, "What is man?" and he answers (40:6), man is "grass"—"all flesh is grass, and all the goodliness thereof is as the flower of the field." Ask David, "What is man?" He answers (Psalm 62:9), man is "a lie," not a liar only, or a deceiver, but "a lie," and a deceit. The sinful nature of man is an enemy to the nature of God and would pull God out of heaven; yet God even at that time is raising man to heaven; sin would lessen the great God, and yet God greatens sinful man. JOS. CARYL

Oh, the grandeur and littleness, the excellence and the corruption, the majesty and meanness of man! PASCAL

Vs. 5. *For Thou hast made him a little lower than the angels.* In order of dignity, man stood next to the angels, and a little lower than they; in the Lord Jesus this was accomplished, for He was made a little lower than the angels by the suffering of death. C. H. S.

It is a mysterious thing, and one to which we scarcely dare allude, that there has arisen a Redeemer of fallen men, but not of fallen angels. We would build no theory on so awful and inscrutable a truth; but is it too much to say that the interference on the behalf of man and the non-interference on the behalf of angels, gives ground for the persuasion, that men occupy at least not a lower place than angels in the love and the solicitude of their Maker?

The Redeemer is represented as submitting to be humbled—"made a little lower than the angels"—for the sake or with a view to the glory that was to be the recompense of His sufferings. This is a very important representation—one that should be most attentively considered; and from it may be drawn, we think, a strong and clear argument for the divinity of Christ.

We could never see how it could be humility in any creature, whatever the dignity of his condition, to assume the office of a Mediator and to work out our reconciliation. We do not forget to how extreme degradation a Mediator must consent to be reduced, and through what suffering and ignominy He could alone achieve our redemption; but neither do we forget the unmeasured exaltation which was to be the Mediator's reward, and which, if Scripture be true, was to make Him far higher than the highest of principalities and powers; and we know not where would have been the amazing humility, where the unparalleled condescension, had any mere creature consented to take the office on the prospect of such a recompense. HENRY MELVILL

# PSALM 9

Vs. 1. *I will praise Thee, O Lord.* It sometimes needs all our determination to face the foe and bless the Lord in the teeth of His enemies; vowing that whoever else may be silent we shall bless His name; here however, the overthrow of the foe is viewed as complete and the song flows with sacred fulness of delight. It is our duty to praise the Lord; let us perform it as a privilege.

*With my whole heart.* Half heart is no heart. C. H.S.

Half-heartedness and the depreciation of Divine grace go hand in hand. E. W. HENGSTENBERG

Vs. 1. *I will show forth all Thy marvelous works.* Gratitude for one mercy refreshes the memory as to thousands of others. One silver link in the chain draws up a long series of tender remembrances. Here is eternal work for us, for there can be no end to the showing forth of all His deeds of love. C. H. S.

When we have received any special good thing from the Lord, it is well, according as we have opportunities, to tell others of it. When the woman who had lost one of her ten pieces of silver found the missing portion of her money, she gathered her neighbors and her friends together, saying, "Rejoice with me, for I have found the piece which I had lost."

Who knows so much of the marvelous works of God as His own people? If they be silent, how can we expect the world to see what He has done? Let us not be ashamed to glorify God, by telling what we know and feel He has done; let us watch our opportunity to bring out distinctly the fact of His acting; let us feel delighted at having an opportunity, from our own experience, of telling what must turn to His praise; and them that honor God, God will honor in turn; if we be willing to talk of His deeds, He will give us enough to talk about. P. B. POWER, in *"I Wills" of the Psalms*

Vs. 2. *I will be glad and rejoice in Thee.* God loveth a cheerful giver, whether it be the gold of his purse or the gold of his mouth which he presents upon His altar.

*I will sing praise to Thy Name, O Thou most High.* Songs are the fitting expressions of inward thankfulness, and it were well if we indulged ourselves and honored our Lord with more of them. Mr. B. P. Power has well said, "The sailors give a cheery cry as they weigh anchor, the ploughman whistles in the morning as he drives his team; the milkmaid sings her rustic song as she sets about her early task; when the soldiers are leaving friends behind them, they do not march out to the tune of the 'Dead March in Saul,' but to the quick notes of some lively air. A praising spirit would do for us all that their songs and music do for them; and if only we could determine to praise the Lord, we should surmount many a difficulty which our low spirits never would have been equal to, and we should do double the work which can be done if the heart be languid in its beating, if we be crushed and trodden down in soul. As the evil spirit in Saul yielded in the olden time to the influence of the harp of the son of Jesse, so would the spirit of melancholy often take flight from us, if only we would take up the song of praise." C. H. S.

Vs. 4. *For Thou hast maintained my right and my cause.* If we seek to maintain the cause and honor of our Lord we may suffer reproach and misrepresentation, but it is a rich comfort to remember that He Who sits in the throne knows our hearts and will not leave us to the ignorance and ungenerous judgment of erring man. C. H. S.

Vs. 8. *And He shall judge the world in righteousness, He shall minister judgment to the people in uprightness.* How the prospect of appearing before the impartial tribunal of the Great King should act as a check to us when tempted to sin and as a comfort when we are slandered or oppressed! C. H. S.

Of all things, the guilty conscience cannot abide to hear of this day, for they know that when they hear of it, they hear of their own condemnation. I think if there were a general collection made through the whole world that there might be no judgment-day, then God would be so rich that the world would go a-begging and be a waste wilderness. HENRY SMITH

Vs. 9. *The Lord also will be a refuge for the oppressed, a refuge in times of trouble.* It is reported of the Egyptians that, living in the fens, and being vexed with gnats, they used to sleep in high towers, whereby those creatures not being able to soar so high, they are delivered from the biting of them: so would it be with us when bitten with cares and fear, did we but run to God for refuge and rest confident of His help. JOHN TRAPP

Vs. 10. *And they that know Thy Name will put their trust in Thee.* Faith is an intelligent grace; though there can be knowledge without faith, yet there can be no faith without knowledge. They say ignorance is the mother of devotion; but sure where the sun is set in the understanding, it must needs be night in the affections. So necessary is knowledge to the being of faith, that the Scriptures do sometimes baptize faith with the name of knowledge. Isa. 53:11: "By His knowledge shall My righteous Servant justify many." Knowledge is put there for faith. THOS. WATSON

They can do no otherwise who savingly know God's sweet attributes and noble acts for His people. We never trust a man till we know him, and bad men are better known than trusted. Not so the Lord; for where His name is ointment poured forth, the virgins love Him, rejoice in Him, and repose upon Him. JOHN TRAPP

Vs. 12. *When He maketh inquisition for blood, He remembereth them.* O persecutors, there is a time a-coming when God will make a strict enquiry after the blood of Hooper, Bradford, Latimer, Taylor, Ridley, etc. There is a time a-coming, wherein God will enquire who silenced and suspended such-and-such ministers, and who stopped the months of such-and-such, and who imprisoned, confined, and banished such-and-such, who were once burning and shining lights, and who were willing to spend and be spent that sinners might be saved and that Christ might be glorified. There is a time, when the Lord will make a very narrow enquiry into all the actions and practices of ecclesiastical courts, high commissions, committees, assizes, etc., and deal with persecutors as they have dealt with His people. THOS. BROOKS

There is *vox sanguinis,* a voice of blood; and "He that planted the ear, shall He not hear?" It covered the old world with waters. The earth is filled with cruelty; it was *vox sanguinis* that cried, and the heavens heard the earth, and the windws of heaven opened to let fall judgment and vengeance upon it. EDWARD MARBURY

*He forgetteth not the cry of the humble.* Prayer is a haven to the shipwrecked man, an anchor to them that are sinking in the waves, a staff to the limbs that totter, a mine of jewels to the poor, a healer of diseases, and a guardian of health. Prayer at once secures the continuance of our blessings and dissipates the clouds of our calamities. O blessed prayer! thou art the unwearied conqueror of human woes, the firm foundation of human happiness, the source of ever-enduring joy, the mother of philosophy. The man who can pray truly, though languishing in extremest indigence, is richer than all beside, whilst the wretch who never bowed the knee, though proudly sitting as monarch of all nations, is of all men most destitute. CHRYSOSTOM

Vs. 13. *Have mercy upon me, O Lord.* Just as Luther used to call some texts little Bibles, so we may call this sentence a little prayerbook; for it has in it the soul and marrow of prayer. C. H. S.

Vs. 14. *That I may show forth all Thy praise.* We must not overlook David's object in desiring mercy; it is God's glory. Saints are not so selfish as to look only to self; they desire mercy's diamond that they may let others see it flash and sparkle, and may admire Him who gives such priceless gems to His beloved. C. H. S.

Verses 15-17. It will much increase the torment of the damned in that their torments will be as large and strong as their understandings and affections, which will cause those violent passions to be still working. Were their loss never so great, and their sense of it never so passionate, yet if they could but lose the use of their memory, those passions would die, and that loss being forgotten, would little trouble them. But as they cannot lay by their life and being, though then they would account annihilation a singular mercy, so neither can they lay aside any part of their being. Understanding, conscience, affections, memory, must all live to torment them, which should have helped to their happiness. And as by these they should have fed upon the love of God, and drawn forth perpetually the joys of His presence, so by these must they now feed upon the wrath of God, and draw forth continually the dolours of His absence.

Now they have no leisure to consider, nor any room in their memories for the things of another life. Ah, then they shall have leisure enough, they shall be where they shall have nothing else to do but consider it: their memories shall have no other employment to hinder them; it shall even be engraven upon the tables of their hearts. RICHARD BAXTER

Vs. 16. *The wicked is snared in the work of his own hands.* The wages that sin bargains with the sinner are life, pleasure, and profit; but the wages it pays him with are death, torment, and destruction. He that would understand the falsehood and deceit of sin must compare its promises and its payment together. ROBERT SOUTH

Not only do we read it in the Word of God, but all history, all experience, records the same righteous justice of God in snaring the wicked in the work of their own hands. Perhaps the most striking instance on record, next to Haman on his own gallows, is one connected with the horrors of the French Revolution, in which we are told that, "within nine months of the death of the queen Marie Antoinette by the guillotine, every one implicated in her untimely end, her accusers, the judges, the jury, the prosecutors, the witnesses, all, every one at least whose fate is known, perished by the same instrument as their innocent victim." "In the net which they had laid for her was their own foot taken—into the pit which they digged for her did they themselves fall." BARTON BOUCHIER

Vs. 17. *The wicked shall be turned into hell.* The ungodly at death must undergo God's fury and indignation. I have read of a loadstone in Ethiopia which hath two corners, with one it draws the iron to it, with the other it puts the iron from it: so God hath two hands, of mercy and justice; with the one He will draw the godly to heaven, with the other He will thrust the sinner to hell; and oh, how dreadful is that place! It is called a fiery lake (Rev. 20:15); a lake, to denote the plenty of torments in hell; a fiery lake, to show the fierceness of them: fire is the most torturing element. THOS. WATSON

*And all the nations that forget God.* There are whole nations of such; the forgetters of God are far more numerous than the profane or profligate and according to the very forceful expression of the Hebrew, the nethermost hell will be the place into which all of them shall be hurled headlong. Forgetfulness seems a small sin, but it brings eternal wrath upon the man who lives and dies in it. C. H. S.

Remembrance of Him is the well-spring of virtue; forgetfulness of Him, the fountain of vice. GEORGE HORNE

Vs. 18. *The expectation of the poor shall not perish forever.* A heathen could say, when a bird, scared by a hawk, flew into his bosom, "I will not betray thee unto thy enemy, seeing thou comest for sanctuary unto me." How much less will God yield up a soul unto its enemy, when it takes sanctuary in His name, saying, "Lord, I have no confidence in myself or any other: into Thy hands I commit my cause myself and rely on Thee." This dependence of a soul undoubtedly will awaken the almighty power of God for such a one's defense. He hath sworn the greatest oath that can come out of His blessed lips, even by Himself, that such as thus fly for refuge to hope in Him shall have strong consolation (Heb. 6:17). WM. GURNALL

Vs. 19. *Arise, O Lord; let not man prevail: let the heathen be judged in Thy sight.* What does this mean? Are we to consider the Psalmist as praying for the destruction of his enemies, as pronouncing a malediction, a curse upon them? No; these are not the words of one who is wishing that mischief may happen to his enemies; they are the words of a prophet, of one who is foretelling, in Scripture language, the evil that must befall them on account of their sins. AUGUSTINE

Vs. 20. *That the nations may know themselves to be but men.* One would think that men would not grow so vain as to deny themselves to be but men, but it appears to be a lesson which only a divine Schoolmaster can teach to some proud spirits. Crowns leave their wearers *but men,* degrees of eminent learning make their owners not more than *men,* valor and conquest cannot elevate beyond the dead level of *but men*; and all the wealth of Croesus, the wisdom of Solon, the power of Alexander, the eloquence of Demosthenes, if added together, would leave the possessor but a man. May we ever remember this, lest like those in the text, we should be *put in fear.* C. H. S.

The original is *enosh;* and therefore it is a prayer that they may know themselves to be but miserable, frail, and dying men. The word is in the singular number, but it is used collectively. JOHN CALVIN

# PSALM 10

There is not, in my judgment, a Psalm which describes the mind, the manners, the works, the words, the feelings, and the fate of the ungodly with so much propriety, fulness, and light, as this Psalm. So that, if in any respect there has not been enough said heretofore, or if there shall be anything wanting in the Psalms that shall follow, we may here find a perfect image and representation of iniquity. This Psalm, therefore, is a type, form, and description of that man, who, though he may be in the sight of himself and of men more excellent than Peter himself, is detestable in the eyes of God; and this it was that moved Augustine and those who followed him to understand the Psalm of Antichrist. MARTIN LUTHER

Vs. 1. *Why standest Thou afar off, O Lord?* The presence of God is the joy of His people, but any suspicion of His absence is distracting beyond measure. Let us, then, ever remember that the Lord is nigh us. The refiner is never far from the mouth of the furnace when his gold is in the fire, and the Son of God is always walking in the midst of the flames when His holy children are cast into them. C. H. S.

*Why hidest Thou Thyself in times of trouble?* It is not the trouble, but the hiding of our Father's face, which cuts us to the quick. If we need an answer to the question, "Why hidest Thou Thyself?" it is to be found in the fact that there is a "needs-be," not only for trial, but for heaviness of heart under trial (I Pet. 1:6); but how could this be the case if the Lord should shine upon us while He is afflicting us? Should the parent comfort his child while he is correcting him, where would be the use of the chastening? A smiling face and a rod are not fit companions. God bares the back that the blow may be felt; for it is only *felt* affliction which can become *blest* affliction. If we were carried in the arms of God over every stream, where would be the trial, and where the experience, which trouble is meant to teach us?

If the Lord did not hide Himself it would not be a time of trouble at all. As well ask why the sun does not shine at night when for certain there could be no night if it did. C. H. S.

"Times of trouble" should be times of confidence; fixedness of heart on God would prevent fears of heart. "Trusting in the Lord, his heart is established; he shall not be afraid." Otherwise without it we shall be as light as a weathercock, moved with every blast of evil tidings, our hopes will swim or sink according to the news we hear. Unbelief doth only discourage God from showing His power in taking our part. STEPHEN CHARNOCK

Vs. 2. *The wicked in his pride doth persecute the poor.* The accusation divides itself into two distinct charges—pride and tyranny; the one the root and cause of the other. Pride is the egg of persecution. C. H. S.

"Pride" is a vice which cleaveth so fast unto the hearts of men, that if we were to strip ourselves of all faults one by one, we should undoubtedly find it the very last and hardest to put off. RICHARD HOOKER

*Let them be taken in the devices that they have imagined.* The prayer is reasonable, just, and natural. Even our enemies themselves being judges, it is but right that men should be done by as they wished to do to others. We only weigh you in your own scales, and measure your corn with your own bushel. There are none who will dispute the justice of God when He shall hang every

Haman on his own gallows and cast all the enemies of His Daniels into their own den of lions. C. H. S.

Vs. 3. *For the wicked boasteth of his heart's desire.* The evidence is very full and conclusive upon the matter of pride, and no jury could hesitate to give a verdict against the prisoner at the bar. The first witness testifies that he is a boaster. Bragging sinners are the worst and most contemptible of men, especially when their filthy desires—too filthy to be carried into act—become the theme of their boastings.

*And blesseth the covetous, whom the Lord abhorreth.* Another witness desires to be sworn and heard. This time, the impudence of the proud rebel is even more apparent; for he "blesseth the covetous, whom the Lord abhorreth." This is insolence, which is pride unmasked. The only sinners who are received as respectable are covetous men. If a man is a fornicator, or a drunkard, we put him out of the church; but who ever read of church discipline against that idolatrous wretch—the covetous man? Let us tremble lest we be found to be partakers of this atrocious sin of pride, "blessing the covetous, whom Jehovah abhorreth." C. H. S.

Christ knew what He spake when He said, "No man can serve two masters." As the angel and the devil strove for the body of Moses (Jude 9) not who should have a part, but who should have the whole, so they strive still for our souls, who shall have all. HENRY SMITH

Vs. 4. *The wicked, through the pride of his countenance, will not seek after God.* A brazen face and a broken heart never go together. We are not quite sure that the Athenians were wise when they ordained that men should be tried in the dark lest their countenances should weigh with the judges; for there is much more to be learned from the motions of the muscles of the face than from the words of the lips. Honesty shines in the face, but villainy peeps out at the eyes. C. H. S.

Thousands will die and be damned rather than they will have a pardon upon the sole account of Christ's merits and obedience. When will men be contented with God's way of saving them by the blood of the everlasting covenant? Wilt thou be damned unless thou mayest be thine own Savior? Art thou so proud as that thou wilt not be beholden to God? Thou wilt deserve, or have nothing. What shall I say? Poor thou art, and yet proud; thou hast nothing but wretchedness and misery, and yet thou are talking of a purchase. He that is proud of his clothes and parentage is not so contemptible in God's eyes as he that is proud of his abilities and so scorns to submit to God's methods for His salvation by Christ, and by His righteousness alone. LEWIS STUCKLEY

The pride of the wicked is the principal reason why they will not seek after the knowledge of God. Pride consists in an unduly exalted opinion of oneself. It is, therefore, impatient of a rival, hates a superior, and cannot endure a master. It is evident that nothing can be more painful to a proud heart than the thoughts of such a being as God. Such a being pride can contemplate only with feelings of dread, aversion, and abhorrence. It must look upon Him as its natural enemy, the great enemy, Whom it has to fear.

Pride plunged Satan from heaven into hell; it banished our first parents from paradise; and it will, in a similar manner, ruin all who indulge in it. It keeps us in ignorance of God; shuts us out from His favor; prevents us from resembling Him. Beware of pride! Beware lest you indulge it imperceptibly, for it is perhaps, of all sins, the most secret, subtle, and insinuating. EDWARD PAYSON

*God is not in all his thoughts.* Amid heaps of chaff there was not a grain of wheat. The only place where God is not is in the thoughts of the wicked. This is a damning accusation; for where the God of heaven is not, the lord of hell is reigning and raging; and if God be not in our thoughts, our thoughts will bring us to perdition. C. H. S.

Some read it, "No God in all his crafty, presumptuous purposes"; others, "All his thoughts are, there is no God." THOS. GOODWIN

Trifles possess us, but *God is not in all our thoughts,*—seldom the sole object of them. We have durable thoughts of transitory things and flitting thoughts of a durable and eternal good. STEPHEN CHARNOCK

Vs. 5. *Thy judgments are far above out of His sight.* He looks high but not high enough. As God is forgotten, so are His judgments. He is not able to comprehend the things of God; a swine may sooner look through a telescope at the stars than this man study the Word of God to understand the righteousness of the Lord. C. H. S.

Vs. 6. *He hath said in his heart, I shall not be moved: for I shall never be in adversity.* Oh, impertinence run to seed! The man thinks himself immutable, and omnipotent, too, for he is never to be in adversity. C. H. S.

Pompey, when he had in vain assaulted a city and could not take it by force, devised this strategem in way of agreement: he told them he would leave the siege and make peace with them upon condition that they would let in a few weak, sick, and wounded soldiers among them to be cured. They let in the soldiers, and when the city was secure, the soldiers let in Pompey's army. A carnal, settled security will let in a whole army of lusts into the soul. THOMAS BROOKS

Vs. 7. *His mouth is full of cursing and deceit and fraud.* There is not only a little evil there, but his mouth is full of it. A three-headed serpent hath stowed away its coils and venom within the den of his black mouth. C. H. S.

Vs. 8. *He sitteth in the lurking places of the villages: in the secret place doth he murder the innocent: his eyes are privily set against the poor.* Despite the bragging of this base wretch, it seems that he is as cowardly as he is cruel. He acts the part of the highwayman who springs upon the unsuspecting traveler in some desolate part of the road. C. H. S.

The Arab robber lurks like a wolf among these sand-heaps and often springs out suddenly upon the solitary traveler, robs him in a trice, and then plunges again into the wilderness of sand-hills and reedy downs, where pursuit is fruitless. W. M. THOMPSON in *The Land and the Book*

The extirpation of true religion is the great object of the enemies of truth and righteousness; and there is nothing to which they will not stoop in order to effect that object. JOHN MORRISON

Vs. 9. *He lieth in wait secretly as a lion in his den: he lieth in wait to catch the poor: he doth catch the poor, when he draweth him into his net.* Oppression turns princes into roaring lions and judges into ravening wolves. It is an unnatural sin, against the light of nature. No creatures do oppress them of their own kind. Look upon the birds of prey, as upon eagles, vultures, hawks, and you shall never find them preying upon their own kind. Look upon the beasts of the forest, as upon the lion, the tiger, the wolf, the bear; and you shall ever find them favorable to their own kind; and yet men unnaturally prey upon one another, like the fish in the sea, the great swallowing up the small. THOS. BROOKS

Vs. 10. *He croucheth, and humbleth himself.* You shall see his holiness, the pope, washing the pilgrims' feet, if such a stratagem be necessary to act on the minds of the deluded multitude; or you shall see him sitting on a throne of purple, if he wishes to awe and control the kings of the earth. JOHN MORISON

Vs. 11. *He hath said in his heart, God hath forgotten: He hideth His face: He will never see it.* As upon the former count, so upon this one; a witness is forthcoming who has been listening at the keyhole of the heart. This cruel man comforts himself with the idea that God is blind, or at least forgetful: a fond and foolish fancy, indeed. C. H. S.

The old sins forgotten by men stick fast in an infinite understanding. Time cannot raze out that which hath been known from eternity. Why should they be forgotten many years after they were acted, since they were foreknown in an eternity before they were committed, or the criminal capable to practice them? We may well say that God foreknows nothing that shall be done to the end of the world, as that He forgets anything that hath been done from the beginning of the world. STEPHEN CHARNOCK

God forbears punishing; therefore men forbear repenting. The bee naturally gives honey, but stings only when it is angered. THOS. WATSON

Because justice seems to wink, men suppose her blind; because she delays punishment, they imagine she denies to punish them; because she does not always reprove them for their sins, they suppose she always approves of their sins. But let such know that the silent arrow can destroy as well as the roaring cannon. Though the patience of God be lasting, yet it is not everlasting. WM. SECKER

Vs. 13. *Wherefore doth the wicked contemn God?* In these verses the description of the wicked is condensed, and the evil of his character is traced to its source, viz., atheistic ideas with regard to the government of the world.

*He hath said in his heart, Thou will not require it.* If there were no hell for other men, there ought to be one for those who question the justice of it. C. H. S.

What, do you think that God doth not remember our sins which we do not regard? for while we sin the score runs on, and the Judge setteth down all in the table of remembrance, and His scroll reacheth up to heaven. HENRY SMITH

Vs. 14. *Thou hast seen it; for Thou beholdest mischief and spite, to requite it with Thy hand.* Wanton mischief shall meet with woeful misery, and those who harbor spite shall inherit sorrow. C. H. S.

Vs. 16. *The Lord is King forever and ever: the heathen are perished out of His hand.* Such confidence and faith must appear to the world strange and unaccountable. It is like what his fellow-citizens may be supposed to have felt (if the story be true) toward that man of whom it is recorded, that his powers of vision were so extraordinary, that he could distinctly see the fleet of the Carthaginians entering the harbor of Carthage, while he stood himself at Lilyboeum, in Sicily. A man seeing across an ocean and able to tell of objects so far off, he could feast his vision on what others saw not!

Even thus does faith now stand at its Lilyboeum and see the long-tossed fleet entering safely the desired haven, enjoying the bliss of that still distant day, as if it was already come. ANDREW A. BONAR

Vs. 17. *Lord, Thou hast heard the desire of the humble: Thou wilt prepare their heart, Thou wilt cause Thine ear to hear.* There is a kind of omnipotency in prayer as having an interest and prevalency with God's omnipotency. It hath loosed iron chains (Acts 16:25-26); it hath opened iron gates (Acts 12:5-10); it hath unlocked the windows of heaven (I Kings 18:41); it hath broken the bars of death (John 11:40-43).

Satan hath three titles given in the Scriptures, setting forth his malignity against the church of God: a dragon, to note his malice; a serpent, to note his subtlety; and a lion, to note his strength. But none of all these can stand before prayer. The greatest malice of Haman sinks under the prayer of Esther; the deepest policy, the counsel of Ahithophel, withers before the prayer of David; the largest army, a host of a thousand Ethiopians, run away like cowards before the prayer of Asa. EDW. REYNOLDS

# PSALM 11

David, at the different periods of his life, was placed in almost every situation in which a believer, whether rich or poor, can be placed; in these heavenly compositions, he delineates all the workings of the heart.

To assist us to remember this short but sweet Psalm, we shall give it the name of "the Song of the Stedfast." C. H. S.

David's friends, or those professing to be so, advised him to flee to his native mountains for a time and remain in retirement till the king should show himself more favorable. David does not at that time accept the counsel, though afterwards he seems to have followed it. This Psalm applies itself to the establishment of the church against the calumnies of the world and the compromising counsel of man, in that confidence which is to be placed in God the Judge of all. W. WILSON

Notice how remarkably the whole Psalm corresponds with the deliverance of Lot from Sodom. This verse, with the angel's exhortation, "Escape to the mountains, lest thou be consumed," and Lot's reply, "I cannot escape to the mountains, lest some evil take me and I die" (Gen. 19:17-19). And again, "*The Lord's seat is in heaven, and upon the ungodly He shall rain snares, fire, brimstone, storm, and tempest,*" with "Then the Lord rained upon Sodom and Gomorrah brimstone and fire out of heaven": and again, "*His countenance will behold the thing that is just,*" with "delivered just Lot . . . for that righteous man vexed his righteous soul with their ungodly deeds" (II Pet. 2:7-8). CASSIODORUS in *John Mason Neale's Commentary on the Psalms, from Primitive and Medieval Writers.*

The combatants at the Lake Thrasymene are said to have been so engrossed with the conflict that neither party perceived the convulsions of nature that shook the ground. From a nobler cause, it is thus with the soldiers of the Lamb. They believe and, therefore, make no haste; nay, they can scarcely be said to feel earth's convulsions as other men, because their eager hope presses forward to the issue of the advent of the Lord. ANDREW A. BONAR

Vs. 1-3. These verses contain an account of a temptation to distrust God, with which David was, upon some unmentioned occasion, greatly exercised. It may be, that in the days when he was in Saul's court, he was advised to flee at a time when this flight would have been charged against him as a breach of duty to the king or a proof of personal cowardice. His case was like that of Nehemiah, when his enemies, under the garb of friendship, hoped to entrap him by advising him to escape for his life. C. H. S.

Vs. 1. *In the Lord put I my trust: how say ye to my soul, Flee as a bird to your mountain?* When Satan cannot overthrow us by presumption, how craftily will he seek to ruin us by distrust! He will employ our dearest friends to argue us out of our confidence, and he will use such plausible logic that unless we once for all assert our immovable trust in Jehovah, he will make us like the timid bird which flies to the mountains whenever danger presents itself. C. H. S.

We may observe that David is much pleased with the metaphor in frequently comparing himself to a bird, and that of several sorts: first, to an eagle (Ps.

103:5), "My youth is renewed like the eagle's"; sometimes to an owl (Ps. 102:6), "I am like an owl in the desert"; sometimes to a pelican, in the same verse, "Like a pelican in the wilderness"; sometimes to a sparrow (Ps. 102:7), "I watch, and am as a sparrow"; sometimes to a partridge, "As when one doth hunt a partridge."

Some will say, "How is it possible that birds of so different a feather should all so fly together as to meet in the character of David?" To whom we answer that no two men can more differ one from another than the same servant of God at several times differeth from himself.

Those his words, *Why say ye to my soul, Flee as a bird to your mountain?* import some passion, at leastwise, a disgust of the advice. It is answered, David was not offended with the counsel but with the manner of the propounding thereof. His enemies did it ironically, in a gibing, jeering way, as if his flying thither were to no purpose, and he unlikely to find there the safety he sought for. Thus, when the chief priests mocked our Savior (Matt. 27:43), "He trusted in God, let Him deliver Him now if He will have Him." Christ trusted in God never a whit the less for the fleere and flout which their profaneness was pleased to bestow upon Him. Otherwise, if men's mocks should make us to undervalue good counsel, we might in this age be mocked out of our God, and Christ, and Scripture, and heaven; the apostle Jude, verse 18, having foretold that in the last times there should be mockers, walking after their own lusts. THOMAS FULLER

It is as great an offence to make a new, as to deny the true God. "Whom have I in heaven but thee," amongst those thousands of angels and saints, what Michael or Gabriel, what Moses or Samuel, what Peter, what Paul? "and there is none in earth that I desire in comparison of Thee." JOHN KING

In temptations of inward trouble and terror, it is not convenient to dispute the matter with Satan. RICHARD GILPIN

The shadow will not cool except in it. What good to have the shadow, though of a mighty rock, when we sit in the open sun, to have almighty power engaged for us, and we to throw ourselves out of it, by bold sallies in the mouth of temptation? The saints' falls have been when they have run out of their trench and stronghold; for, like the conies, they are a weak people in themselves, and their strength lies in the rock of God's almightiness, which is their habitation. WILLIAM GURNALL

Vs. 2. *The wicked bend their bow, they make ready their arrow upon the string.* The bow is bent, the arrow is fitted to the string: "Flee, flee, thou defenceless bird, thy safety lies in flight; begone, for thine enemies will send their shafts into thy heart; haste, haste, for soon wilt thou be destroyed!" David seems to have felt the force of the advice, for it came home to his soul; but yet he would not yield, but would rather dare the danger than exhibit a distrust in the Lord, his God. C. H. S.

The plottings of the chief priests and Pharisees that they might take Jesus by subtlety and kill Him: they bent their bow when they hired Judas Iscariot for the betrayal of his Master; they made ready their arrows within the quiver when they sought "false witnesses against Jesus to put Him to death" (Matt. 26:59). MICHAEL AYGAUN, *in J. M. Neale's Commentary*

Vs. 3. *If the foundations be destroyed, what can the righteous do?* Is it possible that the foundations of religion should be destroyed? Can God be in so long a sleep, yea, so long a lethargy, as patiently to permit the ruins thereof? If He looks on, and yet doth not see these foundations when destroyed, where then is His omniscience? If He seeth it, and cannot help it, where then is His omnipotence? If He seeth it, can help it and will not, where then is His goodness and mercy?

We answer negatively that it is impossible that the foundations of religion should ever be totally and finally destroyed, either in relation to the church in general or in reference to every true and lively member thereof. For the reason is that we have an express promise of Christ.—Matt. 16:18: "The gates of hell shall not prevail against it. THOMAS FULLER

*If.* It is the only word of comfort in the text that what is said is not *positive* but *suppositive.* Well, it is good to know the worst of things, that we may provide ourselves accordingly; and therefore let us behold this doleful case, not as doubtful, but as done; not as feared, but felt; not as suspected, but at this time really come to pass. THOMAS FULLER

First a sad case supposed, *If the foundations be destroyed.* Secondly, a sad question propounded, *What can the righteous do?* Thirdly, a sad answer implied, namely, that they can do just nothing, as to the point of reestablishing the destroyed foundation. THOMAS FULLER

His answer to the question, "What can the righteous do?" would be the counter-question, "What cannot they do?" When prayer engages God on our side, and when faith secures the fulfillment of the promise, what cause can there be for flight, however cruel and mighty our enemies? C.H. S.

*What CAN the righteous do?* The *can* of the righteous is a limited *can,* confined to the rule of God's Word; they *can* do nothing but what they *can* lawfully do (II Cor. 13:8). For we *can* do nothing against the truth, but for the truth. Wicked men can do anything; their conscience, which is so wide that it is none at all, will bear them out to act anything how unlawful soever, to stab, poison, massacre, by any means, at any time, in any place, whosoever standeth betwixt them and the effecting of their desires.

Not so the righteous; they have a rule whereby to walk, which they will not, they must not, they dare not, cross. If therefore a righteous man were assured, that by the breach of one of God's commandments he might restore decayed religion and resettle it *statu quo prius,* his hands, head, and heart are tied up, he *can* do nothing, because their damnation is just who say (Rom. 3:8): "Let us do evil that good may come thereof." THOMAS FULLER

Sinning times have ever been the saints' praying times. Yes, this they may and should do, "fast and pray." There is yet a God in heaven to be sought to, when a people's deliverance is thrown beyond the help of human policy or power. WILLIAM GURNALL

Vs. 4. *The Lord is in His holy temple.* The heavens are above our heads in all regions of the earth, and so is the Lord ever near to us in every state and condition. This is a very strong reason why we should not adopt the vile suggestions of distrust. There is One Who pleads His precious blood in our behalf in the temple above, and there is One upon the throne Who is never deaf to the intercession of His Son. Why, then, should we fear? What plots can men devise which Jesus will not discover?

*The Lord's throne is in heaven.* If we trust this King of kings, is not this enough? Cannot He deliver us without our cowardly retreat? Yes, blessed be the Lord our God, we can salute Him as Jehovah-nissi; in His Name we set up our banners, and, instead of flight, we once more raise the shout of war. C. H. S.

*His eyes behold.* God searcheth not as man searcheth, by enquiring into that which before was hid from him; His searching is no more but His beholding; He seeth the heart, He beholdeth the reins; God's very sight is searching. RICHARD ALLEINE

In Rev. 1:14, where Christ is described, it is said, *His eyes are as a flame of fire:* you know the property of fire is to search and make trial of those things which are exposed unto it, and to separate the dross from the pure metal: so, God's eye is like fire, to try and examine the actions of men. He is a God that can look through all those fig-leaves of outward profession and discern the nakedness of your duties through them. EZEKIEL HOPKINS

Take God into thy counsel. Heaven overlooks hell. God at any time can tell thee what plots are hatching there against thee. WILLIAM GURNALL

*His eyelids try the children of men.* He narrowly inspects their actions, words, and thoughts. As men, when intently and narrowly inspecting some very minute object, almost close their eyelids to exclude every other object, so will the Lord look all men through and through. God sees each man as much and as perfectly as if there were no other creature in the universe. C. H. S.

This phrase is a metaphor taken from men, that contract the eyelids when they would wisely and accurately behold a thing: it is not a transient and careless look. STEPHEN CHARNOCK

*His eyelids try, the children of men,* as a judge tries a guilty person with his eye and reads the characters of his wickedness printed in his face. At that great gaol-delivery described in Rev. 6:16, all the prisoners cry out to be hid from the face of Him that sat upon the throne. Wickedness cannot endure to be under the observation of any eye, much less of the eye of justice. It is very hard not to show the guilt of the heart in the face, and it is as hard to have it seen there. JOSEPH CARYL

Vs. 5. *The Lord trieth the righteous.* He doth not hate them, but only tries them. C. H. S.

Except our sins, there is not such plenty of anything in all the world as there is of troubles which come from sin, as one heavy messenger came to Job after another. Since we are not in paradise, but in the wilderness, we must look for one trouble after another. As a bear came to David after a lion, and a giant after a bear, and a king after a giant, and Philistines after a king, so, when believers have fought with poverty, they shall fight with infamy; when they have fought with infamy, they shall fight with sickness; they shall be like a laborer who is never out of work. HENRY SMITH

Vs. 6. *Upon the wicked He shall rain snares.* No snares hold us so fast as those of our own sins; they keep down our heads and stoop us that we cannot look up; a very little ease they are to him that hath not a seared conscience. SAMUEL PAGE

*And an horrible tempest.* Some expositors think that in the term "horrible tempest" there is in the Hebrew an allusion to that burning, suffocating wind, which blows across the Arabian deserts and is known by the name of *simoom.* "A burning storm," Lowth calls it, while another great commentator reads it "wrathwind"; in either version the language is full of terrors.

*This shall be the portion of their cup.* A drop of hell is terrible, but what must a full cup of torment be? Think of it—a cup of misery, but not a drop of mercy. O people of God, how foolish is it to fear the faces of men who shall soon be faggots in the fire of hell. Think of their end, their fearful end, and all fear of them must be changed into contempt of their threatenings and pity for their miserable estate. C. H. S.

Vs. 7. *For the righteous Lord loveth righteousness.* It is not only His office to defend it but His nature to love it.

*His countenance doth behold the upright.* Mammon, the flesh, the devil, will all whisper in our ear, "Flee as a bird to your mountain"; but let us come forth and defy them all. "Resist the devil, and he will flee from you." There is no room or reason for retreat. Advance! Let the vanguard push on! To the front! all ye powers and passions of our soul. On! on! in Gods Name, on! for "the Lord of hosts is with us; the God of Jacob is our refuge." C. H. S.

He looks upon him with a smiling eye, and therefore He cannot favorably look upon an unrighteous person; so that this necessity is not founded only in the command of God that we should be renewed, but in the very nature of the thing, because God, in regard of His holiness, cannot converse with an impure creature. God must change His nature or the sinner's nature must be changed. Wolves and sheep, darkness and light, can never agree. God cannot love a sinner as a sinner, because He hates impurity by a necessity of nature as well as a choice of will. It is as impossible for Him to love it as to cease to be holy. STEPHEN CHARNOCK

## PSALM 12

Title: This Psalm is headed "To the Chief Musician upon Sheminith, a Psalm of David," which title is identical with that of the Sixth Psalm, except that *Neginoth* is here omitted. The subject will be better before the mind's eye if we entitle this Psalm: "Good Thoughts in Bad Times." It is supposed to have been written while Saul was persecuting David and those who favored his cause.

Vs. 1. *Help, Lord.* The Psalmist sees the extreme danger of his position, for a man had better be among lions than among liars; he feels his own inability to deal with such sons of Belial, for "he who shall touch them must be fenced with iron." He therefore turns himself to his all-sufficient Helper, the Lord, Whose help is never denied to His servants and Whose aid is enough for all their needs.

As small ships can sail into harbors which larger vessels, drawing more water, cannot enter, so our brief cries and short petitions may trade with heaven when our soul is wind-bound, and business-bound, as to longer exercises of devotion, and when the stream of grace seems at too low an ebb to float a more laborious supplication. C. H. S.

'Twas high time to call to heaven for help, when Saul cried, "Go, kill me up the priests of Jehovah" (the occasion as it is thought of making this Psalm), and therein committed the sin against the Holy Ghost, as some grave divines are of opinion. JOHN TRAPP

*For the godly man ceaseth.* The death, departure, or decline of godly men should be a trumpet-call for more prayer.

*The faithful fail from among the children of men.* When godliness goes, faithfulness inevitably follows; without fear of God, men have no love of truth. David, amid the general misrule, did not betake himself to seditious plottings, but to solemn petitionings; nor did he join with the multitude to do evil, but took up the arms of prayer to withstand their attacks upon virtue. C. H. S.

Does thy neighbor or thy friend find thee faithful to him? What does our daily intercourse witness? Is not the attempt to speak what is agreeable oft made at the expense of truth. CHARLES BRIDGES

Vs. 2. *They speak vanity every one with his neighbor.* Compliments and fawning congratulations are hateful to honest men; they know that if they take they must give them, and they scorn to do either.

*With flattering lips and with a double heart do they speak.* He who puffs up another's heart has nothing better than wind in his own. C. H. S.

There is no such stuff to make a cloak of as religion; nothing so fashionable, nothing so profitable: it is a livery wherein a wise man may serve two masters, God and the world, and make a gainful service by either. I serve both, and in both myself, by prevaricating with both. Before man none serves his God with more severe devotion; for which, among the best of men, I work my own ends, and serve myself. In private, I serve the world; not with so strict devotion, but with more delight; where fulfilling of her servants' lusts, I work my end and serve myself.

The house of prayer, who more frequents than I? In all Christian duties, who more forward than I? I fast with those who fast that I may eat with those that eat. I mourn with those that mourn. No hand more open to the cause than mine, and in their families none prays longer and with louder zeal. Thus when the opinion of a holy life hath cried the goodness of my conscience up, my trade can lack no custom, my wares can want no price, my words can need no credit, my actions can lack no praise.

If I am covetous, it is interpreted providence; if miserable, it is counted temperance; if melancholy, it is construed godly sorrow; if merry, it is voted spiritual joy; if I be rich, it is thought the blessing of a godly life; if poor, supposed the fruit of conscionable dealing; if I be well spoken of, it is the merit of holy conversation; if ill, it is the malice of malignants.

Thus I sail with every wind, and have my end in all conditions. This cloak in summer keeps me cool, in winter warm, and hides the nasty bag of all my secret lusts. Under this cloak I walk in public fairly with applause, and in private sin securely without offence, and officiate wisely without discovery. I compass sea and land to make a proselyte; and no sooner made, but he makes me. At a fast I cry Geneva, and at a feast, I cry Rome.

If I be poor, I counterfeit abundance to save my credit; if rich, I dissemble poverty to save charges. I most frequent schismatical lectures which I find most profitable; from thence learning to divulge and maintain new doctrines; they maintain me in suppers thrice a week. I use the help of a lie sometimes, as a new stratagem to uphold the gospel; and I color oppression with God's judgments executed upon the wicked. Charity I hold an extraordinary duty; therefore not ordinarily to be performed. What I openly reprove abroad, for my own profit, that I secretly act at home, for my own pleasure. But stay, I see a handwriting in my heart which damps my soul. It is charactered in these sad words, "Woe be to you, hypocrites" (Matt. 23:13). FRANCIS QUARLES' *Hypocrite's Soliloquy*

The world indeed says that society could not exist if there were perfect truthfulness and candor between man and man; but, oh, what a picture does it present of the social edifice, that its walls can be cemented and kept together only by flattery and falsehood! BARTON BOUCHIER

The philosopher Bion, being asked what animal he thought the most hurtful, replied, "That of wild creatures, a tyrant, and of tame ones, a flatterer." *The Book of Symbols*

*They speak with a double heart.* The original is, "A heart and a heart"; one for the church, another for the change; one for Sundays, another for working-days; one for the king, another for the pope. A man without a heart is a wonder, but a man with two hearts is a monster. It is said of Judas, "There were many hearts in one man": and we read of the saints, "There was one heart in many men" (Acts 4:32). A special blessing! THOMAS ADAMS

When men cease to be faithful to their God, he who expects to find them so to each other will be much disappointed. GEORGE HORNE

Vs. 3. *The Lord shall cut off all flattering lips, and the tongue that speaketh proud things.* Strange it is that the easy yoke of the Lord should so gall the shoulders of the proud, while the iron bands of Satan they bind about themselves as chains of honor.

One generally imagines that flatterers are such mean parasites, so cringing and fawning, that they cannot be proud; but the wise man will tell you that while all pride is truly meanness, there is in the very lowest meanness no small degree of pride. Caesar's horse is even more proud of carrying Caesar than Caesar is of riding him. None are so detestably domineering as the little creatures who creep into offices by cringing to the great; those are bad times, indeed, in which these obnoxious beings are numerous and powerful. C. H. S.

Vs. 4. *Who have said, With our tongue will we prevail.* From the time of Tertullus to that of Julian the Apostate, every species of oratory, learning, wit, was lavished against the church of God. MICHAEL AYGUAN, in *J. M. Neale's Commentary*

*Our lips are our own.* If we have to do with God, we must quit claim to ourselves and look on God as our owner. JOHN HOWE

Vs. 5. *The oppression of the poor.* Poverty and want and misery should be motives to pity; but oppressors make them the whetstones of their cruelty and severity, and therefore the Lord will plead the cause of His poor, oppressed people against their oppressors without fee or fear; yea, He will plead their cause with pestilence, blood, and fire. THOMAS BROOKS

Vs. 6. *The words of the Lord are pure words: as silver tried in a furnace of earth, purified seven times.* Man's words are yea and nay, but the Lord's promises are yea and amen. In the original there is an allusion to the most severely purifying process known to the ancients, through which silver was passed when the greatest possible purity was desired; the dross was all consumed, and only the bright and precious metal remained; so clear and free from all alloy of error or unfaithfulness is the book of the words of the Lord. The Bible has passed through the furnace of persecution, literary criticism, philosophic doubt, and scientific discovery, and has lost nothing but those human interpretations which clung to it as alloy to precious ore. C. H. S.

They that purify silver to the purpose used to put it in the fire again and again, that it may be thoroughly tried. The doctrine of God's free grace hath been tried over, and over, and over again. Pelagius begins, and he mingles his dross with it: he saith, grace is nothing but nature in man. Well, his doctrine was purified, and a great deal of dross purged out.

Then come the semi-Pelagians, and they part stakes; they say, nature can do nothing without grace, but they make nature to concur with grace, and to have an influence as well as grace; and the dross of that was burnt up. The Papists take up the same quarrel, but will neither be Pelagians nor semi-Pelagians, yet still mingle dross.

The Arminians come and they refine popery in that point anew; still they mingle dross. God will have this truth tried seven times in the fire, till He hath brought it forth as pure as pure may be. And I say it is because that truth is thus precious. THOMAS GOODWIN

The Scripture is the sun; the church is the clock. The sun we know to be sure, and regularly constant in his motions; the clock, as it may fall out, may go too fast or too slow. As then, we should condemn him of folly that should profess to trust the clock rather than the sun, so we cannot but justly tax the credulity of those who would rather trust to the church than to the Scripture. BISHOP HALL

"When Voltaire reads a book, he makes it what he pleases, and then writes against what he has made," says Montesquieu of Voltaire. GARDINER SPRING

"The Word of the Lord is tried; he is a buckler to all those that trust in him" (Prov. 30:5); as pure gold suffers no loss by the fire, so the promises suffer no loss when they are tried, but stand to us in our greateset troubles. THOMAS MANTON

Vs. 8. *The wicked walk on every side, when the vilest men are exalted.* As a warm sun brings out noxious flies, so does a sinner in honor foster vice everywhere. C. H. S.

# PSALM 13

We have been wont to call this the "How-Long Psalm." We had almost said the Howling Psalm, from the incessant repetition of the cry, "How long?"

Vs. 1. *How long?* This question is repeated no less than four times. It betokens very intense desire for deliverance and great anguish of heart. And what if there be some impatience mingled therewith; is not this the more true a portrait of our own experience? It is not easy to prevent desires from degenerating into impatience. Long sorrow seems to argue abounding corruption; for the gold which is long in the fire must have had much dross to be consumed; hence the question "How long?" may suggest deep searching of the heart.

*How long wilt Thou forget me?* Ah, David! how like a fool thou talkest! Can God forget? Can Omniscience fail in memory? Above all, can Jehovah's heart forget His own beloved child? Ah, brethren, let us drive away the thought, and hear the voice of our covenant God by the mouth of the prophet, "Behold, I have graven thee upon the palms of My hands; thy walls are continually before Me."

*Forever.* Oh, dark thought! It was surely bad enough to suspect a temporary forgetfulness, but shall we ask the ungracious question and imagine that the Lord will forever cast away His people? No, His anger may endure for a night, but His love shall abide eternally. C. H. S.

*How long wilt Thou hide Thy face from me?* What is that accursed thing in our hearts or in our lives for which God hides His face and frowns upon us? TIMOTHY ROGERS

As night and shadows are good for flowers, and moonlight and dews are better than continual sun, so is Christ's absence of special use, and that it hath some nourishing virtue in it, and giveth sap to humility, and putteth an edge on hunger, and furnisheth a fair field to faith to put forth itself, and to exercise its fingers in gripping it seeth not what, that I know. SAMUEL RUTHERFORD

Verses 1-2. That which the French proverb hath of sickness is true of all evils, that they come on horseback and go away on foot. JOSEPH HALL.

The Christian, while in this world, lives in an unwholesome climate; one while, the delights of it deaden and dull his love to Christ; another while, the trouble he meets in it damps his faith on the promise. WILLIAM GURNALL

Vs. 2. *How long?* There are many situations of the believer in this life in which the words of this Psalm may be a consolation and help to revive sinking faith. A certain man lay at the Pool of Bethesda who had an infirmity thirty and eight years (John 5:5). A woman had a spirit of infirmity eighteen years, before she was "loosed" (Luke 13:11). Lazarus, all his life long labored under disease and poverty, till he was released by death and transferred to Abraham's bosom (Luke 16:20-22). Let everyone, then, who may be tempted to use the complaints of this Psalm, assure his heart that God does not forget His people, help will come at last, and, in the meantime, all things shall work together for good to them that love Him. W. WILSON

Thus the careful reader will remark that the question, "How long?" is put in four shapes. The writer's grief is viewed, as it seems to be, as it is, as it affects himself within, and his foes without. We are all prone to play most on the worst string. We set up monumental stones over the graves of our joys, but who thinks of erecting monuments of praise for mercies received? We write four books of Lamentations and only one of Canticles, and are far more at home in wailing out a *Miserere* than in chanting a *Te Deum.*

Vs. 5. *But I have trusted in Thy mercy; my heart shall rejoice in Thy salvation.* What a change is here! Lo, the rain is over and gone, and the time of the singing of birds is come. David's heart was more often out of tune than his harp. He begins many of his Psalms sighing, and ends them singing. C. H. .S

Vs. 6. *I will sing unto the Lord, because He hath dealt bountifully with me.* The world wonders how we can be so merry under such extreme miseries; but our God is Omnipotent, Who turns misery into felicity. Believe me, there is no such joy in the world as the people of God have under the cross of Christ. I speak by experience, and therefore, believe me, and fear nothing that the world can do unto you, for when they imprison our bodies, they set our souls at liberty to converse with God; when they cast us down, they lift us up; when they kill us, then do they send us to everlasting life. What greater glory can there be than to be made conformable to our head, Christ? And this is done by affliction. Oh good God, what am I, upon whom Thou shouldest bestow so great a mercy? JOHN TRAPP

I never knew what it was for God to stand by me at all turns, and at every offer of Satan to afflict me, etc., as I have found Him since I came in hither; for look how fears have presented themselves, so have supports and encouragements; yea, when I have started even as it were at nothing else but my shadow, yet God, as being very tender of me, hath not suffered me to be molested, but would with one Scripture or another strengthen me against all; insomuch that I have often said, Were it lawful, I could pray for greater trouble, for the greater comfort's sake. JOHN BUNYAN

# PSALM 14

As no distinguishing title is given to this Psalm, we would suggest as an assistance to the memory, the heading "Concerning Practical Atheism." C. H. S.

There is a peculiar mark put upon this Psalm, in that it is twice in the Book of Psalm. The Fourteenth Psalm and the Fifty-Third Psalm are the same, with the alteration of one or two expressions at most. JOHN OWEN

Vs. 1. *The fool.* The atheist is the fool preëminently and a fool universally. He would not deny God if he were not a fool by nature, and having denied God it is no marvel that he becomes a fool in practice. Sin is always folly, and as it is the height of sin to attack the very existence of the Most High, so is it also the greatest imaginable folly. One fool makes hundreds, and a noisy blasphemer spreads his horrible doctrines as lepers spread the plague.

Ainsworth, in his *Annotations,* tells us that the word here used is *Nabal,* which has the signification of fading, dying, or falling away, as a withered leaf or flower; it is a title given to the foolish man as having lost the juice and sap of wisdom, reason, honesty, and godliness. Trapp hits the mark when he calls him "that sapless fellow, that carcass of a man, that walking sepulcher of himself, in whom all religion and right reason is withered and wasted, dried up and decayed." Some translate it the *apostate,* and others *the wretch.* With what earnestness we should shun the appearance of doubt as to the presence, activity, power, and love of God, for all such mistrust is of the nature of folly, and who among us would wish to be ranked with the fool in the text? Yet let us not forget that all unregenerate men are more or less such fools. C. H. S.

*"The fool,"* a term in Scripture signifying a wicked man, is used also by the heathen philosophers to signify a vicious person. It also signifies the extinction of life in men, animals, and plants; so the word is taken (Isa. 40:7), "the flower fadeth" (Isa. 28:1), a plant that hath lost all that juice that made it lovely and useful. So, a fool is one that hath lost his wisdom and right notion of God and divine things, which were communicated to man by creation; one dead in sin, yet one not so much void of rational faculties as of grace in those faculties; not one that wants reason but abuses his reason. STEPHEN CHARNOCK

*The fool hath said in his heart, There is no God.* How terrible the depravity which makes the whole race adopt this as their hearts' desire, "no God!" C. H. S.

The devils believe and acknowledge four articles of our faith (Matt. 8:29): (1) They acknowledge God; (2) Christ; (3) the day of judgment; (4) that they shall be tormented then; so that he that does not believe that there is a God is more vile than a devil. To deny there is a God is a sort of atheism that is not to be found in hell.

*On earth are atheists many,*
*In hell there is not any.*

—T. BROOKS

A man may better believe there is no such man as himself and that he is not in being, than that there is no God; for himself can cease to be, and once was not, and shall be changed from what he is, and in very many periods of his life knows not that he is; and so it is every night with him when he sleeps; but none of these can happen to God; and if he knows it not, he is a fool.

In distresses, the atheist must be of all creatures the most helpless and forlorn. About thirty years ago, I was a shipboard with one of these vermin, when there arose a brisk gale, which could frighten nobody but himself. Upon the rolling of the ship he fell upon his knees and confessed to the chaplain that he had been a vile atheist and had denied a supreme Being ever since he came to his estate.

The good man was astonished, and a report immediately ran through the ship that there was an atheist upon the upper deck. Several of the common seamen, who had never heard the word before, thought it had been some strange fish; but they were more surprised when they saw it was a man and heard out of his own mouth "that he never believed till that day that there was a God."

As he lay in the agonies of confession, one of the honest tars whispered to the boatswain "that it would be a good deed to heave him overboard." But we were now within sight of port, when of a sudden the wind fell, and the penitent relapsed, begging of all of us that were present as we were gentlemen not to say anything of what had passed.

He had not been ashore above two days when one of the company began to rally him upon his devotion on shipboard, which the other denied in so high terms that it produced the lie on both sides and ended in a duel. The atheist was run through the body, and after some loss of blood, became as good a Christian as he was at sea till he found that his wound was not mortal. He is at present one of the age and now writing a pamphlet against several received opinions concerning the existence of fairies. JOSEPH ADDISON, *in The Tattler.*

*The owlet, Atheism,*
*Sailing on obscene wings across the Moon,*
*Drops his blue-fringed lids, and shuts them close,*
*And hooting at the glorious sun in heaven,*
*Cries out, "Where is it?"*

—SAMUEL TAYLOR COLERIDGE.

So the text yields these three points: Who is he? A *fool.* What he saith? *No God.* How he speaks it: *In his heart.* It is not the natural but the moral fool that David means, the wicked and ungracious person, for so is the sense of the original term. What hath this fool done? Surely nothing; he hath only said. What hath he *said?* Nay, nothing either; he hath only *thought:* for to *say in heart,* is but to *think.* RICHARD CLERKE (*one of the translators of our English Bible*)

*There is none that doeth good.* Save only where grace reigns, there is none that doeth good; humanity, fallen and debased, is a desert without an oasis, a night without a star, a dunghill without a jewel, a hell without a bottom. C. H. S.

Vs. 3. *They are altogether become filthy.* The only reason why we do not more clearly see this foulness is because we are accustomed to it, just as those who work daily among offensive odors at last cease to smell them. C. H. S.

*Nothing is left, nothing, for future times*
*To add to the full catalogue of crimes;*
*The baffled sons must feel the same desires,*
*And act the same mad follies as their sires,*
*Vice has attained its zenith.*

—JUVENAL, *Sat. 1*

He has put it positively, he repeats it negatively, *There is none that doeth good, no, not one.* The Holy Spirit is not content with saying all and altogether, but adds the crushing threefold negative, *none, no, not one.*

Vs. 4. *Who eat up my people as they eat bread.* As pikes in a pond eat up little fish, as eagles prey on smaller birds, as wolves rend the sheep of the pasture, so sinners naturally and as a matter of course, persecute, malign, and mock the followers of the Lord Jesus. C. H. S.

Wicked men will run the hazard of damning their own souls rather than not fling a dagger at the apple of God's eye. LEWIS STUCKLEY

When you can find a serpent without a sting, or a leopard without spots, then you may expect to find a wicked world without hatred to the saints. If the world hated Christ, no wonder that it hates us. "The world hated Me before it hated you" (John 15:18). Why should any hate Christ? This blessed Dove had no gall, this Rose of Sharon did send forth a most sweet perfume; but this shows the world's baseness, it is a Christ-hating and a saint-eating world. THOMAS WATSON

Vs. 6. *Ye have shamed the counsel of the poor, because the Lord is his refuge.* This sweetly illustrates God's care of His poor, not merely the poor in spirit, but literally the poor and lowly ones, the oppressed and the injured. It is this character of God which is so conspicuously delineated in His Word. We may look through all the Shasters and Vedas of the Hindoo, the Koran of the Mahomedan, the legislation of the Greek, and the code of the Roman, aye, and the Talmud of the Jew, the bitterest of all; and not in one single line or page shall we find a trace of that tenderness, compassion, or sympathy for the wrongs, and oppressions, and trials, and sorrows of God's poor, which the Christian's Bible evidences in almost every page. BARTON BOUCHIER

The wise man trusts in his wisdom, the strong man in his strength, the rich man in his riches; but this trusting in God is the foolishest thing in the world. JOHN OWEN

Vs. 7. *Oh that the salvation of Israel were come out of Zion! when the Lord bringeth back the captivity of His people, Jacob shall rejoice, and Israel shall be glad.* Natural enough is this closing prayer, for what would so effectually convince atheists, overthrow persecutors, stay sin, and secure the godly, as the manifest appearance of Israel's great salvation? The coming of Messiah was the desire of the godly in all ages, and though He has already come with a sin-offering to purge away iniquity, we look for Him to come a second time, to come without a sin-offering unto salvation. C. H. S.

Affliction is as it were the sauce of prayer, as hunger is unto meat. Truly their prayer is usually unsavory who are without afflictions, and many of them do not pray truly, but do rather counterfeit a prayer, or pray for custom. WOLFGANG MUSCULUS

*The captivity* of our souls to the law of concupiscence, of our bodies to the law of death; the captivity of our senses to fear; the captivity, the conclusion of which is so beautifully expressed by one of our greatest poets, namely, GILES FLETCHER, in his *Christ's Triumph Over Death:*

*No sorrow now hangs clouding on their brow;*
*No bloodless malady impales their face;*
*No age drops on their heads his silver snow;*
*No nakedness their bodies doth embase;*
*No poverty themselves and theirs disgrace;*
*No fear of death the joy of life devours;*
*No unchaste sleep their precious time deflowers;*
*No loss, no grief, no change, wait on their wingèd hours.*

—JOHN MASON NEALE, *in loc.*

## PSALM 15

This Psalm of David bears no dedicatory title at all indicative of the occasion upon which it was written, but it is exceedingly probable that, together with the Twenty-Fourth Psalm, to which it bears a striking resemblance, its composition was in some way connected with the removal of the ark to the holy hill of Zion.

We shall call the Psalm, "The Question and Answer." The first verse asks the question; the rest of the verses answer it.

Vs. 1. *Lord, who shall abide in Thy tabernacle? who shall dwell in Thy holy hill?* Where angels bow with veiled faces, how shall man be able to worship at all? C. H. S.

*Now, who is he? Say, if you can,*
*Who so shall gain the firm abode?*
*Pilate shall say, "Behold the Man!"*
*And John, "Behold the Lamb of God!"*

—JOHN BARCLAY, *quoted by A. A. Bonar, in loc.*

Vs. 2. *He that walketh uprightly, and worketh righteousness, and speaketh the truth in his heart.* Observe the accepted man's *walk, work,* and *word.* Walking is of far more importance than talking. He only is right who is upright in walk and downright in honesty. His faith shows itself by good works, and therefore is no dead faith. God's house is a hive for workers, not a nest for drones. C. H. S.

When the wheels of a clock move within, the hands on the dial will move without. When the heart of a man is sound in conversion, then the life will be fair in profession. When the conduit is walled in, how shall we judge of the spring but by the waters which run through the pipes. WILLIAM SECKER

*And worketh righteousness.* A righteous man may make a righteous work, but no work of an unrighteous man can make him righteous. THOMAS BOSTON

Jacob's ladder had stairs, upon which he saw none standing still, but all either ascending, or else descending by it. Ascend you likewise to the top of the ladder, to heaven, and there you shall hear one say, "My Father doth now work, and I work also." THOMAS PLAYFERE

But here observe, David saith, "that worketh righteousness"; not that talks about, thinks about, or hears of, righteousness; because "not the hearers of the law, but the doers of the law, shall be justified." The only work that we must hope will be considered and accounted of, is the work of righteousness: all other works that either urge or allure us on under a show of godliness, are a thing of nought. MARTIN LUTHER

*And speaketh the truth in his heart.* Anatomists have observed that the tongue in man is tied with a double string to the heart. THOMAS BOSTON

I am thankful for any conviction and sense I have of the evil of lying; Lord, increase my abhorrence of it. I would endeavor to cleanse myself from all filthiness: there never will be a mortified tongue while there is an unmortified heart. BENJAMIN BENNET'S *"Christian Oratory"*

Vs. 3. *He that backbiteth not with his tongue, nor doeth evil to his neighbor, nor taketh up a reproach against his neighbor.* All slanderers are the devil's bellows to blow up contention, but those are the worst which blow at the back of the fire.

Trapp says that "the tale-bearer carrieth the devil in his tongue, and the tale-hearer carries the devil in his ear."

"Show that man out!" we should say of a drunkard, yet it is very questionable if his unmannerly behavior will do us so much mischief as the tale-bearer's insinuating story. "Call for a policeman!" we say if we see a thief at his business; ought we to feel no indignation when we hear a gossip at her work? "Mad dog! Mad dog!" is a terrible hue and cry, but there are few curs whose bite is so dangerous as a busybody's tongue. "Fire! fire!" is an alarming note, but the tale-bearer's tongue is set on fire of hell, and those who indulge it had better mend their manners or they may find that there is fire in hell for unbridled tongues. C. H. S.

And this were the more tolerable if it were only the fault of ungodly men, of strangers and enemies of religion; for so saith the proverb, "Wickedness proceedeth from the wicked." When a man's heart is full of hell, it is not unreasonable to expect that his tongue should be set on fire of hell; and it is no wonder to hear such persons reproach good men, yea, even for their goodness. But alas! the disease doth not rest here, this plague is not only among the Egyptians but Israelites, too. Pity your brethren; let it suffice that godly ministers and Christians are loaded with reproaches by wicked men—there is no need that you should combine with them in this diabolical work. MATTHEW POOLE

The viper woundeth none but such as it biteth; the venomous herbs or roots kill none but such as taste, or handle, or smell them, and so come near unto them; but the poison of slanderous tongues is much more rank and deadly; for that hurteth and slayeth, woundeth and killeth, not only near, but afar off; not only at hand, but by distance of place removed; not only at home, but abroad; not only in our own nation, but in foreign countries; and spareth neither quick nor dead. RICHARD TURNBULL

Verses 3, 4, 5. What care I to see a man run after a sermon, if he cozens and cheats as soon as he comes home? He that has not religion to govern his morality is not a dram better than my mastiff-dog; so long as you stroke him, and please him, and do not pinch him, he will play with you as finely as may be, he is a very good moral mastiff; but if you hurt him, he will fly in your face, and tear out your throat. JOHN SELDON

Vs. 4. *In whose eyes a vile person is contemned; but he honoreth them that fear the Lord.* A sinner in a golden chain and silken robes is no more to be compared with a saint in rags than a rushlight in a silver candlestick with the sun behind a cloud. C. H. S.

To contemn the wicked and honor the godly are opposite the one to the other. God hateth no man, nay, He hateth nothing at all in this whole universal world, but only sin. PETER BARO

Augustine, as Posidonius writeth, showing what hatred he had to tale-bearers and false reporters of others, had two verses written over his table; by translation these:

> *He that doth love with bitter speech the absent to defame,*
> *Must surely know that at this board no place is for the same.*
>
> —RICHARD TURNBULL

*He that sweareth to his own hurt, and changeth not.*

> *His words are bonds, his oaths are oracles;*
> *His love sincere, his thoughts immaculate;*
> *His tears pure messengers, sent from his heart;*
> *His heart as far from fraud as heaven from earth.*
>
> —WILLIAM SHAKESPEARE

Vs. 5. *The sorrows of hell compassed me about.* The Puritanic divines are almost all of them against the taking of any interest upon money and go the length of saying that one penny per cent per annum will shut a man out of heaven if persisted in. The demanding of excessive and grinding interest is a sin to be detested; the taking of the usual and current interest in a commercial country is not contrary to the law of love. C. H. S.

By usury is generally understood the gain of anything above the principal, or that which was lent, exacted only in consideration of the loan, whether it be in money, corn, wares, or the like. It is most commonly taken for an unlawful profit which a person makes of his money or good. ALEXANDER CRUDEN

There is no worse species of usury than an unjust way of making bargains, where equity is disregarded on both sides. Let us, then, remember that all bargains, wherein one party unrighteously strives to make gain by the loss of the other party, whatever name may be given to them, are here condemned.

It may be asked, whether all kinds of usury are to be put into this denunciation and regarded as alike unlawful? If we condemn all without distinction, there is danger lest many, seeing themselves brought into such a strait as to find that sin must be incurred, in whatever way they can turn themselves, may be rendered bolder by despair, and may rush headlong into all kinds of usury without choice or discrimination. On the other hand, whenever we concede that something may be lawfully done in this way, many will give themselves loose reins, thinking that a liberty to exercise usury, without control or moderation has been granted them.

It is not without cause that God has in Lev. 25:35-36, forbidden usury, adding this reason: "And if thy brother be waxen poor, and fallen in decay with thee; then thou shalt relieve him: yea, though he be a stranger, or a sojourner; that he may live with thee. Take thou no usury of him, or increase." We see that the end for which the law was framed was that man should not cruelly oppress the poor, who ought rather to receive sympathy and compassion.

Whence it follows, that the gain which he who lends his money upon interest acquires without doing injury to anyone, is not to be included under the head of unlawful usury. The Hebrew word "*neshek*" which David employs, being derived from another word which signifies *to bite*, sufficiently shows that usuries are condemned in so far as they involve in them, or lead to, a license of robbing or plundering our fellowmen. In short, provided we had engraven on our hearts the rule of equity which Christ prescribes in Matt. 7:12, "Therefore, all things whatsoever ye would that men should do to you, do ye even so to them," it would not be necessary to enter into lengthened dispute concerning usury. JOHN CALVIN, *in loc.*

*He that doeth these things shall never be moved.* 'Tis not he that hears much or talks much of religion; no, nor he that preaches and prays much, nor he that thinks much of these things, and means well; but 'tis he that *doeth these things*—that is actually employed about them—that is the religious and truly godly man.

'Tis not, I say, a formal professor, a confidant solifidian, a wild opinionist, a high-flown perfectist; it is not a constant hearer, or a mighty talker, or a laborious teacher, or a gifted brother, or a simple well-wisher must pass, but 'tis the honest and sincere doer of these things that will abide the test and stand the trial; when all other flashy pretences shall, in those searching flames, be burnt and consumed like "hay and stubble," as the Apostle expresses it.

To wear Christ's livery and to do Him no service is but to mock a gracious Master; to own Him in our profession and deny Him in our practice, is, with

Judas, to betray Him with a kiss of homage; with the rude soldiers to bow the knee before Him, and, in the meantime to beat His sacred head with His reeden scepter, and with Pilate to crown Him with thorns, to crucify the Lord, and write over His head, "King of the Jews": in a word, to grieve Him with our honors and wound Him with our acknowledgments.

A Christian profession without a life answerable will be so far from saving anyone, that 'twill highly aggravate his condemnation; when a dissembled friendship at the great day of discoveries shall be looked upon as the worst of enmities. A mere outside formality of worship is at best but Prometheus' sacrifice, a skeleton of bones and a religious cheat. *Condensed from* ADAM LITTLETON

For were it enough to read or hear these precepts, then should an infinite number of vain and wicked persons enter into, and continue in the church, which notwithstanding have no place therein; for there are very few, or none at all, which have not read, or at least have not heard these things, yet they will not do them. RICHARD TURNBULL

# PSALM 16

Title: Michtam of David." This is usually understood to mean the Golden Psalm. Ainsworth calls it "David's jewel, or notable song," The Psalm of the Precious Secret.

We are not left to human interpreters for the key to this golden mystery, for, speaking by the Holy Ghost, Peter tells us, "David speaketh concerning Him" (Acts 2:25). The Apostle Paul, led by the same infallible inspiration, quotes from this Psalm and testifies that David wrote of the man through whom is preached unto us the forgiveness of sins (Acts 13:35-38). It has been the usual plan of commentators to apply the Psalm both to David, to the saints, and to the Lord Jesus, but we shall venture to believe that in it "Christ is all"; since in the ninth and tenth verses, like the apostles on the mount, we can see "no man but Jesus only." C. H. S.

Vs. 1. *"Preserve me,"* keep, or save me, or as Horsley thinks, "guard me," even as body-guards surround their monarch, or as shepherds protect their flocks. One of the great names of God is "the Preserver of men" (Job 7:20), and this gracious office the Father exercised toward our Mediator and Representative. It had been promised to the Lord Jesus in express words, that He should be preserved (Isa. 49:7-8). C. H. S.

Vs. 2. *O my soul, thou hast said unto the Lord, Thou art my Lord.* In His inmost heart, the Lord Jesus bowed Himself to do service to His heavenly Father, and before the throne of Jehovah His soul vowed allegiance to the Lord for our sakes. C. H. S.

*My goodness extended not to Thee.* Although the life-work and death agony of the Son did reflect unparalleled luster upon every attribute of God, yet the Most Blessed and Infinitely Happy God stood in no need of the obedience and death of His Son; it was for our sakes that the work of redemption was undertaken and not because of any lack or want on the part of the Most High. How modestly does the Savior here estimate His own goodness! C. H. S.

I think the words should be understood of what the Messiah was doing for men. My goodness, *tobhathi,* "my bounty" is not to Thee. What I am doing can add nothing to Thy Divinity; Thou art not providing this astonishing sacrifice because Thou canst derive any excellence from it; but this bounty extends to the saints—to all the spirit of just men made perfect, whose bodies are still in the earth; and to the excellent, *addirey,* "the noble or supereminent ones," those who through faith and patience inherit the promises. ADAM CLARKE

Oh, what shall I render unto Thee, my God, for all Thy benefits toward me? What shall I repay? Alas! I can do Thee no good, for mine imperfect goodness cannot pleasure Thee Who art most perfect and goodness itself; my well-doing can do Thee no good, my wickedness can do Thee no harm. I receive all good from Thee, but no good can I return to Thee; wherefore I acknowledge Thee to be most rich, and myself to be most beggarly; so far off is it that Thou standest in any need of me. RICHARD GREENHAM

Verses 2-3. *My goodness extendeth not to Thee; but to the saints.* Some children do not indeed take after their earthly parents, as Cicero's son, who had nothing of his father but his name; but God's children all partake of their heavenly Father's nature. WILLIAM GURNALL

Vs. 3. *But to the saints that are in the earth, and to the excellent.* These sanctified ones, although still upon the earth, partake of the results of Jesus' mediatorial work, and by His goodness are made what they are. The peculiar people, zealous for good works and hallowed to sacred service, are arrayed in the Saviour's righteousness and washed in His blood and so receive of the goodness treasured up in Him; these are the persons who are profited by the work of the Man Christ Jesus; but that work added nothing to the nature, virtue, or happiness of God, Who is blessed forevermore.

Poor believers are God's receivers and have a warrant from the Crown to receive the revenue of our offering in the King's Name. Saints departed, we cannot bless; even prayer for them is of no service; but while they are here we should practically prove our love to them, even as our Master did, for they are the excellent of the earth. C. H. S.

We know the New Testament outshines the Old as much as the sun outshines the moon. If we then live in a more glorious dispensation, should we not maintain a more glorious conversation? . . . *The excellent.* Were the sun to give no more light than a star, you could not believe he was the regent of the day; were he to transmit no more heat than a glowworm, you would question his being the source of elementary heat. Were God to do no more than a creature, where would His Godhead be? Were a man to do no more than a brute, where would his manhood be? Were not a saint to excel a sinner, where would his sanctity be? WILLIAM SECKER

Ingo, an ancient king of the Draves, who making a stately feast, appointed his nobles, at that time pagans, to sit in the hall below, and commanded certain poor Christians to be brought up into his presence-chamber, to sit with him at his table, to eat and drink of his kingly cheer, at which many wondering, he said, he accounted Christians, though ever so poor, a greater ornament to his table, and more worthy of his company than the greatest peers unconverted to the Christian faith; for when these might be thrust down to hell, those might be his comforts and fellow princes in heaven. Although you see the stars sometimes by their reflections in a puddle, in the bottom of a well, or in a stinking ditch, yet the stars have their situation in heaven. So, although you see a godly man in a poor, miserable, low, despised condition, for the things of this world, yet he is fixed in heaven, in the region of heaven: "Who hath raised us up," saith the apostle, "and made us sit together in heavenly places in Christ Jesus." CHARLES BRADBURY'S *"Cabinet of Jewels"*

Vs. 4. *Their sorrows shall be multiplied that hasten after another god.* Professed believers are often slow toward the true Lord, but sinners *hasten after another god.* They run like madmen where we creep like snails. Let their zeal rebuke our tardiness. Yet theirs is a case in which the more they haste the worse they speed, for their sorrows are multiplied by their diligence in multiplying their sins. Matthew Henry says, "That they who multiply gods multiply griefs to themselves; for whosoever thinks one god too little will find two too many, and yet hundreds not enough."

The cruelties and hardships which men endure for their false gods is wonderful to contemplate; our missionary reports are a noteworthy comment on this passage; but perhaps our own experience is an equally vivid exposition; for when we have given our heart to idols, sooner or later we have had to smart for it.

Moses broke the golden calf and ground it to powder and cast it into the water of which he made Israel to drink, and so shall our cherished idols become bitter portions for us unless we at once forsake them.

Sin and the Savior have no communion. He came to destroy, not to patronize or be allied with the works of the devil. Hence He refused the testimony of unclean spirits as to His Divinity, for in nothing would He have fellowship with darkness. We should be careful above measure not to connect ourselves in the remotest degree with falsehood in religion.

*Their drink offerings of blood will I not offer.* The old proverb says, "It is not safe to eat at the devil's mess, though the spoon be ever so long."

The mere mentioning of ill names, it were well to avoid—*nor take up their names into my lips.* If we allow poison upon the lip, it may ere long penetrate to the inwards, and it is well to keep out of the mouth that which we would shut out from the heart. If the church would enjoy union with Christ, she must break all bonds of impiety and keep herself pure from all the pollutions of carnal will-worship, which now pollute the service of God. C. H. S.

A sin rolled under the tongue becomes soft and supple, and the throat is so short and slippery a passage that insensibly it may slide down from the mouth into the stomach; and contemplative wantonness quickly turns into practical uncleanness. THOMAS FULLER

Vs. 5. *The Lord is the portion of mine inheritance and of my cup.* With what confidence and bounding joy does Jesus turn to Jehovah, Whom His soul possessed and delighted in! Content beyond measure with His portion in the Lord His God, He had not a single desire with which to hunt after other gods.

Vs. 6. *The lines are fallen unto me in pleasant places; yea, I have a goodly heritage.* Jesus found the way of obedience to lead into "pleasant places." Notwithstanding all the sorrows which marred His countenance, He exclaimed, "Lo, I come; in the volume of the book it is written of Me, I delight to do Thy will, O my God: yea, Thy law is within My heart." It may seem strange, but while no other man was ever so thoroughly acquainted with grief, it is our belief that no other man ever experienced so much joy and delight in service, for no other served so faithfully and with such great results in view as His recompense of reward.

All the saints can use the language of this verse, and the more thoroughly they can enter into its contented, grateful, joyful spirit, the better for themselves and the more glorious to their God. Discontented spirits are as unlike Jesus as the croaking raven is unlike the cooing dove. Martyrs have been happy in dungeons.

Mr. Greenham was bold enough to say, "They never felt God's love or tasted forgiveness of sins who are discontented." Some divines think that discontent was the first sin, the rock which wrecked our race in paradise; certainly there can be no paradise where this evil spirit has power. Its slime will poison all the flowers of the garden. C. H. S.

Bitter herbs will go down very well when a man has such delicious "meats which the world knows not of." The sense of our Father's love is like honey at the end of every rod; it turns stone into bread, and water into wine, and the valley of trouble into a door of hope; it makes the biggest evils seem as if they were none, or better than none; for it makes our deserts like the garden of the Lord, and when we are upon the cross for Christ, as if we were in paradise with Christ. TIMOTHY CRUSO

Vs. 7. *My reins also instruct me in the night seasons.* Great generals fight their battles in their own mind long before the trumpet sounds, and so did our Lord win our battle on His knees before He gained it on the cross. He who learns from God and so gets the seed will soon find wisdom within himself growing in the garden of his soul: "Thine ears shall hear a voice behind thee, saying, This is the way, walk ye in it, when ye turn to the right hand and when ye turn to the left." The night season which the sinner chooses for his sins is the hallowed hour of quiet when believers hear the soft still voices of heaven and of the heavenly life within themselves.

Verses 8-11. The fear of death at one time cast its dark shadow over the soul of the Redeemer, and we read that "He was heard in that He feared." There appeared unto Him an angel, strengthening Him; then hope shone full upon our Lord's soul, and, as recorded in these verses, He surveyed the future with holy confidence because He had a continued eye to Jehovah, and enjoyed His perpetual presence. He felt that, thus sustained, He could never be driven from His life's grand design; nor was He, for He stayed not His hand till He could say, "It is finished." What an infinite mercy was this for us!

To recognize the presence of the Lord is the duty of every believer—*I have set the Lord always before me.* And to trust the Lord as our champion and guard is the privilege of every saint; *because He is at my right hand, I shall not be moved.* C. H. S.

Vs. 8. A faithful Christian man, whether he abound in wealth or be pinched with poverty, whether he be of high or low degree in this world, ought continually to have his faith and hope surely built and grounded upon Christ, and to have his heart and mind fast fixed and settled in Him, and to follow Him through thick and thin, through fire and water, through wars and peace, through hunger and cold, through friends and foes, through a thousand perils and dangers, through the surges and waves of envy, malice, hatred, evil speeches, railing sentences, contempt of the world, flesh, and devil, and even in death itself, be it ever so bitter, cruel, and tyrannical, yet never to lose sight and view of Christ, never to give over faith, hope, and trust in Him. ROBERT CAWDRAY

The laden cloud soon drops into rain; the piece charged soon goes off when fire is put to it. A meditating soul is in *proxima potentia* to prayer. WILLIAM GURNALL

Enoch walked so much with God that he walked as God: he did not "walk" (which kind of walking the Apostle reproves, I Cor. 3:3) "as men." He walked so little like the world, that his stay was little in the world. JOSEPH CARYL

Vs. 9. *My heart is glad, and my glory rejoiceth.* His inward joy was not able to contain itself. We testify our pleasure on lower occasions, even at the gratification of our senses; when our ear is filled with harmonious melody, when our eye is fixed upon admirable and beauteous objects, when our smell is recreated with agreeable odors, and our taste also by the delicacy and rareness of provisions; and much more will our soul show its delight, when its faculties, that are of a more exquisite constitution, meet with things that are in all respects agreeable and pleasant to them; and in God they meet with all those: with His light our understanding is refreshed, and so is our will with His goodness and His love. TIMOTHY ROGERS

Vs. 10. *Thou wilt not leave my soul in hell.* Christ, in soul, descended into hell, when as our surety He submitted Himself to bear those hellish sorrows (or equivalent to them), which we were bound by our sins to suffer forever. Thus Christ descended into hell when He was alive, not when He was dead. Thus His soul was in hell when in the garden He did sweat blood, and on the cross when He cried so lamentably, "My God, My God, why hast Thou forsaken Me?" (Matt. 26:38). NICHOLAS BYFIELD'S "*Exposition of the Creed*"

*Neither wilt Thou suffer Thine Holy One to see corruption.* Into the outer prison of the grace, His body might go, but into the inner prison of corruption

He could not enter. This is noble encouragement to all the saints; die they must, but rise they shall, and though in their case they shall see corruption, yet they shall rise to everlasting life. Christ's resurrection is the cause, the earnest, the guarantee, and the emblem of the rising of all His people. C. H. S.

Vs. 11. *Thou wilt show me the path of life.* In this verse are four things observable: 1. A Guide—Thou; 2. a Traveler—me; 3. a way—the path; 4. the end—life, described after; for that which follows is but the description of this life.

The Guide we find named in the first verse—Jehovah. Here we may begin, as we ought in all holy exercises, with adoration. The traveler. Having found the Guide, we shall not long seek for one who wants Him; for, see, here is a man out of his way. As there is but one Guide, so he speaks in the person but of one traveler. It is to show his confidence.

But let us now see what he will show us: "the path." We must know, that as men have many paths out of their highway—the world—but they all end in destruction; so God hath many paths out of His highway the Word, but they all end in salvation. WILLIAM AUSTIN

*In Thy presence is fulness of joy; at Thy right hand there are pleasures forevermore.* Trapp's note on the heavenly verse which closes the Psalm is a sweet morsel, which may serve for a contemplation and yield a foretaste of our inheritance. He writes, "Here is as much said as can be, but words are too weak to utter it. For quality there is in heaven joy and pleasures; for quantity, a fullness, a torrent whereat they drink without let or loathing; for constancy, it is at God's right hand, Who is stronger than all, neither can any take us out of His hand; it is a constant happiness without intermission: and for perpetuity it is forevermore. Heaven's joys are without measure, mixture, or end." C. H. S.

All we here present for the present are but mere strangers in the midst of danger, we are losing ourselves and losing our lives in the land of the dying. But ere long, we may find our lives and ourselves again in heaven with the Lord of life, being found of Him in the land of the living. If when we die, we be in the Lord of life, our souls are sure to be bound up in the bundle of life, that so when we live again we may be sure to find them in the life of the Lord.

Now we have but a dram, but a scruple, but a grain of happiness, to an ounce, to a pound, to a thousand weight of heaviness; now we have but a drop of joy to an ocean of sorrow; but a moment of ease to an age of pain; but then, we shall have endless ease without any pain, true happiness without any heaviness, the greatest measure of felicity without the least of misery, the fullest measure of joy that may be, without any mixture of grief. Here, therefore (as St. Gregory the divine adviseth us), let us ease our heaviest loads of sufferings, and sweeten our bitterest cups of sorrows with the continual meditation and constant expectation of the fullness of joy in the presence of God, and of the pleasure at His right hand forevermore.

*In Thy presence is*—there it is, not there it was, nor there it may be, nor there it will be, but there it is—there it is without cessation or intercision, there it always hath been, and is and must be. For what does any man here present wish for more than joy? And what measure of joy can any man wish for more than fullness of joy? *The Consummation of Felicity, by* EDWARD WILLAN

In heaven they are free from want; they can want nothing there unless it be want itself. They may find the want of evil, but never feel the evil of want. Evil is but the want of good, and the want of evil is but the absence of want. Here some men eat their meat without any hunger, whilst others hunger without any meat to eat, and some men drink extremely without any thirst, whilst others thirst extremely without any drink. But in the glorious presence of God, not anyone can be pampered with too much, nor anyone be pined with too little. EDWARD WILLAN

In this life our joy is mixed with sorrow like a prick under the rose. Jacob had joy when his sons returned home from Egypt with the sacks full of corn, but much sorrow when he perceived the silver in the sack's mouth. David had much joy in bringing up the ark of God, but at the same time great sorrow for the breach made upon Uzza. This is the Lord's great wisdom to temper and moderate our joy.

As men of a weak constitution must have their wine qualified with water for fear of distemper, so we must in this life (such is our weakness), have our joy mixed with sorrow, lest we turn giddy and insolent. Here our joy is mixed with fear (Psalm 2). "Rejoice with trembling"; the women departed from the sepulcher of our Lord "with fear and great joy" (Matt. 28:8).

As our joy here is mixed with fears, so with sorrow also. Sound believers do look up to Christ crucified and do rejoice in His incomparable love, that such a Person should have died such a death for such as were enemies to God by sinful inclinations and wicked works; they look down also upon their own sins that have wounded and crucified the Lord of glory, and this breaketh the heart. WILLIAM COLVILL'S *"Refreshing Streams"*

Mark, for quality, there are pleasures; for quantity, fullness; for dignity, at God's right hand; for eternity, forevermore. And millions of years multiplied by millions make not up one minute to this eternity of joy that the saints shall have in heaven. In heaven there shall be no sin to take away your joy, nor no devil to take away your joy; nor no man to take away your joy. "Your joy no man taketh from you" (John 16:22). The joys of heaven never fade, never wither, never die, nor never are lessened nor interrupted. The joy of the saints in heaven is a constant joy, an everlasting joy, in the root and in the cause, and in the matter of it and in the objects of it. "Their joy lasts forever whose objects remain forever"; so Christ (Heb. 13:8). THOMAS BBOOKS

## PSALM 17

Title and Subject: "A Prayer of David." David would not have been a man after God's own heart if he had not been a man of prayer. He was a master in the sacred art of supplication. He flew to prayer in all times of need as a pilot speeds to the harbor in the stress of tempest. We have in the present plaintive song "An Appeal to Heaven" from the persecutions of earth. C. H. S.

Though the other Psalms contain divers prayers mixed with other matters, this is a supplication through its whole course. THE VENERABLE BEDE

Divisions: There are no very clear lines of demarcation between the parts; but we prefer the division adopted by that precious old commentator, David Dickson. In verses 1-4, David craves justice in the controversy between him and his oppressors. In verses 5 and 6, he requests of the Lord grace to act rightly while under the trial. From verse 7-12, he seeks protection from his foes, whom he graphically describes; and in verses 13 and 14, pleads that they may be disappointed; closing the whole in the most comfortable confidence that all would certainly be well with himself at the last. C. H. S.

Vs. 1. *Hear the right, O Lord.* He that has the worst cause makes the most noise; hence the oppressed soul is apprehensive that its voice may be drowned, and therefore pleads in this one verse for a hearing no less than three times. There is more fear that we will not hear the Lord than that the Lord will not hear us. C. H. S.

*Attend unto my cry.* A real hearty, bitter, piteous cry might almost melt a rock; there can be no fear of its prevalence with our heavenly Father. If our prayer should, like the infant's cry, be more natural than intelligent, and more earnest than elegant, it will be none the less eloquent with God. There is a mighty power in a child's cry to prevail with a parent's heart. C. H. S.

*Give ear unto my prayer.* The reduplication here used is neither superstition nor tautology but is like the repeated blow of a hammer hitting the same nail on the head to fix it the more effectually or the continued knocking of a beggar at the gate who cannot be denied an alms. C. H. S.

This petition repeated thrice indicates a great power of feeling and many tears; because the craft of the ungodly, in truth, grieves and afflicts the spiritual man more than their power and violence, for we can get a knowledge of open force and violence, and, when we see the danger, can in some way guard against it. MARTIN LUTHER

*That goeth not out of feigned lips.* He who would feign and flatter had better try his craft with a fool like himself, for to deceive the all-seeing One is as impossible as to take the moon in a net or to lead the sun into a snare. He who would deceive God is himself already grossly deceived. Our sincerity in prayer has no merit in it any more than the earnestness of a mendicant in the street; but at the same time the Lord has regard to it, through Jesus, and will not long refuse His ear to an honest and fervent petitioner. C. H. S.

There are such things as "*feigned lips*"; a contradiction between the heart and the tongue, a clamor in the voice and scoffing in the soul. STEPHEN CHARNOCK

It is observable that the eagle soareth on high, little intending to fly to heaven, but to gain her prey; and so it is that many do carry a great deal of seeming devotion in lifting up their eyes towards heaven; but they do it only to accomplish with more ease, safety, and applause, their wicked and damnable designs here on earth; such as without are Catos, within Neros; hear them, no man better; search and try them, no man worse; they have Jacob's voice, but Esau's hands; they profess like saints, but practice like Satans; they have their long prayers, but short prayings; they are like apothecaries' gallipots—having without the title of some excellent preservative, but within they are full of deadly poison; counterfeit holiness is their cloak for all manner of villainies. PETER BALES, in *Spencer's "Things New and Old"*

Vs. 2. *Let my sentence come forth from Thy presence.* With Jesus as our complete and all-glorious righteousness, we need not fear though the day of judgment should commence at once and hell open her mouth at our feet, but might joyfully prove the truth of our hymn-writers holy boast:

*Bold shall I stand in that great day;*
*For who aught to my charge shall lay?*
*While, through Thy blood, absolved I am*
*From sin's tremendous curse and shame.*
C. H. S.

Verses 3, 4, 5. Where there is true grace, there is hatred of all sin. STEPHEN CHARNOCK

Vs. 3. *Thou hast tried me, and shalt find nothing.* Surely the Psalmist means nothing hypocritical or wicked in the sense in which his slanderers accused him; for if the Lord should put the best of His people into the crucible, the dross would be a fearful sight and would make penitence open her sluices wide. Assayers very soon detect the presence of alloy, and when the Chief of all assayers shall, at the last, say of us that He has found nothing, it will be a glorious hour indeed—"They are without fault before the throne of God." Even here, as viewed in our covenant Head, the Lord sees no sin in Jacob nor perverseness in Israel; even the all-detecting glance of Omniscience can see no flaw where the great Substitute covers all with beauty and perfection.

*I am purposed that my mouth shall not transgress.* The number of diseases of the tongue is as many as the diseases of all the rest of the man put together, and they are more inveterate. It needs more than a purpose to keep this nimble offender within its proper range. Lion-taming and serpent charming are not to be mentioned in the same day as tongue taming, for the tongue can no man tame.

David desired in all respects to tune his lips to the sweet and simple music of truth. Notwithstanding all this, David was slandered, as if to show us that the purest innocence will be bemired by malice. There is no sunshine without a shadow, no ripe fruit unpecked by the birds. C. H. S.

Vs. 4. *Concerning the works of men, by the Word of Thy lips I have kept me from the paths of the destroyer.* I must ascribe it to the good Word of God; it is this I consult with, and by it I am kept from those foul ways whereinto others that make no use of the Word for their defence are carried by Satan, the destroyer. Can we go against sin and Satan with a better weapon than Christ used to vanquish the tempter with? Christ could with one beam shot from His deity (if He had pleased to exert it) have as easily laid the bold fiend at His foot, as afterward He did them that came to attack Him; but He chose rather to conceal the majesty of His divinity and let Satan come up closer to Him, that so He might confound him with the Word and thereby give him a proof of that sword of His saints, which He was to leave them for their defence against the same enemy. WILLIAM GURNALL

"I write unto you, young men, because ye are strong." Where lies their strength? "And the Word of God abideth in you, and ye have overcome the wicked one" (I John 2:14). THOMAS MANTON

Vs. 5. Plato said to one of his disciples, "When men speak ill of thee, live so that no one will believe them."

*Hold up my goings*—as a careful driver holds up his horse when going down hill. We have all sorts of paces, both fast and slow, and the road is never long of one sort, but with God to hold up our goings, nothing in the pace or in the road can cast down.

*In Thy paths.* We cannot keep from evil without keeping to good.

*That my footsteps slip not.* Yes, the road is good, but our feet are evil, and therefore slip, even on the King's highway. One may trip over an ordinance as well as over a temptation. C. H. S.

It was Beza's prayer, and let it be ours, "Lord, perfect what Thou hast begun in me, that I may not suffer shipwreck when I am almost at the haven." THOMAS WATSON

Vs. 6. *I have called upon Thee, for Thou wilt hear me.* God will not only hear our cry, but also hear us before we cry, and will help us. T. PLAYFERE

I have called upon Thee formerly; therefore, Lord, hear me now. Tradesmen are willing to oblige those that have been long their customers. MATTHEW HENRY

Vs. 8. *Keep me as the apple of the eye.* The all-wise Creator has placed the eye in a well-protected position; it stands surrounded by projecting bones like Jerusalem encircled by mountains. Moreover, its great Author has surrounded it with many tunics of inward covering besides the hedge of the eyebrows, the curtain of the eyelids, and the fence of the eyelashes; and, in addition to this, he has given to every man so high a value for his eyes and so quick an apprehension of danger that no member of the body is more faithfully cared for than the organ of sight. C. H. S.

Does it not appear to thee to be a work of Providence, that considering the weakness of the eye, He has protected it with eyelids, as with doors, which whenever there is occasion to use it are opened and are again closed in sleep? And that it may not receive injury from the winds, he has planted on it eyelashes like a strainer; and over the eyes has disposed the eyebrows like a penthouse, so that the sweat from the head may do no mischief. SOCRATES, *in Xenophon*

Vs. 9. *From the wicked that oppress me, from my deadly enemies, who compass me about.* The foes of a believer's soul are mortal foes most emphatically, for they who war against our faith aim at the very life of our life. Deadly sins are deadly enemies, and what sin is there which hath not death in its bowels?

Vs. 10. *They are inclosed in their own fat.* Luxury and gluttony beget vainglorious fatness of heart, which shuts up its gates against all compassionate emotions and reasonable judgments. The old proverb says that "full bellies make empty skulls," and it is yet more true that they frequently make empty hearts.

*With their mouth they speak proudly.* He who adores himself will have no heart to adore the Lord. Full of selfish pleasure within his heart, the wicked man fills his mouth with boastful and arrogant expressions. Prosperity and vanity often lodge together. Woe to the fed ox when it bellows at its owner; the poleaxe is not far off. C. H. S.

Vs. 11. *They have set their eyes bowing to the earth.* It is an allusion, as I conceive, to hunters, who go poring upon the ground to prick the hare, or to find the print of the hare's claw when the hounds are at a loss and can make nothing of it by the scent. JOSEPH CARYL

Vs. 13. *The wicked, which is Thy sword.* The devil and his instruments both are God's instruments; therefore "the wicked" are called His "sword." The devil and his whole council are but fools to God; nay, their wisdom foolishness. WILLIAM GURNALL

Vs. 14. *From men of the world, which have their portion in this life.* Luther was always afraid lest he should have his portion here, and therefore frequently gave away sums of money which had been presented to him. We cannot have earth and heaven too for our choice and portion; wise men choose that which will last the longest. C. H. S.

God gives wicked men a portion here to show unto them what little good there is in all these things and to show the world what little good there is in all the things that are here below in the world.

Certainly, if they were much good they should never have them; it is an argument there is no great excellency in the strength of body, for an ox hath it more than you; an argument there is no great excellency in agility of body, for a dog hath it more than you; an argument no great excellency in gay clothes, for a peacock hath them more than you; an argument there is not any great excellency in gold and silver, for the Indians that know not God have them more than you; and if these things had any great worth in them, certainly God would never give them to wicked men—a certain argument.

As for outward things, crabs, the Lord suffers the swine of the world to come grunting and take them up; but when He comes to His choice mercies in His Christ, there He makes a distinction. Oh, this is precious fruit! A blacksmith that is working upon iron, though a great many cinders and little bits of iron fly up and down, regards them not; but a goldsmith that is working upon gold preserves every rag and every dust of gold; and a lapidary that is working upon precious stones, every little bit he will be sure to preserve; a carpenter that is only hewing of timber, regards it not much if chips fly up and down; but it is not so with a lapidary. So these things are but as chips and cinders, and such kind of things as those are, and therefore God gives a portion to wicked men out of them. JEREMIAH BURROUGHS

The earth and the commodities thereof God distributeth without respect of persons, even to them that are His children by creation only, and not by adoption. MILES SMITH

There is yet another thing to be seen far more monstrous in this creature; that whereas he is endued with reason and counsel, and knoweth that this life is like unto a shadow, to a dream, to a tale that is told, to a watch in the night, to smoke, to chaff which the wind scattereth, to a water-bubble, and such-like fading things; and that life to come shall never have end; yet nevertheless, he setteth his whole mind most carefully upon this present life, which is today, and tomorrow is not; but of the life which is everlasting he doth not so much as think. If this be not a monster, I know not what may be called monstrous. THOMAS TYMME

What wicked men possess of this world is all that ever they can hope for: why should we grudge them filled bags, or swelling titles! it is their whole portion; they now receive their good things.

Whereas thou, O Christian, who possessest nothing, art heir-apparent of heaven, co-heir with Jesus Christ, Who is the Heir of all things, and hast an infinite mass of riches laid up for thee; so great and infinite, that all the stars of heaven are too few to account it by: you have no reason to complain of being kept short; for all that God hath is yours, whether prosperity or adversity, life or death, all is yours. What God gives is for your comfort; what He denies or takes away is for your trial: it is for the increase of those graces which are far more gracious than any temporal enjoyment. If, by seeing wicked and ungodly men flow in wealth and ease, when thou art forced to struggle against the inconveniences and difficulties of a poor estate, thou hast learnt a holy contempt and disdain of the world, believe it, God hath herein given thee more than if He had given thee the world itself. EZEKIEL HOPKINS

A master or lord pays his servant his present wages, while he cuts his son short in his allowance during his nonage, that he may learn to depend upon his father for the inheritance.

Surely (are many ready to argue) if God did not love me He would not give me such a portion in the world. Deceive not thyself in a matter of so great concernment. Thou mayest as well say God loved Judas because he had the bags, or Dives because he fared deliciously, who are now roaring in hell. JOHN FROST

*Whose belly Thou fillest with Thy hid treasure.* A generous man does not deny dogs their bones; and our generous God gives even His enemies enough to fill them, if they were not so unreasonable as never to be content. Gold and silver which are locked up in the dark treasuries of the earth are given to the wicked liberally, and they therefore roll in all manner of carnal delights. C. H. S.

Wicked men may have the earth and the fullness of it, the earth, and all that is earthly; their bellies are filled by God Himself with hidden treasure. JOSEPH CRAYL

The hearts of the saints only are filled with the "hidden manna," but the bellies of the wicked are often filled with hidden treasure; that is, with those dainties and good things which are virtually hidden in, and formally spring out of, the belly and bowels of the earth. JOSEPH CARYL

*They are full of children.* Margin, "their children are full." The obvious signification is, that they have enough for themselves and for their children. ALBERT BARNES

Vs. 15. *As for me, I will behold Thy face in righteousness: I shall be satisfied, when I awake, with Thy likeness.* Glimpses of glory good men have here below to stay their sacred hunger, but the full feast awaits them in the upper skies. Compared with this deep, ineffable, eternal fullness of delight, the joys of the worldling are as a glowworm to the sun, or the drop of a bucket to the ocean. C. H. S.

Now the scaffolding is kept around men long after the fresco is commenced to be painted; and wondrous disclosures will be made when God shall take down this scaffolding body and reveal what you have been doing.

Your portrait and mine are being painted, and God by wondrous strokes and influences is working us up to His own ideal. Over and above what you are doing for yourself, God is working to make you like Him. And the wondrous declaration is, that when you stand before God and see what has been done for you, you shall be *satisfied.* Oh, word that has been wandering solitary and without a habitation ever since the world began and the morning stars sang together for joy! Has there even been a human creature that could stand on earth while clothed in the flesh and say, "I am satisfied?" HENRY WARD BEECHER, *in "Royal Truths"*

Even under the weight and combination of so many sore evils, David carries himself as one that is neither hopeless nor forsaken, yea, lays his estate in the balance against theirs, and in this low ebb of his, vies with them for happiness. WILLIAM SPURSTOW

When a Roman conqueror had been at war and won great victories, he would return to Rome with his soldiers, enter privately into his house, and enjoy himself till the next day, when he would go out of the city to reënter it publicly in triumph. Now, the saints, as it were, enter privately into heaven without their bodies; but on the last day, when their bodies wake up, they will enter into their triumphal chariots. Methinks I see that grand procession, when Jesus Christ first of all, with many crowns on His head, with His bright, glorious, immortal body, shall lead the way. "I shall be satisfied" in that glorious day when all the angels of God shall come to see the triumphs of Jesus, and when His people shall be victorious with Him. SPURGEON'S SERMONS

Let a man who is thirsty be brought to an ocean of pure water, and he has enough. If there be enough in God to satisfy the angels, then sure there is enough to satisfy us. Fresh joys spring continually from His face; and He is as much to be desired after millions of years by glorified souls as at the first moment. If there be so much delight in God, when we see Him only by faith (I Pet. 1:8), what will the joy of vision be, when we shall see Him face to face! If the saints have found so much delight in God while they were suffering, oh, what joy and delight will they have when they are being crowned! Who would put anything in balance with Deity? Who would weigh a feather against a mountain of gold? God excels all other things more infinitely than the sun the light of a taper. THOMAS WATSON

They say the Gauls, when they first tasted of the wines of Italy, were so taken with their lusciousness and sweetness that they could not be content to trade thither for this wine but resolved they would conquer the land where they grew. Thus the sincere soul thinks it not enough to receive a little now and then of grace and comfort from heaven, by trading and holding commerce at a distance with God in His ordinances here below but projects and mediates a conquest of that Holy Land and blessed place from which such rich commodities come, that he may drink the wine of that kingdom in that kingdom. WILLIAM GURNALL

There is a threefold meaning in this verse; 1. The saints will greatly delight in the glorious state in which they will rise. 2. They will greatly delight in Jesus, in Whom, and by Whom, resurrection and immortality are brought to light; and 3. They will delight greatly in beholding the blessed and reconciled countenance of Jehovah, the Father, Whom no eye of flesh can see. BENJAMIN WEISS, *in loc.*

# PSALM 18

We will call it "The Grateful Retrospect." C. H. S.

It is a magnificent eucharistic ode. JOHN BROWN

Kitto, in *The Pictorial Bible,* has the following note upon II Samuel 22: "This is the same as the Eighteenth Psalm."

The proof of the grandeur of this Psalm is in the fact that it has borne the test of almost every translation and made doggerel erect itself and become divine. Perhaps the great charm of it, apart from the poetry of the descent, exquisite and subtle alteration of the I and *Thou.* GEORGE GILFILLAN, *in The Bards of the Bible*

He that would be wise, let him read the Proverbs; he that would be holy, let him read the Psalms. Holy David, being near the shore, here looks on his former dangers and deliverances with a thankful heart and writes this Psalm to bless the Lord: as if each of you that are grown into years should review your lives and observe the wonderful goodness and providence of God towards you; and then sit down and write a modest memorial of His most remarkable mercies, for the comfort of yourselves and posterity; an excellent practice.

After David had heaped on God all the sweet names he could devise (vs. 2), as the true saint thinks he can never speak too well of God, or too ill of himself, then he begins his narrative. 1. Of his dangers (vs. 4); 2. Of his retreat, and that was, earnest prayer to God (vs. 6). The mother trifles while the child whimpers, but when he raises his note—strains every nerve and cries every vein—then she throws all aside, and gives him his desire. While our prayers are only whispers, our God can take his rest; but when we fall to crying, "Now will I arise, saith the Lord." 3. Of his rescue (verses 7-20). 4. Of the reason of this gracious dealing of God with him (vs. 20, etc.). RICHARD STEELE'S *Plain Discourse upon Uprightness*

Vs. 1. *I will love Thee, O Lord.* I will love heartily, with my inmost bowels. Our triune God deserves the warmest love of all our hearts. C. H. S.

Verses 1-2. God hath, as it were, made Himself over to believers. It is God Himself Who is the salvation and the portion of His people. That which faith pitcheth most upon is God Himself; He shall be my salvation, let me have Him, and that is salvation enough; He is my life, He is my comfort, He is my riches, He is my honor, and He is my all.

It pleased holy David more that God was his strength than that He gave him strength; that God was his deliverer, than that he was delivered; that God was his fortress, his buckler, his horn, his high tower, than that He gave him the effect of all these. It pleased David, and it pleases all the saints more that God is their salvation, whether temporal or eternal, than that He save them: the saints look more at God than at all that is God's. JOSEPH CARYL

Vs. 2. *The Lord is my rock, and my fortress.* Dwelling among the crags and mountain fastnesses of Judea, David had escaped the malice of Saul, and here he compares his God to such a place of concealment and security.

*My strength.* This word is really *My rock,* in the sense of strength and immobility; my sure, unchanging, eternal confidence and support. Thus the word "rock" occurs twice, but it is no tautology, for the first time it is a rock for concealment, but here a rock for firmness and immutability.

*My buckler,* warding off the blows of my enemy, shielding me from arrow or sword.

Here are many words, but none too many; we might profitably examine each one of them had we leisure, but summing up the whole, we may conclude with Calvin, that David here equips the faithful from head to foot.

Vs. 4. *The floods of ungodly men made me afraid.* On the night of the lamentable accident at the Surrey Music Hall, the floods of Belial were let loose, and the subsequent remarks of a large portion of the press were exceedingly malicious and wicked; our soul was afraid as we stood encompassed with the sorrows of death and the blasphemies of the cruel. But, oh, what mercy was there in it all, and what honey of goodness was extracted by our Lord out of this lion of affliction! C. H. S.

There is no metaphor of more frequent occurrence with the sacred poets than that which represents dreadful and unexpected calamities under the image of overwhelming waters. This image seems to have been especially familiar with the Hebrews, inasmuch as it was derived from the peculiar habit and nature of their own country. They had continually before their eyes the river Jordan, annually overflowing its banks. ROBERT LOWTH (BISHOP)

Vs. 5. *The sorrows of hell compassed me about.* A cordon of devils hemmed in the hunted man of God; every way of escape was closed up. Satan knows how to blockade our coasts with the iron war-ships of sorrow, but, blessed be God, the port of all prayer is still open, and grace can run the blockade bearing messages from earth to heaven and blessings in return from heaven to earth.

According to the four metaphors which he employs, he was bound like a malefactor for execution; overwhelmed like a shipwrecked mariner; surrounded and standing at bay like a hunted stag; and captured in a net like a trembling bird. What more of terror and distress could meet upon one poor, defenseless head? C. H. S.

*The snares of death prevented me.* The English word "prevent" has changed its meaning in some measure since our Authorized Translation of the Bible was made. Its original meaning is to "come before." JOHN BROWN

Vs. 6. *In my distress.* If you listen even to David's harp, you shall hear as many hearse-like airs as carols; and the pencil of the Holy Spirit hath labored more in describing the afflictions of Job than the felicities of Solomon. We see, in needleworks and embroideries, it is more pleasing to have a lively work upon a sad and solemn ground than to have a dark and melancholy work upon a lightsome ground; judge, therefore, of the pleasures of the heart by the pleasures of the eye. Certainly virtue is like precious odors—most fragrant when they are crushed; for prosperity doth best discover vice, but adversity doth best discover virtue. FRANCIS BACON

Verses 6-7. The prayer of a single saint is sometimes followed with wonderful effects; what then can a thundering legion of such praying souls do? The Queen of Scots professed she was more afraid of the prayers of Mr. Knox than of an army of ten thousand men. JOHN FLAVEL

Vs. 7. *Then the earth shook and trembled.* Observe how the most solid and immovable things feel the force of supplication. Prayer has shaken houses, opened prison doors, and made stout hearts to quail. Prayer rings the alarm bell, and the Master of the house arise to the rescue, shaking all things beneath His tread.

Vs. 8. *There went up a smoke out of His nostrils.* A violent Oriental method of expressing fierce wrath. Since the breath from the nostrils is heated by strong emotion, the figure portrays the almighty Deliverer as pouring forth smoke in the heat of His wrath and the impetuousness of His zeal.

*And fire out of His mouth devoured.* This fire was no temporary one, but steady and lasting. C. H. S.

Verses 8-19. Since man heeds heaven more in anger than in blessing, and regards God more when He descends on earth in the storm than in the rainbow, David describes the blessed condescension of God by the figure of a tempest. AUGUSTUS F. THOLUCK

Vs. 10. When God comes to punish His foes and rescue His people, nothing has ever surprised His friends or foes more than the admirable swiftness with which He moves and acts: He flies *upon the wings of the wind.* WILLIAM S. PLUMER

Vs. 11. *Thick clouds of the skies.* Blessed is the darkness which encurtains my God; if I may not see Him, it is sweet to know that He is working in secret for my eternal good. Even fools can believe that God is abroad in the sunshine and the calm, but faith is wise and discerns Him in the terrible darkness and threatening storm.

Vs. 13. *The Lord also thundered in the heavens, and the Highest gave His voice.* How will men bear to hear it at the last when addressed to them in proclamation of their doom, for even now their hearts are in their mouths if they do but hear it muttering from afar? In all this terror, David found a theme for song, and thus every believer finds even in the terrors of God a subject for holy praise.

*Hailstones and coals of fire.* Horne remarks that "every thunderstorm should remind us of that exhibition of power and vengeance which is hereafter to accompany the general resurrection."

Vs. 18. *They prevented me in the day of my calamity: but the Lord was my stay.* What a blessed "but" which cuts the Gordian knot and slays the hundred-headed hydra! There is no fear of deliverance when our stay is in Jehovah. C. H. S.

When Henry the Eighth had spoken and written bitterly against Luther, saith Luther, "Tell the Henries, the bishops, the Turks, and the devil himself, do what they can, we are the children of the kingdom, worshipers of the true God, whom they, and such as they, spit upon and crucified." CHARLES BRADBURY

Vs. 19. *He brought me forth also into a large place.* The Lord does not leave His work half done, for having routed the foe, He leads out the captive into liberty.

*He delivered me, because He delighted in me.* Why Jehovah should delight in us is an answerless question, a mystery which angels cannot solve. Believer, sit down, and inwardly digest the instructive sentence now before us, and learn to view the uncaused love of God as the cause of all the lovingkindness of which we are the partakers. C. H. S.

Vs. 20. *The Lord rewarded me according to my righteousness.* Viewing this Psalm as prophetic of the Messiah, these strongly expressed claims to righteousness are readily understood, for His garments were white as snow; but considered as the language of David, they have perplexed many. David's early troubles arose from the wicked malice of envious Saul, who no doubt prosecuted his persecutions under cover of charges brought against the character of "the man after God's own heart." These charges David declares to have been utterly false and asserts that he possessed a grace-given righteousness which the Lord had graciously rewarded in defiance of all his calumniators. Before God, the man after Gods own heart was a humble sinner, but before his slanderers he could with unblushing face speak of the *cleanness of his hands* and the righteousness of his life. It is not at all an opposition to the doctrine of salvation by grace, and no sort of evidence of a pharisaic spirit, when a gracious man, having been slandered, stoutly maintains his integrity and vigorously defends his character.

Vs. 21. There is *I have* and *I have not,* both of which must be blended in a truly sanctified life; constraining and restraining grace must each take its share. C. H. S.

*I have not wickedly departed from my God.* The false-hearted men in the world look not upon God alone but upon something else together with God; as Herod regarded John, but regarded his Herodias more; and the young man in the gospel, comes to Christ, yet he looks after his estate; and Judas followed Christ, yet looks after the bag; this is to *depart wickedly* from God. WILLIAM STRONG

Vs. 23. *I was also upright before Him, and I kept myself from mine iniquity.* David's impetuous temper might have led him to slay Saul when he had him in his power, but grace enabled him to keep his hands clean of the blood of his enemy. C. H. S.

As in the hive there is one master-bee; so in the heart there is one master-sin; there is one sin which is not only near to a man as the garment but dear to him as the right eye. The devil can hold a man as fast by this one link as by a whole chain of vices. The fowler hath the bird fast enough by one wing. An upright Christian takes the sacrificing knife of mortification and runs it through his dearest sin. THOMAS WATSON

Vs. 24. *Therefore hath the Lord recompensed me according to my righteousness, according to the cleanness of my hands in His eyesight.* God first gives us holiness and then rewards us for it. The prize is awarded the flower at the show, but the gardener reared it; the child wins the prize from the schoolmaster, but the real honor of his schooling lies with the master, although instead of receiving, he gives the reward. C. H. S.

Verses 24-27. Even as the sun, which, unto eyes being sound and without disease, is very pleasant, and wholesome, but unto the same eyes, when they are feeble, sore, and weak, is very troublesome and hurtful, yet the sun is ever all one and the selfsame that was before; so God, Who hath even shown Himself benign and bountiful to those who are kind and tender-hearted towards His saints, and are merciful to those who show mercy. But unto the same men, when they fall into wickedness and grow to be full of beastly cruelty, the Lord showeth Himself to be very wrathful and angry, and yet is one and the same immutable God from everlasting to everlasting. ROBERT CAWDRAY

Vs. 25. *With an upright man Thou wilt show Thyself upright.* "Noah was a just man and perfect in his generations, and Noah walked with God. And Noah found grace in the eyes of the Lord. These are the generations of Noah; Noah begat three sons." Noah, Noah, Noah, I love the sound of thy name; and so are all your names precious to God, though hated by men, if the name of God be dear and sweet to you.

Unto an hypocrite there be "gods many and lords many," and he must have an heart for each, but to the upright there is but one God the Father, and one Lord Jesus Christ, and one heart will serve them both. He that fixes his heart upon the creatures, for every creature he must have an heart, and the dividing of his heart destroys him (Hos. 10:2). Worldly profits knock at the door, he must have an heart for them; carnal pleasures present themselves, he must have an heart for them also; sinful preferments appear, they must have an heart, too. The upright man hath made choice of God and hath enough. RICHARD STEELE

Vs. 28. *For Thou wilt light my candle.* Candles lit by God, the devil cannot blow out.

Vs. 29. *For by Thee I have run through a troop; and by my God have I leaped over a wall.* Such feats we have already performed, hewing our way at a run through hosts of difficulties and scaling impossibilities at a leap. God's warriors may expect to have a taste of every form of fighting and must by the power of faith determine to quit themselves like men.

Vs. 31. *Who is God save the Lord?* His God, as Matthew Henry says, is a none-such. Who else creates, sustains, foresees, and overrules? Who but He is perfect in every attribute and glorious in every act? C. H. S.

Here first in the Psalms, occurs the name *Eloah,* rendered *God.* It occurs more than fifty times in the Scripture, but only four times in the Psalms. It is the singular of Elohim. Many have supposed that this name specially refers to God as an object of religious worship. That idea may well be prominent in this place. WILLIAM S. PLUMER

Vs. 33. *He maketh my feet like hinds' feet, and setteth me upon my high places.* Pursuing his foes the warrior had been swift of foot as a young roe, but, instead of taking pleasure in the legs of a man, he ascribes the boon of swiftness to the Lord alone.

Vs. 34. *So that a bow of steel is broken by mine arms.* A bow of brass is probably meant, and these bows could scarcely be bent by the arms alone; the archer had to gain the assistance of his foot; it was, therefore, a great feat of strength to bend the bow, so far as even to snap it by halves.

Jesus not only destroyed the fiery suggestions of Satan, but He broke his arguments with which He shot them, by using Holy Scripture against him; by the same means we may win a like triumph, breaking the bow and cutting the spear in sunder by the sharp edge of revealed truth. Probably David had by nature a vigorous bodily frame; but it is even more likely that, like Samson, he was at times clothed with more than common strength; at any rate, he ascribes the honor of his feats entirely to his God. Let us never wickedly rob the Lord of His due, but faithfully give unto Him the glory which is due unto His Name.

Vs. 35. *Thou hast also given me the shield of Thy salvation.* Above all we must take the shield of faith, for nothing else can quench Satan's fiery darts.

*Thy gentleness hath made me great.* There are several readings of this sentence. The word is capable of being translated, "Thy *goodness* hath made me great." Certain learned annotators tell us that the text means, "Thy *humility* hath made me great." "Thy *condescension*" may, perhaps, serve as a comprehensive reading, combining the ideas which we have already mentioned, as well as that of humility. It is God's making Himself little which is the cause of our being made great. We are so little that if God should manifest His greatness without condescension, we should be trampled under His feet; but God, Who must stoop to view the skies and bow to see what angels do, looks to the lowly and contrite, and makes them great.

Vs. 36. *Thou hast enlarged my steps.* It is no small mercy to be brought into full Christian liberty and enlargement, but it is a greater favor still to be enabled to walk worthily in such liberty, not being permitted to slip with our feet. C. H. S.

Verses 37-38.

*Oh, I have seen the day,*
*When with a single word,*
*God helping me to say,*
*"My trust is in the Lord";*
*My soul has quelled a thousand foes,*
*Fearless of all that could oppose.*

—WILLIAM COWPER.

Verses 39-40. It is impossible to be too frequent in the duty of ascribing all our victories to the God of our salvation.

Vs. 41. *They cried, but there was none to save them; even unto the Lord, but He answered them not.* Prayer is so notable a weapon that even the wicked will take to it in their fits of desperation. Bad men have appealed to God against God's own servants, but all in vain. There are prayers to God which are no better than blasphemy, which bring no comfortable reply, but rather provoke the Lord to greater wrath. C. H. S.

Of Antiochus, though he vowed in his last illness, "that also he would become a Jew himself, and go through all the world, that was inhabited, and declare the power of God, yet," continues the historian, "for all this his pains would not cease, for the just judgment of God was come upon him." JOHN LORINUS, *and* REMIGIUS, *quoted by J. M. Neale*

Vs. 42. *Then did I beat them small as the dust before the wind: I did cast them out as the dirt in the streets.*

*Hell and my sins resist my course,*
*But hell and sin are vanquish'd foes,*
*My Jesus nail'd them to His cross,*
*And sung the triumph when He rose.*
C. H. S.

To cast forth anyone, therefore, as the dirt of the streets, is a strong image of contempt and rejection. JOHN KITTO

Vs. 43. *Thou hast made me the head of the heathen: a people whom I have not known shall serve me.* Surely there is far more of Jesus than of David here.

Vs. 44. *As soon as they hear of me, they shall obey me.* "Love at first sight" is no uncommon thing when Jesus is the wooer. He can write Caesar's message without boasting; His Gospel is in some cases no sooner heard than believed. What inducements to spread abroad the doctrine of the cross!

Vs. 45. *The strangers shall fade away.* Those who are strangers to Jesus are strangers to all lasting happiness; those must soon fade who refuse to be watered from the river of life. C. H. S.

*They shall be afraid out of their close places.* One Jewish scholar interprets it, "They shall fear for the prisons in which I will throw them and keep them confined." JOHN BROWN

Vs. 46. *The Lord liveth.* We serve no inanimate, imaginary, or dying God. He only hath immortality. Like royal subjects, let us cry, "Live on, O God. Long live the King of kings." C. H. S.

Do you not see young heirs to great estates act and spend accordingly? And, why shall you, being the King of heaven's son, be lean and ragged from day to day, as though you were not worth a groat?

A woman, truly godly for the main, having buried a child, and sitting alone in sadness, did yet bear up her heart with the expression, "God lives"; and having parted with another, still she redoubled, "Comforts die, but God lives." At last her dear husband dies, and she sat oppressed and most overwhelmed with sorrow. A little child she had yet surviving, having observed what before she spoke to comfort herself, comes to her and saith, "Is God dead, Mother? is God dead?" This reached her heart, and by God's blessing recovered her former confidence in her God, who is a living God. Thus, Christians, argue down your discouraged and disquieted spirits as David did. OLIVER HEYWOOD'S "*Sure Mercies of David.*"

*Let the God of my salvation be exalted.* We should publish abroad the story of the covenant and the cross, the Father's election, the Son's redemption, and the Spirit's regeneration.

Vs. 47. *It is God that avengeth me, and subdueth the people under me.* That sinners perish is in itself a painful consideration, but that the Lord's law is avenged upon those who break it is to the devout mind a theme for thankfulness. C. H. S.

*It is God.* Sir, this is none other than the hand of God; and to Him alone belongs the glory, wherein none are to share with Him. The General served you with all faithfulness and honor; and the best commendation I can give him is that I dare say he attributes all to God, and would rather perish than assume to himself. *Written to the Speaker of the House of Commons, after the Battle of Naseby, by* OLIVER CROMWELL

Vs. 49. *Therefore will I give thanks unto Thee, O Lord, among the heathen, and sing praises unto Thy Name.* For fighting with others, he did overcome all others; but singing, and delighting himself, he did overcome himself. THOMAS PLAYFERE

# PSALM 19

He is wisest who reads both the world-book and the Word-book as two volumes of the same work and feels concerning them, "My Father wrote them both." C. H. S.

This Psalm forms a perfect contrast with the Eighth Psalm, evidently composed in the evening, and should be read in connection with it, as it was probably written nearly at the same time, and as both are songs of praise derived from natural phenomena, and therefore peculiarly appropriate to rural or pastoral life. JOHN MASON GOOD

As Aristotle had two sorts of books of writings, one called *exoterical,* for his common auditors, another *acromatical,* for his private scholars and familiar acquaintance; so God hath two sorts of books, as David intimates in this Psalm; namely, the book of His creatures, as a commonplace book for all men in the world (verses 1-6), and the book of His Scriptures as a statute-book for His domestic auditory, the church (verses 7-8).

So, *the heavens declare,* that is, they make men declare the glory of God by their admirable structure, motions, and influence. The preaching of the heavens is wonderful in three respects: 1. As preaching all the night and all the day without intermission (verse 2); 2. As preaching in every kind of language (verse 3); 3. As preaching in every part of the world, and in every parish of every part, and in every place of every parish (verse 4). They be diligent pastors, as preaching at all times; and learned pastors, as preaching in all tongues; and catholic pastors, as preaching in all towns.

This is God's primer, as it were, for all sorts of people. Heathen men read in his primer, but Christian men are well acquainted with His Bible. JOHN BOYS

Vs. 1. *The heavens declare the glory of God.* The book of nature has three leaves—heaven, earth, and sea—of which heaven is the first and the most glorious, and by its aid we are able to see the beauties of the other two. He who begins to read creation by studying the stars begins the book at the right place.

The *heavens* are plural for their variety, comprising the watery heavens with their clouds of countless forms, the aerial heavens with their calms and tempests, the solar heavens with all the glories of the day, and the starry heavens with all the marvels of the night; what the heaven of heavens must be hath not entered into the heart of man, but there in chief all things are telling the glory of God. It is not merely glory that the heavens declare, but the *glory of God.*

*The firmament showeth His handywork;* not handy, in the vulgar use of that term, but hand-work. The expanse is full of the works of the Lord's skilful, creating hands. In the expanse above us God flies, as it were, His starry flag to show that the King is at home and hangs out His escutcheon that atheists may see how He despises their denunciations of Him. He who looks up to the firmament and then writes himself down an atheist brands himself at the same moment as an idiot or a liar. C. H. S.

The heavens discover His wisdom, His power, His goodness; and so there is not any one creature, though ever so little, but we are to admire the Creator in it. As a chamber hung round about with looking-glasses represents the face upon every turn, thus all the world doth the mercy and the bounty of God;

though that be visible, yet it discovers an invisible God and His invisible properties. ANTHONY BURGESS

During the French revolution, Jean Bon St. Andre, the Vendean revolutionist, said to a peasant, "I will have all your steeples pulled down, that you may no longer have any object by which you may be reminded of your old superstitions." "But," replied the peasant, "you cannot help leaving us the stars." JOHN BATES' "*Cyclopedia of Moral and Religious Truths*"

Verses 1-2. The literal reading of the first and second verses may be thus given:

*The heavens are TELLING the glory of God,*
*The firmament DISPLAYING the work of His hands;*
*Day unto day WELLETH forth speech,*
*Night unto night BREATHETH OUT knowledge.*

—HENRY CRAIK.

Verses 1-4. Though all preachers on earth should grow silent, and every human mouth cease from publishing the glory of God, the heavens above will never cease to declare and proclaim His majesty and glory. Though nature be hushed and quiet when the sun in his glory has reached the zenith on the azure sky—though the world keep her silent festival, when the stars shine brightest at night—yet, says the Psalmist, *they speak;* aye, holy silence itself is a speech, provided there be the ear to hear it. AUGUSTUS T. THOLUCK

Vs. 2. *Day unto day uttereth speech, and night unto night showeth knowledge.* As if one day took up the story where the other left it, and each night passed over the wondrous tale to the next. C. H. S.

One day telleth another, is one day teacheth another. JOHN BOYS

Vs. 3. *There is no speech.* I will not say the voice of God was not heard; it spoke in the very stillness as loud as in roaring thunder. JOHN GADSBY

Verses 4-6. The commencing of the gospel dispensation as it was introduced by Christ is called the Sun of Righteousness rising (Mal. 4:2). But this gospel dispensation commences with the resurrection of Christ. Here the Psalmist says that God has placed a tabernacle for the sun in the heavens: so God the Father had prepared an abode in heaven for Jesus Christ; He had set a throne for Him there, to which He ascended after He rose. So Christ when He rose from the grave ascended up to the height of heaven, and far above all heavens, but at the end of the gospel day will descend again to the earth. It is here said that the risen sun "rejoiceth as a strong man to run a race." So Christ, when He rose, rose as a man of war, as the Lord strong and mighty, the Lord mighty in battle. JONATHAN EDWARDS

Vs. 5. *Which is as a bridegroom;* Christ is the bridegroom, man's nature the bride, the conjunction and blessed union of both in one person in His marriage. The best way to reconcile two disagreeing families is to make some marriage between them: even so, the Word became flesh and dwelt among us in the world that He might hereby make our peace, reconciling God to man and man to God. My sin is His sin, and His righteousness is my righteousness. He Who knew no sin, for my sake was made sin; and I, contrariwise, having no good thing, am made the righteousness of God in Him. JOHN BOYS

Vs. 6. *And there is nothing hid from the heat thereof.* The bowels of the earth are stored with the ancient produce of the solar rays, and even yet earth's inmost caverns feel their power. Where light is shut out, yet heat and other more subtle influences find their way.

God's way of grace is sublime and broad and full of His glory; in all its displays it is to be admired and studied with diligence. Jesus, like a sun, dwells in the midst of revelation, tabernacling among men in all His brightness;

rejoicing, as the Bridegroom of His church, to reveal Himself to men; and, like a champion, to win unto Himself renown. He makes a circuit of mercy, blessing the remotest corners of the earth.

The earth receives its heat from the sun, and by conduction, a part of it enters the crust of our globe. By convection, another portion is carried to the atmosphere, which it warms. Another portion is radiated into space, according to laws yet imperfectly understood, but which are evidently connected with the color, chemical composition, and mechanical structure of parts of the earth's surface. EDWIN SIDNEY, in *"Conversations on the Bible and Science"*

It is not solely on the mountain top that Christ shines, as in the day before He was fully risen, when His rays, although unseen by the rest of the world, formed a glory round the heads of His prophets, who saw Him while to the chief part of mankind He was still lying below the horizon. Now, however, that He is risen, He pours His light through the valley, as well as over the mountain; nor is there anyone, at least in these countries, who does not catch some gleams of that light, except those who burrow and hide themselves in the dark caverns of sin.

Not only does He enlighten the understanding, but He also softens and melts, and warms the heart, so that it shall love the truth, and calls forth fruit from it, and ripens the fruit He has called forth; and that too on the lowliest plant which creeps along the ground, as well as the loftiest tree. JULIUS CHARLES HARE

Vs. 7. *The law of the Lord is perfect;* by which he means not merely the law of Moses but the doctrine of God, the whole run and rule of sacred Writ. There are no redundancies and no omissions in the Word of God and in the plan of grace; why then do men try to paint this lily and gild this refined gold? The gospel is perfect in all its parts, and perfect as a whole: it is a crime to add to it, treason to alter it, and felony to take from it.

*Converting the soul.* The great means of the conversion of sinners is the Word of God, and the more closely we keep to it in our ministry the more likely are we to be successful. It is God's Word rather than man's comment on God's Word which is made mighty with souls.

Vs. 8. *The statutes of the Lord are right, rejoicing the heart.* Mark the progress; he who was converted was next made wise and is now made happy; that truth which makes the heart right then gives joy to the right heart. C. H. S.

How odious is the profaneness of those Christians who neglect the Holy Scriptures and give themselves to reading other books! How many precious hours do many spend, and that not only on work days, but holy days, in foolish romances, fabulous histories, lascivious poems! And why this, but that they may be cheered and delighted, when as full joy is only to be had in these Holy Books. Other books may comfort against outward trouble, but not against inward fears; they may rejoice the mind, but cannot quiet the conscience; they may kindle some flashy sparkles of joy, but they cannot warm the soul with a lasting fire of solid consolations.

If ever God gives you a spiritual ear to judge of things aright, you will then acknowledge there are no bells like to those of Aaron's, no harp like to that of David's, no trumpet like to that of Isaiah's, no pipes like to those of the Apostle's; and, you will confess with Petrus Damianus, that those writings of heathen orators, philosophers, poets, which formerly were so pleasing, are now dull and harsh in comparison of the comfort of the Scriptures. NATHANAEL HARDY

*Enlightening the eyes.* Whether the eye be dim with sorrow or with sin, the Scripture is a skilful oculist and makes the eye clear and bright. Look at the sun and it puts out your eyes, look at the more than sunlight of Revelation, and it enlightens them; the purity of snow causes snow-blindness to the Alpine traveler, but the purity of God's truth has the contrary effect and cures the natural blindness of the soul. It is well again to observe the gradation; the convert becomes a disciple and next a rejoicing soul, he now obtains a discerning eye, and as a spiritual man discerneth all things, though he himself is discerned of no man.

Vs. 9. *Enduring forever.* When the governments of nations are shaken with revolution, and ancient constitutions are being repealed, it is comforting to know that the throne of God is unshaken and His law unaltered.

Vs. 10. *More to be desired are they than gold, yea, than much fine gold.* The metaphor is one which gathers force as it is brought out—gold—fine gold—much fine gold; it is good, better, best, and therefore it is not only to be desired with a miser's avidity but with more than that. Men speak of solid gold, but what is so solid as solid truth? For love of gold pleasure is forsworn, ease renounced, and life endangered; shall we not be ready to do as much for love of truth? C. H. S.

*Sweeter also than honey and the honeycomb.* There is no difference made amongst us between the delicacy of honey in the comb and that which is separated from it. SAMUEL BURDER, in *"Oriental Customs"*

Vs. 11. *Moreover by them is Thy servant warned.* A certain Jew had formed a design to poison Luther, but was disappointed by a faithful friend, who sent Luther a portrait of the man, with a warning against him. By this, Luther knew the murderer and escaped his hands. Thus the Word of God, O Christian, shows thee the face of those lusts which Satan employs to destroy thy comforts and poison thy soul. G. S. BOWES, in *"Illustrative Gatherings for Preachers and Teachers*

*In keeping of them there is great reward.* There is a wage, and a great one; though we earn no wages of debt, we win great wages of grace. C. H. S.

Not only for keeping, but in keeping of them, there is great reward. THOMAS BROOKS

Vs. 12. *Who can understand his errors?* He best knows himself who best knows the Word, but even such an one will be in a maze of wonder as to what he does not know, rather than on the mount of congratulation as to what he does know. C. H. S.

None can understand his errors to the depth and bottom. In this question there are two considerables: 1. A Concession. 2. A Confession. The Scriptures affirm that "All we like sheep have gone astray." The whole man in nature is like a tree nipped at root, which brings forth worm-eaten fruits. The whole man in life is like an instrument out of tune, which jars at every stroke. If we cannot understand them, certainly they are very many. ROBERT ABBOT

If a man repent not until he have made confession of all his sins in the ear of his ghostly father, if a man cannot have absolution of his sins until his sins be told by tale and number in the priest's ear; in that, as David saith, none can understand, much less, then, utter all his sins. Alas! shall not a man by this doctrine be utterly driven from repentance? JOHN BRADFORD (*Martyr*)

"The heart of man is desperately wicked, who can know it?" OBADIAH SEDGWICK

No arithmetic can number our sins. Before we can recount a thousand we shall commit ten thousand more. THOMAS ADAMS

*Cleanse Thou me from secret faults.* Secret sins, like private conspirators, must be hunted out, or they may do deadly mischief; it is well to be much in prayer concerning them. In the Lutheran Council of the Church of Rome, a decree was passed that every true believer must confess his sins, all of them, once in a year to the priest, and they affixed to it this declaration, that there is no hope of pardon but in complying with that decree. What can equal the absurdity of such a decree as that? Do they suppose that they can tell their sins as easily as they can count their fingers? C. H. S.

"O wretched man [saith Paul], who shall deliver me?" Verily brethren, it was not sin abroad, but at home: it was not sin without, but at this time sin within; it was not Paul's sinning with man, but Paul's sinning within Paul. As Rebekah was weary of her life, not as we read for any foreign disquietments, but because of domestic troubles: "The daughters of Heth" within the house made her "weary of her life"; so the private and secret birth of corruption within Paul—the workings of that—that was the cause of his trouble, that was the ground of his exclamation and desires, "Who shall deliver me?" OBADIAH SEDGWICK

Some can see and will not, as Balaam; some would see, and cannot, as the eunuch; some neither will nor can, as Pharaoh; some both can and will, as David. THOMAS ADAMS

The law of the Lord is so holy that forgiveness must be prayed for, even for hidden sins. (Note—This was a principal text of the Reformers against the auricular confession of the Roman Catholics. T. C. BARTH'S *"Bible Manual"*

If a man's sin breaks out there is a minister at hand, a friend near, and others to reprove, to warn, to direct; but when he is the artificer of his lusts, he bars himself of all public remedy and takes great order and care to damn his soul by covering his *secret sins* with some plausible varnish which may beget a good opinion in others of his ways. OBADIAH SEDGWICK

There is a singular poem by Hood, called "The Dream of Eugene Aram"—a most remarkable piece it is indeed, illustrating the point on which we are now dwelling. Aram had murdered a man and cast his body into the river—"a sluggish water, black as ink, the depth was so extreme." The next morning he visited the scene of his guilt—

*And sought the black accursed pool,*
*With a wild misgiving eye;*
*And he saw the dead in the river bed,*
*For the faithless stream was dry.*

Next he covered the corpse with heaps of leaves, but a mighty wind swept through the wood and left the secret bare before the sun—

*Then down I cast me on my face*
*And first began to weep,*
*For I knew my secret then was one*
*That earth refused to keep;*
*On land or sea though it should be*
*Ten thousand fathoms deep.*

In plaintive notes, he prophesies his own discovery. He buried his victim in a cave, and trod him down with stones, but when years had run their weary round, the foul deed was discovered and the murderer put to death.

Hypocrisy is a hard game to play at, for it is one deceiver against many observers. Secret sinner! if thou wantest the foretaste of damnation upon earth, continue in thy secret sins; for no man is more miserable than he who sinneth secretly, and yet trieth to preserve a character. Yon stag, followed by the hungry hounds, with open mouths, is far more happy than the man who is pursued by his sins. SPURGEON'S SERMON on "*Secret Sins*"

When Satan tempts us, it is but like the casting of fire into tinder, that presently catcheth: our hearts kindle upon the least spark that falls; as a vessel that is brimful of water, upon the least jog, runs over. And hence it is, that many times small temptations and very petty occasions draw forth great corruptions: as a vessel, that is full of new liquor, upon the least vent given, works over into foam and froth. EZEKIEL HOPKINS

The Scripture doth often command that duty of searching and trying, of examining and communing with our hearts. ANTHONY BURGESS

Verses 12-13. He that will sin, and when he hath done will say—not to comfort his soul against Satan, but to flatter himself in his sin—that it is but an infirmity; for aught I know, he may go to hell for his infirmities.

David saith not *cleanse, but keep back Thy servant from presumptuous sins.* We may, then, be kept from them. Daily get your pardon. Except we be kept back from them they will *have dominion over us.* It follows, "*then shall I be upright;* so that the man in whom gross or presumptuous sin or sins have no dominion, he is an upright man. RICHARD CAPEL

Vs. 13. *Keep back Thy servant.* It is an evil man's cross to be restrained and a good man's joy to be kept back from sin. An evil man is kept back from sin, as a friend from a friend, as a lover from his lover, with knit affections and projects of meeting; but a good man is kept back from sin, as a man from his deadly enemy, whose presence he hates, and with desires of his ruin and destruction. It is the good man's misery that he hath yet a heart to be more tamed and mastered; it is an evil man's vexation and discontent that still, or at any time, he is held in by cord and bridle. OBADIAH SEDGWICK

It is not our grace, our prayer, our watchfulness keeps us, but it is the power of God, His right arm, supports us. ANTHONY BURGESS

God keeps back His servants from sin: 1. By preventing grace; 2. By assisting grace; 3. By quickening grace; 4. By directing grace; and 5. By doing grace. *Condensed from* OBADIAH SEDGWICK

*From presumptuous sins.* Presumptuous sins are peculiarly dangerous. It is remarkable that though an atonement was provided under the Jewish law for every kind of sin, there was this one exception: "But the soul that sinneth presumptuously shall have no atonement; it shall be cut off from the midst of my people." Presumptuous sinners, dying without pardon, must expect to receive a double portion of the wrath of God and a more terrible portion of eternal punishment in the pit that is digged for the wicked. C. H. S.

The Rabbins distinguish all sins unto those committed ignorantly and presumptuously. BENJAMIN KENNICOTT

When sin grows up from act to delight, from delight to new acts, from repetition of sinful acts to vicious indulgence, to habit and custom and a second nature, so that anything that toucheth upon it is grievous, and strikes to the man's heart; when it has gotten into God's place, and requires to be loved with the whole strength, makes grace strike sail, and other vices do it homage, demands all his concerns to be sacrificed to it and to be served with his reputation, his fortunes, his parts, his body and soul, to the irreparable loss of his time and eternity both—this is the height of its dominion—then sin becomes "exceedingly sinful." ADAM LITTLETON

David prays that God would keep him back from *presumptuous sins,* from known and evident sins, such as proceed from the choice of the perverse will against the enlightened mind. ALEXANDER CRUDEN

*Let them not have dominion over me.* Any small sin may get the upper hand of the sinner and bring him under in time, but a presumptuous sin worketh a great alteration in the state of the soul at once, and by one single act advanceth marvelously, weakening the spirit, and giving a mighty advantage to the flesh, even to the hazard of a complete conquest. ROBERT SANDERSON

First David prays, *Lord, keep me from secret sins,* which he maketh sins of ignorance, and then next he prays against *presumptuous sins,* which, as the opposition shows, are sins against knowledge; for says he, "if they get dominion over me, I shall not be free from that great offence," that is, that unpardonable sin which shall never be forgiven. For to commit that sin, but two things are required—light in the mind, and malice in the heart; not malice alone, unless there be light, for then that Apostle had sinned it, so as knowledge is the parent of it, it is "after receiving the knowledge of the truth" (Heb. 10:27-28). THOMAS GOODWIN

Happy souls, who, under a sense of peace through the blood of Jesus, are daily praying to be kept by the grace of the Spirit. Such truly know themselves, see their danger of falling, will not, dare not palliate or lessen the odious nature and hateful deformity of their sin. They will not give a softer name to sin than it deserves lest they depreciate the infinite value of that precious blood which Jesus shed to atone its guilt. Alas! the most exalted saint, the most established believer, if left to himself, how soon might the blackest crimes, the most *presumptuous sins,* get the *dominion* over him! WILLIAM MASON, in "*A Spiritual Treasury for the Children of God*"

*Then shall I be upright, and I shall be innocent from the great transgression.* He shudders at the thought of the unpardonable sin. Secret sin is a stepping-stone to presumptuous sin, and that is the vestibule of "the sin which is unto death." He who tempts the devil to tempt him is in a path which will lead him from bad to worse, and from the worse to the worst. C. H. S.

It is in the motions of a tempted soul to sin, as in the motions of a stone falling from the brow of a hill; it is easily stopped at first, but when once it is set a-going, who shall stay it? And therefore it is the greatest wisdom in the world to observe the first motions of the heart, to check and stop it there. G. H. SALTER

Take special heed of those sins that come near to the sin against the Holy Ghost; and these are, hypocrisy, taking only the outward profession of religion, and so dissembling and mocking of God; sinning wilfully against conviction of conscience, and against great light and knowledge, sinning presumptuously, with a high hand. These sins, though none of them are the direct sin against the Holy Ghost, yet they will come very near to it. ROBERT RUSSELL

Vs. 14. *Let the words of my mouth, and the meditation of my heart, be acceptable in Thy sight, O Lord, my Strength, and my Redeemer.* Words of the mouth are mockery if the heart does not meditate. C. H. S.

But, Lord, what are my words? what are my thoughts? Both are wicked, my heart a corrupt fountain, and my tongue an unclean stream; and shall I bring such a sacrifice to God? The halt, the lame, the blind, though otherwise the beasts be clean, yet are they sacrifices abominable to God: how much more if we offer those beasts which are unclean? And yet, Lord, my sacrifice is no better, faltering words, wandering thoughts, are neither of them presentable to Thee; how much less evil thoughts, and idle words? Yet such are the best of mine. What remedy? If any, it is in Thee, O Lord, that I must find it, and for it now do I seek unto Thee. Thou only, O Lord, canst hallow my tongue, and hallow my heart that my tongue may speak, and my heart think that which may *be acceptable unto Thee,* yea, that which may be Thy delight. ARTHUR LAKE (BISHOP), in "*Divine Meditations*"

## PSALM 20

Subject: We have before us a national anthem fitted to be sung at the outbreak of war, when the monarch was girding on his sword for the fight. If David had not been vexed with wars, we might never have been favored with such Psalms as this. There is a needs-be for the trials of one saint, that he may yield consolation to others.

Vs. 1. *The Lord hear thee in the day of trouble.* What a mercy that we may pray in the day of trouble, and what a still more blessed privilege that no trouble can prevent the Lord from hearing us! Troubles roar like thunder, but the believer's voice will be heard above the storm. C. H. S.

All the days of Christ were days of trouble. He was a brother born for adversity, a Man of sorrows and acquainted with griefs. . . . But more particularly it was a "day of trouble" with Him when He was in the Garden, heavy and sore amazed, and His sweat was, as it were, drops of blood falling on the ground, and His soul was exceeding sorrowful, even unto death; but more especially this was His case when He hung upon the cross . . . when He bore all the sins of His people, endured the wrath of His Father, and was forsaken by Him. *Condensed from* JOHN GILL

And who is there of the sons of men to whom a "day of trouble" does not come, whose path is not darkened at times, or with whom is it unclouded sunshine from the cradle to the grave? "Few plants," says old Jacomb, "have both the morning and the evening sun"; and one far older than he said, "Man is born to trouble." BARTON BOUCHIER

*The Name of the God of Jacob defend thee.* The more that they know of His name, that is, of His goodness, mercy, truth, power, wisdom, justice, etc., so may they the more boldly pray unto Him, not doubting but that He will be answerable unto His name . . . For as among men, according to the good name that they have for liberty and pity, so will men be ready to come unto them in their need, and the poor will say, "I will go to such an house, for they have a good name." NICHOLAS BOWND

I was once goaded by a poor, silly Irish papist to try it, who told me, in his consummate ignorance and bigotry, that if a priest would but give him a drop of holy water, and make a circle with it around a field full of wild beasts, they would not hurt him. I retired in disgust at the abominable trickery of such villains, reflecting, what a fool I am that I cannot put such trust in my God as this poor deluded man puts in his priest and a drop of holy water! JOSEPH IRONS

Vs. 2. *Send Thee help from the sanctuary.* Men of the world despise sanctuary help, but our hearts have learned to prize it beyond all material aid. They seek help out of the armory, or the treasury, or the buttery, but we turn to the sanctuary. C. H. S.

Here we see the nature of true faith, that it causeth us to see help in heaven, and so to pray for it when there is none to be seen in the earth.

And this is the difference between faith and unbelief; that the very unbelievers can by reason conceive of help, so long as they have any means to help them; but if they fail they can see none at all; so they are like unto those that are purblind, who can see nothing but near at hand. But faith seeth afar off, even into heaven, so that it is "the evidence of things that are not seen." NICHOLAS BOWND

Vs. 3. *Remember all thy offerings, and accept thy burnt sacrifice. Selah.* Before war kings offered sacrifice, upon the acceptance of which they depended for success; our blessed Lord presented Himself as a victim, and was a sweet savor unto the Most High, and then He met and routed the embattled legions of hell. C. H. S.

*All Thy offerings.* The humiliation that brought Him from heaven to earth; the patient tabernacling in the womb of the holy Virgin; the poor nativity; the hard manger; ox and ass for courtiers; the weary flight into Egypt; the poor cottage in Nazareth; the doing all good, and bearing all evil; the miracles, the sermons, the teachings; the being called a man gluttonous and a wine-bibber, the friend of publicans and sinners; the attribution of His wondrous deeds to Beelzebub.

*And accept Thy burnt sacrifices.* As every part of the victim was consumed in a burnt sacrifice, so what limb, what sense of our dear Lord did not agonize in His passion? The thorny crown on His head; the nails in His hands and feet; the reproaches that filled His ears; the gloating multitude on whom His dying gaze rested; the vinegar and the gall; the evil odors of the hill of death and corruption. The ploughers ploughed upon His back, and made long furrows; His most sacred face was smitten with the palm of the hand, His head with the reed. DIONYSIUS and GERHOHUS, *quoted by* J. M. NEALE

*Accept:* Hebrew "turn to ashes," by fire from heaven, in token of His acceptance, as was usual. MATTHEW POOLE

Vs. 5. *We will rejoice in Thy salvation.* We should fixedly resolve that come what may, we will rejoice in the saving arm of the Lord Jesus. The people in this Psalm, before their king went to battle, felt sure of victory, and therefore began to rejoice beforehand; how much more ought we to do this who have seen the victory completely won! Unbelief begins weeping for the funeral before the man is dead; why should not faith command piping before the dance of victory begins? C. H. S.

*In the Name of our God.* As those cried (Judg. 7:20): "The sword of the Lord and of Gideon"; and as we have it in Josh. 6:20: "And the people shouted, and the walls of Jericho fell down"; and King Abiah, crying out with his men in the same, killed five hundred thousand of the children of Israel.

So now also, according to the military custom in our day, the soldiers boast in the name and glory of their general in order to encourage themselves against their enemies. And it is just this custom that the present verse is now teaching, only in a godly and religious manner. MARTIN LUTHER

Vs. 6. *He will hear him.* I would be glad of the prayers of all the churches of Christ; oh, that there were not a saint on earth but that I were by name in his morning and evening prayer (whosoever thou art that readest, I beseech thee pray for me); but above all, let me have a property in those prayers and intercessions that are proper only to Christ; I am sure then I would never miscarry: Christ's prayers are heavenly, glorious, and very effectual. ISAAC AMBROSE

Vs. 7. *Some trust in chariots, and some in horses: but we will remember the Name of the Lord our God.* Chariots and horses make an imposing show, and with their rattling and dust and fine caparisons make so great a figure that vain man is much taken with them; yet the discerning eye of faith sees more in an invisible God than in all these. The most dreaded war-engine of David's day was the war-chariot, armed with scythes, which mowed down men like grass: this was the boast and glory of the neighboring nations; but the saints considered the name of Jehovah to be a far better defense.

The name of our God is Jehovah, and this should never be forgotten; the self-existent, independent, immutable, ever-present, all-filling I AM. Let us adore that matchless Name and never dishonor it by distrust or creature confidence. C. H. S.

About Michaelmas I was in the utmost extremity, and having gone out in the very fine weather, I contemplated the azure heavens, and my heart was so strengthened in faith (which I do not ascribe to my own powers, but solely to the grace of God), that I thought within myself, "What an excellent thing it is when we have nothing, and can rely upon nothing, but yet are acquainted with the living God, Who made heaven and earth, and place our confidence alone in Him, which enables us to be so tranquil even in necessity!"

Although I was well aware that I required something that very day, yet my heart was so strong in faith that I was cheerful and of good courage. On coming home, I was immediately waited upon by the overseer of the workmen and masons, who, as it was Saturday, required money to pay their wages. He expected the money to be ready, which he wished to go and pay, but enquired, however, whether I had received anything. "Has anything arrived?" asked he. I answered, "No, but I have faith in God."

Scarcely had I uttered the words when a student was announced who brought me thirty dollars from someone whom he would not name. I then went into the room again and asked the other how much he required for the workman's wages? He answered, "Thirty dollars." "Here they are," said I, and enquired at the same time if he needed anymore? He said, "No," which very much strengthened the faith of both of us, since we so visibly saw the miraculous hand of God, Who sent it at the very moment when it was needed. AUGUSTUS HERMAN FRANKE

Vs. 8. *They are brought down and fallen.* The world, death, Satan, and sin, shall all be trampled beneath the feet of the champions of faith; while those who rely upon an arm of flesh shall be ashamed and confounded forever. C. H. S.

# PSALM 21

If we pray today for a benefit and receive it, we must, ere the sun goes down, praise God for that mercy or we deserve to be denied the next time. It has been called David's triumphant song, and we may remember it as "The Royal Triumphal Ode." "The king" is most prominent throughout, and we shall read it to true profit if our meditation of Him shall be sweet while perusing it. C. H. S.

I am persuaded that there is not one who consents to the application of the preceding Psalm to Christ in His trouble, who will fail to recognize in this, Christ in His triumph.

There He was in the dark valley—the Valley of Achor: now He is on the Mount of Zion; there He was enduring sorrow and travail: now He remembers no more the anguish, for joy that a spiritual seed is born into the world; there He was beset with deadly enemies, who encompassed Him on every side: but here He has entered upon that which is written in Ps. 78:65-66: "Then the Lord awaked as one out of sleep, and like a mighty man that shouteth by reason of wine. And he smote His enemies in the hinder parts: He put them to a perpetual reproach." HAMILTON VERSCHOYLE

Vs. 1. *The king shall joy in Thy strength, O Lord.* Jesus is a royal Personage. The question, "Art Thou a king then?" received a full answer from the Savior's lips: "Thou sayest that I am a king. To this end was I born, and for this purpose came I into this world, that I might bear witness unto the truth."

He is not merely a king, but *the* King; King over minds and hearts, reigning with a dominion of love before which all other rule is but mere brute force. He was proclaimed King even on the cross, for there, indeed, to the eye of faith, He reigned as on a throne, blessing with more than imperial munificence the needy sons of earth. C. H. S.

*Thy strength . . . Thy salvation.* Not in strength alone is there matter of joy, every way considered. No, not in God's strength, if it have not salvation behind it. Strength, not to smite us down, but strength to deliver; this is the joyful side. Now turn it the other way. As strength, if it end in salvation, is just cause for joy, so salvation, if it go with strength, makes joy yet more joyful; for it becomes a strong salvation, a mighty deliverance. LANCELOT ANDREWES, in *"Conspiracie of the Gowries"*

The joy here spoken of is described by a note of exclamation and a word of wonder: *How greatly!* The rejoicing of our risen Lord must, like His agony, be unutterable. If the mountains of His joy rise in proportion to the depth of the valleys of His grief, then His sacred bliss is high as the seventh heaven. For the joy which was set before Him He endured the cross, despising the shame, and now that joy daily grows, for He rests in His love and rejoices over His redeemed with singing, as in due order they are brought to find their salvation in His blood.

Let us with our Lord rejoice in salvation, as coming from God, as coming to us, as extending itself to others, and as soon to encompass all lands. We need not be afraid of too much rejoicing in this respect; this solid foundation will well sustain the loftiest edifice of joy. The shoutings of the early Methodists in the excitement of the joy were far more pardonable than our own lukewarmness. Our joy should have some sort of inexpressibleness in it. C. H. S.

*And hast not withholden the request of his lips.* What is in the well of the heart is sure to come up in the bucket of the lips, and those are the only true prayers where the heart's desire is first, and the lip's request follows after.

Vs. 3. *For Thou preventest him with the blessings of goodness.* The word "prevent" formerly signified to precede or go before, and assuredly Jehovah preceded His Son with blessings. Before He died saints were saved by the anticipated merit of His death; before He came believers saw His day and were glad; and He Himself had His delights with the sons of men.

The Father is so willing to give blessings through His Son that instead of His being constrained to bestow His grace, He outstrips the mediatorial march of mercy. "I say not that I will pray the Father for you, for the Father Himself loveth you." Before Jesus calls the Father answers, and while He is yet speaking He hears. Mercies may be bought with blood, but they are also freely given. The love of Jehovah is not caused by the Redeemer's sacrifice, but that love, with its blessings of goodness, preceded the great atonement, and provided it for our salvation.

Reader, it will be a happy thing for thee if, like thy Lord, thou canst see both providence and grace preceding thee, forestalling thy needs, and preparing thy path. Mercy, in the case of many of us, ran before our desires and prayers, and it ever outruns our endeavors and expectancies, and even our hopes are left to lag behind. Prevenient grace deserves a song; we may make one out of this sentence; let us cry. C. H. S.

As if he should say, "Lord, I never asked a kingdom, I never thought of a kingdom, but Thou hast prevented me with the blessings of Thy goodness." From whence I take up this note or doctrine, that it is a sweet thing and worthy of all our thankful acknowledgements, to be prevented with the blessings of God's goodness or God's good blessings.

It is no new thing for God to walk in a way of preventing love and mercy with the children of men. Thus He hath always dealt, doth deal, and will deal; thus He hath always dealt with the world, with the nations of the world, with great towns and places, with families, and with particular souls.

And pray tell me what do you think of that whole chapter of Luke—the fifteenth? There are three parables: the Parable of the Lost Groat, of the Lost Sheep, and of the Lost Son. The woman lost her groat and swept to find it; but did the groat make first toward the woman or the woman make after the groat first?

The shepherd lost his sheep, but did the sheep make first after the shepherd or the shepherd after the sheep? Indeed, it is said concerning the lost son, that he first takes up a resolution, "I will return home to my father," but when his father saw him afar off, he ran and met him, and embraced him and welcomed him home. Why? But to show that the work of grace and mercy shall be all along carried in a way of preventing love. *Condensed from* WILLIAM BRIDGE

A large portion of our blessing is given us before our asking or seeking. Existence, reason, intellect, a birth in a Christian land, the calling of our nation to the knowledge of Christ, and Christ Himself, with many other things, are unsought bestowed on men, as was David's right to the throne on him. No one ever asked for a Savior till God of His own motion promised "the seed of the woman." WILLIAM S. PLUMER

*Thou settest a crown of pure gold on His head.* Jesus wore the thorn-crown, but now wears the glory-crown. It is a "crown," indicating royal nature, imperial power, deserved honor, glorious conquest, and divine government.

Napoleon crowned himself, but Jehovah crowned the Lord Jesus; the empire of the one melted in an hour, but the Other has an abiding dominion. C. H. S.

Vs. 4. *He asked life of Thee.* Hezekiah asked but one life, and God gave him fifteen years, which we reckon at two lives and more. He giveth liberally and like Himself; as great Alexander did when he gave the poor beggar a city; and when he sent his schoolmaster a ship full of frankincense and bade him sacrifice freely. JOHN TRAPP

Vs. 5. *His glory is great in Thy salvation.* Lord, Who is like unto Thee? Solomon in all his glory could not be compared with Thee, Thou once despised Man of Nazareth! C. H. S.

I remember one dying and hearing some discourse of Jesus Christ. "Oh," said she, "speak more of this—let me hear more of this—be not weary of telling His praise; I long to see Him. How should I but long to hear of Him?" Surely I cannot say too much of Jesus Christ. On this blessed subject, no man can possibly hyperbolize. Had I the tongues of men and angels, I could never fully set forth Christ. It involves an eternal contradiction, that the creature can see to the bottom of the Creator.

Suppose all the sands on the seashore, all the flowers, herbs, leaves, twigs of trees in woods and forests, all the stars of heaven, were all rational creatures; and had that wisdom, and tongues of angels to speak of the loveliness, beauty, glory, and excellency of Christ, as gone to heaven, and sitting at the right hand of His Father, they would, in all their expressions, stay millions of miles on this side Jesus Christ. ISAAC AMBROSE

*Honor and majesty hast Thou laid upon Him.* If there be a far more exceeding and eternal weight of glory for His humble followers, what must there be for our Lord Himself? The whole weight of sin was laid upon Him; it is but meet that the full measure of the glory of bearing it away should be laid upon the same Beloved Person. A glory commensurate with His shame He must and will receive, for well has He earned it. It is not possible for us to honor Jesus too much; what our God delights to do, we may certainly do to our utmost. C. H. S.

Happy he who hath a bone, or an arm, to put the crown upon the head of our highest King, whose chariot is paved with love. Were there ten thousand millions of heavens created above these highest heavens, and again as many above them, and as many above them, till angels were wearied with counting, it were but too low a seat to fix the princely throne of that Lord Jesus (whose ye are) above them all. SAMUEL RUTHERFORD

Vs. 7. *Through the mercy of the most High He shall not be moved.* Eternal mercy secures the mediatorial throne of Jesus. He Who is most High in every sense engages all His infinite perfections to maintain the throne of grace upon which our king in Zion reigns. He was not moved from His purpose, nor in His sufferings, nor by His enemies, nor shall He be moved from the completion of His designs. He is the same yesterday, today, and forever. C. H. S.

Vs. 8. Who may abide the day of His coming? If Joseph's brethren were so terrified that they "could not answer him" when he said, "I am Joseph your brother," how will it be with sinners when they shall hear the voice of the Son of God, when He shall triumph over them in His wrath, and say unto them, "I am He" Whom ye despised; "I am He" Whom ye have offended; "I am He" Whom ye have crucified?

If these words, "I am He," overthrew the soldiers in the Garden of Olives (John 18:6), though spoken with extreme gentleness, how will it be when His indignation bursts forth, when it falls upon His enemies like a thunderbolt and reduces them into dust? Then will they cry out in terror and say to the mountains, "Fall on us, and hide us from the face of Him that sitteth on the throne and from the wrath of the Lamb" (Rev. 6:16). JAMES NOUET

Vs. 9. *Thou shalt make them as a fiery oven in the time of Thine anger.* Like faggots cast into an oven, they shall burn furiously beneath the anger of the Lord; "they shall be cast into a furnace of fire, there shall be weeping and gnashing of teeth."

These are terrible words, and those teachers do not well who endeavor by their sophistical reasonings to weaken their force. Reader, never tolerate slight thoughts of hell or you will soon have low thoughts of sin. The hell of sinners must be fearful beyond all conception or such language as the present would not be used. Who would have the Son of God to be his enemy when such an overthrow awaits His foes?

The expression, "the time of Thine anger," reminds us that as now is the time of His grace, so there will be a set time for His wrath. The judge goes upon assize at an appointed time. There is a day of vengeance of our God; let those who despise the day of grace remember this day of wrath. C. H. S.

They shall not only be cast into a furnace of fire (Matt. 13:42), but He shall make them themselves as a fiery oven or furnace, they shall be their own tormentors; the reflections and terrors of their own consciences will be their hell. Those that might have had Christ to rule and save them, but rejected Him, and fought against Him, even the remembrance of that will be enough to make them to eternity a fiery oven to themselves. MATTHEW HENRY

No power can rescue us from God's anger, no ransom but Christ's blood redeem us. God's will being set afoot, all His attributes follow; if His will say, "Be angry," His eye seeks out the object of His anger and finds it; His wisdom tempers the cup, His hand whets the sword, His arm strikes the blow. Thus you see there is a time of God's anger for sin, because He will have it so. JOHN CRAGGE

Vs. 11. *For they intended evil against Thee.* God takes notice of intentions. He who would but could not is as guilty as he who did. Christ's church and cause are not only attacked by those who do not understand it, but there are many who have the light and yet hate it.

Intentional evil has a virus in it which is not found in sins of ignorance; now as ungodly men with malice aforethought attack the gospel of Christ, their crime is great, and their punishment will be proportionate. The words *against Thee* show us that he who intends evil against the poorest believer means ill to the King Himself: let persecutors beware.

*They imagined a mischievous device, which they are not able to perform.* Want of power is the clog on the foot of the haters of the Lord Jesus. They have the wickedness to imagine, and the cunning to devise, and the malice to plot mischief, but blessed be God, they fail in ability; yet they shall be judged as to their hearts, and the will shall be taken for the deed in the great day of account. C. H. S.

# PSALM 22

Title: *Aijeleth Shahar.* The title of the Twenty-Second Psalm is "Aijeleth Shahar"—*the morning hart.* The whole Psalm refers to Christ, containing much that cannot be applied to another: parting His garments, casting lots for His vesture, etc.

He is described as a kindly, meek, and beautiful hart started by the huntsman at the dawn of the day. Herod began hunting Him down as soon as He appeared. Poverty, the hatred of men, and the temptation of Satan, joined in the pursuit. There always was some "dog" or "bull" or "unicorn" ready to attack Him. After His first sermon, the huntsmen gathered about Him, but He was too fleet of foot and escaped.

Christ found Calvary a craggy, jagged, and fearful hill—"a mountain of division." Hence He was driven by the huntsmen to the edges of the awful precipices yawning destruction from below, while He was surrounded and held at bay by all the beasts of prey and monsters of the infernal forest. The "unicorn" and the "bulls of Bashan" gored Him with their horns; the great "lion" roared at Him; and the "dog" fastened himself upon Him.

But He foiled them all. In His own time He bowed His head and gave up the ghost. He was buried in a new grave and His assailants reckoned upon complete victory. They had not considered that He was a "morning hart." Surely enough, at the appointed time, did He escape from the hunter's net and stand forth on the mountains of Israel alive and never, never to die again.

Now He is with Mary in the garden, giving evidence of His own resurrection; in a moment He is at Emmaus, encouraging the too timid and bewildered disciples. Nor does it cost Him any trouble to go thence to Galilee to His friends, and again to the Mount of Olives, "on the mountains of spices," carrying with Him the day-dawn, robed in life and beauty forevermore. CHRISTMAS EVANS.

Subject: This is beyond all others "The Psalm of The Cross." It may have been actually repeated word by word by our Lord when hanging on the tree; it would be too bold to say that it was so, but even a casual reader may see that it might have been. It begins with, "My God, my God, why hast Thou forsaken Me?" and ends, according to some, in the original, with, "It is finished." For plaintive expressions uprising from unutterable depths of woe, we may say of this Psalm, "There is none like it."

It is the photograph of our Lord's saddest hours, the record of His dying words, the lachrymatory of His last tears, the memorial of His expiring joys. David and his afflictions may be here in a very modified sense, but, as the star is concealed by the light of the sun, he who sees Jesus will probably neither see nor care to see David.

Before us we have a description both of the darkness and of glory of the cross, the sufferings of Christ and the glory which shall follow. Oh, for grace to draw near and see this great sight! We should read reverently, putting off our shoes from off our feet, as Moses did at the burning bush, for if there be holy ground anywhere in Scripture it is in this Psalm. C. H. S.

Vs. 1. *My God, my God.* Let us gaze with holy wonder and mark the flashes of light amid the awful darkness of that midday-midnight. First, our Lord's faith beams forth and deserves our reverent imitation; He keeps His hold upon His God with both hands and cries twice, *My God, my God!* The spirit of adoption was strong within the suffering Son of man, and He felt no doubt about His interest in His God. Oh, that we could imitate this cleaving to an afflicting God! Nor does the sufferer distrust the power of God to sustain Him, for the title used—*El*—signifies strength and is the Name of the mighty God.

*Why hast Thou forsaken Me?* We must lay the emphasis on every word of this saddest of all utterances.

*Why?* What is the great cause of such a strange fact as for God to leave His own Son at such a time and in such a plight? There was no cause in Him; why then was He deserted?

*Hast.* It is done, and the Savior is feeling its dread effect as He asks the question; it is surely true, but how mysterious! It was no threatening of forsaking which made the great Surety cry aloud. He endured that forsaking in very deed.

*Thou.* I can understand why traitorous Judas and timid Peter should be gone, but Thou, my God, my faithful Friend, how canst Thou leave Me? This is the worst of all, yea, worse than all put together. Hell itself has for its fiercest flame the separation of the soul from God.

*Forsaken.* If Thou hadst chastened I might bear it, for Thy face would shine; but to forsake Me utterly, ah! why is this?

*Me.* Thine innocent, obedient, suffering Son—why leavest Thou Me to perish? A sight of self seen by penitence, and of Jesus on the cross seen by faith, will best expound this question. Jesus is forsaken because our sins had separated between us and our God. C. H. S.

*Why?* Not the *Why* of impatience or despair, not the sinful questioning of one whose heart rebels against his chastening, but rather the cry of a lost child who cannot understand why his father has left him, and who longs to see his father's face again. J. J. STEWART PEROWNE

Oh! how will our very hearts melt with love when we remember that as we have been distressed for our sins against Him; so He was in greater agonies for us! We have had gall and wormwood, but He tasted a more bitter cup. The anger of God has dried up our spirits, but He was scorched with a more flaming wrath.

He was under violent pain in the garden and on the cross; ineffable was the sorrow that He felt, being forsaken of His Father, deserted by His disciples, affronted and reproached by His enemies, and under a curse for us. This Sun was under a doleful eclipse, this living Lord was pleased to die, and in His death was under the frowns of an angry God. TIMOTHY ROGERS

Vs. 2. *O my God, I cry in the daytime, but Thou hearest not.* For our prayers to appear to be unheard is no new trial. Jesus felt it before us, and it is observable that He still held fast His believing hold on God, and cried still, *My God.* On the other hand, His faith did not render Him less importunate, for amid the hurry and horror of that dismal day He ceased not His cry, even as in Gethemane He had agonized all through the gloomy night.

Our Lord continued to pray even though no comfortable answer came, and in this He set us an example of obedience to His own words, "Men ought always to pray, and not to faint." No daylight is too glaring, and no midnight too dark to pray in; and no delay or apparent denial, however grievous, should tempt us to forbear from importunate pleading. C. H. S.

Verses 2-3. They that have conduit-water come into their houses, if no water come they do not conclude the spring to be dry, but the pipes to be stopped or broken. If prayer speed not, we must be sure that the fault is not with God but in ourselves; were we but ripe for mercy, He is ready to extend it to us, and even waits for the purpose. JOHN TRAPP

Vs. 3. *But Thou art holy, O Thou that inhabitest the praises of Israel.* If we cannot perceive any ground for the delay in answering prayer, we must leave the riddle unsolved, but we must not fly in God's face in order to invent an answer. The argument is: Thou art holy; oh, why is it that Thou dost disregard Thy holy One in His hour of sharpest anguish? We may not question the holiness of God, but we may argue from it and use it as a plea in our petitions. C. H. S.

Here is the triumph of faith—the Savior stood like a rock in the wide ocean of temptation. High as the billows rose, so did His faith, like the coral rock, wax greater and stronger till it became an island of salvation to our ship-wrecked souls. It is as if He had said, "It matters not what I endure. Storms may howl upon Me, men despise, devils tempt, circumstances overpower, and God Himself forsake Me; still God is holy; there is no unrighteousness in Him." JOHN STEVENSON

Does it seem strange that the heart in its darkness and sorrow should find comfort in this attribute of God? No, for God's holiness is but another aspect of His faithfulness and mercy. And in that remarkable name, "the Holy One of Israel," we are taught that He Who is the *holy* God is also the God Who has made a covenant with His chosen. J. J. STEWART PEROWNE

Were temptations ever so black, faith will not hearken to an ill word spoken against God, but will justify God alway. DAVID DICKSON

Vs. 4. *Our fathers trusted in Thee: they trusted, and Thou didst deliver them.* This is the rule of life with all the chosen family. Three times over is it mentioned, they *trusted,* and *trusted,* and *trusted,* and never left off trusting, for it was their very life; and they fared well too, for *Thou didst deliver them.*

The experience of other saints may be a great consolation to us when in deep waters if faith can be sure that their deliverance will be ours; but when we feel ourselves sinking, it is poor comfort to know that others are swimming.

The use of the plural pronoun *our* shows how one with His people Jesus was even on the cross. We say, "Our Father which art in heaven," and He calls those "our fathers" through whom we came into the world, although He was without father as to the flesh.

Vs. 6. *But I am a worm, and no man.* This verse is a miracle in language. How could the Lord of glory be brought to such abasement as to be not only lower than the angels but even lower than men? What a contrast between "I AM" and *I am a worm!* yet such a double nature was found in the person of our Lord Jesus when bleeding on the tree.

He felt Himself to be comparable to a helpless, powerless, down-trodden worm, passive while crushed and unnoticed and despised by those who trod upon Him. He selects the weakest of creatures, which is all flesh, and becomes, when trodden upon, writhing, quivering flesh, utterly devoid of any might except strength to suffer.

This was a true likeness of Himself when His body and soul had become a mass of misery—the very essence of agony—in the dying pangs of crucifixion. Man by nature is but a worm; but our Lord puts Himself even beneath man, on account of the scorn which was heaped upon Him and the weakness which He felt, and therefore He adds, *and no man.* C. H. S.

He, coming to perform the great work of our redemption, did cover and hide His Godhead within the worm of His human nature. The grand water-serpent, Leviathan, the devil, thinking to swallow the worm of His humanity, was caught upon the hook of His Divinity. This hook stuck in his jaws, and tore him very sore. By thinking to destroy Christ, he destroyed his own kingdom, and lost his own power for ever. LANCELOT ANDREWES

So trodden under foot, trampled upon, maltreated, buffeted, and spit upon, mocked and tormented, as to seem more like a worm than a man. Behold what great contempt hath the Lord of Majesty endured, that His confusion may be our glory; His punishment our heavenly bliss! Without ceasing impress this spectacle, O Christian, on thy soul! DIONYSIUS, *quoted by* ISAAC WILLIAMS

Vs. 7. *All they that see Me laugh Me to scorn: they shoot out the lip, they shake the head.* Priests and people, Jews and Gentiles, soldiers and civilians, all united in the general scoff, and that at the time when He was prostrate in weakness and ready to die. Which shall we wonder at the most, the cruelty of man or the love of the bleeding Savior? How can we ever complain of ridicule after this?

Men made faces at Him before Whom angels veil their faces and adore. The basest signs of disgrace which disdain could devise were maliciously cast at Him. C. H. S.

Imagine this dreadful scene. Behold this motley multitude of rich and poor, of Jews and Gentiles! Some stand in groups and gaze. Some recline at ease and stare. Others move about in restless gratification at the event. There is a look of satisfaction on every countenance. None are silent. The velocity of speech seems tardy. The theme is far too great for one member to utter. Every lip, and head, and finger, is now a tongue.

The rough soldiers, too, are busied in their coarse way. The work of blood is over. Refreshment had become necessary. Their usual beverage of vinegar and water is supplied them. As they severally are satisfied, they approach the cross, hold some forth to the Savior, and bid Him drink as they withdraw it (Luke 23:36). They know He must be suffering an intense thirst; they therefore aggravate it with the mockery of refreshment.

Cruel Romans! and ye, O regicidal Jews! Was not death enough? Must mockery and scorn be added? On this sad day, Christ made you one indeed! Dreadful unity—which constituted you the joint mockers and murderers of the Lord of glory! JOHN STEVENSON

Vs. 8. *He trusted on the Lord that He would deliver Him: let Him deliver Him, seeing He delighted in Him.* Here the taunt is cruelly aimed at the sufferer's faith in God, which is the tenderest point in a good man's soul, the very apple of his eye. They must have learned the diabolical art from Satan himself, for they made rare proficiency in it.

Vs. 9. *But Thou art He that took me out of the womb.* The destitute state of Joseph and Mary, far away from friends and home, led them to see the cherishing hand of God in the safe delivery of the mother, and the happy birth of the child; that Child now fighting the great battle of His life, uses the mercy of His nativity as an argument with God. Faith finds weapons everywhere. He who wills to believe shall never lack reasons for believing. C. H. S.

*Thou didst make me hope when I was upon my mother's breasts.* Was our Lord so early a believer? Was He one of those babes and sucklings out of whose mouths strength is ordained? So it would seem; and if so, what a plea for help! Early piety gives peculiar comfort in our after trials, for surely He Who loved us when we were children is too faithful to cast us off in our riper years. C. H. S.

Vs. 10. *Thou art my God from my mother's belly.* Our birth was our weakest and most perilous period of existence; if we were then secured by Omnipotent tenderness, surely we have no cause to suspect that divine goodness will fail us now. He Who was our God when we left our mother will be with us till we return to Mother Earth and will keep us from perishing in the belly of hell.

Vs. 12. *Many bulls have compassed Me: strong bulls of Bashan have beset Me round.* The mighty ones in the crowd are here marked by the tearful eye of their victim. The priests, elders, scribes, Pharisees, rulers, and captains bellowed round the cross like wild cattle, fed in the fat and solitary pastures of Bashan, full of strength and fury; they stamped and foamed around the innocent One, and longed to gore Him to death with their cruelties. Conceive of the Lord Jesus as a helpless, unarmed, naked man, cast into the midst of a herd of infuriated wild bulls. C. H. S.

Verses 12-13. "Bashan" was a fertile country (Num. 32:4), and the cattle there fed were fat and "strong" (Deut. 32:14). Like them, the Jews in that good land "waxed fat and kicked," grew proud and rebelled; forsook God "that made them, and lightly esteemed the rock of their salvation." GEORGE HORNE

Vs. 14. *I am poured out like water:* that is, in the thought of my enemies, I am utterly destroyed. "For we must needs die, and are as water spilt on the ground, which cannot be gathered up again" (II Sam. 14:14). "What marvel," asks St. Bernard, "that the Name of the Bridegroom should be as ointment poured forth, when He Himself, for the greatness of His love, was poured forth like water!" J. M. NEALE

*All My bones are out of joint.* The rack is devised as a most exquisite pain, even for terror. And the cross is a rack, whereon He was stretched till, saith the Psalm, *all His bones were out of joint.* But even to stand, as He hung, three long hours together, holding up but the arms at length, I have heard it avowed of some that have felt it, to be a pain scarce incredible.

But the hands and the feet being so cruelly nailed (part, of all other, most sensible, by reason of the texture of sinews there in them most) it could not but make His pain out of measure painful. LANCELOT ANDREWES

*My heart is like wax; it is melted in the midst of My bowels.* Dr. Gill wisely observes, "if the heart of Christ, the Lion of the tribe of Judah, melted at it, what heart can endure, or hands be strong, when God deals with them in His wrath?"

Vs. 16. *For dogs have compassed Me.* Hunters frequently surround their game with a circle and gradually encompass them with an ever-narrowing ring of dogs and men. Such a picture is before us. In the center stands, not a panting stag, but a bleeding, fainting man, and around Him are the enraged and unpitying wretches who have hounded Him to His doom. Here we have the "hind of the morning" of Whom the Psalm so plaintively sings, hunted by bloodhounds, all thirsting to devour Him.

*The assembly of the wicked have inclosed Me.* Thus the Jewish people were unchurched, and that which called itself an assembly of the righteous is justly for its sins marked upon the forehead as an assembly of the wicked. This is not the only occasion when professed churches of God have become synagogues of Satan and have persecuted the Holy One and the Just. C. H. S.

*They pierced My hands and My feet.* It was much for the Son of God to be bound, more to be beaten, most of all to be slain; but what shall I say to this, that He was crucified? That was the most vile and ignominious; it was also a cruel and cursed kind of death, which yet He refused not; and here we have a clear testimony for His cross. JOHN TRAPP

The tearing asunder of the tender fibers of the hands and feet, the lacerating of so many nerves, and bursting so many blood-vessels, must be productive of intense agony. The nerves of the hand and foot are intimately connected, through the arm and leg, with the nerves of the whole body; their laceration therefore must be felt over the entire frame. Witness the melancholy result of even a needle's puncture in even one of the remotest nerves. A spasm is not infrequently produced by it in the muscles of the face, which locks the jaws inseparably.

When, therefore, the hands and feet of our blessed Lord were transfixed with nails, He must have felt the sharpest pangs shoot through every part of His body. Supported only by His lacerated limbs, and suspended from His pierced hands, our Lord had nearly six hours' torment to endure. JOHN STEVENSON

Vs. 17. *I may tell all My bones.* Oh, that we cared less for the body's enjoyment and ease and more for our Father's business! It were better to count the bones of an emaciated body than to bring leanness into our souls.

*They look and stare upon Me.* Let us blush for human nature and mourn in sympathy with our Redeemer's shame. The first Adam made us all naked, and therefore the second Adam became naked that He might clothe our naked souls. C. H. S.

Oh, how different is that look which the awakened sinner directs to Calvary, when faith lifts up her eye to Him Who agonized, and bled, and died, for the guilty! And what gratitude should perishing men feel, that from Him that hangs upon the accursed tree there is heard proceeding the inviting sound, "Look unto Me, and be ye saved, all ye ends of the earth, for I am God, and besides Me there is none else." JOHN MORISON

Vs. 18. *They part My garments among them, and cast lots upon My vesture.* It may be noted that the habit of gambling is of all others the most hardening, for men could practice it even at the cross-foot while besprinkled with the blood of the Crucified. No Christian will endure the rattle of the dice when he thinks of this. C. H. S.

Trifling as this act of casting lots for our Lord's vesture may appear, it is most significant. It contains a double lesson. It teaches us how greatly that seamless shirt was valued; how little He to Whom it had belonged. It seemed to say, this garment is more valuable than its owner. As it was said of the thirty pieces of silver, "A goodly price at which I was prized at of them"; so may we say regarding the casting of the lot, "How cheaply Christ was held!" JOHN STEVENSON

Vs. 21. *Save Me from the lion's mouth.* Satan is called a lion, and that fitly; for he hath all the properties of the lion: as bold as a lion, as strong as a lion, as furious as a lion, as terrible as the roaring of a lion. Yea, worse: the lion wants subtlety and suspicion; herein the devil is beyond the lion. The lion will spare the prostrate; the devil spares none.

The lion is full and forbears; the devil is full and devours. He seeks all; let not the simple say, "He will take no notice of me"; nor the subtle, "He cannot overreach me"; nor the noble say, "He will not presume to meddle with me"; nor the rich, "He dares not contest with me"; for he seeks to devour all. He is our common adversary; therefore let us cease all quarrels amongst ourselves, and fight with him. THOMAS ADAMS

Verses 21-22. The transition is very marked; from a horrible tempest all is changed into calm. The darkness of Calvary at length passed away from the face of nature and from the soul of the Redeemer and, beholding the light of His triumph and its future results, the Savior smiled.

Vs. 22. *I will declare Thy Name unto My brethren.* Among His first resurrection words were these, "Go to My brethren." In the verse before us, Jesus anticipates happiness in having communication with His people; He purposes to be their teacher and minister, and fixes His mind upon the subject of His discourse. We may learn from this resolution of our Lord that one of the most excellent methods of showing our thankfulness for deliverances is to tell to our brethren what the Lord has done for us. We mention our sorrows readily enough; why are we so slow in declaring our deliverances? C. H. S.

*My brethren.* This gives evidence of the low condescension of the Son of God, and also of the high exaltation of sons of men; for the Son of God to be a brother to sons of men is a great degree of humiliation, and for sons of men to be made brethren with the Son of God is a high degree of exaltation; for Christ's brethren are in that respect sons of God, heirs of salvation, or kings, not earthly, but heavenly; not temporary, but everlasting kings . . . This respect of Christ to His brethren is a great encouragement and comfort to such as are despised and scorned by men of this world for Christ's professing of them. WILLIAM GOUGE

Vs. 24. *For He hath not despised nor abhorred the affliction of the afflicted.* 'Tis true that justice demanded that Christ should bear the burden which as a substitute He undertook to carry, but Jehovah always loved Him and in love laid that load upon Him with a view to His ultimate glory and to the accomplishment of the dearest wish of His heart.

*But when He cried unto Him, He heard.*

*None that approach His throne shall find*
*A God unfaithful or unkind.*

Vs. 25. *My praise shall be of Thee in the great congregation.* The word in the original is "from Thee"—true praise is of celestial origin. The rarest harmonies of music are nothing unless they are sincerely consecrated to God by hearts sanctified by the Spirit.

Vs. 26. *The meek shall eat and be satisfied.* Mark how the dying Lover of our souls solaces Himself with the result of His death! The spiritually poor find a feast in Jesus; they feed upon Him to the satisfaction of their hearts; they were famished until He gave Himself for them: but now they are filled with royal dainties. C. H. S.

*They shall praise the Lord that seek Him: your heart shall live forever.* Now, I would fain know the man that ever went about to form such laws as should bind the hearts of men or prepare such rewards as should reach the souls and consciences of men!

Truly, if any mortal man should make a law that his subjects should love him with all their hearts and souls, and not dare, upon peril of his greatest indignation, to entertain a traitorous thought against his royal person, but presently confess it to him, or else he would be avenged on him, he would deserve to be more laughed at for his pride and folly than Xerxes for casting his fetters into the Hellespont to chain the waves into his obedience; or Caligula, that threatened the air if it durst rain when he was at his pastimes, who durst not himself so much as look into the air when it thundered.

Certainly a madhouse would be more fit for such a person than a throne, who should so far forfeit his reason as to think that the thoughts and hearts of men were within his jurisdiction. WILLIAM GURNALL

Vs. 27. *All the ends of the world shall remember and turn unto the Lord: and all kindreds of the nations shall worship before Thee.* The nature of true conversion: It is to *remember—to turn to the Lord*—and to *worship before Him.* This is a plain and simple process. Perhaps the first religious exercise of mind of which we are conscious is reflection. A state of unregeneracy is a state of forgetfulness. God is forgotten. Sinners have lost all just sense of His glory, authority, mercy, and judgment; living as if there is no God, or as if they thought there is none.

But if ever we are brought to be the subjects of true conversion, we shall be brought to remember these things. This divine change is fitly expressed by the case of the Prodigal, who is said to have come to himself, or to his right mind.

But further, true conversion consists not only in remembering, but in *turning to the Lord.* This part of the passage is expressive of a cordial relinquishment of our idols, whatever they have been, and an acquiescence in the gospel way of salvation by Christ alone. Once more, true conversion to Christ will be accompanied with the *worship* of Him. *Condensed from Andrew Fuller*

*All the ends of the world shall remember.* This is a remarkable expression. It implies that man has forgotten God. It represents all the successive generations of the world as but one, and then it exhibits that one generation, as if it had been once in paradise suddenly remembering the Lord Whom it had known there but had long forgoteten. The converted nations, we learn by this verse, will not only obtain remembrance of their past loss but will also be filled with the knowledge of the present duty. JOHN STEVENSON

Vs. 29. *None can keep alive his own soul.* This is the stern counterpart of the gospel message of "look and live." There is no salvation out of Christ. We must hold life and have life as Christ's gift, or we shall die eternally. This is very solid evangelical doctrine and should be proclaimed in every corner of the earth, that like a great hammer it may break in pieces all self-confidence. C. H. S.

## PSALM 23

There is no inspired title to this Psalm, and none is needed, for it records no special event and needs no other key than that which every Christian may find in his own bosom. It is David's "Heavenly Pastoral"; a surpassing ode, which none of the daughters of music can excel. The clarion of war here gives place to the pipe of peace, and he who so lately bewailed the woes of the Shepherd tunefully rehearses the joys of the flock.

This is the pearl of Psalms, whose soft and pure radiance delights every eye; a pearl of which Helicon need not be ashamed, though Jordan claims it. Of this delightful song, it may be affirmed that its piety and its poetry are equal, its sweetness and its spirituality are unsurpassed.

The position of this Psalm is worthy of notice. It follows the Twenty-Second, which is peculiarly the "Psalm of the Cross." There are no green pastures, no still waters on the other side of the Twenty-Second Psalm. It is only after we have read, "My God, my God, why hast Thou forsaken Me?" that we come to "The Lord is my Shepherd." We must by experience know the value of the Blood-shedding and see the sword awakened against the Shepherd before we shall be able truly to know the sweetness of the good Shepherd's care.

It has been said that what the nightingale is among birds, that is this Divine ode among the Psalms, for it has sung sweetly in the ear of many a mourner in his night of weeping and has bidden him hope for a morning of joy. I will venture to compare it also to the lark, which sings as it mounts, and mounts as it sings, until it is out of sight, and even then is not out of hearing. C. H. S.

Augustine is said to have beheld, in a dream, the One Hundred and Nineteenth Psalm rising before him as a tree of life in the midst of the paradise of God. This Twenty-Third may be compared to the fairest flowers that grew around it. The former has ever been likened to the sun amidst the stars—surely this is like the richest of the constellations, even the Pleiades themselves! John Stoughton in *"The Songs of Christ's Flock"*

Some pious souls are troubled because they cannot at all times, or often, use, in its joyous import, the language of this Psalm. Such should remember that David, though he lived long, never wrote but one Twenty-Third Psalm. William S. Plumer

Vs. 1. *The Lord is my shepherd.* It is well to know, as certainly as David did, that we belong to the Lord. There is a noble note of confidence about this sentence. There is no "if" nor "but," nor even "I hope so"; but he says, "The Lord is my shepherd." We must cultivate the spirit of assured dependence upon our heavenly Father.

The sweetest word of the whole is that monosyllable, *My.* He does not say, "The Lord is the shepherd of the world at large, and leadeth forth the multitude as His flock," but "The Lord is my shepherd"; if He be a shepherd to no one else, He is a shepherd to me; He cares for me, watches over me, and preserves me. The words are in the present tense. Whatever be the believer's position, he is even now under the pastoral care of Jehovah. C. H. S.

Satan deals seemingly sweet that he may draw you into sin, but in the end he will be really bitter to you. Christ, indeed, is seemingly bitter to keep you from sin, hedging up your way with thorns. But He will be really sweet if you come into His flock, even notwithstanding your sins. It may be now Satan smiles and is pleasant to you while you sin; but you know, he will be bitter in the end. He that sings siren-like now will devour lion-like at last. He will torment you and vex you and be burning and bitterness to you.

Oh, come in, therefore, to Jesus Christ; let Him be now the Shepherd of thy soul. And know then, He will be sweet in endeavoring to keep thee from sin before thou commit it; and He will be sweet in delivering thee from sin after thou hast committed it. Oh, that this thought—that Jesus Christ is sweet in His carriage unto all His members, unto all His flock, especially the sinning ones, might persuade the hearts of some sinners to come in unto His fold. JOHN DURANT

I notice that some of the flock keep near the shepherd and follow whithersoever he goes without the least hesitation, while others stray about on either side, or loiter far behind; and he often turns around and scolds them in a sharp, stern cry, or sends a stone after them. I saw him lame one just now. Not altogether unlike the good Shepherd.

And when the thief and the robber come (and come they do), the faithful shepherd has often to put his life in his hand to defend his flock. I have known more than one case in which he had literally to lay it down in the contest. A poor, faithful fellow last spring, between Tiberias and Tabor, instead of fleeing, actually fought three Bedawin robbers until he was hacked to pieces with their khanjars and died among the sheep he was defending.

Some sheep always keep near the shepherd and are his special favorites. Each of them has a name to which it answers joyfully, and the kind shepherd is ever distributing to such, choice portions which he gathers for that purpose. There are the contented and happy ones. They are in no danger of getting lost or into mischief nor do wild beasts or thieves come near them.

The great body, however, are mere worldlings, intent upon their mere pleasures or selfish interests. They run from bush to bush, searching for variety or delicacies, and only now and then lift their heads to see where the shepherd is, or, rather where the general flock is, lest they get so far away as to occasion a remark in their little community or rebuke from their keeper.

Others, again, are restless and discontented, jumping into everbody's field, climbing into bushes, and even into leaning trees, whence they often fall and break their limbs. These cost the good shepherd incessant trouble. W. M. THOMSON, in *"The Land and the Book"*

The next words are a sort of inference from the first statement—they are sententious and positive—*I shall not want.* I might want otherwise, but when the Lord is my Shepherd He is able to supply all my needs, and He is certainly willing to do so, for His heart is full of love, and therefore *I shall not want.* I shall not lack for temporal things. Does He not feed the ravens and cause the lilies to grow? How, then, can He leave His children to starve? I shall not want for spirituals; I know that His grace will be sufficient for me. C. H. S.

"I want nothing": thus it may be equally well rendered, though in our version it is in the future tense. J. R. MACDUFF, in *"The Shepherd and His Flock"*

Only he who can want does not want; and he who cannot, does. You tell me that a godly man wants these and these things, which the wicked man hath; but I tell you he can no more be said to *want* them than a butcher may be said to want Homer, or such another thing, because his disposition is such, that he makes no use of those things which you usually mean. 'Tis but only necessary things that he cares for, and those are not many. Even so it is when we say that a godly man wanteth nothing. For though in regard of unnecessary goods he be "as having nothing," yet in regard of others he is as if he possessed all things. He wants nothing that is necessary either for his glorifying of God (being able to do that best in and by his afflictions), or for God's glorifying of him, and making him happy, having God Himself for his portion and supply of his wants, Who is abundantly sufficient at all times, for all persons, in all conditions. ZACHARY BOGAN

How *can* we want. When united to Him, we have a right to use all His riches. Our wealth is His riches and glory. With Him nothing can be withheld. Eternal life is ours, with the promise that all shall be added; all He knows we want. THEODOSIA A. HOWARD, *Viscountess Powerscourt in "Letters" etc., edited by Robert Daly*

In the tenth chapter of John's Gospel, you will find six marks of Christ's sheep: 1. They know their Shepherd; 2. They know His voice; 3. They hear Him calling them each by name; 4. They love Him; 5. They trust Him; 6. They follow Him. *In "The Shepherd King," by the Authoress of "The Folded Lamb"* (MRS. ROGERS)

Vs. 2. *He maketh me to lie down in green pastures: He leadeth me beside the still waters.* The Christian life has two elements in it, the contemplative and the active, and both of these are richly provided for. First, the contemplative, *He maketh me to lie down in green pastures.* What are these *green pastures* but the Scriptures of truth—always fresh, always rich, and never exhausted? There is no fear of biting the bare ground where the grass is long enough for the flock to lie down in it. Sweet and full are the doctrines of the Gospel; fit food for souls, as tender grass is natural nutriment for sheep.

The second part of a vigorous Christian's life consists in gracious activity. We not only think, but we act. We are not always lying down to feed but are journeying onward toward perfection; hence we read, *He leadeth me beside the still waters.* What are these *still waters* but the influences and graces of His blessed Spirit? His Spirit attends us in various operations, like waters—in the plural—to cleanse, to refresh, to fertilize, to cherish. C. H. S.

*Lie down—leadeth.* Sitting Mary and stirring Martha are emblems of contemplation and action, and they dwell in one house, so must these in one heart. NATHANAEL HARDY

This short but touching epitaph is frequently seen in the catacombs at Rome, *In Christo, in pace*—("In Christ, in peace"). Realize the constant presence of the Shepherd of peace. J. R. MACDUFF

*Green pastures.* Here are many pastures, and every pasture rich so that it can never be eaten bare; here are many streams, and every stream so deep and wide that it can never be drawn dry. The sheep have been eating in these pastures ever since Christ had a church on earth, and yet they are as full of grass as ever. The sheep have been drinking at these streams ever since Adam, and yet they are brim full to this very day, and they will so continue till the sheep are above the use of them in heaven! RALPH ROBINSON

Vs. 3. *He restoreth my soul.* When the soul grows sorrowful, He revives it; when it is sinful, He sanctifies it; when it is weak, He strengthens it. *He* does it. His ministers could not do it if He did not. His Word would not avail by itself. "He restoreth my soul." Are any of us low in grace? Do we feel that our spirituality is at its lowest ebb? He Who turns the ebb into the flood can soon restore our soul. Pray to Him, then, for the blessing—"Restore Thou me, Thou Shepherd of my soul!" C. H. S.

He restores it to its original purity, that was now grown foul and black with sin; for also, what good were it to have "green" pastures and a black soul! He "restores" it to its natural temper in affections, that was grown distempered with violence of passions; for, alas! what good were it to have "still" waters and turbulent spirits!

He "restores" it indeed to life, that was grown before in a manner quite dead; and who could "restore my soul" to life, but He only that is the Good Shepherd and gave His life for His sheep? SIR RICHARD BAKER

*Paths of righteousness.* Alas! O Lord, these "paths of righteousness" have a long time so little been frequented that prints of a path are almost clean worn out; that it is a hard matter now, but to find where the paths lie and if we can find them, yet they are so narrow and so full of ruts, that without special assistance it is an impossible thing not to fall or go astray. SIR RICHARD BAKER

Vs. 4. *Yea, though I walk through the valley of the shadow of death, I will fear no evil.* This unspeakably delightful verse has been sung on many a dying bed and has helped to make the dark valley bright times out of mind. Every word in it has a wealth of meaning.

"Yea, though I *walk,*" as if the believer did not quicken his pace when he came to die, but still calmly walked with God. To walk indicates the steady advance of a soul which knows its road, knows its end, resolves to follow the path, feels quite safe, and is therefore perfectly calm and composed. The dying saint is not in a flurry, he does not run as though he were alarmed, nor stand still as though he would go no further; he is not confounded nor ashamed, and therefore keeps to his old pace.

Observe that it is not walking *in* the valley, but *through* the valley. We go through the dark tunnel of death and emerge into the light of immortality. We do not die; we do but sleep to wake in glory. Death is not the house but the porch, not the goal but the passage to it. The dying article is called a *valley.* And then, it is not "the valley of death," but "the valley *of the shadow* of death," for death in its substance has been removed, and only the shadow of it remains. Someone has said that when there is a shadow there must be light somewhere, and so there is. Death stands by the side of the highway in which we have to travel, and the light of heaven shining upon him throws a shadow across our path; let us then rejoice that there is light beyond.

Nobody is afraid of a shadow, for a shadow cannot stop a man's pathway even for a moment. The shadow of a dog cannot bite; the shadow of a sword cannot kill; the shadow of death cannot destroy us. Let us not, therefore, be afraid.

*I will fear no evil.* He does not say there shall not be any evil; he had got beyond even that high assurance, and knew that Jesus had put all evil away; but "*I* will *fear* no evil"; as if even his fears, those shadows of evil, were gone forever.

The worst evils of life are those which do not exist except in our imagination. If we had no trouble but real troubles, we should not have a tenth part of our present sorrows. We feel a thousand deaths in fearing one, but the Psalmist was cured of the disease of fearing. C. H. S.

Thus is this bodily death a door for entering into life, and therefore not so much dreadful, if it be rightly considered, as it is comfortable; not a mischief, but a remedy for all mischief; no enemy, but a friend; not a cruel tyrant, but a gentle guide; leading us not to mortality, but to immortality; not to sorrow and pain, but to joy and pleasure, and that to endure forever. *Homily against the Fear of Death*

Though I were called to such a sight as Ezekiel's vision, a valley full of dead men's bones; though the king of terrors should ride in awful pomp through the streets, slaying heaps upon heaps, and thousands should fall at my side, and ten thousands at my right hand, I will fear no evil.

Though he should level his fatal arrows at the little circle of my associates, and put lover and friend far from me, and mine acquaintance into darkness, I will fear no evil. Yea, though I myself should feel his arrow sticking fast in me, the poison drinking up my spirits; though I should in consequence of that fatal seizure, sicken and languish, and have all the symptoms of approaching dissolution, still I will fear no evil.

Nature, indeed, may start back and tremble, but I trust that He Who knows the flesh to be weak will pity and pardon these struggles. However, I may be afraid of the agonies of dying; I will fear no evil in death. The venom of his sting is taken away. The point of his arrow is blunted so that it can pierce no deeper than the body. My soul is invulnerable. I can smile at the shaking of his spear; look unmoved on the ravages which the unrelenting destroyer is making on my tabernacle; and long for the happy period when he shall have made a breach wide enough for my heaven-aspiring spirit to fly away and be at rest. SAMUEL LAVINGTON

"I want to talk to you about heaven," said a dying parent to a member of his family. "We may not be spared to each other long. May we meet around the throne of glory, one family in heaven!"

Overpowered at the thought, his beloved daughter exclaimed, "Surely you do not think there is any danger?" Calmly and beautifully, he replied, "Danger, my darling! Oh, do not use that word! There can be no danger to the Christian, whatever may happen! All is right! All is well! God is love! All is well! Everlastingly well!" JOHN STEVENSON

When a carnal man's heart is ready to die within him, and, with Nabal, to become like a stone, how cheerfully then can those look that have God for their friend! Which of the valiant ones of the world can outface death, look joyfully into eternity? Which of them can hug a fagot, embrace the flames? This the saint can do, and more, too; for he can look infinite justice in the face with a cheerful heart; he can hear of hell with joy and thankfulness; he can think of the day of judgment with great delight and comfort.

I again challenge all the world to produce one out of all their merry companies, one that can do all this. Come, muster up all your joyful blades together; call for your harps and viols; add what you will to make the concert complete; bring in your richest wines; come, lay your heads together, and study what may still add to your comfort. Well, is it done? Now, come away, sinner, this night thy soul must appear before God.

Well, now, what say you, man? What! doth your courage fail you? Now, call for your merry companions and let them cheer thy heart. Now, call for a cup, a whore; never be daunted, man. Shall one of thy courage quail, that could make a mock at the threatening of the almighty God? What, so boon and jolly but now, and now down in the mouth! Here's a sudden change, indeed.

Where are thy merry companions, I say again? All fled? Where are thy darling pleasures? Have all forsaken thee? Why shouldst thou be dejected; there's a poor man in rags that's smiling? What! art thou quite bereft of all comfort? What's the matter, man? What's the matter? There's a question with all my heart, to ask a man that must appear before God tomorrow morning. Well, then, it seems your heart misgives you. What then did you mean to talk of joys and pleasures? Are they all come to this?

Why, there stands one that now hath his heart as full of comfort as ever it can hold, and the very thoughts of eternity, which do so daunt your soul, raise his! And would you know the reason? He knows he is going to his Friend; nay, his Friend bears him company through that dirty lane. Behold, how good and how pleasant a thing it is for God and the soul to dwell together in unity! This it is to have God for a Friend. "Oh, blessed is the soul that is in such a case; yea, blessed is the soul whose God is the Lord." JAMES JANEWAY

It hath been an ancient proverb, when a man had done some great matter, he was said to have "plucked a lion by the beard"; when a lion is dead, even to little children it hath been an easy matter.

As boys, when they see a bear, a lion, or a wolf dead in the streets, they will pull off their hair, insult over them, and deal with them as they please; they will trample upon their bodies, and do that unto them being dead which they durst not in the least measure venture upon whilst they are alive.

Such a thing is death, a furious beast, a ramping lion, a devouring wolf, the *helluo generis humani* (eater-up of mankind), yet Christ hath laid him at his length, hath been the death of death, so that God's children triumph over him, such as those refined ones in the ore of the church, those martyrs of the primitive times, who cheerfully offered themselves to the fire, and to the sword, and to all the violence of this hungry beast; and have played upon him, scorned and derided him, by the faith that they had in the life of Christ, Who hath subdued him to Himself (I Cor. 15). MARTIN DAY

The Psalmist will trust, even though all be unknown. Here, surely, there is trust the most complete. We dread the unknown far above anything that we can see; a little noise in the dark will terrify, when even great dangers which are visible do not affright: the unknown, with its mystery and uncertainty often fills the heart with anxiety, if not with foreboding and gloom.

Here, the Psalmist takes the highest form of the unknown, the aspect which is most terrible to man, and says, that even in the midst of it he will trust. What could be so wholly beyond the reach of human experience or speculation, or even imagination, as "the valley of the shadow of death," with all that belonged to it? but the Psalmist makes no reservation against it; he will trust where he cannot see.

How often are we terrified at the unknown; even as the disciples were, "who feared as they entered the cloud"! How often is the uncertainty of the future as harder trial to our faith than the pressure of some present ill! Many dear children of God can trust Him in all known evils; but why those fears and forebodings, and sinkings of heart, if they trust Him equally for the unknown? PHILIP BENNETT POWER

*Thou art with me.* Do you know the sweetness, the security, the strength of "Thou art with me"? When anticipating the solemn hour of death, when the soul is ready to halt and ask, How shall it then be? can you turn in soul-affection to your God and say, "There is nothing in death to harm me, while Thy love is left to me"? Can you say, "O death, where is thy sting"?

It is said, when a bee has left its sting in anyone, it has no more power to hurt. Death has left its sting in the humanity of Christ and has no more power to harm His child. Christ's victory over the grave is His people's. "At that moment I am with you," whispers Christ; "the same arm you have proved strong and faithful all the way up through the wilderness, which has never failed, though you have been often forced to lean on it all your weakness." VISCOUNT POWERSCOURT

*Thy rod and Thy staff they comfort me.* Many persons profess to receive much comfort from the hope that they shall not die. Certainly there will be some who will be "alive and remain" at the coming of the Lord, but is there so very much advantage in such an escape from death as to make it the object of Christian desire?

A wise man might prefer of the two to die, for those who shall not die, but who "shall be caught up together with the Lord in the air," will be losers rather than gainers. They will lose that actual fellowship with Christ in the tomb which dying saints have, and we are expressly told they shall have no preference beyond those who are asleep.

Let us be of Paul's mind when he said that "to die is gain," and think of "departing to be with Christ which is far better." This Twenty-Third Psalm is not worn out, and it is as sweet in a believer's ear now as it was in David's time, let novelty-hunters say what they will. C. H. S.

Not long before he died, he blessed God for the assurance of his love, and said he could now as easily die as shut his eyes; and added, "Here am I longing to be silent in the dust and enjoying Christ in glory. I long to be in the arms of Jesus. It is not worth while to weep for me." Then, remembering how busy the devil had been about him, he was exceedingly thankful to God for His goodness in rebuking him. MEMOIR OF JAMES JANEWAY

When Mrs. Hervey, the wife of a missionary in Bombay, was dying, a friend said to her that he hoped the Savior would be with her as she walked through the dark valley of the shadow of death. "If this," said she, "is the dark valley, it has not a dark spot in it; all is light." She had, during most of her sickness, bright views of the perfections of God. "His awful holiness," she said, "appeared the most lovely of all His attributes." At one time she said she wanted words to express her views of the glory and majesty of Christ. "It seems," said she, "that if all other glory were annihilated and nothing left but His bare Self, it would be enough; it would be a universe of glory!

Vs. 5. *Thou preparest a table before me in the presence of mine enemies.* The good man has his enemies. He would not be like his Lord if he had not. If we were without enemies we might fear that we were not the friends of God, for the friendship of the world is enmity to God. Yet see the quietude of the godly man in spite of, and in the sight of, his enemies. How refreshing is his calm bravery! "Thou preparest a table before me." When a soldier is in the presence of his enemies, if he eats at all he snatches a hasty meal and away he hastens to the fight.

But observe, "Thou *preparest* a table," just as a servant does when she unfolds the damask cloth and displays the ornaments of the feast on an ordinary peaceful occasion. Nothing is hurried, there is no confusion, no disturbance, the enemy is at the door, and yet God prepares a table, and the Christian sits down and eats as if everything were in perfect peace. Oh! the peace which Jehovah gives to His people, even in the midst of the most trying circumstances! C. H. S.

An effectual impediment must not only have contrariety in it, but superiority: a drop of water cannot put out a fire, for though it hath a contrary nature, yet it hath not greater power. Now the malice and contrivances of evil men are too short and weak for the divine intention of blessing, which is accompanied with an almighty arm. Evil men are but men, and God is a God; and being but men, they can do no more than men. *Condensed from* OBADIAH SEDGWICK

*Thou anointest my head with oil.* A priest without oil misses the chief qualification for his office, and the Christian priest lacks his chief fitness for service when he is devoid of new grace from on high.

*My cup runneth over.* He had not only enough, a cup full, but more than enough, a cup which overflowed. A poor man may say this as well as those in higher circumstances. "What, all this, and Jesus Christ, too"? said a poor cottager as she broke a piece of bread and filled a glass with cold water. Whereas a man may be ever so wealthy, but if he be discontented, his cup cannot run

over; it is cracked and leaks. Content is the philosopher's stone which turns all it touches into gold; happy is he who has found it. Content is more than a kingdom; it is another word for happiness. C. H. S.

He had not only a fullness of abundance but of redundance. Those that have this happiness must carry their cup upright and see that it overflow into their poor brethren's emptier vessels. JOHN TRAPP

Wherefore doth the Lord make your cup run over but that other men's lips might taste the liquor? The showers that fall upon the highest mountains should glide into the lowest valleys. "Give, and it shall be given you," is a maxim little believed (Luke 6:38). WILLIAM SECKER

Or as it is in the Vulgate: "And my inebriating chalice, how excellent it is!" With this cup were the martyrs inebriated, when, going forth to their passion, they recognized not those that belonged to them; not their weeping wife, not their children, not their relations; while they gave thanks and said, "I will take the cup of salvation!" AUGUSTINE

Vs. 6. *I will dwell in the house of the Lord forever.* A wicked man, it may be, will turn into God's house, and say a prayer, etc., but the prophet would (and so all godly men must) dwell there forever; his soul lieth always at the throne of grace begging for grace.

A wicked man prayeth as the cock croweth; the cock crows and ceaseth, and crows again, and ceaseth again, and thinks not of crowing till he crows again: so a wicked man prays and ceaseth, prays and ceaseth again; his mind is never busied to think whether his prayers speed or no; he thinks it is good religion for him to pray, and therefore he takes for granted that his prayers speed, though in very deed God never hears his prayers, nor no more respects them than he respects the lowing of oxen or the grunting of hogs. WILLIAM FENNER, in *"The Sacrifice of the Faithful"*

# PSALM 24

Title: "A Psalm of David." From the title we learn nothing but the authorship: but this is interesting and leads us to observe the wondrous operations of the Spirit upon the mind of Israel's sweet singer, enabling him to touch the mournful string in Psalm Twenty-Two, to pour forth gentle notes of peace in Psalm Twenty-Three, and here to utter majestic and triumphant strains. We can do or sing all things when the Lord strengtheneth us.

This sacred hymn was probably written to be sung when the ark of the covenant was taken up from the house of Obed-edom to remain within curtains upon the hill of Zion. We will call it "The Song of the Ascension." This Psalm makes a pair with the Fifteenth Psalm. C. H. S.

How others may think upon this point, I cannot say, nor pretend to describe, but for my own part, I have no notion of hearing or of any man's ever having seen or heard, anything so great, so solemn, so celestial, on this side the gates of heaven. PATRICK DELANY.

Vs. 1. *The earth is the Lord's, and the fulness thereof; the world, and they that dwell therein.* How very different is this from the ignorant Jewish notion of God which prevailed in our Savior's day! The Jews said, "The holy land is God's and the seed of Abraham are His only people"; but their great Monarch had long before instructed them, "The earth is the Lord's, and the fulness thereof." The whole round world is claimed for Jehovah, "and they that dwell therein" are declared to be His subjects.

When we consider the bigotry of the Jewish people at the time of Christ and how angry they were with our Lord for saying that many widows were in Israel but unto none of them was the prophet sent save only to the widow of Sarepta, and that there were many lepers in Israel but none of them was healed except Naaman the Syrian. . . . . .

When we recollect, too, how angry they were at the mention of Paul's being sent to the Gentiles, we are amazed that they should have remained in such blindness, and yet have sung this Psalm, which shows so clearly that God is not the God of the Jews only, but of the Gentiles also.

What a rebuke is this to those wiseacres who speak of the Negro and other despised races as though they were not cared for by the God of heaven! If a man be but a man, the Lord claims him, and who dares to brand him as a mere piece of merchandise? The meanest of men is a dweller in the world, and therefore belongs to Jehovah. Jesus Christ has made an end of the exclusiveness of nationalities. There is neither barbarian, Scythian, bond nor free; but we are all one in Christ Jesus.

Man lives upon "the earth" and parcels out its soil among his mimic kings and autocrats; but the earth is not man's. He is but a tenant at will, a leaseholder upon most precarious tenure, liable to instantaneous ejectment. The great Landowner and true Proprietor holds His court above the clouds and laughs at the title-deeds of worms of the dust.

The earth is full of God; He made it full and He keeps it full, notwithstanding all the demands which living creatures make upon its stores. The sea is full despite all the clouds which rise from it; the air is full notwithstanding all the lives which breathe it; the soil is full though millions of plants derive their nourishment from it. C. H. S.

*The earth is the Lord's,* that is, Christ's, Who is the "Lord of lords" (Rev. 19:16); for the whole world and all things therein are His by a twofold title. First, by donation of God His Father, having "all power given unto Him in heaven and in earth" (Matt. 28:18), even whatsoever things the Father hath are His (John 16:15); and so consequently "made Heir of all things" (Heb. 1:2).

Second, the earth is Christ's and all that therein is by right of creation, for "He founded it," saith our prophet, and that after a wonderful manner, "upon the seas and floods.". . . . All things then are Christ's, in respect of creation, "by Whom all things were made" (John 1:3); in respect of sustentation, as upholding all things by His mighty Word (Heb. 1:3); in respect of administration, as reaching from one end to another, and ordering all things sweetly (Wis. 8:1): in one word—"Of Him, and through Him, and to Him, are all things (Rom. 11:36). JOHN BOYS

St. Chrysostom, suffering under the Empress Eudoxia, tells his friend Cyriacus how he armed himself beforehand: "I thought, will she banish me? 'The earth is the Lord's and the fulness thereof.' Take away my goods? 'Naked came I into the world, and naked must I return.' Will she stone me? I remembered Stephen. Behead me? John Baptist came into my mind," etc.

Thus it should be with everyone that intends to live and die comfortably: they must, as we say, lay up something for a rainy day; they must stock themselves with graces, store up promises, and furnish themselves with experiences of God's lovingkindness to others and themselves, too, that so, when the evil day cometh, they may have much good coming thereby. JOHN SPENCER

"Light is the countenance of the Eternal," sung the setting sun: "I am the hem of His garment," responded the soft and rosy twilight. The clouds gathered themselves together and said, "We are His nocturnal tent." And the waters in the clouds, and the hollow voices of the thunders, joined in the lofty chorus, "The voice of the Eternal is upon the waters, the God of glory thundereth in the heavens, the Lord is upon many waters."

"He flieth upon my wings," whispered the winds, and the gentle air added, "I am the breath of God, the aspirations of His benign presence." We hear the songs of praise," said the parched earth; "all around is praise; I alone am sad and silent." Then the falling dew replied, "I will nourish thee, so that thou shalt be refreshed and rejoice, and thy infants shall bloom like the young rose." "Joyfully we bloom," sang the refreshed meads; the full ears of corn waved as they sang, "We are the blessing of God, the hosts of God against famine."

"We bless Thee from above," said the gentle moon; "We, too, bless Thee," responded the stars; and the lightsome grasshopper chirped, "Me, too, He blesses in the pearly dew-drop." "He quenched my thirst," said the roe; "and refreshed me," continued the stag; "and grants us our food," said the beasts of the forest; "and clothes my lambs," gratefully added the sheep.

"He heard me," croaked the raven, "when I was forsaken and alone"; "He heard me," said the wild goat of the rocks, "when my time came, and I brought forth." And the turtle-dove cooed, and the swallow and other birds joined the song, "We have found our nests, our houses, we dwell upon the altar of the Lord, and sleep under the shadow of His wing in tranquility and peace."

"And peace," replied the night, and echo prolonged the sound, when chanticleer awoke the dawn and crowed with joy, "Open the portals, set wide the gates of the world! The King of glory approached. Awake! Arise, ye sons of men, give praises and thanks unto the Lord, for the King of glory approaches!"

The sun arose, and David awoke from his melodious rapture. But as long as he lived, the strains of Creation's harmony remained in his soul, and daily he recalled them from the strings of his harp. *From the "Legend of the Songs of the Night," in the Talmud, quoted in "Biblical Antiquities" by* F. A. Cox

Vs. 2. *He hath established it upon the floods.* The world is Jehovah's because from generation to generation He preserves and upholds it, having settled its foundations. Providence and Creation are the two legal seals upon the title-deeds of the great Owner of all things. He Who built the house and bears up its foundation has surely a first claim upon it. Let it be noted, however, upon what insecure foundations all terrestrial things are founded. Founded on the seas! Established on the floods!

Blessed be God, the Christian has another world to look forward to, and rests his hopes upon a more stable foundation than this poor world affords. They who trust in worldly things build upon the sea; but we have laid our hopes, by God's grace, upon the Rock of Ages; we are resting upon the promise of an immutable God; we are depending on the constancy of a faithful Redeemer.

Vs. 3. *Who shall ascend into the hill of the Lord?* It is uphill work for the creature to reach the Creator. Where is the mighty climber who can scale the towering heights? Nor is it height alone; it is glory, too. Whose eye shall see the King in His beauty and dwell in His palace? C. H. S.

To be of the number of Christ's true, faithful servants is no slight work; 'tis a fight, 'tis a race, 'tis a continual warfare; fastings and watchings, and cold and nakedness, and hunger and thirst, bonds, imprisonments, dangers and distresses, ignominy and reproach, afflictions and persecutions, the world's hatred and our friends' neglect, all that we call hard or difficult is to be found in the way we are to go.

A man cannot leave a lust, shake off bad company, quit a course of sin, enter upon a way of virtue, profess his religion, or stand to it, cannot ascend the spiritual hill, but he will meet some or other of these to contest and strive with. But not only to ascend, but to stand there, as the word signifies; to continue at so high a pitch, to be constant in truth and piety, that will be hard indeed, and bring more difficulties to contest with. MARK FRANK

Vs. 4. *He that hath clean hands, and a pure heart.* Outward, practical holiness is a very precious mark of grace. To wash in water with Pilate is nothing, but to wash in innocency is all-important. It is to be feared that many professors have perverted the doctrine of justification by faith in such a way as to treat good works with contempt; if so, they will receive everlasting contempt at the last great day. It is vain to prate of inward experience unless the daily life is free from impurity, dishonesty, violence, and oppression.

But "clean hands" would not suffice unless they were connected with "a pure heart." True religion is heart-work. We may wash the outside of the cup and the platter as long as we please, but if the inward parts be filthy, we are filthy altogether in the sight of God, for our hearts are more truly ourselves than our hands are. We may lose our hands and yet live, but we could not lose our heart and still live; the very life of our being lies in the inner nature, and hence the imperative need of purity within. Dirt in the heart throws dust in the eyes. C. H. S.

Shall I tell you then, who is a moral man in the sight of God? It is he that bows to the divine law as the supreme rule of right; he that is influenced by a governing regard to God in all his actions; he that obeys other commands spontaneously because he has obeyed the first and great command, "Give me thy heart." His conduct is not conformed to custom or expediency, but to one consistent, immutable standard of duty.

Take this man into a court of justice and call on him to testify and he will not bear false witness. Give him the charge of untold treasures; he will not steal. Trust him with the dearest interests of yourself or family; you are safe, because he has a living principle of truth and integrity in his bosom. He is as worthy of confidence in the dark as at noonday; for he is a moral man, not because reputation or interest demands it, not because the eye of public observation is fixed upon him, but because the love and fear of God have predominant ascendency in his heart. EBENEZER PORTER

*Who hath not lifted up his soul unto vanity.* If we suck our consolation from the breasts of the world, we prove ourselves to be its homeborn children. Does the world satisfy these? Then thou hast thy reward and thy portion in this life; make much of it, for thou shalt know no other joy. C. H. S.

*Who hath not lifted up his soul unto vanity* is read by Arius Montanus, "He that hath not received his soul in vain." Oh! How many receive their souls in vain, making no more use of them than the swine, of whom the philosopher observes, their souls are only for salt to keep their bodies from stinking. Who would not grieve to think that so choice a piece should be employed about so vain a use! GEORGE SWINNOCK

Now we come to the four conditions requisite to render such an ascent possible: 1. Abstinence from evil doing: "He that hath clean hands." 2. Abstinence from evil thought: "and a pure heart." 3. Who does that duty which he is sent into the world to do: "That hath not lift up his mind unto vanity"; or, as it is in the Vulgate, "Who hath not received his soul in vain." And, 4. Remembers the vows by which he is bound to God: "nor sworn to deceive."

And in the fullest sense, there was but One in Whom all these things were fulfilled; so that in reply to the question, "Who shall ascend into the hill of the Lord?" He might well answer, "No man hath ascended up to heaven, but He that came down from heaven, even the Son of man which is in heaven" (John 3:13). "Therefore it is well written," says St. Bernard, "that such an High Priest became us, because He knows the difficulty of that ascent to the celestial mountain, He knows the weakness of us that have to ascend." LORINUS AND BERNARD, *quoted by J. M. Neale.*

Heaven is not won with good words and a fair profession. The doing Christian is the man that shall stand when the empty boaster of his faith shall fall. The great talkers of religion are often the least doers. His religion is in vain whose profession brings not letters testimonial from a holy life. WILLIAM GURNALL

Vs. 5. *He shall receive . . . righteousness.* As for our own righteousness which we have without Him, Isaiah telleth us, "It is a defiled cloth"; and St. Paul, that it is but "dung." Two very homely comparisons, but they be the Holy Ghost's own; yet nothing so homely as in the original, where they be so odious, as what manner of defiled cloth or what kind of dung we have not dared to translate. Our own then being no better, we are driven to seek for it elsewhere.

*He shall receive his righteousness,* saith the prophet; and "the gift of righteousness," saith the Apostle (Phil. 3:8-9; Rom. 5:17). It is then another, to be given us, and to be received by us, which we must seek for.

And whither shall we go for it? Job alone dispatcheth this point (ch. 15:15; 4:18; 25:5). Not to the heavens or stars; they are unclean in his sight. Not to the saints, for in them he found folly. Not to the angels, for neither in them found he steadfastness. Now, if none of these will serve, we see a necessary reason why Jehovah must be a part of this Name—"the Lord our righteousness" (Jer. 23:6). LANCELOT ANDREWES

Vs. 6. *This is the generation of them that seek Him, that seek Thy face, O Jacob.* These are the regeneration, these are in the line of grace; these are the legitimate seed. Yet they are only seekers; hence learn that true seekers are very dear in God's esteem and are entered upon His register.

Even seeking has a sanctifying influence; what a consecrating power must lie in finding and enjoying the Lord's face and favor! To desire communion with God is a purifying thing. Oh, to hunger and thirst more and more after a clear vision of the face of God; this will lead us to purge ourselves from all filthiness and to walk with heavenly circumspection. C. H. S.

Christians must be seekers. This is the generation of seekers. All mankind, if ever they will come to heaven, they must be a generation of seekers. Heaven is a generation of finders, of possessors, of enjoyers, seekers of God. But here we are a generation of seekers. RICHARD SIBBES

By the demonstrative pronoun "this," the psalmist erases from the catalogue of the servants of God all counterfeit Israelites who, trusting only to their circumcision and the sacrifice of beasts, have no concern about offering themselves to God; and yet, at the same time, they rashly thrust themselves into the church. JOHN CALVIN

Vs. 7. These last verses reveal to us the great Representative Man, Who answered to the full character laid down, and therefore by His own right ascended the holy hill of Zion. Our Lord Jesus Christ could ascend into the hill of the Lord because His hands were clean and His heart was pure, and if we by faith in Him are conformed to His image, we shall enter, too. C. H. S.

*Lift up your heads, O ye gates; and be ye lift up, ye everlasting doors; and the King of glory shall come in.* In the Gospel history, we find that Christ had a threefold entertainment among men. Some received Him into house, not into heart, as Simon the Pharisee (Luke 7:44), who gave him no kiss nor water to his feet; some into heart, but not into house, as the faithful centurion (Matt. 8:34); some both into house and heart, as Lazarus, Mary, Martha (John 3:15; Luke 10:38). JOHN BOYS

Because the door of men's hearts is locked, and barred, and bolted, and men are in a deep sleep and will not hear the knocking that is at the gate, though it be loud, though it be a king; therefore David knocks again, "Lift up, ye everlasting doors." "Why, what haste?" saith the sinner. "What haste?" Why, here's the King at your gates; and that not an ordinary king either; He is a glorious King, that will honor you so far, if you open quickly, as to lodge within, to take up His abode in your house to dwell with you.

But the soul for all this doth not yet open but stands still questioning, as if it were an enemy rather than a friend that stood there, and asks, "*Who is this King of glory?*" Who? He answers again, *It is the Lord of Hosts;* He, that if you will not open quickly and thankfully, too, can easily pull your house down about your ears; He is the Lord of hosts, that King Who hath a mighty army always at His command, who stand ready for their commission, and then you should know who it is you might have had for your friend. "Lift up, therefore, your heads, O ye gates."

Open quickly, ye that had rather have God for your friend than for your enemy. Oh, why should not the soul of every sinner cry out, Lord, the door is locked, and Thou hast the key; I have been trying what I can do, but the wards are so rusty, that I cannot possibly turn the key"?

But, Lord, throw the door off the hinges, anything in the world, so Thou wilt but come in and dwell here. Come, O mighty God, break through doors of iron, and bars of brass, and make way for Thyself by Thy love and power. Come, Lord, and make Thyself welcome; all that I have is at thy service; oh, fit my soul to entertain Thee! JAMES JANEWAY

He hath left with us the earnest of the Spirit and taken from us the earnest of our flesh, which He hath carried into heaven as a pledge that the whole shall follow after. TERTULLIAN

Christ is gone to heaven as a victor; leading sin, Satan, death, hell, and all His enemies in triumph at His chariot wheels. He has not only overcome His enemies for Himself, but for all His people, whom He will make conquerors, yea, "more than conquerors." As He has overcome, so shall they also overcome; and as He is gone to heaven a victor, they shall follow in triumph. HENRY PENDLEBURY

This Ark, which has saved the world from destruction, after floating on a deluge of blood, rests at length on the mountain. This innocent Joseph, whose virtue had been oppressed by the synagogue, is brought out of the dungeon to receive a crown. This invincible Samson has carried away the gates of hell, and goes in triumph to the everlasting hills.

This victorious Joshua has passed over Jordan with the ark of the covenant and takes possession of the land of the living. This Sun of righteousness, which had gone down ten degrees, returns backward to the place which it had left. He Who was "a worm" at His birth, a Lamb in His passion, and a Lion in His resurrection, now ascends as an Eagle to heaven, and encourages us to follow Him thither. *From "The Life of Jesus Christ in Glory," translated from the French of* JAMES NOUET

Verses 7-8. O my soul, how should this heighten thy joy and enlarge thy comforts, in that Christ is now received up into glory? Every sight of Christ is glorious, and in every sight thou shouldst wait on the Lord Jesus Christ for some glorious manifestations of Himself. Come, live up to the rate of this great mystery; view Christ as entering into glory, and thou wilt find the same sparkles of glory on thy heart. Oh, this sight is a transforming sight: "We all, with open face beholding as in a glass the glory of the Lord, are changed into the same image from glory to glory, even as by the Spirit of the Lord" (II Cor. 3:18). ISAAC AMBROSE

Verses 7-8. And know, O all ye faithful and obedient ones, for your courage and comfort, Who, and of what quality this glorious King, the Lord Jesus is, Whom the world despises but you honor. Why, He is the Almighty God, of power all-sufficient to preserve and defend His people and church, that in trust of Him do love and serve Him, against all the strength and power of men and devils that do or shall malign or oppose themselves against them, and to put them to the foil, as we His Israel in the letter, have found by experience for your instruction and corroboration that are His people in spirit. GEORGE ABBOT, in *"Brief Notes upon the Whole Book of Psalms"*

Verses 7-10. Certainly, if, when He brought His only-begotten Son into the world, He said, "Let all the angels worship Him," much more now that He "ascends on high, and hath led captivity captive, hath He given Him a Name above all names, that at the Name of Jesus all knees should bow." And if the holy angels did so carol at His birth, in the very entrance into that state of humiliation and infirmity, with what triumph did they receive Him now returning from the perfect achievement of man's redemption? JOSEPH HALL

Verses 7-10. There was something like triumph when He entered into Jerusalem. All the city was moved, saying, "Who is this?" And the multitude answered, "It is Jesus, the prophet of Nazareth"; and the very children sang, "Hosanna to the Son of David: blessed be He that cometh in the Name of the Lord; Hosanna in the highest!"

How much greater then must be the triumph of His entry into the heavenly Jerusalem! Would not all the city be "moved" in this case saying, "Who is this?" See thousands of angels attending Him, and ten thousand times ten thousand come forth to meet Him! The entrance of the ark into the city of David was but a shadow of this, and the responsive strains which were sung on that occasion would on this be much more applicable. ANDREW FULLER

Verses 7-10. Alone He rose from the dead: alone, as far as man could see, He went up to heaven. Thus He showed Himself "the Lord mighty in battle," mighty in that single combat which He, as our Champion, our David, victoriously maintained against our great enemy. But when He shall come down and go up the second time, He will show Himself "the Lord of hosts." Instead of coming down alone in mysterious silence, as in His wonderful incarnation, He will be followed by all the armies of heaven. "The Lord my God will come, and all His saints with Him." "The Lord cometh with ten thousand of His saints." "The Son of man will come in the glory of His Father, and all the holy angels with Him." "Thousand thousands will stand around Him, and ten thousand times ten thousand will minister unto Him."

Instead of the silence of that quiet chamber at Nazareth, and of the holy Virgin's womb, there will be the voice of the archangel, and the trump of God accompanying Him. JOHN KEBLE

Vs. 8. The watchers at the gate, hearing the song, look over the battlements and ask, *Who is this King of glory?* A question full of meaning and worthy of the meditations of eternity. Who is He in person, nature, character, office, and work? What is His pedigree? What His rank and what His race?

The answer given in a mighty wave of music is, *The Lord strong and mighty, the Lord mighty in battle.* We know the might of Jesus by the battles which He has fought, the victories which He has won over sin, and death, and hell, and we clap our hands as we see Him leading captivity captive in the majesty of His strength. Oh, for a heart to sing His praises! Mighty Hero, be Thou crowned for ever King of kings and Lord of lords.

Vs. 9. Dear reader, it is possible that you are saying, "I shall never enter into the heaven of God, for I have neither clean hands nor a pure heart"! Look, then, to Christ, Who has already climbed the holy hill. He has entered as the forerunner of those who trust Him. Follow in His footsteps and repose upon His merit. He rides triumphantly into heaven, and you shall ride there, too, if you trust Him.

"But how can I get the character described?" say you. The Spirit of God will give you that. He will create in you a new heart and a right spirit. Faith in Jesus is the work of the Holy Spirit and has all virtues wrapped up in it. Faith stands by the fountain filled with blood, and as she washes therein, clean hands and a pure heart, a holy soul and a truthful tongue was given to her. C. H. S.

# PSALM 25

Title: "A Psalm of David." David is pictured in this Psalm as in a faithful miniature. His holy trust, his many conflicts, his great transgression, his bitter repentance, and his deep distresses are all here; so that we see the very heart of "the man after God's own heart." It is evidently a composition of David's later days, for he mentions the sins of his youth, and from its painful references to the craft and cruelty of his many foes, it will not be too speculative a theory to refer it to the period when Absalom was heading the great rebellion against him. This has been styled the second of the seven Penitential Psalms. It is the mark of a true saint that his sorrows remind him of his sins, and his sorrow for sin drives him to his God. C. H. S.

In these four Psalms, which immediately follow one another, we may find the soul of David presented in all the several postures of piety-lying, standing, sitting, kneeling. In the Twenty-Second Pealm, he is lying all along, falling flat on his face, low groveling on the ground, even almost entering into a degree of despair; speaking of himself in the history of Christ in the mystery, "My God, why hast Thou forsaken me?"

In the Twenty-Third Psalm, he is standing, and through God's favor, in despite of his foes, trampling and triumphing over all opposition: "The Lord is my shepherd, therefore shall I lack nothing."

In the Twenty-Fourth Psalm, he is sitting, like a doctor in his chair or a professor in his place, reading a lecture of divinity and describing the character of that man—how he must be accomplished—"who shall ascend into the holy hill," and hereafter be partaker of happiness.

In this Twenty-Fifth Psalm, he is kneeling, with hands and voice lifted up to God, and on these two hinges the whole Psalm turneth; the one is a hearty beseeching of God's mercy, the other a humble bemoaning of his own misery. Thomas Fuller

Vs. 1. *Unto Thee, O Lord, do I lift up my soul.* See how the holy soul flies to its God like a dove to its cote. When the storm-winds are out, the Lord's vessels put about and make for their well-remembered harbor of refuge. What a mercy that the Lord will condescend to hear our cries in time of trouble, although we may have almost forgotten Him in our hours of fancied prosperity! Very often the soul cannot rise; she has lost her wings, and is heavy and earth-bound; more like a burrowing mole than a soaring eagle. At such dull seasons we must not give over prayer, but must, by God's assistance, exert all our powers to lift up our hearts. Let faith be the lever and grace be the arm, and the dead lump will yet be stirred.

But what a lift it has sometimes proved! With all our tugging and straining, we have been utterly defeated, until the heavenly loadstone of our Saviour's love has displayed its omnipotent attractions, and then our hearts have gone up to our Beloved like mounting flames of fire. C. H. S.

The lifting up of the heart presupposeth a former dejection of his soul. The soul of man is pressed down with sin and with the cares of this world, which, as lead doth the net, draweth it so down, that it cannot mount above till God send spiritual prayers, as cork to the net, to exalt it; which arise out of faith, as the flame doth out of the fire, and which must be free of secular cares, and all things pressing down, which showeth unto us that worldlings can no more pray than a mole is able to fly. But Christians are as eagles which mount upward.

Seeing then the heart of man by nature is fixed to the earth, and of itself is no more able to rise therefrom than a stone which is fixed in the ground, till God raises it by His power, Word, and workmen; it should be our principal petition to the Lord that it would please Him to draw us, that we might run after Him; that He would exalt and lift up our hearts to heaven, that they may not lie still in the puddle of this earth. ARCHIBALD SYMSON

A godly man prays as a builder builds. Now, a builder first layeth a foundation, and because he cannot finish in one day, he comes the second day and finds the frame standing that he made the first day, and then he adds a second day's work; and then he comes a third day and finds his two former days' work standing; then he proceeds to a third day's work, and makes walls to it, and so he goes on till his building be finished.

So prayer is the building of the soul till it reach up to heaven; therefore, a godly heart prays and reacheth higher and higher in prayer till at last his prayers reach up to God. WILLIAM FENNER

A prayer without the intention of the affection is like a body without a soul. And yet their devotion is a mere outside, saith one—a brainless head and a soulless body: "This people draweth nigh to me with their lips, but their heart is far from me" (Isa. 29:13). A carnal man can as little lift up his heart in prayer as a mole can fly. A David finds it a hard task; since the best heart is lumpish, and naturally beareth downwards, as the poise of a clock, as the lead of a net. Let us therefore "lay aside every weight, and the sin that doth so easily beset us" and pray to God to draw us up to Himself, as the loadstone doth the iron. JOHN TRAPP

Vs. 2. *O my God, I trust in Thee.* Faith is the cable which binds our boat to the shore, and by pulling at it we draw ourselves to the land; faith unites us to God, and then draws us near to Him. As long as the anchor of faith holds there is no fear in the worst tempest; if that should fail us there would be no hope left. We must see to it that our faith is sound and strong, for otherwise prayer cannot prevail with God. Woe to the warrior who throws away his shield; what defence can be found for him who finds no defence in his God? C. H. S.

Vs. 3. *Yea, let none that wait on Thee be ashamed.* Suffering enlarges the heart by creating the power to sympathize. If we pray eagerly for ourselves, we shall not long be able to forget our fellow-sufferers. None pity the poor like those who have been or are still poor; none have such tenderness for the sick as those who have been long in ill health themselves. We ought to be grateful for occasional griefs if they preserve us from chronic hard-heartedness; for of all afflictions, an unkind heart is the worst; it is a plague to its possessor and a torment to those around him.

*Let them be ashamed which transgress without cause.* David had given his enemies no provocation; their hatred was wanton. Sinners have no justifiable reason or valid excuse for transgressing; they benefit no one, not even themselves by their sins; the law against which they transgress is not harsh or unjust; God is not a tyrannical ruler; providence is not a bondage: men sin because they will sin, not because it is either profitable or reasonable to do so.

Hence, shame is their fitting reward. May they blush with penitential shame now, or else they will not be able to escape the everlasting contempt and the bitter shame which is the promotion of fools in the world to come. C. H. S.

Let shame be sent to the right owner, even to those that deal disloyally, unprovoked on my part. And so it was; for Ahithophel hanged himself; Absalom was trussed up by the hand of God and dispatched by Joab; the people that conspired with him partly perished by the sword and partly fled home, much ashamed of their enterprise. Oh, the power of prayer! What may not the saints have for asking? JOHN TRAPP

Vs. 4. *Show me Thy ways, O Lord: teach me Thy paths.* There are the "ways" of men and the "ways" of God; the "paths" of sin and the "paths" of righteousness: there are "Thy ways" and there are my ways; Thine the ways of truth, mine the ways of error; Thine which are good in Thine eyes, and mine which are good in mine eyes; Thine which lead to heaven, and mine which lead to hell. Wherefore, "Show me Thy ways, O Lord; teach me Thy paths," lest I mistake mine own ways for Thine; yea, lead me in the truth, and teach me, lest I turn out of Thy ways into mine own: "show me Thy ways," by the ministry of Thy Word; "teach me Thy paths," in the guidance of Thy Spirit; "lead me in Thy truth," by the assistance of Thy grace. ROBERT MOSSOM

Vss. 4, 5, 9. Do what you know, and God will teach you what to do. Do what you know to be your present duty, and God will acquaint you with your future duty as it comes to be present. Make it your business to avoid known omissions, and God will keep you from feared commissions. SAMUEL ANNESLEY, in *"Morning Exercises at Cripplegate"*

Vs. 5. *Lead me in Thy truth, and teach me.* David knew much, but he felt his ignorance and desired to be still in the Lord's school; four times over in these two verses he applies for a scholarship in the college of grace. It were well for many professors if instead of following their own devices and cutting out new paths of thought for themselves, they would enquire for the good old ways of God's own truth and beseech the Holy Ghost to give them sanctified understandings and teachable spirits. C. H. S.

The soul that is unsatiable in prayer, he proceeds, he gets near to God, he gains something, he winds up his heart higher. As a child that seeth the mother have an apple in her hand, and it would fain have it, it will come and pull at the mother's hand for it: now she lets go one finger, and yet she holds it, and then he pulls again; and then she lets go another finger, and yet she keeps it, and then the child pulls again, and will never leave pulling and crying till it hath got it from its mother.

So a child of God, seeing all graces to be in God, he draws near to the throne of grace, begging for it, and by his earnest and faithful prayers he opens the hands of God to him; God dealing as parents to their children, holds them off for a while; not that He is unwilling to give, but to make them more earnest with God; to draw them the nearer to Himself. WILLIAM FENNER

*For Thou art the God of my salvation.* The Three-One Jehovah is the Author and Perfecter of salvation to His people. Reader, is He the God of *your* salvation? Do you find in the Father's election, in the Son's atonement, and in the Spirit's quickening, all the grounds of your eternal hopes? If so, you may use this as an argument for obtaining further blessings; if the Lord has ordained to save you, surely He will not refuse to instruct you in His ways. It is a happy thing when we can address the Lord with the confidence which David here manifests; it gives us great power in prayer and comfort in trial. C. H. S.

*On Thee do I wait all the day.* To wait on God, is: 1. To live a life of desire towards God; to wait on Him as the beggar waits on his benefactor, with earnest desire to receive supplies from him, as the sick and sore at Bethesda's Pool waited for the stirring of the water and attended in the porches with desire to be helped in and healed. 2. It is to live a life in God, as the lover waits on his beloved. Desire is love in motion, as a bird upon the wing; delight is love at rest, as a bird upon the nest; now, though our desire must still be so towards

God, as that we must be wishing for more of God, yet our delight must be so in God, as that we must never wish for more than God. *Condensed from* MATTHEW HENRY, on *"Communion with God"*

*On Thee do I wait,* wait to hear the secret voice of Thy Spirit, speaking peace unto my conscience; wait to feel the reviving vigor of Thy grace, quickening mine obedience; wait to see the subduing power of Thy Holy Spirit quelling my rebellious sin; wait to feel the cheering virtue of Thy heavenly comforts, refreshing my fainting soul; for all these Thy blessings. ROBERT MOSSOM

Vs. 6. *Remember, O Lord, Thy tender mercies and Thy loving-kindnesses.* There is a holy boldness which ventures thus to deal with the Most High. Let us cultivate it. But there is also an unholy unbelief which suggests our fears. Let us strive against it with all our might. What gems are those two expressions: "Tender mercies and loving-kindnesses"! They are the virgin honey of language; for sweetness no words can excel them; but as for the gracious favors which are intended by them, language fails to describe them. C. H. S.

Oh, how does one deep call upon another! The depth of my multiplied miseries calls, loudly calls, upon the depth of Thy manifold mercies; even that mercy whereby Thou dost pardon my sin and help mine infirmities; that mercy whereby Thou dost sanctify me by Thy grace and comfort me by Thy Spirit; that mercy whereby Thou dost deliver me from hell and possess me of heaven. "Remember, O Lord," all those Thy mercies, Thy tender mercies, which have been "of old" unto Thy saints. ROBERT MOSSOM

*For they have been ever of old.* A more correct translation would be "from eternity." David was a sound believer in the doctrine of God's eternal love. The Lord's loving-kindnesses are no novelties. When we plead with Him to bestow them upon us, we can urge use and custom of the most ancient kind. In courts of law men make much of precedents, and we may plead them at the throne of grace. "Faith," saith Dickson, "must make use of experiences and read them over unto God, out of the register of a sanctified memory, as a recorder to Him Who cannot forget." C. H. S.

Divine love is an eternal fountain that never leaves running while a vessel is empty or capable of holding more; and it stands open to all comers: therefore, come; and if ye have not sufficient of your own, go and borrow vessels, empty vessels, not a few; "pay your debts out of it, and live on the rest" (II Kings 4:7) to eternity. ELISHA COLES on *God's Sovereignty*

Vs. 7. *Remember not the sins of my youth.* The world winks at the sins of young men, and yet they are none so little after all; the bones of our youthful feastings at Satan's table will stick painfully in our throats when we are old men. He who presumes upon his youth is poisoning his old age. How large a tear may wet this page as some of us reflect upon the past! C. H. S.

Before we come to the principal point, we must first clear the text from the incumbrance of a double objection. The first is this: It may seem (may some say) very improbable that David should have any sins of his youth, if we consider the principals whereupon his youth was past.

The first was poverty. We read that his father Jesse passed for an old man, we read not that he passed for a rich man; and probably his seven sons were the principal part of his wealth.

Secondly, painfulness. David, though the youngest, was not made a darling, but a drudge; sent by his father to follow the ewes big with young, where he may seem to have learned innocence and simplicity from the sheep he kept.

Thirdly, piety (Ps. 71:5), "for Thou art my hope, O Lord God; Thou art my trust from my youth." And again in the seventeenth verse of the same Psalm, "O God, Thou hast taught me from my youth." David began to be good betimes, a young saint, and yet crossed that pestilent proverb, was no old devil. And what is more still, he was constantly in the furnace of affliction. Ps. 88:15: "Even from my youth up, Thy terrors have I suffered with a troubled mind."

The question then will be this: How could that water be corrupted which was daily clarified? How could that steel gather rust which was duly filed? How could David's soul in his youth be sooty with sin, which was constantly scoured with suffering? But the answer is easy; for though David for the main was a man after God's own heart (the best transcript of the best copy), yet he, especially in his youth had his faults and infirmities, yea, his sins and transgressions.

If David's youth, which was poor, painful, and pious, was guilty of sins, what shall we say of such whose education hath been wealthy, wanton, and wicked? And I report the rest to be acted with shame, sorrow, and silence in every man's conscience. THOMAS FULLER

*Nor my transgressions.* Another word for the same evils. Sincere penitents cannot get through their confessions at a gallop; they are constrained to use many bemoanings, for their swarming sins smite them with so innumerable griefs.

A painful sense of any one sin provokes the believer to repentance for the whole mass of his iniquities. Nothing but the fullest and clearest pardon will satisfy a thoroughly awakened conscience. David would have his sins not only forgiven but forgotten.

*According to Thy mercy remember Thou me for Thy goodness' sake, O Lord.* David and the dying thief breathe the same prayer, and doubtless they grounded it upon the same plea, viz., the free grace and unmerited goodness of Jehovah. We dare not ask to have our portion measured from the balances of justice, but we pray to be dealt with by the hand of mercy.

Vs. 8. *Good and upright is the Lord: therefore will He teach sinners in the way.* It is no less true than wonderful that through the atonement the justice of God pleads as strongly as His grace for the salvation of the sinners whom Jesus died to save. Moreover, as a good man naturally endeavors to make others like himself, so will the Lord our God in His compassion bring sinners into the way of holiness and conform them to His own image; thus the goodness of our God leads us to expect the reclaiming of sinful men.

We may not conclude from God's goodness that He will save those sinners who continue to wander in their own ways, but we may be assured that He will renew transgressors' hearts and guide them into the way of holiness. Let those who desire to be delivered from sin take comfort from this: God Himself will condescend to be the teacher of sinners. What a ragged school is this for God to teach in! God's teaching is practical; He teaches sinners not only the doctrine, but *the way.* C. H. S.

As election is the effect of God's sovereignty, our pardon the fruit of His mercy, our knowledge a stream from His wisdom, our strength an impression of His power; so our purity is a beam from His holiness. STEPHEN CHARNOCK

Vs. 10. *All the paths of the Lord.* How frequent, how deeply indented and how multiplied are those tracks to every family and individual! Where ever we go, we see that God's mercy and truth have been there by the deep tracks they have left behind them. ADAM CLARKE

Vs. 11. *For Thy Name's sake, O Lord, pardon mine iniquity: for it is great.* Here is a blessed, never-failing plea. Not for our sakes or our merit's sake, but to glorify Thy mercy and to show forth the glory of Thy divine attributes.

*Pardon mine iniquity.* It is confessed; it is abhorred; it is consuming my heart with grief. Lord, forgive it; let Thine own lips pronounce absolution. *For it is great.* It weighs so heavily upon me that I pray Thee remove it. Its greatness is no difficulty with Thee, for Thou art a great God, but the misery which it causes to me is my argument with Thee for speedy pardon.

Lord, the patient is sore sick; therefore heal him. To pardon a great sinner will bring Thee great glory; therefore for Thy Name's sake pardon me. Observe how this verse illustrates the logic of faith, which is clean contrary to that of a legal spirit; faith looks not for merit in the creature, but hath regard to the goodness of the Creator; and instead of being staggered by the demerits of sin, it looks to the precious blood and pleads all the more vigorously because of the urgency of the case. C. H. S.

Among all divine works, there is none which more setteth forth His glory than this of remission. Sin, by committing it, brings God a great deal of dishonor, and yet, by forgiving it, God raiseth to Himself a great deal of honor. Since God forgiveth sins for His Name's sake, He will be ready to forgive many sins as well as few, great and small; indeed, the more and greater our sins are, the greater is the forgiveness, and consequently, the greater is God's glory; and therefore David, upon this consideration of God's name and glory, maketh the greatness of his iniquity a motive of forgiveness.

Indeed, to run into gross sins that God may glorify Himself by forgiving them, is an odious presumption, but to hope that those gross sins we have run into may, and will, be forgiven by God to us, being truly penitent, for His name's sake, is a well grounded expectation, and such as may support our spirits against the strongest temptations to despair. NATHANAEL HARDY

He pleads the greatness of his sin, and not the smallness of it: he enforces his prayer with this consideration, that his sins are very heinous. When a beggar begs for bread, he will plead the greatness of his poverty and necessity. When a man in distress cries for pity, what more suitable plea can be urged than the extremity of his case? And God allows such a plea as this: for He is moved to mercy towards us by nothing in us but the miserableness of our case.

It is the honor of Christ to save the greatest sinners when they come to Him, as it is the honor of a physician that he cures the most desperate diseases or wounds. Therefore, no doubt, Christ will be willing to save the greatest sinners if they come to Him; for He will not be backward to glorify Himself and to commend the value and virtue of His own blood. Seeing He hath so laid out Himself to redeem sinners, He will not be unwilling to show that He is able to redeem to the uttermost. JONATHAN EDWARDS

1. Sinners that come to God for pardon do look upon their sins as great sins, because against a great God, great in power, great in justice, great in holiness, I am a worm, and yet sin, and that boldly against a God so great; for a worm to lift up himself against a great and infinite God; oh, this makes every little sin great and calls for great vengeance from so great a God!

2. Because they have sinned against great patience, despising the goodness, forbearance, and longsuffering of God, which is called "treasuring up wrath" (Rom. 2:4-5). 3. Sins do appear great because against great mercies. O, against how many mercies and kindnesses do sinners sin and turn all the mercies of God into sin!

4. That which greatens sin in the eyes of poor sinners that cry for pardon is that they have sinned against great light—light in the conscience; this heightens sin exceedingly, especially to such as are under gospel means; and is indeed the sin of all in this nation.

Yet we do not find that David's youth was notoriously sinful; but inasmuch as he spent not his youth to get knowledge and to serve the Lord fully, 'twas his burden and complaint before the Lord; much more such whose youth was spent in nothing but vanity, profaneness, lying, swearing, profaning of the Sabbath, sports, pastimes, excess of riot, and the like, when God lays it in upon their consciences, must be grievous and abominable to their souls. ANTHONY PALMER in *"The Gospel New-Creature"*

"Oh," says Pharaoh, "take away these filthy frogs, this dreadful thunder!" But what says holy David? "Lord, take away the iniquity of Thy servant!" The one would be freed from punishment, the effect of sin; the other from sin, the cause of punishment. And it is most true that a true Christian man is more troubled at sin than at frogs and thunder; he sees more filthiness in sin than in frogs and toads, more horror than in thunder and lightning. JEREMIAH DYKE'S *"Worthy Communicant"*

Pharaoh more lamented the hard strokes that were upon him than the hard heart which was within him. Esau mourned not because he sold the birthright, which was his sin, but because he lost the blessing, which was his punishment.

This is like weeping with an onion; the eye sheds tears because it smarts. A mariner casts overboard that cargo in a tempest which he courts the return of when the winds are silenced. Many complain more of the sorrows to which they are born than of the sins with which they were born; they tremble more at the vengeance of sin than at the venom of sin; one delights them, the other affrights them. WILLIAM SECKER

Vs. 12. *He that feareth the Lord.* Present fear begetteth eternal security: fear God, which is above all, and no need to fear man at all. AUGUSTINE

*Him shall he teach in the way that he shall choose.* Those whose hearts are right shall not err for want of heavenly direction. Where God sanctifies the heart, He enlightens the head. We all wish to choose our way; but what a mercy is it when the Lord directs that choice and makes free-will to be good-will! If we make our will God's will, God will let us have our will.

God does not violate our will, but leaves much to our choice; nevertheless, He instructs our wills, and so we choose that which is well pleasing in His sight. The will should be subject to law; there is a way which we should choose, but so ignorant are we that we need to be taught and so wilful that none but God Himself can teach us effectually. C. H. S.

Vs. 13. He who fears God has nothing else to fear. *His soul shall dwell at ease.* He shall lodge in the chamber of content. One may sleep as soundly in the little bed in the corner as in the Great Bed of Ware; it is not abundance but content that gives true ease. C. H. S.

The holy fear of God shall destroy all sinful fears of men, even as Moses' serpent devoured all those serpents of the magicians. ROBERT MOSSOM

Vs. 14. *The secret of the Lord is with them that fear Him.* Some read it "the friendship": it signifies familiar intercourse, confidential intimacy, and select fellowship. This is a great secret. Carnal minds cannot guess what is intended by it, and even believers cannot explain it in words, for it must be felt to be known.

The higher spiritual life is necessarily a path which the eagle's eye hath not known, and which the lion's whelp has not traveled; neither natural wisdom nor strength can force a door into this inner chamber. Saints have the key of heaven's hieroglyphics; they can unriddle celestial enigmas. They are initiated into the fellowship of the skies; they have heard words which it is not possible for them to repeat to their fellows. C. H. S.

There is a vital sense in which "the natural man discerneth not the things of the Spirit of God" and in which all the realities of Christian experience are utterly hid from his perceptions. To speak to him of communion with God, of the sense of pardon, of the lively expectation of heaven, of the witness of the Holy Ghost, of the struggles of the spiritual life, would be like reasoning with a blind man about colors, or with one deaf about musical harmony. JOHN MORISON

Ay, but you will say, do not many carnal men know the gospel, and discourse of things in it, through strength of learning, etc.? I answer out of the text (Col. 1:26-27), that though they may know the things which the gospel reveals, yet not the riches and glory of them, that same rich knowledge spoken of in the Word, they want, and therefore know them not; as a child and jeweler looking upon a pearl, both look upon it, and call it by the same name; but the child yet knows it not as a pearl in the worth and riches of it as the jeweler doth, and therefore cannot be said to know it. THOMAS GOODWIN

Walking with God is the best way to know the mind of God; friends who walk together impart their secrets one to another: *The secret of the Lord is with them that fear Him.* Noah walked with God, and the Lord revealed a great secret to him, of destroying the old world, and having him in the ark.

Abraham walked with God, and God made him one of His privy council: "Shall I hide from Abraham that thing which I do?" (Gen. 24:40 and 18:17). God doth sometimes sweetly unbosom Himself to the soul in prayer, and in the Holy Supper, as Christ made Himself known to the disciples in the breaking of bread (Luke 24:35). THOMAS WATSON

Vs. 15. *Mine eyes are ever toward the Lord.* The writer claims to be fixed in his trust and constant in his expectation; he looks in confidence and waits in hope. We may add to this look of faith and hope the obedient look of service, the humble look of reverence, the admiring look of wonder, the studious look of meditation, and the tender look of affection. Happy are those whose eyes are never removed from their God. "The eye," says Solomon, "is never satisfied with seeing," but this sight is the most satisfying in the world.

*For He shall pluck my feet out of the net.* Observe the conflicting condition in which a gracious soul may be placed, his eyes are in heaven and yet his feet are sometimes in a net; his nobler nature ceases not to behold the glories of God, while his baser parts are enduring the miseries of the world. C. H. S.

An unfortunate dove, whose feet are taken in the snare of the fowler, is a fine emblem of the soul, entangled in the cares or pleasures of the world; from which she desires, through the power of grace, to fly away, and to be at rest with her glorified Redeemer. GEORGE HORNE

Vs. 16. His own eyes were fixed upon God, but he feared that the Lord had averted His face from him in anger. Oftentimes unbelief suggests that God has turned His back upon us. If we know that we turn to God, we need not fear that He will turn from us, but may boldly cry, *Turn Thee unto me.*

Vs. 17. *The troubles of my heart are enlarged.* When trouble penetrates the heart, it is trouble indeed. In the case before us, the heart was swollen with grief like a lake surcharged with water by enormous floods; this is used as an argument for deliverance, and it is a potent one. When the darkest hour of the night arrives, we may expect the dawn; when the sea is at its lowest ebb, the tide must surely turn; and when our troubles are enlarged to the greatest degree, then we may hopefully pray, *O bring Thou me out of my distresses.* C. H. S.

Let no good man be surprised that his affliction is great and to him of an unaccountable character. It has always been so with God's people. The road to heaven is soaked with the tears and blood of the saints. WILLIAM S. PLUMER

We may not complain of God, but we may complain to God. With submission to His holy will, we may earnestly cry for help and deliverance. WILLIAM S. PLUMER

Vs. 18. *Look upon mine affliction and my pain; and forgive all my sins.* Note the many trials of the saints; here we have no less than six words all descriptive of woe: "Desolate, and afflicted, troubles enlarged, distresses, affliction, and pain." But not yet more the submissive and believing spirit of a true saint; all he asks for is, "Lord, look upon my evil plight." He does not dictate or even express a complaint; a look from God will content him and, that being granted, he asks no more.

Even more noteworthy is the way in which the believer under affliction discovers the true source of all mischief and lays the axe at the root of it. *Forgive all my sins is* the cry of a soul that is more sick of sin than of pain and would sooner be forgiven than healed. Blessed is the man to whom sin is more unbearable than disease; he shall not be long before the Lord shall both forgive his iniquity and heal his diseases. Men are slow to see the intimate connection between sin and sorrow, a grace-taught heart alone feels it. C. H. S.

It is for the sickness of the soul that God visits with the sickness of the body. He aims at the cure of the soul in the touch of the body. And, therefore, in this case, when God visits with sickness, we should think our work is more in heaven with God than with men or physic. RICHARD SIBBES

Vs. 19. *Consided mine enemies.* Or look upon them; but with another kind of look; as He looked through the pillar of fire upon the Egyptians and troubled them (Exod. 14:24), with a look of wrath and vengeance. JOHN GILL

God needeth not hound out many creatures to punish man; he doeth that on himself. There is no kind of creature so hurtful to itself as he. Some hurt other kinds and spare their own, but mankind in all sorts of injuries destroyeth itself. Man to man is more crafty than a fox, more cruel than a tiger, and more fierce than a lion, and in a word, if he be left to himself, man unto man is a devil. WILLIAM STRUTHER'S *"Christian Observations"*

Vs. 20. *O keep my soul* out of evil, *and deliver me* when I fall into it. This is another version of the prayer, "Lead us not into temptation, but deliver us from evil."

*Let me not be ashamed.* This is the one fear which like a ghost haunted the Psalmist's mind. He trembled lest his faith should become the subject of ridicule through the extremity of his affliction. Noble hearts can brook anything but shame. David was of such a chivalrous spirit that he could endure any torment rather than to be put to dishonor. C. H. S.

## PSALM 26

Title: "A Psalm of David." The sweet singer of Israel is before us in this Psalm as one enduring reproach; in this he was the type of the great Son of David and is an encouraging example to us to carry the burden of slander to the throne of grace. It is an ingenious surmise that this appeal to heaven was written by David at the time of the assassination of Ish-bosheth by Baanah and Rechab to protest his innocence of all participation in that treacherous murder. The tenor of the Psalm certainly agrees with the supposed occasion, but it is not possible with such a slender clue to go beyond conjecture.

Vs. 1. *Judge me, O Lord.* Such an appeal as this is not to be rashly made on any occasion; and as to the whole of our walk and conversation, it should never be made at all except as we are justified in Christ Jesus: a far more fitting prayer for a sinful mortal is the petition, Enter not into judgment with Thy servant." C. H. S.

As an instance of appeal to heaven, we quote that mighty preacher of the Word, George Whitefield: "However some may account me a mountebank and an enthusiast, one that is only going to make you methodically mad; they may breathe out their invectives against me, yet Christ knows all; He takes notice of it, and I shall leave it to Him to plead my cause, for He is a gracious Master. I have already found Him so, and am sure He will continue so. Vengeance is His, and He will repay it." George Whitefield

*For I have walked in mine integrity.* He held integrity as his principle and walked in it as his practice. David had not used any traitorous or unrighteous means to gain the crown or to keep it; he was conscious of having been guided by the noblest principles of honor in all his actions with regard to Saul and his family.

What a comfort it is to have the approbation of one's own conscience! If there be peace within the soul, the blustering storms of slander which howl around us are of little consideration. When the little bird in my bosom sings a merry song it is no matter to me if a thousand owls hoot at me from without.

*I have trusted also in the Lord.* Why should I steal when God has promised to supply my need? Why should I avenge myself when I know that the Lord has espoused my cause? Confidence in God is a most effectual security against sin.

*Therefore I shall not slide.* Slippery as the way is, so that I walk like a man upon ice, yet faith keeps my heels from tripping and will continue to do so. The doubtful ways of policy are sure sooner or later to give a fall to those who run therein, but the ways of honesty, though often rough, are always safe. We cannot trust in God if we walk crookedly; but straight paths and simple faith bring the pilgrim happily to his journey's end. C. H. S.

Vs. 2. The Psalmist uses three words: "*examine,*" "*prove,*" "*try.*" These words are designed to include all the modes in which the reality of anything is tested; and they imply together that he wished the most thorough investigation to be made; he did not shrink from any test. Albert Barnes

*Examine—prove—try.* As gold by fire is severed and parted from dross, so singleness of heart and true Christian simplicity is best seen and made most evident in troubles and affliction. In prosperity, every man will seem godly, but afflictions do draw out of the heart whatsoever is there, whether it be good or bad. Robert Cawdray

Vs. 3. *And I have walked in Thy truth.* Some talk of truth; it is better to walk in it. Some vow to do well in future, but their resolutions come to nothing; only the regenerate man can say, "I have *walked* in Thy truth." C. H. S.

Verses 3-4. God will not shake the wicked by the hand, as the Vulgate reads (Job 8:20), neither must the godly man. David proves the sincerity of his course by his care to avoid such society. GEORGE SWINNOCK

Vs. 4. *I have not sat with vain persons.* So far from being himself an open offender against the laws of God, the Psalmist had not even associated with the lovers of evil. He had kept aloof from the men of Belial. A man is known by his company, and if we have kept ourselves apart from the wicked, it will always be evidence in our favor should our character be impugned. He who was never in the parish is not likely to have stolen the corn. He who never went to sea is clearly not the man who scuttled the ship.

True citizens have no dealings with traitors. David had no seat in the parliament of triflers. They were not his boon companions at feasts nor his advisers in council nor his associates in conversation. We must needs see, and speak, and trade, with men of the world, but we must on no account take our rest and solace in their empty society. Not only the profane, but the vain are to be shunned by us. All those who live for this life only are vain, chaffy, frothy men, quite unworthy of a Christian's friendship. C. H. S.

What do Christ's doves among birds of prey? What do virgins among harlots? The company of the wicked is very defiling; it is like going among them that have the plague. "They were mingled among the heathen and learned their works." If you mingle bright armor with rusty, the bright armor will not brighten the rusty, but the rusty armor will spoil the bright. Pharaoh taught Joseph to swear, but Joseph did not teach Pharaoh to pray. THOMAS WATSON

*Neither will I go in with dissemblers.* The congregation of the hypocrites is not one with which we should cultivate communion; their ultimate rendezvous will be the lowest pit of hell. Let us drop their acquaintance now, for we shall not desire it soon. They hang their heads around their necks and carry the devil in their hearts. C. H. S.

The hypocrite has much angel without, more devil within. He fries in words, and freezes in works; speaks by ells, doth good by inches. He is a stinking dunghill covered over with snow; a loose-hung mill that keeps great clacking but grinds no grist; a lying hen that cackles when she hath not laid. THOMAS ADAMS

Verses 4-5. "It is difficult (saith a late ingenious writer) even to a miracle to keep God's commandments and evil company, too. LEWIS STUCKLEY

Vs. 5. *I have hated the congregation of evil doers.* A severe sentence, but not too severe. A man who does not hate evil terribly does not love good heartily. Men, as men, we must always love, for they are our neighbors, and therefore to be loved as ourselves; but evil doers, as such, are traitors to the great King, and no loyal subject can love traitors. What God hates, we must hate. The congregation, or assembly, of evil doers signifies violent men in alliance and conclave for the overthrow of the innocent; such synagogues of Satan are to be held in abhorrence.

What a sad reflection it is that there should be a congregation of evil doers as well as a congregation of the upright, a church of Satan as well as a church of God; a seed of the serpent as well as a seed of the woman; an old Babylon as well as a new Jerusalem; a great whore sitting upon many waters, to be judged in wrath, as well as a chaste bride of the Lamb to be crowned at His coming. C. H. S.

The hatred of God's enemies, *quá* his enemies—"yea, I hate them right sore" so entirely opposed to the indifferentism of the present day, has always been one distinguishing mark of His ancient servants. Witness Phinehas (Ps. 106:31): "And that was counted unto him for righteousness unto all generations for evermore"; Samuel with Agag; Elias with the priests of Baal. And notice the commendation of the angel of Ephesus, "Thou canst not bear them that are evil" (Rev. 2:2). J. M. NEALE

*And will not sit with the wicked.* Saints have a seat at another table and will never leave the King's dainties for the husks of the swinetrough. Better to sit with the blind, and the halt, and the lame, at the table of mercy, than with the wicked in their feasts of ungodliness, yea, better to sit on Job's dunghill than on Pharaoh's throne. Let each reader see well to his company, for such as we keep in this world, we are likely to keep in the next. C. H. S.

How few consider how they harden wicked men by an intimacy with them, whereas withdrawment from them might be a means to make them ashamed! Whilst we are merry and jovial with them, we make them believe their condition is not deplorable, their danger is not great; whereas if we shunned them as we would a bowed wall, whilst they remain enemies to the Lord, this might do them good, for the startling of them, and rousing of them out of the unhappy security and strong delusions wherein they are held. LEWIS STUCKLEY

Vs. 6. *I will wash my hands in innocency: so will I compass Thine altar, O Lord.* Whatever Rome's physiologists pretend for the power of nature and of free will, we wretched sinners are taught to conceive more truly of our own infirmity. Christ's own apostle, stout Thomas, failed in the faith of His resurrection; Peter (whose chair is now the pretended seat of infallibility) denied his Master; David, "a man after God's own heart," hath need of washing; and who can say, "I am pure in the sight of the Lord"? Certainly, O Lord, no flesh is righteous in Thy sight. ISAAC BARGRAVE

Vs. 7. *And tell of all Thy wondrous works.* God's people should not be tongue-tied. The wonders of divine grace are enough to make the tongue of the dumb sing. God's works of love are wondrous if we consider the unworthiness of their objects, the costliness of their method, and the glory of their result. And as men find great pleasure in discoursing upon things remarkable and astonishing, so the saints rejoice to tell of the great things which the Lord hath done for them. C. H. S.

Vs. 8. *Lord, I have loved the habitation of Thy house.* "I have in my congregation," said a venerable minister of the gospel, "a worthy aged woman, who has for many years been so deaf as not to distinguish the loudest sound, and yet she is always one of the first in the meeting.

"On asking the reason of her constant attendance (as it was impossible for her to hear my voice), she answered, 'Though I cannot hear you, I come to God's house because I love it, and would be found in His ways; and He gives me many a sweet thought upon the text when it is pointed out to me: another reason is, because I am in the best company there, in the more immediate presence of God, and among His saints, the honorable of the earth. I am not satisfied with serving God in private; it is my duty and privilege to honor Him regularly in public.' " What a reproof this is to those who have their hearing and yet always come to a place of worship late or not at all! K. ARVINE

Vs. 9. *Gather not my soul with sinners.* "Oh, do not gather my soul with sinners" for the wine-press of Thine eternal anger! Marcion, the heretic, seeing Polycarp, wondered that he would not own him. "Do you not know me, Polycarp?" "Yea," saith Polycarp, "I know thee to be the firstborn of the devil," and so despised him. GEORGE SWINNOCK

Death is God's gathering time, wherein He gets the souls belonging to Him and the devil those belonging to him. They did go long together, but then they are parted; and the saints are taken home to the congregation of saints, and sinners to the congregation of sinners. And it concerns us to say, "Gather not my soul with sinners." Whoever be our people here, God's people or the devil's, death will gather our souls to them.

It is a horrible thing to be gathered with sinners in the other world. To think of our souls being gathered with them there may make the hair of one's head stand up.

Many now like no gathering like the gathering with sinners; it is the very delight of their hearts; it makes a brave, jovial life in their eyes. And it is a pain to them to be gathered with saints, to be detained before the Lord on a Sabbath-day.

But to be gathered with them in the other world is a horror to all sorts. 1. The saints have a horror of it, as in the text. To think to be staked down in their company in the other world would be a hell of itself to the godly. David never had such a horror of the society of the diseased, the persecuted, etc., as of sinners. He is content to be gathered with saints of whatever condition; but, "Lord," says he, "gather not my soul with sinners." 2. The wicked themselves have a horror of it. Num. 23:10: "Let me die the death of the righteous," said the wicked Balaam, "and let my last end be like his." Though they would be content to live with them or be with them in life, their consciences bear witness that they have a horror of being with them in death. They would live with sinners, but they would die with saints. A poor, unreasonable, self-condemning thought. THOMAS BOSTON

Vs. 10. *Bribes.*

*What makes all doctrines plain and clear?*
*Above two hundred pounds a year,*
*And that which was proved true before*
*Proved false again? Two hundred more.*

SAMUEL BUTLER *in "Hudibras," Part III, Canto I.*

## PSALM 27

The Psalm may with profit be read in a threefold way, as the language of David, of the church, and of the Lord Jesus. The plenitude of Scripture will thus appear the more wonderful. C. H. S.

Vs. 1. *The Lord is my light and my salvation.* Where there is not enough light to see our own darkness and to long for the Lord Jesus, there is no evidence of salvation. Salvation finds us in the dark, but does not leave us there. It is not said merely that the Lord gives light, but that He "is" light; not that He gives salvation, but that He "is" salvation. C. H. S.

Alice Driver, martyr, at her examination put all the doctors to silence, so that they had not a word to say, but one looked upon another; then she said, "Have you no more to say? God be honored, you be not able to resist the Spirt of God in me, a poor woman. I was an honest poor man's daughter, never brought up at the University as you have been; but I have driven the plough many a time before my father, I thank God; yet, notwithstanding, in the defense of God's truth, and in the cause of my Master, Christ, by His grace I will set my foot against the foot of any of you all, in the maintenance and defense of the same; and if I had a thousand lives they should go for payment thereof." So the Chancellor condemned her, and she returned to the prison joyful. CHAS. BRADBURY

There is a great difference between the *light* and the eye that sees it. A blind man may know a great deal about the shining of the sun, but it does not shine for him—it gives him no light. So, to know that "God is light" is one thing (I John 1:5) and to be able to say, "The Lord is *my* light," is quite another thing. When He is thus "our light," then He is "our salvation" also. He is pledged to guide us right; not only to show us sin but to save us from it, not only to make us see God's hatred of sin and His curse upon it, but also to draw us unto God's love and to take away the curse. *From Sacramental Meditations*

"Adorable Sun," cried St. Bernard, "I cannot walk without Thee; enlighten my steps and furnish this barren and ignorant mind with thoughts worthy of Thee. Adorable fullness of light and heat, be thou the true noon day of my soul; exterminate its darkness, disperse its clouds; burn, dry up and consume all its filth and impurities. Divine Sun, rise upon my mind and never set." JEAN AVRILLON

*Of whom shall I be afraid?* A question which is its own answer. The powers of darkness are not to be feared, for the Lord, our Light, destroys them; and the damnation of hell is not to be dreaded by us, for the Lord is our salvation. C. H. S.

I have no notion of a timid, disingenuous profession of Christ. Such preachers and professors are like a rat playing at hide-and-seek behind a wainscot, who puts his head through a hole to see if the coast is clear and ventures out if nobody is in the way, but slinks back again if danger appears. We cannot be honest to Christ except we are bold for Him. He is either worth *all* we can lose for Him or He is worth *nothing.* H. G. SALTER

Vs. 2. *When the wicked.* It is a hopeful sign for us when the wicked hate us; if our foes were godly men it would be a sore sorrow, but as for the wicked, their hatred is better than their love. C. H. S.

There is no such dainty dish to a malicious stomach as the flesh of an enemy; it goes down without chewing, and they swallow it up whole like cormorants. Sir Richard Baker

As the great fishes eat up the little ones, so great men they make no more conscience of eating up other men than of eating bread. R. Sibbes

Vultures have an antipathy against sweet smells; so in the wicked there is an antipathy against the people of God; they hate the sweet perfumes of their graces. Thomas Watson

There was great wisdom in the prayer of John Wesley, "Lord if I must contend, let it not be with Thy people." When we have for foes and enemies those who hate good men, we have at least this consolation, that God is not on their side, and therefore it is essentially weak. Wm. Plumer

Vs. 3. *Though an host should encamp against me, my heart shall not fear.* The encamping host often inspires greater dread than the same host in actual affray. Young tells us of some "who feel a thousand deaths in fearing one." C. H. S.

Happily for me, ye cannot blacken me before God, and His esteem alone makes amends to me, and rewards me, for all your contempt. Jean Avrillon

Where there is no confidence *in* God, there will be no continuance *with* God. When the wind of faith ceases to fill the sails, the ship of obedience ceases to plough the seas. Wm. Secker

Vs. 4. *One thing.* The man of one book is eminent, the man of one pursuit is successful. Let all our affections be bound up in one affection and that affection set upon heavenly things. C. H. S.

I understand thus much in a generality, which is clear that he means a communion and fellowship with God, which is that *one thing,* which if a Christian had, he needs desire no more. John Stoughton

*Have I desired.* What we cannot at once attain, it is well to desire. God judges us very much by the desire of our hearts. He who rides a lame horse is not blamed by his master for want of speed, if he makes all the haste he can, and would make more if he could; God takes the will for the deed with His children. C. H. S.

*Of the Lord.* This is the right target for desires; this is the well into which to dip our buckets; this is the door to knock at, the bank to draw upon; desire of men, and lie on the dunghill with Lazarus: desire of the Lord, and be carried of angels into Arabahm's bosom. Under David's painful circumstances, we might have expected him to desire repose, safety, and a thousand other good things, but, no, he has set his heart on the pearl, and leaves the rest. C. H. S.

*That will I seek after.* Holy desires must lead to resolute action. The old proverb says, "Wishers and woulders are never good housekeepers." C. H. S.

*To behold the beauty of the Lord.* We must not enter the assemblies of the saints in order to see and be seen or merely to hear the minister. Better far—behold it by faith! What a sight will that be when every faithful follower of Jesus shall behold "the King in His beauty!" Oh, for that infinitely blessed vision! C. H. S.

Tell me, if there be, if there can be, any greater request to be made. This "*one thing*" that David desires is in effect that *unum necessarium* that Christ speaks of in the Gospel; which Mary makes choice of there, as David doth here. Sir Richard Baker

Another thing, which we may call an element of beauty in God, is the combination of His various attributes in one harmonious whole. The colors of the rainbow are beautiful when taken one by one: but there is a beauty in the rainbow, which arises not from any single tint. Holiness is beautiful; mercy is beautiful; truth is beautiful. ANDREW GRAY

Vs. 5. *For in the time of trouble He shall hide me in His pavilion.* He shall give me the best of shelter in the worst of danger. *In the secret of His tabernacle shall He hide me.* No one of old dared to enter the most holy place on pain of death; and if the Lord has hidden His people there, what foe shall venture to molest them? C. H. S.

Vs. 7. *Hear, O Lord, when I cry with my voice.* The voice which in the last verse was tuned to music is here turned to crying. Pharisees care not a fig for the Lord's hearing them, so long as they are heard of men. C. H. S.

Vs. 8. *When Thou saidst, Seek ye My face; my heart said unto Thee, Thy face, Lord, will I seek.* Oh, for more of this holy readiness! Would to God that we were more plastic to the Divine hand, more sensitive of the touch of God's Spirit. C. H. S.

*God is willing to be known.* He is willing to open and discover Himself; God delights not to hide Himself. God stands not upon state, as some emperors do that think their presence diminisheth respect. God is no such God, but He may be searched into. Man, if any weakness be discovered, we can soon search into the depth of his excellency; but with God it is clean otherwise. The more we know of Him, the more we shall admire Him. I desire to be made known and lay open myself to you. As if God were a God that delighted to hide Himself. No; the fault is altogether in us. *Seek ye My face.* He desires to reveal Himself. RICHARD SIBBES

*When Thou saidst.* Let there be a prayer, and there is a prayer; that is, He pours upon a man a spirit of grace and supplication, a praying disposition; He puts in motives, suggests arguments and pleas to God. THOMAS GOODWIN

Well may this be pleaded, in that God useth not so to stir up and strengthen us to seek Him, but when He intendeth to be found of us. Ps. 10:17: "Thou hast heard the desire of the humble: Thou wilt prepare their heart, Thou wilt cause Thine ear to hear." Jer. 29:13: "And ye shall seek Me and find Me, when ye shall search for Me with all your heart." THOMAS COBBET

*My heart said unto Thee.* The heart is between God and our obedience, as it were, an ambassador. It understands from God what God would have done, and then it lays a command upon the whole man. The heart and conscience of man is partly Divine, partly human. RICHARD SIBBES

*Put not Thy servant away in anger.* God puts away many in anger for their supposed goodness, but not any at all for their confessed badness. JOHN TRAPP

*Thy servant.* It is a blessed and happy thing to be God's true *servant.* Consider what the Queen of Sheba said of Solomon's servants (I Kings 10:8): "Happy are these thy servants." THOMAS PIERSON

Vs. 10. *When my father and my mother forsake me.* These dear relations will be the last to desert me, but if the milk of human kindness should dry up even from their breasts, there is a Father Who never forgets. C. H. S.

*Then the Lord will take me up.* Those are His *love,* His *wisdom,* His *power,* His *eternity,* and all in His nature. To which *four,* add His *promise,* and you have the fullness of all the assurance that can be desired. ROBERT SANDERSON

Vs. 11. *Lead me in a plain path, because of mine enemies.* If a man traveling in the King's highway be robbed between sun and sun, satisfaction is recoverable upon the county where the robbery was made; but if he takes his journey in the night, being an unseasonable time, then it is at his own peril, he must take what falls. So, if a man keep in *God's ways,* he shall be sure of God's protection; but if he stray out of them, he exposeth himself to danger. ROBERT SKINNER

*Because of mine enemies.* It is wonderful to observe how honest simplicity baffles and outwits the craftiness of wickedness. Truth is wisdom. "Honesty is the best policy." C. H. S.

Believers condemn those by their lives who condemn them by their lips. Christian, if you dwell in the open tent of licentiousness, the wicked shall not walk backward, like modest Shem and Japheth, to cover your shame: but they will walk forward, like cursed Ham, to publish it. Thus they make use of your weakness as a plea for their wickedness. Men are merciless in their censures of Christians; they have no sympathy for their infirmity. While a saint is a *dove* in the eyes of God, he is only a *raven* in the estimation of sinners. WM. SECKER

Vs. 12. *For false witnesses are risen up against me.* Slander is an old-fashioned weapon out of the armory of hell and is still in plentiful use; and no matter how holy a man may be, there will be some who will defame him. It is their vital breath to hate the good. C. H. S.

Vs. 13. *I had fainted.* You may as well doubt that all the waters of the ocean cannot fill a spoon as that the divine fullness cannot be enough to you, if you should have nothing left in this world. One drop of Divine sweetness is enough to make one in the very agony of the cruelest death to cry out with joy, "The bitterness of death is past." His *goodness* makes Him willing to do. His *goodness* sets His mighty power a-work for His suffering saints. DAVID CLARKSON

Vs. 14. *Wait on the Lord.* Wait at His door with prayer; wait at His foot with humility; wait at His table with service; wait at His window with expectancy. C. H. S.

*Stand but your ground, your ghostly foes will fly—*
*Hell trembles at a heaven-directed eye;*
*Choose rather to defend than to assail—*
*Self-confidence will in the conflict fail:*
*When you are challenged, you may dangers meet—*
*True courage is a fixed, not sudden heat;*
*Is always humble, lives in self-distrust,*
*And will itself into no danger thrust.*
*Devote yourself to God, and you will find*
*God fights the battles of a will resigned.*
*Love Jesus! love will no base fear endure—*
*Love Jesus! and of conquest rest secure.*

THOMAS KEN

# PSALM 28

The thorn at the breast of the nightingale was said by the old naturalists to make it sing. David's griefs made him eloquent in holy Psalmody. C. H. S.

Vs. 1. *Unto Thee will I cry, O Lord my rock.* It will be in vain to call to the rocks in the day of judgment, but our Rock attends to our cries. C. H. S.

It is of the utmost importance that we should have a *definite object* on which to fix our thoughts. "Call unto *Me,* and I will answer thee, and shew thee great and mighty things, which thou knowest not." One looking down upon him, listening to him, feeling for him, preparing to answer him. Dear reader, in the time of your trouble, do not roam; do not let your thoughts wander as though they were looking for someone on whom to fix. "Unto *Thee* will I cry." . . . . Oh! happy is that man who feels and knows that when trouble comes he cannot be bewildered and confused by the stroke, no matter how heavy it may be. PHILIP BENNETT POWER

*My rock.* "Christ in His person, Christ in the love of His heart, and Christ in the power of His arm, is the Rock on which I rest." K. ARVINE

*Be not silent to me.* His silence is equally full of awe to an eager suppliant. What a dreadful case should we be in if the Lord should become forever silent to our prayers! C. H. S.

What do we desire God to say? We want Him to let us know that He hears us; we want to hear Him speak as distinctly to us as we feel that we have spoken to Him. "It is said," said Rutherford, speaking of the Savior's delay in responding to the request of the Syrophoenician woman, "He answered not a word," but it is not said, 'He *heard* not a word.' Christ often heareth when He doth not answer—His *not* answering *is an answer,* and speaks thus—'pray on, go on and cry, for the Lord holdeth His door fast bolted,' not to keep you out, but that you may knock, and knock, and it shall be opened. PHILIP BENNETT POWER

*Lest . . . I become like them that go down into the pit.* With secret horror I daily hear them blaspheming the ineffable gifts of Thy grace and ridiculing the faith and fervor of the godly as mere imbecility of mind. I fear that insensibly I may become such a self-deceiver as to disguise my criminal timidity by the name of prudence. I know that it is impossible both to please a corrupt world and a holy God, and yet I so far lose sight of this truth. Strengthen me, O Lord, against these declensions so injurious to Thy glory, so fatal to the fidelity which is due to Thee. JEAN MASSILLON

Vs. 2. *Hear the voice of my supplications!* A silent prayer may have a louder voice than the cries of those priests who sought to awaken Baal with their shouts. C. H. S.

*When I lift up my hands toward Thy holy oracle.* We stretch out empty hands, for we are beggars; we lift them up, for we seek heavenly supplies; we lift them towards the mercy seat of Jesus. C. H. S.

Vs. 3. *Draw me not away with the wicked.* They shall be dragged off to hell like felons of old drawn on a hurdle to Tyburn, like logs drawn to the fire, like fagots to the oven. David fears lest he should be bound up in their bundle, drawn to their doom.

*Which speak peace to their neighbors, but mischief is in their hearts.* Soft words, oily with pretended love. It were better to be shut up in a pit with serpents than to be compelled to live with liars. C. H. S.

Dissembled love is worse than hatred; counterfeiting of friendship is no better than a lie. THOMAS WATSON

Vs. 4. Ungodly reader, what will be your lot when the Lord deals with you? Our "endeavors" are taken as facts; God takes the will for the deed and punishes or rewards accordingly. C. H. S.

*Give them according to their deeds.* It is unquestionable that if the flesh move us to seek revenge, the desire is wicked in the sight of God. He forbids us to imprecate evil upon our enemies in revenge. The holy prophet is not inflamed here by his own private sorrow to devote his enemies to destruction; but laying aside the desire of the flesh, he gives judgment concerning the matter itself. Before a man can, therefore, denounce vengeance against the wicked, he must first shake himself free from all improper feelings in his own mind, which happened even to Christ's disciples. In short, David, being free from every evil passion, pleads here not so much his own cause as the cause of God. JOHN CALVIN

Great God, Thou hast from the beginning been only occupied in saving men. The very benevolence towards mankind solicits Thy thunders against these corrupters of society. They labor incessantly to put men far away from Thee, O my God, and in return Thou wilt put them far away from Thee forever and have the desperate consolation of being such themselves to all eternity. Frightful necessity of hating Thee forever! JEAN MASSILLON

*Render to them their desert.* Meditate on God's righteousness, that it is not only His will, but His nature to punish sin. God cannot but hate sin, because He is holy; and He cannot but punish sin. God must not forego His own nature to gratify our humors. CHRISTOPHER FOWLER

He prayeth against his enemies, being led by the infallible Spirit of prophecy, looking through these men to the enemies of Christ and of His people in all ages. DAVID DICKSON

*Give them—render them—He shall destroy them.* If, therefore, the verbs, in all such passages, were uniformily rendered in the "future," they would appear clearly to be what they are, namely, prophecies of the divine judgments which have been since executed against the Jews. GEORGE HORNE

Vs. 6. *Blessed be the Lord.* Our Psalm was prayer up to this point, and now it turns to praise. They who pray well will soon praise well: prayer and praise are the two lips of the soul; two altars; two of Solomon's lilies. C. H. S.

Vs. 7. *The Lord is my strength.* If he have *strength* added to him, if the burden be doubled, yet his *strength* be trebled, the burden will not be heavier, but lighter. If we cannot bear them with our own strength, why may we not bear them with the strength of Jesus Christ! Can we have the strength of Christ? Yes; that very strength is made over to us by faith, therefore, is Christ's strength ours, made over unto us. ISAAC AMBROSE

*Therefore my heart greatly rejoiceth; and with my song will I praise Him.* Observe the adverb *greatly*—we need not be afraid of being too full of rejoicing at the remembrance of grace received. Let us greatly rejoice in Him. It were well if we were more like the singing lark and less like the croaking raven. When God blesses us, we should bless Him with all our heart. C. H. S.

Vs. 8. *The Lord is their strength.* Not mine only, but the strength of every believer. For we are sure there is enough for all and enough for each. MATTHEW HENRY

# PSALM 29

This Psalm is meant to express the glory of God as heard in the pealing thunder. The verses march to the tune of thunderbolts. True ministers are sons of thunder, and the voice of God in Christ Jesus is full of majesty. Thus we have God's works and God's Word joined together. C. H. S.

*Whole Psalm:* In this Psalm, the strength of Jehovah is celebrated; and the exemplification of it is evidently taken from a thunderstorm in Lebanon. From the mountains, the storm sweeps down into the plains. ROBERT MURRAY M'CHEYNE

There is no phenomenon in nature so awful as a thunderstorm. The Twenty-Ninth Psalm derives a sacred vitality and power from the presence of Jehovah in each successive peal. JAMES HAMILTON, D.D.

One ought to realize an Oriental storm rightly to appreciate the feelings of the bard; with a power which suggested the end of the world. AUGUSTUS F. THOLUCK

Vs. 1. *Give unto the Lord.* Neither men nor angels can confer anything upon Jehovah, but they should recognize His glory and might. Natural causes, as men call them, are God in action, and we must not ascribe power to them. C. H. S.

This showeth how unwilling such are usually to give God His right. JOHN TRAPP

Vs. 2. *Give unto the Lord the glory due unto His Name.* A third time the admonition is given, for men are backward in glorifying God, and especially great men. Unbelief and distrust, complaining and murmuring, rob God of His honor. C. H. S.

Which yet you cannot do, for His name is above all praise; but you must aim at it. JOHN TRAPP

*Worship the Lord.* Why is the Lord to be worshipped? Why must He have such high honors?

Vs. 1-2. A sincere Christian aims to glorify God, to exalt God, and to lift up God in the world. He that sets up the glory of God as his chief end will find that his chief end will by degrees eat out all low and base ends. Where the glory of God is kept up as a man's greatest end, there all bye and base ends will be kept at an under. THOMAS BROOKS

Vs. 3. *The voice of the Lord is upon the waters.* No sight more alarming than the flash of lightning around the mast of the ship.

*The glory of God thundereth.* Thunder is in truth no mere electric phenomenon but is caused by the interposition of God Himself. Electricity of itself can do nothing; it must be called and sent upon its errand: and until the Almighty Lord commissions it, its bolt of fire is inert and powerless. As well might a rock of granite or a bar of iron fly in the midst of heaven as the lightning go without being sent by the great First Cause. C. H. S.

Yes, great God, this heart hitherto so dry, so arid, so hard; this rock which Thou hast struck a second time, will not resist Thee any longer, for out of it there now gushes healthful waters in abundance. The selfsame voice of God which overturns the mountains, thunders, lightens, and divides the heaven above the sinner, now commands the clouds to pour forth showers of blessings, changing the desert of his soul into a field producing a hundredfold; that voice I hear. J. B. MASSILLON

The natural powers of matter and laws of motion are indeed the effects of God's acting upon matter. Consequently there is no such thing as the cause of nature or the power of nature. SAMUEL CLARKE

Vs. 4. *The voice of the Lord is powerful.* As the voice of God in nature is so powerful, so is it in grace; the reader will do well to draw a parallel, and he will find much in the Gospel which may be illustrated by the thunder of the Lord in the tempest. See that ye refuse not Him that speaketh. If His voice be thus mighty, what must His hand be! C. H. S.

Chaos knows not how to resist Thee, it hears Thy voice obediently, but the obdurate heart repels Thee, and Thy mighty voice too often calls to it in vain. Thou art not so great and wonderful in creating worlds out of nothing as Thou art when Thou dost command a rebel heart to arise from its abyss of sin, and to run in the ways of Thy commandments. J. B. MASSILLON

*The voice of the Lord is full of majesty.* The King of kings speaks like a king. As when a lion roareth, all the beasts of the forest are still, so is the earth hushed and mute while Jehovah thundereth marvellously. C. H. S.

Oh, may the evangelical "Boanerges" so cause the glorious sound of the gospel to be heard under the whole heaven that the world may again be made sensible thereof; before the voice of the Son of Man, which hath so often called sinners to repentance, shall call them to judgment. GEORGE HORNE

Vs. 5. *The voice of Jehovah.* It is a diabolical science, however, which fixes our contemplations on the works of nature and turns them away from God. If anyone who wished to know a man should take no notice of his face, but should fix his eyes only on the points of his nails, his folly might justly be derided. JOHN CALVIN

*The cedars of Lebanon.* These mighty trees of God, which for ages have stood the force of the tempest, are the first objects of the fury of the lightning, which is well known to visit first the highest objects. ROBERT MURRAY M'CHEYNE

Vs. 6. *He maketh them also to skip like a calf; Lebanon and Sirion like a young unicorn.* The voice of our dying Lord rent the rocks and opened the graves: His living voice still works the like wonders. C. H. S.

Any beast in the forest, He brings to the sorrows of their new birth, to repentance and gospel humiliation, and in doing this, He opens the hearts of men, which are as thick set and full grown with vanity, pride, hypocrisy, self-love, and self-sufficiency, as also with wantoness and sensuality, as any forest is overgrown with thickets of trees and bushes, which deny all passage through, till cleared away with burning down or cutting up. JOSEPH CARYL

Vs. 7. *The voice of the Lord divideth the flames of fire.* The same power of God goeth forth by His Word, "quick and powerful, and sharper than any two-edged sword," penetrating, melting, enlightening, and inflaming the hearts of men. GEORGE HORNE

"The voice of Jehovah sendeth out divided flames of fire." This is very descriptive of the Divine action at Pentecost, sending forth *divided flames,* in the tongues of fire which were divided off from one heavenly source or fountain of flame, and sat upon the heads of the Apostles, and which filled them with the fire of holy zeal and love. CHRISTOPHER WORDSWORTH

Vs. 8. *The voice of the Lord shaketh the wilderness.* Yet even there, great God, where I believed that I had found an asylum inaccessible to Thine eternal mercy, wherein I could sin with impunity, even there, in that wilderness, Thy voice arrested me and laid me at Thy feet. J. B. MASSILLON

Vs. 9. *The voice of the Lord maketh the hinds to calve.* Our first parents sought a refuge among the trees but the voice of the Lord soon found them out and made their hearts to tremble. The gospel has a like revealing power in dark hearts and bids the soul tremble before the Lord. C. H. S.

Doth the Lord take care of *hinds?* then certainly He takes care of those that particularly belong to Him. JOSEPH CARYL

*And in His temple doth every one speak of His glory.* There is far more royal power in the thunder of the Word than in the word of thunder. This terrifieth only to conviction, but that terrifieth to salvation. JOSEPH CARYL

Vs. 11. *The Lord will give strength unto His people; the Lord will bless His people with peace.* Power was displayed in the hurricane whose course this Psalm so grandly pictures; in the cool calm after the storm, that power is promised to be the strength of the chosen. C. H. S.

First, the gospel puts that price into his hand which will assuredly purchase it; it is peace of conscience, because peace of conscience is but a discharge under God's hand, that the debt due to divine justice is fully paid. Secondly, every true believer hath peace of conscience in the promise, that we count as good as ready money. It is worth your reading the whole Psalm to see what weight the Lord gives to this sweet promise. The Psalm is spent in showing what great things God can do, and that with no more trouble to Himself than a word. This God that doth all this promiseth to *bless His people with peace.* A sad peace, were it not, to have quiet streets, but cutting of throats in our houses? yet infinitely more sad to have peace both in our streets and houses, but war and blood in our guilty consciences. "Peace I leave with you, My peace I give unto you."

Thirdly, it is called "the peaceable fruit of righteousness." It shoots as naturally from holiness as any fruit in its kind doth from the seed proper to it. WILLIAM GURNALL

## PSALM 30

Title: "A Psalm and Song at the Dedication of the House of David"; or rather, "A Psalm; a Song of Dedication for the House, by David." A song of faith since the house of Jehovah, here intended, David never lived to see. A Psalm of praise, since a sore judgment had been stayed and a great sin forgiven.

Vs. 1. *I will extol Thee.* I will have high and honorable conceptions of Thee and give them utterance in my best music. Others may forget Thee, murmur at Thee, despise Thee, blaspheme Thee, but "I will extol Thee," for I have been favored above all others.

*For Thou hast lifted me up.* Here is an antithesis, "I will exalt Thee, for Thou hast exalted me." Grace has uplifted us from the pit of hell, from the ditch of sin, from the Slough of Despond, from the bed of sickness, from the bondage of doubts and fears: have we no song to offer for all this? How high has our Lord lifted us? Lifted us up into the children's place, to be adopted into the family; lifted us up into union with Christ, "to sit together with Him in heavenly places." Lift high the Name of our God, for He has lifted us above the stars. C. H. S.

The verb is used, in its original meaning, to denote *the reciprocating motion of the buckets of a well,* one descending as the other rises, and vice versa; and is here applied with admirable propriety to point out the various reciprocations and changes of David's fortunes as described in this Psalm, as to prosperity and adversity. SAMUEL CHANDLER

*And hast not made my foes to rejoice over me.* Oh, happy they whom the Lord keeps so consistent in character that the lynx eyes of the world can see no real fault in them. Is this our case? Let us ascribe all the glory to Him Who has sustained us in our integrity.

Vs. 2. *O Lord my God, I cried unto Thee, and Thou hast healed me.* If our watch is out of order, we take it to the watchmaker; if body or soul be in an evil plight, let us resort to Him Who created them and has unfailing skill to put them in right condition. As for our spiritual diseases, nothing can heal these evils but the touch of the Lord Christ: if we do but touch the hem of His garment, we shall be made whole, while if we embrace all other physicians in our arms, they can do us no service.

Vs. 3. *O Lord, Thou hast brought up my soul from the grave.* Mark, it is not, "I hope so"; but it is, "Thou hast; Thou hast; Thou hast"—three times over. David is quite sure, beyond a doubt, that God has done great things for him, whereof he is exceeding glad.

Vs. 4. *Sing unto the Lord, O ye saints of His.* David would not fill his choir with reprobates but with sanctified persons who could sing from their hearts. He calls to you, ye people of God, because ye are saints: and if sinners are wickedly silent, let your holiness constrain you to sing. You are His saints—chosen, blood-bought, called, and set apart for God; sanctified on purpose that you should offer the daily sacrifice of praise. Abound ye in this heavenly duty. C. H. S.

Vs. 5. *His anger.* Oh, admire and wonder forever at the sovereign, distinguishing grace of God. Are you that are at ease better than many of His people that are now thrown into a fiery furnace? Have you less dross than they? Have they sinned, think you, at a higher rate than you have ever done? He is angry with them for their lukewarmness, for their backsliding; and have your hearts always burned with love?

Have your feet always kept His way and not declined? Have you never wandered? Have you never turned aside to the right hand or to the left? Surely you have; and therefore, what a mercy is it, that He is not angry with you as well as with them. TIMOTHY ROGERS

*In His favor is life.* If a damned soul should be admitted to the fruition of all the pleasure of eternal life without the favor of God, heaven would be hell to him. It is not the dark and horrid house of woe that maketh a soul miserable in hell, but God's displeasure.

If an elect soul should be cast thither and retain the favor of God, hell would be an heaven to him, and his joy could not all the devils of hell take from him; his night would be turned into day. EDWARD MARBURY

*Weeping may endure for a night, but joy cometh in the morning.* When the Sun of Righteousness comes, we wipe our eyes, and joy chases out intruding sorrow. Who would not be joyful that knows Jesus? The first beams of the morning bring us comfort when Jesus is the day-dawn, and all believers know it to be so. Mourning only lasts till morning: when the night is gone the gloom shall vanish. This is adduced as a reason for saintly singing, and forcible reason it is; short nights and merry days call for the psaltery and harp. C. H. S.

How heavily does any trouble weigh on us at night! Our wearied nerve and brain seem unable to bear up under the pressure. Our pulse throbs, and the fevered, restless body refuses to help in the work of endurance. After such a night of struggle, and the heavy sleep of exhaustion, we awake with a vague sense of trouble. Why were we so helpless and despairing? Things do not look so now—sad indeed still, but endurable—hard, but no longer impossible—bad enough perhaps, but we despair no more. *Weeping may endure for a night, but joy cometh in the morning.*

And so, when life with its struggles and toils and sins, bringing us perpetual conflict, ends at last in the fierce struggle of death, then God "giveth His beloved sleep." They sleep in Jesus and awake to the joy of a morning which shall know no wane—the morning of joy.

The Sun of Righteousness is beaming on them. Light is now on all their ways. And they can only wonder when they recall the despair and darkness and toil and violence of their earthly life, and say, as they have often said on earth, "Weeping has endured only for the night, and now it is morning, and joy has come!" And our sorrows, our doubts our difficulties, our long looks forward, with despair of enduring strength for so long a night of trial—where are they? Shall we not feel as is so beautifully described in the words of one of our hymns—

*When in our Father's happy land*
*We meet our own once more,*
*Then we shall scarcely understand*
*Why we have wept before.*

MARY B. M. DUNCAN

Their mourning shall last but till morning. God will turn their winter's night into a summer's day, their sighing into singing their grief into gladness, their mourning into music, their bitter into sweet, their wilderness into a paradise.

It is best and most for the health of the soul that the south wind of mercy, and the north wind of adversity, doth blow upon it; and though every wind that blows shall blow good to the saints, yet certainly their sins die most, and their graces thrive best, when they are under the drying, nipping north wind of calamity, as well as under the warm, cherishing south wind of mercy and prosperity. THOMAS BROOKS

Vs. 6. *In my prosperity.* When all his foes were quiet, and his rebellious son dead and buried, then was the time of peril. Many a vessel founders in a calm. No temptation is so bad as tranquillity. C. H. S.

We are never in greater danger than in the sunshine of prosperity. To be always indulged of God and never to taste of trouble is rather a token of God's neglect rather than of His tender love. WILLIAM STRUTHER

*I said, I shall never be moved.* Ah, David, you said more than was wise to say, or even to think, for God has founded the world upon the floods, to show us what a poor, mutable, movable, inconstant world it is. Unhappy he who builds upon it! He builds himself a dungeon for his hopes.

Vs. 7. *Lord, by Thy favor, Thou hast made my mountain to stand strong.* His state he compares to a mountain, a molehill would have been nearer—we never think too little of ourselves. He boasted that his mountain stood strong, and yet he had before in Psalm 29, spoken of Sirion and Lebanon as moving like young unicorns.

Was David's state more firm than Lebanon? Ah, vain conceit, too common to us all! How soon the bubble bursts when God's people get conceit into their heads and fancy that they are to enjoy immutability beneath the stars and constancy upon this whirling orb. How touchingly and teachingly God corrected His servant's mistake!

*Thou didst hide Thy face, and I was troubled.* There was no need to come to blows, a hidden face was enough. This proves, first, that David was a genuine saint, for no hiding of God's face on earth would trouble a sinner; and, secondly, that the joy of the saint is dependent upon the presence of his Lord. C. H. S.

Enjoyments beget confidence; confidence brings forth carelessness; carelessness makes God withdraw, and gives opportunity to Satan to work unseen. And thus, as armies after victory growing secure, are oft surprised; so are we oft after our spiritual advancements thrown down. RICHARD GILPIN

No verse can more plainly teach us that glorious and comforting truth on which the Mediaeval writers especially love to dwell, that it is the looking or not looking of God upon His creatures that forms the happiness or the misery of that creature. JOHN MASON NEALE

If God be thy portion, then there is no loss in all the world that lies so hard and so heavy upon thee as the loss of thy God. The Hebrew word *bahal* signifies to be greatly troubled, to be sorely terrified, as you may see in that I Sam. 28:21: "And the woman came to Saul, and saw that he was sore troubled." Here is the same Hebrew word, *bahal.* THOMAS BROOKS

Vs. 8. *I cried to Thee, O Lord.* Prayer is the unfailing resource of God's people. If they are driven to their wits' end, they may still go to the mercy-seat. When an earthquake makes our mountain tremble, the throne of grace still stands firm, and we may come to it. Let us never forget to pray, and let us never doubt the success of prayer. The hand which wounds can heal: let us turn to Him who smites us, and He will be entreated of us.

Prayer is better solace than Cain's building a city or Saul's seeking for music. Mirth and carnal amusements are a sorry prescription for a mind distracted and despairing: prayer will succeed where all else fails. C. H. S.

Vs. 9. *What profit is there in my blood?* So then, poor saints of God when they come and tell the Lord in their prayers that indeed He may condemn or confound or cut or cast them off; He may continue to frown upon them; He may deny such-and-such requests of theirs, for such-and-such just causes in them; but what will He gain thereby?

He may gain many praises, etc., by hearing them and helping them; but what good will it do Him to see them oppressed by the enemies of their souls? or what delight would it be to Him to see them sighing and sinking and fainting under sad pressures, etc.? This is an allowed and a very successful kind of pleading. THOMAS COBBET

*Shall the dust praise Thee?* Can any number be sufficient to praise Thee? Can there ever be mouths enough to declare Thy truth? And may not I make one—a sinful one I know—but yet one in number, if Thou be pleased to spare me from descending into the pit? SIR RICHARD BAKER

Prayer that is likely to prevail with God must be argumentative. God loves to have us plead with Him and overcome Him with arguments in prayer. THOMAS WATSON

Vs. 10. *Lord, be Thou my helper.* Another compact, expressive ever-fitting prayer. It is suitable to hundreds of the cases of the Lord's people; it is well becoming in the minister when he is going to preach, to the sufferer upon the bed of pain, to the toiler in the field of service, to the believer under temptation, to the man of God under adversity; when God helps, difficulties vanish. C. H. S.

Vs. 11. *Thou hast turned for me my mourning into dancing: Thou hast put off my sackcloth, and girded me with gladness.* This might be true of David, delivered from his calamity; it was true of Christ, arising from the tomb, to die no more; it is true of the penitent, exchanging his sackcloth for the garments of salvation; and it will be verified in us all, at the last day, when we shall put off the dishonors of the grave to shine in glory everlasting. GEORGE HORNE

Vs. 12. *To the end that my glory may sing praise to Thee, and not be silent. O Lord my God, I will give thanks unto Thee forever.* To the end—namely, with this view and intent—*that my glory*—that is, my tongue or my soul—*may sing praise to Thee, and not be silent.* It would be a shameful crime if, after receiving God's mercies, we should forget to praise Him.

God would not have our tongues lie idle while so many themes for gratitude are spread on every hand. He would have no dumb children in the house. They are all to sing in heaven and therefore they should all sing on earth. Let us sing with the poet:

*I would begin the music here,*
*And so my soul should rise:*
*Oh, for some heavenly notes to bear*
*My passions to the skies.*

C. H. S.

The prophet in this Psalm begins with the anger of God but ends with His favor: as of old, when they entered into the tabernacle they did at first see unpleasant things, as the knives of the sacrifices, the blood of victims, the fire that burned upon the altar, which consumed the offerings; but when they passed a little farther there was the holy place, the candlestick of gold, the show-bread, and the altar of gold on which they offered perfumes; and in fine, there was the Holy of Holies, and the ark of the covenant, and the mercy-seat, and the cherubims, which was called the face of God. TIMOTHY ROGERS

What is praise? The rent we owe to God; and the larger the farm the greater the rent should be. G. S. BOWES

## PSALM 31

Some have thought that the occasion in his troubled life which led to this Psalm was the treachery of the men of Keilah, and we have felt much inclined to this conjecture; but after reflection it seems to us that its very mournful tone and its allusion to his iniquity demand a later date, and it may be more satisfactory to illustrate it by the period when Absalom had rebelled and his courtiers were fled from him, while lying lips spread a thousand malicious rumors against him.

Vs. 1. *Let me never be ashamed.* How can the Lord permit the man to be ultimately put to shame who depends alone upon Him? This would not be dealing like a God of truth and grace. It would bring dishonor upon God Himself if faith were not in the end rewarded. It will be an ill day indeed for religion when trust in God brings no consolation and no assistance. C. H. S.

Vs. 2. *Bow down Thine ear.* Listen to my complaint. Put Thy ear to my lips, that Thou mayest hear all that my feebleness is capable of uttering. We generally put our ear near to the lips of the sick and dying that we may hear what they say. To this the text appears to allude. ADAM CLARKE

*For an house of defense to save me.* How very simply does the good man pray, and yet with what weight of meaning! He uses no ornamental flourishes; he is too deeply in earnest to be otherwise than plain: it were well if all who engage in public prayer would observe the same rule.

Vs. 3. *For Thou art my rock and my fortress.* The two personal pronouns, like sure nails, lay hold upon the faithfulness of the Lord. Oh, for grace to have our heart fixed in firm, unstaggering belief in God!

*Therefore for Thy Name's sake lead me, and guide me.* It is not possible that the Lord should suffer His own honor to be tarnished, but this would certainly be the case if those who trusted Him should perish. This was Joshua's plea, "What wilt Thou do unto Thy great Name?" C. H. S.

If merely a creature's honor, the credit of ministers, or the glory of angels were involved, man's salvation would indeed be uncertain. But every step involves the honor of God. We plead for *His Name's sake.* WILLIAM S. PLUMER

Vs. 4. *For Thou art my strength.* Omnipotence cuts the net which policy weaves. When we poor, puny things are in the net, God is not. In the old fable the mouse set free the lion; here the lion liberates the mouse.

Vs. 5. *Into Thine hand I commit my spirit.* These living words of David were our Lord's dying words and have been frequently used by holy men in their hour of departure. Be assured that they are good, choice, wise, and solemn words; we may use them now and in the last tremendous hour. C. H. S.

These were the last words of Polycarp, of Bernard, of Huss, of Jerome of Prague, of Luther, Melanchthon, and many others. "Blessed are they," says Luther, "who die not only for the Lord as martyrs, not only in the Lord, as all believers, but likewise with the Lord, as breathing forth their lives in these words, 'Into Thine hand I commit my spirit'." J. J. STEWART PEROWNE

I commend and offer up into Thy most sacred hands, O my God, what I am, which Thou knowest far better than I can know, weak, wretched, wounded, fickle, blind, deaf, dumb, poor, bare of every good, nothing, yea, less than nothing, on account of my sins, and more miserable than I can either know or express.

Do Thou, Lord God, receive me and make me to become what He, the Divine Lamb, would have me to be. I commend, I offer up, I deliver over into Thy Divine hands, all my affairs, my cares, my affections, my success, my comforts, my labors, and everything which Thou knowest to be coming upon me. FRA THOMÉ DE JESU

With loud voice, He exclaimed it to the world, which will forever and ever sink into the heathenish consciousness of death, of the fear of death, of despair of immortality and resurrection, because it forever and ever allows the consciousness of the personality of God, and of personal union with Him, to be obscured and shaken. J. P. LANGE, D.D., in *"The Life of the Lord Jesus Christ"*

*Thou hast redeemed me, O Lord God of truth.* Redemption is a solid basis for confidence. David had not known Calvary as we have done, but temporal redemption cheered him; and shall not eternal redemption yet more sweetly console us?

Vs. 6. *I have hated them that regard lying vanities.* Those who will not lean upon the true arm of strength are sure to make to themselves vain confidences. Many must have a god, and if he will not adore the only living and true God, he makes a fool of himself, and pays superstitious regard to a lie, and waits with anxious hope upon a base delusion. Men who make gods of their riches, their persons, their wits, or anything else, are to be shunned by those whose faith rests upon God in Christ Jesus; and so far from being envied, they are to be pitied as depending upon utter vanities. C. H. S.

The Romanists feign miracles of the saints to make them, as they suppose, the more glorious. They say that the house wherein the Virgin Mary was when the angel Gabriel came unto her was, many hundred years after, translated, first out of Galilee into Dalmatia, above two thousand miles, and thence over the sea into Italy, where also it removed from one place to another, till at length it found a place where to abide, and many most miraculous cures, they say, were wrought by it, and that the very trees when it came, did bow unto it.

Infinite stories they have of this nature, especially in the Legend of Saints, which they call "The Golden Legend," a book so full of gross stuff that Ludovicus Vives, a Papist, but learned and ingenous, with great indignation cried out, "What can be more abominable than that book?" and he wondered why they should call it "golden," when as he that wrote it was a man "of an iron mouth and of a leaden heart."

"You may now, everywhere," saith Erasmus, "see held out for gain, Mary's milk, which they honor almost as much as Christ's consecrated body; prodigious oil; so many pieces of the cross, that if they were all gathered together a great ship would scarce carry them.

"Here Francis' hood set forth to view; there the innermost garment of the Virgin Mary; in one place Anna's comb; in another place, Joseph's stocking; in another place, Thomas of Canterbury's shoe; in another place, Christ's foreskin, which, though it be a thing uncertain, they worship more religiously than Christ's whole person.

"Neither do they bring forth these things as things that may be tolerated, and to please the common people, but all religion almost is placed in them." CHRISTOPHER CARTWRIGHT

*But I trust in the Lord.* This might be very unfashionable, but the Psalmist dared to be singular. Bad example should not make us less decided for the truth, but the rather in the midst of general defection we should grow the more bold. This adherence to his trust in Jehovah is the great plea employed all along: the troubled one flies into the arms of his God and ventures everything upon the Divine faithfulness.

Vs. 7. *I will be glad and rejoice in Thy mercy.* These two words, *glad* and *rejoice,* are an instructive reduplication. We need not stint ourselves in our holy triumph. This wine we may drink in bowls without fear of excess.

*Thou hast known my soul in adversities.* God owns His saints when others are ashamed to acknowledge them; He never refuses to know His friends. He thinks not the worse of them for the rags and tatters. He does not misjudge them and cast them off when their faces are lean with sickness or their hearts heavy with despondency. C. H. S.

Yes; though we have lost our rich attire and come to Him in rags; though our forms be wasted because of grief and waxed old (Ps. 6:7; Luth. Ver); though sickness and sorrow have consumed our beauty like a moth (Ps. 39:11); though blushes, and tears, and dust, overspread our face (Ps. 69:7), He still recognizes and is not ashamed to own us. Comfort yourself with this, for what harm will it do you at last, though men disown, if God the Lord have not forgotten you? CHRISTIAN SCRIVER

Vs. 8. *Thou hast set my feet in a large room.* Blessed be God for liberty: civil liberty is valuable, religious liberty is precious, spiritual liberty is priceless.

Vs. 9. *Have mercy upon me, O Lord, for I am in trouble.* This first sentence pithily comprehends all that follows; it is the text for his lamenting discourse. Misery moves mercy—no more reasoning is needed. "Have mercy" is the prayer; the argument is as prevalent as it is plain and personal, "I am in trouble."

*Mine eye is consumed with grief.* Tears draw their salt from our strength, and floods of them are very apt to consume the source from which they spring. Dim and sunken eyes are plain indicators of failing health. God would have us tell Him the symptoms of our disease not for His information but to show our sense of need.

*Yea, my soul and my belly (or body).* Soul and body are so intimately united that one cannot decline without the other feeling it. We, in these days, are not strangers to the double sinking which David describes; we have been faint with physical suffering and distracted with mental distress: when two such seas meet, it is well for us that the Pilot at the helm is at home in the midst of the water-floods and makes storms to become the triumph of His art.

Vs. 10. *For my life is spent with grief, and my years with sighing.* Grief is a sad market to spend all our wealth of life in, but a far more profitable trade may be driven there than in Vanity Fair; it is better to go to the house of mourning than the house of feasting. Black is good wear. The salt of tears is a healthy medicine. Better spend our years in sighing than in sinning.

*My strength faileth because of mine iniquity.* It is profitable trouble which leads us to trouble ourselves about our iniquity. Was this the Psalmist's foulest crime which now gnawed at his heart and devoured his strength? Very probably it was so. C. H. S.

I find that when the saints are under trial and well humbled, little sins raise great cries in the conscience; but in prosperity, conscience is a pope that gives dispensations and great latitude to our hearts. The cross is therefore as needful as the crown is glorious. SAMUEL RUTHERFORD

Vs. 11. *I was a reproach among all mine enemies.* They were pleased to have something to throw at me; my mournful estate was music to them, because they maliciously interpreted it to be a judgment from heaven upon me. Reproach is little thought of by those who are not called to endure it, but he who passes under its lash knows how deep it wounds. The best of men may have the bitterest foes and be subjected to the most cruel taunts. C. H. S.

If anyone strives after patience and humility, he is a hypocrite. If he allows himself in the pleasures of this world, he is a glutton. If he seeks justice, he is impatient; if he seeks it not, he is a fool. If he would be prudent, he is stingy; if he would make others happy, he is dissolute. If he gives himself up to prayer, he is vainglorious.

And this is the great loss of the church, that by means like these many are held back from goodness! which the Psalmist lamenting says, "I became a reproof among all mine enemies. CHRYSOSTOM, *quoted by J. M. Neale*

*But especially among my neighbors.* Those who are nearest can stab the sharpest. We feel most the slights of those who should have shown us sympathy.

*And a fear to mine acquaintance.* The more intimate before, the more distant did they become. Our Lord was denied by Peter, betrayed by Judas, and forsaken by all in the hour of His utmost need. All the herd turn against a wounded deer. The milk of human kindness curdles when a despised believer is the victim of slanderous accusations.

*They that did see me without fled from me.* How villainous a thing is slander which can thus make an eminent saint, once the admiration of his people, to become the general butt, the universal aversion of mankind!

Vs. 12. *I am forgotten as a dead man is out of mind.* A man had better be dead than be smothered in slander. Of the dead we say nothing but good, but in the Psalmist's case they said nothing but evil.

*I am like a broken vessel.* Let us see herein the portrait of the King of kings in His humiliation, when He made Himself of no reputation and took upon Him the form of a servant.

Vs. 13. *For I have heard the slander of many.* One slanderous viper is death to all comfort—what must be the venom of the whole brood? C. H. S.

From my very childhood, when I was first sensible of the concernments of men's souls, I was possessed with some admiration to find that everywhere the religious, godly sort of people, who did but exercise a serious care of their own and other men's salvation, were made the wonder and obloquy of the world, especially of the most vicious and flagitious men; so that they that professed the same articles of faith, the same commandments of God to be their law, and the same petitions of the Lord's Prayer to be their desire, and so professed the same religion, did everywhere revile those that endeavored to live in good earnest in what they said.

If religion be bad, and our faith be not true, why do these men profess it? If it be true and good, why do they hate and revile them that would live in the serious practice of it, if they will not practice it themselves? But we must not expect reason when sin and sensuality have made men unreasonable.

But I must profess that since I observed the course of the world, and the concord of the Word and providence of God, I took it for a notable proof of man's fall, and of the truth of the Scripture, and of the supernatural original of true sanctification, to find such a universal enmity between the holy and the serpentine seed, and to find Cain and Abel's case so ordinarily exemplified, and he that is born after the flesh persecuting him that is born after the Spirit. And methinks to this day it is a great and visible help for the confirmation of our Christian faith. RICHARD BAXTER

*While they took counsel together against me, they devised to take away my life.* Better fall into the power of a lion than under the will of malicious persecutors, for the beast may spare its prey if it be fed to the full, but malice is unrelenting and cruel as a wolf. Of all fiends, the most cruel is envy.

Vs. 14. *I said, Thou art my God.* He proclaimed aloud his determined allegiance to Jehovah. He was no fair-weather believer; he could hold to his faith in a sharp frost and wrap it about him as a garment fitted to keep out all the ills of time.

He who can say what David did, need not envy Cicero his eloquence. "Thou art my God," has more sweetness in it than any other utterance which human speech can frame. Note that this adhesive faith is here mentioned as an argument with God to honor His own promise by sending a speedy deliverance. C. H. S.

How much it is more worth than ten thousand mines of gold to be able to say, "God is mine!" God's servant is apprehensive of it, and he seeth no defect, but this may be complete happiness to him, and therefore he delights in it and comforts himself with it.

As he did sometime who was a great courtier in King Cyrus' court, and one in favor with him; he was to bestow his daughter in marriage to a very great man, and of himself he had no great means; and therefore one said to him, "O Sir, where will you have the means to bestow a dowry upon your daughter proportionate to her degree? Where are your riches?" He answered, "What need I care? Cyrus is my friend."

But may not we say much more, where the Lord is our Friend, that hath those excellent and glorious attributes that cannot come short in any wants, or to make us happy, especially we being capable of it, and made proportionable. JOHN STOUGHTON'S *"Righteous Man's Plea to True Happiness"*

Vs. 15. *My times are in Thy hand.* It is said there is a moon to control the tides of every sea; is there not a master power for souls? It may not always be so, apparently, in the more earthly lives, but it is so in the heavenly; not more surely does the moon sway tides than God sways souls. The hand of Jesus is the hand which rules our times. He regulates our life-clock. Christ for and Christ in us. *My* times in *His* hand. My life can be no more in vain than was my Savior's life in vain. E. PAXTON HOOD, in *"Dark Sayings on a Harp"*

*Deliver me from the hand of mine enemies, and from them that persecute me.* It is lawful to desire escape from persecution if it be the Lord's will.

Vs. 16. *Make Thy face to shine upon Thy servant.* Give me the sunshine of heaven in my soul, and I will defy the tempests of earth. Permit me to enjoy a sense of Thy favor, O Lord, and a consciousness that Thou art pleased with my manner of life, and all men may frown and slander as they will.

Vs. 18. *Let the lying lips be put to silence; which speak grievous things, proudly and contemptuously against the righteous.* Proud thoughts of self are generally attended by debasing estimates of others. The more room we take upon ourselves, the less we can afford our neighbors. What wickedness it is that unworthy characters should always be the loudest in railing at good men! They have no power to appreciate moral worth of which they are utterly destitute, and yet they have the effrontery to mount the judgment-seat and judge the men compared with whom they are as so much draff. C. H. S.

In that venerable and original monument of the Vaudois Church entitled "The Golden Lesson," of the date 1100, we met with a verse, which has been thus translated:

*If there be anyone who loves and fears Jesus Christ,*
*Who will not curse, nor swear, nor lie,*
*Nor be unchaste, nor kill, nor take what is another's,*
*Nor take vengeance on his enemies;*
*They say that he is a Vaudes, and worthy of punishment.*

ANTOINE MONASTIER, in *A History of Vaudois Church*

Vs. 19. *Oh how great is Thy goodness.* He does not tell us how great was God's goodness, for he could not; there are no measures which can set forth the immeasurable goodness of Jehovah, Who is goodness itself. Holy amazement uses interjections where adjectives utterly fail. Notes of exclamation suit us when words of explanation are of no avail. If we cannot measure, we can marvel.

Vs. 20. *Thou shalt hide them in the secret of Thy presence from the pride of man.* Dwellers at the foot of the cross of Christ grow callous to the sneers of the haughty. The wounds of Jesus distil a balsam which heals all the scars which the jagged weapons of contempt can inflict upon us; in fact, when armed with the same mind which was in Christ Jesus, the heart is invulnerable to all the darts of pride.

Vs. 21. *Blessed be the Lord.* When the Lord blesses us, we cannot do less than bless Him in return.

Vs. 22. *I said in my haste, I am cut off from before Thine eyes,* etc. We generally speak amiss when we are in a hurry. Hasty words are but for a moment on the tongue, but they often lie for years on the conscience. C. H. S.

Oh! what love is due from us to Christ, that has pleaded for us when we ourselves had nothing to say! That has brought us out of a den of lions, and from the jaws of the roaring lion!

To say, as Mrs. Sarah Wright did, "I have obtained mercy, that thought my time of mercy past forever; I have hope of heaven, that thought I was already damned by unbelief; I said many a time, there is no hope in mine end, and I thought I saw it; I was so desperate, I cared not what became of me.

"Oft was I at the very brink of death and hell, even at the very gates of both, and then Christ shut them. I was as Daniel in the lion's den, and He stopped those lions, and delivered me.

"The goodness of God is unsearchable; how great is the excellency of His majesty, that yet He would look upon such a one as I; that He has given me peace that was full of terror, and walked continually as amidst fire and brimstone. Timothy Rogers

Vs. 23. *O love the Lord, all ye His saints.* If saints do not love the Lord, who will? Love is the universal debt of all the saved family; who would wish to be exonerated from its payment? Reasons for love are given, for believing love is not blind. C. H. S.

Vs. 23. *And plentifully rewardeth the proud doer.* The next query is, how God rewardeth the proud doer. (1) By way of *retaliation*—for Adonibezek that would be cutting off thumbs, had his thumbs cut off (Judges 1:7). So the poor Jews that cried so loud, "Crucify Him, crucify Him," were so many of them crucified, that if you believe Josephus, there was not wood enough to make crosses nor in the usual place room enough to set up the crosses when they were made. Snares are made and pits are digged by the proud for themselves commonly, to which the Scripture throughout gives abundant testimony.

(2) By shameful *disappointments,* seldom reaping what they sow, nor eating what they catch in hunting, which is most clear in the Jewish state when Christ was among them. Judas betrayed Him to get money and hardly lived long enough to spend it. Pilate, to please Cæsar, withstands all counsels against it, and gives way to that murder by which he ruined both himself and Cæsar. Hugh Peters

Vs. 24. *Be of good courage.* Christian courage may thus be described. It is the undaunted audacity of a sanctified heart in adventuring upon difficulties and undergoing hardships for a good cause upon the call of God.

The boldness that is in brutes is spoken of as a piece of this same courage that God is pleased to give to men (Ezek. 3:9). This is the Lord's promise—"As an adamant harder than flint have I made thy forehead." The word "harder" is the same in the Hebrew that is here in my text—*fortiorem petra*—the rock that is not afraid of any weather, summer or winter, sun and showers, heat and cold, frost and snow; it blusheth not, shrinketh not, it changeth not its complexion, it is still the same.

Beloved, valor doth not consist in a piercing eye, in a terrible look, in big words; but it consists in the mettle, the vigor that is within the bosom. The *root* whence courage ariseth is *love to God:* all the saints of God that love the Lord be of good courage. The love of Christ constraineth me to make these bold and brave adventures, saith the Apostle (II Cor. 5:14). The *rule*, whereby it is directed, is the *Word of God*—what the Lord hath pleased to leave on record for a Christian's guidance in holy pages (I Chron. 22:12-13). And the *end*, to which it refers, is *God.* For every sanctified man, being a self-denying and a God-advancing man, his God is his center, wherein his actings, his undertakings rest; and his soul is not, yea, it cannot be satisfied but in God. SIMEON ASH'S "SERMON *Preached before the Commanders of the Military Forces of the Renowned Citie of London*"

To massacre fleshly lusts is (as it were) for a man to mangle and dismember his own body; it is a work painful and grievous, as for a man to cut off his own feet, to chop off his own hands, and to pick out his own eyes, as Christ and the Apostle Paul do express it. SIMEON ASH

# PSALM 32

Title: "A Psalm of David, Maschil." That David wrote this gloriously evangelic Psalm is proved not only by this heading but by the words of the Apostle Paul in Rom. 4:6-8; "Even as David also describeth the blessedness of the man unto whom God imputeth righteousness without works," etc. Probably his deep repentance over his great sin was followed by such blissful peace that he was led to pour out his spirit in the soft music of this choice song. In the order of history, it seems to follow the Fifty-First. C. H. S.

This is a mark of a true penitent when he hath been a stumbling-block to others, to be as careful to raise them up by his repentance as he was hurtful to them by his sin; and I never think that man truly penitent who is ashamed to teach sinners repentance by his own particular proof.

The Samaritan woman, when she was converted, left her bucket at the well, entered the city, and said, "Come forth, yonder is a man who hath told me all that I have done." And our Savior saith to St. Peter, "When thou art converted, strengthen thy brethren" (John 4:29; Luke 22:32).

St. Paul, also after his conversion, is not ashamed to call himself chiefest of all sinners and to teach others to repent of their sins by repenting of his own. Happy, and thrice happy, is the man who can build so much as he hath cast down. ARCHIBALD SYMSON

It is told of Luther that one day being asked which of all the Psalms were the best, he made answer, *Psalmi Paulini,* and when his friends pressed to know which these might be, he said, "The 32nd, the 51st, the 130th, and 143d. For they all teach that the forgiveness of our sins comes without the law and without works to the man who believes, and therefore I call them Pauline Psalms." LUTHER'S *Table Talk*

The Penitential Psalms: When Galileo was imprisoned by the Inquisition at Rome for asserting the Copernican system, he was enjoined, as a penance, to repeat the Seven Penitential Psalms every week for three years.

This must have been intended as extorting a sort of confession from him of his guilt and acknowledgment of the justice of his sentence; and in which there certainly was some cleverness, and indeed, humor, however adding to the iniquity (or foolishness) of the proceeding. Otherwise it is not easy to understand what idea of painfulness or punishment the good fathers could attach to a devotional exercise such as this, which, in whatever way, could only have been agreeable and consoling to their prisoner. M. MONTAGUE, in *"The Seven Penitential Psalms in Verse . . . with an Appendix and Notes"*

Vs. 1. *Blessed.* Like the Sermon on the Mount, this Psalm begins with beatitudes. This is the second Psalm of benediction. The First Psalm describes the result of holy blessedness, the Thirty-Second details the cause of it. The first pictures the tree in full growth: this depicts it in its first planting and watering. C. H. S.

*Blessed,* or, O blessed man; or, oh, the felicities of that man! ROBERT LEIGHTON

Notice, this is the first Psalm, except the first of all, which begins with "blessedness." In the First Psalm we have the blessing of innocence, or rather, of Him Who only was innocent: here we have the blessing of repentance, as the next happiest state to that of sinlessness. LORINUS, in *Neale's Commentary*

*Blessed is he whose transgression is forgiven.* A full, instantaneous, irreversible pardon of transgression turns the poor sinner's hell into heaven and makes the heir of wrath a partaker in blessing. The word rendered forgiven is, in the original, "taken off," or "taken away," as a burden is lifted or a barrier removed. What a lift is here! It cost our Savior a sweat of blood to bear our load, yea, it cost Him His life to bear it quite away. Samson carried the gates of Gaza, but what was that to the weight which Jesus bore on our behalf? C. H. S.

Holy David, in the front of this Psalm, shows us wherein true happiness consists: not in beauty, honor, riches (the world's trinity), but in the forgiveness of sin. Paul cries out, "I obtained mercy" (I Tim. 1:13). The Greek signifies, "I was be-mercied"; he who is pardoned is all bestrewed with mercy. When the Lord pardons a sinner, He doth not pay a debt but gives a legacy.

God, in forgiving sin, remits the guilt and penalty. Guilt cries for justice: no sooner had Adam eaten the apple, but he saw the flaming sword, and heard the curse; but in remission God doth indulge the sinner; He seems to say thus to him: "Though thou art fallen into the hands of My justice, and deservest to die, yet I will absolve thee, and whatever is charged upon thee shall be discharged. THOMAS WATSON

*Whose sin is covered.* Covered by God, as the ark was covered by the mercy-seat, as Noah was covered from the flood, as the Egyptians were covered by the depths of the sea. What a cover must that be which hides away forever from the sight of the all-seeing God all the filthiness of the flesh and of the spirit! He who has once seen sin in its horrible deformity will appreciate the happiness of seeing it no more forever. C. H. S.

Get your sins hid. There is a covering of sin which proves a curse (Prov. 28:13). "He that covereth his sins shall not prosper." There is a *covering* it, by not confessing it, or which is worse, by denying it—Gehazi's covering—a covering of sin by a lie; and there is also a covering of sin by justifying ourselves in it. I have not done this thing; or, I did not evil in it.

All these are evil coverings: he that thus covereth his sin shall not prosper. But there is a blessed covering of sin: forgiveness of sin is the hiding it out of sight, and that's the blessedness. RICHARD ALLEINE

Verses 1-2. In these verses four evils are mentioned: 1. *Transgression, pesha;* 2. *sin, chataah;* 3. *iniquity, avon;* 4. *guile, remiyah.* The first signifies the passing over a boundary, doing what is prohibited. The second signifies the missing of a mark, not doing what was commanded; but it is often taken to express sinfulness, or sin in the nature, producing transgression in the life.

The third signifies what is turned out of its proper course or situation; anything morally distorted or perverted; iniquity, what is contrary to equity or justice. The fourth signifies fraud, deceit, guile, etc. To remove these evils, three acts are mentioned: forgiving, covering, and not imputing. ADAM CLARKE

Verses 1-2, 6-7. Who is blessed? Not he who cloaks, conceals, confesses not his sin. As long as David was in this state, he was miserable. There was guile in his spirit (2), misery in his heart, his very bones waxed old, his moisture was dried up as the drought in summer (3, 4).

Who is blessed? He that is without sin, he who sins not, he who grieves no more by his sin the bosom on which he reclines. This is superlative blessedness, its highest element the happiness of heaven. To be like God, to yield implicit, ready, full, perfect obedience, the obedience of the heart, of our entire being; this is to be blessed above all blessedness. JAMES HARRINGTON EVANS, M.A.

Vs. 2. *Blessed is the man unto whom the Lord imputeth not iniquity.* Note the three words so often used to denote our disobedience: transgression, sin, and iniquity, are the three-headed dog at the gates of hell, but our glorious Lord has silenced his barkings forever against His own believing ones. The trinity of sin is overcome by the Trinity of heaven.

*And in whose spirit there is no guile.* Free from guilt, free from guile. Those who are justified from fault are sanctified from falsehood. A liar is not a forgiven soul. Treachery, double-dealing, chicanery, dissimulation, are lineaments of the devil's children, but he who is washed from sin is truthful, honest, simple, and childlike. C. H. S.

When once pardon is realized, the believer has courage to be truthful before God: he can afford to have done with guile in the spirit. Who would not declare all his debts when they are certain to be discharged by another? Who would not declare his malady when he was sure of a cure?

True faith knows not only that "guile" before God is impossible, but also that it is no longer necessary. The believer has nothing to conceal: he sees himself as before God, stripped and laid open, and bare; and if he has learned to see himself as he is, so also has he learned to see God as He reveals Himself. J. W. REEVE, M. A., in *"Lectures on the Thirty-second Psalm"*

"Here is water," said the eunuch, "what doth hinder me to be baptized?" (Acts 8:36). Now, mark Philip's answer, verse 37: "If thou believest with all thine heart, thou mayest;" as if he had said, "Nothing but an hypocritical heart can hinder thee. It is the false heart only that finds the doors of mercy shut." WILLIAM GURNALL

Vs. 3. *My bones waxed old.* What a killing thing is sin! It is a pestilent disease! A fire in the bones! While we smother our sin it rages within, and like a gathering wound swells horribly and torments terribly.

*Through my roaring all the day long.* None know the pangs of conviction but those who have endured them. The rack, the wheel, the flaming fagot are ease compared with the Tophet which a guilty conscience kindles within the breast: better suffer all the diseases which flesh is heir to, than lie under the crushing sense of the wrath of Almighty God. The Spanish inquisition with all its tortures was nothing to the inquest which conscience holds within the heart.

Vs. 4. *For day and night Thy hand was heavy upon me.* God's finger can crush us—what must His hand be, and that pressing heavily and continuously! Under terrors of conscience, men have little rest by night, for the grim thoughts of the day dog them to their chambers and haunt their dreams, or else they lie awake in a cold sweat of dread. God's hand is very helpful when it uplifts, but it is awful when it presses down: better a world on the shoulder, like Atlas, than God's hand on the heart, like David. C. H. S.

*The drought of summer.* During the twelve years from 1846 to 1859 only two slight showers fell in Jerusalem between the months of May and October. One fell in July, 1858, another in June, 1859. DR. WHITTY'S *"Water Supply of Jerusalem," quoted in Kitto's Cyclopedia*

If God striketh those so sore whom He favoreth, how sharply and sore will He strike them whom He favoreth not. GREGORY

Verses 4-5. If our offences have been not gnats, but camels, our sorrow must not be a drop, but an ocean. Scarlet sins call for bloody tears; and if Peter sin heinously he must weep bitterly. If, then, thy former life hath been a cord of iniquity, twisted with many threads, a writing full of great blots, a course spotted with various and grievous sins, multiply thy confessions and enlarge thy humiliation; double thy fastings and treble thy prayers; pour out thy tears, and fetch deep sighs.

In a word, iterate and aggravate thy acknowledgments, though yet, as the Apostle saith in another case, I say in this, "Grieve not as without hope," that upon thy sincere and suitable repentance divine goodness will forgive thee thy sins. NATHANAEL HARDY

Vs. 5. *I said, I will confess my transgressions unto the Lord; and Thou forgavest the iniquity of my sin.* With men, a free confession makes way for a condemnation; but with God, the more a sinner bemoans his offence the more he extenuates the anger of his Judge. Sin cannot but call for justice, as it is an offence against God; yet, when once 'tis a wound to the soul, it moveth him to mercy and clemency. ISAAC CRAVEN'S SERMON AT PAUL'S CROSS

This sin seems very probably to have been his adultery with Bath-sheba and murder of Uriah. Now David, to make the pardoning mercy of God more illustrious, saith he did not only forgive his sin, but the iniquity of his sin; and what was that? Surely the worst that can be said of that, his complicated sin, is that there was so much hypocrisy in it, he woefully juggled with God and man in it; this, I do not doubt to say, was the iniquity of his sin, and put a color deeper on it than the blood which he shed.

Were there not other false steps which David took beside this? Doth the Spirit of God, by excepting this, declare His approbation of all that else he ever did? No, surely the Spirit of God records other sins that escaped this eminent servant of the Lord; but all those are drowned here, and this mentioned is the only stain of his life.

But why? Surely because there appeared less sincerity, yea, more hypocrisy in this one sin than in all his others put together; though David in them was wrong as to the matter of his actions, yet his heart was more right in the manner of committing them. WILLIAM GURNALL

Vs. 6. *For this shall every one that is godly pray unto Thee,* saith David. *For this!* What? Because of his sins. And who? Not the wickedest, but the *godly,* in this respect, have cause to pray. And for what should he pray? Surely, for renewed pardon, for increase of grace, and for the perfection of glory. We cannot say we have no sin. Oh, then, let us pray with David, "Enter not into judgment with Thy servant, O Lord!" NATHANAEL HARDY

*In a time when Thou mayest be found.* There is, however, a set time for prayer beyond which it will be unavailing; between the time of sin and the day of punishment mercy rules the hour, and God may be found, but when once the sentence has gone forth, pleading will be useless, for the Lord will not be found by the condemned soul. C. H. S.

*Surely in the floods of great waters they shall not come nigh unto him.* The effects of prayer heretofore have been wonderful. Prayer hath shut up the windows of heaven that it should not rain and again hath opened them that the earth might give her increase.

Prayer hath stayed the swift course of the sun and caused it to go backward fifteen degrees. Prayer hath held God's hands that He could not strike when He was ready to plague His people. Prayer without any other help or means hath thrown down the strong walls of Jericho. Prayer hath divided the sea that the floods thereof could not come near the Israelites. In this place it delivereth the faithful man from all the dangers of this world. THOMAS PLAYFERE

Fire and water have no mercy, we say. But of the two, water is the worst. For any fire may be quenched with water; but the force of water, if it begins to be violent, cannot by any power of man be resisted.

*Him.* For philosophy defineth *him,* that is, a man, by his reason, and the moral virtues of the mind; but Divinity defineth a Christian man by his faith, and his conjunction thereby with Christ. THOMAS PLAYFERE

Vs. 7. *Thou art my hiding place.* Observe that the same man who in the fourth verse was oppressed by the presence of God here finds a shelter in Him. See what honest confession and full forgiveness will do! The gospel of substitution makes Him to be our refuge who otherwise would have been our Judge. C. H. S.

Suppose a traveler upon a bleak and exposed heath to be alarmed by the approach of a storm. He looks out for shelter. But if his eye discern a place to hide him from the storm, does he stand still and say, "I see there is a shelter, and therefore I may remain where I am"? Does he not betake himself to it? Does he not run in order to escape the stormy wind and tempest? It was a "hiding-place" before; but it was his hiding-place only when he ran into it and was safe. Had he not gone into it, though it might have been a protection to a thousand other travelers who resorted there, to him it would have been as if no such place existed.

Who does not see at once, from this simple illustration that the blessings of the gospel are such only in their being appropriated to the soul? The physician can cure only by being applied to; the medicine can heal only by being taken; money can enrich only by being possessed; and the merchantman in the parable would have been none the wealthier for discovering that there was a "pearl of great price" had he not made it his.

So with the salvation of the gospel: if Christ is the "Balm in Gilead," apply the remedy; if He is the "Physician there," go to Him; if He is the "pearl of great price," sell all that you have and buy it; and if He is the "hiding-place," run into it and be safe; there will be no solid joy and peace in the mind until He is your "hiding-place." FOUNTAIN ELWIN

*Thou shalt preserve me from trouble.* Trouble shall do me no real harm when the Lord is with me; rather it shall bring me much benefit, like the file which clears away the rust, but does not destroy the metal. Observe the three tenses; we have noticed the sorrowful past, the last sentence was a joyful present, this is a cheerful future. C. H. S.

God uses both these ways in behalf of His servants—sometimes to suspend the working of that that should work their torment, as He suspended the rage of the lions for Daniel and the heat of the fire in the furnace for the others; sometimes by imprinting a holy stupefaction and insensibleness in the person that suffers; so St. Laurence was not only patient, but merry and facetious when he lay broiling upon the fire, and so we read of many other martyrs that have been less moved, less affected with their torments than their executioners or their persecutors have been. JOHN DONNE

Vs. 8. This threefold repetition, *I will instruct thee, I will teach thee, I will guide thee,* teaches us three properties of a good teacher. First, to make the people understand the way of salvation; second, to go before them; third, to watch over them and their ways. ARCHIBALD SYMSON

*I will guide thee with Mine eye.* Marg., "I will counsel thee, Mine eye shall be upon thee." The margin expresses the sense of the Hebrew. The literal meaning is, "I will counsel thee; Mine eyes shall be upon thee." De Wette: "My eye shall be directed towards thee."

The idea is that of one who is telling another what way he is to take in order that he may reach a certain place; and he says he will watch him, or will keep an eye upon him; he will not let him go wrong. ALBERT BARNES

Vs. 9. *Be ye not as the horse, or as the mule.* According to the several natures of these two beasts, the fathers and other expositors have made several interpretations, at least, several allusions. They consider the horse and the mule to admit any rider, any burden, without discretion or difference, without debate or consideration; they never ask whether their rider be noble or base, nor whether their load be gold for the treasure or roots for the market. And those expositors find the same indifference in an habitual sinner to any kind of sin; whether he sin for pleasure, or sin for profit, or sin but for company, still he sins. JOHN DONNE

*Whose mouth must be held in with bit and bridle, lest they come near unto thee.* Those cutting bits of affliction show how hard-mouthed we are; those bridles of infirmity manifest our headstrong and wilful manners. We should not be treated like mules if there was not so much of the ass about us.

Vs. 10. *Many sorrows shall be to the wicked.* He who sows sins will reap sorrow in heavy sheaves. Sorrows of conscience, of disappointment, of terror, are the sinner's sure heritage in time, and then forever sorrows of remorse and despair.

*But he that trusteth in the Lord, mercy shall compass him about.* The wicked have a hive of wasps around them, many sorrows; but we have a swarm of bees storing honey for us. C. H. S.

He shall be surrounded with mercy as one is surrounded by the air or by the sunlight. He shall find mercy and favor everywhere—at home, abroad; by day, by night; in society, in solitude; in sickness, in health; in life, in death; in time, in eternity. He shall walk amid mercies; he shall die amidst mercies; he shall live in a better world in the midst of eternal mercies. ALBERT BARNES

"Mark that text," said Richard Adkins to his grandson Abel, who was reading to him the Thirty-Second Psalm. "Mark that text, 'He that trusteth in the Lord, mercy shall compass him about.' I read it in my youth and believed it; and now I read it in my old age, thank God, I know it to be true. Oh! it is a blessed thing in the midst of the joys and sorrows of the world, Abel, to trust in the Lord." *The Christian Treasury*

Vs. 11. *Be glad.* Happiness is not only our privilege but our duty. Truly we serve a generous God, since He makes it a part of our obedience to be joyful. How sinful are our rebellious murmurings! How natural does it seem that a man blest with forgiveness should be glad! We read of one who died at the foot of the scaffold of overjoy at the receipt of his monarch's pardon; and shall we receive the free pardon of the King of kings and yet pine in inexcusable sorrow?

*And shout for joy, all ye that are upright in heart.* It is to be feared that the church of the present day, through a craving for excessive propriety, is growing too artificial; so that enquirers' cries and believers' shouts would be silenced if they were heard in our assemblies. This may be better than boisterous fanaticism, but there is as much danger in the one direction as the other.

For our part, we are touched to the heart by a little sacred excess, and when godly men in their joy o'erleap the narrow bounds of decorum, we do not, like Michal, Saul's daughter, eye them with a sneering heart. C. H. S.

When the poet Carpani enquired of his friend Haydn how it happened that his church music was so cheerful, the great composer made a most beautiful reply. "I cannot," he said, "make it otherwise. I write according to the thoughts I feel: when I think upon God, my heart is so full of joy that the notes dance and leap, as it were, from my pen: and, since God has given me a cheerful heart, it will be pardoned me that I serve Him with a cheerful spirit. JOHN WHITECROSS' ANECDOTES

# PSALM 33

Title: This song of praise bears no title or indication of authorship; to teach us, says Dickson, "to look upon Holy Scripture as altogether inspired of God, and not put price upon it for the writers thereof."

The praise of Jehovah is the subject of this sacred song. C. H. S.

How absurdly have the philosophers treated of the origin of the world! How few of them have reasoned conclusively on this important subject! Our prophet solves the important question by one single principle; and what is more remarkable, this principle, which is nobly expressed, carries the clearest evidence with it.

The principle is this: "By the Word of the Lord were the heavens made; and all the host of them by the breath of His mouth" (verse 6). This is the most rational account that was ever given of the creation of the world. The world is the work of a self-efficient will, and it is this principle alone that can account for its creation.

The doctrine of providence expressed in these words, "God considereth the works of the inhabitants of the earth," is a necessary consequence of His principle, "God fashioneth their hearts alike"; and this principle is a necessary consequence of that which the Psalmist had before laid down to account for the origin of the world.

One of the most specious objections that has ever been opposed to the doctrine of providence is a contrast between the grandeur of God and the meanness of men. How can such an insignificant creature as man be the object of the care and attention of such a magnificent being as God?

No objection can be more specious, or, in appearance, more invincible. The distance between the meanest insect and the mightiest monarch, who treads and crushes reptiles to death without the least regard for them, is a very imperfect image of the distance between God and man. That which proves that it would be beneath the dignity of a monarch to observe the motions of ants, or worms, to interest himself in their actions, to punish, or to reward them, seems to demonstrate that God would degrade Himself were He to observe, to direct, to punish, to reward mankind, who are infinitely inferior to Him.

But one fact is sufficient to answer this specious objection: that is, that God has created mankind. Does God degrade Himself more by governing than by creating mankind? JAMES SAURIN

Vs. 1. *Rejoice in the Lord.* To rejoice in temporal comforts is dangerous, to rejoice in self is foolish, to rejoice in sin is fatal, but to rejoice in God is heavenly. He who would have a double heaven must begin below to rejoice like those above. C. H. S.

The Hebrew verb, according to the etymologists, originally means to dance for joy, and is therefore a very strong expression for the liveliest exultation. J. A. ALEXANDER

Rejoice not in yourselves, for that is not safe, but *in the Lord.* AUGUSTINE

*For praise is comely for the upright.* Praise is not comely from unpardoned professional singers; it is like a jewel of gold in a swine's snout. Crooked hearts make crooked music, but the upright are the Lord's delight. Praise is the dress of saints in heaven; it is meet that they should fit it on below. C. H. S.

Praise is not comely for any but the godly. A profane man stuck with God's praise is like a dunghill stuck with flowers. Praise in the mouth of a sinner is like an oracle in the mouth of a fool: how uncomely is it for him to praise God, whose whole life is a dishonoring of God? THOMAS WATSON

He pleaseth God whom God pleaseth. AUGUSTINE

Vs. 3. *Sing unto Him.* Singing is the music of saints. (1) They have performed this duty in their greatest numbers (Ps. 147:1-2). (2) In their greatest straits (Isa. 26:19). (3) In their greatest flight (Isa. 42:10-11). (4) In their greatest deliverances. (5) In their greatest plenties (Isa. 65:14). JOHN WELLS, in *"Morning Exercises"*

*Play skilfully.* It is wretched to hear God praised in a slovenly manner. He deserves the best that we have. Every Christian should endeavor to sing according to the rules of the art, so that he may keep time and tune with the congregation. The sweetest tunes and the sweetest voices, with the sweetest words, are all too little for the Lord, our God; let us not offer Him limping rhymes set to harsh tunes and growled out by discordant voices. C. H. S.

*With a loud noise.* Heartiness should be conspicuous in divine worship. Well-bred whispers are disreputable here. It is not that the Lord cannot hear us, but that it is natural for great exultation to express itself in the loudest manner. Men shout at the sight of their kings: shall we offer no loud hosannas to the Son of David? C. H. S.

Vs. 4. *For the Word of the Lord is right; and all His works are done in truth.* God writes with a pen that never blots, speaks with a tongue that never slips, acts with a hand which never fails. Bless His Name!

Vs. 5. *The earth is full of the goodness the Lord.* Come hither, astronomers, geologists, naturalists, botanists, chemists, miners, yea, all of you who study the works of God, for all your truthful stories confirm this declaration. From the midge in the sunbeam to leviathan in the ocean, all creatures own the bounty of the Creator. Even the pathless desert blazes with some undiscovered mercy, and the caverns of ocean conceal the treasures of love. Earth might have been as full of terror as of grace, but instead thereof it teems and overflows with kindness.

He who cannot see it and yet lives in it as the fish lives in the water deserves to die. If earth be full of mercy, what must heaven be where goodness concentrates its beams? C. H. S.

Vs. 6. It is interesting to note the mention of the Spirit in the clause: *and all the host of them by the breath of His mouth.* The word *breath* is the same as is elsewhere rendered "Spirit." Thus the three persons of the Godhead unite in creating all things. How easy for the Lord to make the most ponderous orbs and the most glorious angels! A word, a breath could do it. It is as easy for God to create the universe as for man to breathe, nay, far easier, for man breathes not independently but borrows the breath in his nostrils from his Maker.

Vs. 7. *He layeth up the depth in storehouses.* May not the text refer to the clouds, and the magazines of hail and snow, and rain—those treasuries of merciful wealth for the fields of earth? These aqueous masses are not piled away as in lumber rooms, but in storehouses for future beneficial use. Abundant tenderness is seen in the foresight of our heavenly Joseph, whose granaries are already filled against earth's time of need. These stores might have been, as once they were, the ammunition of vengeance; they are now a part of the commissariat of mercy. C. H. S.

Vs. 8. *Let all the earth fear the Lord.* Let them not fear another instead of Him. Doth a wild beast rage? Fear God. Doth a serpent lie in wait? Fear God. Doth man hate thee? Fear God. Doth the devil fight against thee? Fear God. For the whole creation is under Him Whom thou art commanded to fear. AUGUSTINE

Vs. 9. *He commanded, and it stood fast.* Happy is the man who has learned to lean his all upon the sure Word of Him Who built the skies! C. H. S.

Vs. 10. *The Lord bringeth the counsel of the heathen to nought.* The more the Pharisees of old and their successors, the prelates of late, opposed the truth, the more it prevailed. The Reformation in Germany was much furthered by the Papists' opposition; yea, when two kings (amongst many others), wrote against Luther, namely, Henry VIII of England and Ludovicus of Hungary, this kingly title being entered into the controversy (making men more curious to examine the matter), stirred up a general inclination towards Luther's opinions. RICHARD YOUNGE'S CHRISTIAN LIBRARY

*He maketh the devices of the people of none effect.* Their persecutions, slanders, falsehoods, are like puff-balls flung against a granite wall—they produce no result at all; for the Lord overrules the evil, and brings good out of it. The cause of God is never in danger: infernal craft is outwitted by Infinite wisdom, and Satanic malice held in check by boundless power. C. H. S.

Vs. 11. *The counsel of the Lord standeth forever, the thoughts of His heart to all generations.* The wheels in a watch or a clock move contrary one to another, some one way, some another, yet all serve the intent of the workman, to show the time, or to make the clock strike.

So in the world, the providence of God may seem to run cross to His promises; one man takes this way, another runs that way; good men go one way, wicked men another, yet all in conclusion accomplish the will, and center in the purpose of God, the great Creator of all things. RICHARD SIBBES

Vs. 12. *Blessed . . . the people whom He hath chosen for His own inheritance.* A man may have his name set down in chronicles, yet lost; wrought in durable marble, yet perish; set upon a monument equal to a Colossus, yet be ignominious; inscribed on the hospital gates, yet go to hell; written in the front of his own house, yet another come to possess it; all these are but writings in the dust, or upon the waters, where the characters perish so soon as they are made; they no more prove a man happy than the fool could prove Pontius Pilate happy because his name was written in the creed.

But the true comfort is this, when a man by assurance can conclude with his own soul that his name is written in those eternal leaves of heaven, in the book of God's election, which shall never be wrapped up in the cloudy sheets of darkness but remain legible to all eternity. THOMAS ADAMS

I have sometimes compared the great men of the world and the good men of the world to the consonants and vowels in the alphabet. The consonants are the most and the biggest letters; they take up most room and carry the greatest bulk; but, believe it, the vowels though they are the fewest and least of all the letters, yet they are most useful; they give the greatest sound of all; there is no pronunciation without vowels.

O beloved, though the great men of the world take up room, and make a show above others, yet they are but consonants, a company of mute and dumb consonants for the most part; the good men, they are the vowels that are of the greatest use and most concernment at every turn: a good man to help with his prayers; a good man to advise with his counsels; a good man to interpose with his authority; this is the loss we lament, we have lost a good man; death has blotted out a vowel.

I fear there will be much silence where he is lacking; silence in the bed, and silence in the house, and silence in the shop, and silence in the church, and silence in the parish, for he was everywhere a vowel, a good man in every respect. JOHN KITCHIN, M.A., *in a Funeral Sermon*

Vs. 15. *He considereth all their works.* Two men give to the poor, one seeketh his reward in heaven, the other the praise of men. Thou, in two, seest one thing; God understandeth two. For He understandeth what is within, and knoweth what is within; their ends He seeth, their base intentions He seeth. "He understandeth all their works." AUGUSTINE

Vs. 16. *There is no king saved by the multitude of an host.* Mortal power is a fiction, and those who trust in it are dupes. Serried ranks of armed men have failed to maintain an empire, or even to save their monarch's life when a decree from the court of heaven has gone forth for the empire's overthrow. C. H. S.

At the Battle of Arbela, the Persian hosts numbered between five hundred thousand and a million men, but they were utterly put to the rout by Alexander's band of fifty thousand; and the once mighty Darius was soon vanquished.

Napoleon led more than half a million of men into Russia, but the terrible winter left the army a mere wreck, and their leader was soon a prisoner on the lone rock of St. Helena. All along the line of history, this verse has been verified. The strongest battalions melt like snowflakes when God is against them. C. H. S.

Vs. 18. *The eye of the Lord is upon.* Look upon the sun, how it casts light and heat upon the whole world in its general course, how it shineth upon the good and the bad with an equal influence; but let its beams be but concentrated in a burning-glass; then it sets fire on the object only, and passeth by all others.

Thus God, in the creation, looketh upon all His works with a general love—*erant omnia valde bona*—they pleased Him very well. Oh! but when He is pleased to cast the beams of His love, and cause them to shine upon His elect through Christ, then it is that their hearts burn within them, then it is that their affections are inflamed; whereas others are but as it were a little warmed, have a little shine of common graces cast upon them. RICHARD HOLDSWORTH

Vs. 19. *To deliver their soul from death.* The Lord's hand goes with His eye; His sovereignty preserves those whom He graciously observes. Rescues and restorations hedge about the lives of the saints; death cannot touch them till the King signs His warrant and gives him leave, and even then His touch is not so much mortal as immortal; He doth not so much kill us as kill our mortality. C. H. S.

Vs. 20. *Our soul.* Not our souls, but *our soul,* as if they all had only one. And what is the language of God by the prophet? "I will give them one heart and one way." And thus the two disciples going to Emmaus exclaimed, upon their discovery and surprise, "Did not our heart burn within us?"

And thus in the beginning of the gospel it was said, "The multitude of them that believed were of one heart, and of one soul." We have seen several drops of water on the table, by being brought to touch, running into one. If Christians were better acquainted with each other, they would easily unite. WILLIAM JAY

*Our soul waiteth for the Lord: He is our help and our shield.* There is an excellent story of a young man that was at sea in a mighty, raging tempest; and when all the passengers were at their wits' end for fear, he only was merry; and when he was asked the reason of his mirth, he answered, "That the pilot of the ship was his father, and he knew his father would have a care of him."

The great and wise God, Who is our Father, hath from all eternity decreed what shall be the issue of all wars, what the event of all troubles; He is our Pilot, He sits at the stern; and though the ship of the church or state be in a sinking condition, yet be of good comfort, our Pilot will have a care of us.

There is nothing done in the lower house of Parliament on earth but what is first decreed in the higher house in heaven. All the lesser wheels are ordered and overruled by the upper. "Are not five sparrows," saith Christ, "sold for a farthing?" One sparrow is not worth half a farthing. And there's no man shall have half a farthing's worth of harm more than God hath decreed from all eternity. EDMUND CALAMY

## PSALM 34

Title: "A Psalm of David, when he changed his behavior before Abimelech; who drove him away, and he departed." Of this transaction, which reflects no credit upon David's memory, we have a brief account in I Sam. 21. Although the gratitude of the Psalmist prompted him thankfully to record the goodness of the Lord in vouchsafing an undeserved deliverance, yet he weaves none of the incidents of the escape into the narrative but dwells only on the grand fact of his being heard in the hour of peril.

We may learn from his example not to parade our sins before others, as certain vainglorious professors are wont to do who seem as proud of their sins as old Greenwich pensioners of their battles and their wounds. David played the fool with singular dexterity, but he was not so real a fool as to sing of his own exploits of folly.

Vs. 1. *I will bless the Lord at all times.* He who praises God for mercies shall never want a mercy for which to praise. To bless the Lord is never unseasonable. C. H. S.

Mr. Bradford, martyr, speaking of Queen Mary, at whose cruel mercy he then lay, said, "If the queen be pleased to release me, I will thank her; if she will imprison me, I will thank her; if she will burn me, I will thank her," etc. So saith a believing soul: "Let God do with me what He will, I will be thankful." SAMUEL CLARKE'S *"Mirrour"*

Vs. 2. *My soul shall make her boast in the Lord.* Boasting is a very natural propensity, and if it were used as in this case, the more it were indulged the better. The exultation of this verse is no mere tongue bragging; *the soul* is in it, the boasting is meant and felt before it is expressed. What scope there is for holy boasting in Jehovah! C. H. S.

Vs. 4. *I sought the Lord, and He heard me.* God expects to hear from you before you can expect to hear from Him. If you restrain prayer, it is no wonder the mercy promised is retained. Meditation is like the lawyer's studying the case in order to his pleading at the bar; when, therefore, thou hast viewed the promise and affected thy heart with the riches of it, then fly thee to the throne of grace and spread it before the Lord. WILLIAM GURNALL

Vs. 5. *They looked unto Him.* The more we can think upon our Lord and the less upon ourselves, the better. Looking to Him, as He is seated upon the right hand of the throne of God, will keep our heads and especially our hearts steady when going through the deep waters of affliction.

Often have I thought of this when crossing the water opposite the old place of Langholm. I found, when I looked down on the water, I got dizzy; I therefore fixed my eyes upon a steady object on the other side and got comfortably through. DAVID SMITH

Vs. 6. *This poor man cried.* His prayer was a cry, for brevity and bitterness, for earnestness and simplicity, for artlessness and grief; it was a poor man's cry, but it was none the less powerful with heaven, for *the Lord heard him,* and to be heard of God is to be delivered; and so it is added, the Lord *saved him out of all his troubles.*

At once and altogether David was clean rid of all his woes. The Lord sweeps our griefs away as men destroy a hive of hornets or as the winds clear away the mists. Prayer can clear us of troubles as easily as the Lord made riddance of the frogs and flies of Egypt when Moses entreated him. C. H. S.

An arrow drawn with full strength hath a speedier issue; therefore, the prayers of the saints are expressed by crying in Scripture. SAMUEL RUTHERFORD

Vs. 7. *The angel of the Lord encampeth round about them that fear Him, and delivereth them.* I will not rub the questions, whether these angels can contract themselves and whether they can subsist in a point and so stand together the better in so great a number; neither will I trouble myself to examine whether they are in such-and-such a place in their substance or only in their virtue and operation. But this the godly man may assure himself of, that whensoever he shall want their help, in spite of doors, and locks, and bars, he may have it in a moment's warning. ZACHARY BOGAN

Vs. 8. *O taste and see that the Lord is good.* Our senses help our understandings; we cannot by the most rational discourse perceive what the sweetness of honey is; taste it and you shall perceive it. RICHARD ALLEINE, in *"Heaven Opened"*

It is not enough for thee to see it afar off, and not have it, as Dives did; or to have it in thee, and not to taste it, as Samson's lion had great store of honey in him, but tasted no sweetness of it; but thou must as well have it as see it, and as well taste it as have it. THOMAS PLAYFERE

Be unwilling that all the good gifts of God should be swallowed without taste, or maliciously forgotten, but use your palate, know them, and consider them. D. H. MOLLERUS

Vs. 10. *But they that seek the Lord shall not want any good thing.* There shall be no silver lacking in Benjamin's sack while Joseph has it to throw in. Grace is not such a beggarly visitant as will not pay its own way. When the best of beings is adored, the best of blessings are enjoyed. WILLIAM SECKER

Want sanctified is a notable means to bring to repentance, to work in us amendment of life; it stirs up prayer; it weans from the love of the world; it keeps us always prepared for the spiritual combat, discovers whether we be true believers or hypocrites, prevents greater evils of sin and punishment to come; it makes us humble, conformable to Christ, our Head, increaseth our faith, our joy, and thankfulness, our spiritual wisdom, and likewise our patience, as I have largely shown in another treatise. RICHARD YOUNG, in *"Poor's Advocate"*

I remember as I came through the country, that there was a poor widow woman, whose husband fell at Bothwell: the bloody soldiers came to plunder her house, telling her they would take all she had. "We will leave thee nothing," said they, "either to put in thee, or on thee." "I care not," said she, "I will not want as long as God is in the heavens." That was a believer indeed. ALEXANDER PEDEN'S SERMON

Take a survey of heaven and earth and all things therein, and whatsoever upon sure ground appears good, ask it confidently of Christ; His love will not deny it. If it were good for you that there were no sin, no devil, no affliction, no destruction, the love of Christ would instantly abolish these. Nay, if the possession of all the kingdoms of the world were absolutely good for any saint, the love of Christ would instantly crown him monarch of them. DAVID CLARKSON

Vs. 11. *Come, ye children.* When God had created the heavens and the earth, the first thing He did was to adorn the world with light and separate it from the darkness. Happy is that child on whom the light of saving knowledge begins to dawn early. God, in the law, required the firstborn, and the first-fruits, so He doth still our first days, to be offered to Him. NATHANAEL HARDY

David, in this latter part of the Psalm, undertakes to teach children; though a man of war and anointed to be king, he did not think it below him: though now he had his head so full of cares, and his hands of business, yet he could find heart and time to give good counsel to young people from his own experience. MATTHEW HENRY

Observe I. What He expects from them, *Hearken unto Me,* leave your play, lay by your toys, and hear what I have to say to you; not only give Me the hearing, but observe and obey Me. II. What He undertakes to teach them, *The fear of the Lord,* inclusive of all the duties of religion.

David was a famous musician, a statesman, a soldier, but he doth not say to his children, "I will teach you to play upon the harp, or to handle the sword or spear, or draw the bow," or "I will teach you the maxims of state policy," but "I will teach you *the fear of the Lord,*" which is better than all arts and sciences, better than all burnt-offerings and sacrifices. That is it which we should be solicitous both to learn ourselves and teach our children. MATTHEW HENRY

The Master of Sentences dwells, from this verse, on the four kinds of fear: mundane, servile, initial, filial. *Mundane,* when we fear to commit sin, simply lest we should lose some worldly advantage or incur some worldly inconvenience. *Servile,* when we fear to commit sin, simply because of hell torments due to it. *Initial,* when we fear to commit it, lest we should lose the happiness of heaven. *Filial,* when we fear, only and entirely because we dread to offend that God Whom we love with all our hearts.

"Human fear is full of bitterness; divine fear of sweetness: the one drives to slavery, the other allures to liberty; the one dreads the prison of Gehenna, the other opens the kingdom of heaven," says Cassiodorus. J. M. NEALE

Vs. 14. *Do good.* Negative goodness is not sufficient to entitle us to heaven. There are some in the world whose religion runs all upon negatives; they are not drunkards, they are not swearers, and for this they do bless themselves.

See how the Pharisee vapors (Luke 18:11), "God, I thank Thee that I am not as other men are, extortioners, unjust, adulterers," etc. Alas! the not being scandalous will no more make a Christian than a cipher will make a sum.

We are bid, not only to *cease from evil,* but to *do good.* It will be a poor plea at last—"Lord, I kept myself from being spotted with gross sin: I did no hurt." But what good is there in thee? It is not enough for the servant of the vineyard that he doth no hurt there, he doth not break the trees or destroy the hedges; if he doth not work in the vineyard, he loseth his pay.

It is not enough for us to say at the last day, "We have done no hurt; we have lived in no gross sin"; but what good have we done in the vineyard? Where is the grace we have gotten? If we cannot show this, we shall lose our pay and miss of salvation. THOMAS WATSON

*Seek peace.* Anger is murder to one's own self as well as to its objects.

*And pursue it.* Hunt after it; chase it with eager desire. It may soon be lost, indeed—nothing is harder to retain—but do your best, and if enmity should arise let it be no fault of yours. Follow after peace when it shuns you; be resolved not to be of a contentious spirit. The peace which you thus promote will be returned into your own bosom and be a perennial spring of comfort to you. C. H. S.

The most desirable things are not the easiest to be obtained. What is more lovely to the imagination than the tranquillity of peace? But this great blessing does not voluntarily present itself: it must be sought. Even when sought, it often eludes the grasp: it flies away and must be pursued. *Condensed from* DR. WATERLAND'S SERMON, in *J. R. Pitman's Course of Sermons on the Psalms*

Vs. 18. *The Lord is nigh unto them that are of a broken heart.* Near in friendship to accept and console. Broken hearts think God far away, when He is really most near them; their eyes are holden so that they see not their best friend. C. H. S.

Consider the advantages of this broken heart. A broken heart is acceptable and well-pleasing to God (Ps. 51:17). It makes up many defects in your service and duties (Ps. 51:17). It makes the soul a fit receptacle for God to dwell in (Isa. 57:15). It brings God near to men (Ps. 34:18). It lays you open to Christ's sweet healing (Ezek. 34:16). Yea, it puts you in the right road to heaven, where all your wounds and bruises will be cured (Rev. 22:2). JOHN SPALDING, in *"Synaxis Sacra, or a Collection of Sermons,"* etc.

We are apt to overlook men in proportion as they are humbled beneath us; God regards them in that proportion. Vessels of honor are made of that clay which is *broken* into the smallest parts. GEORGE HORNE

O poor sinner, thou hast an unsupportable burden of sin and guilt lying on thy soul, ready to press thee down to hell, and yet thou feelest it not; thou hast the wrath of God hanging over thy head by the twined thread of a short life, which it may be thou mayest not be free from one year, nay, perhaps not one month, but thou seest it not: if thou didst but see it, then thou wouldest cry out as he did in Bosworth field, "A horse! a horse! a kingdom for a horse!" So thou wouldest cry out, "None but Christ! Nothing but Christ! Ten thousand worlds for Christ!" JAMES NALTON

*A contrite spirit—dakkeey ruach—*"the beaten-out spirit." In both words the hammer is necessarily implied; in breaking to pieces the ore first, and then plating out the metal when it has been separated from the ore. This will call to the reader's remembrance Jer. 23:29: "Is not My word like as a fire? saith the Lord: and like a hammer that breaketh the rock in pieces?" ADAM CLARKE

Vs. 19. *The Lord delivereth him out of them all.* The lawyer can deliver his client but from strife, the physician can deliver his patient but from sickness, the master can deliver his servant but from bondage, but the Lord delivereth us from all. As when Moses came to deliver the Israelites, he would not leave a hoof behind him, so when the Lord cometh to deliver the righteous, He will not leave a trouble behind him. He who saith, "I put away all thine iniquities," will also say, "I put away all thine infirmities." HENRY SMITH

Vs. 20. *He keepeth all His bones: not one of them is broken.* Eternity will heal all their wounds. Not a bone of the mystical body of Christ shall be broken, even as His corporeal frame was preserved intact. Divine love watches over every believer as it did over Jesus; no fatal injury shall happen to us. We shall neither be halt nor maimed in the kingdom, but shall be presented after life's trials are over without spot or wrinkle or any such thing, being preserved in Christ Jesus and kept by the power of God through faith unto salvation. C. H. S.

Christ's bones were in themselves breakable but could not actually be broken by all the violence in the world because God had fore-decreed, "A bone of Him shall not be broken." So we confess God's children mortal; but all the power of devil or man may not, must not, cannot, kill them before their conversion according to God's election of them to life, which must be fully accomplished. THOMAS FULLER

# PSALM 35

Title: "A Psalm of David." Here is all we know concerning this Psalm, but internal evidence seems to fix the date of its composition in those troublous times when Saul hunted David over hill and dale and when those who fawned upon the cruel king slandered the innocent object of his wrath, or it may be referred to the unquiet days of frequent insurrections in David's old age. The whole Psalm is the appeal to heaven of a bold heart and a clear conscience irritated beyond measure by oppression and malice. Beyond a doubt, David's Lord may be seen here by the spiritual eye. C. H. S.

Bonar entitles this Psalm, "The awful utterance of the Righteous One regarding those that hate Him without cause"; and he makes the following remarks thereupon: "On that day when their views of justice shall be far clearer and fuller than now, we shall be able to understand how Samuel could hew Agag in pieces, and the godly hosts of Israel slay utterly in Canaan man and woman and child, at God's command. We shall be able, not only fully to agree in the doom, 'Let them be confounded,' etc., but even to sing, 'Amen, Hallelujah,' over the smoke of torment (Rev. 19:1-2)."

We should in some measure now be able to use every verse of this Psalm in the spirit in which the Judge speaks it, we feeling ourselves His assessors in judging the world (I Cor. 6:2). We shall, at all events, be able to use it on that day when what is written here shall be accomplished. ANDREW A. BONAR

Vs. 1. *Plead my cause, O God, with them that strive with me.* Doth the world condemn thee for thy zeal in the service of God? Reproachfully scorn thee for thy care to maintain good works? not blush to traduce thee with imputations of preciseness, conceited singularity, Pharisaical hypocrisy?

Oh, but if thy conscience condemn thee not all this while, if that be rectified by the sacred Word of God, if thou aim at His glory in pursuing thine own salvation, and side not with the disturbers of the church, go on, good Christian, in the practice of piety, discourage not thyself in thy laudable endeavors, but recount with comfort that the Lord is thy Judge (I Cor. 4:4). ISAAC CRAVEN'S SERMON AT PAUL'S CROSS

Vs. 3. *Draw out also the spear, and stop the way against them that persecute me.* To stave off trouble is no mean act of lovingkindness. As when some valiant warrior with his lance blocks up a defile, and keeps back a host until his weaker brethren have made good their escape, so does the Lord often hold the believer's foes at bay until the good man has taken breath, or clean fled from his foes. C. H. S.

*Say unto my soul, I am thy salvation.* Observe that salvation may be made sure to a man. David would never pray for that which could not be, nor would Peter charge us with a duty which stood not in possibility to be performed. II Peter 1:10: "Make your election sure."

And to stop the bawling throats of all cavilling adversaries, Paul directly proves it: "Know ye not your own selves, how that Jesus Christ is in you, except ye be reprobates?" (II Cor. 13:5). We may then know that Christ is in us. If Christ be in us, we are in Christ; if we be in Christ, we cannot be condemned, for (Rom.8:1), "There is no damnation to them which are in Christ Jesus." THOMAS ADAMS

If God speak comfort, let hell roar horror. There is no vexation to the vexation of the soul; so no consolation to the consolation of the soul . . . Let this teach us to make much of this *My*. Luther says there is great divinity in pronouns. The assurance that God will save some is a faithful incident to devils. The very reprobates may believe that there is a book of election; but God never told them that their names were written there. The hungry beggar at the feast-house gate smells good cheer, but the master doth not say, "This is provided for thee." It is small comfort to the harborless wretch to pass through a goodly city and see many glorious buildings, when he cannot say, "I have a place here."

The beauty of that excellent city Jerusalem, built with sapphires, emeralds, chrysolites, and such precious stones, the foundation and walls whereof are perfect gold (Revelation 21), affords a soul no comfort, unless he can say, "I have a mansion in it." The all-sufficient merits of Christ do thee no good unless He be thy Savior. The world fails, the flesh fails, the devil kills. Only the Lord saves. What? Salvation. A special good thing; every man's desire. "I will give thee a lordship," said God to Esau. "I will give thee a kingdom," saith God to Saul. "I will give thee an apostleship," saith God to Judas. But, "I will be thy salvation," He says to David, and to none but saints. *Condensed from* THOMAS ADAMS

Vs. 4. *Let them be confounded and put to shame that seek after my soul.* There is nothing malicious here; the slandered man simply craves for justice, and the petition is natural and justifiable. Guided by God's good Spirit, the Psalmist foretells the everlasting confusion of all the haters of the righteous.

Shameful disappointment shall be the portion of the enemies of the gospel, nor would the most tender-hearted Christian have it otherwise; viewing sinners as men, we love them and seek their good, but regarding them as enemies of God, we cannot think of them with anything but detestation and a loyal desire for the confusion of their devices.

No loyal subject can wish well to rebels. Squeamish sentimentality may object to the strong language here used, but in their hearts all good men wish confusion to mischief-makers. C. H. S.

Verses 4, 8, 26. How are we to account for such prayers for vengeance? We find them chiefly in four Psalms—the seventh, thirty-fifth, sixty-ninth, and one-hundred and ninth, and the imprecations in these form a terrible climax. In the last, no less than thirty anathemas have been counted. Are these the mere outbursts of passionate and unsanctified feeling or are they the legitimate expression of a righteous indignation? An uninstructed fastidiousness, it is well known, has made many persons recoil from reading these Psalms at all.

Now, the real source of the difficulty lies in our not observing and bearing in mind the essential difference between the Old Testament and the New. The older dispensation was in every sense a sterner one than the new. The spirit of Elias, though not an evil spirit, was not the spirit of Christ. "The Son of man came not to destroy men's lives, but to save them" (Luke 9:56). J. J. STEWART PEROWNE

David was about as devoid of vindictiveness as any public character who can well be named. His conduct in relation to Saul, from first to last, displayed a singularly noble spirit, far removed from anything like the lust of vengeance; and the meekness with which he endured the bitter reproaches of Shimei, bore witness to the same spirit after his accession to the throne. . . .

He can affirm regarding his implacable enemies, "O Lord my God, if I have done this; if there be iniquity in my hands; if I have rewarded evil unto him that was at peace with me; (yea, I have delivered him that without cause is mine enemy:) let the enemy persecute my soul, and take it; yea, let him tread down my life upon the earth" (Ps. 7:3-5).

Surely one ought to think twice before putting on the imprecations an interpretation which would make them utterly incongruous with these appeals, uttered almost in the same breath. WILLIAM BINNIE, D.D.

Vs. 7. *For without cause have they hid from me their net in a pit, which without cause they have digged for my soul.* Twice does David assert in one verse that his adversaries plotted against him *without cause.* Net-making and pit-digging require time and labor, and both of these the wicked will expend cheerfully if they may but overthrow the people of God.

Vs. 8. *And let his net that he hath hid catch himself: into that very destruction let him fall.* There is a *lex talionis* with God which often works most wonderfully. Men set traps and catch their own fingers. They throw up stones, and they fall upon their own heads. How often Satan outwits himself and burns his fingers with his own coals!

This will doubtless be one of the aggravations of hell, that men will torment themselves with what were once the fond devices of their rebellious minds. They curse and are cursed; they kick the pricks and tear themselves; they pour forth floods of fire, and it burns them within and without. C. H. S.

By giving Ahithophel rope enough, the Lord preserved David from perishing. Who will not admire that Goliath should be slain with his own sword, and that proud Haman should hold Mordecai's stirrup and be the herald of his honor? The wicked shall be undone by their own doings; all the arrows that they shoot at the righteous shall fall upon their own pates.

Maxentious built a false bridge to drown Constantine but was drowned himself. Henry the Third of France was stabbed in the very same chamber where he had helped to contrive the cruel massacre of the French Protestants. And his brother, Charles the Ninth who delighted in the blood of the saints, had blood given him to drink, for he was worthy. *Condensed from* THOMAS BROOKS

Vs. 11. *False witnesses did rise up.* This is the old device of the ungodly, and we must not wonder if it be used against us as against our Master. To please Saul, there were always men to be found mean enough to impeach David.

*They laid to my charge things that I knew not.* He had not even a thought of sedition; he was loyal even to excess; yet they accused him of conspiring against the Lord's anointed. He was not only innocent but ignorant of the fault alleged. It is well when our hands are so clean that no trace of dirt is upon them. C. H. S.

You will say, "Why does God permit wicked people to lay to the charge of the godly such things as they are clear of? God if He pleased could prevent it, and stop the mouths of the wicked, that they should not be able to speak against His children."

Answer: As all things work for the best to them that love God, so this works for the good of God's people. God doth permit it for the good of His people, and thus He frustrates the hopes of the wicked: they intend evil against the godly, and God disposes of it for good. As Joseph said to his brethren, "You intended evil against me, and God disposed of it for good."

There is a fourfold good that God brings out of it to His people.

First, God doth by this means humble them, and brings them to examine what is amiss.

Secondly, God doth by this means bring them oftener upon their knees, to seek unto Him, to plead their cause, and to clear their innocency. How oft did the prophet speak unto God when the wicked did falsely accuse him!

Thirdly, God doth use the reproach of the wicked as a preventing medicine against that crime which the wicked lay to their charge. The godly have unrenewed nature as well as renewed, and if God should leave them ever so little to themselves, they are not their own keepers they might fall into that sin which the wicked lay to their charge: and every godly man and woman may say when they are falsely accused, "It is God's mercy that I did not fall into that sin they lay to my charge."

Fourthly, God doth by this means teach them how to judge of others when they are falsely accused. For the time to come they will not receive a false report against their neighbor; they will know the truth of a thing before they believe it, and they know how to comfort others in the like condition. ZEPHANIAH SMYTH'S SERMON *"The Malignant's Plot"*

Vs. 12. *They rewarded me evil for good.* For the good David did in killing Goliath, and slaying his ten thousands of Philistines, and thereby saving his king and country, Saul and his courtiers envied him and sought to slay him: so our Lord Jesus Christ, for all the good He did to the Jews, by healing their bodies and diseases and preaching the Gospel to them for the benefit of their souls, was rewarded with reproaches and persecutions, and at last with the shameful death of the cross; and in like manner are His people used, but this is an evil that shall not go unpunished (see Prov. 17:13). JOHN GILL

*And my prayer returned into mine own bosom.* Prayer is never lost: if it bless not those for whom intercession is made, it shall bless the intercessors. Clouds do not always descend in showers upon the same spot from which the vapors ascended, but they come down somewhere; and even so do supplications in some place or other yield their showers of mercy. If our dove find no rest for the sole of her foot among our enemies, it shall fly into our bosoms and bring an olive branch of peace in its mouth. C. H. S.

Vs. 14. *His mother.* Mahomet was once asked what relation had the strongest claim upon our affection and respect; when he instantly replied, "The mother, the mother, the mother."

Vs. 15. *But in mine adversity they rejoiced.* In my halting, they were delighted. My lameness was sport to them. Danger was near, and they sang songs over my expected defeat. How glad are the wicked to see a good man limp! C. H. S.

Do not glory in your neighbor's ruins. The fire-fly leaps and dances in the fire, and so do many wicked men rejoice in the sufferings of others. Such as rejoice in the suffering of others are sick of the devil's disease; but from that disease the Lord deliver all your souls. We must not pray with him in the tragedy, that it may rain calamities; nor with Clemens' Gnostic, "Give me calamities that I may glory in them." There cannot be a greater evidence of a wicked heart than for a man to be merry because others are in misery. "He that is glad at calamities (that is, at the calamities of others) shall not be unpunished" (Prov. 17:5). THOMAS BROOKS

Marvelous prophecy of the cross! second only, if indeed second, to that in the Twenty-Second Psalm. Still closer to the history if we take the Vulgate: "The scourges were gathered together upon me." Even so, O Lord Jesus, the ploughers ploughed upon Thy back, and made long furrows: precious furrows for us, where are sown patience for the present life and glory in the next; where are sown hope that maketh not ashamed and love that many waters cannot quench. LEWIS de GRENADA

*Yea, the abjects gathered themselves together against me.* How unanimous are the powers of evil; how heartily do men serve the devil and none decline his service because they are not endowed with great abilities!

*They did tear me, and ceased not.* It is such dainty work to tear to pieces a good man's character that when slanderers have their hand in they are loath to leave off. A pack of dogs tearing their prey is nothing compared with a set of malicious gossips mauling the reputation of a worthy man. That lovers of the Gospel are not at this time rent and torn as in the old days of Mary is to be attributed to the providence of God rather than to the gentleness of men.

Vs. 16. *With hypocritical mockers in feasts, they gnashed upon me with their teeth.* Very forcibly might our Lord have used the words of these verses! Let us not forget to see the Despised and Rejected of men here painted to the life. Calvary and the ribald crew around the cross seem brought before our eyes. C. H. S.

Some cannot be merry, but it must be with Scripture; if they want a little diversion, the saints must be the subject of their discourses! they can vent their profane jests upon the Word of God; this is their pastime over their cups upon the ale-bench. How ready they are with their contumelious reflections; they have learnt their father's dialect, they are accusers of the brethren, their speech betrays them to be Hellians. OLIVER HEYWOOD

Vs. 17. *Lord, how long wilt Thou look on?* Why be a mere spectator? Who so neglectful of Thy servant? Art Thou indifferent? Carest Thou not that we perish? We may thus reason with the Lord. He permits us this familiarity.

Vs. 18. *I will give Thee thanks in the great congregation.* Most men publish their griefs; good men should proclaim their mercies.

Vs. 19. *Neither let them wink with the eye that hate me without a cause.* To cause hatred is the mark of the wicked; to suffer it causelessly is the lot of the righteous. C. H. S.

Vs. 21. *And said, Aha, aha, our eye hath seen it.* Glad to find out a fault or a misfortune or to swear they had seen evil where there was none. Malice has but one eye; it is blind to all virtue in its enemy. Eyes can generally see what hearts wish. A man with a mote in his eye sees a spot in the sun. How like a man to an ass when he brays over another's misfortunes! How like to a devil when he laughs a hyena-laugh over a good man's slip! C. H. S.

Vs. 23. *My God and my Lord.* The cry of Thomas when he saw the wounds of Jesus. If he did not count our Lord to be divine, neither does David here ascribe deity to Jehovah, for there is no difference except in the order of the words and the tongue in which they were spoken; the meaning is identical.

What words they are, with their two eyes seeing Jehovah in two aspects, yet as one, grasping him with two hands in the double "my" to one heart, for the word is but one, bowing before him on both knees to worship him in lowliest reverence.

Well might Nouet, in his exposition of the words as used by Thomas, exclaim, "O sweet word, I will say it all my life long; I will say it in the hour of death; I will say it in eternity." C. H. S.

Vs. 27. *Let the Lord be magnified, which hath pleasure in the prosperity of His servants.* The Romans, being in great distress, were put so hard to it that they were fain to take the weapons out of the temples of their gods to fight with their enemies, and so they overcame them.

So when the people of God have been hard put to it by reason of afflictions and persecutions, the weapons that they have fled to have been prayers and tears, and with these they have overcome their persecutors. THOMAS BROOKS

Vs. 28. *My tongue shall speak of Thy righteousness and of Thy praise all the day long.* See now I have made a discourse something longer; ye are wearied. Who endureth to praise God all the day long? I will suggest a remedy whereby thou mayest praise God all the day long if thou wilt. Whatever thou dost, do well, and thou hast praised God. AUGUSTINE

## PSALM 36

It is The Song of Happy Service: such a one as all may join in who bear the easy yoke of Jesus. The wicked are contrasted with the righteous, and the great Lord of devout men is heartily extolled; thus obedience to so good a Master is indirectly insisted on, and rebellion against Him is plainly condemned.

Vs. 1. *The transgression of the wicked saith within my heart, that there is no fear of God before his eyes.* Men's sins have a voice to godly ears. They are the outer index of an inner evil. Wickedness is the fruit of an atheistic root. If God be everywhere, and I fear Him, how can I dare to break His laws in His very presence? C. H. S.

"Not having the fear of God before his eyes," has become inwoven into proceedings in criminal courts. When a man has no fear of God, he is prepared for any crime. WILLIAM S. PLUMER

Vs. 2. *For he flattereth himself in his own eyes.* God-fearing men see their sins and bewail them. Where the reverse is the case, we may be sure there is no fear of God. To smooth over one's own conduct to one's conscience (which is the meaning of the Hebrew) is to smooth one's own path to hell.

He had not God before his eyes in holy awe, therefore he puts himself there in unholy admiration. He who makes little of God makes much of himself. They who forget adoration fall into adulation. The eyes must see something, and if they admire not God, they will flatter self. C. H. S.

Some sinners flatter themselves that they are already converted. They sit down and rest in a false hope, persuading themselves that all their sins are pardoned; that God loves them; that they shall go to heaven when they die; and that they need trouble themselves no more. "Because thou sayest, I am rich, and increased with goods, and have need of nothing; and knowest not that thou art wretched, and miserable, and poor, and blind, and naked" (Rev. 3:17). *Condensed from* JONATHAN EDWARDS

Vs. 3. *The words of his mouth are iniquity and deceit.* This pair of hell dogs generally hunt together, and what one does not catch the other will; if iniquity cannot win by oppression, deceit will gain by chicanery. When the heart is so corrupt as to flatter itself, the tongue follows suit. The open sepulcher of the throat reveals the foulness of the inner nature. C. H. S.

Verses 3-4:

*Yet did he spare his sleep, and hear the clock*
*Number the midnight watches, on his bed*
*Devising mischief more; and early rose,*
*And made most hellish meals of good men's names.*
*From door to door you might have seen him speed,*
*Or placed amid a group of gaping fools.*
*Peace fled the neighborhood in which he made*
*His haunts; and, like a moral pestilence,*
*Before his breath the healthy shoots and blooms*
*Of social joy and happiness decayed.*
*Fools only in his company were seen,*
*And those forsaken of God, and to themselves*
*Given up. The prudent shunned him and his house*
*As one who had a deadly moral plague.*

ROBERT POLLOK

Vs. 4. *He deviseth mischief upon his bed.* His place of rest becomes the place for plotting. His bed is a hotbed for poisonous weeds. He hath the devil for his bedfellow, who lies abed and schemes how to sin. God is far from him. C. H. S.

As the man that feareth God communeth with his heart upon his bed, that he may not sin, no, not in his heart; so the man that feareth not God deviseth how he may plot and perform sin willingly. DAVID DICKSON

Most diligently does Ayguan follow up the Scriptural expressions concerning a bed and tell us that there are six different beds of wickedness—that of luxury, that of avarice, of ambition, of greediness, of torpor, and of cruelty, and he illustrates them all by examples from Scripture. J. M. NEALE

From the baseness of the wicked, the Psalmist turns his contemplation to the glory of God. Contrasts are impressive.

Vs. 5. *Thy mercy, O Lord, is in the heavens.* When we can measure the heavens, then shall we bound the mercy of the Lord. Towards His own servants especially, in the salvation of the Lord Jesus, He has displayed grace higher than the heaven of heavens and wider than the universe. Oh, that the atheist could but see this, how earnestly would he long to become a servant of Jehovah! C. H. S.

When men sin so impudently, who does not admire the divine longsuffering? SEBASTIAN MUNSTER

*Thy faithfulness reacheth unto the clouds.* Far, far above all comprehension is the truth and faithfulness of God. He never fails, nor forgets, nor falters, nor forfeits His Word. C. H. S.

Vs. 6. *Thy righteousness is like the great mountains.* Firm and unmoved, lofty and sublime. As winds and hurricanes shake not an Alp, so the righteousness of God is never in any degree affected by circumstances; He is always just. Who can bribe the Judge of all the earth, or who can, by threatening, compel Him to pervert judgment? Not even to save His elect would the Lord suffer His righteousness to be set aside. Right across the path of every unholy man who dreams of heaven stand the towering Andes of divine righteousness, which no unregenerate sinner can ever climb. C. H. S.

*Thy judgments are a great deep.* God's dealings with men are not to be fathomed by every boaster who demands to see a why for every wherefore. The Lord is not to be questioned by us as to why this and why that. He has reasons, but He does not choose to submit them to our foolish consideration.

Vs. 7. *Therefore the children of men put their trust under the shadow of Thy wings.* Oh, that more of Adam's race knew the excellency of the heavenly shelter! It made Jesus weep to see how they refused it: our tears may well lament the same evil. C. H. S.

*In lonesome cell, guarded and strong I lie,*
*Bound by Christ's love, His truth to testify,*
*Though walls be thick, the door no hand unclose,*
*God is my strength, my solace, and repose.*

*In a letter to* JERONIUS SEGERSON, *written in the prison at Antwerp to his wife, named Lysken, who likewise lay a prisoner there*

Vs. 8. *They shall be abundantly satisfied.* As God expects the best from us, so He gives the best to us. GEORGE SWINNOCK

*Satisfied with the fatness of Thy house.* I once heard a father tell that when he removed his family to a new residence where the accommodation was much more ample, the substance much more rich and varied than that to which they had previously been accustomed, his youngest son, yet a lisping infant, ran round every room and scanned every article with ecstasy, calling out in childish wonder at every new sight, "Is this ours, Father? and is this ours?"

The child did not say "yours"; and I observed that the father while he told the story was not offended with the freedom. You could read in his glistening eye that the infant's confidence in appropriating as his own all that his father had was an important element in his satisfaction.

Such, I suppose, will be the surprise, and joy, and appropriating confidence with which the child of our Father's family will count all his own when he is removed from the comparative mean condition of things present and enters the Infinite things to come.

When the glories of heaven burst upon his view, he does not stand at a distance like a stranger saying, "O God, these are Thine." He bounds forward to touch and taste every provision which those blessed mansions contain, exclaiming as he looks in the Father's face, "Father, this and this is ours!" The dear child is glad of all the Father's riches, and the Father is gladder of His dear child. WILLIAM ARNOT

*Thou shalt make them drink of the river of Thy pleasures.* Hath the child, then, any cause, when his Father keeps so rare and costly a table, to leave such dainties and go a-begging up and down the country for scraps and fragments? GEORGE SWINNOCK

*Pleasures.* Delights, the same word as is translated "Eden" in Genesis, only it is here in the plural number. DALMAN HAPSTONE, M.A.

Vs. 9. *For with Thee is the fountain of life.* This verse is made of simple words, but like the first chapter of John's Gospel, it is very deep. From the Lord, as from an independent self-sufficient spring, all creature life proceeds, by Him it is sustained, through Him alone can it be perfected. Life is in the creature, but the fountain of it is only in the Creator. C. H. S.

These are some of the most wonderful words in the Old Testament. Their fulness of meaning no commentary can ever exhaust. They are, in fact, the kernel and the anticipation of much of the profoundest teaching of St. John. J. J. STEWART PEROWNE

*In Thy light shall we see light.* In spiritual things, the knowledge of God sheds a light on all other subjects. We need no candle to see the sun; we see it by its own radiance and then see everything else by the same luster. We never see Jesus by the light of self, but self in the light of Jesus. Vain are they who look to learning and human wit; one ray from the throne of God is better than the noonday splendor of created wisdom. Lord, give me the sun, and let those who will delight in the wax candles of superstition and the phosphorescence of corrupt philosophy. C. H. S.

That glorious sight which Daniel saw took strength from him (Dan. 10:8). The object, being without him, drew out all his spirits to behold and admire it and so weaken him; but in heaven, our God, Whom we shall see and know, will be within us to strengthen us; then shall we live because we see His face. It will be also a comforting light, like the light of the morning to the wearied watchman, who longed after it in the nighttime. WILLIAM COLVILLE

The light of nature is like a spark, the light of the gospel a lamp, the light of grace a star, but the light of glory the sun itself. The higher our ascent, the greater our light; God dwelleth "in the light which no man can approach unto" (I Tim. 6:16) no man, while he carries mortality and sin about him; but when those two corrupt and incapable qualities shall be put off, then shall we be brought to that light.

We are now glad of the sun and stars over our heads, to give us light: what light and delight shall that be when these are under our feet! That light must needs go as far beyond their light as they now go beyond us. THOMAS ADAMS

There is a great boast of light in the world, and there is some ground for it in natural things; but, as of old, the world by wisdom knew not God, so of late. If ever we know God, it must be through the medium of His Word. ANDREW FULLER

We shall know vastly and inconceivably more in the first moment after we come to heaven than we are capable of attaining here throughout all our days. TIMOTHY CRUSO

In this communion of God, what can we want? Why, God shall be all and in all to us; He shall be beauty for the eye, music for the ear, honey for the taste, the full content and satisfaction of our desires, and that immediately from Himself. EDMUND PINCHBECK, in *"The Fountain of Life:" a Funeral Sermon*

Vs. 10. *And Thy righteousness to the upright in heart.* The worst thing to be feared by the man of God is to be forsaken of heaven, hence this prayer; but the fear is groundless, hence the peace which faith brings to us. Learn from this verse, that although a continuance of mercy is guaranteed in the covenant, we are yet to make it a matter of prayer. For this good thing will the Lord be enquired of.

Vs. 11. *Let not the foot of pride come against me.* Good men may well be afraid of proud men, for the serpent's seed will never cease to bite the heel of the godly. C. H. S.

## PSALM 37

Subject: The great riddle of the prosperity of the wicked and the affliction of the righteous, which has perplexed so many, is here dealt with in the light of the future; and fretfulness and repining are most impressively forbidden.

It is a Psalm in which the Lord hushes most sweetly the too common repinings of His people and calms their minds as to His present dealings with His own chosen flock and the wolves by whom they are surrounded. It contains eight great precepts, is twice illustrated by autobiographical statements, and abounds in remarkable contrasts. C. H. S.

This Psalm may well be styled, "The good man's cordial in bad times; a sovereign plaister for the plague of discontent; or, a choice antidote against the poison of impatience." NATHANIEL HARDY, *in a Funeral Sermon*

Vs. 1. *Fret not thyself because of evildoers.* To fret is to worry, to have the heart-burn, to fume, to become vexed. Nature is very apt to kindle a fire of jealousy when it sees law-breakers riding on horses and obedient subjects walking in the mire. It seems hard to carnal judgments that the best meat should go to the dogs, while loving children pine for want of it.

*Neither be thou envious against the workers of iniquity.* Who envies the fat bullock the ribbons and garlands which decorate him as he is led to the shambles? Yet the case is a parallel one; for ungodly rich men are but as beasts fattened for the slaughter. C. H. S.

Queen Elizabeth envied the milk-maid when she was in prison; but if she had known what a glorious reign she should have had afterwards for forty-four years, she would not have envied her.

And as little needeth a godly man, though in misery, to envy a wicked man in the ruff of all his prosperity and jollity, considering what he hath in hand much more what he hath in hope. JOHN TRAPP

What good doth all their prosperity do them? It does but hasten their ruin, not their reward. The ox that is the laboring ox is the longer lived than the ox that is put into the pasture; the very putting of him there doth but hasten his slaughter; and when God puts the wicked men into fat pastures, into places of honor and power, it is but to hasten their ruin. LUDOVIC DE CARBONE, *quoted by John Spencer*

Vs. 2. *And wither as the green herb.* How complete an end is made of the man whose boasts had no end! Is it worth while to waste ourselves in fretting about the insect of an hour, an ephemera which in the same day is born and dies? Within believers there is a living and incorruptible seed which liveth and abideth forever; why should they envy mere flesh, and the glory of it, which are but as grass, and the flower thereof?

Vs. 4. *Delight thyself also in the Lord.* In a certain sense, imitate the wicked; they delight in their portion—take care to delight in yours, and so far from envying you will pity them. There is no room for fretting if we remember that God is ours. C. H. S.

And consider that your condition on earth is such as exposes you to many sufferings and hardships, which, by your not delighting in Him, you can never be sure to avoid (for they are things common to men), but which by your delighting in Him, you may be easily able to endure.

Besides all this, seriously consider that you must die. You can make no shift to avoid that. How easily tolerable and pleasant will it be to think, then, of going to Him with Whom you have lived in a delightful communion before! And how dreadful to appear before Him to Whom your own heart shall accuse you to have been (against all His importunities and allurements) a disaffected stranger. JOHN HOWE'S "*Treatise of Delight in God*"

Vs. 5. *Commit thy way unto the Lord,* is rendered by the Vulgate, *Revela viam Domino,* "reveal thy way"; and by St. Ambrose, understood of revealing our sins to God. Indeed, since it is impossible to cover, why should we not discover, our sins? Conceal not that which God knoweth already and would have thee to make known. It is a very ill office to be the devil's secretary. Oh, break thy league with Satan by revealing his secrets, thy sins, to God. NATHANIEL HARDY

*Trust also in Him; and He shall bring it to pass.* The ploughman sows and harrows and then leaves the harvest to God. What can he do else? He cannot cover the heavens with clouds, or command the rain, or bring forth the sun, or create the dew. He does well to leave the whole matter with God; and so to all of us it is truest wisdom, having obediently trusted in God, to leave results in His hands and expect a blessed issue.

Vs. 6. *And He shall bring forth thy righteousness as the light.* The more we fret in this case, the worse for us. Our strength is to sit still. The Lord will clear the slandered. If we look to His honor, He will see to ours. It is wonderful how, when faith learns to endure calumny with composure, the filth does not defile her, but falls off like snowballs from a wall of granite. C. H. S.

Vs. 7. *Rest in the Lord.* "Hold thee still" (so it may be translated). And this is the hardest precept that is given to man; insomuch that the most difficult precept of action sinks into nothing when compared with this command to inaction. JEROME

The Hebrew word rendered *silent* is *dom,* from which the English word *dumb* appears to be derived. The silence here enjoined is opposed to murmuring or complaining. JAMES ANDERSON, in *Calvin's Commentary*

Vs. 8. *Fret not thyself in any wise to do evil.* Evil may be done by fretting at the prosperity of wicked men, or by imitating them, doing as they do, in hope of being prosperous as they are. JOHN GILL

Vs. 9. *But those that wait upon the Lord, they shall inherit the earth.* Passion, according to Bunyan's parable, has his good things first, and they are soon over; Patience has his good things last, and they last forever.

Vs. 10. *For yet a little while, and the wicked shall not be.* O wherefore, tried believer, dost thou envy one who in a little while will lie lower than the dust?

*Yea, thou shalt diligently consider his place, and it shall not be.* His house shall be empty, his chair of office vacant, his estate without an owner; he shall be utterly blotted out, perhaps cut off by his own debauchery, or brought to a deathbed of penury by his own extravagance. Gone like a passing cloud—forgotten as a dream—where are his boastings and hectorings, and where the pomp which made poor mortals think the sinner blest? C. H. S.

Vs. 11. *The meek shall inherit the earth.* Not the hot, stirring spirits who bustle for the world shall have it, but the meek, who are thrust up and down from corner to corner, and hardly suffered to remain anywhere quietly in it. This earth, which they seem most deprived of, they only shall have and enjoy. JOHN PENNINGTON

Vs. 13. *The Lord shall laugh at him.* Lest the flesh should still murmur and complain, demanding why God should only laugh at the wicked, and not rather take vengeance upon them, the reason is added, that He sees the day of their destruction at hand. *"For He seeth that his day is coming."* JOHN CALVIN

*For He seeth that his day is coming.* The evil man does not see how close his destruction is upon his heels; he boasts of crushing others when the foot of justice is already uplifted to trample him as the mire of the streets. Sinners, in the hand of an angry God, and yet plotting against His children! Poor souls, thus to run upon the point of Jehovah's spear. C. H. S.

His dismal day, his death's day, which will also be his doom's day. JOHN TRAPP

Vs. 16. *A little that the righteous man hath is better than the riches of many wicked.* We would sooner hunger with John than feast with Herod; better to feed on scant fare with the prophets in Obadiah's cave than riot with the priests of Baal. A man's happiness consists not in the heaps of gold which he has in store. Content finds *multum in parvo,* while for a wicked heart the whole world is too little. C. H. S.

Oh, what comfort is it to taste the sweetness of Christ's love in every enjoyment! When we can say, "Christ loved me, and gave Himself for me, that I might enjoy these blessings," oh, how will this raise the value of every common mercy. DAVID CLARKSON

As the waters which flow from the hills of some of the islands of Molucca taste of the cinnamon and cloves which grow there, so should Thy gift, though it were but water, taste of the good-will and special grace of the Giver. GEORGE SWINNOCK

'Tis as possible for a wicked man to fill his body with air and his chest with grace, as his mind with wealth. 'Tis with them as with a ship; it may be over-laden with silver and gold, even unto sinking, and yet have compass and sides to hold ten times more. So here, a covetous wretch, though he have enough to sink him, yet he shall never have enough to satisfy him. JOHN GLASCOCK'S SERMON, entitled *"Mary's Choice"*

Verses 16-17. Never let a Christian murmur because he hath but little, but rather let him be still a-blessing of that God that hath blest his little, and that will bless his little to him. THOMAS BROOKS

Vs. 18. *The Lord knoweth the days of the upright.* Depositeth their days, lays them up in safety for them: for such is the original idea of the Hebrew. JOHN FRY

Vs. 20. *But the wicked shall perish.* Whatever phantom light may mock their present, their future is black with dark, substantial night. C. H. S.

*Into smoke shall they consume.* "What hath pride profited us? or what hath our boasting of riches given us?" Such are the things, they shall speak who are in hell and who have sinned. For the hope of the ungodly is like a dry thistledown by the wind carried away, or the thin foam spread upon the billows, or as a smoke floated hither and thither by the wind, or as the remembrance of a wayfaring man for a day. WOUTER OF STOELWYK

Vs. 25. *Nor his seed begging bread.* If any say that David himself begged—he asked bread of Abimelech and of Nabal—I answer, it is a good rule, and it resolves the case; transitory cases and sudden accidents make no beggars: we must not say, "David was a beggar, or begged his bread," because once he was in a strait and asked bread of Abimelech and in a second strait sent to Nabal.

In such sudden cases, the richest man in the world may be put to ask a piece of bread. A good man may fall into such wants, but good men are rarely, if ever or at all, left in them. JOSEPH CARYL

Verses 25-26. The good man *is ever merciful, and lendeth; and his seed is blessed.* What the worldling thinks shall make his posterity poor, God saith shall make the good man's rich. The precept gives a promise of mercy to obedience, not confined to the obedient man's self, but extended to his seed, and that even to a thousand generations (Exod. 20:6).

Trust, then, Christ with thy children; when thy friends shall fail, usury bear no date, oppression be condemned to hell, thyself rotten to the dust, the world itself turned and burned into cinders, still "Jesus Christ is the same, yesterday, and today, and forever. THOMAS ADAMS

Vs. 34. *Wait on the Lord.* He that truly trusts in God will stay God's time, and use God's means, and walk in God's way, though it seem round about. DAVID CLARKSON

*Wait . . . keep.* While we are waiting, let us take heed of wavering. Go not a step out of God's way, though a lion be in the way; avoid not duty to meet with safety; keep God's highway, the good old way (Jer. 6:16), the way which is paved with holiness. "And an highway shall be there, and a way, and it shall be called The way of holiness" (Isa. 35:8).

Avoid crooked paths, take heed of turning to the left hand, lest you be set on the left hand. Sin doth cross our hopes, it barricades up our way; a man may as well expect to find heaven in hell as in a sinful way. THOMAS WATSON

Vs. 35. *I have seen the wicked in great power* [terrible, fierce, violent], *and spreading himself like a green bay tree* (a tree in its native soil, vigorous, and luxuriant, that had never been transplanted). A striking figure of the ungodly man of the world, firmly rooted in earthly things—his native soil grown proud and wanton in his prosperity, without fear or apprehension of any reverse. WILLIAM WILSON

And why like a green bay-tree? Because in the winter, when all other trees —as the vine-trees, fig-tree, apple-tree, etc., which are more profitable trees— are withered and naked, yet the bay-tree continueth as green in the winter as the summer.

So fareth it with wicked men; when the children of God, in the storms of persecutions and afflictions and miseries, seem withered, and, as it were, dead, yet the wicked all that time flourish, and do appear green in the eyes of the world: they wallow in worldly wealth, but it is for their destruction; they wax fat, but it is for the day of slaughter.

It was the case of Hophni and Phinehas: the Lord gave them enough and suffered them to go on and prosper in their wickedness; but what was the reason? Because He would destroy them. J. GORE'S SERMON AT ST. PAUL'S

Vs. 36. *Yea, I sought him, but he could not be found.* Moved by curiosity, if we enquire for the ungodly, they have left no trace; like birds of ill omen, none desire to remember them. Some of the humblest of the godly are immortalized, their names are imperishably fragrant in the church, while of the ablest of infidels and blasphemers hardly their names are remembered beyond a few years. Men who were in everybody's mouths but yesterday are forgotten tomorrow, for only virtue is immortal. C. H. S.

Vs. 37. *Mark, . . . and behold.* If Christ would have Mary's name remembered in the Gospel until the world's end for one box of ointment poured on His head, we cannot imagine that He would have the many pious and charitable deeds of His servants to be buried in oblivion. NATHANIEL HARDY

*The perfect man.* Thus every saint is perfect in comparison to the wicked among whom he liveth. In this respect, it is said of Noah, "That he was a perfect man in his generations"; his grace compared with the wickedness of the old world well deserving the name of perfection; indeed every upright man is perfect in comparison of them who are openly bad, or but openly good; stained with wickedness, or but painted with holiness. NATHANIEL HARDY

*Mark the perfect man, and behold the upright: for the end of that man is peace.* The text may be divided into these two parts. Here is, 1. The godly man's property; and 2. The godly man's privilege. His property is perfection; his privilege is peace. Here is the saint's character and the saint's crown: he is characterized by uprightness or sincerity and crowned with peace.

Here is the Christian's way and his end, his motion, and his rest. His way is holiness, his end happiness; his motion is towards perfection and in uprightness; his rest is peace at his journey's end. JOHN WHITLOCK, *in a Funeral Sermon entitled "The Upright Man and His Happy End"*

To die well, be sure to live well; we must not think to have Lazarus' death, and Dives' life; like him in Plutarch that would live with Croesus, as he said, but he would die with Socrates.

No, Balaam's wishes are foolish and fruitless: if you would die well, Christians, you must have a care to live well: if you would die quietly, you must live strictly; if you would die comfortably, you must live conformably; if you would die happily, you must live holily. JOHN KITCHEN, M.A.

Vs. 40. *And the Lord shall help them.* He *shall,* He *shall,* He *shall.* Oh, the rhetoric of God! the safety of the saints! the certainty of the promises! JOHN TRAPP

*And save them, because they trust in Him.* Faith shall insure the safety of the elect. It is the mark of the sheep by which they shall be separated from the goats. Not their merit, but their believing, shall distinguish them. C. H. S.

Luther closes his *Exposition of the Psalm* with the words, "Oh, shame on our faithlessness, mistrust, and vile unbelief, that we do not believe such rich, powerful, consolatory, declarations of God, and take up so readily with little grounds of offence, whenever we but hear the wicked speeches of the ungodly. Help, O God, that we may once attain to right faith. Amen."

## PSALM 38

Title: "A Psalm of David, to bring to remembrance." David felt as if he had been forgotten of his God, and, therefore, he recounted his sorrows and cried mightily for help under them. The same title is given to Psalm 70, where in like manner, the Psalmist pours out his complaint before the Lord. It would be foolish to make a guess as to the point in David's history when this was written; it may be a commemoration of his own sickness and endurance of cruelty; it may, on the other hand, have been composed by him for the use of sick and slandered saints without special reference to himself.

Among the things which David brought to his own remembrance, the first and foremost were: (1) his past trials and his past deliverances. The great point, however, in David's Psalm is to bring to remembrance; (2) the depravity of our nature. There is, perhaps, no Psalm which more fully than this describes human nature as seen in the light which God, the Holy Ghost, casts upon it in the time when He convinces us of sin.

I am persuaded that the description here does not tally with any known disease of the body. It is very like leprosy, but it has about it certain features which cannot be found to meet in any leprosy described either by ancient or modern writers.

The fact is, it is a spiritual leprosy, it is an inward disease which is here described, and David paints it to the very life, and he would have us to recollect this. C. H. S.

Vs. 1. *O Lord, rebuke me not in Thy wrath.* Rebuked I must be, for I am an erring child and Thou a careful Father, but throw not too much anger into the tones of Thy voice; deal gently although I have sinned grievously. The anger of others I can bear, but not Thine. C. H. S.

Vs. 2. *Thine arrows stick fast.* They are arrows, indeed, that are feathered with swiftness and headed with sharpness; and to give them a force in flying, they are shot, I may say, out of His cross-bow, I am sure His bow of crosses; for no arrows can fly so fast, none pierce so deep, as the crosses and afflictions with which He hath surprised me.

Oh, then, as thou hast stretched forth Thine arm of anger, O God, to shoot these arrows at me, so stretch forth Thine arm of mercy to draw them forth, that I may rather sing hymns than dirges unto Thee; and that Thou mayest show Thy power, as well in pardoning as Thou hast done in condemning. Sir Richard Baker

Arrows are (1) swift, (2) secret, (3) sharp, (4) killing instruments. They are instruments drawing blood and drinking blood, even unto drunkenness (Deut. 32:42); afflictions are like arrows in all these properties. Joseph Caryl

Vs. 3. *Thine anger . . . my sin.* I, alas! am as an anvil under two hammers; one of Thine anger, another of my sin; both of them beating incessantly upon me; the hammer of Thine anger bèating upon my flesh and making that unsound; the hammer of my sin beating upon my bones and making them unquiet; although indeed both beat upon both; but Thine anger more upon my flesh, as being more sensible; my sin more upon my bones, as being more obdurate.

God's anger and sin are the two efficient causes of all misery; but the procatarctic cause indeed is sin: God's anger, like the house that Samson pulled upon his own head, falls not upon us but when we pull it upon ourselves by sin. Sir Richard Baker

*Neither is there any rest in my bones because of my sin.* A Christian in this life is like quicksilver, which hath a principle of motion in itself, but not of rest: we are never quiet, but as the ball upon the racket, or the ship upon the waves.

As long as we have sin, this is like quicksilver: a child of God is full of motion and disquiet. . . We are here in a perpetual hurry, in a constant fluctuation; our life is like the tide, sometimes ebbing, sometimes flowing. Here is no rest; and the reason is because we are out of center.

Everything is in motion till it comes at the center; Christ is the center of the soul; the needle of the compass trembles till it comes to the North Pole. THOMAS WATSON

Learn here of beggars how to procure succor and relief. Lay open thy sores, make known thy need, discover all thy misery, make not thy case better than it is. Beggars by experience find that the more miserable they appear to be, the more they are pitied, the more succored. WILLIAM GOUGE

Vs. 4. *As an heavy burden they are too heavy for me.* It is well when sin is an intolerable load, and when the remembrance of our sins burdens us beyond endurance. This verse is the genuine cry of one who feels himself undone by his transgression and as yet sees not the great sacrifice. C. H. S.

No strength is so great but it may be overburdened; though Samson went light away with the gates of Gaza, yet when a whole house fell upon him, it crushed him to death.

And such, alas! am I; I have had sin as a burden upon me ever since I was born, but bore it a long time as light as Samson did the gates of Gaza; but now that I have pulled a whole house of sin upon me, how can I choose but be crushed to death with so great a weight? And crushed, O my soul, thou shouldst be indeed, if God for all His anger did not take some pity on thee, and for all His displeasure did not stay His hand from further chastening thee. SIR RICHARD BAKER

It is of singular use to us, that the backslidings of the holy men of God are recorded in Holy Writ. Spots appear nowhere more disagreeable than when seen in a most beautiful face or on the cleanest garment.

And it is expedient to have a perfect knowledge of the filthiness of sin. We also learn from them to think humbly of ourselves, to depend on the grace of God, to keep a stricter eye upon ourselves, lest perhaps we fall into the same or more grievous sins (Gal. 6:1). HERMAN WITSIUS, D.D.

Vs. 5. *My wounds stink and are corrupt because of my foolishness.* Conscience lays on stripe after stripe till the swelling becomes a wound and suppurates, and the corruption within grows offensive. What a horrible creature man appears to be to his own consciousness when his depravity and vileness are fully opened up by the law of God, applied by the Holy Spirit!

Even the most filthy diseases cannot be so foul as sin. No ulcers, cancers, or putrifying sores, can match the unutterable vileness and pollution of iniquity. Our own perceptions have made us feel this. We write what we do know, and testify what we have seen; and even now we shudder to think that so much of evil should lie festering deep within our nature. C. H. S.

Could the grave hold Lazarus when Thou didst but open Thy mouth to call him forth? No more can the corruption of my sores be any hindrance to their healing when Thy pleasure is to have them be cured. SIR RICHARD BAKER

Verses 5-6. Wherever God intends to reveal His Son with power, wherever He intends to make the gospel to be "a sinful sound," He makes the conscience feel and groan under the burden of sin. And sure am I that when a man is laboring under the burden of sin, he will be full of complaint. The Bible records hundreds of the complaints of God's people under the burden of sin.

Spiritual complaint then is a mark of spiritual life and is one which God recognizes as such. "I have surely heard Ephraim bemoaning himself" (Jer. 31:18). It shows that he has something to mourn over; something to make him groan, being burdened; that sin has been opened up to him in its hateful malignancy; that it is a trouble and distress to his soul; that he cannot roll it like a sweet morsel under his tongue; but that it is found out by the penetrating eye, and punished by the chastening hand of God. J. C. PHILPOT

Vs. 6. *I am troubled; I am bowed down greatly; I go mourning all the day long.* Let a man see and feel himself under the bonds of guilt, in danger of hell, under the power of his lusts, enmity against God, and God a stranger to him; let but the sense of this condition lie upon his heart, and let him go on in his jollity if he can.

What a woful creature doth a man see himself now to be! He envies the happiness of the beasts that are filled and play in their pastures. We have heard of him who when he saw a toad, stood weeping, because God had made him a man, so excellent a creature, and not a toad, so abominable: the goodness of God, then, it seems, as he apprehended it, made him weep; but this man meets a toad, and he weeps also, but why? because he is a man, who thinks his estate infinitely worse than the condition of a toad, and if it were possible to attain it, would change states with the toad, that hath no guilt of sin, fears no wrath of God, is not under power of lusts or creatures; God is no enemy to it, which is his miserable state. GILES FIRMIN

Vs. 7. *A loathsome disease.* In many things, our estimates are extravagant; but we never overestimate the evil of sin. It is as corrupting as it is damning. It covers the soul with plague-spots, with leprosy (Isa. 1:5-6). WILLIAM S. PLUMER

Vs. 8. *I am feeble.* The original is "benumbed," or frozen, such strange incongruities and contradictions meet in a distracted mind and a sick body—it appears to itself to be alternately parched with heat and pinched with cold.

Like souls in the popish-fabled purgatory, tossed from burning furnaces into thick ice, so tormented hearts rush from one extreme to the other, with equal torture in each. A heat of fear, a chill of horror, a flaming desire, a horrible insensibility—by these successive miseries a convinced sinner is brought to death's door. C. H. S.

*I have roared,* etc. It is difficult for a true penitent, in the bitterness of his soul, to go over the life which he has dragged on in sinfulness without groaning and sighing from the bottom of his heart. But happy are these groans, happy these sobs, since they flow from the influence of grace and from the breath of the Holy Spirit, Who Himself in an ineffable manner groans in us and with us and Who forms these groans in our hearts by penitence and love! JEAN BAPTISTE ELIAS AVRILLON

Vs. 9. *My groaning is not hid from Thee.* Secret tears for secret sins are an excellent sign of a holy heart and a healing balsam for broken spirits. SAMUEL LEE

Vs. 11. *My lovers and my friends stand aloof from my sore.* It is very hard when those who should be the first to come to the rescue are the first to desert us. In times of deep soul trouble, even the most affectionate friends cannot enter into the sufferer's case. Let them be as anxious as they may, the sores of a tender conscience they cannot bind up. Oh, the loneliness of a soul passing under the convincing power of the Holy Ghost! C. H. S.

The proof of affection is seen by deeds. I hear the name of kinsman and friend; I see no deed. To Thee, therefore, I flee, Whose Word is deed; for I need Thy help. *From the Latin of* A. RIVETUS

Vs. 13. *But I, as a deaf man, heard not; and I was as a dumb man that openeth not his mouth.* Oh, how happy should we be, if we could always do that which we know is best to be done, and if our wills were as ready to act as our reason is able to enact; we should then decline many rocks we now run upon; we should then avoid many errors we now run into. To be deaf and dumb are indeed great inabilities and defects when they be natural; but when they be voluntary, and I may say artificial, they are then great abilities, or rather perfections. SIR RICHARD BAKER

Vs. 15. *For in Thee, O Lord, do I hope: Thou wilt hear, O Lord my God.* A man that is to go down into a deep pit, he does not throw himself head long into it, or leap down at all adventures, but fastens a rope at top upon a cross beam or some sure place, and so lets himself down by degrees.

So let thyself down into the consideration of thy sin, hanging upon Christ; and when thou art gone so low that thou canst endure no longer, but art ready to be overcome with the horror and darkness of thy miserable estate, dwell not too long at the gates of hell, lest the devil pull thee in, but wind thyself up again by renewed acts of faith, and "fly for refuge unto the hope that is set before thee" (Heb. 6:18). THOMAS COLE, in "*Morning Exercises*"

Vs. 16. *When my foot slippeth, they magnify themselves against me.* The least flaw in a saint is sure to be noticed; long before it comes to a fall the enemy begins to rail, the merest trip of the foot sets all the dogs of hell barking. How careful ought we to be and how importunate in prayer for upholding grace! We do not wish, like blind Samson, to make sport for our enemies; let us then beware of the treacherous Delilah of sin, by whose means our eyes may soon be put out. C. H. S.

Vs. 17. *For I am ready to halt:* to show my infirmity in my trials and afflictions, as Jacob halted after his wrestling with God (Gen. 32:31). In the Greek, *I am ready for scourges,* that is, to suffer correction and punishment for my sins: so the Chaldee saith, for *calamity.* HENRY AINSWORTH

Vs. 18. *For I will declare mine iniquity.* When sorrow leads to hearty and penitent acknowledgment of sin, it is blessed sorrow, a thing to thank God for most devoutly.

*I will be sorry for my sin.* To be sorry for sin is no atonement for it, but it is the right spirit in which to repair to Jesus, Who is the reconciliation and the Savior. A man is near to the end of his trouble when he comes to an end with his sins.

Vs. 19. *But mine enemies are lively, and they are strong.* However weak and dying the righteous man may be, the evils which oppose him are sure to be lively enough. Neither the world, the flesh, nor the devil are ever afflicted with debility or inertness; this trinity of evils labor with mighty unremitting energy to overthrow us.

If the devil were sick, or our lusts feeble, or Madame Bubble infirm, we might slacken prayer; but with such lively and vigorous enemies, we must not cease to cry mightily unto our God.

Vs. 20. *Because I follow the thing that good is.* If men hate us for this reason, we may rejoice to bear it: their wrath is the unconscious homage which vice renders to virtue. This verse is not inconsistent with the writer's previous confession; we may feel equally guilty before God and yet be entirely innocent of any wrong to our fellowmen. It is one thing to acknowledge the truth, quite another thing to submit to be belied. The Lord may smite me justly, and yet I may be able to say to my fellowman, "Why smitest thou me?" C. H. S.

# PSALM 39

The Psalmist, bowed down with sickness and sorrow, is burdened with unbelieving thoughts he resolves to stifle, lest any evil should come from their expression (verses 1-2). But silence creates an insupportable grief, which at last demands utterance and obtains it in the prayer of verses 3-6, which is almost a complaint and a sigh for death, or at best a very desponding picture of human life. In verses 7-17 the tone is more submissive, and the recognition of the divine hand more distinct; the cloud has evidently passed, and the mourner's heart is relieved. C. H. S.

The most beautiful of all the elegies in the Psalter. H. EWALD

Vs. 1. *I said.* I steadily resolved and registered a determination. In his great perplexity, his greatest fear was lest he should sin; and, therefore, he cast about for the most likely method for avoiding it, and he determined to be silent. It is right excellent when a man can strengthen himself in a good course by the remembrance of a well and wisely-formed resolve. C. H. S.

*I said, I will take heed,* etc. Socrates reports of one Pambo, an honest, well-meaning man, who came to his friend, desiring him to teach him one of David's Psalms. He read to him this verse. He answered, "This one verse is enough, if I learn it well." Nineteen years after, he said in all that time he had hardly learned that one verse. SAMUEL PAGE

*That I sin not with my tongue.* Tongue sins are great sins; like sparks of fire, ill-words spread and do great damage. If believers utter hard words of God in times of depression, the ungodly will take them up and use them as a justification for their sinful courses. If a man's own children rail at him, no wonder his enemies' mouths are full of abuse. C. H. S.

Man's mouth, though it be but a little hole, will hold a world full of sin. For there is not any sin forbidden in the law or gospel which is not spoken by the tongue as well as thought in the heart or done in the life. Is it not then almost as difficult to rule the tongue as to rule the world? EDWARD REYNER

*I will keep my mouth with a bridle,* or more accurately, with a muzzle. The original does not so much mean a bridle to check the tongue as a muzzle to stop it altogether. David was not quite so wise as our translation would make him; if he had resolved to be very guarded in his speech, it would have been altogether commendable; but when he went so far as to condemn himself to entire silence, "even from good," there must have been at least a little sullenness in his soul. In trying to avoid one fault, he fell into another. To use the tongue against God is a sin of commission, but not to use it at all involves an evident sin of omission. Commendable virtues may be followed so eagerly that we may fall into vices; to avoid Scylla we run into Charybdis.

*While the wicked is before me.* This qualifies the silence and almost screens it from criticism, for bad men are so sure to misuse even our holiest speech that it is as well not to cast any of our pearls before such swine. The firmest believers are exercised with unbelief, and it would be doing the devil's work with a vengeance if they were to publish abroad all their questionings and suspicions. If I have the fever myself, there is no reason why I should communicate it to my neighbors. If any on board the vessel of my soul are diseased, I will put my heart in quarantine and allow none to go on shore in the boat of speech till I have a clean bill of health. C. H. S.

It is a vexation to be tied to hear so much impertinent babbling in the world but profitable to discern and abhor it. A wonder that men can cast out so much wind, and the more they have to utter, the more they are prodigal of their own breath and of the patience of others and careless of their own reckoning. WILLIAM STRUTHER

Vs. 2. *I was dumb with silence.* There is a seven-fold silence: 1. A stoical silence. 2. A politic silence. 3. A foolish silence. 4. A sullen silence. 5. A forced silence. 6. A despairing silence. 7. A prudent, a holy, a gracious silence. THOMAS BROOKS

*I held my peace.* A Christian, being asked what fruit he had by Christ: "Is not this fruit," said he, "not to be moved at your reproaches?" In cases of this nature, we must refer all to God. CHRISTOPHER SUTTON, B.D., in *Disce Vivere*

Verses 2-9. An invalid who had been ordered a couple of pills, took them very absurdly, for, in place of swallowing them at once, he rolled them about in his mouth, ground them to pieces, and so tasted their full bitterness.

Gotthold was present and thus mused: The insults and calumnies of a slanderer and adversary are bitter pills; all do not understand the art of swallowing without chewing them.

To the Christian, however, they are wholesome in many ways. They remind him of his guilt; they try his meekness and patience; they show him what he needs to guard against; and at last they redound to his honor and glory in the sight of Him for Whose sake they were endured.

In respect of the pills of slander, however, as well as the others, it is advisable not to roll them about continually in our minds or judge of them according to the flesh and the world's opinion. This will only increase their bitterness, spread the savor of it to the tongue, and fill the heart with proportional enmity. The true way is to swallow, keep silence, and forget. CHRISTIAN SCRIVER

Vs. 3. *My heart was hot within me.* The friction of inward thoughts produced an intense mental heat. The door of his heart was shut, and with the fire of sorrow burning within, the chamber of his soul soon grew unbearable with heat. Silence is an awful thing for a sufferer; it is the surest method to produce madness.

*While I was musing the fire burned.* While his heart was musing, it was fusing, for the subject was confusing. C. H. S.

What a blessed (shall I say duty or) privilege is prayer! Now, meditation is a help to prayer. Gersom calls it the nurse of prayer. Meditation is like oil to the lamp; the lamp of prayer will soon go out unless meditation cherish and support it.

Meditation and prayer are like two turtles; if you separate one the other dies. A cunning angler observes the time and season when the fish bite the best, and then he throws in the angle; when the heart is warmed by meditation, now is the best season to throw in the angle of prayer and fish for mercy.

After Isaac had been in the field meditating, he was fit for prayer when he came home. When the gun is full of powder, it is fittest to discharge. So when the mind is full of good thoughts, a Christian is fittest by prayer to discharge; now he sends up whole volleys of sighs and groans to heaven.

Meditation hath a double benefit in it—it pours in and pours out; first, it pours good thoughts into the mind, and then it pours out those thoughts again into prayer; meditation first furnisheth with matter to pray and then it furnisheth with a heart to pray. THOMAS WATSON

Meditate so long till thou findest thy heart grow warm in this duty. If, when a man is cold, you ask how long he should stand by the fire? Sure, till he be thoroughly warm and made fit for his work.

So, Christian, thy heart is cold; never a day, no, not the hottest day in summer, but it freezeth there; now, stand at the fire of meditation till thou findest thy affections warmed and thou art made fit for spiritual service. THOMAS WATSON

When the careful magistrates, or officers, of a city break into a suspected house in the night-time, the great question is, "What company have you here?" So when God breaks in upon our dark hearts, the enquiry is, "What thoughts have you here? Why do thoughts arise in your minds? Are ye not become judges of evil thoughts?" (Luke 24:38; James 2:4). FAITHFUL TEAT

*I spake.* The muzzled tongue burst all its bonds. The gag was hurled away. Misery, like murder, will out. You can silence praise, but anguish is clamorous. Resolve or no resolve, heed or no heed, sin or no sin, the impetuous torrent forced for itself a channel and swept away every restraint. C. H. S.

Vs. 4. *Make me to know mine end.* The Psalmist would know more of the shortness of life that he might better bear its transient ills, and herein we may safely kneel with him, uttering the same petition. That there is no end to its misery is the hell of hell; that there is an end to life's sorrow is the hope of all who have a hope beyond the grave. God is the best teacher of the divine philosophy, which looks for an expected end. They who see death through the Lord's glass see a fair sight, which makes them forget the evil of life in foreseeing the end of life. C. H. S.

*That I may know how frail I am,* or when I shall cease to be. Alas, poor human nature, dear as life is, man quarrels with God at such a rate that he would sooner cease to be than bear the Lord's appointment. Such pettishness in a saint! Let us wait till we are in a like position, and we shall do no better. The ship on the stocks wonders that the barque springs a leak, but when it has tried the high seas, it marvels that its timbers hold together in such storms. David's case is not recorded for our imitation but for our learning. C. H. S.

Between Walsall and Iretsy, in Cheshire, is a house built in 1636, of thick oak framework, filled in with brick. Over the window of the taproom is still legible, cut in the oak, a Latin inscription, the sense of which is: "You would weep if you know that your life was limited to one month, yet you laugh while you know not but it may be restricted to a day."

How sad the thought, that with this silent monitor, this truthful sermon before their very eyes, numbers have reveled in soul-destructive inebriation! And yet this is but a likeness of what we see constantly about us. *Quoted in a Monthly Periodical*

Vs. 5. *And mine age is as nothing before Thee.* So short as not to amount to an entity. Think of eternity, and an angel is as a new-born babe, the world a fresh blown bubble, the sun a spark just fallen from the fire, and man a nullity. Before the Eternal, all the age of frail man is less than one ticking of a clock. C. H. S.

If a man be so diminutive a creature compared with the fabric of that great world, and the world itself so little that it cannot contain the Lord, so little and light that He feels not the weight thereof upon the tip of His finger, man will well merit the name "nothing" when he is placed before the Lord. EDMUND LAYFIELDE

*Verily every man at his best state is altogether vanity.* This is the surest truth, that nothing about man is either sure or true. Take man at his best, he is but a man, and man is a mere breath, unsubstantial as the wind. Man is settled, as the margin has it, and by divine decree it is settled that he shall not be settled. He is constant only in inconstancy. His vanity is his only verity; his best, of which he is vain, is but vain. C. H. S.

*Selah.* This is mentioned seventy-four times in the Scripture, whereof seventy-one in the Book of Psalms, and thrice in the Prophet Habakkuk, which is written psalm-wise. EDMUND LAYFIELDE

Vs. 6. *Surely every man walketh in a vain show.* Worldly men walk like travelers in a mirage, deluded, duped, deceived, soon to be filled with disappointment and despair.

*Surely they are disquieted in vain.* Read well this text and then listen to the clamor of the market, the hum of the exchange, the din of the city streets, and remember that all this noise (for so the word means), this breach of quiet, is made about unsubstantial, fleeting vanities. Broken rest, anxious fear, overworked brain, failing mind, lunacy, these are the steps in the process of disquieting with many, and all to be rich or, in other words, to load oneself with the thick clay; clay, too, which a man must leave so soon. C. H. S.

Every carnal man walks *in a vain show,* and yet how vain is he of his show of vanity! He is *disquieted in vain,* and it is only vanity which disquiets him. He labors all his life for the profits of riches, and yet in death his riches will not profit him. He that views an ox grazing in a fat pasture concludes that he is but preparing for the day of slaughter. WILLIAM SECKER

*He heapeth up riches, and knoweth not who shall gather them.* Men rise up early and sit up late to build a house, and then the stranger tramps along its passages, laughs in its chambers, and forgetful of its first builder, calls it all his own. Here is one of the evils under the sun for which no remedy can be prescribed. C. H. S.

The world's trinity consists: 1. In fruitless honors: what appears to them to be substantial honors are but *a vain show.* 2. In needless cares. *They are disquieted in vain.* Imaginary cares are substituted for real ones. 3. In useless riches; such as yield no lasting satisfaction to themselves, or in their descent to others. G. ROGERS

*Tomorrow, and tomorrow, and tomorrow,*
*Creeps in this petty pace from day to day,*
*To the last syllable of recorded time;*
*And all our yesterdays have lighted fools*
*The way to dusty death. Out, out, brief candle!*
*Life's but a walking shadow; a poor player,*
*That struts and frets his hour upon the stage,*
*And then is heard no more; it is a tale*
*Told by an idiot, full of sound and fury,*
*Signifying nothing.*

WILLIAM SHAKESPEARE

Vs. 8. *Deliver me from all my transgressions.* How fair a sign it is when the Psalmist no longer harps upon his sorrows but begs freedom from his sins! What is sorrow when compared with sin! Let but the poison of sin be gone from the cup, and we need not fear its gall, for the bitter will act medicinally. None can deliver a man from his transgression but the blessed One Who is called Jesus, because He saves His people from their sins. C. H. S.

*Make me not the reproach of the foolish.* For the fleshly pleasures of a few days to have bartered thine eternal jewel! For a few grains of yellow earth to have missed the city with streets of gold and gates of several pearls! O fool, beyond all folly! O madman, beyond all insanity! Truly we have need to pray with all earnestness, *Make me not the reproach of the foolish.* ORIGEN, *quoted by J. M. Neale*

Vs. 9. *I was dumb, I opened not my mouth; because Thou didst it.* God is training up His children here. This is the true character of His dealings with them. The education of His saints is the object He has in view. It is training for the kingdom; it is education for eternity. . . . It is the discipline of love. Every step of it is kindness. There is no wrath nor vengeance in any part of the process. The discipline of the school may be harsh and stern; but that of the family is love.

The aged saint was in prison "for the Word of God, and for the testimony of Jesus Christ." The bleeding head of his martyred son, Richard Cameron, was brought to him by his unfeeling persecutors, and he was asked derisively if he knew it. "I know it, I know it," said the father, as he kissed the mangled forehead of his fair-haired son—"it is my son's, my own dear son's! It is the Lord! good is the will of the Lord, Who cannot wrong me or mine, but Who hath made goodness and mercy to follow us all our days." HORATIUS BONAR, in *"The Night of Weeping"*

If the King of kings lays His hand on our backs, let us, beloved, lay our hands on our mouths. NICHOLAS ESTWICK, B.D.

I wondered once at providence, and called white providence black and unjust, that I should be smothered in a town where no soul will take Christ off my hand. But providence hath another luster with God than with my bleared eyes. I proclaim myself a blind body, who knoweth no black and white, in the unco (strange) course of God's providence.

Suppose that Christ should set hell where heaven is, and devils up in glory beside the elect angels (which yet cannot be), I would I had a heart to acquiesce in His way without further dispute. I see that Infinite wisdom is the mother of His judgments, and that His ways pass finding out. SAMUEL RUTHERFORD

A little girl, in the providence of God, was born deaf and dumb. She was received and instructed at an institution established for these afflicted ones. A visitor was one day requested to examine the children thus sadly laid aside from childhood's common joys. Several questions were asked and quickly answered by means of a slate and pencil.

At length the gentleman wrote, "Why were you born deaf and dumb?" A look of anguish clouded for the moment the expressive face of the little girl; but it quickly passed, as she took her slate and wrote, "Even so, Father; for so it seemeth good in Thy sight." MRS. ROGERS, in *"The Shepherd King"*

Vs. 10. *I am consumed by the blow of Thine hand.* Good pleas may be found in our weakness and distress. It is well to show our Father the bruises which His scourge has made, for peradventure His fatherly pity will bind His hands and move Him to comfort us in His bosom. It is not to consume us, but to consume our sins, that the Lord aims at in His chastisements.

Vs. 11. *When Thou with rebukes dost correct man for iniquity.* God does not trifle with His rod; He uses it because of sin, and with a view to whip us from it; hence He means His strokes to be felt, and felt they are.

*Thou makest his beauty to consume away like a moth.* As the moth frets the substance of the fabric, mars all its beauty, and leaves it worn out and worthless, so do the chastisements of God discover to us our folly, weakness, and nothingness, and make us feel ourselves to be as worn-out vestures, worthless, and useless. Beauty must be a poor thing when a moth can consume it and a rebuke can mar it. C. H. S.

The moths of the East are very large and beautiful, but short lived. After a few showers these splendid insects may be seen fluttering in every breeze, but the dry weather, and their numerous enemies, soon consign them to the common lot. Thus the beauty of man consumes away like that of this gay rover, dressed in his robes of purple, and scarlet, and green. JOHN KITTO

Butterflies live only for twenty-four hours. What a tragedy if for one it should be a rainy day. ANON

*Surely every man is vanity.* What is greatness? Can we predicate it of man, independently of his qualities as an immortal being? or of his actions, independently of principles and motives? Then the glitter of nobility is not superior to the plumage of the peacock; nor the valor of Alexander to the fury of a tiger; nor the sensual delights of Epicurus to those of any animal that roams the forest. EBENEZER PORTER, D.D., in *Lectures on Homiletics*

Vs. 12. *Hear my prayer, O Lord.* Now, in this prayer of David, we find three things, which are the chief qualifications of all acceptable prayers. The first is humility. The second qualification of this prayer is fervency and importunity. The third is faith. "He who comes to God must believe that He is, and that He is a rewarder of them that diligently seek Him" (Heb. 11:6). And, certainly, as he that comes to God must believe this, so he that believes this cannot but come to God. *Condensed from* ROBERT LEIGHTON

*Hold not Thy peace at my tears.* Tears speak more eloquently than ten thousand tongues; they act as keys upon the wards of tender hearts, and mercy denies them nothing, if through them the weeper looks to richer drops, even to the blood of Jesus.

*For I am a stranger with Thee, and a sojourner.* Not *to* Thee, but *with* Thee. Like Thee, my Lord, a stranger among the sons of men, an alien from my mother's children. God made the world, sustains it, and owns it, and yet men treat Him as though He were a foreign intruder; and as they treat the Master, so do they deal with the servants. " 'Tis no surprising thing that we should be unknown." These words may also mean, "I share the hospitality of God," like a stranger entertained by a generous host. C. H. S.

How settled soever their condition be, yet this is the temper of the saints upon earth—to count themselves but strangers. All men indeed are strangers and sojourners, but the saints do best discern it, and most freely acknowledge it.

Wicked men have no firm dwelling upon earth, but that is against their intentions; their inward thought and desire is that they may abide forever. They are strangers against their wills; their abode is uncertain in the world; and they cannot help it. THOMAS MANTON

Vs. 13. *O spare me, that I may recover strength, before I go hence and be no more.* Man in his corrupt state is like Nebuchadnezzar—he hath a beast's heart that craves no more than the satisfaction of his sensual appetite; but when renewed by grace, then his understanding returns to him.

David was not yet recovered out of that sin which had brought him exceeding low, as you may perceive (vss. 10-11). And the good man cannot think of dying with any willingness till his heart be in a holier frame: and for the peace of the gospel, serenity of conscience, and inward joy; alas! all unholiness is to it as poison is to the spirits which drink them up. WILLIAM GURNALL

# PSALM 40

Subject: Jesus is evidently here, and although it might not be a violent wrestling of language to see both David and his Lord, both Christ and the church, the double comment might involve itself in obscurity, and therefore we shall let the sun shine even though this should conceal the stars. Even if the New Testament were not so express upon it, we should have concluded that David spoke of our Lord in verses 6-9, but the apostle in Heb. 10:5-9 puts all conjecture out of court and confines the meaning to Him Who came into the world to do the Father's will.

Vs. 1. *I waited patiently for the Lord.* Patient waiting upon God was a special characteristic of our Lord Jesus. Impatience never lingered in His heart, much less escaped His lips. All through His agony in the Garden, His trial of cruel mockings before Herod and Pilate, and His passion on the tree, He waited in omnipotence of patience.

No glance of wrath, no word of murmuring, no deed of vengeance came from God's patient Lamb; He waited and waited on; was patient, and patient to perfection, far excelling all others who have according to their measure glorified God in the fires. Job on the dunghill does not equal Jesus on the cross. The Christ of God wears the imperial crown among the patient. Did the Only Begotten wait, and shall we be petulant and rebellious? C. H. S.

*I waited patiently.* Rather *anxiously;* the original has it, *waiting I waited;* a Hebraism, which signifies vehement solicitude. DANIEL CRESSWELL

Our Lord's patience under suffering was an element of perfection in His work. Had He become impatient, as we often do, and lost heart, His atonement would have been vitiated. Well may we rejoice that in the midst of all His temptations and in the thickest of the battle against sin and Satan, He remained patient and willing to finish the work which His Father had given Him to do. JAMES FRAME

Vs. 2. *An horrible pit.* Some of the pits referred to in the Bible were prisons, one such I saw at Athens, and another at Rome. To these there were no openings, except a hole at the top which served for both door and window. The bottoms of these pits were necessarily in a filthy and revolting state, and sometimes deep in mud.—JOHN GADSBY

*Out of the miry clay.* Once give man a good foothold, and a burden is greatly lightened, but to be loaded and to be placed on slimy, slippery clay, is to be tried doubly.

Vs. 3. *And He hath put a new song in my mouth, even praise unto our God.* At the Passover, before His passion, our Lord sang one of the grand old Psalms of praise; but what is the music of His heart now, in the midst of His redeemed! What a song is that in which His glad heart forever leads the chorus of the elect! Not Miriam's tabor, nor Moses' triumphant hymn o'er Miriam's chivalry can for a moment rival that ever new and exulting song.

Justice magnified and grace victorious; hell subdued and heaven glorified; death destroyed and immortality established; sin o'erthrown and righteousness resplendent; what a theme for a hymn in that day when our Lord drinketh the red wine new with us all in our heavenly Father's kingdom! C. H. S.

*Many shall see it, and fear, and shall trust in the Lord.* But while the sinner only sees and fears, he is but in the initial stage of conversion, only in a state of readiness to flee from the city of destruction. He may have set out on his pilgrimage, but he has not yet reached his Father to receive the kiss of welcome and forgiveness.

The consummating step has not yet been taken. He has seen indeed; he has feared, too; but he still requires to trust, to trust in the Lord, and banish all his fears. This is the culminating point in the great change; and, unless this be reached, the other experiences will either die away, like an untimely blossom, or they will only be fuel to the unquenchable fire. JAMES FRAME

Vs. 4. *Blessed is that man that maketh the Lord his trust.* Faith obtaineth promises. A simple, single-eyed confidence in God is the sure mark of blessedness. A man may be as poor as Lazarus, as hated as Mordecai, as sick as Hezekiah, as lonely as Elijah, but while his hand of faith can keep its hold on God, none of his outward afflictions can prevent his being numbered among the blessed.

*Nor such as turn aside to lies.* We must never pay deference to apostates, time-servers, and false teachers; they are an ill leaven, and the more we purge ourselves of them the better; they are blessed whom God preserves from all error in creed and practice. Verily, were the archfiend of hell to start a carriage and pair, and live like a lord, he would have thousands who would court his acquaintance.

Vs. 6. Here we enter upon one of the most wonderful passages in the whole of the Old Testament, a passage in which the incarnate Son of God is seen not through a glass darkly, but as it were face to face.

*Sacrifice and offering Thou didst not desire.* In themselves considered, and for their own sakes, the Lord saw nothing satisfactory in the various offerings of the ceremonial law. Neither the victim pouring forth its blood, nor the fine flour rising in smoke from the altar, could yield content to Jehovah's mind; He cared not for the flesh of bulls or of goats, neither had He pleasure in corn and wine and oil.

Typically these offerings had their worth, but when Jesus, the Antitype, came into the world, they ceased to be of value, as candles are of no estimation when the sun has arisen. C. H. S.

*Mine ears hast Thou opened.* The literal translation is, *mine ears hast Thou digged* (or *pierced*) *through;* which may well be interpreted as meaning, "Thou hast accepted me as Thy slave," an allusion to the custom (Exod. 21:6) of masters boring the ear of a slave who had refused his offered freedom, in token of retaining him. DANIEL CRESSWELL

*Burnt offering and sin offering hast Thou not required.* We learn from this verse that Jehovah values far more the obedience of the heart than all the imposing performances of ritualistic worship; and that our expiation from sin comes not to us as the result of an elaborate ceremonial, but as the effect of our great Substitute's obedience to the will of Jehovah.

Vs. 7. *Lo, I come.* Behold, O heavens, and thou earth, and ye places under the earth! Here is something worthy of your intensest gaze. Sit ye down and watch with earnestness, for the invisible God comes in the likeness of sinful flesh, and as an infant the Infinite hangs at a virgin's breast!

Immanuel did not send, but *came;* He came in His own personality, in all that constituted His essential self. He came forth from the ivory palaces to the abodes of misery; He came promptly at the destined hour; He came with sacred alacrity as one freely offering Himself. C. H. S.

As His name is above every name, so this coming of His is above every coming. We sometimes call our own births, I confess, a coming into the world; but properly, none ever came into the world, but He. For, 1. He only truly can be said to come, Who is before He comes; so were not we, only He so.

2. He only strictly comes who comes willingly; our crying and struggling at our entrance into the world shows how unwilling we come into it. He alone it is that sings out, *Lo, I come.* 3. He only properly comes who comes from some place or other. Alas! we had none to come from but the womb of nothing. He only had a place to be in before He came. MARK FRANK

Vs. 8. *I delight to do Thy will, O my God.* Did Christ find pleasure in abasement and torment, in suffering and dying for me, and can I find no pleasure in praying, hearing, meditating, and enjoying the sweet duties of communion with Him? Did He come so cheerfully to die for me, and do I go so dead-heartedly to prayers and sacraments to enjoy fellowship with Him? Was it a pleasure to Him to shed His blood, and is it none to me to apply it, and reap the benefits of it?

Oh, let there be no more grumblings, lazy excuses, shiftings of duty, or dead-hearted and listless performances of them, after such an example as this. Be ready to do the will of God; be ye also ready to suffer it. And as to sufferings for Christ, they should not be grievous to Christians that know how cheerfully Christ came from the bosom of the Father to die for them.

What have we to leave or lose in comparison with Him? What are our sufferings to Christ's? Alas! there is no comparison; there was more bitterness in one drop of His sufferings than in a sea of ours. To conclude: your delight and readiness in the paths of obedience is the very measure of your sanctification. *Condensed from* JOHN FLAVEL

It was Jesus Who was the doer of the work. The Father willed it; but He did not do it. It was Jesus Who did it, Who wrought it out; Who brought it in; Who carried it within the veil, and laid it as an acceptable and meritorious offering at the feet of His well-pleased Father.

The work then is done; it is finished. We need not attempt to do it. We cannot do it. We cannot do that which is already done; and we could not do it, though it were yet undone. There is much that man can do, but he cannot make a propitiation. JAMES FRAME

*Yea, Thy law is within my heart.* No outward, formal devotion was rendered by Christ; His heart was in His work, holiness was His element, the Father's will His meat and drink. We must each of us be like our Lord in this, or we shall lack the evidence of being His disciples. Where there is no heart work, no pleasure, no delight in God's law, there can be no acceptance. C. H. S.

He was as willing to bleed and die for thee as thou art to eat when hungry. He was delighted as much to be scourged, wounded, crucified, as thou delightest in meat, when most delicious. DAVID CLARKSON

Vs. 9. *I have preached righteousness.* It is Jesus Who speaks, and He speaks of Himself as a Preacher. He was a preacher, and a great preacher, too. He was great: 1. In genuine eloquence. All the handmaids of the choicest rhetoric ministered to Him as He spoke. His mind touched the minds of His auditors on all sides.

2. He was great in knowledge. Many who have an astonishing command of words, and who can use their words with astonishing rhetorical adroitness, spoil their influence by their "lack of knowledge." They go blundering onward when they attempt to think for themselves or to guide their hearers into fields of thought which have not been tracked by minds of the pioneer order. 3. He was great also in goodness. There is a greatness in goodness, and the greatness of goodness is an important element in the greatness of a preacher.

4. Another element still in the greatness of Jesus as a Preacher, consisted in the greatness of His essential dignity. He was God as well as man. Such was Christ as a Preacher. True He was more than a preacher; He was likewise a Pattern, and a Priest, and a Propitiator; and as pattern, priest, and propiti-

ator, He stands without a peer. But He was a Preacher, too, and as a Preacher, He has never had, and never will have an equal. *Condensed from* JAMES FRAME

*Lo, I have not refrained my lips, O Lord, Thou knowest.* Never either from love of ease, or fear of men, did the Great Teacher's lips become closed. He was instant in season and out of season. The poor listened to Him, and princes heard His rebuke; Publicans rejoiced at Him, and Pharisees raged, but to them both He proclaimed the truth from heaven. C. H. S.

Verses 9-10. *I have published . . . I would not refrain . . . I have not covered . . . I have uttered . . . I have not hid.* Words are heaped upon words to express the eager forwardness of a heart burning to show forth its gratitude. No elaborate description could so well have given us the likeness of One Whose "life was a thanksgiving." J. J. STEWART PEROWNE

Vs. 10. *I have not hid.* This intimates that whoever undertook to preach the gospel of Christ would be in great temptation to hide it, and conceal it, because it must be preached with great contention, and in the face of great opposition. MATTHEW HENRY

*I have not concealed Thy lovingkindness and Thy truth from the great congregation.* The tender as well as the stern attributes of God, our Lord Jesus fully unveiled. Concealment was far from the Great Apostle of our profession. Cowardice He never exhibited, hesitancy never weakened His language.

He Who as a child of twelve years spake in the temple among the doctors, and afterwards preached to five thousand at Gennesaret, and to the vast crowds at Jerusalem on that great day, the last day of the feast, was always ready to proclaim the name of the Lord and could never be charged with unholy silence.

Vs. 12. *Mine iniquities have taken hold upon me, so that I am not able to look up.* He had no sin, but sins were laid on Him, and He took them as if they were His. "He was made sin for us." O my soul, what would thy sins have done for thee eternally if the Friend of sinners had not condescended to take them all upon Himself?

*They are more than the hairs of mine head.*

*Sins against a holy God;*
*Sins against His righteous laws;*
*Sins against His love, His blood;*
*Sins against His Name and cause;*
*Sins immense as is the sea—*
*Hide me, O Gethsemane!*

C. H. S.

The Apostle makes every sin tenfold (James 2:10). That which seems one to us, according to the sense of the law and the account of God, is multiplied by ten. He breaks every command by sinning directly against one, and so sins ten times at once; besides that swarm of sinful circumstances and aggravations which surround every act in such numbers, as atoms use to surround your body in a dusty room; you may more easily number these than those.

And though some count these but fractions, incomplete sins, yet even from hence it is more difficult to take an account of their number. And, which is more for astonishment, pick out the best religious duty that ever you performed, and even in that performance you may find such a swarm of sins as cannot be numbered.

In the best prayer that ever you put up to God, irreverence, lukewarmness, unbelief, spiritual pride, self-seeking, hypocrisy, distractions, etc., and many more, that an enlightened soul grieves and bewails; and yet there are many more that the pure eye of God discerns than any man does take notice of. DAVID CLARKSON

Vs. 13. The remaining verses of this Psalm are almost exactly identical with Psalm 70.

Vs. 14. *Let them be ashamed and confounded together that seek after my soul to destroy it.* It is to the infinite confusion of Satan that his attempts to destroy the Savior destroyed himself; the diabolical conclave who plotted in council are now all alike put to shame, for the Lord Jesus has met them at all points and turned all their wisdom into foolishness.

Vs. 15. *For a reward of their shame that say unto me, Aha, aha.* Do wicked men today pour shame upon the name of the Redeemer? Their desolation shall avenge Him of His adversaries! Jesus is the gentle Lamb to all who seek mercy through His blood; but let despisers beware, for He is the Lion of the tribe of Judah, and "who shall rouse Him up?" O ungodly reader, if such a person glance over this page, beware of persecuting Christ and His people, for God will surely avenge His own elect. Your "ahas" will cost you dear. It is hard for you to kick against the pricks.

Vs. 16. *Let all those that seek Thee rejoice and be glad in Thee.* He groaned that we might sing and was covered with a bloody sweat that we might be anointed with the oil of gladness. C. H. S.

Vs. 17. *Yet the Lord thinketh upon me.* He that turns the hearts of kings like rivers at His pleasure turns all the little brooks in the world into what scorched and parched ground He pleases. SAMUEL LEE

There are three things in God's thinking upon us that are solacing and delightful. Observe the *frequency* of His thoughts. Indeed, they are incessant. You have a friend whom you esteemed and love. You wish to live in his mind. You say when you part and when you write, "Think of me." You give him, perhaps, a token to revive his remembrance.

But the dearest connection in the world cannot be always thinking upon you. Half his time he is in a state of unconsciousness; and how much during the other half is he engrossed! But there is no remission in the Lord's thoughts.

Observe in the next place, the *wisdom* of His thoughts. You have a dear child, absent from you, and you follow him in your mind. But you know not his present circumstances. You left him in such a place; but where is he now? You left him in such a condition; but what is he now?

Perhaps while you are thinking upon his health, he is groaning under a bruised limb or a painful disorder. Perhaps while you are thinking of his safety, some enemy is taking advantage of his innocency. Perhaps while you are rejoicing in his prudence, he is going to take a step that will involve him for life.

But when God thinketh upon you, He is perfectly acquainted with your situation, your dangers, your wants.

Again, observe the *efficiency* of His thoughts. He Who thinks upon you is a God at hand and not afar off; He has all events under His control; He is the God of all grace. WILLIAM JAY

In Dr. Malan's memoir, the editor, one of his sons, thus writes of his brother Jocelyn, who was for some years prior to his death the subject of intense bodily sufferings: "One striking feature in his character was his holy fear of God and reverence for His will."

One day I was repeating a verse from the Psalms: *As for me, I am poor and needy, but the Lord careth for me: Thou art my helper and deliverer; O Lord, make no long tarrying.* He said, "Mamma, I love that verse, all but the last bit, it looks like a murmur against God. He never 'tarries' in my case." *From "The Life, Labors, and Writings of* CÆSAR MALAN," *by one of His sons*

# PSALM 41

Jesus Christ, betrayed of Judas Iscariot, is evidently the great theme of this Psalm but, we think, not exclusively. He is the antitype of David, and all His people are in their measure like Him, hence words suitable to the Great Representative are most applicable to those who are in Him.

Such as receive a vile return for long kindness to others may read this song with much comfort, for they will see that it is, alas, too common for the best of men to be rewarded for their holy charity with cruelty and scorn; and when they have been humbled by falling into sin, advantage has been taken of their low estate, their good deeds have been forgotten, and the vilest spite has been vented upon them.

Vs. 1. *Blessed is he that considereth the poor.* Such as have been made partakers of divine grace receive a tenderer nature and are not hardened against their own flesh and blood; they undertake the cause of the downtrodden and turn their minds seriously to the promotion of their welfare. They do not toss them a penny and go on their way, but enquire into their sorrows, sift out their cause, study the best ways for their relief, and practically come to their rescue. C. H. S.

Not the poor of the world in common, nor poor saints in particular, but some single poor man; for the word is in the singular number, and designs our Lord Jesus Christ, Who, in the last verse of the preceding Psalm, is said to be poor and needy. JOHN GILL

To give money is not to do all the work and labor of benevolence. You must go to the poor man's sick-bed. You must lend your hand to the work of assistance. This is true and unsophisticated goodness. *From a Sermon by* THOMAS CHALMERS

A Piedmontese nobleman into whose company I fell, at Turin, told me the following story: "I was weary of life, and after a day such as few have known, and none would wish to remember, was hurrying along the street to the river, when I felt a sudden check; I turned and beheld a little boy who had caught the skirt of my cloak in his anxiety to solicit my notice. His look and manner were irresistible. No less so was the lesson he had learnt—'There are six of us, and we are dying for want of food.'

"'Why should I not,' said I, to myself, 'relieve this wretched family? I have the means, and it will not delay me many minutes. But what if it does?' The scene of misery he conducted to me I cannot describe. I threw them my purse, and their burst of gratitude overcame me. It filled my eyes; it went as a cordial to my heart. 'I will call again tomorrow,' I cried. 'Fool that I was to think of leaving a world where such pleasure was to be had, and so cheaply!'" SAMUEL ROGERS, in "*Italy*"

*An ardent spirit dwells with Christian love,*
*The eagle's vigor in the pitying dove.*
*'Tis not enough that we with sorrow sigh,*
*That we the wants of pleading man supply,*
*That we in sympathy with sufferers feel,*
*Nor hear a grief without a wish to heal:*
*Not these suffice—to sickness, pain, and woe,*
*The Christian spirit loves with aid to go:*
*Will not be sought, waits not for want to plead,*
*But seeks the duty—nay, prevents the need;*
*Her utmost aid to every ill applies,*
*And plants relief for coming miseries.* GEORGE CRABBE

How foolish are they that fear to lose their wealth by giving it and fear not to lose themselves by keeping it! He that lays up his gold may be a good jailer, but he that lays it out is a good steward. Do good while it is in your power; relieve the oppressed, succor the fatherless, while your estates are your own; when you are dead your riches belong to others. One light carried before a man is more serviceable than twenty carried after him. In your compassion to the distressed, or for pious uses, let your hands be your executors and your eyes your overseers. FRANCIS RAWORTH, in a *Funeral Sermon*

*The Lord will deliver him in time of trouble.* The promise is not that the generous saint shall have no trouble but that he shall be preserved in it and in due time brought out of it. How true was this of our Lord! never trouble deeper nor triumph brighter than His, and glory be to His name, He secures the ultimate victory of all His blood-bought ones.

Selfishness bears in itself a curse; it is a cancer in the heart; while liberality is happiness, and maketh fat the bones. In dark days, we cannot rest upon the supposed merit of almsgiving, but still the music of memory brings with it no mean solace when it tells of widows and orphans whom we have succored and prisoners and sick folk to whom we have ministered. C. H. S.

Verses 1, 5. *He that considereth. Mine enemies.* Strigelius has observed, there is a perpetual antithesis in this Psalm between the few who have a due regard to the poor in spirit and the many who afflict or desert them. W. WILSON

Vs. 2. *The Lord will preserve him and keep him alive.* The miser, like the hog, is of no use till he is dead—then let him die; the righteous, like the ox, is of service during life—then let him live.

*And he shall be blessed upon the earth.*

*There was a man, and some did count him mad,*
*The more he gave away the more he had.*

Vs. 3. *The Lord will strengthen him upon the bed of languishing.* The everlasting arms shall stay up his soul as friendly hands and downy pillows stay up the body of the sick. How tender and sympathizing is this image; how near it brings our God to our infirmities and sicknesses! Who ever heard this of the old heathen Jove, or of the gods of India, or China?

This is the language peculiar to the God of Israel; He it is Who deigns to become nurse and attendant upon good men. If He smites with one hand, He sustains with the other. Oh, it is blessed fainting when one falls upon the Lord's own bosom and is upborne thereby! C. H. S.

*Thou wilt make all his bed in his sickness.* But, oh! how shall God make my bed, who have no bed of mine own to make? Thou fool, He can make thy not having a bed to be a bed unto thee. When Jacob slept on the ground, who would not have had his hard lodging, therewithal to have his heavenly dream? THOMAS FULLER

When I visted one day, as he was dying, my beloved friend, Benjamin Parsons, I said, "How are you today, Sir?" He said, "My head is resting very sweetly on three pillows—Infinite power, Infinite love, and Infinite wisdom." PAXTON HOOD, in "*Dark Sayings on a Harp*"

Vs. 4. *For I have sinned against Thee.* Sin and suffering are inevitable companions. Observe that by the Psalmist, sin was felt to be mainly evil because directed against God. This is of the essence of true repentance. Applying the petition to David and other sinful believers, how strangely evangelical is the argument: heal me, not for I am innocent, but *I have sinned.* How contrary is this to all self-righteous pleading! How consonant with grace! How inconsistent with merit!

Even the fact that the confessing penitent had remembered the poor is but obliquely urged, but a direct appeal is made to Mercy on the ground of great sin. O trembling reader, here is a divinely revealed precedent for thee, be not slow to follow it. C. H. S.

Saul and Judas each said, "I have sinned"; but David says, "I have sinned against Thee." WILLIAM S. PLUMER

Vs. 5. *When shall he die, and his name perish?* If persecutors could have their way, the church should have but one neck, and that should be on the block. Thieves would fain blow out all candles. The lights of the world are not the delights of the world. Poor, blind bats, they fly at the lamp and try to dash it down. C. H. S.

It is the *name,* the character, and privileges of a true servant of God that calls out the hatred of ungodly men, and they would gladly extirpate Him from their sight. W. WILSON

Vs. 6. *And if he come to see me, he speaketh vanity.* His visits of sympathy are visitations of mockery. When the fox calls on the sick lamb, his words are soft but he licks his lips in hope of the carcass.

*His heart gathered iniquity to itself.* Like will to like. The bird makes its nest of feathers. Out of the sweetest flowers, chemists can distil poison, and from the purest words and deeds malice can gather groundwork for caluminous report. It is perfectly marvelous how spite spins webs out of no materials whatever. C. H. S.

I remember a pretty apologue that Bromiard tells: A fowler, in a sharp, frosty morning, having taken many little birds for which he had long watched, began to take up his nets and, nipping the birds on the head, laid them down.

A young thrush, espying the tears trickling down his cheeks by reason of the extreme cold, said to her mother that certainly the man was very merciful and compassionate who wept so bitterly over the calamity of the poor birds. But her mother told her more wisely, that she might better judge of the man's disposition by his hand than by his eye; and if the hands do strike treacherously, he can never be admitted to friendship who speaks fairly and weeps pitifully. JEREMY TAYLOR

Vs. 7. *All that hate me whisper together against me.* The spy meets his comrades in conclave and sets them all a whispering. Why could they not speak out? Were they afraid of the sick warrior? Or were their designs so treacherous that they must needs be hatched in secrecy?

Mark the unanimity of the wicked—*all.* How heartily the dogs unite to hunt the stag! Would God we were half as united in holy labor as persecutors in their malicious projects, and were half as wise as they are crafty, for their whispering was craft as well as cowardice, the conspiracy must not be known till all is ready.

Vs. 9. *Yea, mine own familiar friend.* "The man of my peace," so runs the original, with whom I had no differences, with whom I was in league, who had aforetime ministered to my peace and comfort. This was Ahithophel to David, and Iscariot with our Lord.

Judas was an apostle, admitted to the privacy of the Great Teacher, bearing His secret thoughts, and, as it were, allowed to read His very heart. *Et tu Brute?* said the expiring Cæsar. The kiss of the traitor wounded our Lord's heart as much as the nail wounded His hand. C. H. S.

The sufferings of the church, like those of her Redeemer, generally begin at home: her open enemies can do her no harm until her pretended friends have delivered her into their hands; and, unnatural as it may seem, they who have waxed fat upon her bounty are sometimes the first to "lift the heel" against her. GEORGE HORNE

Vs. 11. *By this I know that Thou favorest me.* As Mary and Martha put Christ in mind but of two things; the first was, that Christ loved their brother Lazarus; the second was, that Lazarus was sick; "He whom Thou lovest is sick": it was no need to tell Him what He should do, for they knew He would do what might be done for him because He loved him.

So we may say to the Lord, when we are sure that He loveth us: "Lord, he whom Thou loveth wanteth this or that for his body or his soul." We need not then appoint Him what to do, or when, or how; for look what He seeth most convenient for us, and for His own glory, He will surely do it. WILLIAM BURTON

*Because mine enemy doth not triumph over me.* When God doth deliver us from the hands of our enemies, or any trouble else, we may persuade ourselves thereby, He hath a favor unto us, as David did.

But then it may be demanded, if God doth love His church, why doth He suffer His church to be troubled and molested with enemies? The reason is this—because by this means His love may be made more manifest in saving and delivering them. For as a sure friend is not known but in time of need, so God's goodness and love is never so well perceived as it is in helping of us when we cannot help ourselves. WILLIAM BURTON

Vs. 12. *And as for me, Thou upholdest me in mine integrity.* We are like those glasses without feet, which can only be upright while they are held in the hand; we fall, and spill, and spoil all, if left to ourselves. The Lord should be praised every day if we are preserved from gross sin. When others sin, they show us what we should be but for grace. "He today and I tomorrow," was the exclamation of a holy man whenever he saw another falling into sin. C. H. S.

This same integrity is like Noah's ark, wherein he was preserved when others perished, being without it. It is like the red thread, which the spies of Joshua gave to Rahab, it was a charter whereby she claimed her life when the rest were destroyed, which had not the like.

So is this integrity of small reckoning, I confess, with the men of this world, which think that there is no other heaven but earth; but as Rahab's thread was better to her than all her goods, and substance when the sword came, so this is better to God's children than all the world when death comes. WILLIAM BURTON

Vs. 13. The Psalm ends with a doxology. *Blessed be the Lord,* i.e., let Him be glorified. The blessing at the beginning from the mouth of God is returned from the mouth of His servant. We cannot add to the Lord's blessedness, but we can pour out our grateful wishes, and these He accepts, as we receive little presents of flowers from children who love us. C. H. S.

## HERE ENDETH THE FIRST BOOK OF THE PSALMS

# PSALM 42

Title: It is always edifying to listen to the experience of a thoroughly gracious and much afflicted saint.

Although David is not mentioned as the author, this Psalm must be the offspring of his pen; it is so Davidic, it smells of the son of Jesse; it bears the marks of his style and experience in every letter. We could sooner doubt the authorship of the second part of *Pilgrim's Progress* than question David's title to be the composer of this Psalm. C. H. S.

*Sons of Korah.* Mediaeval writers remark how here, as so often, it was the will of God to raise up saints where they could have been least looked for. Who should imagine that from the posterity of him who said, "Ye take too much upon you, ye sons of Aaron," should have risen those whose sweet Psalms would be the heritage of the church of God to the end of time? J. M. NEALE

Subject: It is the cry of a man far removed from the outward ordinances and worship of God, sighing for the long-loved house of his God; and at the same time it is the voice of a spiritual believer, under depressions, longing for the renewal of the divine presence, struggling with doubts and fears, but yet holding his ground by faith in the living God.

Vs. 1. *As the hart panteth after the water brooks, so panteth my soul after Thee, O God.* Debarred from public worship, David was heartsick. Ease he did not seek; honor he did not covet; but the enjoyment of communion with God was an urgent need of his soul. He viewed it not merely as the sweetest of all luxuries but as an absolute necessity, like water to a stag.

Give him his God, and he is as content as the poor deer, which at length slakes its thirst and is perfectly happy; but deny him his Lord, and his heart heaves, his bosom palpitates, his whole frame is convulsed, like one who gasps for breath or pants with long running.

Dear reader, dost thou know what this is, by personally having felt the same? It is a sweet bitterness. The next best thing to living in the light of the Lord's love is to be unhappy till we have it, and to pant hourly after it—hourly, did I say? Thirst is a perpetual appetite, and not to be forgotten, and even thus continual is the heart's longing after God.

When it is as natural for us to long for God as for an animal to thirst, it is well with our souls, however painful our feelings. We may learn from this verse that the eagerness of our desires may be pleaded with God, and the more so because there are special promises for the importunate and fervent. C. H. S.

Little do the drunkards think that take so much pleasure in frequenting the houses of Bacchus, that the godly take a great deal more, and have a great deal more joy in frequenting the houses of God. ZACHARY BOGAN

Vs. 2. *My soul thirsteth for God.* See that your heart rest not short of Christ in any duty. Let go your hold of no duty until you find something of Christ in it; and until you get not only an handful, but an armful (with old Simeon, Luke 2:28); yea, a heartful of the blessed and beautiful babe of Bethlehem therein. Indeed you should have commerce with heaven, and communion with Christ in duty, which is therefore called the presence of God, or your appearing before Him.

Augustine said he loved not Tully's elegant orations (as formerly) because he could not find Christ in them: nor doth a gracious soul love empty duties.

Rhetorical flowers and flourishes, expressions without impressions in praying or preaching, are not true bread, but a tinkling cymbal to it. CHRISTOPHER NESS'S *"Chrystal Mirrour"*

*For the living God.* A dead God is a mere mockery; we loathe such a monstrous deity; but the ever-living God, the perennial fountain of life and light and love, is our soul's desire.

*When shall I come and appear before God?* "To see the face of God" is a nearer translation of the Hebrews; but the two ideas may be combined—he would see his God and be seen of Him: this is worth thirsting after! C. H. S.

A wicked man can never say in good earnest, *When shall I come and appear before God?* because he shall do so too soon, and before he would, as the devils that said Christ came "to torment them before their time." Ask a thief and a malefactor whether he would willingly appear before the judge. No, I warrant you, not he; he had rather there were no judge at all to appear before. And so it is with worldly men in regard of God—they desire rather to be hidden from Him. THOMAS HORTON

If you attempt to put a little child off with toys and fine things, it will not be pleased long; it will cry for its mother's breast. So, let a man come into the pulpit with pretty Latin and Greek sentences and fine stories; these will not content a hungry soul. He must have the sincere milk of the Word to feed upon. OLIVER HEYWOOD

Vs. 3. *My tears have been my meat day and night.* Salt meats, but healthful to the soul. When a man comes to tears, constant tears, plenteous tears, tears that fill his cup and trencher, he is in earnest indeed. Perhaps it was well for him that the heart could open the safety valves; there is a dry grief far more terrible than showery sorrows.

*While they continually say unto me, Where is thy God?* The wicked know that our worst misfortune would be to lose God's favor; hence their diabolical malice leads them to declare that such is the case. C. H. S.

What is become of your God that you bragged so of, and thought yourselves so happy in, as if He had been nobody's God but yours? We may learn hence the disposition of wicked men. It is a character of a poisonful, cursed disposition to upbraid a man with his religion.

*Where is thy God?* So the devil dealt with the Head of the church, our blessed Savior Himself, when he came to tempt Him. "If Thou be the Son of God, command these stones to be made bread" (Matt. 4:3). He comes with an "if"; he labored to shake Him in His Sonship. The devil, since he was divided from God Himself eternally, is become a spirit of division; he labors to divide even God the Father from His own Son—"If thou be the Son of God?"

So he labors to sever Christians from their Head, Christ. *Where is thy God?* There was his scope, to breed division if he could, between his heart and God, that he might call God into jealousy, as if he had not regarded him: thou hast taken a great deal of pains in serving thy God; thou seest how He regards thee now. *Where is thy God?* RICHARD SIBBES

Vs. 4. *I pour out my soul.* The very soul of prayer lies in the pouring out of the soul before God. THOMAS BROOKS

*For I had gone with the multitude, I went with them to the house of God, with the voice of joy and praise, with a multitude that kept holyday.* What a degradation to supplant the intelligent song of the whole congregation by the theatrical prettiness of a quartet, the refined niceties of a choir, or the blowing off of wind from inanimate bellows and pipes! We might as well pray by machinery as praise by it. C. H. S.

The gracious God is pleased to esteem it His glory to have many beggars thronging at the beautiful gate of His temple, for spiritual and corporal alms.

What an honor is it to our great Landlord that multitudes of tenants flock together to His house to pay their rent of thanks and worship for their all which they hold of Him! GEORGE SWINNOCK

Vs. 5. *Why art thou cast down, O my soul?* To search out the cause of our sorrow is often the best surgery for grief. Self-ignorance is not bliss; in this case it is misery. The mist of ignorance magnifies the causes of our alarm; a clearer view will make monsters dwindle into trifles. C. H. S.

Think of this, ye that feel the heaviness of your soul; think of it, ye that do not, for ye may feel it. Know there is a sorrow "that worketh repentance not to be repented of." Know again there is a sorrow "that worketh death."

Rmember that there were tears that got sinful Mary heaven; remember again, there were tears that got sinful Esau nothing. For as in martyrdom, it is not the sword, the boiling lead, or fire, not what we suffer, but *why*, that justifies them. BRIAN DUPPA, *in a Sermon entitled "The Soule's Soliloquie"*

Wicked men oppressed David, and the devil tempted him; yet he chides his own heart and nothing else. David did not chide at Saul, nor chide at Absalom; but he chides and checks his own heart. *Why art thou cast down, O my soul?* Though the devil and wicked men, the one do tempt, the other do oppress as instruments of punishment for sin; yet we with David are to chide our own hearts. CHRISTOPHER LOVE, *in "The Dejected Soul's Cure"*

*Why art thou disquieted?* more literally, *tumultuated,* a word frequently applied to the roaring and tumult and tossing of the sea. See Isa. 17:12; Jer. 5:22; 6:23; 51:55. HENRY MARCH

*Hope thou in God.* Hope never affords more joy than in affliction. It is on a watery cloud that the sun paints those curious colors in the rainbow . . . There are two graces, which Christ useth above any other, to fill the soul with joy—faith and hope, because these two fetch all their wine of joy without dour. Faith tells the soul what Christ hath done for it; and so comforts it; hope revives the soul with the news of what Christ will do: both draw at one tap—Christ and His promise. *Condensed from* WILLIAM GURNALL

*I shall yet praise Him for the help of His countenance.* When it may be said, "He whom God loveth is sick," then it may be said, "This sickness is not unto death"; and though it be to the first death, yet not to the second.

Who would think when Jonah was in the sea (Jonah 3), that he would preach at Nineveh? Who would think when Nebuchadnezzar was in the forest (Daniel 4), that he should reign again in Babel? Who would think when Joseph was banished of his brethren, that his brethren should seek unto him like his servants?

Who would think when Job scraped his sores upon the dunghill, all his houses were burned, all his cattle stolen, and all his children dead, that he should be richer than ever he was? These are the acts of mercy which make the righteous sing, "The Lord hath triumphed valiantly" (Exod. 15:21). HENRY SMITH

Think it not enough to silence thy heart from quarreling with God, but leave not till thou canst bring it sweetly to rely on God. Holy David drove it thus far, he did not only chide his soul for being disquieted, but he charges it to trust in God. WILLIAM GURNALL

Verses 5, 11. It is not so much the weight of the burden as the soreness of the back that troubles the poor beast: so it is not so much the weight of outward evils as the inward soreness of a galled conscience, not purified nor healed by faith, that vexeth and troubleth the poor creature. MATTHEW LAWRENCE in *"The Use and Practice of Faith"*

The foolish bird, who being in a room whose door is locked and the casements shut, beateth herself against the wall and windows, breaking her feathers and bruising her body, whereas, would she stay till the passages were by the keeper opened, she might depart, being not at all wounded; even so falleth it out with us.

When the Lord doth shut us up, and straiten our liberty for a time, we would fain make way for ourselves, having many devices in our hearts to break through the walls of His providence; whereas, if we would stay His leisure, depend on His promise, and submit ourselves to be disposed of by His hand, we might with more ease endure this prison, and with less hurt at the last be set at liberty. For God is in one mind, and who can change Him? He will bring to pass that thing that He hath decreed upon us. JOHN BARLOW'S SERMON

If you would get assurance, spend more time in strengthening your evidences for heaven than in questioning of them. It is the great fault of many Christians: they will spend much time in questioning, and not in strengthening their comforts. They will reason themselves into unbelief, and say, "Lord, why should I believe?" CHRISTOPHER LOVE

Vs. 6. *My God.* Astonishing expression! Who shall dare to say to the Creator of the ends of the earth, the Majesty in the heavens, *My God?* An exile, a wanderer, an outcast; a man forsaken, despised, reviled; a soul cast down and disquieted: he shall dare. By what right? Of covenant. HENRY MARCH

*Therefore will I remember Thee.* It is great wisdom to store up in memory our choice occasions of converse with heaven; we may want them another day, when the Lord is slow in bringing back His banished ones, and our soul is aching with fear. Oh, never-to-be-forgotten Valley of Achor, thou art a door of hope! Fair days, now gone, ye have left a light behind you which cheers our present gloom. C. H. S.

Vs. 7. *Deep calleth unto deep at the noise of Thy waterspouts.* Here he has conjoined two awful and terrific phenomena of nature. It is a fact well ascertained by the evidence of travelers that the falling of waterspouts is not uncommon on the coast of Judea. It should seem that they are occasioned by the congregating of great masses of cloud, whose waters concentrating to a point, pour themselves down in a tremendous column, accompanied with a roaring noise.

Now, the image conceived in the mind of the Psalmist seems to be that of the rushing of this vast waterspout down into the sea, already agitated, and increasing the turbulence and disorder of its waves. An awful picture! Especially if there be added to it the ideas of a black, tempestuous sky, and the deafening roar occasioned by the tumult. What would be the situation of a vessel in the midst of such a tempest, the deluge pouring down from above, and all around her the furious ocean heaving its tremendous surges—how ungovernable, how helpless, how next to impossible that she should escape foundering except by some almost miraculous interference!

Yet to such a situation does David here compare the state of his soul when submersed, as it were, under a sea of afflictions; "all Thy waves and Thy billows are gone over me." How pungent must his sense of grief have been to occasion him to make use of such a comparison, so strongly expressive of the utmost danger and terror! HENRY MARCH

*All Thy waves and Thy billows are gone over me.* Atlantic rollers, sweeping in ceaseless succession over one's head, waterspouts coming nearer and nearer, and all the ocean in uproar around the weary swimmer; most of the heirs of heaven can realize the description, for they have experienced the like.

This is a deep experience unknown to babes in grace, but common enough to such as do business on great waters of affliction: to such it is some comfort to remember that the waves and billows are the Lord's. "Thy waves and Thy billows," says David, "they are all sent, and directed by Him, and achieve His designs, and the child of God, knowing this, is the more resigned."

Vs. 8. *Yet the Lord will command His lovingkindness in the daytime.* No day shall ever dawn on an heir of grace and find him altogether forsaken of his Lord: the Lord reigneth, and as a sovereign He will with authortiy command mercy to be reserved for His chosen. C. H. S.

His expression is remarkable; he does not say simply that the Lord will bestow, but, *command His loving kindness.* As the gift bestowed is grace—free favor to the unworthy; so the manner of bestowing it is sovereign. It is given by decree; it is a royal donative. And if He commands the blessing, who shall hinder its reception? HENRY MARCH

*And in the night.* To tell you the truth, I think the night is the merriest time that the godly man hath, and the saddest for the wicked man (who, though he make use of darkness to hide his sin, yet is he afraid, because of that very thing in which his safety consists). ZACHARY BOGAN

*And my prayer unto the God of my life.* Here may be seen that David's religion was a religion of prayer after deliverance, as well as before. The selfish who cry out in trouble will have done with their prayers when the trouble is over.

With David, it was the very reverse. Deliverance from trouble would strengthen his confidence in God, embolden his addresses to him, and furnish him with new arguments. . . . There is great need of prayer after deliverance; for the time of deliverance is often a time of temptation; the soul being elated, and thrown off its guard. HENRY MARCH

Vs. 9. *Why go I mourning because of the oppression of the enemy?* It is a pitiable thing for any man to have a limb amputated, but when we know that the operation was needful to save life, we are glad to hear that it has been successfully performed; even thus as trial unfolds, the design of the Lord in sending it becomes far more easy to bear.

Vs. 10. *While they say daily unto me, Where is thy God?* Such was the malice of David's foes, that having thought of the cruel question, they said it, said it daily, repeated it to him, and that for a length of time; surely the continual yapping of these curs at his heel was enough to madden him, and perhaps would have done so had he not resorted to prayer and made the persecutions of his enemies a plea with his Lord. C. H. S.

David might rather have said to them, "Where are your eyes? where is your sight? for God is not only in heaven, but in me." Though David was shut out from the sanctuary, yet David's soul was a sanctuary for God; for God is not tied to a sanctuary made with hands. God hath two sanctuaries: He hath two heavens—the heaven of heavens and a broken spirit. RICHARD SIBBES

Forest-flies, small as they are, drive the noble war-horse mad; therefore David says, *As with a sword in my bones, mine enemies reproach me; while they say daily unto me, Where is thy God?* FREDERICK WILLIAM ROBERTSON

Vs. 11. *Hope.* Hope is like the sun, which, as we journey towards it, casts the shadow of our burden behind it. SAMUEL SMILES

*God . . . is the health of my countenance.* The health and life of thy grace lie both of them, not in thy grace, saith faith, but in God, Who is thy God; therefore I shall yet live and praise Him. I do not wonder that the weak Christian is melancholy and sad when he sees his sickly face in any other glass than this. WILLIAM GURNALL

Hast thou seen the sun shine forth in February, and the sky blue, and the hedgerows bursting into bud, and the primrose peeping beneath the bank, and the birds singing in the bushes? Thou hast thought that spring was already come in its beauty, and sweet odors. But a few days, and the clouds returned, and the atmosphere was chilled, and the birds were mute, and snow was on the ground, and thou hast said that spring would never come.

And thus sometimes the young convert finds his fears removed, and the comforts of the gospel shed abroad in his heart, and praise and thanksgiving, and a new song put in his mouth. And he deems unadvisedly that his troubles are past forever. But awhile and his doubts return, and his comforts die away, and his light is taken from him, and his spirit is overwhelmed, and he is fain to conclude that salvation and all its blessings are not for him. But the spring, though late, shall break at last. H. G. SALTER'S *"Book of Illustrations"*

## PSALM 43

Subject: On account of the similarity of the structure of this Psalm to that of Psalm 42, it has been supposed to be a fragment wrongly separated from the preceding song; but it is always dangerous to allow these theories of error in Holy Scripture, and in this instance it would be very difficult to show just cause for such an admission.

Vs. 1. *Judge me, O God.* I can laugh at human misrepresentation if my conscience knows that Thou art on my side.

*And plead my cause against an ungodly nation.* When people are ungodly, no wonder that they are unjust; those who are not true to God Himself cannot be expected to deal rightly with His people. Hating the King, they will not love His subjects. Popular opinion weighs with many, but divine opinion is far more weighty with the gracious few. One good word from God outweighs ten thousand railing speeches of men. He bears a brazen shield before him whose reliance in all things is upon his God; the arrows of calumny fall harmlessly from such a buckler. C. H. S.

Now, God cannot in justice punish twice; therefore, seeing Christ was wounded, believers must be healed (Isaiah 53). Believers have God's righteousness imputed to them (II Corinthians 5); therefore, God must deal with believers as He will deal with His own righteousness. *Condensed from* NATHANAEL HOMES

*O deliver me from the deceitful and unjust man.* Deceit and injustice are boon companions: he who fawns will not fear to slander. From two such devils none can deliver us but God.

Vs. 2. *Why dost Thou cast me off?* There are many reasons why the Lord might cast us off, but no reason shall prevail to make Him do so. He hath not cast off His people, though He for awhile treats them as cast-offs. Learn from this question that it is well to enquire into dark providences, but we must enquire of God, not of our own fears. He Who is the Author of a mysterious trial can best expound it to us.

*Blind unbelief is sure to err,*
*And scan His work in vain;*
*God is His own interpreter*
*And He will make it plain.*

C. H. S.

Vs. 3. *Light and truth.* "In the day that thou eatest thereof, thou shalt surely die!" Adam ate, and in that day became the subject of sin and death. This was truth executing judgment. But light arose around the darkness; beams of mercy tempered the heavy cloud. The promise of the Great Deliverer was given; then faithfulness was enlisted on the side of grace and became engaged for its bestowment; "mercy and truth met together; righteousness and peace kissed each other." Since then, all humble and trusting souls have beheld them united and have made their union the ground of their confidence and joy. HENRY MARCH

*Let them lead me.* Be these my star to guide me to my rest. Be these my Alpine guides to conduct me over mountains and precipices to the abodes of grace.

*Let them bring me unto Thy holy hill, and to Thy tabernacles.* We seek not light to sin by nor truth to be exalted by it, but that they may become our practical guides to the nearest communion with God. C. H. S.

Vs. 4. *Then will I go unto the altar of God.* Toward this altar all the rays of the light of divine favor and grace, and of divine truth and holiness, have from eternity converged; and from this point they shine forth toward and upon the soul and heart of the poor, far-off penitent, attracting him to that altar where he may meet his God. JOHN OFFORD

*Unto God my exceeding joy.* It was not the altar as such that the Psalmist cared for; he was no believer in the heathenism of ritualism: his soul desired spiritual fellowship, fellowship with God Himself in very deed. What are all the rites of worship unless the Lord be in them; what, indeed, but empty shells and dry husks? C. H. S.

Vs. 5. *Hope in God.* The worldling's motto is, "a bird in the hand." "Give me today," say they, "and take tomorrow whoso will." But the word of believers is, *spero meliora*—my hopes are better than my present possessions. ELNATHAN PARR

# PSALM 44

Title: "To the Chief Musician for the sons of Korah, Maschil." The title is similar to the Forty-Second, and although this is no proof that it is by the same author, it makes it highly probable. No other writer should be sought for to father any of the Psalms when David will suffice, and therefore we are loath to ascribe this sacred song to any but the great Psalmist, yet as we hardly know any period of his life which it would fairly describe, we feel compelled to look elsewhere. The last verses remind us of Milton's famous lines on the massacre of the Protestants among the mountains of Piedmont. C. H. S.

S. Ambrose observes that in former Psalms we have seen a prophecy of Christ's passion, resurrection, and ascension, and of the coming of the Holy Ghost, and that here we are taught that we ourselves must be ready to struggle and suffer in order that these things may profit us. Human will must work together with divine grace. CHRISTOPHER WORDSWORTH

Vs. 1. *We have heard with our ears, O God.* To hear with the ears affects us more sensitively than to read with the eyes; we ought to note this and seize every possible opportunity of telling abroad the gospel of our Lord Jesus *viva voce,* since this is the most telling mode of communication.

*Our fathers have told us.* When fathers are tongue-tied religiously with their offspring, need they wonder if their children's hearts remain sin-tied? Religious conversation need not be dull, and indeed it could not be if, as in this case, it dealt more with facts and less with opinions. C. H. S.

*What work Thou didst.* Why only *work* in the singular, when such innumerable deliverances had been wrought by Him, from the passage of the Red Sea to the destruction of the hundred and eighty-five thousand in the camp of the Assyrians? Because all these were but types of that one great work, that one stretching forth of the Lord's hand, when Satan was vanquished, death destroyed, and the kingdom of heaven opened to all believers. AMBROSE

While the songs of other nations sing of the heroism of their ancestors, the songs of Israel celebrate the works of God. AUGUSTUS F. THOLUCK

Vs. 2. *How Thou didst afflict the people and cast them out.* How fair is Mercy when she stands by the side of justice! Bright beams the star of grace amid the night of wrath! It is a solemn thought that the greatness of divine love has its counterpart in the greatness of His indignation.

Vs. 3. *For they got not the land in possession by their own sword.* The passage may be viewed as a beautiful parable of the work of salvation; men are not saved without prayer, repentance, etc., but none of these save a man; salvation is altogether of the Lord. Canaan was not conquered without the armies of Israel, but equally true is it that it was not conquered by them; the Lord was the conqueror, and the people were but instruments in His hands.

Vs. 5. *Through Thy Name will we tread them under that rise up against us.* Mark well that all the conquests of these believers are said to be "through Thee," "through Thy Name"; never let us forget this, lest going a warfare at our own charges, we fail most ignominiously. Let us not, however, fall into the equally dangerous sin of distrust, for the Lord can make the weakest of us equal to any emergency.

Vs. 6. *For I will not trust in my bow, neither shall my sword save me.* Arm of flesh, how dare I trust thee? How dare I bring upon myself the curse of those who rely upon man? C. H. S.

The less confidence we have in ourselves or in anything beside God, the more evidence have we of the sincerity of our faith in God. DAVID DICKSON

Vs. 8. *In God we boast all the day long.* What a blessed boasting is this! It is the only sort of boasting that is bearable. All other manna bred worms and stank except that which was laid up before the Lord, and all other boasting is loathsome save this glorying in the Lord, which is laudable and pleasing.

Vs. 11. *And hast scattered us among the heathen.* All this is ascribed to the Lord, as being allowed by Him, and even appointed by His decree. It is well to trace the hand of God in our sorrows, for it is surely there. C. H. S.

Vs. 12. *Thou sellest Thy people for nought.* Referring to the siege of Jerusalem by Titus, Eusebius says: "Many were sold for a small price; there were many to be sold, but few to buy."

Vs. 13. *A scorn and a derision to them that are round about us.* To be a derision to both strong and weak, superiors, equals, and inferiors, is hard to bear. The tooth of scoffing bites to the bone.

Vs. 14. *Thou makest us a byword among the heathen, a shaking of the head among the people.* The world knows not its nobility; it has no eye for true excellence: it found a cross for the Master and cannot be expected to award crowns to His disciples.

Vs. 17. *All this is come upon us; yet have we not forgotten Thee.* When in the midst of many griefs, we can still cling to God in loving obedience, it must be well with us. True fidelity can endure rough usage. Those who follow God for what they get will leave Him when persecution is stirred up, but not so the sincere believer; he will not forget his God, even though the worst come to the worst. C. H. S.

Eusebius, narrating the cruelties inflicted upon the Christians by the Eastern tyrant, Maximinus, says: "He prevailed against all sorts of people, the Christians only excepted, who contemned death and despised his tyranny.

"The men endured burning, beheading, crucifying, ravenous devouring of beasts, drowning in the sea, maiming and broiling of the members, goring and digging out of the eyes, mangling of the whole body; moreover, famine and imprisonment: to be short, they suffered every kind of torment for the service of God rather than they would leave the worship of God and embrace the adoration of idols.

"Women also, not inferior to men through the power of the Word of God, put on manly courage, whereof some suffered the torments with men, some attained unto the like masteries of virtue." *From "The Ecclesiastical History of Eusebius Pamphilus"*

Verses 17-19. Neither the persecuting hand of men nor the chastising hand of God relaxed ancient, singular saints. Believers resemble the moon, which emerges from her eclipse by keeping her motion, and ceases not to shine because the dogs bark at her. Shall we cease to be professors because others will not cease to be persecutors? WILLIAM SECKER

Vs. 18. *Our heart is not turned back.* Serious piety has become a ludicrous subject with which the wanton wits of this atheistical world sport themselves. JOHN FLAVEL

Our understandings and minds are the same as they were in a summer's day, though now we be in a winter's storm; though now we be afflicted, tossed, broken, and persecuted, yet notwithstanding, *Our heart is not* turned back, our mind, will, affections, and conscience, our whole soul, is the same now as before. THOMAS BROOKS

Vs. 19. *Though Thou hast sore broken us in the place of dragons.* To be true to a smiting God, even when the blows lay our joys in ruinous heaps, is to be such as the Lord delighteth in. Better to be broken by God than from God.

Vs. 20. *If we have forgotten the Name of our God.* This would be the first step in apostasy; men first forget the true and then adore the false. C. H. S.

Vs. 21. *For He knoweth the secrets of the heart.* A godly man dares not sin secretly. He knows that God sees in secret. As God cannot be deceived by our subtlety, so He cannot be excluded by our secrecy. THOMAS WATSON

Vs. 22. *Yea, for Thy sake are we killed all the day long,* etc. We wander in the woods; they hunt us with dogs. They lead us away, seized and bound, as lambs that open not their mouths. They cry out against us as seditious persons and heretics. We are brought like sheep to the slaughter. Many sit oppressed, and in bonds which even decay their bodies. Some have sunk under their sufferings and died without fault.

Here is the patience of the saints in the earth. We must be tried by suffering here. The faithful have they hanged on trees, strangled, hewn in pieces, secretly and openly drowned. Not only men, but likwise women and maidens have borne witness to the truth, that Jesus Christ is the Truth, the only Way to eternal life. *From "A Martyrology of the Churches of Christ, commonly called Baptists, edited by E. B. Underhill"*

*We are counted as sheep for the slaughter.* From Piedmont and Smithfield, from St. Bartholomew's massacre and the dragoonades of Claverhouse, this appeal goes up to heaven, while the souls under the altar continue their solemn cry for vengeance. Not long shall the church plead in this fashion; her shame shall be recompensed, her triumph shall dawn. C. H. S.

Vs. 23. *Awake, why sleepest Thou, O Lord?* and Psalm 121:4, "Behold He that keepeth Israel shall neither slumber nor sleep." If God at no time sleep, why doth the church call on Him so often to awake? If He must be awakened from sleep, why doth the Psalmist say He never sleeps? Are not these places contradictory?

Answer: It is one thing what the afflicted church cries in the heat of her sufferings; another thing what the Spirit of truth speaks for the comfort of the saints. It is ordinary for the best of saints and martyrs during the storm to go to God as Peter did to Christ at sea (sleeping in the stern of the ship), with such importunity in prayer as if the Lord were no more sensible of their agony than Jonah was of the mariners' misery, ready to perish in the turbulent ocean, and he cried out, "What meanest Thou, O sleeper? Arise!" Saints are so familiar with God in prayer, as if they were at His bedside. WILLIAM STREAT *in "The Dividing of the Hoof"*

*Cast us not off for ever.* At the thought of what the saints have endured from their haughty enemies, we join our voices in the great martyr cry with the bard of Paradise:

*Avenge, O Lord, Thy slaughtered saints, whose bones*
*Lie scattered on the Alpine mountains cold;*
*Even those who kept Thy truth so pure of old,*
*When all our fathers worshiped stocks and stones,*
*Forget not: in Thy book record their groans*
*Who were Thy sheep.*

MILTON *on "Massacre of Piedmont"*

# PSALM 45

Special singers are appointed for so divine a hymn. King Jesus deserves to be praised not with random, ranting ravings, but with the sweetest and most skillful music of the best trained choristers.

Subject: Some here see Solomon and Pharaoh's daughter only—they are short-sighted; others see both Solomon and Christ—they are cross-eyed; well-focused spiritual eyes see here Jesus only, or if Solomon be present at all, it must be like those hazy shadows of passers-by which cross the face of the camera and therefore are dimly traceable upon a photographic landscape. "The King," the God Whose throne is forever and ever, is no mere mortal, and His everlasting dominion is not bounded by Lebanon and Egypt's river. This is no wedding song of earthly nuptials, but an epithalamium for the heavenly Bridegroom and His elect spouse.

Vs. 1. *My heart is inditing a good matter.* It is a sad thing when the heart is cold with a good matter, and worse when it is warm with a bad matter, but incomparably well when a warm heart and a good matter meet together. C. H. S.

It is reported of Origen, saith Erasmus, that he was ever earnest, but most of all when he discoursed of Christ. Of Johannes Mollias, a Bononian, it is said, that whenever he spake of Jesus Christ, his eyes dropped, for he was fraught with a mighty fervency of God's Holy Spirit; and like the Baptist, he was first a burning (boiling or bubbling), and then a shining light. JOHN TRAPP

Vs. 2. *Thou.* As though the King Himself had suddenly appeared before him, the Psalmist lost in admiration of His Person, turns from his preface to address his Lord. A loving heart has the power to realize its object. The eyes of a true heart see more than the eyes of the head.

Moreover, Jesus reveals Himself when we are pouring forth our affections towards Him. It is usually the case that when we are ready, Christ appears. If our heart is warm, it is an index that the sun is shining, and when we enjoy his heat, we shall soon behold his light.

*Thou art fairer than the children of men.* In Person, but especially in mind and character, the King of saints is peerless in beauty. The Hebrew word is doubled, "Beautiful, beautiful, art Thou." Jesus is so emphatically lovely that words must be doubled, strained, yea, exhausted before He can be described. C. H. S.

Thus he begins to set forth His beauty, wherein is the delightfulness of any person; so is it with the soul when God hath made known to man his own filthiness and uncomeliness through sin, and that only by Jesus sin is taken away; oh, how beautiful is this face, the first sight of Him! RICHARD COORE, *in "Christ Set Forth"*

Fair in His manhood; had He not been so, says S. Jerome, had there not been something admirable in His countenance and presence, some heavenly beauty, the Apostles and the whole world (as the Pharisees themselves confess) would not so suddenly have gone after Him. Fair in His transfiguration, white as the light, or as the snow, His face glittering as the sun (Matt. 17:2), even to the ravishing the very soul of S. Peter, that "he knew not what he said," could let his eyes dwell upon that face forever and never come down the mount again.

Fair in His passion. No uncomeliness in His nakedness; His very wounds and the bloody prints of the whips and scourges drew an *ecce* from the mouth of Pilate: "Behold the Man!" the sweetness of His countenance and carriage in the midst of filth and spittle, whips and buffets. MARK FRANK

O fair sun, and fair moon, and fair stars, and fair flowers, and fair roses, and fair lilies; but O ten thousand thousand times fairer Lord Jesus! Alas! I have wronged Him in making the comparison this way. O black sun and moon! but, O fair Lord Jesus! O black flowers, and black lilies, and roses! but, O fair, fair, ever fair, Lord Jesus! O black heaven! but, O fair Christ! O black angels! but O surpassingly fair Lord Jesus! SAMUEL RUTHERFORD

In one Christ we may contemplate and must confess all the beauty and loveliness both of heaven and earth; the beauty of heaven is God, the beauty of earth is man; the beauty of heaven and earth together is this God-man. EDWARD HYDE, D.D.

"I have a passion," observed Count Zinzendorf in one of his discourses to the congregation at Herrnhut; "and it is He—He only."

*Grace is poured into Thy lips.* One word from Himself dissolved the heart of Saul of Tarsus and turned him into an Apostle; another word raised up John the Divine when fainting in the Isle of Patmos. Oftentimes a sentence from His lips has turned our own midnight into morning, our winter into spring. C. H. S.

Never were there such words of love and sweetness spoken by any man as by Him; never was there such a loving and tender heart as the heart of Jesus Christ: "Grace was poured into His lips." Certainly never were there such words of love, sweetness, and tenderness spoken here upon this earth as those last words of His which were uttered a little before His sufferings and are recorded in the 13th, 14th, 15th, 16th, and 17th chapters of John. Read over all the books of love and friendship that were ever written by any of the sons of men; they do all come far short of those melting strains of love that are there expressed. JOHN ROW

Vs. 3. *Thy sword.* The Word of God is compared to such a weapon, for the apostle informs us that it is quick, or living, and powerful, and sharper than any two-edged sword, piercing even to the dividing asunder of the soul and spirit, and of the joints and marrow, and laying open the thoughts and intents of the heart.

It must be observed, however, that this description of the Word of God is applicable to it only when Christ girds it on and employs it as His sword. Of what use is a sword, even though it be the sword of Goliath, while it lies still in its scabbard or is grasped by the powerless hand of an infant?

Armed with this weapon, the Captain of our salvation cuts His way to the sinner with infinite ease, though surrounded by rocks and mountains, scatters His strongholds and refuges of lies, and with a mighty blow cleaves asunder his heart of adamant and lays him prostrate and trembling at His feet.

Since such are the effects of this weapon in the hand of Christ, it is with the utmost propriety that the Psalmist begins by requesting Him to gird it on, and not suffer it to be inactive in its scabbard, or powerless in the feeble grasp of His ministers. EWARD PAYSON

*With Thy glory and Thy majesty.* Our precious Christ can never be made too much of. Heaven itself is but just good enough for Him. All the pomp that angels and archangels, and thrones, and dominions, and principalities, and powers can pour at His feet is too little for Him. Only His own essential glory is such as fully answers to the desire of His people, who can never enough extol Him.

Vs. 5. *In the heart of the King's enemies.* Our Captain aims at men's hearts rather than their heads, and He hits them, too; point-blank are His shots, and they enter deep into the vital part of man's nature. Whether for love or vengeance, Christ never misses sin, and when His arrows stick, they cause a smart not soon forgotten, a wound which only He can heal. Jesus' arrows of conviction are sharp in the quiver of His Word and sharp when on the bow of His ministers.

*Whereby the people fall under Thee.* There is no standing against the Son of God when His bow of might is in His hands. Terrible will be that hour when His bow shall be made quite naked and bolts of devouring fire shall be hurled upon His adversaries; then shall princes fall and nations perish.

Vs. 6. *Thy throne, O God, is forever and ever.* To whom can this be spoken but our Lord? The Psalmist cannot restrain his adoration. His enlightened eyes see in the royal Husband of the church, God, God to be adored, God reigning, God reigning everlastingly. Blessed sight! Blind are the eyes that cannot see God in Christ Jesus!

*The scepter of Thy kingdom is a right scepter.* He is the lawful monarch of all things that be. His rule is founded in right, its law is right, its result is right. Our King is no usurper and no oppressor. Even when He shall break His enemies with a rod of iron, He will do no man wrong; His vengeance and His grace are both in conformity with justice.

Hence we trust Him without suspicion; He cannot err; no affliction is too severe, for He sends it; no judgment too harsh, for He ordains it. O blessed hands of Jesus! the reigning power is safe with you. All the just rejoice in the government of the King Who reigns in righteousness. C. H. S.

Vs. 7. *Thou lovest righteousness, and hatest wickedness.* Many a one loves righteousness but would not be its champion; such a love is not Christ's love. Many a one hates iniquity, not for its own sake, but for the sake of its consequences; such a hate is not Christ's hate.

To be like Christ, we must love righteousness as He loved and hate wickedness as He hated. To love and hate as He loves and hates is to be perfect as He is perfect. The perfection of this love and hate is moral perfection. George Harpur

*Therefore.* He says not, "Wherefore He anointed Thee in order to Thy being God, or King, or Son, or Word"; for so He was before, and is forever, as has been shown; but rather, "Since Thou art God and King, therefore Thou wast anointed, since none but Thou couldst unite man to the Holy Ghost, Thou the image of the Father, in which we were made in the beginning: for Thine is even the Spirit." Athanasius

Vs. 10. *Hearken, O daughter, and consider.* Ever is this the great duty of the church. Faith cometh by hearing and confirmation by consideration. No precept can be more worthy of the attention of those who are honored to be espoused unto Christ than that which follows.

*Forget also thine own people, and thy father's house.* The house of our nativity is the house of sin—we were shapen in iniquity; the carnal mind is enmity against God; we must come forth of the house of fallen nature, for it is built in the City of Destruction. Not that natural ties are broken by grace, but ties of the sinful nature, bonds of graceless affinity. We have much to forget as well as to learn, and the unlearning is so difficult that only diligent hearing, and considering, and bending of the whole soul to it, can accomplish the work; and even these would be too feeble did not divine grace assist.

Yet why should we remember the Egypt from which we came out? Are the leeks and the garlic, and the onions anything, when the iron bondage, and the slavish tasks, and the death-dealing Pharaoh of hell are remembered? We part with folly for wisdom; with bubbles for eternal joys; with deceit for truth; with misery for bliss; with idols for the living God.

Oh, that Christians were more mindful of the divine precept here recorded; but, alas! worldliness abounds; the church is defiled; and the glory of the great King is veiled. Only when the whole church leads the separated life will the full splendor and power of Christianity shine forth upon the world. C. H. S.

"Three 'alls' I expect you to part with," saith Christ: 1. All your sinful lusts, all the ways of the old Adam, our Father's house. Ever since Adam's apostasy, God and man have parted houses. Ever since, our Father's house is a house of ill manners, a house of sin and wickedness.

2. All your worldly advantages. "If any man come unto Me, and hate not his father, and mother, and wife, and children, and brethren, and sisters, yea, and his own life also, he cannot be My disciple." He that hath all these must be ready to part with all; they are joined not disjunctively but copulatively.

3. All self, self-will, self-righteousness, self-sufficiencies, self-confidences, and self-seekings. LEWIS STUCKLEY

If thou be on the mountain, have no love to look back to Sodom. If thou be in the ark, fly not back to the world, as the raven did. If thou be set on Canaan, forget the flesh-pots of Egypt. If marching against Midian, forget stooping to the waters of Harod (Judges 7).

If on the house-top, forget that is below thee (Mark 13:15). If thy hand be put to the plough, forget that is behind thee (Luke 9:62). Themistocles desired rather to learn the art of forgetfulness than of memory. Philosophy is an art of remembering; divinity includes in it an art of forgetting.

The first lesson that Socrates taught his soldiers was, "Remember"; for he thought that knowledge was nothing else but a calling to remembrance of those things the mind knew ere it knew the body. But the first lesson that Christ teacheth His scholars is, *Forget: Forget thine own people;* "Repent" (Matt. 4: 17); first, "eschew evil" (I Pet. 3:11). THOMAS ADAMS

Vs. 11. *So shall the King greatly desire thy beauty.* No great and lasting revival of religion can be granted us till the professed lovers of Jesus prove their affection by coming out from an ungodly world, being separated, and touching not the unclean thing. C. H. S.

This is a most sweet promise. For the Holy Spirit knoweth that this monster, Monk, sticks fast in our heart—that we want to be pure and without spot before God. Thus, under Popery, all my temptation was this. I used to say, "that I would willingly go to the sacrament if I were but worthy."

Thus we seek, naturally, a purity in ourselves; and we examine our whole life and want to find a purity in ourselves, that we might have no need of grace, but might be pronounced righteous upon the grounds of our own merit. . . . Thou wilt certainly never become righteous by thyself and thine own works works.

The sum of the whole therefore is this: That our beauty does not consist in our own virtues, nor even in the gifts which we have received from God, by which we put forth virtues, and do all those things which pertain unto the life of the law; but in this—our apprehending Christ and believing in Him. Then it is that we are truly beautiful: and it is this beauty alone that Christ looks upon, and upon no other. MARTIN LUTHER

Vs. 12. *And the daughter of Tyre shall be there with a gift.* The power of missions abroad lies at home: a holy church will be a powerful church. Nor shall there be lack of treasure in her coffers when grace is in her heart; the free gifts of a willing people shall enable the workers for God to carry on their sacred enterprises without stint. C. H. S.

Vs. 13. *Within.* The ark was pitched within with the same pitch with which it was pitched without withal; such is the sincere man, within and without alike, inside and outside, all one.

Yea, he is rather better than he shows, as the *king's daughter*, whose outside might sometimes be sackcloth, yet was *all glorious within, and her inward garments of wrought gold.* Or as the temple, outwardly nothing but wood and stone to be seen, inwardly all rich and beautiful, especially the sanctum sanctorum (when the veil was drawn) was all gold. The very floor, as well as the roof, was overlaid with gold (I Kings 6:30). JOHN SHEFFIELD

Vs. 15. *With gladness and rejoicing shall they be brought.* The saints themselves shall rejoice unspeakably when they shall enter into the King's palace and be forever with the Lord (I Thess. 4:17). Indeed, there will be joy on all hands, except among the devils and damned, who shall gnash their teeth with envy at the everlasting advancement and glory of believers. JOHN FLAVEL

*They shall be brought.* Reader! do not fail to observe the manner of expression—the church is brought—she doth not come of herself. No, she must be convinced, converted, made willing. No one can come to Christ, except the Father, Who hath sent Christ, draw him (John 6:44). ROBERT HAWKER

# PSALM 46

Title: "To the Chief Musician." He who could sing other Psalms so well was fitly entrusted with this noble ode. Trifles may be left to commoner songsters, but the most skilful musician in Israel must be charged with the due performance of this song, with the most harmonious voices and choicest music.

Subject: "Happen what may, the Lord's people are happy and secure; this is the doctrine of the Psalm, and it might, to help our memories, be called "The Song of Holy Confidence," were it not that from the great Reformer's love to this soul-stirring hymn it will probably be best remembered as Luther's Psalm. C. H. S.

We sing this Psalm to the praise of God because God is with us and powerfully and miraculously preserves and defends His church and His Word against all fanatical spirits, against the gates of hell, against the implacable hatred of the devil, and against all the assaults of the world, the flesh, and sin. MARTIN LUTHER

Luther and his companions, with all their bold readiness for danger and death in the cause of truth, had times when their feelings were akin to those of a divine singer, who said, "Why art thou cast down, O my soul?" But in such hours, the unflinching Reformer would cheerily say to his friend Melanchthon, "Come, Philip, let us sing the Forty-Sixth Psalm; and they could sing it in Luther's own characteristic version:

*A sure stronghold our God is He,*
*A timely shield and weapon;*
*Our help He'll be, and set us free*
*From every ill can happen.*

*And were the world with devils filled,*
*All eager to devour us,*
*Our souls to fear shall little yield,*
*They cannot overpower us.*

S. W. CHRISTOPHERS *in "Hymn Writers and Their Hymns"*

Vs. 1. *God is our refuge and strength.* Not our armies or our fortresses. Israel's boast is in Jehovah, the only living and true God. Others vaunt their impregnable castles placed on inaccessible rocks and secured with gates of iron, but God is a far better refuge from distress than all these: and when the time comes to carry the war into the enemy's territories, the Lord stands His people in better stead than all the valor of legions or the boasted strength of chariot and horses.

"He is my refuge and strength." Do not forget the fact that God is our refuge just now, in the immediate present, as truly as when David penned the word. God alone is our all in all. All other refuges are refuges of lies. all other strength is weakness, for power belongeth unto God: but as God is all-sufficient, our defence and might are equal to all emergencies. C. H. S.

It begins abruptly, but nobly; ye may trust in whom and in what ye please; but *God* [*Elohim*]*is our refuge and strength. A very present help.* A help found to be very powerful and effectual in straits and difficulties. The words are very emphatic: *ezrah betsaroth nimtsa meod,* "He is found an exceeding, or superlative, help in difficulties." Such we have found Him, and therefore celebrate His praise. ADAM CLARKE

Vs. 2. *Therefore will not we fear.* With God on our side, how irrational would fear be! Where He is, all power is, and all love; why therefore should we quail? C. H. S.

*Though the earth be removed.* John Wesley preached in Hyde-Park on the occasion of the earthquake felt in London, March 8, 1750, and repeated these words.

*And though the mountains be carried into the midst of the sea.* Let the worst come to the worst, the child of God should never give way to mistrust; since God remaineth faithful, there can be no danger to His cause or people. When the elements shall melt with fervent heat, and the heavens and the earth shall pass away in the last general conflagration, we shall serenely behold "the wreck of matter, and the crash of worlds," for even then our refuge shall preserve us from all evil, our strength shall prepare us for all good.

Vs. 4. *There is a river.* Divine grace like a smoothly flowing, fertilizing, full and never-failing river, yields refreshment and consolation to believers.

*The streams whereof,* in their various influences, for they are many, *shall make glad the city of God* by assuring the citizens that Zion's Lord will unfailingly supply all their needs. The streams are not transient, like Cherith; nor muddy, like the Nile; nor furious, like Kishon; nor treacherous, like Job's deceitful brooks; neither are their waters "naught" like those of Jericho—they are clear, cool, fresh, abundant, and gladdening.

The great fear of an Eastern city in time of war was lest the water supply should be cut off during a siege; if that were secured the city could hold out against attacks for an indefinite period. In this verse, Jerusalem, which represents the church of God, is described as well supplied with water, to set forth the fact that in seasons of trial all-sufficient grace will be given to enable us to endure unto the end. C. H. S.

What is the river that makes glad the city of God? I answer, God Himself is the river, as in the following verse, "God is in the midst of her."

1. God, the *Father,* is the river: "For my people have committed two evils; they have forsaken me the fountain of living waters, and hewed them out cisterns, broken cisterns, that can hold no water" (Jer. 2:13).

2. God, the *Son,* is the river, the fountain of salvation: "In that day there shall be a fountain opened to the house of David, and the inhabitants of Jerusalem for sin and for uncleanness" (Zech. 13:1).

3. God, the *Spirit,* is the river: "He that believeth on Me, as the Scripture hath said, out of his belly shall flow rivers of living water." "Whosoever drinketh of the water that I shall give him shall never thirst; but the water that I shall give him shall be in him a well of water springing up into everlasting life" (John 7:38; 4:14).

What are the streams of this river? Answer—the perfections of God, the fullness of Christ, the operations of the Spirit, and these running in the channel of the covenant of promise. RALPH ERSKINE

*The city.* The church of God is like a city: 1. Because a city is a place of security. 2. A place of *society:* what one wants another supplies; they have mutual fellowship. 3. A place of *unity,* that people may therein live in peace and concord. 4. A place of *trade* and *traffic.* Here is the market of free grace: "Ho, every one that thirsteth," etc. Here is the pearl of great price exposed for sale.

5. A place of *freedom* and *liberty,* freedom from the guilt of sin, wrath of God, curse of the law, present evil world, bondage to Satan, etc., etc. 6. A place of *order* and *regularity;* it hath its constitutions and ordinances. 7. A place of *rest,* and commodious to live in, and thus it is opposed to the wilderness. 8. A place of *privileges.* 9. A place of *pomp* and *splendor;* there is the king, the court,

the throne. 10. A place of *pleasure* and *beauty* (Psalm 48:2). RALPH ERSKINE

*The holy place of the tabernacles of the Most High.* To be a temple for the Holy Ghost is the delightful portion of each saint; to be the living temple for the Lord our God is also the high honor of the church in her corporate capacity. We have not a great God in nature and a little God in grace; no, the church contains as clear and convincing a revelation of God as the works of nature, and even more amazing in the excellent glory which shines between the cherubim overshadowing that mercy-seat which is the center and gathering place of the people of the living God. C. H. S.

Vs. 5. *God is in the midst of her.* His help is therefore sure and near. Is she besieged, then He is Himself besieged within her, and we may be certain that He will break forth upon His adversaries. How near is the Lord to the distresses of His saints, since He sojourns in their midst! C. H. S.

The church spreads because her *God is in the midst of her.* When at any time she has forgotten her dependence on the invisible intercession of her Head, and the gracious energy of His Spirit, she has found herself shorn of the locks of her great strength and has become the laughing stock of the Philistines. WILLIAM BINNIE, D.D.

The enemies of the church may toss her as waves, but they shall not split her as rocks. She may be dipped in water as a feather, but shall not sink therein as lead. He that is a well of water within her to keep her from fainting, will also prove a wall of fire about her to preserve her from falling. Tried she may be, but destroyed she cannot be. Her foundation is the Rock of Ages, and her defense the everlasting Arms. WILLIAM SECKER

When the Papists were in their ruff, and Melanchthon began sometimes to fear lest the infant Reformation should be stifled in the birth, Luther was wont to comfort him with these words: "If we perish, Christ must fall too ('He is in the midst of us'), and if it must be so, be it so; I had rather perish with Christ, that great Ruler of the world, than prosper with Cæsar. JOHN COLLINGS

*God shall help her, and that right early.* The Lord is up betimes. We are slow to meet Him, but He is never tardy in helping us. Impatience complains of divine delays, but in very deed the Lord is not slack concerning His promise. Man's haste is often folly, but God's apparent delays are ever wise, and, when rightly viewed, are no delays at all. C. H. S.

Therefore, notice that all the great deliverances wrought in Holy Scripture were wrought so early as to have been brought to pass in the middle of the night. So Gideon, with his pitchers and lamps against the Midianites; so Saul, when he went forth against Nahash, the Ammonite; so Joshua, when he went up to succor Gibeon; so Samson, when he carried off in triumph the gates of Gaza; so also the associate kings, under the guidance of Elisha, in their expedition against the Moabites, when they, according to God's command, filled the wilderness with ditches and then beheld their enemies drawn to their destruction by the reflection of the rising sun upon the water. MICHAEL AYGUAN

*Right early,* rather, with the margin, *when the morning appeareth.* The restoration of the Jews will be one of the first things at the season of the second advent. It will be accomplished in the very dawning of that day, "when the Sun of Righteousness will rise with healing on His wings. SAMUEL HORSLEY

Vs. 6. *The heathen raged.* The nations were in a furious uproar; they gathered against the city of the Lord like wolves ravenous for their prey; they foamed and roared and swelled like a tempestuous sea.

*The kingdoms were moved.* A general confusion seized upon society; the fierce invaders convulsed their own dominions by draining the population to urge on the war, and they desolated other territories by their devastating march to

Jerusalem. Crowns fell from royal heads, ancient thrones rocked like trees driven of the tempest, powerful empires fell like pines uprooted by the blast: everything was in disorder, and dismay seized on all who knew not the Lord.

*He uttered His voice, the earth melted.* How mighty is a word from God! How mighty the Incarnate Word. Oh, that such a word would come from the excellent glory even now to melt all hearts in love to Jesus and to end forever all the persecutions, wars, and rebellions of men! C. H. S.

Vs. 7. *Our refuge.* "The conies are but a feeble folk, yet make they their houses in the rocks." They are safe in the rock if they can get thither, though never so weak in themselves. So the church, though pursued by bloody enemies, and though weak in herself, if yet she get under the wing of the God of Jacob, she may be fearless, for she is safe there. *He is our refuge.*

It were to undervalue God, if we should fear the creatures, when He is with us. Antigonus, when he overheard his soldiers reckoning how many their enemies were, he steps in unto them suddenly, demanding, "And how many do you reckon me for?" JOHN STRICKLAND

Vs. 8. *Come, behold the works of the Lord.* It were well if we also carefully noted the providential dealings of our covenant God and were quick to perceive His hand in the battles of His church. Whenever we read history, it should be with this verse sounding in our ears. We should read the newspaper in the same spirit, to see how the Head of the church rules the nations for His people's good, as Joseph governed Egypt for the sake of Israel. C. H. S.

God looks that His works should be well observed, and especially when He hath wrought any great deliverance for His people. Of all things, He cannot abide to be forgotten. JOHN TRAPP

*What desolations He hath made in the earth.* The destroyers He destroys, the desolators He desolates. How forcible is the verse at this date! The ruined cities of Assyria, Babylon, Petra, Bashan, Canaan, are our instructors, and in tables of stone record the doings of the Lord. In every place where His cause and crown have been disregarded, ruin has surely followed; sin has been a blight on nations and left their palaces to lie in heaps.

*Ye gloomy piles, ye tombs of living men,*
*Ye sepulchers of womanhood, or worse;*
*Ye refuges of lies, soon may ye fall,*
*And 'mid your ruins may the owl, and bat,*
*And dragon find congenial resting-place.*

C. H. S.

We are here first invited to a tragical sight. We are carried into the *camera di morte,* to see the ghastly visage of deaths and desolations all the world over; than which nothing can be more horrible and dreadful. You are called out to see piles of dead carcasses; to see whole basketfuls of heads, as was presented to Jehu: a woeful spectacle, but a necessary one.

See, therefore, *what desolations the Lord hath wrought in all the earth.* Desolations by wars: how many fields have been drenched with blood, and composted with carcasses; how many millions of men have been cut off in all ages by the edge of the sword!

Desolations by famine; wherein men have been forced to make their bodies one another's sepulchers, and mothers to devour their children of a span long. Desolations by plague and pestilence; which have swept away, as our story tells us, eight hundred thousand in one city. JOSEPH HALL

Vs. 9. *He burneth the chariot in the fire.* How glorious will the ultimate victory of Jesus be in the day of His appearing, when every enemy shall lick the dust!

Vs. 10. *Be still, and know that I am God.* Hold off your hands, ye enemies! Sit down and wait in patience, ye believers! Acknowledge that Jehovah is God, ye who feel the terrors of His wrath! Adore Him, and Him only, ye who partake in the protections of His grace. Since none can worthily proclaim His nature, let "expressive silence muse His praise." The boasts of the ungodly and the timorous forebodings of the saints should certainly be hushed by a sight of what the Lord has done in past ages. C. H. S.

As if the Lord has said, "Not a word, do not strive nor reply; whatever you see, hold your peace; know that I, being God, give no account of any of My matters." JOSEPH CARYL

Many give way to quarreling with God, and consider not the hazard thereof. Beware of it, for it is dreadful thing to quarrel with God: who may say unto Him, "What doest Thou?" It is a good account of Aaron, that when God made fire to destroy his sons, he held his peace. Let us then, while we bear the yoke, "sit alone and keep silence, and put our mouths in the dust, if so be there may be hope" (Lam. 3:28-29).

Ye know, the murmuring of the children of Israel cost them very dear. *Be still,* that is, beware of murmuring against me, saith the Lord. God gives not an account of His matters to any; because there may be many things ye cannot see through; and therefore ye may think it better to have wanted them, and much more, for the credit of God and the church. I say, God gives not an account of His matters to any. Beware, then, of drawing rash conclusions. RICHARD CAMERON'S SERMON *preached three days before he was killed at Airsmoss*

The reason why the presumptuous sinner fears so little, and the despairing soul so much, is for want of knowing God as great; therefore, to cure them both, the serious consideration of God, under this notion, is propounded: *Be still, and know that I am God;* as if He had said, "Know, O ye wicked, that I am God, Who can avenge Myself when I please upon you, and cease to provoke Me by your sins, to your own confusion; and again, know, ye trembling souls, that I am God; and therefore able to pardon the greatest sins, and cease to dishonor Me by your unbelieving thoughts of me." WILLIAM GURNALL

The sole consideration that God is God, sufficient to still all objections to His sovereignty. JONATHAN EDWARDS

Vs. 11. *The Lord of hosts is with us.* On Tuesday, Mr. Wesley could with difficulty be understood, though he often attempted to speak. At last, with all the strength that he had, he cried out, "The best of all is, God is with us."

Again raising his hand, and waving it in triumph, he exclaimed with thrilling effect, "The best of all is, God is with us." These words seem to express the leading feature of his whole life. God had been with him from early childhood; His providence had guided him through all the devious wanderings of human life; and now, when he was entering the "valley of the shadow of death," the same hand sustained him. *From "Wesley and His Coadjutors," by* REV. W. C. LARRABEE, A.M., *Edited by Rev. B. F. Tefft, Cincinnati*

## PSALM 47

Title: "To the Chief Musician." Many songs were dedicated to this leader of the chorus, but he was not overloaded thereby. God's service is such delight that it cannot weary us; and that choicest part of it, the singing of His praises, is so pleasurable that we cannot have too much of it. Our ear has grown accustomed to the ring of David's compositions, and we are morally certain that we hear it in this Psalm. Every expert would detect here the autography of the Son of Jesse, or we are greatly mistaken. C. H. S.

Some have applied this Psalm to Christ's ascension; but it speaks of His Second Coming. The Mighty One is seated peacefully on His throne. We are referred back to Psalm 45. ANDREW A. BONAR

Vs. 1. *Clap your hands, all ye people.* The most natural and most enthusiastic tokens of exultation are to be used in view of the victories of the Lord and His universal reign. Our joy in God may be demonstrative, and yet He will not censure it.

The joy is to extend to all nations; Israel may lead the van, but all the Gentiles are to follow in the march of triumph, for they have an equal share in that kingdom where there is neither Greek nor Jew, but Christ is all and in all. C. H. S.

*O clap your hands, all ye people; shout unto God with the voice of triumph.* This should be done, 1. Cheerfully, *Clap your hands,* for this is a sign of inward joy (Nah. 3:19). 2. Universally: "O clap your hands, *all ye people.*" 3. Vocally: *Shout unto God with the voice of triumph.* 4. Frequently: *Sing praises to God, sing praises, sing praises unto our King, sing praises* (verse 6); and again, *sing praises* (verse 7). It cannot be done too frequently. 5. Knowingly and discreetly: "Sing ye praises with understanding"; know the reason why ye are to praise Him. ADAM CLARKE

Such expressions of pious and devout affection as to some may seem indecent and imprudent, yet ought not to be hastily censured and condemned, much less ridiculed; because if they come from an upright heart, God will accept the strength of the affection, and excuse the weakness of the expression of it. MATTHEW HENRY

The voice of melody is not so much to be uttered with the tongue as with the hands; that is, it is our deeds not our words by which God is here to be praised. Even as it was in Him Whose pattern we are to follow: "Jesus began both to do and to teach." J. M. NEALE

Vs. 2. *For the Lord,* or Jehovah, the Self-existent and only God; *Most High,* most great in power, lofty in dominion, eminent in wisdom, elevated in glory, *is terrible.* Omnipotence, which is terrible to crush, is almighty to protect.

*He is a great King over all the earth.* Our God is no local deity, no petty ruler of a tribe; in infinite majesty He rules the mightiest realm as absolute Arbiter of destiny, sole Monarch of all lands, King of kings, and Lord of lords. Not a hamlet or an islet is excluded from His dominion. How glorious will that era be when this is seen and known of all; when in the person of Jesus all flesh shall behold the glory of the Lord!

Vs. 4. *He shall choose our inheritance for us.* We submit our will, our choice, our desire, wholly to Him. Our heritage here and hereafter we leave to Him, let Him do with us as seemeth Him good. C. H. S.

It is reported of a woman who, being sick, was asked whether she was willing to live or die; she answered, "Which God pleases." "But," said one, "if God should refer it to you, which would you choose?" "Truly," replied she, "I would refer it to Him again."

Thus that man obtains his will of God, whose will is subjected to God. We are not to be troubled that we have no more from God, but we are to be troubled that we do no more for God. Christians, if the Lord be well pleased with your persons, should not you be well pleased with your conditions? There is more reason that you should be pleased with them than that He should be pleased with you.

Believers should be like sheep, which change their pastures at the will of the shepherd; or like vessels in a house, which stand to be filled or emptied at the pleasure of their owner. He that sails upon the sea of this world in his own bottom, will sink at last into a bottomless ocean. Never were any their own carvers, but they were sure to cut their own fingers. WILLIAM SECKER

It may be thou art godly and poor. 'Tis well; but canst thou tell whether, if thou wert not poor, thou wouldst be godly? Surely God knows us better than we ourselves do, and therefore can best fit the estate to the person. GILES FLETCHER

*The excellency of Jacob whom He loved.* Our beauty, our boast, our best treasure, lies in having such a God to trust in, such a God to love us.

Vs. 5. *God is gone up with a shout.* Faith hears the people already shouting. The command of the first verse is here regarded as a fact. The fight is over, the conqueror ascends to His triumphal chariot, and rides up to the gates of the city which is made resplendent with the joy of His return.

The words are fully applicable to the ascension of the Redeemer. We doubt not that angels and glorified spirits welcomed Him with acclamations. He came not without song, shall we imagine that He returned in silence?

*The Lord with the sound of a trumpet.* Jesus is Jehovah. The joyful strain of the trumpet betokens the splendor of His triumph.

Vs. 7. *For God is the King of all the earth.* The Jews of our Savior's time resented this truth, but had their hearts been right they would have rejoiced in it. They would have kept their God to themselves, and not even have allowed the Gentile dogs to eat the crumbs from under His table. Alas! how selfishness turns honey into wormwood.

*Sing ye praises with understanding.* It is to be feared from the slovenly way in which some make a noise in singing that they fancy any sound will do. On the other hand, from the great attention paid by some to the mere music, we feel sadly sure that the sense has no effect upon them. Is it not a sin to be tickling men's ears with sounds when we profess to be adoring the Lord? What has a sensuous delight in organs, anthems, etc., to do with devotion? Do not men mistake physical effects for spiritual impulses? Do they not often offer to God strains far more calculated for human amusement than for divine acceptance? And understanding enlightened of the Holy Spirit is then and then only fully capable of offering worthy praise. C. H. S.

If we do not understand what we sing, it argues carelessness of spirit, or hardness of heart; and this makes the service impertinent. Upon this the worthy Davenant cries out, "Adieu to the bellowing of the Papists, who sing in an unknown tongue." God will not understand us in that service which we understand not ourselves. One of the first pieces of the creation was light, and this must break out in every duty. JOHN WELLS, *in "Morning Exercises"*

Vs. 8. *He sitteth upon the throne of His holiness.* Unmoved, He occupies an undisputed throne, Whose decrees, acts, and commands are holiness itself. What other throne is like this? Never was it stained with injustice, or defiled with sin. Neither is He Who sits upon it dismayed nor in a dilemma. He sits in serenity, for He knows His own power and sees that His purposes will not miscarry. Here is reason enough for holy song. C. H. S.

# PSALM 48

Title: "A Song and Psalm for the Sons of Korah." A song for joyfulness and a Psalm for reverence. Alas! every song is not a Psalm, for poets are not all heaven-born, and every Psalm is not a song, for in coming before God we have to utter mournful confessions as well as exulting praises.

Subject: It would be idle dogmatically to attribute this song to any one event of Jewish history. Its author and date are unknown. It records the withdrawal of certain confederate kings from Jerusalem, their courage failing them before striking a blow.

Vs. 1. *Great is the Lord.* How great Jehovah is essentially none can conceive; but we can all see that He is great in the deliverance of His people, great in their esteem who are delivered, and great in the hearts of those enemies whom He scatters by their own fears. Instead of the mad cry of Ephesus, "Great is Diana," we bear the reasonable, demonstrable, self-evident testimony, "Great is Jehovah." C. H. S.

Greater (Job 33:12). Greatest of all (Ps. 95:3). Greatness itself (Ps. 95:3). A degree He is above the superlative. JOHN TRAPP

Vs. 2. *The joy of the whole earth, is Mount Zion.* Jerusalem was the world's star; whatever light lingered on earth was borrowed from the oracles preserved by Israel. C. H. S.

When I stood that morning on the brow of Olivet, and looked down on the city crowning those battlemented heights, encircled by those deep and dark ravines, I involuntarily exclaimed, *Beautiful for situation, the joy of the whole earth, is mount Zion, on the sides of the north, the city of the great King.* And as I gazed, the red rays of the rising sun shed a halo round the top of the castle of David; then they tipped with gold each tapering minaret, and gilded each dome of mosque and church, and at length, bathed in one flood of ruddy light the terraced roofs of the city, and the grass and foliage, the cupolas, pavements, and colossal walls of the Haram. No human being could be disappointed who first saw Jerusalem from Olivet. J. L. PORTER

Vs. 5. *They saw it, and so they marvelled.* They came, they saw, but they did not conquer. There was no *veni, vidi, vici* for them. No sooner did they perceive that the Lord was in the Holy City than they took to their heels. Before the Lord came to blows with them, they were faint-hearted and beat a retreat. C. H. S.

Verses 5-6. The potentates of the world saw the miracles of the Apostles, the courage and constancy of the martyrs, and the daily increase of the church, notwithstanding all their persecutions; they beheld with astonishment the rapid progress of the faith through the Roman Empire; they called upon their gods, but their gods could not help themselves; idolatry expired at the foot of the victorious cross. GEORGE HORNE

Vs. 7. *Thou breakest the ships of Tarshish with an east wind.* Speculative heresies, pretending to bring us wealth from afar, are constantly assailing the church, but the breath of the Lord soon drives them to destruction. The church too often relies on the wisdom of men, and these human helps are soon shipwrecked; yet the church itself is safe beneath the care of her God and King.

Vs. 9. *We have thought.* Holy men are thoughtful men; they do not suffer God's wonders to pass before their eyes and melt into forgetfulness, but they meditate deeply upon them.

*Of Thy lovingkindness, O God.* What a delightful subject! Devout minds never tire of so divine a theme.

*In the midst of Thy temple.* Memories of mercy should be associated with continuance of praise. Hard by the table of show-bread commemorating His bounty, should stand the altar of incense denoting our praise.

Vs. 10. *According to Thy Name, O God, so is Thy praise unto the ends of the earth.* Great fame is due to His great Name. The glory of Jehovah's exploits overleaps the boundaries of earth; angels behold with wonder, and from every star delighted intelligences proclaim His fame beyond the ends of the earth.

What if men are silent, yet the woods, and seas, and mountains, with all their countless tribes, and all the unseen spirits that walk them, are full of the divine praise. As in a shell we listen to the murmurs of the sea, so in the convolutions of creation we hear the praises of God.

*Thy right hand is full of righteousness.* Thy scepter and Thy sword, Thy government and Thy vengeance, are altogether just. Thy hand is never empty, but full of energy, of bounty, and of equity. Neither saint nor sinner shall find the Lord to be an empty-handed God; He will in both cases deal out righteousness to the full: to the one, through Jesus, He will be just to forgive, to the other just to condemn.

Vs. 13. *Mark ye well her bulwarks.* The security of the people of God is not a doctrine to be kept in the background. It may be safely taught, and frequently pondered. Only to base hearts will that glorious truth prove harmful. The sons of perdition make a stumbling-stone even of the Lord Jesus Himself; it is little wonder that they pervert the truth of God concerning the final perseverance of the saints. C. H. S.

Vs. 14. *This God is our God forever and ever.* What a portion then is that of the believer! The landlord cannot say of his fields, "These are mine forever and ever." The king cannot say of his crown, "This is mine forever and ever." These possessions shall soon change masters; these possessors shall soon mingle with the dust, and even the graves they shall occupy may not long be theirs.

But it is the singular, the supreme happiness of every Christian to say, or to have the right to say, "This glorious God with all His divine perfections is my God, forever and ever, and even death itself shall not separate me from His love." GEORGE BURDER

God is not only a satisfying portion, filling every crevice of thy soul with the light of joy and comfort; and a sanctifying portion, elevating thy soul to its primitive and original perfection; and a universal portion; not health, or wealth, or friends, or honors, or liberty, or life, or house, or wife, or child, or pardon, or peace, or glory, or earth, or heaven, but all these and infinitely more, but also He is an eternal portion. This God would be thy God *forever and ever.* Oh, sweet word *ever!* Thou art the crown of the saints' crown, and the glory of their glory. GEORGE SWINNOCK

# PSALM 49

Vs. 2. *Both low and high, rich and poor, together.* Our preaching ought to have a voice for all classes, and all should have an ear for it. To suit our word to the rich alone is wicked sycophancy, and to aim only at pleasing the poor is to act the part of a demagogue. Truth may be so spoken as to command the ear of all, and wise men seek to learn that acceptable style. Rich and poor must soon meet together in the grave; they may well be content to meet together now. In the congregation of the dead all differences of rank will be obliterated; they ought not now to be obstructions to united instructions.

Vs. 3. *And the meditation of my heart shall be of understanding.* The same Spirit Who made the ancient seers eloquent also made them thoughtful. The help of the Holy Spirit was never meant to supersede the use of our own mental powers. The Holy Spirit does not make us speak as Balaam's ass, which merely uttered sounds, but never meditated: but He first leads us to consider and reflect, and then He gives us the tongue of fire to speak with power.

Vs. 5. *Wherefore should I fear in the days of evil, when the iniquity of my heels shall compass me about?* The man of God looks calmly forward to dark times when those evils which have dogged his heels shall gain a temporary advantage over him. Iniquitous men, here called in the abstract *iniquity,* lie in wait for the righteous, as serpents that aim at the heels of travellers. C. H. S.

Vs. 6. *They that trust in their wealth, and boast themselves in the multitude of their riches.* Who knocks more boldly at heaven-gate to be let in than they whom Christ will reject as workers of iniquity? Oh, what delusion is this! Caligula never made himself more ridiculous than when he would be honored as a God, while he lived more like a devil. Before you would have others take you for Christians, for God's sake prove yourselves men and not beasts, as you do by your brutish lives. Talk not of your hopes of salvation so long as the marks of damnation are seen upon your flagitious lives.

That friar was far more sound in his judgment in this point, who, preaching at Rome one Lent, when some cardinals and many other great ones were present, began his sermon thus abruptly and ironically, "Saint Peter was a fool, Saint Paul was a fool, and all the primitive Christians were fools; for they thought the way to heaven was by prayers, and tears, watchings and fastings, severities of mortification, and denying the pomp and glory of this world; whereas you here in Rome spend your time in balls and masks, live in pomp and pride, lust and luxury, and yet count yourselves good Christians, and hope to be saved; but at last you will prove the fools, and they will be found to have been the wise men." WILLIAM GURNALL'S *Funeral Sermon for Lady Mary Vere*

Vs. 7. *None of them can by any means redeem his brother.* With all their riches, the whole of them put together could not rescue a comrade from the chill grasp of death. They boast of what they will do with us, let them see to themselves. Let them weigh their gold in the scales of death, and see how much they can buy therewith from the worm and the grave. C. H. S.

Vs. 8. *For the redemption of their soul is precious, and it ceaseth forever.* In this judgment, tears will not prevail, prayers will not be heard, promises will not be admitted, repentance will be too late, and as for riches, honorable titles, scepters, and diadems, these will profit much less. THOMAS TYMME

Vs. 9. No price could secure for any man *That he should still live forever, and not see corruption.* Mad are men now after gold; what would they be if it could buy the elixir of immortality? Gold is lavished out of the bag to cheat the worm of the poor body by embalming it, or enshrining it in a coffin of lead, but it is a miserable business, a very burlesque and comedy. As for the soul, it is too subtle a thing to be detained when it hears the divine command to soar through tracks unknown. Never, therefore, will we fear those base nibblers at our heels, whose boasted treasure proves to be so powerless to save.

Vs. 10. *Likewise the fool and the brutish person perish.* Folly has no immunity from death. Off goes the jester's cap, as well as the student's gown. Jollity cannot laugh off the dying hour; Death, who visits the university, does not spare the tavern.

Vs. 11. *Their inward thought is, that their houses shall continue forever, and their dwelling places to all generations.* He is very foolish who is more a fool in his inmost thought than he dare be in his speech. Such rotten fruit, rotten at the core, are worldlings. Down deep in their hearts, though they dare not say so, they fancy that earthly goods are real and enduring. Foolish dreamers! The frequent dilapidations of their castles and manor-houses should teach them better, but still they cherish the delusion. They cannot tell the mirage from the true streams of water; they fancy rainbows to be stable, and clouds to be the everlasting hills. C. H. S.

Christians! many may (orator like), declaim against the vanity of the creature, and speak as basely of money as others do, and say, "We know it is but a little refined earth"; but their hearts close with it, they are loath to part with it for God's sake, or upon God's declared will. As he that speaketh good words of God, is not said to trust in God; so speaking bad words of worldly riches doth not exempt us from trusting them. There is a difference between declaiming as an orator and acting like a Christian. THOMAS MANTON

*They call their lands after their own names.* Common enough is this practice. His grounds are made to bear the groundling's name; he might as well write it on the water. Men have even called countries by their own names, but what are they the better for the idle compliment, even if men perpetuate their nomenclature?

Vs. 12. *Nevertheless man being in honor abideth not.* He is but a lodger for the hour and does not stay a night: even when he dwells in marble halls, his notice to quit is written out. Eminence is evermore in imminence of peril. The hero of the hour lasts but for an hour. Scepters fall from the paralyzed hands which once grasped them, and coronets slip away from skulls when the life is departed. C. H. S.

The Rabbins read it thus: "Adam, being in honor, *lodged not one night.*" The Hebrew word for *abide* signifies "to stay or lodge all night." Adam, then, it seems, did not take up one night's lodging in Paradise. THOMAS WATSON'S *"Body of Divinity"*

*He is like the beasts that perish.* He is not like the sheep which are preserved of the Great Shepherd, but like the hunted beast which is doomed to die. He lives a brutish life and dies a brutish death. Wallowing in riches, surfeited with pleasure, he is fatted for the slaughter, and dies like the ox in the shambles. Alas! that so noble a creature should use his life so unworthily and end it so disgracefully. So far as this world is concerned, wherein doth the death of many men differ from the death of a dog? They go down

*To the vile dust from whence they sprung,*
*Unwept, unhonour'd, and unsung.*

What room is there, then, for fear to the godly when such natural brute beasts assail them? Should they not in patience possess their souls? C. H. S.

Vs. 13. *This their way is their folly.* The folly of man seldom appears more than in being busy about nothing, in making a great cry where there is little wool; like that empty fellow that showed himself to Alexander—having spent much time, and taken much pains at it beforehand—and boasted that he could throw a pea through a little hole, expecting a great reward; but the king gave him only a bushel of peas, for a recompense suitable to his diligent negligence, or his busy idleness. GEORGE SWINNOCK

Vs. 14. *Death shall feed on them.* Death, like a grim shepherd, leads them on, and conducts them to the place of their eternal pasturage, where all is barrenness and misery.

*The upright shall have dominion over them in the morning.* The poor saints were once the tail, but at the day-break they shall be the head. Sinners rule till night-fall; their honors wither in the evening, and in the morning they find their position utterly reversed. The sweetest reflection to the upright is that "the morning" here intended begins an endless, changeless day. C. H. S.

*Their beauty shall consume in the grave.* Where is their pomp, their delicacy and niceness? All these things are vanished away like the smoke, and there is now nothing left but dust, horror, and stink. The soul, being dissolved, there lieth upon the ground not a human body, but a dead carcase without life, without sense, without strength, and so fearful to look upon that the sight thereof may hardly be endured. THOMAS TYMME

Ah! the melancholy, confused heap of the ruins of mankind, what a terrible carnage is made of the human race! And what a solemn and awful theater of mortality, covered with the disordered remains of our fellow-creatures, presents itself to our minds!

There lie the bones of a proud monarch, who fancied himself a little god, mingled with the ashes of his poorest subjects! Death seized him in the height of his vanity; he was just returning from a conquest, and his haughty mind was swelled with his power and greatness, when one of these fatal arrows pierced his heart and at once finished all his perishing thoughts and contrivances; then the dream of glory vanished and all his empire was confined to the grave.

There a body that was so much doted on, and solicitously cared for, and the beauty and shape whereof were so foolishly admired, now noisome and rotten; nothing but vermin are now fond of it, so affecting a change hath death made upon it. Look, next to this, upon the inglorious ashes of a rich, covetous wretch, whose soul was glued to this world and hugged itself in its treasures; with what mighty throes and convulsions did death tear him from this earth? How did his hands cling to his gold! with what vehement desires did he fasten on his silver, all of them weak and fruitless! WILLIAM DUNLOP

Vs. 15. *But God will redeem my soul from the power of the grave.* Forth from that temporary resting-place we shall come in due time, quickened by divine energy. Like our risen Head, we cannot be holden by the bands of the grave; redemption has emancipated us from the slavery of death. No redemption could man find in riches, but God has found it in the blood of His dear Son. C. H. S.

*For He shall receive me.* This short half-verse, is, as Bottcher remarks, the more weighty from its very shortness. The same expression occurs again (73:24), "Thou shalt take me," the original of both being Gen. 5:24, where it is used of the translation of Enoch, "He was not, for God took him." J. J. STEWART PEROWNE

Vs. 16. *Be not thou afraid when one is made rich.* Let it not give thee any concern to see the godless prosper. Raise no questions as to divine justice;

suffer no foreboding to cloud thy mind. Temporal prosperity is too small a matter to be worth fretting about; let the dogs have their bones, and the swine their draff.

*When the glory of his house is increased.* Though the sinner and his family are in great esteem, and stand exceedingly high, never mind; all things will be righted in due time. Only those whose judgment is worthless will esteem men the more because their lands are broader; those who are highly estimated for such unreasonable reasons will find their level ere long, when truth and righteousness come to the fore.

Vs. 17. *For when he dieth he shall carry nothing away.* He has but a leasehold of his acres, and death ends his tenure. Through the river of death a man must pass naked. Not a rag of all his raiment, not a coin of all his treasure, not a jot of all his honor, can the dying worldling carry with him. Why then fret ourselves about so fleeting a prosperity? C. H. S.

Rich men are but like hailstones; they make a noise in the world, as the other rattle on the tiles of a house; down they fall, lie still, and melt away. Man's life is like the banks of a river, his temporal estate is the stream: time will moulder away the banks, but the stream stays not for that, it glides away continually. THOMAS ADAMS

*His glory shall not descend after him* As he goes down, down, down forever, none of his honor or possessions will follow him. Patents of nobility are invalid in the sepulcher. His worship, his honor, his lordship, and his grace, will alike find their titles ridiculous in the tomb. Hell knows no aristocracy. Your dainty and delicate sinners shall find that eternal burnings have no respect for their affectations and refinements. C. H. S.

Death takes the sinner by the throat and "hauls him down stairs to the grave." The indulgence in any sinful propensity has this downward, deathly tendency. Every lust, whether for riches or honors, for gambling, wine, or women, leads the deluded, wretched votary step by step to the chambers of death. There is no hope in the dread prospect; trouble and anguish possess the spirit. Hast thou escaped, O my soul, from the net of the infernal fowler? Never forget that it is as a brand snatched from the burning. Oh, to grace how great a debtor! GEORGE OFFOR'S *note in "The Works of John Bunyan"*

Vs. 18. *Though while he lived he blessed his soul.* He pronounced himself happy. He had his good things in this life. His chief end and aim were to bless himself. He was charged with the adulations of flatterers.

*Men will praise thee, when thou doest well to thyself.* The generality of men worship success, however it may be gained. The color of the winning horse is no matter; it is the winner, and that is enough. "Take care of Number One" is the world's proverbial philosophy, and he who gives heed to it is "a clever fellow," "a fine man of business," "a shrewd, common-sense tradesman," "a man with his head put on the right way." The banker rots as fast as the shoeblack, and the peer becomes as putrid as the pauper. Alas! poor wealth, thou art but the rainbow coloring of the bubble, the tint which yellows the morning mist but adds no substance to it.

So ends the minstrel's lay. Comforting as the theme is to the righteous, it is full of warning to the worldly. Hear ye it, O ye rich and poor. Give ear to it, ye nations of the earth. C. H. S.

## PSALM 50

Title: "A Psalm of Asaph." This is the first of the Psalm of Asaph, but whether it was the production of that eminent musician, or merely dedicated to him, we cannot tell. The titles of twelve Psalms bear his name, but it could not in all of them be meant to ascribe their authorship to him, for several of these Psalms are of too late a date to have been composed by the same writer as the others. C. H. S.

Vs. 3. *Our God shall come!* May our God come! A prayer for the hastening of His advent, as in the Apocalypse (22:20). POOL'S SYNOPSIS

*A fire shall devour before Him.* As He gave His law in fire, so in fire shall He require it. JOHN TRAPP

Vs. 5. *Gather My saints together unto Me.* Go, ye swift-winged messengers, and separate the precious from the vile. Gather out the wheat of the heavenly garner. Let the long-scattered, but elect people, known by My separating grace to be My sanctified ones, be now assembled in one place.

All are not saints who seem to be so—a severance must be made; therefore let all who profess to be saints be gathered before My throne of judgment, and let them hear the Word which will search and try the whole, that the false may be convicted and the true revealed. C. H. S.

Remember this important truth, that Christians are called by the Gospel to be saints; that you are Christians, not so much by your orthodoxy as by your holiness; that you are saints no further than as you are holy in all manner of conversation.

The people of God furnish an evidence of being saints by their godly conduct. "By their fruits," not by their feelings; not by their lips, not by their general profession, but, "By their fruits shall ye know them." The character of the saints is evidenced by divine consecration. The people of God are called holy inasmuch as they are dedicated to God. It is the duty and the privilege of saints to consecrate themselves to the service of God. Even a heathen philosopher could say, "I lend myself to the world, but I give myself to the gods." But we possess more light and knowledge, and are therefore laid under greater obligations than was Seneca. *Condensed from* J. SIBREE'S *"Sermon Preached at the Reopening of Surrey Chapel"*

*Those that have made a covenant with Me by sacrifice:* this is the grand test, and yet some have dared to imitate it. The covenant was ratified by the slaying of victims, the cutting and dividing of offerings; this the righteous have done by accepting with true faith the great propitiatory sacrifice, and this the pretenders have done in merely outward form. Let them be gathered before the throne for trial and testing, and as many as have really ratified the covenant by faith in the Lord Jesus shall be attested before all worlds as the objects of distinguishing grace, while formalists shall learn that outward sacrifices are all in vain. Oh, solemn assize, how does my soul bow in awe at the prospect thereof!

The address which follows, beginning with the seventh verse, is directed to the professed people of God. It is clearly, in the first place, meant for Israel; but is equally applicable to the visible church of God in every age. It declares the futility of external worship when spiritual faith is absent and the mere outward ceremonial is rested in.

Vs. 9. *I will take no bullock out of Thy house.* Foolishly they dreamed that bullocks with horns and hoofs could please the Lord, when indeed He sought for hearts and souls. Impiously they fancied that Jehovah needed these supplies, and that if they fed His altar with their fat beasts, He would be content. What He intended for their instruction, they made their confidence. They remembered not that "to obey is better than sacrifice, and to hearken than the fat of rams." C. H. S.

Vs. 11-12. We show our scorn of God's sufficiency by secret thoughts of meriting from Him by any religious act, as though God could be indebted to us, and obliged by us. As though our devotions could bring a blessedness to God more than He essentially hath; when indeed "our goodness extends not to Him." STEPHEN CHARNOCK

Vs. 12. *If I were hungry, I would not tell thee.* Strange conception, a hungry God! Yet if such an absurd ideal could be truth, and if the Lord hungered for meat, He would not ask it of men. He could provide for Himself out of His own possessions; He would not turn suppliant to His own creatures. Even under the grossest idea of God, faith in outward ceremonies is ridiculous.

Do men fancy that the Lord needs banners, and music, and incense, and fine linen? If He did, the stars would emblazon His standard, the winds and the waves become His orchestra, ten thousand times ten thousand flowers would breathe forth perfume, the snow should be His alb, the rainbow His girdle, the clouds of light His mantle. O fools and slow of heart, ye worship ye know not what!

Vs. 13. *Will I eat the flesh of bulls, or drink the blood of goats?* Are you so infatuated as to think this? Is the great I AM subject to corporeal wants, and are they to be thus grossly satisfied? Heathens thought thus of their idols, but dare ye think thus of the God Who made the heavens and the earth? Can ye have fallen so low as to think thus of Me, O Israel? What vivid reasoning is here! How the fire flashes dart into the idiot faces of trusters in outward forms!

Ye dupes of Rome, can ye read this and be unmoved? The expostulation is indignant; the questions utterly confound; the conclusion is inevitable; heart worship only can be acceptable with the true God. It is inconceivable that outward things can gratify Him, except so far as through them our faith and love express themselves.

Vs. 14. *Offer unto God thanksgiving.* No longer look at your sacrifices as in themselves gifts pleasing to Me, but present them as the tributes of your gratitude; it is then that I will accept them, but not while your souls have no love and no thankfulness to offer Me.

Vs. 15. *And call upon Me in the day of trouble.* O blessed verse! Is this then true sacrifice? Is it an offering to ask an alms of heaven? It is even so. The King Himself so regards it. For herein is faith manifested, herein is love proved, for in the hour of peril we fly to those we love. Who shall say that Old Testament saints did not know the gospel? Its very spirit and essence breathes like frankincense all around this holy Psalm.

*And thou shalt glorify Me.* Thus we see what is true ritual. Here we read inspired rubrics. Spiritual worship is the great, the essential matter; all else without it is rather provoking than pleasing to God. As helps to the soul, outward offerings were precious, but when men went not beyond them, even their hallowed things were profaned in the view of heaven. C. H. S.

Prayer is like the ring which Queen Elizabeth gave to the Earl of Essex, bidding him if he were in any distress send that ring to her and she would help him. God commandeth His people if they be in any perplexity to send this ring to Him: *Call upon Me in the day of trouble: I will deliver thee, and thou shalt glorify Me.* GEORGE SWINNOCK

Who will scrape to a keeper for a piece of venison who may have free access to the master of the game to ask and have? Hanker not after other helpers, rely on Him only, fully trusting Him in the use of such means as He prescribeth and affordeth. God is jealous, will have no co-rival, nor allow thee (in this case) two strings to thy bow. He Who worketh all in all must be unto thee all in all; of, through, and to Whom are all things, to Him be all praise forever (Rom. 11: 36). GEORGE GIPPS, *in "A Sermon Preached [before God, and from Him] to the Honourable House of Commons"*

God withholds from them that ask not, lest He should give to them that desire not (Augustine). David was confident that by God's power he should spring over a wall; yet not without putting his own strength and agility to it. Those things we pray for, we must work for (Augustine). THOMAS ADAMS

Here, beginning with the sixteenth verse, the Lord turns to the manifestly wicked among His people; and such there were even in the highest places of His sanctuary. If moral formalists had been rebuked, how much more these immoral pretenders to fellowship with heaven? If the lack of heart spoiled the worship of the more decent and virtuous, how much more would violations of the law, committed with a high hand, corrupt the sacrifices of the wicked?

Vs. 16. *But unto the wicked God saith, What hast thou to do to declare My statutes?* You violate openly My moral law, and yet are great sticklers for My ceremonial commands! What have you to do with them? What interest can you have in them? Do you dare to teach my law to others and profane it yourselves? What impudence, what blasphemy is this! You count up your holy days, you contend for rituals, you fight for externals, and yet the weightier matters of the law ye despise! Ye blind guides, ye strain out gnats and swallow camels; your hypocrisy is written on your foreheads and manifest to all. C. H. S.

"As snow in summer, and as rain in harvest, so honor is not seemly for a fool." Is it not? No wonder then that divine wisdom requires us ourselves to put off the old man (as snakes put off their skins) before we take on us the most honorable office of reproving sin. DANIEL BURGESS, *in "The Golden Snuffers"*

*The wicked.* By whom are meant, not openly profane sinners; but men under a profession of religion, and indeed who were teachers of others, as appears from the following expostulations with them: the Scribes, Pharisees, and doctors among the Jews, are designed, and so Kimchi interprets it of their wise men, who learnt and taught the law, but did not act according to it. JOHN GILL

*Or that thou shouldest take My covenant in thy mouth.* Ye talk of being in covenant with Me and yet trample My holiness beneath your feet as swine trample upon pearls; think ye that I can brook this? Your mouths are full of lying and slander, and yet ye mouth My words as if they were fit morsels for such as you! How horrible an evil it is that to this day we see men explaining doctrines who despise precepts! They make grace a coverlet for sin and even judge themselves to be sound in the faith, while they are rotten in life. We need the grace of the doctrines as much as the doctrines of grace, and without it an apostle is but a Judas, and a fairspoken professor is an arrant enemy of the cross of Christ. C. H. S.

Observe what follows, and His meaning is expounded: *Seeing thou hatest to be reformed.* As if God has said, "Thou wicked man, who protectest thy sin, and holdest it close, refusing to return and hating to reform; what hast thou to do to meddle with My covenant? Lay off thy defiled hands. He that is resolved to hold his sin takes hold of the covenant in vain, or rather he lets it go, while he seems to hold it. Woe unto those who sue for mercy while they neglect duty. JOSEPH CARYL

When a minister does not do what he teaches, this makes him a vile person; nay, this makes him ridiculous, like Lucian's apothecary, who had medicines in his shop to cure the cough, and told others that he had them, and yet was troubled with it himself. WILLIAM FENNER

Vs. 17. *Seeing thou hatest instruction.* Profane professors are often too wise to learn, too besotted with conceit to be taught of God.

*And castest My words behind thee.* Despising them, throwing them away as worthless, putting them out of sight as obnoxious. Many boasters of the law did this practically; and in these last days there are pickers and choosers of God's words who cannot endure the practical part of the Scripture; they are disgusted at duty, they abhor responsibility, they disembowel texts of their plain meanings, they wrest the Scriptures to their own destruction. It is an ill sign when a man dares not look a Scripture in the face, and an evidence of brazen impudence when he tries to make it mean something less condemnatory of his sins and endeavor to prove it to be less sweeping in its demands. C. H. S.

Vs. 18. *When thou sawest a thief, then thou consentedst with him; or didst run with him.* This was literally true of the Scribes and Pharisees; they devoured widows' houses, and robbed them of their substance, under a pretext of long prayers; they consented to the deeds of Barabbas, a robber, when they preferred him to Jesus Christ; and they joined with the thieves on the cross in reviling Him; and, in a spiritual sense, they stole away the Word of the Lord, every man from his neighbor; took away the key of knowledge from the people, and put false glosses upon the sacred writings. JOHN GILL

*And hast been partaker with adulterers.* How plainly all this declares that without holiness no man shall see the Lord! No amount of ceremonial or theological accuracy can cover dishonesty and fornication: these filthy things must be either purged from us by the blood of Jesus or they will kindle a fire in God's anger which will burn even to the lowest hell.

Vs. 19. *Thou givest thy mouth to evil.* Sins against the ninth commandment are here mentioned. The man who surrenders himself to the habit of slander is a vile hypocrite if he associates himself with the people of God. A man's health is readily judged by his tongue. A foul mouth, a foul heart. Some slander almost as often as they breathe, and yet are great upholders of the church, and great sticklers for holiness. To what depths will not they go in evil, who delight in spreading it with their tongues?

*And thy tongue frameth deceit.* This is a more deliberate sort of slander, where the man dexterously elaborates false witness and concocts methods of defamation. There is an ingenuity of calumny in some men, and, alas! even in some who are thought to be followers of the Lord Jesus. They manufacture falsehoods, weave them in their loom, hammer them on their anvil, and then retail their wares in every company.

Are these accepted with God? Though they bring their wealth to the altar, and speak eloquently of truth and of salvation, have they any favor with God? We should blaspheme the holy God if we were to think so. They are corrupt in His sight, a stench in His nostrils. He will cast all liars into hell. Let them preach, and pray, and sacrifice as they will; till they become truthful, the God of truth loathes them utterly.

Vs. 20. *Thou slanderest thine own mother's son.* The wretched slanderer knows no claims of kindred. He stabs his brother in the dark and aims a blow at him who came forth of the same womb; yet he wraps himself in the robe of hypocrisy and dreams that he is a favorite of heaven, an accepted worshiper of the Lord.

Are such monsters to be met with nowadays? Alas! they pollute our churches still, and are roots of bitterness, spots in our solemn feasts, wandering stars, for whom is reserved the blackness of darkness for ever.

Perhaps some such may read these lines, but they will probably read them in vain; their eyes are too dim to see their own condition, their hearts are waxen gross, their ears are dull of hearing; they are given up to a strong delusion to believe a lie, that they may be damned.

Vs. 21. *Thou thoughtest that I was altogether such an one as thyself.* The inference drawn from the Lord's patience was infamous; the respited culprit thought his Judge to be one of the same order as himself. He offered sacrifice, and deemed it accepted; he continued in sin, and remained unpunished, and therefore he rudely said, "Why need believe these crazy prophets? God cares not how we live so long as we pay our tithes. Little does He consider how we get the plunder, so long as we bring a bullock to His altar." What will not men imagine of the Lord? At one time they liken the glory of Israel to a calf, and anon unto their brutish selves. C. H. S.

Such is the blindness and corruption of our nature that we have very deformed and misshapen thoughts of Him, till with the eye of faith we see His face in the glass of the Word; and therefore Mr. Perkins affirms that all men who ever came of Adam (Christ alone excepted) are by nature atheists; because at the same time that they acknowledge God, they deny His power, presence, and justice, and allow Him to be only what pleaseth themselves.

Indeed, it is natural for every man to desire to accommodate his lusts with such conception of God as may be most favorable to and suit best with them. God charges some for this: *Thou thoughtest that I was altogether such an one as thyself.* Sinners do with God as the Ethiopians do with angels, whom they picture with black faces that they may be like themselves. WILLIAM GURNALL

This men do when they plead for sins as little, as venial, as that which is below God to take notice of; because they themselves think it so, therefore God must think it so, too. Man, with a giant-like pride, would climb into the throne of the Almighty and establish a contradiction to the will of God by making his own will and not God's the square and rule of his actions. This principle commenced and took date in Paradise, when Adam would not depend upon the will of God revealed to him but upon himself and his own will, and thereby makes himself as God. STEPHEN CHARNOCK

*And set them in order before thine eyes:* as if He should say, "Thou thoughtest all thy sins were scattered and dispersed; that there was not a sin to be found; that they should never be rallied and brought together; but I assure thee I will make an army of those sins, a complete army of them, I will set them in rank and file before thine eyes; and see how thou canst behold, much less contend with, such an host as they."

If an army of divine terrors be so fearful, what will an army of black, hellish sins be when God shall bring whole regiments of sins against you—here a regiment of oaths, there a regiment of lies, there a third of false dealings, here a troop of filthy actions, and there a legion of unclean or profane thoughts, all at once fighting against thy life and everlasting peace? JOSEPH CARYL

Atheists do mock at those Scriptures which tell us that we shall give account of all our deeds; but God shall make them find the truth of it in that day of their reckoning. It is as easy for Him to make their forgetful minds remember as to create the minds in them. When He applieth His register to their forgetful spirits, they shall see all their forgotten sins.

When the printer presseth clean paper upon his oiled irons, it receiveth the print of every letter: so when God shall stamp their minds with His register, they shall see all their former sins in a view. The hand was ever writing against Belshazzar, as he was ever sinning, though he saw it not until the cup was filled: so is it to the wicked; their sins are numbered, and themselves weighed, and see not till they be divided by a fearful wakening. WILLIAM STRUTHER

Vs. 22. *Now consider this, ye that forget God,* etc. What is less than a grain of sand? Yet when it comes to be multiplied, what is heavier than the sands of the sea? A little sum multiplied rises high; so a little sin unrepented of will damn us, as one leak in the ship, if it be not well looked to, will drown us. THOMAS WATSON

Vs. 23. *Whoso offereth praise glorifieth Me.* Thanksgiving is a God-exalting work. Though nothing can add the least cubit to God's essential glory, yet praise exalts Him in the eyes of others. THOMAS WATSON

# PSALM 51

Title: "To the chief Musician." Therefore, not written for private meditation only, but for the public service of song. Suitable for the loneliness of individual penitence, this matchless Psalm is equally well adapted for an assembly of the poor in spirit. "A Psalm of David." It is a marvel, but nevertheless a fact, that writers have been found to deny David's authorship of this Psalm, but their objections are frivolous; the Psalm is David-like all over. It would be far easier to imitate Milton, Shakespeare, or Tennyson, than David. His style is altogether *sui generis,* and it is as easily distinguishable as the touch of Rafael or the coloring of Rubens.

The great sin of David is not to be excused, but it is well to remember that his case has an exceptional collection of specialties in it. He was a man of very strong passions, a soldier, and an Oriental monarch having despotic power; no other king of his time would have felt any compunction for having acted as he did, and hence there were not around him those restraints of custom and association which, when broken through, render the offence the more monstrous.

He never hints at any form of extenuation, nor do we mention these facts in order to apologize for his sin, which was detestable to the last degree; but for the warning of others, that they reflect that the licentiousness in themselves at this day might have even a graver guilt in it than in the erring King of Israel. When we remember his sin, let us dwell most upon his penitence, and upon the long series of chastisements which rendered the after part of his life such a mournful history. C. H. S.

This Psalm is the brightest gem in the whole Book and contains instruction so large and doctrine so precious that the tongue of angels could not do justice to the full development. VICTORINUS STRIGELIUS

This Psalm is often and fitly called "The Sinner's Guide." In some of its versions, it often helps the returning sinner. Athanasius recommends to some Christians, to whom he was writing, to repeat it when they awake at night. All evangelical churches are familiar with it. Luther says, "There is no other Psalm which is oftener sung or prayed in the church." This is the first Psalm in which we have the word *Spirit* used in application to the Holy Ghost. WILLIAM S. PLUMER

This is the most deeply affecting of all the Psalms, and I am sure the one most applicable to me. It seems to have been the effusion of a soul smarting under the sense of a recent and great transgression. My God, whether recent or not, give me to feel the enormity of my manifold offences and remember not against me the sins of my youth. THOMAS CHALMERS

Vs. 1. *Have mercy upon me, O God.* He appeals at once to the mercy of God, even before he mentions his sin. The sight of mercy is good for eyes that are sore with penitential weeping. Pardon of sin must ever be an act of pure mercy, and therefore to that attribute the awakened sinner flies. C. H. S.

I dare not say *my* God, for that were presumption. I have lost Thee by sin, I have alienated myself from Thee by following the enemy, and therefore am unclean. I dare not approach Thee, but standing afar off and lifting up my voice with great devotion and contrition of heart, I cry and say, *Have mercy upon me, O God. From "A Commentary on the Seven Penitential Psalms," Chiefly from Ancient Sources, by the* RIGHT REV. A. P. FORBES, *Bishop of Brechin*

*According unto the multitude.* Men are greatly terrified at the multitude of their sins, but here is a comfort—our God hath multitudes of mercies. If our sins be in number as the hairs of our head, God's mercies are as the stars of heaven; and as He is an infinite God, so His mercies are infinite; yea, so far are His mercies above our sins, as He Himself is above us poor sinners. ARCHIBALD SYMSON

Vs. 2. *Wash me thoroughly from mine iniquity.* The dye is in itself immovable, and I, the sinner, have lain long in it, till the crimson is ingrained; but, Lord, wash, and wash, and wash again, till the last stain is gone and not a trace of my defilement is left. The hypocrite is content if his garments be washed; but the true suppliant cries, "Wash me." The one sin against Bathsheba, served to show the Psalmist the whole mountain of his iniquity, of which that foul deed was but one falling stone. He desires to be rid of the whole mass of his filthiness, which though once so little observed, had then become a hideous and haunting terror to his mind. C. H. S.

Hence we learn what a vile, filthy, and miserable thing sin is in the sight of God: it staineth a man's body, it staineth a man's soul, it maketh him more vile than the vilest creature that lives: no toad is so vile and loathsome in the sight of man as a sinner stained and defiled with sin is in the sight of God till he be cleansed and washed from it in the blood of Christ. SAMUEL SMITH

*And cleanse me from my sin.* This is a more general expression; as if the Psalmist said, "Lord, if washing will not do, try some other process; if water avails not, let fire, let anything be tried, so that I may but be purified. Rid me of my sin by some means, by any means, by every means, only do purify me completely, and leave no guilt upon my soul." It is not the punishment he cries out against, but the sin.

Many a murderer is more alarmed at the gallows than at the murder which brought him to it. The thief loves the plunder, though he fears the prison. Not so David: he is sick of sin as sin; his loudest outcries are against the evil of his transgression and not against the painful consequences of it. When we deal seriously with our sin, God will deal gently with us. When we hate what the Lord hates, He will soon make an end of it, to our joy and peace. C. H. S.

Sin is filthy to think of, filthy to speak of, filthy to hear of, filthy to do; in a word, there is nothing in it but vileness. ARCHIBALD SYMSON

Vs. 3. *For I acknowledge my transgressions.* He seems to say, "I make a full confession of them." Not that this is my plea in seeking forgiveness, but it is a clear evidence that I need mercy and am utterly unable to look for any other quarter for help.

*And my sin is ever before me.* My sin as a whole is never out of my mind; it continually oppresses my spirit. I lay it before Thee because it is ever before me: Lord, put it away both from Thee and me. To an awakened conscience, pain on account of sin is not transient and occasional, but intense and permanent, and this is no sign of divine wrath but rather a sure preface of abounding favor. C. H. S.

David owneth his sin and confesseth it his own. Here is our natural wealth: what can we call our own but sin? Our food and raiment, the necessaries of life, are borrowings. We came hungry and naked into the world; we brought none of these with us and we deserved none of them here. Our sin came with us, as David after confesseth. We have right of inheritance in sin, taking it by traduction and transmission from our parents: we have right of possession. So Job: "Thou makest me to possess the sins of my youth." SAMUEL PAGE

Vs. 4. *Against Thee, Thee only, have I sinned.* A sin of infirmity may admit apology; a sin of ignorance may find out excuse; but a sin of defiance can find no defense. SIR RICHARD BAKER

There is a godly sorrow which leads a man to life; and this sorrow is wrought in a man by the Spirit of God, and in the heart of the godly; that he mourns for sin because it has displeased God, Who is so dear and so sweet a Father to him. And suppose he had neither a heaven to lose, nor a hell to gain, yet he is sad and sorrowful in heart because he has grieved God. JOHN WELCH

*And done evil in Thy sight.* To commit treason in the very court of the king and before his eye is impudence indeed: David felt that his sin was committed in all its filthiness while Jehovah Himself looked on. None but a child of God cares for the eye of God, but where there is grace in the soul it reflects a fearful guilt upon every evil act, when we remember that the God Whom we offend was present when the trespass was committed.

Vs. 5. *Behold, I was shapen in iniquity.* He is thunderstruck at the discovery of his inbred sin and proceeds to set it forth. This was not intended to justify himself, but it rather meant to complete the confession. It is as if he said, "Not only have I sinned this once, but I am in my very nature a sinner. The fountain of my life is polluted as well as its streams. My birth-tendencies are out of the square of equity; I naturally lean to forbidden things. Mine is a constitutional disease, rendering my very person obnoxious to Thy wrath."

*And in sin did my mother conceive me.* He goes back to the earliest moment of his being, not to traduce his mother, but acknowledge the deep taproots of his sin. It is a wicked wresting of Scripture to deny that original sin and natural depravity are here taught. Surely men who cavil at this doctrine have need to be taught of the Holy Spirit what be the first principles of the faith. C. H. S.

Verses 5-6. It was a *behold* of astonishment at himself, as before the great and holy God; and therefore it was he seconds and follows it with another *behold* made unto God: *Behold, Thou desirest truth in the inward parts.* And it is as if he had said in both, "Oh, how am I in every way overwhelmed, whilst with one eye cast on myself I see how infinitely corrupt I am in the very constitution of my nature; and with the other eye I behold and consider what an infinite holy God Thou art in Thy nature and being, and what an holiness it is which Thou requirest. I am utterly overwhelmed in the intuition of both these, and able to behold no more, nor look up unto Thee, O holy God!" THOMAS GOODWIN.

Vs. 6. *Thou desirest truth in the inward parts.* Reality, sincerity, true holiness, heart-fidelity, these are the demands of God. He cares not for the pretence of purity; He looks to the mind, heart, and soul. Always has the Holy One of Israel estimated men by their inner nature and not by their outward professions; to Him the inward is as visible as the outward, and He rightly judges that the essential character of an action lies in the motive of him who works it.

Vs. 7. *Purge me with hyssop.* Give me the reality which legal ceremonies symbolize. This passage may be read as the voice of faith as well as a prayer, and so it runs—"Thou wilt purge me with hyssop, *and I shall be clean.*" Foul as I am, there is such power in the divine propitiation that my sin shall vanish away.

*And I shall be whiter than snow.* None but Thyself can whiten me, but Thou canst in grace outdo nature itself in its purest state. Snow soon gathers smoke and dust; it melts and disappears; Thou canst give me an enduring purity. Though snow is white below as well as on the surface, Thou canst work the like inward purity in me and make me so clean that only an hyperbole can set forth my immaculate condition. Lord, do this; my faith believes Thou wilt, and well she knows Thou canst.

Scarcely does Holy Scripture contain a verse more full of faith than this. Considering the nature of the sin and the deep sense of the Psalmist had of it, it is a glorious faith to be able to see in the blood sufficient, nay, all-sufficient merit entirely to purge it away. C. H. S.

But how is this possible? All the dyers upon earth cannot dye a red into a white; and how, then, is it possible that my sins which are as red as scarlet should ever be made as white as snow? Indeed such retrogradation is no work of human art; it must be only His doing Who brought the sun ten degrees back in the dial of Ahaz: for God hath a nitre of grace that can bring not only the redness of scarlet sins, but even the blackness of deadly sins into its native purity and whiteness again.

Yet such whiteness as is manifest in snow will not serve, for I may be as white as snow and yet a leper still; as it is said of Gehazi that "he went from Elisha a leper as white as snow"; it must be therefore *whiter than snow.* And such a whiteness it is that God's washing works upon us, makes within us; for no snow is so white in the eyes of men as a soul cleansed from sin in the sight of God. SIR RICHARD BAKER

Vs. 8. *Make me to hear joy and gladness.* As a Christian is the most sorrowful man in the world, so there is none more glad than he; for the cause of his joy is greatest. In respect his misery was greatest, his delivery greatest, therefore his joy greatest. ARCHIBALD SYMSON.

*That the bones which Thou hast broken may rejoice.* He groaned under no mere flesh wounds; his firmest and yet tenderest powers were "broken in pieces all asunder"; his manhood had become a dislocated, mangled, quivering sensibility. Yet if he who crushed would cure, every wound would become a new mouth for song, every bone quivering before with agony would become equally sensible of intense delight.

The figure is bold, and so is the suppliant. He is requesting a great thing; he seeks joy for a sinful heart, music for crushed bones. Preposterous prayer anywhere but at the throne of God! Preposterous there most of all, but for the cross where Jehovah Jesus bore our sins in His own body on the tree. C. H. S.

Vs. 9. *Hide Thy face from my sins.* He said in the third verse that his sin was always in his sight, and now he prays that God would put it out of His sight. This is a very good order. If we hold our sins in our eyes to pursue them, God will cast them behind His back to pardon them; if we remember them and repent, He will forget them and forgive. WILLIAM COWPER

*Blot out all mine iniquities.* If God hide not His face from our sin, He must hide it forever from us; and if He blot not out our sins, He must blot our names out of His book of life.

Vs. 10. *Create!* What! has sin so destroyed us that the Creator must be called in again? What ruin then doth evil work among mankind! *Create in me.* I, in my outward fabric, still exist; but I am empty, desert, void. Come, then, and let Thy power be seen in a new creation within my old fallen self. Thou didst make a man in the world at first; Lord, make a new man in me.

*A clean heart.* In the seventh verse he asked to be clean; now he seeks a heart suitable to that cleanliness; but he does not say, "Make my old heart clean"; he is too experienced in the hopelessness of the old nature. He would have the old man buried as a dead thing, and a new creation brought in to fill its place. None but God can create either a new heart or a new earth.

Vs. 11. *Cast me not away from Thy presence.* Throw me not away as worthless; banish me not, like Cain, from Thy face and favor. Permit me to sit among those who share Thy love, though I only be suffered to keep the door. I deserve to be forever denied admission to Thy courts; but, O good Lord, permit me still the privilege which is dear as life itself to me.

Vs. 12. *Restore unto me the joy of Thy salvation.* None but God can give back this joy; He can do it; we may ask it; He will do it for His own glory and our benefit. This joy comes not first, but follows pardon and purity: in such order it is safe, in any other it is vain presumption or idiotic delirium. C. H. S.

It is no small comfort to a man that hath lost his receipt for a debt paid when he remembers that the man he deals with is a good and just man, though his discharge is not presently to be found. That God Whom thou hast to deal with is very gracious; what thou hast lost, He is ready to restore (the evidence of thy grace I mean). WILLIAM GURNALL

How can God restore that which He took not away? For can I charge God with the taking away the joy of His salvation from me? O gracious God, I charge not Thee with taking it, but myself with losing it. SIR RICHARD BAKER

*Uphold me with Thy free spirit.* I am tempted to think that I am now an established Christian, that I have overcome this or that lust so long that I have got into the habit of the opposite grace, so that there is no fear; I may venture very near the temptation, nearer than other men.

This is a lie of Satan. I might as well speak of gunpowder getting by habit a power of resisting fire, so as not to catch the spark. As long as powder is wet, it resists the spark, but when it becomes dry it is ready to explode at the first touch. As long as the Spirit dwells in my heart, He deadens me to sin; so that if lawfully called through temptation, I may reckon upon God's carrying me through. But when the Spirit leaves me, I am like dry gunpowder. Oh, for a sense of this! ROBERT MURRAY M'CHEYNE

A loving mother chooses a fitting place and a fitting time to let her child fall; it is learning to walk, it is getting over-confident, it may come to a dangerous place, and if possessed of all this confidence, may fall and destroy itself. So she permits it to fall at such a place and in such a way as that it may be hurt, wholesomely hurt, but not dangerously so. It has now lost its confidence and clings all the more fondly and trustingly to the strong hand that is able to hold up all its goings.

So this David, this little child of the great God, has fallen; it is a sore fall, all his bones are broken, but it has been a precious and a profitable lesson to him; he has no confidence any longer in himself; his trust is not now in an arm of flesh. *Uphold me with Thy free spirit.* THOMAS ALEXANDER

Vs. 13. *Then will I teach transgressors Thy ways.* Reclaimed poachers make the best gamekeepers. Huntingdon's degree of S.S., or Sinner Saved, is more needful for soul-winning evangelists than either M.A. or D.D. The pardoned sinner's matter will be good, for he has been taught in the school of experience, and his manner will be telling, for he will speak sympathetically, as one who has felt what he declares. The audience the Psalmist would choose is memorable—he would instruct transgressors like himself; others might despise them, but "a fellow-feeling makes us wondrous kind." If unworthy to edify saints, he would creep in along with the sinners and humbly tell them of divine love.

Vs. 14. *Deliver me from bloodguiltiness.* He had been the means of the death of Uriah, the Hittite, a faithful and attached follower, and he now confesses that fact. Besides, his sin of adultery was a capital offense, and he puts himself down as one worthy to die the death. Honest penitents do not fetch a compass and confess their sins in an elegant periphrasis, but they come to the point, call a spade a spade, and make a clean breast of all. What other course is rational in dealing with the Omniscient?

*O God, Thou God of my salvation.* He had not ventured to come so near before. It had been, *O God* up till now, but here he cries, *Thou God of my salvation.* Faith grows by the exercise of prayer. He confesses sin more plainly in this verse than before, and yet he deals with God more confidently: growing upward and downward at the same time are perfectly consistent. None but the King can remit the death penalty; it is therefore a joy to faith that God is King, and that He is the author and finisher of our salvation.

*And my tongue shall sing aloud of Thy righteousness.* One would rather have expected him to say, "I will sing of Thy mercy"; but David can see the divine way of justification, that righteousness of God which Paul afterwards spoke of by which the ungodly are justified, and he vows to sing, yea, and to sing lustily of that righteous way of mercy.

After all, it is the righteousness of divine mercy which is its greatest wonder. Note how David would preach in the last verse, and now here he would sing. We can never do too much for the Lord, to Whom we owe more than all. If we could be preacher, precentor, doorkeeper, pewopener, footwasher, and all in one, all would be too little to show forth all our gratitude. A great sinner pardoned makes a great singer. Sin has a loud voice, and so should our thankfulness have. We shall not sing our own praises if we be saved, but our theme will be the Lord, our righteousness, in Whose merits we stand righteously accepted.

Vs. 15. *And my mouth shall show forth Thy praise.* If God opens the mouth He is sure to have the fruit of it. According to the porter at the gate is the nature of that which comes out of man's lips; when vanity, anger, falsehood, or lust unbar the door, the foulest villanies troop out. C. H. S.

If we desire to be doorkeepers in God's house, let us entreat God first to be a doorkeeper in our house, that He would shut the wicket of our mouth against unsavory speeches and open the door of our lips, "that our mouth shall show forth His praise." This was David's prayer and ought to be thy practice, wherein observe three points especially: Who, *the Lord;* what *open my lips;* why, *that my mouth shall show forth Thy praise.* JOHN BOYS

He prays that his lips may be opened; in other words, that God would afford him matter of praise. The meaning usually attached to the expression is that God would so direct his tongue by the Spirit as to fit him for singing His praises. But though it is true that God must supply us with words, and that if He do not, we cannot fail to be silent in His praise, David seems rather to intimate that his mouth must be shut until God called him to the exercise of thanksgiving by extending pardon. JOHN CALVIN

Verses 16-17. Is a thing that is broken good for anything? Can we drink in a broken glass? Or can we lean upon a broken staff? But though other things may be the worse for breaking, yet a heart is never at the best till it be broken; for till it be broken we cannot see what is in it; though God loves a whole heart in affection, yet He loves a broken heart in sacrifice. SIR RICHARD BAKER

Vs. 17. *The sacrifices of God are a broken spirit.* When the heart mourns for sin, Thou art better pleased than when the bullock bleeds beneath the axe. C. H. S.

# PSALM 52

Title: "To the Chief Musician." Even short Psalms, if they record but one instance of the goodness of the Lord, and rebuke but briefly the pride of man, are worthy of our best minstrelsy. When we see that each Psalm is dedicated to "the chief musician," it should make us value our Psalmody and forbid us to praise the Lord carelessly. "Maschil." An instructive. Even the malice of a Doeg may furnish instruction to a David. "A Psalm of David." He was the prime object of Doeg's doggish hatred, and therefore the most fitting person to draw from the incident the lesson concealed within it.

Vs. 1. *Why boasteth thou thyself in mischief, O mighty man?* Doeg had small matter for boasting in having procured the slaughter of a band of defenseless priests. A mighty man indeed to kill men who never touched a sword! He ought to have been ashamed of his cowardice. He had no room for exultation! Honorable titles are but irony where the wearer is mean and cruel. C. H. S.

*The goodness of God endureth continually.* He contrasts the goodness of God with the might and wealth of Doeg, and the foundation of his goodness of God, enduring forever and showing itself effectual. HERMANN VENEMA

Vs. 2. *Like a sharp razor.* The smooth, adroit manner of executing a wicked device neither hides nor abates its wickedness. Murder with *a sharp razor* is as wicked as murder with a meat-axe or bludgeon. A lie very ingeniously framed and rehearsed in an oily manner is as great a sin and in the end will be seen to be as great a folly as the most bungling attempt at deception. WILLIAM S. PLUMER

Vs. 3. *Selah.* Let us pause and look at the proud, blustering liar. Doeg is gone, but other dogs bark at the Lord's people. Saul's cattle-master is buried, but the devil still has his drovers, who fain would hurry the saints like sheep to the slaughter.

Vs. 4. *Thou lovest.* Thou hast a taste, a gusto for evil language.

*All devouring words.* There are words that, like boa-constrictors, swallow men whole, or like lions, rend men to pieces; these words evil minds are fond of. Their oratory is evermore furious and bloody. That which will most readily provoke the lowest passions they are sure to employ, and they think such pandering to the madness of the wicked to be eloquence of a high order.

*O thou deceitful tongue.* Men can manage to say a great many furious things and yet cover all over with the pretext of justice. They claim that they are jealous for the right, but the truth is they are determined to put down truth and holiness and craftily go about it under this transparent pretense.

Vs. 7. *Lo.* Look ye here, and read the epitaph of a mighty man, who lorded it proudly during his little hour and set his heel upon the necks of the Lord's chosen.

*This is the man that made not God his strength.* Behold the man, the great, vainglorious man! He found a fortress, but not in God; he gloried in his might, but not in the Almighty. Where is he now? How has it fared with him in the hour of his need? Behold his ruin, and be instructed.

*But trusted in the abundance of his riches, and strengthened himself in his wickedness.* The substance he had gathered and the mischiefs he had wrought were his boast and glory. Wealth and wickedness are dreadful companions; when combined they make a monster. When the devil is master of money-bags, he is a devil indeed. Beelzebub and Mammon together heat the furnace seven times hotter for the child of God, but in the end they shall work out their own destruction. Wherever we see today a man great in sin and substance, we shall do well to anticipate his end and view this verse as the divine in memoriam. C. H. S.

# PSALM 53

Title: "To the Chief Musician." If the leader of the choir is privileged to sing the jubilates of divine grace, he must not disdain to chant the miseries of human depravity. This is the second time he has had the same Psalm entrusted to him (see Psalm 14), and he must, therefore, be the more careful in singing it.

"Upon Mahalath." The word "Mahalath" appears to signify, in some forms of it, "disease," and truly this Psalm is "The Song of Man's Disease"—the mortal, hereditary taint of sin. It is not a copy of the Fourteenth Psalm emended and revised by a foreign hand; it is another edition by the same author emphasized in certain parts and rewritten for another purpose.

Subject: The evil nature of man is here brought before our view a second time in almost the same inspired words. All repetitions are not vain repetitions. We are slow to learn and need line upon line. David, after a long life, found men no better than they were in his youth. C. H. S.

Probably the two Psalms refer to different periods: the Fourteenth, to the earlier portion of the world, or of Jewish history; the fifty-third, to a later, perhaps a still future time. Jehovah, through Christ, is frequently said to turn to the world to see what its condition is and always with the same result. "All flesh had corrupted its way" in the days of Noah, and "when the Son of Man cometh" again, it is intimated that He will scarcely "find faith on the earth." The two Psalms also apply to different persons. R. H. RYLAND, *in "The Psalms Restored to Messiah"*

The state of the earth ought to be deeply felt by us. The world lying in wickedness should occupy much of our thoughts. The enormous guilt, the inconceivable pollution, the ineffably provoking atheism of this fallen province of God's dominion might be a theme for our ceaseless meditation and mourning. To impress it the more on us, therefore, the Psalm repeats what has been already sung in Psalm 14. ANDREW A. BONAR

This Psalm is a variation of Psalm 14. In each of these two Psalms, the name of God occurs seven times. In Psalm 14, it is three times *Elohim* and four times *Jehovah;* in the present Psalm it is seven times *Elohim.* CHRISTOPHER WORDSWORTH

1. The fact of sin. God is a witness to it.
2. The fault of sin. It is iniquity (verses 1, 4).
3. The fountain of sin. How comes it that men are so bad?
4. The folly of sin. He is a fool who harbors such corrupt thoughts.
5. The filthiness of sin. What neatness soever proud sinners pretend to, it is certain that wickedness is the greatest nastiness in the world.
6. The fruit of sin. See to what a degree of barbarity it brings men at last!
7. The fear and shame that attends sin (verse 5). MATTHEW HENRY

Vs. 1. *The fool hath said in his heart, There is no God.* And this he does because he is a fool. Being a fool, he speaks according to his nature; being a great fool, he meddles with a great subject and comes to a wild conclusion. The atheist is, morally as well as mentally, a fool, a fool in the heart as well as in the head; a fool in morals as well as in philosophy. With the denial of God as a starting-point, we may well conclude that the fool's progress is a rapid, riotous, raving, ruinous one. He who begins at impiety is ready for anything. "No God," being interpreted, means no law, no order, no restraint to lust, no limit to passion. C. H. S.

It is in his heart he says this; this is the secret desire of every unconverted bosom. If the breast of God were within the reach of men, it would be stabbed a million times in one moment. When God was manifest in the flesh, He was altogether lovely; He did no sin; He went about continually doing good: and yet they took Him and hung Him on a tree; they mocked Him and spat upon Him. And this is the way men would do with God again.

Learn—1st. The fearful depravity of your heart. I venture to say there is not an unconverted man present who has the most distant idea of the monstrous wickedness that is now within his breast. Stop till you are in hell, and it will break out unrestrained. But still let me tell you what it is—you have a heart that would kill God if you could. If the bosom of God were now within your reach, and one blow would rid the universe of God, you have a heart fit to do the deed. 2d. The amazing love of Christ—"While we were enemies, Christ died for us." ROBERT MURRAY M'CHEYNE

*Corrupt are they* They are rotten. It is idle to compliment them as sincere doubters and amiable thinkers—they are putrid. There is too much dainty dealing nowadays with atheism; it is not a harmless error, it is an offensive, putrid sin, and righteous men should look upon it in that light. All men being more or less atheistic in spirit are also in that degree corrupt; their heart is foul, their moral nature is decayed. C. H. S.

*And have done abominable iniquity.* If all men are not outwardly vicious, it is to be accounted for by the power of other and better principles, but left to itself the "No God" spirit so universal in mankind would produce nothing but the most loathsome actions. C. H. S.

*There is none that doeth good.* The one typical fool is reproduced in the whole race; without a single exception men have forgotten the right way. This accusation twice made in the Psalm, and repeated a third time by the inspired Apostle Paul, is an indictment most solemn and sweeping, but He Who makes it cannot err, He knows what is in man; neither will He lay more to man's charge than He can prove. C. H. S.

Vs. 2. *God looked down from heaven upon the children of men, to see if there were any that did understand, that did seek God.* He did so in ages past, and He has continued His steadfast gaze from His all-surveying observatory. Had there been one understanding man, one true lover of his God, the divine eye would have discovered him.

Those pure heathens and admirable savages that men talk so much of do not appear to have been visible to the eye of Omniscience, the fact being that they live nowhere but in the realm of fiction. The Lord did not look for great grace but only for sincerity and right desire, but these He found not. He saw all nations, and all men in all nations, and all hearts in all men, and all motions of all hearts, but He saw neither a clear head nor a clean heart among them all. Where God's eyes see no favorable sign we may rest assured there is none. C. H. S.

Vs. 3. *They are altogether become filthy—"neelachu."* They are become sour and rancid; a metaphor taken from milk that has fermented and turned sour, rancid and worthless. ADAM CLARKE

*There is none that doeth good, no, not one.* The fallen race of man, left to its own energy, has not produced a single lover of God or doer of holiness, nor will it ever do so. Grace must interpose or not one specimen of humanity will be found to follow after the good and true. This is God's verdict after looking down upon the race. Who shall gainsay it? C. H. S.

Evil men are not only guilty of sins of commission, having done abominable iniquity, but they are guilty of many sins of omission. In fact, they have never done one holy act. They may be moral, decent, amiable, they may belong to the church; but *there is none that doeth good, no, not one.* WM. S. PLUMER

Vs. 4. *Have the workers of iniquity no knowledge?* Conscience is a means to curb and restrain, control and rebuke corrupt nature, and the swelling forms of it. It is not there as a native inhabitant but as a garrison planted in a rebellious town by the great Governor of the world, to keep the rebellion of the inhabitants within compass, who else would break forth into present confusion. THOS. GOODWIN

*Who eat up my people as they eat bread. C'est, n'en font non plus de conscience, que de manger un morceau de pain.* (That is, they have no more scruple in doing this than in eating a morsel of bread.)—*French Margin*

Vs. 5. *There were they in great fear, where no fear was.* David sees the end of the ungodly and the ultimate triumph of the spiritual seed. The rebellious march in fury against the gracious, but suddenly they are seized with a causeless panic. The once fearless boasters tremble like the leaves of the aspen, frightened at their own shadows. In this sentence and this verse, this Psalm differs much from the fourteenth. C. H. S.

Behold how fearful a hell a wounded conscience is. NICHOLAS GIBBINS

## PSALM 54

Monotony is often the death of congregational praise. Providence is varied and so should our recording songs be.

From verses 1 to 3, where the *Selah* makes a pause for us, the Psalmist pleads with God, and then in the rest of the song, laying aside all doubt, he chants a hymn of joyful triumph. The vigor of faith is the death of anxiety and the birth of security. C. H. S.

He durst not lift up his hands even against the enemies of God (yet what durst not David do?) till he had first lifted them up in humble supplication to the Lord, his strength. J. DOLBEN

Vs. 1. *Save me, O God.* Thou art my Savior; all around me are my foes and their eager helpers. No shelter is permitted me. Every land rejects me and denies me rest. But Thou, O God, wilt give me refuge, and deliver me from all my enemies. C. H. S.

Vs. 2. *Hear my prayer, O God.* This has ever been the defense of saints. As long as God hath an open ear, we cannot be shut up in trouble. All other weapons may be useless, but all-prayer is evermore available. But what is prayer if God hear not? C. H. S.

Vs. 3. *For strangers are risen up against me.* Let them leave off meddling and mind their own concerns. C. H. S.

*And oppressors seek after my soul.* Kings generally coin their own likeness. C. H. S.

*They have not set God before them.* They had no more regard for right and justice than if they knew no God or cared for none. David felt that atheism lay at the bottom of the enmity which pursued him. Good men are hated for God's sake, and this is a good plea for them to urge in prayer.

*Selah.* Enough of this. C. H. S.

Vs. 4. "Behold," says he, "I produce a certain fact, well-known, demonstrated by a new proof, and worthy of all attention; for the particle *behold* contains this breadth of meaning." HERMANN VENEMA

*Behold, God is mine helper.* He saw enemies everywhere, and now to his joy as he looks upon the band of his defenders, he sees One Whose aid is better than all the help of men; he is overwhelmed with joy at recognizing his divine Champion and cries, *Behold.* And is not this a theme for pious exultation in all time, that the great God protects us, His own people: what matters the number or violence of our foes when He uplifts the shield of His omnipotence to guard us and the sword of His power to aid us? Little care we for the defiance of the foe while we have the defence of God. C. H. S.

There is more joy in God's felt presence than grief in felt trouble; for "Behold, God is mine Helper," was more comfortable to David than his friends' unkindness, and strangers' malice was grievous. DAVID DICKSON

*The Lord is with them that uphold my soul.* It is a great mercy to have some friends left us, but a greater mercy still to see the Lord among them, for like so many cyphers, our friends stand for nothing till the Lord sets Himself as a great Unit in the front of them.

Vs. 6. *I will freely sacrifice unto Thee.* Spontaneously will I bring my free-will offerings. So certain is he of deliverance, that he offers a vow by anticipation. His overflowing gratitude would load the altars of God with victims cheerfully presented. The more we receive, the more we ought to render. The spontaneousness of our gifts is a great element in their acceptance; "the Lord loveth a cheerful giver." C. H. S.

## PSALM 55

It would be idle to fix a time and find an occasion for this Psalm with any dogmatism. It reads like a song of the time of Absalom and Ahithophel. C. H. S.

A prayer of the Man Christ in His humiliation, despised and rejected of men, when He was made sin for His people, that they might be made the righteousness of God in Him, when He was about to suffer their punishment, pay their debt, and discharge their ransom. JOHN NOBLE COLEMAN

Vs. 1. *Give ear to my prayer, O God.* But note well that it is never the bare act of prayer which satisfies the godly; they crave an audience with heaven and an answer from the throne, and nothing less will content them.

Vs. 2. *Attend unto me, and hear me.* This is the third time he prays the same prayer. He is in earnest, in deep and bitter earnest. If his God do not hear, he feels that all is over with him. He begs for his God to be a Listener and an Answerer.

*I mourn in my complaint and make a noise.* What a comfort that we may be thus familiar with our God! We may not complain of Him, but we may complain to Him. Our rambling thoughts when we are distracted with grief, we may bring before Him, and that too in utterances rather to be called "a noise" than language. "Groanings that cannot be uttered" are often prayers which cannot be refused. Our Lord Himself used strong crying and tears and was heard in that He feared.

Vs. 3. *And in wrath they hate me.* With a hearty ill-will they detested the holy man. It was no sleeping animosity, but a moral rancor which reigned in their bosoms. The reader needs not that we show how applicable this is to our Lord.

Vs. 4. *And the terrors of death are fallen upon me.* Think of our Lord in the garden, with His "soul exceeding sorrowful even unto death," and you have a parallel to the griefs of the Psalmist. Perchance, dear reader, if as yet thou hast not trodden this gloomy way, thou wilt do so soon; then be sure to mark the footprints of thy Lord in this miry part of the road. C. H. S.

Whilst the Christian is looking only to his own habits and temper, he may and will be always wretched; but if he looks to the great Surety, Christ Jesus, his gloomy prospect will soon be turned to joy. Were our faith more frequently in exercise, we should be enabled to look beyond the dreary mansions of the grave with a hope full of immortality. *Condensed from a Sermon by* JOHN GROVE

The fear of death is upon all flesh. It is no sign of manhood to be without it. To overcome it in the way of duty is courage; to meet death with patience is faith; but not to fear it is either a gift of special grace or a dangerous insensibility. HENRY EDW. MANNING

Vs. 5. *Fearfulness and trembling are come upon me.* The sly, mysterious whisperings of slander often cause a noble mind more fear than open antagonism; we can be brave against an open foe, but cowardly, plotting conspiracies bewilder and distract us. C. H. S.

Fearfulness. How natural is this description! He is *in distress,* he *mourns, makes a noise, sobs,* and *sighs,* his heart *is wounded,* he expects nothing but *death;* this produces *fear,* this produces *tremor,* which terminates in that *deep apprehension* of *approaching* and *inevitable ruin* that *overwhelms* him with *horror.* No man ever described a wounded heart like David. ADAM CLARKE

Vs. 6. *And I said, Oh, that I had wings like a dove! for then would I fly away, and be at rest.* It is cowardly to shun the battle which God would have us fight. We had better face the danger, for we have no armor for our backs. He had need of a swifter conveyance than doves' pinions who would outfly slander; he may be at rest who does not fly but commends his case to his God.

Some of the most astounding sermons ever delivered have been preached on this text, which was a very favorite one with the old divines.

They ransacked Pliny and Aldrovandus for the most outrageous fables about doves, their eyes, their livers, their crops, and even their dung, and then went on to find emblems of Christians in every fact and fable.

Griffith Williams, at considerable length, enlarges upon the fact that David did not desire wings like a grasshopper to hop from flower to flower, as those hasty souls who leap in religion, but do not run with perseverance; nor like an ostrich which keeps to the earth, though it be a bird, as hypocrites do who never mount towards heavenly things; nor like an eagle, or a peacock, or a beetle, or a crow, or a kite, or a bat; and after he has shown in many ways the similarity between the godly and doves he refers to Hugo Cardinalis, and others for more.

We do not think it would be to edification to load these pages with such eccentricities and conceits. This one single sentence from Bishop Patrick is worth them all, "He rather wished than hoped to escape." He saw no way of escape except by some improbable or impossible means. C. H. S.

Wherever the Psalmist cast his eye, the inscription was vanity and vexation. A deluge of sin and misery covered the world, so that like Noah's dove he could find no rest for the sole of his foot below, therefore does he direct his course toward heaven, and say, *Oh that I had wings like a dove! for then would I fly away, and be at rest.* THOS. SHARP, in "*Divine Comforts*"

When the Gauls had tasted the wine of Italy, they asked where the grapes grew and would never be quiet till they came there. Thus may you cry, *Oh, that I had wings like a dove! for then would I fly away, and be at rest.* A believer is willing to lose the world for the enjoyment of grace; and he is willing to leave the world for the fruition of glory. WM. SECKER

Vs. 8. *I would hasten my escape from the windy storm and tempest.* There was a windy storm and tempest without, and which is worse, a tumult and combustion within in his thoughts. A man may escape from external confusions, but how shall he fly from himself? THOS. SHARP

Vs. 11. *Wickedness is in the midst thereof.* The very heart of the city was base. In her places of authority, crime went hand-in-hand with calamity. All the wilder and more wicked elements were uppermost; the *canaille* were commanders; the scum floated uppermost; justice was at a discount; the population was utterly demoralized; prosperity had vanished and order with it.

*Deceit and guile depart not from her streets.* In all the places of concourse, crafty tongues were busy persuading the people with cozening phrases. Crafty demagogues led the people by the nose. Their good king was defamed in all ways, and when they saw him go away, they fell to reviling the governors of their own choosing. The forum was the fortress of fraud, the congress was the convention of cunning. Alas, poor Jerusalem, to be thus the victim of sin and shame! Virtue reviled and vice regnant! Her solemn assemblies broken up, her priests fled, her king banished, and troops of reckless villains parading her streets, sunning themselves on her walls, and vomiting their blasphemies in her sacred shrines. Here was cause enough for the sorrow which so plaintively utters itself in these verses.

Vs. 12. The reader will do well to observe how accurately the Psalmist described his own Psalm when he said, "I mourn in my complaint," or rather

"Give loose to my thoughts," for he proceeds from one point of his sorrow to another, wandering on like one in a maze making few pauses, and giving no distinct intimations that he is changing the subject.

*For it was not an enemy that reproached me; then could I have borne it.* None are such real enemies as false friends. Reproaches from those who have been intimate with us, and trusted by us, cut us to the quick; and they are usually so well acquainted with our peculiar weaknesses that they know how to touch us where we are most sensitive, and to speak so as to do us most damage. We can bear from Shimei what we cannot endure from Ahithophel.

*Neither was it he that hated me that did magnify himself against me; then I would have hid myself from him.* If our enemies proudly boast over us, we nerve our souls for resistance, but when those who pretend to love us leer at us with contempt, whither shall we go? Our blessed Lord had to endure at its worst the deceit and faithlessness of a favored disciple; let us not marvel when we are called to tread the road which is marked by His pierced feet. C. H. S.

Vs. 13. *But it was Thou.* How justly might the Lord have pointed at Judas and said, *But thou;* but His gentler spirit warned the son of perdition in the mildest manner, and had not Iscariot been tenfold a child of hell, he would have relinquished his detestable purpose. C. H. S.

Vs. 14. *And walked unto the house of God in company.* There is a measure of impiety of a detestable sort in the deceit which debases the union of men who make professions of godliness. Shall the very altar of God be defiled with hypocrisy? Shall the gatherings of the temple be polluted by the presence of treachery? All this was true of Ahithophel, and in a measure of Judas. His union with the Lord was on the score of faith; they were joined in the holiest of enterprises; he had been sent on the most gracious of errands. His co-operation with Jesus to serve his own abominable ends stamped him as the firstborn of hell. Better had it been for him had he never been born.

Let all deceitful professors be warned by his doom, for like Ahithophel, he went to his own place by his own hand, and retains a horrible preeminence in the calendar of notorious crime. Here was one source of heart-break for the Redeemer, and it is shared in by His followers. Of the serpent's brood, some vipers still remain, who will sting the hand that cherished them and sell for silver those who raised them to the position which rendered it possible for them to be so abominably treacherous. C. H. S.

Vs. 15. *Let death seize upon them.* Traitors such as these deserve to die; there is no living with them. Earth is polluted by their tread; if spies are shot, much more these sneaking villains. C. H. S.

This prayer is a prophecy of the utter, the final, the everlasting ruin of all those who, whether secretly or openly, oppose and rebel against the Lord's Messiah. MATTHEW HENRY

*Let them go down quick into hell.* While in the vigor of life, into *sheol* let them sink, let them suddenly exchange the enjoyment of the quick or living for the sepulchers of the dead. There is, however, no need to read this verse as an imprecation; it is rather a confident expectation, or prophecy.

*For wickedness is in their dwellings, and among them.* There is justice in the universe; love itself demands it; pity to rebels against God, as such, is no virtue—we pray for them as creatures; we abhor them as enemies of God. We need in these days far more to guard against the disguised iniquity which sympathizes with evil and counts punishment to be cruelty than against the harshness of a former age. C. H. S.

Vs. 17. *Evening and morning and at noon, will I pray.* Often, but none too often. Seasons of great need call for frequent seasons of devotion. The three periods chosen are most fitting: to begin, continue, and end the day with God is supreme wisdom. Where time has naturally set up a boundary, there let us set up an altar-stone. The Psalmist means that he will always pray; he will run a line of prayer right along the day and track the sun with his petitions. Day and night he saw his enemies busy (verse 10), and therefore he would meet their activity by continuous prayer. C. H. S.

This was the custom of the pious Hebrews (see Dan. 6:10). The Hebrews began their day in the evening, and hence David mentions the evening first. The rabbins say men should pray three times each day because the day changes three times. This was observed in the primitive church; but the times in different places were various.

The old Psalter gives this a curious turn: "At *even* I sall tell his louing (*praise*) what tim Christ was on the Crosse; and at *morn* I sall schew his louing, what tim he ros fra dede. And sua he sall here my voice at *midday*, that is sitand at the right hand of his fader, wheder he stegh (ascended) at midday." ADAM CLARKE

If our poor, frail bodies need refreshment from food three times a day, who that knows his own weakness will say that we need not as frequent refreshment for our poor, frail spirits? WM. S. PLUMER

Vs. 19. *God shall hear, and afflict them.* They make a noise as well as I, and God will hear them. The voice of slander, malice, and pride is not alone heard by those whom it grieves. It reaches heaven; it penetrates the Divine ear; it demands vengeance and shall have it.

*Because they have no changes, therefore they fear not God.* His own reverential feeling causes him to remember the daring godlessness of the wicked; he feels that his trials have driven him to his God, and he declares that their uninterrupted prosperity was the cause of their living in such neglect of the Most High. It is a very manifest fact that long-continued ease and pleasure are sure to produce the worst influences upon graceless men: though troubles do not convert them, yet the absence of them makes their corrupt nature more readily develop itself. Stagnant water becomes putrid. Summer heat breeds noxious insects. He who is without trouble is often without God. It is a forcible proof of human depravity that man turns the mercy of God into nutriment for sin: the Lord save us from this. C. H. S.

Vs. 21. *The words of his mouth were smoother than butter.* He lauded and larded the man he hoped to devour. He buttered him with flattery and then battered him with malice. Beware of a man who has too much honey on his tongue; a trap is to be suspected where the bait is so tempting. Soft, smooth, oily words are most plentiful where truth and sincerity are most scarce. C. H. S.

Vs. 22. *Cast thy burden upon the Lord, and He shall sustain thee:* He shall *never suffer the righteous to be moved.* The remedy which the Psalm suggests, and, perhaps, the only resource in a difficulty of the kind, where the enemies of true religion are fighting under the semblance of friendship, is announced in an oracular voice from God: "Cast thy care upon Jehovah, for He will sustain thee; He will not suffer the just one to be tossed about forever." R. H. RYLAND

God delights not to see tears in thine eyes or paleness in thy countenance; thy groans and sighs make no music in His ears. He had rather that thou wouldst free thyself of thy burden by casting it upon Him, that He might rejoice in thy joy and comfort. SAMUEL BLACKERBY

# PSALM 56

We have here the songs of God's servant, who rejoices once more to return from banishment and to leave those dangerous places where he was compelled to hold his peace even from good. There is such deep, spiritual knowledge in this Psalm that we might say of it, "Blessed art thou David Bar-jonas, for flesh and blood hath not revealed this unto thee." C. H. S.

Vs. 1. *Be merciful unto me, O God.* This is to me the one source of all my expectations, the one fountain of all promises: *Miserere mei, Deus, miserere mei.* BERNARD

*For man would swallow me up.* He is but Thy creature, a mere man, yet like a monster he is eager for blood; he pants, he gapes for me; he would not merely wound me, or feed on my substance, but he would fain swallow me altogether, and so make an end of me. The open mouths of sinners when they rage against us should open our mouths in prayer. C. H. S.

*Scoop me up* (as the Hebrew word soundeth); make but one draught of me, or suck me in as a whirlpool; swallow me up as a ravenous wild beast. JOHN TRAPP

Vs. 2. *Mine enemies would daily swallow me up.* Their appetite for blood never fails them. With them there is no truce or armistice. They are many, but one mind animates them. Nothing I can do can make them relent. Unless they can quite devour me, they will never be content. The ogres of nursery tales exist in reality in the enemies of the church, who would crush the bones of the godly and make a mouthful of them if they could.

*For they be many that fight against me.* Sinners are gregarious creatures. Persecutors hunt in packs. These wolves of the church seldom come down upon us singly. C. H. S.

Vs. 3. *What time I am afraid, I will trust in Thee.* David was no braggart; he does not claim never to be afraid; he was no brutish Stoic free from fear because of the lack of tenderness. David's intelligence deprived him of the stupid needlessness of ignorance; he saw the imminence of his peril and was afraid. We are men, and therefore liable to overthrow; we are feeble, and therefore unable to prevent it; we are sinful men, and therefore deserving it, and for all these reasons we are afraid.

But the condition of the Psalmist's mind was complex—he feared, but that fear did not fill the whole area of his mind, for he adds, *I will trust in Thee.* It is possible, then, for fear and faith to occupy the mind at the same moment. We are strange beings, and our experience in the divine life is stranger still. We are often in a twilight, where light and darkness are both present, and it is hard to tell which predominates.

It is a blessed fear which drives us to trust. Unregenerate fear drives from God; gracious fear drives to Him. If I fear man, I have only to trust God, and I have the best antidote. C. H. S.

There is nothing like faith to help at a pinch; faith dissolves doubts as the sun drives away the mists. And that you may not be put out, know that your time for believing is always. There are times when some graces may be out of use, but there is no time wherein faith can be said to be so. Wherefore, faith must be always in exercise.

Faith is the eye, is the mouth, is the hand, and one of these is of use all the day long. Faith is to see, to receive, to work, or to eat; and a Christian should be seeing or receiving, or working, or feeding all day long. Let it rain, let blow, let it thunder, let it lighten, a Christian must still believe. "At what time," said the good man, "I am afraid, I will trust in Thee." JOHN BUNYAN

A divine spark may live in a smoke of doubts without a speedy rising into a flame. When grace is at the bottom of doubting, there will be reliance on Christ and lively petition to Him. Peter's faith staggers when he began to sink, but he casts a look and sends forth a cry to his Savior, acknowledging His sufficiency (Matt. 14:30), "Lord, save me." STEPHEN CHARNOCK

It is a good maxim with which to go into a world of danger; a good maxim to go to sea with; a good maxim in a storm; a good maxim when in danger on land; a good maxim when we are sick; a good maxim when we think of death and judgment—*What time I am afraid, I will trust in Thee.* ALBERT BARNES

Vs. 4. *In God I will praise His word.* Faith brings forth praises. He who can trust will soon sing. C. H. S.

*I will not fear what flesh can do unto me.* Again, thou oughtest not to fear flesh. Our Savior (Matthew 10) thrice, in the compass of six verses, commands us not to fear man: if thy heart quail at him, how wilt thou behave thyself in the list against Satan, whose little finger is heavier than man's loins? The Romans had *arma proelusoria,* weapons rebated, or cudgels, which they were tried at before they came to the sharp.

If thou canst not bear a bruise in thy flesh from man's cudgels and blunt weapons, what wilt thou do when thou shalt have Satan's sword in thy side? God counts Himself reproached when His children fear a sorry man; therefore, we are bid sanctify the Lord, not to fear their fear. WILLIAM GURNALL

Eusebius tells us of a notable speech that Ignatius used when he was in his enemies' hands, not long before he was to suffer, which argued a raised spirit to a wonderful height above the world and above himself. "I care," says he, "for nothing visible or invisible, that I might get Christ. Let fire, the cross, the letting out of beasts upon me, breaking of my bones, the tearing of my members, the grinding of my whole body, and the torments of the devils come upon me, so be it I may get Christ." *From* JEREMIAH BURROUGHS' *"Moses, His Self-denyall"*

*Fear of man*—grim idol, bloody mouthed; many souls has he devoured and trampled down into hell! His eyes are full of hatred to Christ's disciples. Scoffs and jeers lurk in his eyes. The laugh of the scorner growls in his throat. Cast down this idol. This keeps some of you from secret prayer, from worshiping God in your family, from going to lay your case before ministers, from openly confessing Christ. You that have felt God's love and Spirit, dash this idol to pieces. "Who are thou, that thou shouldest be afraid of a man that shall die?" "Fear not, thou worm Jacob." "What have I to do any more with idols?" ROBERT MURRAY M'CHEYNE

Vs. 5. *Every day they wrest my words.* This is a common mode of warfare among the ungodly. They put our language on the rack; they extort meanings from it which it cannot be made fairly to contain. Thus our Savior's prophecy concerning the temple of His body, and countless accusations against His servants, were founded on wilful perversions. They who do this every day become great adepts in the art. A wolf can always find in a lamb's discourse a reason for eating him. Prayers are blasphemies if you choose to read them the wrong way upwards. C. H. S.

*All their thoughts are against me for evil.* No mixture of good will tone down their malice. Whether they viewed him as a king, a Psalmist, a man, a father, a warrior, a sufferer, it was all the same—they saw through colored glass and could not think a generous thought towards him. Even those actions of his which were an undoubted blessing to the commonwealth they endeavored to undervalue. O, foul spring, from which never a drop of pure water can come! C. H. S.

Vs. 6. *They hide themselves.* Men of malice are men of cowardice.

Vs. 8. *Put Thou my tears into Thy bottle.* There is no allusion to the little complimentary lachrymatories for fashionable and fanciful Romans; it is a robuster metaphor by far; such floods of tears had David wept that a leathern bottle would scarce hold them. C. H. S.

It is the witty observation by one that God is said in Scripture to have a bag and a bottle, a bag for our sins and a bottle for our tears; and that we should help to fill this, as we have that. There is an allusion here in the original that cannot be Englished. JOHN TRAPP

It was a precious ointment wherewith the woman in the Pharisee's house (it is thought Mary Magdalene) anointed the feet of Christ; but her tears wherewith she washed them were more worth than her spikenard. ABRAHAM WRIGHT, *in "A Practical Commentary or Exposition upon the Book of Psalms"*

Vs. 9. *When I cry.* The cry of faith and prayer to God is more dreadful to our spirtual foes than the war-whoop of the Indian is to his surprised brother savage. ADAM CLARKE

Vs. 13. *That I may walk before God in the light of the living.* Here is the loftiest reach of a good man's ambition, to dwell with God, to walk in righteousness before Him, to rejoice in His presence, and in the light and glory which it yields. C. H. S.

# PSALM 57

This petition is a very sententious prayer, as full as it is brief, and well worthy to be the motto for a sacred song. David had said, "Destroy not," in reference to Saul, when he had him in his power, and now he takes pleasure in employing the same words in supplication to God. We may infer from the spirit of the Lord's prayer that the Lord will spare us as we spare our foes. There are four of these "Destroy not" Psalms, namely, the 57th, 58th, 59th, and 75th. C. H. S.

Mystically, this hymn may be construed of Christ, Who was in the days of His flesh assaulted by the tyranny both of spiritual and temporal enemies. His temporal enemies, Herod and Pontius Pilate, with the Gentiles and people of Israel, furiously raged and took counsel together against Him. The chief priests and princes were, saith Hierome, like *lions,* and the people like the *whelps of lions,* all of them in a readiness to devour His soul. The rulers *laid a net for His feet* in their captious interrogatories, asking (Matt. 22:17), "Is it lawful to give tribute unto Cæsar, or not?" and (John 8:5) whether the woman taken in the very act of adultery should be stoned to death or no.

The people were *set on fire,* when as they raged against Him, and *their teeth and tongues were spears and swords* in crying, "Crucify him, crucify him." His spiritual enemies also sought to *swallow Him up;* His *soul* was *among lions* all the days of His life, at the hour of His death especially. The devil in tempting and troubling Him had *laid a snare for His feet;* and death, in *digging a pit* for Him, had thought to *devour* Him. As David was in the *cave,* so Christ, the Son of David, was in the *grave.* JOHN BOYS

Vs. 1. *Be merciful unto me, O God.* This excellent Psalm was composed by David when there was enough to discompose the best man in the world. JOHN FLAVEL

*Yea, in the shadow of Thy wings will I make my refuge.* Not in the cave alone would he hide, but in the cleft of the Rock of Ages. C. H. S.

*Until these calamities be overpast.* Athanasius said of Julian, furiously raging against the Lord's Anointed, *Nubecula est, cito transibit*—he is a little cloud; he will soon pass away. JOHN BOYS

Vs. 2. *I will cry.* He is quite safe, but yet he prays, for faith is never dumb. We pray because we believe.

Vs. 3. *And save me from the reproach of him that would swallow me up.* O dog of hell, I am not only delivered from thy bite but even from thy bark. Our foes shall not have the power to sneer at us, their cruel jests and taunting gibes shall be ended by the message from heaven, which shall forever save us. C. H. S.

If I were to take you to my house and say that I had an exquisitely fat man and wished you to join me in eating him, your indigation could be restrained by nothing. You would pronounce me to be crazy. There is not in New York a man so mean that he would not put down a man who should propose to have a banquet off from a fellow-man, cutting steaks out of him, and eating them.

And that is nothing but feasting on the human body, while they all will sit down and take a man's soul, and look for the tender loins, and invite their neighbors in to partake of the little tidbits. They will take a man's honor and name and broil them over the coals of their indigation, and fill the whole room with the aroma thereof, and give their neighbor a piece, and watch him, and wink as he tastes it.

You all eat men up—you eat the souls, the finest elements of men. You are more than glad if you can whisper a word that is derogatory to a neighbor, or his wife, or his daughter. The morsel is too exquisite to be lost. Here is the soul of a person, here is a person's hope for this world and the world to come, and you have it on your fork, and you cannot refrain from tasting it and give it to someone else to taste.

You are cannibals, eating men's honor and name and rejoicing in it—and that, too, when you do not always know that the things charged against them are true; when in ninety-nine cases out of a hundred the probabilities are that they are not true. HENRY WARD BEECHER

*Selah.* Such mercy may well make us pause to meditate and give thanks. Rest, singer, for God has given thee rest!

*God shall send forth His mercy and His truth.* He asked for mercy, and truth came with it. Thus evermore doth God give us more than we ask or think. His attributes, like angels on the wing, are ever ready to come to the rescue of His chosen. C. H. S.

Vs. 4. *My soul is among lions.* Eleven popes had that name, whereof all, excepting two or three, were roaring lions in their bulls, and ravening lions in seeking after their prey. JOHN BOYS

*And I lie even among them that are set on fire.* Like the bush in Horeb, the believer is often in the midst of flames, but never consumed. It is a mighty triumph of faith when we can lie down even among firebrands and find rest, because God is our defense. C. H. S.

The horrors of a lion's den, the burning of a fiery furnace, and the cruel onset of war, are the striking images by which David here describes the peril and wretchedness of his present condition. JOHN MORISON

Vs. 6. *They have digged a pit before me, into the midst whereof they are fallen themselves. Selah.* Evil is a stream which one day flows back to its source. *Selah.* We may sit down at the pit's mouth and view with wonder the just retaliations of providence. C. H. S.

Vs. 7. *My heart is fixed.* One would have thought he would have said, "My heart is fluttered"; but no, he is calm, firm, happy, resolute, established. When the central axle is secure, the whole wheel is right. If our great bower anchor holds, the ship cannot drive.

*O God, my heart is fixed.* I am resolved to trust Thee, to serve Thee, and to praise Thee. Twice does he declare this to the glory of God, Who thus comforts the souls of His servants. Reader, it is surely well with thee if thy once roving heart is now firmly fixed upon God and the proclamation of His glory.

*I will sing and give praise.* Vocally and instrumentally will I celebrate Thy worship. With lip and with heart will I ascribe honor to Thee. Satan shall not stop me, nor Saul, nor the Philistines. I will make Adullam ring with music, and all the caverns thereof echo with joyous song. Believer, make a firm decree that your soul in all seasons shall magnify the Lord.

*Sing, though sense and carnal reason*
*Fain would stop the joyful song:*
*Sing, and count it highest treason*
*For a saint to hold his tongue.*

C. H. S.

Whether saints conquer or are conquered, they still sing on. Blessed be God for that. Let sinners tremble at contending with men of a spirit so heavenly. WM. S. PLUMER

Sincerity makes the Christian sing when he hath nothing to his supper. David was in none of the best case when in the cave, yet we never find him merrier: his heart makes sweeter music than ever his harp did. WM. GURNALL

Vs. 8. *Awake up, my glory; awake, psaltery and harp.* We must sing *with excited grace.* Not only with grace habitual, but with excited and actual: the musical instrument delights not but when it is played upon. In this duty we must follow Paul's advice to Timothy (II Tim. 1:16), stir up the grace that is in us, and cry out as David, *Awake love, awake delight.*

The clock must be wound before it can guide our time; the bird pleaseth not in her nest, but in her notes; the chimes only make music while they are going. Let us therefore beg the Spirit to blow upon our garden, that the spices thereof may flow out, when we set upon this joyous service. God loves active grace in duty, that the soul should be ready trimmed when it presents itself to Christ in any worship. JOHN WELLS, *in "Morning Exercises"*

Vs. 10. *And Thy truth unto the clouds.* Upon the cloud, He sets the seal of His truth, the rainbow, which ratifies His covenant; in the cloud He hides His rain and snow, which prove His truth by bringing to us seedtime and harvest, cold and heat. C. H. S.

Vs. 11. *Be Thou exalted, O God, above the heavens: let Thy glory be above all the earth.* Greater words of prayer than these never came from human lips. Heaven and earth have, as they imply, a mutually interwoven history, and the blessed, glorious end of this is the sunrise of the divine Glory over both. FRANZ DELITZSCH

# PSALM 58

This is the fourth of the Psalms of the Golden Secret and the second of the "Destroy Nots." These names, if they serve for nothing else, may be useful to aid the memory. Men give names to their horses, jewels, and other valuables, and these names are meant not so much to describe as to distinguish them, and in some cases to set forth the owner's high esteem of his treasure; after the same fashion, the Oriental poet gave a title to the song he loved, and so aided his memory, and expressed his estimation of the strain. We are not always to look for a meaning in these superscriptions but to treat them as we would the titles of poems or the names of tunes.

Vs. 1. *Do ye indeed speak righteousness, O congregation?* "What everybody says must be true" is a lying proverb based upon the presumption which comes of large combinations. Have we not all agreed to hound the man to the death, and who dare hint that so many great ones can be mistaken? Yet the persecuted one lays the axe at the root by requiring his judges to answer the question whether or not they were acting according to justice. It were well if men would sometimes pause and candidly consider this. Some of those who surrounded Saul were rather passive than active persecutors; they held their tongues when the object of royal hate was slandered. He who refrains from defending the right is himself an accomplice in the wrong. C. H. S.

Vs. 2. *Yea, in heart ye work wickedness; ye weigh the violence of your hands in the earth.* See what a generation saints have to deal with! Such were the foes of our Lord, a generation of vipers, an evil and adulterous generation; they sought to kill Him because He was righteousness itself, yet they masked their hatred to His goodness by charging Him with sin. C. H. S.

The Psalmist doth not say they had wickedness in their heart, but they did work it there: the heart is a shop within, an underground shop; there they did closely contrive, forge, and hammer out their wicked purposes, and fit them into actions; *yea, they weigh the violence of their hands in the earth.* That's an allusion to merchants, who buy and sell by weight; they weigh their commodity to an ounce; they do not give it out in gross, but by exact weight. Thus saith the Psalmist, *they weigh the violence of their hands;* they do not oppress grossly, but with a kind of exactness and skill, they sit down and consider what and how much violence they may use in such a case, or how much such a person can endure, or such a season may bear. JOSEPH CARYL

The principles of the wicked are even worse than their practices: premeditated violence is doubly guilty. GEORGE ROGERS

Vs. 3. *The wicked are estranged from the womb: they go astray as soon as they be born, speaking lies.* It is small wonder that some men persecute the righteous seed of the woman, since all of them are of the serpent's brood, and enmity is set between them. No sooner born than alienated from God—what a condition to be found in! He who starts early in the morning will go far before night. To be untruthful is one of the surest proofs of a fallen state, and since falsehood is universal, so also is human depravity. C. H. S.

How early men do sin! How late they do repent! *As soon as they are born* "they go astray," but if left to themselves they will not return till they die; they will never return. JOSEPH CARYL

Of all sins, no sin can call Satan father like to lying. All the corruption that is in us came from Satan, but yet this sin of forging and lying is from the devil more than any; tastes of the devil more than any. As we are in body, subject to all diseases, but yet, some to one sickness rather than to another: so in the soul, all are apt enough to all sin, and some rather to one vice than to another; but all are much inclined to lying. RICHARD CAPEL in *"Temptations, their Nature, Danger, Cure"*

The youngest serpent can convey poison to anything which it bites; and the suffering in all cases is great, though the bite is seldom fatal. JOSEPH ROBERTS, *in "Oriental Illustrations of the Sacred Scriptures"*

Vs. 4. *Their poison is like the poison of a serpent.* There is such a thing as poison; but where to be found? Wheresoever it is, in man who would look for it? God made man's body of the dust; He mingled no poison with it. He inspireth his soul from heaven; He breathes no poison with it. He feeds him with bread; He conveys no poison with it. Whence is the poison? Matt. 13:27: "Didst not thou, O Lord, sow good seed in thy field?" "From whence then hath it tares?" Whence? "The enemy hath done this." We may perceive the devil in it. That great serpent, the red dragon, hath poured into wicked hearts this poison. His own poison, wickedness. "When he pours in sin, he pours in poison."

Sin is poison. Original pravity is called corruption; actual poison. The violence and virulence of this venomous quality comes not at first. No man becomes worst at the first dash. We are born corrupt, we have made ourselves poisonous. There be three degrees, as it were so many ages, in sin. First—secret sin; an ulcer lying in the bones, but skinned over with hypocrisy. Secondly—open sin, bursting forth into manifest villany. The former is corruption, the second is eruption. Thirdly—frequented and confirmed sin, and that is rank poison, envenoming soul and body. THOS. ADAMS

*They are like the deaf adder that stoppeth her ear.* The point of the rebuke is, the pathen, or "adder," here in question, could hear in some degree but would not; just as the unrighteous judges, or persecutors of David could hear with their outward ears such appeals as he makes in verses 1, 2, but would not. A. R. FAUSSET

Vs. 5. *Which will not hearken to the voice of charmers, charming never so wisely.* Ungodly men are not to be won to right by arguments the most logical or appeals the most pathetic. Try all your arts, ye preachers of the Word! Lay yourselves out to meet the prejudices and tastes of sinners, and ye shall yet have to cry, "Who hath believed our report?" It is not in your music but in the sinner's ear that the cause of failure lies, and it is only the power of God that can remove it.

Vs. 6. *Break their teeth, O God, in their mouth.* Treat them as the snake-charmers do their serpents—extract their fangs, break their teeth.

Vs. 7. *Let them melt away as waters which run continually.* Begone, ye foul streams; the sooner ye are forgotten the better for the universe.

Vs. 8. *As a snail which melteth, let every one of them pass away.* As the snail makes its own way by its slime, and so dissolves as it goes, or as its shell is often found empty, as though the inhabitant had melted away, so shall the malicious eat out their own strength while they proceed upon their malevolent designs, and shall themselves disappear.

*Like the untimely birth of a woman, that they may not see the sun.* They are as if thy had never been. Their character is shapeless, hideous, revolting. They are fitter to be hidden away in an unknown grave than to be reckoned among men. Their life comes never to ripeness, their aims are abortive, their only achievement is to have brought misery to others and horror to themselves.

Such men as Herod, Judas, Alva, Bonner, had it not been better for them if they had never been born? Better for the mothers who bore them? Better for the lands they cursed? Better for the earth in which their putrid carcasses are hidden from the sun? Every unregenerate man is an abortion. He misses the true form of God-made manhood; he corrupts in the darkness of sin; he never sees or shall see the light of God in purity, in heaven. C. H. S.

The wicked are all, so to speak, human abortions; they are and forever remain defective beings who have not accomplished the great purpose of their existence. Heaven is the one end for which man is created, and he who falls short of it does not attain the purpose of his being; he is an eternal abortion. O. PRESCOTT HILLER

Vs. 9. *He shall take them away as with a whirlwind.* Cook, fire, pot, meat, and all disappear at once, whirled away to destruction.

*Both living, and in his wrath.* In the very midst of the man's life, and in the fury of his rage against the righteous, the persecutor is overwhelmed with a tornado, his designs are baffled, his contrivances defeated, and himself destroyed. The passage is difficult, but this is probably its meaning, and a very terrible one it is. The malicious wretch puts on his great seething pot, he gathers his fuel, he means to play the cannibal with the godly; but he reckons without his host, or rather without the Lord of hosts, and the unexpected tempest removes all trace of him, and his fire, and his feast, and that in a moment.

Vs. 10. *The righteous shall rejoice when he seeth the vengeance.* We shall at the last say "Amen" to the condemnation of the wicked and feel no disposition to question the ways of God with the impenitent. C. H. S.

No doubt, at the sight of Sodom, Gomorrah, Admah, and Zeboim destroyed, angels saw cause to rejoice and sing, "Hallelujah." Wickedness was swept away; earth was lightened of a burden; justice, the justice of God, was highly exalted; love to His other creatures was displayed in freeing them from the neighborhood of hellish contaminations. On the same principles (entering, however, yet deeper into the mind of the Father, and sympathizing to the full in His justice), the Lord Jesus Himself, and each one of His members shall cry "Hallelujah," over Antichrist's ruined hosts. ANDREW A. BONAR

*He shall wash his feet in the blood of the wicked.* The damnation of sinners shall not mar the happiness of the saints. C. H. S.

## PSALM 59

Whom God preserves, Satan cannot destroy. The Lord can even preserve the lives of His prophets by the very ravens that would naturally pick out their eyes. David always found a friend to help him when his case was peculiarly dangerous, and that friend was in his enemy's household; in this instance it was Michal, Saul's daughter, as on former occasions it had been Jonathan, Saul's son. "Michtam of David." This is the fifth of the Golden Secrets of David: God's chosen people have many such.

Vs. 1. *Deliver me from mine enemies, O my God.* He was to be taken dead or alive, well or ill, and carried to the slaughter. Unbelief would have suggested that prayer was a waste of breath, but not so thought the good man, for he makes it his sole resort. Note how he sets the title, *My God*, over against the word *mine enemies.* This is the right method of effectually catching and quenching the fiery darts of the enemy upon the shield of faith. C. H. S.

There are two pleas which the Psalmist makes use of; one was, that God was *his God* (vs. 1); the other was the *power* and *strength* of his *enemies.* JOHN HILL, *in "Sermons on Several Occasions"*

Vs. 2. *Deliver me, defend me, deliver me, save me.* Saul had more cause to fear than David had, for the invincible weapon of prayer was being used against him, and heaven was being aroused to give him battle.

Vs. 3. *For lo, they lie in wait for my soul.* While the enemy lies waiting in the posture of a beast, we wait before God in the posture of prayer, for God waits to be gracious to us and terrible towards our foes.

*The mighty are gathered against me.* None of them were absent from the muster when a saint was to be murdered. They were too fond of such sport to be away. C. H. S.

*The mighty are gathered against me* is rendered by Chandler, *The mighty are turned aside to lay snares against me.*

Vs. 4. *They run and prepare themselves without my fault.* To a brave man, the danger causes little distress of mind compared with the injustice to which he is subjected. C. H. S.

Verses 3-4. He pleads his own innocency, not as to God, but as to his persecutors. Note, 1. The innocency of the godly will not secure them from the malignity of the wicked. Those that are harmless like doves, yet for Christ's sake are hated of all men, as if they were noxious like serpents, and obnoxious accordingly.

2. Though our innocency will not secure us from troubles, yet it will greatly support and comfort us under our troubles. The testimony of our conscience for us, that we have behaved ourselves well toward those that have behaved themselves ill towards us, will be very much our rejoicing in the day of evil. If we are conscious to ourselves of our innocency, we may with humble confidence appeal to God and beg of Him to plead our injured cause, which He will do in due time. MATTHEW HENRY

Vs. 5. 1. *God of hosts,* and therefore *able;* 2. *God of Israel,* and therefore *willing.* ANDREW A. BONAR

*Awake to visit.* What a forceful petition is contained in these words! Actively punish, in wisdom judge, with force chastise.

*Be not merciful to any wicked transgressors.* Be merciful to them as men, but not as transgressors; if they continue hardened in their sin, do not wink at their oppression. To wink at sin in transgressors will be to leave the righteous under their power; therefore do not pass by their offences, but deal out the due reward. C. H. S.

Vs. 6. *They make a noise like a dog, and go round about the city.* David compares his foes to Eastern dogs—despised, unowned, loathesome, degraded, lean, and hungry, and he represents them as howling with disappointment because they cannot find the food they seek.

Saul's watchmen and the cruel king himself must have raved and raged fiercely when they found the image and the pillow of goats' hair in the bed instead of David. Vain were their watchings, the victim had been delivered, and that by the daughter of the man who desired his blood. Go, ye dogs, to your kennels and gnaw your bones, for this good man is not meat for your jaws. C. H. S.

The whole city rang with one vast riot. Down below me, at Tophane; over about Stamboul; far away at Scutari; the whole sixty thousand dogs that are said to overrun Constantinople appeared engaged in the most active extermination of each other, without a moment's cessation. The yelping, howling, barking, growling, and snarling, were all merged into one uniform and continuous even sound, as the noise of frogs becomes when heard at a distance.

For hours there was no lull. I went to sleep and woke again, and still, with my windows open, I heard the same tumult going on; nor was it until daybreak that anything like tranquility was restored. ALBERT SMITH, *in "A Month at Constantinople"*

Verses 6-7. 1. They are diligent about it, *They return at evening.* 2. *Mad,* and set to do it. *They make a noise like a dog,* and threaten boldly. 3. Unwearied and obdurate in their purpose: *They go round about the city.* 4. Impudent, and brag what they will do to me: *Behold, they belch out with their mouth.* 5. And their words are bloody: *Swords are in their lips.* ADAM CLARKE

Vs. 7. *Behold, they belch out with their mouth.* Their malicious speech gushes from them as from a bubbling fountain. The wicked are voluble in slander; their vocabulary of abuse is copious, and as detestable as it is abundant. What torrents of wrathful imprecation will they pour on the godly! They need no prompters, their feelings force for themselves their own vent, and fashion their own expressions.

*Swords are in their lips.* They speak daggers. Their words pierce like rapiers and cleave like cutlasses. As the cushion of a lion's paw conceals his claw, so their soft, ruby lips contain bloody words.

*For who, say they, doth hear?* They are free from all restraint, they fear no God in heaven, and the government on earth is with them. When men have none to call them to account, there is no accounting for what they will do. David called them dogs, and no doubt a pretty pack they were, a cursed, cursing company of curs. C. H. S.

Vs. 9. *Will I wait upon thee,* lit., I will *keep watch* to thee," alluding to the title, When Saul sent, and they *watched* the house to *kill* him. David sets *watching before God,* against their *watching to kill* him. A. R. FAUSSET

How weak soever the believer finds himself, and how powerful soever he perceives his enemy to be, it is all one to him, he hath no more to do but to put faith at work and to wait till God works. DAVID DICKSON

Vs. 10. *The God of my mercy shall prevent me.* It is a great word that (I Pet. 5:10), *the God of all grace.* God has in Him all sorts of grace for His saints. He hath pardoning, quickening, strengthening, comforting, and preserving grace. His mercy is rich mercy, abundant mercy, inexhaustible mercy, sure mercy. A man's riches are his glory; God glories in His mercy; it is His delight, He rests in it; and so may we, because there is an infinite inconceivable fullness of it in *Him* (II Cor. 1:3). God is not called the Author of our mercies but the *Father* of them; to show how freely they come from Him. *Condensed from John Hill's Sermon*

*God shall let me see my desire upon mine enemies.* Observe that the words, *My desire*, are not in the original. From the Hebrew, we are taught that David expected to see his enemies without fear. God will enable His servant to gaze steadily upon the foe without trepidation; he shall be calm and self-possessed in the hour of peril; and ere long he shall look down on the same foes discomfited, overthrown, destroyed. C. H. S.

So Christ looked upon His murderers. So Stephen was enabled to do when they *gnashed upon him with their teeth.* "All that sat in the council looking steadfastly upon him, saw his face as it had been the face of angel" (Acts 6:15). CHRISTOPHER WORDSWORTH

Vs. 11. *Slay them not, lest my people forget.* It argues great faith on David's part that even while his house was surrounded by his enemies, he is yet so fully sure of their overthrow, and so completely realizes it in his own mind, that he puts in a detailed petition that they may not be too soon or too fully exterminated.

God's victory over the craft and cruelty of the wicked is so easy and so glorious that it seems a pity to end the conflict too soon. To sweep away the plotters all at once were to end the great drama of retribution too abruptly. Nay, let the righteous be buffeted a little longer, and let the boasting oppressor puff and brag through his little hour, it will help to keep Israel in mind of the Lord's justice and make the brave party who side with God's champion accustomed to divine interpositions. It were a pity for good men to be without detractors, seeing that virtue shines the brighter for the foil of slander. Enemies help to keep the Lord's servants awake. A lively, vexatious devil is less to be dreaded than a sleepy, forgetful spirit, which is given to slumber.

Vs. 12. *For the sin of their mouth and the words of their lips let them even be taken in their pride.* Sins of the lips are real sins and punishable sins. Men must not think because their hatred gets no further than railing and blasphemy that therefore they shall be excused. He who takes the will for the deed will take the word for the deed and deal with men accordingly. Wretches who are persecutors in talk, burners and stabbers with the tongue, shall have a reckoning for their would-be transgressions. Pride, though it show not itself in clothes but only in speech, is a sin; and persecuting pride, though it pile no fagots at Smithfield, but only revile with its lips, shall have to answer for it among the unholy crew of inquisitors.

*And for cursing and lying which they speak.* Sins, like hounds, often hunt in couples. He who is not ashamed to curse before God will be sure to lie unto men. Every swearer is a liar. Persecution leads on to perjury. They lie and swear to it. C. H. S.

Albeit the persecutors do not accomplish their purpose against the righteous; yet their pride, their brags, their lies, their slanders, their curses against the godly are a sufficient ditty for damnation and wrath to come upon them. DAVID DICKSON

Vs. 13. *Consume them in wrath, consume them, that they may not be.* If they could be reformed, it would be infinitely better; but if they cannot, if they must and will continue to be like mad dogs in a city, then let them cease to be. Who can desire to see such a generation perpetuated?

*And let them know;* i. e., let all the nations know, *that God ruleth in Jacob unto the ends of the earth.* The overthrow of a Napoleon is a homily for all monarchs; the death of a Tom Paine a warning to all infidels; the siege of Paris a sermon to all cities. C. H. S.

Vs. 14. *And at evening let them return; and let them make a noise like a dog, and go round about the city.* He laughs to think that all the city would know how they were deceived, and all Israel would ring with the story of the image and the goats' hair in the bed. Nothing was more a subject of Oriental merriment than a case in which the crafty are deceived, and nothing more makes a man the object of derision than to be outwitted by a woman, as in this instance Saul and his base minions were by Michal. C. H. S.

At Tyre, as in most Eastern towns, the familiar words came to us with all their true and forcible meaning. The wolfish, hungry, masterless dogs which "go about the cities (of Alexandria, for instance), gathering in packs like jackals, prowling about for offal, and grudging if they be not satisfied"; or the famished outcasts, like our dogs at Tyre, prowling "outside" the city. To these we may apply the highly unfavorable definitions of Scripture, which every Englishman and Englishwoman must indignantly disclaim on behalf of the loyal, faithful, patient creatures who watch beside our homes like sentinels, and guard our flocks like shepherds, and welcome us with ecstatic joy when we come home again, and sometimes will even die rather than desert a master's grave. *From "Wanderings over Bible Lands and Seas"*

Those that repent of their sins when they are in trouble, *mourn like doves;* those whose hearts are hardened when they are in trouble, *make a noise like dogs.* MATTHEW HENRY

Vs. 15. *Let them wander up and down for meat, and grudge if they be not satisfied.* See the restlessness of wicked men; this will increase as their enmity to God increases, and in hell it will be their infinite torment. What is the state of the lost, but the condition of an ambitious camp of rebels who have espoused a hopeless cause and will not give it up but are impelled by their raging passions to rave on against the cause of God, of truth, and of His people. C. H. S.

## PSALM 60

Title. Here is a lengthy title, but it helps us very much to expound the Psalm. "To the Chief Musician upon Shushan-eduth, or the Lily of Testimony." The Forty-Fifth was on the lilies and represented the kingly warrior in His beauty going forth to war; here we see Him dividing the spoil and bearing testimony to the glory of God. C. H. S.

*Shushan-eduth. The lilies of the testimony*—means that this Psalm has for its chief subject something very lovely and cheering in the law, namely, the words of promise quoted in the beginning of verse six. T. C. BARTH'S *"Bible Manual"*

*The Valley of Salt.* The ridge of Usdum exhibits more distinctly its peculiar formation; the main body of the mountain being a solid mass of rock salt. EDWARD ROBINSON'S *"Biblical Researches in Palestine"*

Vs. 1. David found himself the possessor of a tottering throne, troubled with the double evil faction at home and invasion from abroad. He traced at once the evil to its true source and began at the fountainhead. His were politics of piety, which after all are the wisest most profound. C. H. S.

*O God, Thou hast cast us off.* The word here used means properly to be foul, rancid, offensive; and then to treat anything as if it were foul or rancid; to repel, to spurn, to cast away. It is strong language, meaning that God had seemed to treat them as if they were loathsome or offensive to Him. ALBERT BARNES

*Thou hast scattered us.* These first two verses, with their depressing confession, must be regarded as greatly enhancing the power of the faith, which in the after verses rejoices in better days through the Lord's gracious return unto His people.

*Thou hast been displeased.* Had we pleased Thee, Thou wouldst have pleased us; but as we have walked contrary to Thee, Thou hast walked contrary to us. C. H. S.

Vs. 2. *Heal the breaches thereof.* As a house in time of earthquake is shaken, and the walls begin to crack and gape with threatening fissures, so it was with the kingdom. C. H. S.

Vs. 3. *Thou hast showed Thy people hard things.* God will be sure to plough His own ground, whatsoever becometh of the waste; and to weed His own garden, though the rest of the world should be let alone to grow wild. JOHN TRAPP

*The wine of astonishment. Intoxicating wine.* Hebrew, "Wine of staggering," that is, which causeth staggering, or, in other words intoxicating. Some render, "wine of stupor," or stupefying. Symmachus, "wine of agitation," and this sense I have adopted, which is also that of the Syriac. BENJAMIN BOOTHROYD

Vs. 4. *Thou hast given a banner to them that fear Thee, that it may be displayed because of the truth.* The Lord has given us the standard of the gospel; let us live to uphold it, and if needful die to defend it. To publish the gospel is a sacred duty, to be ashamed of it a deadly sin. The truth of God was involved in the triumph of David's armies. He had promised them victory; and so in the proclamation of the gospel we need feel no hesitancy, for as surely as God is true, He will give success to His own word. C. H .S.

Vs. 6. *God hath spoken in His holiness.* Faith is never happier than when it can fall back upon the promise of God. She sets this over against all discouraging circumstances; let outward providences say what they will, the voice of a faithful God drowns every sound of fear. God had promised Israel victory, and David the kingdom; the holiness of God secured the fulfillment of His own covenant, and therefore the King spake confidently. The goodly land had been secured to the tribes by the promise made to Abraham, and that divine grant was an abundantly sufficient warrant for the belief that Israel's arms would be successful in battle. Believer, make good use of this and banish doubts while promises remain.

*I will rejoice*, or, "I will triumph." Faith regards the promise not as fiction, but fact, and therefore drinks in joy from it and grasps victory by it. "God hath spoken; I will rejoice"; here is a motto fit for every soldier of the cross.

*I will divide Shechem, and mete out the Valley of Succoth.* When God has spoken, His divine *shall*, our *I will*, becomes no idle boast, but the fit echo of the Lord's decree. Believer, up and take possession of covenant mercies; *Divide Shechem, and mete out the Valley of Succoth.* Let not Canaanitish doubts and legalisms keep thee out of the inheritance of grace. C. H. S.

Vs. 7. *Judah is my lawgiver.* To all claims of Rome, or Oxford, or the councils of men, we pay no attention; we are free from all other ecclesiastical rule but that of Christ. C. H. S.

Vs. 8. *Moab is my washpot.* A mere pot to hold the dirty water after my feet have been washed in it. Once she defiled Israel, according to the counsel of Balaam, the son of Beor; but she shall be no longer able to perpetrate such baseness; she shall be a washpot for those whom she sought to pollute. C. H. S.

*Over Edom will I cast out my shoe.* He need not draw a sword to smite his now crippled and utterly despondent adversary, for if he dared revolt, he would only need to throw his slipper at him, and he would tremble. Easily are we victors when Omnipotence leads the way. C. H. S.

*Philistia, triumph thou because of me.* So utterly hopeless is the cause of hell when the Lord comes forth to the battle, that even the weakest daughter of Zion may shake her head at the enemy and laugh him to scorn. C. H. S.

Vs. 11. *For vain is the help of man.* As they had lately experimented in Saul, a king of their own choosing, but not able to save them from those proud Philistines. JOHN TRAPP

# PSALM 61

Subject and Division: This Psalm is a pearl. It is little, but precious. To many a mourner, it has furnished utterance when the mind could not have devised a speech for itself. It was evidently composed by David after he had come to the throne (see verse 6). The second verse leads us to believe that it was written during the Psalmist's enforced exile from the tabernacle, which was the visible abode of God: if so, the period of Absalom's rebellion has been most suitably suggested as the date of its authorship, and Delitzsch is correct in entitling it, "Prayer and thanksgiving of an expelled King on his way back to his throne." C. H. S.

Vs. 1. *Hear my cry, O God.* He was in terrible earnest; he shouted; he lifted up his voice on high. Pharisees may rest in their prayers; true believers are eager for an answer to them: ritualists may be satisfied when they have "said or sung" their litanies and collects, but living children of God will never rest till their supplications have entered the ears of the Lord God of Sabaoth. C. H. S.

*Attend unto my prayer.* Aquinas saith that some read the words thus, (*Intende ad cantica mea*), attend unto my songs—and so the words may be safely read, from the Hebrew word, *ranah,* which signifies to shout or shrill out for joy—to note that the prayers of the saints are like pleasant songs and delightful ditties in the ears of God. No mirth, no music, can be so pleasing to us as the prayers of the saints are pleasing to God (Cant. 2:14; Ps. 141:2). THOMAS BROOKS

Vs. 2. *From the end of the earth will I cry unto Thee.* No spot is too dreary, no condition too deplorable; whether it be the world's end or life's end, prayer is equally available. To pray in some circumstances needs resolve, and the Psalmist here expresses it, *I will cry.* It was a wise resolution, for had he ceased to pray he would have become the victim of despair; there is an end to a man when he makes an end to prayer.

*When my heart is overwhelmed.* It is hard to pray when the very heart is drowning, yet gracious men plead best at such times. Tribulation brings us to God and brings God to us. Faith's greatest triumphs are achieved in her heaviest trials. It is all over with me, affliction is all over me; it encompasses me as a cloud, it swallows me up like a sea, it shuts me in with thick darkness, yet God is near, near enough to hear my voice, and I will call Him. C. H. S.

When the action of the heart is paralyzed, even temporally, it will tell upon all the members, a chill there sends its cold vibration through every limb; Satan knows this well, and so all his dealings are heart dealings, efforts to paralyze the very spring of life itself. PHILLIP BENNETT POWER

*Lead me to the Rock that is higher than I.* There is a mint of meaning in this brief prayer. Our experience leads us to understand this verse right well, for the time was with us when we were in such amazement of soul by reason of sin that although we knew the Lord Jesus to be a sure salvation for sinners, yet we could not come at Him by reason of our many doubts and forebodings. C. H. S.

It is more the image of one overtaken by the tide, as he is hastening onwards to get beyond its reach, and yet with every step he sees it rolling nearer and nearer to him; he hears its angry roar, the loosening sand sinks beneath his tread—a few minutes more, and the waves will be around him; despair hath *overwhelmed his heart;* when in the very depths of his agony he sees a point of rock high above the waves. "Oh, that I could reach it and be safe!" And then comes the cry, the agonizing cry to Him that is mighty to save, *Lead me to the Rock that is higher than I.* It is the sinner's cry to the sinner's Savior. BARTON BOUCHIER, *in "Manna in the Heart; or Daily Comments on the Book of Psalms"*

Vs. 3. *For Thou hast been a shelter for me, and a strong tower from the enemy.* Experience is the nurse of faith. Sweet is it beyond expression to remember the lovingkindness of the Lord in our former days, for He is unchangeable and therefore will continue to guard us from all evil.

Vs. 4. *I will abide in Thy tabernacle forever.* Hewers of wood and drawers of water in the tents of Jehovah are more to be envied than the princes who riot in the pavilions of kings. The best of all is that our residence with God is not for a limited period of time but for ages; yea, for ages of ages, for time and for eternity: this is our highest and most heavenly privilege: *I will abide in Thy tabernacle forever.*

*I will trust in the covert of Thy wings.* Oh, for more trust; it cannot be too implicit; such a covert invites us to the most unbroken repose. C. H. S.

Vs. 5. *Thou hast given me the heritage of those that fear Thy name.* If we suffer, it is the heritage of the saints; if we are persecuted, are in poverty or in temptation, all this is contained in the title-deeds of the heritage of the chosen. Those we are to sup with we may well be content to dine with. We have the same inheritance as the Firstborn Himself; what better is cnceivable?

Saints are described as fearing the name of God; they are reverent worshipers; they stand in awe of the Lord's authority; they are afraid of offending Him; they feel their own nothingness in the sight of the infinite One. To share with such men, to be treated by God with the same favor as He metes out to them, is matter for endless thanksgiving. All the privileges of all the saints are also the privilege of each one. C. H. S.

Vs. 7. *He shall abide before God forever: O prepare mercy and truth, which may preserve him.* Though this is true of David in a modified sense, we prefer to view the Lord Jesus as here intended as the lineal descendant of David and the Representative of his royal race. Jesus is enthroned before God to eternity; here is our safety, dignity, and delight. As men cry, "Long live the king," so we hail with acclamation our enthroned Immanuel, and cry, *Let mercy and truth preserve Him.* C. H. S.

Vs. 8. *So will I sing praise unto Thy name forever.* There should be a parallel between our supplications and our thanksgivings. We ought not to leap in prayer and limp in praise. C. H. S.

# PSALM 62

Title: "To the Chief Musician, to Jeduthun." This is the second Psalm which is dedicated to Jeduthun, or Ethan, the former one being the Thirty-Ninth, a Psalm which is almost a twin with this in many respects, containing in the original the word translated *only* four times as this does six. C. H. S.

There is in it throughout not one single word (and this is a rare occurrence), in which the prophet expresses *fear* or *dejection.* MOSES AMYRAUT

Athanasius says of this Psalm: "Against all attempts upon thy body, thy state, thy soul, thy fame, temptations, tribulations, machinations, defamations, say this Psalm." JOHN DONNE

Vs. 1. *Truly my soul waiteth upon God: from Him cometh my salvation.* To wait upon God, and for God, is the habitual position of faith; to wait on Him truly is sincerity; to wait on Him only is spiritual chastity. The original is, "only to God is my soul silence." The proverb that speech is silver but silence is gold is more than true in this case. No eloquence in the world is half so full of meaning as the patient silence of a child of God. If to wait on God be worship, to wait on the creature is idolatry; if to wait on God alone be true faith, to associate an arm of flesh with Him is audacious unbelief. C. H. S.

There was a time when I used greatly to wonder at these words of Luther:

*Bear and forbear, and silent be,*
*Tell to no man thy misery;*
*Yield not in trouble to dismay,*
*God can deliver any day.*

I wondered because we feel the outpouring of grief into the heart of a friend to be so sweet. At the same time, he who talks much of his troubles to men is apt to fall into a way of saying too little of them to God; while, on the other hand, he who has often experienced the blessed alleviation which flows from silent converse with the Eternal, loses much of his desire for the sympathy of his fellows. "Talking of trouble makes it double." AUGUSTUS F. THOLUCK, *in "Hours of Christian Devotion"*

Vs. 2. *He only is my rock and my salvation.* David had often lain concealed in rocky caverns, and here he compares his God to such a secure refuge.

*I shall not be greatly moved.* "Moved," as one says, "but not removed." Moved like a ship at anchor, which swings with the tide but is not swept away by the tempest. When a man knows assuredly that the Lord is his salvation, he cannot be very much cast down: it would need more than all the devils in hell greatly to alarm a heart which knows God to be its salvation. C. H. S.

The mortified man sings and is not light, and weeps and is not sad, is zealous in God's cause, and yet composed in spirit; he is not so eager on anything but he can quit it for God. Ah! few can act but they over act. ALEXANDER CARMICHAEL, *in "The Believer's Mortification of Sin"*

Vs. 3. *How long will ye imagine mischief against a man?* He marvels at their dogged perseverance in malice after so many failures and with certain defeat before them. It is a marvel that men will readily enough continue in vain and sinful courses, and yet to persevere in grace is so great a difficulty as to be an impossibility, were it not for divine assistance. If there were any shame in Satan, or in his children, they would be ashamed of the dastardly manner in which they have waged war against the seed of the woman. Ten thousand to one has not seemed to them too mean an advantage; there is not a drop of chivalrous blood in all their veins.

*As a bowing wall shall ye be, and as a tottering fence.* They expect men to bow to them, and quake for fear in their presence; but men made bold by faith see nothing in them to honor, and very, very much to despise. It is never well on our part to think highly of ungodly persons whatever their position, they are near their destruction, they totter to their fall; it will be our wisdom to keep our distance, for no one is advantaged by being near a falling wall; if it does not crush with its weight, it may stifle with its dust. C. H. S.

Vs. 4. *They delight in lies.* To lie is bad enough, but to delight in it is one of the blackest marks of infamy.

*They bless with their mouth, but they curse inwardly.* Flattery has ever been a favorite weapon with the enemies of good men; they can curse bitterly enough when it serves their turn; meanwhile, since it answers their purpose, they mask their wrath, and with smooth words pretend to bless those whom they would willingly tear in pieces. C. H. S.

Vs. 5. *My soul, wait thou only upon God.* Be still silent, O my soul! submit thyself completely, trust immovably, wait patiently. Be like thy Lord, conquer by the passive resistance of victorious patience: thou canst only achieve this as thou shalt be inwardly persuaded of God's presence, and as thou waitest solely and alone on Him. Unmingled faith is undismayed. C. H. S.

They trust no God *at all* who trust Him not *alone*. He that stands with one foot on a rock and another foot upon a quicksand will sink and perish as certainly as he that standeth with both feet upon a quicksand. JOHN TRAPP

*For my expectation is from Him.* We expect from God because we believe in Him. Expectation is the child of prayer and faith and is owned of the Lord as an acceptable grace. C. H. S.

Vs. 7. *In God is my salvation and my glory.* Wherein should we glory but in Him Who saves us? Our honor may well be left with Him who secures our souls. To find all in God and to glory that it is so is one of the sure marks of an enlightened soul. C. H. S.

On the shields of the Greeks, Neptune was depicted; on the shields of the Trojans, Minerva; because in them they put their confidence, and in their protection deemed themselves secure. Now, Christ is the insignia of our shields. THOMAS LE BLANC

*The rock of my strength, and my refuge is in God.* Observe how the Psalmist brands his own initials upon every name which he rejoicingly gives to his God—*my* expectation, *my* rock, *my* salvation, *my* glory, *my* strength, *my* refuge; it is the word *my* which puts the honey into the comb. C. H. S.

Vs. 8. *Trust in Him at all times.* Faith is an abiding duty, a perpetual privilege. We should trust when we can see as well as when we are utterly in the dark. C. H. S.

In a word, trust in God is that high act or exercise of faith whereby the soul, looking upon God and casting itself on His goodness, power, promises, faithfulness, and providence, is lifted up above carnal fears and discouragements; above perplexing doubts and disquietments; either for the obtaining and continuance of that which is good, or for the preventing or removing of that which is evil. THOMAS LYE, *in "The Morning Exercises at Cripplegate"*

*Trust in Him at all times; ye people, pour out your heart before Him.* According to our love, so is our faith and trust in God; and according to our trust, such is our freedom at the throne of grace. Trust in Him, and pour out your hearts before Him; pour them out like water, in joyful tears. For when the stone in the heart is melted by mercy, the eyes will issue like a fountain of tears. SAMUEL LEE

Make Him your Counsellor and Friend; you cannot please Him better than when your hearts rely wholly upon Him. You may tell Him, if you please, you have been so foolish as to look to this friend and the other for relief, and found none; and you now come to Him, Who commands you to *"pour out your heart before Him."* JOHN BERRIDGE

Pour it out as water; not as milk, whose color remains. Not as wine, whose savor remains. Not as honey, whose taste remains. But as water, of which, when it is poured out, nothing remains. So let sin be poured out of the heart, that no color of it may remain in external marks, no savor in our words, no taste in our affections. THOMAS LE BLANC

Vs. 9. *Surely men of low degree are vanity.* Here the word is *only* again; men of low degree are only vanity, nothing more. They cry "Hosanna" today, and "Crucify Him" tomorrow. The instability of popular applause is a proverb; as well build a house with smoke as find comfort in the adulation of the multitude. As the first son of Adam was called "Abel," or "vanity," so here we are taught that all the sons of Adam are Abels.

*And men of high degree are a lie.* For this reason are they a lie; because they promise so much, and in the end, when relied upon, yield nothing but disappointment.

*To be laid in the balance, they are altogether lighter than vanity.* A feather has some weight in the scale; vanity has none, and creature confidence has less than that: yet such is the universal infatuation that mankind prefer an arm of flesh to the power of the invisible but almighty Creator; and even God's own children are too apt to be bitten with this madness. C. H. S.

Vanity is nothing, but there is a condition worse than nothing. Confidence in the things or persons of this world, but most of all a confidence in ourselves, will bring us at last to that state wherein we would fain be nothing, and cannot. JOHN DONNE

If there were any one among men immortal, not liable to sin, or change, whom it were impossible for anyone to overcome, but who was strong as an angel, such a one might be something; but inasmuch as everyone is a man, a sinner, mortal, weak, liable to sickness and death, exposed to pain and terror, like Pharaoh, even from the most insignificant animals, and liable to so many miseries that it is impossible to count them, the conclusion must be a valid one: "Man is nothing." ARNDT

Vs. 10. *Trust not in oppression, and become not vain in robbery.* Wealth ill gotten is the trust only of fools, for the deadly pest lies in it; it is full of canker, it reeks with God's curse. C. H. S.

He that putteth his trust for salvation in any other save in God, loses not only his salvation but also robs God of His glory and does God manifest wrong, as much as lieth in Him; as the wicked people amongst the Jews did, who said as long as they honored and trusted unto the queen of heaven, all things prospered with them; but when they hearkened to the true preachers of God's Word, all things came into a worse state, and they were overwhelmed with scarcity and trouble (Hosea 2; Jeremiah 44).

He also that puts his trust and confidence in any learning or doctrine beside God's Word, not only falls into error and loses the truth; but also as much as lies in him, he robs God's Book of His sufficient truth and verity and ascribes it to the book of men's decrees; which is as much wrong to God and His Book as may be thought or done. JOHN HOOPER

*If riches increase, set not your heart upon them.* To bow an immortal spirit to the constant contemplation of fading possessions is extreme folly. Shall those who call the Lord their glory, glory in yellow earth? Shall the image and superscription of Caesar deprive them of communion with Him Who is the image of the invisible God? As we must not rest in men, so neither must we repose in money. Gain and fame are only so much foam of the sea. C. H. S.

"The lust of riches," says Valerian, "stirs with its stimulus the hearts of men, as oxen perpetually plough the soil." Hugo, on Isaiah says: "The more deeply riches are sown in the heart through love, the more deeply will they pierce through grief." THOMAS LE BLANC

Oh, how many have riches served as Absalom's mule served her master, whom she lurched, and left, in his greatest need, hanging betwixt heaven and earth, as if rejected of both! A spark of fire may set them on flying, a thief may steal them, a wicked servant may embezzle and purloin them, a pirate or shipwreck at sea, a robber or bad debtor at land; yea, an hundred ways sets them packing. They are as the apples of Sodom, that look fair yet crumble away with the least touch—golden delusions, a mere mathematical scheme or fancy of man's brain (I Cor. 7:31). CHRISTOPHER LOVE, *in "A Chrystal Mirrour, or Christian Looking-Glass"*

Verses 10-13. Our estimate of man depends upon our estimate of God. AUGUSTUS F. THOLUCK

Vs. 11. *Twice have I heard this.* He hears twice in the best sense who hears with his heart as well as his ears. C. H. S.

*Power belongeth unto God.* What need is there to press people to believe it? Great need; because this is the great thing we are apt to question in cases of difficulty. Faith is never quite laid by till the soul questions the power of God. So the life and vigor of faith is very much concerned in the belief of God's power.

God is much displeased, even with His own children, when His power is questioned by them. For this God takes up Moses' short: "Is the Lord's hand waxen short?" (Num. 11:23). For this also Christ rebuked Martha very sharply: "Said I not unto thee, that if thou wouldst believe, thou shouldst see the glory of God?" (John 11:40). Yea, God is so tender of the glory of His power that He hath sharply chastened His dear children when their faith staggered in this matter; as we see in Zacharias, who, for questioning the power of God, was immediately stricken dumb upon the place. WILLIAM WISHEART

Verses 11-12. I confess I wonder to find so constantly in Scripture that the inspired writers put "merciful" and "mighty," "terrible," and "great," all together: you shall find it so. Neh. 1:5: "O Lord God of heaven, the great and terrible God, that keepeth covenant and mercy," etc. You have it also in Dan. 9:4, in his solemn prayer: "O Lord," says he, "the great and dreadful God, keeping the covenant and mercy," etc. Thus mercy, and great, and terrible are constantly joined together. THOMAS GOODWIN

Vs. 12. *Also unto Thee, O Lord, belongeth mercy.* God is so full of mercy that it belongs to Him, as if all the mercy in the universe came from God and still was claimed by Him as His possession. C. H. S.

# PSALM 63

Title: "A Psalm of David, when he was in the wilderness of Judah." This was probably written while David was fleeing from Absalom; certainly at the time he wrote it he was king (verse 11), and hard pressed by those who sought his life.

The distinguishing word of this Psalm is "Early." When the bed is the softest, we are most tempted to rise at lazy hours, but when comfort is gone, and the couch is hard, if we rise the earlier to seek the Lord, we have much for which to thank the wilderness. C. H. S.

There are Psalms proper for a wilderness; and we have reason to thank God it is the wilderness of Judah we are in, not the wilderness of Sin. MATTHEW HENRY

Hagar saw God in the wilderness and called a well by the name derived from that vision *Beer-lahai-roi* (Gen. 16:13-14). Moses saw God in the wilderness (Exod. 3:1-4). Elijah saw God in the wilderness (I Kings 19:4-18). David saw God in the wilderness. The Christian church will see God in the wilderness (Rev. 12:6-14). Every devout soul which has loved to see God in His house will be refreshed by visions of God in the wilderness of solitude, sorrow, sickness, and death. CHRISTOPHER WORDSWORTH

It was the favorite Psalm of M. Schade, the famous preacher in Berlin, which he daily prayed with such earnestness and appropriation to himself, that it was impossible to hear it without emotion. E. W. HENTSTENBERG

Vs. 1. *O God, thou art my God;* or, "O God, thou art my Mighty One." The last Psalm left the echo of power wringing in the ear, and it is here remembered. C. H. S.

*O God.* This is a serious word; pity it should ever be used as a by-word. MATTHEW HENRY

In the Hebrew, this Psalm begins *Elohim, Eli.* Now, *Elohim* is plural and *Eli* is singular, to express the mystery of the Trinity, the mystery of the Unity, the distinct subsistence of the (three) hypostases and their consubstantiality. *Psalterium Quin. Fabri stapulensis*

*Early will I seek Thee.* Possession breeds desire. Full assurance is no hindrance to diligence but is the mainspring of it. How can I seek another man's God? But it is with ardent desire that I seek after Him Whom I know to be my own. Observe the eagerness implied in the time mentioned; he will not wait for noon or the cool eventide; he is up at cockcrowing to meet his God.

*My soul thirsteth for Thee.* Thirst is an insatiable longing after that which is one of the most essential supports of life; there is no reasoning with it, no forgetting it, no despising it, no overcoming it by stoical indifference. Thirst will be heard; the whole man must yield to its power; even thus is it with that divine desire which the grace of God creates in regenerate men. C. H. S.

Oh, that Christ would come near, and stand still, and give me leave to look upon Him! for to look seemeth the poor man's privilege, since he may, for nothing and without hire, behold the sun. SAMUEL RUTHERFORD

Vs. 2. *To see Thy power and Thy glory, so as I have seen Thee in the sanctuary.* Our misery is that we thirst so little for these sublime things and so much for the mocking trifles of time and sense. The sight of God was enough for David, but nothing short of that would content him. C. H. S.

It is, or should be, the desire of every Christian to see and enjoy more and more of the glory of God. A view of the divine glory crucifies our lusts and puts the corruptions of our heart to death. JOHN ANGELL JAMES

Vs. 3. *Because Thy lovingkindness is better than life.* To dwell with God is better than life at its best; life at ease, in a palace, in health, in honor, in wealth, in pleasure; yea, a thousand lives are not equal to the eternal life which abides in Jehovah's smile. C. H. S.

Divine favor is better than life; yea, it is better than many lives put together. Now you know at what a high rate men value their lives; they will bleed, sweat, vomit, purge, part with an estate, yea, with a limb, yea, limbs, to preserve their lives. Now, though life be so dear and precious to a man, yet a deserted soul prizes the returnings of divine favor upon him above life, yea, above many lives. Many men have been weary of their lives, as is evident in Scripture and history; but no man was ever found that was weary of the love and favor of God. No man sets so high a price upon the sun as he that hath long lain in a dark dungeon. THOMAS BROOKS

What so desirable as life if a man have no place in the heart of God? This is the greatest temporal blessing, and nothing can outdo it but the favor of the God of our life; and this excels indeed. What comparison is there between the breath in our nostrils and the favor of an eternal God? TIMOTHY CRUSO

*My lips shall praise Thee.* Is it possible that any man should love another and not commend him nor speak of him? If thou hast but a hawk or a hound that thou lovest, thou wilt commend it; and can it stand with love to Christ, yet seldom or never to speak of Him nor of His love, never to commend Him unto others, that they may fall in love with Him also? I tell you, it will be one main reason why you desire to live, that you may make the Lord Jesus known to your children, friends, acquaintance, that so in the ages to come His name might ring and His memorial might be of sweet odor from generation to generation. THOMAS SHEPPARD *in "The Sound Believer"*

Vs. 4. *I will lift up my hands in Thy name.* No hands need hang down when God draws near in love. The name of Jesus has often made lame men leap as a hart and it has made sad men clap their hands for joy. C. H. S.

Vs. 5. *My soul shall be satisfied as with marrow and fatness.* It oftentimes so fell out that David had nothing but the bare ground for his bed, and the stones for his pillows, and the hedges for his curtains, and the heavens for his canopy; yet, in this condition, God was sweeter than marrow and fatness to him. THOMAS BROOKS

When the Lord puts His Spirit within us, then our starving souls begin to be feasted; for this blessed Spirit shows us the things of Christ and applies Him to us; by which means we are enabled to eat His flesh and drink His blood. And after the Holy Ghost is thus given, He is never taken away. *Outline of a Sermon by* JOHN FRASER

Vs. 7. *Because Thou hast been my help.* This is the grand use of memory, to furnish us with proofs of the Lord's faithfulness and lead us onward to a growing confidence in Him. C. H. S.

The surest way, and the nearest way, to lay hold upon God is the consideration of that which He hath done already, which was David's way here; because, says he, this was God's way before, therefore will I look for God in this way still. I cannot have better security for present nor future than God's former mercies exhibited to me. ABRAHAM WRIGHT

God helps His people; namely, to bear patiently those crosses which He lays upon them. He takes part with them in their sufferings, and in all their afflictions is afflicted Himself, as sometimes He expresses it. He lays no more upon them than He does help them and enable them to endure. THOMAS HORTON

*Therefore in the shadow of Thy wings will I rejoice.* The very shade of God is sweet to a believer. C. H. S.

As a bird sheltered in the rich foliage from the heat of the sun sings its merry notes; so he celebrates his songs of praise from the shadow of the wings of God. AUGUSTUS F. THOLUCK

Vs. 8. *My soul followeth hard after Thee.* This is the language of a good man in his worst frames; for when he has lost his nearness to God, he will be uneasy till he has again obtained it and will follow after it with all his might. It is also his language in his best frames; for when he knows and enjoys most of God, he wants to know and enjoy more. Not earth nor heaven merely is the object of pursuit, but God Himself. *Condensed from Benjamin Beddome's Sermon, "The Christian's Pursuit" in "Short Discourses"*

The primary sense is *agglutinavit,* to glue together; from thence it signifies figuratively to *associate,* to adhere to, to be united with; and particularly to be firmly united with strong affection. "Therefore shall a man leave his father and mother, and cleave to his wife"; properly, be closely united and compacted with his wife, with the most permanent affection. SAMUEL CHANDLER

The cleaving of David's spirit was a glueing of the Lord's Spirit; a marriage of the Lord's making is altogether incapable of the devil's breaking. ALEXANDER PRINGLE, *in "A Stay in Trouble; or, the Saint's Rest in the Evil Day"*

Vs. 9. *Shall go into the lower parts of the earth.* Every blow aimed against the godly will recoil on the persecutor; he who smites a believer drives a nail in his own coffin.

Vs. 10. *They shall be a portion for foxes.* Too mean to be fit food for the lions, the foxes shall sniff around their corpses, and the jackals shall hold carnival over their carcasses. C. H. S.

Is it not against the law of nature that men should become beasts' meat; yea, the meat of such beasts as are carrion, and not man's meat? Questionless it is, yet Nature giveth her consent to this kind of punishment of unnatural crimes. For it is consonant to reason that the law of nature should be broken in their punishment who brake it in their sin; that they who devoured men like beasts should be devoured of beasts like men; that they who with their hands offered unnatural violence to their Sovereign should suffer the like by the claws and teeth of wild beasts, their slaves; that they who bear a fox in their breast in their life, should be entombed in the belly of a fox at their death.

St. Austin, expounding this whole prophecy of Christ, yieldeth a special reason for this judgment of God by which the Jews were condemned to foxes. The Jews, saith he, therefore killed Christ that they might not lose their country; but, indeed, they therefore lost their country because they killed Christ; because they refused the Lamb and chose Herod the fox before Him, therefore by the just retribution of the Almighty, they were allotted to the foxes for their portion. DANIEL FEATLEY, *in "Clavis Mystica"*

What a doom is that which David pronounces upon those who seek the soul of the righteous to destroy it: *They shall be a portion for foxes;* by which *jackals* are meant, as I suppose. These sinister, guilty, woe-begone brutes, when pressed with hunger, gather in gangs among the graves, and yell in rage, and fight like fiends over their midnight orgies; but on the battle-field is their great carnival. Oh! let me never even dream that anyone dear to me has fallen by the sword and lies there to be torn, and gnawed at, and dragged about by these hideous howlers. W. M. THOMSON, *in "The Land and the Book"*

Vs. 11 *But the mouth of them that speak lies shall be stopped.* And the sooner the better. If shame will not do it, nor fear, nor reason, then let them be stopped with the sexton's shovel-full of earth; for a liar is a human devil, he is the curse of men, and accursed of God, who has comprehensively said, "All liars shall have their part in the lake which burneth with fire and brimstone." See the difference between the mouth that praises God and the mouth that forges lies: the first shall never be stopped, but shall sing on forever; the second shall be made speechless at the bar of God. C. H. S.

## PSALM 64

A Psalm of David. His life was one of conflict, and very seldom does he finish a Psalm without mentioning his enemies; in this instance his thoughts are wholly occupied with prayer against them. C. H. S.

This Psalm is applied by R. Obadiah to Haman and Mordecai. The enemy is Haman, the perfect man shot at is Mordecai. JOHN GILL

A cry of God's elect when persecuted for righteousness' sake. ARTHUR PRIDHAM, *in "Notes and Reflections on the Psalms"*

Vs. 1. *Hear my voice, O God, in my prayer.* We do not read that Moses had spoken with his lips at the Red Sea, and yet the Lord said to him, "Why criest thou unto Me?" Prayers which are unheard on earth may be among the best heard in heaven. It is our duty to note how constantly David turns to prayer; it is his battle axe and weapon of war. C. H. S.

Vs. 3. *Who whet their tongue like a sword.* The verb means, says Parkhurst, "to whet, sharpen," which is performed by reiterated motion or friction; and by a beautiful metaphor it is applied to a wicked tongue. It has, however, been rendered "vibrate," as it is certain a serpent does his tongue. RICHARD MANT

The ingenuity of man has been wonderfully tasked and exercised in two things, inventing destructive weapons of war and devising various methods of ruining men by wicked words. The list of the former is found in military writings. But the various forms of evil speaking can hardly be catalogued.

Evil speakers have arrows, sharp, barbed, dipped in poison. They have "swords, flaming swords, two-edged swords, drawn swords, drawn in anger, with which they cut and wound and kill the good name of their neighbor." Sins of the tongue are commonly cruel, very cruel. When slander is secret, as it commonly is, you cannot defend yourself from its assaults. Its canons are infernal. One of them is, "If a lie will do better than the truth, tell a lie." Another is, "Heap on reproach; some of it will stick." WILLIAM S. PLUMER

*And bend their bows to shoot their arrows, even bitter words.* They studiously and with force prepare their speech as bended bows, and then with cool, deliberate aim, they let fly the shaft which they have dipped in bitterness. To sting to inflict anguish, to destroy, is their one design. C. H. S.

Verses 3-4. We saw in the Museum at Venice an instrument with which one of the old Italian tyrants was accustomed to shoot poisoned needles at the objects of his wanton malignity. We thought of gossips, backbiters, and secret slanderers, and wished that their mischievous devices might come to a speedy end. Their weapons of inuendo, shrug, and whisper, appear to be as insignificant as needles; but the venom which they instil is deadly to many a reputation. C. H. S., *in "Feathers for Arrows; or Illustrations for Preachers and Teachers"*

How much, then, doth it concern every man to walk circumspectly; to give no just cause of reproach, not to make himself a scorn to the fools of the world; but, if they will reproach (as certainly they will), let it be for forwardness in God's ways, and not for sin, that so the reproach may fall upon their own heads, and their scandalous language into their own throats. JEREMIAH BURROUGHS

Verses 3, 7-8. The most mischievous weapons of the wicked are words, "even bitter words"; but the Word is the chief weapon of the Holy Spirit: and as with this sword the great Captain foiled the tempter in the wilderness, so may we vanquish "the workers of iniquity" with the true Jerusalem blade. J. L. K.

Vs. 4. *That they may shoot in secret at the perfect.* Sincere and upright conduct will not secure us from the assaults of slander. The devil shot at our Lord Himself, and we may rest assured he has a fiery dart in reserve for us. C. H. S.

Who would have thought to have found a devil in Peter, tempting his Master, or suspected that Abraham should be his instrument to betray his beloved wife into the hands of a sin? Yet it was so. Nay, sometimes he is so secret that he borrows God's bow to shoot his arrows from, and the poor Christian is abused, thinking it is God Who chides and is angry, when it is the devil who tempts him to think so, and only counterfeits God's voice. WILLIAM GURNALL

*Suddenly do they shoot at him, and fear not.* We have seen in daily life the arrow of calumny wounding its victim sorely; and yet we have not been able to discover the quarter from which the weapon was shot, not to detect the hand which forged the arrowhead or tinged it with the poison.

Is it possible for justice to invent a punishment sufficiently severe to meet the case of the dastard who defiles my good name and remains himself in concealment? An open liar is an angel compared with this demon. Vipers and cobras are harmless and amiable creatures compared with such a reptile. The devil himself might blush at being the father of so base an offspring. C. H. S.

Vs. 5. *They encourage themselves in an evil matter.* Good men are frequently discouraged and not infrequently discourage one another, but the children of darkness are wise in their generation and keep their spirits up, and each one has a cheering word to say to his fellow villain.

*They commune of laying snares privily.* They know the benefit of cooperation and are not sparing in it; they pour their experience into one common fund; they teach each other fresh methods.

*They say, Who shall see them?* They forget the all-seeing eye and the all-discovering hand, which are ever hard by them. Therefore, fear not, ye tremblers; for the Lord is at your right hand, and ye shall not be hurt of the enemy. C. H. S.

Vs. 6. *They search out iniquities.* Sad indeed it is that to ruin a good man the evil-disposed will often show as much avidity as if they were searching after treasure. C. H. S.

It is a sign that malice boils up to a great height in men's hearts when they are so active to find matter against their neighbors. Love would rather not see or hear of others' failings; or if it doth and must, busieth itself in healing and reforming them to the utmost of its power. JOHN MILWARD *in "Morning Exercises"*

Vs. 8. *So they shall make their own tongue to fall upon themselves.* Their slander shall recoil. Their curses shall come home to roost. Their tongue shall cut their throats. C. H. S.

"Words are but wind," is the common saying, but they are such wind as will either blow the soul to its haven of rest, if holy, wholesome, savory, spiritual, and tending to edification, or else sink it into the Dead Sea and bottomless gulf of eternal misery, if idle, profane, frothy, and unprofitable. EDWARD REYNER in *"Rules for the Government of the Tongue"*

*All that see them shall flee away.* Who cares to go near to Herod when the worms are eating him? or to be in the same chariot with Pharaoh when the waves roar around him? Those who crowded around a powerful persecutor and cringed at his feet are among the first to desert him in the day of wrath. Woe unto you, ye liars! Who will desire fellowship with you in your seething lake of fire?

Vs. 9. *And all men shall fear, and shall declare the work of God.* So strange, so pointed, so terrible shall be the Lord's overthrow of the malicious, that it shall be spoken of in all companies. C. H. S.

# PSALM 65

This is a charming Psalm. Coming after the previous sad ones, it seems like the morning after the darkness of night. There is a dewy freshness about it, and from the ninth verse to the end there is a sweet succession of landscape pictures that remind one of the loveliness of spring; and truly it is a description, in natural figures, of that happy state of men's minds, which will be the result of the "Day-Spring's visiting us from on high" (Luke 1-7-8). O. PRESCOTT HILLER

Vs. 1. *Praise waiteth for Thee, O God, in Zion.* Those who have seen in Zion the blood of sprinkling, and know themselves to belong to the church of the first-born, can never think of her without presenting humble praise to Zion's God.

We shall continue to wait on, tuning our harps, amid the tears of earth; but, oh, what harmonies will those be which we will pour forth when the home-bringing is come and the King shall appear in His glory. Certainly when the soul is most filled with adoring awe, she is least content with her own expressions and feels most deeply how inadequate are all mortal songs to proclaim the divine goodness. C. H. S.

The soul is often put to a nonplus in crying up the grace of God and wants words to express its greatness. ALEXANDER CARMICHAEL

*To Thee belongeth silence-praise.* Praise without any tumult. (Alexander.) It has been said, "The most intense feeling is the most calm, being condensed by repression." And Hooker says of prayer, "The very silence which our unworthiness putteth us unto doth itself make request for us, and that in the confidence of His grace. Looking inwardly, we are stricken dumb; looking upward, we speak and prevail." Horsley renders it, "Upon Thee is the repose of prayer." ANDREW A. BONAR

Atheneus says, silence is a divine thing; and Thomas à Kempis calls silence the nutriment of devotion. THOMAS LE BLANC

Vs. 2. *O Thou that hearest prayer.* This is Thy name, Thy nature, Thy glory. God not only has heard, but is now hearing prayer, and always must hear prayer, since He is an immutable Being and never changes in His attributes. David evidently believed in a personal God and did not adore a mere idea or abstraction.

*Unto Thee shall all flesh come.* To come to God is the life of true religion; we come weeping in conversion, hoping in supplication, rejoicing in praise, and delighting in service. False gods must in due time lose their deluded votaries, for man when enlightened will not be longer befooled; but each one who tries the true God is encouraged by his own success to persuade others also, and so the kingdom of God comes to men, and men come to it. C. H. S.

As sure as God is the true God, so sure is it that none who sought Him diligently departed from Him without a reward. You may as well doubt that He is God, as doubt that He will not reward, not hear prayer. DAVID CLARKSON

Vs. 3. *Iniquities prevail against me.* Our sins would, but for grace, prevail against us in the court of divine justice, in the court of conscience, and in the battle of life. Unhappy is the man who despises these enemies, and worse still is he who counts them his friends who slander and accuse him.

*As for our transgressions, Thou shalt purge them away.* What a comfort that iniquities that prevail against us do not prevail against God! They would keep us away from God, but He sweeps them away from before Himself and us. It is worthy of note that as the priest washed in the laver before he sacrificed, so David leads us to obtain purification from sin before we enter upon the service of song. When we have washed our robes and made them white in His blood, then shall we acceptably sing, "Worthy is the Lamb that was slain."

Vs. 4. *Blessed is the man whom Thou choosest, and causest to approach unto Thee.* Christ, Whom God chose, and of Whom He said, "This is My beloved Son in Whom I am well pleased," is, indeed, "over all, God blessed forever"; but in Him His elect are blessed, too. For His sake, not for our own, are we chosen; in Him, not in ourselves, are we received by God, being accepted in the Beloved; and, therefore, in Him are we blessed: He is our blessing. *From "A Plain Commentary on the Book of Psalms"*

To crown all, we do not come nigh in peril of dire destruction, as Nadab and Abihu did, but we approach as chosen and accepted ones, to become dwellers in the divine household: this is heaped-up blessedness, vast beyond conception. C. H. S.

Vs. 5. *By terrible things in righteousness wilt Thou answer us, O God of our salvation.* We seek sanctification, and trial will be the reply: we ask for more faith, and more affliction is the result: we pray for the spread of the gospel, and persecution scatters us. Nevertheless, it is good to ask on, for nothing which the Lord grants in His love can do us any harm. Terrible things will turn out to be blessed things after all, where they come in answer to prayer. C. H. S.

You pray for pardon; that is pleasing to God, yet rightly understand not pleasing to the flesh; it mortifies corruption, breaks the heart, engages to a holy life. Now, God is terrible to sinful flesh: so far as He appears, it dies. Jacob, therefore, whilst he conquered God in prayer, himself was overcome, signified by that touch upon his thigh put out of joint, where the chiefest stress in wrestling lies. When we are weak, then are we strong; because, as God appears, we die unto ourselves and live in Him. WILLIAM CARTER, *in a Fast Sermon entitled, "Light in Darkness"*

*Who art the confidence of all the ends of the earth.* The stability of the mountains is ascribed not to certain physical laws but to the power of God. Without God's own immediate power, the laws of nature could not produce their effect. How consoling and satisfactory is this view of Divine Providence compared with that of an infidel philosophy that forbids us to go further back than to the power of certain physical laws, which it grants, indeed, were at first established by God, but which can now perform their office without Him. ALEXANDER CARSON

*And of them that are afar off upon the sea.* If the land gave Moses elders, the sea gave Jesus apostles. Noah, when all was ocean, was as calm with God as Abraham in his tent. Faith is a plant of universal growth; it is a tree of life on shore and a plant of renown at sea; and, blessed be God, those who exercise faith in Him anywhere shall find that He is swift and strong to answer their prayers. C. H. S.

Vs. 6. *Which by His strength setteth fast the mountains.* Philosophers of the forget-God school are too much engrossed with their laws of upheaval to think of the Upheaver. Their theories of volcanic action and glacier action, etc., etc., are frequently used as bolts and bars to shut the Lord out of His own world. Let me forever be just such an unphilosophic simpleton as David was, for he was nearer akin to Solomon than any of our modern theorists. C. H. S.

*Being girded with power.* Let us learn that we poor, puny ones, if we wish for true establishment, must go to the strong for strength. Without Him, the everlasting hills would crumble; how much more shall all our plans, projects, and labors come to decay. Repose, O believer, where the mountains find their bases—viz., in the undiminished might of the Lord God. C. H. S.

Vs. 7. *And the tumult of the people.* Human society owes its preservation to the continued power of God: evil passions would secure its instant dissolution; envy, ambition, and cruelty would create anarchy tomorrow, if God did not prevent; whereof we have had clear proof in the various French revolutions.

Vs. 9. *Thou visitest the earth, and waterest it.* He is represented here as going around the earth, as a gardener surveys his garden, and as giving water to every plant that requires it, and that not in small quantities, but until the earth is drenched and soaked with a rich supply of refreshment. O Lord, in this manner visit Thy church, and my poor, parched and withering piety. Make Thy grace to overflow towards my graces; water me, for no plant of Thy garden needs it more. C. H. S.

The sun rises and sets so surely; the seasons run on amid all their changes with such inimitable truth, that we take as a matter of course that which is amazing beyond all stretch of imagination, and good beyond the widest expansion of the noblest human heart. Let a moment's failure of His power, of His watchfulness, or of His will to do good, occur, and what a sweep of death and annihilation through the universe! How stars would reel, planets expire, and nations perish! But from age to age, no such catastrophe occurs, even in the midst of national crimes, and of atheism that denies the hand that made and feeds it. WILLIAM HOWITT, *in "The Year-Book of the Country"*

God is intelligent, loving, and free; God rules in all, over all, and above all. He is not displaced or supplanted by the forces and agencies which He employs; He is not absorbed by care of other worlds; He is not indifferent toward the earth. SAMUEL MARTIN, *in "Rain upon the Mown Grass, and other Sermons"*

*Thou preparest them corn.* As surely as the manna was prepared of God for the tribes, so certainly is corn made and sent by God for our daily use. What is the difference whether we gather wheat-ears or manna, and what matters it if the first comes upward to us, and the second downward? God is as much present beneath as above; it is as great a marvel that food should rise out of the dust as that it should fall from the skies. C. H. S.

Vs. 11. *And Thy paths drop fatness.* It was said of the Tartar hordes that grass grew no more where their horses' feet had trodden; so, on the contrary, it may be said that the march of Jehovah, the Fertilizer, may be traced by the abundance which He creates.

Vs. 12. *They drop upon the pastures of the wilderness.* Ten thousand oases smile while the Lord of mercy passes by. The birds of the air, the wild goats, and the fleet stags rejoice as they drink from the pools, new filled from heaven. The most lonely and solitary souls, God will visit in love.

Vs. 13. *They also sing.* Nature has no discords. Her airs are melodious, her chorus is full of harmony. All, all is for the Lord; the world is a hymn to the Eternal. Blessed is he who, hearing, joins in it, and makes one singer in the mighty chorus. C. H. S.

# PSALM 66

He hath need to be a man of great skill, worthily to sing such a Psalm as this: the best music in the world would be honored by marriage with such expressions. We do not know who is its author, but we see no reason to doubt that David wrote it. C. H. S.

Vs. 1. *Make a joyful noise unto God, all ye lands.* We need not so much noise as *joyful* noise. God is to be praised with the voice, and the heart should go therewith in holy exultation. All praise from all nations should be rendered unto the Lord. Happy the day when no shouts shall be presented to Juggernaut or Boodh, but all the earth shall adore the Creator thereof. C. H. S.

Vs. 2. *Sing forth the honor of His name.* To give glory to God is but to restore to Him His own. It is our glory to be able to give God glory; and all our true glory should be ascribed unto God, for it is His glory. C. H. S.

Vs. 3. *Say unto God.* Devotion, unless it be resolutely directed to the Lord, is no better than whistling to the wind.

*Through the greatness of Thy power shall Thine enemies submit themselves unto Thee.* Power brings a man to his knee, but love alone wins his heart. Pharaoh said he would let Israel go, but he lied unto God; he submitted in word but not in deed. Tens of thousands, both in earth and hell, are rendering this constrained homage to the Almighty; they only submit because they cannot do otherwise; it is not their loyalty, but His power which keeps them subjects of His boundless dominion. C. H. S.

Those for whom God has done most, the angels, turned enemies first; vex not thou thyself, if those whom thou has loved best hate thee deadliest—God Himself hath enemies. Our Savior, Christ, never expostulated for Himself; never said, "Why scourge ye Me? Why spit you upon Me? Why crucify ye Me?" As long as their rage determined in His person, He opened not His mouth; when Saul extended the violence to the church, to His servants, then Christ came to that, "Saul, Saul, why persecutest thou Me?" *Condensed from* JOHN DONNE

The earthquakes in New England occasioned a kind of religious panic. A writer, who was then one of the ministers of Boston, informs us that immediately after the great earthquake, as it was called, a great number of his flock came and expressed a wish to unite themselves with the church. But, on conversing with them, he could find no evidence of improvement in their religious views or feelings, no convictions of their own sinfulness; nothing, in short, but a kind of superstitious fear occasioned by a belief that the end of the world was at hand. All their replies proved that they had not found God, though they had seen *the greatness of His power* in the earthquake. EDWARD PAYSON

Vs. 4. *All the earth shall worship Thee, and shall sing unto Thee.* What a change shall have taken place when singing shall displace sighing, and music shall thrust out misery!

*Selah.* No meditation can be more joyous than that excited by the prospect of a world reconciled to its Creator. C. H. S.

Vs. 6. *There did we rejoice in Him.* A much greater miracle is that men should pass over the bitter sea of this life and cross the river of mortality that never ceases to run and which swallows up and drowns so many and still come safe and alive to the land of eternal promise, and there rejoice in God Himself, beholding Him face to face; and yet this greater miracle is so accomplished by God that many pass through this sea as if it were dry land and cross this river with dry feet. ROBERT BELLARMINE

Vs. 7. *His eyes behold the nations.* This should give check to much iniquity. Can a man's conscience easily and delightfully swallow that which he is sensible falls under the cognizance of God when it is hateful to the eye of His holiness and renders the action odious to Him? STEPHEN CHARNOCK

*Let not the rebellious exalt themselves.* The proudest have no cause to be proud. Could they see themselves as God sees them, they would shrivel into nothing. O proud rebels, remember that the Lord aims His arrows at the high-soaring eagles and brings them down from their nest among the stars. C. H. S.

Vs. 8. *And make the voice of His praise to be heard.* Whoever else may sing with bated breath, do you be sure to give full tongue and volume to the song. Compel unwilling ears to hear the praises of your covenant God.

Vs. 9. *And suffereth not our feet to be moved.* If God has enabled us not only to keep our life, but our position, we are bound to give Him double praise. Living and standing is the saints' condition through divine grace. Immortal and immovable are those whom God preserves.

Vs. 10. *For Thou, O God, hast proved us.* God had one Son without sin, but He never had a son without trial. The day may come when we shall make hymns out of our grief and sing all the more sweetly because our mouth's have been purified with bitter draughts. C. H. S.

It is not known what corn will yield till it comes to the flail; nor what grapes till they come to the press. Grace is hid in nature as sweet water in rose-leaves. JOHN TRAPP

*As silver is tried.* To assay silver requires great personal care in the operator. "The principle of assaying gold and silver is very simple theoretically, but in practice great experience is necessary to insure accuracy; and there is no branch of business which demands more personal and undivided attention. The result is liable to the influence of so many contingencies that no assayer who regards his reputation will delegate the principal processes to one not equally skilled with himself. *Encycl. Britan.*

To assay silver requires a skilfully constructed furnace. C. H. S.

Vs. 11. *Thou laidst affliction upon our loins.* We, too, often forget that God lays our afflictions upon us; if we remembered this fact, we should more patiently submit to the pressure which now pains us. The time will come when, for every ounce of present burden, we shall receive a far more exceeding and eternal weight of glory.

Vs. 12. *Thou hast caused men to ride over our heads.* Nothing is too bad for the servants of God when they fall into the hands of proud persecutors. C. H. S.

The greatest danger that befalls man comes whence it should least come, from man himself. Lions fight not with lions; serpents spend not their venom on serpents; but man is the main suborner of mischief to his own kind. THOMAS ADAMS

God works in the same action with others, not after the same manner. In the affliction of Job there were three agents—God, Satan, and the Sabeans. The devil works on his body, the Sabeans on his goods; yet Job confesseth a third party: "The Lord gives, and the Lord takes away." Here oppressors trample on the godly, and God is said to cause it. He causeth affliction for trial (so verses 10-11: "Thou hast tried us," etc.); they work it for malice; neither can God be accused nor they excused. THOMAS ADAMS

*We went through fire and water.* The fires of the brick-kiln and the waters of the Nile did their worst to destroy the chosen race; hard labor and child-murder were both tried by the tyrant, but Israel went through both ordeals unharmed, and even thus the church of God has outlived, and will outlive, all the artifices and cruelties of man. The fire is not kindled which can burn the woman's seed, neither does the dragon know how to vomit a flood which shall suffice to drown it. C. H. S.

The children of Israel when they had escaped the Red Sea, and had seen their enemies, the Egyptians dead, they thought all was cocksure, and therefore sang songs of rejoicing for the victory. But what followed within a while? The Lord stirred up another enemy against them, from out their bowels, as it were, which was hunger, and this pinched them sorer, they thought, than the Egyptian. But was this the last? No; after the hunger came thirst, and this made them to murmur as much as the former; and after the thirst came fiery serpents, and fire and pestilence, and Amalekites, and Midianites, and what not? MILES SMITH

*But Thou broughtest us out in a wealthy place.*

*The path of sorrow and that path alone,*
*Leads to the land where sorrow is unknown.*

The depth of our griefs bear no proportion to the height of our bliss. With patience, we will endure the present gloom, for the morning cometh. Over the hills, faith sees the daybreak, in whose light we shall enter into our wealthy place. C. H. S.

So this strain of David's music, or Psalmody, consists of two notes—one mournful, the other mirthful; the one a touch of distress, the other of redress: which directs our course to an observation of misery and of mercy; of grievous misery, of gracious mercy. THOMAS ADAMS

The deliverer is great, the deliverance is certain, the distress grievous, the exaltation glorious. There is yet a first word, that like a key unlocks this golden gate of mercy, a veruntamen:—BUT. This is *vox respirationis,* a gasp that fetcheth back again the very life of comfort. *But Thou broughtest,* etc. We were fearfully endangered into the hand of our enemies; they rode and trode upon us and drove us through hard perplexities. *But Thou,* etc. If there had been a full point or period at our misery, if those gulfs of persecution had quite swallowed us, and all our light of comfort had been thus smothered and extinguished, we might have cried, "Our hope, our help is quite gone. He had mocked us that would have spoken, 'Be of good cheer'." This same *but* is like a happy oar that turns our vessel from the rocks of despair and lands it at the haven of comfort. THOMAS ADAMS

The margin saith, *into a moist place.* They were in fire and water before. Fire is the extremity of heat and dryness; water is the extremity of moistness and coldness. A *moist place* notes a due temperament of heat and cold. JOSEPH CARYL

Vs. 13. *I will go into Thy house with burnt offerings.* Even the thankful heart dares not come to God without a victim of grateful praise; of this as well as of every other form of worship, we may say, "The blood is the life thereof." Reader, never attempt to come before God without Jesus, the divinely promised, given, and accepted burnt offering. C. H. S.

For ourselves, be we sure that the best sacrifice we can give to God is obedience; not a dead beast, but a living soul. Let this be our burnt-offering, our holocaust, a sanctified body and mind given up to the Lord (Rom. 12:1-2). First, the heart: "My son, give Me thy heart." Is not the heart enough? No, the hand also (Isa. 1:16). Wash the hands from blood and pollution. Is not the hand enough? No, the foot also: "Remove thy foot from evil." Is not the foot enough? No, the lips also: "Guard the doors of thy mouth" (Ps. 34:14); "Refrain thy tongue from evil." Is not thy tongue enough? No, the ear also: "Let him that hath ears to hear, hear." Is not the ear enough? No, the eye also: "Let thine eyes be towards the Lord." Is not all this sufficient? No, give body and spirit (I Cor. 6:20): "Ye are bought with a price: therefore glorify God in your body, and in your spirit, which are God's."

When the eyes abhor lustful objects, the ear slanders, the foot erring paths, the hands wrong and violence, the tongue flattery and blasphemy, the heart pride and hypocrisy; this is thy holocaust, thy whole burnt-offering. THOMAS ADAMS

Vs. 14. *Which my lips have uttered.* Extreme distress burst open the door of his lips and out rushed the vow like a long pent-up torrent which had at last found a vent. What we were so eager to vow, we should be equally earnest to perform; but alas! many a vow runs so fast in words that it lames itself for deeds.

*When I was in trouble.* All men have trouble, but they act not in the same manner while under it; the profane take to swearing and the godly to praying. Both bad and good have been known to resort to vowing, but the one is a liar unto God and the other a conscientious respecter of His word. C. H. S.

V. 15. *I will offer unto Thee burnt sacrifices of fatlings.* The good man will give his best things to God. He who is miserly with God is a wretch indeed.

Vs. 16. *Come and hear.* Before, they were bidden to come and see. Hearing is faith's seeing. Mercy comes to us by way of ear-gate. "Hear, and your soul shall live."

*And I will declare what He hath done for my soul.* To declare man's doings is needless; they are too trivial, and, besides, there are trumpeters enough of man's trumpery deeds; but to declare the gracious acts of God is instructive, consoling, inspiriting, and beneficial in many respects. Let each man speak for himself, for a personal witness is the surest and most forcible; second-hand experience is like "cauld kale het again"; it lacks the flavor of first-hand interest. We must not be egotists, but we must be egotists when we bear witness for the Lord. C. H. S.

The principal end he should have in view when he declares his experience is the glory of that God Who hath dealt so bountifully with him. And with what luster doth the glory of God shine when His children are ready to acknowledge that He never called them out to any duty but His grace was sufficient for them.

What! are we ashamed of the noblest, the most interesting subject? It is but a poor sign that we have felt anything of it, if we think it unnecessary to declare it to our fellow-Christians. What think you? Suppose any two of us were cast upon a barbarous shore, where we neither understand the language nor the customs of the inhabitants and were treated by them with reproach and cruelty; do you think we should not esteem it a happiness that we could unburden ourselves to each other and communicate our griefs and troubles? And shall we think it less so, while we are in such a world as this, in a strange land, and at a distance from our Father's house? Shall we neglect conversing with each other? No; let our conversation not only be in heaven, but about spiritual and heavenly things. SAMUEL WILSON, *in "Sermons on Various Subjects"*

Vs. 17. *I cried unto Him with my mouth, and He was extolled with my tongue.* Observe that the Psalmist did both cry and speak; the Lord has cast the dumb devil out of His children, and those of them who are least fluent with their tongues are often the most eloquent with their hearts. C. H. S.

It is a proof that prayer has proceeded from unworthy motives when the blessings which succeed it are not acknowledged with as much fervency as when they were originally implored. The ten lepers all cried for mercy, and all obtained it, but only one returned to render thanks. JOHN MORISON

Let the praise of God be in thy tongue, under thy tongue, and upon thy tongue, that it may shine before all men, and that they may see that thy heart is good. THOMAS LE BLANC

Vs. 18. *If I regard iniquity in my heart, the Lord will not hear me.* Nothing hinders prayer like iniquity harbored in the breast; as with Cain, so with us—sin lieth at the door, and blocks the passage. If thou listen to the devil, God will not listen to thee. If thou refusest to hear God's commands, He will surely refuse to hear thy prayers. An imperfect petition God will hear for Christ's sake, but not one which is wilfully miswritten by a traitor's hand. For God to accept our devotions while we are delighting in sin would be to make Himself the God of hypocrites, which is a fitter name for Satan than for the Holy One of Israel. C. H. S.

The very supposition implies the possibility that such may be the state even of believers; and there is abundant reason to fear that it is in this way their prayers are so often hindered and their supplications so frequently remain unanswered. ROBERT GORDON

So long, therefore, as the love of sin possesses our hearts, our love to spiritual things is dull, heavy, inactive, and our prayers for them must needs be answerable. Oh, the wretched fallacy that the soul will here put upon itself! At the same time it will love its sin and pray against it; at the same time it will entreat for grace with a desire not to prevail. So, then, while we regard iniquity, how is it possible for us to regard spiritual things, the only lawful object of our prayers? And, if we regard them not, how can we be urgent with God for the giving of them? And where there is no fervency on our part, no wonder if there is no answer on God's. ROBERT SOUTH

They regard iniquity in the heart who entertain and indulge the desire of sin, although in the course of providence they may be restrained from the actual commission of it. I am persuaded the instances are not rare of men feeding upon sinful desires, even when through want of opportunity, through the fear of man, or through some partial restraint of conscience, they dare not carry them into execution.

Many can remember their sins without sorrow, they can speak of them without shame, and sometimes even with a mixture of boasting and vain glory. Did you never hear them recall their past follies and speak of them with such relish that it seems to be more to renew the pleasure than to regret the sin?

Sin is so abominable a thing, so dishonoring to God, and so destructive to the souls of men, that no real Christian can witness it without concern. JOHN WITHERSPOON, *in a Sermon entitled "The Petitions of the Insincere Unavailing"*

Vs. 19. *He hath attended to the voice of my prayer.* Love of sin is a plague spot, a condemning mark, a killing sign, but those prayers which evidently live and prevail with God most clearly arise from a heart which is free from dalliance with evil. C. H. S.

Vs. 20. *Blessed be God, which hath not turned away my prayer, nor His mercy from me.* Thus David had deceived, but not wronged me. I looked that he should have clapped the crown on his own, and he puts it on God's head. I will learn this excellent logic; for I like David's better than Aristotle's syllogisms, that whatsoever the premises be, I make God's glory the conclusion. THOMAS FULLER

## PSALM 67

No author's name is given, but he would be a bold man who should attempt to prove that David did not write it.

Vs. 1. *God be merciful unto us, and bless us; and cause His face to shine upon us.* Forgiveness of sin is always the first link in the chain of mercies experienced by us. Mercy is a foundation attribute in our salvation. C. H. S.

God forgives, then He gives; till He be merciful to pardon our sins through Christ, He cannot bless or look kindly on us sinners. All our enjoyments are but blessings in bullion, till gospel grace and pardoning mercy stamp and make them current. God cannot so much as bear any good will to us till Christ makes peace for us. WILLIAM GURNALL

*God be merciful unto us.* Hugo attributes these words to penitents; *Bless us,* to those setting out in the Christian life; *Cause His face to shine upon us,* to those who have attained, or the sanctified. The first seek for pardon, the second for justifying peace, the third for edification and the grace of contemplation. LORINUS

Vs. 2. *That Thy way may be known upon earth, Thy saving health among all nations.* Despite the gloomy notions of some, we cling to the belief that the kingdom of Christ will embrace the whole habitable globe and that all flesh shall see the salvation of God: for this glorious consummation we agonize in prayer. C. H. S.

If, therefore, thou continuest still in thy brutish ignorance, and knowest not so much as Who Christ is, and what He hath done for the salvation of poor sinners, and what thou must do to get interest in Him, thou art far enough from believing. If the day be not broke in thy soul, much less is the Sun of Righteousness arisen by faith in thy soul. WILLIAM GURNALL

*Thy way;* that is, Thy will, Thy word, Thy works. JOHN BOYS

Vs. 3. *Let the people praise Thee.* Mark the sweet order of the blessed Spirit: first, mercy; then, knowledge; last of all, praising of God. JOHN BOYS

There is a constant circular course and recourse from the sea unto the sea; so there is between God and us; the more we praise Him, the more our blessings come down; and the more blessings come down, the more we praise Him again; so that we do not so much bless God as bless ourselves. When the springs lie low, we pour a little water into the pump, not to enrich the fountain, but to bring up more for ourselves. THOMAS MANTON

Vs. 4. *O let the nations be glad and sing for joy.* Nothing creates gladness so speedily, surely, and abidingly as the salvation of God. Nations never will be glad till they follow the leadership of the great Shepherd. Some sing for form, others for show, some as a duty, others as an amusement, but to sing from the heart because overflowing joy must find a vent, this is to sing indeed. Whole nations will do this when Jesus reigns over them in the power of His grace.

Vs. 6. *Then shall the earth yield her increase; and God, even our own God, shall bless us.* We never love God aright till we know Him to be ours, and the more we love Him the more we long to be fully assured that He is ours. What dearer name can we give to Him than "mine own God"! The spouse in the song has no sweeter canticle than "My Beloved is mine and I am His." C. H. S.

Whatever the details and steps of the work of redemption, all must be traced up to this original fountain, the sovereign grace and mercy of our God. . . . The eternal, free, unchangeable, inexhaustible mercy of our God revealed through His dear Son Jesus Christ; this is the fountain-head of the blessed increase here foretold.

The order in which this increase is granted may next be considered. It is the divine plan first to choose His people and bless them and then to make them a blessing, as we see in Abraham, the father of the faithful.

The world craves and will crave more and more for righteous government. The Lord has promised to supply this natural want of the human heart, though He take vengeance on His hardened enemies. Even in the coming of the Lord to judgment, goodness will so finally triumph that the nations are to be glad and sing for joy.

Men now live as without God in the world, full though it be of proofs of His wisdom and love . . . What a change when every social circle shall be a fellowship of saints, and all bent to one great purpose—the divine glory and the blessedness of each other. Much praise, much zeal, much reverence, much humility, will distinguish his servants. Faith, hope, and love, will all be in the fullest exercise. Christ will be all and in all, and every power will be consecrated to Him. This is the best increase the earth yields to God.

The perpetuity of this increase has to be added to this glory. This is according to the promise made to the Wonderful, Counsellor, the Mighty God, the Everlasting Father, the Prince of Peace. *Condensed from Edward Bickersteth's in the "Bloomsbury Lent Lectures"*

# PSALM 68

It is a most soul-stirring hymn. The first verses were often the battle-song of the Covenanters and Ironsides; and the whole Psalm fitly pictures the way of the Lord Jesus among His saints and His ascent to glory. The Psalm is at once surpassingly excellent and difficult. Its darkness in some stanzas is utterly impenetrable. Well does a German critic speak of it as a Titan very hard to master. C. H. S.

By many critics, esteemed the loftiest effusion of David's lyrical muse. WILLIAM BINNIE

To judge from the antiquity of its language, the concise description, the thoroughly fresh, forcible, and occasional artlessly ironical expression of its poetry, we consider this poem as one of the most ancient monuments of Hebrew poetry. BOETTCHER

Vs. 1. *Let God arise.* The ark would have been a poor leader if the Lord had not been present with the symbol. Before we move, we should always desire to see the Lord lead the way.

*Let His enemies be scattered.* Our glorious Captain of the vanguard clears the way readily, however many may seek to obstruct it; He has but to arise, and they flee. He has easily overthrown His foes in days of yore, and will do so all through the ages to come. Sin, death, and hell know the terror of His arm; their ranks are broken at His approach. Our enemies are His enemies, and in this is our confidence of victory.

*Let them also that hate Him flee before Him.* To hate the infinitely good God is infamous, and the worst punishment is not too severe. He comes, He sees, He conquers. How fitting a prayer is this for the commencement of a revival! How it suggests the true mode of conducting one: the Lord leads the way, His people follow, the enemies flee. C. H. S.

It was no easy work to rescue souls from Satan's grasp or to lay low the prison-house of darkness. The enemy rushed on, clad in his fiercest armor, wild in his keenest rage, wily in his deadliest crafts. Malignant passions maddened in opposing breasts. But still the Ark moved on. The cross gave aid, not injury. The grave could not detain. Death could not vanquish. The gates of hell fly open. And now, from glory's throne, He cheers His humble followers in their desert march. Their toils, their conflicts, and their fears are many. As of old the ark was victory, so Jesus is victory now. HENRY LAW, *in "Christ is All, The Gospel of the Old Testament"*

Verses 1-3. The words of the text contain a prayer for the second advent of the Lord Jesus Christ. As members of the Christian church, we continually profess our faith in the second coming of Christ; and, it may be, that we sometimes meditate upon His glorious appearance; but have we, like David, adopted it as one of the subjects of our addresses at the throne of grace? . . . Has our faith ever enabled us to take up the language of the text, and say, *Let God arise, let His enemies be scattered: let them also that hate Him flee before Him?* Never shall the honor of Christ be complete, nor His people happy, nor the righteous be glad and rejoice exceedingly, until God arise and His enemies be scattered. ALEXANDER M'CAUL, *in "Plain Sermons on Subjects Practical and Prophetic"*

Vs. 2. *As smoke is driven away.* They fume in pride; they darken the sky with their malice; they mount higher and higher in arrogance; they defile wherever they prevail. Lord, let Thy breath, Thy Spirit, Thy Providence, make them to vanish forever from the march of Thy people. Philosophic skepticism is flimsy and as foul as smoke; may the Lord deliver His church from the reek of it. C. H. S.

"Their end was bitter as the smoke," said an aged teacher. "What meanest thou, O Master?" asked his young disciple. "I was thinking of the end of the unrighteous," replied the old man, "and of how too often I, like the Psalmist, have been envious when they were in prosperity. Their lives have seemed so bright and glowing that I have thought they resembled the blaze of a cheerful fire on a winter's night. But, as I have watched them, they have suddenly vanished like the flame that fades into black and bitter smoke; and I have ceased to envy them. Trust not, O my scholar, only to that which appears brilliant; but watch also for its ending, lest thou be deceived." HUBERT BOWER, *in "Parables and Similitudes of the Christian Life"*

*As wax melteth before the fire, so let the wicked perish at the presence of God.* It is hard when by itself, but put it to the fire, how soft it is. Wicked men are haughty till they come into contact with the Lord, and then they faint for fear. Rome, like the candles on her altars, shall dissolve, and with equal certainty shall infidelity disappear. C. H. S.

Vs. 4. *Sing unto God, sing praises to His name.* Sing not for ostentation, but devotion; not to be heard of men, but of the Lord Himself.

*And rejoice before Him.* We ought to avoid dullness in our worship. Our songs should be weighty with solemnity, but not heavy with sadness. Angels are nearer the throne than we, but their deepest awe is consonant with the purest bliss. C. H. S.

Vs. 6. *But the rebellious dwell in a dry land.* Even where God is revealed on the mercy-seat, some men persist in rebellion, and such need not wonder if they find no peace, no comfort, no joy, even where all these abound. Of the most soul-satisfying of sacred ordinances, these witless rebels cry, "What a weariness it is!" and, under the most soul-sustaining ministry, they complain of "the foolishness of preaching." When a man has a rebellious heart, he must of necessity find all around him a dry land. C. H. S.

Vs. 8. *The earth shook, the heavens also dropped at the presence of God: even Sinai itself was moved at the presence of God, the God of Israel.* This passage is so sublime that it would be difficult to find its equal. May the reader's heart adore the God before Whom the unconscious earth and sky act as if they recognized their Maker and were moved with a tremor of reverence. C. H. S.

Vs. 10. *Thou, O God, hast prepared of Thy goodness for the poor.* Within the guarded circle, there was plenty for all; all were poor in themselves, yet there were no beggars in all the camp, for celestial fare was to be had for the gathering. We, too, still dwell within the circling protection of the Most High, and find goodness made ready for us: although poor and needy by nature, we are enriched by grace; divine preparations in the decree, the covenant, the atonement, providence, and the Spirit's work, have made ready for us a fullness of the blessing of the Lord. C. H. S.

Cs. 11. *The Lord gave the word: great was the company of those that published it.* The ten thousand maids of Israel, like good handmaids of the Lord, aroused the sleepers, called in the wanderers, and bade the valiant men hasten to the fray. Oh, for the like zeal in the church of today, that when the gospel is published, both men and women may eagerly spread the glad tidings of great joy. C. H. S.

You shall find, when the enemies of the church are destroyed, that God hath many preachers made that do teach His praises. The word which you read *company,* in the Hebrew it is "army"—"great was the army of preachers." An army of preachers is a great matter; nay it is a great matter to have seven or eight good preachers in a great army; but to have a whole army of preachers, that is glorious. Now, my brethren, it is much to have a preaching army; but if this army will with heart and soul preach of God's praise, oh, that is a blessed thing. WILLIAM BRIDGE, *in "The True Soldier's Convoy"*

Vs. 13. It would neither be profitable nor possible to give the reader all the conjectures with which learned men have illustrated or darkened this passage. C. H. S.

*Though ye have lien among the pots.* It is a hard passage, a nut for the learned to crack. If we knew all that was known when this ancient hymn was composed, the allusion would no doubt strike us as being beautifully appropriate, but as we do not, we will let it rest among the unriddled things. Of making many conjectures there is no end, but the sense seems to be, that from the lowest condition the Lord would lift up His people into joy, liberty, wealth, and beauty. C. H. S.

Though ye had been treated by the Egyptians as a company of contemptible shepherds, and were held in abomination by them as such (see Gen. 46:34). WILLIAM GREEN, *in "A New Translation of the Psalms, with Notes"* etc.

A sharp remonstrance. Will ye lie at ease, in the quiet of your pastoral life, as the dove with unsoiled plumage in her peaceful nest, while your brethren are in the tumult and dust of the conflict! THOMAS J. CONANT

*Though ye have lien among the pots, yet shall ye be as the wings of a dove covered with silver, and her feathers with yellow gold.* Miss Whately, in her work, *Ragged Life in Egypt,* describing some of the sights witnessed from the flat roofs of the houses in Cairo, among other interesting objects, states: "The roofs are usually in a great state of litter, and were it not that Hasna, the seller of *geeleh,* gets a palm-branch, and makes a clearance once in a while, her roof would assuredly give way under the accumulation of rubbish.

"One thing never seemed cleared away, and that was the heaps of old broken pitchers, sherds, and pots, that in these and similar houses are piled in some corner; and there is a curious observation in connection with this. A little before sunset, numbers of pigeons suddenly emerge from behind the pitchers and other rubbish, where they have been sleeping in the heat of the day, or pecking about to find food. They dart upwards, and careen through the air in large circles, their outspread wings catching the bright glow of the sun's slanting rays, so that they really resemble bright yellow gold; then, as they wheel round, and are seen against the light, they appear as if turned into molten silver, most of them being pure white, or else very light colored.

"This may seem fanciful, but the effect of light in these regions is difficult to describe to those who have not seen it; and evening after evening, we watched the circling flight of the doves, and always observed the same appearance. It was beautiful to see these birds, rising clean and unsoiled, as doves always do, from the dust and dirt in which they had been hidden, and soaring aloft in the sky till nearly out of sight among the bright sunset clouds.

Thus a believer, who leaves behind him the corruptions of the world, and is rendered bright by the Sun of Righteousness shining upon his soul, rises higher and higher, nearer and nearer to the light, till, lost to the view of those who stay behind, he has passed into the unknown brightness above! MISS WHATELY, in *Ragged Life in Egypt*

Vs. 14. *When the Almighty scattered kings in it, it was white as snow in Salmon.* A traveler informed the writer that on a raw and gusty day he saw the side of what he supposed to be Mount Salmon suddenly swept bare by a gust of wind, so that the snow was driven hither and thither into the air like the down of thistles or the spray of the sea: thus did the Omnipotent one scatter all the potentates that defied Israel. Whatever may be the precise meaning, it was intended to portray the glory and completeness of the divine triumph over the greatest foes. In this let all believers rejoice.

Vs. 16. *This is the hill which God desireth to dwell in.* Elohim makes Zion His abode, yea, Jehovah resides there.

*Yea, the Lord will dwell in it forever.* Spiritually the Lord abides eternally in Zion, His chosen church, and it was Zion's glory to be typical thereof. C. H. S.

Vs. 17. *The Lord is among them, as in Sinai, in the holy place.* The presence of God is the strength of the church; all power is ours when God is ours. Twenty thousand chariots shall bear the gospel to the ends of the earth; and myriads of agencies shall work for its success. C. H. S.

And, on the other hand, "How fearful a thing it is to fall into the hands of the living God," Who hath all these chariots and horsemen at His command to execute His will and vengeance on those that neglect, hate, and oppose Him. JOHN EVERARD, *in "Militia Coelestis, or the Heavenly Host"*

Vs. 18. *Thou hast ascended on high.* The ark was conducted to the summit of Zion. The antitype of the ark, the Lord Jesus, has ascended into the heavens with signal marks of triumph.

*Thou hast led captivity captive.* As great conquerors of old led whole nations into captivity, so Jesus leads forth from the territory of His foe a vast company as the trophies of His mighty grace. The Lord Jesus destroys His foes with their own weapons; He puts death to death, entombs the grave, and leads captivity captive. C. H. S.

*Thou hast ascended on high,* etc. There was a glorious fulfillment immediately after His ascension, in a rich profusion of gifts and graces to His church, like David's presents. Here it is *received;* in Ephesians, *gave.* He received that He might give; received the spoil that He might distribute it. But, as I wish to appropriate the passage to the work allotted me, the whole of that to which I would at this time call your attention will be contained in the following paragraph entitled, "The great blessings of the Christian ministry."

1. Ministers are received for, and are given to, you by Christ. As men, and as sinful men, ministers are as nothing, and wish not to make anything of themselves; but, as the gifts of Christ, it becomes you to make much of them. If you love Christ, you will make much of your minister on account of his being *His* gift —a gift designed to supply Christ's absence in a sort. He is gone ("ascended"), but He gives you His servants. By-and-by you hope to be with Him, but as yet you are as sheep in the wilderness. He gives you a shepherd. 2. If you fear God, you will be afraid of treating your pastor amiss, seeing he is the gift of Christ. God took it ill of Israel for despising Moses (Num. 12:8). He is *My servant.* ANDREW FULLER'S *Sketch of a Sermon, addressed on the Ordination of Mr. Carey*

Yet I say that, mystically, this Psalm is a triumphal song penned by king David upon the foresight of Jesus Christ arising from the dead and with great joy and triumph ascending up into heaven, and thence sending His Holy Spirit unto His apostles and disciples; and, having overcome all His enemies, collecting by the ministry of His preachers, His churches and chosen people together, and so guiding and defending them here in this life, until He doth receive them into eternal glory. GRIFFITH WILLIAMS

The ancient prophecy of David is fulfilled here on the foot of Mount Olivet. To take "captivity captive" signifies that Christ conquered the allied principalities and powers, the devil, sin, death, and hell; that He deprived them of the instruments wherewith they enslaved men. He not only silenced the cannon on the spiritual Gibraltar, but He took rock fortification, and all. He not only silenced the horrible and destructive battlements of the powerful and compactly united ghostly enemies, but He threw down the towers, razed the castles, and took away the keys of the dungeons.

He had no sooner left the grave, than He began to distribute His gifts, and did so all along the road on His way to His Father's house; and, especially after He entered the heaven of heavens, did He shower down gifts unto men, as a mighty conqueror loaded with treasures with which to enrich and adorn His followers and people. CHRISTMAS EVANS

The Apostle (Eph. 4:8) does not quote the words of the Psalm literally, but according to the sense. The phrase, *Thou hast received gifts,* as applied to Christ at His glorification, could only be for the purpose of distribution, and hence the Apostle quotes them in this sense, *He gave gifts to men.* This Hebrew phrase may be rendered either, "Thou hast received gifts in the human nature," or, "Thou hast received gifts for the sake of man" (see Gen. 18:28; II Kings 14:6). The Apostle uses the words in the sense of the purpose for which the gifts were received, and there is no contradiction between the Psalmist and the Apostle.

Thus the difficulties of this quotation vanish when we examine them closely, and the Old and New Testaments are in complete harmony. Rosenmuller expounds Psalm 18, and never mentions the name of Christ; and the neologists in general see no Messiah in the Old Testament. To these, indeed, (Eph. 4:8) if they had had modesty, would present a formidable obstacle. Paul asserts the Psalm belongs to Christ, and they assert he is mistaken, and that he has perverted (De Wette) and destroyed its meaning. WILLIAM GRAHAM, in "*Lectures on St. Paul's Epistle to the Ephesians*"

Above all, consider the reasons of this gift in reference to thyself: the gift of the Holy Ghost. Was it not to make thee a temple and receptacle of the Holy Ghost? Stand a while on this! Admire, O my soul, at the condescending, glorious, and unspeakable love of Christ in this! It was infinite love to come down into our nature when He was incarnate; but this is more, to come down into thy heart by His Holy Spirit: He came near to us then, but as if that were not near enough, He comes nearer now, for now He unites Himself unto thy person, now He comes and dwells in thy soul by His Holy Spirit. ISAAC AMBROSE

It may be laid down as an incontrovertible truth, that David, in reigning over God's ancient people, shadowed forth the beginning of Christ's eternal kingdom. This must appear evident to everyone who remembers the promise made to him of a never-failing succession, and which received its verification in the person of Christ. As God illustrated His power in David by exalting him with the view of delivering His people, so has He maginfied His name in His only begotten Son.

It was not Himself that God enriched with the spoils of the enemy, but His people; and neither did Christ seek or need to seek His advancement, but made His enemies tributary, that He might adorn His church with the spoil. From the close union subsisting between the head and members, to say that God manifest in the flesh received gifts from the captives is one and the same thing with saying that He distributed them to His church. By His ascension to heaven, the glory of His divinity has been only more illustriously displayed; and, though no longer present with us in the flesh, our souls receive spiritual nourishment from His body and blood, and we find, notwithstanding distance of place, that His flesh is meat indeed and His blood drink indeed. JOHN CALVIN

*Yea for the rebellious also.* I feared also that this was the mark that the Lord did set on Cain, even continual fear and trembling under the heavy load of guilt that he had charged upon him for the blood of his brother Abel. Thus did I wind and twine and shrink under the burden that was upon me, which burden also did so oppress me, that I could neither stand, nor go, nor lie, either at rest or quiet.

Yet that saying would sometimes come to my mind, "He hath received gifts for the rebellious" (Ps. 68:18). "The rebellious," thought I; why surely, they are such as once were under subjection to their Prince, even those who, after they have sworn subjection to His government, have taken up arms against Him; and this, thought I, is my very condition; once I loved Him, feared Him, served Him; but now I am a rebel; I have sold Him. I have said, let Him go if He will; but yet He has gifts for rebels, and then why not for me? JOHN BUNYAN, *in "Grace Abounding"*

Vs. 19. *Who daily loadeth us with benefits.* God's benefits are not few nor light; they are loads. Neither are they intermittent, but they come "daily"; nor are they confined to one or two favorites, for all Israel can say, "He loadeth us with benefits." C. H. S.

Though some may have more than others, yet every one hath his load, as much as he can carry. Every vessel cannot bear up with the like sail, and therefore God, to keep us from oversetting, puts on so much as will safest bring us to heaven, our desired port. EZEKIEL HOPKINS

There are but three loads whereof man is capable from God—favors, precepts, punishments. When we might therefore have expected judgments, behold benefits; and those, not sparingly hand-fulled out to us, but dealt to us by the whole load.

Where shall we begin to survey this vast load of mercies? Were it no more but that he hath given us a world to live in, a life to enjoy, air to breathe in, earth to tread on, fire to warm us, water to cool and cleanse us, clothes to cover us, food to nourish us, sleep to refresh us, houses to shelter us, variety of creatures to serve and delight us; here were a just load.

But, if from what God hath done for us as men, we look to what He hath done for us as Christians; that He hath embraced us with an everlasting love, that He hath moulded us anew, enlivened us by His Spirit, fed us by His word and sacraments, clothed us with His merits, bought us with His blood, becoming vile to make us glorious, a curse, to invest us with blessedness; in a word, that He hath given Himself to us, His Son for us; *oh, the height, and depth, and breadth* of the rich mercies of our God! Oh, the boundless, topless, bottomless, load of divine benefits, whose immensity reaches from the center of this earth to the unlimited extent of the very empyreal heavens! JOSEPH HALL

Vs. 20. *Our God is the God of salvation*" (that is of deliverance, of outward deliverance); *and unto God the Lord belong the issues from death,* or the goings out from death! that is, God hath all ways that lead out from death in His own keeping; He keepeth the key of the door that lets us out from death. God keepeth all the passages; when men think they have shut us up in the jaws of death, He can open them and deliver us. JOSEPH CARYL

Vs. 21. *But God shall wound the head of His enemies.* Headstrong sinners will find that Providence overcomes them despite their strong heads. At the second coming of the Lord Jesus, His enemies will find His judgments to be beyond conception, terrible.

Vs. 22. *The Lord said, I will bring again from Bashan, I will bring My people again from the depths of the sea.* As there is no resisting Israel's God, so is there no escape from Him; neither the heights of Bashan nor the depths of the great sea can shelter from His eye of detection and His hand of justice.

Vs. 23. *That thy foot may be dipped in the blood of thine enemies, and the tongue of thy dogs in the same.* To us, except in a spiritual sense, the verse sounds harshly; but read it with an inner sense, and we also desire the utter and crushing defeat of all evil, and that wrong and sin may be the objects of profound contempt. C. H. S.

Vs. 26. *Bless ye God.* Bless Him; He "healeth all thy diseases," etc. (Psalm 103). This is an employment that fits for heaven. The tears of a mourner in God's house were supposed to defile His altar. We may mourn for sin; but a fretful spirit, discontented and unthankful, defiles God's altar still. ANDREW FULLER

Vs. 28. *Thy God hath commanded thy strength. Thy strength* is thy best—all that is within thee; all that thou canst do, and be, and become; and all that thou hast—the two mites, if these be all, and the alabaster box of spikenard, very costly, if this be thy possession . . . By that which God is in Himself, by that which God is in us, by law on the heart, and by law oral and written, by the new kingdom of His love, and by all His benefits, *Thy God commands thy strength.*

He speaks from the beginning, and from the end of time, from the midst of chaos, and from the new heavens and new earth, from Bethel and from Gethsemane, from Sinai and from Calvary, and He saith to us all, "My son, give Me thine heart," consecrate to Me thy best, and devote to Me thy strength. SAMUEL MARTIN

*Strengthen, O God, that which Thou hast wrought for us.* We expect God to bless His own work. He has never left any work unfinished yet, and He never will. "When we were without strength, in due time Christ died for the ungodly"; and now, being reconciled to God, we may look to Him to perfect that which concerneth us, since He never forsakes the work of His own hands. C. H. S.

Vs. 30. *The multitude of the bulls.* Popish bulls and imperial edicts have dashed against the Lord's church, but they have not prevailed against her, and they never shall. C. H. S.

*With the calves of the people.* The gospel, like the ark, has nothing to fear from great or small; it is a stone upon which everyone that stumbleth shall be broken. C. H. S.

*Till every one submit himself with pieces of silver.* The taxation of sin is infinitely more exacting than the tribute of religion. The little finger of lust is heavier than the loins of the law. Pieces of silver given to God are replaced with pieces of gold. C. H. S.

*Scatter thou the people that delight in war.* The church of God never wanted enemies, never will. "There is no peace to the wicked," saith God: "there shall be no peace to the godly," say the wicked. The wicked shall have no peace which God can give; the godly shall have no peace which the wicked can take away. THOMAS WALL

When the enemies of God rise up against His church, it is time for the church to fall down to God, to implore His aid against those enemies. Holy prayers are more powerful than profane swords. THOMAS WALL, *in "A Comment on the Times"*

Vs. 31. *Princes shall come out of Egypt; Ethiopia shall soon stretch out her hands unto God.* Hasten, O Lord, this day, when both the civilization and the barbarism of the earth shall adore Thee, Egypt and Ethiopia blending with glad accord in Thy worship! Here is the confidence of thy saints, even Thy promise; hasten it in Thine own time, good Lord.

Vs. 32. *Sing unto God, ye kingdoms of the earth.* Happy are men that God is One Who is consistently the object of joyous worship, for not such are the demons of the heathen. C. H. S.

*O sing praises unto the Lord.* Again and again is God to be magnified; we have too much sinning against God but cannot have too much singing to God. C. H. S.

Vs. 33. *And that a mighty voice;* or, *a voice of strength;* a strong and powerful voice, such as the gospel is, when accompanied with the power and Spirit of God. It is a soul-shaking and awakening voice; it is a heart-melting and a heart-breaking one; it is a quickening and an enlightening voice; it quickens dead sinners, gives life unto them, and the entrance of it gives light to dark minds; it is a soul-charming and alluring one; it draws to Christ, engages the affections to Him, and fills with unspeakable delight and pleasure. JOHN GILL

The power of Christ's voice, when He was on earth, appeared by the effects which followed, when He said, "Young man, arise"; "Lazarus, come forth": "Peace, be still"; and it will yet further appear when "all that are in the graves shall hear the voice of the Son of man and come forth." GEORGE HORNE

Vs. 34. *Ascribe ye strength unto God.* Let us never by our doubts or our daring defiances appear to deny power unto God; on the contrary, by yielding to Him and trusting in Him, let our hearts acknowledge His might. When we are reconciled to God, His omnipotence is an attribute of which we sing with delight. C. H. S.

# PSALM 69

In the Forty-First they were golden lilies, dropping sweet-smelling myrrh, and blooming in the fair gardens which skirt the ivory palaces: in this we have the lily among thorns, the lily of the valley, fair and beautiful, blooming in the Garden of Gethsemane. If any enquire, "Of whom speaketh the psalmist this? of himself, or of some other man?" we would reply, "Of himself and of some other man." Who that other is, we need not be long in discovering; it is the Crucified alone Who can say, "In My thirst they gave Me vinegar to drink." His footprints all through this sorrowful song have been pointed out by the Holy Spirit in the New Testament, and therefore we believe, and are sure, that the Son of man is here. Yet it seems to be the intention of the Spirit, while He gives us personal types and so shows the likeness to the firstborn which exists in the heirs of salvation, to set forth also the disparities between the best of the sons of men and the Son of God, for there are verses here which we dare not apply to our Lord; we almost shudder when we see our brethren attempting to do so, as for instance, verse 5. C. H. S.

This has usually been regarded as a Messianic Psalm. No portion of the Old Testament Scriptures is more frequently quoted in the New, with the exception of Psalm 22. J. J. STEWART PEROWNE

Vs. 1. *Save me, O God.* "He saved others, Himself He cannot save." With strong cryings and tears, He offered up prayers and supplications unto Him that was able to save Him from death, and was heard in that He feared. Thus David had prayed, and here his Son and Lord utters the same cry. It is remarkable that such a scene of woe should be presented to us immediately after the jubilant ascension hymn of the last Psalm, but this only shows how interwoven are the glories and the sorrows of our ever-blessed Redeemer.

*For the waters are come in unto My soul.* Bodily anguish is not His first complaint; He begins not with the gall which embittered His lips, but with the mighty griefs which broke into His heart. All the sea outside a vessel is less to be feared than that which finds its way into the hold. In all this, He has sympathy with us and is able to succor us when we, like Peter, beginning to sink, cry to Him, "Lord, save, or we perish."

Vs. 2. *I sink in deep mire, where there is no standing.* Everything gave way under the Sufferer; He could not get foothold for support—this is a worse fate than drowning. Sin is as mire for its filthiness, and the holy soul of the Savior must have loathed even that connection with it which was necessary for its expiation. C. H. S.

*I sink, . . . there is no standing.* I saw indeed there was cause of rejoicing for those that held to Jesus; but as for me, I had cut myself off by my transgressions and left myself neither foothold nor handhold, amongst all the stays and props in the precious Word of life. And truly I did now feel myself to sink into a gulf, as an house whose foundation is destroyed; I did liken myself, in this condition, unto the case of a child that was fallen into a mill-pit, who, though it could make some shift to scrabble and sprawl in the water, yet, because it could find neither hold for hand nor foot, therefore, at last, it must die in that condition. JOHN BUNYAN

*I am come into deep waters, where the floods overflow me.* Our Lord was no faint-hearted sentimentalist; His were real woes, and though He bore them heroically, yet were they terrible even to Him. He stemmed the torrent of almighty wrath that we might forever rest in Jehovah's love. C. H. S.

Vs. 3. *My throat is dried.* Few, very few, of His saints follow their Lord in prayer so far as this. We are, it is to be feared, more likely to be hoarse with talking frivolities to men than by pleading with God; yet our sinful nature demands more prayer than His perfect humanity might seem to need. His prayers should shame us into fervor.

*Mine eyes fail while I wait for my God.* There are times when we should pray till the throat is dry, and watch till the eyes grow dim. Only thus can we have fellowship with Him in His sufferings. What! can we not watch with Him one hour? Does the flesh shrink back? O cruel flesh, to be so tender of thyself and so ungenerous to thy Lord! C. H. S.

O pitiable sight! that that sight should fail, by which Jesus saw the multitudes and, therefore, ascended the Mount to give the precepts of the New Testament; by which, beholding Peter and Andrew, He called them; by which, looking upon the man sitting at the receipt of custom, He called and made an evangelist; by which, gazing upon the city, He wept over it . . . With eyes Thou didst look upon Simon, when Thou didst say, *Thou art the son of Jonas; thou shalt be called Cephas.* With these eyes Thou didst gaze upon the woman who was a sinner, to whom Thou didst say, *Thy faith hath saved thee; go in peace.* Turn these eyes upon us, and never turn them away from our continual prayers. GERHOHUS

Vs. 4. *They that hate Me without a cause are more than the hairs of Mine head.* "This is the heir, let us kill Him that the inheritance may be ours," was the unanimous resolve of all the keepers of the Jewish vineyard; while the Gentiles outside the walls of the Garden furnished the instruments for His murder and actually did the deed. C. H. S.

It is well known that Tertullian relates of Socrates, when his wife met him after his condemnation, and addressed him with a woman's tears: "Thou art unjustly condemned, Socrates." His reply was, "Wouldest thou have me justly?" LORINUS

*Then I restored that which I took not away.* In reference to our Lord, it may be truly said that He restores what He took not away; for He gives back to the injured honor of God a recompense, and to man his lost happiness, though the insult of the one and the fall of the other were neither of them, in any sense His doings. Usually, when the ruler sins, the people suffer, but here the proverb is reversed—the sheep go astray and their wanderings are laid at the Shepherd's door. C. H. S.

The devil took away by arrogating in heaven what was not his when he boasted that he was like the Most High, and for this he pays a righteous penalty . . . Adam also took away what was not his own, when, by the enticement of the devil, "You will be as gods," he sought after a likeness to God, by yielding to the deception of the woman.

But the Lord Jesus thought it not robbery to be equal with God . . . And yet His enemies said, "Let Him be crucified, for He hath made Himself the Son of God." GERHOHUS

Vs. 5. *O God, Thou knowest my foolishness.* David might well say this, but not David's Lord; unless it be understood as an appeal to God as to His freedom from the folly which men imputed to Him when they said He was mad. That which was foolishness to men was superlative wisdom before God. How often might we use these words in their natural sense, and if we were not such fools as to be blind to our own folly, this confession would be frequently on our lips. C. H. S.

*And my sins are not hid from Thee.* That prayer which has no confession in it may please a Pharisee's pride but will never bring down justification. C. H. S.

Vs. 6. *Let not them that wait on Thee, O Lord God of hosts, be ashamed for my sake.* Unbelievers are ready enough to catch at anything which may turn humble faith into ridicule; therefore, O God of all the armies of Israel, let not my case cause the enemy to blaspheme—such is the spirit of this verse. C. H. S.

*Let not those that seek Thee be confounded for my sake, O God of Israel.* In the depths of tribulation, no repining word escaped him, for there was no repining in his heart. The Lord of martyrs witnessed a good confession. He was strengthened in the hour of peril and came off more than a conqueror, as we also shall do if we hold fast our confidence even to the end. C. H. S.

Vs. 7. *Because for Thy sake I have borne reproach.* Because He undertook to do the Father's will, and teach His truth, the people were angry; because He declared Himself to be the Son of God, the priesthood raved. They could find no real fault in Him but were forced to hatch up a lying accusation before they could commence their sham trial of Him. The bottom of the quarrel was that God was with Him, and He with God, while the Scribes and Pharisees sought only their own honor. C. H. S.

*Shame hath covered My face.* There is nothing that a noble nature more abhors than shame, for honor is a spark of God's image; and the more of God's image there is in anyone, the more is shame abhorred by him. What must it be then to Christ, Who because He was to satisfy God in point of honor debased by man's sin, therefore of all punishments besides, He suffered most of shame; it being also (as was said) one of the greatest punishments in hell. THOMAS GOODWIN

Vs. 8. *I am become a stranger unto My brethren.* The Jews, His brethren in race, rejected Him; His family, His brethren by blood, were offended at Him; His disciples, His brethren in spirit, forsook Him and fled; one of them sold Him and another denied Him with oaths and cursings.

*And an alien unto My mother's children.* May none of us ever act as if we were strangers to Him; never may we treat Him as if He were an alien to us: rather let us resolve to be crucified with Him, and may grace turn the resolve into fact. C. H. S.

Vs. 9. *For the zeal of thine house hath eaten me up.* Zeal for God is so little understood by men of the world that it always draws down opposition upon those who are inspired with it; they are always sure to be accused of sinister motives, or of hypocrisy, or of being out of their senses. When zeal eats us up, ungodly men seek to eat us up, too, and this was preeminently the case with our Lord, because His holy jealousy was preeminent. C. H. S.

How industrious was Calvin in the Lord's vineyard! When his friends persuaded him for his health's sake to remit a little of his labor, saith he, "Would you have the Lord find me idle when He comes?" Luther spent three hours a day in prayer. It is said of holy Bradford, preaching, reading, and prayer, was his whole life. "I rejoice," said bishop Jewel, "that my body is exhausted in the labors of my holy calling."

How violent were the blessed martyrs! They wore their fetters as ornaments; they snatched up torments as crowns, and embraced the flames as cheerfully as Elijah did the fiery chariot that came to fetch him to heaven. "Let racks, fires, pullies, and all manner of torments come, so I may win Christ," said Ignatius. These pious souls "resisted unto blood." How should this provoke our zeal! Write after these fair copies. THOMAS WATSON

*Zeal, reproaches.* I remember Moulin, speaking of the French Protestants, saith, "When Pápists hurt us for reading the Scriptures, we burn with zeal to be reading of them; but now persecution is over, our Bibles are like old almanacs." In times of greatest affliction and persecution for holiness' sake, a Christian hath, first a good captain to lead and encourage him; secondly, a righteous cause to prompt and embolden him; thirdly, a gracious God to relieve and succor him; fourthly, a glorious heaven to receive and reward him; and, certainly, these things cannot but mightily raise him and inflame him under the greatest opposition and persecution. THOMAS BROOKS

Vs. 10. *When I wept, and chastened my soul with fasting, that was to my reproach.* Our Savior wept much in secret for our sins, and no doubt His private soul-chastenings on our behalf were very frequent. Lone mountains and desert places saw repeated agonies, which, if they could disclose them, would astonish us indeed. The emaciation which these exercises wrought in our Lord made Him appear nearly fifty years old when He was but little over thirty; this which was to His honor was used as a matter of reproach against Him. C. H. S.

Behold here, virtue is accounted vice; truth, blasphemy; wisdom, folly. Behold, the peace-maker of the world is judged a seditious person; the fulfiller of the law, a breaker of the law; our Savior, a sinner; our God, a devil. SIR JOHN HAYWARD, in *"The Sanctuary of a Troubled Soul"*

Vs. 12. *And I was the song of the drunkards.* The ungodly know no merrier jest than that in which the name of the holy is traduced. The flavor of slander is piquante and gives a relish to the revelers' wine. The saints are ever choice subjects for satire. Butler's *Hudibras* owed more of its popularity to its irreligious banter than to any intrinsic cleverness. What amazing sin that He Whom seraphs worship with veiled faces should be a scornful proverb among the most abandoned of men!

*The by-word of the passing throng,*
*The ruler's scoff, the drunkard's song.*
C. H. S.

Holy walking is the drunkard's song, as David was; and so preciseness and strictness of walking is ordinarily: the world cannot bear the burning and shining conversations of some of the saints; they are so cuttingly reproved by them, that with those heathens, they curse the sun, that by its shining doth scorch them. JOHN MURCOT

"Unless they scoff and jeer the ways and servants of God" (as Mr. Greenham saith), "the fools cannot tell how to be merry"; and then the devil is merry with them for company. ANTHONY TUCKNEY, *in "A Good Day Well Improved"*

Vs. 13. *O God, in the multitude of Thy mercy, hear me.* To misery, no attribute is more sweet than mercy, and when sorrows multiply, the multitude of mercy is much prized. C. H. S.

*Heavier the cross, the heartier prayer;*
*The bruised herbs most fragrant are.*
*If sky and wind were always fair,*
*The sailor would not watch the star;*
*And David's Psalms had ne'er been sung*
*If grief his heart had never wrung.*
*From the German*

Vs. 17. *Hear me speedily.* Our Lord was the perfection of patience, yet He cried urgently for speedy mercy; and therein He gives us liberty to do the same, so long as we did, "Nevertheless, not as I will, but as Thou wilt."

Vs. 18. *Draw nigh unto my soul.* The near approach of God is all the sufferer needs; one smile of heaven will still the rage of hell.

Vs. 19. *Mine adversaries are all before Thee.* The whole lewd and loud company is now present to Thine eye: Judas and his treachery; Herod and his cunning; Caiaphas and his counsel; Pilate and his vacillation; Jews, priests, people, rulers, all, Thou seest and wilt judge.

Vs. 21. *And in My thirst they gave Me vinegar to drink.* A criminal's draught was offered to our innocent Lord, a bitter portion to our dying Master. Sorry entertainment had earth for her King and Savior. How often have our sins filled the gall-cup for our Redeemer! While we blame the Jews, let us not excuse ourselves. C. H. S.

Verse 22. The imprecations in this verse and those following it are revolting only when considered as the expression of malignant selfishness. If uttered by God, they shock no reader's sensibilities, nor should they when considered as the language of an ideal person, representing the whole class of righteous sufferers and particularly Him, Who, though He prayed for His murderers while dying (Luke 23:24), had before applied the words of this very passage to the unbelieving Jews (Matt. 23:38), as Paul did afterwards (Rom. 11:9-10).

The general doctrine of providential retribution, far from being confined to the Old Testament, is distinctly taught in many of our Savior's parables (see Matt. 21:41; 22:7; 24:51). JOSEPH ADDISON ALEXANDER

*Let their table become a snare.* That is, for a recompense for their inhumanity and cruelty towards me. Michaelis shows how exactly these combinations were fulfilled in the history of the final siege of Jerusalem by the Romans. Many thousands of the Jews had assembled in the city to eat the paschal lamb, when Titus unexpectedly made an assault upon them. In this siege, the greater part of the inhabitants of Jerusalem miserably perished. WILLIAM WALFORD

Vs. 23 *Let their eyes be darkened, that they see not.* Eyes which see no beauty in the Lord Jesus but flash wrath upon Him may well grow yet more dim, till death spiritual leads to death eternal.

Vs. 24. *Pour out Thine indignation upon them.* What can be too severe a penalty for those who reject the incarnate God and refuse to obey the commands of His mercy? They deserve to be flooded with wrath, and they shall be; for upon all who rebel against the Savior, Christ the Lord, "the wrath is come to the uttermost" (I Thess. 2:16). God's indignation is no trifle; the anger of a holy, just, omnipotent, and infinite Being is above all things to be dreaded; even a drop of it consumes, but to have it poured upon us is inconceivably dreadful. O God, who knoweth the power of Thine anger?

Vs. 27. *Add iniquity unto their iniquity.* Unbelievers will add sin to sin, and so, punishment to punishment. This is the severest imprecation or prophecy of all. C. H. S.

Sin, carried far enough, becomes its own punishment. Let but a voracious glutton be bound to sit at a well-furnished table but two hours after he had filled his stomach, he would account it an intolerable penance. Let but the drunkard be forced to drink on with those that can drink him down, how is he a burden to himself and a scorn to his fellow drunkards! Let but a lazy sluggard be confined three days to his bed, and how weary will he be of his bed of down! How is the idle person more weary of his idleness than another is of work! SAMUEL ANNESLEY, *in "Morning Exercises"*

*And let them not come into Thy righteousness.* Those who choose evil shall have their choice. Men who hate divine mercy shall not have it forced upon them. C. H. S.

Vs. 28. *Let them be blotted out of the book of the living, and not be written with the righteous.* We come to the question, whether to be written in heaven be an infallible assurance of salvation, or whether any there registered may come to be blotted out? The truth is, that none written in heaven can ever be lost; yet they object against this verse.

Hence, they infer, that some names once there recorded are afterwards put out; but this opinion casteth a double aspersion on God Himself. Either it makes

Him ignorant of future things, as if He foresaw not the end of elect and reprobate, and so were deceived in decreeing some to be saved that shall not be saved; or, that His decree is mutable, in excluding those upon their sins whom He hath formerly chosen. From both these weaknesses St. Paul vindicates Him (II Tim. 2:19): "The foundation of God standeth sure, having this seal, the Lord knoweth them that are His."

Augustine says, we must not so take it, that God first writes and then dasheth out. For if a Pilate could say, "What I have written, I have written," and it shall stand; shall God say, "What I have written, I will wipe out, and it shall not stand?"

They are written, then, according to their own hope that presumed their names there, and are blotted out when it is manifest to themselves that their names never had any such honor of inscription. This even that Psalm strengthens whence they fetch their opposition: *Let them be blotted out of the book of the living, and not be written with the righteous.*

So that to be blotted out of that book, it is, indeed, never to be written there. To be wiped out in the end is but a declaration that such were not written in the beginning. THOMAS ADAMS

Vs. 29. *But I am poor and sorrowful.* No man was ever poorer or more sorrowful than Jesus of Nazareth, yet His cry out of the depths was heard, and He was uplifted to the highest glory.

*Let Thy salvation, O God, set me up on high.* O ye poor and sorrowful ones, lift up your heads, for as with your Lord, so shall it be with you. You are trodden down today as the mire of the streets, but you shall ride upon the high places of the earth ere long; and even now ye are raised up together and made to sit together in the heavenlies in Christ Jesus. C. H. S.

Vs. 31. *This also shall please the Lord better than an ox or bullock that hath horns and hoofs.* The *opus operatum,* which our ritualists think so much of, the Lord puffs at. The horning and hoofing are nothing to Him, though to Jewish ritualists there were great points, and matters for critical examination; our modern rabbis are just as precise as to the mingling of water with their wine, the baking of their wafers, the cut of their vestments, and the performance of genuflections towards the right quarter of the compass. O fools, and slow of heart to perceive all that the Lord has declared. C. H. S.

# PSALM 70

Title: "To the Chief Musician, A Psalm of David." So far the title corresponds with Psalm XL, of which this is a copy with variations. David appears to have written the full-length Psalm and also to have made this excerpt from it and altered it to suit the occasion. It is a fit pendant to Psalm LXIX and a suitable preface to Psalm LXXI. To bring to remembrance: this is the poor man's memorial. C. H. S.

Vs. 3. *For a reward of their shame that say, Aha, aha.* They thought to shame the godly, but it was their shame and shall be their shame forever. How fond men are of taunts, and if they are meaningless aha's, more like animal cries than human words, it matters nothing, so long as they are a vent for scorn and sting the victim. Rest assured, the enemies of Christ and His people shall have wages for their work; they shall be paid in their own coin; they loved scoffing, and they shall be filled with it—yea, they shall become a proverb and a by-word forever. C. H. S.

O miracle of mercy! He Who deserved the hallelujahs of an intelligent universe and the special hosannahs of all the children of men, had first to anticipate and then to endure from the mouths of the very rebels whom He came to bless and to save, the malicious tauntings of "Aha, aha." JAMES FRAME

Vs. 5. *O Lord, make no tarrying.* His prayer for Himself, like His prayer for His foes and for His friends, was answered. The Lord made no tarrying.

Ere four and twenty hours had rolled past, His rescued spirit was in Paradise, and the crucified thief was with Him. Oh, what a change! The morning saw Him condemned at the bar of an earthly tribunal, sentenced to death, and nailed to the bitter tree; before the evening shadowed the hill of Calvary, He was nestling in the bosom of God and had become the great center of attraction and of admiration to all the holy intelligences of the universe.

The morning saw Him led out through the gate of the Jerusalem below, surrounded by a ribald crowd, whose hootings rung in His ear; but ere the night fell, He had passed through the gate of Jerusalem above, and His tread was upon the streets of gold, and angel anthems rose high through the dome of heaven, and joy filled the heart of God. JAMES FRAME

# PSALM 71

There is no title to this Psalm, and hence some conjecture that Psalm LXX is intended to be a prelude to it and has been broken off from it. Such imaginings have no value with us. We have already met with five Psalms without title, which are, nevertheless, as complete as those which bear them.

We have here "The Prayer of the Aged Believer," who in holy confidence of faith, strengthened by a long and remarkable experience, pleads against his enemies and asks further blessings for himself. Anticipating a gracious reply, he promises to magnify the Lord exceedingly. C. H. S.

It will be asked how Christ could use such verses as verses 9 and 18, since these look forward apparently to the frailty of age. The reply to this difficulty is, that these expressions are used by Him in sympathy with His members, and in His own case denote the state equivalent to age. His old age was, ere He reached three and thirty years, as John 8:57 is supposed to imply: for "worn-out men live fast" ANDREW A. BONAR

Vs. 3. *Thou hast given commandment to save me.* Destruction cannot destroy us; famine cannot starve us; but we laugh at both, while God's mandate shields us. C. H. S.

Vs. 4. *The cruel man* is literally the leavened man, leavened with hatred of truth and enmity to God; and, therefore, a violent opposer of His people. So, in I Cor. 5:8, we are cautioned against the "leaven of malice and wickedness," which, in accordance with the figure, may pervade the whole natural character of an ungodly man, his faculties and affections. W. WILSON

Vs. 5. *Thou art my hope.* Each yearning of our hearts, each ray of hope which gleams upon us, each touch which thrills us, each voice which whispers in our inmost hearts of the good things laid up in store for us, if we will love God, are the light of Christ enlightening us, the touch of Christ raising us to new life, the voice of Christ, "Whoso cometh to Me, I will in no wise cast out"; it is "Christ in us, the hope of glory," drawing us up by His Spirit Who dwelleth in us, unto Himself, our hope.

For our hope is not the glory of heaven, not joy, not peace, not rest from labor, not fullness of our wishes, nor sweet contentment of the whole soul, nor understanding of all mysteries and all knowledge, not only a torrent of delight; it is "Christ our God," "the hope of glory."

Nothing which God could create is what we hope for; nothing which God could give us out of Himself, no created glory, or bliss, or beauty, or majesty, or riches. What we hope for is our redeeming God Himself, His love, His bliss, the joy of our Lord Himself, Who hath so loved us, to be our joy and our portion forever. E. B. PUSEY

*Thou art my trust from my youth.* Even Seneca, a heathen, could say: "Youth well spent is the greatest comfort of old age." When the proconsul bade Polycarp deny Christ and swear by the emperor, he answered: "I have served Christ these eighty-six years, and He hath not once injured me, and shall I now deny Him?" OLIVER HEYWOOD

Vs. 7. *I am as a wonder unto many.* "To thousand eyes a mark and gaze am I." The saints are men wondered at; often their dark side is gloomy even to amazement, while their bright side is glorious even to astonishment. The believer is a riddle, an enigma puzzling the unspiritual; he is a monster warring with those delights of the flesh, which are the all in all of other men; he is a prodigy, unaccountable to the judgments of ungodly men; a wonder gazed at, feared, and, by-and-by, contemptuously derided. Few understand us; many are surprised at us. C. H. S.

The Messiah did not attract the admiring gaze of mankind. He did arrest attention; He did excite "wonder"; but it was not the wonder of admiration. A few whose eyes God had opened, saw, indeed, in some measure, the real grandeur there was amid all this apparent meanness. They "beheld His glory—the glory as of the Only Begotten of the Father"; a glory that bedimmed all created luster.

But the great body of those who beheld Him were "astonished" at Him. His external appearance, especially when contrasted with His claim to Messiahship, shocked them. The Galilean peasant— the Nazarene carpenter—the son of Joseph, claiming God for His own Father—declaring Himself the "bread of life," and "the light of the world," and asserting that the destinies of eternity hung on the reception or rejection of Him and His message; all this excited a mingled emotion of amazement and indignation, scorn and horror, in the bosom of the great majority of his countrymen. He was a "wonder," a prodigy unto many. JOHN BROWN, *in "The Sufferings and Glories of the Messiah"*

Vs. 8. *Let my mouth be filled with Thy praise and with Thy honor all the day.* What a blessed mouthful! A man never grows nauseated, though the flavor of it be all day in his mouth. God's bread is always in our mouths; so should His praise be. He fills us with good; let us be also filled with gratitude. This would leave no room for murmuring or backbiting; therefore, may we well join with holy David in this sacred wish. C. H. S.

Vs. 9. *Cast me not off in the time of old age.* Old age robs us of personal beauty and deprives us of strength for active service; but it does not lower us in the love and favor of God. C. H. S.

It is not unnatural or improper for a man who sees old age coming upon him to pray for special grace, and special strength, to enable him to meet what he cannot ward off, and what he cannot but dread; for who can look upon the infirmities of old age, as coming upon himself, but with sad and pensive feelings.

Who would wish to be an old man? Who can look upon a man tottering with years, and broken down with infirmities; a man whose sight and hearing are gone; a man who is alone amidst the graves of all the friends that he had in early life; a man who is a burden to himself, and to the world; a man who has reached the "last scene of all that ends in strange, eventful history"—that scene of

*Second childishness, and mere oblivion,*
*Sans teeth, sans eyes, sans taste, sans everything.*

ALBERT BARNES

*Forsake me not when my strength faileth.* June 28. This day I enter on my eighty-sixth year. I now find I grow old: (1) My sight is decayed, so that I cannot read small print, unless in a strong light. (2) My strength is decayed, so that I walk much slower than I did some years since. (3) My memory of names, whether persons or places, is decayed, till I stop a little to recollect them.

What I should be afraid of, is, if I took thought for the morrow, that my body should weigh down my mind, and create either stubbornness, by the decrease of my understanding, or peevishness, by the increase of bodily infirmities; but Thou shalt answer for me, O Lord, my God. JOHN WESLEY

Vs. 11. *Saying, God hath forsaken him.* Oh, bitter taunt! There is no worse arrow in all the quivers of hell. Our Lord felt this barbed shaft, and it is no marvel if His disciples feel the same. Were this exclamation the truth, it were indeed an ill day for us; but, glory be to God, it is a barefaced lie.

Vs. 14. *But I will hope continually.* When I cannot rejoice in what I have, I will look forward to what shall be mine and will still rejoice. C. H. S.

Vs. 15. *I know not the numbers.* David began his arithmetic, in the 14th verse, with addition: "I will yet praise Thee more and more"; but he is fairly beaten in this first rule of sacred mathematics. His calculation fails him; the mere enumeration of the Lord's mercies overwhelms his mind; he owns his inadequacy. Reckon either by time, by place, or by value, and the salvation of God baffles all powers of estimation. C. H. S.

Vs. 17. *Thou hast taught me from my youth.* Jerome, in his Epistle to Nepotianus, says: "As fire in green wood is stifled, so wisdom in youth, impeded by temptations and concupiscence, does not unfold its brightness unless by hard work, and steady application and prayer, the incentives of youth are inwardly repelled. Plato says that there is nothing more divine than the education of children. Socrates says that God is the mind of the universe. Without Him, therefore, all are demented; but with Him, and through Him, in a single moment they become wise. THOMAS LE BLANC

Those that are wicked are but as weeds upon a dunghill, but you that are godly are as plants in God's own orchard. In the last of the Romans (verse 7) we find that Andronicus and Junia are commended because they were in Christ before Paul: "They were in Christ before me."

It is an honorable thing to be in Christ before others; this is honorable when you are young; and then going on in the ways of godliness all your young time, and so in your middle age, and till you come to be old. JEREMIAH BURROUGHS

*And hitherto have I declared Thy wondrous works.* A sacred conservatism is much needed in these days, when men are giving up old lights for new. We mean both to learn and to teach the wonders of redeeming love, till we can discover something nobler or more soul-satisfying; for this reason we hope that our grey heads will be found in the same road as we have trodden, even from our beardless youth. C. H. S.

Vs. 18. *Now also when I am old and greyheaded, O God, forsake me not.* Come, let me knock at your hearts; are none of you old professors, like old hollow oaks, who stand in the woods among professors still, and keep their stand of profession still, and go to ordinances, etc.; but the "rain they drink in," as the Apostle's word is serves to no other end but to rot them. "These are nigh unto cursing."

Oh, have you green fruits still growing on you, as quickly and lively affections to God and Christ, and faith and love, as at the first, and more abounding? Oh, bless God, you are so near the haven, and lift up your hearts, your redemption draws near; and, withal, raise your confidence, that that God of grace, Who hath called you into His eternal glory, will keep you for it, and possess you of it shortly. THOMAS GOODWIN

*Forsake me not; until.* Apostasy in old age is fearful. He that climbs almost to the top of a tower, then slipping back, hath the greater fall. The patient almost recovered, is more deadly sick by a relapse. THOMAS ADAMS

Vs. 23. *And my soul, which Thou hast redeemed.* Soul-singing is the soul of singing. Till men are redeemed, they are like instruments out of tune; but when once the precious blood has set them at liberty, then are they fitted to magnify the Lord Who bought them. Our being bought with a price is a more than sufficient reason for our dedicating ourselves to the earnest worship of God, our Savior.

Vs. 24. *My tongue also shall talk of Thy righteousness all the day long.* I will talk to myself, and to Thee, my God, and to my fellow-men: my theme shall be Thy way of justifying sinners, the glorious display of Thy righteousness and grace in Thy dear Son; and this most fresh and never-to-be-exhausted subject shall be ever with me, from the rising of the sun to the going down of the same.

Others talk of their beloveds, and they shall be made to hear of mine. I will become an incessant talker, while this matter lies on my heart, for in all company, this subject will be in season. C. H. S.

# PSALM 72

It is pretty certain that the title declares Solomon to be the author of this Psalm, and yet from verse 20 it would seem that David uttered it in prayer before he died. Jesus is here, beyond all doubt, in the glory of His reign, both as He now is and as He shall be revealed in the latter-day glory. C. H. S.

So clear are the traces of Solomon's pen that Calvin, whose sagacity in this kind of criticism has never been excelled, although he thought himself obliged, by the note at the end of the Psalm, to attribute the substance of it to David, felt Solomon's touch so sensibly that he threw out the conjecture that the prayer was the father's, but that it was afterwards thrown into the lyrical form by the son. WILLIAM BINNIE

Vs. 3. *And the little hills, by righteousness.* In a spirtual sense, peace is given to the heart by the righteousness of Christ; and all the powers and passions of the soul are filled with a holy calm, when the way of salvation, by a divine righteousness, is revealed. Then do we go forth with joy, and are led forth with peace; the mountains and the hills break forth before us into singing.

Vs. 5. *They shall fear Thee as long as the sun and moon endure.* His kingdom, moreover, is no house of cards, or dynasty of days; it is as lasting as the lights of heaven; days and nights will cease before He abdicates His throne. Neither sun nor moon as yet manifest any failure in their radiance, nor are there any signs of decrepitude in the kingdom of Jesus; on the contrary, it is but in its youth, and is evidently the coming power, the rising sun.

*Throughout all generations.* Each generation shall have a regeneration in its midst, let pope and devil do what they may. Even at this hour we have before us the tokens of His eternal power; since He ascended to His throne, eighteen hundred years ago, His dominion has not been overturned, though the mightiest of empires have gone like visions of the night. We see on the shore of time the wrecks of the Cæsars, the relics of the Moguls, and the last remnants of the Ottomans. Charlemagne, Maximilian, Napoleon, how they flit like shadows before us! They were and are not; but Jesus forever *is.* As for the houses of Hohenzollern, Guelph, or Hapsburg, they have their hour; but the Son of David has all hours and ages as His own. C. H. S.

Vs. 6. *He shall come down like rain upon the mown grass: as showers that water the earth.* Each crystal drop of rain tells of heavenly mercy which forgets not the parched plains: Jesus is all grace, all that He does is love, and His presence among men is joy. We need to preach Him more, for no shower can so refresh the nations. Philosophic preaching mocks men as with a dust shower, but the gospel meets the case of fallen humanity, and happiness flourishes beneath its genial power. Come down, O Lord, upon my soul, and my heart shall blossom with Thy praise. C. H. S.

Christless souls are like the dry ground; without the moisture of saving grace their hearts are hard; neither rods, mercies, nor sermons, make impression upon them. Why? They are without Christ, the fountain of grace and spiritual influences. Before the fall, man's soul was like a well-watered garden—beautiful, green, and fragrant; but his apostasy from God, in Adam our first head, the springs of grace and holiness are quite dried up in his soul; and there is no curing of this drought but by the soul's union with a new head. JOHN WILLISON

Vs. 7. *Righteous. Peace.* Do you ask what He is individually? The answer is, "King of righteousness": a Being loving righteousness, working righteousness, promoting righteousness, procuring righteousness, imparting righteousness to those whom He saves, perfectly sinless, and the enemy and abolisher of all sin.

Do you ask what He is practically and in relation to the effect of His reign? The answer is, "King of Peace": a Sovereign Whose kingdom is a shelter for all who are miserable, a covert for all who are persecuted, a resting-place for all who are weary, a home for the destitute, and a refuge for the lost. CHARLES STANFORD

Vs. 8. *He shall have dominion also from sea to sea, and from the river unto the ends of the earth.* We are encouraged by such a passage as this to look for the Savior's universal reign; whether before or after His personal advent, we leave for the discussion of others. In this Psalm, at least, we see a personal monarch, and He is the central figure, the focus of all the glory; not His servant, but Himself do we see possessing the dominion and dispensing the government. Personal pronouns referring to our great King are constantly occurring in this Psalm; *He* has dominion, kings fall down before *Him,* and serve *Him;* for *He* delivers, *He* spares, *He* saves, *He* lives, and daily is *He* praised. C. H. S.

Vs. 12. *When He crieth.* A cry is the native language of a spiritually needy soul; it has done with fine phrases and long orations, and it takes to sobs and moans; and so, indeed, it grasps the most potent of all weapons, for heaven always yields to such artillery.

*The poor also, and him that hath no helper.* The proverb says, "God helps those that help themselves"; but it is yet more true that Jesus helps those who cannot help themselves nor find help in others. All helpless ones are under the especial care of Zion's compassionate King; let them hasten to put themselves in fellowship with Him. Let them look to Him, for He is looking for them.

Vs. 13. *And shall save the souls of the needy.* Scipio used to say that he would rather save a single citizen than slay a thousand enemies. Of this mind ought all princes to be towards their subjects; but this affection and love rose to the highest excellence and power in the breast of Christ. So ardent is His love for His own, that He suffers not one of them to perish, but leads them to full salvation, and, opposing Himself to both devils and tyrants who seek to destroy their souls, He constrains their fury and confounds their rage. MOLLERUS

Vs. 14. *And precious shall their blood be in His sight.* The Angolani so despised their slaves that they would sometimes give as many as twenty-two for one hunting dog. . . . But Christ prefers the soul of one of His servants to the whole world, since He died that it might be made more capable of entering into eternal felicity.

For breaking one goblet, the Roman cast his slave into the pond to be devoured by the muraenae. But the Son of God came down from heaven to earth to deliver mankind, His vile, ungrateful, faithless servants, from the pangs of the serpent, like the golden fleece, and save them as Jonah from the whale. Is not their blood precious in His sight? THOMAS LE BLANC

Vs. 15. *He shall live.* Alexander the Great acknowledged at death that he was a frail and feeble man. "Lo! I," said he, "am dying, whom you falsely called a god." But Christ proved that He was God when, by His own death, He overcame, and, as I may say, slew death. THOMAS LE BLANC

Vs. 16. *An handful of corn.* Doubtless it has been familiar to you to see corn merchants carrying small bags with them, containing just a handful of corn, which they exhibit as specimens of the store which they have for sale.

Now, let me beg of every one of you to carry a small bag with this precious corn of the gospel. When you write a letter, drop in a word for Christ; it may be a seed that will take root. . . . Speak a word for Christ wherever you go; it may be seed productive of a great deal of fruit. Drop a tract on the counter, or in a house; it may be a seed productive of a plenteous harvest. The most difficult place, the steepest mountain, the spot where there is the least hope of producing fruit, is to be the first place of attack; and the more labor there is required, the more is to be given, in the distribution of the seeds. JAMES SHERMAN

Verses 18-19. As Quesnel well observes, these verses explain themselves. They call rather for profound gratitude and emotion of heart than for an exercise of the understanding; they are rather to be used for adoration than for exposition. It is, and ever will be, the acme of our desires and the climax of our prayers, to behold Jesus exalted King of kings and Lord of lords. C. H. S.

Vs. 19. *Amen, and Amen.* Rabbi Jehudah the Holy said, "He that said *Amen* in this world is worthy to say it in the world to come. David, therefore, utters *Amen* twice in this Psalm, to show that one 'Amen' belongs to this world, the other to that which is to come. He who saith 'Amen' devoutly is greater than he who uttereth the prayers, for the prayers are but the letter, and the Amen is the seal. The scribe writeth the letters; the prince alone seals them." NEALE AND LITTLEDALE

## HERE ENDETH BOOK II OF THE BOOK OF PSALMS

# PSALM 73

Subject: Curiously enough, this Seventy-Third Psalm corresponds in subject with the Thirty-Seventh: it will help the memory of the young to notice the reverse figures. The theme is that ancient stumbling-block of good men, which Job's friends could not get over; viz., the present prosperity of wicked men and the sorrows of the godly. Heathen philosophers have puzzled themselves about this, while to believers it has too often been a temptation. C. H. S.

The Seventy-Third Psalm is a very striking record of the mental struggle which an eminently pious Jew underwent when he contemplated the respective conditions of the righteous and the wicked. He relates the most fatal shock which his faith had received when he contrasted the prosperity of the wicked, who, though they proudly contemned God and man, prospered in the world and increased in riches, with his own lot, who, though he had cleansed his heart and washed his hands in innocency, had been "plagued all the day long and chastened every morning." THOMAS THOMASON PEROWNE, *in "'The Essential Coherence of the Old and New Testaments"*

In Psalm Seventy-Three, the soul looks out and reasons on what it sees there; namely, successful wickedness and suffering righteousness. What is the conclusion? "I have cleansed my heart in vain." So much for looking about.

In Psalm Seventy-Seven, the soul looks in and reasons on what it finds there. What is the conclusion? "Hath God forgotten to be gracious?" So much for looking in. Where, then, should we look? Look up, straight up, and believe what you see there. What will be the conclusion? You will understand the "end" of man and trace the "way" of God. *From "Things New and Old, a Monthly Magazine"*

Vs. 1. *Truly:* it's but a particle; but the smallest fillings of gold are gathered up. Little pearls are of great price. And this small particle is not of small use, being rightly applied and improved. Take it (as our translators gave it us) as a *note of asseveration. Truly.* It's a word of faith, opposite to the Psalmist's sense and Satan's injections. SIMEON ASH, *in a Sermon entitled "God's Incomparable Goodness unto Israel"*

*Truly God is good to Israel, even to such as are of a clean heart.* Whatever may or may not be the truth about mysterious and inscrutable things, there are certainties somewhere; experience has placed some tangible facts within our grasp; let us, then, cling to these, and they will prevent our being carried away by these hurricanes of infidelity which still come from the wilderness, and like whirlwinds, smite the four corners of our house and threaten to overthrow it.

O my God, however puzzled I may be, let me never think ill of Thee. If I cannot understand Thee, let me never cease to believe in Thee. It must be so; it cannot be otherwise; Thou art good to those whom Thou hast made good; and where Thou hast renewed the heart, Thou wilt not leave it to its enemies. C. H. S.

Notwithstanding the variety and frequency of the saint's sufferings, *yet God is good.* Though sorrow salutes them every morning at their first awaking and trouble attends them to bed at night, *yet God is good.* Though temptations many and terrible make batteries and breeches upon their spirits, *yet God is good to Israel.* The administrations of God are not according to the sad surmises of His people's misgiving hearts. For, though they through diffidence are apt often to give up their holy labors as lost, and all their conscientious care and carriage as utterly cast away, *yet God is good to Israel.* SIMEON ASH, *in a Sermon entitled, "God's Incomparable Goodness unto Israel"*

We see how emphatic is this exclamation of the Psalmist! He does not ascend into the chair to dispute after the manner of the philosophers and to deliver his discourse in a style of studied oratory; but as if he had escaped from hell, he proclaims with a loud voice, and with impassioned feeling, that he had obtained the victory. JOHN CALVIN

*Yet sure the goods are good: I would think so,*
*If they would give me leave!*
*But virtue in distress, and vice in triumph,*
*Make atheists of mankind.*

DRYDEN

Let the devil and his instruments say what they will to the contrary, I will never believe them; I have said it before, and I see no reason to reverse my sentence: *Truly God is good.* Though sometimes He may hide His face for awhile, yet He doth that in faithfulness and love; there is kindness in His very scourges, and love bound up in His rods. JAMES JANEWAY

Vs. 2. Here begins the narrative of a great soul-battle, a spiritual marathon, a hard and well-fought field in which the half-defeated became in the end wholly victorious. C. H. S.

Let such as fear God and begin to look aside on the things of this world know it will be hard even for them to hold out in faith and in the fear of God in time of trial. Remember the example of David; he was a man that had spent much time in travelling towards heaven; yet, looking but a little aside upon the glittering show of this world, had very near lost his way, his feet were almost gone, his steps had well-nigh slipt. EDWARD ELTON

*My feet were almost gone.* Errors of heart and head soon affect the conduct. There is an intimate connection between his heart and the feet. Asaph could barely stand, his uprightness was going, his knees were bowing like a falling wall. When men doubt the righteousness of God, their own integrity begins to waver. C. H. S.

There is to be noted that the prophet said he was almost gone, and not altogether. Here is the presence, providence, strength, safeguard, and keeping of man by Almighty God, marvelously set forth. That although we are tempted and brought even to the very point to perpetrate and do all mischief, yet He stays us and keeps us, that the temptation shall not overcome us. JOHN HOOPER

Verses 2-14. But the prosperity of wicked and unjust men, both in public and in private life, who, though not leading a happy life in reality, are yet thought to do so in common opinion, being praised improperly in the works of poets, and all kinds of books, may lead you—and I am not surprised at your mistake—to a belief that the gods care nothing for the affairs of men. These matters disturb you. Being led astray by foolish thoughts, and yet not able to think ill of the gods, you have arrived at your present state of mind, so as to think that the gods do indeed exist, but that they despise and neglect human affairs. PLATO

Vs. 3. *For I was envious at the foolish.* It is a pitiful thing that an heir of heaven should have to confess, "I was envious," but worse still that he should have to put it, "I was envious at the foolish." Yet this acknowledgment is, we fear, due from most of us. C. H. S.

Who would envy a malefactor's going up a high ladder and being mounted above the rest of the people when it is only for a little and in order to his being turned over and hanged? That is just the case of wicked men who are mounted up high in prosperity; for it is so only that they may be cast down deeper into destruction. JOHN WILLISON

The sneering jest of Dionysius the younger, a tyrant of Sicily, when after having robbed the Temple of Syracuse, he had a prosperous voyage with the plunder, is well known. "See you not," says he to those who were with him, "how the gods favor the sacrilegious?"

In the same way, the prosperity of the wicked is taken as an encouragement to commit sin; for we are ready to imagine that, since God grants them so much of the good things of this life, they are the objects of His approbation and favor. We see how their prosperous condition wounded David to the heart, leading him almost to think that there was nothing better for him than to join himself to their company, and to follow their course of life. JOHN CALVIN

*When I saw the prosperity of the wicked.* Prosperity it seems is a dangerous weapon, and none but the innocent should dare to use it. The Psalmist himself, before he thought upon this, began to envy the prosperity of wicked men. WILLIAM CROUCH, *in "The Enormous Sin of Covetousness Detected"*

Socrates, being asked what would be vexatious to good men, replied, "The prosperity of the bad." What would vex the bad? "The prosperity of the good." THOMAS LE BLANC

Diogenes, the cynic, seeing Harpalus, a vicious fellow, still thriving in the world, he was bold to say that wicked Harpalus' living long in prosperity was an argument that God had cast off His care of the world, that He cared not which end went forward.

But he was a heathen. Yet, for all that, the lights of the sanctuary have burnt dim; stars of no small magnitude have twinkled; men of eminent parts, famous in their generation for religion and piety, have staggered in their judgment to see the flourishing estate of the wicked. It made Job to complain, and Jeremiah to expostulate with God; and David was even ready to sink in seeing the prosperity of the ungodly men: to see the one in wealth, the other in want; the one honorable, the other despised; the one upon a throne, the other on a dunghill. JOHN DONNE

Vs. 4. *For there are no bands in their death.* The notion is still prevalent that a quiet death means a happy hereafter. The Psalmist had observed that the very reverse is true. Careless persons become case-hardened and continue presumptuously secure, even to the last. C. H. S.

Men may die like lambs and yet have their places forever with the goats. MATTHEW HENRY

Vs. 5. *They are not in trouble as other men,* for God has given them over to the desires of their own hearts, that they who are filthy may be filthy still: like a sick man, are they to whom a wise physician forbids nothing, since the disease is incurable. GERHOHUS

*Neither are they plagued like other men.* Fierce trials do not arise to assail them: they smart not under the divine rod. While many saints are both poor and afflicted, the prosperous sinner is neither. He is worse than other men, and yet he is better off; he ploughs least, and yet has the most fodder. He deserves the hottest hell, and yet the warmest nest.

Vs. 6. *Therefore pride compasseth them about as a chain; violence covereth them as a garment.* They brag and bully, bluster and browbeat, as if they had taken out a license to ride roughshod over all mankind. C. H. S.

A chain of pearl doth not better become their necks, nor the richest robes adorn their backs, than sin doth, in their judgments, become and suit their souls; they glory in their shame. Plato saith of Protagoras that he boasted, whereas he had lived sixty years, he had spent forty years in corrupting youth. They brag of that which they ought to bewail. GEORGE SWINNOCK

Vs. 8. *They are corrupt, and speak wickedly concerning oppression.* Work them like horses and feed them like dogs; and if they dare complain, send them to the prison or let them die in the workhouse. There is still too much of this wicked talk abroad, and although the working classes have their faults, and many of them very grave and serious ones, too, yet there is a race of men who habitually speak of them as if they were an inferior order of animals. C. H. S.

These giants, or rather inhuman monsters, of whom David speaks, on the contrary, not only imagine that they are exempted from subjection to any law, but, unmindful of their own weakness, foam furiously, as if there were no distinction between good and evil, between right and wrong. JOHN CALVIN

Vs. 12. *Behold these are the ungodly, who prosper in the world.* Look! See! Consider! Here is the standing enigma! The crux of Providence! The stumbling-block of faith! Here are the unjust rewarded and indulged, and that not for a day or an hour, but in perpetuity. From their youth up these men, who deserve perdition, revel in prosperity. They deserve to be hung in chains, and chains are hung about their necks; they are worthy to be chased from the world, and yet the world becomes all their own. Poor, purblind sense cries, "Behold this! Wonder and be amazed, and make this square with providential justice, if you can." C. H. S.

*They increase in riches;* or, strength. Both wealth and health are their dowry. No bad debts and bankruptcies weigh them down, but robbery and usury pile up their substance. Money runs to money; gold pieces fly in flocks; the rich grow richer; the proud grow prouder. Lord, how is this? Thy poor servants who become yet poorer and groan under their burdens, are made to wonder at Thy mysterious ways. C. H. S.

Vs. 13. *Verily I have cleansed my heart in vain.* Thus foolishly will the wisest of men argue when faith is napping. Asaph was a seer, but he could not see when reason left him in the dark. C. H. S.

*And washed my hands in innocency.* Asaph had been as careful of his hands as of his heart; he had guarded his outer as well as his inner life, and it was a bitter thought that all this was useless and left him in even a worse condition than foul-handed, black-hearted worldlings. Surely, the horrible character of the conclusion must have helped to render it untenable; it could not be so while God was God. It smelt too strong of a lie to be tolerated long in the good man's soul; hence, in a verse or two, we see his mind turning in another direction. C. H. S.

Vs. 14. *For all day long have I been plagued, and chastened every morning,* saith the Psalmist. . . . As sure, or as soon as I rise I have a whipping, and my breakfast is bread of sorrow and the water of adversity. . . . Our lives are full of afflictions; and it is as great a part of a Christian's skill to know afflictions as to know mercies; to know when God smites, as to know when He girds us; and it is our sin to overlook mercies. JOSEPH CARYL

The way to heaven is an *afflicted way,* a perplexed, persecuted way, crushed close together with crosses, as was the Israelites' way in the wilderness, or that of Jonathan and his armor-bearer, that had a sharp rock on the one side and a sharp rock on the other. And, whilst they crept upon all four, flinty stones were under them, briars and thorns on either hand of them; mountains, crags, and promontories over them; so heaven is caught by pains, by patience, by violence, affliction being our inseparable companion. "The cross way is the highway to heaven," said that martyr (Bradford); and another, "If there be any way to heaven on horseback, it is by the cross." To hell a man may go without a staff, as we say; the way thereto is easy, steep, strawed with roses; 'tis but a yielding to Satan, a passing from sin to sin, from evil purposes to evil practices, from practice to custom, etc. JOHN TRAPP

Vs. 15. *I should offend against the generation of Thy children.* Woe unto the man by whom offence cometh! Rash, undigested, ill-considered speech, is responsible for much of the heart-burning and trouble in the churches. Would to God that, like Asaph, men would bridle their tongues. Where we have any suspicion of being wrong, it is better to be silent; it can do no harm to be quiet, and it may do serious damage to spread abroad our hastily formed opinions. C. H. S.

Vs. 17. *Then understood I their end.* No envy gnaws now at his heart, but a holy horror both of their impending doom, and of their present guilt fills his soul. He recoils from being dealt with in the same manner as the proud sinners, whom he just now regarded with admiration. C. H. S.

*Then understood I.* There is a famous story of providence in Bradwardine to this purpose. A certain hermit that was much tempted and was utterly unsatisfied concerning the providence of God, resolved to journey from place to place till he met with some who could satisfy him. An angel in the shape of a man joined himself with him as he was journeying, telling him that he was sent from God to satisfy him in his doubts of providence.

The first night they lodged at the house of a very holy man, and they spent their time in discourses of heaven and praises of God, and were entertained with a great deal of freedom and joy. In the morning, when they departed, the angel took with him a great cup of gold.

The next night they came to the house of another holy man, who made them very welcome and exceedingly rejoiced in their society and discourse; the angel, notwithstanding, at his departure killed an infant in the cradle, which was his only son, he having been for many years before childless, and, therefore, was a very fond father of this child.

The third night they came to another house, where they had like free entertainment as before. The master of the family had a steward whom he highly prized and told them how happy he accounted himself in having such a faithful servant. Next morning he sent this, his steward, with them part of the way to direct them therein. As they were going over the bridge, the angel flung the steward into the river and drowned him.

The last night they came to a very wicked man's house, where they had very untoward entertainment, yet the angel, next morning, gave him the cup of gold. All this being done, the angel asked the hermit whether he understood those things. He answered, his doubts of providence were increased, not resolved, for he could not understand why he should deal so hardly with those holy men who received them with so much love and joy, and yet give such a gift to that wicked man who used them so unworthily.

The angel said, "I will now expound these things unto you. The first house where we came, the master of it was a holy man; yet, drinking in that cup every morning, it being too large, it did somewhat unfit him for holy duties, though not so much that others or himself did perceive it; so I took it away, since it is better for him to lose the cup of gold than his temperance.

"The master of the family where we lay the second night was a man given much to prayer and meditation, and spent much time in holy duties, and was very liberal to the poor all the time he was childless; but as soon as he had a son he grew so fond of it, and spent so much time in playing with it, that he exceedingly neglected his former holy exercise, and gave but little to the poor, thinking he could never lay up enough for his child; therefore, I have taken the infant to heaven and left him to serve God better upon earth.

"The steward whom I did drown had plotted to kill his master the night following; and as to that wicked man to whom I gave the cup of gold, he was to have nothing in the other world; I therefore gave him something in this, which, notwithstanding, will prove a snare to him, for he will be more intemperate; and let him that is filthy, be filthy still."

The truth of this story I affirm not, but the moral is very good, for it shows that God is an indulgent Father to the saints when He most afflicts them; and that when He sets the wicked on high He sets them also in slippery places and their prosperity is their ruin (Prov. 1:32). THOMAS WHITE, *in "A Treatise of the Power of Godliness"*

Vs. 18. *Thou castedst them down into destruction.* Eternal punishment will be all the more terrible in contrast with the former prosperity of those who are ripening for it. Taken as a whole, the case of the ungodly is horrible throughout; and their worldly joy instead of diminishing the horror, actually renders the effect the more awful, even as the vivid lightning amid the storm does not brighten but intensify the thick darkness which lowers around. The ascent to the fatal gallows of Haman was an essential ingredient in the terror of the sentence—"hang him thereon." If the wicked had not been raised so high they could not have fallen so low. C. H. S.

Vs. 19. *They are utterly consumed with terrors.* Like blasted trees consumed by the lightning, they are monuments of vengeance; like the ruins of Babylon they reveal, in the greatness of their desolation, the judgments of the Lord against all those that unduly exalt themselves. The momentary glory of the graceless is in a moment effaced, their loftiness is in an instant consumed. C. H. S.

An English merchant that lived at Dantzic, now with God, told us this story, and it was true. A friend of his (a merchant also), upon what grounds I know not, went to a convent and dined with some friars. His entertainment was very noble. After he had dined and seen all, the merchant fell to commending their pleasant lives. "Yea," said one of the friars to him, "we live gallantly indeed, had we anybody to go to hell for us when we die." GILES FIRMIN, *in "The Real Christian, or, A Treatise of Effectual Calling"*

Vs. 20. *As a dream when one awaketh.* The conception is rather subtle but seems to have been shrewdly penetrated by Shakespere, who makes the Plantagenet prince (affecting, perhaps, the airs of a ruler in God's stead) say to his discarded favorite:

*I have long dreamt of such a kind of man,*
*So surfeit swelled, so old and so profane,*
*But being awake I do despise my dream.*

*—Henry IV*

C. B. CAYLEY, *in "The Psalms in Metre"*

Vs. 21. *Thus my heart was grieved.* Alexander reads it, "My heart is soured." His spirit had become embittered; he had judged in a harsh, crabbed, surly manner. He had become atrabilarious, full of black bile, melancholy, and choleric; he had poisoned his own life at the fountain-head, and made all its streams to be bitter as gall. C. H. S.

Vs. 22. *I was as a beast before Thee.* I permitted my mind to be wholly occupied with *sensible things*, like the beasts that perish, and did not look into a future state, nor did I consider nor submit to the wise designs of an unerring providence. ADAM CLARKE

The original has in it no word of comparison; it ought to be rather translated, *I was a very beast before Thee,* and we are told that the Hebrew word being in the plural number, gives it a peculiar emphasis, indicating some monstrous or astonishing beast. It is the word used by Job which is interpreted "behemoth."

"I was a very monster before Thee," not only a beast, but one of the most brutish of all beasts, one of the most stubborn and intractable of all beasts. I think no man can go much lower than this in humble confession. This is a description of human nature and of the old man in the renewed saint which is not to be excelled. C. H. S.

Tully writes very copiously in setting forth the good service which he did the Roman state, but not a word of his covetousness, of his affecting popular applause, of his pride and vain glory, of his mean extraction and the like. Whereas, clean contrary, Moses sets down the sin and punishment of his own sister, the idolatry and superstition of Aaron his brother, and his own fault in his preposterous striking the rock, for which he was excluded the Land of Canaan. THOMAS FULLER

Vs. 23. *Nevertheless I am continually with Thee.* He does not give up his faith, though he confesses his folly. Sin may distress us, and yet we may be in communion with God. It is a sin beloved and delighted in which separates us from the Lord, but when we bewail it heartily, the Lord will not withdraw from us. C. H. S.

Vs. 25. *Whom have I in heaven but Thee? and there is none upon earth that I desire beside Thee.* How small is the number of those who keep their affections fixed on God alone! We see how superstition joins to him many others as rivals for our affections. While the Papists admit in word that all things depend upon God, they are, nevertheless, constantly seeking to obtain help from this and the other quarter independent of Him. JOHN CALVIN

*Whom have I in heaven but Thee?* saith David. What are saints? What are angels to a soul without God? 'Tis true of things as well as of persons. What have we in heaven but God? What's joy without God? What's glory without God? What's all the furniture and riches, all the delicacies, yea, all the diadems of heaven, without the God of heaven? If God should say to the saints, "Here is heaven, take it amongst you, but I will withdraw Myself," how would they weep over heaven itself, and make it a Baca, a valley of tears indeed? Heaven is not heaven unless we enjoy God. 'Tis the presence of God which makes heaven: glory is but our nearest being unto God. JOSEPH CARYL

Verses 25-26. Gotthold was invited to an entertainment and had the hope held out that he would meet with a friend whom he loved and in whose society he took the greatest delight. On joining the party, however, he learned that, owing to some unforeseen occurrence, this friend was not to be present, and felt too much chagrined to take any share in the hilarity.

The circumstance afterwards led him into the following train of thought: The pious soul, that sincerely loves and fervently longs for the Lord Jesus, experiences what I lately did. She seeks her Beloved in all places, objects, and events. If she finds Him, who is happier? If she find Him not, who more disconsolate? Ah! Lord Jesus, Thou best of friends, Thou art the object of my love; my soul seeketh Thee; my heart longeth after Thee. What care I for the world with all its pleasures and pomps, its power and glory, unless I find Thee in it?

What care I for the daintiest food, the sweetest drinks, and the merriest company, unless Thou art present, and unless I can dip my morsel in Thy wounds, sweeten my draught with Thy grace, and hear Thy pleasant words. Verily, my Savior, were I even in heaven, and did not find Thee there, it would seem to me no heaven at all. Wherefore, Lord Jesus, when with tears, sighs, yearnings of heart, and patient hope I seek Thee, hide not Thyself from me, but suffer me to find Thee; for, "Lord! whom have I in heaven but Thee; and there is none upon earth that I desire beside Thee. My flesh and my heart faileth: but God is the strength of my heart, and my portion forever." CHRISTIAN SCRIVER

Vs. 26. Oh, strange logic! Grace hath learned to deduce strong conclusions out of weak premises, and happy out of sad. If the major be, *My flesh and my heart faileth; and the minor,* "There is no blossom in the fig-tree, nor fruit in the vine," etc.; yet his conclusion is firm and undeniable: *The Lord is the strength of my heart, and my portion forever;* or, "Yet will I rejoice in the God of my salvation." And if there be more in the conclusion than in the premises, it is the better; God comes even in the conclusion. JOHN SHEFFIELD, *in "The Rising Sun"*

Of all seasons, the Christian hath most need of succor at his dying hour. Then he must take his leave of all his comforts on earth, and then he shall be sure of the sharpest conflicts from hell, and, therefore it is impossible that he should hold out without extraordinary help from heaven. But the Psalmist had armor of proof ready wherewith to encounter his last enemy. As weak and fearful a child as he was, he durst venture a walk in the dark entry of death, having his Father by the hand: "Though I walk through the valley of the shadow of death, I will fear no evil: for Thou art with me; Thy rod and Thy staff they comfort me" (Psalm 23). Though at the troubles of my life, and my trial at death, my heart is ready to fail me, yet I have a strong cordial which will cheer me in my saddest condition: *God is the strength of my heart.*

*And my portion forever.* Without alteration, this God will be my God forever and ever, my Guide and aid unto death; nay, death, which dissolveth so many bonds, and untieth such close knots, shall never part me and my portion, but give me a perfect and everlasting possession of it. GEORGE SWINNOCK

Vs. 27. *For, lo, they that are far from Thee shall perish. Thou hast destroyed all them that go a whoring from Thee.* Mere heathens, who are far from God, perish in due season; but those who, being His professed people, act unfaithfully to their profession, shall come under active condemnation, and be crushed beneath His wrath. We read examples of this in Israel's history; may we never create fresh instances in our own persons. C. H. S.

Vs. 28. *To draw near to God.* It is not one isolated act. It is not merely turning to God and saying, "I have come to Him." The expression is, "Draw." It is not a single act; it is the drawing, the coming, the habitual walk, going on, and on, and on, so long as we are on earth. It is, therefore, an habitual religion which must be pressed and enforced upon us. MONTAGU VILLIERS

The Epicurean, says Augustine, is wont to say, "It is good for me to enjoy the pleasures of the flesh": the Stoic is wont to say, "For me it is good to enjoy the pleasures of the mind": the Apostle used to say (not in words, but in sense), "It is good for me to cleave to God." LORINUS

## PSALM 74

Title: "Maschil of Asaph." An instructive Psalm by Asaph. The history of the suffering church is always edifying; when we see how the faithful trusted and wrestled with their God in times of dire distress, we are thereby taught how to behave ourselves under similar circumstances; we learn, moreover, that when the fiery trial befalls us, no strange things have happened unto us, we are following the trail of the host of God. C. H. S.

There is one singularity in this Psalm which reminds one strongly of Psalm 44: there is not one mention of national or personal sin throughout, no allusion to the Lord's righteous dealing in their punishment, no supplication for pardon and forgiveness; and yet one can hardly doubt that the writer of the Psalm, be he who he may, must have felt it as keenly as Jeremiah, Ezekiel, Daniel, or any other prophet of the captivity, the sins and iniquities which had brought all this sore evil upon them.

But still, though there be expostulation, there is no complaint; though there be mourning, there is no murmuring; there is far more the cry of a smitten child, wondering why, and grieving that his father's face is so turned away from him in displeasure, and a father's hand so heavy on the child of his love.

Or, as we might almost say, it is like the cry of one of those martyred ones beneath the altar, wondering at the Lord's continued endurance of His heritage thus trampled under foot of the marauder and oppressor, and exclaiming, "How long, O Lord, how long?" And yet it is the appeal of one who was still a sufferer, still groaning under the pressure of his calamities, "Why hast Thou cast us off forever? We see not our signs; there is no more any prophet among us." BARTON BOUCHIER

Vs. 1. *O God, why hast Thou cast us off forever?* To cast us off at all were hard, but when Thou dost for so long a time desert Thy people, it is an evil beyond all endurance—the very chief of woes and abyss of misery. Sin is usually at the bottom of all the hidings of the Lord's face; let us ask the Lord to reveal the special form of it to us, that we may repent of it, overcome it, and henceforth forsake it. C. H. S.

*The sheep of Thy pasture.* There is nothing more imbecile than a sheep: simple, frugal, gentle, tame, patient, prolific, timid, domesticated, stupid, useful. Therefore, while the name of sheep is here used, it is suggested how pressing the necessity is for divine assistance and how well-befitting the Most High it would be to make their cause His own. LORINUS

Vs. 3. *Lift up Thy feet.* Abu Walid renders it, *Tread hard upon Thine enemies.* The Jewish Arab, *Show forth Thy punishment,* adding in a note that the *lifting up the feet* implies punishment, the bringing under by force being usually expressed by *treading under the feet.* HENRY HAMMOND

Verses 4-7. (*The persecution under Antiochus,* B.C. 168.) Athenæus proceeded to Jerusalem, where with the assistance of the garrison, he prohibited and suppressed every observance of the Jewish religion, forced the people to profane the Sabbath, to eat swine's flesh and other unclean food, and expressly forbade the national rite of circumcision.

The Temple was dedicated to Jupiter Olympius: the statue of that deity was erected on part of the altar of burnt-offerings, and sacrifice duly performed . . . As a last insult, the feasts of the Bacchanalia, the license of which, as they were celebrated in the later ages of Greece, shocked the severe virtue of the older Romans, were substituted for the national Festival of Tabernacles.

The reluctant Jews were forced to join in these riotous orgies, and to carry the ivy, the insignia of the god. So near was the Jewish nation, and the worship of Jehovah, to total extermination. HENRY HART MILMAN, *in "A History of the Jews"*

Vs. 5. *A man was famous according as he had lifted up axes upon the thick trees.* Once men were renowned for felling the cedars and preparing them for building the Temple, but now the axe finds other work, and men are as proud of destroying as their fathers were of erection.

Thus in the olden times our sires dealt sturdy blows against the forests of error and labored hard to lay the axe at the root of the trees; but alas! their sons appear to be quite as diligent to destroy the truth and to overthrow all that their fathers built up. Oh, for the good old times again! Oh, for an hour of Luther's hatchet, or Calvin's mighty axe! C. H. S.

Vs. 7. *They have cast fire into Thy sanctuary.* Those who hate God are never sparing of the most cruel weapons. To this day, the enmity of the human heart is quite as great as ever; and, if providence did not restrain, the saints would still be as fuel for the flames. C. H. S.

Vs. 8. *They said in their hearts, Let us destroy them together.* Pharaoh's policy to stamp out the nation has been a precedent for others, yet the Jews survive, and will: the bush though burning has not been consumed. Even thus the church of Christ has gone through baptisms of blood and fire, but it is all the brighter for them. C. H. S.

Vs. 10. *Shall the enemy blaspheme Thy name forever?* The sinner never leaves his sin till sin first leaves him: did not death put a stop to his sin, he would never cease from sin. Every impenitent sinner would sin to the days of eternity, if he might live to the days of eternity. C. H. S.

*O God, how long shall the adversary reproach? shall the enemy blaspheme Thy name forever?* I have read of the crocodile, that he knows no *maximum quod sic,* he is always growing bigger and bigger, and never comes to a certain pitch of monstrosity so long as he lives. *Quamdiu vivit crescit.* Every habituated sinner would, if he were let alone, be such a monster, perpetually growing worse and worse. THOMAS BROOKS

Vs. 14. *And gavest him to be meat to the people inhabiting the wilderness.* Not only did the wild beasts feed upon the carcasses of the Egyptians, but the dwellers along the shores stripped the bodies and enriched themselves with the spoil. Israel, too, grew rich with the relics of her drowned adversaries.

How often so great afflictions work our lasting good. Leviathan, who would have devoured us, is himself devoured, and out of the monster we gather sweetness. Let us not give way to fear; hydra-headed evils shall be slain, and monstrous difficulties shall be overcome, and all things shall work our lasting good. C. H. S.

Vs. 16. *Thou hast prepared the light.* Light is *life:* the merest insect could not live without light; and even blind natures receive, in those organs which are not the property of vision, the assurance of its benignant operations. Light is *order:* and at its wand and command the separation takes place, and dark and light pair off into their separate ranks.

Light is *beauty:* whether in the refulgence of the moon; the chill sparkle of the stars; the unrivalled play of colors in the attenuated film of the soap-bubble, at once the toy of childhood and the tool of the sage; the rich play of tints in the mother-of-pearl, or the rich, gorgeous rays in the plumes of birds.

Light is *purity:* forms that rankle out of the glance of its clear, steady beam, contract around themselves loathsomeness and disgust, and become the seats of foulness and shame. Light is *growth:* where it is, we know that nature pursues her work in life and in vigor; light gives vitality to the sap; light removes obstructions from the pathway of the growing agencies, while, in its absence, forms become stunted and gnarled and impaired.

Light is *health:* as it darts its clear and brilliant points to and fro, it brings in its train those blessings of elasticity and energy, which give the fullness of being—which is perfect health to the expanding forms. There is a fine consistency, when Scripture makes light to contain, as it were, the seeds of all things, and when the prelude of all creation is made to be those words, "God said, Let there be light." E. PAXTON HOOD

Vs. 17. *Thou hast set all the borders of the earth.* The man must be blind indeed that does not see the wise purpose of the Great Author of nature, in thus diversifying the surface of the earth. Were the earth an even plain, how much beauty would it lose? Besides, this variety of valley and mountain is very favorable to the health of living creatures, and were there no hills, the earth would be less peopled with men and animals. There would be fewer plants, fewer simples, and trees. We should be deprived of metals and minerals: the vapors would not be condensed nor should we have either springs or rivers.

Must we not then acknowledge that the whole plan of the earth, its form, its inward and outward construction, are all regulated according to the wisest laws, which all combine towards the pleasure and happiness of mankind? O Thou supreme Author of nature, Thou hast done all things well! Whichever way I turn my eyes, whether I penetrate into the interior structure of the globe Thou hast appointed me to inhabit, or whether I examine its surface, I everywhere discover marks of profound wisdom and infinite goodness. CHRISTOPHER CHRISTIAN STURM

Vs. 18. *And that the foolish people have blasphemed Thy name.* The meanness of the enemy is here pleaded. Sinners are fools, and shall fools be allowed to insult the Lord and oppress His people; shall the abjects curse the Lord and defy Him to His face? When error grows too bold, its day is near and its fall certain. Arrogance forshadows ripeness of evil, and the next step is rottenness. Instead of being alarmed when bad men grow worse and more audacious, we may reasonably take heart, for the hour of their judgment is evidently near. C. H. S.

Vs. 20. The sick man, if he be in danger of death, suspects not his ignorant neighbors, but his skillful physician. He that is oppressed in his estate, when the sentence goes against him, suspects none more than the advocate or the judge. We know God is best able to help us; our corruption, therefore, makes us to suspect Him most, if our troubles continue. FRANCIS TAYLOR

*Cruelty.* Heathenism is cruel. It is not changed in character since the days when parents made their children to pass through fire to Moloch. JOHN HAMBLETON

Much of this Psalm has passed over our mind while beholding the idolatries of Rome (the author visited Rome in November and December, 1871, while this portion of the TREASURY OF DAVID was in progress), and remembering her bloody persecution of the saints. O Lord, how long shall it be ere Thou wilt ease Thyself of those profane wretches, the priests, and cast the harlot of Babylon into the ditch of corruption? May Thy church never cease to plead with Thee till judgment shall be executed and the Lord avenged upon Antichrist. C. H. S.

# PSALM 75

The destruction of Sennacherib's army is a notable illustration of this sacred song. A hymn to God and a song for His saints. Happy were the people who, having found a Milton in David, had an almost equal songster in Asaph: happiest of all, because these poets were not inspired by earth's Castalian fount, but drank of "the fount of every blessing."

Vs. 1. *Unto Thee, O God, do we give thanks.* As the smiling flowers gratefully reflect in their lovely colors the various constituents of the solar ray, so should gratitude spring up in our hearts after the smiles of God's providence. C. H. S.

*For that Thy Name is near Thy wondrous works declare.* We sing not of a hidden God Who sleeps and leaves the church to her fate, but of One Who ever in our darkest days is most near, a very present help in trouble. "Near is His Name." Baal is on a journey, but Jehovah dwells in His church. Glory be unto the Lord, Whose perpetual deeds of grace and majesty are the sure tokens of His being with us always, even unto the end of the world.

Vs. 3. *The earth and all the inhabitants thereof are dissolved.* When anarchy is abroad, and tyrants are in power, everything is unloosed, dissolution threatens all things, the solid mountains of government melt as wax; but even then the Lord upholds and sustains the right.

*I bear up the pillars of it.* Hence, there is no real cause for fear. While the pillars stand, and stand they must for God upholds them, the house will brave out the storm. In the day of the Lord's appearing a general melting will take place, but in that day our covenant God will be the sure support of our confidence. C. H. S.

Vs. 4. *Fools.* The ungodly are spiritual fools. If one had a child very beautiful, yet if he were a fool, the parent would have little joy in him. The Scripture hath dressed the sinner in a fool's coat: and let me tell you, better be a fool void of reason than a fool void of grace: this is the devil's fool (Prov. 14:9).

Is not he a fool who refuseth a rich portion? God offers Christ and salvation, but the sinner refuseth this portion: "Israel would none of Me" (Ps. 81:11). Is not he a fool who preferreth an annuity before an inheritance? Is not he a fool who tends his mortal part and neglects his angelical part? As if one should paint the wall of his house and let the timber rot. Is not he a fool who will feed the devil with his soul?

As that emperor who fed his lion with a pheasant, is not he a fool who lays a snare for himself? (Prov. 1:18). Who consults his own shame? (Hab. 2:10). Who loves death? (Prov. 8:36). THOMAS WATSON

Vs. 5. *Speak not with a stiff neck.* Impudence before God is madness. The outstretched neck of insolent pride is sure to provoke his axe. Those who carry their heads high shall find that they will be lifted yet higher, as Haman was upon the gallows which he had prepared for the righteous man.

Silence, thou silly boaster! Silence! or God will answer thee. Who art thou, thou worm, that thou shouldst arrogantly object against thy Maker's laws and cavil at His truth? Be hushed, thou vainglorious prater, or vengeance shall silence thee to thine eternal confusion. C. H. S.

Vs. 6. *For promotion cometh neither from the east, nor from the west, nor from the south.* Men forget that all things are ordained in heaven; they see but the human force, and the carnal passion, but the unseen Lord is more real far than these. He is at work behind and within the cloud. The foolish dream that He is not, but He is near even now, and on the way to bring in His hand that cup of spiced wine of vengeance, one draught of which shall stagger all His foes. C. H. S.

A godless man is like the Arabian desert, of no profit to himself or his neighbors; like evershifting sands being tossed to and fro by his own wayward passions; heated with the suns of turbulence, self-will, and recklessness, he is a desert, a waste where God will not vouchsafe the light of His countenance for promotion. *Condensed from a Sermon by* GREGORY BATEMAN

Vs. 7. *But God is the judge.* Even now, He is actually judging. His seat is not vacant; His authority is not abdicated; the Lord reigneth evermore.

*He putteth down one, and setteth up another.* Empires rise and fall at His bidding. A dungeon here, and there a throne, His will assigns. Assyria yields to Babylon, and Babylon to the Medes. Kings are but puppets in His hand; they serve His purpose when they rise and when they fall.

A certain author has issued a work called "Historic Ninepins," a fit name of scorn for all the great ones of the earth. God only is; all power belongs to Him; all else is shadow, coming and going, unsubstantial, misty, dream-like. C. H. S.

Vs. 8. *Full of mixture.* It is mixed with the wrath of God, the malice of Satan, the anguish of soul, the gall of sin, the tears of despair. "The cup is all bitter, and full of sorrow," saith Augustine: the godly do often taste the top, and feel the bitterness, but then it is suddenly snatched from them; but the ungodly shall drink the very grounds and extremest poison. THOMAS ADAMS

*But the dregs thereof, all the wicked of the earth shall wring them out, and drink them.* Even to the bitter end must wrath proceed. They must drink on and on forever, even to the bottom where lie the lees of deep damnation; these they must suck up and still must they drain the cup. Oh, the anguish and the heart-break of the day of wrath!

Mark well, it is for all the wicked; all hell for all the ungodly; the dregs for the dregs; bitters for the bitter; wrath for the heirs of wrath. Righteousness is conspicuous, but over all terror spreads a tenfold night, cheerless, without a star. Oh, happy they who drink the cup of godly sorrow and the cup of salvation; these, though now despised, will then be envied by the very men who trod them under foot. C. H. S.

They have not only the cup, but the dregs of the cup, that is, the worst of the cup; for as in a good cup, the deeper the sweeter; so in an evil cup, the deeper the worse: the dregs are the worst, the bottom is the bitterest of a bitter cup. JOSEPH CARYL

This memorable ode may be sung in times of great depression, when prayer has performed her errand at the mercy-seat, and when faith is watching for speedy deliverance. It is a song of the second advent, "Concerning the Nearness of the Judge with the Cup of Wrath." C. H. S.

## PSALM 76

Here faith sings of triumphs achieved. The present Psalm is a most jubilant war song, a pæan to the King of kings, the hymn of a theocratic nation to its Divine Ruler. We have no need to mark divisions in a song where the unity is so well preserved.

Vs. 1. *In Judah is God known: His name is great in Israel.* Dark is the outer world, but within the favored circle Jehovah is revealed and is the adoration of all who behold Him. The world knows Him not, and therefore blasphemes Him, but His church is full of ardor to proclaim His fame unto the ends of the earth. C. H. S.

There He is known as a *King* in His courts, for the glory and beauty which He there manifesteth; as a *Teacher* in His school, for the wisdom and knowledge which He there dispenseth; as a *Dweller* in His house, for the holy orders He there prescribeth, and gracious rule and dominion He there erecteth and beareth in the souls of His servants; as a *Bridegroom* in the banqueting house, for the spiritual dainties He there maketh, for the clear and open manifestation of Himself, and love and comforts He there ministereth to His spiritual friends and guests. ALEXANDER GROSSE

Vs. 4. *Thou art more glorious and excellent than the mountains of prey.* What are the honors of war but brags of murder? What the fame of conquerors but the reek of manslaughter? But the Lord is glorious in holiness, and His terrible deeds are done in justice for the defence of the weak and the deliverance of the enslaved. Mere power may be glorious, but it is not excellent: when we behold the mighty acts of the Lord, we see a perfect blending of the two qualities. C. H. S.

Vs. 5. *The stouthearted are spoiled.* Daring men, who fear nothing, are turned into Magor-missabibs—fear round about; their stout hearts are taken from them, and then they are so far from being a terror to other men, that they run from the shadow of a man; their courage is down; they cannot give a child a confident look, much less look dangers or enemies in the face. JOSEPH CARYL

Verses 5-6.

*For the Angel of Death spread his wings on the blast,*
*And breathed in the face of the foe as he passed;*
*And the eyes of the sleepers waxed deadly and chill,*
*And their hearts but once heaved, and forever were still!*

*And there lay the steed with his nostril all wide,*
*But through it there rolled not the breath of his pride:*
*And the foam of his gasping lay white on the turf,*
*And cold as the spray of the rock-beating surf.*

*And there lay the rider distorted and pale,*
*With the dew on his brow and the rust on his mail;*
*And the tents were all silent, the banners alone,*
*The lances unlifted, the trumpet unblown.*

GEORGE GORDON, LORD BYRON

Vs. 7. *Thou, even Thou, art to be feared.* Not Sennacherib, nor Nisroch his god, but Jehovah alone, Who with a silent rebuke had withered all the monarch's host.

*Fear Him, ye saints, and then ye shall*
*Have nothing else to fear.*

The fear of man is a snare, but the fear of God is a great virtue and has great power for good over the human mind. God is to be feared profoundly, continually, and alone. C. H. S.

*Who may stand?* Who? Shall angels? They are but like refracted beams or rays; if God should hide His face, they would cease to shine. Shall man? His glory and pomp, like the colors in the rainbow, vanish away, when God puts forth in anger the brightness of His face. Shall devils? If He speak the word, they are tumbled down from heaven like lightning. JOHN CRAGGE'S *"Cabinet of Spiritual Jewells"*

Vs. 8. *Thou didst cause judgment to be heard from heaven.* So complete an overthrow was evidently a judgment from heaven; those who saw it not, yet heard the report of it, and said, "This is the finger of God." Man will not hear God's voice if he can help it, but God takes care to cause it to be heard. The echoes of that judgment executed on the haughty Assyrian are heard still, and will ring on down all the ages, to the praise of divine justice. C. H. S.

Vs. 10. *Surely the wrath of man shall praise Thee.* It shall not only be overcome, but rendered subservient to Thy glory. Man, with his breath of threatening, is but blowing the trumpet of the Lord's eternal fame. Furious winds often drive vessels the more swiftly into port. The devil blows the fire and melts the iron, and then the Lord fashions it for His own purposes. Let men and devils rage as they may; they cannot do otherwise than subserve the divine purposes. C. H. S.

In the Septuagint it is, "The wrath of man shall keep holy day to Thee, shall increase a festival for Thee." God many times gets up in the world on Satan's shoulders. THOMAS MANTON

How contemptibly doth the Spirit of God speak of man and of the power of man in Scripture? "Cease ye from man, whose breath is in his nostrils; for wherein is he to be accounted of?" The wrath of man, when it is lengthened out to its utmost boundaries, can only go to the length of killing the body, or of the breaking the sheath of clay in which the soul lodges, and then it can do no more. EBENEZER ERSKINE

*The remainder of wrath shalt Thou restrain.* Malice is tethered and cannot break its bounds. The fire which cannot be utilized shall be dampened. Some read it "Thou shalt gird," as if the Lord girded on the wrath of man as a sword to be used in the hand of God to scourge others. The verse clearly teaches that even the most rampant evil is under the control of the Lord, and will in the end be overruled for His praise. C. H. S.

But what becomes of that wrath that is left? God shall "restrain" it. The word signifies to *gird up.* However God may see fit to slacken the bridle of His providence and suffer wicked men to vent their wrath and enmity, as far as it shall contribute to His glory; yet the superplus and the remainder of His wrath that is not for His glory and His people's profit, God will gird it up, that they shall not get it vented . . . If any wrath of man remain beyond what shall bring in a revenue of praise unto God, He will restrain it, and bind it up like the waters of a mill. EBENEZER ERSKINE

Vs. 11. *Let all that be round about Him bring presents unto Him that ought to be feared.* He who deserves to be praised as our God does, should not have mere verbal homage, but substantial tribute. Dread Sovereign, behold I give myself to Thee.

Vs. 12. *He shall cut off the spirit of princes.* Their courage, skill, and life are in His hands, and He can remove them as a gardener cuts off a slip from a plant. None are great in His hand. Caesars and Napoleons fall under His power as the boughs of the tree beneath the woodman's axe. C. H. S.

The Lord *cuts off the spirit of princes;* the word is, He *slips off*, as one should slip off a flower between one's fingers, or as one should slip off a bunch of grapes from a vine, so soon is it done. How great uncertainty have many great ones, by their miserable experience, found in their outward glory and worldly felicity! What a change hath a little time made in all their honors, riches, and delights!

That victorious emperor, Henry the Fourth, who had fought two-and-fifty pitched battles, fell to that poverty before he died, that he was forced to petition to be a prebend in the church of Spier, to maintain him in his old age.

And Procopius reports of King Gillimer, who was a potent king of the Vandals, who was so low brought, as to intreat his friend to send him a sponge, a loaf of bread, and a harp; a sponge to dry up his tears, a loaf of bread to maintain his life, and a harp to solace himself in his misery.

Philip de Comines reports of a Duke of Exeter, who though he had married Edward the Fourth's sister, yet he saw him in the Low Countries begging barefoot. Bellisarius, the chief man living in his time, having his eyes put out, was led at last in a string crying, "Give a halfpenny to Bellisarius." JEREMIAH BURROUGHS

*He is terrible to the kings of the earth.* While they are terrible to others, He is terrible to them. If they oppose themselves to His people, He will make short work of them; they shall perish before the terror of His arm, "for the Lord is a man of war, the Lord is His name." Rejoice before Him, all ye who adore the God of Jacob. C. H. S.

# PSALM 77

"A Psalm of Asaph." Asaph was a man of exercised mind and often touched the minor key; he was thoughtful, contemplative, believing, but withal there was a dash of sadness about him and this imparted a tonic flavor to his songs.

Vs. 1. *I cried unto God with my voice.* This Psalm has much sadness in it, but we may be sure it will end well, for it begins with prayer, and prayer never has an ill issue. Asaph did not run to man but to the Lord, and to Him he went, not with studied, stately, stilted words, but with a cry, the natural, unaffected, unfeigned expression of pain. He used his voice also, for though vocal utterance is not necessary to the life of prayer, it often seems forced upon us by the energy of our desires. Sometimes the soul feels compelled to use the voice, for thus it finds a freer vent for its agony. It is a comfort to hear the alarm-bell ringing when the house is invaded by thieves. C. H. S.

In the beginning of the Psalm, before speaking of his sorrows, he hastens to show the necessary and most efficacious remedy for allaying sorrow. He says that he did not, as many do, out of their impatience of grief or murmuring, either accuse God of cruelty or tyranny, or utter blasphemous words by which dishonor might fall upon God, or by indulging in sorrow and distrust hasten his own destruction, or fill the air with vain complainings, but fled straight to God and to Him unburdened his sorrow, and sought that He would not shut him out from that grace which most effectually heals his griefs. MOLLERUS

*And He gave ear unto me.* At the second knock, the door of grace flew open: *the Lord heard me.* JOHN COLLINGS

Vs. 2. *In the day of my trouble I sought the Lord.* Days of trouble must be days of prayer; in days of inward trouble, especially when God seems to have withdrawn from us, we must seek Him, and seek till we find Him. In the day of his trouble, he did not seek for the diversions of business recreation to shake off his trouble that way, but he sought God, and His favor, and grace. Those that are under trouble of mind must not think to drink it away, or laugh it away, but pray it away. MATTHEW HENRY

Vs. 3. There are moments in the life of all believers when God and His ways become unintelligible to them. They get lost in profound meditation, and nothing is left them but a desponding sigh. But we know from Paul the Apostle that the Holy Spirit intercedes for believers with God when they cannot utter their sighs (Rom. 8:26). AUGUSTUS F. THOLUCK

Vs. 4. *I am so troubled that I cannot speak.* Great griefs are dumb. Deep streams brawl not among the pebbles like the shallow brooklets which live on passing showers. Words fail the man whose heart fails him. He had cried to God, but he could not speak to man; what a mercy it is that if we can do the first, we need not despair though the second should be quite out of our power. Sleepless and speechless Asaph was reduced to great extremities, and yet he rallied, and even so shall we. C. H. S.

Sometimes our grief is so violent that it finds no vent, it strangles us, and we are overcome. It is with us in our desertions as with a man that gets a slight hurt; at first he walks up and down, but not looking betimes to prevent a growing mischief, the neglected wound begins to fester, or to gangrene, and brings him to greater pain and loss.

So it is with us many times in our spiritual sadness; when we are first troubled, we pray and pour out our souls before the Lord; but afterwards the waters of our grief drown our cries and we are so overwhelmed that if we might have all the world we cannot pray, or at least we can find no enlargement, no life, no pleasure in our prayers; and God Himself seems to take no delight in them, and that makes us more sad (Psalm 22:1). TIMOTHY ROGERS, in *"A Discourse on Trouble of Mind and the Disease of Melancholy"*

Tears have a tongue, and grammar, and language, that our Father knoweth. Babes have no prayer for the breast, but weeping: the mother can read hunger in weeping. SAMUEL RUTHERFORD

If, through all thy discouragements, thy condition prove worse and worse, so thou canst not pray, but are struck dumb when thou comest into His presence, as David, then fall a-making signs when thou canst not speak; groan, sigh, sob, "chatter," as Hezekiah did; bemoan thyself for thine unworthiness, and desire Christ to speak thy requests for thee, and God to hear Him for thee. THOMAS GOODWIN

Vs. 5. *I have considered the days of old, the years of ancient times.* If no good was in the present, memory ransacked the past to find consolation. She fain would borrow a light from the altars of yesterday to light the gloom of today. It is our duty to search for comfort, and not in sullen indolence yield to despair. C. H. S.

Vs. 6. *I call to remembrance my song in the night.* No doubt Paul and Silas remembered their song in the night when imprisoned at Philippi; and it afforded them encouragement under subsequent trials. And cannot many of you, my brethren, in like manner, remember the supports and consolations you have enjoyed in former difficulties and how the Lord turned the shadow of death into morning? JOHN RYLAND

*I commune with mine own heart.* He did not cease from introspection, for he was resolved to find the bottom of his sorrow and trace it to its fountain-head. He made sure work of it by talking, not with his mind only, but with his inmost heart; it was heart work with him. He was no idler, no melancholy trifler; he was up and at it, resolutely resolved that he would not tamely die of despair but would fight for his hope to the last moment of life. C. H. S.

Vs. 9. *Hath God forgotten to be gracious?* O my God, I sin against Thy justice hourly, and Thy mercy interposes for my remission: but, oh, keep me from sinning against Thy mercy. What plea can I hope for when I have made my advocate my enemy? JOSEPH HALL

The poor child crieth after the mother. What shall I do for my mother! Oh, my mother, my mother, what shall I do for my mother! And it may be the mother stands behind the back of the child, only she hides herself to try the affection of the child.

So the poor soul cries after God, and complains, "Oh, my Father! my Father! Where is my heavenly Father? Hath He forgotten to be gracious? Hath He shut up His loving-kindness in displeasure?" when (all the while), God is nearer than they think for, shining upon them in "a spirit of grace and supplications," with sighs and "groans that cannot be uttered." MATTHEW LAWRENCE

*Hath He in anger shut up His tender mercies?* Are the pipes of goodness choked up so that love can no more flow through them? Do the bowels of Jehovah no longer yearn towards His own beloved children?

Thus with cord after cord, unbelief is smitten and driven out of the soul; it raises questions, and we will meet it with questions. It makes us think and act ridiculously, and we will heap scorn upon it. The argument of this passage assumes very much the form of a *reductio ad absurdum.* Strip it naked and mistrust is a monstrous piece of folly. *Selah.* Here rest awhile, for the battle of questions needs a lull. C. H. S.

Vs. 10. *And I said, This is my infirmity.* He has won the day; he talks reasonably now and surveys the field with a cooler mind. He confesses that unbelief is an infirmity, a weakness, a folly, a sin. He may also be understood to mean, "This is my appointed sorrow," I will bear it without complaint. When we perceive that our affliction is meted out by the Lord and is the ordained portion of our cup, we become reconciled to it and no longer rebel against the inevitable. Why should we not be content if it be the Lord's will? What He arranges, it is not for us to cavil at. C. H. S.

An infirmity is this—when the bent and inclination of the soul is right, but either through some violence of corruption or strength of temptation, a man is diverted and turned out of the way. As the needle in the seaman's compass, you know if it be right it will stand always northwards, the bent of it will be toward the North Pole, but being jogged and troubled, it may sometimes be put out of frame and order, yet the bent and inclination of it is still northward; this is an infirmity. JAMES NALTON

Verses 10-11. *This is my infirmity; but I will remember the years of the right hand of the Most High. I will remember Thy wonders of old.* Therefore, Christian, when thou art in the depths of affliction, and Satan tempts thee to asperse God, as if He were forgetful of thee, stop his mouth with this: "No Satan, God hath not forgotten to do for me, but I have forgotten what He hath done for me, or else I could not question His fatherly care at present over me." Go, Christian, play over thy own lessons; praise God for past mercies, and it will not be long before thou hast a new song put into thy mouth for a present mercy.

Sometimes a little writing is found in a man's study that helps to save his estate, for want of which he had gone to prison; and some one experience remembered keeps the soul from despair, a prison which the devil longs to have the Christian in.

The hound, when he hath lost his scent, hunts backward and so recovers it and pursues his game with louder cry than ever. Thus, Christian, when thy hope is at a loss, and thou questionest thy salvation in another world, then look backward and see what God hath already done for thee. WILLIAM GURNALL

Vs. 11. *I will remember the works of the Lord: surely I will remember Thy wonders of old.* Whatever else may glide into oblivion, the marvelous works of the Lord in the ancient days must not be suffered to be forgotten. Memory is a fit handmaid for faith. When faith has its seven years of famine, memory like Joseph in Egypt opens her granaries. C. H. S.

*The works of the Lord . . . Thy wonders.* The Psalmist does not mean to draw a distinction between the works and the wonders of God; but, rather, to state that all God's works are wonders. All, whether in providence or grace—all God's works are wonderful! If we take the individual experience of the Christian, of what is that experience made up? Of wonders.

The work of his conversion, wonderful!—arrested in a course of thoughtlessness and impiety; graciously sought and gently compelled to be at peace with God, Whose wrath he had provoked. The communication of knowledge, wonderful! —Deity and eternity gradually piled up; the Bible taken page by page, and each page made a volume which no searching can exhaust.

The assistance in warfare, wonderful!—himself a child of corruption, yet enabled to grapple with the world, the flesh, and the devil, and often to trample them under foot. The solaces in affliction, wonderful!— sorrow sanctified so as to minister to joy, and a harvest of gladness reaped from a field which has been watered with tears. The foretastes of heaven, wonderful!—angels bringing down the clusters of the land, and the spirit walking with lightsome tread the crystal river and the streets of gold. All wonderful! HENRY MELVILL

Vs. 13. *Thy way, O God, is in the sanctuary.* Although the works of God are in part manifest to us, yet all our knowledge of them comes far short of their immeasurable height. Besides, it is to be observed that none enjoy the least taste of His works but those who by faith rise up to heaven. And yet, the utmost point to which we can ever attain is, to contemplate with admiration and reverence the hidden wisdom and power of God, which, while they shine forth in His works, yet far surpass the limited powers of our understanding. JOHN CALVIN

Vs. 15. *The sons of Jacob and Joseph.* Was it Joseph, or was it Jacob that begat the children of Israel? Certainly Jacob begat; but as Joseph nourished them, they are called by his name also. TALMUD

Vs. 16. *The waters saw Thee, O God, the waters saw Thee; they were afraid.* The water saw its God but man refuses to discern Him; it was afraid, but proud sinners are rebellious and fear not the Lord. C. H. S.

Verses 16-18. The waters saw Thee, but men do not see Thee. The depths were troubled, but men say in their heart, "There is no God." The clouds poured out water, but men pour not out cries and tears unto God. The skies send out a sound, but men say not, "Where is God, my Maker?"

Thine arrows also went abroad, but no arrows of contrition and supplication are sent back by men in return. The voice of Thy thunder was in the heaven, but men hear not the louder thunders of the law. The lightnings lightened the world, but the light of truth shines in darkness, and the darkness comprehendeth it not. The earth trembled and shook, but human hearts remain unmoved. GEORGE ROGERS

Vs. 20. *Thou leddest Thy people like a flock by the hand of Moses and Aaron.* What a transition from tempest to peace, from wrath to love! Quietly as a flock, Israel was guided on, by human agency which veiled the excessive glory of the divine presence. The smiter of Egypt was the shepherd of Israel. He drove His foes before Him but went before His people. Heaven and earth fought on His side against the sons of Ham, but they were equally subservient to the interests of the sons of Jacob.

Therefore, with devout joy and full of consolation, we close this Psalm; the song of one who forgot how to speak and yet learned to sing far more sweetly than his fellows. C. H. S.

The Psalmist has reached the climax of his strain, he has found relief from his sorrow by forcing his thoughts into another channel, by dwelling on all God's mightiest wonders of old; and there he must end: in his present intensity of passion he cannot trust himself to draw forth in detail any mere lessons of comfort. There are seasons when even the holiest faith cannot bear to listen to words of reasoning; though it can still find a support whereon to rest, in the simple contemplation, in all their native grandeur, of the deeds that God hath wrought. JOSEPH FRANCIS THRUPP

# PSALM 78

Vs. 1. *Give ear, O My people, to My law: incline your ears to the words of My mouth.* When God gives His truth a tongue and sends forth His messengers trained to declare His word with power, it is the least we can do to give them our ears and the earnest obedience of our hearts. As the officer of an army commences his drill by calling for "attention," even so every trained soldier of Christ is called upon to give ear to His words. Men lend their ears to music; how much more then should they listen to the harmonies of the gospel; they sit enthralled in the presence of an orator; how much rather should they yield to the eloquence of heaven! C. H. S.

Inclining the ears does not denote any ordinary sort of hearing, but such as a disciple renders to the words of his master, with submission and reverence of mind, silent and earnest, that whatever is enunciated for the purpose of instruction may be heard and properly understood, and nothing be allowed to escape.

He is a hearer of a different stamp, who hears carelessly, not for the purpose of learning or imitation, but to criticize, to make merry, to indulge animosity, or to kill time. MUSCULUS

Vs. 2. *I will utter dark sayings of old;* enigmas of antiquity, riddles of yore. The mind of the poet-prophet was so full of ancient lore that he poured it forth in a copious stream of song, while beneath the gushing flood lay pearls and gems of spiritual truth capable of enriching those who could dive into the depths and bring them up.

The letter of this song is precious, but the inner sense is beyond all price. Whereas the first verse called for attention, the second justifies the demand by hinting that the outer sense conceals an inner and hidden meaning, which only the thoughtful will be able to perceive. C. H. S.

Vs. 4. *Showing to the generation to come the praises of the Lord, and His strength, and His wonderful works that He hath done.* We dare not follow the vain and vicious traditions of the apostate Church of Rome, neither would we compare the fallible record of the best human memories with the infallible written Word, yet would we fain see oral tradition practiced by every Christian in his family, and children taught cheerfully by word of mouth by their own mothers and fathers, as well as by the printed pages of what they too often regard as dull, dry task books. What happy hours and pleasant evenings have children had at their parents' knees as they have listened to some "sweet story of old." Reader, if you have children, mind you do not fail in this duty. C. H. S.

Verses 4-6. The cloth that is dyed in the wool will keep color best. Disciples in youth will prove angels in age. Use and experience strengthen and confirm in any art or science. The longer thy child hath been brought up in Christ's school, the more able he will be to find out Satan's wiles and fallacies and to avoid them. The longer he hath been at the trade the more skill and delight will he have in worshipping and enjoying the blessed God. The tree when it is old stands strongly against the wind, just as it was set when it was young.

The children of Merindal so answered one another in the matters of religion, before the persecuting Bishop of Cavailon, that a stander-by said unto the bishop, I must needs confess I have often been at the disputations of the doctors in the Sorbonne, but I never learned so much as by these children. Seven children at one time suffered martyrdom with Symphrosia, a godly matron, their mother. Such a blessing doth often accompany religious breeding; therefore, Julian the apostate, to hinder the growth and increase of Christianity, would not suffer children to be taught either human or divine learning.

Philip was glad that Alexander was born whilst Aristotle lived that he might be instructed by Aristotle in philosophy. It is no mean mercy that thy children are born in the days of the gospel, and in a valley of vision, a land of light, where they may be instructed in Christianity. Oh, do not fail, therefore, to acquaint thy children with the nature of God, the natures and offices of Christ, their own natural sinfulness and misery, the way and means of their recovery, the end and errand for which they were sent into the world, the necessity of regeneration and a holy life, if ever they would escape eternal death! Alas! how is it possible they should ever arrive at heaven if they know not the way thither? GEORGE SWINNOCK

Vs. 8. *And might not be as their fathers, a stubborn and rebellious generation.* There was room for improvement. Fathers stubborn in their own way, and rebellious against God's way, are sorry examples for their children; and it is earnestly desired that better instruction may bring forth a better race. It is common in some regions for men to count their family custom as the very best rule; but disobedience is not to be excused because it is hereditary. The leprosy was none the less loathsome because it had been long in the family.

Vs. 14. *And all the night with a light of fire.* So constant was the care of the Great Shepherd that all night and every night the token of His presence was with His people. That cloud which was a shade by day was as a sun by night. Even thus the grace which cools and calms our joys, soothes and solaces our sorrows. What a mercy to have a light of fire with us amid the lonely horrors of the wilderness of affliction. Our God has been all this to us, and shall we prove unfaithful to Him? We have felt Him to be both shade and light, according as our changing circumstances have required.

*"He hath been our joy in woe,*
*Cheer'd our heart when it was low,*
*And, with warnings softly sad,*
*Calm'd our heart when it was glad."*

C. H. S.

Vs. 16. *He brought streams also out of the rock, and caused waters to run down like rivers.* The supply of water was as plenteous in quantity as it was miraculous in origin. Torrents, not driblets, came from the rocks. Streams followed the camp; the supply was not for an hour or a day. This was a marvel of goodness.

If we contemplate the aboundings of divine grace, we shall be lost in admiration. Mighty rivers of love have flowed for us in the wilderness. Alas, great God! our return has not been commensurate therewith, but far otherwise. C. H. S.

"Where sin abounded, grace did much more abound." The second murmuring for water at Kadesh seems to have been a more aggravated act of rebellion than the former, and yet the water is given in greater abundance. Oh, the freeness of the sovereign grace of God! W. WILSON

Vs. 17. *And they sinned yet more against Him.* It was bad enough to mistrust their God for necessaries but to revolt against Him in a greedy rage for superfluities was far worse. Ever is it the nature of the disease of sin to proceed from bad to worse; men never weary of sinning but rather increase their speed in the race of iniquity. C. H. S.

He does not say that they sinned only, but that they sinned against God. *And they sinned yet more against Him,* namely *God.* Against what God? Against Him Who had delivered them by great and unheard of wonders out of Egypt, Who had led them as free men across the Red Sea with a dry foot, Who had continued to lead and to protect them with pillars of cloud and fire by day and night and had given them to drink abundantly of water drawn from the arid rock.

Against this God, they had added sin to sin. Simply to sin is human, and happens to the saints even after they have received grace: but to sin against God argues a singular degree of impiety. MUSCULUS

Vs. 18. *And they tempted God in their heart.* He was not tempted, for He cannot be tempted by any, but they acted in a manner calculated to tempt Him, and it is always just to charge that upon men which is the obvious tendency of their conduct.

Christ cannot die again, and yet many crucify Him afresh, because such would be the legitimate result of their behavior if its effects were not prevented by other forces. The sinners in the wilderness would have had the Lord change His wise proceedings to humor their whims, hence they are said to tempt Him. C. H. S.

*Asking meat for their lust.* God had given them meat for their hunger in the manna, wholesome, pleasant food, and in abundance; He had given them meat for their faith, out of the heads of Leviathan which He brake in pieces (Ps. 74:14). But all this would not serve, they must have meat *"for their lust"*; dainties and varieties to gratify a luxurious appetite. Nothing is more provoking to God than our quarreling with our allotment, and indulging the desires of the flesh. MATTHEW HENRY

Vs. 19. *Yea, they spake against God; they said, Can God furnish a table in the wilderness?* It is particularly to be observed that the sin of which the children of Israel were on this occasion guilty, was not in wishing for bread and water, but in thinking for one moment that after the Lord had brought them out of Egypt, He would suffer them for the lack of any needful thing to come short of Canaan. It was no sin to be hungry and thirsty; it was a necessity of nature.

There is nothing living that does not desire and require food: when we do not, we are dead, and that they did so was no sin. Their sin was *to doubt either that God could or would support them in the wilderness, or allow those who followed His leadings to lack any good thing.* This was their sin. It was just the same with the Christian now. These Israelites did not more literally require a supply of daily food for their bodies, than does the Christian for his soul. Not to do so is a sign of death, and the living soul would soon die without it.

And so far from its being a sin, our Lord has pronounced that man blessed who hungers and thirsts after righteousness, adding the most precious promise, that all such shall be satisfied. But it is a sin, and very great sin, should this food not be perceptibly, and to the evidence of our senses, immediately supplied, to murmur and be fearful. It was for the trial of their faith that these things happened to the Israelites, as do the trials of all Christians in all ages: and it is "after we have suffered a while" that we may expect to be established, strengthened, settled. BROWNLOW NORTH, *in "Ourselves; a Picture Sketched from the History of the Children of Israel"*

Verses 19-20. After all their experience, they doubted the divine omnipotence, as if it were to be regarded as nothing, when it refused to gratify their lusts. Unbelief is so deeply rooted in the human heart, that when God performs miracles on earth, unbelief doubts whether He can perform them in heaven, and when He does them in heaven, whether He can do them on earth. AUGUSTUS F. THOLUCK

Vs. 20. *Can He give bread also?* Who will say that a man is thankful to his friend for a past kindness, if he nourishes an ill opinion of him for the future? This was all that ungrateful Israel returned to God, for His miraculously broaching the rock to quench their thirst: "Behold, He smote the rock"—*Can he give bread also?*

Oh, how sad is this, that after God hath entertained a soul at His table with choice mercies and deliverances, these should be so ill husbanded, that not a bit of them should be left to give faith a meal, to keep the heart from fainting, when God comes not so fast to deliver as desired. He is the most thankful man that treasures up the mercies of God in his memory, and can feed his faith with what God hath done for him, so as to walk in the strength thereof in present straits. WILLIAM GURNALL

Vs. 22. *Because they believed not in God, and trusted not in His salvation.* This is the master sin, the crying sin. Like Jeroboam, the son of Nebat, it sins and makes Israel to sin; it is in itself evil and the parent of evils. It was this sin which shut Israel out of Canaan, and it shuts myriads out of heaven. God is ready to save, combining power with willingness, but rebellious man will not trust his Saviour, and therefore is condemned already.

In the text, it appears as if all Israel's other sins were as nothing compared with this; this is the peculiar spot which the Lord points at, the special provocation which angered Him. From this let every unbeliever learn to tremble more at his unbelief than at anything else. If he be no fornicator, or thief, or liar, let him reflect that it is quite enough to condemn him that he trust not in God's salvation.

Vs. 24. *And had rained down manna upon them to eat.* There was so much of it, the skies poured with food, the clouds burst with provender. It was fit food, proper not for looking at but for eating; they could eat it as they gathered it. Mysterious though it was, so that they called it manna, or "what is it?" yet it was eminently adopted for human nourishment; and as it was both abundant and adapted, so also was it available! They had not far to fetch it, it was nigh them, and they had only to gather it up.

O Lord Jesus, Thou blessed manna of heaven, how all this agrees with Thee! We will even now feed on Thee as our spiritual meat and will pray Thee to chase away all wicked unbelief from us. Our fathers ate manna and doubted; we feed upon Thee and are filled with assurance. C. H. S.

Vs. 27. *He rained flesh also upon them as dust.* First, He rained bread and then flesh, when He might have rained fire and brimstone. The words indicate speed and abundance of the descending quails. C. H. S.

*And feathered fowls like as the sand of the sea.* There was no counting them. By a remarkable providence, if not by miracle, enormous numbers of migratory birds were caused to alight around the tents of the tribes. It was, however, a doubtful blessing, as easily acquired and superabounding riches generally are. The Lord save us from meat which is seasoned with divine wrath. C. H. S.

Vs. 30. *They were not estranged from their lust.* This implies that they were still burning with their lust. If it is objected that this does not agree with the preceding sentence, where it is said, that "they did eat, and were thoroughly filled," I would answer that if, as is well known, the minds of men are not kept within the bounds of reason and temperance, they become insatiable; and, therefore, a great abundance will not extinguish the fire of a depraved appetite. JOHN CALVIN

Consider that there is more real satisfaction in mortifying lusts than in making provision for them or in fulfilling them: there's more true pleasure in crossing and pinching our flesh than in gratifying it; were there any true pleasure in sin, hell would not be hell, for the more sin, the more joy. You cannot satisfy one lust if you would do your utmost, and make yourself ever so absolute a slave to it; you think if you had your heart's desire, you would be at rest: you much mistake; they had it. ALEXANDER CARMICHAEL

Vs. 31. *Slew the fattest of them.* They were fed as sheep for the slaughter. The butcher takes the fattest first. We may suppose there were some pious and contented Israelites that did eat moderately of the quails and were never the worse; for it was not the meat that poisoned them, but their own lust. Let epicures and sensualists here read their doom; they who make *a god of their belly, their end is destruction* (Phil. 3:19). MATTHEW HENRY

Verses 31-34. None so prodigiously wicked as those who are fed high with carnal pleasures. They are to the ungodly as the dung and ordure is to the swine which grows fat by lying in it; so their hearts grow gross and fat; their consciences more stupid and senseless in sin by them; whereas the comforts and delights that God gives unto a holy soul by the creature, turn to spiritual nourishment to His graces, and draw these forth into exercise, as they do others' lusts. WILLIAM GURNALL

Vs. 32. *For all this they sinned still, and believed not for His wondrous works.* Continuance in sin and in unbelief go together. Had they believed they would not have sinned, had they not been blinded by sin they would have believed. There is a reflex action between faith and character. How can the lover of sin believe? How, on the other hand, can the unbeliever cease from sin? God's ways with us in providence are in themselves both convincing and converting, but unrenewed nature refuses to be either convinced or converted by them. C. H. S.

"Men are not always in a mood to be convinced." It is not want of evidence, but the want of right disposition that keeps men from believing God. WILLIAM S. PLUMER

Experience ought to strengthen faith; but there must be present faith to use experience. J. N. DARBY, *in "Practical Reflections on the Psalms"*

Vs. 33. *And their years in trouble.* Weary marches were their trouble and to come to no resting-place was their vanity. Innumerable graves we left along the track of Israel, and if any ask, "Who slew all these?" the answer must be, "They could not enter because of unbelief."

Doubtless much of the vexation and failure of many lives results from their being sapped by unbelief and honeycombed by evil passions. None live so fruitlessly and so wretchedly as those who allow sense and sight to override faith and their reason and appetite to domineer over their fear of God. Our days go fast enough according to the ordinary lapse of time, but the Lord can make them rust away at a bitterer rate, till we feel as if sorrow actually ate out the heart of our life and like a canker devoured our existence. Such was the punishment of rebellious Israel, the Lord grant it may not be ours. C. H. S.

Vs. 34. *When He slew them, then they sought Him.* Like whipped curs, they licked their Master's feet. They obeyed only so long as they felt the whip about their loins. Hard are the hearts which only death can move. While thousands died around them, the people of Israel became suddenly religious, and repaired to the tabernacle door, like sheep who run in a mass while the black dog drives them, but scatter and wander when the shepherd whistles him off.

Vs. 35. *And they remembered that God was their rock, and the high God their Redeemer.* Alas, poor man, how readily dost thou forget thy God! Shame on thee, ungrateful worm, to have no sense of favors a few days after they have been received. Will nothing make thee keep in memory the mercy of thy God except the utter withdrawal of it? C. H. S.

Vs. 36. *Nevertheless they did flatter Him with their mouth.* Bad were they at their best. False on their knees, liars in their prayers. Mouth worship must be very detestable to God when dissociated from the heart: other kings love flattery, but the King of kings abhors it.

Since the sharpest afflictions only extort from carnal men a feigned submission to God, there is proof positive that the heart is desperately set on mischief, and that sin is ingrained in our very nature. If you beat a tiger with many stripes, you cannot turn him into a sheep. The devil cannot be whipped out of human nature, though another devil, namely, hypocrisy may be whipped into it. Piety produced by the damps of sorrow and the heats of terror is of mushroom growth; it is rapid in its upspringing—"they enquired early after God"—but it is a mere unsubstantial fungus of unabiding excitement. C. H. S.

But could they flatter God? Man is flattered when that is ascribed to him which he hath not, or when he is applauded for what he hath, beyond the worth of it. God cannot be flattered thus: He is as much beyond flatterings as He is beyond sufferings.

The Jews, then, are said to flatter God, not because they applauded Him by fair speeches more than was His due, but because by fair speeches they hoped to prevent what they themselves did deserve; or they flattered God with their own promises, not with His praises. They sinned against Him, and He slew them; and when the sword found them, they sought God; they creeped to Him and fawned upon Him; they came as with ropes about their necks, confessing they were worthy to die, yet humbly begging for life: and if God would but humbly sheathe His sword and spare them, O what manner of men they would be in all holy conversation and godliness.

Thus, "they flattered God with their mouth, while their hearts were not right"; they made great shows of repentance and turning to God, but they meant no such thing: this was their flattery. Neither can the Lord be flattered any other way. And as He cannot be flattered by overpraising Him, so His person cannot be unduly honored by over-respecting Him. JOSEPH CARYL

*And they lied unto Him with their tongues.* Their godly speech was cant, their praise mere wind, their prayer a fraud. Their skin-deep repentance was a film too thin to conceal the deadly wound of sin. This teaches us to place small reliance upon professions of repentance made by dying men, or upon such even in others when the basis is evidently slavish fear, and nothing more. Any thief will whine out repentance if he thinks the judge will thereby be moved to let him go scot free. C. H. S.

The heart is the metal of the bell, the tongue is but the clapper; when the metal of the bell is right and good (as silver) such will the sound be; if the metal of the bell be cracked, or lead, the sound will soon discover it to a judicious ear.

God can see the diseases and spots of the heart upon the tongue. As Jacob said to his mother, "If I dissemble, my father will find me out, and I shall meet with a curse instead of a blessing." GEORGE SWINNOCK

Verses 36-38. If God would not leave the show and semblance of contrition without a recompense, will He be unmindful of real penitence? If *many a time turned He His anger away* from those who "*did but flatter Him with their mouths,* and lied unto Him with their tongues," has He nothing in store for those who are humble in spirit and who come to Him with a sacrifice of a broken heart?

Oh! the turning away of temporal wrath because idols were outwardly abandoned, this is a mighty pledge that eternal wrath will be averted if we are inwardly stricken and flee for refuge to the Savior. God must have eternal good in store for His friends, if even His enemies are recompensed with temporal good.

Yes, as I mark the Philistines and the Ammonites oppressing the idolatrous Israelites and then see the oppressors driven back in return even for heartless service, oh! I learn that true penitence for sin and true faith in the sacrifice of Jesus Christ will cause all enemies to be scattered; I return from the contemplation of the backsliding people, emancipated notwithstanding the known hollowness of their vows, I return assured that a kingdom which neither Philistine nor Ammonite can invade, shall be the portion of all who seek deliverance through Christ. HENRY MELVILL

Vs. 37. *For their heart was not right with Him.* There was no depth in their repentance; it was not heart work. They were fickle as a weathercock; every wind turned them; their mind was not settled upon God.

*Neither were they stedfast in His covenant.* Their promises were no sooner made than broken, as if only made in mockery. Good resolutions call at their hearts as men do at inns; they tarried awhile and then took their leave. They were hot today for holiness, but cold towards it tomorrow. Variable as the hues of the dolphin, they changed from reverence to rebellion, from thankfulness to murmuring. One day they gave their gold to build a tabernacle for Jehovah, and the next they plucked off their ear-rings to make a golden calf. Surely the heart is a chameleon. Proteus had not so many changes. As in the ague we both burn and freeze, so do inconstant natures in their religion. C. H. S.

Vs. 41. *And limited the Holy One of Israel.* Doubted His power and so limited Him, dictated to His wisdom, and so did the same. To chalk out a path for God is arrogant impiety. The Holy One must do right, the covenant God of Israel must be true, it is profanity itself to say unto Him Thou shalt do this or that, or otherwise I will not worship Thee. Not thus is the eternal God to be led by a string by His impotent creature. He is the Lord, and He will do as seemeth Him good. C. H. S.

Here, then, is an awful charge, and mysterious it seems to us as awful. How dreadful that man, the worm, should arrogate to himself that, to say to Him that made him, "Thus far shalt Thou go and no farther." Amazing, I say, the charge! to contact the dimensions and operations of the Deity. Amazing insolence, to draw a boundary line beyond which the Creator Himself must not pass, to define and prescribe to the Lawgiver of nature Himself the pathway of His providence! The turpitude is immense.

But we know, my friends, that the crime is not uncommon; and one of the natural results of sin seems to be this—that the sinful spirit, whether of man or of the lost archangel, unable to shake the firm foundations of the eternal Throne, amuses its malignity and seeks a temporary cessation from its withering cares in putting up barriers on the outskirts and frontiers of the Almighty empire, vainly hoping to annoy the Possessor of the throne they cannot disturb. E. PAXTON HOOD

God cannot bear it with patience, that we should limit Him, either to the time or manner or means of help. He complains of the Jews for this presumption, *they limited the Holy One of Israel.* It is insufferable to circumscribe an infinite wisdom and power. He will work, but when He pleases, and how He pleases, and by what instruments He pleases, and if He please, without instruments, and if He please by weak and improbable, by despised and exploded instruments. JOSEPH CARYL, *in a "Sermon before the House of Commons" entitled "The Works of Ephesus"*

*Limited.* In the only other place where the Hebrew word occurs (Ezra 9:4), it means to set a mark upon a person, which some apply here, in the figurative sense of stigmatizing or insulting. JOSEPH ADDISON ALEXANDER

Vs. 42. *They remembered not His hand, nor the day when He delivered them from the enemy.* Because Israel forgot the first deliverance, they went on frowardly in the way of evil. Because a Christian sometimes stops short of the cross in his spiritual conflicts, he fails to defeat the enemy and remains unfruitful and unhappy, until by some special intervention of the great Restorer, he is again brought, in spirit, to that place where God first met him and welcomed him in Jesus in the fullness of forgiveness and of peace. No intermediate experience, how truthful soever in its character, will meet his case.

It is at the cross alone that we regain a thorough right-mindedness about ourselves as well as about God. If we would glorify Him, we must "hold fast the beginning of our confidence stedfast unto the end" (Heb. 3:14). ARTHUR PRIDHAM

Eaten bread is soon forgotten. Nothing so soon grows stale as a favor. JOHN TRAPP

Verses 43-51. Moses wrought wonders destructive, Christ wonders preservative: he turned water into blood, Christ water into wine; he brought flies and frogs and locusts and caterpillars, destroying the fruits of the earth and annoying it; Christ increased a little of these fruits, five loaves and a few fishes, by blessing them, so that He herewith fed five thousand men: Moses smote both men and cattle with hail, and thunder and lightning, that they died, Christ made some alive that were dead, and saved from death the diseased and sick.

Moses was an instrument to bring all manner of wrath and evil angels amongst them, Christ cast out devils, and did all manner of good, giving sight to the blind, hearing to the deaf, speech to the dumb, limbs to the lame, and cleansing to the leper, and when the sea was tempestuous appeasing it; Moses slew their firstborn, thus causing an horrible cry in all the land of Egypt; Christ saveth all the firstborn, or by saving makes them so; for thus they are called (Heb. 12: 23). JOHN MAYER

Vs. 44. *And had turned their rivers into blood.* The waters had been made the means of the destruction of Israel's newborn infants, and now they do as it were betray the crime—they blush for it, they avenge it on the murderers. The Nile was the vitality of Egypt, its true life blood, but at God's command it became a flowing curse; every drop of it was a horror, poison to drink, and terror to gaze on.

How soon might the Almighty One do this with the Thames or the Seine. Sometimes He has allowed men, who were His rod, to make rivers crimson with gore, and this is a severe judgment; but the event now before us was more mysterious, more general, more complete, and must, therefore, have been a plague of the first magnitude.

*And their flood, that they could not drink.* Lesser streams partook of the curse, reservoirs and canals felt the evil; God does nothing by halves. All Egypt boasted of the sweet waters of their river, but they were made to loathe it more than they had ever loved it. Our mercies may soon become our miseries if the Lord shall deal with us in wrath. C. H. S.

They looked upon their river not only as consecrated to a deity; but if we may believe some authors, as their chief national god; and worshipped it accordingly.

They must have felt the utmost astonishment and horror when they beheld their sacred stream changed and polluted and the divinity whom they worshipped so shamefully soiled and debased. And these appearances must have had a salutary effect upon the Israelites; as they were hence warned not to accede to this species of idolatry; but to have it ever in contempt, as well as abhorrence. It is to be observed, that God might, if it had been the divine pleasure, have many different ways tainted and polluted the streams of Egypt. But He thought proper to change it to blood.

Now the Egyptians, and especially their priests, were particularly nice and delicate in their outward habit and rites; and there was nothing which they abhorred more than blood, they seldom admitted any bloody sacrifices; and with the least stain of gore they would have thought themselves deeply polluted. Their affectation of purity was so great that they could not bear to come within contact with a foreigner, or even to handle his clothes, but to touch a dead body was an abomination and required to be immediately expiated.

On these accounts, the priests were continually making ablutions. There were four stated times, twice in the day and as often in the night, at which they were obliged to bathe themselves. Many accidents caused them to repeat it much oftener. Hence this evil brought upon them must have been severely felt, as "there was blood throughout all the land of Egypt" (Exod. 7:21). JACOB BRYANT, *in "Observations upon the Plagues Inflicted upon the Egyptians"*

Vs. 45. *And frogs, which destroyed them.* How great is that God Who thus by a minute can crush the magnificent. These creatures swarmed everywhere when they were alive, until the people felt ready to die at the sight; and when the reptiles died, the heaps of their bodies made the land to stink so foully that a pestilence was imminent.

Thus not only did earth and air send forth armies of horrible life, but the water also added its legions of loathsomeness. It seemed as if the Nile was first made nauseous and then caused to leave its bed altogether, crawling and leaping in the form of frogs. Those who contend with the Almighty little know what arrows are in His quiver; surprising sin shall be visited with surprising punishment. C. H. S.

Vs. 49. *He cast upon them the fierceness of His anger, wrath, and indignation, and trouble.* His last arrow was the sharpest. He reserved the strong wine of His indignation to the last. Note how the Psalmist piles up the words, and well he might; for blow followed blow, each one more staggering than its predecessor, and then the crushing stroke was reserved for the end. C. H. S.

*By sending evil angels among them.* Messengers of evil entered their houses at midnight and smote the dearest objects of their love. The angels were evil to them, though good enough in themselves; those who to the heirs of salvation are ministers of grace are, to the heirs of wrath, executioners of judgment. C. H. S.

When God sends angels, they are sure to come, and if He bids them slay, they will not spare. See how sin sets all the powers of heaven in array against man; he has no friend left in the universe when God is his enemy. C. H. S.

That the devil and his angels are so very evil, that for them everlasting fire is prepared, no believer is ignorant: but that there should be sent by means of them an infliction from the Lord God upon certain whom He judgeth to be deserving of this punishment, seemeth to be a hard thing to those who are little prone to consider how the perfect justice of God doth use well even evil things.

For these, indeed, as far as regardeth their substance, what other person but Himself hath made? But evil He hath not made them; yet He doth use them, inasmuch as He is good, conveniently and justly; just as on the other hand unrighteous men do use his good creatures in evil manner: God, therefore, doth use evil angels not only to punish evil men, as in the case of all those concerning whom the Psalm doth speak, as in the case of king Ahab, whom a spirit of lying by the will of God did beguile, in order that he might fall in war; but also to prove and make manifest good men, as He did in the case of Job. AUGUSTINE

Vs. 51. *And smote all the firstborn in Egypt.* No exceptions were made, the monarch bewailed his heir as did the menial at the mill. They smote the Lord's firstborn, even Israel, and He smites theirs.

*The chief of their strength in the tabernacles of Ham.* Swinging his scythe over the field, death topped off the highest flowers. The tents of Ham knew each one its own peculiar sorrow, and were made to sympathize with the sorrows which had been ruthlessly inflicted upon the habitations of Israel. Thus curses come home to roost. Oppressors are repaid in their own coin, without the discount of a penny. C. H. S.

The sun of the last day of the sojourn of Israel in Egypt had set. It was the fourth day after the interview with Moses. Pharaoh, his princes, and the priests of his idols would doubtless take courage from this unwonted delay. Jehovah and His ministers are beaten at length, for now the gods of Egypt prevail against them. The triumph would be celebrated in pomps and sacrifices, in feasts and dances. Nothing is more likely than that the banquet halls of Pharaoh at Rameses were blazing with lamps, and that he and his princes were pouring forth libations of wine to their gods, and concerting schemes amid their revelry, for the perpetuation of the thraldom of Israel.

Pharaoh Sethos started from his couch that night yelling in fierce and bitter agony, and gnawing at the sharp arrow that was rankling in his vitals, like a wounded lion. His son, his firstborn, his only son, just arrived at man's estate, just crowned king of Egypt, and associated with his father in the cares of sovereignty, writhed before him in mortal throes, "and died."

His transports of grief were reechoed, and with no feigned voice, by the princes, the councillors, and the priests that partook of his revelry. Each one rends his garments and clasps to his bosom the quivering corpse of his firstborn son. On that fearful night "there was a great cry throughout all the land of Egypt," but if we have rightly read its history, the loudest, wildest wail of remorseful anguish would arise from Pharaoh's banquet hall! WILLIAM OSBURN, *in "Israel in Egypt"*

Vs. 56. *And kept not His testimonies.* They were true to nothing but hereditary treachery; steadfast in nothing but in falsehood. They knew His truth and forgot it, His will and disobeyed it, His grace and perverted it to an occasion for greater transgression. Reader, dost thou need a looking-glass? See, here is one which suits the present expositor well; does it not also reflect thine image?

Vs. 57. *And dealt unfaithfully like their fathers,* proving themselves legitimate by manifesting the treachery of their sires. They were a new generation, but not a new nation—another race yet not another. Evil propensities are transmitted; the birth follows the progenitor; the wild ass breeds wild asses; the children of the raven fly to the carrion. Human nature does not improve; the new editions contain all the errata of the first, and sometimes fresh errors are imported. C. H. S.

*They were turned aside like a deceitful bow.* When the bow is unbent, the rift it hath may be undiscerned, but go to use it by drawing the arrow to the head, and it flies in pieces; thus doth a false heart when put to the trial.

As the ape in the fable, dressed like a man, when nuts are thrown before her, cannot dissemble her nature any longer but shows herself an ape indeed; a false heart betrays itself before it is aware, when a fair occasion is presented for its lust; whereas sincerity keeps the soul pure in the face of temptation. WILLIAM GURNALL

Vs. 58. *And moved Him to jealousy with their graven images.* This was but one more step; they manufactured symbols of the invisible God, for they lusted after something tangible and visible to which they could show reverence. This also is the crying sin of modern times. Do we not hear and see superstition abounding? Images, pictures, crucifixes, and a host of visible things are had in religious honor, and worst of all men now-a-days worship what they eat, and call that God which passes into their belly, and thence into baser places still.

Surely the Lord is very patient, or He would visit the earth for this worst and basest of idolatry. He is a jealous God and abhors to see Himself dishonored by any form of representation which can come from man's hands.

Vs. 59. *And greatly abhorred Israel.* If Dagon sit aloft in any soul, the ark of God is not there. Where the Lord dwells, no image of jealousy will be tolerated. A visible church will soon become a visible curse if idols be set up in it, and then the pruning knife will remove it as a dead branch from the vine. C. H. S.

Vs. 61. *And His glory into the enemy's hand.* This was a fearful downfall for the favored nation, and it was followed by dire judgments of most appalling nature. When God is gone, all is gone. No calamity can equal the withdrawal of the divine presence from a people. O Israel, how art thou brought low! Who shall help thee now that thy God has left thee!

Vs. 64. *Their priests fell by the sword.* Hophni and Phineas were slain; they were among the chief in sin, and, therefore, they perished with the rest. Priesthood is no shelter for transgressors: the jewelled breastplate cannot turn aside the arrows of judgment. C. H. S.

Vs. 70. *He took him from the sheepfolds.* The art of feeding cattle and the art of ruling men are sisters, saith Basil. JOHN TRAPP

Vs. 71. *From following the ewes great with young.* It hath been reported that a learned doctor of Oxford hung up his leathern breeches in his study for a memorial to visitors of his mean origin; the truth I avouch not, but history tells us of Agathocles, who arose from a potter to be King of Sicily and would be served in no other plate at his table but earthenware, to mind him of his former drudgery.

'Twere well if some would remember whose shoes they have cleaned, whose coats they have carried, and whose money they have borrowed, and deal gratefully with their creditors, as the good Lord Cromwell did by the Florentine merchant in the time of Henry the Eighth, when Wolsey, like a butcher, forgot the king, his master.

'Twas otherwise with holy David, who being in kingly dignity, graciously calls to mind his following the ewes great with young, when now feeding the sheep of Israel. His golden scepter points at his wooden hook, and he plays the old lessons of his oaten pipe upon his Algum harp, and spreads his Bethlehem tent within his marble palace on Mount Zion. SAMUEL LEE

## PSALM 79

A Psalm of complaint such as Jeremiah might have written amid the ruins of the beloved city. It evidently treats of times of invasion, oppression, and national overthrow.

Vs. 1. *O God, the heathen are come into Thine inheritance.* It is with the cry of amazement at sacrilegious intrusion; as if the poet were struck with horror.

*Thy holy Temple have they defiled.* It is an awful thing when wicked men are found in the church and numbered with her ministry.

*They have laid Jerusalem on heaps.* It is sad to see the foe in our own house, but worse to meet him in the house of God; they strike hardest who smite at our religion. C. H. S.

Verses 1-4. In that last and most fearful destruction, when the eagles of Rome were gathered round the doomed city, and the Temple of which God had said, "Let us depart hence"; when one stone was not to be left upon another, when the fire was to consume the sanctuary, and the foundations of Zion were to be ploughed up; when Jerusalem was to be filled with slain, and the sons of Judah were to be crucified round her walls in such thick multitudes that no more room was left for death; when insult and shame and scorn was the lot of the child of Israel, as he wandered an outcast, a fugitive in all lands; when all these bitter and deadly things came upon Jerusalem, it was as a punishment for many and long-repeated crimes; it was the accomplishment of a warning which had been often sent in vain. Yea, fiercely did thy foes assault thee, O Jerusalem, but thy sins more fiercely still! *"Plain Commentary"*

Verses 1, 4-5. Entering the inhabited part of the old city, and winding through some crooked, filthy lanes, I suddenly found myself on turning a sharp corner, in a spot of singular interest; the "Jews' place of Wailing." Old men were there—pale, haggard, careworn men, tottering on pilgrim staves; and little girls with white faces, and lustrous black eyes, gazing wistfully now at their parents, now at the old wall. Some were on their knees chanting mournfully from a Book of Hebrew prayers, swaying their bodies to and fro; some were prostrate on the ground, pressing forehead and lips to the earth; some were close to the wall, burying their faces in the rents and crannies of the old stones; some were kissing them; some had their arms spread out as if they would clasp them to their bosoms; some were bathing them with tears, and all the while sobbing as if their hearts would burst. It was a sad and touching spectacle.

Eighteen centuries of exile and woe have not dulled their hearts' affections or deadened their feelings of devotion. Here we see them assembled from the ends of the earth—poor, despised, down-trodden outcasts—amid the desolations of their fatherland, beside the dishonored ruins of their ancient sanctuary—chanting, now in accents of deep pathos, and now of wild woe, the prophetic words of their own Psalmist: *O God, the heathen are come into Thine inheritance; Thy holy temple have they defiled. . . . We are become a reproach to our neighbors, a scorn and derision to them that are round about us. How long, Lord? wilt Thou be angry forever?* J. L. PORTER, *in "The Giant Cities of Bashan'*

Verses 2-3. (The following extract is from the writings of a godly monk, who applies the language of the Psalm to the persecutions of his time. He wrote at Rome during the period of the Reformation and was evidently a favorer of the

Gospel.) At this day what river is there, what brook, in this our afflicted Europe (if it is still ours) that we have not seen flowing with the blood of Christians?

Hast Thou ever seen so dire a spectacle? They have piled up in heaps the dead bodies of Thy servants to be devoured by birds: the unburied remains of Thy saints, I say, they have given to the beasts of the earth. What greater cruelty could ever be committed? So great was the effusion of human blood at that time, that the rivulets, yea, rather, the rivers around the entire circuit of the city flowed with it. GIAMBATTISTA FOLENGO

Vs. 3. *And there was none to bury them.* Has it come to this, that there are none to bury the dead of Thy family, O Lord? Can none be found to grant a shovelful of earth with which to cover up the poor bodies of Thy murdered saints? What woe is here! How glad should we be that we live in so quiet an age, when the blast of the trumpet is no more heard in our streets.

Vs. 4. *A scorn and derision to them that are round about us.* To find mirth in others' miseries and to exult over the ills of others is worthy only of the devil and of them whose father he is. C. H. S.

This was more grievous to them than stripes or wounds, saith Chrysostom, because these being inflicted upon the body are divided after a sort betwixt soul and body, but scorns and reproaches do wound the soul only. *Habet quendam aculeum contumelia*—they leave a sting behind them, as Cicero observeth. JOHN TRAPP

It is the height of reproach a father casts upon his child when he commands his slave to beat him. Of all outward judgments, this is the sorest, to have strangers rule over us, as being made up of shame and cruelty. If once the heathen come into God's inheritance, no wonder the church complains that she is "become a reproach to her neighbors, a shame and derision to all round about her." ABRAHAM WRIGHT

Vs. 6. *Pour out Thy wrath upon the heathen that have not known Thee, and upon the kingdoms that have not called upon Thy Name.* Neglect of prayer by unbelievers is threatened with punishment. The prophet's imprecation is the same in effect with a threatening (see Jer. 10:25), and same imprecation (Ps. 79:6). The prophets would not have used such an imprecation against those that call not upon God, but that their neglect of calling on His name makes them liable to His wrath and fury; and no neglect makes men liable to the wrath of God but the neglect of duty. DAVID CLARKSON

Vs. 8. *O remember not against us former iniquities.* Sins accumulate against nations. Generations lay up stores of transgressions to be visited upon their successors; hence this urgent prayer. In Josiah's days, the most earnest repentance was not able to avert the doom which former long years of idolatry had sealed against Judah. C. H. S.

The Jews have a saying that there is no punishment happens to Israel but there is an ounce in it for the sin of the calf; their meaning is that this always is remembered and visited according to Exod. 32:34; the phrase may take in all the sins of former persons, their ancestors, and of former times, from age to age, they had continued in, which had brought ruin upon them; and all their own sins of nature and of youth, all past ones to the present time. JOHN GILL

Old debts vex most; the delay of payment increases them by interest upon interest; and the return of them being unexpected, a person is least provided for them. We count old sores, breaking forth, incurable. Augustus wondered at a person sleeping quietly that was very much in debt, and sent for his pillow, saying, "Surely there is some strange virtue in it, that makes him rest so secure." ELIAS PLEDGER, *in "Morning Exercises"*

Vs. 9. *God of our salvation.* If human reason were to judge of the many and great blows wherewith God so often smote and wasted His people, it would call God, not the Savior of the people, but the destroyer and oppressor. But the faith of the Prophet judges far otherwise of God and sees even in an angry and pursuing God the salvation of His people.

The gods of the nations, though they do not afflict even in temporal things, are gods not of the salvation of their worshippers, but of their perdition. But our God, even when He is most severely angry, and smites, is not the God of destruction, but of salvation. MUSCULUS

*And deliver us, and purge away our sins, for Thy name's sake.* Sin, the root of the evil, is seen and confessed; pardon of sin is sought as well as removal of chastisement, and both are asked not as matters of right but as gifts of grace. God's Name is a second time brought into the pleading. Believers will find it their wisdom to use very frequently this noble plea: it is the great gun of the battle, the mightiest weapon in the armory of prayer. C. H. S.

God is free to choose what suits His own heart best and most conduceth to the exalting of His great Name: and He delights more in the mercy shown to one than in the blood of all the damned that are made a sacrifice to His justice. And, indeed, He had a higher end in their damnation than their suffering; and that was the enhancing of the glory of His mercy, in His saved ones. WILLIAM GURNALL

Vs. 11. *Let the sighing of the prisoner come before Thee.* When the captive gazes through the bars of iron which night and day stand like mute sentinels before the narrow window of his cell, and when his eyes fall upon the green fields and groves beyond, he sighs and turns away from the scene with a wish. He spake not a word, yet he wished. That sigh was a wish that he could be set free.

And such sighs as these are heard by God. Your longings, your sorrows, when they are not fulfilled, your sad thoughts—"Oh! when shall I be delivered from the burden of my sin, and from the coldness of my heart!"—all these wishes were your sighs, and they have been heard on high. PHILIP BENNETT POWER

*According to the greatness of Thy power preserve Thou those that are appointed to die.* Men and devils may consign us to perdition, while sickness drags us to the grave, and sorrow sinks us in the dust; but, there is One who can keep our soul alive, ay, and bring it up again from the depths of despair. A lamb shall live between the lion's jaws if the Lord wills it. Even in the sharnel, life shall vanquish death if God be near. C. H. S.

Ought not pious people more closely to imitate their heavenly Father in caring for those who have been condemned to die? An eminent Christian lady keeps a record of all who have been sentenced to death, so far as she hears of them, and prays for them every day till their end come. Is not such conduct in sympathy with the heart of God! WILLIAM S. PLUMER

# PSALM 80

Title: "To the Chief Musician upon Shoshannim-Eduth." For the fourth time we have a song upon Shoshannim, or the lilies; the former ones being Psalms 45, 60, and 69. Why this title is given it would be difficult to say in every case, but the delightfully poetical form of the present Psalm may well justify the charming title. The Psalm is a testimony of the church as a "lily among the thorns." C. H. S.

Vs. 1. The prophet does not nakedly begin his prayer, but mingles therewith certain titles, by which he most aptly addresses God and urges his cause. He does not say, "O Thou Who sustainest and governest all things which are in heaven and earth, Who hast placed Thy dwelling-place above the heaven of heavens; but Thou Who art the Shepherd of Israel, Thou that leadest Joseph like a flock, Thou that dwellest between Cheribim." Those things which enhance the favor and providence of God revealed to Israel, he brings to remembrance that he might nourish and strengthen confidence in prayer.

Let us learn from this example to feed and fortify our confidence in praying to God, with the mark of that divine and paternal kindness revealed to us in Christ, our Shepherd and propitiation. MUSCULUS

*O Shepherd of Israel, Thou that leadest Joseph like a flock.* Now, can you watch such a scene and not think of that Shepherd Who leadeth Joseph like a flock, and of another river which all His sheep must cross? He, too, goes before, and, as in the case of the flock, they who keep near Him fear no evil. They hear His sweet voice saying, "When thou passest through the waters, I will be with thee; and through the rivers, they shall not overflow thee." With eye fastened on Him, they scarcely see the stream or feel its cold and threatening waves.

The great majority, however, "linger, shivering on the brink, and fear to launch away." They lag behind, look down upon the dark river, and, like Peter on stormy Gennesaret, when faith failed, they begin to sink. Then they cry for help, but not in vain. The Good Shepherd hastens to their rescue, and none of all His flock can ever perish. Even the weakest lambkins are carried safely over.

I once saw flocks crossing the Jordan "to Canaan's fair and happy land," and there the scene was even more striking and impressive. The river was broader, the current stronger, and the flocks larger, while the shepherds were more picturesque and Biblical. The catastrophe, too, with which many more sheep were threatened—of being swept down into that mysterious sea of death, which swallows up the Jordan itself—was more solemn and suggestive. W. M. THOMSON, *in "The Land and the Book"*

*Thou that leadest Joseph like a flock.* Thou that leadest Joseph like a flock art considered by the unbelieving to have no thoughts for our affairs; therefore, stretch forth Thine hand for our assistance that the mouth of them that speak iniquities may be shut. We seek not gold and riches or the dignities of this world, but we long for Thy light, we desire more ardently to know Thee; therefore "shine forth." SAVONAROLA

*Thou that dwellest between the cherubims, shine forth.* Our greatest dread is the withdrawal of the Lord's presence, and our brightest hope is the prospect of His return.

Vs. 2. *Before Ephraim and Benjamin and Manasseh stir up Thy strength, and come and save us.* It is wise to mention the names of the Lord's people in prayer, for they are precious to Him. Jesus bears the names of His people on His breast-plate. Just as the mention of the names of his children has power with a father, so is it with the Lord. C. H. S.

Vs. 3. *Turn us, and cause Thy face to shine.* To Thyself, convert us from the earthly to the heavenly; convert our rebellious wills to Thee, and when we are converted, show Thy countenance that we may know Thee; show Thy power that we may fear Thee; show Thy wisdom that we may reverence Thee; show Thy goodness that we may love Thee; show them once, show them a second time, show them always, that through tribulation we may pass with a happy face and be saved. When Thou dost save, we shall be saved; when Thou withdrawest Thy hand, we cannot be saved. SAVONAROLA

*And we shall be saved.* All that is wanted for salvation is the Lord's favor. One glance of His gracious eye would transform Tophet into Paradise. No matter how fierce the foe or dire the captivity, the shining face of God ensures both victory and liberty. This verse is a very useful prayer. Since we, too, often turn aside, let us often with our lips and heart cry, "Turn us again, O God, and cause Thy face to shine, and we shall be saved."

Vs. 4. *O Lord God of hosts, how long wilt Thou be angry against the prayer of Thy people?* That God should be angry with us when sinning seems natural enough, but that He should be angry even with our prayers is a bitter grief. C. H. S.

God hath not only the chariots and horsemen of heaven to defend His prophet; but even the basest, the most indocible, and despicable creatures, wherewith to confound His enemies. If Goliath stalk forth to defy the God of Israel, he shall be confuted with a pebble. If Herod swells up to a god, God will set His vermin on him, and all the king's guard cannot save him from them. You have heard of rats that could not be beaten off till they had destroyed that covetous prelate; and of the fly that killed Pope Adrian. God hath more ways to punish than He hath creatures.

His anger, therefore, seems so much the more fearful, as it is presented to us under so great a title: *"the Lord God of hosts" is angry.* They talk of Tamerlane that he could daunt his enemies with the very look of his countenance. Oh! then what terror dwells in the countenance of an offended God. THOMAS ADAMS

Vs. 5. *Thou feedest them with the bread of tears.* Their meat is seasoned with brine distilled from weeping eyes. Their meals, which were once such pleasant seasons of social merriment, are now like funeral feasts to which each man contributes his bitter morsel. Thy people ate bread of wheat before, but now they receive from Thine own hand no better diet than bread of tears.

*And givest them tears to drink in great measure.* Tear-bread is even more the fruit of the curse than to eat bread in the sweat of one's face, but it shall by divine love be turned into a greater blessing by ministering to our spiritual health.

Vs. 6. *And our enemies laugh among themselves.* They find mirth in our misery, comedy in our tragedy, salt for their wit in the brine of our tears, amusement in our amazement. It is devilish to sport with another's griefs; but it is the constant habit of the world which lieth in the wicked one to make merry with the saints' tribulations; the seed of the serpent follow their progenitor and rejoice in evil. C. H. S.

Vs. 7. *Turn us again, O God of hosts.* See verse 3 and observe that there it was only, *Turn us again, O God;* here *O God of hosts;* and verse 19, *O Lord God of hosts.* As the bird by much waving gathereth wind under the wing, and mounteth higher, so doth faith in prayer. JOHN TRAPP

Vs. 12. *Why hast Thou then broken down her hedges?* All who keep not Thy precepts, who know not the way of God, open sinners, disreputable, these are the men that are chosen to minister at the altar, to these are benefices given, these gather her grapes for themselves, not for Thee. They regard not Thy poor; they feed not the hungry; they clothe not the naked; they help not the stranger; they defend not the widow and orphan; they eat up the lamb of the flock, and the fatted calf from the midst of the herd.

They sing to the sound of psaltery and organ, like David; they think they have the instruments of song, arranged in choirs, praising God with the lips, but in heart they are far from God. Drinking wine in cups, perfumed with the richest odors, they suffer nothing for the grief of Joseph; with no pity are they moved for the needy and poor.

Today in the theatre, tomorrow in the bishop's chair. Today at the custom-house, tomorrow a canon in the choir. Today a soldier, tomorrow a priest. They have transgressed Thy way, and turned to Thy vine: not, indeed that they might cultivate her for Thee, but that they might gather her grapes for themselves. SAVONAROLA

Vs. 13. *The boar out of the wood doth waste it.* No image of a destructive enemy could be more appropriate than that which is used. We have read of the little foxes that spoil the vines, but the wild boar is a much more destructive enemy, breaking its way through fences, rooting up the ground, tearing down the vines themselves, and treading them under its feet.

Indeed, the inhabitants of countries where the wild boar flourishes would as soon face a lion as one of these animals, the stroke of whose razor-like tusks is made with lightning swiftness, and which is sufficient to rip up a horse and cut a dog nearly asunder. J. G. WOOD, *in "Bible Animals"*

According to the Talmud, the middle letter of the word rendered *wood,* in this verse, is the middle letter of the Hebrew Psalter. DANIEL CRESSWELL

Vs. 14. *Visit this vine.* Still it has roots; still some branches are living. In the beginning of the world it began, and never has failed and never will. For Thou hast said, "Lo, I am with you always, even unto the end of the world." It may be diminished, it can never utterly fail. This vine is the vine which Thou hast planted. There is one Spirit, one faith, one baptism, one God, and Lord of all, Who is all in all.

Visit, then, this vine, for Thy visitation preserves her spirit; visit by Thy grace, by Thy presence, by Thy Holy Spirit. Visit with Thy rod and with Thy staff; for Thy rod and Thy staff comfort her. Visit with Thy scourge that she may be chastened and purified, for the time of pruning comes. Cast out the stones, gather up the dry branches, and bind them in bundles for burning. Raise her up, cut off the superfluous shoots, make fast her supports, enrich the soil, build up the fence, and visit this vine, as now Thou visitest the earth and waterest it. SAVONAROLA

Vs. 17. *Let Thy hand be upon the man of Thy right hand, upon the Son of man Whom Thou madest strong for Thyself.* Nations rise or fall largely through the instrumentality of individuals: by a Napoleon the kingdoms are scourged, and by a Wellington nations are saved from the tyrant. It is by the Man Christ Jesus that fallen Israel is yet to rise, and indeed through Him, Who deigns to call Himself the Son of man, the world is to be delivered from the domain of Satan and the curse of sin. O Lord, fulfill Thy promise to the Man of Thy right hand, Who participates in Thy glory, and give Him to see the pleasure of the Lord prospering in His hand. C. H. S.

Now, since Christ is called *the Man of God's right hand,* this says that He is the object of His warmest and most honorable regards. In Him He is well pleased, and in token of this, He has set Him in the most honorable place. He is the

Son of man, Whom the Father made to stand strong for Himself, *i.e.*, to support the honor and dignity of the divine character amidst a perverse and crooked generation: the consideration of the Father's right hand being upon Him, or of the Father's satisfaction in Him as our Surety, serves to animate and embolden our addresses to His throne, and is the keenest incitement to put in practice that resolution, "Henceforth, will we not go back from Thee." Alexander Pirie

Vs. 19. *Cause Thy face to shine; and we shall be saved.* Even we who were so destroyed. No extremity is too great for the power of God. He is able to save at the last point, and that, too, by simply turning His smiling face upon His afflicted. Men can do little with their arm, but God can do all things with a glance. Oh, to live forever in the light of Jehovah's countenance. C. H. S.

During distress, God comes; and when He comes, it is no more distress. Gaelic Proverb

# PSALM 81

Vs. 1. *Sing aloud.* No dullness should ever stupefy our Psalmody or half-heartedness cause it to limp along. Sing aloud, ye debtors to sovereign grace. Your hearts are profoundly grateful; let your voices express your thankfulness.

*Make a joyful noise unto the God of Jacob.* It is to be regretted that the niceties of modern singing frighten our congregations from joining lustily in the hymns. For our part, we delight in full bursts of praise and had rather discover the ruggedness of a want of musical training than miss the heartiness of universal congregational song. The gentility, which lisps the tune in well-bred whispers or leaves the singing altogether to the choir, is very like a mockery of worship.

The gods of Greece and Rome may be worshipped well enough with classical music, but Jehovah can only be adored with the heart, and that music is the best for His service which gives the heart most play. C. H. S.

Vs. 4. *For this was a statute for Israel, and a law of the God of Jacob.* When it can be proved that the observance of Christmas, Whitsuntide, and other Popish festivals was ever instituted by a divine statute, we also will attend to them, but not till then.

It is as much our duty to reject the traditions of men as to observe the ordinances of the Lord. We ask concerning every rite and rubric, "Is this a law of the God of Jacob?" and if it be not clearly so, it is of no authority with us who walk in Christian liberty. C. H. S.

Vs. 7. *I proved thee at the waters of Meribah.* The story of Israel is only our own history in another shape. God has heard us, delivered us, liberated us, and too often our unbelief makes the wretched return of mistrust, murmuring, and rebellion. Great is our sin; great is the mercy of our God: let us reflect upon both and pause a while.

*Selah.* Hurried reading is of little benefit; to sit down a while and meditate is very profitable. C. H. S.

Vs. 9. *There shall no strange god be in thee.* No alien god is to be tolerated in Israel's tents.

*Neither shalt thou worship any strange god.* Where false gods are, their worship is sure to follow. Man is so desperate an idolator that the image is always a strong temptation: while the nests are there the birds will be eager to return. C. H. S.

Vs. 10. *Open thy mouth wide.* When the good man gets near to God, he has much business to transact with Him, many complaints to make, and many blessings to implore; and, as such seasons do not frequently occur, he's the more careful to improve them. He then pours out his whole soul, and is at no loss for words; for when the heart is full, the tongue overflows. Sorrow and distress will even make those eloquent who are naturally slow of speech.

Open thy mouth wide, then, O Christian; stretch out thy desires to the uttermost, grasp heaven and earth in thy boundless wishes, and believe there is enough in God to afford thee full satisfaction. Not only come, but come with boldness to the throne of grace: it is erected for sinners, even the chief of sinners. Come to it then, and wait at it, till you obtain mercy and find grace to help in time of need. Those who expect most from God are likely to receive the most. The desire of the righteous, let it be ever so extensive, shall be granted. BENJAMIN BEDDOME

The custom is said still to exist in Persia that when the king wishes to do a visitor, an ambassador for instance, especial honor, he desires him to open his mouth wide; and the king then crams it as full of sweetmeats as it will hold; and sometimes even with jewels. Curious as this custom is, it is doubtless referred to in Ps. 81:10: *Open thy mouth wide, and I will fill it;* not with baubels of jewels, but with far richer treasure. JOHN GADSBY

Vs. 11. *My people would not hearken to My voice; and Israel would none of Me.* Know, sinner, that if at last thou missest heaven, which God forbid! the Lord can wash His hands over your head and clear Himself of your blood: thy damnation will be laid at thine own door: it will then appear there was no cheat in the promise, no sophistry in the Gospel, but thou didst voluntarily put eternal life from thee, whatever thy lying lips uttered to the contrary: "My people would have none of Me." So that, when the jury shall sit on thy murdered soul, to inquire how thou camest to thy miserable end, thou wilt be found guilty of thy own damnation. No one loseth God, but he that is willing to part with Him. WILLIAM GURNALL

Vs. 12. *So I gave them up unto their own hearts' lust, and they walked in their own counsels.* No punishment is more just or more severe than this. If men will not be checked, but madly take the bit between their teeth and refuse obedience, who shall wonder if the reins are thrown upon their necks and they are let alone to work out their own destruction. It were better to be given up to lions than to our hearts' lusts.

Men, deserted of restraining grace, sin with deliberation; they consult, and debate, and consider, and then elect evil rather than good, with malice aforethought and in cool blood. It is remarkable obduracy of rebellion when men not only run into sin through passion but calmly "walk in their own counsels" of iniquity. C. H. S.

A man may be given up to Satan for the destruction of the flesh that the soul may be saved, but to be given up to sin is a thousand times worse, because that is the fruit of divine anger in order to the damnation of the soul; here God wounds like an enemy and like a cruel one, and we may boldly say, God never punished any man or woman with this spiritual judgment in kindness and love. JOHN SHOWER, *in "The Day of Grace"*

Let it be your great and constant care and endeavor to get the Spirit's leading continued to you. You have it; pray keep it. Can it be well with a Christian when this is suspended or withdrawn from him? How does he wander and bewilder himself when the Spirit does not guide him! How backward is he to good, when the Spirit does not bend and incline him thereunto! How unable to go, when the Spirit does not uphold him! What vile lusts and passions rule him when the Spirit does not put forth His holy and gracious government over him!

Oh, it is of infinite concern to all that belong to God to preserve and secure to themselves the Spirit's leading! Take a good man without this, and he is like a ship without a pilot, a blind man without a guide, a poor child that has none to sustain it, the rude multitude that have none to keep them in any order. What a sad difference is there in the same person as to what he is when the Spirit leads him and as to what he is when the Spirit leaves him! THOMAS JACOMBE, *in "Morning Exercises"*

Such and no better is the issue when God gives a people up to their own counsels; then they soon become a very chaos and run themselves into a ruinous heap. As good have no counsel from man as none but man's. JOSEPH CARYL

God's leaving one soul to one lust is far worse than leaving him to all the lions in the world. Alas, it will tear the soul worse than a lion can do the body, and rend it in pieces when there is none to deliver it. God's giving them up to their own wills, that they walked in their own counsels, is in effect a giving them up to eternal wrath and woe. George Swinnock

Our first corruption was our own act, not God's work; we owe our creation to God, our corruption to ourselves. Now, since God will govern His creature, I do not see how it can be otherwise than according to the present nature of the creature, unless God be pleased to alter that nature. God forces no man against his nature; He doth not force the will in conversion, but graciously and powerfully inclines it. He doth never force nor incline the will to sin but leaves it to the corrupt habits it hath settled in itself.

As when a clock or watch hath some fault in any of the wheels, the man that winds it up, or putting his hand upon the wheels moves them, he is the cause of the motion, but it is the flaw in it, a deficiency of something, is the cause of its erroneous motion; that error was not from the person that made it, or the person that winds it up and sets it going, but from some other cause; yet till it be mended it will not go otherwise, so long as it is set upon motion.

Our motion is from God (Acts 17:28). "In Him we move"—but not the disorder of that motion. It is the fullness of a man's stomach at sea is the cause of his sickness and not the pilot's government of the ship.

God doth not infuse the lust or excite it, though He doth present the object about which the lust is exercised. God delivered up Christ to the Jews, He presented Him to them, but never commanded them to crucify Him, nor infused that malice into them, nor quickened it; but He, seeing such a frame, withdrew His restraining grace, and left them to the conduct of their own vitiated wills. All the corruption in the world ariseth from lust in us, not from the object which God in His providence presents to us (II Pet. 1:4): "The corruption that is in the world through lust." Stephen Charnock

Vs. 13. *Walked in My ways.* None are found in the ways of God but those who have hearkened to His words. W. Wilson

Vs. 16. *Honey out of the rock.* The rock spiritually and mystically designs Christ, the Rock of salvation (I Cor. 10:4); the *"honey"* out of the rock, the fullness of grace in Him, and the blessings of it, the sure mercies of David, and the precious promises of the everlasting covenant; and the Gospel, which is sweeter than the honey or the honey-comb, and with these such are filled and satisfied who hearken to Christ and walk in His ways; for, as the whole of what is here said shows what Israel lost by disobedience, it clearly suggests what such enjoy who hear and obey. John Gill

# PSALM 82

Title and Subject: "A Psalm of Asaph." This poet of the Temple here acts as a preacher to the court and to the magistracy. Men who do one thing well are generally equal to another; he who writes good verse is not unlikely to be able to preach. What preaching it would have been had Milton entered the pulpit, or had Virgil been an apostle! C. H. S.

Vs. 3. *Defend the poor and fatherless: do justice to the afflicted and needy.* It is said of Francis the First, of France, that when a woman kneeled to him to beg justice, he bade her stand up; for, said he, "Woman, it is justice that I owe thee, and justice thou shalt have; if thou beg anything of me, let it be mercy." WILLIAM PRICE

Vs. 4. *Deliver the poor and needy: rid them out of the hand of the wicked.* It is a brave thing when a judge can liberate a victim like a fly from the spider's web, and a horrible case when magistrate and plunderer are in league. Law has too often been an instrument for vengeance in the hand of unscrupulous men, an instrument as deadly as poison or the dagger. It is for the judge to prevent such villainy. C. H. S.

Vs. 5. *They know not, neither will they understand,* etc. Every judge must have in him (as Baldus actually said) two kinds of salt; the first is sal scientiae, that he may know his duty; the second is sal conscientiae, that he may do his duty. JOHN BOYS, *in "The Judge's Charge"*

Vs. 6. *I have said, Ye are gods; and all of you are children of the most High.* No one needs to be told that this old doctrine of the divine right of rulers has been woefully abused. Sycophantic divines have often made of it a flattering unction for the ears of princes; teaching them that they owed no obedience to the laws; that they were responsible to none but God for their administration; that any attempt on the part of the people to curb their tyranny or to depose them from their seats when milder measures failed was rebellion against God, Whose vicegerents they were.

Even now, the same doctrine occasionally makes itself heard from the pulpit and the press; and thus men attempt to subject the consciences of the people to the caprice of tyrants. Let it be carefully observed that the harp of Asaph lends no sanction to this "right divine of kings to govern wrong."

But while care ought to be taken to guard the divine right of civil government from abuse, the right itself is not to be forgotten. The state is an ordinance of God, having, like the family, its foundation in the very constitution of human nature. WILLIAM BINNIE

Vs. 7. *"But ye shall die like men.* What sarcasm it seems! Great as the office made the men, they were still but men, and must die. To every judge this verse is a memento mori! He must leave the bench to stand at the bar and on the way must put off the ermine to put on the shroud.

*And fall like one of the princes.* How quickly death unrobes the great. What a leveler he is. He is no advocate for liberty, but in promoting equality and fraternity, he is a masterly democrat. Great men die as common men do. As their blood is the same, so the stroke which lets out their life produces the same pains and throes. No places are too high for death's arrows: he brings down his birds from the tallest trees. It is time that all men considered this. C. H. S.

The prince in his lofty palace, the beggar in his lowly cottage, have double difference, local and ceremonial height and lowness; yet meet at the grave and are mingled in ashes. We walk in this world as a man in a field of snow; all the way appears smooth, yet cannot we be sure of any step.

All are like actors on a stage; some have one part and some another. Death is still busy amongst us; here drops one of the players. We bury him with sorrow, and to our scene again: then falls another, yea, all, one after another, till death be left upon the stage. Death is that damp which puts out all the dim lights of vanity. Yet man is easier to believe that all the world shall die, than to suspect himself. THOMAS ADAMS

The meditation of death would pull down the plumes of pride; thou art but dust animated; shall dust and ashes be proud? Thou hast a grassy body, and shall shortly be mowed down: "I have said, ye are gods"; but lest they should grow proud, he adds a corrective: "ye shall die like men"; ye are dying gods. THOMAS WATSON

# PSALM 83

Title: "A Psalm, or Song of Asaph." This is the last occasion upon which we shall meet with this eloquent writer. Asaph the seer is well aware of the serious dangers arising from the powerful confederate nations, but his soul in faith stays itself upon Jehovah, while as a poet-preacher he excites his countrymen to prayer by means of this sacred lyric. C. H. S.

Vs. 1. *Keep not Thou silence, O God: hold not Thy peace, and be not still, O God.* In Scripture there are three reasons why the Lord keeps silence when His people are in danger and sits still when there is most need to give help and assistance. One is, the Lord doth it to try their faith, as we clearly see (Matt. 8:24) where it is said that our Lord Jesus Christ was asleep. Truly, the Lord will not suffer to be overwhelmed, that is certain, but He will suffer them to come very near, that the waves cover them, and fear and horror shall cover their souls, and all to try their faith.

2. I find another reason in Isaiah 59, and that is, the Lord doth keep silence in the midst of the troubles of His people, to try men's uprightness, and discover who will stick to God, and His cause, and His people, out of uprightness of heart. For if God should always appear for His cause, God and His cause should have many favorites and friends; but sometimes God leaves His cause, and leaves His people, and leaves His gospel, and His ordinances to the wide world, to see who will plead for it and stick to it.

3. There is a third reason: God, as it were, keeps silence in the midst of the greatest troubles, that He may, as it were, gather the wicked into one fagot, into one bundle, that they may be destroyed together. GUALTER (WALTER) CRADOCK, *in "Divine Drops"*

Is the Lord silent? Then be not thou silent; but cry unto Him till He breaks the silence. STARKE, in *Lange's Bibelwerk*

Vs. 2. *Thine enemies make a tumult.* The adversaries of the church are usually a noisy and a boastful crew. Their pride is a brass which always sounds, a cymbal which is ever tinkling. C. H. S.

Vs. 3. *They have taken crafty counsel against Thy people, and consulted against Thy hidden ones.* The less the world knows thee, the better for thee; thou mayst be satisfied with this one thing—God knows them that are His: not lost, although hidden is the symbol of a Christian. FRISCH, *in Lange's Bibelwerk*

Vs. 4. *They have said, Come, and let us cut them off from being a nation.* Easier said than done. Yet it shows how thorough-going are the foes of the church. Theirs was the policy of extermination. They laid the axe at the root of the matter. Rome has always loved this method of warfare, and hence she has gloated over the massacre of Bartholomew and the murders of the Inquisition. C. H. S.

Vs. 5. *They have consulted together with one consent.* Do the enemies of the church act with one consent to destroy it? Are the kings of the earth of one mind to give their power and honor to the beast? And shall not the church's friends be unanimous in serving her interests? If Herod and Pilate are made friends that they may join in crucifying Christ, sure Paul and Barnabas, Paul and Peter, will soon be made friends, that they may join in preaching Christ. MATTHEW HENRY

Though there may fall out a private grudge betwixt such as are wicked, yet they will all agree and unite against the saints: if two greyhounds are snarling at a bone, yet put up a hare between them, and they will leave the bone and follow after the hare; so, if wicked men have private differences amongst themselves, yet if the godly be near them, they will leave snarling at one another—and will pursue after the godly. THOMAS WATSON

Vs. 6. *Of Moab.* Born of incest, but yet a near kinsman, the feud of Moab against Israel was very bitter. Little could righteous Lot have dreamed that his unhallowed seed would be such unrelenting enemies of his uncle Abraham's posterity.

Vs. 8. *Assur also is joined with them.* Herod and Pilate are friends, if Jesus is to be crucified. Romanism and Ritualism make common cause against the gospel.

*Selah.* There was good reason for a pause when the nation was in such jeopardy: and yet it needs faith to make a pause, for unbelief is always in a hurry.

Vs. 9. *As to Sisera, as to Jabin, at the brook of Kison.* When God wills it, a brook can be as deadly as a sea. Kison was as terrible to Jabin as was the Red Sea to Pharaoh. How easily can the Lord smite the enemies of His people! God of Gideon and of Barak, wilt Thou not again avenge Thine heritage of their bloodthirsty foes? C. H. S.

Vs. 10. *They became as dung for the earth.* In the year 1830, it is estimated that more than a million bushels of "human and inhuman bones" were imported from the continent of Europe into the port of Hull.

The neighborhood of Leipsic, Austerlitz, Waterloo, etc., where the principal battles were fought some fifteen or twenty years before, were swept alike of the bones of the hero and the horse which he rode.

Thus collected from every quarter, they were shipped to Hull, and thence forwarded to the Yorkshire bone-grinders, who, by steam-engines and powerful machinery, reduced them to a granulary state.

In this condition they were sent chiefly to Doncaster, one of the largest agricultural markets of the country, and were there sold to the farmers to manure their lands. The oily substance gradually evolving as the bone calcines, makes better manure than almost any other substance—particularly human bones. K. ARVINE

Vs. 11. *Make their nobles like Oreb, and like Zeeb: yea, all their princes as Zebah, and as Zalmunna.* The Psalmist, seeing these four culprits hanging in history upon a lofty gallows, earnestly asks that others of a like character may, for truth and righteousness' sake, share their fate. C. H. S.

Vs. 14. *As the fire burneth a wood, and as the flame setteth the mountains on fire.* Let us pray the divine aid to break the power and enmity of the natural man; that it may yield unto the Word of grace; and let the wood, hay, and stubble of all false doctrine perish before the brightness of the face of God. EDWARD WALTER

Vs. 17. *Let them be confounded and troubled forever; yea, let them be put to shame, and perish.* What a terrible doom it will be to the enemies of God to be "confounded, and troubled forever"—to see all their schemes and hopes defeated, and their bodies and souls full of anguish without end: from such a shameful perishing, may our souls be delivered. C. H. S.

Vs. 18. *That men may know that Thou, Whose name alone is JEHOVAH,* etc. Early English History informs us that some bloodthirsty persecutors were marching on a band of Christians. The Christians, seeing them approaching, marched out towards them, and at the top of their voices shouted, "Hallelujah, hallelujah!" (Praise Jehovah). The name of the Lord being presented, the rage of the persecutors abated.

Josephus says that the Great Alexander, when on his triumphal march, being met near Jerusalem by the Jewish high priest, on whose mitre was engraved the name of Jehovah, "approached by himself and adored that name" and was disarmed of his hostile intent.

There was significance and power in the glorious old name as written by the Jews. But the name of Jesus is now far more mighty in the world than was the name Jehovah in these earlier ages. *The Dictionary of Illustrations*

## PSALM 84

It matters little when this Psalm was written, or by whom; for our part it exhales to us a Davidic perfume; it smells of the mountain heather and the lone places of the wilderness, where King David must have often lodged during his many wars. This sacred ode is one of the choicest of the collection; it has a mild radiance about it, entitling it to be called "The Pearl of Psalms."

If the twenty-third be the most popular, the One Hundred And Third the most joyful, the One Hundred And Nineteenth the most deeply experimental, the Fifty-First the most plaintive, this is one of the most sweet of the Psalms of Peace. C. H. S.

Vs. 1. *How amiable are Thy tabernacles.* Here the gospel trumpet is blown, and its joyful sound echoed forth, and songs of love and grace are sung by all believers; besides, what makes these tabernacles still more lovely are, the presence of God here, so that they are no other than the house of God, the gate of heaven; the provisions that are here made, and the company that is here enjoyed. JOHN GILL

Vs. 2. *My heart and my flesh crieth out for the living God.* The Psalmist declared that he could not remain silent in his desires, but began to cry out for God and His house; he wept, he sighed, he pleaded for the privilege. Some need to be whipped to church, while here is David crying for it. He needed no clatter of bells from the belfry to ring him in; he carried his bell in his own bosom: holy appetite is a better call to worship than a full chime. C. H. S.

*Crieth.* The word that is here rendered "crieth" is from "Ramag" that signifies to shout, shrill, or cry out, as soldiers do at the beginning of a battle when they cry out, "Fall on, fall on, fall on," or when they cry out after a victory, "Victory, victory, victory!" The Hebrew word notes a strong cry, or to cry as a child cries when it is sadly hungry, for now every whit of the child cries, hands cry, and face cries, and feet cry. THOMAS BROOKS

Vs. 3. *The sparrow hath found an house,* etc. The tender care of God over the least of His creatures is here most touchingly alluded to.

They enjoyed the rich provisions of His tender care; He thought of everything for their need, but there was no fellowship between them and the great Giver. From this, O my soul, thou mayest learn a useful lesson. Never rest satisfied with merely frequenting such places or with having certain privileges there; but rise in spirit and seek and find and enjoy direct communion with the living God through Jesus Christ our Lord. The heart of David turns to God Himself. "My heart and my flesh crieth out for the living God." *Things New and Old.*

Vs. 4. *They will be still praising Thee.* Communion is the mother of adoration. They fail to praise the Lord who wander far from Him, but those who dwell in Him are always magnifying Him. C. H. S.

As having hearts full of heaven, and consciences full of comfort. There cannot but be music in the temple of the Holy Ghost. JOHN TRAPP

Vs. 5. *Blessed is the man whose strength is in Thee.* Neither prayer nor praise, nor the hearing of the Word will be pleasant or profitable to persons who have left their hearts behind them. A company of pilgrims who had left their hearts at home would be no better than a caravan of carcasses, quite unfit to blend with living saints in adoring the living God. C. H. S.

*In whose heart are the ways.* The natural heart is a pathless wilderness full of cliffs and precipices. When the heart is renewed by grace, a road is made, a highway is prepared for our God. (See Isa. 40:3-4). FREDERICK FYSH

Vs. 6. *Make it a well.* That which seemed an impediment turns to a furtherance; at least, no misery can be so great, no estate so barren, but a godly heart can make it a well, out of which to draw forth water of comfort; either water to cleanse, and make it a way to repentance; or water to cool, and make it a way to patience; or water to moisten, and make it a way of growing in grace; and if the well happen to be dry, and afford no water from below, yet the rain shall fill their pools, and supply them with water from above. SIR RICHARD BAKER

Vs. 7. *Every one of them in Zion appeareth before God.* So shall it ever be with true spiritual pilgrims. The grace of God will always prove sufficient to preserve them, safe and blameless, to His heavenly kingdom and glory—troubles shall not overwhelm them—temptations not wholly overcome them—spiritual enemies shall not destroy them. They are kept by the power of God, through faith unto salvation, ready to be revealed in the last time. WILLIAM MAKELVIE

Vs. 10. *I had rather be a doorkeeper in the house of my God, than to dwell in the tents of wickedness.* Every man has his choice, and this is ours. God's worst is better than the devil's best. God's doorstep is a happier rest than downy couches within the pavilions of royal sinners, though we might lie there for a lifetime of luxury. C. H. S.

Another sign of God's children is, to delight to be much in God's presence. Children are to be in the presence of their father; where the King is, there is the court; where the presence of God is, there is heaven. God is in a special manner present in His ordinances; they are the Ark of His presence. THOMAS WATSON

Vs. 11. *For the Lord God is a sun and shield.* As a sun, God shows me myself; as a shield, God shows me Himself. The sun discloses mine own nothingness; the shield, divine sufficiency. The one enables me to discern that I deserve nothing but wrath and can earn nothing but shame; the other, that I have a title to immortality and may lay claim to an enduring inheritance in heaven.

I learn, in short, from God as "a Sun," that if I have "wages," I must have eternal death; but from God as "a Shield," that if I will receive the "free gift" I may have "eternal life." Whom then shall I fear? Myself—confessedly my worst enemy? "The Sun" makes a man start from himself; the "Shield" assures him that he shall be protected against himself and builded up "for a habitation of God through the Spirit." HENRY MELVILL

Hear, O my soul, *the Lord is a shield.* Light and strength are conjoined; none can miscarry under His conduct, nor have any reason to be discouraged. With this He comforteth Abraham. Gen. 15:1: "Fear not: I am Thy shield." DANIEL WILCOX

Why need a saint fear darkness when he has such a Sun to guide him? Or dread dangers when he has such a Shield to guard him? WILLIAM SECKER

# PSALM 85

Subject and Occasion: It is the prayer of a patriot for his afflicted country, in which he pleads the Lord's former mercies and by faith forsees brighter days. We believe that David wrote it, but many question that assertion. Certain interpreters appear to grudge the Psalmist David the authorship of any of the Psalms and refer the sacred songs by wholesale to the times of Hezekiah, Josiah, the Captivity, and the Maccabees. It is remarkable that, as a rule, the more skeptical a writer is, the more resolute is he to have done with David; while the purely evangelic annotators are for the most part content to leave the royal poet in the chair of authorship.

Vs. 2. *Thou hast forgiven the iniquity of Thy people.* Often and often had He done this, pausing to pardon even when His sword was bared to punish. Who is a pardoning God like Thee, O Jehovah? Who is so slow to anger, so ready to forgive? Every believer in Jesus enjoys the blessing of pardoned sin, and he should regard this priceless boon as the pledge of all other needed mercies. C. H. S.

Thou hast borne, or carried away, the iniquity. An allusion to the ceremony of the scape-goat. ADAM CLARKE

*Thou hast covered all their sin.* When God is said to cover sin, He does so, not as one would cover a sore with a plaster, thereby merely hiding it only; but He covers it with a plaster that effectually cures and removes it altogether. BELLARMINE

Vs. 4. *Turn us, O God of our salvation.* Conversion is the dawn of salvation. To turn a heart to God is as difficult as to make the world revolve upon its axis.

Vs. 5. *Wilt Thou be angry with us forever?* That our enemies should be always wroth is natural, but wilt Thou, our God, be always incensed against us? Every word is an argument. Men in distress never waste words.

Vs. 6. *That Thy people may rejoice in Thee.* A genuine revival without joy in the Lord is as impossible as spring without flowers or day-dawn without light. If, either in our own souls or in the hearts of others, we see declension, it becomes us to be much in the use of this prayer, and if on the other hand we are enjoying visitations of the Spirit and bedewings of grace, let us abound in holy joy and make it our constant delight to joy in God. C. H. S.

Bernard, in his Fifteenth Sermon on Canticles, says, "Jesus is honey in the mouth, melody in the ear, joy in the heart. Is any among us sad? Let Jesus enter the heart, and thence spring to the countenance, and behold, before the rising brightness of His name, every cloud is scattered, serenity returns."

Origen in his Tenth Homiletic on Genesis, has the remark, Abraham rejoiced not in present things, neither in the riches of the words, nor deeds of time. But do you wish to hear whence he drew his joy? Listen to the Lord speaking to the Jews (John 8:56): "Your father, Abraham rejoiced to see my day: and he saw it, and was glad"; hope heaped up his joys. LE BLANC

Truly sin kills. Men are dead in trespasses and sins, dead in law, dead in their affections, dead in a loss of comfortable communion with God. Probably the greatest practical heresy of each age is a low idea of our undone condition under the guilt and dominion of sin. While this prevails, we shall be slow to cry for reviving or quickening. What sinners and churches need is quickening by the Holy Ghost. WILLIAM S. PLUMER

Vs. 8. *I will hear.* The eye as a mere organ of sense must give place to the ear. Therefore it is wittily observed that our Savior, commanding the abscession of the offending hand, foot, and eye (Mark 9:43-47), yet never spake of the ear.

If thy hand, thy foot, or thine eye, cause thee to offend, deprive thyself of them; but part not with thine ear, for that is an organ to derive unto thy soul's salvation.

As Christ says there, a man may enter into heaven lamed in his feet, as Mephibosheth, blind in his sight, as Barzillai, maimed in his hand, as the dry-handed man in the gospel; but if there be not an ear to hear of the way, there will be no foot to enter into heaven.

Bernard hath this description of a good ear: Which willingly hears what is taught, wisely understands what it heareth, and obediently practices what it understandeth. O give me such an ear, and I will hang on it jewels of gold, ornaments of praise. THOMAS ADAMS

*But let them not turn again to folly.* Backsliders should study this verse with the utmost care; it will console them and yet warn them, draw them back to their allegiance, and at the same time inspire them with a wholesome fear of going further astray, To turn again to folly is worse than being foolish for once; it argues wilfulness and obstinacy, and it involves the soul in sevenfold sin. There is no fool like the man who will be a fool, cost him what it may.

Vs. 9. *Surely His salvation is nigh them that fear Him.* If to seeking sinners salvation is nigh, it is assuredly very nigh to those who have once enjoyed it and have lost its present enjoyment by their folly; they have but to turn unto the Lord, and they shall enjoy it again. C. H. S.

Vs. 10. *Mercy and truth are met together; righteousness and peace have kissed each other.* God is as true as if He had fulfilled every letter of His threatenings, as righteous as if He had never spoken peace to a sinner's conscience; His love in undiminished splendor shines forth, but no other of His ever-blessed characteristics is eclipsed thereby.

It is the custom of modern thinkers (?) to make sport of this representation of the result of our Lord's substitutionary atonement; but had they ever been themselves made to feel the weight of sin upon a spiritually awakened conscience, they would cease from their vain ridicule.

Their doctrine of atonement has well been described by Dr. Duncan as the admission "that the Lord Jesus Christ did something or other, which somehow or other, was in some way or other connected with man's salvation." This is their substitute for substitution. Our facts are infinitely superior to their dreams, and yet they sneer. It is but natural that natural men should do so. We cannot expect animals to set much store by the discoveries of science, neither can we hope to see unspiritual men rightly estimate the solution of spiritual problems—they are far above and out of their sight. Meanwhile it remains for those who rejoice in the great reconciliation to continue both to wonder and adore. C. H. S.

These four divine attributes parted at the fall of Adam and met again at the birth of Christ. GEORGE HORNE

It was good for Joseph that he was a captive; good for Naaman that he was a leper; good for Bartimæus that he was blind, and for David that he was in trouble. Bradford thanked God more for his prison than for any parlour or pleasure. All things are for the best unto the faithful, and so God's *mercy and truth are met together; righteousness and peace have kissed each other.* JOHN BOYS

Vs. 11. *And righteousness shall look down from heaven,* as if it threw up the windows and leaned out to gaze upon a penitent people, whom it could not have looked upon before without an indignation which would have been fatal to them.

This is a delicious scene. Earth yielding flowers of truth, and heaven shining with stars of holiness; the spheres echoing to each other, or being mirrors of each other's beauties. "Earth carpeted with truth and canopied with righteousness" shall be a nether heaven. When God looks down in grace, man sends his heart upward in obedience. C. H. S.

Vs. 12. It has sometimes been objected that the Christian doctrine of a millennium cannot be true, for the earth could not support the teeming millions that would naturally be found upon it, if wars and vices should cease to waste its population.

But omitting other and pertinent answers that have been given, we find one here that covers the whole ground, *the earth shall yield her increase.* Now and then the season is unusually propitious, and we have a specimen of what God can do when He chooses. He can without any miracle make it many times more fruitful than it has ever been. WILLIAM S. PLUMER

Vs. 13. *Shall set us in the way of His steps.* It is reported in the Bohemian history that St. Wenceslaus, their king, one winter night going to his devotions, in a remote church, barefooted in the snow and sharpness of unequal and pointed ice, his servant Podavivus, who waited upon his master's piety, and endeavored to imitate his affections, began to faint through the violence of the snow and cold; till the king commanded him to follow him, and see his feet in the same footsteps, which his feet should mark for him: the servant did so, and either fancied a cure, or found one; for he followed his prince, helped forward with shame and zeal to his imitation, and by the forming of footsteps for him in the snow.

In the same manner does the blessed Jesus; for, since our way is troublesome, obscure, full of objection and danger, apt to be mistaken, and to affright our industry, He commands us to mark His footsteps, to tread where His feet have stood, and not only invites us forward by the argument of His example, but He hath trodden down much of the difficulty and made the way easier and fit for our feet.

For He knows our infirmities, and Himself hath felt their experience in all things but in the neighborhoods of sin; and therefore He hath proportioned a way and a path to our strength and capacities, and, like Jacob, hath marched softly and in evenness with the children and the cattle to entertain us by the comforts of His company and the influence of a perpetual guide. JEREMY TAYLOR

# PSALM 86

Title: "A Prayer of David." We have here one of the five Psalms entitled Tephillahs, or prayers. This Psalm consists of praise as well as prayer, but it is in all parts so directly addressed to God that it is most fitly called "a prayer." A prayer is none the less but all the more a prayer because veins of praise run through it. This Psalm would seem to have been specially known as David's prayer; even as the Nineteenth is "the prayer of Moses."

The name of God occurs very frequently in this Psalm. Sometimes it is Jehovah, but more commonly Adonai, which it is believed by many learned scholars was written by the Jewish transcribers instead of the sublimer title, because their superstitious dread led them to do so: we, laboring under no such tormenting fear, rejoice in Jehovah, our God. It is singular that those who were so afraid of their God, that they dared not write His name, had yet so little godly fear, that they dared to alter His Word. C. H. S.

Christ prays throughout the whole of this Psalm. All the words are spoken exclusively by Christ, Who is both God and man. *Psalt. Cassiodori*

In this Psalm, Christ, the Son of God and Son of Man, one God with the Father, one man with men, to Whom we pray as God, prays in the form of a servant. For He prays for us, and He prays in us, and He is prayed to by us. He prays for us as our Priest. He prays in us as our Head. He is prayed to by us as our God. *Psalt. Pet. Lombard*

Vs. 1. *Bow down Thine ear, O Lord, hear me.* In condescension to my littleness, and in pity to my weakness, "bow down Thine ear, O Lord." When our prayers are lowly by reason of our humility, or feeble by reason of our sickness, or without wing by reason of our despondency, the Lord will bow down to them, the infinitely exalted Jehovah will have respect unto them.

*For I am poor and needy.* Of all the despicable sinners, those are the worst who use the language of spiritual poverty while they think themselves to be rich and increased with goods.

Vs. 2. *For I am holy: O Thou my God, save Thy servant that trusteth in Thee.* Lest any man should suppose that David trusted in his own holiness he immediately declared his trust in the Lord, and begged to be saved as one who was not holy in the sense of being perfect, but was even yet in need of the very elements of salvation. C. H. S.

They that are holy, yet must not trust in themselves, or in their own righteousness, but only in God and His grace. MATTHEW HENRY

Vs. 4. *Unto Thee, O Lord, do I lift up my soul.* As the heliotrope looks to the sun for its smile, so turn I my heart to Thee. Thou art as the brazen serpent to my sick nature, and I lift up my soul's eye to Thee, that I may live. I know that the nearer I am to Thee the greater is my joy; therefore be pleased to draw me nearer while I am laboring to draw near.

It is not easy to lift up a soul at all; it needs a strong shoulder at the wheel when a heart sticks in the miry clay of despondency: it is less easy to lift a soul up to the Lord, for the height is great as well as the weight oppressive; but the Lord will take the will for the deed and come in with a hand of Almighty grace to raise His poor servant out of the earth and up to heaven. C. H. S.

If thou hadst corn in thy rooms below, thou wouldest take it up higher lest it should grow rotten. Wouldest thou remove thy corn, and dost thou suffer thy heart to rot on the earth? Thou wouldest take thy corn up higher: lift up thy heart to heaven.

"And how can I," dost thou say? What ropes are needed? What machines? What ladders? Thy affections are the steps; thy will the way. By loving, thou mountest; by neglect, thou descendest.

Standing on the earth, thou art in heaven, if thou lovest God. For the heart is not so raised as the body is raised: the body to be lifted up changes its place: the heart to be lifted up changes its will. AUGUSTINE

Vs. 6. *Attend to the voice of my supplications.* Here are repetitions, but not vain repetitions. When a child cries, it repeats the same note, but it is equally in earnest every time, and so was it with the suppliant here. C. H. S.

Vs. 7. *In the day of my trouble I will call upon Thee: for Thou wilt answer me.* There can be no reason for praying if there be no expectation of the Lord's answering. Who would make a conscience of pleading with the winds or find a solace in supplicating the waves? The mercy seat is a mockery if there be no hearing nor answering. David, as the following verses show, believed the Lord to be a living and potent God, and indeed to be "God alone," and it was on that account that he resolved in every hour of trouble to call upon Him. C. H. S.

Vs. 8. *Neither are there any works like unto Thy works.* What have the false gods ever made or unmade? What miracles have they wrought? When did they divide a sea or march through a wilderness scattering bread from the skies? O Jehovah, in Thy person and in Thy works, Thou art as far above all gods as the heavens are above the nethermost abyss. C. H. S.

Vs. 10. *Thou art God alone.* Alone wast Thou God before Thy creatures were; alone in Godhead still art Thou now that Thou hast given life to throngs of beings; alone forever shalt Thou be, for none can ever rival Thee. True religion makes no compromises; it does not admit Baal or Dagon to be a god; it is exclusive and monopolizing, claiming for Jehovah nothing less than all.

The vaunted liberality of certain professors of modern thought is not to be cultivated by believers in the truth. "Philosophic breadth" aims at building a Pantheon and piles a Pandemonium; it is not for us to be helpers in such an evil work. C. H. S.

Vs. 11. *Teach me.* It is the fashion in the present day to talk of man's enlightenment and to represent human nature as upheaving under its load, as straining towards a knowledge of truth; such is not in reality the case, and whenever there is an effort in the mind untaught of the Spirit, it is directed towards God as the great moral and not as the great spiritual Being. A man untaught of the Holy Ghost may long to know a moral, he can never desire to know a spiritual Being. JOHN HYATT

*I will walk in Thy truth.* Conform to Scripture. Let us lead Scripture lives. Oh, that the Bible might be seen to be printed in our lives! Do what the Word commands. Obedience is an excellent way of commenting upon the Bible.

Let the Word be the sun-dial by which you set your life. What are we the better for having the Scriptures, if we do not direct all our speeches and actions according to it?

What is a carpenter better for his rule about him, if he sticks it at his back and never makes use of it for measuring and squaring? So, what are we the better for the rule of the Word, if we do not make use of it, and regulate our lives by it? THOMAS WATSON

Vs. 12. *I will praise Thee, O Lord my God, with all my heart.* When my heart is one, I will give Thee all of it. Praise should never be rendered with less than all our heart, and soul, and strength, or it will be both unreal and unacceptable. C. H. S.

Vs. 13. *And Thou hast delivered my soul from the lowest hell.* There are some alive now who can use this language unfeignedly, and he who pens these lines most humbly confesses that he is one. Left to myself to indulge my passions, to rush onward with my natural vehemence, and defy the Lord with recklessness of levity, what a candidate for the lowest abyss should I have made myself by this time.

For me, there was but one alternative, great mercy or the lowest hell. With my whole heart do I sing, "Great is Thy mercy towards me, and Thou hast delivered my soul from the lowest hell." C. H. S.

Vs. 16. *O turn unto me, and have mercy upon me.* Let the justiciaries deduce arguments from their own present merits, my soul from God's former mercies. Thou, O Lord, madest me good, restoredst me when I was evil; therefore have mercy upon me, miserable sinner, and give me Thy salvation.

Thus Paul grounded his assurance; because the Lord had stood with him, and delivered him out of the lion's mouth; therefore the Lord shall deliver me still, from every evil work, and preserve me unto His heavenly kingdom (II Tim. 4:17-18). THOMAS ADAMS

# PSALM 87

Subject and Division: The song is in honor of Zion, or Jerusalem, and it treats of God's favor to that city among the mountains, the prophecies which made it illustrious, and the honor of being a native of it. Many conceive that it was written at the founding of David's city of Zion, but does not the mention of Babylon imply a later date? It would seem to have been written after Jerusalem and the Temple had been built and had enjoyed a history of which glorious things could be spoken.

Vs. 1. *His foundation is in the holy mountains.* Sudden passion is evil, but bursts of holy joy are most precious.

Not on the sand of carnal policy, nor in the morass of human kingdoms, has the Lord founded His church, but on His own power and godhead, which are pledged for the establishment of His beloved church, which is to Him the chief of all His works. Rome stands on her seven hills and has never lacked a poet's tongue to sing her glories, but more glorious far art Thou, O Zion, among the eternal mountains of God: while pen can write or mouth can speak, Thy praises shall never lie buried in inglorious silence. C. H. S.

The sure decree, the divine perfections, the promise of Him that cannot lie, the oath and covenant of God, and the incarnate Son Himself, are the holy mountains, the perpetual hills, whose summits are gloriously crowned by the city of the Great King. There the city sits securely, beautiful for situation, the joy of the whole earth. ANDREW GRAY

Vs. 2. *The Lord loveth the gates of Zion more than all the dwellings of Jacob.* Some absent themselves from public worship under pretense that they can serve the Lord at home as well as in private. How many are apt to say they see not but their time may be as well spent at home, in praying, reading some good book, or discoursing on some profitable subject, as in the use of ordinances in public assemblies! DAVID CLARKSON

Vs. 7. *All my springs are in Thee.* The springs of my faith and all my graces; the springs of my life and all my pleasures; the springs of my activity and all its right doings; the springs of my hope, and all its heavenly anticipations, all lie in Thee, my Lord.

Without Thy Spirit I should be as a dry well, a mocking cistern, destitute of power to bless myself or others. O Lord, I am assured that I belong to the regenerate whose life is in Thee, for I feel that I cannot live without Thee; therefore, with all Thy joyful people will I sing Thy praises. C. H. S.

## PSALM 88

Title: "A Song or Psalm for the sons of Korah." This sad complaint reads very little like a Song, nor can we conceive how it could be called by a name which denotes a song of praise or triumph; yet perhaps it was intentionally so called to show how faith "glories in tribulations also." Assuredly, if ever there was a song of sorrow and a Psalm of sadness, this is one. C. H. S.

In verses 10-12, we have the sustaining hope of resurrection. Yes, God's wonders shall be known at the grave's mouth. God's righteousness in giving what satisfied justice in behalf of Messiah's members, has been manifested gloriously, so that resurrection must follow, and the land of forgetfulness must give up its dead.

O morning of surpassing bliss, hasten on! Messiah has risen; when shall all that are His arise? Till that day dawn, they must take up their Head's plaintive expostulations and remind their God in Heman's strains of what He has yet to accomplish. "Wilt Thou show wonders to the dead?" etc. ANDREW A. BONAR

Vs. 1. *O Lord God of my salvation.* While a man can see God as his Savior, it is not altogether midnight with him. While the living God can be spoken of as the life of our salvation, our hope will not quite expire. It is one of the characteristics of true faith that she turns to Jehovah, the saving God, when all other confidences have proved liars unto her. C. H. S.

*I have cried day and night before Thee.* Day and night are both suitable to prayer; it is no work of darkness, therefore let us go with Daniel and pray when men can see us; yet, since supplication needs no light, let us accompany Jacob and wrestle at Jabbok till the day breaketh. Evil is transformed to good when it drives us to prayer. C. H. S.

Vs. 3. *For my soul is full of troubles.* I am satiated and nauseated with them. Like a vessel full to the brim with vinegar, my heart is filled up with adversity till it can hold no more. He had his house full and his hands full of sorrow; but, worse than that, he had his heart full of it.

Trouble in the soul is the soul of trouble. A little soul trouble is painful; what must it be to be sated with it? And how much worse still to have your prayers return empty when your soul remains full of grief. C. H. S.

*And my life draweth nigh unto the grave.* Are good men ever permitted to suffer thus? Indeed they are; and some of them are even all their lifetime subject to bondage. O Lord, be pleased to set free Thy prisoners of hope! Let none of Thy mourners imagine that a strange thing has happened unto him, but rather rejoice as he sees the footprints of brethren who have trodden this desert before.

Vs. 4. *I am as a man that hath no strength.* I have but the name to live; my constitution is broken up; I can scarce crawl about my sickroom, my mind is even weaker than my body, and my faith weakest of all. The sons and daughters of sorrow will need but little explanation of these sentences; they are to such tried ones as household words. C. H. S.

Vs. 5. *Like the slain that lie in the grave, whom Thou rememberest no more.* He felt as if he were as utterly forgotten as those whose carcasses are left to rot on the battle-field. As when a soldier, mortally wounded, bleeds unheeded amid the heaps of slain, and remains to his last expiring groan unpitied and unsuccored, so did Heman sigh out his soul in loneliest sorrow, feeling as if even God Himself had quite forgotten him. How low the spirits of good and brave men will sometimes sink! Under the influence of certain disorders everything will wear a somber aspect, and the heart will dive into the profoundest deeps of misery.

It is all very well for those who are in robust health and full of spirits to blame those whose lives are sicklied o'er with the pale cast of melancholy, but the evil is as real as a gaping wound, and all the more hard to bear because it lies so much in the region of the soul that to the inexperienced it appears to be a mere matter of fancy and diseased imagination.

Reader, never ridicule the nervous and hypochondriacal, their pain is real; though much of the evil lies in the imagination, it is not imaginary. C. H. S.

*Cut off from Thy hand.* Beware how you ever look upon yourself as cut off from life and from enjoyment; you are not cut off, only taken apart, laid aside, it may be but for a season, or it may be for life; but still you are part of the body of which Christ is the Head.

Your feet may be set fast; they may have run with great activity, and you sorrow now, because they can run no more. But do not sorrow thus; do not envy those who are running; you have a work to do; it may be the work of the head, or of the eye, it surely is whatever work God gives to you. It may be the work of lying still, of not stirring hand or foot, of scarcely speaking, scarcely showing life.

Fear not: if He, your heavenly Master, has given it to you to do, it is His work, and He will bless it. Do not repine. Do not say, "This is work, and this is not"; how do you know?

What work, think you, was Daniel doing in the lion's den? or Shadrach, Meshach, and Abednego in the fiery furnace? Their work was glorious, "laudable, and honorable"; they were glorifying God in suffering. *From "Sickness, its Trials and Blessings" (Anon.)*

Vs. 6. *Thou hast laid me in the lowest pit, in darkness, in the deeps.* The flesh can bear only a certain number of wounds and no more, but the soul can bleed in ten thousand ways, and die over and over again each hour.

Vs. 7. *Thy wrath lieth hard upon me.* Dreadful plight this, the worst in which a man can be found. Wrath is heavy in itself; God's wrath is crushing beyond conception, and when that presses hard, the soul is oppressed indeed. The wrath of God is the very hell of hell, and when it weighs upon the conscience, a man feels a torment such as only that of damned spirits can exceed. C. H. S.

Vs. 8. *Thou hast put away mine acquaintance far from me.* There are times when an unspeakable sadness steals upon me, an immense loneliness takes possession of my soul, a longing perchance for some vanished hand and voice to comfort me as of old, a desolation without form and void, that wraps me in its folds and darkens my inmost being. It was not thus in the first days of my illness.

Even to those who love me most, my pain and helplessness is now an accustomed thing, while to me it keeps its keen edge of suffering, but little dulled by use. My ills to them are a tedious oft-told tale which comes with something of a dull reiterance.

It has become almost a matter of course that in the pleasant plan I should be left out, that in the pleasant walk, I should be left behind; a matter of course that the pleasures of life should pass me by with folded hand and averted face; and sickness, and monotonous days, and grey shadows should be my portion.

My God, my God, to whom can I turn for comfort but unto Thee, Thou Who didst drink the bitter cup of human loneliness to the dregs that Thou mightest make Thyself a brother to the lonely, a merciful and faithful High Priest to the desolate soul; Thou Who alone canst pass within, the doors being shut to all human aid, into that secret place of thunder, where the tempest-tossed soul suffers and struggles alone; Thou Who alone canst command the winds and tempests, and say unto the sea, "Be still!" and unto the wind, "Blow not!" and there shall be a great calm.

As a child alone in the dark cries out for Thee, cries for Thine embracing arms, for Thy voice of comfort, for Thy pierced heart on which to rest my aching head, and feel that Love is near. *From "Christ, the Consoler, A Book of Comfort for the Sick"* (Anon.)

*Thou hast made me an abomination unto them.* The mass of men who gather around a man and flatter him are like tame leopards; when they lick his hand, it is well for him to remember that with equal gusto they would drink his blood. C. H. S.

Vs. 11. *In the grave.* Here is a striking figure of what a living soul feels under the manifestations of the deep corruptions of his heart. All his good words, once so esteemed; and all his good works, once so prized; and all his prayers, and all his faith, and hope and love, and all the imaginations of his heart, are not merely paralyzed and dead, not merely reduced to a state of utter helplessness, but also in soul-feeling turned into rottenness and corruption.

When we feel this, we are spiritually brought where Heman was, when he said, "Shall Thy lovingkindness be declared in the grave?" What! wilt Thou manifest Thy love to a stinking corpse?

What! is Thy love to be shed abroad in a heart full of pollution and putrefaction? Is Thy lovingkindness to come forth from Thy glorious sanctuary, where Thou sittest enthroned in majesty, and holiness, and purity—is it to leave that eternal abode of ineffable light and glory and enter into the dark, polluted, and loathsome "grave"?

What! is Thy lovingkindness to come out of the sanctuary into the charnel-house? Shall it be "declared" there—revealed there—spoken there—manifested there—known there? For nothing else but the declaration of it there will do.

He does not say, "Shall Thy lovingkindness be declared in the Scriptures?" "Shall Thy lovingkindness be declared in Christ?" "Shall Thy lovingkindness be declared by the mouth of ministers?" "Shall Thy lovingkindness be declared in holy and pure hearts?"—but he says, "Shall Thy lovingkindness be declared," uttered, spoken, revealed, manifested, "in the grave?" where everything is contrary to it, where everything is unworthy of it—the last of all places fit for the lovingkindness of an all-pure God to enter. J. C. PHILPOT

Vs. 12. *Shall Thy wonders be known in the dark?* If not here permitted to prove their goodness of Jehovah, how could the singer do so in the land of darkness and death shade? Could his tongue, when turned into a clod, charm the dull, cold ear of death? Is not a living dog better than a dead lion and a living believer of more value to the cause of God on earth than all the departed put together? C. H. S.

Vs. 14. *Why hidest Thou Thy face from me?* Wilt Thou not so much as look upon me? Canst Thou not afford me a solitary smile? Why this severity to one who has in brighter days basked in the light of Thy favor?

We may put these questions to the Lord, nay, we ought to do so. It is not undue familiarity, but holy boldness. It may help us to remove the evil which provokes the Lord to jealousy, if we seriously beg Him to show us wherefore He contends with us.

He cannot act towards us in other than a right and gracious manner, therefore for every stroke of His rod there is a sufficient reason in the judgment of His loving heart; let us try to learn that reason and profit by it. C. H. S.

Vs. 15. *I am afflicted and ready to die from my youth up.* How much some suffer! I have seen a child, who at the age of twenty months had probably suffered more bodily pain than the whole congregation of a thousand souls, where its parents worshiped. WILLIAM S. PLUMER

Even in tender infancy, the sufferings of the Redeemer began, and he complains, *I am afflicted and ready to die from my youth up.* Perhaps these scorching beams beat upon his infant brow, and this sand-laden breeze dried up his infant lips, while the heat of the curse of God began to melt his heart within. Even in the desert, we see the surety-ship of Jesus. R. M. MCCHEYNE'S *"Narrative of a Mission of Inquiry to the Jews"*

*While I suffer Thy terrors I am distracted.* How near akin to madness soul-depression sometimes may be it is not our province to decide; but we speak what we do know when we say that a feather-weight might be sufficient to turn the scale at times. Thank God, O ye tempted ones who yet retain your reason! Thank Him that the devil himself cannot add that feather while the Lord stands by to adjust all things. C. H. S.

O Lord, the monotony of my changeless days oppresses me, the constant weariness of my body weighs me down. I am weary of gazing on the same dull objects: I am tired of going through the same dull round day after day; the very inanimate things about my room and the patterns on the walls, seem quickened with the waste of my life, and, through the power of association, my own thoughts and my own pain come back upon me from them with a dull reverberation.

"My heart is too tired to hope; I dare not look forward to the future; I expect nothing from the days to come, and yet my heart sinks at the thought of the grey waste of years before me; and I wonder how I shall endure, whether I shall faint by the way, before I reach my far-off home." *From "Christ, the Consoler"*

Vs. 18. *Lover and friend hast Thou put far from me.* Lonely sorrow falls to the lot of not a few; let them not repine, but enter herein into close communion with that dearest Lover and Friend Who is never far from His tried ones. C. H. S.

*And mine acquaintance into darkness.* To be discountenanced or coldly treated by Christian friends, is often a consequence of a believer's having forfeited his spiritual comfort. When the Lord is angry with His rebellious child, and is chastening him, He not only giveth Satan leave to trouble him, but permitteth some of the saints who are acquainted with him, to discountenance him, and by their cold treatment of him, to add to his grief.

When the father of a family resolves the more effectually to correct his obstinate child, he will say to the rest of the household, "Do not be familiar with him; show him no countenance; put him to shame."

In like manner, when the Lord is smiting, especially with spiritual trouble, His disobedient child, He, as it were, saith to others of His children, "Have for a season no familiarity with him; treat him with coldness and neglect; in order that he may be ashamed, and humbled for his iniquity." Job, under his grievous affliction, complained thus, "He hath put my brethren far from me, and mine acquaintance are verily estranged from me." JOHN COLQUHOUN

(We have not attempted to interpret this Psalm concerning our Lord, but we fully believe that where the members are, the Head is to be seen preeminently. To have given a double exposition under each verse would have been difficult and confusing; we have therefore left the Messianic references to be pointed out in the Notes, where, if God, the Holy Ghost, be pleased to illustrate the page, we have gathered up more than enough to lead each devout reader to behold Jesus, the Man of sorrows and the acquaintance of grief.) C. H. S.

# PSALM 89

We have now reached the majestic Covenant Psalm, which, according to the Jewish arrangement, closes the third book of the Psalms. It is the utterance of a believer in presence of great national disaster, pleading with his God, urging the grand argument of covenant engagements and expecting deliverance and help because of the faithfulness of Jehovah. C. H. S.

The present Psalm makes a pair with the preceding one. It is a spiritual Allegro to that Penseroso . . . That Psalm was a dirge of Passion-Tide, this Psalm is a carol of Christmas. CHRISTOPHER WORDSWORTH

Vs. 1. This one short verse contains the summary, pith, and argument of the whole long Psalm; wherein observe "The Song's Ditty," the lovingkindness and truth of the Lord, manifested unto the whole world generally, to David's house (that is, the church) especially. The "Singer's Duty," magnifying the mercies of God always, even from one generation to another. JOHN BOYS

*I will sing.* We think when we are in trouble we get ease by complaining: but we do more, we get joy, by praising. Let our complaints therefore be turned into thanksgiving; and in these verses we find that which will be a matter of praise and thanksgiving for us in the worst of times, whether upon a personal or public account. MATTHEW HENRY

*With my mouth will I make known Thy faithfulness to all generations.* Because God is, and ever will be, faithful, we have a theme for song which will not be out of date for future generations; it will never be worn out, never be disproved, never be unnecessary, never be an idle subject, valueless to mankind. C. H. S.

The author has heard continual praises from a tongue half eaten away with cancer. What use, beloved reader, are you making of your tongue? PHILIP BENNETT POWER

Vs. 2. *Mercy shall be built up forever.* The elect constitute and form one grand house of mercy. This house, contrary to the fate of all sublunary buildings, will never fall down, nor ever be taken down. As nothing can be added to it, so nothing can be diminished from it. Fire cannot injure it; storms cannot overthrow it; age cannot impair it.

It stands on a rock, and is immovable as the rock on which it stands—the threefold rock of God's inviolable decree, of Christ's finished redemption, and of the Spirit's never-failing faithfulness. AUGUSTUS MONTAGUE TOPLADY

Vs. 3. *I have made a covenant with my chosen, I have sworn unto David my servant.* In Christ Jesus, there is a covenant established with all the Lord's chosen, and they are by grace led to be the Lord's servants and then are ordained kings and priests by Christ Jesus. How sweet it is to see the Lord, not only making a covenant but owning to it in after days, and bearing witness to His own oath; this ought to be solid ground for faith, and Ethan, the Ezrahite, evidently thought it so. C. H. S.

Vs. 5. *Thy wonders,* etc. It is a wonderful salvation, it is such a salvation as the angels desire to pry into it; and it is such a salvation that all the prophets desire to pry into it; it is almost six thousand years since all the angels in heaven fell into a sea of wonder at this great salvation; it is almost six thousand years since Abel fell into a sea of wonder at this great salvation; and what think ye is his exercise this day? He is even wondering at this great salvation. ANDREW GRAY

Vs. 6. *Who can be compared?* The Dutch have translated these words, "Who can be shadowed with Him?" that is, they are not worthy to be accounted shadows unto such a comparison with Him. THOMAS GOODWIN

Vs. 7. *God is greatly to be feared in the assembly of the saints.* Those saints of His who walk close with Him have a daunting power in their appearance. I appeal to guilty consciences, to apostates, to professors who have secret haunts of wickedness: sometime when you come but into the presence of one who is a truly gracious godly man or woman whom your conscience tells you walks close to God, doth not even the very sight of such an one terrify you? JEREMIAH BURROUGHS

*And to be had in reverence of all them that are about Him.* The nearer they are, the more they adore. If mere creatures are struck with awe, the courtiers and favorites of heaven must be yet more reverent in the presence of the great King, God's children are those who most earnestly pray, "Hallowed be Thy name." Irreverence is rebellion. C. H. S.

Vs. 14. *Justice and judgment are the habitation of Thy throne.* Now, saith the Psalmist, justice and judgment are the pillars upon which God's throne standeth, as Calvin expoundeth it, the robe and diadem, the purple and scepter, the regalia with which God's throne is adorned. GEORGE SWINNOCK

*Justice,* which defends His subjects, and does every one right. *Judgment,* which restrains rebels, and keeps off injuries. *Mercy,* which shows compassion, pardons, supports the weak. *Truth,* that performs whatsoever He promiseth. WILLIAM NICHOLSON

*Mercy and truth shall go before Thy face.* Thus has the poet sung the glories of the covenant God. It was meet that before he poured forth his lament he should record his praise, lest his sorrow should seem to have withered his faith. Before we argue our case before the Lord, it is most becoming to acknowledge that we know Him to be supremely great and good, whatever may be the appearance of His providence; this is such a course as every wise man will take who desires to have an answer of peace in the day of trouble. C. H. S.

Truth goes before the face of God, because God keeps it ever before His eyes, to mould His actions thereby. Pindar calls truth the daughter of God. Epaminondas, the Theban general, cultivated truth so studiously that he is reported never to have spoken a falsehood even in jest. In the courts of kings, this is a rare virtue. LE BLANC

Mercy in promising; truth in performing. Truth in being as good as thy word; mercy, in being better. MATTHEW HENRY

Vs. 15. *They shall walk, O Lord, in the light of Thy countenance.* While the sun shines, men walk without stumbling as to their feet, and when the Lord smiles on us, we live without grief as to our souls. C. H. S.

They are totally mistaken who suppose that *the light of God's countenance,* and the privileges of the gospel, and the comforts of the Spirit, conduce to make us indolent and inactive in the way of duty. The text cuts up this surmise by the roots. For, it does not say they shall sit down in the light of Thy countenance; or they shall lie down in the light of Thy countenance; but "they shall *walk* in the light of Thy countenance."

What is walking? It is a progressive motion from one point of space to another. And what is that holy walking which God's Spirit enables all His people to observe? It is a continued, progressive motion from sin to holiness; from all that is evil, to every good word and work.

And the self-same "light of God's countenance" in which you, O believer, are enabled to walk, and which at first gave you spiritual feet wherewith to walk, will keep you in a walking and in a working state, to the end of your warfare. AUGUSTUS MONTAGUE TOPLADY

Vs. 16. *And in Thy righteousness shall they be exalted.* This is an incredible paradox to a blind world, that the believer who is sitting at this moment upon the dunghill of this earth, should at the same time be sitting in heaven with and in Christ, his glorious Head and Representative (Eph. 2:6). EBENEZER ERSKINE

Vs. 19. *I have exalted one chosen out of the people.* David was God's elect, elect out of the people as one of themselves, and elect to the highest position in the state. In his extraction, election, and exaltation, he was an eminent type of the Lord Jesus, Who is the Man of the people, the chosen of God, and the King of His church.

Whom God exalts, let us exalt. Woe unto those who despise him; they are guilty of contempt of court before the Lord of Hosts, as well as of rejecting the Son of God. C. H. S.

Vs. 22. *The enemy shall not exact upon him; nor the son of wickedness afflict him.* Who does not in all this see a type of the Lord Jesus, Who though He was once seized for our debts and also evil entreated by the ungodly, is now so exalted that He can never be exacted upon anymore, neither can the fiercest of His enemies vex Him again. No Judas can now betray Him to death; no Pilate can deliver Him to be crucified. Satan cannot tempt Him, and our sins cannot burden Him. C. H. S.

Vs. 25. *I will set His hand also in the sea, and His right hand in the rivers.* A certain artist was in the habit of saying that he should represent Alexander in such a manner, that in one hand he should hold a city and from the other pour a river. Christ is represented here as of immense stature, higher than all mountains, with one hand holding the earth, and the other the sea, while from Eastern sea to Western, He extends His arms. LE BLANC

Vs. 26. *He shall cry unto me, Thou art my Father.* When did David call God his Father? It is striking that we do not find anywhere in the Old Testament that the patriarchs or prophets called God their Father. You do not find them addressing Him as Father: they did not know Him as such.

This verse is unintelligible in reference to David; but in regard to the true David, it is exactly what he did say, "My Father, and your Father; my God, and your God." Never until Christ uttered these words, never until He appeared on earth in humanity as the Son of God, did any man or any child of humanity address God in this endearing character.

It was after Christ said, "I ascend unto My Father, and your Father," that believers were enabled to look up to God and to say, "Abba Father." Here you see distinctly that this applies to Christ. He was the first to say this: David did not say it.

If there were no other proof in the whole Psalm, that one clause would be a demonstration to me that no other man than the Lord Jesus Christ can be here spoken of. CAPEL MOLYNEUX

Vs. 28. *And my covenant shall stand fast with Him.* With Jesus, the covenant is ratified both by blood of sacrifice and by oath of God; it cannot be canceled or altered, but is an eternal verity, resting upon the veracity of One Who cannot lie. What exultation fills our hearts as we see that the covenant of grace is sure to all the seed, because it stands fast with Him with whom we are indissolubly united.

Vs. 29. *His seed also will I make to endure forever.* David's seed lives on in the person of the Lord Jesus, and the seed of Jesus in the persons of believers. Saints are a race that neither death nor hell can kill. Rome and its priests, with their inquisition and other infernal cruelties, have labored to exterminate the covenant seed, but "vain is their rage, their efforts vain." As long as God lives, His people must live. C. H. S.

Vs. 30. *If his children forsake my law.* How astonished many would be if they knew what the real case was of those perhaps whom they admire, and think highly advanced and exalted in the Divine life, if they were to know the falls the wretched falls, falls in heart, in word, and in practice; if they were to know the deep distress that the children of God, who are far advanced as they suppose in the divine life, are continually suffering from the effect of such transgression! CAPEL MOLYNEUX

Vs. 33. *Nor suffer my faithfulness to fail.* Man's faith may fail him sometimes, but God's faithfulness never fails him: God will not suffer His faithfulness to fail. God's operations may have an aspect that way; the devil's temptations and our unbelieving hearts may not only make us think so, but persuade us it is so. Whereas, it cannot be so, for the Lord will not suffer it, He will not make a lie in His truth or faithfulness; so the Hebrew is: He is a God that cannot lie, He is Truth, speaks truth, and not one of His promises can or shall fail; which may afford strong consolation unto all that are under any promise of God. WILLIAM GREENHILL

Vs. 34. *My covenant will I not break.* It is His own covenant. He devised it, drew up the draft of it, and voluntarily entered into it; He therefore thinks much of it. It is not a man's covenant, but the Lord claims it as His own. It is an evil thing among men for one to be a "covenant-breaker," and such an opprobrious epithet shall never be applicable to the Most High. C. H. S.

Vs. 36. *His seed shall endure forever.* David's line in the person of Jesus is an endless one, and the race of Jesus, as represented in successive generations of believers, shows no sign of failure. No power, human or Satanic, can break the Christian succession; as saints die, others shall rise up to fill their places, so that till the last day, the day of doom, Jesus shall have a seed to serve Him. C. H. S.

Vs. 37. *And as a faithful witness in heaven.* The Jews, when they behold the rainbow, are said to bless God, Who remembers His covenant and is faithful to His promise. And the tradition of this, its designation to proclaim comfort to mankind, was strong among the heathens: for, according to the mythology of the Greeks, the "rainbow" was the daughter of "wonder," "a sign to mortal men," and regarded, upon its appearance, as a messenger of the celestial deities.

Thus Homer, with remarkable conformity to the Scripture account, speaks of the "rainbow," which "Jove hath set in the cloud, a sign to men." RICHARD MANT

Vs. 40. *Hedges* and *strongholds.* Both of these may refer to the appointments of a vineyard, in which the king was the vine. It was usually fenced around with a stone wall, and in it was a small house or tower wherein a keeper was set to keep away intruders.

When the wall, or hedge, was thrown down, every passerby plucked at the fruit, and when the tower was gone the vineyard was left open to the neighbors, who could do as they would with the vines. When the church is no longer separated from the world, and her divine Keeper has no more a dwelling-place within her, her plight is wretched indeed. C. H. S.

Vs. 41. *All that pass by the way spoil him.* Idle passers-by who have nothing else to do must needs have a pluck at this vine, and they do it without difficulty, since the hedges are gone. Woe is the day when every petty reasoner has an argument against religion, and men in their cups are fluent with objections against the gospel of Jesus.

Although Jesus on the cross is nothing to them, and they pass Him by without inquiring into what He has done for them, yet they can loiter as long as you will, if there be but the hope of driving another nail into His hands and helping to crucify the Lord afresh. They will not touch Him with the finger of faith but they pluck at Him with the hand of malice.

Vs. 43. *And hast not made him to stand in the battle.* Courage and decision are more needed now than ever, for charity towards heresy is the fashionable vice, and indifference to all truth, under the name of liberal-mindedness, is the crowning virtue of the age. The Lord send us men of the school of Elias, or, at least, of Luther and Knox. C. H. S.

Verses 46-47. This undoubtedly sounds like the voice of one who knows no hereafter. The Psalmist speaks as if all his hopes were bound by the grave; as if the overthrow of the united kingdom of Judah and Ephraim had bereft him of all his joy; and as if he knew no future kingdom to compensate him with its hopes.

But it would be doing cruel injustice to take him thus at his word. What we hear is the language of passion, not of sedate conviction. This is well expressed by John Howe in a famous sermon. "The expostulation (he observes) was somewhat passionate, and did proceed upon the sudden view of this disconsolate case, very abstractly considered, and by itself only; and the Psalmist did not, at that instant, look beyond it to a better and more comfortable scene of things.

"An eye bleared with present sorrow sees not far, nor comprehends so much at one view, as it would at another time, or as it doth presently when the tear is wiped out and its own beams have cleared it up." WILLIAM BINNIE

Vs. 47. *Wherefore hast Thou made all men in vain?* When I consider the millions of distorted existences; and the many millions!—the greater number of the world by far—who wander Christless, loveless, hopeless, over the broad highway of it; when I consider life in many of the awakened as a restless dream, as children beating the curtain and crying in the night; when I consider how many questions recur for ever to us; and will not be silenced, and cannot be answered; when I consider the vanity of the philosopher's inquisitiveness, and the end of Royalty in the tomb; when I look round on the region of my own joys, and know how short their lease is, and that their very ineffableness is a blight upon them; when I consider how little the best can do, and that none can do anything well; and finally, when I consider the immeasurable immensity of thought within, unfulfilled, and the goading restlessness, I can almost exclaim with our unhappy poet, (Byron):

*Count all the joys thine hours have seen,*
*Count all thy days from anguish free,*
*And know, whatever thou hast been,*
*'Twere something better not to be.*

E. PAXTON HOOD, *in "Dark Sayings on a Harp"*

Vs. 48:

*The boast of heraldry, the pomp of power,*
*And all that beauty, all that wealth e'er gave,*
*Await alike th' inevitable hour—*
*The paths of glory lead but to the grave.*

*Can storied urn, or animated bust,*
*Back to its mansions call the fleeting breath?*
*Can Honor's voice provoke the silent dust,*
*Or Flatt'ry soothe the dull cold ear of Death?*

THOMAS GRAY

Vs. 51. *Wherewith they have reproached the footsteps of Thine anointed.* Tracking Him and finding occasion to blaspheme at every turn; not only watching His words and actions, but even His harmless steps. Neither Christ nor His church can please the world, whichever way we turn scoffers will rail.

Does this verse refer to the oft-repeated sarcasm, "Where is the promise of His coming?" Is the reproach aimed at the delays of the Messiah, those long-expected footfalls which as yet are unheard? O Lord, how long shall this threadbare taunt continue? How long? How long? C. H. S.

HERE ENDETH BOOK III OF THE BOOK OF PSALMS

# PSALM 90

Title: "A Prayer of Moses the man of God." Many attempts have been made to prove that Moses did not write this Psalm, but we remain unmoved in the conviction that he did so. The condition of Israel in the wilderness is so preeminently illustrative of each verse, and the turns, expressions, and words are so similar to many in the Pentateuch, that the difficulties suggested are, to our mind, light as air in comparison with the internal evidence in favor of its Mosaic origin. Moses was mighty in word as well as deed, and this Psalm we believe to be one of his weighty utterances worthy to stand side by side with his glorious oration recorded in Deuteronomy.

This is the oldest of the Psalms and stands between two books of Psalms as a composition unique in its grandeur and alone in its sublime antiquity. Many generations of mourners have listened to this Psalm when standing around the open grave, and have been consoled thereby even when they have not perceived its special application to Israel in the wilderness and have failed to remember the far higher ground upon which believers now stand. C. H. S.

The Ninetieth Psalm might be cited as perhaps the most sublime of human compositions—the deepest in feeling—the loftiest in theologic conception—the most magnificent in its imagery. True is it in its report of human life—as troubled, transitory, and sinful. True in its conception of the Eternal—the Sovereign and the Judge; and yet the refuge and hope of men, who, notwithstanding the most severe trials of their faith, lose not their confidence in Him; but who, in the firmness of faith, pray for, as if they were predicting, a near-at-hand season of refreshment.

No taint is there in this Psalm of the pride and petulance—the half-uttered blasphemy—the malign disputing or arraignment of the justice or goodness of God, which have so often shed a venomous color upon the language of those who have writhed in anguish, personal or relative. ISAAC TAYLOR

Vs. 1. *Lord, Thou hast been our dwelling place in all generations.* Moses, in effect, says—wanderers though we be in the howling wilderness, yet we find a home in Thee, even as our forefathers did when they came out of Ur of the Chaldees and dwelt in tents among the Canaanites.

Not in the tabernacle or the temple do we dwell, but in God Himself; and this we have always done since there was a church in the world. We have not shifted our abode. Kings' palaces have vanished beneath the crumbling hand of time—they have been burned with fire and buried beneath mountains of ruins, but the imperial race of heaven has never lost its regal habitation. C. H. S.

It is a remarkable expression, the like of which is nowhere in sacred Scripture, that God is a Dwelling-Place. Scripture in other places says the very opposite; it calls men temples of God, in whom God dwells; "the temple of God is holy," says Paul, "which temple ye are." Moses inverts this, and affirms we are inhabitants and masters in this house.

When a monk, it often happened to me when I read this Psalm, that I was compelled to lay the book out of my hand. But I knew not that these terrors were not addressed to an awakened mind. I knew not that Moses was speaking to a most obdurate and proud multitude, which neither understood nor cared for the anger of God, nor were humbled by their calamities, or even in prospect of death. MARTIN LUTHER

Vs. 2. *Before the mountains were brought forth.* Before those elder giants had struggled forth from nature's womb, as her dread firstborn, the Lord was glorious and self-sufficient. Mountains to Him, though hoar with the snows of ages, are but new-born babes, young things whose birth was but yesterday, mere novelties of an hour. C. H. S.

*Or ever Thou hadst formed the earth and the world.* Such a God (he says) have we, such a God do we worship, to such a God do we pray, at Whose command all created things sprang into being. Why, then, should we fear if this God favors us? Why should we tremble at the anger of the whole world? If He is our dwelling-place, shall we not be safe though the heavens should go to wrack? For we have a Lord greater than all the world. We have a Lord so mighty that at His Word all things sprang into being.

And yet we are so faint hearted that if the anger of a single prince or king, nay, even of a single neighbor, is to be borne, we tremble and droop in spirit. Yet in comparison with this King, all things beside in the whole world are but as the lightest dust which a slight breath moves from its place and suffers not to be still. In this way, this description of God is consolatory, and trembling spirits ought to look to this consolation in their temptations and dangers. MARTIN LUTHER

Vs. 3. *Thou turnest man to destruction,* or "to dust." Man's body is resolved into its elements, and is as though it had been crushed and ground to powder. C. H. S.

Augustine says, "We walk amid perils." If we were glass vases we might fear less dangers. What is there more fragile than a vase of glass? And yet it is preserved and lasts for centuries: we therefore are more frail and infirm. LE BLANC

*And sayest, Return, ye children of men,* i.e., return even to the dust out of which ye were taken. The frailty of man is thus forcibly set forth; God creates him out of the dust, and back to dust he goes at the word of his Creator. God resolves, and man dissolves. A word created, and a word destroys.

Observe how the action of God is recognized; man is not said to die because of the decree of faith, or the action of inevitable law, but the Lord is made the agent of all, His hand turns and His voice speaks; without these we should not die; no power on earth or hell could kill us.

*An angel's arm can't save me from the grave,*
*Myriads of angels can't confine me there.*

C. H. S.

Vs. 4. *A thousand years,* etc. As to a very rich man, a thousand sovereigns are as one penny; so, to the eternal God, a thousand years are as one day. JOHN ALBERT BENGEL

The Holy Ghost expresseth Himself according to the manner of men, to give us some notion of an infinite duration by a resemblance suited to our capacity. If a thousand years be but as a day to the life of God, then as a year is to the life of man, so are three hundred and sixty-five thousand years to the life of God; and as seventy years are to the life of man, so are twenty-five million five hundred and fifty thousand years to the life of God.

Yet still, since there is no proportion between time and eternity, we must dart our thoughts beyond all these, for years and days measure only the duration of created things, and of those only that are material and corporeal, subject to the motion of the heavens, which makes days and years. STEPHEN CHARNOCK

*And as a watch in the night,* a time which is no sooner come than gone. There is scarce time enough in a thousand years for the angels to change watches; when their millennium of service is almost over, it seems as though the watch were newly set.

We are dreaming through the long night of time, but God is ever keeping watch, and a thousand years are as nothing to Him. A host of days and nights must be combined to make up a thousand years to us, but to God, that space of time does not make up a whole night but only a brief portion of it. If a thousand years be to God as a single night-watch, what must be the life-time of the Eternal! C. H. S.

The ages and the dispensations, the promise to Adam, the engagement with Noah, the oath to Abraham, the covenant with Moses—these were but watches through which the children of men had to wait amid the darkness of things created until the morning should dawn of things uncreated. Now is "the night far spent, and the day at hand." *Plain Commentary*

Vs. 5. *They are as a sleep.* How many errors are we subject to in sleep? In sleep, the prisoner many times dreams that he is at liberty; he that is at liberty, that he is is in prison; he that is hungry, that he is feeding daintily; he that is in want, that he is in great abundance; he that abounds, that he is in great want.

How many in their sleep have thought they have gotten that which they shall be better for forever, and when they are even in the hope of present possessing some such goodly matter, or beginning to enjoy it, or in the midst of their joy, they suddenly awaked, and then all is gone with them, and their golden fancies vanish away in an instant. So for evil and sorrow as well. And is it not just so in the life of man? WILLIAM BRADSHAW

*In the morning they are like grass which groweth up.* As grass is green in the morning and hay at night, so men are changed from health to corruption in a few hours. We are not cedars, or oaks, but only poor grass, which is vigorous in the spring but lasts not a summer through. What is there upon earth more frail than we!

Vs. 6. *In the evening it is cut down, and withereth.* The scythe ends the blossoming of the field-flowers, and the dews at night weep their fall. Here is the history of the grass—sown, grown, blown, mown, gone; and the history of man is not much more. C. H. S.

Vs. 7. *For we are consumed by Thine anger.* This is a point disputed by philosophers. They seek for the cause of death, since indeed proofs of immortality that cannot be despised exist in nature.

The prophet replies that the chief cause must not be sought in the material, either in a defect of the fluids, or in a failure of the natural heat; but that God being offended at the sins of men, hath subjected this nature to death and other infinite calamities.

Therefore, our sins are the causes which have brought down this destruction. Hence, he says, "In Thine anger we vanish away." MOLLERUS

Vs. 8. *Thou hast set our iniquities before Thee.* Hence these tears! Sin seen by God must work death; it is only by the covering blood of atonement that life comes to any of us. When God was overthrowing the tribes in the wilderness, He had their iniquities before Him, and therefore dealt with them in severity. He could not have their iniquities before Him and not smite them.

*Our secret sins in the light of Thy countenance.* Rebellion in the light of justice is black, but in the light of love it is devilish. How can we grieve so good a God? The children of Israel had been brought out of Egypt with a high hand, fed in the wilderness with a liberal hand, and guided with a tender hand, and their sins were peculiarly atrocious.

We, too, having been redeemed by the blood of Jesus and saved by abounding grace, will be verily guilty if we forsake the Lord. What manner of persons ought we to be? How ought we to pray for cleansing from secret faults? C. H. S.

My hearers, if you are willing to see your sins in their true colors; if you would rightly estimate their number, magnitude, and criminality, bring them into the hallowed place, where nothing is seen but the brightness of unsullied purity, and the splendors of uncreated glory; where the sun itself would appear only as a dark spot; and there, in the midst of this circle of seraphic intelligences, with the infinite God pouring all the light of His countenance round you, review your lives, contemplate your offences, and see how they appear.

Recollect that the God in Whose presence you are is the Being Who forbids sin, the Being of Whose eternal law sin is the transgression, and against Whom every sin is committed. EDWARD PAYSON

Vs. 9. *As a tale that is told.* The Chaldee has it, "Like the breath of our mouth in winter." DANIEL CRESSWELL

What are we but a vain dream that hath no existence or being, a mere phantasm or apparition that cannot be held, a ship sailing in the sea which leaves no impression or trace behind it, a dust, a vapor, a morning dew, a flower flourishing one day and fading another, yea, the same day behold it springing and withered.

But my text adds another metaphor from the flying of a bird, "and we fly away," not go and run but fly, the quickest motion that any corporeal creature hath. Our life is like the flight of a bird, 'tis here now and 'tis gone out of sight suddenly.

The Prophet, therefore, speaking of the speedy departure of Ephraim's glory, expresseth it thus, "It shall flee away like a bird" (Hos. 9:11); and Solomon saith the like of riches, "They make themselves wings and flee away like an eagle toward heaven" (Prov. 23:5). David wished for the wings of a dove that he might flee away and be at rest, and good cause he had for it, for this life is not more short than miserable. THOMAS WASHBOURNE

The Hebrew is different from all the Versions. "We consume our years (*kemo hegeh*) like a groan." We live a dying, whining, complaining life, and at last a groan is its termination! ADAM CLARKE

The Vulgate translation has, "Our years pass away like those of a spider." It implies that our life is as frail as the thread of a spider's web. Constituted most curiously the spider's web is; but what more fragile? In what is there more wisdom than in the complicated frame of the human body; and what more easily destroyed? Glass is granite compared with flesh; and vapors are rocks compared with life. C. H. S.

Vs. 10. *And if by reason of strength they be fourscore years, yet is their strength labor and sorrow.* The unusual strength which overleaps the bounds of threescore and ten only lands the aged man in a region where life is a weariness and a woe. The strength of old age, its very prime and pride, are but labor and sorrow; what must its weakness be? What panting for breath! What toiling to move! What a failing of the senses! What a crushing sense of weakness! The evil days are come and the years wherein a man cries, "I have no pleasure in them." The sun is setting and the heat of the day is over, but sweet is the calm and cool of the eventide; and the fair day melts away, not into a dark and dreary night, but into a glorious, unclouded, eternal day. The mortal fades to make room for the immortal; the old man falls asleep to wake up in the region of perennial youth.

*For it is soon cut off, and we fly away.* The cable is broken and the vessel sails upon the sea of eternity; the chain is snapped, and the eagle mounts to its native air above the clouds. Moses mourned for men as he thus sung: and well he might, as all his comrades fell at his side. C. H. S.

At the Witan, or council assembled at Edwin of Northumbria at Godmundingham (modern name Godmanham), to debate on the mission of Paulinus, the King was thus addressed by a heathen Thane, one of his chief men: "The present life of man, O King, may be likened to what often happens when thou art sitting at supper with thy thanes and nobles in winter-time. A fire blazes on the hearth and warms the chamber; outside rages a storm of wind and snow; a sparrow flies in at one door of thy hall, and quickly passes out at the other.

"For a moment and while it is within, it is unharmed by the wintry blast, but this brief season of happiness over, it returns to that wintry blast whence it came, and vanishes from thy sight.

"Such is the brief life of man: we know not what went before it, and we are utterly ignorant as to what shall follow it. If, therefore, this new doctrine contain anything more certain, it justly deserves to be followed." BEDE'S CHRONICLE

Vs. 11. *Who knoweth the power of Thine anger?* None at all; and unless the power of that can be known, it must abide as unspeakable as the love of Christ, which passeth knowledge. JOHN BUNYAN

Moses, I think, here means that it is a holy awe of God, and that alone, which makes us truly and deeply feel His anger. We see that the reprobate, although they are severely punished, only chafe upon the bit, or kick against God, or become exasperated, or are stupefied, as if they were hardened against all calamities; so far are they from being subdued. And though they are full of trouble, and cry aloud, yet the divine anger does not so penetrate their hearts as to abate their pride and fierceness.

The minds of the godly alone are wounded with the wrath of God; nor do they wait for His thunder-bolts, to which the reprobate hold out their hard and iron necks, but they tremble the very moment when God moves only His little finger. This I consider to be the true meaning of the prophet. JOHN CALVIN

No man knows the power of God's anger, because that power has never yet put itself forth to its full stretch. Is there, then, no measure of God's wrath—no standard by which we may estimate its intenseness? There is no fixed measure or standard, but there is a variable one. The wicked man's fear of God is a measure of the wrath of God. There is such a fear and such a dread of that God into Whose immediate presence he feels himself about to be ushered, that even they who love Him best, and charm Him most, shrink from the wildness of His gaze and the fearfulness of His speech. HENRY MELVILL

*Even according to Thy fear, so is Thy wrath.* Holy Scripture, when it depicts God's wrath against sin, never uses an hyperbole; it would be impossible to exaggerate it. Whatever feelings of pious awe and holy trembling may move the tender heart, it is never too much moved; apart from other considerations, the great truth of the divine anger, when most powerfully felt, never impresses the mind with a solemnity in excess of the legitimate result of such a contemplation. What the power of God's anger is in hell, and what it would be on earth, were it not in mercy restrained, no man living can rightly conceive.

Modern thinkers rail at Milton and Dante, Bunyan and Baxter, for their terrible imagery; but the truth is that no vision of poet, or denunciation of holy seer, can ever reach to the dread height of this great argument, much less go beyond it. C. H. S.

Fear is but a mirror, which you may lengthen indefinitely, and widen indefinitely, and wrath lengthens with the lengthening and widens with the widening, still crowding the mirror with new and fierce forms of wasting and woe. We caution you, then, against ever cherishing the flattering notion that fear can exaggerate God's wrath. We tell you that when fear has done its worst, it can in no degree come up to the wrath which it images. HENRY MELVILL

Vs. 12. *So teach us to number our days.* Moses sends you to God for teaching. "Teach Thou us; not as the world teacheth—teach Thou us." No meaner Master; no inferior school; not Moses himself except as he speaks God's Word and becomes the schoolmaster to bring us to Christ; not the prophets, not apostles themselves, neither "holy men of old," except as they "spake and were moved by the Holy Ghost."

This knowledge comes not from flesh and blood, but from God. "So teach Thou us." And so David says, "Teach me Thy way, O Lord, and I will walk in Thy truth." And hence our Lord's promise to His disciples, "The Holy Ghost, He shall teach you all things." CHARLES RICHARD SUMNER

*Improve Time in time, while the Time doth last,*
*For all Time is no time, when the Time is past.*

*From Richard Pigot's "Life of Man, symbolized by the Months of the Year."*

Number we our days by our daily prayers—number we them by our daily obedience and daily acts of love—number we them by the memories that they bring of holy men who have entered into their Savior's peace, and by the hopes which are woven with them of glory and of grace won for us! *Plain Commentary*

*That we may apply our hearts unto wisdom.* A short life should be wisely spent. We have not enough time at our disposal to justify us in misspending a single quarter of an hour. Neither are we sure of enough of life to justify us in procrastinating for a moment. If we were wise in heart, we should see this, but mere head wisdom will not guide us aright. C. H. S.

St. Austin says, "We can never do that, except we number every day as our last day." Many put far the evil day. They refuse to leave the earth when earth is about to take its leave of them. WILLIAM SECKER

Even as you see the wicked, because they apply their hearts to wickedness, how fast they proceed, how easily and how quickly they become perfect swearers, expert drunkards, cunning deceivers, so if ye could apply your hearts as thoroughly to knowledge and goodness, you might become like the Apostle which teacheth you.

Thus we have learned how to apply knowledge that it may do us good; not to our ears, like them which hear sermons only, nor to our tongues, like them which make table-talk of religion, but to our hearts, that we may say with the virgin, "My heart doth magnify the Lord" (Luke 1), and the heart will apply it to the ear and to the tongue, as Christ saith, "Out of the abundance of the heart the mouth speaketh" (Matt. 12:34). HENRY SMITH

Of all arithmetical rules, this is the hardest—to number our days. Men can number their herds and droves of oxen and of sheep; they can estimate the revenues of their manors and farms; they can with a little pains number and tell their coins; and yet they are persuaded that their days are infinite and innumerable and therefore do never begin to number them. THOMAS TYMME

What! is there not enough to make us feel our frailty without an actual, supernatural impression? What! are there not lessons enough of that frailty without any new teaching from above?

Go into your churchyards—all ages speak to all ranks. Can we need more to prove to us the uncertainty of life? Go into mourning families—and where are they not to be found?—in this it is the old, in that it is the young, whom death has removed—and is there not eloquence in tears to persuade us that we are mortal?

Can it be that in treading every day on the dust of our fathers and meeting every day with funerals of our brethren, we shall not yet be practically taught to number our days, unless God print the truth on our hearts, through some special operation of His Spirit?

The chief pursuit of life should be the attainment of an experimental knowledge of Christ, by Whom "kings reign and princes decree justice; whose delights are with the sons of men, and Who crieth, Whoso findeth Me findeth life, and shall obtain favor of the Lord; come, eat of My bread and drink of the wine which I have mingled."

David in the Psalms, and Solomon, his son, in the Proverbs, have predictively manifested Messiah as the hypostatic wisdom, "Whose goings forth have been from of old, from everlasting." J. N. COLEMAN

Vs. 14. *O satisfy us early with Thy mercy.* Since they must die and die so soon, the Psalmist pleads for speedy mercy upon himself and his brethren. Good men know how to turn the darkest trials into arguments at the throne of grace. He who has but the heart to pray need never be without pleas in prayer. The only satisfying food for the Lord's people is the favor of God; this Moses earnestly seeks for, and as the manna fell in the morning, he beseeches the Lord to send at once His satisfying favor, that all through the little day of life they might be filled therewith. C. H. S.

A poor, hungry soul lying under sense of wrath, will promise to itself happiness forever if it can but once again find what it hath sometime felt; that is, one sweet fill of God's sensible mercy towards it. DAVID DICKSON

That is everywhere and evermore the cry of humanity. And what a strange cry it is, when you think of it, brethren! Man is the offspring of God: the bearer of His image; he stands at the head of the terrestrial creation; on earth he is peerless; he possesses wondrous capacities of thought, and feeling, and action.

The world and all that is in it has been formed in a complete and beautiful adaptation to his being. Nature seems to be ever calling to him with a thousand voices, to be glad and rejoice; and yet he is unsatisfied, discontented, miserable!

This is a most strange thing—strange, that is, on any theory respecting man's character and condition, but that which is supplied by the Bible; and it is not only a testimony to the ruin of his nature, but also to the insufficiency of everything earthly to meet his cravings. CHARLES M. MERRY

Vs. 15. *Make us glad according to the days wherein Thou hast afflicted us, and the years wherein we have seen evil.* None can gladden the heart as Thou canst, O Lord; therefore as Thou hast made us sad, be pleased to make us glad. Fill the other scale. Proportion Thy dispensations. Give us the lamb, since Thou has sent us the bitter herbs. Make our days as long as our nights.

The prayer is original, childlike, and full of meaning; it is, moreover, based upon a great principle in providential goodness by which the Lord puts the good over against the evil in due measure. Great trial enables us to bear great joy and may be regarded as the herald of extraordinary grace. God, Who is great in justice when He chastens, will not be little in mercy when He blesses; He will be great all through: let us appeal to Him with unstaggering faith. C. H. S.

Vs. 16. *And Thy glory unto their children.* How eagerly do good men plead for their children! They can bear very much personal affliction if they may but be sure that their children will know the glory of God and thereby be led to serve Him. We are content with the work if our children may but see the glory which will result from it: we sow joyfully if they may reap. C. H. S.

Vs. 17. *And establish Thou the work of our hands upon us; yea, the work of our hands establish Thou it."* We come and go, but the Lord's work abides. We are content to die so long as Jesus lives and His kingdom grows. Since the Lord abides forever the same, we trust our work in His hands and feel that since it is far more His work than ours, He will secure it immortality. When we have withered like grass, our holy service, like gold, silver, and precious stones, will survive the fire. C. H. S.

# PSALM 91

This Psalm is without a title, and we have no means of ascertaining either the name of its writer or the date of its composition with certainty. The Jewish doctors consider that when the author's name is not mentioned, we may assign the Psalm to the last-named writer; and, if so, this is another Psalm of Moses, the man of God. Many expressions here used are similar to those of Moses in Deuteronomy, and the internal evidence, from the peculiar idioms, would point towards him as the composer.

In the whole collection, there is not a more cheering Psalm; its tone is elevated and sustained throughout—faith is at its best—and speaks nobly. A German physician was wont to speak of it as the best preservative in times of cholera, and in truth it is a heavenly medicine against plague and pest. He who can live in its spirit will be fearless, even if once again London should become a lazar-house and the graves be gorged with carcases. C. H. S.

It is one of the most excellent works of this kind which has ever appeared. It is impossible to imagine anything more solid, more beautiful, more profound, or more ornamented. Could the Latin or any modern language express thoroughly all the beauties and elegancies as well as the words of the sentences, it would not be difficult to persuade the reader that we have no poem, either in Greek or Latin, comparable to this Hebrew ode. SIMON de MUIS

Psalm 90 spoke of man withering away beneath God's anger against sin. Psalm 91 tells of a Man Who is able to tread the lion and adder under His feet. Undoubtedly the Tempter was right in referring this Psalm to "the Son of God" (Matt. 4:6). WILLIAM KAY

Vs. 1. *He that dwelleth in the secret place of the Most High.* The blessings here promised are not for all believers but for those who live in close fellowship with God. Every child of God looks towards the inner sanctuary and the mercy-seat, yet all do not dwell in the most holy place; they run to it at times and enjoy occasional approaches, but they do not habitually reside in the mysterious presence. C. H. S.

*He.* No matter who he may be, rich or poor, learned or unlearned, patrician or plebian, young or old, for "God is no respecter of persons," but "He is rich to all that call upon Him." BELLARMINE

*Shall abide under the shadow of the Almighty.* No shelter can be imagined at all comparable to the protection of Jehovah's own shadow. The Almighty Himself is where His shadow is, and hence those who dwell in His secret place are shielded by Himself. What a shade in the day of noxious heat! What a refuge in the hour of deadly storm! Communion with God is safety. The more closely we cling to our Almighty Father, the more confident may we be. C. H. S.

We read of a stag that roamed about in the greatest security by reason of its having a label on its neck, "Touch me not, I belong to Cæsar": thus the true servants of God are always safe, even among lions, bears, serpents, fire, water, thunder, and tempests; for all creatures know and reverence the shadow of God. BELLARMINE

Vs. 2. *I will say of the Lord, He is my refuge and my fortress.* It is but poor comfort to say, 'The Lord is a refuge,' but to say He is *my* refuge is the essence of consolation. Those who believe should also speak—"I will say," for such bold avowals honor God and lead others to seek the same confidence.

Men are apt to proclaim their doubts, and even to boast of them; indeed there is a party nowadays of the most audacious pretenders to culture and thought who glory in casting suspicion upon everything; hence it becomes the duty of all true believers to speak out and testify with calm courage to their own well-grounded reliance upon their God. C. H. S.

*My God; in Him will I trust.* Now he can say no more; "my God" means all, and more than all, that heart can conceive by way of security. We have trusted in God; let us trust Him still. He has never failed us; why then should we suspect Him? To trust in man is natural to fallen nature; to trust in God should be as natural to regenerated nature. C. H. S.

Vs. 3. *He shall deliver thee from the snare of the fowler.* Are not the riches of this world, then, the snare of the devil? Alas! how few we find who can boast of freedom from this snare, how many who grieve that they seem to themselves too little involved in the net, and who still labor and toil with all their strength to involve and entangle themselves more and more.

Ye who have left all and followed the Son of man Who has not where to lay His head, rejoice and say, *He hath delivered me from the snare of the fowler.* BERNARD

*And from the noisome pestilence.* He Who is a Spirit can protect us from evil spirits. He Who is mysterious can rescue us from mysterious dangers. He Who is immortal can redeem us from mortal sickness.

There is a deadly pestilence of error; we are safe from that if we dwell in communion with God of truth; there is a fatal pestilence of sin, we shall not be infected by it if we abide with the thrice Holy One; there is also a pestilence of disease, and even from that calamity our faith will win immunity if it be of that high order which abides in God, walks on in calm serenity, and ventures all things for duty's sake. C. H. S.

Lord Craven lived in London when that sad calamity, the plague, raged. His house was in that part of the town called Craven Buildings. On the plague growing epidemic, his Lordship, to avoid the danger, resolved to go to his seat in the country.

His coach and six were accordingly at the door, his baggage put up, and all things in readiness for the journey. As he was walking through his hall with his hat on, his cane under his arm, and putting on his gloves, in order to step into his carriage, he overheard his Negro, who served him as postillion, saying to another servant, "I suppose, by my Lord's quitting London to avoid the plague, that his God lives in the country and not in town."

The poor Negro said this in the simplicity of his heart, as really believing a plurality of gods. The speech, however, struck Lord Craven very sensibly, and made him pause. "My God," thought he, "lives everywhere, and can preserve me in town as well as in the country. I will even stay where I am. The ignorance of that Negro has just now preached to me a very useful sermon. Lord, pardon this unbelief, and that distrust of Thy providence, which made me think of running from Thy hand."

He immediately ordered his horses to be taken from the coach and the baggage to be taken in. He continued in London, was remarkably useful among his sick neighbors, and never caught the infection. *Whitecross' Anecdotes*

Vs. 4. *He shall cover thee with His feathers, and under His wings shalt thou trust.* A wonderful expression! Had it been invented by an uninspired man, it would have verged upon blasphemy, for who should dare to apply such words to the infinite Jehovah? But as He Himself authorized, yea, dictated the language, we have here a transcendent condescension such as it becomes us to admire and adore.

Doth the Lord speak of His feathers as though He likened Himself to a bird? Who will not see herein a matchless love, a divine tenderness, which should both woo and win our confidence? Even as a hen covereth her chickens, so doth the Lord protect the souls which dwell in Him.

*His truth*—His true promise, and His faithfulness to His promise, *shall be thy shield and buckler.* To quench fiery darts, the truth is a most effectual shield, and to blunt all swords, it is an equally effectual coat of mail. Let us go forth to battle thus harnessed for the war, and we shall be safe in the thickest of the fight. C. H. S.

Vs. 5. *Nor for the arrow that flieth by day.* When Satan's quiver shall be empty, thou shalt remain uninjured by his craft and cruelty; yea, his broken darts shall be to thee as trophies of the truth and power of the Lord, thy God. C. H. S.

Vs. 6. *Not for the destruction that wasteth at noonday.* Famine may starve, or bloody war devour, earthquake may overturn and tempest may smite, but amid all, the man who has sought the mercy seat and is sheltered beneath the wings which overshadow it, shall abide in perfect peace. Remember that the voice which saith, "Thou shalt not fear," is that of God Himself, Who hereby pledges His Word for the safety of those who abide under His shadow, nay, not for their safety only, but for their serenity. So far shall they be from being injured that they shall not even be made to fear the ills which are around them, since the Lord protects them. C. H. S.

Vs. 7. *It shall not come nigh thee.* How true is this of the plague of moral evil, of heresy, and of backsliding. Whole nations are infected, yet the man who communes with God is not affected by the contagion; he holds the truth when falsehood is all the fashion.

Professors all around him are plague-smitten, the church is wasted, the very life of religion decays, but in the same place and time, in fellowship with God, the believer renews his youth, and his soul knows no sickness. In a measure, this also is true of physical evil; the Lord still puts a difference between Israel and Egypt in the day of His plagues. Sennacherib's army is blasted, but Jerusalem is in health. C. H. S.

As good may be locally near us, and yet virtually far from us, so may evil. The multitude thronged Christ in the Gospel, and yet but one touched Him so as to receive good; so Christ can keep us in a throng of dangers, that not one shall touch us to our hurt. JOSEPH CARYL

Vs. 9. *Because thou hast made the Lord, which is my refuge, even the most High, thy habitation.* Our safety lies not simply upon this, because God is a refuge, and is an habitation, but "Because thou hast made the Lord which is my refuge, thy habitation, there shall no evil befall thee," etc.

It is therefore the making of God our habitation upon which our safety lies; and this is the way to make God an habitation, thus to pitch and cast ourselves by faith upon His power and providence. JEREMIAH DYKE

Verses 9-10. Before expounding these verses, I cannot refrain from recording a personal incident illustrating their power to soothe the heart, when they are applied by the Holy Spirit.

In the year 1854, when I had scarcely been in London twelve months, the neighborhood in which I labored was visited by Asiatic cholera, and my congregation suffered from its inroads. Family after family summoned me to the bedside of the smitten, and almost every day I was called to visit the grave.

I gave myself up with youthful ardor to the visitation of the sick, and was sent for from all corners of the district by persons of all ranks and religions.

I became weary in body and sick at heart. My friends seemed to be falling one by one, and I felt or fancied that I was sickening like those around me. A little more work and weeping would have laid me low among the rest; I felt that my burden was heavier than I could bear, and I was ready to sink under it.

As God would have it, I was returning mournfully home from a funeral, when my curiosity led me to read a paper which was wafered up in a shoemaker's window in the Dover Road. It did not look like a trade announcement, nor was it, for it bore in a good bold handwriting these words: *Because thou hast made the Lord, which is my refuge, even the most High, thy habitation; there shall no evil befall thee, neither shall any plague come nigh thy dwelling.*

The effect upon my heart was immediate. Faith appropriated the passage as her own. I felt secure, refreshed, girt with immortality. I went on with my visitation of the dying in a calm and peaceful spirit; I felt no fear of evil, and I suffered no harm. The providence which moved the tradesman to place those verses in his window I gratefully acknowledge, and in the remembrance of its marvelous power, I adore the Lord, my God. C. H. S.

Austin had appointed to go to a certain town to visit the Christians there and to give them a sermon or more. The day and place were known to his enemies, who set armed men to lie in wait for him by the way which he was to pass and kill him.

As God would have it, the guide whom the people had sent with him to prevent his going out of the right way mistook, and led him into a bypath, yet brought him at last to his journey's end. Which when the people understood, as also the adversaries' disappointment, they adored the providence of God and gave Him thanks for that great deliverance. JOHN ARROWSMITH

Verses 9-14. Dependence on Christ is not the cause of His hiding us, but it is the qualification of the person that shall be hid. RALPH ROBINSON

Vs. 10. Sin, which has kindled a fire in hell, is kindling fires on earth continually. And when they break out, everyone is asking how they happened. Amos replies, "Shall there be evil in a city, and the Lord hath not done it?" And when desolation is made by fire, Isaiah declares, The Lord hath "consumed us, because of our iniquities."

Many years ago my house was oft threatened to be destroyed, but the Lord insured it, by giving me the tenth verse of the Ninety-First Psalm; and the Lord's providence is the best insurance. JOHN BERRIDGE

Vs. 11. *For He shall give His angels charge over thee.* Not one guardian angel, as some fondly dream, but all the angels are here alluded to. They are the body-guard of the princes of the blood imperial of heaven, and they have received commission from their Lord and ours to watch carefully over all the interests of the faithful. C. H. S.

When Satan tempted Christ in the wilderness, he alleged but one sentence of Scripture for himself (Matt. 4:6), and that Psalm out of which he borrowed it made so plain against him that he was fain to pick here a word and there a word and leave out that which went before and skip in the midst, and omit that which came after, or else he had marred his cause.

The Scripture is so holy, and pure, and true, that no word nor syllable thereof can make for the devil, or for sinners, or for heretics: yet, as the devil alleged Scripture, though it made not for him but against him, so do the libertines, and epicures, and heretics, as though they had learned at his school. HENRY SMITH

Vs. 12. *Lest thou dash thy foot against a stone.* And these angels, seeing we are so dear to God, that for our sakes He spared not His own Son, take this charge with all their hearts upon them, and omit nothing of their duty from our birth to the end of our life. HENRY LAWRENCE, *in "A Treatise of our Communion and Warre with Angells"*

Vs. 13. *The young lion and the dragon shalt thou trample under feet.* To men who dwell in God, the most evil forces become harmless; they wear a charmed life and defy the deadliest ills. Their feet come into contact with the worst of foes. Even Satan himself nibbles at their heel, but in Christ Jesus they have the assured hope of bruising Satan under their feet shortly.

The people of God are the real "George and the dragon," the true lion-kings and serpent-tamers. Their dominion over the powers of darkness makes them cry, "Lord, even the devils are subject unto us through Thy word."

Vs. 14. *Because he hath set his love upon Me, therefore will I deliver him.* When the heart is enamored of the Lord, all taken up with Him, and intensely attached to Him, the Lord will recognize the sacred flame and preserve the man who bears it in his bosom. C. H. S.

He does not say, "Because he is without sin; because he has perfectly kept all my precepts; because he has merit and is worthy to be delivered and guarded." But he produces those qualities which are even found in the weak, the imperfect, and those still exposed to sin in the flesh, namely, adhesion, knowledge of His name, and prayer. MUSCULUS

Vs. 15. *He shall call upon Me, and I will answer him.* Saints are first called of God, and then they call upon God; such calls as theirs always obtain answers.

It is better for me, O Lord, to be troubled, whilst only Thou art with me, than to reign without Thee, to feast without Thee, to be honored without Thee. It is good rather to be embraced by Thee in trouble, to have Thee in the furnace with me, than to be without Thee even in heaven. For what have I in heaven, and without Thee what do I desire upon earth? The furnace tries the gold, and the temptation of trouble just men. BERNARD

*I will deliver him, and honor him.* Believers are not delivered or preserved in a way which lowers them, and makes them feel themselves degraded; far from it, the Lord's salvation bestows honor upon those it delivers. God first gives us conquering grace, and then rewards us for it. C. H. S.

Vs. 16. *With long life will I satisfy him.*

*We live in deeds, not years; in thoughts, not breaths;*
*In feelings, not in figures on a dial.*
*We should count time by heart-throbs. He most lives*
*Who thinks most, feels noblest, acts the best.*

—PHILIP JAMES BAILEY, *in "Festus"*

*And shew him My salvation.* The last, greatest, climax of blessing, including and concluding all! What God does is perfectly done. Hitherto has His servant caught glimpses of the "great salvation." The Spirit has revealed step by step of it, as he was able to bear it. The Word has taught him, and he has rejoiced in His light. But all was seen in part and known in part. But when God has satisfied His servant with length of days, and time for him is over, eternity begun, He will "show him His salvation." All will be plain. All will be known. God will be revealed in His love and His glory. And we shall know all things, even as we are known! MARY B. M. DUNCAN

## PSALM 92

Title: "A Psalm or Song for the Sabbath Day." This admirable composition is both a Psalm and a Song, full of equal measures of solemnity and joy; and it was intended to be sung upon the day of rest. The subject is the praise of God; praise is Sabbatic work, the joyful occupation of resting hearts. No one acquainted with David's style will hesitate to ascribe to him the authorship of this divine hymn; the ravings of the Rabbis who speak of its being composed by Adam only need to be mentioned to be dismissed. Adam in Paradise had neither harps to play upon nor wicked men to contend with.

Vs. 1. *It is a good thing to give thanks unto the Lord,* or Jehovah. It is good ethically, for it is the Lord's right; it is good emotionally, for it is pleasant to the heart; it is good practically, for it leads others to render the same homage. We thank men when they oblige us: how much more ought we to bless the Lord when He benefits us! Devout praise is always good; it is never out of season, never superfluous, but it is especially suitable to the Sabbath; a Sabbath without thanksgiving is a Sabbath profaned. C. H. S.

Giving of thanks is more noble and perfect in itself than petition; because in petition often our own good is eyed and regarded, but in giving of thanks only God's honor.

The Lord Jesus said, "It is more blessed to give than to receive." Now, a subordinate end of petition is to receive some good from God, but the sole end of thanks is to give glory unto God. WILLIAM AMES, *in "Medulla Theologica"*

*And to sing praises.* Singing is the music of saints. (1) They have performed this duty in their greatest numbers (Ps. 149:1). (2) In their greatest straits (Isa. 26:19). (3) In their greatest flight (Isa. 42:10-11). (4) In their greatest deliverances (Isa. 65:14). (5) In their greatest plenties. In all these changes, singing hath been their stated duty and delight. JOHN WELLS, *in "The Morning Exercises"*

Vs. 2. *In the morning.* The Brahmins rise three hours before the sun, to pray. The Indians would esteem it a great sin to eat in the morning before praying to their gods. The ancient Romans considered it impious if they had not a little chamber, in their house, appropriated to prayer. Let us take a lesson from these Turks and heathen; their zealous ardor ought to shame us. Because we possess the true light, should their zeal surpass ours? FREDERIC ARNDT, *in "Lights in the Morning"*

*Every night,* clouded or clear, moonlit or dark, calm or tempestuous, is alike suitable for a song upon the faithfulness of God, since in all seasons, and under all circumstances, it abides the same, and is the mainstay of the believer's consolation. Shame on us that we are so backward in magnifying the Lord, Who in the daytime scatters bounteous love, and in the night season walks His rounds of watching care. C. H. S.

Vs. 3. *Upon an instrument of ten strings, and upon the psaltery; upon the harp with a solemn sound.* In Augustine to Ambrose there is the following passage bearing on this same subject: "Sometimes, from over jealousy, I would entirely put from me and from the church the melodies of the sweet chants that we use in the Psalter, lest our ears seduce us; and the way of Athanasius, bishop of Alexandria, seems the safe one, who, as I have often heard, made the reader chant with so slight a change of voice, that it was more like speaking than singing. And yet, when I call to mind the tears I shed when I heard the chants of Thy church in the infancy of my recovered faith, and reflect that I was affected, not by the mere music, but by the subject, brought out as it were by clear voices and appropriate tune, in turn, I confess how useful is the practice." C. H. S.

Vs. 5. *And Thy thoughts are very deep.* Redemption is grand beyond conception, and the thoughts of love which planned it are infinite. Man is superficial, God is inscrutable; man is shallow, God is deep. Dive as we may, we shall never fathom the mysterious plan or exhaust the boundless wisdom of the all-comprehending mind of the Lord. We stand by the fathomless sea of divine wisdom and exclaim with holy awe, "O the depth!" C. H. S.

Verily, my brethren, there is no sea so deep as these thoughts of God, Who maketh the wicked flourish and the good suffer: nothing so profound, nothing so deep; therein every unbelieving soul is wrecked, in that depth, in that profundity. Dost thou wish to cross this depth? Remove not from the wood of Christ's cross; and thou shalt not sink: hold thyself fast to Christ. AUGUSTINE

Vs. 6. *A brutish man knoweth not; neither doth a fool understand this.* In this and the following verses, the effect of the Psalm is heightened by contrast; the shadows are thrown in to bring out the lights more prominently.

What a stoop from the preceding verse; from the saint to the brute, from the worshiper to the boor, from the Psalmist to the fool! Yet, alas, the character described here is no uncommon one. The boorish, or boarish man, for such is almost the very Hebrew word, sees nothing in nature; and if it be pointed out to him, his foolish mind will not comprehend it.

He may be a philosopher and yet be such a brutish being that he will not own the existence of a Maker for the ten thousand matchless creations around him, which wear, even upon their surface, the evidences of profound design. The unbelieving heart, let it boast as it will, does not know; and with all its parade of intellect, it does not understand.

A man must either be a saint or a brute, he has no other choice; his type must be the adoring seraph or the ungrateful swine. So far from paying respect to great thinkers who will not own the glory or being of God, we ought to regard them as comparable to the beasts which perish, only vastly lower than mere brutes, because their degrading condition is of their own choosing.

O God, how sorrowful a thing it is that men whom Thou hast so largely gifted, and made in Thine own image, should so brutify themselves that they will neither see nor understand what Thou hast made so clear. Well might an eccentric writer say, "God made man a little lower than the angels at first, and he has been trying to get lower ever since." C. H. S.

Expressively he wrote: "The man-brute will not know; the fool will not understand this," viz., that when the wicked spring up with rapid and apparently vigorous growth as the summer flowers in Palestine, it is that they may ripen for a swift destruction.

The man-brute precisely translates the Hebrew words; one whom God has endowed with manhood, but who has debased himself to brutehood; a man as being of God's creation in His own image, but a brute as being self-moulded (shall we say self-made?) into the image of the baser animals! HENRY COWLES

A sottish sensualist, who hath his soul for salt only, to keep his body from putrefying (as we say of swine) he takes no knowledge of God's great works, but grunts and goes his ways, contenting himself with a natural use of the creatures, as beasts do. JOHN TRAPP

A man may be frightfully successful in such a process of destruction if long enough continued, upon his own nature. "Who can read without indignation of Kant," remarks De Quincey, "that at his own table in social sincerity and confidential talk, let him say what he would in his books, he exulted in the prospect of absolute and ultimate annihilation; that he planted his glory in the grave, and was ambitious of rotting forever!

"The King of Prussia, though a personal friend of Kant's, found himself obliged to level his state thunders at some of his doctrines, and terrified him in his advance; else I am persuaded that Kant would have formally delivered Atheism from the professor's chair and would have enthroned the horrid ghoulish creed, which privately he professed, in the University of Konigsberg. It required the artillery of a great king to make him pause.

"The fact is, that as the stomach has been known by means of its natural secretion, to attack not only whatsoever alien body is introduced within it, but also (as John Hunter first showed), sometimes to attack itself and its own organic structure; so, and with the same preternatural extension of instinct, did Kant carry forward his destroying functions, until he turned them upon his own hopes, and the pledges of his own superiority to the dog, the ape, the worm." GEORGE B. CHEEVER, *in "Voices of Nature"*

Vs. 9. *All the workers of iniquity shall be scattered.* The grass cannot resist the scythe, but falls in withering ranks, even so are the ungodly cut down and swept away in process of time, while the Lord Whom they despised sits unmoved upon the throne of His infinite dominion.

Terrible as this fact is, no true-hearted man would wish to have it otherwise. Treason against the great Monarch of the universe ought not to go unpunished; such wanton wickedness richly merits the severest doom. C. H. S.

Vs. 11. *And mine ears shall hear my desire of the wicked that rise up against me.* The holy Psalmist had seen the beginning of the ungodly and expected to see their end; he felt sure that God would right all wrongs and clear His Providence from the charge of favoring the unjust; this confidence he here expresses, and sits down contentedly to wait the issues of the future. C. H. S.

Vs. 12. *The righteous shall flourish like the palm tree.* This song now contrasts the condition of the righteous with that of the graceless. The wicked "spring as the grass," but *the righteous shall flourish like the palm tree,* whose growth may not be so rapid but whose endurance for centuries is in fine contrast with the transitory verdure of the meadow.

When we see a noble palm standing erect, sending all its strength upward in one bold column, and growing amid the dearth and drought of the desert, we have a fine picture of the godly man, who in his uprightness aims alone at the glory of God; and, independent of outward circumstances, is made by divine grace to live and thrive where all things else perish. C. H. S.

The young Christian is lovely, like a tree in the blossoms of spring: the aged Christian is valuable, like a tree in autumn, bending with ripe fruit. We, therefore, look for something superior in old disciples. More deadness to the world, the vanity of which they have had more opportunities to see; more meekness of wisdom; more disposition to make sacrifices for the sake of peace; more maturity of judgment in divine things; more confidence in God; more richness of experience. WILLIAM JAY

The palm tree grows from the sand, but the sand is not its food; water from below feeds its tap roots, though the heavens above be brass. Some Christians grow, not as the lily (Hos. 14:5), by green pastures, or the willow by watercourses (Isa. 44:4), but as the palm of the desert; so Joseph among the cat-worshipers of Egypt, Daniel in voluptuous Babylon. Faith's penetrating root reaches the fountains of living waters.

The palm tree is beautiful, with its tall and verdant canopy, and the silvery flashes of its waving plumes; so the Christian virtues are not like the creeper or bramble, tending downwards, their palm branches shoot upwards, and seek the things above where Christ dwells (Col. 3:1): some trees are crooked and gnarled, but the Christian is a tall palm as a son of the light (Matt. 3:12; Phil. 2:15). The Jews were called a crooked generation (Deut. 32:5), and Satan a crooked serpent (Isa. 27), but the Christian is upright like the palm.

The palm tree is very useful. The Hindus reckon it has 360 uses. Its shadow shelters, its fruit refreshes the weary traveler, it points out the place of water: such was Barnabas, a son of consolation (Acts 4:36); such Lydia, Dorcas, and others, who on the King's highway showed the way to heaven, as Philip did to the Ethiopian eunuch (Acts 9:34). Jericho was called the City of Palms (Deut. 34:3).

The palm tree produces even to old age. The best dates are produced when the tree is from thirty to one hundred years old; three hundred pounds of dates are annually yielded: so the Christian grows happier and more useful as he becomes older. Knowing his own faults more, he is more mellow to others: he is like the sun setting, beautiful, mild, and large, looking like Elim, where the wearied Jews found twelve wells and seventy palm trees. J. LONG, *in "Scripture Truth in Oriental Dress"*

Verses 12-15. The life and greenness of the branches is an honor to the root by which they live. Spiritual greenness and fruitfulness is in a believer an honor to Jesus Christ, Who is his life. The fullness of Christ is manifested by the fruitfulness of a Christian. RALPH ROBINSON

Vs. 14. *They shall still bring forth fruit in old age; they shall be fat and flourishing.* Constancy is an ingredient in the obedience Christ requires. His trees bring forth fruit in old age. Age makes other things decay, but makes a Christian flourish. Some are like hot horses, mettlesome at the beginning of a journey and tired a long time before they come to their journey's end.

A good disciple, as he would not have from God a temporary happiness, so he would not give to God a temporary obedience; as he would have His glory last as long as God lives, so he would have his obedience last as long as he lives. Judas had a fair beginning but destroyed all in the end by betraying his Master. STEPHEN CHARNOCK

# PSALM 93

This brief Psalm is without title or name of author, but its subject is obvious enough, being stated in the very first line. It is the Psalm of Omnipotent Sovereignty: Jehovah, despite all opposition, reigns supreme. Possibly at the time this sacred ode was written, the nation was in danger from its enemies, and the hopes of the people of God were encouraged by remembering that the Lord was still King. What sweeter and surer consolation could they desire? C. H. S.

This is one of those magnificent Psalms which describe Jehovah's reign. Even Jewish interpreters say of them: "These all treat of the things which will take place in the times of Messiah."

What matters the opinion of men—who may be for and who against me; who may be with me, or who may leave me? Who would speak of prospects or probabilities, of the support to be derived from wealth or power, or of the defections of friends on whose sympathy and help we had counted? "Jehovah reigneth!" There is light here across my every path, provided I follow Christ, walking in the narrow way. Only let me be sure that, in any and every respect, I am on the Lord's side and in the Lord's way, and I ask no more. ALFRED EDERSHEIM, in *"The Golden Diary of Heart Converse with Jesus in the Book of Psalms"*

Vs. 1. *The Lord reigneth.* The very first words of this Psalm seem to indicate a morning of calm repose after a night of storm, a day of stillness after the tumult of battle. *The Lord reigneth.* "He hath put all enemies under His feet." BARTON BOUCHIER

*The Lord is clothed with strength.* May the Lord appear in His church, in our day, in manifest majesty and might, saving sinners, slaying errors, and honoring His own Name. Oh, for a day of the Son of man, in which the King immortal and almighty shall stand upon His glorious high throne, to be feared in the great congregation, and admired by all them that believe. C. H. S.

Vs. 2. *Of old.* The Italian, *from all eternity:* Hebrew, *from then;* an Hebrew phrase to signify an eternity without any beginning (Prov. 8:22); as eternity without end is signified by another term, which is as much as, *until then.* DIODATI

Vs. 3. *The floods have lifted up their voice; the floods lift up their waves.* Sometimes men are furious in words—they lift up their voice, and at other times they rise to acts of violence—they lift up their waves; but the Lord has control over them in either case.

The ungodly are all foam and fury, noise and bluster, during their little hour, and then the tide turns or the storm is hushed, and we hear no more of them; while the kingdom of the Eternal abides in the grandeur of its power.

The whole Psalm is most impressive and is calculated to comfort the distressed, confirm the timorous, and assist the devout. O Thou Who art so great and gracious a King, reign over us forever! We do not desire to question or restrain Thy power; such is Thy character that we rejoice to see Thee exercise the rights of an absolute monarch. All power is in Thine hands, and we rejoice to have it so. Hosanna! Hosanna! C. H. S.

# PSALM 94

Subject: The writer sees evil-doers in power and smarts under their oppressions. His sense of the divine sovereignty, of which he had been singing in the previous Psalm, leads him to appeal to God as the great Judge of the earth; this he does with much vehemence and importunity, evidently tingling under the lash of the oppressor.

Confident in God's existence, and assured of His personal observation of the doings of men, the Psalmist rebukes his atheistic adversaries and proclaims his triumph in his God: he also interprets the severe dispensation of Providence to be in very deed most instructive chastisements, and so he counts those happy who endure them.

The Psalm is another pathetic form of the old enigma: "Wherefore do the wicked prosper?" It is another instance of a good man perplexed by the prosperity of the ungodly, cheering his heart by remembering that there is, after all, a King in heaven, by Whom all things are overruled for good. C. H. S.

Vs. 1. *O Lord God, to Whom vengeance belongeth; O God, to Whom vengeance belongeth, show Thyself:* or, God of retributions, Jehovah, God of retributions, shine forth! A very natural prayer when innocence is trampled down and wickedness exalted on high. If the execution of justice be a right thing—and who can deny the fact?—then it must be a very proper thing to desire it; not out of private revenge, in which case a man would hardly dare to appeal to God, but out of sympathy with right, and pity for those who are made wrongfully to suffer. C. H. S.

I do not think that we sufficiently attend to the distinction that exists between revenge and vengeance. "Revenge," says Dr. Johnson, "is an act of passion, vengeance of justice; injuries are revenged, crimes avenged." BARTON BOUCHIER

Vs. 3. *Lord, how long shall the wicked, how long shall the wicked triumph?* Twice he saith it, because the wicked boast day after day, with such insolency and outrage, as if they were above control. JOHN TRAPP

What answer shall we give, what date shall we put to this "How long?" The answer is given in verse 23, "He shall bring upon them their own iniquity, and shall cut them off in their own wickedness," etc. As if he had said, "Except the Lord cut them off in their wickedness, they will never leave off doing wickedly." They are men of such a kind that there is no curing of them, they will never have done doing mischief until they be cut off by death, therefore God threatens death to deter men from sin.

A godly man saith, "If God kill me, yet will I trust in Him"; and some wicked men say (in effect, if not in the letter), "Till God kills us, we will sin against Him." JOSEPH CARYL

Vs. 4. *How long shall they utter and speak hard things?* The ungodly are not content with deeds of injustice, but they add hard speeches, boasting, threatening, and insulting over the saints. Will the Lord forever endure this? Will He leave His own children much longer to be the prey of their enemies? Will not the insolent speeches of His adversaries and theirs at last provoke His justice to interfere?

Words often wound more than swords; they are as hard to the heart as stones to the flesh; and these are poured forth by the ungodly in redundance, for such is the force of the word translated *utter;* and they use them so commonly that they become their common speech (they utter and speak them)— will this always be endured? C. H. S.

Vs. 7. *Yet they say, the Lord shall not see.* This was the reason of their arrogance and the climax of their wickedness: they were blindly wicked because they dreamed of a blind God.

When men believe that the eyes of God are dim, there is no reason to wonder that they give full license to their brutal passions. The persons mentioned above not only cherished an infidel unbelief, but dared to avow it, uttering the monstrous doctrine that God is too far away to take notice of the actions of men. C. H. S.

Vs. 8. *Understand, ye brutish among the people.* When a man has done with God, he has done with his manhood, and has fallen to the level of the ox and the ass, yea, beneath them, for "the ox knoweth his owner, and the ass his master's crib." Instead of being humbled in the presence of scientific infidels, we ought to pity them; they affect to look down upon us, but we have far more cause to look down upon them. C. H. S.

Verses 8-11. We may observe that this dreadful disease is ascribed to mankind in general. "The Lord knoweth the thoughts of man, that they are vanity." The Psalmist had been setting forth the vanity and unreasonableness of the thoughts of some of the children of men; and immediately upon it he observes that this vanity and foolishness of thought is common and natural to mankind.

From these particulars, we may fairly deduce the following doctrinal observation: That there is an extreme and brutish blindness in things of religion, which naturally possesses the hearts of mankind. JONATHAN EDWARDS

Vs. 9. *He that planted the ear, shall He not hear?* He fashioned that marvelous organ and fixed it in the most convenient place near to the brain, and is He deaf Himself? Is He capable of such design and invention, and yet can He not discern what is done in the world which He made? He made you hear; can He not Himself hear? Unanswerable question! It overwhelms the skeptic and covers him with confusion. C. H. S.

Shall the Author of these senses be senseless? Our God is not as that Jupiter of Crete, who was pictured without ears and could not be at leisure to attend upon small matters. JOHN TRAPP

*He that formed the eye, shall He not see?* We can understand the mechanism of the eye, we can comprehend the wisdom that devised it; but the preparation of materials, and the adjustment of parts, speak of a power and skill to which man can never hope to attain.

When he sees his most cunning workmanship surpassed both in plan and execution, shall he fail to recognize design? Shall we fail to recognize a Builder when we contemplate such a work? P. A. CHADBOURNE, *in "Lectures on Natural Theology; or, Nature and the Bible from the same Author," New York*

He Who made the sun itself and causes it to revolve, being a small portion of His works if compared with the whole, is He unable to perceive all things? EPICTETUS

That is wise counsel of the Rabbins, that the three best safeguards against falling into sin are to remember, first, that there is an Ear which hears everything; secondly, that there is an Eye which sees everything; thirdly, that there is a Hand which writes everything in the Book of Knowledge, which shall be opened at the judgment. J. M. NEALE

Vs. 10. *He that teacheth man knowledge,* and then it comes to a pause, which the translators have supplied with the words, "*shall not He know?*" but no such words are in the original, where the sentence comes to an abrupt end, as if the inference were too natural to need to be stated and the writer had lost patience with the brutish men with whom he had argued.

The earnest believer often feels as if he could say, "Go to, you are not worth arguing with! If you were reasonable men, these things would be too obvious to need to be stated in your hearing. I forbear." Man's knowledge comes from God. Science in its first principles was taught to our progenitor Adam, and all after advances have been due to divine aid; does not the Author and Revealer of all knowledge Himself know? C. H. S.

Vs. 11. *The Lord knoweth the thoughts.* The thoughts of man's heart—what millions are there of them in a day! The twinkling of the eye is not so sudden a thing as the twinkling of a thought; yet those thousands and thousands of thoughts which pass from thee, that thou canst not reckon, they are all known to God. ANTHONY BURGESS

*They are vanity.* If during our state of childhood and youth only vanity had been ascribed to our thoughts, it would have been less surprising. This is a truth of which numberless parents have painful proof; yea, and of which children themselves, as they grow up to maturity, are generally conscious. Vanity at this period, however, admits of some apology. The obstinacy and folly of some young people, while they provoke disgust, often excite a tear of pity. But the charge is exhibited against man. "Man at his best estate is altogether vanity." ANDREW FULLER

*They are vanity.* The Syriac version is, "For they are a vapor." Compare James 4:14. JOHN GILL

Vs. 12. *Blessed is the man whom Thou chastenest, O Lord.* The Psalmist's mind is growing quiet. He no longer complains to God or argues with men but tunes his harp to softer melodies, for his faith perceives that with the most afflicted believer all is well. C. H. S.

If by outward afflictions thy soul be brought more under the inward teachings of God, doubtless thy afflictions are in love. All the chastening in the world, without divine teaching, will never make a man blessed; that man that finds correction attended with instruction, and lashing with lessoning, is a happy man.

If God, by the affliction that is upon thee, shall teach thee how to loathe sin more, how to trample upon the world more, and how to walk with God more, thy afflictions are in love. If God shall teach thee by afflictions how to die to sin more, and how to die to thy relations more, and how to die to thy self-interest more, thy afflictions are in love.

If God shall teach thee by afflictions how to live to Christ more, how to lift up Christ more, and how to long for Christ more, thy afflictions are in love. If God shall teach thee by afflictions to get assurance of a better life, and to be still in a gracious readiness and preparedness for the day of thy death, thy afflictions are in love.

If God shall teach thee by afflictions how to mind heaven more, and how to fit for heaven more, thy afflictions are in love. If God by afflictions shall teach thy proud heart how to lie more low, and thy hard heart how to grow more humble, and thy censorious heart how to grow more charitable, and thy carnal heart how to grow more spiritual, and thy forward heart how to grow more quiet, etc., thy afflictions are in love.

Pambo, an illiterate dunce, as the historian terms him, was a-learning that one lesson, "I said I will take heed to my ways, that I sin not with my tongue," nineteen years, and yet had not learned it. Ah! it is to be feared that there are many who have been in this school of affliction above this nineteen years and yet have not learned any saving lesson all this while. Surely their afflictions are not in love, but in wrath.

Where God loves, He afflicts in love, and wherever God afflicts in love, there He will first and last teach such souls such lessons as shall do them good to all eternity. THOMAS BROOKS

If we have nothing but the rod, we profit not by the rod; yea, if we have nothing but the Word, we shall never profit by the Word. It is the Spirit given with the Word, and the Spirit given with the rod, by which we profit under both, or either. Chastening and divine teaching must go together, else there will be no profit by chastening. JOSEPH CARYL

God sees that the sorrows of life are very good for us; for, as seeds that are deepest covered with snow in winter flourish most in spring; or as the wind by beating down the flame raiseth it higher and hotter; and as when we would have fires flame the more, we sprinkle water upon them; even so, when the Lord would increase our joy and thankfulness, He allays it with the tears of affliction. H. G. SALTER

Vs. 13. *That Thou mayest give him rest from the days of adversity, until the pit be digged for the wicked.* The mighty Hunter is preparing the pit for the brutish ones; they are prowling about at this time, and tearing the sheep, but they will soon be captured and destroyed; therefore the people of the Lord learn to rest in days of adversity and tarry the leisure of their God.

Wicked men may not yet be ripe for punishment nor punishment ready for them: hell is a prepared place for a prepared people; as days of grace ripen saints for glory, so days of wantonness help sinners to rot into the corruption of eternal destruction. C. H. S.

*Rest.* Let there be a revival of the passive virtues. Mr. Hume calls them the "monkish virtues." Many speak of them slightingly, especially as compared with the dashing qualities so highly esteemed in the world. But quietness of mind and of spirit, like a broken heart, is of great price in the sight of God. Some seem to have forgotten that silence and meekness are graces. WILLIAM S. PLUMER

Behold, thou hast the counsel of God, and the reason why He spareth the wicked; the pit is being digged for the sinner. Thou wishest to bury him at once: the pit is as yet being dug for him: do not be in haste to bury him. AUGUSTINE

Vs. 16. *Who will rise up for me against the evildoers? or who will stand up for me against the workers of iniquity?* Where are our Luthers and our Calvins? A false charity has enfeebled the most of the valiant men of Israel. Our John Knox would be worth a mint at this hour, but where is he? Our grand consolation is that the God of Knox and Luther is yet with us and in due time will call out His chosen champions. C. H. S.

Vs. 19. *Thy comforts delight my soul.* The little world within is, like the great world without, full of confusion and strife; but when Jesus enters it and whispers, "Peace be unto you," there is a calm, yea, a rapture of bliss. Let us turn away from the mournful contemplation of the oppression of man and the present predominance of the wicked to that sanctuary of pure rest which is found in the God of all comfort. C. H. S.

*Thy comforts*—the comforts we get from the Lord Jesus Christ; from looking at Him, considering Him; thinking of His person, and offices, and blood, and righteousness, and intercession, and exaltation, and glory, and His second coming; our meeting Him, seeing Him, being like Him.

*Thy comforts*—the comforts which come from the Holy Spirit, "the Comforter": when He opens the Scriptures to us, or speaks through ceremonies and ordinances, or witnesses within us of our adoption of God; shining in on His own work of grace in our hearts; enabling us to see that work, and to see in it God's peculiar, eternal love to us; not opening to us the Book of life, and showing us our names there, but doing something that makes us almost as joyful as though that Book were opened to us; showing us the hand of God in our own souls—His converting, saving hand—His hand apprehending us as His own; making us feel as it were, His grasp of love, and feel, too, that it is a grasp which He will never loosen. CHARLES BRADLEY

Xerxes offered great rewards to him that could find out a new pleasure; but the comforts of the Spirit are satisfactory, they recruit the heart. There is as much difference between heavenly comforts and earthly as between a banquet that is eaten and one that is painted on the wall. THOMAS WATSON

Vs. 20. *The throne of iniquity . . . which frameth mischief by a law.* The first pretext of wicked men to color their proceedings against innocent men is their throne; the second is the law; and the third is their council. What tyrant could ask more? But God has prepared an awful hell for impenitent tyrants, and they will be in it long before they now expect to leave the world. WILLIAM NICHOLSON

Vs. 21. *And condemn the innocent blood.* They are great at slander and false accusation, nor do they stick at murder; no crime is too great for them, if only they can trample on the servants of the Lord. This description is historically true in reference to persecuting times; it has been fulfilled in England, and may be again if popery is to advance in future time at the same rate as in the past few years. C. H. S.

Vs. 23. *He shall bring upon them their own iniquity.* It is an ill work wicked ones are about: they make fetters for their own feet and build houses for to fall upon their own heads; so mischievous is the nature of sin that it damnifies and destroys the parents of it. WILLIAM GREENHILL

# PSALM 95

This Psalm has no title, and all we know of its authorship is that Paul quotes it as "in David" (Heb. 4:7). It is true that this may merely signify that it is to be found in the collection known as David's Psalms; but if such were the Apostle's meaning, it would have been more natural for him to have written, "saying in the Psalms"; we therefore incline to the belief that David was the actual author of this poem. We will call it "The Psalm of the Provocation." C. H. S.

This Psalm is twice quoted in the Epistle to the Hebrews as a warning to the Jewish Christians at Jerusalem, in the writer's day, that they should not falter in the faith and despise God's promises as their forefathers had done in the wilderness, lest they should fail of entering into His rest. CHRISTOPHER WORDSWORTH

Vs. 1. *O come, let us sing unto the Lord.* Other nations sing unto their gods; let us sing unto Jehovah. We love Him, we admire Him, we reverence Him; let us express our feelings with the choicest sounds, using our noblest faculty for its noblest end. C. H. S.

If it be so that one *come, let us* go further than twenty times *go and do,* how careful should such be whom God hath raised to eminence of place that their examples be Jacob's ladders to help men to heaven, not Jeroboam's stumbling-blocks to lie in their way and make Israel to sin. CHARLES HERLE

Vs. 2. *Let us come before His presence with thanksgiving.* Here is probably a reference to the peculiar presence of God in the Holy of Holies above the mercy-seat, and also to the glory which shone forth out of the cloud which rested above the tabernacle. Everywhere God is present, but there is a peculiar presence of grace and glory into which men should never come without the profoundest reverence. Our worship should have reference to the past as well as to the future; if we do not bless the Lord for what we have already received, how can we reasonably look for more?

*And make a joyful noise unto Him with Psalms.* We should shout as exultingly as those do who triumph in war and as solemnly as those whose utterance is a Psalm. It is not always easy to unite enthusiasm with reverence, and it is a frequent fault to destroy one of these qualities while straining after the other. It is to be feared that this is too much overlooked in ordinary services. People are so impressed with the idea that they ought to be serious that they put on the aspect of misery and quite forget that joy is as much a characteristic of true worship as solemnity itself. C. H. S.

Vs. 5. *The sea is His.* This was seen to be true at the Red Sea when the waters saw their God and obediently stood aside to open a pathway for His people. It was not Edom's Sea, though it was red, nor Egypt's sea, though it washed her shores. The Lord on high reigned supreme over the flood as King forever and ever.

*And His hands formed the dry land.* Come ye, then, who dwell on this fair world, and worship Him Who is conspicuous where'er ye tread! Count it all as the floor of a temple where the footprints of the present Deity are visible before your eyes if ye do but care to see. The argument is overpowering if the heart be right; the command to adore is alike the inference of reason and the impulse of faith. C. H. S.

Vs. 6. *O come, let us worship and bow down: let us kneel before the Lord our Maker.* As suppliants must we come; joyful, but not presumptuous; familiar as children before a father, yet reverential as creatures before their Maker. Posture is not everything, yet is it something; prayer is heard when knees cannot bend, but it is seemly that an adoring heart should show its awe by prostrating the body and bending the knee. C. H. S.

Not before a crucifix, not before a rotten image, not before a fair picture of a foul saint: these are not our makers; we made them, they made not us.

Our God, unto Whom we must sing, in Whom we must rejoice, before Whom we must worship, "is a great King above all gods": He is no god of lead, no god of bread, no brazen god, no wooden god; we must not fall down and worship our *Lady,* but our *Lord;* not any *martyr,* but our *Maker;* not any *saint,* but our *Savior.* JOHN BOYS

Vs. 7. *For He is our God.* Here is the master reason for worship. Jehovah has entered into covenant with us, and from all the world beside has chosen us to be His own elect. If others refuse Him homage, we at least will render it cheerfully. He is ours, and our God; ours, therefore will we love Him; our God, therefore will we worship Him. Happy is that man who can sincerely believe that this sentence is true in reference to himself.

But what is this warning which follows? Alas, it was sorrowfully needed by the Lord's ancient people and is not one whit the less required by ourselves. The favored nation grew deaf to their Lord's command and proved not to be truly His sheep, of whom it is written, "My sheep hear My voice": will this turn out to be our character also? God forbid.

*Today if ye will hear His voice.* Dreadful *if.* Many would not hear; they put off the claims of love and provoked their God. "Today," in the hour of grace, in the day of mercy, we are tried as to whether we have an ear for the voice of our Creator.

Nothing is said of tomorrow, "He limiteth a certain day," He presses for immediate attention, for our own sakes He asks instantaneous obedience. Shall we yield it? The Holy Ghost saith "Today." Will we grieve Him by delay? C. H. S.

If we put off repentance another day, we have a day more to repent of and a day less to repent in. W. MASON

He that hath promised pardon on our repentance hath not promised to preserve our lives till we repent. FRANCIS QUARLES

You cannot repent too soon, because you do not know how soon it may be too late. THOMAS FULLER

Oh! what an *if* is here! what a reproach is here to those that hear Him not! "My sheep hear My voice, and I know them, and they follow Me"; "but ye will not come to Me that ye might have life." And yet there is mercy; there is still salvation, if ye will hear that voice. BARTON BOUCHIER

And yet, as S. Bernard tells us, there is no difficulty at all in hearing it; on the contrary, the difficulty is to stop our ears effectually against it, so clear is it in enunciation, so constant in appeal.

Yet there are men who do not hear, from divers causes: because they are far off; because they are deaf; because they sleep; because they turn their heads aside; because they stop their ears; because they hurry away to avoid hearing; because they are dead; all of them types of various forms and degrees of unbelief. BERNARD AND HUGO CARDINALS, in *Neale and Littledale*

Verses 7-8. You will never know how easy the yoke of Christ is till it is bound about your necks, nor how light His burden is till you have taken it up. While you judge of holiness at a distance, as a thing without you and contrary to you, you will never like it.

Come a little nearer to it; do but take it in, actually engage in it, and you will find religion carries meat in its mouth; it is of a reviving, nourishing, strengthening nature. It brings that along with it that enables the soul cheerfully to go through with it. THOMAS COLE, *in the "Morning Exercises"*

Vs. 8. *Harden not your heart."* If ye will hear, learn to fear also. The sea and the land obey Him; do not prove more obstinate than they! We cannot soften our hearts, but we can harden them, and the consequences will be fatal. Today is too good a day to be profaned by the hardening of our hearts against our own mercies. While mercy reigns, let not obduracy rebel. C. H. S.

An old man, one day taking a child on his knee, entreated him to seek God now—to pray to Him, and to love Him; when the child, looking up at him, asked, "But why do not you seek God?" The old man, deeply affected, answered, "I would, child; but my heart is hard—my heart is hard." ARVINES ANECDOTES

Vs. 9. *Your fathers tempted Me.* In short, unbelief of every kind and every degree may be said to tempt God. For not to believe upon the evidence which He has seen fit to give is to provoke Him to give more, offering our possible assent if proof were increased as an inducement to Him to go beyond what His wisdom has prescribed. You cannot mistrust God and not accuse Him of want either of power or of goodness. HENRY MELVILL

*Proved Me.* If we were for ever testing the love of our wife or husband, and remained unconvinced after years of faithfulness, we should wear out the utmost human patience. Friendship only flourishes in the atmosphere of confidence; suspicion is deadly to it: shall the Lord God, true and immutable, be day after day suspected by His own people? Will not this provoke Him to anger? C. H. S.

*Proved Me,* put Me to the proof of My existence, presence, and power, by requiring Me to work, *i.e.,* to act in an extraordinary manner. And this desire, unreasonable as it was, I gratified. J. A. ALEXANDER

*And saw My work.* They tested Him again and again, throughout forty years, though each time His work was conclusive evidence of His faithfulness. Nothing could convince them for long. Fickleness is bound up in the heart of man, unbelief is our besetting sin; we must for ever be seeing or we waver in our believing. This is no mean offence and will bring with it no small punishment. C. H. S.

Vs. 10. *Forty years long was I grieved with this generation.* The impression upon the divine Mind is most vivid. He sees them before Him now and calls them "this generation." He does not leave His prophets to upbraid the sin, but Himself utters the complaint and declares that He was grieved, nauseated, and disgusted. C. H. S.

Oh, the desperate presumption of man, that he should offend his Maker "forty years"! Oh, the patience and longsuffering of his Maker, that He should allow him forty years to offend in! Sin begins in the "heart," by its desires wandering and going astray after forbidden objects; whence follows inattention to the "ways" of God, to His dispensations, and our own duty. Lust in the heart, like vapor in the stomach, soon affects the head and clouds the understanding. GEORGE HORNE

*Was I grieved.* The word is a strong word, expressive of loathing and disgust. J. J. S. PEROWNE

*And said, It is a people that do err in their heart, and they have not known My ways.* The heart is the mainspring of the man, and if it be not in order, the entire nature is thrown out of gear. If sin were only skin deep, it might be a slight matter; but since it had defiled the soul, the case is bad indeed.

Forty years of providential wisdom, yea, and even a longer period of experience, have failed to teach them serenity of assurance and firmness of reliance. There is ground for much searching of heart concerning this. Many treat unbelief as a minor fault; they even regard it rather as an infirmity than a crime. But the Lord thinketh not so.

Faith is Jehovah's due, especially from those who claim to be the people of His pasture and yet more emphatically from those whose long life has been crowded with evidences of His goodness: unbelief insults one of the dearest attributes of Deity. It does so needlessly and without the slightest ground and in defiance of all-sufficient arguments, weighty with the eloquence of love. Let us, in reading this Psalm, examine ourselves and lay these things to heart. C. H. S.

Verses 10-11. *And said.* Mark the gradation, first grief or disgust with those who erred made Him *say;* then anger felt more heavily against those who did not believe made Him *swear.* The people had been called "sheep" in verse 7. To sheep, the highest good is rest, but into this rest they were never to come, for they had not known or delighted in the ways in which the good Shepherd desired to lead them. JOHN ALBERT BENGEL

Vs. 11. *Unto whom I sware in My wrath that they should not enter into My rest.* There can be no rest to an unbelieving heart. If manna and miracles could not satisfy Israel, neither would they have been content with the land which flowed with milk and honey. Solemn warning this to all who leave the way of faith for paths of petulant murmuring and mistrust. The rebels of old could not enter in because of unbelief. "Let us therefore fear, lest, a promise being left us of entering into His rest, any of us should even seem to come short of it." C. H. S.

It is terrible to hear an oath from the mouth of a poor mortal, but from the mouth of an omnipotent God, it does not only terrify, but confound. An oath from God is truth delivered in anger; truth, as I may so speak, with a vengeance. When God speaks, it is the creature's duty to hear; but when He swears, to tremble. ROBERT SOUTH

# PSALM 96

Subject: This Psalm is evidently taken from that sacred song which was composed by David at the time when "the ark of God was set in the midst of the tent which David had prepared for it, and they offered burnt sacrifices and peace offerings before God." See the sixteenth chapter of the First Book of the Chronicles. It is a grand missionary hymn, and it is a wonder that Jews can read it and yet remain exclusive.

Divisions: We will make none, for the song is one and indivisible, a garment of praise without seam, woven from the top throughout. C. H. S.

The mother teaches her child to lisp a hymn before he comprehends its full scope and meaning. And so here, in this holy Psalm, the Jerusalem from above, the mother of us all, trains us to the utterance of a song suitable to seasons of millennial glory, when the Moloch of oppression, the Mammon of our avarice, the Ashtaroth of fiery lust, every erring creed, every false religion, shall have given place to the worship of the one true and living God—to the faith and love of Christ. "Let the peoples praise Thee, O God; let all the peoples praise Thee." W. H. GOOLD, *in "The Mission Hymn of the Hebrew Church: a Sermon"*

Vs. 1. *O sing unto the Lord a new song.* New joys are filling the hearts of men, for the glad tidings of blessing to all people are proclaimed; therefore let them sing a new song. Angels inaugurated the new dispensation with new songs, and shall not we take up the strain?

The song is for Jehovah alone, the hymns which chanted the praises of Jupiter and Neptune, Vishnoo and Siva, are hushed for ever; Bacchanalian shouts are silenced; lascivious sonnets are no more. Unto the One only God all music is to be dedicated. Mourning is over, and the time of singing of hearts has come. C. H. S.

*Sing unto the Lord, all the earth.* National jealousies are dead; a Jew invites the Gentiles to adore, and joins with them, so that all the earth may lift up one common Psalm as with one heart and voice unto Jehovah, Who hath visited it with His salvation.

No corner of the world is to be discordant, no race of heathen to be dumb. All the earth Jehovah made, and all the earth must sing to Him. As the sun shines on all lands, so are all lands to delight in the light of the Sun of Righteousness. E Pluribus Unum—out of many, one song shall come forth. The multitudinous languages of the sons of Adam, who were scattered at Babel, will blend in the same song when the people are gathered at Zion.

Nor men alone, but the earth itself is to praise its Maker. Made subject to vanity for a while by a sad necessity, the creation itself also is to be delivered from the bondage of corruption and brought into the glorious liberty of the children of God, so that sea and forest, field and flood, are to be joyful before the Lord.

Is this a dream? Then let us dream again. Blessed are the eyes which shall see the kingdom and the ears which shall hear its songs. Hasten Thine advent, good Lord! Yea, send forth speedily the rod of Thy strength out of Zion, that the nations may bow before the Lord and His Anointed. C. H. S.

"A new song," unknown to you before. Come, all ye nations of the wide earth, who, up to this hour, have been giving your worship to dead gods that were no gods at all; come and give your hearts to the true and only God in this new song! HENRY COWLES

We find it thrice said, *sing unto the Lord,* that we may understand that we are to sing unto Him with mind, and tongue, and deed. For all these things must be joined together, and the life ought to correspond with the mouth and mind. As Abbott Absolom says, "When the speech does not jar with the life, there is sweet harmony." LE BLANC

Vs. 2. *Sing unto the Lord, bless His name.* Thrice is the name of the Lord repeated, and not without meaning. Is it not unto the Three-One Lord that the enlightened nations will sing? Unitarianism is the religion of units; it is too cold to warm the world to worship; the sacred fire of adoration only burns with vehement flame where the Trinity is believed in and beloved.

*Show forth His salvation from day to day.* Each day brings us deeper experience of our saving God; each day shows us anew how deeply men need His salvation; each day reveals the power of the Gospel; each day the Spirit strives with the sons of men; therefore, never pausing, be it ours to tell out the glorious message of free grace.

Let those do this who know for themselves what His salvation means; they can bear witness that there is salvation in none other, and that in Him salvation to the uttermost is to be found. Let them show it forth till the echo flies around the spacious earth and all the armies of the sky unite to magnify the God Who hath displayed His saving health among all people. C. H. S.

Vs. 3. *Declare His glory among the heathen.* His glory shines from every ray of light that reaches us from a thousand stars; it sparkles from the mountain-tops that reflect the earliest and retain the last rays of the rising and the setting sun; it spreads over the expanse of the sea, and speaks in the murmur of its restless waves; it girdles the earth with a zone of light, and flings over it an aureole of beauty. We cannot augment it; we cannot add one ray of light to the faintness of a distant star nor give wings to an apterous insect, nor change a white hair into black. We can unfold, but not create; we can adore, but not increase; we can recognize the footprints of Deity, but not add to them. JOHN CUMMING, *in "From Patmos to Paradise"*

It is a part of the commission given to ministers of the gospel not only to teach their congregations concerning Christ, but also to have a care that they who never did hear of Him may know what He is, what He hath done and suffered, and what good may be had by His mediation. Nothing so glorious to God, nothing so wonderful in itself, as is the salvation of man by Christ; to behold God saving His enemies by the incarnation, sufferings, and obedience of Christ, the eternal Son of God: *Declare His glory among the heathen, His wonders among all people.* DAVID DICKSON

*His wonders among all people.* The gospel is a mass of wonders; its history is full of wonders, and it is in itself far more marvelous than miracles themselves. In the Person of His Son, the Lord has displayed wonders of love, wisdom, grace, and power. All glory be unto His name; who can refuse to tell out the story of redeeming grace and dying love? C. H. S.

What a wonderful person He is, for He is God manifest in the flesh; what wonderful love He has shown in His incarnation, obedience, sufferings, and death; what amazing miracles He wrought, and what a wonderful work He performed; the work of our redemption, the wonder of men and angels!

Declare His wonderful resurrection from the dead, His ascension to heaven, sitting at the right hand of God, and intercession for His people; the wonderful effusion of His Spirit, and the conquests of His grace, and the enlargement of His kingdom in the world; as also what wonders will be wrought by Him when He appears a second time; how the dead will be raised and all will be judged. JOHN GILL

Vs. 4. *For the Lord is great and greatly to be praised.* Praise should be proportionate to its object; therefore let it be infinite when rendered unto the Lord. We cannot praise Him too much, too often, too zealously, too carefully, too joyfully. C. H. S.

*He is to be feared above all gods.* Holy fear is the beginning of the graces, and yet it is the accompaniment of their highest range. Fear of God is the blush upon the face of holiness enhancing its beauty. C. H. S.

Vs. 6. *Honor and majesty are before Him.* Men can but mimic these things; their pompous pageants are but the pretense of greatness. Honor and majesty are with Him, and with Him alone. C. H. S.

Vs. 7. *Give unto the Lord glory and strength,* that is to say, recognize the glory and power of Jehovah and ascribe them unto Him in your solemn hymns. Who is glorious but the Lord? Who is strong save our God? Ye great nations, who count yourselves both famous and mighty, cease your boastings! Ye monarchs, who are styled imperial and puissant, humble yourselves in the dust before the only Potentate. Glory and strength are nowhere to be found save with the Lord; all others possess but the semblance thereof. Well did Massillon declare, "God alone is great." C. H. S.

Vs. 8. *Give unto the Lord the glory due unto His name.* But who can do that to the full? Can all the nations of the earth put together discharge the mighty debt? All conceivable honor is due to our Creator, Preserver, Benefactor, and Redeemer, and however much of zealous homage we may offer to Him, we cannot give Him more than His due. If we cannot bring in the full revenue which He justly claims, at least let us not fail from want of honest endeavor. C. H. S.

Is all the glory due unto God's name, and ought it, in strict justice, to have been ascribed unto Him by men, ever since man began to exist? How immeasurably great then is the debt which our world has contracted and under the burden of which it now groans!

During every day and every hour which has elapsed since the apostasy of man, this debt has been increasing; for every day and every hour all men ought to have given unto Jehovah the glory which is due to His name. But no man has ever done this fully. And a vast proportion of our race have never done it at all.

Now, the difference between the tribute which men ought to have paid to God and that which they actually have paid constitutes the debt of which we are speaking. How vast, then; how incalculable is it! EDWARD PAYSON

Vs. 9. *O worship the Lord in the beauty of holiness.* Worship must not be rendered to God in a slovenly, sinful, superficial manner. C. H. S.

Shall I call holiness an attribute? Is it not rather the glorious combination of all His attributes into one perfect whole? As all His attributes proceed from the Absolute, so all again converge and meet in holiness.

As from the insufferable white light of the Absolute they all seem to diverge and separate into prismatic hues, so they all seem again to converge and meet and combine in the dazzling white radiance of His holiness.

This, therefore, is rather the intense whiteness, purity, clearness, the infinite luster and splendor of His perfect nature—like a gem without flaw, without stain, and without color. All of His attributes are glorious, but in this we have a combination of all into a still more glorious whole. It is for this reason that it is so frequently in Scripture associated with the divine beauty. JOSEPH LE COUTE, *in "Religion and Science"*

*Fear before Him, all the earth.* Men of the world ridiculed "the Quakers" for trembling when under the power of the Holy Spirit; had they been able to discern the majesty of the Eternal, they would have quaked also. There is a sacred trembling, which is quite consistent with joy; the heart may even quiver with an awful excess of delight.

The sight of the King in His beauty caused no alarm to John in Patmos, and yet it made him fall at His feet as dead. Oh, to behold Him and worship Him with prostrate awe and sacred fear! C. H. S.

Vs. 10. *Say among the heathen that the Lord reigneth.* The dominion of Jehovah Jesus is not irksome; His rule is fraught with untold blessings; His yoke is easy, and His burden is light. C. H. S.

Vs. 11. *Let the sea roar.*

*Thou paragon of elemental powers,*
*Mystery of waters—never-slumbering sea!*
*Impassioned orator with lips sublime,*
*Whose waves are arguments which prove a God!*

ROBERT MONTGOMERY

Vs. 13. *For He cometh to judge the earth.* All the world will be under the jurisdiction of this great Judge, and before His bar all will be summoned to appear. At this moment He is on the road, and the hour of His coming draweth nigh. His great assize is proclaimed. Hear ye not the trumpets? His foot is on the threshold. C. H. S.

That is, to put the earth in order, to be its Gideon and Samson, to be its Ruler, to fulfill all that the Book of Judges delineates of a judge's office. It is, as Hengstenberg says, "a gracious judging," not a time of mere adjudication of causes or pronouncing sentences—it is a day of jubilee.

It is the happiest day our world has ever seen. Who would not long for it? Who is there that does not pray for it? It is the day of the Judge's glory, as well as of our world's freedom—the day when "the judgment of this world" (John 12:31 and 16:11), which His cross began and made sure, is completed by the total suppression of Satan's reign and the removal of the curse.

All this is anticipated here; and so we entitle this Psalm, *The glory due to Him Who cometh to judge the earth.* ANDREW A. BONAR

# PSALM 97

Subject: As the last Psalm sung the praises of the Lord in connection with the proclamation of the Gospel among the Gentiles, so this appears to foreshadow the mighty working of the Holy Ghost in subduing the colossal systems of error and casting down the idol gods.

One Psalm in this series is said to be "in David," and we believe that the rest are in the same place and by the same author. The matter is not important, and we only mention it because it seems to be the pride of certain critics to set up new theories; and there are readers who imagine this to be a sure proof of prodigious learning. We do not believe that their theories are worth the paper they are written upon. C. H. S.

Vs. 1. *The Lord reigneth; let the earth rejoice; let the multitude of isles be glad thereof.* This is the watchword of this Psalm—Jehovah reigns. It is also the essence of the gospel proclamation and the foundation of the gospel kingdom. Jesus has come, and all power is given to Him in heaven and in earth; therefore men are bidden to yield Him their obedient faith. Saints draw comfort from these words, and only rebels cavil at them. C. H. S.

As though he should say, "'Let nothing fear but hell: let nothing be disquieted but devils." Let the lowest, the poorest of the people of God, though but earth, yet let them rejoice in this, *The Lord reigneth.*

God will take all the power and authority into His own hands. He will not be any longer under men but above all men. It's time He should be so; it's reason He should be so; it's just He should be so. Everything now must bow, stoop, and submit to the law, and rule, and will of God. No man shall any longer say, it shall be so, because it is my will to have it so: there shall not be found an heart, or tongue, that shall move against the dominion of the Lord. WILLIAM SEDGWICK, *in "Some Flashes of Lightnings of the Son of Man"*

He Who stood before the judge, He Who received the blows, He Who was scourged, He Who was spit upon, He Who was crowned with thorns, He Who was struck with fists, He Who hung upon the cross, He Who as He hung upon the wood was mocked, He Who died upon the cross, He Who was pierced with the spear, He Who was buried, Himself rose from the dead. *The Lord reigneth.* Let kingdoms rage as much as they can; what can they do to the King of kingdoms, the Lord of all kings, the Creator of all worlds? AUGUSTINE

I am glad that Christ is the Lord of all, for otherwise I should utterly have been out of hope, saith Miconius in an epistle to Calvin, upon a view of the church's enemies. JOHN TRAPP

When Bulstrode Whitelock was embarked as Cromwell's envoy to Sweden, in 1635, he was much disturbed in mind, as he rested at Harwich the preceding night, which was very stormy, he thought upon the distracted state of the nation.

It happened that a confidential servant slept in an adjacent bed, who finding that his master could not sleep, at length said:

"Pray, sir, will you give me leave to ask you a question?"

"Certainly."

"Pray, sir, do you think God governed the world very well before you came into it?"

"Undoubtedly."

"And pray, sir, do you think that He will govern it quite as well when you are gone out of it?"

"Certainly."

"Then, pray, sir, excuse me, but do not you think you may trust Him to govern it quite as well as long as you live?"

To this question Whitelock had nothing to reply: but turning about, soon fell fast asleep, till he was summoned to embark. G. S. BOWES, in *"Illustrative Gatherings"*

Vs. 2. *Clouds and darkness are round about Him.* Around the history of His church, dark clouds of persecution hover, and an awful gloom at times settles down; still the Lord is there; and though men for a while see not the bright light in the clouds, it bursts forth in due season to the confusion of the adversaries of the Gospel.

This passage should teach us the impertinence of attempting to pry into the essence of the Godhead, the vanity of all endeavors to understand the mystery of the Trinity in unity, the arrogance of arraigning the Most High before the bar of human reason, the folly of dictating to the Eternal One the manner in which He should proceed.

Wisdom veils her face and adores the mercy which conceals the divine purpose; folly rushes in and perishes, blinded first, and by-and-by consumed by the blaze of glory. C. H. S.

*Righteousness and judgment are the habitation of His throne.* When the roll of the decrees and the books of the divine providence shall be opened, no eye shall there discern one word that should be blotted out, one syllable of error, one line of injustice, one letter of unholiness. Of none but the Lord of all can this be said. C. H. S.

Vs. 3. *A fire goeth before Him.* This divine flame goes still before the face of the Lord in His coming to every faithful soul, as it kindles with longing for Him, and burns up all its sins therewith, as He heaps His coals of fire upon its head, to soften and purify it.

"It must needs be," teaches a great saint, "that the fervor of holy desire must go before His face to every soul to which He means to come, a flame which shall burn up all the mildew of sin and make ready a place for the Lord.

"And then the soul knows that the Lord is at hand, when it feels itself kindled with that fire, and it saith with the prophet, "My heart was hot within me; then spake I with my tongue'" (Psalm 39:3). *Augustine and others, quoted by* NEALE AND LITTLEDALE

Vs. 4. *The earth saw, and trembled.* Nothing ever caused such a shaking and commotion as the proclamation of the Gospel; nothing was more majestic than its course; it turned the world upside down, leveled the mountains, and filled up the valleys. Jesus came, He saw, He conquered.

When the Holy Ghost rested upon His servants, their course was like that of a mighty storm, the truth flashed with the force and speed of a thunderbolt, and philosophers and priests, princes and people, were utterly confounded, and altogether powerless to withstand it. It shall be so again. Faith even now sets the world on fire and rocks the nations to and fro. C. H. S.

Vs. 5. *At the presence of the Lord of the whole earth.* Oh, for the presence of the Lord after this sort with His church at this hour! It is our one and only need. With it the mountains of difficulty would flee away and all obstacles would disappear. Oh, that Thou wouldest rend the heavens and come down, that the mountains might flow down at Thy presence, O Lord. C. H. S.

Vs. 7. *Confounded be all they that serve graven images, that boast themselves of idols.* They shall be so; shame shall cover their faces; they shall blush to think of their former besotted boastings. When a man gravely worships what has been engraved by a man's hand and puts his trust in a mere nothing and nonentity, he is indeed brutish, and when he is converted from such absurdity, he may well be ashamed. A man who worships an image is but the image of a man; his senses must have left him. He who boasts of an idol makes an idle boast.

*Worship Him, all ye gods.* Bow down yourselves, ye fancied gods. Let Jove do homage to Jehovah; let Thor lay down his hammer at the foot of the cross and Juggernaut remove his blood-stained car out of the road of Immanuel. If the false gods are thus bidden to worship the coming Lord, how much more shall they adore Him who are godlike creatures in heaven, even the angelic spirits? C. H. S.

Vs. 10. *Ye that love the Lord, hate evil.* For He hates it, His fire consumes it, His lightnings blast it, His presence shakes it out of its place, and His glory confounds all the lovers of it. We cannot love God without hating that which He hates. We are not only to avoid evil, and to refuse to countenance it, but we must be in arms against it, and bear towards it a hearty indignation. C. H. S.

It is evident that our conversation is sound when we loathe and hate sin from the heart: a man may know his hatred of evil to be true, first, if it be universal: he that hates sin truly, hates all sin.

Secondly, true hatred is fixed; there is no appeasing it but by abolishing the thing hated. Thirdly, hatred is a more rooted affection than anger: anger may be appeased, but hatred remains and sets itself against the whole kind. Fourthly, if our hatred be true, we hate all evil, in ourselves first, and then in others; he that hates a toad would hate it most in his own bosom. Many, like Judah, are severe in censuring others (Gen. 38:24), but partial to themselves.

Fifthly, He that hates sin truly, hates the greatest sin in the greatest measure; He hates all evil in a just proportion. Sixthly, our hatred is right if we can endure admonition and reproof for sin and not be enraged; therefore, those that swell against reproof do not appear to hate sin. Richard Sibbes

*Hate evil.*

Lucian: I am declared enemy of all false pretense, all quackery, all lies, and all puffing. I am a lover of truth, of beauty, or undisguised nature; in short, of everything that is lovely.

Philosophy: To love and to hate, they say, spring from one and the same source.

Lucian: That, O Philosophy, must be best known to you. My business is to hate the bad, and to love and commend the good; and that I stick to. Lucian, *Piscat, c. 8*

*He preserveth the souls of His saints.* Let us observe that there are two parts of divine protection—preservation and deliverance. Preservation is keeping lest we should be imperilled: deliverance has reference to those already involved in perils. The shepherd keeps his sheep lest they should fall among wolves; but if perchance they should fall into the clutches of the wolf, he pursues and delivers.

Both parts, the Prophet exhibits, persuading us that it is the Lord Who keeps the souls of His saints lest they fall into the hands of the wicked; and if they should fall, He will deliver them. Musculus

*He delivereth them out of the hand of the wicked.* It is not consistent with the glory of His name to give over to the power of His foes those whom His grace has made His friends. He may leave the bodies of His persecuted saints in the hand of the wicked, but not their souls; these are very dear to Him, and He preserves them safe in His bosom. This foretells for the church a season of battling with the powers of darkness, but the Lord will preserve it and bring it forth to the light. C. H. S.

Vs. 11. *Light is sown for the righteous.* We must remember that "light is sown for the righteous"; that its more or less rapid germination and development depend upon the nature of the soil on which it falls and the circumstances that influence it; that, like seed, it at first lies concealed in the dark furrow, under the cheerless clod, in the cold, ungenial winter.

Even then, while shining in the darkness, while struggling with doubts and difficulties of the mind and heart, it is nevertheless the source of much comfort, and in its slow, quickening, and hidden growth the cause of lively hope and of bright anticipation of that time when it shall blossom and ripen in the summer-time of heaven—shine more and more unto the perfect day. HUGH MACMILLAN, *in "The Ministry of Nature"*

The righteous man's harvest is secret and hidden if we consider where it is growing. One close is, *the secret purpose of God;* and who can understand it? A second is, *His Word;* and how hardly is that to be searched into? A third is, *a man's own heart;* and is not that both secret and deceitful? And last of all, the very principal part of the harvest is hid *with Christ in heaven;* and when He appears, it will appear what it shall be. JOHN BARLOW

*And gladness for the upright in heart.* Those who are right-hearted shall also be glad-hearted. Right leads to light. In the furrows of integrity lie the seeds of happiness, which shall develop into a harvest of bliss. God has lightning for sinners and light for saints. The gospel of Jesus, wherever it goes, sows the whole earth with joy for believers, for these are the men who are righteous before the Lord. C. H. S.

Vs. 12. *And give thanks at the remembrance of His holiness.* An unholy gospel is no gospel. The holiness of the religion of Jesus is its glory, it is that which makes it glad tidings, since while man is left in his sins no bliss can be his portion. Salvation from sin is the priceless gift of our thrice holy God; therefore let us magnify Him forever and ever. He will fill the world with holiness, and so with happiness; therefore let us glory in His holy name, world without end. Amen. C. H. S.

# PSALM 98

Title and Subject: The present Psalm is a sort of Coronation Hymn, officially proclaiming the conquering Messiah as Monarch over the nations, with blast of trumpets, clapping of hands, and celebration of triumphs. It is a singularly bold and lively song. The critics have fully established the fact that similar expressions occur in Isaiah, but we see no force in the inference that therefore it was written by him; on this principle half the books in the English language might be attributed to Shakespeare. C. H. S.

This Psalm is an evident prophecy of Christ's coming to save the world; and what is here foretold by David is, in the Blessed Virgin's Song, chanted forth as being accomplished. David is the *Voice*, and Mary is the *Echo*.

1. David: "O sing unto the Lord a new song" (The Voice).
   Mary: "My soul doth magnify the Lord" (The Echo).
2. David: "He hath done marvelous things" (The Voice).
   Mary: "He that is mighty hath done great things" (The Echo).
3. David: "With His own right hand and holy arm hath He gotten Himself the victory" (The Voice).
   Mary: "He hath showed strength with His arm, and scattered the proud in the imagination of their hearts" (The Echo).
4. David: "The Lord hath made known His salvation; His righteousness hath He openly showed," etc. (The Voice).
   Mary: "His mercy is on them that fear Him, from generation to generation" (The Echo).
5. David: "He hath remembered His mercy and His truth toward the house of Israel" The Voice).
   Mary: "He hath holpen His servant Israel, in remembrance of His mercy" (The Echo).

These parallels are very striking; and it seems as if Mary had this Psalm in her eye when she composed her song of triumph. ADAM CLARKE

Vs. 1. *O sing unto the Lord a new song; for He hath done marvelous things.* Jesus, our King, has lived a marvelous life, died a marvelous death, risen by a marvelous resurrection, and ascended marvelously into heaven.

By His divine power, He has sent forth the Holy Spirit doing marvels, and by that sacred energy His disciples have also wrought marvelous things and astonished all the earth. Idols have fallen, superstitions have withered, systems of error have fled, and empires of cruelty have perished.

For all this, He deserves the highest praise. His acts have proved His Deity, Jesus is Jehovah, and therefore we sing unto Him as the Lord. C. H. S.

This is a man's end, to seek God in this life, to see God in the next; to be a subject in the kingdom of grace, and a saint in the kingdom of glory. JOHN BOYS

He has opened His greatness and goodness in the work of redemption. What marvels has not Christ done? 1. He was conceived by the Holy Ghost. 2. Born of a virgin. 3. Healed all manner of diseases. 4. Fed thousands with a few loaves and fishes. 5. Raised the dead. 6. And what was more marvelous, died Himself. 7. Rose again by His own power. 8. Ascended to heaven. 9. Sent down the Holy Ghost. 10. And made His apostles and their testimony the instruments of enlightening and ultimately converting the world. ADAM CLARKE

*His right hand, and His holy arm, hath gotten Him the victory.* Jesus never stops to use policy or brute force; His unsullied perfections secure to Him a real and lasting victory over all the powers of evil, and that victory will be gained as dexterously and easily as when a warrior strikes his adversary with his right hand and stretches him prone upon the earth. Glory be unto the Conqueror; let new songs be chanted to His praise. C. H. S.

A clergyman in the county of Tyrone had, for some weeks, observed a little ragged boy come every Sunday and place himself in the center of the aisle, directly opposite the pulpit, where he seemed exceedingly attentive to the services.

He was desirous of knowing who the child was, and for this purpose hastened out, after the sermon, several times, but never could see him, as he vanished the moment service was over and no one knew whence he came or anything about him.

At length the boy was missed from his usual situation in the church for some weeks. At this time a man called on the minister and told him a person very ill was desirous of seeing him; but added, "I am really ashamed to ask you to go so far; but it is a child of mine, and he refuses to have anyone but you; he is altogether an extraordinary boy and talks a great deal about things that I do not understand."

The clergyman promised to go, and went, though the rain poured down in torrents, and he had six miles of rugged mountain country to pass. On arriving where he was directed, he saw a most wretched cabin indeed, and the man he had seen in the morning was waiting at the door. He was shown in and found the inside of the hovel as miserable as the outside.

In a corner, on a little straw, he beheld a person stretched out whom he recognized as the little boy who had so regularly attended his church. As he approached the wretched bed, the child raised himself up, and, stretching forth his arms, said, *His own right hand and His holy arm hath gotten Him the victory*, and immediately he expired. K. ARVINE

Vs. 3. *All the ends of the earth have seen the salvation of our God.* Pentecost deserves a new song as well as the passion and the resurrection; let our hearts exult as we remember it. Our God, our own forever blessed God, has been honored by those who once bowed down before dumb idols; His salvation has not only been heard of but seen among all people; it has been experienced as well as explained; His Son is the actual Redeemer of a multitude out of all nations. C. H. S.

Vs. 4. *Make a joyful noise unto the Lord, all the earth.* If ever men shout for joy, it should be when the Lord comes among them in the proclamation of His gospel reign. John Wesley said to his people, "Sing lustily, and with a good courage. Beware of singing as if you were half dead or half asleep; but lift up your voice with strength. Be no more afraid of your voice now, nor more ashamed of its being heard, than when you sang the songs of Satan." C. H. S.

Vs. 5. *With the harp.* God, Who accepts the unlettered ditty of a ploughman, does not reject the smooth verse of a Cowper or the sublime strains of a Milton. All repetitions are not vain repetitions; in sacred song there should be graceful repeats; they render the sense emphatic and help to fire the soul; even preachers do not amiss when they dwell on a word and sound it out again and again till dull ears feel its emphasis. C. H. S.

*The voice of a Psalm.* Jerome tells us that in his day the Psalms were to be heard in the fields and vineyards of Palestine, and that they fell sweetly on the ear, mingling with the song of birds and the scent of flowers in spring.

The ploughman, as he guided his plough, chanted the hallelujah, and the reaper, the vine-dresser, and the shepherd sang the songs of David. "These," he says, "are our love songs; these the instruments of our agriculture."

Sidonius Apollinaris makes his boatmen, as they urge their heavily-laden barge up stream, sing Psalms, till the river banks echo again with the hallelujah, and beautifully applies the custom, in a figure, to the voyage of the Christian life. J. J. S. PEROWNE

The singing of these Psalms became so popular that D'Israeli suggests that "it first conveyed to the sullen fancy of the austere Calvin the project" of introducing the singing of Psalms into his Genevan discipline. "This infectious frenzy of Psalm-singing," as Warton almost blasphemously describes it, rapidly propagated itself through Germany as well as France, and passed over to England.

D'Israeli says, with a sneer, that in the time of the Commonwealth, "Psalms were now sung at Lord Mayor's dinners and city feasts; soldiers sang them on their march and at parade; and a few houses which had windows fronting the streets, but had their evening Psalms." We can only add, would to God it were so again. C. H. S.

Vs. 6. *With trumpets.* Origen calls the writings of the evangelists and the apostles trumpets at whose blast all the structures of idolatry and the dogmas of the philosophers were utterly overthrown. He teaches likewise that by the sound of the trumpets is prefigured the trumpet of the universal judgment, at which the world shall fall in ruin, and whose sound shall be joy to the just and lamentation to the unjust. LORINUS

Verses 7-8. The setting forth the praise of Christ for the redemption of sinners may not only furnish work to all reasonable creatures but also if every drop of water in the sea, and in every river and flood, every fish in the sea, every fowl of the air, every living creature on the earth, and whatsoever else is in the world: if they all had reason and ability to express themselves: yea, and if all the hills were able by motion and gesticulation to communicate their joy one to another; there is work for them all to set out the praise of Christ. DAVID DICKSON

Vs. 9. *Before the Lord; for He cometh to judge the earth.* Stiller music such as made the stars twinkle with their soft kind eyes suited His first coming at Bethlehem, but His second advent calls for trumpets, for He is a judge; and for all earth's acclamations, for He has put on His royal splendor. The rule of Christ is the joy of nature. All things bless His throne, yea, and the very coming of it.

As the dawn sets the earth weeping for joy at the rising of the sun till the dewdrops stand in her eyes, so should the approach of Jesus' universal reign make all creation glad.

*With righteousness shall He judge the world, and the people with equity.* If ever there was a thing to rejoice in upon this poor, travailing earth, it is the coming of such a Deliverer, the ascension to the universal throne of such a Governor. All hail Jesus! all hail! Our soul faints with delight at the sound of Thine approaching chariots, and can only cry, "Come quickly. Even so, come quickly, Lord Jesus!" C. H. S.

Oh, what a store of comfort for the downtrodden, the enslaved, the needy, is laid up in the announcement that the Lord is coming to be the avenger of all such! Well may all the creatures be invited to clap their hands for joy at the thought that He has taken this work in hand; that He sitteth upon the floods; and that the storms that agitate the nations are the chariot in which He rides to take possession of the earth and make it an abode of righteousness and peace. WILLIAM BINNIE

This may be called the Sanctus, or "The Holy, Holy, Holy Psalm," for the word "holy" is the conclusion and the refrain of its three main divisions. Its subject is the holiness of the divine government, the sanctity of the mediatorial reign. C. H. S.

This Psalm has three parts, in which the Lord is celebrated as He Who is to come, as He Who is, and as He Who was. JOHN ALBERT BENGEL

There are three Psalms which begin with the words, "The Lord [Jehovah] reigneth" (Pss. 93, 97, 99). This is the third and last of these Psalms; and it is remarkable that in this Psalm the words *He is holy,* are repeated three times (verses 3, 5, 9).

Thus this Psalm is one of the links in the chain which connects the first revelation of God in Genesis with the full manifestation of the doctrine of the blessed Trinity, which is revealed in the commission of the risen Savior to His Apostles: "Go ye, and make disciples of all nations, baptizing them into the name of the Father, and of the Son, and of the Holy Ghost," and which prepares the faithful to join in the heavenly hallelujah of the church glorified. "Holy, holy, holy, Lord God Almighty, which was, and is, and is to come."

The other links in this chain in the Old Testament are: the Aaronic benediction in Num. 6:24-27; and the Seraphic Trisagion in Isa. 6:1-3. CHRISTOPHER WORDSWORTH

Vs. 1. *Let the people tremble.* Saints quiver with devout emotion and sinners quiver with terror when the rule of Jehovah is fully perceived and felt. It is not a light or trifling matter; it is a truth which, above all others, should stir the depths of our nature. C. H. S.

Vs. 2. *And He is high above all the people;* towering above their highest thoughts and loftiest conceptions. The highest are not high to Him yet, blessed be His name, the lowliest are not despised by Him. In such a God we rejoice. His greatness and loftiness are exceedingly delightful in our esteem. The more He is honored and exalted in the hearts of men, the more exultant are His people.

If Israel delighted in Saul because he was head and shoulders above the people, how much more should we exult in our God and King, Who is as high above us as the heavens are above the earth? C. H. S.

Vs. 3. *Let them praise Thy great and terrible name.* Many profess to admire the milder beams of the sun of righteousness but burn with rebellion against its more flaming radiance: so it ought not to be: we are bound to praise a terrible God and worship Him Who casts the wicked down to hell.

Did not Israel praise Him "Who overthrew Pharaoh and his hosts in the Red Sea, for His mercy endureth forever"! The terrible Avenger is to be praised as well as the loving Redeemer. Against this, the sympathy of man's evil heart with sin rebels; it cries out for an effeminate God in whom pity has strangled justice. C. H. S.

The Father's name is *great,* for He is the source, the Creator, the Lord of all; the Son's Name is *terrible,* for He is to be our Judge; the name of the Holy Ghost is *holy,* for He it is Who bestows hallowing and sanctification. HUGO CARDINALIS, GENEBRARDUS, AND BALTHAZAR CORDERIUS, *in Neale's Commentary*

The misery of sin consists not merely in its consequences, but in its very nature, which is to separate between God and our souls and to shut us out from God, and

God from us. ALFRED ELDERSHEIM, *in "The Golden Diary of Heart Converse with Jesus in the Book of Psalms"*

Vs. 5. *For He is holy.* Holiness is the harmony of all the virtues. The Lord has not one glorious attribute alone, or in excess, but all glories are in Him as a whole; this is the crown of His honor and the honor of His crown. His power is not His choicest jewel, nor His sovereignty, but His holiness.

The gods of the heathen were, according to their own votaries, lustful, cruel, and brutish; their only claim to reverence lay in their supposed potency over human destinies: who would not far rather adore Jehovah, Whose character is unsullied purity, unswerving justice, unbending truth, unbounded love, in a word, perfect holiness? C. H. S.

Vs. 5. *For He is holy.* Holiness is the harmony of all the virtues. The Lord a virtue all too rare in these our days; men run after their own views and opinions and make light of the truth of God; hence it is that they fail in prayer, and scoffers have even dared to say that prayer avails not at all. May the good Lord bring back His people to reverence His Word, and then will He also have respect unto the voice of their cry. C. H. S.

Vs. 8. *Thou answeredst them . . . forgavest them.* Oh, the blessed assurance that nothing can disturb our standing in the covenant. Answer and forgiveness are certain, though vengeance is taken of our inventions. How every word and expression here seems to go right to our hearts! The very designation of our sins and punishments is so true.

Yet, withal, we are not shut out from God. We are able to speak to and to hear Him; we receive what we need, and much more; and, above all, we have the sweet, abiding sense of forgiveness, notwithstanding "our inventions." When we smart under chastisements or disappointments, we know that it is the fire which burns up the hay, wood, and stubble—a Father's dealings in compassion and mercy.

We willingly, we gladly take these chastisements, which now are to us fresh pledges of our safety. For safe, eternally safe, remains the foundation, and unclosed the way of access. Oh, surely with all our heart do we accord: *Exalt Jehovah our God, and worship at His holy hill; for Jehovah our God is holy.* ALFRED EDERSHEIM

*Thou tookest vengeance of their inventions.* It is not a light punishment, but a "vengeance," "he takes on their inventions"; to manifest that He hates sin as sin, and not because the worst persons commit it.

Perhaps had a profane man touched the ark, the hand of God had not so suddenly reached him. But when Uzzah, a man zealous for Him, as may be supposed by his care for the support of the tottering ark, would step out of his place, He strikes him down for his disobedient action, by the side of the ark, which he would indirectly (as not being a Levite) sustain (II Sam. 6:7).

Nor did our Savior so sharply reprove the Pharisees and turn so short from them as He did from Peter, when he gave a carnal advice, and contrary to that wherein was to be the greatest manifestation of God's holiness, viz., the death of Christ (Matt. 16:23). He calls him "Satan," a name sharper than the title of the devil's children wherewith He marked the Pharisees, and given ((besides him) to none but Judas, who made a profession of love to Him and was outwardly ranked in the number of His disciples.

A gardener hates a weed the more for being in the bed with the most precious flowers. STEPHEN CHARNOCK

## PSALM 100

Title: "A Psalm of Praise"; or rather, of thanksgiving. This is the only Psalm bearing this precise inscription. It is all ablaze with grateful adoration, and has for this reason been a great favorite with the people of God ever since it was written. C. H. S.

This Psalm contains a promise of Christianity, as winter at its close contains the promise of spring. The trees are ready to bud, the flowers are just hidden by the light soil, the clouds are heavy with rain, the sun shines in his strength; only a genial wind from the south is wanted to give a new life to all things. *The Speaker's Commentary*

Vs. 1. *Make a joyful noise unto the Lord, all ye lands.* Our happy God should be worshiped by a happy people; a cheerful spirit is in keeping with His nature, His acts, and the gratitude which we should cherish for His mercies.

Vs. 2. *Serve the Lord with gladness.* The invitation to worship here given is not a melancholy one, as though adoration were a funeral solemnity, but a cheery, gladsome exhortation, as though we were bidden to a marriage feast. C. H. S.

It is a sign the oil of grace hath been poured into the heart "when the oil of gladness" shines on the countenance. Cheerfulness credits religion. THOMAS WATSON

Can you bear to be waited upon by a servant who goes moping and dejected to his every task? You would rather have no servant at all than one who evidently finds your service cheerless and irksome. GEORGE BOWEN

*Come before His presence with singing.* How a certain society of brethren can find it in their hearts to forbid singing in public worship is a riddle which we cannot solve. We feel inclined to say with Dr. Watts:

*Let those refuse to sing*
*Who never knew our God;*
*But favorites of the heavenly king*
*Must speak His praise abroad.*

C. H. S.

Vs. 3. *Know ye that the Lord He is God.* "Man, know thyself," is a wise aphorism, yet to know our God is truer wisdom; and it is very questionable whether a man can know himself until he knows his God. Jehovah is God in the fullest, most absolute, and most exclusive sense. He is God alone; to know Him in that character and prove our knowledge by obedience, trust, submission, zeal, and love is an attainment which only grace can bestow. C. H. S.

From the reasons of this exhortation, learn, that such is our natural atheism, that we have need again and again to be instructed, that the Lord is God; of Whom, and through Whom, and for Whom are all things. DAVID DICKSON

*It is He that hath made us, and not we ourselves.* To disclaim honor for ourselves is as necessary a part of true reverence as to ascribe glory to the Lord. For our part, we find it far more easy to believe that the Lord made us than that we were developed by a long chain of natural selections from floating atoms which fashioned themselves. C. H. S.

He made all without the help or concurrence of any other. There was none that assisted Him or did the least cooperate with Him in the work of creation . . . Those that assist and concur with another in the making of a thing may claim a share in it; but here lies no such claim in this case, where the Lord alone did all, alone made all. All is His only. DAVID CLARKSON

Many a one has drawn balsamic consolation from these words; as for instance Melanchthon when disconsolately sorrowful over the body of his son in Dresden on the twelfth of July, 1559. But, in "He made us and we are His," there is also a rich mine of comfort and of admonition, for the Creator is also the Owner, His heart clings to His creature, and the creature owes itself entirely to Him, without Whom it would not have had a being, and would not continue in being. F. DELITZSCH

The Masorites, by altering one letter in the Hebrew, read it, "He made us, and His we are," or "to Him we belong." Put both the readings together, and we learn that because God "made us, and not we ourselves," therefore we are not our own but His. MATTHEW HENRY

Vs. 5. *For the Lord is good.* This sums up His character and contains a mass of reasons for praise. He is good, gracious, kind, bountiful, loving; yea, God is love.

*His mercy is everlasting.* God is not mere justice, stern and cold; He has bowels of compassion and wills not the sinner's death.

*And His truth endureth to all generations.* It were well if the truth of divine faithfulness were more fully remembered by some theologians; it would overturn their belief in the final fall of believers and teach them a more consolatory system. C. H. S.

# PSALM 101

Title: "A Psalm of David." This is just such a Psalm as the man after God's own heart would compose when he was about to become a king in Israel. It is David all over, straight-forward, resolute, devout; there is no trace of policy or vacillation—the Lord has appointed him to be king, and he knows it; therefore he purposes in all things to behave as becomes a monarch whom the Lord Himself has chosen.

If we call this "The Psalm of Pious Resolutions," we shall perhaps remember it all the more readily. After songs of praise a Psalm of practice not only makes variety but comes in most fittingly. We never praise the Lord better than when we do those things which are pleasing in His sight. C. H. S.

This is the Psalm which the old expositors used to designate "The Mirror for Magistrates"; and an excellent mirror it is. It would mightily accelerate the coming of the time when every nation shall be Christ's possession and every capital a "City of the Lord," if all magistrates could be persuaded to dress themselves by it every time they go forth to perform the functions of their godlike office. WILLIAM BINNIE

Eyring, in his *Life of Ernest the Pious* (Duke of Saxegotha), relates that he sent an unfaithful minister a copy of the One Hundred First Psalm, and that it became a proverb in the country when an official had done anything wrong: "He will certainly soon receive the Prince's Psalm to read." F. DELITZSCH

The One Hundred First Psalm was one beloved by the noblest of Russian princes, Vladimir Monomachos; and by the gentlest of English reformers, Nicholas Ridley. But it was its first leap into life that has carried it so far into the future.

It is full of a stern exclusiveness, of a noble intolerance, not against theological error, not against uncourtly manners, not against political insubordination, but against the proud heart, the high look, the secret slanderer, the deceitful worker, the teller of lies. These are the outlaws from king David's court; these are the rebels and heretics whom he would not suffer to dwell in his house or tarry in his sight. ARTHUR PENRHYN STANLEY, *in "Lectures on the History of the Jewish Church"*

Vs. 1. *I will sing of mercy and judgment.* We ought as much to bless the Lord for the judgment with which He chastens our sin as for the mercy with which He forgives it; there is as much love in the blows of His hand as in the kisses of His mouth. C. H. S.

Oh, how fair a thing is this mercy in the time of anguish and trouble! It is like a cloud of rain that cometh in the time of drought. But this mercy, here spoken of in the first part of our prophet's song, stretcheth further; unfolding itself in clemency, in courtesy, and in compassion. In clemency, pardoning malefactors; in compassion, by relieving the afflicted; in courtesy, towards all. GEORGE HAKEWILL, OR HAKEWELL

Is there a child of God that can look into the varied record of his heart or of his outward history, and not see goodness and severity, severity and goodness, tracking him all his journey through? Has he ever had a cup so bitter that he could say, "There is no mercy here"? Has he ever had a lot so bright that he could say, "There is no chastisement or correction here"?

Has he ever had any bad tidings, and there have been no good tidings set over against them to relieve them? Has he ever had a sky so dark that he could see in it no star, or a cloud so unchequered that he could trace no rainbow of promise there? HUGH STOWELL

Vs. 2. *O when wilt Thou come unto me?* If God be with us, we shall neither err in judgment nor transgress in character; His presence brings us both wisdom and holiness; away from God, we are away from safety.

*I will walk within my house with a perfect heart.* Reader, how fares it with your family? Do you sing in the choir and sin in the chamber? Are you a saint abroad and a devil at home? For shame! What we are at home, that we are indeed. He cannot be a good king whose palace is the haunt of vice, nor he a true saint whose habitation is a scene of strife, nor he a faithful minister whose household dreads his appearance at the fireside. C. H. S.

He is a bad husband that hath money to spend among the company abroad, but none to lay in provisions to keep his family at home. And can he be a good Christian that spends all his religion abroad and leaves none for his nearest relations at home? WILLIAM GURNALL

It is easier for most men to walk with a perfect heart in the church, or even in the world, than in their own families. How many are as meek as lambs among others, when at home they are wasps or tigers! ADAM CLARKE

Vs. 3. *Wicked thing.* The original hath it, if we will render it word for word, "I will set no word of Belial before mine eyes." But *word* is figuratively there put for *thing;* as likewise Ps. 41:8; and so is it rendered both by Montanus in the margin, and in the text by Junius; howbeit, in his comment upon this Psalm, he precisely follows the original, applying it against sycophants and flatterers, the mice and moths of court. GEORGE HAKEWILL

*I hate the work of them that turn aside.* He was warmly against it; he did not view it with indifference, but with utter scorn and abhorrence. Hatred of sin is a good sentinel for the door of virtue. C. H. S.

*It shall not cleave to me.* A bird may light upon a man's house; but he may choose whether she shall nestle or breed there, or no: and the devil or his instruments may represent a wicked object to a man's sight; but he may choose whether he will entertain or embrace it or no. For a man to set wicked things before his eyes is nothing else but to sin of set purpose, to set himself to sin, or to sell himself to sin, as Ahab did (I Kings 21). GEORGE HAKEWILL

Vs. 4. *A froward heart.* The original sense of "froward" is *torsit, contorsit* (contortion), to twist together, and denotes, when applied to men, persons at a perverse, subtle disposition, that can twist and twine themselves into all manner of shapes, and who have no truth and honor to be depended on. SAMUEL CHANDLER

Vs. 5. *Whoso privily slandereth his neighbor, him will I cut off.* To give one's neighbor a stab in the dark is one of the most atrocious of crimes and cannot be too heartily reprobated, yet such as are guilty of it often find patronage in high places and are considered to be men of penetration, trusty ones who have a keen eye and take care to keep their lords well posted up. C. H. S.

Vs. 6. *He that walketh in a perfect way, he shall serve me.* What I wish myself to be, that I desire my servant to be. Employers are to a great degree responsible for their servants, and it is customary to blame a master if he retains in his service persons of notorious character; therefore, lest we become partakers of other men's sins, we shall do well to decline the services of bad characters. C. H. S.

## PSALM 102

Subject: This is a patriot's lament over his country's distress. He arrays himself in the griefs of his nation as in a garment of sackcloth and casts her dust and ashes upon his head as the ensigns and causes of his sorrow. He has his own private woes and personal enemies; he is, moreover, sore afflicted in body by sickness, but the miseries of his people cause him a far more bitter anguish, and this he pours out in an earnest, pathetic lamentation. Not, however, without hope does the patriot mourn; he has faith in God and looks for the resurrection of the nation through the omnipotent favor of the Lord.

The word rendered "complaint" has in it none of the idea of fault-finding or repining, but should rather be rendered "moaning"—the expression of pain, not of rebellion. To help the memory, we will call this Psalm "The Patriot's Plaint." C. H. S.

Title: *A Prayer*, etc. The prayer following is longer than ours. When Satan, the Law-Adversary, doth extend his pleas against us, it is meet that we should enlarge our counter pleas for our own souls; as the powers of darkness do lengthen and multiply their wrestlings, so must we our counter wrestlings of prayer (Eph. 6:12, 18). THOMAS COBBET

Here is no lazy, slothful, lip-labor, stinted forms of prayer, no empty sounds of verbal expressions, which can never procure her a comfortable answer from her God, or the least ease to her burdened soul; but poured-out prayers as Hannah (I Sam. 1:15) and Jeremy (Lam. 2:12), pressed forth with vehemence of spirit and heart pangs of inward grief: thus the Lord deals with His church and people; ere He pours out cups of consolation, they must pour out tears in great measure. FINIENS CANUS VOVE

Vs. 1. *Hear my prayers, O Lord.* Or, O Jehovah. Sincere suppliants are not content with praying for praying's sake; they desire really to reach the ear and heart of the great God. It is a great relief in time of distress to acquaint others with our trouble. We are eased by their hearing our lamentation. But it is the sweetest solace of all to have God Himself as a sympathizing listener to our plaint. That He is such is no dream, or fiction, but an assured fact.

It would be the direst of all our woes if we could be indisputably convinced that with God there is neither hearing nor answering; he who could argue us into so dreary a belief would do us no better service than if he had read us our death-warrants. Better die than be denied the mercy-seat. As well be atheists at once as believe in an unhearing, unfeeling God. C. H. S.

Verses 1-2. Note, David sent his prayer as a sacred ambassador to God. Now there are three things requisite to make an embassy prosperous. The ambassador must be regarded with favorable eye: he must be heard with a ready ear: he must speedily return when his demands are conceded. These three things David, as a suppliant, asks from God, his King. LE BLANC

Vs. 2. *In the day when I call answer me speedily.* It is a proverb concerning favors from human hands that "he gives twice who gives quickly," because a gift is enhanced in value by arriving in a time of urgent necessity; and we may be sure that our heavenly Patron will grant us the best of gifts in the best manner, granting us grace to help in time of need. When answers come upon the heels of our prayers, they are all the more striking, more consoling, and more encouraging. C. H. S.

Vs. 3. *For my days are consumed like smoke.* The metaphor is very admirably chosen, for, to the unhappy, life seems not merely to be frail, but to be surrounded by so much that is darkening, defiling, blinding, and depressing, that, sitting down in despair, they compare themselves to men wandering in a dense fog and themselves so dried up thereby that they are little better than pillars of smoke. C. H. S.

Vs. 4. *So that I forget to eat my bread.* As the smitten flower no longer drinks in the dew or draws up nutriment from the soil, so a heart parched with intense grief often refuses consolation for itself and nourishment for the bodily frame and descends at a doubly rapid rate into weakness, despondency, and dismay.

The case here described is by no means rare. We have frequently met with individuals so disordered by sorrow that their memory has failed them even upon such pressing matters as their meals, and we must confess that we have passed through the same condition ourselves. One sharp pang has filled the soul, monopolized the mind, and driven everything else into the background, so that such common matters as eating and drinking have been utterly despised, and the appointed hours of refreshment have gone by unheeded, leaving no manifest faintness of body but an increased weariness of heart. C. H. S.

But as the vigor of the heart breeds plenty of spirits, which convey to all the parts, gives everyone a natural appetite; so when the heart is blasted and withered like grass, and that there is no more any vigor in it, the spirits are presently at a stand, and then no marvel if the stomach lose its appetite and forget to eat bread. SIR R. BAKER

Vs. 5. *By reason of the voice of my groaning my bones cleave to my skin.* That grief readily causes the body to pine away is very well known. It is related of Cardinal Wolsey, by an eye-witness, that when he heard that his master's favor was turned from him, he was wrung with such an agony of grief, which continued a whole night, that in the morning his face was dwindled away into half its usual dimensions. C. H. S.

Vs. 6. *I am like an owl of the desert.* The Psalmist likens himself to two birds which were commonly used as emblems of gloom and wretchedness; on other occasions he had been as the eagle, but the griefs of his people had pulled him down, the brightness was gone from his eye, and the beauty from his person.

Were there more of this holy sorrow, we should soon see the Lord returning to build up His church. It is ill for men to be playing the peacock with worldly pride when the ills of the times should make them as mournful as the pelican; and it is a terrible thing to see men flocking like vultures to devour the prey of a decaying church, when they ought rather to be lamenting among her ruins, like the owl. C. H. S.

*Save that from yonder ivy-mantled tower,*
*The moping owl does to the moon complain*
*Of such as, wand'ring near her secret bow'r,*
*Molest her ancient solitary reign.*

THOMAS GRAY

Vs. 7. *I watch, and am like a sparrow alone upon the house top.* Christians of an earnest, watchful kind often find themselves among those who have no sympathy with them; even in the church they look in vain for kindred spirits; then so they persevere in their prayers and labors, but feel themselves to be as lonely as the poor bird which looks from the ridge of the roof and meets with no friendly greeting from any of its kind. C. H. S.

But little do men perceive what solitude is, and how far it extendeth; for a crowd is not company, and faces are but a gallery of pictures, and talk but a tinkling cymbal where there is no love. FRANCIS BACON

Vs. 8. *Mine enemies reproach me.* It is true what Plutarch writes, that men are more touched with reproaches than with other injuries; affliction, too, gives a keener edge to calumny, for the afflicted are more fitting objects of pity than of mockery. MOLLERUS

If I be where they are, they rail at me to my face; and if I be not amongst them, they revile me behind my back; and they do it not by starts and fits, that might give me some breathing time; but they are spitting their poison *all the day long;* and not single and one by one, that might leave hope of resisting; but they make combinations, and enter leagues against me; and to make their leagues the stronger, and less subject to dissolving, they bind themselves by oath, and take the sacrament upon it.

And now sum up all these miseries and afflictions; begin with my fasting; then take my groaning; then add my watching; then the shame of being wondered at in company; then the discomfort of sitting disconsolate alone; and, lastly, add to these the spite and malice of my enemies; and what marvel, then, if these miseries joined all together make me altogether miserable; what marvel if I be nothing but skin and bone, when no flesh that were wise would ever stay upon a body to endure such misery. SIR R. BAKER

Vs. 9. *I have mingled my drink with weeping.* No man certainly commits sin but with a design of pleasure; but sin will not be so committed; for whosoever commit sin, let them be sure at some time or other to find a thousand times more trouble about it than ever they found pleasure in it. For all sin is a kind of surfeit, and there is no way to keep it from being mortal but by this strict diet of eating ashes like bread and mingling his drink with tears.

O my soul, if these be works of repentance in David, where shall we find a penitent in the world besides himself? To talk of repentance is obvious in everyone's mouth; but where is any that eats ashes like bread and mingles his drink with tears? SIR R. BAKER

Vs. 11. *And I am withered like grass.* There are times when through depression of spirit a man feels as if all life were gone from him and existence had become merely a breathing death. Heart-break has a marvelously withering influence over our entire system; our flesh at its best is but as grass, and when it is wounded with sharp sorrows, its beauty fades, and it becomes a shriveled, dried, uncomely thing.

Vs. 13. *For the time to favor her, yea, the set time, is come.* When God's own time is come, neither Rome, nor the devil, nor persecutors, nor atheists, can prevent the kingdom of Christ from extending its bounds. It is God's work to do it—He must "arise"; He will do it, but He has His own appointed season; and meanwhile we must, with holy anxiety and believing expectation, wait upon Him. C. H. S.

That is God's set time when the church is most believing, most humble, most affectionate to God's interest in it, and most sincere. Without faith we are not fit to desire mercy; without humility we are not fit to receive it; without affection we are not fit to value it; without sincerity we are not fit to improve it. Times of extremity contribute to the growth and exercise of these qualifications. STEPHEN CHARNOCK

Vs. 16. *When the Lord shall build up Zion, He shall appear in His glory.* The sun is ever glorious in the most cloudy day but appears not so till it hath scattered the clouds that muffle it up from the sight of the lower world: God is glorious when the world sees Him not: but His declarative glory then appears when the glory of His mercy, truth, and faithfulness break forth in His people's salvation.

Now, what shame must this cover thy face with, O Christian, if thou shouldest not sincerely aim at thy God's glory, Who loves thee, yea, all His children so dearly, as to ship His own glory and your happiness in one bottom, that He cannot now lose the one and save the other! WILLIAM GURNALL

Vs. 17. *The prayer of the destitute.* A man that is destitute knows how to pray. He needs not any instructor. His miseries indoctrinate him wonderfully in the art of offering prayer. Let us know ourselves destitute, that we may know how to pray; destitute of strength, of wisdom, of due influence, of true happiness, of proper faith, of thorough consecration, of the knowledge of the Scriptures, of righteousness.

Give all thy trashy gold—trashy while it is with thee—give it to My poor; and I will give thee true gold, namely, a sense of thy misery and meanness; a longing for grace, purity, usefulness; a love of thy fellowmen; and My love shed abroad in thy heart. GEORGE BOWEN

Vs. 21. *To declare the Name of the Lord in Zion, and His praise in Jerusalem.* To communicate to others what God has done for us personally and for the church at large is so evidently our duty that we ought not to need urging to fulfill it. God has ever an eye to the glory of His grace in all that He does, and we ought not wilfully to defraud Him of the revenue of His praise. C. H. S.

Vs. 24. *O my God.* The leaving out one word in a will may mar the estate and disappoint all a man's hopes; the want of this one word, *my* (God) is the wicked man's loss of heaven, and the dagger which will pierce his heart in hell to all eternity.

The pronoun *my* is as much worth to the soul as the boundless portion. All our comfort is locked up in that private cabinet. When God saith to the soul, as Ahab to Benhadad, "Behold, I am thine, and all that I have," who can tell how the heart leaps for joy in, and expires almost in desires after Him upon such news!

Luther saith, "Much religion lieth in pronouns." All our consolation, indeed, consisteth in this pronoun. It is the cup which holdeth all our cordial waters. All the joys of the believer are hung upon this one string; breaketh that asunder, and all is lost. I have sometimes thought how David rolls it as a lump of sugar under his tongue, as one loth to lose its sweetness too soon: "I will love Thee, O Lord, my strength, my buckler, and the horn of my salvation, and my high tower" (Ps. 18:1-2). This pronoun is the door at which the King of saints entereth into our hearts with His whole train of delights and comforts. GEORGE SWINNOCK

*Thy years are throughout all generations.* Thou livest, Lord; let me live also. A fullness of existence is with Thee; let me partake therein. Note the contrast between himself pining and ready to expire, and his God living on in the fullness of strength forever and ever; this contrast is full of consolatory power to the man whose heart is stayed upon the Lord. Blessed be His Name, He faileth not, and, therefore, our hope shall not fail us; neither will we despair for ourselves or for His church. C. H. S.

The Psalmist says of Christ, *Thy years are throughout all generations* (Ps. 102:24); which Psalm the Apostle quoteth of Him (Heb. 1:10). Let us trace His existence punctually through all times. Let us go from point to point and see how in particulars the Scriptures accord with it.

We find Him to have existed just afore He came into the world, the instance of His conception (Heb. 10:5) in these words, "Wherefore when He cometh into the world, He saith, A body hast Thou prepared Me."

We find Him existing in Moses' time, both because it was He that was tempted in the wilderness, "Neither let us tempt Christ as some of them also tempted, and were destroyed of serpents" (I Cor. 10:9); and it was Christ that was the Person said to be tempted by them, as well as now by us, as the words, "as they also," evidently show.

We find Him existing in and afore Abraham's time: "Verily, verily I say unto you, Before Abraham was, I am" (John 8:58).

We find Him existing in the days of Noah (I Pet. 3:19). He says of Christ, that He was "put to death in the flesh, but quickened in the Spirit."

He was extant at the beginning of the world, "In the beginning was the Word." In which words, there being no predicate or attribute affirmed of this word, the sentence or affirmation is terminated or ended merely with His existence: "He was," and He was then, "in the beginning." He says not that He was *made* in the beginning, but that "He was in the beginning." *Condensed from T. Goodwin's Treatise on "The Knowledge of God the Father, and His Son Jesus Christ"*

Vs. 26. *As a vesture shalt Thou change them, and they shall be changed,* not abolished. The concupiscence shall pass, not the essence; the form, not the nature. In the altering of an old garment, we destroy it not, but trim it, refresh it, and make it seem new. They pass; they do not perish; the dross is purged, the metal stays. The corrupt quality shall be renewed, and all things restored to that original beauty wherein they were created.

The end of all things is at hand (I Pet. 4:7): an end of us, an end of our days, an end of our ways, and end of our thoughts. If a man could say as Job's messenger, "I alone am escaped," it were somewhat; or might find an ark with Noah. But there is no ark to defend them from that heat, but only the bosom of Jesus Christ. THOMAS ADAMS

We have thus passed through the cloud, and in the next Psalm we shall bask in the sunshine. Such is the chequered experience of the believer. Paul, in the seventh of Romans, cries and groans, and then in the eighth rejoices and leaps for joy; and so, from the moaning of the Hundred and Second Psalm, we now advance to the songs and dancing of the Hundred and Third, blessing the Lord, that "though weeping may endure for a night, joy cometh in the morning." C. H. S.

# PSALM 103

How often have saints in Scotland sung this Psalm in days when they celebrated the Lord's Supper! It is thereby specially known in our land. It is connected also with a remarkable case in the days of John Knox.

Elizabeth Adamson, a woman who attended on his preaching, "because he more fully opened the fountain of God's mercies than others did," was led to Christ and to rest, on hearing this Psalm, after enduring such agony of soul that she said, concerning racking pains of body, "A thousand years of this torment, and ten times more joined, are not to be compared to a quarter of an hour of my soul's trouble."

She asked for this Psalm again before departing: "It was in receiving it that my troubled soul first tasted God's mercy, which is now sweeter to me than if all the kingdoms of the earth were given me to possess." ANDREW A. BONAR

Vs. 1. *And all that is within me, bless His holy name.* Halfhearted, ill-conceived, unintelligent praises are not such as we should render to our loving Lord. If the law of justice demanded all our heart and soul and mind for the Creator, much more may the law of gratitude put in a comprehensive claim for the homage of our whole being to the God of grace. C. H. S.

Let your conscience "bless the Lord" by unvarying fidelity. Let your judgment bless Him by pure and holy musings.

Let your affections praise Him by loving whatsoever He loves. Let your desires bless Him by seeking only His glory. Let your memory bless Him by not forgetting any of His benefits. Let your thoughts bless Him by meditating on His excellencies.

Let your hope praise Him by longing and looking for the glory that is to be revealed. Let your every sense bless Him by its fealty, your every word by its truth, and your every act by its integrity. JOHN STEVENSON

Verses 1-2. The well is seldom so full that water will at first pumping flow forth; neither is the heart commonly so spiritual, after our best care in our worldly converse (much less when we somewhat overdo therein) as to pour itself into God's bosom freely, without something to raise and elevate it; yea, often, the springs of grace lie so low, that pumping only will not fetch the heart up to a praying frame but arguments must be poured into the soul before the affections rise. WILLIAM GURNALL

Verses 1-3.

*If there be passions in my soul,*
*(And passions, Lord, there be);*
*Let them be all at Thy control,*
*My gracious Lord, for Thee.*

WILLIAM JAY

Vs. 2. *And forget not all His benefits.* Remember how the Persian king, when he could not sleep, read the chronicles of the empire, and discovered that one who had saved his life had never been rewarded. How quickly did he do him honor! The Lord has saved us with a great salvation; shall we render no recompense?

The name of *ingrate* is one of the most shameful that a man can wear; surely we cannot be content to run the risk of such a brand. Let us awake then and with intense enthusiasm bless Jehovah.

Vs. 3. *Who forgiveth all thine iniquities.* Here David begins his list of blessings received, which he rehearses as themes and arguments for praise. He selects a few of the choicest pearls from the casket of divine love, threads them on the string of memory, and hangs them about the neck of gratitude. C. H. S.

In this lovely and well-known Psalm, we have great fullness of expression, in reference to the vital subject of redemption. "Who forgiveth *all* thine iniquities." It is not *some* or "*many* of thine iniquities." This would never do. If so much as the very smallest iniquity in thought, word, or act, were left unforgiven, we should be just as badly off, just as far from God, just as unfit for heaven, just as exposed to hell, as though the whole weight of our sins were yet upon us. Let the reader ponder this deeply.

It does not say, "Who forgiveth thine iniquities previous to conversion." There is no such notion as this in Scripture. When God forgives, He forgives like Himself. The source, the channel, the power, and the standard of forgiveness are all divine. When God cancels a man's sins, He does so according to the measure in which Christ bore those sins. Now, Christ not only bore some or many of the believer's sins, He bore them *all,* and, therefore, God forgives *all.*

God's forgiveness stretches to the length of Christ's atonement; and Christ's atonement stretches to the length of every one of the believer's sins, past, present, and future. "The blood of Jesus Christ His Son cleanseth us from all sin" (I John 1). "*Things New and Old*"

*Who healeth all thy diseases.*

*In Him is only good,*
*In me is only ill,*
*My ill but draws His goodness forth,*
*And me He loveth still.*

God gives efficacy to medicine for the body, and His grace sanctifies the soul. Spiritually we are daily under His care, and He visits us, as the surgeon does his patient; healing still (for that is the exact word) each malady as it arises. No disease of our soul baffles His skill; He goes on healing all; and He will do so till the last trace of taint has gone from our nature. The two *alls* of this verse are further reasons for *all* that is within us praising the Lord. C. H. S.

In one of the prisons of a certain country was a man who had committed high treason: for this crime he was in due time tried, and, being found guilty, was condemned to die. But more than this; he was afflicted with an inward disease which generally proves mortal.

Now, we may say truly that this man is doubly dead; that his life is forfeited twice over: the laws of his country have pronounced him guilty of death, and therefore his life is forfeited once to the laws of his country, and, if he had not died in this way, he must die of his disease; he is, therefore, "twice dead."

Now suppose that the sovereign of that country had made up his mind to wish to save that prisoner's life; could he save it? He could indeed take off the penalty of the law; he could give him a free pardon, and so restore the life, as sure as it is forfeited by the just sentence of the law; but, unless he could also send a physician who could cure the man of his disease, he would die by that, and his pardon would only lengthen out for a few weeks or months a miserable existence.

And if this disease were not only a mortal disease but an infectious one, likely to spread itself by the breath of the patient, and a contagious one, likely to spread by the touch of the patient's body or clothes, then it would be dangerous to others to come near that man; and unless he were cured, and thoroughly and entirely cured, the man, though pardoned, would still be a fit inmate only for the pest-house and could not be received into the houses of the healthy.

You have seen such a case as this, brethren; you are at this very moment, perhaps, sitting close by a person in this case; yes, and perhaps you are in this very case yourself! Perhaps, do I say? I should say, you are in this very case, unless you are really and truly a Christian, a believer in Christ Jesus. W. WELDON CHAMPNEYS

The body experienceth the melancholy consequences of Adam's offence, and is subject to many infirmities; but the soul is subject to as many. What is pride, but lunacy; what is anger, but a fever; what is avarice, but a dropsy; what is lust, but a leprosy; what is sloth, but a dead palsy? Perhaps there are spiritual maladies similar to all corporeal ones. GEORGE HORNE

Must not that needs be a monstrous face, wherein the blueness which should be in the veins is in the lips, the redness which should be in the cheeks, in the nose; the hair that should grow on the head, on the face? And must not our souls' needs seem ugly in the sight of God, who have grief growing there where joy should, and joy where grief should? We love what we should hate and hate where we should love; we fear where no fear is, and fear not where we ought to fear; and all our affections either mistake their object or exceed their due measure. THOMAS FULLER

Vs. 4. *Who crowneth thee with lovingkindness and tender mercies.* Our sin deprived us of all our honors, a bill of attainder was issued against us as traitors; but He Who removed the sentence of death by redeeming us from destruction restores to us more than all our former honors by crowning us anew. Shall God crown us and shall we not crown Him? Up, my soul, and cast thy crown at His feet, and in lowliest reverence worship Him, Who has so greatly exalted thee as to lift thee from the dunghill and set thee among princes. C. H. S.

I do not know that I can do better than tell you a little incident that took place in my native town of Stirling. Workmen were blasting the castle rock near where it abuts upon a walk that lies open to the street. The train was laid and lit and an explosion was momentarily expected.

Suddenly, trotting round the great wall of the cliff, came a little child going straight to where the match burned. The men shouted (it was mercy) and by their very terror in shouting, alarmed and bewildered the poor little thing. By this time the mother also had come round: in a moment saw the danger; opened wide her arms, and cried from her very heart, "Come to me, my darling" (that was tender mercy).

Instantly, with eager, pattering feet, and little arms opened to her arms, and tear-filled eyes answering to her eyes, the little thing ran back and away and stopped not until she was clasped in her mother's bosom—wealth of sunny hair loosened on it, and lips coral red pressed to mother's pallid lip of fear—as the motherly heart gave way to tears, in the thought of so imperiled an escape: for it was barely by a second, as the roar of the shattered rock told. ALEXANDER B. GROSART, *in "The Pastor and Helper of Joy"*

Vs. 5. *Who satisfieth thy mouth with good things,* or rather "filling with good thy soul." No man is ever filled to satisfaction but a believer, and only God Himself can satisfy even him.

*So that thy youth is renewed like the eagle's.* He who sat moping with the owl in the last Psalm here flies on high with the eagle: the Lord works marvelous changes in us, and we learn by such experiences to bless His holy name. To grow from a sparrow to an eagle and leave the wilderness of the pelican to mount among the stars is enough to make any man cry, "Bless the Lord, O my soul." C. H. S.

The fairest part of life the sensual man sees soon behind him, the spiritual man always in prospect; and like the eagle, this last can often from the low atmosphere round him soar to the pure, clear ether, whence already from afar the image, nay, the ineffable reality, shows him a more than earthly joy. J. J. VAN OOSTERZEE, *in "The Year of Salvation"*

Vs. 8. *Plenteous in mercy.* The commodity which we stand in need of is mercy and the pardon of our sins, because we have been unholy and ungodly creatures; this commodity is abundantly in God. There it is treasured up as waters are in the storehouse of the sea; there is no end of the treasures of His grace, mercy, pardon, and compassion.

There is no man, being in want, but had rather go to a rich man's door to be relieved than to the door of a poor man, if he knoweth the rich man to be as liberal and as bountifully disposed as the poor man can be. JOHN GOODWIN, *on "Being Filled with the Spirit"*

Vs. 9. *Neither will He keep His anger forever.* He bears no grudges. The Lord would not have His people harbor resentments, and in His own course of action He sets them a grand example. When the Lord has chastened His child, He has done with His anger: He is not punishing as a judge, else might His wrath burn on, but He is acting as a father, and, therefore, after a few blows, He ends the matter and presses His beloved one to His bosom as if nothing had happened.

Or if the offence lies too deep in the offender's nature to be thus overcome, He continues to correct, but He never ceases to love, and He does not suffer His anger with His people to pass into the next world, but receives His erring child into His glory. C. H. S.

Vs. 10. *He hath not dealt with us after our sins; nor rewarded us according to our iniquities.* Else had Israel perished outright, and we also had long ago been consigned to the lowest hell. We ought to praise the Lord for what He has not done as well as for what He has wrought for us; even the negative side deserves our adoring gratitude.

Up to this moment, at our very worst estate, we have never suffered as we deserved to suffer; our daily lot has not been apportioned upon the rule of what we merited, but on the far different measure of undeserved kindness. Shall we not bless the Lord? Every power of our being might have been rent with anguish instead of which we are all in the enjoyment of comparative happiness, and many of us are exceedingly favored with inward joy; let then every faculty, yea, all that is within us, bless His holy name. C. H. S.

Why is it that God hath not dealt with us after our sins? Is it not because He hath dealt with another after our sins? Another Who took our sins upon Him; of Whom it is said, that "God chastened Him in His fierce wrath"? and why did He chasten Him, but for our sins? O gracious God, Thou art too just to take revenge twice for the same faults; and therefore, having turned Thy fierce wrath upon Him, Thou wilt not turn it upon us too; but having rewarded Him according to our iniquities, Thou wilt now reward us according to His merits. SIR R. BAKER

Vs. 11. *For as the heaven is high above the earth, so great is His mercy toward them that fear Him.* Godly fear is one of the first products of the divine life in us. It is the beginning of wisdom, yet it fully ensures to its possessor all the benefits of divine mercy, and is, indeed, here and elsewhere, employed to set forth the whole of true religion. C. H. S.

Vs. 12. *As far as the east is from the west, so far hath He removed our transgressions from us.* O glorious verse, no word even upon the inspired page can excel it! Sin is removed from us by a miracle of love! What a load to move, and yet is it removed so far that the distance is incalculable. Fly as far as the wing of imagination can bear you, and if you journey through space eastward, you are farther from the west at every beat of your wing. If sin be removed so far, then we may be sure that the scent, the trace, the very memory of it must be entirely gone.

If this be the distance of its removal, there is no shade of fear of its ever being brought back again; even Satan himself could not achieve such a task. Our sins are gone; Jesus has borne them away. Far as the place of sunrise is removed from yonder west, where the sun sinks when his day's journey is done, so far were our sins carried by our scapegoat nineteen centuries ago, and now if they be sought for, they shall not be found, yea, they shall not be, saith the Lord.

Come, my soul, awaken thyself thoroughly and glorify the Lord for this richest of blessings. Hallelujah. The Lord alone could remove sin at all, and He has done it in a godlike fashion, making a final sweep of all our transgressions. C. H. S.

When sin is pardoned, it is never charged again; the guilt of it can no more return than east can become west, or west become east. STEPHEN CHARNOCK

Vs. 13. *As a father pitieth his children.* The father pitieth his children that are weak in knowledge, and instructs them, pities them when they are froward, and bears with them; pities them when they are sick, and comforts them; when they are fallen, and helps them up again; when they have offended, and upon their submission, forgives them; when they are wronged, and rights them. Thus, "the Lord pitieth them that fear Him." MATTHEW HENRY

*Them that fear Him.* The fear of God is that deference to God which leads you to subordinate your will to His; makes you intent on pleasing Him; penitent in view of past wilfulness; happy in His present smile; transported by His love; hopeful of His glory. GEORGE BOWEN

Vs. 14. *He knoweth our frame; He remembereth that we are dust.* Not like some unskilled empiric, who hath but one receipt for all, strong or weak, young or old; but as a wise physician considers his patient, and then writes his bill. Men and devils are but God's apothecaries, they make not our physic, but give what God prescribes. Balaam loved Balak's fee well enough but could not go a hair's breadth beyond God's commission. WILLIAM GURNALL

Verses 14, 16. *We are dust.* I never see one of those spiral pillars of dust which, like a mimic simoon, rush along the road upon a windy day, without thinking, "There is an image of life." Dust and a breath!

Observe how the apparent "pillar" is but a condition, an active condition, of the particles of dust, and those particles continually changing. The form depends upon the incessant movement. The heavy sand floats on the impalpable air while it partakes its motion; let that cease, and it falls.

So the dull clods of the field, smitten by force, take wings and soar in life, partake for a time its rapid course, and then, the force exhausted, fall back into their former state. A whirl, a flux, maintained by forces without, and ceasing when they are withdrawn; that is our life. JAMES HINTON, *in "Thoughts on Health and some of its Conditions"*

Vs. 15. *As for man, his days are as grass.* He lives on the grass and lives like the grass. Corn is but educated grass, and man, who feeds on it, partakes of its nature. The grass lives, grows, flowers, falls beneath the scythe, dries up, and is removed from the field: read this sentence over again, and you will find it the history of man. If he lives out his little day, he is cut down at last, and it is far more likely that he will wither before he comes to maturity or be plucked away of a sudden, long before he has fulfilled his time.

*As a flower of the field, so he flourisheth.* A large congregation, in many-colored attire, always reminds us of a meadow bright with many hues; and the comparison becomes sadly true when we reflect, that as the grass and its goodliness soon pass away, even so will those we gaze upon, and all their visible beauty.

Vs. 16. *For the wind passeth over it, and it is gone.* Only a little wind is needed, not even a scythe is demanded, a breath can do it, for the flower is so frail. C. H. S.

A breath of air, a gentle wind passes over him and he is gone. It would not be so strange if a tempest, a whirlwind, passing over should sweep him away. The Psalmist means much more than this. The gentlest touch, the whispering breeze, bears him off. He soon becomes a stranger, no more known in the little space he once filled, going out and coming in. HENRY COWLES

The blasting effect which seems to be here alluded to, of certain pestilential winds upon the animal frame, is by no means exaggerated by the comparison to the sudden fading of a flower. Maillet describes hundreds of persons in a caravan as stifled on the spot by the fire and dust, of which the deadly wind, that sometimes prevails in the eastern deserts, seems to be composed.

And Sir John Chardin describes this wind "as making a great hissing noise," and says that "it appears red and fiery, and kills those whom it strikes by a kind of stifling them, especially when it happens in the day time. RICHARD MANT

Vs. 17. *But the mercy of the Lord is from everlasting to everlasting upon them that fear Him.* Blessed *but!* How vast the contrast between the fading flower and the everlasting God! How wonderful that His mercy should link our frailty with His eternity and make us everlasting, too! From old eternity the Lord viewed His people as objects of mercy, and as such chose them to become partakers of His grace; the doctrine of eternal election is most delightful to those who have light to see it and love wherewith to accept it. It is a theme for deepest thought and highest joy. C. H. S.

From everlasting, by predestination; to everlasting, by glorification: the one without beginning, the other without end. BERNARD

Vs. 19. *His kingdom ruleth over all.* He hath a raven for Elijah, a gourd for Jonah, a dog for Lazarus. Makes the leviathan, the hugest living creature, preserve His prophet. That a terrible lion should be killed, as was by Samson; or not kill, as they forbore Daniel; or kill and not eat, as that prophet (I Kings 13): here was the Lord.

Over metals; He makes iron to swim, stones to cleave asunder. Over the devils; they must obey Him though unwillingly. But they continually rebel against Him and break His will? They do indeed against His complacency, not against His permission.

There is then no time, not the hour of death; no place, not the sorest torment; no creature, not the devil; but the Lord can deliver us from them. Therefore, at all times, in all places, and against all creatures, let us trust in Him for deliverance. THOMAS ADAMS

When Melanchthon was extremely solicitous about the affairs of the church in his days, Luther would have him admonished in these terms, *Monendus est Philippus ut desinat esse rector mundi:* Let not Philip make himself any longer governor of the world. DAVID CLARKSON

Vs. 20. *Angels, that excel in strength, that do His commandments, hearkening to the voice of His Word.* They who do the will of God faithfully and obediently, have God for them; and then what can be against them? Then work itself strengthens them, and is like a tide bearing them onward; because it is His work.

They, on the other hand, who run counter to the will of God, have God against them; and then what can be for them? Can a man push back the sea? can he lay hold on the sun, and drag him out of his course? Then may he hope to be strong, when he is fighting against the will of God? JULIUS CHARLES HARE

Vs. 22. *Bless the Lord, all His works in all places of His dominion.* See how finite man can awaken unbounded praise! Man is but little, yet, placing his hands upon the keys of the great organ of the universe, he wakes it to thunders of adoration! Redeemed man is the voice of nature, the priest in the temple of creation, the precentor in the worship of the universe.

Oh, that all the Lord's works on earth were delivered from the vanity to which they were made subject and brought into the glorious liberty of the children of God: the time is hastening on and will most surely come; then will all the Lord's works bless Him indeed. The immutable promise is ripening, the sure mercy is on its way. Hasten, ye winged hours! C. H. S.

# PSALM 104

The poem contains a complete cosmos: sea and land, cloud and sunlight, plant and animal, light and darkness, life and death, are all proved to be expressive of the presence of the Lord. Traces of the six days of creation are very evident, and though the creation of man, which was the crowning work of the sixth day, is not mentioned, this is accounted for from the fact that man is himself the singer. It is a poet's version of Genesis.

We have no information as to the author, but the Septuagint assigns it to David, and we see no reason for ascribing it to anyone else. His spirit, style, and manner of writing are very manifest therein, and if the Psalm must be ascribed to another, it must be to a mind remarkably similar, and we could only suggest the wise son of David—Solomon, the poet-preacher, to whose notes upon natural history in the Proverbs some of the verses bear a striking likeness. C. H. S.

Vs. 1. *Bless the Lord, O my soul.* This Psalm begins and ends like the Hundred and Third. When we magnify the Lord, let us do it heartily: our best is far beneath His worthiness; let us not dishonor Him by rendering to Him half-hearted worship. C. H. S.

A good man's work lieth most within doors; he is more taken up with his own soul than with all the world besides; neither can he ever be alone so long as he hath God and his own heart to converse with. JOHN TRAPP

*O Lord my God, Thou art very great.* God was great on Sinai, yet the opening words of His law were, "I am the Lord thy God"; His greatness is no reason why faith should not put in her claim and call Him all her own. It is not "the universe is very great!" but, "Thou art very great." Many stay at the creature, and so become idolatrous in spirit; to pass onward to the Creator Himself is true wisdom. C. H. S.

Vs. 2. *Who coverest Thyself with light as with a garment.* Wrapping the light about Him as a monarch puts on His robe. The conception is sublime: but it makes us feel how altogether inconceivable the personal glory of the Lord must be; if light itself is but His garment and veil, what must be the blazing splendor of His own essential being! C. H. S.

The first creation of God in the works of the days was the light of sense; the last was the light of reason; and His Sabbath work ever since is the illumination of the spirit. FRANCIS BACON

Vs. 4. *Who maketh His angels spirits.* God is a Spirit, and He is waited upon by spirits in His royal courts. Angels are like winds for mystery, force, and invisibility, and no doubt the winds themselves are often the angels, or messengers of God.

*His ministers a flaming fire.* That the passage refers to angels, is clear from Heb. 1:7; and it was most proper to mention them here in connection with light and the heavens, and immediately after the robes and palace of the Great King. C. H. S.

Fire is expressive of irresistible power, immaculate holiness, and ardent emotion. It is remarkable that the seraphim, one class at least of these ministers, have their name from a root signifying to burn; and the altar, from which one of them took the live coal (Isa. 6:6), is the symbol of the highest form of holy love. JAMES G. MURPHY

*Who laid the foundations of the earth.* Thus the commencement of creation is described in almost the very words employed by the Lord Himself in Job 38:4: "Where wast thou when I laid the foundations of the earth?" C. H. S.

*That it should not be removed forever.* The language is, of course, poetical, but the fact is none the less wonderful: the earth is so placed in space that it remains as stable as if it were a fixture. What power must there be in that Hand which has caused so vast a body to know its orbit and to move so smoothly in it! What engineer can save every part of his machinery from an occasional jar, jerk, or friction? Yet to our great world in its complicated motions, no such thing has ever occurred. "O Lord, my God, Thou art very great." C. H. S.

The stability of the earth is of God, as much as the being and existence of it. There have been many earthquakes, or movings of the earth in several parts of it, but the whole body of the earth was never removed so much as one hair's breadth out of its place since the foundations thereof were laid. Archimedes, the great mathematician, said, "If you will give me a place to set my engine on, I will remove the earth." It was a great brag; but the Lord hath laid it too fast for man's removing. He, Himself can make it quake and shake; He can move it when He pleaseth; but He never hath nor will remove it. J. CARYL

It has also been asked whether the velocity of the earth's rotation has changed, or, which comes to the same thing, if the length of the sidereal day and that of the solar day deduced from it have varied within the historical period. Laplace has replied to this question, and his demonstration shows that it has not varied the one hundredth of a second during the last two thousand years. AMEDEE GUILLEMIN

Vs. 8. *They go up by the mountains.* The Targum is, "They ascend out of the deep to the mountains"; that is, the waters, when they went off the earth at the divine orders, steered their course up the mountains and then went down by the valleys to the place appointed for them; they went over hills and dales; nothing could stop them or retard their course till they came to their proper place; which is another instance of the Almighty Power of the Son of God. JOHN GILL

*They go down by the valleys unto the place which Thou hast founded for them.* They are as willing to descend in rain, and brooks, and torrents as they were eager to ascend in mists. The loyalty of the mighty waters to the laws of their God is most notable; the fierce flood, the boisterous rapid, the tremendous torrent, are only forms of that gentle dew which trembles on the tiny blade of grass, and in those ruder shapes they are equally obedient to the laws which their Maker has impressed upon them. C. H. S.

Vs. 9. *Thou hast set a bound that they may not pass over; that they turn not again to cover the earth.* That bound has once been passed, but it shall never be so again. The deluge was caused by the suspension of the divine mandate which held the floods in check: they knew their old supremacy and hastened to reassert it, but now the covenant promise forever prevents a return of that revolt of the waves. Jehovah's Word bounds the ocean, using only a narrow belt of sand to confine it to its own limits: that apparently feeble restraint answers every purpose, for the sea is obedient as a little child to the bidding of its Maker. Destruction lies asleep in the bed of the ocean, and though our sins might well arouse it, yet are its bands made strong by covenant mercy, so that it cannot break loose again upon the guilty sons of men. C. H. S.

Some great princes, heated with rage and drunken with pride, have cast shackles into the sea, as threatening it with imprisonment and bondage if it would not be quiet; but the sea would not be bound by them; they have also awarded so many strokes to be given the sea as a punishment of its contumacy and rebellion against either their commands or their designs. How ridiculously ambitious have they been who would needs pretend to such a dominion! Many princes have had great power at and upon the sea, but there was never any prince had any power over the sea; that's a flower belonging to no crown but the crown of heaven. JOSEPH CARYL

Vs. 11. *They give drink to every beast of the field.* Who else would water them if the Lord did not? C. H. S.

*The wild asses quench their thirst.* Though bit or bridle of man they will not brook, and man denounces them as unteachable, they learn of the Lord and know better far than man where flows the cooling crystal of which they must drink or die. They are only asses, and wild, yet our heavenly Father careth for them. Must everything exist for man or else be wasted? It is not true that flowers which blush unseen by human eye are wasting their sweetness, for the bee finds them out, and other winged wanderers live on their luscious juices. Man is but one creature of the many whom the heavenly Father feedeth and watereth. C. H. S.

Vs. 12. *The fowls which sing among the branches.* The music of birds was the first song of thanksgiving which was offered from the earth before man was formed. JOHN WESLEY

But the nightingale, another of my airy creatures, breathes such sweet, loud music out of her little instrumental throat that it makes mankind to think miracles are not ceased. He that at midnight, when the very laborer sleeps securely, should hear, as I have very often, the clear airs, the sweet descants, the natural rising and falling, the doubling and redoubling of her voice, might well be lifted above the earth, and say, "Lord, what music hast Thou provided for the saints in heaven, when Thou affordest bad men such music on earth?" IZAAK WALTON

Vs. 14. *He causeth the grass to grow.* Surely it should humble men to know that all human power united cannot make anything, not even the grass, to grow. WILLIAM S. PLUMER

*That He may bring forth food out of the earth.* How great is that God Who from among the sepulchers finds the support of life, and out of the ground which was cursed brings forth the blessings of corn and wine and oil. C. H. S.

It is the most indispensable and necessary means of nourishment, of which we never tire, whilst other food, the sweeter it is, the more easily it surfeits: everybody, the child and the old man, the beggar and the king, like bread. We remember the unfortunate man who was cast on the desert isle, famishing with hunger, and who cried at the sight of a handful of gold, "Ah, it is only gold!" He would willingly have exchanged for a handful of bread, this to him, useless material, which in the mind of most men is above all price. Oh, let us never sin against God by lightly esteeming bread! FREDERICK ARNDT

Vs. 15. *And wine that maketh glad the heart of man.* Of this he must himself bear the blame; he deserves to be miserable who turns even blessings into curses. C. H. S.

*And bread which strengtheneth man's heart.* Men have more courage after they are fed: many a depressed spirit has been comforted by a good, substantial meal. We ought to bless God for strength of heart as well as force of limb, since if we possess them, they are both the bounties of His kindness. C. H. S.

The ancients made much use of oil to beautify their persons. We read of "oil to make man's face to shine." Ruth anointed herself for decoration (Ruth 3:3) and the woman of Tekoah and the prophet Daniel omitted the use of oil for the contrary reason (II Sam. 14:3; Dan. 10:3). The custom is also mentioned in Matt. 6:17; Luke 7:46. AMBROSE SERLE

It is not without reason that instead of the word "Adam" which was used in vs. 14, there is here employed the word meaning an infirm and feeble man, because he mentions those nourishments of which there was no need before the fall and which are specially suitable to nourish and exhilarate feeble man. VENEMA

Vs. 16. *The trees of the Lord are full of sap; the cedars of Lebanon, which He hath planted.* The trees uncared for by man are yet so full of sap, we may rest assured that the people of God who by faith live upon the Lord alone shall be equally well sustained. Planted by grace, and owing all to our heavenly Father's care, we may defy the hurricane and laugh at the fear of drought, for none that trust in Him shall ever be left unwatered. C. H. S.

The transition which the prophet makes from men to trees is as if he had said, "It is not to be wondered at, if God so bountifully nourishes men, who are created after His own image, since He does not grudge to extend His care even to trees." By "the trees of the Lord" is meant those which are high and of surpassing beauty; for God's blessing is more conspicuous in them. It seems scarcely possible for any juice of the earth to reach so great a height, and yet they renew their foliage every year. JOHN CALVIN

Vs. 18. *The high hills are a refuge for the wild goats.* There is scarcely any doubt that the "Azel" of the Old Testament is the "Arabian Ibex," or "Beden." This animal is very closely allied to the Ibex of the Alps. The agility of the Beden is extraordinary. Living in the highest and most craggy parts of the mountain ridge, it flings itself from spot to spot with a recklessness that startles one who has not been accustomed to the animal and the wonderful certainty of its foot.

It will, for example, dash at the face of a perpendicular precipice that looks as smooth as a brick wall for the purpose of reaching a tiny ledge which is hardly perceptible and which is some fifteen feet or so above the spot whence the animal sprang. Its eye, however, has marked certain little cracks and projections on the face of the rock, and as the animal makes its leap, it takes these little points of vantage in rapid succession, just touching them as it passes upwards, and by the slight stroke of its foot keeping up the original impulse of its leap.

Similarly, the ibex comes sliding and leaping down precipitous sides of the mountains, sometimes halting with all the four feet drawn together on a little projection scarcely larger than a penny, and sometimes springing boldly over a wild crevasse and alighting with exact precision upon a projecting piece of rock that seems scarcely large enough to sustain a rat comfortably. J. G. WOOD

Vs. 19. *He appointed the moon for seasons.* Never let us regard the moon's motions as the inevitable result of inanimate impersonal law but as the appointment of our God. C. H. S.

Vs. 20. *Thou makest darkness, and it is night.* Let us see God's hand in the veiling of the sun, and never fear either natural or providential darkness, since both are of the Lord's own making. C. H. S.

*Wherein all the beasts of the forest do creep forth.* Darkness is fitter for beasts than man; and those men are most brutish who love darkness rather than light. C. H. S.

Vs. 21. *The young lions roar after their prey, and seek their meat from God.* They, after their own fashion, express their desires for food, and the expression of desire is a kind of prayer. Out of this fact comes the devout thought of the wild beast's appealing to its Maker for food. What they have in their own language asked for they go forth to seek; being in this thing far wiser than many men who offer formal prayers not half so earnest as those of the young lions and then neglect the means in the use of which the object of their petitions might be gained. The lions roar and seek; too many are liars before God and roar but never seek. C. H. S.

The roaring of the young lions, like the crying of the ravens, is interpreted, asking their meat of God. Doth God put this construction upon the language of mere nature, even in venomous creatures, and shall He not much more interpret favorably the language of grace in His own people, though it be weak and broken groanings which cannot be uttered? MATTHEW HENRY

Vs. 22. *The sun ariseth.* Were it not that we have seen the sun rise so often, we should think it the greatest of miracles and the most amazing of blessings. C. H. S.

*They gather themselves together, and lay them down in their dens.* There was One Who in this respect was poorer than lions and foxes, for He had not where to lay His head: all were provided for except their incarnate Provider. Blessed Lord, Thou hast stooped beneath the conditions of the brutes to lift up worse than brutish men!

The sun suffices to do it. He is the true lion-tamer. They gather themselves together as though they were so many sheep, and in their own retreats they keep themselves prisoners till returning darkness gives them another leave to range. By simply majestic means, the divine purposes are accomplished. In like manner, even the devils are subject unto our Lord Jesus, and by the simple spread of the light of the gospel, these roaring demons are chased out of the world.

No need for miracles or displays of physical power, the Sun of Righteousness arises, and the devil and the false gods and superstitions and errors of men all seek their hiding places in the dark places of the earth among the moles and the bats. C. H. S.

In order to keep the wild beasts shut up within their dens, the only means which God employs is to inspire them with terror simply by the light of the sun. This instance of divine goodness the prophet commends the more on account of its necessity; for were it otherwise, men would have no liberty to go forth to engage in the labors and business of life. JOHN CALVIN

Vs. 23. Man alone, among all creatures, in distinction from the involuntary instruments of the Almighty, has a real daily work. He has a definite part to play in life and can recognize it. CARL BERNHARD MOLL

Vs. 24. *O Lord, how manifold are Thy works!* They are not only many for number, but manifold for variety. Mineral, vegetable, animal—what a range of works is suggested by these three names! C. H. S.

If the number of the creatures be so exceeding great, how great, nay, immense, must needs be the power and wisdom of Him Who formed them all! For (that I may borrow the words of a noble and excellent author) as it argues and manifests more skill by far in an artificer to be able to frame both clocks and watches, and pumps and mills, and granadoes and rockets, than He could display in His wisdom in forming such a vast multitude of different sorts of creatures, and all with admirable and irreprovable art, than if He had created but a few.

The infinitely wise Creator hath shown in many instances that He is not confined to one only instrument for the working one effect, but can perform the same thing by divers means. So, though feathers seem necessary for flying, yet hath He enabled several creatures to fly without them, as two sorts of fishes, one sort of lizard, and the bat, not to mention the numerous tribes of flying insects. In like manner, though the air-bladder in fishes seems necessary for swimming, yet some are so formed as to swim without it.

Again, the great use and convenience, the beauty and variety of so many springs and fountains, so many brooks and rivers, so many lakes and standing pools of water, and these so scattered and dispersed all the earth over, that no great part of it is destitute of them, without which it must, without a supply other ways, be desolate and void of inhabitants, afford abundant arguments of wisdom and counsel: that springs should break forth on the sides of mountains most remote from the sea: that there should way be made for rivers through straits and rocks, and subterraneous vaults, so that one would think that nature had cut a way on purpose to derive the water, which else would overflow and drown whole countries. JOHN RAY

Vs. 25. *So is this great and wide sea.* The heathen made a sea a different province from the land and gave the command thereof to Neptune, but we know of a surety that Jehovah rules the waves. *Wherein are things creeping innumerable, both small and great beasts.* Read "moving things and animals small and great," and you have the true sense. The number of minute forms of animal life is indeed beyond all reckoning: when a single phosphorescent wave may bear millions of infusoria, and around a fragment of rock armies of microscopic beings may gather, we renounce all idea of applying arithmetic to such a case. C. H. S.

*Things innumerable.* The waters teem with more life than the land. Beneath a surface less varied than that of the continents, the sea enfolds in its bosom an exuberance of life of which no other region of the globe can afford the faintest idea.

Charles Darwin truly says that the terrestrial forests do not contain anything like the number of animals as those of the sea. The ocean, which is for man the element of death, is for myriads of animals a home of life and health. There is joy in its waves, there is happiness upon its shores, and heavenly blue everywhere. MOQUIN TANDON

Vs. 26. *Ships.* The original of ships was doubtless Noah's ark, so that they owe their first draught to God Himself. JOHN GILL

Dreadful and tempestuous as the sea may appear, and uncontrollable in its billows and surges, it is only the field of sport, the playground, the bowling green, to those huge marine monsters. ADAM CLARKE

*Leviathan . . . made to play therein.* With such wonderful strength is the tail of the whale endowed, that the largest of these animals, measuring some eighty feet in length, are able by its aid to leap clear out of the water, as if they were little fish leaping after flies. This movement is technically termed "breaching," and the sound which is produced by the huge carcass as it falls upon the water is so powerful as to be heard for a distance of several miles. J. G. WOOD

He is made to "play in the sea"; he hath nothing to do as man hath, that "goes forth to his work"; he hath nothing to fear as the beasts have, that lie down in their dens; and therefore he plays with the waters: it is pity any of the children of men, that have nobler powers, and were made for nobler purposes, should live as if they were sent into the world like the leviathan into the waters, to play therein, spending all their time in pastime. MATTHEW HENRY

Vs. 28. *That Thou givest them they gather.* When we see the chickens picking up the corn which the housewife scatters from her lap, we have an apt illustration of the manner in which the Lord supplies the needs of all living things—He gives, and they gather. C. H. S.

*Thou openest Thine hand, they are filled with good.* What should we do if that hand were closed? There would be no need to strike a blow; the mere closing of it would produce death by famine. Let us praise the open-handed Lord, Whose providence and grace satisfy our mouths with good things. C. H. S.

The general principle of the text is, God gives to His creatures and His creatures gather. That general principle we shall apply to our own case as men and women; for it is as true of us as it is of the fish of the sea, and the cattle on the hills: "That Thou givest them they gather."

We have only to gather, for God gives. In temporal things God gives us day by day our daily bread, and our business is simply to gather it. As to spirituals, the principle is true, most emphatically, we have, in the matter of grace, only to gather what God gives.

The natural man thinks that he has to earn divine favor; that he has to purchase the blessing of heaven; but he is in grave error: the soul has only to receive that which Jesus freely gives.

We can only gather what God gives; however eager we may be, there is the end of the matter. The diligent bird shall not be able to gather more than the Lord has given it; neither shall the most avaricious and covetous man. "It is vain for you to rise up early and to sit up late, to eat the bread of carefulness; for so He giveth His beloved sleep."

We must gather what God gives or else we shall get no good by His bountiful giving. God feeds the creeping things innumerable, but each creature collects the provender for itself. The huge leviathan receives his vast provision, but he must go ploughing through the boundless meadows and gather up the myriads of minute objects which supply his need. The fish must leap up to catch the fly, the swallow must hawk for its food, the young lions must hunt for their prey.

The fourth turn of the text gives us the sweet thought that we may gather what He gives. We have divine permission to enjoy freely what the Lord bestows.

The last thing is, God will always give us something to gather. It is written, "The Lord will provide." Thus is it also in spiritual things. If you are willing to gather, God will always give. C. H. S.

Vs. 29. *They are troubled.* They are confounded; they are overwhelmed with terror and amazement. The word "troubled" by no means conveys the sense of the original word, *bahal*—which means properly to tremble; to be in trepidation; to be filled with terror; to be amazed; to be confounded. It is that kind of consternation which one has when all support and protection are withdrawn and when inevitable ruin stares one in the face. So when God turns away, all their support is gone, all their resources fail, and they must die. They are represented as conscious of this; or this is what would occur if they were conscious. ALBERT BARNES

*Thou takest away their breath, they die, and return to their dust.* Note here that death is caused by the act of God, "Thou takest away their breath"; we are immortal till He bids us die, and so are even the little sparrows, who fall not to the ground without our Father. C. H. S.

Vs. 30. *Thou sendest forth Thy spirit, they are created: and Thou renewest the face of the earth.* The works of the Lord are majestically simple and are performed with royal ease—a breath creates, and its withdrawal destroys. C. H. S.

Vs. 32. *He looketh on the earth, and it trembleth: He toucheth the hills, and they smoke.* Even our God is a consuming fire. Woe unto those who shall provoke Him to frown upon them; they shall perish at the touch of His hand. If sinners were not altogether insensible, a glance of the Lord's eye would make them tremble, and the touches of His hand in affliction would set their hearts on fire with repentance. "Of reason all things show some sign" except man's unfeeling heart. C. H. S.

This is the philosophy of Scripture: this, then, shall be my philosophy. Never was a sentence uttered by uninspired man so sublime as this sentence. The thought is grand beyond conception; and the expression clothes the thought with suitable external majesty. The sublimity of the expression in this passage arises from the infinite disproportion between the means and the end. An earthly sovereign looks with anger, and his courtiers tremble. God looks on the earth, and it trembles to its foundation. He touches the mountains, and the volcano smokes, vomiting forth torrents of lava. How chill and withering is the breath of that noxious philosophy that would detach our minds from viewing God in His works of Providence! This malaria destroys all spiritual life. ALEXANDER CARSON

Vs. 33. *I will sing praise to my God while I have my being.* We never sing so well as when we know that we have an interest in the good things of which we sing and a relationship to the God Whom we praise. C. H. S.

Vs. 34. *My meditation of Him shall be sweet.* Meditation is the soul of religion. It is the tree of life in the midst of the garden of piety, and very refreshing is its fruit to the soul which feeds thereon. C. H. S.

A Christian needs to study nothing but *Christ;* there is enough in Christ to take up his study and contemplation all his days; and the more we study Christ, the more we may study Him; there will be new wonders still appearing in Him. JOHN ROW

The last words ever written by Henry Martyn, dying among Mohammedans in Persia, was: "I sat in the orchard and thought with sweet comfort and peace of my God, in solitude my company, my Friend and Comforter." C. H. S.

I must meditate on Christ. Let philosophers soar in their contemplations, and walk among the stars; what are the stars to Christ, the Sun of righteousness, the brightness of the Father's glory, and the express image of His Person? God manifest in the flesh is a theme which angels rejoice to contemplate. SAMUEL LAVINGTON

Vs. 35. *Let the sinners be consumed out of the earth.* It fell to my lot some years ago to undertake a walk of some miles, on a summer morning, along a seashore of surpassing beauty. It was the Lord's Day, and the language of the Hundred and Fourth Psalm rose spontaneously in my mind as one scene after another unfolded itself before the eye.

About half way to my destination, the road lay through a dirty hamlet, and my meditations were rudely interrupted by the brawling of some people, who looked as if they had been spending the night in a drunken debauch.

Well, I thought, the Psalmist must have had some such unpleasant experience. He must have fallen in with people, located in some scene of natural beauty, who, instead of being a holy priesthood to give voice to nature in praise of her Creator, instead of being, in the pure and holy tenor of their lives, the heavenliest note of the general song—filled it with a harsh discord.

His prayer is the vehement expression of a desire that the earth may no longer be marred by the presence of wicked men—that they may be utterly consumed and may give place to men animated with the fear of God, just and holy men, men that shall be a crown of beauty on the head of this fair creation. If this be the right explanation of the Psalmist's prayer, it is not only justifiable, but there is something wrong in our meditations on nature if we are not disposed to join in it. WILLIAM BINNIE

*Praise ye the Lord.* This is the first time that we meet with "Hallelujah"; and it comes in here upon occasion of the destruction of the wicked; and the last time we meet with it, it is upon the like occasion, when the New Testament Babylon is consumed, this is the burthen of song—"Hallelujah" (Rev. 19:1, 3-4, 6). MATTHEW HENRY

This Psalm is an inspired "Oratorio of Creation." CHRISTOPHER WORDSWORTH

We are astonished to find in a lyrical poem of such a limited compass, the whole universe—the heavens and the earth—sketched with a few bold touches. A. VON HUMBOLDT

## PSALM 105

This historical Psalm was evidently composed by King David, for the first fifteen verses of it were used as a hymn at the carrying up of the ark from the house of Obed-edom, and we read in I Chron. 16:7, "Then on that day David delivered first this Psalm to thank the Lord, into the hand of Asaph and his brethren."

Our last Psalm sang the opening chapters of Genesis, and this takes up its closing chapters and conducts us into Exodus and Numbers.

We are now among the long Psalms, as at other times we have been among the short ones. These varying lengths of the sacred poems should teach us not to lay down any law either of brevity or prolixity in either prayer or praise. C. H. S.

Vs. 2. *Talk ye of all His wondrous works.* Who have so many of these to boast of as Christians? Christianity is a tissue of miracles; and every part of the work of grace on the soul is a miracle. Genuine Christian converts may talk of miracles from morning to night; and they should talk of them, and recommend to others their miracle-working God and Savior. ADAM CLARKE

Vs. 3. *Glory ye in His holy name.* Make it a matter of joy that you have such a God. His character and attributes are such as will never make you blush to call Him your God. Every deed of His will bear the strictest scrutiny; His name is holy, His character is holy, His law is holy, His government is holy, His influence is holy.

*And those who find Thee find a bliss,*
*Nor tongue nor pen can show:*
*The love of Jesus what it is,*
*None but His loved ones know.*

C. H. S.

Vs. 4. *Seek the Lord, and His strength: seek His face evermore.* First we seek Him, then His strength, and then His face; from the personal reverence, we pass on to the imparted power, and then to the conscious favor. This seeking must never cease—the more we know the more we must seek to know. C. H. S.

It is added "evermore," lest they should imagine that they had performed their duty if they assembled twice or three times in the year at the tabernacle and observed the external rites according to the Law. MOLLERUS

Vs. 5. *Remember.* How others may be affected, I do not ask. For myself, I confess, that there is no care or sorrow by which I am so severely harassed as when I feel myself guilty of ingratitude to my most kind Lord. It not seldom appears to be a fault so inexplicable that I am alarmed when I read these words, inasmuch as I consider them addressed to myself and others like me. Remember, O ye forgetful, thoughtless, and ungrateful, the works of God, which He hath done to us, with so many signs and proofs of His goodness. What more could He have done which He hath not done? FOLENGIUS

*His wonders, and the judgments of His mouth.* As the Word of God is the salvation of His saints, so is it the destruction of the ungodly: out of His mouth goeth a two-edged sword with which He will slay the wicked. C. H. S.

Vs. 6. *O ye seed of Abraham His servant, ye children of Jacob His chosen.* Election is not a couch for ease, but an argument for seven-fold diligence. If God has set His choice upon us, let us aim to be choice men. C. H. S.

Vs. 7. *He is the Lord our God.* Blessed be His name. Jehovah condescends to be our God. This sentence contains a greater wealth of meaning than all the eloquence of orators can compass, and there is more joy in it than in all the sonnets of them that make merry.

*His judgments are in all the earth.* It is wonderful that the Jewish people should have become so exclusive and have so utterly lost the missionary spirit, for their sacred literature is full of the broad and generous sympathies which are so consistent with the worship of "the God of the whole earth."

Nor is it less painful to observe that among a certain class of believers in God's election of grace there lingers a hard exclusive spirit fatal to compassion and zeal. It would be well for these also to remember that their Redeemer is "the Savior of all men, specially of them that believe." C. H. S.

Vs. 8. *The word which He commanded to a thousand generations.* This is only an amplification of the former statement, and serves to set before us the immutable fidelity of the Lord during the changing generations of men. His judgments are threatened upon the third and fourth generations of them that hate Him, but His love runs on forever, even to "a thousand generations." C. H. S.

Vs. 11. *The lot of your inheritance.* (Literally, "the cord of your inheritance"). This is an expression taken from the ancient method of measuring land by the cord, or line; whence the measuring cord is metonymically put for the part measured, and divided by the cord. Thus, the lines, "the cords are fallen unto me in pleasant places," i.e., as the Psalmist explains it: "I have a goodly heritage" (Ps. 16:6). SAMUEL CHANDLER

Vs. 11-12. *When they were but a few men in number; yea, very few, and strangers in it.* The blessings promised to the seed of Abraham were not dependent upon the number of his descendants or their position in this world. The covenant was made with one man, and consequently the number could never be less, and that one man was not the owner of a foot of soil in all the land, save only a cave in which to bury his dead, and therefore his seed could not have less inheritance than he.

The smallness of a church, and the poverty of its members, are not barriers to the divine blessing, if it be sought earnestly by pleading the promise. Were not the apostles few, and the disciples feeble when the good work began? Neither because we are strangers and foreigners here below, as our fathers were, are we in any the more danger; we are like sheep in the midst of wolves, but the wolves cannot hurt us, for our Shepherd is near. C. H. S.

Vs. 12, 14-15. One would think that all the world would have been upon them; but here was the protection; God has a negative voice, *He suffered no man to do them wrong.* Many had (as we say) an aching tooth at the people of God, their finger itched to be dealing with them, and the text shows four advantages the world had against them. First, "They were few." Secondly, "very few." Thirdly, "strangers." Fourthly, unsettled. What hindered their enemies? It was the Lord's negative voice.

*He reproved kings for their sakes; saying, Touch not Mine anointed, and do My prophets no harm.* We see an instance of this (Gen. 35:5) when Jacob and his family journeyed; "the terror of God was upon the cities that were round about them, and they did not pursue after the sons of Jacob." They had a mind to pursue after them, to revenge the slaughter of the Shechemites; but God said, "Pursue not," and then they could not pursue, they must stay at home. And when His people, the Jews, were safe in Canaan, He encouraged them to come up freely to worship at Jerusalem by this assurance, "No man shall desire the land, when thou shalt go up to appear before the Lord Thy God, thrice in the year" (Exod. 34:24). God can stop not only hands from spoiling but hearts from desiring. JOSEPH CARYL

Vs. 14-15. Here is the great danger to kings and states, to deal with his saints otherwise than well. Which appeareth many ways; for He doth not only in words give a charge not to touch them, but He carries it in a high way (for so God will do when He pleads their cause). Touch them not; as if He had said, "Let Me see if you dare so much as touch them; and it is with an intimation of the highest threatening if they should; upon your peril if you do so; for that is the scope of such a speech."

And accordingly, in deeds, He made this good; for the text saith He suffered no man to do them wrong; not that He did altogether prevent all wrong and injuries, for they received many as they went through those lands; but at no time did He let it go unpunished. THOMAS GOODWIN

Vs. 15. *Mine anointed.* Abraham, Isaac, and Jacob had no external anointing. They were, however, called "anointed" because they were separated by God from the multitude of wicked men and endowed with the Spirit and His gifts, of which the oil was an emblem. MOLLERUS

Vs. 16. *Moreover He called for a famine upon the land.* He had only to call for it as a man calls for his servant, and it came at once. How grateful ought we to be that He does not often call in that terrible servant of His, so meager and gaunt, and grim, so pitiless to the women and the children, so bitter to the strong men, who utterly fail before it.

*He brake the whole staff of bread.* Man's feeble life cannot stand without its staff—if bread fail him, he fails. As a cripple with a broken staff falls to the ground, so does man when bread no longer sustains him. C. H. S.

As a master calls for a servant ready to do his bidding. On the contrary, God says (Ezek. 36:29), "I will call for the corn, and will increase it, and lay no famine upon you." Compare the centurion's words as to sickness being Christ's servant, ready to come or go at His call (Matt. 8:8-9). A. R. FAUSSET

Vs. 17. *He sent a man before them, even Joseph.* He was the advance guard and pioneer for the whole clan. His brethren sold him, but God sent him. C. H. S.

*Who was sold for a servant.* Joseph's journey into Egypt was not so costly as Jonah's voyage when he paid his own fare: his free passage was provided by the Midianites, who also secured his introduction to a great officer of state by handing him over as a slave. His way to a position in which he could feed his family lay through the pit, the slaver's caravan, the slave market and the prison, and who shall deny but what it was the right way, the surest way, the wisest way, and perhaps the shortest way.

Yet assuredly it seemed not so. Were we to send a man on such an errand we should furnish him with money—Joseph goes as a pauper; we should clothe him with authority—Joseph goes as a slave; we should leave him at full liberty—Joseph is a bondman: yet money would have been of little use when corn was so dear, authority would have been irritating rather than influential with Pharaoh, and freedom might not have thrown Joseph into connection with Pharaoh's captain and his other servants, and so the knowledge of his skill in interpretation might not have reached the monarch's ear. God's way is the way. Our Lord's path to His mediatorial throne ran by the cross of Calvary; our road to glory runs by the rivers of grief. C. H. S.

Vs. 17, 22. Joseph may be a fit type to us of our spiritual deliverance. Consider him sold into Egypt, not without the determinate counsel of God, Who preordained this to good: "God did send me before you to preserve life" (Gen.

45:5). Here is the difference, the brethren sold Joseph; we sold ourselves. Consider us thus sold unto sin and death; God had a purpose to redeem us; there is election.

Joseph was delivered out of prison, and we ransomed out of the house of bondage; there was redemption. Joseph's cause was made known, and himself acquitted; we could not be found innocent ourselves, but were acquitted in Christ; wherein consists our justification.

Lastly, Joseph was clothed in glorious apparel, and adorned with golden chains, and made to ride in the second chariot of Egypt; so our last step is to be advanced to high honor, even the glory of the celestial court. "This honor have all the saints" (Psalm 149:9). THOMAS ADAMS

Vs. 18. *Whose feet they hurt with fetters.* From this we learn a little more of Joseph's sufferings than we find in the Book of Genesis: inspiration had not ceased, and David was as accurate an historian as Moses, for the same Spirit guided his pen. The iron fetters were preparing him to wear chains of gold and making his feet ready to stand on high places. It is even so with all the Lord's afflicted ones; they, too, shall one day step from their prisons to their thrones. C. H. S.

*His soul came into iron.* Till we have felt it, we cannot conceive that sickness of heart, which at times will steal upon the patient sufferer; that sense of loneliness, that faintness of soul, which comes from hopes deferred and wishes unshared, from the selfishness of brethren and the heartlessness of the world. We ask ourselves, "If the Lord were with me, should I suffer thus, not only the scorn of the learned and the contempt of the great, but even the indifference and neglect of those whom I have served, who yet forget me?" So Joseph might have asked; and so till now may the elect ask, as they stand alone without man's encouragement or sympathy, not turned aside by falsehood or scorn, with their face set as a flint, yet deeply feeling what it costs them. ANDREW JUKES

Vs. 19. Sold into Egypt as as slave, cast into prison through his fidelity to God, the Word of the Lord most powerfully tried his soul. In the gloom of that imprisonment, it was most hard to believe in God's faithfulness, when his affliction had risen from his obedience; and most hard to keep the promise clearly before him, when his mighty trouble would perpetually tempt him to regard it as an idle dream.

We never know our want of faith till some glorious promise rouses the soul into the attitude of belief, and the promise is a trial. Thus Paul with his profound insight into the facts of spiritual experience says, "The Word of the Lord is sharper than a two-edged sword, piercing even to the dividing asunder of soul and spirit, and of the joints and marrow, and is a discerner of the thoughts and intents of the heart." In illustration of this, we may observe that many promises of the Lord come to us as they came to Joseph—like dream-visions of the future.

But I appeal to your experience whether it is not true that such revelations of the promise rapidly become times of trial. Then the mocking voice of unbelief tells us that aspiration is vain. The cold cross-currents of indifference chill the fiery impulses of the heart. We are prisoned like Joseph, by no material bars indeed, but by the invisible bonds of unbelief; and we find it most hard to keep the promise clear and bright, while tempted to believe that our aspirations were merely idle dreams. And there is that arousing, by the promise, of the soul's hidden unbelief, which makes every promise an inevitable trial. *God causes His promises to try us.*

Thus the great idea of an undiscovered land across the wastes of the Atlantic smote the soul of Columbus; but it remained a dreamy faith until by opposition and ridicule he was tempted to regard it as a dream, and then it became heroic endeavor, and the land was found.

Thus with all men of genius. They stand in the front of their age, with thoughts which the world cannot understand; but those thoughts are dreams until suffering and scorn try the men, and then they are awakened into effort to realize them.

Hence God leads us into circumstances in which we are tempted to doubt His promises, that by temptation He may discipline faith into power. There is a wilderness of temptation in every life, and like Christ, we are often led into it, from the solemn hour when we heard the voice, "Thou art My son"; but like Christ, we come forth strong, through the long, silent wrestling with temptation, to do our Father's will.

God sends the Hour of Deliverance: "until the time that His word came." When the discipline was perfected, Joseph came forth ready for his mission. But our deliverance does not always come in this way. Take from the Bible histories the four great methods by which God sends deliverance.

*Sometimes by death.* Thus with Elijah. Weariness, loneliness, failure, had wrung from the strong man the cry, "Take away my life, for I am not better than my fathers." The temptation was becoming too strong, and God sent deliverance in the chariot of fire.

*Sometimes by transforming the height of trial into the height of blessing.* The three youths in Babylon had clenched their nerves for the climax of agony, when the fire became a Paradise. So, now, God makes the climax of trial the herald of spiritual blessedness. By suffering, we are loosened from the bonds of time and sense; there is one near to us like the Son of God; and deliverance has come.

*Sometimes by the glance of love on the falling soul.* Thus with Peter. The temptation was mastering him; one glance of that eye, and he went out weeping and delivered. *Sometimes by continuing the trial, but increasing the power to endure it.* Thus with Paul. After the vision of the third heaven came "the thorn in the flesh." The temptation made him cry thrice to God; the trial remained, but here was the deliverance—"My grace is sufficient for thee." The suffering lost none of its pressure, but he learned to glory in infirmity; and then came his delivering hour. EDWARD LUSCOMBE

*The word of the Lord tried him.* As we try God's Word, so God's Word tries us; and happy if, when we are tried, we come forth as gold; and the trial of our faith proves more precious than that of gold which perisheth, though it be tried with fire. WILLIAM JAY

*Tried Him.* I doubt not that Joseph's brethren were humbled, yet Joseph may be more, he must be cast into the ditch, and into the prison, and the iron must enter not only into his legs, but into his soul. He must be more affected in spirit, because he was to do greater work for God, and was to be raised up higher than the rest, and therefore did need the more ballast. THOMAS SHEPARD

Vs. 19-21. Joseph's feet were hurt in irons, to fit him to tread more delicately in the King's palace at Zoan; and when the Lord's time was come, by the same stairs which winded him into the dungeon, he climbs up into the next chariot to Pharaoh's. Few can bear great and sudden mercies without pride and wantonness, till they are hampered and humbled to carry it moderately. SAMUEL LEE

Vs. 22. *To bind his princes at his pleasure.* What responsibilities and honors loaded the man who had been rejected by his brothers and sold for twenty pieces of silver! What glories crown the head of that greater One Who was "separated from His brethren"! C. H. S.

Vs. 23. *And Jacob sojourned in the land of Ham.* The fairest Goshen in Egypt was not the covenant blessing; neither did the Lord mean His people to think it so; even so to us "earth is our lodge" but only our lodge, for heaven is our home. When we are best housed, we ought still to remember that here we have no continuing city. It were ill news for us if we were doomed to reside in Egypt forever, for all its riches are not worthy to be compared with the reproach of Christ. C. H. S.

The Egyptians were a branch of the race of Ham. They came from Asia through the desert of Syria to settle in the Valley of the Nile. This is a fact clearly established by science and entirely confirms the statements of the Book of Genesis. F. LENORMANT AND E. CHEVALIER

Vs. 25. *He turned their heart to hate His people.* It was His goodness to Israel which called forth the ill-will of the Egyptian court, and so far the Lord caused it, and moreover He made use of this feeling to lead on to the discomfort of His people, and so to their readiness to leave the land to which they had evidently become greatly attached. Thus far but no farther did the Lord turn the hearts of the Egyptians. C. H. S.

God cannot in any sense be the author of sin so far as to be morally responsible for its existence, but it often happens through the evil which is inherent in human nature that the acts of the Lord arouse the ill-feelings of ungodly men. Is the sun to be blamed because while it softens wax it hardens clay? Is the orb of day to be accused of creating the foul exhalations which are drawn by its warmth from the pestilential marsh? The sun causes the reek of the dunghill only in a certain sense, had it been a bed of flowers his beams would have called forth fragrance. C. H. S.

Not by putting this wicked hatred into them, which is not consistent either with the holiness of God's nature, or with the truth of His word, and which was altogether unnecessary, because they had that and all other wickedness in them by nature; but partly by withdrawing the common gifts and operations of his Spirit, and all the restraints and hindrances to it, and wholly leaving them to their own mistakes, and passions, and corrupt affections, which of their own accord were ready to take that course; and partly, by directing and governing that hatred, which was wholly in and from themselves, so as it should fall upon the Israelites rather than upon other people. MATTHEW POOLE

Vs. 27. *They showed His signs among them, and wonders in the land of Ham.* The miracles which were wrought by Moses were the Lord's, not his own: hence they are here called "His signs," as being the marks of Jehovah's presence and power. The plagues were "words of His signs," that is to say, they were speaking marvels, which testified more plainly than words to the omnipotence of Jehovah, to His determination to be obeyed, to His anger at the obstinacy of Pharaoh. C. H. S.

Never were discourses more plain, pointed, personal, or powerful, and yet it took ten of them to accomplish the end designed. In the preaching of the gospel there are words, and signs, and wonders, and these leave men without excuse for their impenitence; to have the kingdom of God come nigh unto them, and yet to remain rebellious is the unhappy sin of obstinate spirits.

Those are wonders of sin who see wonders of grace and yet are unaffected by them: as bad as he was, Pharaoh had not this guilt, for the prodigies which he beheld were marvels of judgment and not of mercy. C. H. S.

Vs. 28. *Darkness.* There is an awful significance in this plague of darkness. The sun was a leading object of devotion among the Egyptians under the name of Osiris. The very name Pharaoh means not only the king, but also the sun, and characterizes the king himself as the representative of the sun and entitled in some sort to divine honors.

But now the very light of the sun has disappeared and primeval chaos seems to have returned. Thus all the forms of Egyptian will-worship were covered with shame and confusion by the plagues. JAMES G. MURPHY

So now the Land of Egypt may have been wrapped about by a thick, palpable cloud, cold, damp, impenetrable: the people would feel it upon their limbs, as swaddling-bands; the sun would be blotted out by it, and all things reduced almost to a state of death—of which this ninth plague was in a certain sense the shadow cast before. THOMAS S. MILLINGTON

Such a cloud would be even more terrible in Egypt, sunny Egypt, than in other countries; for there the sky is almost always clear, and heavy rains unknown. But in any place, and under any conditions, it must have been full of horror and misery. Nothing could represent this more forcibly than the short sentence, "Neither rose any from his place for three days." It was an horror of great darkness; it rested on them like a pall; they knew not what dangers might be around them, what judgment was next to happen: they had not been forewarned of this plague, and they could not tell but it might be only a prelude to some more awful visitation: their soul melted in them, for fear of those things that might come upon them: they dared not more from chamber to chamber, nor even from seat to seat: wherever they chanced to be at the moment when the darkness fell upon them, there they must remain.

Pharaoh might call in vain for his guards; they could not come to him. Moses and Aaron were no longer within reach, for none could go to seek them. Masters could not command their slaves, nor slaves hasten to obey their master's call; the wife could not flee to her husband, nor the child cling to its parents: the same fear was upon all, both high and low; the same paralyzing terror and dismay possessed them every one.

As says the patriarch Job, they "laid hold on horror" (Job 18:20). And this continued for three days and nights: they had no lamps nor torches; either they could not kindle them, or they dared not move to procure them: they were silent in darkness, like men already dead. Hope and expectation of returning light might at first support them; but hope delayed through seventy-two weary hours would presently die out and leave them to despair. The darkness would become more oppressive and intolerable the longer it continued; "felt" upon their bodies as a physical infliction, and "felt" even more in their souls in agonies of fear and apprehension; such a darkness as that which, in the Book of Revelation, the fifth angel pours out upon the seat of the beast—"Whose kingdom was full of darkness; and they gnawed their tongues for pain, and blasphemed the God of heaven because of their pains and their sores, and repented not of their deeds" (Rev. 16:10-11).

If there be any truth in the traditions of the Jews on this subject, there were yet greater alarms under this canopy of darkness, this palpable obscurity, than any which would arise out of the physical infliction. Darkness is a type of Satan's kingdom; and Satan had some liberty in Egypt to walk up and down upon the land and to go to and fro in it. The Jewish rabbis tell us that the devil and his angels were let loose during these three dreadful days; that they had a wider range and greater liberty than usual for working mischief. They describe these evil spirits going among the wretched people, glued to their seats as they were, with terror; frightening them with fearful apparitions; piercing their ears with hideous shrieks and groans; driving them almost to madness with the intensity of their fears; making their flesh creep and the hair of their head to stand on end. Such a climax seems to be referred to by the Psalmist, "He cast upon them the fierceness of His anger, wrath, and indignation, and trouble, by sending evil angels among them." T. S. MILLINGTON

*And they rebelled not against His word.* As Jonah did, who, when he was sent to denounce God's judgments against Nineveh, went to Tarshish. Moses and Aaron were not moved, either with a foolish fear of Pharaoh's wrath or a foolish pity of Egypt's misery, to relax or retard any of the plagues which God ordered them to inflict on the Egyptians; but stretched forth their hand to inflict them as God appointed. They that are instructed to execute judgment will find their remissness construed a rebellion against God's Word. MATTHEW HENRY

Vs. 29. *He turned their waters into blood, and slew their fish.* So that the plague was not a mere coloring of the water with red earth, as some suppose, but the river was offensive and fatal to the fish. C. H. S.

The Nile begins to rise about the end of June and attains its highest point at the end of September. About the commencement of the rise, it assumes a greenish hue, is disagreeable to the taste, unwholesome, and often totally unfit for drinking. It soon, however, becomes red and turbid and continues in this state for three or more weeks. In this condition it is again healthy and fit for use.

The miracle now performed was totally different from this annual change. For (1) it occurred not merely reddened by an admixture of red clay or animalcula; (2) it occurred after the winter, not the summer, solstice; (3) the fish died, a result which did not follow from the periodical change of color; (4) the river stank, and became offensive, which it ceased to be when the ordinary redness made its appearance; (5) the stroke was arrested at the end of seven days, whereas the natural redness continued for at least three weeks; and (6) the change was brought on instantly at the word of command before the eyes of Pharaoh.

The calamity was appalling. The sweet waters of the Nile were common beverage of Egypt. It abounded in all kinds of fish, which formed a principal article of diet for the inhabitants. It was revered as a god by Egypt. But now it was a putrid flood, from which they turned away with loathing. JAMES G. MURPHY

By the miraculous change of the waters into blood, a practical rebuke was given to their superstitions. This sacred and beautiful river, the benefactor and preserver of the country, this birthplace of their chief gods, this abode of their lesser deities, this source of all their prosperity, this center of all their devotion, is turned to blood: the waters stink; the canals and pools, the vessels of wood and vessels of stone, which were replenished from the river, all are alike polluted.

The Nile, according to Pliny, was the "only source from whence the Egyptians obtained water for drinking" (*Hist. Nat.* 76, c.33). This water was considered particularly sweet and refreshing; so much so that the people were in the habit of provoking thirst in order that they might partake more freely of its soft and pleasant draughts. Now it was become abominable to them, and they loathed to drink of it. THOMAS S. MILLINGTON

Vs. 30. *Their land brought forth frogs in abundance.* It is not difficult for an Englishman, in an Eastern wet monsoon, to form a tolerable idea of that plague of Egypt, in which the frogs were in the "houses, bed-chambers, beds and kneading-troughs," of the Egyptians. In the rainy season, myriads of them send forth their constant croak in every direction; and a man not possessed of over-much patience becomes as petulant as was the licentious god and is ready to exclaim,

*Croak, croak! Indeed I shall choke,*
*If you pester and bore my ears anymore*
*With your croak, croak, croak!*

A newcomer, on seeing them leap about the rooms, becomes disgusted and forthwith begins an attack upon them; but the next evening will bring a return of his active visitors. It may appear almost incredible, but in one evening we killed upwards of forty of these guests in the Jaffna mission-house. They had principally concealed themselves in a small tunnel connected with the bathing room, where their noise had become almost insupportable. JOSEPH ROBERTS

*In the chambers of their kings.* Their universal presence must have inspired horror and disgust which would cause sickness and make life a burden; the frogs' swarming even in the king's own chambers was a rebuke to his face, which his pride must have felt. Kings are no more than other men with God, nay less than others when they are first in rebellion; if the frogs had abounded elsewhere, but had been kept out of his select apartments, the monarch would have cared little, for he was a heartless being, but God took care that there should be a special horde of the invaders for the palace; they were more than ordinarily abundant in the chambers of their kings. C. H. S.

God plagued Pharaoh in his bed-chamber: it may be because He would show that His judgments can penetrate the greatest privacy; for the field, and the hall, and the bed-chamber, and the closet are all one to God. JOSIAS SHUTE

Princes and great persons are usually exempted from the reproof of men. As for the laws, ofttimes they are as cobwebs, the great flies break through them. Who dare say to a prince, "Thou art wicked"? Nay, one saith concerning the pope, it is not lawful to say, "What doth he so?" Now, when they are not within the compass of human reproof, God strikes them. J. SHUTE

Vs. 31. *He spake—and there came divers sorts of flies.* Nothing is too small to master man when God commands it to assail him. The sons of Ham had despised the Israelites, and now they were made to loathe themselves. The meanest beggars were more approachable than the proud Egyptians; they were reduced to the meanest condition of filthiness and the most painful state of irritation.

What armies the Lord can send forth when once His right arm is bared for war! And what scorn He pours on proud nations when He fights them, not with angels, but with lice! Pharaoh had little left to be proud of when his own person was invaded by filthy parasites. It was a slap in the face which ought to have humbled his heart, but, alas, man, when he is altogether polluted, still maintains his self-conceit, and when he is the most disgusting object in the universe, he still vaunts himself. Surely pride is moral madness. C. H. S.

As an illustration of the power of flies, we give an extract from Charles Marshall's *Canadian Dominion:* "I have been told by men of unquestioned veracity, that at mid-day the clouds of mosquitoes on the plains would sometimes hide the leaders in a team of four horses from the sight of the driver. Cattle could only be recognized by their shape; all alike becoming black with an impenetrable crust of mosquitoes. The line of the route over the Red River plains would be marked by the carcasses of oxen stung to death by this insignificant foe."

*Lice.* The priests, being polluted by this horrible infection, could not stand to minister before their deities. The people could not, in their uncleanness, be admitted within the precincts of their temples. If they would offer sacrifice, there were no victims fit for the purpose. Even the gods, the oxen, and goats, and cats, were defiled with the vermin.

The Egyptians not only writhed under the loathsome scourge, but felt themselves humbled and disgraced by it. Josephus notices this: "Pharaoh," he says, "was so confounded at this new plague, that, what with the danger, the scandal, and the nastiness of it, he was half sorry for what he had done." The plague assumed the form of a disease, being "in the people" (Exod. 8:17).

As Josephus says again, "The bodies of the people bred them, and they were all covered over with them, gnawing and tearing intolerably, and no remedy, for baths and ointments did no good." But, however distressing to their bodies, the foul and disgraceful character of the plague, and the offence brought upon their religion by the defilement of their deities and the interruption of all their religious ceremonies, was its most offensive feature. T. S. MILLINGTON

Vermin of the kind is one of the common annoyances of Egypt. Herodotus tells us that the priests shave their whole body every other day that no lice or other impure things may adhere to them when they are engaged in the service of the gods. It is manifest that this species of vermin was particularly disgusting to the Egyptians. JAMES G. MURPHY

Vs. 32. *Hail.* Extraordinary reports of the magnitude of hailstones, which have fallen during storms so memorable as to find a place in general history, have come down from the periods of antiquity more or less remote.

According to the "Chronicles," a hailstorm occurred in the reign of Charlemagne, in which hailstones fell which measured fifteen feet in length by six feet in breadth and eleven feet in thickness; and under the reign of Tippoo Saib, hailstones equal in magnitude to elephants are said to have fallen. Setting aside these and like recitals as partaking rather of the character of fable than of history, we shall find sufficient to create astonishment in well authenticated observations on this subject.

In a hailstorm which took place in Flintshire on the ninth of April, 1672, Hailey saw hailstones which weighed five ounces.

On the fourth of May, 1697, Robert Taylor saw fall hailstones measuring fourteen inches in circumference.

In the storm which ravaged Como on the twentieth of August, 1787, Volta saw hailstones which weighed nine ounces.

On the twenty-second of May, 1822, Dr. Noggerath saw fall at Bonn hailstones which weighed from twelve to thirteen ounces.

It appears, therefore, certain that in different countries hailstorms have occurred in which stones weighing from half to three-quarters of a pound have fallen. DIONYSIUS LARDNER

Vs. 34. *Locusts came, and caterpillars, and that without number.* We traveled five days' journey through places wholly waste and destroyed, wherein millet had been sown, which had stalks as great as those we set in our vineyards, and we saw them all broken and beaten down as if a tempest had been there; and this the locusts did. The trees were without leaves, and the bark of them was all devoured; and no grass was there to be seen, for they had eaten up all things. The number of them was so great that I shall not speak of it, because I shall not be believed: but this I will say, that I saw men, women, and children sit as forlorn and dead among the locusts. SAMUEL PURCHAS

A swarm of locusts which was observed in India in 1825 occupied a space of forty English square miles, contained at least forty millions of locusts in one line, and cast a long shadow on the earth.

And Major Moore thus describes an immense army of these animals which ravaged the Mahratta country: "The column they composed extended five hundred miles; and so compact was it when on the wing, that like an eclipse, it completely hid the sun, so that no shadow was cast by any object."

Brown, in his travels in Africa, states that an area of nearly two thousand square miles was literally covered by them; and Kirby and Spence mention that a column of them was so immense that they took four hours to fly over the spot where the observers stood. M. KALISCH

Vs. 34-35. *He spake, and the locusts came, and caterpillars, and that without number. And did eat up all the herbs in their land, and devoured the fruit of their ground.* Nothing escapes these ravenous creatures; they even climb the trees to reach any remnant of foliage which may survive. Commissioned as these were by God, we may be sure they would do their work thoroughly and leave behind them nothing but a desolate wilderness. C. H. S.

Vs. 36. *He smote also all the firstborn in their land, the chief of all their strength.* Now came the master blow. The Lord spoke before, but now He smites; before He only smote vines, but now He strikes men themselves. The glory of the household dies in a single night, the prime and pick of the nation are cut off, the flower of the troops, the heirs of the rich, and the hopes of the poor all die at midnight. C. H. S.

Did you hear that cry? 'Tis the moment of midnight, and some tragedy is enacted in that Egyptian dwelling for such an unearthly shriek! And it is repeated and reechoed, as doors burst open and frantic women rush into the street, and, as the houses of priests and physicians are beset, they only shake their heads in speechless agony and point to the death-sealed features of their own firstborn. Lights are flashing at the palace gates and flitting through the royal chambers; and as king's messengers hasten through the town enquiring where the two venerable Hebrew brothers dwell, the whisper flies, "The prince royal is dead!"

Be off, ye sons of Jacob! Speed from your house of bondage, ye oppressed and injured Israelites! And in their eagerness to "thrust forth" the terrible because Heaven-protected race, they press upon them gold and jewels and bribe them to be gone. JAMES HAMILTON

Vs. 37. *And there was not one feeble person among their tribes.* A great marvel indeed. The number of their army was very great, and yet there was not one in hospital, not one carried in an ambulance or limping in the rear. Poverty and oppression had not enfeebled them.

Jehovah Rophi had healed them; they carried none of the diseases of Egypt with them, and felt none of the exhaustion which sore bondage produces. When God calls His people to a long journey, He fits them for it; in the pilgrimage of life, our strength shall be equal to our day. See the contrast between Egypt and Israel—in Egypt one dead in every house, and among the Israelites not one so much as limping. C. H. S.

When Israel came out of Egypt there were no feeble persons, though there were while dwelling there: so there shall be no feeble saint go to heaven, but they shall be perfect when carried hence by the angels of God, though they complain of feebleness here. "There shall be no more thence an infant of days, nor an old man that hath not filled his days: for the child shall die an hundred years old" (Isa. 45:20). JOHN SHEFFIELD

Vs. 39. *He spread a cloud for a covering.* Never people were so favored. What would not travelers in the desert now give for such a canopy? The sun could not scorch them with its burning ray; their whole camp was screened like a king in his pavilion. Nothing seemed to be too good for God to give His chosen nation; their comfort was studied in every way.

*And fire to give light in the night.* While cities were swathed in darkness, their town of tents enjoyed a light which modern art with all its appliances cannot equal. God Himself was their sun and shield, their glory and their defence. Could they be unbelieving while so graciously shaded or rebellious while they walked at midnight in such a light?

Alas, the tale of their sin is as extraordinary as this story of His love; but this Psalm selects the happier theme and dwells only upon covenant love and faithfulness. Oh, give thanks unto the Lord, for He is good. We, too, have found the Lord all this to us, for He has been our sun and shield and has preserved us alike from the perils of joys and the evils of grief. C. H. S.

Vs. 41. *He opened the rock, and the waters gushed out.* With Moses' rod and His own Word He cleft the rock in the desert, and forth leaped abundant floods for their drinking where they had feared to die of thirst. From most unlikely sources, the all-sufficient God can supply His people's needs; hard rocks become springing fountains at the Lord's command.

*They ran in the dry places like a river.* So that those at a distance from the rock could stoop down and refresh themselves, and the stream flowed on, so that in future journeyings they were supplied. The desert sand would naturally swallow up the streams, and yet it did not so, the refreshing river ran "in the dry places." We know that the rock set forth our Lord Jesus Christ, from Whom there flows a fountain of living waters which shall never be exhausted till the last pilgrim has crossed the Jordan and entered Canaan. C. H. S.

Vs. 45. *That they might observe His statutes, and keep His laws.* Most justly then did the music close with the jubilant but solemn shout of "hallelujah." "Praise ye the Lord." If this history did not make Israel praise God, what would? C. H. S.

The One Hundred Fifth Psalm is a meditation on the covenant as performed on the part of God; the One Hundred Sixth on the covenant as kept by Israel. They both dwell on the predestinating will of God, electing men to holiness and obedience, and the mode in which human sin opposes itself to that will and yet cannot make it void. *Plain Commentary*

# PSALM 106

This Psalm begins and ends with "hallelujah" — "Praise ye the Lord." The space between these two descriptions of praise is filled up with the mournful details of Israel's sin and the extraordinary patience of God; and truly we do well to bless the Lord both at the beginning and the end of our meditations when sin and grace are the themes.

It was probably written by David — at any rate its first and last two verses are to be found in that sacred song which David delivered to Asaph when he brought up the ark of the Lord (I Chron. 16:34-36).

While we are studying this holy Psalm, let us all along see ourselves in the Lord's ancient people, and bemoan our own provocations of the Most High, at the same time admiring His infinite patience and adoring Him because of it. May the Holy Spirit sanctify it to the promotion of humility and gratitude. C. H. S.

Vs. 1. *Praise ye the Lord.* If David were present in churches where quartets and choirs carry on all the singing, he would turn to the congregation and say, "Praise ye the Lord." Our meditation dwells upon human sin; but on all occasions and in all occupations, it is seasonable and profitable to praise the Lord.

*O give thanks unto the Lord; for He is good.* To us needy creatures, the goodness of God is the first attribute which excites praise, and that praise takes the form of gratitude. C. H. S.

*For He is good.* Essentially, solely, and originally; is communicative and diffusive of His goodness; is the Author of all good and no evil; and is gracious and merciful and ready to forgive. JOHN GILL

*For His mercy endureth forever.* The prophet, however, throughout this Psalm celebrates in many instances the way wherein the sinning people were arrested and smitten. And when he proposed that this Psalm should be sung in the church of God, Israel was under the cross and afflictions. Yet he demands that Israel should acknowledge that the Lord is good, that His mercy endureth forever, even in the act of smiting the offender. That therefore alone is a true and full confession of the divine goodness which is made not only in prosperity but also in adversity. MUSCULUS

Vs. 2. *Who can utter?* "Blessed are they that keep judgment." I am of opinion, however, that the prophet had another design, namely, that there is no man who has ever endeavored to concentrate all his energies, both physical and mental, in the praising of God, but will find himself inadequate for so lofty a subject, the transcendant grandeur of which overpowers all our senses. JOHN CALVIN

Vs. 3. "*Blessed are they that keep judgment.* That are of right principles and upright practices; this is real and substantial praising of God. Thanks-doing is the proof of thanksgiving. JOHN TRAPP

Vs. 4. *Remember me, O Lord, with the favor that Thou bearest unto Thy people.* I cannot ask more, nor would I seek less. Treat me as the least of Thy saints are treated, and I am content. It should be enough for us if we fare as the rest of the family. If even Balaam desired no more than to die the death of the righteous, we may be well content both to live as they live and die as they die. This feeling would prevent our wishing to escape trial, persecution, and chastisement; these have fallen to the lot of saints, and why should we escape them? C. H. S.

*O visit me with Thy salvation.* Bring it home to me. Come to my house and to my heart, and give me the salvation which Thou hast prepared and art alone able to bestow. We sometimes hear of a man's dying by the visitation of God, but here is one who knows that he can only live by the visitation of God. Jesus said of Zaccheus, "This day is salvation come to this house," and that was the case because He Himself had come there. There is no salvation apart from the Lord, and He must visit us with it or we shall never obtain it. We are too sick to visit our Great Physician, and therefore He visits us. Visit me, Lord? Can it be? Dare I ask for it? And yet I must, for Thou alone canst bring me salvation: therefore, Lord, I entreat Thee come unto me, and abide with me forever. C. H. S.

Vs. 6. *We have sinned with our fathers.* Here begins a long and particular confession. Confession of sin is the readiest way to secure an answer to the prayer of verse 4; God visits with His salvation the soul which acknowledges its need of a Savior. Men may be said to have sinned with their fathers when they imitate them, when they follow the same objects, and make their own lives to be mere continuations of the follies of their sires. Moreover, Israel was but one nation in all time, and the confession which follows sets forth the national rather than the personal sin of the Lord's people. They enjoyed national privileges, and therefore they shared in national guilt. C. H. S.

*We have committed iniquity, we have done wickedly.* Thus is the confession repeated three times in token of the sincerity and heartiness of it. Sins of omission, commission, and rebellion we ought to acknowledge under distinct heads, that we may show a due sense of the number and heinousness of our offenses. C. H. S.

God tells them they had rebelled of old; "As your fathers did, so do ye" (Acts 8:51). Antiquity is no infallible argument of goodness: though Tertullian says the first things were the best things; and the less they distanced from the beginning, the poorer they were; but he must be understood only of holy customs. For iniquity can plead antiquity: he that commits a new act of murder finds it old in the example of Cain; drunkenness may be fetched from Noah; contempt of parents from Ham; women's lightness from the daughters of Lot.

There is no sin but hath white hairs upon it and is exceeding old. But let us look further back yet, even to Adam; there is the age of sin. This is that St. Paul calls the old man; it is almost as old as the root, but older than all the branches. Therefore, our restitution by Christ to grace is called the new man. THOMAS ADAMS

Vs. 7. *Our fathers understood not Thy wonders in Egypt.* The Israelites saw the miraculous plagues and ignorantly wondered at them: their design of love, their deep moral and spiritual lessons, and their revelation of the divine power and justice they were unable to perceive. A long sojourn among idolaters had blunted the perceptions of the chosen family, and cruel slavery had ground them down into mental sluggishness. C. H. S.

Alas, how many of God's wonders are not understood or misunderstood by us still. We fear the sons are no great improvement upon the sires. We inherit from our fathers much sin and little wisdom; they could only leave us what they themselves possessed. We see from this verse that a want of understanding is no excuse for sin, but is itself one count in the indictment against Israel. C. H. S.

One sin is a step to another more heinous; for not observing, is followed with not remembering, and forgetfulness of duty draweth on disobedience and rebellion. DAVID DICKSON

*They remembered not the multitude of Thy mercies.* What were these fearful forecasts, these amazing bodements of an unavoidable (as they apprehended) ruin, but the overflowings of unbelief, or distrust in God; and this was another provocation. Former mercies are forgotten, yea, eaten up by unbelief, as the seven lean kine in Pharaoh's dream eat up the fat ones, and present difficulties are aggravated by unbelief, as if all the power of God could not remove and overcome them. And will not the Lord (think you) visit in anger such a sin as this? JOSEPH CARYL

*His longsuffering, and His patience.* It was God's patience the ungrateful Israelites sinned against; for they even plied and pursued Him with sin upon sin, one offence following and thronging upon the neck of another, the last account still rising highest, and swelling bigger, till the treasures of grace and pardon were so far drained and exhausted that they provoked God to swear, and what is more, to swear in His wrath, and with a full purpose of revenge, that they should never enter into His rest. ROBERT SOUTH

Vs. 8. *Nevertheless He saved them.* It is said in the verse precedent, "They rebelled at the sea, even at the Red Sea," or, as in the Hebrew, "even in the Red Sea"; when the waters stood like walls on both sides of them; when they saw those walls of waters that never people saw before, and saw the power, the infinite power of God leading them through on dry land; then did they rebel, at the sea, even in the sea; and yet for all this, the Lord saved them with a notwithstanding all this.

And I say, shall the Lord put forth so much of grace upon a people, that were under the law; and not put forth much more of His grace upon those that are under the gospel? WILLIAM BRIDGE

His name is Jehovah-Jireh, in the mount of the Lord it shall be seen, the Lord will provide. Do you need His presence? His name is Jehovah-Shammah, the Lord is there: Immanuel, God with us: look to Him to be with you, for His name's sake. Do you need audience of prayer? His name is the Hearer of prayer.

Do you need strength? His name is the Strength of Israel. Do you need comfort? His name is the Consolation of Israel. Do you need shelter? His name is the City of Refuge. Have you nothing and need all? His name is All in all.

Sit down and devise names to your wants and needs, and you will find He hath a name suitable thereunto; for your supply, He hath wisdom to guide you; and power to keep you; mercy to pity you; grace to adorn you; and glory to crown you. Trust in His name, Who saves for His name's sake. RALPH ERSKINE

Vs. 10. *And He saved them from the hand of him that hated them.* Pharaoh was drowned and the power of Egypt so crippled that throughout the forty years' wanderings of Israel they were never threatened by their old masters. C. H. S.

Vs. 11. *And the waters covered their enemies: there was not one of them left.* The Lord does nothing by halves. What He begins, He carries through to the end. This, again, made Israel's sin the greater, because they saw the thoroughness of the divine justice and the perfection of the divine faithfulness.

In the covering of their enemies, we have a type of the pardon of our sins; they are sunk as in the sea, never to rise again; and, blessed be the Lord, there is "not one of them left." Not one sin of thought, or word, or deed; the blood of Jesus has covered all. "I will cast their iniquities into the depths of the sea. C. H. S.

Vs. 12. *Then believed they His words.* That is to say, they believed the promise when they saw it fulfilled, but not till then. This is mentioned, not to their credit, but to their shame. Those who do not believe the Lord's word till they see it performed are not believers at all. Who would not believe when the fact stares them in the face? The Egyptians would have done as much as this. C. H. S.

*They sang His praise.* How could they do otherwise? Their song was very excellent, and is the type of the song of heaven; but sweet as it was, it was quite as short, and when it was ended, they fell to murmuring. "They sang His praise," but "they soon forgot His works." Between Israel singing and Israel sinning there was scarce a step. Their song was good while it lasted, but it was no sooner begun than over. C. H. S.

Vs. 12-13. *They soon forgat His works.* This was said of that generation of the Israelites which came out of Egypt. The chapter which contains the portion of their history here alluded to begins with rapturous expressions of gratitude and ends with the murmurs of discontent; both uttered by the same lips within the short space of three days. EDWARD PAYSON

Vs. 13. As it is with a sieve, or boulter, the good corn and fine flour goes through, but the light chaff and coarse bran remains behind; or as a strainer, that the sweet liquor is strained out, but the dregs are left behind: or as a grate, that lets the pure water run away, but if there be any straws, sticks, mud or filth, that it holds.

Thus it is with most men's memories; by nature they are but, as it were, pertusa dolia, mere river tubs, especially in good things very treacherous, so that the vain conceits of men are apt to be held in, when divine instructions and gracious promises run through; trifles and toys, and worldly things, they are apt to remember, tenacious enough; but for spiritual things they leak out; like Israel, they soon forget them. WILLIAM GOUGE

Vs. 14-15. *But lusted exceedingly in the wilderness. And He gave them their request.* Though they would not wait God's will, they are hot to have their own. When the most suitable and pleasant food was found them in abundance, it did not please them long, but they grew dainty and sniffed at angel's food and must needs have flesh to eat, which was unhealthy diet for that warm climate and for their easy life.

Prayer may be answered in anger and denied in love. That God gives a man his desire is no proof that he is the object of Divine favor, everything depends upon what that desire is. C. H. S.

Vs. 15. *And He gave them their request.* The throat's pleasure did shut up Paradise, sold the birthright, beheaded the Baptist, and it was the chief of the cooks, Nebuzaradan, that first set fire to the Temple and razed the city. These effects are (1) Grossness; which takes away agility to any good work; which makes a man more like a tun upon two pottle pots.

Caesar said he mistrusted not Antony and Dolabella for any practices, because they were fat; but Casca and Cassius, lean, hollow fellows, who did think too much. The other are the devil's crammed fowls, too fat to lay. THOMAS ADAMS

*But sent leanness into their soul.* Ah, that "but"; It embittered all. The meat was poison to them when it came without a blessing; whatever it might do in fattening the body, it was poor stuff when it made the soul lean. How earnestly might Israel have unprayed her players had she known what would come with their answer! The prayers of lust will have to be wept over. We fret and fume till we have our desire, and we have to be wept over. We fret and fume till we have our desire, and then we have to fret still more because the attainment of it ends in bitter disappointment. C. H. S.

Vs. 16. *They envied Moses also in the camp.* Who can hope to escape envy when the meekest of men was subject to it? How unreasonable was this envy, for Moses was the one man in all the camp who labored hardest and had most to bear. They should have sympathized with him; to envy him was ridiculous. C. H. S.

*And Aaron the saint of the Lord.* By divine choice, Aaron was set apart to be holiness unto the Lord, and instead of thanking God that He had favored them with a high priest by whose intercession their prayers would be presented, they cavilled at the divine election and quarrelled with the man who was to offer sacrifice for them. Thus neither church nor state was ordered aright for them; they would snatch from Moses his scepter, and from Aaron his miter. It is the mark of bad men that they are envious of the good and spiteful against their best benefactors. C. H. S.

Vs. 17. *The earth opened and swallowed up Dathan, and covered the company of Abiram.* Moses had opened the sea for their deliverance, and now that they provoke him, the earth opens for their destruction. It was time that the nakedness of their sins was covered and that the earth should open her mouth to devour those who opened their mouths against the Lord and His servants. C. H. S.

Vs. 19. *They made a calf in Horeb.* In the very place where they had solemnly pledged themselves to obey the Lord, they broke the second, if not the first, of His commandments, and set up the Egyptian symbol of the Ox and bowed before it. The ox image is here sacrastically called "a calf"; idols are worthy of no respect; scorn is never more legitimately used than when it is poured upon all attempts to set forth the invisible God. The Israelites were foolish indeed when they thought they saw the slightest divine glory in a bull, nay, in the mere image of a bull. To believe that the image of a bull could be the image of God must need great credulity.

*And worshipped the molten image.* We have heard the richness of popish paraphernalia much extolled, but an idolatrous image when made of gold is not one jot the less abominable than it would have been had it been made of dross and dung: the beauty of art cannot conceal the deformity of sin. We are told also of the suggestiveness of their symbols, but what of that, when God forbids the use of them? Vain also is it to plead that such worship is hearty. So much the worse. Heartiness in forbidden actions is only an increase of transgression. C. H. S. e

And why a calf? Could they find no fitter resemblance of God amongst all the creatures? Why not rather the lordly lion, to show the sovereignty; vast elephant, the immensity; subtle serpent, the wisdom; long-lived hart, the eternity; swift eagle, the ubiquity of God, rather than the silly, senseless calf, that eateth hay?

But the shape mattereth not much, for if God be made like anything, He may be made like anything, it being as unlawful to fashion Him an angel as a worm, seeing the commandment forbids as well the likeness of things in heaven above as in earth beneath (Exod. 20:4). But probably a calf was preferred before other forms because they had learned it from the Egyptians' worshipping their ox Apis.

Thus the Israelites borrowed (Exod. 12:35) not all gold and silver, but some dross from the Egyptians, whence they fetch the idolatrous forms of their worship. THOMAS FULLER

The local seat of Antichrist (and what seat can that be but Rome?) is called in the Revelation by three names: it is called *Egypt* (Rev. 2:8). It is called *Sodom* in the same verse. It is called *Babylon* in many places of the Revelation. It is called *Babylon,* in regard to her cruelty. It is called *Sodom,* in regard to her filthiness; and *Egypt,* in regard to her idolatry. T. WESTFIELD

It is a hard matter for a man to live in Egypt and not to taste and savor somewhat of the idolatry of Egypt. We had sometime, in England, a proverb about going to Rome. They said, a man that went the first time to Rome, he went to see a wicked man there; he that went the second time to Rome, went to be acquainted with that wicked man there; he that went the third time, brought him home with him. THOMAS WESTFIELD

Vs. 19-22. It is to be hoped, we shall never live to see a time when the miracles of our redemption shall be forgotten; when the return of Jesus Christ from heaven shall be despaired of; and when the people shall solicit their teachers to fabricate a new philosophical deity for them to worship instead of the God of their ancestors, to Whom glory hath been ascribed from generation to generation. GEORGE HORNE

Vs. 20. *Thus they changed their glory into the similitude of an ox that eateth grass.* The Psalmist is very contemptuous, and justly so: irreverence towards idols is an indirect reverence to God. False gods, attempts to represent the true God, and indeed, all material things which are worshiped are so much filth upon the face of the earth, whether they be crosses, crucifixes, virgins, wafers, relics, or even the pope himself. We are by far too mealy-mouthed about these infamous abominations: God abhors them, and so should we. To renounce the glory of spiritual worship for outward pomp and show is the height of folly and deserves to be treated as such. C. H. S.

destruction came at last. For the first wilderness sin, He chastened them, sending leanness into their soul; for the second, He weeded out the offenders, the flame burned up the wicked; for the third, He threatened to destroy them; for the fourth, He lifted up his hand and almost came to blows (Vs. 26); for the fifth He actually smote them, "and the plague brake in among them"; and so the punishment increased with their perserverance in sin. C. H. S.

Vs. 23. *Moses His chosen stood before Him in the breach.* We, through infinite mercy, have had some like Moses and Aaron, to make up our hedges, raise up our foundations, and stop some gaps; but all our gaps are not yet stopped.

Are there not gaps in the hedge of doctrine? If it were not so, how came in such erroneous, blasphemous, and wild opinions amongst us? Are there not gaps in the hedges of civil and ecclesiastical authority? Do not multitudes trample upon magistracy and ministry, all powers, both human and divine?

Are there not gaps in the worship of God? Do not too many tread down all churches, all ordinances, yea, the very Scriptures? Are there not gaps in the hedge of justice through which the bulls of Bashan enter, which oppress the poor, and crush the needy? Amos 4:1: are there not gaps in the hedge of love; is not that bond of perfection broken?

Are there not bitter envyings and strife amongst us; do we not bite and devour one another? Are there not gaps in the hedge of conscience? Is not the peace broken between God and your souls? Doth not Satan come in oft at the gap and disturb you? Are there not gaps also in your several relations whereby he gets advantage? Surely, if our eyes be in our heads, we may see gaps enough. WILLIAM GREENHILL

Vs. 24. *They believed not His word.* This is the root sin. If we do not believe the Lord's Word, we shall think lightly of His promised gifts. "They could not enter in because of unbelief" — this was the key which turned the lock against them. When pilgrims to the Celestial City begin to doubt the Lord of the way, they soon come to think little of the rest at the journey's end, and this is the surest way to make them bad travelers. Israel's unbelief demanded spies to see the land; the report of those spies was of a mingled character, and so a fresh crop of unbelief sprang up with consequences most deplorable. C. H. S.

One great bar to salvation is spiritual sloth. It is said of Israel, "They despised the pleasant land." What should be the reason? Canaan was a paradise of delight, a type of heaven; aye, but they thought it would cost them a great deal of trouble and hazard in the getting, and they would rather go without it; they despised the pleasant land. Are there not millions of us who would rather go sleeping to hell than sweating to heaven?

I have read of certain Spaniards that live near where there is a great store of fish yet are so lazy that they will not be at the pains to catch them, but buy of their neighbors: such a sinful stupidity and sloth is upon the most, that though Christ be near them, though salvation is offered in the gospel, yet they will not work out salvation. THOMAS WATSON

Vs. 28. *They joined themselves also unto Baal-peor.* Ritualism led on to the adoration of false gods. If we choose a false way of worship we shall, ere long, choose to worship a false god. This abomination of the Moabites was an idol in whose worship women gave up their bodies to the most shameless lust. Think of the people of a holy God coming down to this! Perhaps they assisted in necromantic rites which were intended to open a correspondence with departed spirits, thus endeavoring to break the seal of God's providence and burst into the secret chambers which God has shut up. Those who are weary of seeking the living God have often shown a hankering after dark sciences and have sought after fellowship with demons and spirits. To what strong delusions those are often given up who cast off the fear of God! This remark is as much needed now as in days gone by. C. H. S.

Vs. 29. *Thus they provoked Him to anger with their inventions: and the plague brake in upon them.* Their new sins brought on them a disease new to their tribes. When men invent sins, God will not be slow to invent punishments. Their vices were a moral pest, and they were visited with a bodily pest: so the Lord meets like with its like. C. H. S.

Note that it is not said "with their deeds," but with their pursuits (studies). It is one thing simply to do a thing; it is quite another to pursue it earnestly night and day. MUSCULUS

It was Saul's fault. God bade him destroy Amalek altogether, and he would invent a better way, to save some (forsooth) for sacrifice, which God could not think of. And it was St. Peter's fault, when he persuaded Christ from His passion, and found out a better way (as he thought) than Christ could devise. LANCELOT ANDREWS

Vs. 30. *Then stood up Phinehas, and executed judgments and so the plague was stayed.* His honest spirit could not endure that lewdness should be publicly practiced at a time when a fast had been proclaimed. Such daring defiance of God and of all law he could not brook, and so with his sharp javelin, he transfixed two guilty ones in the very act. It was a holy passion which inflamed him, and no enmity to either of the persons whom he slew. C. H. S.

He doth not stand casting of scruples: Who am I to do this? The son of the high priest. My place is all for peace and mercy: it is for me to sacrifice, and pray for the sin of the people, not to sacrifice any of the people for their sin. My duty calls me to appease the anger of God what I may, not to revenge the sins of men; to pray for their conversion, not to work the confusion of any sinner. And who are these? Is not the one a great prince in Israel, the other a princess of Midian? Can the death of two so famous personages go unrevenged? Or, if it be safe and fit, why doth my uncle Moses rather shed his own tears than their blood? I will mourn with the rest; let them revenge whom it concerneth. But the zeal of God hath barred out all weak deliberations; and he holds it now both his duty and his glory to be an executioner of so shameless a pair of offenders. JOSEPH HALL

Mark the mighty principle, which rolled like a torrent in the heart of Phinehas. The Spirit leaves it not obscure. The praise is this, "He was zealous for his God" (Num. 25:13). He could not fold his arms and see God's law insulted, His rule defied, His majesty and empire scorned. The servant's heart blazed in one blaze of godly indignation. He must be up to vindicate his Lord. His fervent love, his bold resolve, fear nothing in a righteous cause. The offending Zimri was a potent prince: nevertheless, he spared him not.

Believer, can you read this and feel no shame? Do your bold efforts testify your zeal? Sinners blaspheme God's name. Do you rebuke? His Sabbaths are profaned. Do you protest? False principles are current. Do you expose the counterfeits? Vice stalks in virtue's garb. Do you tear down the mask? Satan enthralls the world. Do you resist? Nay, rather are you not dozing unconcerned? Whether Christ's cause succeeds, or be cast down, you little care. If righteous zeal girded your loins and braced your nerves and moved the rudder of your heart and swelled your sails of action, would God be so unknown and blasphemy so daring? HENRY LAW

Vs. 31. *And that was counted unto him for righteousness unto all generations forevermore.* He was impelled by motives so pure that what would otherwise have been a deed of blood was justified in the sight of God; nay, more, was made the evidence that Phinehas was righteous. No personal ambition, or private revenge, or selfish passion, or even fanatical bigotry, inspired the man of God, but zeal for God, indignation at open filthiness, and true patriotism urged him on. C. H. S.

Vs. 32. *So that it went ill with Moses for their sakes.* Moses was at last wearied out, and began to grow angry with them, and utterly hopeless of their ever improving. Can we wonder at it, for he was man and not God? After forty years bearing with them the meek man's temper gave way, and he called them rebels and showed unhallowed anger; and therefore he was not permitted to enter the land which he desired to inherit.

Truly, he had a sight of the goodly country from the top of Pisgah, but entrance was denied him, and thus it went ill with him. It was their sin which angered him, but he had to bear the consequences. However clear it may be that others are more guilty than ourselves, we should always remember that this will not screen us, but every man must bear his own burden. C. H. S.

Vs. 33. *Because they provoked his spirit, so that he spake unadvisedly with his lips.* Which seems a small sin compared with that of others, but then it was the sin of Moses, the Lord's chosen servant, who had seen and known so much of the Lord, and therefore it could not be passed by. He did not speak blasphemously or falsely, but only hastily and without care; but this is a serious fault in a lawgiver, and especially in one who speaks for God.

This passage is, to our mind, one of the most terrible in the Bible. Truly we serve a jealous God. Yet He is not a hard master, or austere; we must not think so, but we must the rather be jealous of ourselves and watch that we live the more carefully, and speak the more advisedly, because we serve such a Lord.

We ought also to be very careful how we treat the ministers of the gospel, lest by provoking their spirit we should drive them into any unseemly behavior which should bring upon them the chastisement of the Lord. Little do a murmuring, quarrelsome people dream of the perils in which they involve their pastors by their untoward behavior. C. H. S.

As Abraham was distinguished for his faith, so was Moses for his meekness; for Scripture has declared that he was "very meek, above all the men which were on the face of the earth" (Num. 12:3). Yet, judging from facts recorded of him, we should be inclined to suppose that he was by nature remarkable for sensitiveness and hastiness of temper—that was his one besetting infirmity. ISAAC WILLIAMS

When anyone has run long and run well, how sad it is to stumble within a few steps of the goal! If Moses had an earthly wish, it was to see Israel safe in their inheritance, and his wish was all but consummated. Faith and patience had held out well nigh forty years, and in a few months more the Jordan would be crossed and the work would be finished. And who can tell but this very nearness of the prize helped to create something of a presumptuous confidence? The blood of Moses was hot to begin with, and he was not the meekest of men.

Blessed is the man that feareth alway! Blessed is the man who, although years have passed without an attempt at burglary, still bars his doors and sees his windows fastened!

John Newton remarks, "The grace of God is as necessary to create a right temper in a Christian on the breaking of a china plate as on the death of an only son"; and as no man can tell on any dawning day but what that may be the most trying day in all his life, how wise to pray without ceasing, "Uphold me according unto Thy Word." JAMES HAMILTON

Vs. 34. *They did not destroy the nations, concerning whom the Lord commanded them.* It is a great evil with professors that they are not zealous for the total destruction of all sin within and without. We make alliances of peace where we ought to proclaim war to the knife; we plead our constitutional temperament, our previous habits, the necessity of our circumstances, or some other evil excuse as an apology for being content with a very partial sanctification, if indeed it be sanctification at all.

We are slow also to rebuke sin in others and are ready to spare respectable sins, which like Agag walk with mincing steps. The measure of our destruction of sin is not to be our inclination, or the habit of others, but the Lord's command. We have no warrant for dealing leniently with any sin, be it what it may. C. H. S.

Vs. 35. *But were mingled among the heathen, and learned their works.* Having enough faults of their own, they were yet ready to go to school to the filthy Canaanites and educate themselves still more in the arts of iniquity. It was certain that they could learn no good from men whom the Lord had condemned to utter destruction. Few would wish to go to the condemned cell for learning, yet Israel sat at the feet of accursed Canaan and rose up proficient in every abomination.

This, too, is a grievous but common error among professors: they court worldly company and copy worldly fashions, and yet it is their calling to bear witness against these things. None can tell what evil has come of the folly of worldly conformity. C. H. S.

Vs. 37-38. *Yea, they sacrificed their sons and their daughters unto devils.* This was being snared indeed; they were spell-bound by the cruel superstition and were carried so far as even to become murderers of their own children, in honor of the most detestable deities, which were rather devils than gods. C. H. S.

*And the land was polluted with blood.* The promised land, the Holy Land, which was the glory of all lands, for God was there, was defiled with the reeking gore of innocent babes, and by the blood-red hands of their parents, who slew them in order to pay homage to devils. Alas! Alas! What vexation was this to the Spirit of the Lord. C. H. S.

Vs. 40-41. *Therefore was the wrath of the Lord kindled against His people, insomuch that He abhorred His own inheritance.* The feeling described is like to that of a husband who still loves his guilty wife and yet when he thinks of her lewdness feels his whole nature rising in righteous anger at her, so that the very sight of her afflicts his soul.

*And they that hated them ruled over them.* And who could wonder? Sin never creates true love. They joined the heathen in their wickedness, and they did not win their hearts, but rather provoked their contempt. If we mix with men of the world, they will soon become our masters and our tyrants, and we cannot want worse. C. H. S.

Whenever great love sinks into great hate, it is termed abhorrence. LORINUS

Vs. 43. *And were brought low for their iniquity.* Deeply engrained in their nature must the sin of idolatry have been, or they would not have returned to it with such persistence in the teeth of such penalties; we need not marvel at this, there is a still greater wonder; man prefers sin and hell to heaven and God. C. H. S.

Vs.44. *Nevertheless He regarded their affliction, when He heard their cry.* His fiercest wrath towards His own people is only a temporary flame, but His love burns on forever like the light of His own immortality. C. H. S.

Vs. 48. *Amen.* Martin Luther said once of the Lord's Prayer that "It was the greatest martyr on earth, because it was used so frequently without thought and feeling, without reverence and faith." This quaint remark, as true as it is sad, applies perhaps with still greater force to the word "Amen."

A word which is frequently used without due thoughtfulness, and unaccompanied with the feeling which it is intended to call forth, loses it power from this very familiarity, and though constantly on our lips, lies bedridden in the dormitory of our soul. But it is a great word, this word "Amen"; and Luther has truly said, "As your Amen is, so has been your prayer." ADOLPH SAPHIR

## HERE ENDETH BOOK IV OF THE BOOK OF PSALMS

# PSALM 107

This is a choice song for the "redeemed of the Lord" (Vs. 2). Although it celebrates providential deliverances, and therefore may be sung by any man whose life has been preserved in time of danger; yet under cover of this, it mainly magnifies the Lord for spiritual blessings, of which temporal favors are but types and shadows. The theme is thanksgiving and the motives for it. The construction of the Psalm is highly poetical, and merely as a composition it would be hard to find its compeer among human productions. The bards of the Bible hold no second place among the sons of song.

Vs. 1. *O give thanks unto the Lord.* Unto no duty are we more dull and untoward than to the praise of God and thanksgiving unto Him; neither is there any duty whereunto there is more need that we should be stirred up as this earnest exhortation doth import. DAVID DICKSON

Vs. 2. *Whom He hath redeemed from the hand of the enemy.* What gratitude can suffice for a deliverance from the power of sin, death, and hell? In heaven itself there is no sweeter hymn than that whose burden is, "Thou hast redeemed us unto God by Thy blood." C. H. S.

Vs. 4. *Wandered in the wilderness.* He has lost his way. When he was in the world, he had no difficulties; the path was so broad that he could not mistake it. But when the work of divine grace begins in a sinner's heart, he loses his way. He cannot find his way into the world; God has driven him out of it, as He drove Lot out of Sodom. J. C. PHILPOT

*In a solitary way.* The traveler's way in the wilderness is a waste way, and when he leaves even that poor, barren trail, to get utterly beyond the path of man, he is in a wretched plight indeed. A soul without sympathy is on the borders of hell: a solitary way is the way of despair. C. H. S.

Vs. 6. *Then they cried unto the Lord in their trouble.* Some men will never pray till they are half-starved, and for their best interests it is far better for them to be empty and faint than to be full and stout-hearted. If hunger brings us to our knees, it is more useful to us than feasting; if thirst drives us to the fountain, it is better than the deepest draughts of worldly joys; and if fainting leads to crying, it is better than the strength of the mighty. C. H. S.

In these words we find three things remarkable: first, the condition of God's church and people, trouble and distress: secondly, the practice and the exercise of God's people in this state — *Then they cried unto the Lord:* thirdly, their success, and the good issue of this practice — *And He delivered them.* PETER SMITH

Vs. 7. *And He led them forth by the right way.* There are many wrong ways, but only one right one, and into this none can lead us but God Himself.

*That they might go to a city of habitation.* They found no city to dwell in, but He found one readily enough. What we can do and what God can do are two very different things. C. H. S.

Not a city of inspection! Many (Eternal God, will it be any of this company?) will look in; and "there shall be weeping and wailing and gnashing of teeth, when they shall see Abraham, Isaac, and Jacob in the kingdom of God, and they themselves shut out." Not a city of visitation. Christians shall not only enter but abide. They shall go no more out — it is a "city of habitation." This conveys the idea of repose. WILLIAM JAY

Vs. 8. *Oh that men would praise the Lord.* Hebrew: that they would confess it to the Lord, both in secret, and in society. This is all the rent that God requireth; He is content that we have the comfort of His blessings, so He may have the honor of them. This was all the fee Christ looked for for His cures: go and tell what God hath done for thee. Words seem to be a poor and slight recompense; but Christ, saith Nazienzen, called Himself the Word. JOHN TRAPP

*And for His wonderful works to the children of men.* The children of men are so insignificant, so feeble, and so undeserving, that it is a great wonder that the Lord should do anything for them; but He is not content with doing little works, He puts forth His wisdom, power, and love to perform marvels on the behalf of those who seek Him. In the life of each one of the redeemed, there is a world of wonders, and therefore from each there should resound a world of praises. C. H. S.

Vs. 15. *Oh that men would praise the Lord for His goodness, and for His wonderful works to the children of men!* The sight of such goodness makes a right-minded man long to see the Lord duly honored, for His amazing mercy. When dungeon doors fly open and chains are snapped, who can refuse to adore the glorious goodness of the Lord? It makes the heart sick to think of such gracious mercies remaining unsung: we cannot but plead with men to remember their obligations and extol the Lord, their God. C. H. S.

Vs. 17. *Fools.* There is nothing more foolish than an act of wickedness; there is no wisdom equal to that of obeying God. ALBERT BARNES

Vss. 17 to 20. *He sent His Word, and healed them, and delivered them from their destruction.* Friends may speak, and ministers may speak, yea, angels may speak, and all in vain; the wounds are incurable for all their words; but if God please to speak, the dying soul reviveth. This word is the only balm that can cure the wounded conscience: "He sendeth His Word and healeth them."

Conscience is God's prisoner; He claps it in hold, He layeth it in fetters, that the iron enters the very soul; this He doth by His Word, and truly He only Who shuts up can let out; all the world cannot open the iron gate, knock off the shackles, and set the poor prisoner at liberty, till God speak the word. GEORGE SWINNOCK

Vs. 18. *Their soul abhorreth all manner of meat.* The best of creature-comforts are but vain comforts. What can dainty meat do a man good, when he is sick and ready to die? Then gold and silver, lands and houses, which are the dainty meat of a covetous man, are loathsome to him. *The flesh of Christ is meat indeed* (John 6:55). Feed upon Him by faith, in health and sickness; ye will never loathe Him. His flesh is the true meat of desires, such meat as will fill and fatten us, but never cloy us. JOSEPH CARYL

Vs. 20. *His Word, Who healed them,* was His essential Word, even the Second Person in the Godhead, our Lord Jesus Christ, the Word Who was made flesh and dwelt among us: of this divine Word it was foretold in the Old Testament that He should arise with the glory of the morning sun, bringing healing in His wings for all our maladies; and accordingly the New Testament relates that Jesus went about all Galilee, preaching the gospel of the kingdom and healing all manner of sickness and all manner of disease among the people. He healed the bodily disease miraculously to prove that He was the Almighty Physician of the soul.

And it is remarkable that He never rejected any person who applied to Him for an outward cure, to demonstrate to us that He would never cast out any person who should apply to Him for a spiritual cure. WILLIAM ROMAINE

Vs. 23. *They that go down to the sea in ships.* Navigation was so little practiced among the Israelites that mariners were invested with a high degree of mystery, and their craft was looked upon as one of singular daring and peril.

Tales of the sea thrilled all hearts with awe, and he who had been to Ophir or to Tarshish and had returned alive was looked upon as a man of renown, an ancient mariner to be listened to with reverent attention. Voyages were looked on as descending to an abyss, "going down to the sea in ships"; whereas now our bolder and more accustomed sailors talk of the "high seas." C. H. S.

Vs. 24. *And His wonders in the deep.* All believers have not the same deep experience; but for wise ends, that they may do business for Him, the Lord sends some of His saints to the sea of soul-trouble, and there they see, as others do not, the wonders of divine grace. Sailing over the deeps of inward depravity, the waste waters of poverty, the billows of persecution, and the rough waves of temptation, they need God above all others, and they find Him. C. H. S.

Vs. 28. *Then they cry unto the Lord in their trouble.* Though at their wit's end, they had wit enough to pray; their heart was melted, and it ran out in cries for help. C. H. S.

God bears oftener from an afflicted people than He either does or can from a people that are at ease, quiet, and out of danger. The Prodigal Son was very high and resolved never to return till brought low by pinching and nipping afflictions; then his father had some tidings of him. Hagar was proud in Abraham's house but humbled in the wilderness.

Jonah was asleep in the ship, but awake and at prayer in the whale's belly (Jon. 2:1). Manasses lived in Jerusalem like a libertine, but when bound in chains at Babel, his heart was turned to the Lord (II Chron. 33:11-12). Corporal diseases forced many under the gospel to come to Christ, whereas others that enjoyed bodily health would not acknowledge Him.

One would think that the Lord would abhor to hear those prayers that are made only out of the fear of danger and not out of the love, reality, and sincerity of the heart. If there had not been so many miseries of blindness, lameness, palsies, fevers, etc., in the days of Christ, there would not have been that flocking after Him. DANIEL PELL

Vs. 29. *He maketh the storm a calm.* The image is this. Mankind, before they are redeemed, are like a ship in a stormy sea, agitated with passions, tossed up and down with cares, and so blown about with various temptations that they are never at rest. This is their calmest state in the smiling day of smooth prosperity: but afflictions will come, the afflictions of sin and Satan, and the world will raise a violent storm, which all the wit and strength of man cannot escape. He will soon be swallowed up of the devouring waves: unless that same God Who created the sea speak to it, "Peace, be still."

We are all in the same situation the Apostles were when they were alone in the evening in the midst of the sea, and the wind and the waves were contrary; against which they toiled rowing in vain, until Christ came to them walking upon the sea and commanded the winds to cease and the waves to be still; upon which there was a great calm; for they knew His voice, Who had spoken them into being, and they obeyed. His word is Almighty to compose and still the raging war of the most furious elements.

And He is as Almighty in the spiritual world as He is in the natural. Into whatever soul He enters, He commands all the jarring passions to be still, and there is indeed a blessed calm. Oh, may the Almighty Savior speak thus unto you all, that you may sail on a smooth, unruffled sea, until you arrive safe at the desired haven of eternal rest! WILLIAM ROMAINE

Vs. 30. *Then are they glad because they be quiet.* No one can appreciate this verse unless he has been in a storm at sea. No music can be sweeter than the rattling of the chain as the shipmen let down the anchor; and no place seems more desirable than the little cove, or the wide bay, in which the ship rests in peace.

*So He bringeth them unto their desired haven.* The rougher the voyage, the more the mariners long for port, and heaven becomes more and more a "desired haven" as our trials multiply. C. H. S.

Vs. 32. *Let them exalt Him also in the congregation of the people.* Often when men hear of a narrow escape from shipwreck, they pass over the matter with a careless remark about good luck, but it should never be thus jested with. C. H. S.

Vs. 34. *For the wickedness of them that dwell therein.* If we turn good into evil, can we wonder if the Lord pays us in kind and returns our baseness into our own bosoms? Many a barren church owes its present sad estate to its inconsistent behavior, and many a barren Christian has come into this mournful condition by a careless, unsanctified walk before the Lord. Let not saints who are now useful run the risk of enduring the loss of their mercies, but let them be watchful that all things may go well with them. C. H. S.

Vs. 35. *Dry ground into watersprings.* If God afflict, His justice findeth the cause of it in man; but if He do good to any man, it is of His own good pleasure, without any cause in man: therefore, no reason is given here of this change, as was of the former, but simply, "He turneth dry ground into watersprings." DAVID DICKSON

Vs. 39. *Again, they are minished and brought low through oppression, affliction, and sorrow.* Trials are of various kinds; here we have three words for affliction, and there are numbers more: God has many rods, and we have many smarts, and all because we have many sins. C. H. S.

Vs. 41. *He setteth the poor on high from affliction.* How high? Above the reach of the curse, which shall never touch him; above the power of Satan, which shall never ruin him; above the reigning influence of sin, which "shall not have dominion over him"; above the possibility of being banished from His presence, for "Israel shall be saved in the Lord with an everlasting salvation."

This is the way God sets His people on high, instructing them in the mysteries of His Word and giving them to partake the joys that are contained therein. JOSEPH IRONS

# PSALM 108

A Song, or Psalm, of David. To be sung jubilantly as a national hymn or solemnly as a sacred Psalm. We cannot find it in our heart to dismiss this Psalm by merely referring the reader first to Psalm 42:7-11 and then to Psalm 40:5-12, though it will be at once seen that those two portions of Scripture are almost identical with the verses before us.

It is true that most of the commentators have done so, and we are not so presumptuous as to dispute their wisdom; but we hold for ourselves that the words would not have been repeated if there had not been an object for so doing, and that this object could not have been answered if every hearer of it had said, "Ah, we had that before, and therefore we need not meditate upon it again."

The Holy Spirit is not so short of expressions that He needs to repeat Himself, and the repetition cannot be meant merely to fill the book: there must be some intention in the arrangement of two former divine utterances in a new connection; whether we can discover that intent is another matter. It is at least ours to endeavor to do so, and we may expect divine assistance therein.

We have before us "The Warrior's Morning Song," with which he adores his God and strengthens his heart before entering upon the conflicts of the day. As an old Prussian officer was wont in prayer to invoke the aid of "his Majesty's August Ally," so does David appeal to his God and set up his banner in Jehovah's name.

Some expressions are so admirable that they ought to be used again; who would throw away a cup because he drank from it before? God should be served with the best words, and when we have them, they are surely good enough to be used twice. To use the same words continually and never utter a new song would show great slothfulness and would lead to dead formalism, but we need not regard novelty of language as at all essential to devotion, nor strain after it as an urgent necessity. C. H. S.

Vs. 1. *O God, my heart is fixed.* The wheels of a chariot revolve, but the axletree turns not; the sails of a mill move with the wind, but the mill itself moves not; the earth is carried round its orbit, but its center is fixed. So should a Christian be able, amidst changing scenes and changing fortunes, to say, *O God, my heart is fixed, my heart is fixed.* G. S. BOWES

As we know a garden which is watered with sudden showers is more uncertain in its fruit than when it is refreshed with a constant stream; so when our thoughts are sometimes on good things, and then run off; when they only take a glance of a holy object, and then flit away, there is not so much fruit brought into the soul.

In meditation, then, there must be a fixing of the heart upon the object, a steeping the thoughts, as holy David: *O God, my heart is fixed.* We must view some curious piece and carefully heed every shade, every line and color; as the Virgin Mary kept all these things, and pondered them in her heart.

Indeed, meditation is not only the busying the thoughts but the centering of them, not only the employing of them, but the staking them down upon some spiritual affair. When the soul, meditating upon something divine, saith as the disciples in the Transfiguration (Matt. 17:4), "It is good to be here."
JOHN WELLS

As a man first tuneth his instrument and then playeth on it: so should the holy servant of God first labor to bring his spirit, heart, and affections into a

solid and settled frame for worship, and then go to work. We ourselves must first be stirred up to make the right use of the means, before the means can be fit to stir us up: therefore saith he, "I myself will awake right early."
DAVID DICKSON

*Even with my glory.* With my intellect, my tongue, my poetic faculty, my musical skill, or whatever else causes me to be renowned and confers honor upon me. It is my glory to be able to speak and not to be a dumb animal, therefore my voice shall show forth Thy praise; it is my glory to know God and not to be a heathen, and therefore my instructed intellect shall adore Thee; it is my glory to be a saint, and no more a rebel, therefore the grace I have received shall bless Thee; it is my glory to be immortal and not a mere brute which perisheth, therefore my inmost life shall celebrate Thy majesty. C. H. S.

Vs. 2. With reference to this passage, the Talmud says, "A cithern used to hang above David's bed; and when midnight came, the north wind blew among the strings, so that they sounded of themselves; and forthwith he arose and busied himself with the Tora until the pillar of the dawn ascended." Rashi observes, "The dawn awakes the other kings; but I, said David, will awake the dawn." FRANZ DELITZSCH

Vs. 3. *I will praise Thee, O Lord, among the people.* Whoever may come to hear me, devout or profane, believer or heathen, civilized or barbarian, I shall not cease my music. C. H. S.

Vs. 4. *For Thy mercy is great.* His mercy is great — that mercy sung of lately (Ps. 107:1 and 43). It is "from above the heavens"; i.e., coming down to us as do drops of a fertilizing shower; even as the "peace on earth" of Luke 2:14 was first "peace in heaven" (Luke 19:38). ANDREW A. BONAR

Vs. 5. *Be Thou exalted, O God, above the heavens: and Thy glory above all the earth.* Let Thy praise be according to the greatness of Thy mercy. Ah, if we were to measure our devotion thus, with what ardor should we sing! The whole earth with its overhanging dome would seem too scant an orchestra and all the faculties of all mankind too little for the hallelujah. Angels would be called in to aid us, and surely they would come.

They will come in that day when the whole earth shall be filled with the praises of Jehovah. We long for the time when God shall be universally worshiped and His glory in the gospel shall be everywhere made known. This is a truly missionary prayer.

David had none of the exclusiveness of the modern Jew or the narrow-heartedness of some nominal Christians. For God's sake, that His glory might be everywhere revealed, he longed to see heaven and earth full of the divine praise. Amen, so let it be. C. H. S.

Vs. 9. *Moab is my washpot; over Edom will I cast out my shoe.* This somewhat difficult expression may be thus explained. Moab and Edom were to be reduced to a state of lowest cassalage to the people of God. The one was to be like a pot, or tub, fit only for washing the feet in, while the other was to be like the domestic slave standing by to receive the sandals thrown to him by the person about to perform his ablutions, that he might first put them by in a safe place and then come and wash his master's feet. *Rays from the East*

*Over Edom will I cast out my shoe.* It shall be as the floor upon which the bather throws his sandals; it shall lie beneath his foot, subject to his will and altogether his own. Edom was proud, but David throws his slipper at it; its capital was high, but he casts his sandal over it; it was strong, but he hurls his shoe at it as the gage of battle. He had not entered yet into its rock-built fortresses, but since the Lord was with him, he felt sure that he would do so. Under the leadership of the Almighty, he felt so secure of conquering even fierce Edom itself that he looks upon it as a mere slave, over which he could exult with impunity.

We ought never to fear those who are defending the wrong side, for since God is not with them their wisdom is folly, their strength is weakness, and their glory is their shame. We think too much of God's foes and talk of them with too much respect. Who is this pope of Rome? His Holiness? Call him not so, but call him His Blasphemy! His Profanity! His Impudence! What are he and his cardinals, and his legates, but the image and incarnation of Antichrist, to be in due time cast with the beast and the false prophet into the lake of fire? C. H. S.

Moab, who had enticed Israel to impurity, is made a vessel for its purifying. Edom, descendant of him who despised his birthright, is deprived of his independence; for "flinging a shoe" was a sign of the transference of a prior claim on land (Ruth 4:7). WILLIAM KAY

Vs. 10. The strong city built on the rock, even man's hardened heart, stronger and more stony than the tomb, He had conquered and overcome; and in Him and His might are His people to carry on His warfare, and to cast down all the strongholds of human pride, and human stubbornness, and human unrepentance. *Plain Commentary*

Vs. 11. *Wilt not Thou, O God, Who has cast us off?* This is grand faith which can trust the Lord even when He seems to have cast us off. Some can barely trust Him when He pampers them, and yet David relied upon Him when Israel seemed under a cloud and the Lord had hidden His face. Oh, for more of this real and living faith! The casting off will not last long when faith so gloriously keeps her hold. None but the elect of God have obtained precious faith.

Who will be the means of our obtaining a promised blessing? We need not be discouraged if we perceive no secondary agent, for we may then fall back upon the great Promiser Himself and believe that He Himself will perform His Word unto us. If no one else will lead us into Edom, the Lord Himself will do it, if He has promised it. Or if there must be visible instruments, He will use our hosts, feeble as they are.

We need not that any new agency should be created, God can strengthen our present hosts and enable them to do all that is needed; all that is wanted even for the conquest of a world is that the Lord go forth with such forces as we already have. He can bring us into the strong city even by such weak weapons as we wield today. C. H. S.

*Wilt not Thou, O God?* His hand shall lead him even to Petra, which seems unapproachable by human strength. That marvelous rock-city of the Edomites is surrounded by rocks some of which are three hundred feet high, and a single path twelve feet in width leads to it. The city itself is partly hewn out of the cloven rocks, and its ruins, which however, belong to a later period, fill travelers with amazement. AUGUSTUS F. THOLUCK

Vs. 12. *Give us help from trouble: for vain is the help of man.* We ought to pray with all the more confidence in God when our confidence in man is altogether gone. When the help of man is vain, we shall not find it vain to seek the help of God. C. H. S.

He who would have God's help in any business must quit confidence in man's help; and the seeing of the vanity of man's help must make the believer to trust the more unto, and expect the more confidently God's help, as here is done. DAVID DICKSON

# PSALM 109

"To the Chief Musician"—intended therefore to be sung, and sung in the Temple service! Yet is it by no means easy to imagine the whole nation singing such dreadful imprecations. We ourselves, at any rate, under the gospel dispensation, find it very difficult to infuse into the Psalm a gospel sense or a sense at all compatible with the Christian spirit; and therefore one would think the Jews must have found it hard to chant such strong language without feeling the spirit of revenge excited; and the arousal of that spirit could never have been the object of divine worship in any period of time — under law or under gospel. At the very outset, this title shows that the Psalm has a meaning with which it is fitting for men of God to have fellowship before the throne of the Most High: but what is that meaning? This is a question of no small difficulty, and only a very childlike spirit will ever be able to answer it.

"A Psalm of David"—not, therefore, the ravings of a vicious misanthrope, or the execrations of a hot, revengeful spirit. David would not smite the man who sought his blood; he frequently forgave those who treated him shamefully; and therefore these words cannot be read in a bitter, revengeful sense, for that would be foreign to the character of the son of Jesse.

Unless it can be proved that the religion of the old dispensation was altogether hard, morose, and Draconian, and that David was of a malicious, vindictive spirit, it cannot be conceived that this Psalm contains what one author has ventured to call "a pitiless hate, a refined and insatiable malignity."

To such a suggestion we cannot give place, no, not for an hour. But what else can we make of such strong language? Truly this is one of the hard places of Scripture, a passage which the soul trembles to read; yet as it is a Psalm unto God, and given by inspiration, it is not ours to sit in judgment upon it but to bow our ear to what God, the Lord, would speak to us therein.

This Psalm refers to Judas, for so Peter quoted it; but to ascribe its bitter denunciations to our Lord in the hour of His sufferings is more than we dare to do. These are not consistent with the silent Lamb of God, Who opened not His mouth when led to the slaughter. It may seem very pious to put such words into His mouth; we hope it is our piety which prevents our doing so.

Division. In the first five verses, David humbly pleads with God that he may be delivered from his remorseless and false-hearted enemies. From 6-20, filled with a prophetic furor, which carries him entirely beyond himself, he denounces judgment upon his foes, and then from 21-31 he returns to his communion with God in prayer and praise.

The central portion of the Psalm in which the difficulty lies must be regarded not as the personal wish of the Psalmist in cold blood, but as his prophetic denunciation of such persons as he describes, and emphatically of one special "son of perdition," whom he sees with prescient eye.

We would all pray for the conversion of our worst enemy, and David would have done the same; but viewing the adversaries of the Lord and doers of iniquity as such, and as incorrigible, we cannot wish them well; on the contrary, we desire their overthrow and destruction. The gentlest hearts burn with indignation when they hear of barbarities to women and children, of crafty plots for ruining the innocent, of cruel oppression of helpless orphans, and gratuitous ingratitude to the good and gentle. A curse upon the perpetrators of the atrocities in Turkey may not be less virtuous than a blessing upon the righteous. We wish well to all mankind, and for that very reason we sometimes blaze with indignation against the inhuman wretches by whom every law which protects our fellow creatures is trampled down and every dictate of humanity is set at nought. C. H. S.

Anger against sin and a desire that evildoers may be punished are not opposed to the spirit of the gospel or to that love of enemies which our Lord both enjoined and exemplified. If the emotion of its utterance were essentially sinful, how could Paul wish the enemy of Christ and the perverter of the gospel to be accursed; and especially, how could the spirit of the martyred saints in heaven call on God for vengeance and join to celebrate its final execution?

Yea, resentment against the wicked is so far from being necessarily sinful, that we find it manifested by the Holy and Just One Himself, when in the days of His flesh He looked around on His hearers "with anger, being grieved for the hardness of their hearts"; and when in "the great day of His wrath," He shall say to "all workers of iniquity," "Depart from Me, ye cursed" (Matt. 25:41). BENJAMIN DAVIES

The law of holiness requires us to pray for the fires of divine retribution: the law of love to seek meanwhile to rescue the brand from the burning. The last prayer of the martyr Stephen was answered not by any general averting of doom from a guilty nation but by the conversion of an individual persecutor to the service of God. JOSEPH F. THRUPP

I cannot forbear the following little incident that occurred the other morning at family worship. I happened to be reading one of the imprecatory Psalms, and as I paused to remark, my little boy, a lad of ten years, asked with some earnestness: "Father, do you think it right for a good man to pray for the destruction of his enemies like that?" and at the same time referred me to Christ as praying for His enemies.

I paused a moment to know how to shape the reply so as to fully meet and satisfy his inquiry, and then said, "My son, if an assassin should enter the house by night, and murder your mother, and then escape, and the sheriff and citizens were all out in pursuit, trying to catch him, would you not pray to God that they might succeed and arrest him, and that he might be brought to justice?"

"Oh, yes!" said he, "but I never saw it so before. I did not know that that was the meaning of these Psalms." "Yes," said I, "my son, the men against whom David prays were bloody men, men of falsehood and crime, enemies to the peace of society, seeking his own life, and unless they were arrested and their wicked devices defeated, any innocent persons must suffer." The explanation perfectly satisfied his mind. F. G. HIBBARD

Vs. 2. *For the mouth of the wicked and the mouth of the deceitful are opened against me.* The misery caused to a good man by slanderous reports no heart can imagine but that which is wounded by them: in all Satan's armory there are no worse weapons than deceitful tongues. To have a reputation over which we have watched with daily care suddenly bespattered with the foulest aspersions is painful beyond description; but when wicked and deceitful men get their mouths fully opened, we can hardly expect to escape any more than others. C. H. S.

"Speak," says Arnobius, "to thine own conscience, O man of God, thou who art following Christ; and when the mouth of the wicked and deceitful man is opened concerning thee, rejoice and be secure; because while the mouth of the wicked is opened for thy slander in the earth, the mouth of God is opened for thy praise in heaven." LORINUS

Vs. 3. *They compassed me about also words of hatred.* Turn which way he would, they hedged him in with falsehood, misrepresentation, accusation, and scorn. Whispers, sneers, insinuations, satires, and open charges filled his ear with a perpetual buzz, and all for no reason but sheer hate. Each word was as full of venom as an egg is full of meat: they could not speak without showing their teeth. C. H. S.

Vs. 4. *For my love they are my adversaries.* They hate me because I love them. One of our poets says of the Lord Jesus, "Found guilty of excess of love." Surely it was His only fault.

*But I give myself unto prayer.* He did nothing else but pray. He became prayer as they became malice. This was his answer to his enemies; he appealed from men and their injustice to the Judge of all the earth, Who must do right. True bravery alone can teach a man to leave his traducers unanswered and carry the case unto the Lord.

Men cannot help but reverence the courage that walketh amid calumnies unanswering. C. H. S.

None prove worse enemies than those that have received the greatest kindnesses, when once they turn unkind. As the sharpest vinegar is made of the purest wine, and pleasant meats turn to the bitterest humors in the stomach; so the highest love bestowed upon friends, being ill digested or corrupt, turns to the most unfriendly hatred. ABRAHAM WRIGHT

Persecuted saints are men of prayer, yea, they are as it were made up all of prayer. David prayed before; but, oh, when his enemies fell a persecuting of him, then he gave himself up wholly to prayer. THOMAS BROOKS

A Christian is all over prayer: he prays at rising, at lying down, and as he walks: like a prime favorite at court, who has the key to the privy stairs, and can wake his prince by night. AUGUSTUS M. TOPLADY

Vs. 5. *And they have rewarded me evil for good, and hatred for my love.* It is not for himself that he speaks so much as for all the slandered and the down-trodden, of whom he feels himself to be the representative and mouthpiece. He asks for justice, and as his soul is stung with cruel wrongs, he asks with solemn deliberation, making no stint in his demands. To pity malice would be malice to mankind; to screen the crafty seekers of human blood would be cruelty to the oppressed.

Vengeance is the prerogative of God, and as it would be a boundless calamity if evil were forever to go unpunished, so it is an unspeakable blessing that the Lord will recompense the wicked and cruel man, and there are times and seasons when a good man ought to pray for that blessing. C. H. S.

Vs. 6. *Set thou a wicked man over him.* What worse punishment could a man have? The proud man cannot endure the proud nor the oppressor brook the rule of another like himself. The righteous in their patience find the rule of the wicked a sore bondage; but those who are full of resentful passions and haughty aspirations are slaves indeed when men of their own class have the whip hand of them.

For Herod to be ruled by another Herod would be wretchedness enough, and yet what retribution could be more just? What unrighteous man can complain if he finds himself governed by one of like character? What can the wicked expect but that their rulers should be like themselves? Who does not admire the justice of God when he sees fierce Romans ruled by Tiberius and Nero, and Red Republicans governed by Marat and Robespierre? C. H. S.

*And let Satan stand at his right hand.* Should not like come to like? Should not the father of lies stand near his children? Who is a better right-hand friend for an adversary of the righteous than the great adversary himself? The curse is an awful one, but it is most natural that it should come to pass: those who serve Satan may expect to have his company, his assistance, his temptations, and at last his doom. C. H. S.

Men would have said, "My sin is denounced, not me." What a license would have been given to sin! The depraved nature would have said, "If I am not condemned, but only my sin, I can do as I like; I shall not be called to account for it. I love sin and can go on in it." This is what men would have said. There would have been no effort to get rid of it. Why should there be, if only sin is condemned and not the sinner? But man's sin is identified with himself, and this makes him tremble. God's wrath rests on him because of his sin. Condemnation is awaiting him because of his sin. This makes him anxious to get rid of it. FREDERICK WHITFIELD

Vs. 6-19. These terrible curses are repeated with many words and sentences, that we may know that David has not let these words fall rashly or from any precipitate impulse of mind; but, the Holy Spirit having dictated, He employs this form of execration that it may be a perpetual prophecy or prediction of the bitter pains and destruction of the enemies of the church of God. Nor does David imprecate these punishments so much on his own enemies and Judas the betrayer of Christ; but that similar punishments await all who fight against the kingdom of Christ. MOLLERUS

Vs. 7. *When he shall be judged, let him be condemned. And let his prayer become sin.* It is sin already; let it be so treated. To the injured, it must seem terrible that the black-hearted villain should nevertheless pretend to pray, and very naturally do they beg that he may not be heard, but that his pleadings may be regarded as an addition to his guilt. He has devoured the widow's house, and yet he prays. He has put Naboth to death by false accusation and taken possession of his vineyard, and then he presents prayers to the Almighty. C. H. S.

As the clamors of a condemned malefactor not only find no acceptance but are looked upon as an affront to the court, the prayers of the wicked now become sin, because soured with the leaven of hypocrisy and malice; and so they will in the great day, because then it will be too late to cry, "Lord, Lord, open unto us." MATTHEW HENRY

St. Jerome says that Judas' prayer was turned into sin, by reason of his want of hope when he prayed: and thus it was that in despair he hanged himself. ROBERT BELLARMINE

We should be watchful in prayer lest the most holy worship of God should become an abomination (Isa. 1:15; 66:3; James 4:3; Hos. 7:14; Amos 5:23). If the remedy be poisoned, how shall the diseased be cured? MARTIN GEIER

Vs. 8. *Let his days be few.* Who would desire a persecuting tyrant to live long? As well might we wish length of days to a mad dog. If he will do nothing but mischief, the shortening of his life will be the lengthening of the world's tranquility. "Bloody and deceitful men shall not live out half their days." C. H. S.

Vs. 9. *Let his children be fatherless, and his wife a widow.* The tyrant's sword makes many children fatherless, and who can lament when his barbarities come home to his own family, and they, too, weep and lament! Pity is due to all orphans and widows as such, but a father's atrocious actions may dry up the springs of pity.

Who mourns that Pharaoh's children lost their father or that Sennacherib's wife became a widow? As Agag's sword had made women childless, none wept when Samuel's weapon made his mother childless among women. If Herod had been slain when he had just murdered the innocents at Bethlehem, no man would have lamented it even though Herod's wife would have become a widow.

These awful maledictions are not for common men to use, but for judges, such as David was, to pronounce over the enemies of God and man. Those who regard a sort of effeminate benevolence to all creatures alike as the acme of virtue are very much in favor with this degenerate age; these look for the salvation of the damned, and even pray for the restoration of the devil. It is very possible that if they were less in sympathy with evil, and more in harmony with the thoughts of God, they would be of a far sterner and also of a far better mind.

To us it seems better to agree with God's curses than with the devil's blessings; and when at any time our heart kicks against the terrors of the Lord, we take it as a proof of our need of greater humbling, and confess our sin before our God. C. H. S.

Helpless and shiftless. A sore vexation to many on their deathbeds, and just enough upon graceless persecutors. But happy are they who, when they lie a-dying, can say as Luther did, "Lord God, I thank Thee for my present poverty, but future hopes. I have not an house, lands, possessions, or monies to leave behind me. Thou hast given me wife and children; behold, I return them back to Thee, and beseech Thee to nourish them, teach them, keep them safe, as hitherto Thou hast done, O Thou Father of the fatherless, and Judge of widows. JOHN TRAPP

Vs. 9-10. When we consider of whom this Psalm is used, there will be no difficulty about it. No language could be more awful than that of verses 6 to 19. It embraces almost every misery we can think of. But could any man be in a more wretched condition than Judas was? Could any words be too severe to express the depth of his misery — of him, who, for three whole years, had been the constant attendant of the Savior of mankind; who had witnessed His miracles, and had shared His miraculous powers; who had enjoyed all the warnings, all the reproofs of His love, and then had betrayed Him for thirty pieces of silver? Can we conceive a condition more miserable than that of Judas? F. H. DUNWELL

Vs. 11. *And let the strangers spoil his labor.* Wealth amassed by oppression has seldom lasted to the third generation: it was gathered by wrong and by wrong it is scattered, and who would decree that it should be otherwise? Certainly those who suffer beneath high-handed fraud will not wish to stay the retributions of the Almighty, nor would those who see the poor robbed and trampled on desire to alter the divine arrangements by which such evils are recompensed even in this life. C. H. S.

Vs. 13. *Let his posterity be cut off; and in the generation following let their name be blotted out.* Both from existence and from memory let them pass away till none shall know that such a vile brood ever existed. Who wishes to see the family of Domitian or Julian continued upon earth? Who would mourn if the race of Tom Paine or of Voltaire should come to an utter end? It would be undesirable that the sons of the utterly villainous and bloodthirsty should rise to honor, and if they did, they would only revive the memory of their father's sins. C. H. S.

Vs. 14. This verse is, perhaps, the most terrible of all, but yet as a matter of fact children do procure punishment upon their parents' sins and are often themselves the means of such punishment. We cannot, however, pretend to explain the righteousness of this malediction, though we fully believe in it. We leave it till our heavenly Father is pleased to give us further instruction. Yet, as a man's faults are often learned from his parents, it is not unjust that his consequent crimes should recoil upon him. C. H. S.

Vs. 15. The passage is dark; and we must leave it so. It must be right or it would not be here, but how, we cannot see. Why should we expect to understand all things? Perhaps it is more for our benefit to exercise humility, and reverently worship God over a hard text, than it would be to comprehend all mysteries. C. H. S.

Vs. 15. *Let them be before the Lord continually.* Lafayette, the friend and ally of Washington, was in his youth confined in a French dungeon. In the door of his cell, there was cut a small hole, just big enough for a man's eye; at that hole a sentinel was placed, whose duty it was to watch, moment by moment, till he was relieved by a change of guard. All Lafayette saw was the winking eye, but the eye was always there; look when he would, it met his gaze. In his dreams, he was conscious it was staring at him. "Oh," he says, "it was horrible; there was no escape"; when he lay down and when he rose up, when he ate and when he read, that eye searched him. NEW CYCLOPEDIA OF ILLUSTRATIVE ANECDOTE

Vss. 15, 19 and 29. Strict justice, and nothing more, breathes in every petition. Cannot you say, "Amen!" to all these petitions? Are you not glad when the wicked man falls into the ditch he has made for another's destruction and when his mischief returns upon his own head? But you say, "These petitions are unquestionably just, but why did not the Psalmist ask, not for justice, but for mercy?" The answer is, that in his public capacity, he was bound to think first about justice.

No government could stand upon the basis of forgiveness; justice must always go before mercy. Suppose that in the course of the next session, Parliament should decree that henceforth, instead of justice being shown to thieves by sending them to prison they should be treated charitably and compelled to restore one-half of what they stole — what would honest men say about the government? The thieves would doubtless be very complimentary, but what would honest men say? Why, they would say the government had altogether failed of its function and it would not live to be a week older.

And just so, the Psalmists were bound first of all to seek for the vindication and establishment of justice and truth. Like the magistrates of today, they considered first the well-being of the community. This they had in view in all the calamities they sought to bring upon wrong-doers. R. A. BERTRAM

Vs. 16. *That he might even slay the broken in heart.* He had malice in his heart toward one who was already sufficiently sorrowful, whom it was a superfluity of malignity to attack. Yet no grief excited sympathy in him; no poverty ever moved him to relent. No, he would kill the heart-broken and rob their orphans of their patrimony. To him groans were music, and tears were wine, and drops of blood precious rubies.

Would any man spare such a monster? Will it not be serving the ends of humanity if we wish him gone, gone to the throne of God to receive his reward? If he will turn and repent, well; but if not, such a upas tree ought to be felled and cast into the fire.

As men kill mad dogs if they can, and justly, too, so may we lawfully wish that cruel oppressors of the poor were removed from their place and office and, as an example to others, made to smart for their barbarities. C. H. S.

Vs. 17. *As he delighted not in blessing, so let it be far from him.*

*He was a wolf in clothing of the lamb,*
*That stole into the fold of God, and on*
*The blood of souls, which he did sell to death,*
*Grew fat; and yet, when any would have turned*
*Him out, he cried, "Touch not the priest of God."*
*And that he was anointed, fools believed;*
*But knew, that day, he was the devil's priest,*
*Anointed by the hands of Sin and Death,*
*And set peculiarly apart to ill —*
*While on him smoked the vials of perdition,*
*Poured measureless. Ah, me! What cursing then*
*Was heaped upon his head by ruined souls,*
*That charged him with their murder, as he stood*
*With eye, of all the unredeemed, most sad,*
*Waiting the coming of the Son of Man!*

ROBERT POLLOK

To invoke blessings on such a man would be to participate in his wickedness; therefore, let blessing be far from him, so long as he continues what he now is. C. H. S.

Vs. 20. Thousands of God's people are perplexed with this Psalm, and we fear we have contributed very little towards their enlightenment, and perhaps the notes we have gathered from others, since they display such a variety of view, may only increase the difficulty. What then? Is it not good for us sometimes to be made to feel that we are not yet able to understand all the word and mind of God? A thorough bewilderment, so long as it does not stagger our faith, may be useful to us by confounding our pride, arousing our faculties, and leading us to cry, "What I know not, teach Thou me." C. H. S.

Vs. 21. *But do Thou for me, O God the Lord, for Thy Name's sake.* How eagerly he turns from his enemies to his God! He leaves himself in the Lord's hands, dictating nothing, but quite content so long as his God will but undertake for him. His plea is not his own merit, but the Name. The saints have always felt this to be their most mighty plea. God Himself has performed His grandest deeds of grace for the honor of His Name, and His people know that this is the most potent argument with Him.

*Because Thy mercy is good, deliver Thou me.* Not because I am good, but because Thy mercy is good: see how the saints fetch their pleadings in prayer from the Lord Himself. God's mercy is the star to which the Lord's people turn their eye when they are tossed with tempest and not comforted, for the peculiar bounty and goodness of that mercy have a charm for weary hearts. When man has no mercy, we shall still find it in God. When man would devour, we may look to God to deliver. C. H. S.

He does not say, "For my name," that it may be vindicated from reproach and shame: but "for Thy Name"; as if he would say, "Whatever I may be, O Lord, and whatever may befall me, have respect to Thy Name, have regard to it only. I am not worthy, that I should seek Thy help, but Thy Name is worthy which Thou mayest vindicate from contempt." We learn here with what passion for the glory of the Divine Name they ought to be animated who are peculiarly consecrated to the Name of God. WOLFGANG MUSCULUS

Vs. 21-25. The thunder and lightning are now, as it were, followed by a shower of tears of deep, sorrowful complaint. FRANZ DELITZSCH

Vs. 24. *My knees are weak through fasting.* Either religious fasting, to which he resorted in the dire extremity of his grief, or else through loss of appetite occasioned by distress of mind. Who can eat when every morsel is soured by envy? This is the advantage of the slanderer, that he feels nothing himself, while his sensitive victim can scarcely eat a morsel of bread because of his sensitiveness. However, the good God knoweth all this and will succor His afflicted. C. H. S.

Vs. 27. *That they may know that this is Thy hand.* Dolts as they are, let the mercy shown to me be so conspicuous that they shall be forced to see the Lord's agency in it. Ungodly men will not see God's hand in anything if they can help it, and when they see good men delivered into their power, they become more confirmed than ever in their atheism. C. H. S.

Vs. 28. Men's curses are impotent; God's blessings are omnipotent. *Let them curse.* MATTHEW HENRY

Vs. 29. *Let mine adversaries be clothed with shame.* It is a prophecy as well as a wish and may be read both in the indicative and the imperative. Where sin is the underclothing, shame will soon be the outer vesture. He who would clothe good men with contempt shall himself be clothed with dishonor. C. H. S.

"Mysterious" was the one word written opposite this Psalm in the pocket Bible of a late devout and popular writer. It represents the utter perplexity with which it is very generally regarded. JOSEPH HAMMOND

In this Psalm, David is supposed to refer to Doeg the Edomite or to Ahithopel. It is the most imprecatory of the Psalms and may well be termed "the Iscariot Psalm." PATON J. GLOAG

## PSALM 110

"A Psalm of David." Of the correctness of this title there can be no doubt, since our Lord in Matthew 22 says, "How then doth David in spirit call Him Lord." Yet some critics are so fond of finding new authors for the Psalms that they dare to fly in the face of the Lord Jesus Himself. To escape from finding Jesus here, they read the title, "Psalm of (or concerning) David," as though it was not so much written by him as of him; but he that reads with understanding will see little enough of David here except as the writer. He is not the subject of it even in the smallest degree, but Christ is all. How much was revealed to the patriarch David!

How blind are some modern wise men, even amid the present blaze of light, as compared with this poet-prophet of the darker dispensation! May the Spirit, Who spoke by the man after God's own heart, give us eyes to see the hidden mysteries of this marvelous Psalm, in which every word has an infinity of meaning. C. H. S.

Vs. 1. *The Lord said unto my Lord.* How greatly should we prize the revelation of His private and solemn discourse with the Son, herein made public for the refreshing of His people! Lord, what is man that Thou shouldst thus impart Thy secrets unto him!

*Sit Thou at My right hand, until I make Thine enemies Thy footstool.* Away from the shame and suffering of His earthly life, Jehovah calls the Adonai, our Lord, to the repose and honors of His celestial seat. His work is done, and He may sit; it is well done, and He may sit at His right hand; it will have grand results, and He may therefore quietly wait to see the complete victory which is certain to follow. Therefore, let us never fear as to the future. While we see our Lord and Representative sitting in quiet expectancy, we, too, may sit in the attitude of peaceful assurance and with confidence await the grand outcome of all events. C. H. S.

This putting of Christ's enemies as a stool under His feet, also denotes unto us two things in reference to Christ: first, His rest, and secondly, His triumph. To stand, in the Scripture phrase, denoteth ministry, and to sit, rest; and there is no posture so easy as to sit with a stool under one's feet. Till Christ's enemies then be all under His feet, He is not fully in His rest.

Here they trample upon Christ in His Word, in His ways, in His members; they make the saints bow down for them to go over and make them as the pavements on the ground; they tread under foot the blood of the covenant, and the sanctuary of the Lord, and put Christ to shame; but there their own measure shall be returned into their bosoms; they shall be constrained to confess as Adonibezek, "As I have done, so God hath requited me." *Condensed from Reynolds*

Moreover, because our King has His enemies under His feet, thus shall He also bring all our enemies under our feet, for His victory is ours, God be thanked, Who has given us the victory through Christ our Lord. JOSHUA ARND

Vs. 2. *The rod of Thy strength.* Nor would one err who should call the cross the rod of power; for this rod converted sea and land and filled them with a vast power. Armed with this rod, the Apostles went forth throughout the world and accomplished all they did, beginning at Jerusalem. The cross, which to men seemed the very emblem of shame and weakness, was, in truth, the power of God. J. J. STEWART PEROWNE

*Out of Zion.* We need not say much about how the Omniscience of God is displayed in the wonderful fact, that in the very land of the covenant — in the very midst of that people who rejected and crucified the Savior the first church of Christ on earth was established.

What would cavilers and blasphemers have said had it been otherwise? had the Christian community been formed in any of the heathen countries? Would it not have been considered as a fiction of the idolatrous priests? Israel scattered among the nations, and the church of Christ having begun in Zion at Jerusalem, are the most wonderful and enduring monuments and incontestable witnesses of the truth of Christianity. BENJAMIN WEISS

Vs. 3. *Thy people shall be willing.* Willing to do what? They shall be willing while others are unwilling. The simple term "willing" is very expressive. It denotes the beautiful condition of creatures who suffer themselves to be wrought upon and moved according to the will of God. They suffer God to work in them to will and to do. They are willing to die unto all sin; they are willing to crucify the old man, or self, in order that the new man, or Christ, may be formed in them.

They are willing to be weaned from their own thoughts and purposes that the thoughts and purposes of God may be fulfilled in them. They are willing to be transferred from nature's steps of human descent to God's steps of human ascent.

Or, to abide by the simplicity of our text, God is will, and they are "willing." God will beautify them with salvation, because there is nothing in them to hinder His working. They will be wise; they will be good; they will be lovely; they will be like God; for they are "willing"; and there proceeds from God a mighty spirit, the whole tendency of which is to make His creatures like Himself. JOHN PULSFORD

Am I one of the "willing people"—not only my obedience and allegiance secured from a conviction of the truth, but my heart inclined, and my will renewed? To do the will of God, to bear the will of God, to coincide with the will of God — and that with calm if not cheerful consent of the heart, as seeing Him Who is invisible, and holding fast my living apprehensions of His Person and character?

All unwillingness, whether practical or lurking in the heart, springs from unbelief—from a failure to realize Him or His purposes. The cure, therefore, for all my misery and sin is more faith, more of Christ, and nearer to Him. This let me seek and ask with ever increasing earnestness. ALFRED EDERSHEIM

*In the day of Thy power.* It is an arresting power; it meets the sinner and stays his mad career, as in the case of Saul of Tarsus. It is a convincing power; it teaches the sinner that he is ruined in every respect, and leads him to cry out, "What shall I do to be saved?" It is a life-giving power; it quickens dead souls, and will eventually bring the dead bodies from their graves; "all that are in the graves shall hear the voice of the Son of God and shall live." This is the style of Jehovah: "I will, they shall"; none other dare speak thus. It is also liberating power. "If the Son shall make you free, ye shall be free indeed." THEOPHILUS JONES

*In the beauties of holiness.* God's soldiers can only maintain their war by priestly self-consecration. Conversely: God's priests can only preserve their purity by unintermitted conflict. WILLIAM KAY

Vs. 4. We have now reached the heart of the Psalm, which is also the very center and soul of our faith. Our Lord Jesus is a Priest-King by the ancient oath of Jehovah.

There has never arisen another like to Him since His days, for whenever the kings of Judah attempted to seize the sacerdotal office, they were driven back to their confusion: God would have no king-priest save His Son.

Melchizedek's office was exceptional: none preceded or succeeded him; he comes upon the page of history mysteriously; no pedigree is given, no date of birth, or mention of death; he blesses Abraham, receives tithe, and vanishes from the scene amid honors which show that he was greater than the founder of the chosen nation. He is seen but once, and that once suffices. Aaron and his seed came and went; their imperfect sacrifice continued for many generations, because it had no finality in it and could never make the comers thereunto perfect.

Our Lord Jesus, like Melchizedek, stands forth before us as a Priest of divine ordaining; not made a priest by fleshly birth, as the sons of Aaron; He mentions neither father, mother, nor descent, as His right to the sacred office; He stands upon His personal merits, by Himself alone; as no man came before Him in His work, so none can follow after; His order begins and ends in His own Person, and in Himself it is eternal, "having neither beginning of days nor end of years." The King-Priest has been here and left His blessing upon the believing seed, and now He sits in glory in His complete character, atoning for us by the merit of His blood and exercising all power on our behalf. C. H. S.

At His coronation, we hear nothing, but the Lord said, "Sit Thou on My right hand": the rule of the whole world is imposed upon our Savior by command; and even in this, did Christ show His obedience to His Father that He took upon Him the government of His church.

But at the consecration of Christ, we have a great deal more of ceremony and solemnity. God His Father taketh an oath and particularly expresseth the nature and condition of His office, a priesthood forever after the order of Melchizedek: and He confirmed it unto Him forever, saying, "Thou art a priest forever." DANIEL FEATLEY

What doctrine doth the Scripture afford more comfortable to a drooping soul than this, that God hath sworn His Son a priest forever, to sanctify our persons, and purge our sins, and tender all our petitions to His Father?

What sin is so heinous, for which such a priest cannot satisfy by the oblation of Himself? what cause so desperate, in which such an advocate if He will plead, may not prevail?

We may be sure God will not be hard to be intreated of us, Who Himself hath appointed us such an Intercessor, to Whom He can deny nothing; and to that end hath appointed Him to sit at His right hand to make intercession for us. ABRAHAM WRIGHT

It was wonderful humility in Him to wash His disciples' feet; but in His divine person to wash our unclean souls is as far above human conceit as it seemeth below divine majesty. There is nothing so impure as a foul conscience; no matter so filthy, no corruption so rotten and unsavory as is found in the sores of an exulcerated mind; yet the Son of God vouchsafed to wash and bathe them in His own blood. O bottomless depth of humility and mercy!

Other priests were appointed by men for the service of God, but He was appointed by God for the service and salvation of men: other priests spilt the blood of beasts to save men, but He shed His own blood to save us, more like beasts than men: other priests offered sacrifice for themselves, He offered Himself for a sacrifice.

Other priests were fed by the sacrifices which the people brought, but He feeds us with the sacrifice of His own body and blood: lastly, others were appointed priests but for a time: He was ordained a priest "forever." DANIEL FEATLEY

Vs. 5. This is our consolation which upholds us and makes our heart joyful and glad against the persecution and rage of the world, that we have such a Lord, Who not only delivers us from sin and eternal death but also protects us and delivers us in sufferings and temptations, so that we do not sink under them. And though men rage in a most savage manner against Christians, yet neither the gospel nor Christianity shall perish; but their heads shall be destroyed against it. MARTIN LUTHER

Vs. 6. *He shall wound the heads over many countries.* The monarch of the greatest nation shall not be able to escape the sword of the Lord; nor shall that dread spiritual prince who rules over the children of disobedience be able to escape without a deadly wound. Pope and priest must fall, with Mahomet and other deceivers who are now heads of the people. Jesus must reign, and they must perish. C. H. S.

This Psalm has been well designated the crown of all the Psalms, of which Luther saith that it is worthy to be overlaid with precious jewels. ALFRED EDERSHEIM

The ancients (by Cassiodorus' collection) term this Psalm "the sun of our faith, the treasure of holy writ": short in words, but in sense infinite. Theodoret notes how it is connected with the Psalm going before: "There (saith he) we have His cross and sufferings; here His conquest and trophies." For He cometh forth as the heir apparent of the Almighty, the brightness of His glory, and the express image of His person, graced with: 1. Title, "My Lord." 2. Place, "Sit Thou on My right hand." 3. Power, "Until I make Thine enemies Thy footstool." JOHN PRIDEAUX

# PSALM 111

There is no title to this Psalm, but it is an alphabetical hymn of praise, having for its subject the works of the Lord in creation, providence, and grace. The sweet singer dwells upon the one idea that God should be known by His people, and that this knowledge when turned into practical piety is man's true wisdom and the certain cause of lasting adoration. Many are ignorant of what their Creator has done, and hence they are foolish in heart and silent as to the praises of God: this evil can only be removed by a remembrance of God's works and a diligent study of them; to this, therefore, the Psalm is meant to arouse us. It may be called "The Psalm of God's Works," intended to excite us to the work of praise. C. H. S.

Vs. 1. *Praise ye the Lord.* All ye His saints, unite in adoring Jehovah, Who worketh so gloriously. Do it now; do it always; do it heartily; do it unanimously; do it eternally. Even if others refuse, take care that ye have always a song for your God. C. H. S.

It teaches us, very emphatically, that our preaching, if it is to carry weight and conviction, must be backed and exemplified by our conduct; that we need never expect to persuade others by arguments which are too weak to influence ourselves.

Another inference is similarly suggested — that our own decision should be given without reference to the result of our appeal. The Psalmist did not wait to ascertain whether those whom he addressed would attend to his exhortation, but before he could receive a reply, declared unhesitatingly the course he would himself adopt. W. T. MAUDSON

*With my whole heart.* We see the stress here laid upon a whole heart, and the want of which is the great canker of all vital godliness. Men are ever attempting to unite what the Word of God has declared to be incapable of union — the love of the world and of God — to give half their heart to the world and the other half to God.

Just see the energy, the entireness of every thought and feeling and effort which a man throws into a work in which he is deeply interested; the very phrase we use to describe such an one is, that "he gives his whole mind to it." Attempt to persuade him to divert his energies and divide his time with some other pursuit, and he would wonder at the folly and the ignorance that could suggest such a method of success.

"Just take a hint from Satan," says someone; "see how he plies his powers on the individual as if there were but that one and as if he had nothing else to do but to ruin that one soul." BARTON BOUCHIER

Vs. 2. *The works of the Lord are great.* In design, in size, in number, in excellence, all the works of the Lord are great. Even the little things of God are great. In some point of view or other, each one of the productions of His power or the deeds of His wisdom will appear to be great to the wise in heart. C. H. S.

*Sought out — have pleasure therein.* Philosophy seeks truth, Theology finds it, but Religion possesses it. Human things must be known to be loved, but divine things must be loved to be known. BLAISE PASCAL

Vs. 3. *And His righteousness endureth forever.* The bearing of guilt by our great Substitute proved that not even to effect the purposes of His grace would the Lord forget His righteousness; no future strain upon His justice can ever be equal to that which it has already sustained in the bruising of His dear Son; it must henceforth assuredly endure forever. C. H. S.

Vs. 4. The sweet spices of divine works must be beaten to powder by meditations and then laid up in the cabinet of our memories. Therefore, says the Psalmist here, "God hath made His wonderful works to be remembered"; He gives us the jewels of deliverance, not (because of the commonness of them) to wear them on our shoes, as the Romans did their pearls; much less to tread them under our feet; but rather to tie them as a chain about our necks. ABRAHAM WRIGHT

Vs. 6. *He hath showed His people the power of His works.* So He hath showed His works of power to His people in gospel times, as the miracles of Christ, His resurrection from the dead, redemption by Him, and the work of grace on the hearts of men in all ages. JOHN GILL

Vs. 7. The works of God expound His Word; in His Works is often made visible. That's an excellent expression, "The works of His hands are verity and judgment." The acts of God are verity, that is, God acts His own truths.

As the works of our hands ought to be the verity and judgments of God (every action of a Christian ought to be one of Christ's truths), so it is with God Himself; the works of His hands are His own verity and judgments. When we cannot find the meaning of God in His Word, we may find it in His works: His works are a comment, an infallible comment upon His Word. JOSEPH CARYL

Vs. 9. *Redemption.* Praise our Triune Jehovah for His redemption. Write it down where you may read it. Affix it where you may see it. Engrave it on your heart that you may understand it. It is a word big with importance. In it is enfolded your destinies and those of the church to all future ages.

There are heights in it you never can have scaled and depths you never can have fathomed. You have never taken the wings of the morning and gained the utmost parts of earth to measure the length and breadth of it.

Wear it as a seal on your arm, as a signet on your right hand, for Jesus is the Author of it. Oh, prize it as a precious stone, more precious than rubies. Let it express your best hopes while living and dwell on your trembling lips in the moment of dissolution; for it shall form the chorus of the song of the redeemed throughout eternity. ISAAC SAUNDERS

*Holy and reverend is His name.* Well may He say this. The whole name or character of God is worthy of profoundest awe, for it is perfect and complete, whole or holy. It ought not to be spoken without solemn thought and never heard without profound homage.

His name is to be trembled at; it is something terrible; even those who know Him best rejoice with trembling before Him. How good men can endure to be called "reverend," we know not. Being unable to discover any reason why our fellow-men should reverence us, we half suspect that in other men there is not very much which can entitle them to be called reverend, very reverend, right reverend, and so on. It may seem a trifling matter, but for that very reason we would urge that the foolish custom should be allowed to fall into disuse. C. H. S.

Vs. 10. *The fear of the Lord is the beginning of wisdom: a good understanding have all they that do His commandments.* Practical godliness is the test of wisdom. Men may know and be very orthodox; they may talk and be very eloquent; they may speculate and be very profound; but the best proof of their intelligence must be found in their actually doing the will of the Lord. C. H. S.

Let those that would have their name reverend, labor to be holy as God is holy. JOHN TRAPP

Can it then be said that the non-religious world is without wisdom? Has it no Aristotle, no Socrates, no Tacitus, no Goethe, no Gibbon? Let us understand what wisdom is. It is not any mere amount of knowledge that constitutes wisdom. Appropriate knowledge is essential to wisdom. A man who has not the knowledge appropriate to his position, who does not know himself in his relation to God and to his fellow-men, who is misinformed as to his duties, his dangers, his necessities, though he may have written innumerable works of a most exalted character, yet is he to be set down as a man without wisdom.

What is it to you that your servant is acquainted with mathematics, if he is ignorant of your will and of the way to do it? The genius of a Voltaire, a Spinoza, a Byron, only makes their folly the more striking.

As though a man floating rapidly onward to the falls of Niagara should occupy himself in drawing a very admirable picture of the scenery. Men who are exceedingly great in the world's estimation have made the most signal blunders with regard to the most important things; and it is only because these things are not considered important by the world that the reputation of these men remains.

If you have learned to estimate things in some measure as God estimates them, to desire what He offers, to relinquish what He forbids, and to recognize the duties that He has appointed you, you are in the path of wisdom, and the great men we have been speaking about are far behind you — far from the narrow gate which you have entered. He only is wise who can call Christ the wisdom of God. GEORGE BOWEN

# PSALM 112

The Hundred and Eleventh speaks of the great Father, and this describes His children renewed after His image. The Psalm cannot be viewed as the extolling of man, for it commences with "Praise ye the Lord," and it is intended to give to God all the honor of His grace which is manifested in the sons of God. C. H. S.

Vs. 1. *That delighteth greatly in His commandments.* The Hebrew word *chaphets* is rather emphatical, which is, as it were, to take His pleasure, and I have rendered it to delight Himself. For the prophet makes a distinction between a willing and prompt endeavor to keep the law and that which consists in mere servile and constrained obedience. JOHN CALVIN

Vs. 2. *The generation of the upright shall be blessed.* The godly may be persecuted, but they shall not be forsaken; the curses of men cannot deprive them of the blessing of God, for the words of Balaam are true, "He hath blessed, and I cannot reverse it." To fear God and to walk uprightly is a higher nobility than blood or birth can bestow. C. H. S.

Vs. 3. *Wealth and riches shall be in his house.* If we understand the passage spiritually, it is abundantly true. What wealth can equal that of the love of God? What riches can rival a contented heart? It matters nothing that the roof is thatched and the floor is of cold stone: the heart which is cheered with the favor of heaven is "rich to all the intents of bliss." C. H. S.

Vs. 4. *Light. Darkness.* While we are on earth, we are subject to a threefold "darkness": the darkness of error, the darkness of sorrow, and the darkness of death. To dispel these, God visiteth us, by His Word, with a threefold "light": the light of truth, the light of comfort, and the light of life. GEORGE HORNE

*He is gracious, and full of compassion, and righteous.* This is spoken of God in the fourth verse of the Hundred and Eleventh Psalm, and now the same words are used of His servant: thus we are taught that when God makes a man upright, He makes him like Himself. C. H. S.

Vs. 5. *A good man showeth favor.* Consider that power to do good is a dangerous ability unless we use it. Remember that it is God Who giveth wealth, and that He expecteth some answerable return of it. Live not in such an inhuman manner as if Nabal and Judas were come again into the world. THOMAS TENISON

*He will guide his affairs with discretion.* Alas, some professedly good men act as if they had taken leave of their senses; this is not religion, but stupidity. True religion is sanctified common sense. Attention to the things of heaven does not necessitate the neglect of the affairs of earth; on the contrary, he who has learned how to transact business with God ought to be best able to do business with men. The children of this world often are in their generation wiser than the children of light, but there is no reason why this proverb should continue to be true. C. H. S.

There is a story concerning divers ancient Fathers, that they came to St. Anthony, enquiring of him what virtue did by a direct line lead to perfection, that so a man might shun the snares of Satan. He bade everyone of them speak his opinion; one said watching and sobriety; another said, fasting and discipline; a third said, humble prayer; a fourth said, poverty and obedience; and another said, piety and works of mercy.

But when every one had spoken his mind, his answer was that all these were excellent graces indeed, but discretion was the chief of them all. And so beyond doubt it is; being the very *Auriga virutum,* the guide of all virtuous and religious actions, the moderator and orderer of all the affections; for whatsoever is done with it is virtue, and what without it is vice.

An ounce of discretion is said to be worth a pound of learning. As zeal without knowledge is blind, so knowledge without discretion is lame, like a sword in a madman's hand, able to do much, apt to do nothing. JOHN SPENCER

Vs. 6. *The righteous shall be in everlasting remembrance.* The stately and durable pyramids of Egypt have not transmitted to posterity even the name of those buried in them. And what has even embalming done but tossed them about and exposed them to all the world as spectacles to the curious, of meanness, or horror?

But the piety of Abraham, of Jacob, of David and Samuel, of Hezekiah, Josiah, and others, is celebrated to this very day. So when pyramids shall sink and seas cease to roll, when sun and moon and stars shall be no more, "the righteous shall be in everlasting remembrance. JOHN DUN

Vs. 7. *His heart is fixed.*—established fearlessly. So Moses, with the Red Sea before and the Egyptian foes behind (Exod. 14:13); Jehoshaphat before the Ammonite horde of invaders (II Chron. 20:12, 15, 17); Asa before Zerah, the Ethiopian's "thousand thousand, and three hundred chariots." (II Chron. 14:9-12).

Contrast with the persecuted David's fearless trust, Saul's panic-stricken feeling at the Philistine invasion, inasmuch as he repaired for help to a witch. How bold were the three youths in prospect of Nebuchadnezzar's fiery furnace! How fearless Stephen before the council! Basilius could say, in answer to the threats of Caesar Valens, "such bug-bears should be set before children." Athanasius said of Julian, his persecutor, "He is a mist that will soon disappear." A. R. FAUSSET

Vs. 9. *He hath dispersed, he hath given to the poor.* What he received, he distributed; and distributed to those who most needed it. He was God's reservoir, and forth from his abundance flowed streams of liberality to supply the needy. If this be one of the marks of a man who feareth the Lord, there are some who are strangely destitute of it. They are great at gathering but very slow at dispersing; they enjoy the blessedness of receiving but seldom taste the greater joy of giving. "It is more blessed to give than to receive — perhaps they think that the blessing of receiving is enough for them. C. H. S.

Vs. 10. The tenth and last verse sets forth very forcibly the contrast between the righteous and the ungodly, thus making the blessedness of the godly appear all the more remarkable. Usually we see Ebal and Gerizim, the blessing and the curse, set the one over against the other, to invest both with the greater solemnity.

*The wicked shall see it, and be grieved.* The ungodly shall first see the example of the saints to their own condemnation and shall at last behold the happiness of the godly and to the increase of their eternal misery. The child of wrath shall be obliged to witness the blessedness of the righteous, though the sight shall make him gnaw his own heart. He shall fret and fume, lament and wax angry, but he shall not be able to prevent it, for God's blessing is sure and effectual. C. H. S.

The sight of Christ in glory with His saints will, in an inexpressible manner, torment the crucifiers of the One and the persecutors of the other; as it will show them the hopes and wishes of their adversaries all granted to the full, and all their own "desires" and designs forever at an end; it will excite envy which must prey upon itself, produce a grief which can admit of no comfort, give birth to a worm which can never die, and blow up those fires which nothing can quench. George Horne

It is the property of the devil not to mistake the nature of virtue, and esteem it criminal, but to hate it for this reason, because it is good, and therefore most opposite to his designs. The wicked, as his proper emissaries, resemble him in this, and grieve to have the foulness of their vices made conspicuous by being placed near the light of virtuous example. William Berriman

*He shall gnash with his teeth.* Grind the righteous between his teeth, if that were possible. *And melt away.* The heat of his passion shall melt him like wax, and the sun of God's providence shall dissolve him like snow, and at the last the fire of divine vengeance shall consume him as the fat of rams. How horrible must that life be which like the snail melts as it proceeds, leaving a slimy trail behind. C. H. S.

This Psalm is a banquet of heavenly wisdom; and as Basil speaketh of another part of Scripture, likening it to an apothecary's shop, so may this Book of the Psalms fitly be compared; in which are so many sundry sorts of medicines that every man may have that which is convenient for his disease. T. S.

# PSALM 113

This Psalm is one of pure praise and contains but little which requires exposition; a warm heart full of admiring adoration of the Most High will best of all comprehend this sacred hymn. Its subject is the greatness and condescending goodness of the God of Israel, as exhibited in lifting up the needy from their low estate. It may fitly be sung by the church during a period of revival after it has long been minished and brought low. With this Psalm begins the Hallel, or Hallelujah of the Jews, which was sung at their solemn feasts: we will therefore call it, "The Commencement of the Hallel."

Vs. 1. *Praise ye the Lord.* (Or Hallelujah, praise to Jehovah). Praise is an essential offering at all the solemn feasts of the people of God. Prayer is the myrrh and praise is the frankincense, and both of these must be presented unto the Lord. How can we pray for mercy for the future if we do not bless God for His love in the past? If God's own servants do not praise Him, who will? Ye are a people near unto Him and should be heartiest in your loving gratitude. While they were slaves of Pharaoh, the Israelites uttered groans and sighs by reason of their hard bondage; but now that they had become servants of the Lord, they were to express themselves in songs of joy. The name of Jehovah is thrice used in this verse, and may by us who understand the doctrine of the Trinity in unity be regarded as a thinly-veiled allusion to that holy mystery. Let Father, Son, and Holy Spirit, all be praised as the One, Only, Living, and True God. C. H. S.

The "Hallel" is repeated. This repetition is not without signifiance. It is for the purpose of waking us up out of our torpor. We are all too dull and slow in considering and praising the blessings of God. There is, therefore, necessity for these stimuli. Then this repetition signifies assiduity and perseverance in sounding forth the praises of God. It is not sufficient once and again to praise God, but His praises ought to be always sung in the Church. MOLLERUS

*Ye servants of the Lord.* All men owe this duty to God as being the workmanship of His hands; Christians above other men, as being the sheep of His pasture; preachers of the Word above other Christians as being pastors of His sheep, and so consequently patterns in word, in conversation, in love, in spirit, in faith, in pureness. (I Tim. 4:12). JOHN BOYS

Vs. 2. *Blessed be the name of the Lord.* By mentioning the name, the Psalmist would teach us to bless each of the attributes of the Most High, which are as it were the letters of His name; not quarreling with His justice or His severity, nor servilely dreading His power, but accepting Him as we find Him revealed in the inspired Word and by His own acts, and loving Him and praising Him as such. We must not give the Lord a new name nor invent a new nature, for that would be the setting up of a false god. C. H. S.

Let then, O man, thy laboring soul strive to conceive (for 'tis impossible to express) what an immense debt of gratitude thou owest to Him, Who by His creating goodness called thee out of nothing to make thee a partaker of reason and even a sharer of immortality with Himself. In the whole compass of language what word is expressive enough to paint the black ingratitude of that man who is unaffected by, and entirely regardless of, the goodness of God his Creator and the mercies of Christ? JEREMIAH SEED

*From this time forth and forevermore.* The servants of the Lord are to sing His praises in this life to the world's end; and in the next life, world without end. JOHN BOYS

Vs. 3. *From the rising of the sun unto the going down of the same the Lord's name is to be praised.* It is a marvel of mercy that the sun should rise on the rebellious sons of men, and prepare for the undeserving fruitful seasons and days of pleasantness; let us for this prodigy of goodness praise the Lord of all. From hour to hour let us renew the strain, for each moment brings its mercy. C. H. S.

Vs. 5. *Who is like unto the Lord our God?* The challenge will never be answered. None can be compared with Him for an instant; Israel's God is without parallel; our own God in covenant stands alone, and none can be likened unto Him. Even those whom He has made like Himself in some respects are not like Him in Godhead, for His divine attributes are many of them incommunicable and inimitable. C. H. S.

It is the nature of love that the one whom we love we prefer to all others, and we ask, "Who is like my beloved?" The world has not His like. Thus love thinks ever of one, who in many things is inferior to many others; for in human affairs the judgment of love is blind.

But those who love the Lord their God, though they should glow with more ardent love for Him, and should ask, "Who is as the Lord our God?" in this matter would not be mistaken, but would think altogether most correctly. For there is no being, either in heaven or in earth, who can be in any way likened unto the Lord God. Even love itself cannot conceive, think, speak concerning God Whom we love as He really is. WOLFGANG MUSCULUS.

Vs. 6. *Who humbleth Himself to behold the things that are in heaven, and in the earth!* He dwells so far on high that even to observe heavenly things He must humble Himself. He must stoop to view the skies and bow to see what angels do. What, then, must be His condescension, seeing that He observes the humblest of His servants upon earth and makes them sing for joy like Mary when she said, "Thou hast regarded the low estate of Thine handmaiden." C. H. S.

To see the great King of heaven stooping from His height and condescending Himself to offer terms of reconciliation to His rebellious creatures! To see offended Majesty courting the offenders to accept of pardon! To see God persuading, entreating and beseeching men to return to Him with such earnestness and importunity, as if His very life were bound up in them, and His own happiness depended upon theirs.

To see the adorable Spirit of God, with infinite long-suffering and gentleness, submitting to the contempt and insults of such miserable, despicable wretches as sinful mortals are! Is not this amazing? — VALENTINE NALSON.

Vs. 7. *"He raiseth up the poor out of the dust."* When no hand but His can help He interposes, and the work is done. It is worth while to be cast down to be so divinely raised from the dust. C. H. S.

Perhaps one of the most interesting views of Christianity we can take is its wonderful adaptation to the characters and circumstances of the poor. What an opportunity does it furnish for the manifestation of the bright and mild graces of the Holy Spirit! What sources of comfort does it open to mollify the troubles of life! and how often, in choosing the poor, rich in faith, to make them heirs of the kingdom, does God exalt the poor out of the dust and the needy from the dunghill! RICHARD WATSON

*And lifteth the needy out of the dunghill.* Whereon they lay like worthless refuse, cast off and cast out, left as they thought to rot into destruction, and to be everlastingly forgotten. How great a stoop from the height of His throne to a dunghill! How wonderful that power which occupies itself in lifting up beggars, all befouled with the filthiness in which they lay! For He lifts them out of the dunghill, not disdaining to search them out from amidst the base things of the earth that He may be their means to bring to nought the great ones and pour contempt upon all human glorying.

What a dunghill was that upon which we lay by nature! What a mass of corruption is our original estate! What a heap of loathsomeness we have accumulated by our sinful lives! What reeking abominations surround us in the society of our fellowmen! We could never have risen out of all this by our own efforts; it was a sepulcher in which we saw corruption and were as dead men.

Almighty were the arms which lifted us, which are still lifting us, and will lift us into the perfection of heaven itself. Praise ye the Lord. C. H. S.

Gideon is fetched from threshing, Saul from seeking the asses, and David from keeping the sheep; the Apostles from fishing are sent to be "fishers of men." The treasure of the gospel is put into earthen vessels, and the weak and the foolish ones of the world pitched upon to be preachers of it, to confound the "wise and mighty" (I Cor. 1:27-28), that the excellency of the power may be of God, and all may see that promotion comes from Him. MATTHEW HENRY.

God looketh down from His majestic throne upon you. Amidst the infinite variety of His works, you are not overlooked. Amidst the nobler services of ten thousand times ten thousand saints and angels, not one of your fervent prayers or humble groans escapes His ear. JOB ORTON

Almighty God cannot look above Himself, as having no superiors; nor about Himself, as having no equals; He beholds such as are below Him; and therefore the lower a man is, the nearer unto God; He resists the proud and gives grace to the humble (I Pet. 5:5). JOHN BOYS

These verses are taken almost word for word from the prayer of Hannah (I Sam. 2:8). The transition to the "people" is all the more natural, a Hannah, considering herself at the conclusion as the type of the church, with which every individual among the Israelites felt himself much more closely entwined than can easily be the case among ourselves, draws out of the salvation imparted to herself joyful prospects for the future. E. W. HENGSTENBERG.

Vs. 9. *He maketh the barren woman to keep house, and to be a joyful mother of children.* The strong desire of the Easterners to have children caused the birth of offspring to be hailed as the choicest of favors, while barrenness was regarded as a curse; hence this verse is placed last as if to crown the whole and to serve as a climax to the story of God's mercy.

Nor is this all; each believer in the Lord Jesus must at times have mourned his lamentable barrenness; he has appeared to be a dry tree yielding no fruit to the Lord, and yet when visited by the Holy Ghost, he has found himself suddenly to be like Aaron's rod, which budded, and blossomed, and brought forth almonds.

Or ever we have been aware, our barren heart has kept house, and entertained the Savior, our graces have been multiplied as if many children had come to us at a single birth, and we have exceedingly rejoiced before the Lord. Then have we marveled greatly at the Lord Who dwelleth on high, that He has deigned to visit such poor, worthless things. C. H. S.

The Jews have handed down the tradition, that this Psalm, and those that follow on to the One Hundred Eighteenth, were all sung at the Passover; and they are denominated "The Great Hallel." This tradition shows, at all events, that the ancient Jews preceived in these six Psalms some link of close connection. A. A. BONAR.

# PSALM 114

This sublime "Song of the Exodus" is one and indivisible. True poetry has here reached its climax: no human mind has ever been able to equal, much less to excel, the grandeur of this Psalm. God is spoken of as leading forth His people from Egypt to Canaan and causing the whole earth to be moved at His coming. Things inanimate are represented as imitating the actions of living creatures when the Lord passes by. They are apostrophized and questioned with marvelous force of language, till one seems to look upon the actual scene. The God of Jacob is exalted as having command over river, sea, and mountain, and causing all nature to pay homage and tribute before His glorious majesty. C. H. S.

Vs. 1. *When Israel went out of Egypt.* The song begins with a burst, as if the poetic fury could not be restrained, but overleaped all bounds. The soul elevated and filled with a sense of divine glory cannot wait to fashion a preface, but springs at once into the middle of its theme. They were as one man in their willingness to leave Goshen; numerous as they were, not a single individual stayed behind. Unanimity is a pleasing token of the divine presence, and one of its sweetest fruits. The language of foreign taskmasters is never musical in an exile's ear. How sweet it is to a Christian who has been compelled to hear the filthy conversation of the wicked, when at last he is brought out from their midst to dwell among his own people! C. H. S.

Vs. 2. *Judah was His sanctuary, and Israel His dominion.* The pronoun "His" comes in where we should have looked for the name of God; but the poet is so full of thought concerning the Lord that he forgets to mention His name, like the spouse in the Song, who begins, "Let Him kiss me," or Magdalene when she cried, "Tell me where thou hast laid Him." The whole people were the shrine of Deity, and their camp was one great temple. What a change there must have been for the godly amongst them from the idolatries and blasphemies of the Egyptians to the holy worship and righteous rule of the great King in Jeshurun! They lived in a world of wonders, where God was seen in the wondrous bread they ate and in the water they drank, as well as in the solemn worship of His holy place.

When the Lord is manifestly present in a church, and His gracious rule obediently owned, what a golden age has come, and what honorable privileges His people enjoy! May it be so among us. C. H. S.

Reader, do not fail to remark, when Israel was brought out of Egypt, the Lord set up His tabernacle among them and manifested His presence to them. And what is it now when the Lord Jesus brings out His people from the Egypt of the world? Doth He not fulfil that sweet promise, "Lo, I am with you alway, even unto the end of the world"? Is it not the privilege of His people, to live to Him, to live with Him, and to live upon Him? Doth He not in every act declare, "I will say, it is My people; and they shall say, the Lord is my God"? (Matt. 28:20; Zech. 13:9). ROBERT HAWKER.

Vs. 3. *Jordan was driven back.* This was God's work; the poet does not sing of the suspension of natural laws, or of a singular phenomenon not readily to be explained; but to him the presence of God with His people is everything, and in his lofty song he tells how the river was driven back because the Lord was there.

In this case, poetry is nothing but the literal fact, and the fiction lies on the side of the atheistic critics who will suggest any explanation of the miracle rather than admit that the Lord made bare His holy arm in the eyes of all His people. The division of the sea and the drying up of the river are placed together though forty years intervened, because they were the opening and closing scenes of one great event.

We may thus unite by faith our new birth and our departure out of the world into the promised inheritance, for the God Who led us out of the Egypt of our bondage under sin will also conduct us through the Jordan of death out of our wilderness wanderings in the desert of this tried and changeful life. It is all one and the same deliverance, and the beginning ensures the end. C. H. S.

And now the glorious day was come when, by a stupendous miracle, Jehovah had determined to show how able He was to remove every obstacle in the way of His people and to subdue every enemy before their face. By His appointment, the host, amounting probably to two millions and a half of persons (about the same number as had crossed the Red Sea on foot), had removed to the banks of the river three days before, and now in marching array awaited the signal to cross the stream.

At any time the passage of the river by such a multitude, with their women and children, their flocks and herds, and all their baggage, would have presented formidable difficulties; but now the channel was filled with a deep and impetuous torrent, which overflowed its banks and spread widely on each side, probably extending nearly a mile in width; while in the very sight of the scene were the Canaanitish hosts, who might be expected to pour out from their gates, and exterminate the invading multitude before they could reach the shore. Yet these difficulties were nothing to Almighty Power and only served to heighten the effect of the stupendous miracle about to be wrought.

By the command of Jehovah, the priests, bearing the ark of the covenant, the sacred symbol of the Divine presence, marched more than half a mile in front of the people, who were forbidden to come any nearer to it. Thus it was manifest that Jehovah needed not protection from Israel, but was their guard and guide, since the unarmed priests feared not to separate themselves from the host and to venture with the ark into the river in the face of their enemies.

The passage of this deep and rapid river, remarks Dr. Hales, "at the most unfavorable season, was more manifestly miraculous, if possible, than that of the Red Sea; because here was no natural agency whatever employed; no mighty wind to sweep a passage, as in the former case; no reflux of the tide, on which minute philosophers might fasten to depreciate the miracle.

It seems, therefore, to have been providentially designed to silence cavils respecting the former; and it was done at noon-day, in the face of the sun, and in the presence, we may be sure, of the neighbouring inhabitants, and struck terror into the kings of the Canaanites and Amorites westward of the river." PHILIP HENRY GOSSE

The waters know their Maker: that Jordan which flowed with full streams when Christ went into it to be baptized, now gives way when the same God must pass through it in state: then there was use of His water, now of His sand. I hear no more news of any rod to strike the waters; the presence of the ark of the Lord God, Lord of all the world, is sign enough to these waves, which now, as if a sinew were broken, run back to their issues and dare not so much as wet the feet of the priests that bare it.

How subservient are all the creatures to the God that made them! How glorious a God do we serve; Whom all the powers of the heavens and elements are willingly subject unto, and gladly take that nature which He pleaseth to give them. ABRAHAM WRIGHT

Vs. 4-6. When Christ descends upon the soul in the work of conversion, what strength doth He put forth! The strongholds of sin are battered down; every high thing that exalts itself against the knowledge of Christ is brought into captivity to the obedience of His scepter. (II Cor. 10:4-5). Devils are cast out of the possession which they have kept for many years without the least disturbance. The like is done by Christ in the conversion of a sinner. Jordan is driven back, the whole course of the soul is altered, the mountains skip like rams. There are many mountains in the soul of a sinner, as pride, unbelief, self-conceitedness, atheism, profaneness, etc. These mountains are plucked up by the roots in a moment when Christ begins the work of conversion. RALPH ROBINSON

Vs. 5. *What ailed thee, O thou sea?* Wert thou terribly afraid? Did thy strength fail thee? Did thy very heart dry up? "What ailed thee, O thou sea, that thou fleddest?" Thou were neighbor to the power of Pharaoh, but thou didst never fear his hosts; stormy wind could never prevail against thee so as to divide thee in twain; but when the way of the Lord was in thy great waters, thou was seized with affright, and thou becamest a fugitive from before Him. C. H. S.

Vs. 6. *Ye mountains, that ye skipped like rams; and ye little hills, like lambs.* What ailed ye, that ye were thus moved? There is but one reply: the majesty of God made you to leap. A gracious mind will chide human nature for its strange insensibility, when the sea and the river, the mountains and the hills, are all sensitive to the presence of God.

Man is endowed with reason and intelligence, and yet he sees unmoved that which the material creation beholds with fear. God has come nearer to us than ever He did to Sinai, or to Jordan, for He has assumed our nature, and yet the mass of mankind are neither driven back from their sins nor moved in the paths of obedience. C. H. S.

Vs. 7 *Tremble, thou earth.* Hebrew, "Be in pain," as a travailing woman; for if the giving of the law had such dreadful effects, what should the breaking thereof have? JOHN TRAPP

Vs. 8. *The flint into a fountain of waters.* Our deliverance from under the yoke of sin is strikingly typified in the going up of Israel from Egypt, and so also was the victory of our Lord over the powers of death and hell. The Exodus should therefore be earnestly remembered by Christian hearts.

Did not Moses on the Mount of Transfiguration speak to our Lord of "the exodus" which He should shortly accomplish at Jerusalem; and is it not written of the hosts above that they sing the song of Moses, the servant of God, and of the Lamb? Do we not ourselves expect another coming of the Lord, when before His face heaven and earth shall flee away and there shall be no more sea?

We join then with the singers around the Passover table and make their Hallel ours, for we, too, have been led out of bondage and guided like a flock through a desert land, wherein the Lord supplies our wants with heavenly manna and water from the Rock of ages. Praise ye the Lord. C. H. S.

The remarkable rock in Sinai which tradition regards as the one which Moses smote is at least well chosen in regard to its situation, whatever opinion we may form of the truth of that tradition, which it seems to be the disposition of late travelers to regard with more respect than was formerly entertained.

It is an isolated mass of granite, nearly twenty feet square and high, with its base concealed in the earth — we are left to conjecture to what depth. In the face of the rock are a number of horizontal fissures, at unequal distances from each other; some near the top and others at a little distance from the surface of the ground.

An American traveler says: "The color and whole appearance of the rock are such that, if seen elsewhere, and disconnected from all traditions, no one would hesitate to believe that they had been produced by water flowing from these fissures. I think it would be extremely difficult to form these fissures or produce these appearances by art. It is not less difficult to believe that a natural fountain should flow at the height of a dozen feet out of the face of an isolated rock.

Believing, as I do, that the water was brought out of a rock belonging to this mountain, I can see nothing incredible in the opinion that this is the identical rock, and that these fissures, and the other appearances, should be regarded as evidences of the fact. JOHN KITTO

Shall *the hard rock be turned into a standing water, and the flintstone into a springing well?* and shall not our hard and flinty hearts, in consideration of our own miseries and God's unspeakable mercies in delivering us from evil (if not gush forth into fountains of tears) express so much as a little "standing water" in our eyes?

O Lord, touch Thou the mountains and they shall smoke; touch our lips with a coal from Thine altar, and our mouth shall show forth Thy praise. Smite, Lord, our flinty hearts as hard as the nether millstone, with the hammer of Thy Word, and mollify them also with the drops of Thy mercies and dew of Thy Spirit; make them humble, fleshy, flexible, circumcised, soft, obedient, new, clean, broken, and then "a broken and a contrite heart, O God, shalt Thou not despise."
JOHN BOYS

As I was describing the journey of Israel from Egypt and added the Divine Presence amongst them, I perceived a beauty in this Psalm which was entirely new to me, and which I was going to lose; and that is, that the poet utterly conceals the presence of God in the beginning of it, and rather lets a possessive pronoun go without a substantive, than he will so much as mention anything of divinity there. "Judah was His sanctuary, and Israel His dominion," or kingdom.

The reason now seems evident, and this conduct necessary; for, if God had appeared before, there could be no wonder why the mountains should leap and the sea retire; therefore, that this convulsion of nature may be brought in with due surprise, His name is not mentioned till afterwards; and then with a very agreeable turn of thought, God is introduced at once in all His majesty.
ISAAC WATTS

# PSALM 115

In the former Psalm, the past wonders which God had wrought were recounted to His honor, and in the present Psalm He is entreated to glorify Himself again, because the heathen were presuming upon the absence of miracles, were altogether denying the miracles of former ages, and insulting the people of God with the question, "Where is now their God?"

It grieved the heart of the godly that Jehovah should be thus dishonored, and treating their own condition of reproach as unworthy of notice, they beseech the Lord at least to vindicate His own name. The Psalmist is evidently indignant that the worshippers of foolish idols should be able to put such a taunting question to the people who worshipped the only living and true God; and having spent his indignation in sarcasm upon the images and their makers, he proceeds to exhort the house of Israel to trust in God and and bless His name.

Vs. 1. *Not unto us, O Lord, not unto us, but unto Thy name give glory.* The people undoubtedly wished for relief from the contemptuous insults of idolators, but their main desire was that Jehovah Himself should no longer be the object of heathen insults. The saddest part of all their trouble was that their God was no longer feared and dreaded by their adversaries. When Israel marched into Canaan, a terror was upon all the people round about, because of Jehovah, the mighty God; but this dread the nations had shaken off since there had been of late no remarkable display of miraculous power.

The repetition of the words, "Not unto us," would seem to indicate a very serious desire to renounce any glory which they might at any time have proudly appropriated to themselves, and it also sets forth the vehemence of their wish that God would at any cost to them magnify His own name. In these times, when the first victories of the gospel are only remembered as histories of a dim and distant past, skeptics are apt to boast that the gospel has lost its youthful strength and they even presume to cast a slur upon the name of God Himself. We may therefore rightly entreat the divine interposition that the apparent blot may be removed from His escutcheon, and that His own Word may shine forth gloriously as in the days of old. We may not desire the triumph of our opinions, for our own sakes, or for the honor of a sect, but we may confidently pray for the triumph of truth that God Himself may be honored. C. H. S.

The Psalmist, by this repetition, implies our natural tendency to self-idolatry, and to magnifying of ourselves, and the difficulty of cleansing our hearts from these self-reflections.

If it be angelical to refuse an undue glory stolen from God's throne (Rev. 22:8-9); it is diabolical to accept and cherish it. "To seek our own glory is not glory" (Prov. 25:27). It is vile, and the dishonor of a creature, who, by the law of his creation, is referred to another end. So much as we sacrifice to our own credit, to the dexterity of our hands, or the sagacity of our wit, we detract from God. STEPHEN CHARNOCK

Could we see heaven opened—could we hear its glad and glorious hallelujahs—could we see its innumerable company of angels, and its band of glorified saints, as they cast their crowns before the throne, we should hear as the universal chorus from every lip, "Not unto us, O Lord, not unto us, but unto Thy name give glory, for Thy mercy, and for Thy truth's sake. BARTON BOUCHIER

Vs. 2. *Wherefore should the heathen say, Where is now their God?* Or, more literally, "Where, pray, is their God?" Why should the nations be allowed with a sneer of contempt to question the existence, and mercy, and faithfulness of Jehovah? They are always ready to blaspheme. In our own case, by our own lukewarmness and the neglect of faithful gospel preaching, we have permitted the uprise and spread of modern doubt, and we are bound to confess it with deep sorrow of soul; yet we may not therefore lose heart, but may still plead with God to save His own truth and grace from the contempt of men of the world. Wherefore should the pretended wise men of the period be permitted to say that they doubt the personality of God? Wherefore should they say that answers to prayer are pious delusions, and that the resurrection and the deity of our Lord Jesus are moot points?

Wherefore should they be permitted to speak disparagingly of atonement by blood and by price, and reject utterly the doctrine of the wrath of God against sin, even that wrath which burneth forever and ever? They speak exceeding proudly, and only God can stop their arrogant blusterings: let us by extraordinary intercession prevail upon Him to interpose, by giving to His gospel such a triumphant vindication as shall utterly silence the perverse opposition of ungodly men. C. H. S.

Vs. 3. *But our God is in the heavens.* Where He should be; above the reach of mortal sneers, overhearing all the vain janglings of men, but looking down with silent scorn upon the makers of the babel.

Once they bade His Son come down from the cross and they would believe in Him; now they would have God overstep the ordinary bounds of His providence and come down from heaven to convince them: but other matters occupy His august mind besides the convincement of those who wilfully shut their eyes to the superabundant evidences of His divine power and Godhead, which are all around them. C. H. S.

Vs. 3. *He hath done whatsoever He hath pleased.* We may well endure the jeering question, "Where is now their God?" while we are perfectly sure that His providence is undisturbed, His throne unshaken, and His purposes unchanged. What He hath done He will yet do, His counsel shall stand, and He will do all His pleasure, and at the end of the great drama of human history, the omnipotence of God and His immutability and faithfulness will be more than vindicated to the eternal confusion of His adversaries. C. H. S.

Vs. 4. *Their idols are silver.* They are metal, stone, and wood. They are generally made in the form of man, but can neither see, hear, smell, feel, walk, nor speak. How brutish to trust in such! And next to them, in stupidity and inanity, must they be who form them, with the expectation of deriving any good from them.

So obviously vain was the whole system of idolatry that the more serious heathens ridiculed it, and it was a butt for the jests of their freethinkers and buffoons. How keen are these words of Juvenal! "Dost thou hear, O Jupiter, these things? nor move thy lips when thou oughtest to speak out, whether thou art of marble or of bronze? Or, why do we put the sacred incense on thy altar from the opened paper, and the extracted liver of a calf, and the white caul of a hog? As far as I can discern, there is no difference between thy statue and that of Bathyllus." (Sat. 13:113).

This irony will appear the keener when it is known that Bathyllus was a fiddler and player, whose image, by the order of Polycrates, was erected in the temple of Juno at Samos. ADAM CLARKE

Idolators plead in behalf of their idols, that they are only intended to represent their gods, and to maintain a more abiding sense of their presence. The Spirit, however, does not allow this plea, and treats their images as the very gods they worship. The gods they profess to represent do not really exist, and therefore their worship is altogether vain and foolish.

Must not the same be said of the pretended worship of many in the present day, who would encumber their worship with representative rites and ceremonies, or expressive symbols, or frame to themselves in their imagination a god other than the God of revelation? W. WILSON

Vs. 4-7. The Emperor Theodosius, having commanded the demolition of the heathen temple, Theophilus, the bishop, attended by the soldiers, hastened to ascend the steps and enter the fane. The sight of the image, for a moment, made even the Christian destructives pause. The bishop ordered a soldier to strike without delay. With a hatchet, he smote the statue on the knee.

All waited in some emotion, but there was neither sound nor sign of divine anger. The soldiers next climbed to the head and struck it off. It rolled on the ground. A large family of rats, disturbed in their tranquil abode within the sacred image, poured out from the trembling statue and raced over the temple floor. The people now began to laugh and to destroy with increased zeal. They dragged the fragments of the statue through the streets.

Even the pagans were disgusted with gods who did not defend themselves. The huge edifice was slowly destroyed, and a Christian church was built in its place. There was still some fear among the people that the Nile would show displeasure by refusing its usual inundation. But as the river rose with more than usual fullness and bounty, every anxiety was dispelled. ANDREW REED

Vs. 4-8. Theodoret tells us of S. Publia, the aged abbess of a company of nuns at Antioch, who used to chant, as Julian went by in idolatrous procession, the Psalm, "Their idols are silver and gold, the work of men's hands . . . They that make them are like unto them; so is every one that truseth in them"; and he narrates how the angry Emperor caused his soldiers to buffet her till she bled, unable as he was to endure the sting of the old Hebrew song. NEALE AND LITTLEDALE

Vs. 5. *Eyes have they, but they see not.* They cannot tell who their worshippers may be or what they offer. Certain idols have had jewels in their eyes more precious than a king's ransom, but they were as blind as the rest of the fraternity. A god who has eyes and cannot see is a blind deity; and blindness is a calamity, and not an attribute of godhead. He must be very blind who worships a blind god: we pity a blind man; it is strange to worship a blind image. C. H. S.

Vs. 6. *Noses have they, but they smell not.* The Psalmist seems to heap together these sentences with something of the grim sardonic spirit of Elijah, when he said, "Cry aloud: for he is a god; either he is talking, or he is pursuing, or he is on a journey, or peradventure he sleepeth, and must be awaked." C. H. S.

*They have ears, but they hear not.* Socrates, in contempt of heathen gods, swore by an oak, a goat, a dog; as holding these better gods than those. JOHN TRAPP

Vs. 7. *Feet have they, but they walk not.* They must be lifted into their places or they would never reach their shrines; they must be fastened in their shrines or they would fall; they must be carried or they could never move; they cannot come to the rescue of their friends nor escape the iconoclasm of their foes. The meanest insect has more power of locomotion than the greatest heathen god. C. H. S.

*Neither speak they through their throats.* They cannot even reach so far as the guttural noise of the lowest order of beasts; neither a grunt, nor a growl, nor a groan, nor so much as a mutter, can come from them. C. H. S.

Vs. 8. *They that make them are like unto them.* They that make them images, show their ingenuity, and doubtless are sensible men; but they that make them gods show their stupidity, and are as senseless, blockish things as the idols themselves. MATTHEW HENRY

Every one is just what his God is; whoever serves the Omnipotent is omnipotent with Him: whoever exalts feebleness, in stupid delusion, to be his god, is feeble along with that god. This is an important preservative against fear for those who are sure that they worship the true God. E. W. HENGSTENBERG

*So is every one that trusteth in them.* Those who have sunk so low as to be capable of confiding in idols have reached the extreme of folly and are worthy of as much contempt as their detestable deities. Luther's hard speeches were well deserved by the Papists; they must be mere dolts to worship the rotten relics which are the objects of their veneration.

The god of modern thought exceedingly resembles the deities described in this Psalm. Pantheism is wondrously akin to Polytheism, and yet differs very little from Atheism. The god manufactured by our great thinkers is a mere abstraction: he has no eternal purposes; he does not interpose on the behalf of his people; he cares but very little as to how much man sins, for he has given to the initiated "a larger hope" by which the most incorrigible are to be restored.

He is what the last set of critics chooses to make him; he has said what they choose to say; and he will do what they please to prescribe. Let this creed and its devotees alone, and they will work out their own refutation, for as now their god is fashioned like themselves, they will by degrees fashion themselves like their god. C. H. S.

Vs. 9. *O Israel, trust thou in the Lord.* Whatever our trouble may be, and however fierce the blasphemous language of our enemies, let us not fear nor falter, but confidentally rest in Him Who is able to vindicate His own honor, and protect His own servants. C. H. S.

Vs. 12. *He will bless us; He will bless the house of Israel; He will bless the house of Aaron.* It is His nature to bless; it is His prerogative to bless; it is His glory to bless; it is His delight to bless; He has promised to bless, and therefore be sure of this, that He will bless and bless, and bless without ceasing. C. H. S.

Vs. 17. *The dead praise not the Lord.* The preacher cannot magnify the Lord from his coffin nor the Christian worker further manifest the power of divine grace by daily activity while he lies in the grave.

*Neither any that go down into silence.* The tomb sends forth no voice; from mouldering bones and flesh-consuming worms there arises no sound of gospel ministry nor of gracious song. C. H. S.

Vs. 18. *But we will bless the Lord from this time forth and forevermore.* We who are still living will take care that the praises of God shall not fail among the sons of man. Our afflictions and depressions of spirit shall not cause us to suspend our praises, neither shall old age and increasing infirmities damp the celestial fires, nay, nor shall even death itself cause us to cease from the delightful occupation. The spiritually dead cannot praise God, but the life within us constrains us to do so. C. H. S.

# PSALM 116

Personal love fostered by a personal experience of redemption is the theme of this Psalm, and in it we see the redeemed answered when they pray, preserved in time of trouble, resting in their God, walking at large, sensible of their obligations, conscious that they are not their own but bought with a price, and joining with all the ransomed company to sing hallelujahs unto God. C. H. S.

Vs. 1. *I love the Lord.* A blessed declaration: every believer ought to be able to declare without the slightest hesitation, "I love the Lord." It was required under the law, but was never produced in the heart of man except by the grace of God and upon gospel principles. It is a great thing to say, "I love the Lord"; for the sweetest of all graces and the surest of all evidences of salvation is love. It is great goodness on the part of God that He condescends to be loved by such poor creatures as we are, and it is a sure proof that He has been at work in our heart. C. H. S.

*He hath heard my voice.* But is this such a benefit to us that God hears us? Is His hearing our voice such an argument of His love? Alas! He may hear us, and we be never the better: He may hear our voice, and yet His love to us may be but little, for who will not give a man the hearing though he loved him not at all?

With men, perhaps it may be so, but not with God; for His hearing is not only voluntary but reserved: His ears are not open to every one's cry; indeed, to hear us is in God so great a favor that he may well be counted His favorite whom He vouchsafes to hear: and the rather, for that His hearing is always operative, and with a purpose of helping; so that if He hear my voice, I may be sure He means to grant my supplication; or rather perhaps in David's manner of expressing, and in God's manner of proceeding, to hear my voice is no less in effect than to grant my supplication. SIR RICHARD BAKER

Vs. 2. *Therefore will I call upon Him.* It is love that doth open our mouths, that we may praise God with joyful lips. THOMAS MANTON

When prayer is heard in our feebleness, and answered in the strength and and greatness of God, we are strengthened in the habit of prayer and confirmed in the resolve to make ceaseless intercession. We should not thank a beggar who informed us that because we had granted his request he would never cease to beg of us, and yet doubtless it is acceptable to God that His petitioners should form the resolution to continue in prayer: this shows the greatness of His goodness and the abundance of His patience. C. H. S.

If the hypocrite speed in prayer, and get what he asks, then also he throws up prayer, and will ask no more. If from a sickbed he be raised to health, he leaves prayer behind him, as it were, sick-abed; he grows weak in calling upon God, when at his call God hath given him strength. And thus it is in other instances. When he hath got what he hath a mind to in prayer, he hath no more mind to pray.

Whereas a godly man prays after he hath sped, as he did before, and though he fall not into those troubles again, and so is not occasioned to urge those petitions again which he did in trouble, yet he cannot live without prayer, because he cannot live out of communion with God. JOSEPH CARYL

*As long as I live.* Not on some few days, but every day of my life; for to pray on certain days, and not on all, is the mark of one who loathes and not of one who loves. AMBROSE

Vs. 3. *Gat hold upon me.* When God sends out troubles and afflictions as officers to attack any man, they will find him, and finding him, they will take hold of him. The days of affliction will take hold; there's no striving, no struggling with them, no getting out of their hands. These divine pursuivants will neither be persuaded nor bribed to let you go, till God speak the Word, till God say, "Deliver him; release him." JOSEPH CARYL

Vs. 4. *O Lord, I beseech Thee, deliver my soul.* This form of petition is short, comprehensive, to the point, humble, and earnest. It were well if all our prayers were moulded upon this model; perhaps they would be if we were in similar circumstances to those of the Psalmist, for real trouble produces real prayer. Here we have no multiplicity of words, and no fine arrangement of sentences; everything is simple and natural; there is not a redundant syllable, and yet there is not one lacking. C. H. S.

A short prayer for a so great a suit, and yet as short as it was, it prevailed. If we wondered before at the power of God, we may wonder now at the power of prayer, that can prevail with God, for obtaining of that which in nature is impossible, and to reason is incredible. SIR RICHARD BAKER

Vs. 5. *Gracious is the Lord.* He is gracious in hearing; He is "righteous" in judging; He is "merciful" in pardoning, and how, then, can I doubt of His will to help me? He is righteous to reward according to deserts; He is gracious to reward above deserts; yea, He is merciful to reward without deserts; and how, then, can I doubt of His will to help me? He is gracious, and this shows His bounty; He is righteous, and this shows His justice; yea, He is merciful, and this shows His love; and how, then, can I doubt of His will to help me? SIR RICHARD BAKER

*Yea, our God is merciul.* See how the attribute of righteousness seems to stand between two guards of love: gracious, righteous, merciful. The sword of justice is scabbarded in a jewelled sheath of grace. C. H. S.

Vs. 6. *The Lord preserveth the simple.* Behold here how of all others, they who seem to have least cause to trust on God have most cause to trust on Him. Simple persons, silly wretches, despicable fools in the world's account, who have not subtle brains, or crafty wits to search after indirect means, have, notwithstanding, enough to support them, in the grand fact that they are such as the Lord preserveth. Now, who knoweth not that "It is better to trust in the Lord, than to put confidence in man; it is better trust in the Lord, than to put confidence in princes"? (Ps. 118:8-9). WILLIAM GOUGE

We suppose there are many truths to be apprehended, many principles to be realized before we can be saved. No; "the Lord preserveth the simple." We may be able to reconcile scarcely any of the doctrines of Christianity with each other; we may find ourselves in the greatest perplexity when we examine the evidences on which they rest; we may be exposed to great difficulty when we seek to apply them to practical usefulness; but still we may adopt the language before us: "The Lord preserveth the simple: I was brought low, and He helped me. Return unto thy rest, O my soul." R. S. M.

Simple or foolish, He calls them, because they are generally so esteemed amongst the wise of the world; not that they are so silly as they are esteemed; for if the Lord can judge of wisdom or folly, the only fool is the atheist and profane person; the only wise man in the world is the plain, downright Christian, who keeps himself precisely in all states to that plain, honest course the Lord hath prescribed him. W. SLATER

*I was brought low, and He helped me.* Simple though I was, the Lord did not pass me by. Though reduced in circumstances, slandered in character, depressed in spirit, and sick in body, the Lord helped me. C. H. S.

*I was brought low.* By affliction and trial. The Hebrew literally means to hang down, to be pendulous, to swing, to wave — as a bucket in a well, or as the slender branches of the palm, the willow, etc. Then it means to be slack, feeble, weak, as in sickness, etc. It probably refers to the prostration of strength by disease. "And He helped me." He gave me strength; He restored me.
ALBERT BARNES

Helped me both to bear the worst and to hope the best; helped me to pray, else desire had failed; helped me to wait, else faith had failed. MATTHEW HENRY

Vs. 7. *Return unto thy rest, O my soul.* Even as a bird flies to its nest, so does his soul fly to his God. Whenever a child of God even for a moment loses his peace of mind, he should be concerned to find it again, not by seeking it in the world or in his own experience, but in the Lord alone. When the believer prays, and the Lord inclines His ear, the road to the old rest is before him, let him not be slow to follow it. C. H. S.

Return to that rest which Christ gives to the weary and heavy laden (Matt. 11:28). Return to thy Noah, His name signifies rest, as the dove when she found no rest returned to the ark. I know no word more proper to close our eyes with at night when we go to sleep, nor to close them with at death, that long sleep, than this, "Return unto thy rest, O my soul." MATTHEW HENRY

This is the very word which the angel used to Hagar when she fled from her mistress — "Return" (Gen. 16:9). As Hagar through her mistress' rough dealing with her fled from her, so the soul of this prophet by reason of affliction fell from its former quiet confidence in God. As the angel therefore biddeth Hagar "return to her mistress," so the understanding of this prophet biddeth his soul return to its rest. WILLIAM GOUGE

Vs. 9. *I will walk before the Lord in the land of the living.* O my soul, to walk in the land of the living is to walk in the paths of righteousness: for there is no such death to the soul as sin; no such cause of tears to the eyes as guiltiness of conscience; no such falling of the feet as to fall from God: and therefore, to say the truth, the soul can never return to its rest if we walk not withal in the paths of righteousness; and we cannot well say whether this rest be a cause of the walk, or the walking be a cause of the resting: but this we may say, they are certainly companions the one to the other, which is in effect but this — that justification can never be without sanctification. Peace of conscience and godliness of life can never be one without the other.

Or is it perhaps that David means that land of the living where Enoch and Elias are living with the living God? But if he mean so, how can he speak so confidently, and say, "I will walk in the land of the living"? as though he could come to walk there by his own strength, or at his own pleasure? He therefore gives his reason: "I believed, and therefore I spake," for the voice of faith is strong, and speaks with confidence; and because in faith he believes that he should come to walk in the land of the living, therefore with confidence he speaks it, "I will walk in the land of the living." SIR RICHARD BAKER

To walk in the land of the living is the wicked man's desire, yea, were it possible, he would walk here forever; but for what end? Only to enjoy his lusts, have his fill of pleasure, and increase his wealth: whereas the godly man's aim in desiring to live is that he may "walk before God," advance His glory, and perform His service. Upon this account it is that one hath fitly taken notice how David doth not say, I shall now satiate myself with delights in my royal city, but, "I shall walk before the Lord in the land of the living."
NATHANIEL HARDY

Vs. 10. *I believed, therefore have I spoken.* Concerning the things of God, no man should speak unless he believes; the speech of the waverer is mischievous, but the tongue of the believer is profitable; the most powerful speech which has ever been uttered by the lip of man has emanated from a heart fully persuaded of the truth of God. Not only the Psalmist, but such men as Luther, and Calvin, and other great witnesses for the faith could each one most heartily say, "I believed; therefore have I spoken. C. H. S.

It is not sufficient to believe unless thou also openly confessest before unbelievers, tyrants, and all others. Next to believing, follows confession; and therefore, those who do not make a confession ought to fear; as, on the cantrary, those should hope who speak out what they have believed. PAULUS PALANTERIUS

The heart and tongue should go together. The tongue should always be the heart's interpreter, and the heart should always be the tongue's suggester; what is spoken with the tongue should be first stamped upon the heart and wrought off from it. JOSEPH CARYL

The Apostle takes up that very protestation from David (II Cor. 4:13): "According as it is written, I believed, and therefore have I spoken; we also believe, and therefore speak"; that is, we move others to believe nothing but what we believe, and are fully assured of ourselves. J. CARYL

Christ's word and the cross are companions inseparable. As the shadow followeth the body, so doth the cross follow the word of Christ: and as fire and heat cannot be separated, so cannot the gospel of Christ and the cross be plucked asunder. THOMAS BECON

Vs. 11. *I said in my haste, All men are liars.* In a modified sense, the expression will bear justification, even though hastily uttered, for all men will prove to be liars if we unduly trust in them; some from want of truthfulness and others from want of power. It is much better to be quiet when our spirit is disturbed and hasty, for it is so much easier to say than to unsay; we may repent of our words, but we cannot so recall them as to undo the mischief they have done. If even David had to eat his own words when he spoke in a hurry, none of us can trust our tongue without a bridle. C. H. S.

Vs. 11. If every man be a liar, then David was a liar; therefore he lies when he says every man is a liar — thus contradicting himself and destroying his own position This is answered easily; for when David spoke he did so not as man but from an inspiration of the Holy Ghost. ROBERT BELLARMINE

Vs. 11-15. And now let the world do its worst, and take the lie how it will, for David having Christ on his side, will always be able to make his part good against all the world, for Christ hath overcome the world.

But though all men may be said to be liars, yet not all men in all things; for then David himself should be a liar in this: but all men perhaps in something or other, at some time or other, in some kind or other. Absolute truth is not found in any man, but in that Man only Who was not man only; for if He had been but so, it had not perhaps been found in Him neither, seeing absolute truth and deity are as relatives, never found to be asunder.

*Precious in the sight of the Lord is the death of His saints.* For if it be so great a happiness to be acceptable in His sight, how great a happiness must it be to be precious in His sight? When God, at the creation looked upon all His works, it is said He saw them to be all exceeding good: but it is not said that any of them were precious in His sight. How then comes death to be precious in His sight, that was none of His works but is a destroyer of His works? Is it possible that a thing which destroys His creatures should have a title of more value in His sight than His creatures themselves?

O my soul, this is one of the miracles of His saints, and perhaps one of those which Christ meant, when He said to His apostles, that greater miracles than He did they should do themselves: for what greater miracle than this, that death, which of itself is a thing most vile in the sight of God, yet once embraced by His saints, as it were by their touch only, becomes precious in His sight? To alter a thing from being vile to be precious, is it not a greater miracle than to turn water into wine? Indeed so it is; death doth not damnify His saints, but His saints do dignify death. Death takes nothing away from His saints' happiness, but His saints add luster to death's vileness. If there be glory laid up for them that die in the Lord, much more shall they be glorified that die for the Lord. SIR RICHARD BAKER

Vs. 12. *All His benefits toward me.* What reward shall we give unto the Lord for all the benefits He hath bestowed? From the cheerless gloom of non-existence, He waked us into being; He ennobled us with understanding; He taught us arts to promote the means of life; He commanded the prolific earth to yield its nurture; He bade the animals to own us as their lords.

For us the rains descend; for us the sun sheddeth abroad its creative beams; the mountains rise, the valleys bloom, affording us grateful habitation and a sheltering retreat. For us the rivers flow; for us the fountains murmur; the sea opens its bosom to admit our commerce; the earth exhausts its stores; each new object presents a new enjoyment; all nature pouring her treasures at our feet, through the bounteous grace of Him Who wills that all be ours. . BASIL

As partial obedience is not good, so partial thanks is worthless. An honest soul would not conceal any debt he owes to God, but calls upon itself to give an account for all His benefits. The skipping over one note in a lesson may spoil the grace of the music; unthankfulness for one mercy disparageth our thanks for the rest. WILLIAM GURNALL

Vs. 14. *I will pay my vows.* Foxe, in his *Acts and Monuments,* relates the following concerning the martyr, John Philpot: "He went with the sheriffs to the place of execution; and when he was entering into Smithfield the way was foul, and two officers took him up to bear him to the stake. Then he said merrily, What, will ye make me a pope? I am content to go to my journey's end on foot. But first coming into Smithfield, he kneeled down there, saying these words, I will pay my vows in thee, O Smithfield.

Vs. 15. *Precious in the sight of the Lord is the death of His saints.* They shall not die prematurely; they shall be immortal till their work is done; and when their time shall come to die, then their deaths shall be precious. The Lord watches over their dying beds, smooths their pillows, sustains their hearts, and receives their souls. Those who are redeemed with precious Blood are so dear to God that even their deaths are precious to Him.

The death-beds of saints are very precious to the church; she often learns much from them. They are very precious to all believers, who delight to treasure up the last words of the departed. But they are most of all precious to the Lord Jehovah Himself, Who views the triumphant deaths of His gracious ones with sacred delight.

If we have walked before Him in the land of the living, we need not fear to die before Him when the hour of our departure is at hand. C. H. S.

How much has the cause of religion been promoted by the patient deaths of Ignatius, Polycarp, and Latimer, and Ridley, and Huss, and Jerome of Prague, and the hosts of martyrs! What does not the world owe, and the cause of religion owe, to such scenes as occurred on the deathbeds of Baxter, and Thomas Scott, and Halyburton, and Payson!

What an argument for the truth of religion — what an illustration of its sustaining power — what a source of comfort to those who are about to die — to reflect that religion does not leave the believer when he most needs its support and consolation; that it can sustain us in the severest trial of our condition here; that it can illuminate what seems to us of all places most dark, cheerless, dismal, repulsive — "the valley of the shadow of death." ALBERT BARNES

Their death is precious (jakar); the word of the text is *in pretio fuit, magni estimatum est.* See how the word is translated in other texts. 1. Honorable (*Isa.* 43:4) *jakarta;* "thou was precious in My sight, thou hast been honorable." 2.

Much set by (I Sam. 18:30): "His name was much set by." 3. Dear (Jer. 31:20) *An filius (jakkir) pretiosus mihi Ephraim:* "Is Ephraim my dear son?" 4. Splendid, clear, or glorious (Job. 31:16). *Si vidi lunam (jaker) pretiosam et abeunten:* "the moon walking in brightness." SAMUEL TORSHELL

Death, now, as he hath done also to mine, has paid full many a visit to your house; and in very deed, he has made fell havoc among our comforts. We shall yet be avenged on this enemy—this King of Terrors. I cannot help at times clenching my fist in his face and roaring out in my agony and anguish, "Thou shalt be swallowed up in victory!" There is even, too, in the meantime, this consolation; "O Death, where is thy sting?" JOHN JAMESON

Vs. 16. *O Lord, truly I am Thy servant.* Thou hast made me free, and I am impatient to be bound again. Thou hast broken the bonds of sin; now, Lord, bind me with the cords of love. Thou hast delivered me from the tyranny of Satan; make me as one of Thy hired servants. I owe my liberty, my life, and all that I have, or hope, to Thy generous rescue: and now, O my gracious, my divine Friend and Redeemer, I lay myself and my all at Thy feet. SAMUEL LAVINGTON

The saints have ever had a holy pride in being God's servants; there cannot be a greater honor than to serve such a Master as commands heaven, earth, and hell. Do not think thou dost honor God in serving Him; but this is how God honors thee, in vouchsafing thee to be His servant. THOMAS ADAMS

To have, as it were, high and honorable thoughts of the majesty and greatness of the living God, and a deep and awful impression of the immediate and continual presence of the heart-searching God, this naturally produces the greatest self-abasement and the most unfeigned subjection of spirit before our Maker. JOHN WITHERSPOON

*Thou has loosed my bonds.* Mercies are given to encourage us in God's service, and should be remembered to that end. Rain descends upon the earth, not that it might be more barren, but more fertile. We are but stewards; the mercies we enjoy are not our own, but to be improved for our Master's service.

Great mercies should engage to great obedience. God begins the Decalogue with a memorial of His mercy in bringing the Israelites out of Egypt: "I am the Lord thy God, which brought thee out of the land of Egypt." How effectionately doth the Psalmist own his relation to God as His servant, when he considers how God had loosed his bonds: "O Lord, truly I am Thy servant; Thou hast loosed my bonds!" the remembrance of Thy mercy shall make me know no relation but that of a servant to Thee. It is irrational to encourage ourselves in our way to hell by a remembrance of heaven, to foster a liberty in sin by a consideration of God's bounty. When we remember that all we have or are is the gift of God's liberality, we should think ourselves obliged to honor Him with all that we have, for He is to have honor from all His gifts. STEPHEN CHARNOCK

Vs. 18. *I will pay my vows unto the Lord now in the presence of all His people.* The mercy came in secret, but the praise is rendered in public; the company was, however, select; he did not cast his pearls before swine, but delivered his testimony before those who could understand and appreciate it. C. H. S.

Wicked men are overbold in pouring forth their blasphemies to the dishonor of God; they care not who hear them. They stick not to do it in the midst of cities. Shall they be more audacious to dishonor God than ye, zealous to honor Him? Assuredly Christ will show Himself as forward to confess you, as you are or can be to confess Him (Matt. 10:32). This holy boldness is the ready way to glory. WILLIAM GOUGE

Vs. 19. *In the midst of thee, O Jerusalem.* God's praise is not to be confined to a closet, nor His Name to be whispered in holes and corners, as if we were afraid that men should hear us; but in the thick of the throng, and in the very center of assemblies, we should lift up heart and voice unto the Lord and invite others to join with us in adoring Him. C. H. S.

# PSALM 117

This Psalm, which is very little in its letter, is exceedingly large in its spirit; for, bursting beyond all bounds of race or nationality, it calls upon all mankind to praise the name of the Lord. The same divine Spirit which expatiates in the One Hundred Nineteenth, here condenses His utterances into two short verses, but yet the same infinite fulness is present and perceptible. It may be worth noting that this is at once the shortest chapter of the Scriptures and the central portion of the whole Bible. C. H. S.

Vs. 1. *O Praise the Lord, all ye nations.* This is an exhortation to the Gentiles to glorify Jehovah and a clear proof that the Old Testament spirit differed widely from that narrow and contracted national bigotry with which the Jews of our Lord's Day became so inveterately diseased. C. H. S.

The Psalmist had made an end and yet he had not done; to signify, that when we have said our utmost for God's praise, we must not be content, but begin anew. There is hardly any duty more pressed in the Old Testament upon us, though less practiced, than this of praising God. ABRAHAM WRIGHT

Vs. 2. *For His merciful kindness is great* (*gabar* is strong). It is not only great in bulk or number, but it is powerful; it prevails over sin, Satan, death, and hell. ADAM CLARKE

*The truth of the Lord.* Here, and so in divers other Psalms, God's mercy and truth are joined together; to show that all passages and proceedings, both in ordinances and in providences, whereby He cometh and communicateth Himself to His people, are not only mercy, though that is very sweet, but truth also. Their blessings come to them in the way of promise from God as bound to them by the truth of His covenant. This is soul-satisfying indeed; this turns all that a man hath to cream, when every mercy is a present sent from heaven by virtue of a promise. ABRAHAM WRIGHT

This Psalm, the shortest portion of the Book of God, is quoted, and given much value to, in Romans 15. And upon this it has been profitably observed, "It is a small portion of Scripture, and as such we might easily overlook it. But not so the Holy Ghost. He gleans up this precious little testimony which speaks of grace to the Gentiles and presses it on our attention." BELLETT

In God's worship, it is not always necessary to be long; few words sometimes say what is sufficient, as this short Psalm giveth us to understand.
DAVID DICKSON

This is the shortest, and the next but one is the longest, of the Psalms. There are times for short hymns and long hymns; for short prayers and long prayers; for short sermons and long sermons; for short speeches and long speeches. It is better to be too short than too long, as it can more easily be mended. Short addresses need no formal divisions: long addresses require them, as in the next Psalm but one. G. ROGERS

## PSALM 118

In the Book Ezra (3:10-11) we read that "when the builders laid the foundation of the Temple of the Lord, they set the priests in their apparel with trumpets, and the Levites, the sons of Asaph with cymbals, to praise the Lord, after the ordinance of David, king of Israel. And they sang together by course in praising and giving thanks unto the Lord; because He is good, for His mercy endureth forever toward Israel. And all the people shouted with a great shout, when they praised the Lord, because the foundation of the house of the Lord was laid."

Now the words mentioned in Ezra are the first and last sentences of this Psalm, and we therefore conclude that the people chanted the whole of this sublime song; and, moreover, that the use of this composition on such occasions was ordained by David, whom we conceive to be its author. C. H. S.

Vs. 1. *O give thanks unto the Lord.* Grateful hearts are greedy of men's tongues and would monopolize them all for God's glory. We must never tolerate an instant's unbelief as to the goodness of the Lord; whatever else may be questionable, this is absolutely certain, that Jehovah is good; His dispensations may vary, but His nature is always the same, and always good. It is not only that He was good, and will be good, but He *is* good; let His providence be what it may. Therefore, let us even at this present moment, though the skies be dark with clouds, yet give thanks unto His name. C. H. S.

*Because His mercy endureth forever.* Mercy is a great part of His goodness, and one which more concerns us than any other, for we are sinners and have need of His mercy. Angels may say that He is good, but they need not His mercy and cannot therefore take an equal delight in it; inanimate creation declares that He is good, but it cannot feel His mercy, for it has never transgressed; but man, deeply guilty and graciously forgiven, beholds mercy as the very focus and center of the goodness of the Lord. C. H. S.

Vs. 1-4. Because we hear the sentence so frequently repeated here, that "the mercy of the Lord endureth forever," we are not to think that the Holy Spirit has employed empty tautology, but our great necessity demands it: for in temptations and dangers the flesh begins to doubt of the mercy of God; therefore, nothing should be so frequently impressed on the mind as this, that the mercy of God does not fail, that the eternal Father wearies not in remitting our sins SOLOMON GESNER

Vs. 2, 3, 4. *Now.* Beware of delaying. Delays be dangerous; our hearts will cool and our affections will fall down. It is good, then, to be doing while it is called today, while it is called now. Now, now, now, saith David; there be three nows, and all to teach us that for aught we know, it is now or never, today or not at all; we must praise God while the heart is hot, else our iron will cool. Satan hath little hope to prevail unless he can persuade us to omit our duties when the clock strikes, and therefore his skill is to urge us to put it off till another time as fitter or better. RICHARD CAPEL

Vs. 4. *Let them now that fear the Lord say, that His mercy endureth forever.* In each of the three exhortations, notice carefully the word "now." There is no time like time present for telling out the praises of God. The present exaltation of the Son of David now demands from all who are the subjects of His kingdom continual songs of thanksgiving to Him Who hath set Him on high in the midst of Zion. Now, with us, should mean always. When would it be right to cease from praising God, Whose mercy never ceases? The fourfold testimonies to the everlasting mercy of God which are now before us speak like four evangelists, each one declaring the very pith and marrow of the gospel; and they stand like four angels at the four corners of the earth, holding the winds in their hands, restraining the plagues of the latter days that the mercy and long-suffering of God may endure towards the sons of men.

Here are four cords to bind the sacrifice to the four horns of the altar, and four trumpets with which to proclaim the year of jubilee to every quarter of the world. Let not the reader pass on to the consideration of the rest of the Psalm until he has with all his might lifted up both heart and voice to praise the Lord, "for His mercy endureth forever." C. H. S.

Vs. 5. *I called upon the Lord in distress.* (Or, "out of anguish, I invoked Jah.".) Nothing was left him but prayer, his agony was too great for aught beside; but having the heart and the privilege to pray, he possessed all things. Prayers which come out of distress generally come out of the heart. Prayer may be bitter in the offering, but it will be sweet in the answering. The man of God had called upon the Lord when he was not in distress, and therefore he found it natural and easy to call upon Him when he was in distress. C. H. S.

Saul sought to slay David, but David outlived Saul and sat upon his throne. Scribe and Pharisee, priest and Herodian, united in opposing the Christ of God, but He is exalted on high none the less because of their enmity. The mightiest man is a puny thing when he stands in opposition to God, yea, he shrinks into utter nothingness. C. H. S.

Vs. 6. When inferior natures are backed with a superior, they are full of courage: when the master is by, the dog will venture upon creatures greater than himself and fear not; at another time he will not do it when his master is absent. When God is with us, Who is the supreme, it should make us fearless. It did David: *The Lord is on my side; I will not fear: what can man do unto me?"*

Let him do his worst — frown, threat, plot, arm, strike; the Lord is on my side; He hath a special care for me; He is a shield unto me; I will not fear, but hope; as it is in the next verse, "I shall see my desire on them that hate me." I shall see them changed or ruined. Our help is in the name of the Lord, but our fears are in the name of man. WILLIAM GREENHILL

Vs. 7. *The Lord taketh my part with them that help me: therefore shall I see my desire upon them that hate me.* Our Lord Jesus does at this moment look down upon His adversaries, His enemies are His footstool; He shall look upon them at His second coming, and at the glance of His eyes they shall flee before Him, not being able to endure that look with which He shall read them through and through. C. H. S.

Vs. 8. It may perhaps be considered beneath the dignity and solemnity of our subject to remark that this eighth verse of this Psalm is the middle verse of the Bible. There are, I believe, 31,174 verses in all, and this is the 15,587th. BARTON BOUCHIER

*It is better to trust in the Lord.* All make this acknowledgment, and yet there is scarcely one among a hundred who is fully persuaded that God alone can afford him sufficient help. That man has attained a high rank among the faithful, who resting satisfied in God, never ceases to entertain a lively hope, even when he finds no help upon earth. JOHN CALVIN

Vs. 9. *It is better to trust in the Lord than to put confidence in princes.* A gilded vane turns with the wind as readily as a meaner weathercock. Princes are but men, and the best of men are poor creatures. In many troubles, they cannot help us in the least degree: for instance, in sickness, bereavement, or death; neither can they assist us one jot in reference to our eternal state.

In eternity, a prince's smile goes for nothing; heaven and hell pay no homage to royal authority. The favor of princes is proverbially fickle; the testimonies of worldlings to this effect are abundant.

All of us remember the words put by the world's great poet into the lips of the dying Wolsey; their power lies in their truth:

*O how wretched*
*Is that poor man that hangs on prince's favors!*
*There is, betwixt that smile we would aspire to,*
*That sweet aspect of princes, and their ruin,*
*More pangs and fears than wars or women have;*
*And when he falls, he falls like Lucifer,*
*Never to hope again.* C. H. S.

David knew that by experience, for he confided in Saul, his king; at another time in Achish, the Philistine; at another time in Ahithophel, his own most prudent minister; besides some others; and they all failed him; but he never confided in God without feeling the benefit of it. ROBERT BELLARMINE

"Great men's words," saith one, "are like dead men's shoes; he may go barefoot that waiteth for them." JOHN TRAPP

Vs. 10. *But in the name of the Lord will I destroy them.* It takes grand faith to be calm in the day of actual battle, and especially when that battle waxes hot; but our hero was as calm as if no fight was raging. Napoleon said that God was always on the side of the biggest battalions, but the Psalmist-warrior found that the Lord of hosts was with the solitary champion, and that in His name the battalions were cut to pieces.

There is a grand touch of the ego in the last sentence, but it is so overshadowed with the name of the Lord that there is none too much of it. He recognized his own individuality and asserted it: he did not sit still supinely and leave the work to be done by God by some mysterious means; but he resolved with his own trusty sword to set about the enterprise, and so become in God's hand the instrument of his own deliverance. C. H. S.

Vs. 11. *But in the name of the Lord I will destroy them.* They made the circle three and four times deep, but for all that, he felt confident of victory. It is grand to hear a man speak in this fashion when it is not boasting, but the calm declaration of his heartfelt trust in God. C. H. S.

It is good for some men to have adversaries; for often they more fear to sin, lest they should despise them, than dislike it for conscience, lest God should condemn them. They speak evil of us: if true, let us amend it; if false, condemn it; whether false or true, observe it.

Thus we shall learn good out of their evil; make them our tutors, and give them our pupilage. In all things, let us watch them; in nothing fear them: "which is to them an evident token of perdition, but to you of salvation" (Phil. 1:28). The church is that tower of David; if there be a thousand weapons to wound us, there are a thousand shields to guard us (Cant. 4:4). THOMAS ADAMS

Vs. 12. *For in the name of the Lord I will destroy them.* What wonders have been wrought in the name of the Lord! It is the battle-cry of faith, before which its adversaries fly apace. "The sword of the Lord and of Gideon" brings instant terror into the midst of the foe. The name of the Lord is the one weapon which never fails in the day of battle: he who knows how to use it may chase a thousand with his single arm.

Alas! we too often go to work and to conflict in our own name, and the enemy knows it not, but scornfully enquires, "Who are ye?" Let us take care never to venture into the presence of the foe without first of all arming ourselves with this impenetrable mail. If we knew this name better, and trusted it more, our life would be more fruitful and sublime.

*Jesus, the name high over all,*
*In hell, or earth, or sky,*
*Angels and men before it fall,*
*And devils fear and fly.*

C. H. S.

Vs. 13. *That I might fall.* If our adversaries can do this, they will have succeeded to their heart's content: if we fall into grievous sin, they will be better pleased than even if they had sent the bullet of the assassin into our heart, for a moral death is worse than a physical one. If they can dishonor us, and God in us, their victory will be complete. "Better death than false of faith" is the motto of one of our noble houses, and it may well be ours. C. H. S.

Thou hast indeed. Thou hast done thy part, O Satan, and it has been well done. Thou hast known all my weakest parts; thou hast seen where my armor was not buckled on tightly; and thou hast attacked me at the right time and in the right way.

The great Spanish poet, Calderon, tells of one who wore a heavy suit of armor for a whole year, and laid it by for one hour, and in that hour the enemy came, and the man paid for his negligence with his life. "Blessed is the man that endureth temptation; for when he is tried he shall receive the crown of life, which the Lord hath promised to them that love Him." JOHN MASON NEALE

Vs. 14. *The Lord is my strength and song.* Thus can all the Lord's redeemed say, "Salvation is of the Lord." We cannot endure any doctrine which puts the crown upon the wrong head and defrauds the glorious King of His revenue of praise. C. H. S.

*My strength,* that I am able to resist my enemies; *my salvation,* that I am delivered from my enemies; *my song,* that I may joyfully praise Him and sing of Him after I am delivered. WILLIAM NICHOLSON

Good songs, good promises, good proverbs, good doctrines, are none the worse for age. What was sung just after the passage of the Red Sea is here sung by the Prophet and shall be sung to the end of the world by the saints of the Most High. WILLIAM S. PLUMER

Vs. 16. *The right hand of the Lord doeth valiantly.* The Psalmist speaks in triplets, for he is praising the triune God; his heart is warm and he loves to dwell upon the note; he is not content with the praise he has rendered; he endeavors to utter it each time more fervently and more jubilantly than before. He had dwelt upon the sentence, "they compassed me about," for his peril from encircling armies was fully realized; and now he dwells upon the valor of Jehovah's right hand, for he has as vivid a sense of the presence and majesty of the Lord. How seldom is this the case: the Lord's mercy is forgotten and only the trial is remembered. C. H. S.

Vs. 17. *I shall not die, but live.* David did not look upon himself as immortal, or that he should never die; he knew he was subject to the statute of death: but the meaning is, I shall not die now; I shall not die by the hands of these men; I shall not die the death which they have designed me to. JOSEPH CARYL

The following incident is worth recording: "Wycliffe was now getting old, but the Reformer was worn out rather by the harassing attacks of his foes, and his incessant and ever-growing labors, than with the weight of years, for he was not yet sixty. He fell sick.

With unbounded joy, the friars heard that their great enemy was dying. Of course he was overwhelmed with horror and remorse for the evil he had done them, and they would hasten to his bedside and receive the expression of his penitence and sorrow. In a trice, a little crowd of shaven crowns assembled round the couch of the sick man — delegates from the four orders of friars. They began fair, wishing him health and restoration from his distemper; but speedily changing their tone, they exhorted him, as one on the brink of the grave, to make full confession, and express his unfeigned grief for the injuries he had inflicted on their order.

Wycliffe lay silent till they should have made an end, then, making his servant raise him a little on his pillow, and fixing his keen eyes upon them, he said with a loud voice, "I shall not die, but live, and declare the evil deeds of the friars." The monks rushed in astonishment and confusion from the chamber. J. A. WYLIE

*And declare the works of the Lord.* In the second member of the verse, he points out the proper use of life. God does not prolong the lives of His people that they may pamper themselves with meat and drink, sleep as much as they please, and enjoy every temporal blessing; but to magnify Him for His benefits which He is daily heaping upon them. JOHN CALVIN

According to Matthesius, Luther had this verse written against his study wall.

Vs. 19. *Open to me the gates of righteousness.* The gates won by His righteousness, to Whom we daily say, "Thou only art holy"; the gates which needed the "Via Dolorosa" and the cross, before they could roll back on their hinges. On a certain stormy afternoon, after the sun had been for three hours darkened, the world again heard of that Eden, from which, four thousand years before, Adam had been banished. Verily I say unto thee, this day shalt thou be with Me in Paradise." O blessed malefactor, who thus entered into the heavenly gardens! O happy thief, that thus stole the kingdom of heaven! JOHN M. NEALE.

*I will go into them, and I will praise the Lord.* Alas, there are multitudes who do not care whether the gates of God's house are opened or not; and although they know that they are opened wide, they never care to enter, neither does the thought of praising God so much as cross their minds. The time will come for them when they shall find the gates of heaven shut against them, for those gates are peculiarly the gates of righteousness through which there shall by no means enter anything that defileth. C. H. S.

Vs. 22. *The stone which the builders refused is become the head stone of the corner.* They could see no excellence in Him that they should build upon Him; He could not be made to fit in with their ideal of a national church; He was a stone of another quarry from themselves, and not after their mind nor according to their taste; therefore they cast Him away and poured contempt upon Him, even as Peter said, "This is the stone which was set at nought of you builders"; they reckoned Him to be as nothing, though He is Lord of all. In raising Him from the dead, the Lord God exalted Him to be the head of His church, the very pinnacle of her glory and beauty.

Since then He has become the confidence of the Gentiles, even of them that are afar off upon the sea, and thus He has joined the two walls of Jew and Gentile into one stately temple, and is seen to be the binding corner-stone, making both one. This is a delightful subject for contemplation.

All this is in a very emphatic sense true of our blessed Lord, "The Shepherd, the Stone of Israel." God Himself laid Him where He is, and hid within Him all the precious things of the eternal covenant; and there He shall forever remain, the foundation of all our hopes, the glory of all our joys, the united bond of all our fellowship. He is "the head over all things to the church," and by Him the church is fitly framed together, and groweth unto a holy temple in the Lord. C. H. S.

Still do the builders refuse Him: even to this day the professional teachers of the gospel are far too apt to fly to any and every new philosophy sooner than maintain the simple gospel, which is the essence of Christ: nevertheless, He holds His true position amongst His people, and the foolish builders shall see to their utter confusion that His truth shall be exalted over all.

Those who reject the chosen stone will stumble against Him to their own hurt, and ere long will come His second advent, when He will fall upon them from the heights of heaven and grind them to powder. C. H. S.

There may be wit and learning, and much knowledge of the Scriptures, amongst those that are haters of the Lord Jesus Christ, and of the power of godliness, and corruptors of the worship of God. It is the spirit of humility and obedience, and saving faith, that teach men to esteem Christ and build upon Him. ROBERT LEIGHTON

Vs. 23. *This is the Lord's doing.* Every grain of true faith in this world is a divine creation, and every hour in which the true church subsists is a prolonged miracle. It is not the goodness of human nature, nor the force of reasoning, which exalts Christ and builds up the church, but a power from above. This staggers the adversary, for he cannot understand what it is which baffles him: of the Holy Ghost, he knows nothing. It never ceases to astonish us, as we see, even here below, God by means of weakness defeating power, by the simplicity of His Word baffling the craft of men, and by the invisible influence of His Spirit exalting His Son in human hearts in the teeth of open and determined opposition. It is indeed "marvelous in our eyes," as all God's works must be if men care to study them. In the Hebrew, the passage reads, "It is wonderfully done"; not only is the exaltation of Jesus of Nazareth itself wonderful, but the way in which it is brought about is marvelous: it is wonderfully done. The more we study the history of Christ and His church, the more fully shall we agree with this declaration. C. H. S.

Vs. 24. *Day which the Lord hath made.* Adam introduced a day of sadness, but another day is made by Christ: Abraham saw His day from afar, and was glad; we will walk even now in His light. JOHANN DAVID FRISCH

Vs. 26. *Blessed be He that cometh in the name of the Lord.* In the Psalmist's days, He was the Coming One, and He is still the Coming One, though He hath already come. We are ready with our hosannas both for His first and second advent; our inmost souls thankfully adore and bless Him and invoke upon His head unspeakable joys. C. H. S.

Vs. 27. *God is the Lord, which hath showed us light.* Our knowledge of the glory of God in the face of Jesus Christ came not by the light of nature, nor by reason, nor did it arise from the sparks which we ourselves had kindled, nor did we receive it of men; but the mighty God alone hath showed it to us.

The word rendered "cords" carries with it the idea of wreaths and boughs, so that it was not a cord of hard, rough rope, but a decorated band; even as in our case, though we are bound to the altar of God, it is with the cords of love and the bands of a man, and not by a compulsion which destroys the freedom of the will. There remains a tendency in our nature to start aside from this; it is not fond of the sacrificial knife. In the warmth of our love we come willingly to the altar, but we need constraining power to keep us there in the entirety of our being throughout the whole of life. Happily there is a cord which, twisted around the atonement, or, better still, around the person of our Lord Jesus Christ, Who is our only altar, can hold us, and does hold us: "For the love of Christ constraineth us; because we thus judge, that if one died for all, then all died; and that He died for all, that they that live should not henceforth live unto themselves, but unto Him Who died for them, and rose again."

We are bound to the doctrine of atonement; we are bound to Christ Himself, Who is both altar and sacrifice; we desire to be more bound to Him than ever; our soul finds her liberty in being tethered fast to the altar of the Lord. The American Board of Missions has for its seal an ox, with an altar on one side and a plough on the other, and the motto, "Ready for either" — ready to live and labor, or ready to suffer and die.

We would gladly spend ourselves for the Lord actively, or be spent by Him passively, whichever may be His will; but since we know the rebellion of our corrupt nature, we earnestly pray that we may be kept in this consecrated mind, and that we may never, under discouragements, or through the temptations of the world, be permitted to leave the altar, to which it is our intense desire to be forever fastened.

Such consecration as this, and such desires for its perpetuity, will beseem that day of gladness which the Lord hath made so bright by the glorious triumph of His Son, our Covenant Head, our Well-Beloved. C. H. S.

He did not say: This light came from creature exertion; this light was the produce of my own wisdom; this light was nature transmuted by some action of my own will, and thus gradually rose into existence from long and assiduous cultivation. But he ascribes the whole of that light which he possessed unto God, the Lord, as the sole Author and the only Giver of it. Now, if God, the Lord, has ever showed you and me the same light which He showed His servant of old, we carry about with us more or less of a solemn conviction that we have received this light from Him. J. C. PHILPOT

They are not well-pleasing in the sight of God, except they are bound to the horns of the altar, so as to derive all their acceptance from the altar. Our prayers are only acceptable to God as they are offered through the cross of Jesus. Our praises and thanksgivings are only acceptable to God as they are connected with the cross of Christ and ascend to the Father through the propitiation of His dear Son. And, therefore, every sacrifice of our own comfort, or of our own advantage, of our own time, or of our own money, for the profit of God's children, is only a spiritual and acceptable sacrifice so far as it is bound to the horns of the altar, linked on to the cross of Jesus, and deriving all its fragrance and odor from its connection with the incense there offered by the Lord of life and glory. J. C. PHILPOT

*Bind the sacrifice.* 'Tis a saying among the Hebrews, that the beasts that were offered in sacrifice, they were the most struggling beasts of all the rest; such is the nature of us unthankful beasts, when we should love God again, we are readier to run away from Him; we must be tied to the altar with cords, to draw from us love or fear. ABRAHAM WRIGHT

# PSALM 119

There is no title to this Psalm; neither is any author's name mentioned. It is the longest Psalm, and this is a sufficiently distinctive name for it. Nor is it long only; for it equally excels in breadth of thought, depth of meaning, and height of fervor. Many superficial readers have imagined that it harps upon one string and abounds in pious repetitions and redundancies; but this arises from the shallowness of the reader's own mind: those who have studied this Divine hymn and carefully noted each line of it are amazed at the variety and profundity of the thought. The more one studies it, the fresher it becomes. It contains no idle word; the grapes of this cluster are almost to bursting full with the new wine of the kingdom. Again and again have we cried while studying it, "Oh, the depths!" Yet these depths are hidden beneath an apparent simplicity, as Augustine has well and wisely said, and this makes the exposition all the more difficult.

We believe that David wrote this Psalm. It is Davidic in tone and expression, and it tallies with David's experience in many interesting points.

The one theme is the Word of the Lord. "The most," says Martin Boos, "read their Bibles like cows that stand in the thick grass, and trample under their feet the finest flowers and herbs." It is to be feared that we too often do the like.

This sacred ode is a little Bible, the Scriptures condensed, a mass of Bibline, Holy Writ rewritten in holy emotions and actions. C. H. S.

## NOTES RELATING TO THE PSALM AS A WHOLE

This Psalm is called the "Alphabet of Divine Love," the "Paradise of all the Doctrines," the "Storehouse of the Holy Spirit," the "School of Truth," also the deep mystery of the Scriptures, where the whole moral discipline of all the virtues shines brightly. J. P. PALANTERIUS

It is recorded of the celebrated St. Augustine, who among his voluminous works left a *Comment on the Book of Psalms,* that he delayed to comment on this one till he had finished the whole Psalter; and then yielded only to the long and vehement urgency of his friends, "Because," he says, "as often as I essayed to think thereon, it always exceeded the powers of my intent thought and the utmost grasp of my faculties." W. DEBURGH

In Matthew Henry's *Account of the Life and Death of His father, Philip Henry,* he says: "Once, pressing the study of the Scriptures, he advised us to take a verse of this Psalm every morning to meditate upon, and so go over the Psalm twice in the year; and that, saith he, will bring you to be in love with all the rest of the Scriptures. He often said, "All grace grows as love to the Word of God grows."

In the midst of a London season; in the stir and turmoil of a political crisis (1819); William Wilberforce writes in his Dairy: "Walked from Hyde Park Corner repeating the One Hundred Nineteenth Psalm in great comfort." WILLIAM ALEXANDER, *in* "THE WITNESS OF THE PSALMS"

George Wishart, the chaplain and biographer of *The Great Marquis of Montrose,* as he was called, would have shared the fate of his illustrious patron but for the following singular expedient. When upon the scaffold, he availed himself of the custom of the times, which permitted the condemned to choose a Psalm to be sung. He selected the One Hundred Nineteenth Psalm, and before two-thirds of the Psalm had been sung, a pardon arrived, and his life was preserved. It may not be out of place to add that the George Wishart, Bishop of Edinburgh, above referred to, has been too often confounded with the godly martyr of the same name who lived and died a century previously. C. H. S.

It seems to me to be a collection of David's pious and devout ejaculations, the short and sudden breathings of his soul to God, which he wrote down as they occurred, and towards the latter end of his time gathered them out of his day-book where they lay scattered, added to them many like words, and digested them into this Psalm, in which there is seldom any coherence between the verses. M. HENRY

I know of no part of the Holy Scriptures where the nature and evidence of true and sincere godliness are so fully and largely insisted on and delineated as in the One Hundred Nineteenth Psalm. J. EDWARDS

The name Jehovah occurs twenty-two times in the Psalm. Its theme is the Word of God, which it mentions under one of the ten terms: law, way, testimony, precept, statute, commandments, judgment, word, saying, truth, in every verse except verse one twenty-two. J. D. MURPHY

## EXPOSITION OF VERSES 1 TO 8

These first eight verses are taken up with a contemplation of the blessedness which comes through keeping the statutes of the Lord. Heart-fellowship with God is enjoyed through a love of that Word which is God's way of communing with the soul by His Holy Spirit.

Oh, that every reader may feel the glow which is poured over the verses as they proceed: he will then begin as a reader, but he will soon bow as a suppliant; his study will become an oratory, and his contemplation will warm into adoration.

Vs. 1. *Blessed.* True religion is not cold and dry; it has its exclamations and raptures. We not only judge the keeping of God's law to be a wise and proper thing, but we are warmly enamored of its holiness, and cry out in adoring wonder, "Blessed are the undefiled!" meaning thereby, that we eagerly desire to become such ourselves and wish for no greater happiness than to be perfectly holy.

As David thus begins his Psalm, so should young men begin their lives, so should new converts commence their profession, so should all Christians begin every day. Settle it in your hearts as a first postulate and sure rule of practical science that holiness is happiness.

How easily may defilement come upon us even in our holy things, yea, even in the way! We may even come from public or private worship with defilement upon the conscience gathered when we were on our knees.

The holy life is a walk, a steady progress, a quiet advance, a lasting continuance. Enoch walked with God. Good men always long to do better, and hence they go forward. Good men are never idle, and hence they do not lie down or loiter, but they are still walking onward to their desired end. They are not hurried, and worried, and flurried, and so they keep the even tenor of their way, walking steadily towards heaven.

Rough may be the way, stern the rule, hard the discipline — all these we know and more — but a thousand heaped-up blessednesses are still found in godly living, for which we bless the Lord.

We have in this verse blessed persons who enjoy five blessed things: a blessed way, blessed purity, blessed law, given by a blessed Lord, and a blessed walk therein; to which we may add the blessed testimony of the Holy Ghost given in this very passage that they are in very deed the blessed of the Lord.

Vs. 2. *Blessed are they that keep His testimonies.* What! A second blessing? Yes, they are doubly blessed whose outward life is supported by an inward zeal for God's glory. Blessedness is ascribed to those who treasure up the testimonies of the Lord: in which is implied that they search the Scriptures, that they come to an understanding of them, that they love them, and then that they continue in the practice of them. God's Word is His witness or testimony to grand and important truths which concern Himself and our relation to Him: this we should desire to know; knowing it, we should believe it; believing it, we should love it; and loving it, we should hold it fast against all comers.

We cannot fight a good fight, nor finish our course, unless we keep the faith. To this end the Lord must keep us: only those who are kept by the power of God unto salvation will ever be able to keep His testimonies. C. H. S.

If God's Word were no more than a law, yet were we bound to obey it, because we are His creatures; but since it is also a testimony of His love, wherein as a father He witnesseth His favor towards His children, we are doubly inexcusable if we do not most joyfully embrace it. W. COWPER

*And that seek Him with the whole heart.* See the growth which these sentences indicate: first, in the way, then walking in it, then finding and keeping the treasure of the truth, and to crown all, seeking after the Lord of the way Himself. The blessed man has God already, and for this reason he seeks Him. This may seem a contradiction: it is only a paradox.

God is not truly sought by the cold researches of the brain: we must seek Him with the heart. God is One, and we shall not know Him till our heart is one. A broken heart need not be distressed at this, for no heart is so whole in its seekings after God as a heart which is broken, whereof every fragment sighs and cries after the great Father's face. A heart may be divided and not broken, and it may be broken but not divided; and yet again it may be broken and be whole, and it never can be whole until it is broken. C. H. S.

Vs. 3. *They also do no iniquity.* That is, they make not a trade and common practice thereof. Slip they do, through the infirmity of the flesh, and subtlety of Satan, and the allurements of the world; but they do not ordinarily and customably go forward in unlawful and sinful courses. R. GREENHAM

A wicked man sinneth with deliberation and delight; his bent is to do evil; he makes "provision for lusts" (Rom. 13:14) and "serves" them by a voluntary subjection (Titus 3:3). But those that are renewed by grace are not "debtors" to the flesh; they have taken another debt and obligation, which is to serve the Lord (Rom. 8:12).

If a man be constantly, easily, frequently carried away to sin, it discovers the habit of his soul and the temper of his heart. Meadows may be overflowed, but marsh ground is drowned with every return of the tide. A child of God may be occasionally carried away and act contrary to the inclination of the new nature; but when men are drowned and overcome by the return of every temptation, it argues a habit of sin. T. MANTON

*They walk in His ways.* We must be positively as well as negatively right. The surest way to abstain from evil is to be fully occupied in doing good. C. H. S.

Many men, all their religion runs upon nots: "I am *not* as this publican" (Luke 18:11). That ground is naught, though it brings not forth briars and thorns, if it yields not good increase. Not only the unruly servant is cast into hell, that beat his fellow-servant that ate and drank with the drunken; but the idle servant that wrapped up his talent in a napkin. Meroz is cursed, not for opposing and fighting, but for not helping (Judges 5:23). Dives did not take away food from Lazarus, but he did not give him of his crumbs. Many will say, "I set up no other gods"; say, but dost thou love, reverence, and obey the true God? We do not think of sins of omission. If we are not drunkards, adulterers, and profane persons, we do not think what it is to omit respect to God and reverence for His Holy Majesty. T. MANTON

Vs. 4. *Thou hast commanded us to keep Thy precepts diligently.* Those who are diligent in business rise up early and sit up late and deny themselves much of comfort and repose. They are not soon tired, or if they are, they persevere even with aching brow and weary eye. So should we serve the Lord. Such a Master deserves diligent servants; such service He demands, and will be content with nothing less.

It is no use traveling fast if we are not in the right road. Men have been diligent in a losing business, and the more they have traded, the more they have lost; this is bad enough in commerce; we cannot afford to have it so in our religion. C. H. S.

Vs. 5. *O that my ways were directed to keep Thy statutes!* Our ways are by nature opposed to the way of God and must be turned by the Lord's direction in another direction from that which they originally take, or they will lead us down to destruction. C. H. S.

We might as soon create a world as create in our hearts one pulse of spiritual life. And yet our inability does not cancel our obligation. Our inability is our sin, our guilt, our condemnation, and instead of excusing our condition, stops our mouth, and leaves us destitute of any plea of defense before God. Thus our obligation remains in full force. C. BRIDGES

"The whole life of a good Christian is an holy desire," saith Augustine; and this is always seconded with endeavor, without the which, affection is like Rachel — beautiful, but barren. J. TRAPP

Vs. 6. *Then shall I not be ashamed.*

*I can bear scorpion's stings, tread fields of fire.*
*In frozen gulfs of cold eternal lie;*
*Be toss'd aloft through tracts of endless void,*
*But cannot live in shame.*

JOANNE BAILLIE

*When I have respect unto all Thy commandments.* An abiding sense of duty will make us bold; we shall be afraid to be afraid. No shame in the presence of man will hinder us when the fear of God has taken full possession of our minds. There is nothing to be ashamed of in a holy life; a man may be ashamed of his pride, ashamed of his wealth, ashamed of his own children, but he will never be ashamed of having in all things regarded the will of the Lord, his God. C. H. S.

There can be no true piety except where a man *intends* to keep all the commands of God. If he makes a selection among them, keeping this one or that one, as may be most convenient for him, or as may be most for his interest, or as may be most popular, it is full proof that he knows nothing of the nature of true religion. A child has no proper respect for a parent if he obeys him only as shall suit his whim or his convenience; and no *man* can be a pious man who does not purpose, in all honesty, to keep all the commandments of God; to submit to His will *in everything.* A. BARNES

Saul slew all the Amalekites but one; and that single exception in the path of universal obedience marked the unsoundness of his profession, cost him the loss of his throne, and brought him under the awful displeasure of his God. And thus the foot, or the hand, or the right eye, the corrupt, unmortified members, bring the whole body to hell. Reserves are the canker of Christian sincerity. C. BRIDGES

Vs. 7. *I will praise Thee.* We praise those who can teach a dog, a horse, this or that; but for us ass-colts to learn the will of God, how to walk pleasing before Him, this should be acknowledged of us as a great mercy from God. P. BAYNE

Vs. 8. *O forsake me not utterly.* To be left, that we may discover our weakness, is sufficient trial: to be altogether forsaken would be ruin and death. Hiding the face in a little wrath for a moment brings us very low: an absolute desertion would land us ultimately in the lowest hell. C. H. S.

## EXPOSITION OF VERSES 9 TO 16

Vs. 9. *Wherewithal shall a young man cleanse his way?* How shall he become and remain practically holy? He is but a young man, full of hot passions, and poor in knowledge and experience; how shall he get right and keep right? Never was there a more important question for any man; never was there a fitter time for asking it than at the commencement of life. C. H. S.

A prominent place — one of the twenty-two parts — is assigned to the young men in the One Hundred Nineteenth Psalm. It is meet that it should be so. Youth is the season of impression and improvement. Young men are the future props of society, and the fear of the Lord, which is the beginning of wisdom, must begin in youth. The strength, the aspirations, the unmarred expectations of youth, are in requisition for the world; oh, that they may be consecrated to God!

The very inquiry shows that his heart is not in a corrupt state. Desire is present; direction is required. The inquiry is: How shall a young man make a clean way — a pure line of conduct — through this defiling world? JOHN STEPHEN

*By taking heed thereto according to Thy Word.* Young man, the Bible must be your chart, and you must exercise great watchfulness that your way may be according to its directions. You must take heed to your daily life as well as study your Bible, and you must study your Bible that you may take heed to your daily life. With the greatest care a man will go astray if his map misleads him; but with the most accurate map he will still lose his road if he does not take heed to it. The narrow way was never hit upon by chance, neither did any heedless man ever lead a holy life. We can sin without thought; we have only to neglect the great salvation and ruin our souls; but to obey the Lord and walk uprightly will need all our heart and soul and mind. Let the careless remember this.

A captain may watch from his deck all night; but if he knows nothing of the coast, and has no pilot on board, he may be carefully hastening on to shipwreck. It is not enough to desire to be right; for ignorance may make us think that we are doing God service when we are provoking Him, and the fact of our ignorance will not reverse the character of our action, however much it may mitigate its criminality. C. H. S.

The Word is the only weapon (like Goliath's sword, none to equal this), for the hewing down and cutting off of this stubborn enemy, our lusts. The Word of God can master our lusts when they are in their greatest pride; if ever lust rageth at one time more than another, it is when youthful blood boils in our veins. Youth is giddy, and his lust is hot and impetuous: his sun is climbing higher still, and he thinks it is a great while to night; so that it must be a strong arm that brings a young man off his lusts, who hath his palate at best advantage to taste sensual pleasure. Well, let the Word of God meet this young gallant in all his bravery, with his feast of senual delights before him, and but whisper a few syllables in his ear, give his conscience but a prick with the point of its sword, and it shall make him fly in as great haste from them all, as Absalom's brethren did from the feast when they saw Amnon, their brother, murdered at the table. W. GURNALL

The Scriptures teach us the best way of living, the noblest way of suffering, and the most comfortable way of dying. JOHN FLAVEL

Vs. 10. *With my whole heart have I sought Thee.* The surest mode of cleansing the way of our life is to seek after God Himself, and to endeavor to abide in fellowship with Him.

*O let me not wander from Thy commandments.* We are to be such whole-hearted seekers that we have neither time nor will to be wanderers, and yet with all our whole-heartedness, we are to cultivate a jealous fear lest even then we should wander from the path of holiness.

Two things may be very like and yet altogether different: saints are "strangers" — "I am a stranger in the earth" (verse 19), but they are not wanderers: they are passing through an enemy's country, but their route is direct; they are seeking their Lord while they traverse this foreign land. Their way is hidden from men; but yet they have not lost their way. C. H. S.

Vs. 11. *Thy Word have I hid in my heart.* He did not wear a text *on* his heart as a charm, but he hid it *in* his heart as a rule. C. H. S.

There is a great difference between Christians and worldlings. The worldling hath his treasures in jewels without him; the Christian hath them within. Neither indeed is there any receptacle wherein to receive and keep the word of consolation but the heart only. If thou have it in thy mouth only, it shall be taken from thee; if thou have it in thy book only, thou shalt miss it when thou hast most to do with it; but if thou lay it up in thy heart, as Mary did the words of the angel, no enemy shall ever be able to take it from thee, and thou shalt find it a comfortable treasure in time of thy need. WM. COWPER

This saying, *to hide,* importeth that David studied not to be ambitious to set forth himself and to make glorious show before men; but that he had God for a witness of that secret desire which was within him. JOHN CALVIN

Bernard observes, bodily bread in the cupboard may be eaten of mice, or moulder and waste: but when it is taken down into the body, it is free from such danger. If God enable thee to take thy soulfood into thine heart, it is free from all hazards. GEO. SWINNOCK

*That I might not sin against Thee.* Here was the object aimed at. As one has well said: Here is the best thing — "Thy Word"; hidden in the best place — "in my heart"; for the best of purposes — "that I might not sin against Thee." C. H. S.

Vs. 12. *Blessed art Thou, O Lord.* No sooner is the Word in the heart than a desire arises to mark and learn it. When food is eaten, the next thing is to digest it; and when the Word is received into the soul, the first prayer is — "Lord, teach me its meaning." C. H. S.

*Teach me Thy statutes;* for thus only can I learn the way to be blessed. Thou art so blessed that I am sure Thou wilt delight in blessing others, and this boon I crave of Thee that I may be instructed in Thy commands. Happy men usually rejoice to make others happy, and surely the happy God will willingly impart the holiness which is the fountain of happiness. Faith prompted this prayer and based it, not upon anything in the praying man, but solely upon the perfection of the God to Whom he made supplication. Lord, Thou are blessed; therefore bless me by teaching me. C. H. S.

Whoever reads this Psalm with attention must observe in it one great characteristic, and that is, how decisive are its statements that in keeping the commandments of God nothing can be done by human strength; but that it is He Who must create the will for the performance of such duty. GEO. PHILLIPS

Vs. 13. *With my lips have I declared all the judgments of Thy mouth.* To have been, like Noah, a preacher of righteousness, is a great joy when the floods are rising and the ungodly world is about to be destroyed. C. H. S.

Vs. 14. *I have rejoiced in the way of Thy testimonies, as much as in all riches.* Riches are acquired with difficulty, enjoyed with trembling, and lost with bitterness. BERNARD

Vs. 15. *I will meditate in Thy precepts.* He who has an inward delight in anything will not long withdraw his mind from it. As the miser often returns to look upon his treasure, so does the devout believer by frequent meditation turn over the priceless wealth which he has discovered in the Book of the Lord. To some men, meditation is a task; to the man of cleansed way, it is a joy. C. H. S.

It is not the digging into the golden mine, but the digging long, that finds and fetches up the treasure. It is not the diving into the sea, but staying longer, that gets the greater quantity of pearls. To draw out the golden thread of meditation to its due length till the spiritual ends be attained, this is a rare and happy attainment. NATHANAEL RANEW

Study the Scriptures. If a famous man do but write an excellent book, oh, how we do long to see it! Or suppose I could tell you that there is in France or Germany a book that God Himself wrote, I am confident men may draw all the money out of your purses to get that book. You have it by you: oh, that you would study it!

When the eunuch was riding in his chariot, he was studying the prophet Isaiah. He was not angry when Philip came and, as we would have thought, asked him a bold question: "Understandeth thou what thou readeth?" (Acts 8:27-30); he was glad of it. One great end of the year of release was that the law might be read (Deut. 31:9-13). It is the wisdom of God that speaks in the Scripture (Luke 11:49); therefore, whatever else you mind, really and carefully study the Bible. SAMUEL JACOMB

Vs. 16. *I will delight myself in Thy statutes: I will not forget Thy Word.* I never yet heard of a covetous old man who had forgotten where he had buried his treasure. CICERO DE SENECTUTE

## EXPOSITION OF VERSES 17 TO 24

In this section the trials of the way appear to be manifest to the Psalmist's mind, and he prays accordingly for the help which will meet his case. As in the last eight verses he prayed as a youth newly come into the world, so here he pleads as a servant and a pilgrim who growingly finds himself to be a stranger in an enemy's country. His appeal is to God alone, and his prayer is specially direct and personal. He speaks with the Lord as a man speaketh with his friend.

Vs. 17. *Deal bountifully with Thy servant, that I may live, and keep Thy Word.* We work *for* Him because He works *in us.* Thus we may make a chain out of the opening verses of the three first octaves of this Psalm: verse 1 blesses the holy man; verse 9 asks how we can attain to such holiness; and verse 17 traces such holiness to its secret source and shows us how to keep the blessing. The more a man prizes holiness and the more earnestly he strives after it, the more will he be driven towards God for help therein, for he will plainly perceive that his own strength is insufficient and that he cannot even so much as live without the bounteous assistance of the Lord, his God. C. H. S.

Vs. 18. *Open Thou mine eyes.* Those that vent their own dreams under the name of the Spirit and Divine light; they do not give you *mysteria,* but *monstra,* portentous opinions; they do not show you the wondrous things of God's law, but the prodigies of their own brain; unhappy abortives that die as soon as they come to light. T. MANTON

The Psalmist asks for no new revelation. It was in God's hand to give this, and He did it in His own time to those ancient believers; but to all of them at every time there was enough given for the purposes of life. The request is not for more, but that he may employ well that which he possesses.

This further may be observed, that the Psalmist asks for no new faculty. The eyes are there already, and they need only to be opened. It is not the bestowal of a new and supernatural power which enables a man to read the Bible to profit, but the quickening of a power he already possesses. A man will never grow into the knowledge of God's Word by idly waiting for some new gift of discernment, but by diligently using that which God has already bestowed upon him and using at the same time all other helps that lie within his reach.

The great reason why men do not feel the power and beauty of the Bible is a spiritual one. They do not realize the grand evil which the Bible has come to cure, and they have not a heart to the blessings which it offers to bestow. The film of a fallen nature, self-maintained, is upon their eyes while they read: "The eyes of their understanding are darkened, being alienated from the life of God" (Eph. 4:18). All the natural powers will never find the true key to the Bible till the thoughts of sin and redemption enter the heart and are put in the center of the Book. JOHN KER

*Wondrous things.* Many were the signs and miracles which God wrought in the midst of the people of Israel, which they did not understand. What was the reason? Moses tells us expressly what it was: "Yet the Lord hath not given you an heart to perceive and eyes to see, and ears to hear, unto this day" (Deut. 29:4).

They had sensitive eyes and ears, yea, they had a rational heart or mind; but they wanted a spiritual ear to hear, a spiritual heart or mind to apprehend and improve those wonderful works of God; and these they had not because God had not given them such eyes, ears, and hearts. Wonders without grace cannot open the eyes fully; but grace without wonders can. JOSEPH CARYL

Wherefore useth he this word *wondrous?* It is as if he would have said, "Although the world taketh the law of God to be but a light thing, and it seemeth to be given but as it were for simple souls and young children; yet for all that there seemeth such a wisdom to be in it, as that it surmounteth all the wisdom of the world, and that therein lie hid wonderful secrets." JOHN CALVIN

Verses 18 and 19. "When I cannot have Moses to tell me the meaning," saith Saint Augustine, "give me that Spirit that Thou gavest to Moses." RICHARD STOCK

Vs. 19. *I am a stranger in the earth.* This confession from a solitary wanderer would have had little comparative meaning; but in the mouth of one who was probably surrounded with every source of worldly enjoyment, it shows at once the vanity of "earth's best joys" and the heavenly tendency of the religion of the Bible. C. BRIDGES

A man's greatest care should be for that place where he lives longest; therefore, eternity should be his scope. T. MANTON

When a child is born, it is spoken of sometimes under the designation of "a little stranger"! Friends calling will ask if, as a privilege, they may "see the little stranger." A stranger indeed come from far! From the immensities. From the presence, and touch, and being of God! And going—into the immensities again—into, and through all the unreckonable ages of duration.

But the little stranger grows and in a while begins to take vigorous root. He works, and wins, and builds, and plants, and buys, and holds, and, in his own feeling, becomes so "settled" that he would be almost amused with anyone who should describe him as a stranger now.

And still life goes on, deepening and widening in its flow, and holding in itself manifold and still multiplying elements of interest. Increasingly the man is caught by these — like a ship, from which many anchors are cast into the sea. He strives among the struggling, rejoices with the gay, feels the spur of honor, enters the race of acquisition, does some hard and many kindly things by turns; multiplies his engagements, his relationships, his friends, and then — just when after such preparations, life ought to be fully beginning, and opening itself out into a great, restful, sunny plain — lo! the shadows begin to fall, which tell, too surely, that it is drawing fast to a close.

The voice which, soon or late, everyone must hear, is calling for "the little stranger" who was born not long ago, whose first lesson is over, and who is wanted now to enter by the door called death, into another school. And the stranger is not ready. He has thrown out so many anchors and they have taken such a fast hold of the ground that it will be no slight matter to raise them. He is *settled.* He has no pilgrim's staff at hand; and his eye, familiar enough with surrounding things, is not accustomed to the onward and ascending way, cannot so well measure the mountain altitude, or reckon the far distance.

The progress of time has been much swifter than the progress of his thought. Alas! he has made one long mistake. He has "looked at the things which are seen" and forgotten the things which are not seen. And "the things which are seen" are temporal and go with time into extinction; while "those which are not seen are eternal." And so there is hurry, and confusion, and distress in the last hours, and in the going away. Now, all this may be obviated and escaped, thoroughly, if a man will but say, *I am a stranger in the earth: hide not Thy commandments from me.* A. RALEIGH

Vs. 20. *My soul breaketh for the longing that it hath unto Thy judgments at all times.* The Word of God is a code of justice from which there is no appeal.

*This is the Judge which ends the strife*
*Where wit and reason fail;*
*Our Guide through devious paths of life,*
*Our Shield when doubts assail.* WATTS

David had such reverence for the Word and such a desire to know it and to be conformed to it that his longings caused him a sort of heart-break, which he here pleads before God. Longing is the soul of praying, and when the soul longs till it breaks, it cannot be long before the blessing will be granted. C. H. S.

*At all times.* Some prize the Word in adversity, when they have no other comfort to live upon; then they can be content to study the Word to comfort them in their distress; but when they are well at ease, they despise it. But David made use of it *at all times;* in prosperity, to humble him; in adversity, to comfort him; in the one, to keep him from pride; in the other, to keep him from despair; in affliction, the Word was his cordial; in worldly increase, it was his antidote; and so at all times his heart was carried out to the Word either for one necessity or another. T. MANTON

How few are there even among the servants of God who know anything of the intense feeling of devotion here expressed! Oh, that our cold and stubborn hearts were warmed and subdued by Divine grace, that we might be ready to faint by reason of the longing which we had *at all times* for the judgments of our God. How fitful are our best feelings! If today we ascend the mount of communion with God, tomorrow we are in danger of being again entangled with the things of earth. How happy are they whose hearts are *at all times* filled with longings after fellowship with the great and glorious object of their love! J. MORISON

Vs. 21. *Thou hast rebuked the proud that are cursed.* Proud men are cursed men: nobody blesses them, and they soon become a burden to themselves. In itself, pride is a plague and torment. Even if no curse came from the law of God, there seems to be a law of nature that proud men should be unhappy men. This led David to abhor pride; he dreaded the rebuke of God and the curse of the law. The proud sinners of his day were his enemies, and he felt happy that God was in the quarrel as well as he. C. H. S.

If the proud escape here, as sometimes they do, hereafter they shall not; for, *the proud man is an abomination to the Lord;* (Prov. 16:5). *God cannot endure him;* (Ps. 101:5). And what of that? Thou shalt destroy the proud. The very heathens devised the proud giants struck with thunder from heaven. *And if God spared not the angels,* whom He placed in the highest heavens, *but* for their pride *threw them down headlong to the nethermost hell,* how much less shall He spare the proud dust and ashes of the sons of men, but shall cast them from the height of their earthly altitude to the bottom of that infernal dungeon! "Humility makes men angels; pride makes angels devils," as that father said: I may well add, makes devils of men. "Never soul escaped the revenge of pride," never shall escape it. So sure as God is just, pride shall not go unpunished. Down with your proud plumes, O ye glorious peacocks of the world: look upon your black legs, and your snake-like head: be ashamed of your miserable infirmities: else, God will down with them and yourselves in a fearful revenge. J. HALL

Therefore, proud men may be called God's enemies, because as the covetous pull riches from men, so the proud pull honor from God. HENRY SMITH

Proud men endure the curse of never having friends; not in prosperity, because they know nobody; not in adversity, because then nobody knows them. J. WHITECROSS

*Which do err from Thy commandments.* God rebukes pride even when the multitudes pay homage to it, for He sees in it rebellion against His own majesty, and the seeds of yet further rebellions. It is the sum of sin. C. H. S.

Vs. 22. *Remove from me reproach and contempt.* The best way to deal with slander is to pray about it: God will either remove it or remove the sting from it. Our own attempts at clearing ourselves are usually failures; we are like the boy who wished to remove the blot from his copy and by his bungling made it ten times worse. When we suffer from a libel, it is better to pray about it than go to law over it or even to demand an apology from the inventor. O ye who are reproached, take your matters before the highest court and leave them with the Judge of all the earth. C. H. S.

Vs. 23. *But Thy servant did meditate in Thy statutes.* Who were these malignants that they should rob God of His servant's attention or deprive the Lord's chosen of a moment's devout communion? The rabble of princes were not worth five minutes' thought if those five minutes had to be taken from holy meditation. It is very beautiful to see the two sittings: the princes sitting to reproach David, and David sitting with his God and his Bible, answering his traducers by never answering them at all. Those who feed upon the Word grow strong and peaceful and are by God's grace hidden from the strife of tongues. C. H. S.

As husbandmen, when their ground is overflowed by waters, make ditches and water-furrows to carry it away; so, when our minds and thoughts are overwhelmed with trouble, it is good to divert them to some other matter. T. MANTON

It is impossible to live either *Christianly* or *comfortable* without the daily use of Scripture. It is absolutely necessary for our direction in all our ways before we begin them, and when we have ended them, for the warrant of our approbation of them, for resolving of our doubts, and comforting us in our griefs. Without it our conscience is a blind guide and leadeth us in a mist of ignorance, error, and confusion. W. STRUTHER

If the One Hundred Nineteenth Psalm came from the pen of David, as multitudes believe, then I do not wonder that many have connected its composition with his residence in the school of the prophets at Naioth. The calm in which he then found himself and the studies which he then prosecuted might well have led his musings in the direction of that alphabetic code, while there are in it not a few expressions which, to say the least, may have particular reference to the dangers out of which he had so recently escaped and by which he was *still* threatened. Such, for example, are the following: *Princes also did sit and speak against me: but Thy servant did meditate in Thy statutes. The proud have had me greatly in derision: yet have I not declined from Thy law.* W. M. TAYLOR

## EXPOSITION OF VERSES 25 TO 32

In these verses, we shall see the influence of the Divine Word upon a heart which laments its downward tendencies and is filled with mourning because of its deadening surroundings. C. H. S.

Vs. 25. *My soul cleaveth unto the dust.* Nay, we could never have supposed, when we first heard the Psalm of the Good Shepherd, that it could issue from a heart that panteth after God so often and so bitterly; we could never have imagined that it could become so cold, so dry, so dark within a heart which at an earlier period had tasted so much of the power of that which is to come. O sad hours, when the beams of the sun within seem quenched and nothing but a blood-red disc remains! The fervency of the first love is cooled; earthly cares and sins have, as it were, attached a leaden plummet to the wings of the soul which, God knows, would fain soar upwards. J. J. VAN OOSTERZEE

*Quicken Thou me.* And truly, many times are God's children brought to this estate that they have nothing to uphold them but the Word of God; no sense of mercy, no spiritual disposition; but on the contrary, great darkness, horrible fears and terrors. Only they are sustained by looking to the promise of God and kept in some hope that He will restore them to life again, because it is His praise to finish the work which He begins. W. COWPER

*Quicken Thou me.* This phrase occurs nine times, and only in this Psalm. It is of great importance, as it expresses the spiritual change by which a child of Adam becomes a child of God. Its source is God; the instrument by which it is effected is the Word (verse 50). J. G. MURPHY

Vs. 26. *Thou heardest me.* God's goodness is seen in His hearing what we lay open before Him. If great ones let a poor man tell his tale at large, we count it honorable patience; but it is God's glory to hear our wants, our weakness through sin, the invincibleness of our evils, our utter impotency in ourselves even to seek redress. That mode of procedure would lose the favor of man, but it winneth favor with God. The more humbly we confess all our wants, the more confident we may be that God will hear us. *He teacheth the humble,* for the humble scholar will give to his master the honor of that he learneth. P. BAYNE

*Teach me Thy statutes.* Mercy, which pardons transgression, sets us longing for grace, which prevents transgression. We may boldly ask for more when God has given us much; He Who has washed out the past stain will not refuse that which will preserve us from present and future defilement. C. H. S.

Vs. 28. *My soul melteth for heaviness.* He was dissolving away in tears. The solid strength of his constitution was turning to liquid as if molten by the furnace-heat of his afflictions. Heaviness of heart is a killing thing, and when it abounds, it threatens to turn life into a long death, in which a man seems to drop away in a perpetual drip of grief.

Tears are the distillation of the heart; when a man weeps, he wastes away his soul. Some of us know what great heaviness means, for we have been brought under its power again and again, and often have we felt ourselves to be poured out like water and near to being like water spilt upon the ground, never again to be gathered up. There is one good point in this downcast state, for it is better to be melted with grief than to be hardened by impenitence. C. H. S.

*Strengthen Thou me according unto Thy Word.* Note how David records his inner soul-life. In verse 20, he says, "My soul breaketh"; in verse 25, "My soul cleaveth to the dust"; and here, "My soul melteth." Further on, in verse 81, he cries, "My soul fainteth"; in 109, "My soul is continually in my hand"; in 167, "My soul hath kept Thy testimonies"; and lastly, in 175, "Let my soul live." Some people do not even know that they have a soul. What a difference there is between the spiritually living and the spiritually dead. C. H. S.

*Strengthen Thou me.* Gesenius translates this, *Keep me alive.* This prayer for new strength, or life, is an entreaty that the waste of life through tears might be restored by the life-giving Word. F. G. MARCHANT

Vs. 29. *Remove from me the way of lying.* When any of us shall have had a good beginning, we straightway think that we are at the highest; we never bethink us to pray any more to God, when once He hath showed us favor enough to serve our turns; but if we have done any small deed, we by and by lift up ourselves and wonder at our great virtues, thinking straightway that the devil can win no more of us. J. CALVIN

The whole life of sin is a *lie* from beginning to end. The word *lying* occurs eight times in this Pslam. W. S. PLUMER

*And grant me Thy law graciously.* Holy men cannot review their sins without tears nor weep over them without entreating to be saved from further offending. C. H. S.

Vs. 30. *I have chosen the way of truth.* Here you have the working of a gracious soul. This is more than sitting and hearing the Word—having no objection to what you hear. Such hearing is all that can be affirmed of the generality of gospel hearers, except we add that none are more ready to be caught by false and easy ways of salvation, for they assent to all they hear.

The man of God strikes a higher and more spiritual note—he goes into the *choice* of the thing; he chooses the way of truth; and he cannot but choose it; it is the bent of his renewed nature, the effect indeed of all he has been pleading How act we? The way of truth is all that God has revealed concerning His Son Jesus.

The willing heart chooses this way, and all of it; the bitterness of it, the self-denial of it, as well as the comfort of it; a Savior from sin as well as a Savior from hell; a Savior Whose Spirit can lead from prayerlessness to godliness, from idleness upon the Sabbath day, to a holy keeping of that day, from self-seeking to the seeking of Christ, from slack, inconsistent conduct to a careful observance of all the Lord's will. Where God's people meet, there such will delight to be. Oh, for such to abound among us! JOHN STEPHEN

There are three kinds of truth: truth in heart, truth in word, truth in deed (II Kings 20:3; Zech. 8:16; Heb. 10:22). J. E. VAUX

The choosing Christian is likely to be the sticking Christian; when those that are Christians by chance tack about if the wind turn. M. HENRY

Vs. 31. *I have stuck unto Thy testimonies.* It is not a little remarkable that while the Psalmist says (verse 25), "My soul *cleaveth* into the dust," he should say here, *I have cleaved unto Thy testimonies;* for it is the same original word in both verses. The thing is altogether compatible with the experience of the believer. Within there is the body of indwelling sin and within there is the undying principle of Divine grace.

There is the contest between them—"flesh lusteth against the spirit and the spirit against the flesh" (Gal. 5:17), and the believer is constrained to cry out, "O wretched man that I am" (Rom. 7:24). It is the case; and all believers find it so. While the soul is many times felt cleaving to the dust, the spirit strives to cleave unto God's testimonies.

So the believer prays, "Cause that I be not put to shame." And keeping close to Christ, brethren, you shall not be put to shame, world without end. J. STEPHEN

Vs. 32. *I will run the way of Thy commandments.* When a man hath a mind to do a thing, though he be hindered and jostled, he takes it patiently; he goes on and cannot stay to debate the business. A slow motion is easily stopped, whereas a swift one bears down that which opposeth it; so is it when men run and are not tired in the service of God. Last of all, the prize calls for running: "So run that ye may obtain" (Cor. 8:24) T. MANTON

*When Thou shalt enlarge my heart.* Note how the heart has been spoken of up to this point: "whole heart" (2) "uprightness of heart" (7), "hid in mine heart" (11), "enlarge my heart." There are many more allusions further on, and these all go to show what heart-work David's religion was. It is one of the great lacks of our age that heads count for more than hearts and men are far more ready to learn than to love, though they are by no means eager in either direction. C. H. S.

*Enlarged my heart,* or dilated it, namely, with joy. It is obvious to remark the philosophical propriety with which this expression is applied: since the heart is dilated, and the pulse by consequence becomes strong and full, from the exultation of joy as well as of pride. R. MANT

Surely a temple for the great God (such as our hearts should be) should be fair and ample. If we would have God dwell in our hearts and shed abroad His influence, we should make room for God in our souls by a greater largeness of faith and expectation.

The rich man thought of enlarging his barns when his store was increased upon him (Luke 12); so should we stretch out the curtains of Christ's tent and habitation, have larger expectations of God, if we would receive more from Him. The vessels failed before the oil failed. We are not straitened in God but in ourselves; by the scantiness of our thoughts, we do not make room for Him, nor greaten God: "My soul doth magnify the Lord" (Luke 1:46).

Faith doth greaten God. How can we make God greater than He is? As to the declarative being, we can have greater and larger apprehensions of His greatness, goodness, and truth. T. MANTON

## EXPOSITION OF VERSES 33 TO 40

A sense of dependence and a consciousness of extreme need pervade this section, which is all made up of prayer and plea. C. H. S.

SUBJECT: THE LAW OF JEHOVAH TO BE SET BEFORE THE EYES, THE MIND, THE FEET, AND THE HEART. MR. MARCHANT

Vs. 33. *Teach me, O Lord, the way of Thy statutes.* Child-like, blessed words, from the lips of an old, experienced believer, and he a king, and a man inspired of God. Alas for those who will never be taught. C. H. S.

As the Indian pursues his trail with unerring eye and unfaltering step, so, watching for every deviation which might take us astray, we should pursue the way which leadeth unto life. MR. MARCHANT

Verses 33 to 40. In this part, nine times does the Psalmist send up his petition to his God, and six of these he accompanies with a reason for being heard. These petitions are the utterances of a renewed heart; the man of God could not but give utterance to them — such was the new refining process that had taken place upon him. R. GREENHAM

*And I shall keep it unto the end.* The *end* of which David speaks is the end of life, or the fullness of obedience. He trusted in grace to make him faithful to the utmost, never drawing a line and saying to obedience, "Hitherto shalt thou go, but no further."

The end of our keeping the law will come only when we cease to breathe; no good man will think of marking a date and saying, "It is enough, I may now relax my watch and live after the manner of men." As Christ loves us to the end, so must we serve Him to the end. The end of Divine teaching is that we may persevere to the end. C. H. S.

Vs. 34. *Give me understanding.* This is that which we are indebted to Christ for; for "the Son of God is come, and hath given us an understanding" (I John 5:20). M. HENRY

The understanding is the pilot and guide of the whole man; that faculty which sits at the stern of the soul: but as the most expert guide may mistake in the dark, so may the understanding when it wants the light of knowledge. "Without knowledge the mind cannot be good" (Prov. 19:2); nor the life good; nor the external conditions safe (Eph. 4:18). "My people are destroyed for the lack of knowledge" (Hos. 4:6). *From the "Recommendatory Epistle Prefixed to the Westminster Confession and Catechisms"*

*My whole heart.* When the world, pleasure, ambition, pride, desire of riches, unchaste love, desire a part in us, we may remember we have no affections to dispose of without God's leave. It is all His, and it is sacrilege to rob or detain any part from God. Shall I alienate that which is God's to satisfy the world, the flesh, and the devil? T. MANTON

Verse 35. *Make me to go in the path of Thy commandments; for therein do I delight.* The Psalmist does not ask the Lord to do for him what he ought to do for himself: he wishes himself to "go," or tread, in the path of the command. He asks not to be carried while he lies passive; but to be made "to go." Grace does not treat us as stocks and stones, to be dragged by horses or engines, but as creatures endowed with life, reason, will, and active powers, who are willing and able to go of themselves if once made to do so. C. H. S.

We need not only light to know our way, but a heart to walk in it. It will not answer our duty to have a naked notion of truths unless we embrace and pursue them. So, accordingly, we need a double assistance from God; the mind must be enlightened, the will moved and inclined. The work of a Christian lies not in depth of speculation but in the height of practice. T. MANTON

Vs. 36. *And not to covetousness.* This is the inclination of nature, and grace must put a negative upon it. This vice is as injurious as it is common; it is as mean as it is miserable. It is idolatry, and so it dethrones God; it is selfishness, and so it is cruel to all in its power; it is sordid greed, and so it would sell the Lord Himself for pieces of silver.

It is a degrading, grovelling, hardening, deadening sin, which withers everything around it that is lovely and Christlike. He who is covetous is of the race of Judas and will in all probability turn out to be himself a son of perdition. C. H. S.

It is a handmaid of all sins; for there is no sin which a covetous man will not serve for his gain. We should beware of all sins, but specially of mother-sins. W. COWPER

S. Bonaventura, on our Psalm, says *Covetousness* must be hated, shunned, put away: must be hated, because it attacks the life of nature: must be shunned, because it hinders the life of grace: must be put away, because it obstructs the life of glory. Clemens Alexandrinus says that covetousness is the citadel of the vices, and Ambrose says that it is the loss of the soul. T. LEBLANC

Vs. 37. *Turn away mine eyes from beholding vanity.* Sin first entered man's mind by the eye, and it is still a favorite gate for the incoming of Satan's allurements. Sin is vanity; unjust gain is vanity; self-conceit is vanity; and, indeed, all that is not of God comes under the same head. From all this, we must turn away. C. H. S.

It may seem a strange prayer of David to say, *Turn away mine eyes from seeing vanity;* as though God meddled with our looking; or that we had not power in ourselves to cast our eyes upon what objects we list. But is it not that what we delight in, we delight to look upon? and what we love, we love to be seeing? and so to pray to God that our eyes may not see vanity is as much as to pray for grace that we be not in love with vanity. SIR RICHARD BAKER

An ugly object loses much of its deformity when we look often upon it. Sin follows this general law and is to be avoided altogether, even in its contemplation, if we would be safe. A man should be thankful in this world that he has eyelids; and as he can close his eyes, so he should often do it. A. BARNES

He that feareth burning must take heed of playing with fire: he that feareth drowning must keep out of deep waters. He that feareth the plague, must not go into an infected house. Would they avoid sin who present themselves to the opportunities of it? J. CARYL

It is a most dangerous experiment for a child of God to place himself within the sphere of seductive temptations. Every feeling of duty, every recollection of his own weakness, every remembrance of the failure of others, should induce him to hasten to the greatest possible distance from the scene of unnecessary conflict and danger. J. MORISON

Your eyes, which may be floodgates to pour out tears, should not be casements to let in lusts. A careless eye is an index to a graceless heart. Remember, the whole world died by a wound in the eye. The eye of a Christian should be like sunflowers, which are open to no blaze but that of the sun. WILLIAM SECKER

*Quicken Thou me.* A man that sticks fast in a ditch needs no reason to prove he is in, but remedies to pull him out. Your best course will be to propose the case how you may get rid of this unwelcome guest, spiritual sloth. MR. SIMMONS

*Thy way.* By way of emphasis, in opposition to and exaltation of, above, all other ways. There is a fourfold way: 1, *Via mundi,* the way of the world; and that is *spinosa,* thorny. 2. *Via carnis,* the way of the flesh; and that is *insidiosa,* treacherous. 3. *Via Satana,* the way of the devil; and that is *tenebricosa,* darksome. 4. *Via Domini,* the way of God; and that is *gratiosa,* gracious. SIMMONS

Vs. 38. *Stablish Thy Word unto Thy servant.* Christ was angry with His disciples for not remembering the miracle of the loaves when they fell into a like strait again. "Do ye not yet understand, neither remember the five loaves?"

In teaching a child to spell, we are angry, if, when we have showed him a letter once, twice, and a third time, yet when he meets with it again, still he misseth: so, God is angry with us when we have had experience of His Word in this, that, and the other providence, yet still our doubts return upon us. A. BARNES

*Who is devoted to Thy fear.* We shall never be rooted and grounded in our belief unless we daily practice what we profess to believe. Full assurance is the reward of obedience. Answers to prayer are given to those whose hearts answer to the Lord's command. If we are devoted to God's fear, we shall be delivered from all other fear. C. H. S.

Vs. 39. *For Thy judgments are good.* When men rail at God's government of the world, it is our duty and privilege to stand up for Him and openly to declare before Him, "Thy judgments are good"; and we should do the same when they assail the Bible, the Gospel, the law, or the Name of our Lord Jesus Christ. But we must take heed that they can bring no truthful accusation against us or our testimony will be so much wasted breath. C. H. S.

## EXPOSITION OF VERSES 41 TO 48

The eight verses are one continued pleading for the abiding of grace in his soul, and it is supported by such holy arguments as would only suggest themselves to a spirit burning with love to God. C. H. S.

Verses 41 to 48. This whole section consists of petitions and promises. The petitions are two: verses 41, 43. The promises are six. This, among many, is a difference between godly men and others: all men seek good things from God, but the wicked so seek that they give Him nothing back again, nor yet will promise any sort of return. WILLIAM COWPER

Vs. 41. *Let Thy mercies come also unto me, O Lord.* He desires *mercy* as well as teaching, for he was guilty as well as ignorant. He needed much mercy and varied mercy; hence the request is in the plural. C. H. S.

*Even Thy salvation.* This is the sum and crown of all mercies — deliverance from all evil, both now and forever. Here is the first mention of salvation in the Psalm, and it is joined with mercy: "By grace are ye saved." Salvation is styled "Thy salvation," thus ascribing it wholly to the Lord: "He that is our God is the God of salvation." What a mass of mercies are heaped together in the one salvation of our Lord Jesus! It includes the mercies which spare us before our conversion and lead up to it. Then comes calling mercy, regenerating mercy, converting mercy, justifying mercy, pardoning mercy. Nor can we exclude from complete salvation any of those many mercies which are needed to conduct the believer safe to glory. Salvation is an aggregate of mercies incalculable in number, priceless in value, incessant in application, eternal in endurance. To the God of our mercies be glory, world without end. C. H. S.

Vs. 42. *So shall I have wherewith to answer him that reproacheth me.* This is an unanswerable answer. When God, by granting us salvation, gives to our prayers an answer of peace, we are ready at once to answer the objections of the infidel, the quibbles of the skeptical, and the sneers of the contemptuous. C. H. S.

A man of little learning, except that which he has derived from the Bible, may often thus silence the cavils and reproaches of the learned skeptic; a man of simple-hearted, pure piety, with no weapon but the Word of God, may often thus be better armed than if he had all the arguments of the schools at his command. A. BARNES

Hugo Cardinalis observeth that there are three sorts of blasphemers of the godly — the devils, heretics, and slanderers. The devil must be answered by the internal word of humility; heretics by the external word of wisdom; slanderers by the active word of a good life. R. GREENHAM

*For I trust in Thy Word.* If any reproach us for trusting in God, we reply to them with arguments the most conclusive when we show that God has kept His promises, heard our prayers, and supplied our needs. Even the most skeptical are forced to bow before the logic of facts. C. H. S.

Vs. 43. *And take not the word of truth utterly out of my mouth.* He who has once preached the Gospel from his heart is filled with horror at the idea of being put out of the ministry; he will crave to be allowed a little share in the holy testimony and will reckon his dumb Sabbaths to be days of banishment and punishment. C. H. S.

Eloquence itself becomes dumb if the conscience be evil. The birds of heaven come and take the word out of thy mouth, even as they took the seed of the word from off the rock lest it should bring forth fruit. AMBROSE

Some of us know the painful trial of the indulgence of worldly habits and conversation, when a want of liberty of spirit has hindered us from standing up boldly for our God. We may perhaps allege the plea of bashfulness or judicious caution in excuse for silence; which, however, in many instances, we must regard as a self-deceptive covering for the real cause of restraint — the want of apprehension of the mercy of God to the soul. C. BRIDGES

Vs. 44. *So shall I keep Thy law continually forever and ever.* The language of this verse is very emphatic. Perfect obedience will constitute a large proportion of heavenly happiness to all eternity; and the nearer we approach to it on earth, the more we anticipate the felicity of heaven. *Note in Bagster's Comprehensive Bible*

Vs. 45. *I will walk at liberty: for I seek Thy precepts.* Wherever God pardons sin, He subdues it (Mic. 7:19). Then is the condemning power of sin taken away, when the commanding power of it is taken away. If a malefactor be in prison, how shall he know that his prince hath pardoned him? If a jailer come and knock off his chains and fetters and lets him out of prison, then he may know he is pardoned: so, how shall we know God hath pardoned us? If the fetters of sin be broken off, and we walk at liberty in the ways of God, this is a blessed sign we are pardoned. T. WATSON

There is a state, brethren, when we recognize God but do not love God in Christ. It is that state when we admire what is excellent but are not able to perform it. It is a state when the love of good comes to nothing, dying away in a mere desire. That is a state of nature when we are under the Law and not converted to the love of Christ. And then there is another state, when God writes His law upon our hearts by love instead of fear. The one state is this: "I cannot do the things that I would"; the other state is this: "I will walk at liberty, for I seek Thy commandments." F. W. ROBERTSON

He who goes the beaten and right path will have no brambles hit him across the eyes. SAXON PROVERB

Vs. 46. *I will speak of Thy testimonies also before kings."* Men of greatest holiness have been men of greatest boldness.

Latimer was a man of much holiness, counting the darkness and profaneness of those times wherein he lived, and a man of much courage and boldness; witness his presenting to King Henry the Eighth, for a New Year's gift, a New Testament, wrapped up in a napkin, with this posie, or motto, about it, "Whoremongers and adulterers God will judge." T. BROOKS

Vs. 47. *And I will delight myself in Thy commandments.* He who would preach boldly to others must himself *delight* in the practice of what he preacheth. GEO. HORNE

*Thy commandments, which I have loved.* On the word *loved,* the Carmelite quotes two sayings of ancient philosophers which he commends to the acceptance of those who have learnt the truer philosophy of the Gospel. The first is Aristotle's answer to the question of what profit he had derived from philosophy: "I have learnt to do without constraint that which others do from fear of the law." The second is a very similar saying of Aristippus: "If the laws were lost, all of us would live as we do now that they are in force." And for us the whole verse is summed up in the words of a greater Teacher than they: "If a man love Me, he will keep My words" (John 14:23). NEALE AND LITTLEDALE

Vs. 48. *My hands also will I lift up unto Thy commandments.* But now the world is full of mutilated Christians; either they want an ear and cannot hear God's Word or a tongue and cannot speak of it; or if they have both, they want hands and cannot practice it. W. COWPER

Aben Ezra explains (and perhaps rightly), that the metaphor, in this place, is taken from the action of those who receive anyone whom they are glad or proud to see. DANIEL CRESSWELL

## EXPOSITION OF VERSES 49 TO 56

Vs. 49. *Remember the word unto Thy servant.* There is a world of meaning in the word *remember,* as it is addressed to God; it is used in Scripture in the tenderest sense and suits the sorrowing and the depressed. The Psalmist cried, "Lord, remember David, and all his afflictions": Job also prayed that the Lord would appoint him a set time and remember him. In the present instance the prayer is as personal as the "Remember me" of the thief, for its essence lies in the words — "unto Thy servant." It would be all in vain for us if the promise were remembered to all others if it did not come true to ourselves; but there is no fear, for the Lord has never forgotten a single promise to a single believer. C. H. S.

Those that make God's promises their portion may with humble boldness make them their plea. God gave the promise in which the Psalmist hoped, and the hope by which He embraced the promise. M. HENRY

Vs. 50. *This is my comfort in my affliction: for Thy Word hath quickened me.* The worlding clutches his money-bag and says, "This is my comfort"; the spendthrift points to his gayety, and shouts, "This is my comfort"; the drunkard lifts his glass and sings, "This is my comfort"; but the man whose hope comes from God, feels the life-giving power of the Word of the Lord, and he testifies, "This is my comfort." Paul said, "I know Whom I have believed." Comfort is desirable at all times; but comfort in affliction is like a lamp in a dark place. Some are unable to find comfort at such times; but it is not so with believers, for their Savior has said to them, "I will not leave you comfortless." Some have comfort and no affliction; others have affliction and no comfort; but the saints have comfort in their affliction. C. H. S.

*Comfort. Nechamah,* consolation; whence the name of Nehemiah was derived. The word occurs only in Job 6:9.

Tears are the breeders of spiritual joy. When Hannah had wept, she went away and was no more sad. The bee gathers the best honey from the bitterest herbs. Christ made the best wine of water. T. BROOKS

*Thy Word hath quickened me.* Bless God that He has not only written His Word, but sealed it upon thy heart, and made it effectual. Canst thou say it is of divine inspiration because thou has felt it to be of lively operation? Oh, free grace! That God should send out His Word and heal thee; that He should heal thee and not others! That the same Scripture which to them is a dead letter should be to thee a savor of life. T. WATSON

Vs. 51. *The proud have had me greatly in derision.* Men must have strange eyes to be able to see a farce in faith and a comedy in holiness; yet it is sadly the case that men who are short of wit can generally provoke a broad grin by jesting at a saint. Conceited sinners make footballs of godly men. They call it roaring fun to caricature a faithful member of "The Holy Club"; his methods of careful living are the material for their jokes about "the Methodist"; and his hatred of sin sets their tongues a-wagging at long-faced Puritanism and strait-laced hypocrisy. If David was greatly derided, we may not expect to escape the scorn of the ungodly. There are hosts of proud men still upon the face of the earth, and if they find a believer in affliction, they will be mean enough and cruel enough to make jests at his expense. It is the nature of the son of the bondwoman to mock the child of promise. C. H. S.

The saints of God have complained of this in all ages: David of his busy mockers; the abjects jeered him. Job was disdained of those children whose fathers he would have scorned to set with the dogs of his flock (Job 30:1). Joseph was nicknamed a dreamer, Paul a babbler, Christ Himself a Samaritan, and with intent of disgrace a carpenter . . . Michal was barren, yet she hath too many children that scorn the habit and exercises of holiness. There cannot be a greater argument of a foul soul than the deriding of religious services. Worldly hearts can see nothing in those actions but folly and madness; piety hath no relish, but is distasteful to their palates. T. ADAMS

It is a great thing in a soldier to behave well under fire; but it is a greater thing for a soldier of the cross to be unflinching in the day of his trial. It does not hurt the Christian to have the dogs bark at him. W. S. PLUMER

*Yet have I not declined from Thy law.* Their unhallowed mirth will not harm us if we pay no attention to it, even as the moon suffers nothing from the dogs that bay at her. C. H. S.

Vs. 52. *I remember Thy judgments of old,* O Lord; *and have comforted myself.* The grinning of the proud will not trouble us when we remember how the Lord dealt with their predecessors in bygone periods; He destroyed them at the deluge; He confounded them at Babel; He drowned them at the Red Sea; He drove them out of Canaan: He has in all ages bared His arm against the haughty and broken them as potters' vessels. While in our hearts we humbly drink of the mercy of God in quietude, we are not without comfort in seasons of turmoil and derision; for then we resort to God's justice, and remember how He scoffs at the scoffers: "He that sitteth in the heaven doth laugh, the Lord doth have them in derision." C. H. S.

He remembered that at the beginning, Adam, because of transgression of the divine command, was cast out from dwelling in Paradise; and that Cain, condemned by the authority of the divine sentence, paid the price of his parricidal crime; that Enoch, caught up to heaven because of his devotion, escaped the poison of earthly wickedness: that Noah, because of righteousness the victor of the deluge, became the survivor of the human race; that Abraham, because of faith, diffused the seed of his posterity through the whole earth; that Israel, because of the patient bearing of troubles, consecrated a believing people by the sign of his own name; that David himself, because of gentleness, having had regal honor conferred, was preferred to his elder brothers. AMBROSE

Such as have a disease they call *lienteria,* in which the meat comes up as fast as they eat it, and stays not in the stomach, are not nourished by it. If the Word stays not in the memory, it cannot profit. Some can better remember a piece of news than a line of Scripture; their memories are like those ponds where frogs live but fish die. T. WATSON

Vs. 53. *Horror hath taken hold upon me because of the wicked that forsake Thy law.* Truths which were amusement to them caused amazement to him. He was astonished at their wickedness, stunned by their presumption, alarmed by the expectation of their sudden overthrow, amazed by the terror of their certain doom.

Those who are the firmest believers in the eternal punishment of the wicked are the most grieved at their doom. It is no proof of tenderness to shut one's eyes to the awful doom of the ungodly. Compassion is far better shown in trying to save sinners than in trying to make things pleasant all round. Oh, that we were all more distressed as we think of the portion of the ungodly in the lake of fire! The popular plan is to shut your eyes and forget all about it or pretend to doubt it; but this is not the way of the faithful servant of God. C. H. S.

I have had clear views of *eternity;* have seen the blessedness of the *godly,* in some measure; and have longed to share their happy state, as well as been comfortably satisfied that through grace I shall do so.

But, oh, what anguish is raised in my mind, to think of an *eternity* for those who are *Christless,* for those who are mistaken, and who bring their false hopes to the grave with them! The sight was so dreadful I could by no means bear it: my thoughts recoiled, and I said (under a more affecting sense than ever before), "Who can dwell with everlasting burnings?" D. BRAINERD

Oh, who can express what the state of a soul in such circumstances is! All that we can possibly say about it gives but a very feeble, faint representation of it; it is inexpressible and inconceivable; for who knows the power of God's anger?

How dreadful is the state of those that are daily and hourly in danger of this great wrath and infinite misery! But this is the dismal case of every soul in this congregation that has not been born again, however moral and strict, sober and religious, they may otherwise be. Oh, that you would consider it, whether you be young or old!

There is reason to think that there are many in this congregation now hearing this discourse that will actually be the subjects of this very misery to all eternity. We know not who they are, or in what seats they sit, or what thoughts they now have. It may be they are now at ease and hear all these things without much disturbance and are now flattering themselves that they are not the persons, promising themselves that they shall escape. J. EDWARDS

If we knew that there was one person, and but one, in the whole congregation, that was to be the subject of this misery, what an awful thing would it be to think of! If we knew who it was, what an awful sight would it be to see such a person! How might all the rest of the congregation lift up a lamentable and bitter cry over him! But, alas! instead of one, how many is it likely will remember this discourse in hell! J. EDWARDS

*Because of the wicked that forsake Thy law.* David grieved, not because he was himself attacked; but because the law of God was forsaken; and he bewailed the condemnation of those who so did, because they are lost to God. AMBROSE

Vs. 54. *Thy statutes have been my songs in the house of my pilgrimage.* Saints find horror in sin, and harmony in holiness. The wicked shun the law, and the righteous sing of it. C. H. S.

*Songs.*

*Such songs have power to quiet*
*The restless pulse of care,*
*And come like the benediction*
*That follow after prayer.*

*And the night shall be filled with music,*
*And the cares that infest the day*
*Shall fold their tents like the Arabs,*
*And as silently steal away.*

HENRY WADSWORTH LONGFELLOW

*Songs in the house of my pilgrimage.* Would a prisoner exult at the proclamation of deliverance, and is the redeemed sinner to walk forth from his bondage, unmoved, unaffected, without gratitude or joy? WM. JAY

Sometimes our grief is so great that we cannot sing; then let us pray: sometimes our deliverance so joyful that we must break out in thanksgiving; then let us sing. WM. COWPER

Vs. 55. *I have remembered Thy Name in the night,* and therefore I *have kept Thy law* all day. M. HENRY

*I have remembered Thy Name, O Lord, in the night.* Again this argueth his *fervency* in religion: for as elsewhere he protests that he loved the Word more than his appointed food; so here he protests that he gave up his night's rest that he might meditate in the Word. But now, so far is zeal decayed in professors, that they will not forego their superfluities, far less their needful refreshment, for love of the Word of God. WM. COWPER

*In the night.* First, that is, *continually,* because he remembered God in the day also. Secondly, *sincerely,* because he avoided the applause of men. Thirdly, *cheerfully,* because the heaviness of natural sleep could not overcome him.

All these show that he was *intensely* given to the Word; as we see men of the world will take some part of the night for their delights. And in that he did keep God's testimonies in the night, he showeth that he was the same in secret that he was in the light; whereby he condemned all those that will cover their wickedness with the dark. Let us examine ourselves whether we have broken our sleeps to call upon God, as we have to fulfill our pleasures. R. GREENHAM

Pastor Harms, of Hermansburg, used to preach and pray and instruct his people for nine hours on the Sabbath. And then when his mind was utterly exhausted, and his whole body was thrilling with pain, and he seemed almost dying for the want of rest, he could get no sleep. But he used to say that he loved to lie awake all night in the silence and darkness and think of Jesus. The night put away everything else from his thoughts and left his heart free to commune with the One Whom his soul most devoutly loved and Who visited and comforted His weary disciple in the night watches. D. MARCH

*And have kept Thy law.* If we have no memory for the Name of Jehovah, we are not likely to remember His commandments: if we do not think of Him secretly, we shall not obey Him openly. C. H. S.

Vs. 56. *This I had, because I kept Thy precepts.* The Rabbins have an analogous saying, *The reward of a precept is a precept;* or, *A precept draws a precept;* the meaning of which is, that he who keeps one precept, to him God grants, as if by way of reward, the ability to keep another and more difficult precept. The contrary to this is that other saying of the Rabbins, that *the reward of a sin is a sin;* or *transgression draws transgression.* SIMON DE MUIS

## EXPOSITION OF VERSES 57 TO 64

In this section, the Psalmist seems to take firm hold upon God Himself; appropriating Him (57), crying out for Him (58), returning to Him (59), solacing himself in Him (61-62), associating with His people (63), and sighing for personal experience of His goodness (64). C. H. S.

Vs. 57. *Thou art my portion, O Lord.* A broken sentence. The translators have mended it by insertions, but perhaps it had been better to have left it alone, and then it would have appeared as an exclamation: *My portion, O Lord!* The poet is lost in wonder while he sees that the great and glorious God is all his own! Like the Levites, he took God to be his portion and left other matters to those who coveted them. C. H. S.

The sincerity of this claim may be gathered, because he speaks by way of address to God. He doth not say barely, "He is my portion;" but challengeth God to His face: *"Thou art my portion, O Lord."* Elsewhere it is said: "The Lord is my portion, saith my soul" (Lam. 3:24). There he doth not speak it by way of address to God, but he adds, "saith my soul"; but here to God Himself, Who knows the secrets of the heart.

To speak thus of God to God argues our sincerity, when to God's face we avow our trust and choice; as Peter, "Lord, Thou knowest all things; Thou knowest that I love Thee" (John 21:17). T. MANTON

O sir, if Satan should come to thee with an apple, as once he did to Eve, tell him that "the Lord is your portion"; or with a grape, as once he did to Noah, tell him that "the Lord is your portion"; or with a change of raiment, as once he did to Gehazi, tell him that "the Lord is your portion"; or with a wedge of gold, as once he did to Achan, tell him that "the Lord is your portion"; or with a bag of money, as once he did to Judas, tell him that "the Lord is your portion"; or with a crown, a kingdom, as once he did to Moses, tell him that "the Lord is your portion." T. BROOKS

If God be yours, all His attributes are yours; all His creatures, all His works of providence, shall do you good, as you have need of them. He is an eternal, full, satisfactory portion. He is an ever-living, ever-loving, ever-present Friend; and without Him you are a cursed creature in every condition, and all things will work against you. J. MASON

If there was a moment in the life of David in which one might feel inclined to envy him, it would not be in that flush of youthful victory when Goliath lay prostrate at his feet, nor in that hour of even greater triumph, when the damsels of Israel sang his praise in the dance, saying, "Saul hath slain his thousands, and David his ten thousands"; it would not be on that royal day, when his undisputed claim to the throne of Israel was acknowledged on every side and by every tribe; but it would be in that moment when, with a loving and trustful heart, he looked up to God and said, *Thou art my portion.* B. BOUCHIER

Ss. 58. *Be merciful unto me according to Thy Word.* Here we have his "Be merciful unto me" rising with as much intensity of humble pleading as if he still remained among the most trembling of penitents. The confidence of faith makes us bold in prayer, but it never teaches us to live without prayer or justifies us in being other than humble beggars at mercy's gate. C. H. S.

All comfort must be built upon a Scripture promise, else it is presumption, not true comfort. The promises are *pabulum fidei, et anima fidei,* the food of faith and the soul of faith. As faith is the life of a Christian, so the promises are the life of faith: faith is a dead faith if it hath no promise to quicken it. As the promises are of no use without faith to apply them, so faith is of no use without a promise to lay hold on. EDMUND CALAMY

Vs. 59. *I thought on my ways, and turned my feet unto Thy testimonies.* Action without thought is folly, and thought without action is sloth: to think carefully and then to act promptly is a happy combination. If we can get our feet right as to holy walking, we shall soon get our hearts right as to happy living. C. H. S.

The Hebrew word that is here used for thinking signifies to think on a man's ways accurately, advisedly, seriously, studiously, curiously. This holy man of God thought exactly and curiously on all his purposes and practices, on all his doings and sayings, on all his words and works, and finding too many of them to be short of the rule, yea, to be against the rule, he turned his feet to God's testimonies; having found out his errors, upon a diligent search, a strict scrutiny, he turned over a new leaf and framed his course more exactly by rule.

O Christians! you must look as well to your spiritual wants as to your spiritual enjoyments; you must look as well to your layings out as to your layings up; you must look as well forward to what you should be as backward to what you are. Certainly that Christian will never be eminent in holiness that hath eyes to behold a little holiness and never an eye to see his further want of holiness. T. BROOKS

Poisons may be made medicinable. Let the thoughts of old sins stir up a commotion of anger and hatred. We feel shiverings in our spirits, and a motion in our blood, at the very thought of a bitter potion we have formerly taken. Why may we not do that spiritually, which the very frame and constitution of our bodies doth naturally, upon the calling a loathsome thing to mind? S. CHARNOCK

*And turned my feet unto Thy testimonies.* Mentioning this passage, Philip Henry observed that the great turn to be made in heart and life is from all other things to the Word of God. Conversion turns us to the Word of God, as our touchstone to examine ourselves, our state, our ways, spirits, doctrines, worships, customs; as our glass, to dress by (James 1); as our rule to walk and work by (Gala. 6:16); as our water to wash us (Psalm 119:9); as our fire to warm us (Luke 24); as our food to nourish us (Job 23:12); as our sword to fight with (Eph. 6); as our counsellor in all our doubts (Ps. 119:24); as our cordial, to comfort us; as our heritage to enrich us.

No itinerary to the heavenly city is simpler or fuller than the ready answer made by an English prelate to a scoffer who asked him the way to heaven, "First turn to the right, and keep straight on." NEALE AND LITTLEDALE

Vs. 60. *I made haste, and delayed not.* When anyone is lawfully called either to the study of theology or to the teaching it in the church, he ought not to hesitate, as Moses, or turn away, as Jonah; but, leaving all things, he should obey God, Who calls him; as David says, *I made haste, and delayed not.* (Matt. 4:20; Luke 9:6) SOLOMON GESNER

Faith reasons not with God, asketh no *quids,* no *quares,* no *quomodos,* no whats, no hows, no wherefores: it moveth no questions. It meekly yields assent, and humbly says *Amen* to every Word of God. This is the faith of which our Savior wondered, in the centurion's story. R. CLERKE

Take heed of delays and proscrastination, of putting it off from day to day, by saying there will be time enough hereafter; it will be time enough for me to look after heaven when I have got enough of the world; if I do it in the last year of my life, in the last month of the last year, in the last week of the last month, it will serve.

Oh, take heed of delays; this putting off repentance hath ruined thousands of souls; shun that pit into which many have fallen; shun that rock upon which many have suffered shipwreck; say with David, *I made haste, and delayed not to keep Thy commandments.* JAMES NALTON

Here is the misery; God always comes unseasonably to a carnal heart. It was the devil that said, "Art thou come hither to torment us before the time?" (Matt. 8:29). Good things are a torment to a carnal heart; and they always come out of time. Certainly that is the best time when the Word is pressed upon thy heart with evidence, light, and power, and when God treats with thee about thine eternal peace. T. MANTON

*Delayed. Hithmahmah,* the word used of Lot's lingering, in Gen. 19:16. WM. KAY

Delay in the Lord's errands is next to disobedience, and generally springs out of it, or issues in it. "God commanded me to make haste" (II Chron, 35:21). Let us see to it that we say, *"I made haste, and delayed not to keep Thy commandments.* FRANCES HAVERGAL

Avoid all delay in the performance of this great work of believing in Christ. Until we have performed it, we continue under the power of sin and Satan and under the wrath of God; and there is nothing between hell and us besides the breath of our nostrils.

It is dangerous for Lot to linger in Sodom lest fire and brimstone come down from heaven upon him. The manslayer must fly with all haste to the city of refuge, lest the avenger of blood pursue him while his heart is hot and slay him. We should make haste and not delay to keep God's commandments. W. MARSHALL

Vs. 61. *The bands of the wicked have robbed me.* Aforetime they derided him, and now they have defrauded him. Ungodly men grow worse, and become more and more daring, so that they go from ridicule to robbery. Much of this bold opposition arose from their being banded together: men will dare to do in company what they durst not have thought of alone. David's enemies did their utmost: first the serpents hissed, and then they stung. Since words availed not, the wicked fell to blows. How much the ungodly have plundered the saints in all ages, and how often have righteous borne gladly the spoiling of their gods. C. H. S.

Then said Christian to his fellow, "Now I call to remembrance that which was told me of a thing that happened to a good man hereabout. The name of the man was *Little Faith,* but a good man, and he dwelt in the town of *Sincere.*

"The thing was this: at the entering in of this passage there comes down from *Broadway-gate* a lane called *Dead-man's-lane;* so called because of the murders that are commonly done there. And this *Little Faith,* going on pilgrimage, as we do now, chanced to sit down there and slept.

"Now there happened, at that time, to come down that lane from *Broadway-gate* three sturdy rogues, and their names were *Faint-heart, Mistrust,* and *Guilt* (three brothers), and they, espying *Little Faith,* where he was, came galloping up with speed.

"Now the good man was just awaked from his sleep and was getting up to go on his journey. So they came all up to him, and with threatening language bid him *stand.* At this, *Little Faith* looked as white as a clout, and had neither power to *fight* nor *flie.* Then said *Faint-heart,* 'Deliver thy purse'; and he, making no haste to do it (for he was loth to lose his money). *Mistrust* ran up to him, and thrusting his hand into his pocket, pulled out thence a bag of silver. Then he cried out, '*Thieves! Thieves!*' With that, *Guilt*, with a great club that was in his hand, struck *Little Faith* on the head, and with that blow felled him flat to the ground, where he lay bleeding as one that would bleed to death.

"The place where his jewels were they never ransacked, so those he kept still; but as I was told, the good man was much afflicted for his loss. For the thieves got most of his spending money. That which they got not (as I said) were jewels, also he had a little odd money left, but scarce enough to bring him to his journey's end; nay (if I was not misinformed), he was forced to beg as he went, to keep himself alive (for his jewels he might not sell). But beg, and do what he could he went (as we say) with many a hungry belly, the most part of the rest of the way." JOHN BUNYAN

*But I have not forgotten Thy law.* This was well. Neither his sense of injustice, nor his sorrow at his losses, nor his attempts at defense diverted him from the ways of God. He would not do wrong to prevent the suffering of wrong nor do ill to avenge ill.

He could not be either bribed or bullied into sin. The cordon of the ungodly could not keep God from him, nor him from God: this was because God was his portion, and none could deprive him of it by force or fraud. That is true grace which can endure the test: some are barely gracious among the circle of their friends, but this man was holy amid a ring of foes. C. H. S.

Vs. 62. *At midnight I will rise to give thanks unto Thee because of Thy righteous judgments.* The Psalmist observed posture; he did not lie in bed and praise. There is not much in the position of the body, but there is something, and that something is to be observed whenever it is helpful to devotion and expressive of our diligence or humility. C. H. S.

That which hindered the sleep of ordinary men is either the cares of this world, the impatient resentment of injuries, or the sting of an evil conscience: these keep others waking, but David was awaked by a desire to praise God. T. MANTON

His sincerity, seen in his secrecy. David would profess his faith in God when he had no witness by him; *at midnight* when there was no hazard of ostentation. It was a secret cheerfulness and delighting in God: when alone he could have no respect to the applause of men, but only to approve himself to God, Who seeth in secret. See Christ's direction: "But thou, when thou prayest, enter into thy closet, and when thou hast shut thy door, pray to thy Father which is in secret; and thy Father which seeth in secret shall reward thee openly (Matt. 6:6). Note also Christ's own practice: "Rising up a great while before day, He went out, and departed into a solitary place, and there prayed" (Mark 1:35): before day He went into a desert to pray; both time and place implied secrecy.

The great reverence to be used in secret adoration. David did not only raise up his spirits to praise God, but rise up out of his bed, to bow the knee to Him. Secret duties should be performed with solemnity, not slubbered over. Praise, a special act of adoration, requireth the worship of body and soul. T. MANTON

Vs. 63. *I am a companion of all them that fear Thee.* The last verse said, "I will," and this says, "I am." We can hardly hope to be right in the future unless we are right now. C. H. S.

These two go together — the love of God and the love of His saints. Godly David, when Jonathan was dead, made diligent inquisition: Is there none of Jonathan's posterity to whom I may show kindness for Jonathan's sake? And at length he found a silly, lame Mephibosheth. So if we enquire diligently, "Is there none upon earth to whom I may show kindness for Christ's sake Who is in heaven?" we shall ever find some, to whom whatsoever we do shall be accepted as done to Himself. WM. COWPER

How well would it be for the world if the great potentates of the earth would thus think, speak, and do: *I am a companion of all them that fear Thee.* Self-love reigneth in most men: we love the rich and despise the poor, and so have the faith of our Lord Jesus Christ with respect of persons (James 2:1): therefore, this universality is to be regarded. T. MANTON

Shun the company that shuns God, and keep the company that God keeps. Look on the society of the carnal or profane as infectious, but reckon serious, praying persons the excellent ones of the earth. Such will serve to quicken you when dead and warm you when cold. Make the liveliest of God's people your greatest intimates, and see their love and likeness to Christ be the great motive of your love to them, more than their love or likeness to you. J. WILSON

*And of them that keep Thy precepts.* David was known to be on the godly side, he was ever of the Puritanic party: the men of Belial hated him for this and no doubt despised him for keeping such unfashionable company as that of humble men and women who are strait-laced and religious. C. H. S.

Vs. 64. *The earth, O Lord, is full of Thy mercy.* It is mercy that takes us out of the womb, feeds us in the days of our pilgrimage, furnishes us with spiritual provisions, closes our eyes in peace, and translates us to a secure restingplace. it is the first petitioner's suit, and the first believer's article, the contemplation of Enoch, the confidence of Abraham, the burden of the Prophetic Songs, the glory of all the Apostles, the plea of the penitent, the ecstacies of the reconciled, the believer's hosannah, the angel's hallelujah.

Ordinances, oracles, altars, pulpits, the gates of the grave and the gates of heaven, do all depend upon mercy. It is the loadstar of the wandering, the ransom of the captive, the antidote of the tempted, the prophet of the living, and the effectual comfort of the dying: there would not be one regenerate saint upon earth, nor one glorified saint in heaven, if it were not for mercy. G. S. BOWES

## EXPOSITION OF VERSES 65 TO 72

In this ninth section, the verses all begin with the letter *Teth.* They are the witness of experience, testifying to the goodness of God, the graciousness of His dealings, and the preciousness of His Word. Especially the Psalmist proclaims the excellent uses of adversity and the goodness of God in afflicting him. The sixty-fifth verse is the text of the entire octave. C. H. S.

Vs. 65. *Thou hast dealt well with Thy servant, O Lord, according unto Thy Word.* It is something that God has *dealt* at all with such insignificant and undeserving beings as we are, and it is far more that He has dealt *well* with us, and so well, so wondrously well. C. H. S.

Here is a difference between faith and an accusing conscience: the accusing conscience is afraid to ask more, because it hath abused the former mercies: but faith, assuring us that all God's benefits are tokens of His love bestowed on us according to His Word, is bold to ask for more. R. GREENHAM

"No doubt," said the late Rev. J. Brown, of Haddington, Scotland, "I have met with trials as well as others; yet so kind has God been to me, that I think if He were to give me as many years as I have already lived in the world, I should not desire one single circumstance in my lot changed, except that I wish I had less sin. It might be written on my coffin, 'Here lies one of the cares of Providence, who early wanted both father and mother, and yet never missed them.'" ARVINE'S ANECDOTES

Vs. 66. *Teach me good judgment and knowledge.* Good judgment is the form of goodness which the godly man most needs and most desires, and it is one which the Lord is most ready to bestow. A sight of our errors and a sense of our ignorance should make us teachable.

The Holy Ghost alone can fill us with light and set the understanding upon a proper balance: let us ardently long for His teachings, since it is most desirable. that we should be no longer mere children in knowledge and understanding. C. H. S.

*For I have believed Thy commandments.* Certainly there is a faith in the commandments as well as in the promises. We must believe that God is their Author and that they are the expressions of His commanding and legislative will, which we are bound to obey. Faith must discern the sovereignty and goodness of the Law-maker and believe that His commands are holy, just, and good; it must also teach us that God loves those who keep His law and is angry with those who transgress and that He will see to it that His law is vindicated at the last great day. T. MANTON

Vs. 67. *Before I was afflicted I went astray.* Why is it a little ease works in us so much disease? Can we never rest without rusting? Never be filled without waxing fat? Never rise as to one world without going down as to another! What weak creatures we are to be unable to bear a little pleasure! What base hearts are those which turn the abundance of God's goodness into an occasion for sin. C. H. S.

Not that he wilfully, wickedly, maliciously, and through contempt, departed from his God; this he denies (Ps. 18:21); but through the weakness of the flesh, the prevalence of corruption, and the force of temptation, and very much through a careless, heedless, and negligent frame of spirit, he got out of the right way and wandered from it before he was well aware. The word is used of erring through ignorance (Lev. 5:18).

This was in his time of prosperity, when though he might not, like Jeshurun, wax fat and kick, and forsake and lightly esteem the Rock of his salvation; or fall into temptations and hurtful lusts, and err from the faith, and be pierced with many sorrows; yet he might become inattentive to the duties of religion, and be negligent of them, which is a common case. J. GILL

Prosperity is a more refined and severe test of character than adversity, as one hour of summer sunshine produces greater corruption than the longest winter day. ELIZA COOK

As men clip the feathers of fowls, when they begin to fly too high or too far; even so doth God diminish our riches, etc., that we should not pass our bounds and glory too much of such gifts. OTTO WERMUELLERUS

There are multitudes whom God has afflicted with natural blindness that they might gain spiritual sight; and those who under bodily infirmities and diseases of divers sorts have pined and wasted away this earthly life, gladly laying hold on glory, honor, and immortality instead. W. G. LEWIS

By affliction, God separates the sin which He hates from the soul which He loves. J. MASON

Vs. 68. *Thou art good, and doest good.* All the glory we can give to God is to reflect His own glory upon Himself. We can say no more good of God than God is and does. We believe in His goodness and so honor Him by our faith; we admire that goodness, and so glorify Him by our love; we declare that goodness, and so magnify Him by our testimony.

Vs. 69. *The proud have forged a lie against me.* They first derided him (51), then defrauded him (61), and now they have defamed him. To injure his character, they resorted to falsehood, for they could find nothing against him if they spoke the truth. They forged a lie as a blacksmith beats out a weapon of iron, or they counterfeited the truth as men forge false coin.

Slander is a cheap and handy weapon if the object is the destruction of a gracious reputation; and when many proud ones concoct, exaggerate, and spread abroad a malicious falsehood, they generally succeed in wounding their victim, and it is no fault of theirs if they do not kill him outright.

Oh, the venom which lies under the tongue of a liar! Many a happy life has been embittered by it, and many a good repute has been poisoned as with the deadliest drug. It is painful to the last degree to hear unscrupulous men hammering away at the devil's anvil forging a new calumny; the only help against it is the sweet promise, "No weapon that is formed against thee shall prosper, and every tongue that riseth against thee in judgment thou shalt condemn." C. H. S.

Vatablus translates it, *concinnarunt mendacia.* So Tremellius: *They have trimmed up lies.* As Satan can transform himself into an angel of light, so he can trim up his lies under coverings of truth, to make them the more plausible unto men. And indeed this is no small temptation, when lies made against the godly are trimmed up with the shadows of truth, and wicked men cover their unrighteous dealings with appearances of righteousness.

Thus, not only are the godly unjustly persecuted, but simple ones are made to believe that they have most justly deserved it. In this case, the godly are to to sustain themselves by the testimony of a good conscience. W. COWPER

The metaphor may be like the Greek from sewing or patching up: or, from *smearing,* or *daubing* (Delitzsch, Moll, etc.) a wall, so as to hide the real substance. The Psalmist remains true to God despite the falsehoods with which the proud smear and hide his true fidelity. THE SPEAKER'S COMMENTARY

*But I will keep Thy precepts with my whole heart.* If we try to answer lies by our words, we may be beaten in the battle; but a holy life is an unanswerable refutation of all calumnies. Spite is balked if we persevere in holiness despite all opposition. C. H. S.

Vs. 70. *Their heart is as fat as grease.* A greasy heart is something horrible; it is a fatness which makes a man fatuous, a fatty degeneration of the heart which leads to feebleness and death. The fat in such men is killing the life in them. Dryden wrote:

*O souls! In whom no heavenly fire is found,*
*Fat minds and ever groveling on the ground.*

C. H. S.

The word *tagash* occurs nowhere else in Scriptures, but with the Chaldees *tugesh* signifies *to fatten, to make fat;* also *to make stupid and doltish,* because such the fat oftimes are.

For this reason the proud, who are mentioned in the preceding verse, are described by their fixed resolve in evil, because they are almost insensible; as is to be seen in pigs, who pricked through the skin with a bodkin, and that slowly, as long as the bodkin only touches the fat, do not feel the prick until it reaches to the flesh. Thus the proud, whose great prosperity is elsewhere likened to fatness, have a heart totally insusceptible, which is insensible to the severe reproofs of the divine Word. M. GEIER

As a full stomach loatheth meat and cannot digest it; so wicked men hate the Word; it will not go down with them; it will not gratify their lusts. WM. FENNER

Is not the Psalmist contrasting those who lead an animal, self-indulgent, vicious life, by which body and mind are incapacitated for their proper uses, and those who can *run* in the way of God's commandments, *delight* to do His will, and *meditate* on His precepts? Sloth, fatness, and stupidity, *versus* activity, firm muscles, and mental vigor. Body *versus* mind. Man become as a beast *versus* man retaining the image of God. SIR JAMES RISDON-BENNETT

*But I delight in Thy law.* When law becomes delight, obedience is bliss. Holiness in the heart causes the soul to eat the fat of the land. To have the law for our delight will breed in our hearts the very opposite of the effects of pride: deadness, sensuality and obstinacy will be cured, and we shall become teachable, sensitive, and spiritual. How careful should we be to live under the influence of the divine law that we fall not under the law of sin and death! C. H. S.

Vs. 71. *It is good for me that I have been afflicted.* Our worst is better for us than the sinner's best. C. H. S.

I am mended by my sickness, enriched by my poverty, and strengthened by my weakness, and with S. Bernard desire, *Irascaris mihi Domine,* O Lord, be angry with me.

What fools are we, then, to frown upon our afflictions! These, how crabbed soever, are our best friends. They are not indeed for our pleasure; they are for our profit; their issue makes them worthy of a welcome. What do we care how bitter that potion be that brings health? ABRAHAM WRIGHT

A rare sight it is indeed to see a man coming out of a bed of languishing, or any other furnace of affliction, more like to angels in purity, more like to Christ Who was holy, harmless, undefiled, and separate from sinners; more like unto God Himself, being more exactly righteous in all his ways and more exemplarily holy in all manner of conversation. NATHANAEL VINCENT

As waters are purest when they are in motion, so saints are generally holiest when in affliction. It is well known that by the greatest affliction the Lord has sealed the sweetest instruction. The purest gold is the most pliable. That is the best blade which bends well without retaining its crooked figure. WILLIAM SECKER

In Miss E. J. Whately's very interesting Life of her Father, the celebrated Archbishop of Dublin, a fact is recorded, as told by Dr. Whately, with reference to the introduction of the larchtree into England.

When the plants were first brought, the gardener, hearing that they came from the south of Europe and taking it for granted that they would require warmth, forgetting that they might grow near the snow-line, put them into a hothouse. Day by day they withered, until the gardener in disgust threw them on a dung-heap outside; there they began to revive and bud, and at last grew into trees. They needed the cold.

The great husbandman often saves his plants by throwing them out into the cold. The nipping frosts of trial and affliction are ofttimes needed, if God's larches are to grow. J. W. BARDSLEY

*That I might learn Thy statutes.* To be larded by prosperity is not good for the proud; but for the truth to be learned by adversity is good for the humble. Very little is to be learned without affliction. If we would be scholars, we must be sufferers. God's commands are best read by eyes wet with tears. C. H. S.

"I had never known," said Martin Luther's wife, "what such and such things meant, in such and such Psalms, such complaints and workings of spirit; I had never understood the practice of Christian duties, had not God brought me under some affliction."

It is very true that God's rod is as the schoolmaster's pointer to the child, pointing out the letter, that he may the better notice of it; thus He pointeth out to us many good lessons which we should never otherwise have learned. J. SPENCER

The Christian has reason to thank God that things have not been accommodated to his wishes. When the mist of tears was in his eyes, he looked into the Word of God and saw magnificent things.

When Jonah came up from the depths of ocean, he showed that he had learned the statutes of God. One could not go too deep to get such knowledge as he obtained. Nothing now could hinder him from going to Nineveh. It is just the same as though he had brought up from the deep an army of twelve legions of the most formidable troops. The Word of God, grasped by faith, was all this to him, and more. He still, however, needed further affliction; for there were some statutes not yet learned. Some gourds were to wither. He was to descend into a further vale of humiliation.

Even the profoundest affliction does not, perhaps, teach us everything; a mistake we sometimes make. But why should we compel God to use harsh measures with us? Why not sit at the feet of Jesus and learn quietly what we need to learn? GEO. BOWEN

Vs. 72. *The Law of Thy mouth is better unto me.* The same lips which spoke us into existence have spoken the law by which we are to govern that existence. C. H. S.

The Scripture is the library of the Holy Ghost. The Scripture contains in it the *credenda,* "the things which we are to believe," and the *agenda,* "the things which we are to practice." The Scripture is the compass by which the rudder of our will is to be steered; it is the field in which Christ, the Pearl of price, is hid. The Scripture is both the breeder and feeder of grace. How is the convert born, but by "the Word of truth"? (Jas. 1:18). How doth he grow, but by "the sincere milk of the Word"? (I Pet. 2:2). T. WATSON

A covetous miser could not take such delight in his bags, nor a young heir in a large inheritance, as holy David did in God's Word. O. HEYWOOD

The Word of God must be nearer to us than our friends, dearer to us than our lives, sweeter to us than our liberty, and pleasanter to us than all earthly comforts. J. MASON

In reading a part of the One Hundred and Nineteenth Psalm to Miss Westbrook, who died, she said, "Stop, sir, I never said so much to you before — I never could; but now I *can* say, 'The word of Thy mouth, is dearer to me, than *thousands* of gold and silver.' What can gold and silver do for me now?" GEO. REDFORD

*Is better unto me than thousands of gold and silver.* If a poor man had said this, the world's witlings would have hinted that the grapes are sour, and that men who have no wealth are the first to despise it; but this is the verdict of a man who owned his thousands, and could judge by actual experience of the value of money and the value of truth. C. H. S.

See how this portion of the Psalm is flavored with goodness. God's dealings are good (65), holy judgment is good (66), affliction is good (67), God is good (68), and here the law is not only good, but better than the best of treasure. Lord, make us good, through Thy good Word. C. H. S.

You that are scholars, remember Cranmer and Ridley; the former learned the New Testament by heart in his journey to Rome, the latter in Pembroke-hall walks in Cambridge. Remember what is said of Thomas-à-Kempis — that he found rest nowhere *nisi in angulo, cum libello,* but in a corner with this Book in his hand. And what is said of Beza — that when he was above fourscore years old he could say perfectly by heart any Greek chapter in Paul's Epistles.

Let all men consider that hyperbolical speech of Luther, that he would not live in Paradise without the Word; and with it he could live well enough in hell. This speech of Luther must be understood *cum grano salis.* EDMUND CALAMY

## EXPOSITION OF VERSES 73 TO 80

Its subject would seem to be personal experience and its attractive influence upon others. The prophet is in deep sorrow but looks to be delivered and made a blessing. C. H. S.

Vs. 73-80. The usual account of this section, as given by the mediaeval theologians, is that it is the prayer of man to be restored to his state of original innocence and wisdom by being conformed to the image of Christ.

And this squares with the obvious meaning, which is partly a petition for divine grace and partly and assertion that the example of piety and resignation in trouble is attractive enough to draw men's hearts on towards God, a truth set forth at once by the Passion and by the lives of all those saints who have tried to follow it. NEAL AND LITTLEDALE

Vs. 73. *Give me understanding, that I may learn Thy commandments.* A man without a mind is an idiot, the mere mockery of a man; and a mind without grace is wicked, the sad perversion of a mind. Fools can sin; but only those whc are taught of God can be holy. C. H. S.

The truth is, it is God only that can soundly enlighten our consciences; and therefore let us pray unto Him to do it. All our studying, and hearing, and reading, and conferring will never be able to do it; it is only in the power of Him who made us to do it. He who made our consciences, He only can give them this heavenly light of true knowledge and right understanding; and therefore let us seek earnestly to Him for it. WILLIAM FENNER

Vs. 74. *They that fear Thee will be glad when they see me; because I have hoped in Thy Word.* A hopeful man is a God-send when things are declining or in danger. There are professors whose presence scatters sadness, and the godly quietly steal out of their company: may this never be the case with us. C. H. S.

Vs. 75. *I know,* O Lord, *that Thy judgments are right.* He who would learn most must be thankful for what he already knows. C. H. S.

What, David? what do you know? "I know, O Lord, that Thy judgments are right, and that Thou in faithfulness hast afflicted me."

Fond as I may yet be of other speculations, I would rather, much rather, possess the knowledge of this man in this text than have the largest acquaintance with the whole circle of the sciences, as it is proudly called. J. MARTIN

For in the Psalmist's creed there was no such thing as chance. God ordered all that befell him, and he loved to think so. F. BOURDILLON

*Thou in faithfulness hast afflicted me.* Affliction and trouble are not only consistent with God's love plighted in the covenant of grace; but they are parts and branches of the new-covenant administration. God is not only faithful notwithstanding afflictions, but faithful in sending them. There is a difference between these two; the one is like an exception to the rule, the other makes it a part of the rule. God cannot be faithful without doing all things that tend to our good and eternal welfare. T. MANTON

*Yet, Lord in memory's fondest place*
*I shrine those seasons sad,*
*When looking up, I saw Thy face*
*In kind austereness clad.*

*I would not miss one sigh or tear,*
*Heart pang, or throbbing brow;*
*Sweet was the chastisement severe,*
*And sweet its memory now.*

*Yes! let the fragrant scars abide,*
*Love-tokens in Thy stead,*
*Faint shadows of the spear-pierced side*
*And thorn-encompassed Head.*

*And such Thy tender force be still,*
*When self would swerve or stray,*
*Shaping to truth the froward will*
*Along Thy narrow way.*

J. H. NEWMAN

Vs. 76. *Let, I pray Thee, Thy merciful kindness be for my comfort.* In the former verse, he acknowledged that the Lord had afflicted him; now in this he prayeth the Lord to comfort him. This is strange that a man should seek comfort at the same hand that strikes him; it is the work of faith; nature will never teach us to do it. "Come, and let us return unto the Lord; for He hath spoiled, and He will heal us: He hath wounded, and He will bind us up." W. COWPER

Vs. 77. *Let Thy tender mercies come unto me, that I may live.* Notice, again, the happy combination of the words of our English version. Was there ever a sweeter sound than this — "tender mercies?" He who has been grievously afflicted and yet tenderly succored is the only man who knows the meaning of such choice language. C. H. S.

Alas, many seek the first mercy, of remission; and the second mercy, of consolation in trouble, who are altogether careless of the third mercy, to live well. W. COWPER

Sin is the great hindrance of mercy. We ourselves raise the mists and the clouds which intercept the light of God's countenance; we built up the partition wall which separates between God and us; yet Mercy finds the way.

A man that hath read of honey, or heard of honey, may know the sweetness of it by guess and imagination; but a man that hath tasted of honey knoweth the sweetness of it in truth: so, by reading and hearing of the grace and mercy of God in Christ, we may guess that it is a sweet thing; but he that hath had an experimental proof of the sweet effects and fruits of it in his own heart perceives that all which is spoken of God's pardoning and comforting of sinners is verified in himself. T. MANTON

*For Thy law is my delight.* O blessed faith! He is no mean believer who rejoices in the law even when its broken precepts cause him to suffer. To delight in the Word when it rebukes us is proof that we are profiting under it. Surely this is a plea which will prevail with God, however bitter our griefs may be; if we still delight in the law of the Lord, He cannot let us die; He must and will cast a tender look upon us and comfort our hearts. C. H. S.

A child of God, though he cannot serve the Lord perfectly, yet he serves Him willingly; his will is in the law of the Lord; he is not a pressed soldier, but a volunteer. By the beating of this pulse, we may judge whether there be spiritual life in us or no.

David professeth that God's law was his delight; he had his crown to delight in; he had his music to delight in; but the love he had to God's law did drown all other delights; as the joy of harvest and vintage exceeds the joy of gleaning. T. WATSON

Vs. 78. *Let the proud be ashamed.* Shame is for the proud, for it is a shameful thing to be proud. Shame is not for the holy, for there is nothing in holiness to be ashamed of. C. H. S.

This suggests a word to the wicked. Take heed that by your implacable hatred to the truth and church of God you do not engage her prayers against you.

These imprecatory prayers of the saints, when shot at the right mark, and duly put up, are murdering pieces, and strike dead where they light. "Shall not God avenge His own elect, which cry day and night unto Him, though He bear long with them? I tell you that He will avenge them speedily" (Luke 18:7, 8). They are not empty words — as the imprecations of the wicked poured into the air, and there vanishing with their breath — but are received into heaven, and shall be sent back with thunder and lightning upon the pates of the wicked.

David's prayer unraveled Ahithopel's fine-spun policy and twisted his halter for him. The prayers of the saints are more to be feared — as once a great person said and felt — than an army of twenty thousand men in the field. Esther's fast hastened Haman's ruin, and Hezekiah's against Sennacherib brought his huge host to the slaughter and fetched an angel from heaven to do the execution in one night upon them. W. GURNALL

*I will meditate in Thy precepts.* The verb *asiach,* in the second clause of the verse, may be rendered, *I will speak of,* as well as *I will meditate upon;* implying that when he had obtained the victory, he would proclaim the goodness of God, which he had experienced. *To speak of God's statutes* is equivalent to declaring out of the law how faithfully He guards His saints, how securely He delivers them, and how righteously He avenges their wrongs. J. CALVIN

Vs. 79. *Let those that fear Thee turn unto me, and those that have known Thy testimonies.* David has two descriptions for the saints — they are God-fearing and God-knowing. They possess both devotion and instruction; they have both the spirit and the science of true religion. We neither care for devout dunces nor for intellectual icebergs. C. H. S.

Fear and knowledge do make up a godly man. Knowledge without fear breedeth presumption; and fear without knowledge breedeth superstitution; and blind zeal, as a blind horse, may be full of mettle, but is ever and anon stumbling. Knowledge must direct fear, and fear must season knowledge; then it is a happy mixture and composition. T. MANTON

Vs. 80. *Let my very heart be sound.*

*True-hearted Savior, Thou knowest our story;*
*Weak are the hearts that we lay at Thy fect,*
*Sinful and treacherous! yet for Thy glory,*
*Heal them, and cleanse them from sin and deceit.*

*Half-hearted! false-hearted! Heed we the warning!*
*Only the whole can be perfectly true;*
*Bring the whole offering, all timid thought scorning,*
*True-hearted only if whole-hearted, too.*

*Half-hearted! Savior, shall aught be withholden,*
*Giving Thee part Who has given us all?*
*Blessings outpouring and promises golden,*
*Pledging, with never reserve nor recall.*

FRANCES RIDLEY HAVERGAL

*Ashamed.* It was a saying of Pythagoras, "Reverence thyself; be not ashamed of thyself." God hath a spy and deputy within us, and taketh notice of our conformity and unconformity to His will, and, after sin committed, lasheth the soul with the sense of its own guilt and folly, as the body is lashed with stripes. MANTON

## EXPOSITION OF VERSES 81 TO 88

This portion of the gigantic Psalm sees the Psalmist *in extremis.* His enemies have brought him to the lowest condition of anguish and depression; yet he is faithful to the law and trustful in his God. This octave is the midnight of the Psalm and very dark and black it is. Stars, however, shine out, and the last verse gives promise of the dawn. C. H. S.

Vs. 81. *My soul fainteth for Thy salvation; but I hope.* Believe under a cloud and wait for Him when there is no moonlight nor starlight. Let faith live and breathe and lay hold of the sure salvation of God when clouds and darkness are about you and appearance of rotting in the prison before you.

O stout word of faith, "Though He slay me, yet will I trust in Him!" O sweet epitaph, written upon the grave-stone of a departed believer, namely, "I died hoping, and my dust and ashes believe in life!" Hold fast Christ in the dark; surely ye shall see the salvation of God. SAMUEL RUTHERFORD

Vs. 82. *Mine eyes fail for Thy Word, saying, When wilt Thou comfort me?* To read the Word till the eyes can no longer see is but a small thing compared with watching for the fulfilment of the promise till the inner eyes of expectancy begin to grow dim with hope deferred. We may not set times to God, for this is to limit the Holy One of Israel; yet we may urge our suit with importunity and make fervent enquiry as to why the promise tarries. C. H. S.

Vs. 83. *Yet do I not forget Thy statutes.* Grace is a living power which survives that which would suffocate all other forms of existence. Fire cannot consume it and smoke cannot smother it. A man may be reduced to skin and bone, and all his comfort may be dried out of him, and yet he may hold fast his integrity and glorify his God. C. H. S.

Vs. 85. *Which are not after Thy law.* After God's law they could not be while they were doing such things. Perhaps he refers to the deed more than to the men. "The proud have digged pits for me, which is not after Thy law" — which is against Thy law; and they would seem to do it because it is against Thy law — delighting in wickedness as they do. Such men would seem to imbibe the foul spirit which Milton ascribes to the fallen archangel: "Evil, be thou my good." J. STEPHEN

*The wicked have told me fables, but not as Thy law* (So the Septuagint). The special reason why he desires to be freed from the company of the wicked is, because they always tempt the pious by relating the pleasures of the world, which are nothing but fables, filthy, fleeting pleasures, more fallacious than real — nothing like the grand and solid pleasure that always flows from a pious observance of the law of the Lord. R. BELLARMINE

Vs. 87. *They had almost consumed me upon earth.* His foes had almost destroyed him so as to make him altogether fail. If they could they would have eaten him, or burned him alive; anything so that they could have made a full end of the good man. The lions are chained: they can rage no further than our God permits.

If we are resolved to die sooner than forsake the Lord, we may depend upon it that we shall not die but shall live to see the overthrow of them that hate us. C. H. S.

## EXPOSITION OF VERSES 89 TO 96

Vs. 89. *Forever,* O Lord, *Thy Word is settled in heaven.* Jehovah's Word is not fickle nor uncertain; it is settled, determined, fixed, sure, immovable. Man's teachings change so often that there is never time for them to be settled; but the Lord's Word is from of old the same and will remain unchanged eternally. Some men are never happier than when they are unsettling everything and everybody; but God's mind is not with them. C. H. S.

We have arrived at the center of the Psalm, and the thread of the connection is purposely broken off.

It implieth that as God is eternal, so is His Word, and that it hath a fit representation both in heaven and in earth. That as His Word doth stand fast in heaven, so doth His faithfulness on earth, where the afflictions of the godly seem to contradict it. T. MANTON

Even when patience failed in Job, yet *faith* failed not. Though God kill all other graces and comforts, and my soul, too, yet He shall not kill my faith, says he. If He separate my soul from my body, yet not faith from my soul. And therefore the just lives by faith rather than by other graces, because when all is gone, yet faith remains, and faith remains because the *promise* remains: *Forever,* O Lord, *Thy Word is settled in heaven.* M. LAWRENCE

Vs. 90. *Thou hast established the earth, and it abideth.* When we see the world keeping its place and all its laws abiding the same, we have herein assurance that the Lord will be faithful to His covenant and will not allow the faith of His people to be put to shame. If the earth abideth, the spiritual creation will abide; if God's Word suffices to establish the world, surely it is enough for the establishment of the individual believer. C. H. S.

Vs. 91. *They continue this day according to Thine ordinances.* Man may destroy a plant, but he is powerless to force it into disobedience to the laws given it by the common Creator. Many may forcibly obstruct the path of a growing twig, but it turns quietly aside, and moves patiently and irresistibly on its appointed way. JAMES NEIL

Some of the handsomest flowers in the world, and stranger still, some of the most juicy and succulent plants with which we are acquainted, adorn the arid and desolate sands of the Cape of Good Hope and will not flourish elsewhere. If you twist the branch of a tree so as to turn the under surface of its leaves towards the sky, in a very little while all those leaves will turn down and assume their appointed position.

Wilful man may dare to defy his Maker, and set at nought His wise and merciful commands; but not so all nature besides. Well, indeed, is it for us that His other works have not erred after the pattern of our rebellion; that seed-time and harvest, cold and heat, summer and winter, day and night, with all their accompanying provision, have not ceased; To the precepts imposed upon vegetation when first called into being on creation's third day, it still yields implicit submission, and the tenderest plant will die rather than transgress.

What an awful contrast to this is the conduct of man, God's noblest work, endowed with reason and a never-dying soul, yet too often ruining his health, wasting and destroying his mental power, defiling his immortal spirit, and, in a word, madly endeavoring to frustrate every purpose for which he was framed. JAMES NEIL

*For all are Thy servants.* By that Word which is settled may we be settled; by that voice which establishes the earth may we be established; and by that command which all created things obey may we be made the servants of the Lord God Almighty. C. H. S.

Vs. 92. *Unless Thy law had been my delights, I should then have perished in mine affliction.* In our darkest seasons, nothing has kept us from desperation but the promise of the Lord: yea, at times nothing has stood between us and self-destruction save faith in the eternal Word of God. When worn with pain until the brain has become dazed and the reason well-nigh extinguished, a sweet text has whispered to us its heart-cheering assurance, and our poor struggling mind has reposed upon the bosom of God. That which was our delight in prosperity has been our light in adversity; that which in the day kept us from presuming has in the night kept us from perishing. C. H. S.

The Word of God delighted in is the afflicted saint's antidote against ruin and destruction. The Word of God is the sick saint's salve, the dying saint's cordial, a precious medicine to keep God's people from perishing in time of affliction.

This upheld Jacob from sinking when his brother Esau came furiously marching to destroy him (Gen. 32:12). He pleaded, "And Thou saidst, I will surely do thee good," etc. Thus the promise of God supported him. This also upheld Joshua and enabled him courageously to fight the Lord's battles, because God had said, "He would never leave him nor forsake him" (Josh. 1:5).

Melanchthon saith that the Landgrave of Hesse told him at Dresden that it had been impossible for him to have borne up under the manifold miseries of so long an imprisonment but for the comfort of the Scriptures in his heart. EDMUND CALAMY

The poor widow had received her daily pittance, and she had now come into the shop of the grocer to lay it out to the best advantage. She had but a few coppers in her withered hands. Carefully did she expend her little stock — a pennyworth of this and the other necessary of life nearly exhausted all she had.

She came to the last penny, and with a singular expression of heroic contentment and cheerful resignation on her wrinkled face, she said, "Now I must buy oil with this, that I may see to read my Bible during these long, dark nights, for it is my only comfort now when every other comfort has gone away." ALEXANDER WALLACE

This verse I may call a Perfume against the Plague; The Sick Man's Salve; The Afflicted Man's Consolation; and a blessed Triumph, in and over all troubles. R. GREENHAM

Vs. 94. *I am Thine, save me; for I have sought Thy precepts.* If we have so much love to offer ourselves to God, to become His; much more will the love of God make Him to become ours; for God loves first, and most, and surest. If mine heart rise toward God, much more is the heart of God towards me; because there love is in the fountain. JOSEPH SYMONDS

Vs. 95. *The wicked have waited for me to destroy me.* Daniel's preservation in the lion's den was a great miracle; but it is no less a marvelous work of God that the godly who are the flock of Christ are daily preserved in the midst of the wicked, who are but ravening wolves and thirst for the blood of the saints of God, having a cruel purpose in their heart if they might perform it, utterly to destroy them. W. COWPER

Vs. 96. *I have seen an end of all perfection.* It would be well if some who profess to be perfect could even see the beginning of perfection, for we fear they cannot have begun aright, or they would not talk so exceeding proudly. Is it not the beginning of perfection to lament your imperfection? C. H. S.

A man with the eye of his body may behold an end of many worldly perfections, of many fair estates, great beauties, large parts, hopeful families; but a man with the eye of his soul (or by faith) may see an end of all earthly perfections. He may see the world in a flame, and all its pomp and pride, and glory, and gallantry, and crowns and scepters, and riches, and treasures, turned into ashes. He may see the heavens passing away like a scroll, and the elements melting with fervent heat, and the earth, with the things thereon, consumed; and all its perfections, which men doted so much on, vanish into smoke and nothing.

*Thy commandment is exceeding broad.* Take notice that the law, which is your mark, is *exceeding broad.* And yet not the more easy to be hit; because you must aim to hit it; in every duty of it, with a performance of equal breadth, or else you cannot hit it at all. STEPHEN MARSHALL

## EXPOSITION OF VERSES 97 TO 104

Vs. 97. *O how love I Thy law!"* We love it for its holiness and pine to be holy; we love it for its wisdom and study to be wise; we love it for its perfection and long to be perfect. Those who know the power of the Gospel perceive an infinite loveliness in the Law as they see it fulfilled and embodied in Christ Jesus. C. H. S.

He speaketh not of his knowing, reading, hearing, speaking, or outward practicing of the law, but of *love* to the law: this is more than all the former: all the former may be without this, but this cannot be without the former.

If David were in exile or flight, a man would think that his wife and children, and other friends, as also his country, would have so occupied and fully possessed his heart that there should have been little place for other things therein; but rather he should have said, "Oh, how love I those things! Oh, how is my heart troubled with thoughts of them, and care for them in my great love towards them!"

Moreover, that neither any troubles on the one side, wherewith David was continually exercised; nor his honors, riches, or pleasures, either in possession or in hope on the other side, did extinguish, or cool, or abate his love, is it not a thing of great note?

Christ Himself loved the Word of God more than He loved any riches; for did He not for the performance of the Word submit Himself to such want, that the foxes had holes, and the birds had nests, but He had not whereon to lay His head? and that, although He were the Heir of all things, yet He was ministered unto by certain women? He loved the Word of God more than He loved His mother, brethren and sisters.

Yea, Christ loved the Word of God more than He loved His own life; for did He not lay down His life to fulfill the Word of God? If Christ Jesus Himself loved the Word more than all other things, yea, more than His life, which was more than the life of all angels, was there not great reason why David should love it in like manner? Had not David as much need of it as Christ?

THOMAS STOUGHTON

Were I to enjoy Hezekiah's grant, and to have fifteen years added to my life, I would be much more frequent in my application to the throne of grace. Were I to renew my studies, I would take my leave of those accomplished trifles — the historians, the orators, the poets of antiquity — and devote my attention to the Scriptures of truth. I would sit with much greater assiduity at my divine Master's feet and desire to know nothing but "Jesus Christ, and Him crucified."

This wisdom, whose fruits are peace in life, consolation in death, and everlasting salvation after death — this I would trace — this I would seek — this I would explore through the spacious and delightful fields of the Old and New Testament. JAS. HERVEY

Whoso loveth salvation will love this Word, love to read it, love to hear it; and such as will neither read nor hear it, Christ saith plainly, they are not of God. EDWIN SANDYS

*It is my meditation.* Holy Scripture is not a book for the slothful; it is not a book which can be interpreted without, and apart from and by the deniers of that Holy Spirit by Whom it came. Rather is it a field, upon the surface of which, if sometimes we gather manna easily and without labor, and given, as it were, freely to our hands, yet of which also, many portions are to be cultivated with pains and toil ere they will yield food for the use of man. This bread of life also is to be eaten in the wholesome sweat of our brow. R. C. TRENCH

Vs. 98. *Thou through Thy commandments hast made me wiser than mine enemies.* A thoroughly straightforward man, devoid of all policy, is a terrible puzzle to diplomatists; they suspect him of a subtle duplicity through which they cannot see, while he, indifferent to their suspicions, holds on the even tenor of his way and baffles all their arts. Yes, "honesty is the best policy." He who is taught of God has a practical wisdom such as malice cannot supply to the crafty; while harmless as a dove he also exhibits more than a serpent's wisdom. C. H. S.

*For they are ever with me.* As a soldier in battle must never lay aside his shield, so must we never have the Word of God out of our minds; it must be ever with us. C. H. S.

A good man, wherever he goes, carries his Bible along with him, if not in his hands, yet in his head and in his heart. MATTHEW HENRY

Vs. 99. *I have more understanding than all my teachers.* Even where the preacher is godly, partaker of that grace himself, whereof he is an ambassador to others, it falls out oftentimes that greater measure of light and grace is communicated by his ministry to another than is given to himself; as Augustine first illuminated and converted by Ambrose did far excel, both in knowledge and spiritual grace, him that taught him. And herein God wonderfully shows His glory, that, whosoever be the instrument, He is the dispenser of light and glory, giving more by the instrument than it hath in itself. And this is so far from being to a godly teacher a matter of grief, that it is rather a matter of glory. WM. COWPER

Vs. 100. *I understand . . . because I keep.* It is St. Gregory's observation concerning the two disciples who, whilst Christ talked with them, knew Him not; but in performing an act of hospitality towards Him, to wit, breaking bread with Him, they knew Him, that they were enlightened, not by hearing Him, but by doing Divine precepts. Whosoever therefore will understand, let him first make haste to do what he heareth. NATHANAEL HARDY

Vs. 101. *I have refrained my feet . . . that I might keep Thy Word.* A holy man knows that all sin strikes at the holiness of God, the glory of God, the nature of God, the being of God, and the law of God; and therefore his heart rises against all; he looks upon every sin as the scribes and Pharisees that accused Christ; and as that Judas that betrayed Christ; and as that Pilate that condemned Christ; and as those soldiers that scourged Christ; and as those spears that pierced Christ; and therefore his heart cries out for justice upon all. THOMAS BROOKS

The word *refrained* warns us that we are naturally borne by our feet into the path of every kind of sin and are hurried along it by the rush of human passions, so that even the wise and understanding need to check, recall, and retrace their steps in order that they may keep God's Word and not become castaways.

And further note that the Hebrew verb here translated *refrained* is even stronger in meaning, and denotes I *fettered,* or *imprisoned, my feet,* whereby we may learn that no light resistance is enough to prevent them from leading us astray. AGELLIUS AND GENEBRARDUS, IN NEALE AND LITTLEDALE

Vs. 102. *I have not departed from Thy judgments: for Thou hast taught me.* He who is careful not to go an inch aside will not leave the road. He who never touches the intoxicating cup will never be drunk. He who never utters an idle word will never be profane. If we begin to depart a little, we can never tell where we shall end. C. H. S.

Vs. 103. *Yea, sweeter than honey to my mouth.* When the Psalmist fed on it, he found it sweet; but when he bore witness of it, it became sweeter still. How wise it will be on our part to keep the Word on our palate by meditation and on our tongue by confession! It must be sweet to our taste when we think of it, or it will not be sweet to our mouth when we talk of it. C. H. S.

Vs. 104. *Therefore I hate every false way.* True hearts are not indifferent about falsehood; they grow warm in indignation: as they love the truth, so they hate the lie. Saints have a universal horror of all that is untrue; they tolerate no falsehood or folly; they set their faces against all error of doctrine or wickedness of life. He who is a lover of one sin is in league with the whole army of sins; we must have neither truce nor parley with even one of these Amalekites, for the Lord hath war with them from generation to generation, and so must we.

It is well to be a good hater. And what is that? A hater of no living being, but a hater of "every false way." The way of self-will, of self-righteousness, of worldliness, of pride, of unbelief, of hypocrisy — these are all false ways, and therefore not only to be shunned, but to be abhorred. C. H. S.

A godly man not only doth that which is good, but he delights to do it, his soul cleaves to it; he is in his element when he is doing it; nothing comes more suitably to him than the business of his duty; he loveth to do it, yea, he loveth it when he cannot do it. JOSEPH CARYL

Universality in this is a sure sign of sincerity. Herod spits out some sins when he rolls others as sweet morsels in his mouth. A hypocrite ever leaves the devil some nest-egg to sit upon, though he take many away.

Some men will not buy some commodities because they cannot have them at their own price, but they lay out the same money on others; so hypocrites forbear some sins, yea, are displeased at them, because they cannot have them without disgrace or disease, or some other disadvantage; but they lay out the same love upon other sins which will suit better with their designs.

Some affirm that what the sea loseth in one place it gaineth in another; so what ground the corruption of the unconverted loseth one way, it gaineth another. There is in him some one lust especially which is his favorite; some king sin, like Agag, which must be spared when others are destroyed. "In this the Lord be merciful to Thy servant," saith Naaman. But now the regenerate laboreth to cleanse himself from all pollutions, both of flesh and spirit. (II Cor. 7:1) GEO. SWINNOCK

Hatred is a stabbing, murdering affection; it pursues sin with a hot heart to death, as an avenger of blood, that is to say, of the blood of the soul, which sin would spill, and of the Blood of Christ, which sin hath shed.

Hate sin perfectly and perpetually and then you will not spare it but kill it presently. Till sin be hated, it cannot be mortified; you will not cry against it, as the Jews did against Christ, "Crucify it! Crucify it!" but show indulgence to it as David did to Absalom and say, "Deal gently with the young man — with this or that lust, for my sake." Mercy to sin is cruelty to the soul. EDWARD REYNER

All sin is a *lie.* By it we attempt to cheat God. By it we actually cheat our souls (Prov. 14:12). There is no delusion like the folly of believing that a course of sin will conduce to our happiness. WM. PLUMER

## EXPOSITION OF VERSES 105 TO 112

Vs. 105. *Thy Word is a lamp unto my feet.* Each man should use the Word of God personally, practically, and habitually, that he may see his way and see what lies in it. C. H. S.

What we all want is not to see wonders that daze us and to be rapt in ecstatic visions and splendors, but a little light on the dark and troubled path we have to tread, a lamp that will burn steadfastly and helpfully over the work we have to do. The stars are infinitely more sublime, meteors infinitely more superb and dazzling; and the lamp shining in a dark place is infinitely closer to our practical needs. *From* THE EXPOSITOR

Going two miles into a neighborhood where very few could read to spend an evening in reading to a company who were assembled to listen and about to return by a narrow path through the woods where paths diverged, I was provided with a torch of light wood, or "pitch pine." I objected; it was too small, weighing not over half a pound. "It will light you home," answered my host. I said, "The wind may blow it out." He said, "It will light you home." "But if it should rain?" I again objected. "It will light you home," he insisted.

Contrary to my fears, it gave abundant light to my path all the way home, furnishing an apt illustration, I often think, of the way in which doubting hearts would be led safely along the "narrow way." If they would take the Bible as their guide, it would be a lamp to their feet, leading to the heavenly home. One man had five objections to the Bible. If he would take it as a lamp to his feet, it would "light him home." Another told me he had two faults to find with the Bible. I answered him in the words of my good friend who furnished the torch, "It will light you home." THE AMERICAN MESSENGER

All depends on our way of using the lamp. A man tells that when a boy he was proud to carry the lantern for his Sabbath-school teacher. The way to their school led through unlit, muddy streets. The boy held the lantern far too high, and both sank in the deep mud. "Ah! you must hold the lamp lower," the teacher exclaimed, as they gained a firm footing on the farther side of the slough. The teacher then beautifully explained our text, and the man declares that he never forgot the lesson of that night. You may easily hold the lamp too high; but you can hardly hold it too low. JAMES WELLS

Vs. 106. *I have sworn, and I will perform it.* Frequently renew settled and holy resolutions. A soldier unresolved to fight may easily be defeated. True and sharpened courage treads down those difficulties which would triumph over a cold and wavering spirit. Resolution in a weak man will perform more than strength in a coward. STEPHEN CHARNOCK

Theodoricus, Archbishop of Cologne, when the Emperor Sigismund demanded of him the directest and most compendious way how to attain true happiness, made answer in brief, thus: "Perform when thou art well what thou promisedst when thou wast sick." David did so; he made vows in war, and paid them in peace; and thus should all good men do; not like the cunning devil, of whom the epigrammatist writeth:

The devil was sick, the devil a monk would be;
The devil was well, the *devil* a monk was he.

Nor like unto many now-a-days, that if God's hand do but lie somewhat heavy upon them, oh, what promises, what engagements are there for amendment of life! How like unto marble against rain do they seem to sweat and melt but still retain their hardness! Let but the rod be taken off their backs, or health restored, then, as their bodies live, their vows die; all is forgotten: nay, many times it so falleth out, that they are far worse than ever they were before. JOHN SPENCER

Vs. 107. *Quicken me,* O Lord, *according unto Thy Word.* The Lord has promised, prepared, and provided this blessing of renewed life for all His waiting servants. C. H. S.

Vs. 109. *My soul is continually in my hand.* He lived in the midst of danger. He had to be always fighting for existence — hiding in caves or contending in battles. This is a very uncomfortable and trying state of affairs, and men are apt to think any expedient justifiable by which they can end such a condition: but David did not turn aside to find safety in sin, for he says, *Yet do I not forget Thy law.* They say that all things are fair in love and war; but the holy man thought not so: while he carried his life in his hand, he also carried the law in his heart. C. H. S.

He had his soul in his hand, ready to give whenever God should take it. And this is to be observed, that there is no trouble so ready to take away the life of God's children, as they are ready to give it.

As Elijah came out to the mouth of his cave to meet with the Lord; and Abraham stood in the door of his tent to speak to the angel; so the soul of the godly stands ready in the door of the tabernacle of this body to remove when the Lord shall command it; whereas the soul of the wicked lies back, hiding itself, as Adam among the bushes, and is taken out of the body perforce; as was the soul of that worldling: "This night thy soul shall be required of thee"; but they never sacrifice their souls willingly to the Lord. W. COWPER

If anyone carry in the hand a fragile vessel, made of glass or any other similar material, filled with a precious liquor, especially if the hand be weak, or if from other causes dangers be threatening, he will scarcely be able to avoid the breaking of the vessel and the running out of the liquor.

Such is the condition of my life, which I, set upon by various enemies, carry as it were in my hand; which, therefore, is exposed to such danger, as that I always have death present before my sight, my life hanging on the slenderest thread. ANDREAS RIVETUS

Augustine upon that place doth ingeniously confess that he understood not what David meant by having his soul in his hands; but Jerome, another of the ancients, teacheth us, that it is an Hebraism, signifying a state of extremest peril. The Greeks also have drawn it into a proverb speaking the same thing. J. CARYL

Vs. 110. *The wicked have laid a snare for me.* Wicked men are quite indifferent as to the manner in which they can destroy the good man — they think no more of him than if he were a rabbit or a rat: cunning and treachery are always the allies of malice, and everything like a generous or chivalrous feeling is unknown among the graceless, who treat the godly as if they were vermin to be exterminated. C. H. S.

He calls them *wicked men;* which importeth three things: first, they work wickedness; secondly, they love it; thirdly, they persevere in it. WM. COWPER

In eating, he sets before us gluttony; in love he impels to lust; in labor, sluggishness; in conversing, envy; in governing, covetousness; in correcting, anger; in honor, pride; in the heart, he sets evil thoughts; in the mouth, evil words; in actions, evil works; then awake, he moves us to evil actions; when alseep, to filthy dreams. GIROLAMO SAVONAROLA

*Laid a snare for me: yet I erred not.* It is not the laying the bait hurts the fish, if the fish do not bite. T. WATSON

Vs. 111. *They are the rejoicing of my heart.* He saith not that God's testimonies bring joy, but that they are joy; there is no other joy but the delight in the law of the Lord. For all other joy, the wise king said of laughter, "thou art mad," and of joy, "What is it that thou dost?" (Eccl. 11). True joy is the earnest which we have of heaven, it is the treasure of the soul, and therefore should be laid up in a safe place; and nothing in this world is safe to place it in. ABRAHAM WRIGHT

Vs. 112. *I have inclined mine heart.* The prophet, in order briefly to define what it is to serve God, asserts that he applied not only his hands, eyes, or feet, to the keeping of the law, but that he began with the affection of the heart. JOHN CALVIN

*Unto the end.* Our life on earth is a race; in vain begins he to run swiftly, that fainteth, and gives over before he come to the end. And this was signified (saith Gregory) when in the law the tail of the beast was sacrificed with the rest: perseverance crowneth all. It is good we have begun to do well; let us also strive to persevere to the end. WM. COWPER

## EXPOSITION OF VERSES 113 TO 120

Vs. 113. *I hate vain thoughts: but Thy law do I love.* The opposite of the fixed and infallible law of God is the wavering, changing opinion of men: David had an utter contempt and abhorrence for this; all his reverence and regard went to the sure word of testimony. In proportion to his love to the law was his hate of man's inventions. The thoughts of men are vanity; but the thoughts of God are verity. We hear much in these days of "men of thought," "thoughtful preachers," and "modern thought": what is this but the old pride of the human heart? Vain man would be wise. The Psalmist did not glory in his thoughts; and that which was called "thought" in his day was a thing which he detested. When man thinks his best, his highest thoughts are as far below those of Divine revelation as the earth is beneath the heavens. C. H. S.

The vanity of his heart was a burden to him. A new creature is as careful against wickedness in the head or heart as in the life. A godly man would be purer in the sight of God than in the view of man. He knows none but God can see the wanderings of his heart or the thoughts of his head, yet he is as careful that sins should not rise up as that they should not break out. STEPHEN CHARNOCK

The carnal mind welcomes and delights to dwell upon these congenial imaginations, and to solace itself by ideal indulgences, when opportunity of other gratification is not presented, or when a man dares not commit the actual transgression. But the spiritual mind recoils at them; such thoughts will intrude from time to time, but they are unwelcome and distressing and are immediately thrust out; while other subjects, from the Word of God, are stored up in readiness to occupy the mind more profitably and pleasantly during the hours of leisure and retirement.

There is no better test of our true character than the habitual effect of *vain thoughts* upon our minds — whether we love and indulge them or abhor and watch and pray against them. THOMAS SCOTT

Every dislike of evil is not sufficient; but perfect hatred is required of us against all sorts and degrees of sin. DAVID DICKSON

*Vain thoughts.* The word is used for the *opinions* of men; and may be applied to all heterodox opinions, human doctrines, damnable heresies; such as are inconsistent with the perfections of God, derogate from His grace, and from the Person and offices of Christ; and are contrary to the Word, and which are therefore rejected and abhorred by good men. JOHN GILL

*Vain thoughts.* Hebrew, *seäphim,* haltings between two opinions. (See 1 Kings 18:21) Hence it signifies skeptical doubts. CHRISTOPHER WORDSWORTH

*But Thy law do I love.* Scholars that love learning will be continually hammering upon some notion or other which may further their progress and as greedily clasp it as the iron will its beloved loadstone. He that is "winged with a Divine love" to Christ will have frequent glances and flights toward Him and will start out from his worldly business several times in a day to give Him a visit.

Love, in the very working, is a settling grace; it increaseth our delight in God, partly by the sight of His amiableness, which is cleared to us in the very act of loving; and partly by the recompences He gives to the affectionate carriage of His creatures; both which will prevent the heart's giving entertainment to such loose companions as evil thoughts. STEPHEN CHARNOCK

Mark, he doth not say he is *free* from vain thoughts, but he "hates" them; he likes their company no better than one would a pack of thieves that break into his house. WM. GURNALL

Vs. 114. *I hope in Thy Word.* Of all the ingredients that sweeten the cup of human life, there is none more rich or powerful than *hope.* Its absence embitters the sweetest lot; its presence alleviates the deepest woe. Surround me with all the joys which memory can awaken or possession bestow — without hope, it is not enough.

In the absence of hope there is sadness in past and present joys — sadness in the thought that the past is past and that the present is passing, too. But though you strip me of all the joys the past or the present can confer, if the morrow shineth bright with hope, I am glad amid my woe. Of all the busy motives that stir this teeming earth, hope is the busiest. It is the sweetest balm that soothes our sorrows, the brightest beam that gilds our pleasures.

Hope is the noblest offspring, the firstborn, the last buried child of foreseeing and forecasting man. Without it the unthinking cattle may be content amid present plenty. But without it, reflecting man should not, cannot be truly happy. WM. GRANT

Vs. 115. *Depart from me, ye evil-doers.* As if he had said, talk no more of it, save your breath, I am resolved on my course, I have sworn, and am steadfastly purposed to keep the commandments of my God; with God's help, there will

I hold me, and all the world shall not wrest me from it. ROBERT SANDERSON

It is difficult, even to a miracle, to keep God's commandments and evil company, too; therefore, when David would marry himself to God's commands, to love them, and live with them, for better, for worse, all his days, he is forced to give a bill of divorce to wicked companions, knowing that otherwise the match could never be made. GEO. SWINNOCK

Vs. 116. *And let me not be ashamed of my hope.* We may be ashamed of our thoughts, and our words, and our deeds, for they spring from ourselves; but we never shall be ashamed of our hope, for that springs from the Lord, our God. Such is the frailty of our nature that unless we are continually upheld by grace we shall fall so foully as to be ashamed of ourselves and ashamed of all those glorious hopes which are now the crown and glory of our life.

The man of God had uttered the most positive resolve, but he felt that he could not trust in his own solemn determination: hence these prayers. It is not wrong to make resolutions, but it will be useless to do so unless we salt them well with believing cries to God. David meant to keep the law of the Lord, but he first needed the Lord of the law to keep him. C. H. S.

Vs. 117. *Hold Thou me up.* Three things made David afraid: First, great temptation without; for from every air the wind of temptation blows upon a Christian. Secondly, great corruption within. Thirdly, examples of other worthy men that had fallen before him and are written for us: not that we should learn to fall, but to fear lest we fall. These three should always hold us humble, according to that warning, "Let him that thinketh he standeth take heed lest he fall." WM. COWPER

*Up,* up above the littlenesses in which I have lived too long — above the snares which have so often caught me — above the stumbling-blocks upon which I have so often fallen — above the world — above myself — higher than I have ever reached yet — above the level of my own mortality: worthy of Thee — worthy of the blood, with which I have been bought — nearer to heaven — nearer to Thee — *hold Thou me up.*

There is no elevation like the elevation of abasement. Sometimes by severe discipline to brace up the heart, and strengthen it, and make it independent of external things. Sometimes by heavy affliction, which is the grasp of His hand, that He may hold you tighter. Sometimes by putting into your heart to think the exact thing that you need — to pray the very prayer which He intends at the moment to grant. Sometimes by appearing to let you go, and forsake you, while at the same time — like the Syro-Phoenician woman — He is giving you the wish to hold on that He may give you the more at the last. JAMES VAUGHAN

Vs. 118. *For their deceit is falsehood.* They call it far-seeing policy, but it is absolute falsehood, and it shall be treated as such. Ordinary men call it clever diplomacy, but the man of God calls a spade a spade, and declares it to be falsehood, and nothing less, for he knows that it is so in the sight of God. Men who err from the right road invent pretty excuses with which to deceive themselves and others, and so quiet their consciences and maintain their credits; but their mask of falsehood is too transparent. God treads down falsehoods; they are only fit to be spurned by His feet and crushed into the dust.

How horrified must those be who have spent all their lives in contriving a confectionery religion, and then see it all trodden upon by God as a sham He cannot endure! C. H. S.

He means not here of that deceit whereby the wicked deceive others, but that whereby they deceive themselves. And this is twofold; first, in that they look for a good in sin, which sin deceitfully promiseth, but they shall never find. Next, that they flatter themselves with a vain conceit to escape judgment, which shall assuredly overtake them. WM. COWPER

Vs. 119. *Thou puttest away all the wicked of the earth like dross.* If even a good man feels forced to put away the evil-doers from him, much more must the thrice holy God put away the wicked. C. H. S.

Why are they thus characterized? Because here they flourish; their names "shall be written in the earth" (Jer. 17:13).

Their hearts and minds are in the world (Matt. 6:19-20). It is their natural frame to be worldly, they only savor the things of the world; preferment, honor, greatness, it is their *unum magnum:* here is their pleasure, and here is their portion, their hope, and their happiness. A child of God looketh for another inheritance, immortal and undefiled. T. MANTON

Vs. 120. *My flesh trembleth for fear of Thee.* Instead of exulting over those who fell under God's displeasure, he humbleth himself. What we read and hear of the judgments of God upon wicked people should make us: (1) To reverence His terrible majesty, and to stand in awe of Him. Who is able to stand before this holy Lord God? (I Sam. 6:20), (2) to fear lest we offend Him and become obnoxious to His wrath. Good men have need to be restrained from sin by the terrors of the Lord; especially when judgment begins at the house of God, and hypocrites are discovered, and put away as dross. M. HENRY

## EXPOSITION OF VERSES 121 TO 128

Vs. 123. *Mine eyes fail for Thy salvation.* He wept, waited, and watched for God's saving hand, and these exercises tried the eyes of his faith till they were almost ready to give out. C. H. S.

To the promises of God, he betook himself, and while waiting their accomplishment, and looking with utmost eagerness to the word of God's righteousness, he gives utterances to the desponding sentiment, *Mine eyes fail for Thy salvation.*

Oh, for such warm and anxious desires for that great salvation, which will realize the victory over all our spiritual enemies and enable us to shout triumphantly through all eternity in the Name of our Almighty Deliverer! JOHN MORISON

Vs. 124. *Teach me.* David had Nathan and Gad, the prophets; and beside them, the ordinary Levites to teach him. He read the Word of God diligently and did meditate in the law night and day; but he acknowledged all this was nothing unless God did teach him.

Other teachers speak to the ear, but God speaks to the heart: so Paul preached to Lydia, but God opened her heart. Let us pray for this grace. WM. COWPER

Vs. 126. *It is time for Thee, to work: for they have made void Thy law.* Oh, for another Pentecost with all its wonders to reveal the energy of God to gainsayers and make them see that there is a God in Israel! Man's extremity, whether of need or sin, is God's opportunity. When the earth was without form and void, the Spirit came and moved upon the face of the waters; should He not come when society is returning to a like chaos?

When Israel in Egypt were reduced to the lowest point and it seemed that the covenant would be void, then Moses appeared and wrought mighty miracles; so, too, when the church of God is trampled down and her message is derided, we may expect to see the hand of the Lord stretched out for the revival of religion, the defence of the truth, and the glorifying of the divine Name. C. H. S.

Was ever vessel more hopelessly becalmed in mid-ocean, or did crew ever cry with more frenzy for some favoring breeze than those should cry who man the church of the living God? If God work not, it is certain there is nothing before the church but the prospect of utter discomfiture and overthrow. Greater is the world than the church if God be not in her. But if God be in her, she shall not be moved. May He help her, and that right early!

Sometimes the sleep of the world and the church, too, is so profound that it can be broken only by agencies like the wind, or fire, or earthquake, which made the prophet shiver at the mouth of the cave and without which the voice that followed, so still, so small and tender, would have lost much of its melting and subduing power.

When society has become drugged with the Circean cup of worldliness, and the voices that come from eternity are unheeded, if not unheard, even terror has its merciful mission. The frivolous and superficial hearts of men have to be made serious, their idols have to be broken, their nests have to be stoned or tossed from the trees where they had been made with so much care, and they have to be taught that if this life be all, it is but a phantom and a mockery.

Does the church believe its creed? It writes it, sets it forth, sings it, defends it; but does it believe it, at least with a faith which begets either enthusiasm in itself or respect from the world? Have not the truths which form the methodized symbols of the church become propositions instead of living powers? Do they not lie embalmed with superstitious reverence in the ark of tradition, tenderly cherished for what they have been and done?

But is it not forgotten that if they be truths, they are not dead and cannot die? They are true now, or they were never true; living now, or they never lived. Time cannot touch them, nor human opinion, nor the church's sluggishness or unbelief, for they are emanations from the Divine essence, instinct with His own undecaying life. They are not machinery which may become antiquated and obsolete and displaced by better inventions; they are not methods of policy framed for conditions which are transient, and vanishing with them; they are not scaffolding within which other and higher truth is to be reared from age to age.

They are like Him Who is the end of our conversation, "Jesus Christ, the same yesterday, today, and forever." There is not one of them which, if the faith it awakens were but commensurate with its intrinsic worth, would not clothe the Church with a new and wondrous power. But what would be that power if that faith were to grasp them all? It would be life from the dead. ENOCH MELLOR

*It is time to work,* just as when the attack of some illness is becoming more severe, you hurry to the physician, that he may come more quickly, lest he should later be unable to do any good. So when the prophet saw in the Holy Spirit the rebellion of the people, their luxury, pleasures, deceits, frauds, avarice, drunkenness, he runs for our help to Christ, Whom he knew to be alone able to remedy such sins; implores Him to come, and admits of no delay. AMBROSE, IN NEALE AND LITTLEDALE

Infidelity was never more subtle, more hurtful, more plausible, perhaps more successful, than in the day in which we live. It has left the low grounds of vulgarity and coarseness and ribaldry and entrenched itself upon the lofty heights of criticism, philology, and even science itself. It pervades to a fearful extent our popular literature; it has invested itself with the charms of poetry, to throw its spell over the public mind; it has endeavored to enweave itself with science; and he must be little acquainted with the state of opinion in this land who does not know that it is espoused by a large portion of the cultivated mind of this generation. "It is time for Thee, Lord, to work." JOHN ANGELL JAMES

But our sins are already ripe, yea, rotten ripe, the measure of our iniquities is full up to the brim. Doubtless our land is sunken deep in iniquity; our tongues and works have been against the Lord, to provoke the eyes of His glory; the trial of our countenance doth testify against us (Isa. 3:8-9), yea, we declare our sins as Sodom; we hide them not, the cry of our sins is exceeding grievous, the clamors of them pierce the skies, and with a loud voice roar, saying, "How long, Lord, holy and true? How long ere Thou come to avenge Thyself on such a nation as this?" (Rev. 6:10; Jer. 9:9). GEORGE WEBBE

*It is time for Thee,* Lord. Some read it, and the original will bear it, *It is time to work for Thee,* O Lord; It is time for everyone in his place to appear on the Lord's side, against the threatening growth of profaneness and immorality. We must do what we can for the support of the sinking interests of religion, and, after all, we must beg of God to take the work into His own hands. MATTHEW HENRY

Everything betters a saint. Not only ordinances, word, sacraments, holy society, but even sinners and their very sinning. Even these draw forth their graces into exercise, and put them upon godly, broken-hearted mourning. A saint sails with every wind. As the wicked are hurt by the best things, so the godly are bettered by the worst. Because *they have made void Thy law, therefore do I love Thy commandments.*

Holiness is the more owned by the godly, the more the world despiseth it. The most eminent saints were those of Caesar's (Nero's) house (Phil. 4:22); they who kept God's Name were they who lived where Satan's throne was (Rev. 2:13). Zeal for God grows the hotter by opposition; and thereby the godly most labor to give the glory of God reparation. WM. JENKYN.

Vs. 127. *I love Thy commandments above gold; yea, above fine gold.* The image employed brings before us the picture of the miser; his heart and his treasure are in his gold. With what delight he counts it! With what watchfulness he keeps it, hiding it in safe custody, lest he should be despoiled of that which is dearer to him than life!

Such should Christians be, spiritual misers, counting their treasure is *above fine gold* and "hiding it in their hearts," in safe keeping, where the great despoiler shall not be able to reach it.

Oh Christians! how much more is your portion to you than the miser's treasure! Hide it; watch it; retain it. You need not be afraid of covetousness in spiritual things; rather "covet earnestly" to increase your store; and by living upon it and living in it, it will grow in extent and more precious in value. C. BRIDGES

Vs. 128. *I esteem all Thy precepts concerning all things to be right.* The many *alls* in this verse used (not unlike that in Ezekiel 44:30) showeth the integrity and universality of His obedience. "All" is but a little word, but of large extent. JOHN TRAPP

The upright man squares all his actions by a right rule; carnal reason cannot bias him, corrupt practice cannot sway him, but God's sacred Word directs him. A. WRIGHT

*And I hate every false way.* Love to truth begat hatred of falsehood. This godly man was not indifferent to anything, but that which he did not love he hated. He was no chip in the porridge without flavor; he was a good lover or a good hater, but he was never a waverer. He knew what he felt and expressed it. He was no Gallio, caring for none of the things.

His detestation was as unreserved as his affection; he had not a good word for any practice which would not bear the light of truth. The fact that such large multitudes follow the broad road had no influence upon this holy man except to make him more determined to avoid every form of error and sin. May the Holy Spirit so rule in our hearts that our affections may be in the same decided condition toward the precepts of the Word! C. H. S.

The best trial of our love to God and His Word is the contrary—hatred of sin and impiety: "Ye that love the Lord, hate evil." He that loves a tree hates the worm that consumes it; he that loves a garment hates the moth that eats it; he that loveth life abhorreth death; and he that loves the Lord hates everything that offends Him. Let men take heed to this, who are in love of their sins: how can the love of God be in them? WM. COWPER

The being who loves the good with infinite intensity must hate evil with the same intensity. So far from any incompatibility between this love and this hatred, they are the counterparts of each other — opposite poles of the same moral emotion. JOHN W. HALEY

If Satan get a grip of thee by any one sin, is it not enough to carry thee to damnation? As the butcher carries the beast to the slaughter, sometime bound by all the four feet and sometime by one only; so it is with Satan. Though thou be not a slave to all sins; if thou be a slave to one, the grip he hath of thee, by that one sinful affection, is sufficient to captive thee. WM. COWPER

## EXPOSITION OF VERSES 129 TO 136

All the verses of this section begin with the seventeenth letter of the Hebrew alphabet; but each verse with a different word. WM. S. PLUMER

The seventeenth letter is the letter P. The section is precious, practical, profitable, powerful: peculiarly so. C. H. S.

Vs. 129. *Thy testimonies are wonderful.* Jesus, the eternal Word, is called Wonderful, and all the uttered words of God are wonderful in their degree. Those who know them best wonder at them most.

While we have these holy writings, let us not waste our time, misemploy our thoughts, and prostitute our admiration by doting on human follies and wondering at human trifles. GEO. HORNE

*Therefore doth my soul keep them.* Some men wonder at the Words of God and use them for their speculation; but David was always practical, and the more he wondered the more he obeyed. C. H. S.

David said, *Therefore doth my soul keep them;* and why was this but that he counted them to be wonderful? Can he make a proficiency in any art who doth slight and deprecate it? Prize this Book of God above all other books. T. WATSON

Vs. 130. *The entrance of Thy words giveth light.* Oh, that Thy words, like the beams of the sun, may enter through the window of my understanding and dispel the darkness of my mind! C. H. S.

A Göttingen professor opens a big printed Bible to see if he has eyesight enough to read it and alights on the passage, "I will bring the blind by a way that they knew not," and in reading it the eyes of his understanding are enlightened.

Cromwell's soldier opens his Bible to see how far the musket-ball has pierced and finds it stopped at the verse: "Rejoice, O young man, in thy youth, and let thy heart cheer thee in the days of thy youth; and walk in the ways of thine heart and the sight of thine eyes; but know thou that for all these things God will bring thee into judgment."

And in a frolic, the Kentish soldier opens the Bible which his broken-hearted mother had sent him, and the first sentence that turns up is the text so familiar in boyish days: "Come unto me, all ye that labor and are heavy laden," and the weary profligate repairs for rest to Jesus Christ. JAS. HAMILTON

*It giveth understanding unto the simple.* There are none so knowing that God cannot blind; none so blind and ignorant whose mind and heart He cannot open.

He Who, by His incubation upon the waters at the creation, hatched that rude mass into the beautiful form we now see, and out of that dark chaos made the glorious heavens, and garnished them with so many Orient stars, can move upon thy dark soul and enlighten it, though it be as void of knowledge as the evening of the world's first day was of light.

The schoolmaster sometimes sends home the child and bids his father put him to another trade, because not able, with all his art, to make a scholar of him; but if the Spirit of God be master, thou shalt learn, though a dunce: *The entrance of Thy Words giveth light, it giveth understanding unto the simple.* No sooner is the soul entered into the Spirit's school, than he becomes a proficient. WM. GURNALL

Vs. 131. *I opened my mouth, and panted.* A metaphor taken from men scorched and sweltered with heat, or from those that have run themselves out of breath in following the thing which they would overtake. The former metaphor expressed the vehemency of his love; the other the earnestness of his pursuit: he was like a man grasping for breath, and sucking in the cool air. T. MANTON

Vs. 132. *Look Thou upon me.* If a look from us to God has saving efficacy in it, what may we not expect from a look from God to us?

*And be merciful unto me.* Christ's look at Peter was a look of mercy, and all the looks of the heavenly Father are of the same kind. If He looked in stern justice, His eyes would not endure us, but looking in mercy, He spares and blesses us. C. H. S.

Look on me as on weeping Peter and be merciful unto me as Thou wast to him, who so loved Thy Name as by his triple confession of love to wash out his threefold denial, saying, "Lord, Thou knowest that I love Thee."

*Look upon me,* as on the sinful woman, penitent and weeping, and be merciful unto me, not according to the judgment of the Pharisee who murmured at her, as Judas who was indignant at her, but forgiving me as Thou didst her, "because she loved much," telling me also, "Thy faith hath saved thee; go in peace." NEALE AND LITTLEDALE

Lord, since our looks to Thee are often so slight, so cold, so distant, that no impression is made upon our hearts, do Thou condescend continually to look upon us with mercy and with power. Vouchsafe us such a look as may bring us to ourselves, and touch us with tenderness and contrition in the rememberance of that sin, unbelief, and disobedience, which pierced the hands, the feet, the heart of our dearest Lord and Savior. C. BRIDGES

*As Thou usest to do unto those.* God had one Son without sin, but He never had one without sorrow: "He scourgeth every son whom He receiveth." "Yes," says the suppliant before us, "secure me their everlasting portion, and I am willing to drink of the cup they drank of and to be baptized with the baptism they were baptized with. I want no new, no by-path to glory. I am content to keep the King's highroad. *Be merciful unto me, as Thou usest to do unto those that love Thy Name.* I ask no more." WM. JAY

Vs. 133. *Order my steps in Thy Word.* It is written of Boleslaus, one of the kings of Poland, that he still carries about him the picture of his father, and when he was to do any great work or set upon any design extraordinary, he would look on the picture and pray that he might do nothing unworthy of such a father's name.

Thus it is that the Scriptures are the picture of God's will; therein draws out to the very life. Before a man enter upon or engage himself in any business whatsoever, let him look there and read there what is to be done; what to be undone; and what God commands, let that be done; what He forbids, let that be undone; let the balance of the sanctuary weigh all, the oracles of God decide all, the rule of God's Word be the square of all, and His glory the ultimate of all intendments whatsoever. *From* SPENCER'S "THINGS NEW AND OLD"

*My steps.* Speaking of the steps of the Temple, Bunyan says, "These steps, whether cedar, gold, or stone, yet that which added to their adornment was the wonderment of a Queen. And whatever they were made of, to be sure, they were a shadow of those steps, which we should take to, and in the house of God.

"Steps of God" (Ps. 85:13). "Steps ordered by Him" (Ps. 37:23). "Steps ordered in His Word" (Ps. 119:133). "Steps of faith" (Rom. 4:12). "Steps of the Spirit" (II Cor. 12:18). "Steps of truth" (III John 4). "Steps washed with butter" (Job 29:6). "Steps taken before, or in the presence of God." Steps butted and bounded by a divine rule. These are steps indeed. JOHN BUNYAN

*Let not any iniquity have dominion over me.* I had rather be a prisoner to man all my life than be a bondage to sin one day. He says not, "Let not this and the other hand rule over me"; but "let not *sin* have dominion over me." Well said! There is hope in such a man's condition as long as it is so. MICHAEL BRUCE

Vs. 134. *Deliver me from the oppression of man.* It is a shame that one man should oppress another. Beasts do not usually devour those of the same kind; but usually a man's enemies are those of his own household.

Vs. 135. *Make Thy face to shine upon Thy servant.* O God, Who art the Truth, make me one with Thee in everlasting life! I am often weary of reading and weary of hearing; in Thee alone is the sum of my desire! Let all teachers be silent; let the whole creation be dumb before Thee! and do Thou only speak unto my soul.

Thy ministers can pronounce the words but cannot impart the spirit; they may entertain the fancy with the charms of eloquence but if Thou art silent they do not inflame the heart. They administer the letter, but Thou openest the sense; they utter the mystery, but Thou revealest its meaning; they point out the way of life, but Thou bestowest strength to walk in it; they water, but Thou givest the increase.

Therefore do Thou, O Lord, my God, eternal Truth! speak to my soul! lest, being outwardly warmed, but not inwardly quickened, I die, and be found unfruitful. "Speak, Lord, for Thy servant heareth." THOMAS á KEMPIS

Vs. 136. *Rivers of waters run down mine eyes, because they keep not Thy law.* His grief was such that he could scarcely give it vent; his tears were not mere drops of sorrow but torrents of woe. In this he became like the Lord Jesus, Who beheld the city and wept over it; and like unto Jehovah Himself, Who hath no pleasure in the death of him that dieth but that he turn unto Him and live.

That man is a ripe believer who sorrows because of the sins of others. In verse 120 his flesh trembled at the presence of God, and here it seems to melt and flow away in floods of tears. None are so affected by heavenly things as those who are much in the study of the Word and are thereby taught the truth and essence of things. Carnal men are afraid of brute force and weep over losses and crosses; but spiritual men feel a holy fear of the Lord Himself and most of all lament when they see dishonor cast upon His holy name.

*Lord, let me weep for nought but sin,*
*And after none but Thee,*
*And then I would, O that I might!*
*A constant weeper be.*

Either *because mine eyes keep not Thy law,* so some. The eye is the inlet and outlet of a great deal of sin, and therefore it ought to be a weeping eye. Or rather, *they, i.e., those about me* (ver. 139). Note the sins of sinners are the sorrows of saints. We must mourn for that which we cannot mend. M. HENRY

He that shruggeth when he seeth a snake creeping upon another will much more be afraid when it cometh near to himself. In our own sins we have the advantage of conscience scourging the soul with remorse and shame; in bewailing the sins of others, we have only the reasons of duty and obedience. They that fight abroad out of love to valor and exploits will certainly fight at home out of love to their own safety. T. MANTON

Thus uniformly is the character of God's people represented — not merely as those who are *free* from — but as *those that sigh and cry for — all the abominations that are done in the midst of the land* (Ez. 9:4). And who does not see what an enlarged sphere still presents itself on every side for the unrestrained exercise of Christian compassion? The appalling spectacle of a world apostatized from God, of multitudes sporting with everlasting destruction as if the God of heaven were "a man that he should lie" is surely enough to force "rivers of waters" from the hearts of those that are concerned for His honor.

What a mass of sin ascends as a cloud before the Lord, from a single heart! Add the aggregate of a village — a town — a country — a world every day — every hour — every moment! Well might the *rivers of waters* rise to an overflowing tide, ready to burst its barriers. C. BRIDGES

The vices of the religious are the shame of religion: the sight of this hath made the stoutest champions of Christ melt into tears. David was one of these great worthies of the world, not matchable in his times; yet he weeps.

Did he tear in pieces a bear like a kid? Rescue a lamb with the death of a lion? Foil a mighty giant that had dared the whole army of God? Did he, like a whirlwind, bear and beat down his enemies before him; and now, does he, like a child or a woman, fall a-weeping? Yes, he had heard the name of God blasphemed, seen His holy rites profaned, His statutes vilipended, and violence offered to the pure chastity of that holy virgin, religion; this resolved that valiant heart into tears: *Rivers of waters run down mine eyes.* THOMAS ADAMS

## EXPOSITION OF VERSES 137 TO 144

Vs. 137. *Righteous art Thou,* O Lord. The sinful courses of God's children occasion bitterness enough; they never venture upon sin but with great loss. If Paul give way to little pride, God will humble him. If any give way to sin, their pilgrimage will be made uncomfortable. Eli falls into negligence and indulgence, then is the ark of God taken, his two sons are slain in battle, his daughter-in-law dies, he himself breaks his neck.

Oh, the wonderful tragedies that sin works in the houses of the children of God! David, when he intermeddled with forbidden fruit, was driven from his palace, his concubines defiled, his own son slain; a great many calamities did light upon him. Therefore, the children of God have cause to fear; for the Lord is a just God, and they will find it so.

The hundred and thirty-seventh verse, like the twenty-fifth, is associated with the sorrows of an imperial penitent. When the deposed and captive Emperor Maurice was led out for execution by the usurper Phocas, his five sons were previously murdered one by one in his presence; and at each fatal blow, he patiently exclaimed, *Righteous art Thou, O Lord, and upright are Thy judgments.* NEALE AND LITTLEDALE

*And upright are Thy judgments.* Jehovah both saith and doth that which is right, and that alone. This is a great stay to the soul in time of trouble. C. H. S.

Vs. 138. *Thy testimonies that Thou hast commanded are righteous and very faithful.* Dwell upon that sweet word — *very faithful.* What a mercy that we have a God to deal with Who is scrupulously faithful, true to all the items and details of His promises, punctual to time, steadfast during all time. Well may we risk all upon a Word which is "ever faithful, ever sure." C. H. S.

Men by nature are curious to know their end, rather than careful to mend their life; and for this cause seek answers where they never get good: but if they would know, let them go to the Word and Testimony; they need not to seek any other oracle. If the Word of God testify good things unto them, they have cause to rejoice; if otherwise, it witnesseth evil unto them, let them haste to prevent it, or else it will assuredly overtake them. WM. COWPER

Vs. 139. *My zeal hath consumed me,* etc. Zeal is the heat or intension of the affections; it is a holy warmth, whereby our love and anger are drawn out to the utmost for God and His glory. Now, our love to God and His ways and our hatred of wickedness should be increased because of ungodly men.

Cloudy and dark colors in a table make those that are fresh and lively to appear more beautiful; others' sins should make God and godliness more amiable in thine eyes. Thy heart should take fire by striking on such cold flints. David, by a holy antiperistasis, did kindle from others coldness: *My zeal hath consumed me, because mine enemies have forgotten Thy Words.* Cold blasts make a fire to flame the higher and burn the hotter. GEO. SWINNOCK

Vs. 140. *Thy word is very pure.* It is truth distilled, holiness in its quintessence. In the Word of God, there is no admixture of error or sin. It is pure in its sense, pure in its language, pure in its spirit, pure in its influence, and all this to the very highest degree — *very* pure.

In the original, "tried, refined, purified, like gold in the furnace," absolutely perfect, without the dross of vanity and fallibility which runs through human writings. The more we try the promises, the surer we shall find them. Pure gold is so fixed that Boerhaave informs us of an ounce of it set in the eye of a glass furnace for two months without losing a single grain. GEO. HORNE

A child of God in his best moments does not wish the Word of God brought down to a level with his own imperfect character, but desires rather that his character may be gradually raised to a conformity to that blessed Word. Because it is altogether pure, and because it tends to convey to those who make it their constant study a measure of its own purity, the child of God loves it and delights to meditate in it day and night. J. MORISON

Before I knew the Word of God in spirit and in truth, for its great antiquity, its interesting narratives, its impartial biography, its pure morality, its sublime poetry, in a word, for its beautiful and wonderful variety, I preferred it to all other books; but since I have entered into its spirit, like the Psalmist, I love it above all things for its purity; and desire, whatever else I read, it may tend to increase my knowledge of the Bible and strengthen my affection for its divine and holy truths. SIR WM. JONES

*Therefore Thy servant loveth it,* which is a proof that he himself was pure in heart, for only those who are pure love God's Word because of its purity. His heart was knit to the Word because of its glorious holiness and truth. He admired it, delighted in it, sought to practice it, and longed to come under its purifying power. C. H. S.

Love in God is the fountain of all His benefits extended to us; and love in man is the fountain of all our services and obedience to God. Small sacrifices, flowing from faith and love, are welcome to Him, where greater without these are but abomination to Him. Proofs of both we have in the widow's mite and Cain's rich oblation; whereof the one was rejected, the other received. Happy are we though we cannot say, "We have done as God commands," if out of a good heart we can say, "We love to do what He commands." WM. COWPER

Vs. 141. *I am small and despised: yet do not I forget Thy precepts.* How many a man has been driven to do some ill action in order to reply to the contempt of his enemies: to make himself conspicuous, he has either spoken or acted in a manner which he could not justify.

The first step of defection is to forget what God hath commanded and what we are obliged in duty to do to Him; and upon this easily follows the offending of God by our transgression.

Such beasts as did not chew their cud, under the law were accounted unclean and not meat to be sacrificed unto God: that was but a figure, signifying unto us that a man who hath received good things from God and doth not think upon them cannot feel the sweetness of them and so cannot be thankful to God. WM. COWPER

Vs. 142. *Thy righteousness is an everlasting righteousness.* David here expresses something more than he did in the preceding verse; for there he only said that he reverently served God, although from his rough and hard treatment he might seem to lose his labor; but now when distressed and tormented, he affirms that he finds in the law of God the most soothing delight, which mitigates all griefs, and not only tempers their bitterness but also seasons them with a certain sweetness. Assuredly, when this taste does not exist to afford us delight, nothing is more natural than for us to be swallowed up of sorrow. JOHN CALVIN

Vs. 143. *Have taken hold on me.* Hebrew, *found me.* Like dogs tracking out a wild beast hiding or fleeing. A. R. FAUSSET

*Thy commandments are my delights.* Delight in moral things (saith Aquinas) is the rule by which we may judge of men's goodness or badness. Men are good and bad as the objects of their delight are: they are good who delight in good things, and they are evil who delight in evil things. T. MANTON

Vs. 144. *The righteousness of Thy testimonies is everlasting.* The more we say in praise of Holy Writ, the more we may say and the more we can say. C. H. S.

*Give me understanding and I shall live.* The more the Lord teaches us to admire the eternal rightness of His Word and the more He quickens us to the love of such rightness, the happier and the better we shall be. C. H. S.

As the end for which men are created is not that, like swine or asses, they may stuff their bellies, but that they may exercise themselves in the knowledge and service of God, when they turn away from such employment, their life is worse than a thousand deaths. JOHN CALVIN

## EXPOSITION OF VERSES 145 TO 152

This section is given up to memories of prayer. The Psalmist describes the time and the manner of his devotions and pleads with God for deliverance from his troubles. He who has been with God in the closet will find God with him in the furnace. If we have cried, we shall be answered. Delayed answers may drive us to importunity; but we need not fear the ultimate result, since God's promises are not uncertain, but are "founded forever."

The whole passage shows us; How he prayed (verse 145). What he prayed for (146). When he prayed (147). How long he prayed (148). What he pleaded (149). What happened (150). How he was rescued (151). What was his witness as to the whole matter (152). C. H. S.

Vs. 145. *I cried with my whole heart.* It is well when a man can say as much as this of his prayers: it is to be feared that many cried not to God with their whole heart in all their lives. There may be no beauty of elocution about such prayers, no length of expression, no depth of doctrine, nor accuracy of diction; but if the whole heart be in them they will find their way to the heart of God. C. H. S.

As a man cries most loudly when he cries with all his mouth opened; so a man prays most effectually when he prays with his whole heart. WM. COWPER

God looks not at the elegancy of your prayers, to see how neat they are; nor yet at the geometry of your prayers, to see how long they are; nor yet at the arithmetic of your prayers, to see how many they are; nor yet at the music of your prayers, nor yet at the sweetness of your voice, nor yet at the logic of your prayers; but at the sincerity of your prayers, how hearty they are.

Prayer is only lovely and weighty as the heart is in it, and not otherwise. It is not the lifting up of the voice, nor the wringing of the hands, nor the beating of the breasts, nor an affected tone, nor studied motions, nor seraphical expressions, but the stirrings of the heart that God looks at in prayer. God hears no more than the heart speaks. If the heart be dumb, God will certainly be deaf. No prayer takes with God but that which is the travail of the heart. THOMAS BROOKS

Vs. 146. *I cried unto Thee.* The distressed soul expresses itself in strong cries and tears. Of old they cried unto the Lord, and He heard them in their distress. So Israel at the Red Sea. The men of the Reformation thus expressed themselves in earnest prayer and found relief. Luther, at the Diet of Worms, when remanded for another day, spent the long night in the loud utterance of prayer, that he might appear for his Lord before an august, earthly assembly. JOHN STEPHEN

A crying prayer pierces the depth of heaven. We read not a word that Moses spake, but God was moved by his cry (Exod. 14:15). It means not an obstreperous noise, but melting moans of heart. Yet sometimes the sore and pinching necessities and distresses of spirit extort even vocal cries not displeasant to the inclined ears of God. SAMUEL LEE

Vs. 147. *I prevented the dawning of the morning.* It is a grievous thing if the rays of the rising sun find thee lazy and ashamed in thy bed, and the bright light strike on eyes still weighed down with slumbering sloth. Knowest thou not, O man, that thou owest the daily first-fruits of thy heart and voice to God? Thou hast a daily harvest, a daily revenue.

The Lord Jesus remained all night in prayer, not that He needed its help, but putting an example before thee to imitate. He spent the night in prayer for thee, that thou mightest learn how to ask for thyself. Give Him again, therefore, what He paid for thee. AMBROSE

*And cried.* The first fresh hour of every morning should be dedicated to the Lord, Whose mercy gladdens it with golden light. The eye of day openeth its lids, and in so doing opens the eyes of hosts of heaven-protected slumberers; it is fitting that those eyes should first look up to the great Father of lights, the fount and source of all the good upon which the sunlight gleams.

He who rushes from his bed to his business and waiteth not to worship is as foolish as though he had not put on his clothes, or cleansed his face, and as unwise as though he dashed into battle without arms or armor. Be it ours to bathe in the softly flowing river of communion with God, before the heat of the wilderness and the burden of the way begin to oppress us. C. H. S.

*I hoped in Thy Word.* The student of theology and the minister of the Word should begin the day with prayer, and this chiefly to seek from God, that he may rightly understand the Word of God and be able to teach others. SOLOMON GESNER

Vs. 148. *Mine eyes prevent the night watches, that I might meditate in Thy Word.* The Bible is a book in which we may continually meditate and yet not exhaust its contents. When David expressed himself in the language of our text, Holy Writ — the Word of God — was of course a far smaller volume than it now is, though even now, the Bible is far from a large Book. Yet David could not, so to speak, get to the end of the Book. He might have been studying the Book for years — nay, we are sure that he had been — and yet, as though He were just entering on a new course of reading, with volume upon volume to peruse, he must rise before day to prosecute the study. *Mine eyes prevent the night watches, that I might meditate in Thy Word.* HENRY MELVILL

Vs. 149. O Lord, *quicken me according to Thy judgment.* This is another of David's wise and ardent prayers. He first cried, "Save me"; then, "Hear me"; and now, "Quicken me." This is often the very best way of delivering us from troubles — to give us more life that we may escape from death and to add more strength to that life that we may not be overloaded with its burden. C. H. S.

Vs. 150. *They are far from Thy law.* A mischievous life cannot be an obedient one. Before these men could become persecutors of David, they were obliged to get away from the restraints of God's law. They could not hate a saint and yet love the law. C. H. S.

Vs. 151. *And all Thy commandments are truth.* Virtue is truth in action, and this is what God commands. Sin is falsehood in action, and this is what God forbids. C. H. S.

Vs. 152. *Concerning Thy testimonies, I have known of old that Thou hast founded them forever.* Let "cultured intellects" invent another god, more gentle and effeminate than the God of Abraham; we are well content to worship Jehovah, Who is eternally the same. Things everlastingly established are the joy of established saints. Bubbles please boys, but men prize those things which are solid and substantial with a foundation and a bottom to them which will bear the test of the ages. C. H. S.

## EXPOSITION OF VERSES 153 TO 160

Vs. 153. *Consider mine afflication, and deliver me.* The Psalmist desires two things, and these two things blended: first, a full consideration of his sorrow; secondly, deliverance; and, then, that this deliverance should come with a consideration of his affliction. C. H. S.

We must pray that God will help and deliver us, not after the device of our own brains but after such wise as seemeth best unto His tender wisdom, or else that He will mitigate our pain, that our weakness may not utterly faint. Like as a sick person, although he doubt nothing of the faithfulness and tenderness of his physician yet, for all that, desireth him to handle his wound as tenderly as possible, even so may we call upon God, that, if it be not against His honor and glory, *He will couchsafe to give some mitigation of the pain.* OTTO WERMUELLERUS

Vs. 154. *Plead my cause, and deliver me.* Alexander reads it, "Strive my strife, and redeem me" — that is, stand in my stead, bear my burden, fight my fight, pay my price, and bring me out to liberty. C. H. S.

In this verse are three requests, and all backed with one and the same argument. In the first, he intimateth the right of his cause, and that he was unjustly vexed by wicked men; therefore, as burdened with their calumnies, he desireth God to undertake his defence: *Plead my cause.*

In the second, he representeth the misery and helplessness of his condition; therefore, as oppressed by violence, he saith, *Deliver me;* or, as the words will bear, "Redeem me." In the third, his own weakness, and readiness to faint under this burden; therefore he saith, *Quicken me.* T. MANTON

A wicked woman once brought against Dr. Payson an accusation, under circumstances which seemed to render it impossible that he should escape. She was in the same packet, in which, many months before, he had gone to Boston.

For a time, it seemed almost certain that his character would be ruined. He was cut off from all resources except the throne of grace. He felt that his only hope was in God; and to Him he addressed his fervent prayer. He was heard by the Defender of the innocent. A "compunctious visiting" induced the wretched woman to confess that the whole was a malicious slander. *From* ASA CUMMING'S MEMOIR OF EDWARD PAYSON

Vs. 155. *Salvation is far from the wicked.* In the Name of God consider, were it but the oath of a man, or a company of men that, like those in the Acts, should swear to be the death of such an one, and thou wert the man, would it not fill thee with fear and trembling, night and day, and take away the quiet of thy life till they were made thy friends?

What then are their pillows stuffed with, who can sleep so soundly without any horror or amazement, though they be told that the Almighty God is under an oath of damning them body and soul, without timely repentance? WM. GURNALL

To be saved! What is it to be saved in the fullest and utmost meaning? Who can tell? Eye hath not seen, nor ear heard. It is a rescue, and from such a shipwreck! It is a rest, and in such an unimaginable home! It is to lie down forever in the bosom of God, in an endless rapture of insatiable contentment. FREDERICK W. FABER

Vs. 157. *Yet do I not decline from Thy testimonies.* Some men have been led astray by one enemy, but here is a saint who held on his way in the teeth of many persecutors. There is enough in the testimonies of God to recompense us for pushing forward against all the hosts that may combine against us. So long as they cannot drive or draw us into a spiritual decline our foes have done us no great harm, and they have accomplished nothing by their malice. If we do not decline, they are defeated. If they cannot make us sin, they have missed their mark. Faithfulness to the truth is victory over our enemies. C. H. S.

Vs. 158. *I beheld the transgressors, and was grieved.* Oh, if you have the hearts of Christians or of men in you, let them yearn towards your poor, ignorant, ungodly neighbors. Alas, there is but a step betwixt them and death and hell: many hundred diseases are waiting ready to seize on them, and if they die unregenerate, they are lost forever.

Have you hearts of rock that cannot pity men in such a case as this? If you believe not the Word of God, and the danger of sinners, why are you Christians yourselves? If you do believe it, why do you not bestir yourself to the helping of others? Do you not care who is damned, so you be saved?

Hath God had so much mercy on you and will you have no mercy on your poor neighbors? You need not go far to find objects for your pity; look but into your streets, or into the next house to you, and you will probably find some.

If their houses were on fire, thou wouldst run and help them; and wilt thou not help when their souls are almost at the fire of hell? If thou knewest but a remedy for their diseases thou wouldst tell them, or else thou wouldst judge thyself guilty of their death. RICHARD BAXTER

*And was grieved.* I was sorry to see such sinners. I was sick of them; disgusted with them; I could not endure them. I found no pleasure in them; they were a sad sight to me; however fine their clothing or witty their chattering. Even when they were most mirthful, a sight of them made my heart heavy; I could not tolerate either them or their doings. C. H. S.

*Because they kept not Thy Word.* My grief was occasioned more by their sin against God than by their enmity against myself. I could bear their evil treatment of my words, but not their neglect of Thy Word. Thy Word is so precious to me that those who will not keep it move me to indignation; I cannot keep the company of those who keep not God's Word. That they should have no love for me is a trifle; but to despise the teaching of the Lord is abominable. C. H. S.

I never thought the world had been so wicked when the gospel began as now I see it is; I rather hoped that everyone would have leaped for joy to have found himself freed from the filth of the pope, from his lamentable molestations of poor, troubled consciences, and that through Christ they would by faith obtain the celestial treasure they sought after before with such vast cost and labor, though in vain. And especially I thought the bishops and universities would with joy of heart have received the true doctrines; but I have been lamentably deceived. MARTIN LUTHER

Vs. 159. *Consider,* or see, *how I love Thy precepts.* This is a sure test: many there are who have a warm side towards the promises, but as for the precepts, they cannot endure them.

*Quicken me,* O Lord, *according to Thy loving kindness.* "Quicken me." He prays again the third time, using the same words. We may understand that David felt like one who was half stunned with assaults of his foes, ready to faint under their incessant malice. What he wanted was revival, restoration, renewal; therefore, he pleaded for more life. O Thou Who didst quicken me when I was dead, quicken me again that I may not return to the dead! Quicken me that I may outlive the blows of my enemies, the faintness of my faith, and the swooning of my sorrow.

This time he does not say, "Quicken me according to Thy judgment," but, "Quicken me, O Lord, according to Thy loving kindness." This is the great gun which he brings up last to the conflict: it is his ultimate argument; if this succeed not, he must fail. He has long been knocking at mercy's gate, and with this plea, he strikes his heaviest blow.

When he had fallen into great sin, this was his plea, "Have mercy upon me, O God, according to Thy loving kindness," and now that he is in great trouble, he flies to the same effectual reasoning. Because God is love, He will give us life; because He is kind, He will again kindle the heavenly flame within us. C. H. S.

Vs. 160. *Thy Word is true from the beginning: and every one of Thy righteous judgments endureth forever.* "Forever," and "founded forever." O sweet expression! O grounded comfort! Brethren, get acquainted with God's Word and promise as soon as you can, to maintain that acquaintance everlastingly; and your knowledge of it shall not either go before or go beyond its truth. Know it as soon and as long as you will or can, and you shall never find it tripping or failing; but you may, after long experience of God, say of it, *I have known of old that Thou hast founded it forever.* ANTHONY TUCKNEY

## EXPOSITION OF VERSES 161 TO 168

Vs. 161. *Princes have persecuted me without a cause.* A man expects a fair trial at the hand of his peers: it is ignoble to be prejudiced. C. H. S.

*Without a cause.* I settle it as an established point with me, that the more diligently and faithfully I serve Christ, the greater reproach and the more injury I must expect. I have drunk deep of the cup of slander and reproach, of late, but I am in no wise discouraged; no, nor by, what is much harder to bear, the unsuccessfulness of my endeavors to mend this bad world. PHILIP DODDRIDGE

*But my heart standeth in awe of Thy Word.* Man's wrath, when hottest, is but a temperate climate to the wrath of the living God. They who have felt both have testified as much. Man's wrath cannot hinder the access of God's love to the creature, which hath made the saints sing in the fire in spite of their enemies' teeth. But the creature under God's wrath is like one shut up in a close oven; no crevice is open to let any of the heat out or any refreshing in to him. WM. GURNALL

I would advise you all that come to the reading or hearing of this book, which is the Word of God, the most precious jewel, and most holy relic that remaineth upon earth, that ye bring with you the fear of God, and that ye do it with all due reverence, and use your knowledge thereof, not to vain glory of frivolous disputation, but to the honor of God, increase of virtue, and edification both of yourselves and others. T. CRANMER

They that tremble at the conviction of the Word may triumph in the consolations of it. M. HENRY

Vs. 162. *I rejoice at Thy Word, as one that findeth great spoil.* "Euripides," saith the orator, "hath in his well-composed tragedies more sentiments than sayings"; and Thucydides hath so stuffed every syllable of his history with substance that the one runs parallel along with the other; Lysias' works are so well couched that you cannot take out the least word but you take away the whole sense with it; and Phocion had a special faculty of speaking much in a few words.

The Cretians, in Plato's time (however degenerated in St. Paul's) were more weighty than wordy; Timanthes was famous in this, that in his pictures more things were intended than deciphered; and of Homer it is said that none could ever peer him for poetry.

Then how much more apt and apposite are these high praises to the Book of God, rightly called *the Bible* or *the Book,* as if it were, as indeed it is, both for fitness of terms and fulness of truth, the only book to which (as Luther saith) all the books in the world are but waste paper. It is called *the Word,* by way of eminency, because it must be the butt and boundary of all our words; and *the Scripture,* as the lord paramount above all other words of writings of men collected into volumes. T. ADAMS

Vs. 163. *I hate and abhor lying.* A double expression for an inexpressible loathing. Falsehood in doctrine, in life, or in speech, falsehood in any form or shape, had become utterly detestable to the Psalmist. This was a remarkable state for an Oriental, for generally lying is the delight of Easterns, and the only wrong they see in it is a want of skill in its exercise so that the liar is found out. C. H. S.

A natural man may be angry with his sin, but hate it he cannot; nay, he may leave it, but not loathe it; if he did, he would loathe all sin as well as any one sin. ABRAHAM WRIGHT

*But Thy law do I love,* because it is all truth. His love was as ardent as his hate. True men love truth and hate lying. It is well for us to know which way our hates and loves run, and we may do essential service to others by declaring what are their objects. Both love and hate are contagious, and when they are sanctified, the wider their influence the better. C. H. S.

*Thy law do I love;* nay, as he adds in a later verse, "I love them exceedingly." And so it ever must be, the heart must have some holier object of its affection to fill up the void or there will be no security against a relapse into sin. I might talk forever on the sin, the disgrace, and the danger of lying, and though at the time and for a time my words might have some influence, yet, unless the heart be filled with the love of God and of God's law, the first temptation would prove too powerful.

The Bible teaches us this in a variety of ways. God says to Israel, not only "cease to do evil," but, "learn to do well." And still more pointedly does the Apostle, when he was warring against drunkenness, say, "Be not drunk with wine, wherein its excess, but be filled with the Spirit." BARTON BOUCHIER

Vs. 164. *Seven times a day do I praise Thee.* "As every grace," says Sibbes, "increaseth by exercise of itself, so doth the grace of prayer. By prayer we learn to pray." And thus it was with the Psalmist; he oftentimes anticipated the dawning of the morning for his exercise of prayer; and at midnight frequently arose to pour out his soul in prayer; now he adds that *seven times in a day,* or as we might express it, "at every touch and turn," he finds opportunity for and delight in praise. Oh, for David's spirit and David's practice! BARTON BOUCHIER

Vs. 165. *Great peace have they which love Thy law.* What a charming verse is this! It deals not with those who perfectly keep the law, for where should such men be found, but with those who love it, whose hearts and hands are made to square with its precepts and demands. C. H. S.

Amidst the storms and tempests of the world, there is a perfect calm in the breasts of those who not only do the will of God but "love" to do it.

They are at peace with God by the blood of reconciliation; at peace with themselves, by the answer of a good conscience, and the subjection of those desires which war against the soul; at peace with all men, by the spirit of charity; and the whole creation is so at peace with them that all things work together for their good.

No external troubles can rob them of this *great peace,* no "offences" or stumblingblocks, which are thrown in their way by persecution, or temptation, by the malice of enemies, or by the apostasy of friends, by anything which they see, hear of, or feel, can detain, or divert them from their course. Heavenly love surmounts every obstacle and runs with delight the way of God's commandments. GEO. HORNE

There have been Elis trembling for the ark of God, and Uzzahs putting out their hand in fear that it was going to fall; but in the midst of the deepest troubles through which the church has passed and the fiercest storms that have raged about it, there have been true, faithful men of God who have never despaired.

In every age there have been Luthers and Latimers, who have not only held fast their confidence, but whose peace has deepened with the roaring of the waves. The more they have been forsaken of men, the closer has been their communion with God. And with strong hold of Him and of His promises and hearts that could enter into the secret place of the Most High, although there has been everything without to agitate, threaten, and alarm, they have been guided into perfect peace. JAMES MARTIN

Clearness of conscience is a help to comfortable thoughts. Yet observe that peace is not so much effected as preserved by a good conscience and conversation; for though joy in the Holy Ghost will make its nest nowhere but in a holy soul, yet the blood of Christ only can speak peace; "being justified by faith, we have peace" (Rom. 5:1). An exact life will not make, but keep conscience quiet; an easy shoe does not heal a sore foot, but it keeps a sound one from hurt. OLIVER HEYWOOD

"The pleasures of a good conscience are the Paradise of souls, the joy of angels, a garden of delights, a field of blessing, the temple of Solomon, the court of God, the habitation of the Holy Spirit." OLIVER HEYWOOD

Vs. 166. *I have done Thy commandments.* David calls God's Word "a lamp unto his feet" (verse 105). It was not only a light to his eyes to see by but to his feet to walk by. By practice, we trade with the talent of knowledge and turn it to profit. This is a blessed reading of Scripture, when we fly from the sins which the Word forbids and espouse the doctrines which the Word commands. Reading without practice will be but a torch to light men to hell. T. WATSON

He that has learned the Word of God knows that the law is not made void by faith but established (Rom. 3-31). N. VINCENT

Vs. 168. *I have kept Thy precepts and Thy testimonies; for all my ways are before Thee.* That God seeth the secrets of our heart is a point terrible to the wicked but joyful to the godly. The wicked are sorry that their heart is so open: it is a boiling pot of all mischief, a furnace and forge-house for evil.

It grieveth them that man should hear and see their words and actions; but what a terror is this — that their Judge, Whom they hate, seeth their thought! If they could deny this, they would. But so many of them as are convinced and forced to acknowledge a God are shaken betimes with this also — that He is All-seeing. Others proceed more summarily, and at once deny the Godhead in their heart, and so destroy this conscience of His All-knowledge.

But it is in vain; the more they harden their heart by this godless thought, the more fear is in them; while they choke and check their conscience that it crow not against them, it checketh them with foresight of fearful vengeance and for the present convinceth them of the Omniscience of God, the more they press to suppress it.

But the godly rejoice herein; it is to them a rule to square their thoughts by; they take no liberty of evil thinking, willing, wishing, or affecting, in their hearts. Where that candle shineth, all things are framed as worthy of Him and of His sight, Whom they know to be seeing their heart. WM. STRUTHER

If Alexander's empty chair, which his captains, when they met in counsel, set before them, did awe them so as to keep them in good order; how helpful would it be to set before ourselves the fact that God is looking upon us! WM. GURNALL

## EXPOSITION OF VERSES 169 TO 176

The Psalmist is approaching the end of the Psalm and his petitions gather force and fervency; he seems to break into the inner circle of divine fellowship, and to come even to the feet of the great God, Whose help he is imploring. This nearness creates the most lowly view of himself and leads him to close the Psalm upon his face in deepest self-humiliation, begging to be sought out like a lost sheep. C. H. S.

Vs. 160. *Let my cry come near before Thee,* O Lord. That is, as some will have it, let this whole preceding Psalm, and all the petitions (whereof we have here a repetition) therein contained, be highly accepted in heaven. JOHN TRAPP

The godly, the longer they speak to God, are the more fervent and earnest to speak to Him: so that unless necessity compel them, they desire never to intermit conference with Him. WM. COWPER

*Give me understanding according to Thy Word.* To understand spiritual things is the gift of God. To have a judgment enlightened by heavenly light and conformed to divine truth is a privilege which only grace can give. Many a man who is accounted wise after the manner of this world is a fool according to the Word of the Lord. May we be among those happy children who shall all be taught of the Lord. C. H. S.

Our understanding of the Word of God comes by teaching, but also through experience; we understand hardly anything till we experience it. Such an enlightening experience is the gift of God, and to Him we must look for it in prayer. C. H. S.

*According to Thy Word.* Without this, the wisdom of man is foolishness; and the more subtle he seems to be in his ways, the more deeply he involves himself in the snare of the devil. "They have rejected the Word of the Lord; and what wisdom is in them?" (Jer. 8:9.) ABRAHAM WRIGHT

Vs. 172. *My tongue shall speak of Thy Word.* The worst of us is that for the most part we are full of our own words and speak but little of God's Word. Oh, that we could come to the same resolve as this godly man, and say henceforth, "My tongue shall speak of Thy Word." Then should we break through our sinful silence; we should no more be cowardly and half-hearted, but should be true witnesses for Jesus. C. H. S.

Vs. 173. *I have chosen Thy precepts.* Hath God given you a heart to make choice of His ways? O bless God! There was a time when you went on in giving pleasure to the flesh, and you saw then no better thing than such a kind of life, and the Lord hath been pleased to discover better things to you, so as to make you renounce your former ways, and to make choice of another way, in which your souls have found other manner of comforts, and satisfactions, and contentments than ever you did before.

Bless God as David did: "Blessed be the Lord Who hath given me counsel" . . . Seeing God hath thus inclined your heart to Himself, be forever established in your *choice:* seeing God hath shown to you His ways, as Pilate said in another case, "That I have written I have written": so say you, "That I have chosen I have chosen." JEREMIAH BURROUGHS

Christ loves not melancholy and phlegmatic service; such a temper in acts of obedience is a disgrace to God and to religion: to God, it betrays us to have jealous thoughts of God, as though He were a hard master; to religion, it makes others think duties are drudgeries, and not privileges. STEPHEN CHARNOCK

Vs. 174. *I have longed for Thy salvation, O Lord.* He speaks like old Jacob on his deathbed; indeed, all saints, both in prayer and in death, appear as one, in word, and deed, and mind. C. H. S.

It is mere mockery for a man to say he longeth for bread and prayeth to God every day to give him his daily bread, if he yet walk in no calling, or else seek to get it by fraud and rapine, not staying himself at all upon God's providence. Who will imagine that a man wisheth for health, who either despiseth or neglecteth the means of his recovery? SAMUEL HIERON

God will deliver Noah from the flood, but Noah must be *moved with reverence*, and *prepare the ark* (Heb. 11:7), or else he could not have escaped. He would save Lot from Sodom, but yet Lot must hie him out quickly, and not look behind him till he has entered Zoar (Gen. 19:17). He was pleased to cure Hezekiah of the plague, but yet Hezekiah must take "a lump of figs, and lay it upon his boil" (Isa. 38:21). He vouchsafed to preserve Paul and company at sea, yet the sailors must "abide in the ship," else ye cannot be saved, saith Paul (Acts 27:31). SAMUEL HIERON

Vs. 175. *Let Thy judgments help me.* It is a very profitable doctrine, when things in the world are in a state of great confusion, and when our safety is in danger amid so many and varied storms, to lift up our eyes to the judgments of God, and to seek a remedy in them. JOHN CALVIN

Vs. 176. *I have gone astray like a lost sheep*, etc. And this is all the conclusion — *a lost sheep!* This long Psalm of ascriptions, praises, avowals, resolves, high hopes, ends in this, that he is a perishing sheep. But, stay, there is hope — *Seek Thy servant.*

*I have gone astray like a lost sheep.* The original is of the most extensive range, comprehending all time past, and also the habitual tendencies of the man. The believer feels that he had gone astray when the grace of God found him; that he had gone astray many times had not the grace of God prevented it. JOHN STEPHEN

"All we like sheep have gone astray; we have turned every one to his own way; and the Lord hath laid on Him the iniquity of us all." This would seem to apply to the race of man. Rather is the experience of the Psalmist similar to that described by the Apostle Paul: "I find a law, that when I would do good, evil is present with me. For I delight in the law of God, after the inward man: but I see another law in my members, warring against the law of my mind, and bringing me into captivity to the law of sin which is in my members."

And the Psalmist had the same remedy at the early period as had the Apostle in the later times; for God's salvation is one. The Psalmist's remedy was, "*Seek Thy servant*"; the Apostle's, "O wretched man that I am! who shall deliver me from the body of this death? I thank God through Jesus Christ our Lord." JOHN STEPHEN

Gotthold one day saw a farmer carefully counting his sheep as they came from the field. Happening at the time to be in an anxious and sorrowful mood, he gave vent to his feelings and said: "Why art thou cast down, my soul? and why disquieted with vexing thoughts? Surely thou must be dear to the Most High as his lambs are to this farmer." Art thou not better than many sheep? Is not Jesus Christ thy Shepherd? Has not He risked His Blood and life for thee? Hast thou no interests in His Words: "I give unto My sheep eternal life, and they shall never perish, neither shall any pluck them out of My hand"? (John 10:28).

This man is numbering his flock; and thinkest thou that God does not also count and care for His believing children and elect, especially as His Beloved Son has averred, that the very hairs of our head are all numbered? (Matt 10:30). During the day, I may perhaps have gone out of the way and heedlessly followed my own devices; still, at the approach of evening, when the faithful Shepherd counts His lambs, He will mark my absence and graciously seek and bring me back. Lord Jesus, *I have gone astray like a lost sheep; seek Thy servant; for I do not forget Thy commandments.* CHRISTIAN SCRIVER

Who is called "the man after God's own heart"? David, the Hebrew king, had fallen into sins enough — blackest crimes — there was no want of sin. And, therefore, unbelievers sneer, and ask, "Is this your man after God's own heart?" The sneer, it seems to me, is but a shallow one. What are faults, what are the outward details of a life, if the inner secret of it, the remorse, temptations, the often-baffled, never-ended struggle of it, be forgotten? David's life and history, as written for us in those Psalms of his, I consider to be the truest emblem ever given us for a man's moral progress and warfare here below. All earnest souls will ever discover in it the faithful struggle of an earnest human soul towards what is good and best. Struggle often baffled — sore baffled — driven as into entire wreck; yet a struggle never ended, ever with tears, repentance, true unconquerable purpose begun anew. THOMAS CARLYLE

*For I do not forget Thy commandments.* Yet let the reader remember the first verse of the Psalm while he reads the last: the major blessedness lies not in being restored from wandering but in being upheld in a blameless way even to the end. Be it ours to keep the crown of the causeway, never leaving the King's highway for By-path Meadow or any other flowery path of sin. May the Lord uphold us even to the end. Yet even then we shall not be able to boast with the Pharisee, but shall still pray with the publican, "God be merciful to me a sinner"; and with the Psalmist, "Seek Thy servant." C. H. S.

What an insight into our poor, wayward hearts does this verse give us — not merely liable to wander, but ever wandering, ever losing our way, ever stumbling on the dark mountains, even while cleaving to God's commandments! But at the same time what a prayer does it put into our mouths, *Seek Thy servant* — "I am Thine, save me." Yes, blessed be God! there is One mighty to save. "Kept by the power of God through faith unto salvation." BARTON BOUCHIER

As far as I have been able, as far as I have been aided by the Lord, I have treated throughout, and expounded, this great Psalm. A task which more able and learned expositors have performed, or will perform better; nevertheless, my services were not to be withheld from it on that account, when my brethren earnestly required it of me. AUGUSTINE

# PSALM 120

Suddenly we have left the continent of the vast Hundred and Nineteenth Psalm for the islands and islets of the Songs of Degrees. It may be well to engage in protracted devotion upon a special occasion, but this must cast no slur upon the sacred brevities which sanctify the godly life day by day. He Who inspired the longest Psalm was equally the Author of the short compositions which follow it.

Subject: A certain author supposes that this hymn was sung by an Israelite upon leaving his house to go up to Jerusalem. He thinks that the good man had suffered from the slander of his neighbors and was glad to get away from their gossip and spend his time in the happier engagements of the holy feasts. It may be so, but we hope that pious people were not so foolish as to sing about their bad neighbors when they were leaving them for a few days. C. H. S.

Whole Psalm: Is it any marvel that a Hebrew, with a deep spiritual longing for peace, should cry as he started for the Temple, "Let me get out of all that, at least for a time. Let me quit of this fever and strain, free from the vain turbulence and conflicting noises of the world. Let me rest and recreate myself a while in the sacred asylum and sanctuary of the God of peace. God of peace, grant me Thy peace as I worship in Thy presence; and let me find a bettered world when I come back to it, or at least bring a bettered and more patient heart to its duties and strifes." SAMUEL COX

Vs. 1. *In my distress.* Slander occasions distress of the most grievous kind. Those who have felt the edge of a cruel tongue know assuredly that it is sharper than the sword. Calumny rouses our indignation by a sense of injustice, and yet we find ourselves helpless to fight with the evil or to act in our own defence. C. H. S.

*I cried unto the Lord* (or Jehovah). The wisest course that he could follow. It is of little use to appeal to our fellows on the matter of slander, for the more we stir in it the more it spreads. As well plead with panthers and wolves as with black-hearted traducers. However, when cries to man would be our weakness, cries to God will be our strength. To Whom should children cry but to their Father? C. H. S.

*In my distress I cried unto the Lord.* See the wondrous advantage of trouble — that it makes us call upon God; and again see the wondrous readiness of mercy, that when we call He heareth us! Very blessed are they that mourn while they are traveling the long upward journey from the Galilee of the Gentiles of this lower world to the heavenly Jerusalem, the high and holy city of the saints of God. J. W. BURGON

*In my distress.* God's help is seasonable; it comes when we need it. Christ is a seasonable good . . . For the soul to be dark, and for Christ to enlighten it; for the soul to be dead, and Christ to enliven it; for the soul to be doubting, and for Christ to resolve it; and for the soul to be distressed, and for Christ to relieve it; is not this in season?

For a soul to be hard, and for Christ to soften it; for a soul to be haughty, and for Christ to humble it; for a soul to be tempted, and for Christ to succor it; and for a soul to be wounded, and for Christ to heal it? Is not this in season? R. MAYHEW

Vs. 2. *Deliver my soul, O Lord, from lying lips.* It will need divine power to save a man from these deadly instruments. Lips are soft; but when they are lying lips, they suck away the life of character and are as murderous as razors. C. H. S.

An unbridled tongue is *vehiculum diaboli,* the chariot of the devil, wherein he rides in triumph. Mr. Greenham doth describe the tongue prettily by contraries, or diversities: "It is a little piece of flesh, small in quantity, but mighty in quality; it is soft, but slippery; it goeth lightly, but falleth heavily; it striketh soft, but woundeth sore; it goeth out quickly, but burneth vehemently; it pierceth deep, and therefore not healed speedily; it hath liberty granted easily to go forth, but it will find no means easily to return home; and being once inflamed with Satan's bellows, it is like the fire of hell." EDWARD REYNER

Vs. 3. *Or what shall be done unto thee, thou false tongue?* How shalt thou be visited? The law of retaliation can hardly meet the case, since none can slander the slanderer; he is too black to be blackened; either would any of us blacken him if we could. Wretched being! He fights with weapons which true men cannot touch. Like the cuttlefish, he surrounds himself with an inky blackness into which honest men cannot penetrate.

Like the foul skunk, he emits an odor of falsehood which cannot be endured by the true; and therefore he often escapes, unchastized by those whom he has most injured. His crime, in a certain sense, becomes his shield; men do not care to encounter so base a foe. But what will God do with lying tongues? He has uttered His most terrible threats against them, and He will terribly execute them in due time. C. H. S.

Vs. 3-4. An arrow from the bow of a mighty warrior that flies unseen and unsuspected to its mark and whose presence is only known when it quivers in the victim's heart, not unaptly represents the silent and deadly flight of slander; while the fire which the desert pilgrim kindles on the sand from the dry roots of the juniper, a wood which, of all that are known to him, throws out the fiercest and most continued heat, is not less powerfully descriptive of the intense pain and the lasting injury of a false and malicious tongue. ROBERT NISBET

Vs. 4. *Sharp arrows of the mighty.* What a crime is this to which the All-merciful allots a doom so dreadful! Let us hate it with perfect hatred. It is better to be the victim of slander than to be the author of it. The shafts of calumny will miss the mark, but not so the arrows of God: the coals of malice will cool, but not the fire of justice. Shun slander as you would avoid hell. C. H. S.

He compareth wicked doctrine to an arrow which is not blunt but sharp; and moreover which is cast, not of him that is weak and feeble, but that is strong and mighty; so that there is danger on both sides, as well of the arrow which is sharp and able to pierce, as also of him which with great violence hurleth the same. MARTIN LUTHER

*Arrows. Coals of juniper.* There is a marvelous story in the Midrash which illustrates this very well. Two men in the desert sat down under a juniper tree and gathered sticks of it wherewith they cooked their food. After a year they passed over the same spot where was the dust of what they had the fire, they walked fearlessly upon the dust, and their feet were burned by the "coals" beneath it, which were still unextinguished. H. T. ARMFIELD

Vs. 6. The Arabs are naturally thievish and treacherous; and it sometimes happens that those very persons are overtaken and pillaged in the morning who were entertained the night before with all the instances of friendship and hospitality. Neither are they to be accused for plundering strangers only and attacking almost every person whom they find unarmed and defenceless, but for those many implacable and hereditary animosities which continually subsist among them; literally fulfilling the prophecy of Hagar, that "Ishmael should be a wild man; his hand should be against every man, and every man's hand against him." THOMAS SHAW

Vs. 6. Our Lord was with the wild beasts in the wilderness. There are not a few who would rather face even these than the angry spirits which, alas, are still to be found even in Christian churches. *Wesleyan Methodist Magazine*

Vs. 6-7. The man who hates peace is a dishonor to the race, an enemy to his brother and a traitor to his God. He hates Christ, Who is the Prince of peace. He hates Christians, who are men of peace. N. MCMICHAEL

## PSALM 121

Title: It is a soldier's song as well as a travelers' hymn. There is an ascent in the Psalm itself, which rises to the greatest elevation of restful confidence. C. H. S.

Whole Psalm: It has been said Mr. Romaine read this Psalm every day; and sure it is, that every word in it is calculated to encourage and strengthen our faith and hope in God. SAMUEL EYLES PIERCE

Vs. 1. *I will lift up mine eyes unto the hills, from whence cometh my help.* The holy man who here sings a choice sonnet looked away from the slanderers by whom he was tormented to the Lord, Who saw all from His high places and was ready to pour down succor for His injured servant. C. H. S.

Vs. 2. *My help cometh from the Lord, which made heaven and earth.* He will sooner destroy heaven and earth than permit His people to be destroyed, and the perpetual hills themselves shall bow rather than He shall fail Whose ways are everlasting. We are bound to look beyond heaven and earth to Him Who made them both: it is vain to trust the creatures: it is wise to trust the Creator. C. H. S.

Vs. 3. *He will not suffer thy foot to be moved.* Among the hills and ravines of Palestine, the literal keeping of the feet is a great mercy; but in the slippery ways of a tried and afflicted life, the boon of upholding is of priceless value, for a single false step might cause us a fall fraught with awful danger. C. H. S.

*He that keepeth thee will not slumber.* God is the convoy and bodyguard of His saints. When dangers are awake around us, we are safe, for our Preserver is awake also and will not permit us to be taken unawares. No fatigue or exhaustion can cast our God into sleep; His watchful eyes are never closed. C. H. S.

Vs. 3-8. The everlasting mountains stand fast, and we feel as if, like Mount Zion, they could not be removed forever; but the step of man — how feeble in itself, how liable to stumble or trip even against a pebble in the way! Yet that foot is as firm and immovable in God's protection as the hills themselves. BARTON BOUCHIER

Vs. 3-4. A poor woman, as the Eastern story has it, came to the Sultan one day and asked compensation for the loss of some property. "How did you lose it?" asked the monarch. "I fell asleep," was the reply, "and a robber entered my dwelling." "Why did you fall asleep?" "I fell asleep because I believed that you were awake." The Sultan was so much delighted with the answer of the woman that he ordered her loss to be made up.

But what is true, only by a legal fiction, of human governments, that they never sleep, is true in the most absolute sense with reference to the divine government. We can sleep in safety because our God is ever awake. N. MCMICHAEL

Vs. 4. *He that keepeth Israel shall neither slumber nor sleep.* It is necessary, observes S. Bernard, that "He Who keepeth Israel" should "neither slumber nor sleep," for he who assails Israel neither slumbers nor sleeps. And as the One is anxious about us, so is the other to slay and destroy us, and his one care is that He who has once been turned aside may never come back. NEALE AND LITTLEDALE

Vs. 4. A number of years ago, Captain D. commanded a vessel sailing from Liverpool to New York, and on one voyage he had all his family with him on board the ship.

One night, when all were quietly asleep, there arose a sudden squall of wind, which came sweeping over the waters until it struck the vessel, and instantly threw her on her side, tumbling and crashing everything that was movable and awakening the passengers to a consciousness that they were in imminent peril.

Everyone on board was alarmed and uneasy, and some sprang from their berths and began to dress, that they might be ready for the worst.

Captain D. had a little girl on board, just eight years old, who, of course, awoke with the rest.

"What's the matter?" said the frightened child. They told her a squall had struck the ship. "Is father on deck?" said she. "Yes; father's on deck." The little thing dropped herself on her pillow again without a fear, and in a few moments was sleeping sweetly in spite of winds or waves. *The Biblical Treasury*

Vs. 5. *The Lord is thy Keeper.* What a mint of meaning lies here; the sentence is a mass of bullion, and when coined and stamped with the King's Name it will bear all our expenses between our birthplace on earth and our rest in heaven. Here is a glorious person — Jehovah, assuming a gracious office and fulfilling it in person — Jehovah is thy Keeper, in behalf of a favored individual — thy, and a firm assurance of revelation that it is even so at this hour — Jehovah is thy Keeper. Can we appropriate the divine declaration? If so, we may journey onward to Jerusalem and know no fear; yea, we may journey through the valley of the shadow of death and fear no evil. C. H. S.

*Keeper. Shade.* The titles of God are virtually promises: When He is called a Sun, a Shield, a Strong Tower, a Hiding Place, a Portion. The titles of Christ, Light of the World, Bread of Life, the Way, the Truth, and Life; the titles of the Spirit, the Spirit of Truth, of Holiness, of Glory, of Grace, and Supplication, the sealing, witnessing Spirit; faith may conclude as much out of these as out of promises. Is the Lord a Sun? then He will influence me, etc. Is Christ Life? then He will enliven me, etc. DAVID CLARKSON

*Thy shade upon thy right hand.* That is, always present with thee; or, as the Jewish Arab renders it, "Nigher than thy shadow at, or from thy right hand." THOMAS FENTON

Vs. 6. *Nor the moon by night.* In the cloudless skies of the East, where the moon shines with such exceeding clearness, its effects upon the human frame have been found most injurious. The inhabitants of these countries are most careful in taking precautionary measures before exposing themselves to its influence.

Sleeping much in the open air, they are careful to cover well their heads and faces. It has been proved beyond a doubt that the moon smites as well as the sun, causing blindness for a time, and even distortion of the features.

Sailors are well aware of this fact; and a naval officer relates that he has often, when sailing between the tropics, seen the commanders of vessels waken up young men who have fallen asleep in the moonlight. Indeed he witnessed more than once the effects of a moonstroke, when the mouth was drawn on one side and the sight injured for a time. He was of the opinion that, with long exposure, the mind might become seriously affected. It is supposed that patients suffering under fever and other illnesses are affected by this planet, and the natives of India constantly affirm that they will either get better or worse according to her changes. C. W.

Vs. 7-8. Being then entangled in so many unholy misgivings, and so much inclined to distrust, we are taught from the passage that if a sentence couched in a few words does not suffice us, we should gather together whatever may be found throughout the whole Scriptures concerning the providence of God, until this doctrine — "That God always keeps watch for us" — is deeply rooted in our hearts; so that, depending upon His guardianship alone, we may bid adieu to all the vain confidences of the world. JOHN CALVIN

Vs. 8. *The Lord shall preserve thy going out and thy coming in from this time forth, and even forevermore.* Three times have we the phrase, "Jehovah shall keep," as if the sacred Trinity thus sealed the Word to make it sure: ought not all our fears to be slain by such a threefold flight of arrows? What anxiety can survive this triple promise?

None are so safe as those whom God keeps; none so much in danger as the self-secure. C. H. S.

*From this time forth, and even forevermore.* He has not led me so tenderly thus far to forsake me at the very gate of heaven. ADONIRAM JUDSON

# PSALM 122

Title and Subject: David wrote it for the people to sing at the time of their goings up to the holy feasts at Jerusalem. When they stood within the triple walls, all things around the pilgrims helped to explain the words which they sang within her ramparts of strength. One voice led the Psalm with its personal "I," but ten thousand brethren and companions united with the first musician and swelled the chorus of the strain. C. H. S.

Whole Psalm: Foxe, in his *Acts and Monuments,* relates of Wolfgang Schuch, the martyr, of Lothareng in Germany, that upon hearing the sentence that he was to be burned pronounced upon him, he began to sing the Hundred and Twenty-second Psalm.

Vs. 1. *I was glad when they said unto me, Let us go into the house of the Lord.* Good children are pleased to go home and glad to hear their brothers and sisters call them thither. David's heart was in the worship of God, and he was delighted when he found others inviting him to go where his desires had already gone: it helps the ardor of the most ardent to hear others inviting them to a holy duty. C. H. S.

Gregory Nazianzen writeth that his father being a heathen, and often besought by his wife to become a Christian, had this verse suggested unto him in a dream and was much wrought upon thereby. JOHN TRAPP

Vs. 2. *Our feet shall stand within thy gates, O Jerusalem.* Dr. Clarke, in his travels, speaking of the companions that were traveling from the East to Jerusalem, represents the procession as being very long, and, after climbing over the extended and heavy ranges of hills that bounded the way, some of the foremost at length reached the top of the last hill, and, stretching up their hands in gestures of joy, cried out, "The Holy City! The Holy City!" — and fell down and worshipped; while those who were behind pressed forward to see.

So the dying Christian, when he gets on the last summit of life and stretches his vision to catch a glimpse of the heavenly city, may cry out of its glories and incite those who are behind to press forward to the sight. EDWARD PAYSON

*O Jerusalem.* The Sun of Righteousness has been gradually drawing nearer and nearer, appearing larger and brighter as He approached, and now He fills the whole hemisphere; pouring forth a flood of glory, in which I seem to float like an insect in the beams of the sun; exulting, yet almost trembling, while I gaze on this excessive brightness and wondering with unutterable wonder, why God should deign thus to shine upon a sinful worm. EDWARD PAYSON

Vs. 3. *Jerusalem is builded as a city that is compact together.* There is no joy in going up to a church which is rent with internal dissension: the gladness of holy men is aroused by the adhesiveness of love, the unity of life; it would be their sadness if they saw the church to be a house divided against itself. Some bodies of Christians appear to be periodically blown to fragments, and no gracious man is glad to be in the way when the explosions take place: thither the tribes do not go up, for strife and contention are not attractive forces. C. H. S.

*Jerusalem.* It matters not how wicked or degraded a place may have been in former times, when it is sanctified to the use and service of God, it becomes honorable. Jerusalem was formerly Jebus — a place where the Jebusites committed their abominations and where were all the miseries of those who hasten after another God. But now, since it is devoted to God's service, it is a city — "compact together," "the joy of the whole earth." WILLIAM S. PLUMER

Vs. 6. *Pray for the peace of Jerusalem.* When the Wesleyan Methodists opened a chapel at Painswick, near his own meeting, the late excellent Cornelius Winter prayed three times publicly the preceding Sabbath for their encouragement and success.

When Mr. Hoskins, of Bristol, the Independent minister of Castle-Green, opened a meeting in Temple Street; what did the incomparable Easterbrooke, the Vicar of the parish? The morning it was opened, he was almost the first that entered it. He seated himself near the pulpit. When the service was over, he met the preacher at the foot of the stairs, and shaking him with both hands, said aloud: "I thank you cordially, my dear brother, for coming to my help— here is room enough for us both; and work enough for us both; and much more than we can both accomplish: and I hope the Lord will bless our cooperation in this good cause." WILLIAM JAY

Our praying for the church giveth us a share in all the church's prayers; we have a venture in every ship of prayer that maketh a voyage for heaven, if our hearts be willing to pray for the church; and if not, we have no share in it. JOHN STOUGHTON

Vs. 8. *My brethren.* On another occasion, an elderly native, formerly a cannibal, addressing the church-members, said, "Brethren!" and, pausing for a moment, continued, "Ah! that is a new name; we did not know the true meaning of that word in our heathenism. It is the '*Evangelia a Jesu*' that has taught us the meaning of 'brethren.'" WILLIAM GILL

Vs. 9. *Because of the house of the Lord.* There were synagogues, 480 of them at least, where the rabbis read and the people heard the word which God had in past times spoken unto the fathers by the prophets. The city was indeed in a sense the religion of Israel, incorporated and localized, and the man who loved the one turned daily his face toward the other, saying, "My soul longeth, yea, even fainteth for the courts of Jahveh." A. M. FAIRBAIRN

## PSALM 123

Title: "A Song of Degrees." It has been conjectured that this brief song, or rather sigh, may have first been heard in the days of Nehemiah or under the persecutions of Antiochus. It may be so, but there is no evidence of it; it seems to us quite as probable that afflicted ones in all periods after David's time found this Psalm ready to their hand. If it appears to describe days remote from David, it is all the more evident that the Psalmist was also a prophet and sang what he saw in vision. C. H. S.

Whole Psalm: This Psalm (as ye see) is but short, and therefore a very fit example to show the force of prayer not to consist in many words but in fervency of spirit. For great and weighty matters may be comprised in a few words, if they proceed from the spirit and the unspeakable groanings of the heart, especially when our necessity is such as will not suffer any long prayer. Every prayer is long enough if it be fervent and proceed from a heart that understandeth the necessity of the saints. MARTIN LUTHER

Vs. 1. *Unto Thee lift I up mine eyes.* He who previously lifted his eyes unto the hills now hath raised his heart's eyes to the Lord Himself. *The Venerable Bede*

Praying by the glances of the eye rather than by words; mine afflictions having swollen my heart too big for my mouth. JOHN TRAPP

There are many testimonies in the lifting up of the eyes to heaven. 1. It is the testimony of a believing, humble heart. Infidelity will never carry a man above the earth. Pride can carry a man no higher than the earth, either. 2. It is the testimony of an obedient heart. A man that lifts up his eye to God, he acknowledgeth thus much — Lord, I am Thy servant. 3. It is the testimony of a thankful heart; acknowledging that every good blessing, every perfect gift, is from the hand of God. 4. It is the testimony of a heavenly heart. He that lifts up his eyes to heaven acknowledgeth that he is weary of the earth; his heart is not there; his hope and desire is above. 5. It is the testimony of a devout heart: there is no part of the body besides the tongue that is so great an agent in prayer as the eye. RICHARD HOLDSWORTH

Vs. 2. *As the eyes of servants look unto the hand of their masters.* A traveler says, "I have seen a fine illustration of this passage in a gentleman's house at Damascus. The people of the East do not speak so much or so quick as those in the West and a sign of the hand is frequently the only instructions given to the servants in waiting.

"As soon as we were introduced and seated on the divan, a wave of the master's hand indicated that sherbet was to be served. Another wave brought coffee and pipes; another brought sweetmeats. At another signal, dinner was made ready. The attendants watched their master's eye and hand, to know his will and do it instantly." Such is the attention with which we ought to wait upon the Lord, anxious to fulfill His holy pleasure — our great desire being, "Lord, what wilt Thou have me to do?" *The Sunday at Home*

*Hand.* With the hand we demand, we promise, we call, dismiss, threaten, entreat, supplicate, deny, refuse, interrogate, admire, reckon, confess, repent; express fear, express shame, express doubt; we instruct, command, unite, encourage, swear, testify, accuse, condemn, acquit, insult, despise, defy disdain, flatter, applaud, bless, abase, ridicule, reconcile, recommend exalt, regale, gladden, complain, afflict, discomfort, discourage, astonish; exclaim, indicate silence, and what not? with a variety and a multiplication that keep pace with the tongue. MICHAEL DE MONTAIGNE

*Our eyes wait.* There is good reason: to wait is more than to look: to wait is to look constantly, with patience and submission, by subjecting our affections and wills and desires to God's will; that is to wait. RICHARD HOLDSWORTH

Vs. 3. *For we are exceedingly filled with contempt.* A little contempt they could bear, but now they were satisfied with it and weary of it. Do we wonder at the threefold mention of mercy when this master evil was in the ascendant? Nothing is more wounding, embittering, festering than disdain. When our companions make little of us, we are far too apt to make little of ourselves and of the consolations prepared for us. Oh, to be filled with communion, and then contempt will run off from us and never be able to fill us with its biting vinegar. C. H. S.

Men of the world regard the Temple Pilgrims and their religion with the quiet smile of disdain, wondering that those who have so much to engage them in a present life should be weak enough to concern themselves about frames and feelings, about an unseen God, and unknown eternity; and this is a trial they find it hard to bear. ROBERT NISBET

Vs. 4. *Our soul is exceedingly filled with the scorning of those that are at ease.* They are in easy circumstances; they are easy in heart through a deadened conscience, and so they easily come to mock at holiness; they are easy from needing nothing, and from having no severe toil exacted from them; they are easy as to any anxiety to improve, for their conceit of themselves is boundless.

*And with the contempt of the proud.* Pride is both contemptible and contemptuous. The contempt of the great ones of the earth is often peculiarly acrid: some of them, like a well known statesman, are "masters of gibes and flouts and sneers," and never do they seem so much at home in their acrimony as when a servant of the Lord is the victim of their venom. It is easy enough to write upon this subject, but to be selected as the target of contempt is quite another matter. Great hearts have been broken and brave spirits have been withered beneath the accursed power of falsehood, and the horrible blight of contempt.

For our comfort we may remember that our divine Lord was despised and rejected of men, yet He ceased not from His perfect service till He was exalted to dwell in the heavens. Let us bear our share of this evil which still rages under the sun, and let us firmly believe that the contempt of the ungodly shall turn to our honor in the world to come: even now it serves as a certificate that we are not of the world, for if we were of the world, the world would love us as its own. C. H. S.

## PSALM 124

Whole Psalm: In the year 1582, this Psalm was sung on a remarkable occasion in Edinburgh. An imprisoned minister, John Durie, had been set free and was met and welcomed on entering the town by two hundred of his friends. The number increased till he found himself in the midst of a company of two thousand, who began to sing as they moved up the long High Street, "Now Israel may say," etc.

They sang in four parts with deep solemnity, all joining in the well-known tune and Psalm. They were much moved themselves and so were all who heard; and one of the chief persecutors is said to have been more alarmed at this sight and song than at anything he had seen in Scotland. ANDREW A. BONAR

Vs. 1. *If it had not been the Lord Who was on our side, now may Israel say.* We murmur without being stirred up to it, but our thanksgiving needs a spur, and it is well when some warm-hearted friend bids us say what we feel. Imagine what would have happened if the Lord had left us, and then see what has happened because He has been faithful to us. C. H. S.

Vs. 2. *If it had not been the Lord Who was on our side, when men rose up against us.* There is no doubt as to our Deliverer; we cannot ascribe our salvation to any second cause, for it would not have been equal to the emergency; nothing less than Omnipotence and Omniscience could have wrought our rescue. We set every other claimant on one side and rejoice because the Lord was on our side.

Vs. 3. *Then they had swallowed us up quick, when their wrath was kindled against us.* They were so eager for our destruction that they would have made only one morsel of us and have swallowed us up alive and whole in a single instant. The fury of the enemies of the church is raised to the highest pitch; nothing will content them but the total annihilation of God's chosen. Their wrath is like a fire which is kindled and has taken such firm hold upon the fuel that there is no quenching it.

Anger is never more fiery than when the people of God are its objects. Sparks become flames, and the furnace is heated seven times hotter when God's elect are to be thrust into the blaze. C. H. S.

The word implieth eating with insatiable appetite; every man that eateth must also swallow; but a glutton is rather a swallower than an eater. He throws his meat whole down his throat, and eats (as we may say) without chewing. JOSEPH CARYL

Vs. 4. *The stream had gone over our soul.* When the world's enmity obtains a vent it both rises and rushes, it rages and rolls along, and spares nothing. In the great water-floods of persecution and affliction, who can help but Jehovah? But for Him where would we be at this very hour? We have experienced seasons in which the combined forces of earth and hell must have made an end of us had not omnipotent grace interfered for our rescue. C. H. S.

Vs. 4-5. A familiar but exceedingly apt and most significant figure. Horrible is the sight of a raging conflagration; but far more destructive is a river overflowing its banks and rushing violently on: for it is not possible to restrain it by any strength or power.

As, then, he says, a river is carried along with great impetuosity, and carries away and destroys whatever it meets within its course; thus also is the rage of the enemies of the church not to be withstood by human strength. Hence we should learn to avail ourselves of the protection and help of God. For what else is the church but a little boat fastened to the bank, which is carried away by the force of the waters? or a shrub growing on the bank, which without effort the flood roots up?

Such was the people of Israel in the days of David compared with the surrounding nations. Such in the present day is the church compared with her enemies. Such is each one of us compared with the power of the malignant spirit.

We are as a little shrub, of recent growth and having no firm hold: but he is like the Elbe, overflowing, and with great force overthrowing all things far and wide. We are like a withered leaf, lightly holding to the tree; he is like the north wind, with great force rooting up and throwing down the trees. How, then, can we withstand or defend ourselves by our own power? MARTIN LUTHER

Vs. 7. *Our soul is escaped as a bird out of the snare of the fowlers.* Fowlers have many methods of taking small birds, and Satan has many methods of entrapping souls. Some are decoyed by evil companions; others are enticed by the love of dainties; hunger drives many into the trap, and fright impels numbers to fly into the net. Fowlers know their birds and how to take them; but the birds see not the snare so as to avoid it, and they cannot break it so as to escape from it. Happy is the bird that hath a deliverer strong, and mighty, and ready in the moment of peril: happier still is the soul over which the Lord watches day and night to pluck its feet out of the net. C. H. S.

The soul is surrounded by many dangers. 1. It is ensnared by worldliness, one of the most gigantic dangers against which God's people have specially to guard — an enemy to all spirituality of thought and feeling. 2. It is ensnared by selfishness — a foe to all simple-hearted charity, to all expansive generosity and Christian philanthropy. 3. It is ensnared by unbelief — the enemy of prayer, of ingenuous confidence, of all personal Christian effort. These are not imaginary dangers. We meet them in every-day life. They threaten us at every point and often have we to lament over the havoc they make in our hearts. GEORGE BARLOW

Vs. 8. *The Lord, Who made heaven and earth.* As if the Psalmist had said, "As long as I see heaven and earth, I will never distrust. I hope in that God which made all these things out of nothing; and therefore as long as I see those two great standing monuments of His power before me, heaven and earth, I will never be discouraged."

So the apostle (I Pet. 4:19): "Commit the keeping of your souls to Him in well-doing, as unto a faithful Creator." O Christian, remember when you trust God, you trust an Almighty Creator, Who is able to help, let your case be never so desperate. God could create when He had nothing to work upon, which made one wonder; and He could create when He had nothing to work with, which is another wonder.

What is become of the tools wherewith He made the world? Where is the trowel wherewith He arched the heaven? And the spade wherewith He digged the sea? What had God to work upon or work withal when He made the world? He made it out of nothing. Now, you commit your souls to the same faithful Creator. THOMAS MANTON

The Romans, in a great distress, were put so hard to it that they were fain to take the weapons out of the temples of their gods to fight with them; and so they overcame. And this ought to be the course of every good Christian in times of public distress — to fly to the weapons of the church — prayers and tears. The Spartans' walls were their spears; the Christian's walls are his prayers. His help standeth in the Name of the Lord, Who hath made both heaven and earth. EDMUND CALAMY

*Our help is in the Name of the Lord, Who made heaven and earth.* Thus he setteth the eternal God, the Maker of heaven and earth, against all troubles and dangers, against the floods and overflowings of all temptations, and swallowed up, as it were with one breath, all the raging furies of the whole world, and of hell itself, even as a little drop of water is swallowed up by a mighty, flaming fire: and what is the world with all its force and power in respect of Him that made heaven and earth! THOMAS STINT

# PSALM 125

Faith has praised Jehovah for past deliverances, and here she rises to a confident joy in the present and future safety of believers. She asserts that they shall forever be secure who trust themselves with the Lord. We can imagine the pilgrims chanting this song when perambulating the city walls.

We do not assert that David wrote this Psalm, but we have as much ground for doing so as others have for declaring that it was written after the captivity. It would seem probable that all the Pilgrim Psalms were composed, or at least compiled by the same writer, and as some of them are certainly by David, there is no conclusive reason for taking away the rest from him. C. H. S.

Whole Psalm: This short Psalm may be summed up in those words of the prophet (Isa. 3:10-11), "Say ye to the righteous, that it shall be well with him. Woe unto the wicked! it shall be ill with him." Thus are life and death, the blessing and the curse, set before us often in the Psalms, as well as in the Law and in the Prophets. MATTHEW HENRY

Vs. 1. *They that trust in the Lord shall be as Mount Zion.* What a privilege to be allowed to repose in God! How condescending is Jehovah to become the confidence of His people! To trust elsewhere is vanity; and the more implicit such misplaced trust becomes, the more bitter will be the ensuing disappointment; but to trust in the living God is sanctified common sense, which needs no excuse, its result shall be its best vindication. C. H. S.

*They that trust in the Lord.* Note how he commandeth no work here to be done, but only speaketh of trust. In popery in the time of trouble men were taught to enter into some kind of religion, to fast, to go on pilgrimage, and to do such other foolish works of devotion, which they devised as an high service unto God and thereby thought to make condign satisfaction for sin and to merit eternal life.

But here the Psalmist leadeth us the plain way unto God, pronouncing this to be the chiefest anchor of our salvation — only to hope and trust in the Lord; and declaring that the greatest service that we can do unto God is to trust Him. For this is the nature of God — to create all things of nothing. Therefore, He createth and bringeth forth in death, life; in darkness, light.

Now to believe this is the essential nature and most special property of faith. When God then seeth such a one as agreeth with His own nature, that is, which believeth to find in danger help, in poverty riches, in sin righteousness, and that for God's own mercy's sake in Christ alone, him can God neither hate nor forsake. MARTIN LUTHER

*Shall be as Mount Zion.* Some persons are like the sand — ever shifting and treacherous (see Matt. 7:26). Some are like the sea — restless and unsettled (see Isa. 57:20; Jam. 1:6). Some are like the wind—uncertain and inconstant (see Eph. 4:14). Believers are like a mountain—strong, stable, and secure. To every soul that trusts Him, the Lord says, "Thou art Peter." W. H. J. PAGE

Vs. 2. *As the mountains are round about Jerusalem, so the Lord is round about His people from henceforth even forever.* What a double security the two verses set before us! First, we are established and then entrenched; settled, and then sentineled; made like a mount, and then protected as if by mountains. This is no matter of poetry; it is so in fact; and it is no matter of temporary privilege, but it shall be so forever. The two verses together prove the eternal safety of the saints: they must abide where God has placed them, and God must forever protect them from all evil. It would be difficult to imagine greater safety than is here set forth. C. H. S.

*The Lord is round about His people from henceforth even forever.* What can be spoken more fully, more pathetically? Can any expression of men so set forth the safety of the saints? The Lord is round about them, not to save them from this or that incursion, but from all; not from one or two evils, but from every one whereby they are or may be assaulted. JOHN OWEN

Above us is His heaven; on both sides He is as a wall; under us He is as a strong rock whereupon we stand; so are we everywhere sure and safe. Now, if Satan through these munitions casts his darts at us, it must needs be that the Lord Himself shall be hurt before we take harm. Great is our incredulity if we hear all these things in vain. MARTIN LUTHER

Vs. 3. *For the rod of the wicked shall not rest upon the lot of the righteous.* The people of God are not to expect immunity from trial because the Lord surrounds them, for they may feel the power and persecution of the ungodly. Isaac, even in Abraham's family, was mocked by Ishmael. Assyria laid its scepter even upon Zion itself.

The graceless often bear rule and wield the rod; and when they do so they are pretty sure to make it fall heavily upon the Lord's believing people, so that the godly cry out by reason of their oppressors. Egypt's rod was exceeding heavy upon Israel, but the time came for it to be broken. God has set a limit to the woes of His chosen: the rod may light on their portion, but it shall not *rest* upon it. C. H. S.

*The lot of the righteous.* But the lot of the righteous is faith, and the end of their faith the salvation of their souls. God gives them heaven, not for any foreseen worthiness in the receivers, for no worthiness of our own can make us our father's heirs; but for His own mercy and favor in Christ, preparing heaven for us, and us for heaven. So that upon His decree, it is allotted to us; and unless heaven could lose God, we cannot lose heaven. THOMAS ADAMS

*Lest the righteous put forth their hands unto iniquity.* God (saith Chrysostom) acts like a lutanist, who will not let the strings of His lute be too slack, lest it mar the music, nor suffer them to be too hard stretched or screwed up, lest they break. JOHN TRAPP

Vs. 4. *Those that be good.* O brethren, the good in us is God in us. The inwardness makes the outwardness; the godliness, the beauty. It is indisputable that it is Christ in us that makes all our Christianity. O Christians who have no Christ in them — such Christians are poor, cheap imitations, and hollow shams — and Christ will, with infinite impatience, even infinite love, fling them away. CHARLES STANFORD

*Upright in their hearts.* All true excellence has its seat here. It is not the good action which makes the good man: it is the good man who does the good action. The merit of an action depends entirely upon the motives which have prompted its performance; and, tried by this simple test, how many deeds, which have wrung from the world its admiration and its glory, might well be described in old words, as nothing better than splendid sins. When the heart is wrong, all is wrong. When the heart is right, all is right. N. M'MICHAEL

Vs. 5. *As for such as turn aside unto their crooked ways, the Lord shall lead them forth with the workers of iniquity.* Two kinds of men are always to be found — the upright and the men of crooked ways. Alas, there are some who pass from one class to another, not by a happy conversion, turning from the twisting lanes of deceit into the highway of truth, but by an unhappy declension leaving the main road of honesty and holiness for the by-paths of wickness.

Such apostates have been seen in all ages, and David knew enough of them; he could never forget Saul, and Ahithophel, and others. How sad that men who once walked in the right way should turn aside from it!

All sin will one day be expelled from the universe, even as criminals condemned to die are led out of the city; then shall secret traitors find themselves ejected with open rebels. Divine truth will unveil their hidden pursuits, and lead them forth, and to the surprise of many they shall be set in the same rank with those who avowedly wrought iniquity. C. H. S.

*Crooked ways.* The ways of sinners are *crooked;* they shift from one pursuit to another, and turn hither and thither to deceive; they wind about a thousand ways to conceal their base intentions, to accomplish their iniquitous projects, or to escape the punishment of their crimes; yet disappointment, detection, confusion, and misery, are their inevitable portion. THOMAS SCOTT

*The Lord shall lead them forth with the workers of iniquity.* Sometimes God takes away a barren professor by permitting him to fall into open profaneness. There is one that hath taken up a profession of the worthy Name of the Lord Jesus Christ, but this profession is only a cloak; he secretly practiceth wickedness; he is a glutton, or a drunkard, or covetous, or unclean. Well, saith God, I will loose the reins of this professor, I will give him up to his vile affections. I will loose the reins of his sins before him, he shall be entangled with his filthy lusts; he shall be overcome of ungodly company. Thus they that turn aside to their own crooked ways. JOHN BUNYAN

## PSALM 126

This is the seventh step, and we may therefore expect to meet with some special perfection of joy in it; nor shall we look in vain. We see here not only that Zion abides but that her joy returns after sorrow. Abiding is not enough, fruitfulness is added. The pilgrims went from blessing to blessing in their Psalmody as they proceeded on their holy way. Happy people to whom every ascent was a song, every halt a hymn. Here the truster becomes a sower: faith works by love, obtains a present bliss, and secures a harvest of delight.

The Psalm divides itself into a narrative (1-2), a song (3), a prayer (4), and a promise (5 and 6). C. H. S.

Whole Psalm: In mine opinion, they go near to the sense and true meaning of the Psalm who do refer it to that great and general captivity of mankind under sin, death, and the devil, and to the redemption purchased by the death and blood-shedding of Christ and published in the gospel. For this kind of speech which the prophet useth here is of greater importance than that it may be applied only to Jewish particular captivities.

For what great matter was it for these people of the Jews, being, as it were, a little handful, to be delivered out of temporal captivity, in comparison of the exceeding and incomparable deliverance whereby mankind was set at liberty from the power of their enemies, not temporal, but eternal, even from death, Satan, and hell itself? Wherefore we take this Psalm to be a prophecy of the redemption that should come by Jesus Christ, and the publishing of the gospel, whereby the kingdom of Christ is advanced, and death and the devil with all the powers of darkness are vanquished. THOMAS STINT

Vs. 1. *When the Lord turned again the captivity of Zion, we were like them that dream.* So sudden and so overwhelming was their joy that they felt like men out of themselves, ecstatic, or in a trance. The captivity had been great, and great was the deliverance; for the great God Himself had wrought it: it seemed too good to be actually true.

Let us look to the prison-houses from which we have been set free. Ah, me, what captives we have been! At our first conversion, what a turning again of captivity we experienced! Never shall that hour be forgotten. Joy! Joy! Joy! Since then, from multiplied troubles, from depression of spirit, from miserable backsliding, from grievous doubt, we have been emancipated, and we are not able to describe the bliss which followed each emancipation. C. H. S.

*When the Lord turned again the captivity.* As by the Lord's permission they were led into captivity, so only by His power they were set at liberty. When the Israelites had served in a strange land four hundred years, it was not Moses, but Jehovah, that brought them out of the land of Egypt, and out of the house of bondage. JOHN HUME

*The captivity of Zion.* Why? What was Zion? We know it was but a hill in Jerusalem, on the north side. Why is that hill so honored? No reason in the world but this — that upon it the Temple was built; and so, that Zion is much spoken of, and much made of, it is only for the Temple's sake. LANCELOT ANDREWS (Thus, the hill of Calvary, we honor and make much of only because it was there "The Prince of Glory died." D.O.F.)

*We were like them that dream.* Lorinus seems to excuse this, their distrust, because they were so overravished with joy that they misdoubted the true cause of their joy: like the Apostles, who having Christ after His resurrection standing before them, they were so exceedingly joyed, that rejoicing they wondered and doubted; and like the two Marys when the angel told them of our Savior, Christ's resurrection, they returned from the sepulcher rejoicing and yet withal fearing. It may be they feared the truth of so glad news and doubted lest they were deceived by some apparition. JOHN HUME

Vs. 2. *Then was our mouth filled with laughter, and our tongue with singing.* When at last the tongue could move articulately, it could not be content simply to talk, but it must needs sing; and sing heartily, too, for it was full of singing. Doubtless the former pain added to the zest of the pleasure; the captivity threw a brighter color into the emancipation. The people remembered this joy-flood for years after, and here is the record of it turned into a song.

Note the *when* and the *then.* God's *when* is our *then.* At the moment when He turns our captivity, the heart turns from its sorrow; when He fills us with grace, we are filled with gratitude. We were made to be as them that dream, but we both laughed and sang in our sleep. We are wide awake now, and though we can scarcely realize the blessing, yet we rejoice in it exceedingly. C. H. S.

This is the sense and meaning of the Holy Ghost, that the mouth of such shall be filled with laughter, that is, their mouth shall show forth nothing else but great gladness through the inestimable consolations of the Gospel, with voices of triumph and victory by Christ, overcoming Satan, destroying death, and taking away sins. This was first spoken unto the Jews; for this laughter was first offered to that people, then having the promises. Now He turneth to the Gentiles, whom He calleth to the partaking of this laughter. MARTIN LUTHER

They that were laughed at, now laugh, and a new song is put into their mouths. It was a laughter of joy in God, not scorn of their enemies. MATTHEW HENRY

*And our tongue with singing.* Out of the abundance of the heart the mouth speaks; and if the heart be glad, the tongue is glib. Joy cannot be suppressed in the heart, but it must be expressed with the tongue. JOHN HUME

*Then said they among the heathen, the Lord hath done great things for them.* It is a blessed thing when saints set sinners talking about the lovingkindness of the Lord: and it is equally blessed when the saints, who are hidden away in the world, hear of what the Lord has done for His church, and themselves resolve to come out from their captivity and unite with the Lord's people. C. H. S.

Vs. 3. *The Lord hath done great things for us; whereof we are glad.* I heard one say the other day in prayer, "whereof we desire to be glad." Strange dilution and defilement of Scriptural language! Surely if God has done great things for us we are glad and cannot be otherwise. No doubt such language is meant to be lowly, but in truth it is loathsome. C. H. S.

Vss. 4, 5, 6. The saints are oft feeding their hopes on the carcasses of their slain fears. The time which God chose and the instrument He used to give the captive Jews their gaol delivery and liberty to return home were so incredible to them when it came to pass (like Peter whom the angel had carried out of prison, Acts 12), it was some time before they could come to themselves and resolve whether it was a real truth or but a pleasing dream.

Now, see what effect this strange disappointment of their fears had upon their hope for afterward. It sent them to the throne of grace for the accomplishment of what was so marvelously begun. "The Lord hath done great things for us; whereof we are glad. Turn again our captivity, O Lord" (Verses 3-4). They have got a hand-hold by this experiment of His power and mercy, and they will not now let Him go till they have more; yea, their hope is raised to such a pitch of confidence that they draw a general conclusion from this particular experience for the comfort of themselves or others in any future distress: "They that sow in tears shall reap in joy," etc. (Verses 5-6). WILLIAM GURNALL

Vs. 5. *They that sow in tears shall reap in joy.* Our mouth has never been filled with holy laughter if it had not been first filled with the bitterness of grief. We must sow: we may have to sow in the wet weather of sorrow; but we shall reap, and reap in the bright summer season of joy.

When a man's heart is so stirred that he weeps over the sins of others, he is elect to usefulness. Winners of souls are first weepers for souls. As there is no birth without travail, so is there no spiritual harvest without painful tillage. When our own hearts are broken with grief at man's transgression, we shall break other men's hearts: tears of earnestness beget tears of repentance: "deep calleth unto deep." C. H. S.

In seasons of great scarcity, the poor peasants part in sorrow with every measure of precious seed cast into the ground. It is like taking bread out of the mouths of their children; and in such times many bitter tears are actually shed over it. The distress is frequently so great that government is obliged to furnish seed or none would be sown. W. M. THOMSON

This promise is conveyed under images borrowed from the instructive scenes of agriculture. In the sweat of his brow, the husbandman tills his land, and casts the seed into ground, where for a time it lies dead and buried. A dark and dreary winter succeeds, and all seems to be lost; but at the return of spring, universal nature revives, and the once desolate fields are covered with corn which, when matured by the sun's heat, the cheerful reapers cut down, and it is brought home with triumphant shouts of joy.

Here, O disciple of Jesus, behold an emblem of thy present labor and the future reward! Thou "sowest," perhaps, in "tears"; thou doest thy duty amidst persecution, and affliction, sickness, pain, and sorrow; thou laborest in the church, and no account is made of thy labors, no profit seems likely to arise from them. Nay, thou must thyself drop into the dust of death, and all the storms of that winter must pass over thee, until thy form shall be perished, and thou shalt see corruption. Yet the day is coming when thou shalt "reap in joy," and plentiful shall be thy harvest.

For thus thy blessed Master "went forth weeping," a Man of sorrows and acquainted with grief, "bearing precious seed" and sowing it around Him, till at length His own body was buried, like a grain of wheat, in the furrow of the grave. But He arose, and is now in heaven, from whence He shall "doubtless come again with rejoicing," with the voice of the archangel and the trump of God, "bringing His sheaves with Him." Then shall every man receive the fruit of his works and have praise of God. GEORGE HORNE

They sow *in faith;* and God will bless that seed: it shall grow up to heaven, for it is sown in the side of Jesus Christ, Who is in heaven. "He that believeth on God," this is the seed; "shall have everlasting life" (John 5:24); this is the harvest. *Qui credit quod non videt, videbit quod* credit — he that believes what he doth not see; this is the seed: shall one day see what he hath believed; this is the harvest.

They sow *in obedience:* this is also a blessed seed, that will not fail to prosper wheresoever it is cast. "If ye keep My commandments"; this is the seed: "Ye are become servants to God, and have your fruit unto holiness"; this is the sowing: "and the end everlasting life"; this is the reaping. *Obedientia in terris, regnabit in coelis* — he that serves God on earth, and sows the seed of obedience, shall in heaven reap the harvest of a kingdom.

They sow *in repentance;* To have a good crop on earth, we desire a fair seed-time; but here a wet time of sowing shall bring the best harvest in the barn of heaven.

No worldling, when he sows his seed, thinks he shall lose his seed; he hopes for increase at harvest. Darest thou trust the ground and not God? Sure, God is a better paymaster than the earth: grace doth give a larger recompense than nature. Below, thou mayest receive forty grains for one; but in heaven (by the promise of Christ) a hundred-fold: a "measure heapen, and shaken, and thrust together, and yet running over." "Blessed is he that considereth the poor"; this is the seeding: "the Lord shall deliver him in the time of trouble" (Ps. 41:1); this is the harvest. THOMAS ADAMS

They get the full harvest; and that is gotten at the great and last day. Then we get peace without trouble, joy without grief, profit without loss, pleasure without pain; and then we have a full sight of the face of God. ALEXANDER HENDERSON

Gospel tears are not lost; they are seeds of comfort: while the penitent doth pour out tears, God pours in joy. If thou wouldst be cheerful, saith Chrysostom, be sad. THOMAS WATSON

Vss. 5 and 6. Mind we the undoubted certainty of our harvest verified by divers absolute positive asseverations in the text: *he shall reap; he shall come again; he shall bring his sheaves with him.* Here's no item of contingency or possibility, but all absolute affirmations; and you know heaven and earth shall pass away, but a jot of God's Word shall not fail. Nothing shall prevent the harvest of a laborer in Zion's vineyard. HUMPHREY HARDWICK

Vs. 6. *He that goeth forth and weepeth, bearing precious seed, shall doubtless come again with rejoicing, bringing his sheaves with him. He.* The general assurance is applied to each one in particular. That which is spoken in the previous verse in the plural—"they"—is here repeated in the singular—"he." He leaves his couch to go forth into the frosty air and tread the heavy soil; and as he goes, he weeps because of past failures, or because the ground is so sterile, or the weather so unseasonable, or his corn so scarce, and his enemies so plentiful and so eager to rob him of his reward.

He drops a seed and a tear, a seed and a tear, and so goes on his way. In his basket, he has seed which is precious to him, for he has little of it, and it is his hope for the next year. Each grain leaves his hand with anxious prayer that it may not be lost; he thinks little of himself but much of his seed, and he eagerly asks, "Will it prosper? Shall I receive a reward for my labor?" Yes, good husbandman, *doubtless* you will gather sheaves from your sowing. Because the Lord has written *doubtless,* take heed that you do not doubt.

It is somewhat singular to find this promise of fruitfulness in close contact with return from captivity; and yet it is so in our own experience, for when our own soul is revived, the souls of others are blessed by our labors. If any of us, having been once lonesome and lingering captives, have now returned home, and have become longing and laboring sowers, may the Lord, Who has already delivered us, soon transform us into glad-hearted reapers, and to Him shall be praise forever and ever. Amen. C. H. S.

*Goeth forth.* The church must not only keep this seed in the storehouse for such as come to enquire for it, but must send her sowers forth to cast it among those who are ignorant of its value or too indifferent to ask it at her hands. She must not sit weeping because men will not apply to her, but must go forth and bear the precious seed to the unwilling, the careless, the prejudiced, and the profligate. EDWIN SIDNEY

*Weeping* must not hinder sowing: when we suffer ill we must be doing well. MATTHEW HENRY

*Precious seed.* Seed-corn is always dearest; and when other corn is dear, then it is very dear; yet though never so dear, the husbandman resolves that he must have it; and he will deprive his own belly, and his wife and children of it; and will sow it, going out *weeping* with it. There is also great hazard; for corn, after it is sown, is subject to many dangers. And so is it, indeed, with the children of God in a good cause. Ye must resolve to undergo hazards also, in life, lands, movables, or whatsoever else ye have in this world: rather hazard all these before either religion be in hazard or your own souls. ALEXANDER HENDERSON

Seed was accounted precious when all countries came unto Egypt to buy corn of Joseph, and truly faith must needs be precious, seeing that when Christ comes He shall hardly "find faith upon the earth" (Luke 18:8). JOHN HUME

*Sheaves*. The psalm which begins with "dream" and ends with "sheaves" invites us to think of Joseph; Joseph, "in whom," according to S. Ambrose's beautiful application, "there was revealed the future resurrection of the Lord Jesus, to Whom both His eleven disciples did obeisance when they saw Him gone into Galilee, and to Whom all the saints shall on their resurrection do obeisance, bringing forth the fruit of good works, as it is written, 'He shall doubtless come again with rejoicing, bringing his sheaves with him'." H. T. ARMFIELD

## PSALM 127

The title probably indicates that David wrote it for his wise son, in whom he so greatly rejoiced, and whose name, Jedidiah, or "beloved of the Lord," is introduced into the second verse. The spirit of his name, "Solomon, or peaceable," breathes through the whole of this most charming song.

Vs. 1. *Except the Lord build the house, they labor in vain that build it.* The word *vain* is the key-note here, and we hear it ring out clearly three times. Men desiring to build know that they must labor, and accordingly they put forth all their skill and strength; but let them remember that if Jehovah is not with them their designs will prove failures.

So was it with the Babel builders; they said, "Go to, let us build us a city and tower"; and the Lord returned their words into their own bosoms, saying, "Go to, let us go down and there confound their language." Trowel and hammer, saw and plane, are instruments of vanity unless the Lord be the Master-builder. C. H. S.

*Except the Lord build.* It is a fact that *ben, a son,* and *bath, a daughter,* and *beith, a house,* come from the same root — *banah, to build;* because sons and daughters build up a household, or constitute a *family,* as much and as really as stones and timber constitute a *building.*

Now, it is true that unless the good hand of God be upon us, we cannot prosperously build a place of worship for His Name. Unless we have His blessing, a dwelling-house cannot be comfortably erected. And if His blessing be not on our children, the house (the family) may be built up; but instead of its being the house of God, it will be the synagogue of Satan. All marriages that are not under God's blessing will be a private and public curse. ADAM CLARKE

He is far from thinking that the care and human labor, which is employed in the building of houses and keeping of cities, is to be regarded as useless, because the Lord builds and keeps; since it is then the more especially useful and effectual when the Lord Himself is the Builder and Keeper. The Holy Spirit is not the patron of lazy and inert men; but He directs the minds of those who labor to the providence and power of God. WOLFGANG MUSCULUS

In the beginning of the contest with Britain, when we were sensible of danger, we had daily prayers in this room for the divine protection. Our prayers, sir, were heard, and they were graciously answered. All of us who were engaged in the struggle must have observed frequent instances of a superintending Providence in our favor. To that kind Providence, we owe this happy opportunity of consulting in peace on the means of establishing our future national felicity.

And have we now forgotten this powerful Friend? or do we imagine we no longer need His assistance? I have lived for a long time — (eighty-one years); and the longer I live the more convincing proofs I see of this truth, that God governs in the affairs of man. And if a sparrow cannot fall to the ground without His notice, is it probable that an empire can rise without His aid?

We have been assured, sir, in the sacred writings, that "Except the Lord build the house, they labor in vain that build it." I firmly believe this; and I also believe that without His concurring aid we shall proceed in this political building no better than the builders of Babel: we shall be divided by our little, partial, local interests; our prospects will be confounded; and we ourselves shall become a reproach and a by-word down to future ages.

And what is worse, mankind may hereafter, from this unfortunate instance, despair of establishing government by human wisdom, and leave it to chance, war, or conquest. I therefore beg leave to move that henceforth prayers, implor ing the assistance of Heaven and its blessing on our deliberations, be held in this assembly every morning before we proceed to business; and that one or more of the clergy of this city be requested to officiate in that service. BENJAMIN FRANKLIN

*Except the Lord keep the city, the watchman waketh but in vain.* Note that the Psalmist does not bid the builder cease from laboring, nor suggest that watchmen should neglect their duty, nor that men should show their trust in God by doing nothing: nay, he supposes that they will do all that they can do, and then he forbids their fixing their trust in what they have done and assures them that all creature effort will be in vain unless the Creator puts forth His power to render second causes effectual.

Holy Scripture indorses the order of Cromwell: "Trust in God, and keep your powder dry": only here the sense is varied, and we are told that the dried powder will not win the victory unless we trust in God. Happy is the man who hits the golden mean by so working as to believe in God, and so believing in God as to work without fear. C. H. S.

Vs. 2. *It is vain for you to rise up early, to sit up late, to eat the bread of sorrows.* Hard earned is their food, scantily rationed, and scarcely ever sweetened, but perpetually smeared with sorrow; and all because they have no faith in God and find no joy except in hoarding up the gold which is their only trust. Not thus, not thus, would the Lord have His children live. He would have them, as princes of the blood, lead a happy and restful life. Let them take a fair measure of rest and a due portion of food, for it is for their health.

Of course the true believer will never be lazy or extravagant; if he should be, he will have to suffer for it; but he will not think it needful or right to be worried and miserly. Faith brings calm with it and banishes the disturbers who both by day and night murder peace. C. H. S.

But no man should work beyond his physical and intellectual ability, nor beyond the hours which nature allots. No net result of good to the individual or to the race comes of any artificial prolonging of the day at either end. Early rising, eating one's breakfast by candlelight, and prolonged vigils, the scholar's "midnight oil," are a delusion and a snare. Work while it is day. When the night comes, rest. The other animals do this, and, as races, fare as well as this anxious human race. CHARLES F. DEEMS

The meaning is, that though worldly men fare never so hardly, beat their brains, tire their spirits, rack their consciences, yet many times all is for nothing; either God doth not give them an estate or not the comfort of it.

But His beloved, without any of these racking cares, enjoys contentment; if they have not the world, they have sleep and rest; with silence submitting to the will of God, and with quietness waiting for the blessing of God. Well, then, acknowledge the providence that you may come under the blessing of it: labor *without God* cannot prosper; *against God* and against His will in His Word, will surely miscarry. THOMAS MANTON

*By caring and fretting,*
*By agony and fear,*
*There is of God no getting,*
*But prayer He will hear.*

J. P. LANGE'S

*For so He giveth His beloved sleep.* Note how Jesus slept amid the hurly-burly of a storm at sea. He knew that He was in His Father's hands, and therefore He was so quiet in spirit that the billows rocked Him to sleep: it would be much oftener the same with us if we were more like Him. C. H. S.

Whence proceeds this so great ardor in the unbelieving that they move not a finger without a tumult or bustle; in other words, without tormenting themselves with superfluous cares, but because they attribute nothing to the providence of God! The faithful, on the other hand, although they lead a laborious life, yet follow their vocations with composed and tranquil minds. Thus their hands are not idle, but their minds repose in the stillness of faith, as if they were asleep. JOHN CALVIN

As the Lord *gave* a precious gift to His *beloved,* the first Adam, when he *slept,* by taking a rib from his side, and *building* therefrom a woman, Eve, his bride, the Mother of all living; so, while Christ, the second Adam, the true Jedidiah, the Well-beloved Son of God, was sleeping in death on the cross, God formed for Him, in His death, and by His death, even by the life-giving streams flowing from His own precious side, the church, the spiritual Eve, the Mother of all living; and gave her to Him as His bride. Thus He *built* for Him in His *sleep* the spiritual temple of His church. CHRISTOPHER WORDSWORTH

Quiet sleep is the gift of God, and it is the love of God to give quiet sleep. PHILIP GOODWIN

The world would give its favorites power, wealth, distinction; God gives *sleep.* Could He give anything better? To give sleep when the storm is raging; to give sleep when conscience is arraying a long catalogue of sins; to give sleep when evil angels are trying to overturn our confidence in Christ; to give sleep when death is approaching, when judgment is at hand — oh! what gift could be more suitable? What more worthy of God? Or what more precious to the soul?

Dry your tears, ye that stand around the bed of the dying believer; the parting moment is almost at hand. A cold damp is on the forehead — the eye is fixed — the pulse too feeble to be felt. Are you staggered at such a spectacle? Nay! let faith do its part! The chamber is crowded with glorious forms; angels are waiting there to take charge of the disembodied soul; a hand gentler than any human is closing those eyes; and a voice sweeter than any human is whispering, *Surely the Lord giveth His beloved sleep.* HENRY MELVILL

Go, ye overreaching misers! Go, ye grasping, ambitious men! I envy not your life of inquietude. The sleep of statesmen is often broken; the dream of the miser is always evil; the sleep of the man who loves gain is never hearty; but God *giveth,* by contentment, *His beloved, sleep.* C. H. S.

Vs. 3. *Lo, children are an heritage of the Lord.* This points to another mode of building up a house, namely, by leaving descendants to keep our name and family alive upon the earth. Without this, what is a man's purpose in accumulating wealth? To what purpose does he build a house if he has none in his household to hold the house after him? What boots it that he is the possessor of broad acres if he has no heir? Yet in this matter, a man is powerless without the Lord.

The great Napoleon, with all his sinful care on this point, could not create a dynasty. Hundreds of wealthy persons would give half their estates if they could hear the cry of a babe born of their own bodies. Children are a heritage which Jehovah Himself must give, or a man will die childless, and thus his house will be unbuilt. C. H. S.

If even thou wouldst not part with one of them for thousands of gold and silver, believe that He Who is the fountain of all tenderness regards them with yet deeper love, and will make them now, in thy hour of trial, a means of increasing thy dependence on Him, and soon thy support and pride.

Children! Might another say, as the Psalm referred to them — on their opening promise, the breath of the destroyer has been poured. They are ripening visibly for the grave, and their very smile and caress cause my wounded heart to bleed anew. Yes, mourner; but *God's heritage!* may He not claim His own?

They are in safe keeping when in His, and will soon be restored to thee in the better land, where death will make them ministering angels at His throne; nay, they will be the first to welcome thee to its glories, to love and worship with thee throughout eternity. ROBERT NISBET

*And the fruit of the womb is His reward.* Where society is rightly ordered, children are regarded, not as an incumbrance, but as an inheritance; and they are received, not with regret, but as a reward. C. H. S.

John Howard Hinton's daughter said to him as she knelt by his deathbed: "There is no greater blessing than for children to have godly parents." "And the next," said the dying father, with a beam of gratitude, "for parents to have godly children." MEMOIR IN BAPTIST HANDBOOK

Vs. 4. *As arrows are in the hand of a mighty man; so are children of the youth.* Children born to men in their early days, by God's blessing, become the comfort of their riper years. A man of war is glad of weapons which may fly where he cannot: good sons are their father's arrows, speeding to hit the mark which their sires aim at. What wonders a good man can accomplish if he has affectionate children to second his desires and lend themselves to his designs. C. H. S.

Well doth David call children *arrows;* for if they be well bred, they shoot at their parents enemies; and if they be evil bred, they shoot at their parents. HENRY SMITH

Vs. 5. *Happy is the man that hath his quiver full of them.* Those who have no children bewail the fact; those who have few children see them soon gone, and the house is silent, and their life has lost a charm; those who have many gracious children are upon the whole the happiest. Of course a large number of children means a large number of trials; but when these are met by faith in the Lord it also means a mass of love and a multitude of joys.

Dr. Guthrie used to say, "I am rich in nothing but children." They were eleven in number.

Many children make many prayers, and many prayers bring much blessing. GERMAN PROVERB

The Rev. Moses Browne had twelve children. On one remarking to him, "Sir, you have just as many children as Jacob," he replied, "Yes, and I have Jacob's God to provide for them." G. S. BOWES

I remember a great man coming into my house at Waltham, and seeing all my children standing in the order of their age and stature, said, "These are they that make rich men poor." But he straight received this answer, "Nay, my lord, these are they that make a poor man rich; for there is not one of these whom we would part with for all your wealth."

It is easy to observe that none are so gripple and hardfisted as the childless; thereas those, who, for the maintenance of large families, are inured to frequent disbursements, find such experience of Divine providence in the faithful management of their affairs, as that they lay out with more cheerfulness what they receive. Wherein their care must be abated when God takes it off from them to Himself; and, if they be not wanting to themselves, their faith gives them ease in casting their burden upon Him, Who hath more power and more right to it, since our children are more His than our own. He that feedeth the young ravens, can He fail the best of His creatures? JOSEPH HALL

## PSALM 128

There is clearly an advance in age, for here we go beyond children to children's children; and also a progress in happiness, for children which in the last Psalm were arrows are here olive plants, and instead of speaking "with the enemies in the gate," we close with "peace upon Israel." Thus we rise step by step and sing as we ascend. C. H. S.

Vs. 1. *Blessed is every one that feareth the Lord.* A man's heart will be seen in his walk, and the blessing will come where heart and walk are both with God. Note that the First Psalm links the benediction with the walk in a negative way, "Blessed is that man that walketh *not*," etc.; but here we find it in connection with the positive form of our conversation. To enjoy the Divine blessing, we must be active, and walk; we must be methodical, and walk in certain ways; and we must be godly, and walk in the Lord's way.

God's way are blessed ways; they were cast up by the Blessed One; they were trodden by Him in Whom we are blessed; they are frequented by the blessed; they are provide with means of blessing; they are paved with present blessings, and they lead to eternal blessedness: who would not desire to walk in them? C. H. S.

Whenever you see the household of a married pair continuing to defy every storm, you may be sure that it rests upon a sure foundation, lying beyond the reach of human sense, and that that foundation is *the fear of the Lord.* To the fear of the Lord, therefore, the holy Psalmist has wisely given a place in front of this beautiful Psalm, which celebrates the blessing that descends upon conjugal and domestic life. AUGUSTUS F. THOLUCK

There is a fear of the Lord which hath terror in it and not blessedness. The apprehension with which a warring rebel regards his triumphant and offended sovereign, or the feelings of a fraudulent bankrupt towards a stern creditor, or a conscience-stricken criminal to a righteous judge, are frequently types of men's feelings in regard to God. This evidently cannot be the *fear* which the *blessed* of this Psalm feel. Nor can theirs, on the other hand, be the tormenting fear of self-reproach.

Their fear is that which the believed revelations given of Him in His Word produce. It is the fear which a child feels toward an honored parent—a fear to offend; it is that which they who have been rescued from destruction feel to the benefactor who nobly and at the sacrifice interposed for their safety — a fear to act unworthily of his kindness: it is that which fills the breast of a pardoned and grateful rebel in the presence of a venerated sovereign at whose throne he is permitted to stand in honor — a fear lest he should ever forget his goodness and give him cause to regret it.

Such is the fear of the Christian now: a fear which reverence for majesty, gratitude for mercies, dread of displeasure, desire of approval, and longing for the fellowship of heaven, inspire; the fear of angels and the blessed Son; the fear not of sorrow but of love, which shrinks with instinctive recoil from doing aught that would tend to grieve, or from denying aught that would tend to honor.

Religion is the grand and the only wisdom; and since the beginning, the middle, and the end of it, is the fear of the Lord, blessed is every man that is swayed by it. ROBERT NISBET

Let us take a little of the character of the blessed man. Who is it that is undaunted? *The man that feareth God.* Fear sounds rather contrary to blessedness;

hath an air of misery; but add whom. He that feareth *the* Lord; that touch turns it into gold. He that so fears, fears not: he shall not be afraid; all petty fears are swallowed up in this great fear; and this great fear is as sweet and pleasing as little fears are anxious and vexing. Secure of other things, he can say, "If my God is pleased, no matter who is displeased: no matter who despise me, if He account me His."

Vs. 2. *Thou shalt eat the labor of thine hands.* This must they learn also which are married, that they must labor. For the law of nature requireth that the husband should sustain and nourish his and his children. For after that man and wife do know that they ought, to fear God their Creator, Who not only made them, but gave His blessing also unto His creature; this secondly must they know, that something they must do that they consume not their days in ease and idleness.

Hesiod, the poet, giveth his counsel, that first thou shouldst get thee a house, then a wife, and also an ox to till the ground . . . For albeit that our diligence, care, and travail is not able to maintain our family, yet God useth such as a means by which He will bless us. MARTIN LUTHER

*Happy shalt thou be.* Oh, trust in the Lord for happiness as well as for help! All the springs of happiness are in Him. "Trust" in Him Who giveth us all things richly to enjoy: Who, of His own rich and free mercy, holds them out to us, as in His own hand, that, receiving them as His gifts, and as pledges of His love, we may enjoy all that we possess.

It is His love gives a relish to all we taste, puts life and sweetness into all; while every creature leads us up to the great Creator, and all earth is a scale to heaven. He transfuses the joys that are at His own right hand into all that He bestows on His thankful children, who having fellowship with the Father and His Son Jesus Christ, enjoy Him in all and above all. JOHN WESLEY

*And it shall be well with thee,* or, *good for thee.* If we fear God, we may dismiss all other fear. In walking in God's ways, we shall be under His protection, provision, and approval; danger and destruction shall be far from us: all things shall work out good. In God's view, it would not be a blessed thing for us to live without exertion, nor to eat the unearned bread of dependence: the happiest state on earth is one in which we have something to do, strength to do it with, and a fair return for what we have done. This, with the Divine blessing, is all that we ought to desire, and it is sufficient for any man who fears the Lord and abhors covetousness. Having food and raiment, let us be therewith content.

Vs. 3. *Thy wife.* To reach the full of earthly felicity a man must not be alone. A helpmeet was needed in Paradise, and assuredly she is not less necessary out of it. He that findeth a wife findeth a good thing. It is not every man that feareth the Lord who has a wife; but if he has, she shall share in his blessedness and increase it. C. H. S.

*By the sides of thine house.* She keeps at home, and so keeps the home: It is her husband's house, and she is her husband's; as the text puts it — "thy wife," and "thy house"; but by her loving care, her husband is made so happy that he is glad to own her as an equal proprietor with himself, for he is hers, and the house is hers, too. C. H. S.

The house is her proper place; for she is "the beauty of the House"; there her business lies; there she is safe. The ancients painting them with a snail under their feet, and the Egyptians denying their women shoes, and the Scythians burning the bride's chariot axle-tree at her door, when she was brought to her husband's house, and the angel's asking Abraham where Sarah was (though he knew well enough), that it might be observed, she was "in the tent," do all intimate, that, by the law of nature, and by the rules of religion, the wife ought to keep at home, unless urgent necessity do call her abroad. RICHARD STEELE

*Thy children like olive plants round about thy table.* Our children gather around our table to be fed, and this involves expenses: how much better is this than to see them pining upon beds of sickness, unable to come for their meals! It may help us to value the privileges of our home if we consider where we should be if they were withdrawn. What if the dear partner of our life were removed from the sides of our house to the recesses of the sepulcher? What is the trouble of children compared with the sorrow of their loss? Think, dear father, what would be your grief if you had to cry with Job, "Oh, that I were as in months past, as in the days when God preserved me; when my children were about me." C. H. S.

Before the fall, Paradise was man's home; since the fall, home has been his Paradise. AUGUSTUS WM. HARE

Vs. 4. *Behold, that thus shall the man be blessed.* It is asserted with a note commanding attention: *behold* it by faith in the promise; *behold* it by observation in the performance of the promise; *behold* it with assurance that it shall be so, for God is faithful; and with admiration that it should be so; for we merit no favor, no blessing from Him. MATTHEW HENRY

Vs. 6. *Yea, thou shalt see thy children's children.* This is a great pleasure. Men live their young lives over again in their grandchildren. Does not Solomon say that "children's children are the crown of old men"? So they are. The good man is glad that a pious stock is likely to be continued; he rejoices in the belief that other homes as happy as his own will be built up wherein altars to the glory of God shall smoke with the morning and evening sacrifice. This promise implies long life and that life rendered happy by its being continued in our offspring. It is one token of the immortality of man that he derives joy from extending his life in the lives of his descendants. C. H. S.

Lord, let Thy blessing so accompany my endeavors in their breedings, that all my sons may be Benaiahs, the Lord's building, and then they will all be Abners, their father's light; and that all my daughters may be Bethias, the Lord's daughters, and then they will all be Abigails, their father's joy. GEORGE SWINNOCK

# PSALM 129

Title: "A Song of Degrees." I fail to see how this is a step beyond the previous Psalm; and yet it is clearly the song of an older and more tried individual, who looks back upon a life of affliction in which he suffered all along, even from his youth. Inasmuch as patience is a higher, or at least more difficult, grace than domestic love, the ascent or progress may perhaps be seen in that direction.

Whole Psalm: The following incident in connection with the glorious return of the Vaudois under Henri Arnaud is related in Muston's *Israel of the Alps:* "After these successes, the gallant patriots took an oath of fidelity to each other, and celebrated divine service in one of their own churches, for the first time since their banishment. The enthusiasm of the moment was irrepressible; they chanted the Seventy-Fourth Psalm to the clash of arms; and Henri Arnaud, mounting the pulpit with a sword in one hand and a Bible in the other, preached from the Hundred and Twenty-Ninth Psalm, and once more declared, in the face of heaven, that he would never resume his pastoral office in patience and peace, until he should witness the restoration of his brethren to their ancient and rightful settlements."

Vs. 1. *Many a time have they afflicted me from my youth, may Israel now say.* The song begins abruptly. The poet has been musing, and the fire burns; therefore speaks he with his tongue; he cannot help it; he feels that he must speak, and therefore "may now say" what he has to say. C. H. S.

The earliest years of Israel and of the church of God are spent in trial. Babes in grace are cradled in opposition. No sooner is the manchild born than the dragon is after it. "It is," however, "good for a man that he bear the yoke in his youth," and he shall see it to be so when in after days he tells the tale. C. H. S.

God had one Son, and but one Son, without sin; but never any without sorrow. We may be God's children, and yet still under persecution; His Israel, and afflicted from our youth up. We may feel God's hand as a Father upon us when He strikes us as well as when He strokes us. When He strokes us, it is lest we faint under His hand; and when He strikes us, it is that we should know His hand. ABRAHAM WRIGHT

*They.* The persecutors deserve not a name. The rich man is not named (as Lazarus is) because not worthy (Luke 16). They shall be written in the earth (Jer. 12:13). JOHN TRAPP

History certainly bears ample testimony that the people of God had not to deal with a few enemies but that they were assaulted by almost the whole world; and further, that they were molested not only by external foes but alsc by those of an internal kind, by such as professed to belong to the church JOHN CALVIN

*They afflicted me.* While men know themselves, they *know their sin* also in affliction. What is the natural course and experience of the unbelieving of mankind? Transgression, remorse, and then forgetfulness; new transgression, new sorrow, and again forgetfulness.

How shall this carelessness be broken? How convince them that they stand in need of a Savior as the first and deepest want of their being and that they can only secure deliverance from wrath eternal by a prompt and urgent application to Him? By nothing so effectually as by affliction. God's children, who had forgotten Him, arise and go to their Father when thus smitten by the scourge of sorrow; and no sooner is the penitent, *Father, I have sinned* spoken, than they are clasped in His arms and safe and happy in His love.

It is, further, by affliction that the *world* is known to God's children. God's great rival is the world. The lust of the flesh, pleasure; the lust of the eye, desire; the pride of life, the longing to be deemed superior to those about us — comprise everything man naturally covets. Give us ease, honor, distinction, and all life's good will seem obtained. *But what wilt thou do, when He shall judge thee?* This is a question fitted to alarm the happiest of the children of prosperity.

*From my youth.* The first that ever died, died for religion; so early came martyrdom into the world. John Trapp

Vs. 2. *Many a time.* What afflictions were endured by the Christian church from her youth up! How feeble was that youth! How small the number of the Apostles to whom our Lord gave His Gospel in charge! How destitute were they of human learning, of worldly influence, of secular power! To effect their destruction, and to frustrate their object — the glory of God and the salvation of men — the dungeon and the mine, the rack and the gibbet, were all successively employed. The ploughers ploughed their back, and made long their furrows. Their property was confiscated; their persons were imprisoned; their civil rights were taken from them; their heads rolled on the scaffold; their bodies were consumed at the burning pile; they were thrown, amidst the ringing shouts of the multitude, to the wild beasts of the amphitheatre.

Despite, however, of every opposition, our holy religion took root and grew upward. Not all the fury of ten persecutions could exterminate it from the earth. The teeth of wild beasts could not grind it to powder; the fire could not burn it; the waters could not drown it; the dungeon could not confine it.

Truth is eternal, like the great God from Whose bosom it springs, and therefore it cannot be destroyed. And because Christianity is the truth, and no lie, her enemies have never prevailed against her. W. McMichael

*Yet they have not prevailed against Me.* "Cast down, but not destroyed," is the shout of a victor. Israel has wrestled and has overcome in the struggle. Who wonders? If Israel overcame the angel of the covenant, what man or devil shall vanquish him? C. H. S.

Vs. 3. *The plowers plowed upon my back: they made long their furrows.* While every part of our Lord's sorrows and sufferings is most minutely set forth in the sacred hymns, psalms, and songs, contained in what we style the Book of Psalms, yet we shall never comprehend what our most blessed Lord, in every part of His life, and in His passion and death, underwent for us; may the Lord, the Spirit, imprint this fresh expression used on this subject effectually upon us. Our Lord's words here are very expressive of the violence of His tormentors and their rage against Him, and of the wounds and torments they had inflicted on Him. Samuel Pierce

Vs. 4. *He hath cut asunder the cords of the wicked.* Never has God used a nation to chastize His Israel without destroying that nation when the chastizements has come to a close: He hates those who hurt His people even though He permits their hate to triumph for a while for His own purpose. If any man would have his harness cut, let him begin to plough one of the Lord's fields with the plough of persecution. The shortest way to ruin is to meddle with a saint: the Divine warning is, "He that toucheth you toucheth the apple of His eye." C. H. S.

Vs. 5. *Let them all be confounded and turned back that hate Zion.* Study a chapter from the *Book of Martyrs* and see if you do not feel inclined to read an imprecatory Psalm over Bishop Bonner and Bloody Mary. It may be that some wretched nineteenth century sentimentalist will blame you: if so, read another *over him.* C. H. S.

Vs. 6. *Let them be as the grass upon the housetops, which withereth afore it groweth up.* One of the fathers said of the Apostle Emperor Julian, "That little cloud will soon be gone"; and so it was. Every skeptical system of philosophy has much the same history; and the like may be said of each heresy. Poor, rootless things, they are and are not: they come and go, even though no one rises against them. Evil carries the seeds of dissolution within itself. So let it be. C. H. S.

They are rightly compared to *grass on the housetops;* for more contemptuously the Holy Ghost could not speak of them. For this grass is such that it soon withereth away before the sickle be put into it. Yea, no man thinketh it worthy to be cut down, no man regardeth it, every man suffereth it to brag for a while, and to show itself unto men from the housetops as though it were something when it is nothing.

So the wicked persecutors in the world, which are taken to be mighty and terrible according to the outward show, are of all men most contemptible. For Christians do not once think of plucking them up or cutting them down; they persecute them not, they revenge not their own injuries, but suffer them to increase, to brag and glory as much as they list. For they know that they cannot abide the violence of a vehement wind.

Yea, though all things be in quietness, yet as grass upon the housetops, by little and little, withereth away through the heat of the sun, so tyrannies upon small occasions do perish and soon vanish away. The faithful, therefore, in suffering do prevail, and overcome; but the wicked in doing are overthrown, and miserably perish, as all the histories of all times and ages do plainly witness. MARTIN LUTHER

Vs. 7. *Wherewith the mower filleth not his hand; nor he that bindeth sheaves his bosom.* Easterns carry their corn in their bosoms, but in this case there was nothing to bear home. Thus do the wicked come to nothing. By God's just appointment, they prove a disappointment. Their fire ends in smoke; their verdure turns to vanity; their flourishing is but a form of withering. No one profits by them, least of all are they profitable to themselves. Their aim is bad, their work is worse, their end is worst of all. C. H. S.

Vs. 8. *Neither do they which go by say, The blessing of the Lord be upon you: we bless you in the Name of the Lord.* We dare not use pious expressions as mere compliments, and hence we dare not wish God-speed to evil men lest we be partakers of their evil deeds.

See how godly men are roughly ploughed by their adversaries, and yet a harvest comes of it which endures and produces blessing; while the ungodly, though they flourish for a while and enjoy a complete immunity, dwelling, as they think, quite above the reach of harm, are found in a short time to have gone their way and to have left no trace behind.

Lord, number me with Thy saints. Let me share their grief if I may also partake of their glory. Thus would I make this Psalm my own, and magnify Thy Name, because Thine afflicted ones are not destroyed and Thy persecuted ones are not forsaken. C. H. S.

# PSALM 130

We name this the DeProfundis Psalm: "Out of the depths" is the leading word of it: out of those depths we cry, wail, watch, and hope. In this Psalm we hear of the pearl of redemption (Verses 7 and 8): perhaps the sweet singer would never have found that precious thing had he not been cast into the depths. "Pearls lie deep." C. H. S.

Whole Psalm: The Holy Ghost layeth out here two opposite passions most plainly—fear, in respect of evil-deserving sins, and hope, in regard of undeserved mercies. ALEXANDER ROBERTS

This Psalm, perhaps more than any other, is marked by its mountains: depth; prayer; conviction; light; hope; waiting; watching; longing; confidence; assurance; universal happiness and joy.

Just as the barometer marks the rising of the weather, so does this Psalm, sentence by sentence, record the progress of the soul. And you may test yourself by it, as a rule or measure, and ask yourself at each line, "Have I reached to this? Have I reached to this?" and so take your spiritual gauge. JAMES VAUGHAN

Vs. 1. *Out of the depths have I cried unto Thee, O Lord.* Beneath the floods, prayer lived and struggled; yea, above the roar of the billows rose the cry of faith. It little matters where we are if we can pray; but prayer is never more real and acceptable than when it rises out of the worst places. Deep places beget deep devotion. Depths of earnestness are stirred by depths of tribulation. Diamonds sparkle most amid the darkness. He that prays in the depth will not sink out of his depth. He that cries out of the depths shall soon sing in the heights. C. H. S.

It is cause enough for God not to hear some because they do not cry — cause enough not to hear some that cry because not out of the depths; but when crying and out of the depths are joined together, it was never known that God refused to hear; and therefore now that I cry to Thee out of the depths, be pleased, O God, in Thy great mercy to hear my voice. SIR RICHARD BAKER

When we are in prosperity, our prayers come from our lips; and therefore the Lord is forced to cast us down that our prayers may come from our hearts and that our senses may be wakened from the security in which they are lying. And thus God dealeth with us as men do with such houses that they are minded to build sumptuously and on high; for then they dig deep grounds for the foundation. Thus God, purposing to make a fair show of Daniel, and the three children in Babel; of Joseph in Egypt; of David in Israel; He first threw them into the deep waters of affliction. Daniel is cast into the den of lions; the three children are thrown into the fiery furnace; Joseph is imprisoned; David exiled. Yet all those He exalted and made glorious temples to Himself.

Mark hereby the dullness of our nature, that is such, that God is forced to use sharp remedies to awaken us. Jonah lay sleeping in the ship when the tempest of God's wrath was pursuing him: God, therefore, threw him into the belly of the whale, and the bottom of the deep, that from those deep places he might cry to Him.

When, therefore, we are troubled by heavy sickness, or poverty, or oppressed by the tyranny of men, let us make profit and use thereof, considering that God hath cast His best children into such dangers for their profit; and that it is better to be in deep dangers praying than on the high mountains of vanity playing. ARCHIBALD SYMSON

There are depths after depths of mental darkness, when the soul becomes more and more sorrowful, down to that very depth which is just this side of despair. Earth hollow, heaven empty, the air heavy, every form a deformity, all sounds discord, the past a gloom, the present a puzzle, the future a horror. One more step down, and the man will stand in the chamber of despair, the floor of which is blisteringly hot, while the air is biting cold as the polar atmosphere. To what depths the spirit of a man may fall!

But the most horrible depth into which a man's soul can descend is sin. Sometimes we begin on gradual slopes, and slide so swiftly that we soon reach great depths; depths in which there are horrors that are neither in poverty, nor sorrow, nor mental depression.

It is sin, it is an outrage against God and ourselves. We feel that there is no bottom. Each opening depth reveals a greater deep. This is really the bottomless pit, with everlasting accumulations of speed and perpetual lacerations as we descend. Oh, depths below depths! Oh, falls from light to gloom, from gloom to darkness! Oh, the hell of sin!

What can we do? We can simply cry, cry, cry! But, let us cry to God. Useless, injurious are other cries. They are mere expressions of impotency, or protests against imaginary fate. But the cry of the spirit to the Most High is a manful cry. Out of the depths of all poverty, all sorrow, all mental depression, all sin, cry unto God! *From* "THE STUDY AND THE PULPIT"

But when he crieth from the deep, he riseth from the deep, and his very cry suffereth him not to be long at the bottom. AUGUSTINE

It has been well said that the verse puts before us six conditions of true prayer: it is lowly — "out of the deep"; fervent — "have I called"; directed to God Himself, "unto Thee"; reverent, "O Lord"; awed, "Lord," a solemn title, is again used; one's very own, "hear my voice." NEALE AND LITTLEDALE

Vs. 2. *Lord, hear my voice.* If the Lord were to make an absolute promise to answer all our requests, it might be rather a curse than a blessing, for it would be casting the responsibility of our lives upon ourselves, and we should be placed in a very anxious position: but now the Lord hears our desires, and that is enough; we only wish Him to grant them if His infinite wisdom sees that it would be for our good and for His glory. C. H. S.

Vs. 3. *If Thou, Lord, shouldest mark iniquities, O Lord who shall stand?* If Jah, the All-seeing, should in strict justice call every man to account for every want of conformity to righteousness, where would any one of us be? Truly, He does record all our transgressions; but as yet He does not act upon the record, but lays it aside till another day. If men were to be judged upon no system but that of works, who among us could answer for himself at the Lord's bar and hope to stand clear and accepted? C. H. S.

But doth not the Lord mark iniquity? Doth not He take notice of every sin acted by any of the children of men, especially by His own children? Why, then, doth the Psalmist put it upon an if? "If Thou, Lord, shouldest mark iniquity." 'Tis true, the Lord marks all iniquity to know it, but He doth not mark any iniquity in His children to condemn them for it: so the meaning of the Psalm is that if the Lord should mark sin with a strict and severe eye, as a judge, to charge it upon the person sinning, no man could bear it. JOSEPH CARYL

Let Thine ears be attentive to the voice of my supplication, but let not Thine eyes be intentive to the stains of my sin; for "If Thou, Lord, shouldest mark iniquities, O Lord, who shall stand?" or who shall be able to abide it? Did not the angels fall when Thou markedst their follies? Can flesh, which is but dust, be clean before Thee, when the stars, which are of a far purer substance, are not?

Can anything be clean in Thy sight which is not as clean as Thy sight? and can any cleanness be equal to Thine?

Alas, O Lord, we are neither angels nor stars, and how then can we stand when those fell? How can we be clean when these be impure? If Thou shouldest mark what is done amiss, there would be marking-work enough for Thee as long as the world lasts; for what action of man is free from stain of sin or from defect of righteousness?

Therefore, mark not anything in me, O God, that I have done, but mark that only in me which Thou hast done Thyself. Mark in me Thine own image; and then Thou mayest look upon me, and yet say still, as once Thou saidst, "And all things were very good." SIR RICHARD BAKER

Vss. 3 and 4. These two verses contain the sum of all the Scriptures. In the third is the form of repentance, and in the fourth the mercies of the Lord. These are the two mountains — Gerizim and Ebal — mentioned in Deut. 27:12-13. These are the pillars in Solomon's Temple (I Kings 7:21), called Jachin and Boaz.

We must, with Paul, persuade ourselves that we are come from Mount Sinai to Mount Zion, where mercy is, although some sour grapes must be eaten by the way. Jeremy tasted in his vision first a bitter fig out of one basket, then a sweet fig out of the other. In the days of Moses the waters were first bitter, then sweetened by the sweet wood. And Elisha cast in salt into the pottage of the sons of the prophets; then it became wholesome. ARCHIBALD SYMSON

Vs. 4. *But there is forgiveness with Thee, that Thou mayest be feared.* Blessed, but. Free, full, sovereign pardon is in the hand of the great King: it is His prerogative to forgive, and He delights to exercise it. Because His nature is mercy, and because He has provided a sacrifice for sin, therefore forgiveness is with Him for all that come to Him confessing their sins. If the Lord were to execute justice upon all, there would be none left to fear Him; if all were under apprehension of His deserved wrath, despair would harden them against fearing Him: it is grace which leads the way to a holy regard of God, and a fear of grieving Him. C. H. S.

The hammer of the law may break the icy heart of man with terrors and horrors, and yet it may remain ice still, unchanged; but when the fire of love kindly thaweth its ice, it is changed and dissolved into water; it is no longer ice, but of another nature. GEORGE SWINNOCK

The evangelical doctrine of the gratuitous forgiveness of sins does not of itself beget carelessness, as the Papists falsely allege; but rather a true and genuine fear of God; like as the Psalmist here shows that this is the final cause and effect of the doctrine. SOLOMON GESNER

The man is about to be destroyed, to be swallowed up quick, when suddenly there comes this thrice-blessed "but," which stops the reckless course of ruin, puts forth its strong arm bearing a golden shield between the sinner and destruction, and pronounces these words, "But there is forgiveness with God, that He may be feared." C. H. S.

*That Thou mayest be feared.* This forgiveness, this smile of God, binds the soul to God with a beautiful fear. Fear to lose one glance of love. Fear to lose one work of kindness. Fear to be carried away from the heaven of His presence by an insidious current of worldliness. Fear of slumber. Fear of error. Fear of not enough pleasing Him.

Our duty, then, is to drink deep of God's forgiving love. To be filled with it is to be filled with purity, fervency, and faith. Our sins have to hide their diminished heads and slink away through crevices, when forgiveness—when Christ—enters the soul. GEORGE BOWEN

Vs. 5. *I wait for the Lord, my soul doth wait.* Expecting Him to come to me in love, I quietly wait for His appearing; I wait upon Him in service, and for

Him in faith. For God I wait, and for Him only: if He will manifest Himself, I shall have nothing more to wait for; but until He shall appear for my help, I must wait on, hoping even in the depths. C. H. S.

Oh, how real and instant is the rest found in Jesus! Reposing in Him, however profound the depth of the soul, however dark the clouds that drape it, or surging the waters that overwhelm it, all is sunshine and serenity within. OCTAVIUS WINSLOW

*And in His Word do I hope.* Waiting, we study the Word, believe the Word, hope in the Word, and live on the Word; and all because it is "His Word" — the Word of Him Who never speaks in vain. Jehovah's Word is a firm ground for a waiting soul to rest upon. C. H. S.

Vss. 5 and 6. What comforteth a sick man in time of sickness but hope of health? or a poor man in his distress, but hope of riches? or a prisoner, but hope of liberty? or a banished man, but hope to come home?

All these hopes may fail, as oftentimes wanting a warrant. Albeit a physician may encourage a sick man by his fair words, yet he cannot give him an assurance of his recovery, for his health dependeth on God: friends and courtiers may promise poor men relief, but all men are liars; only God is faithful, Who hath promised.

Therefore, let us fix our faith on God, and our hope in God; for He will stand by His promise. No man hath hoped in Him in vain, neither was ever any disappointed of His hope. ARCHIBALD SYMSON

Vs. 6. *My soul waiteth for the Lord more than they that watch for the morning.* God was no more dreaded by him than light is dreaded by those engaged in a lawful calling. He pined and yearned after his God. C. H. S.

*I say, more than they that watch for the morning,* for must there not be a proportion between the cause and effect? If my cause of watching be more than theirs, should not my watching be more than theirs? They that watch for the morning have good cause, no doubt, to watch for it, that it may bring them the light of day; but have not I more cause to watch, who wait for the Light that lighteth every one that comes into the world?

They that watch for the morning wait but for the rising of the sun to free them from darkness, that hinders their sight; but I wait for the rising of the Sun of righteousness to dispel the horrors of darkness that affright my soul. They watch for the morning that they may have light to walk by; but I wait for the Dayspring from on High to give light to them that sit in darkness and in the shadow of death, and to guide our feet into the way of peace. SIR RICHARD BAKER

In the year 1830, on the night preceding the first of August, the day the slaves in our West Indian Colonies were to come into possession of the freedom promised them, many of them, we are told, never went to bed at all. Thousands, and tens of thousands of them, assembled in their places of worship, engaging in devotional duties, and singing praises to God, waiting for the first streak of the light of the morning of that day on which they were to be made free.

Some of their number were sent to the hills, from which they might obtain the first view of the coming day, and, by a signal, intimate to their brethren down in the valley the dawn of the day that was to make them men, and no longer, as they had hitherto been, mere goods and chattels — men with souls that God had created to live forever. How eagerly must these men have watched for the morning! T. W. AVELING

Vs. 7. *And with Him is plenteous redemption.* The attribute of mercy, and the fact of redemption, are two most sufficient reasons for hoping in Jehovah; and the fact that there is no mercy or deliverance elsewhere should effectually wean the soul from all idolatry. Are not these deep things of God a grand comfort for those who are crying out of the depths? It is not better to be in the depths with David, hoping in God's mercy, than up on the mountain-tops, boasting in our own fancied righteousness? C. H. S.

And such is the redemption that God's mercy procures unto us. It not only delivers us from a dungeon, but puts us in possession of a palace; it not only frees us from eating bread in the sweat of our brows, but it restores us to Paradise, where all fruits are growing of their own accord; it not only clears us from being captives, but endears us to be children; and not only children, but heirs; and not only heirs, but co-heirs with Christ; and who can deny this to be a plenteous redemption?

Or is it said a plenteous redemption in regard of the price that was paid to redeem us? for we are redeemed with a price, not of gold or precious stones, but with the precious blood of the Lamb slain before the foundation of the world. For God so loved the world that He gave His Only Son to be a ransom for us; and this I am sure is a plenteous redemption. SIR RICHARD BAKER

Vs. 8. *Iniquities.* What a graceful and appropriate conclusion of this comprehensive and instructive Psalm! Like the sun, it dawns veiled in cloud; it sets bathed in splendor; it opens with soul-depth; it closes with soul-height. Redemption from all iniquity! It baffles the most descriptive language and distances the highest measurement. The most vivid imagination faints in conceiving it; the most glowing image fails in portraying it; and faith droops her wing in the bold attempt to scale its summit. *He shall redeem Israel from all his iniquities.* The verse is a word-painting of man restored, of Paradise regained. OCTAVIUS WINSLOW

# PSALM 131

Title: "A Song of Degrees of David." It is both by David and of David: he is the author and subject of it, and many incidents of his life may be employed to illustrate it. Comparing all the Psalms to gems, we should liken this to a pearl: how beautifully it will adorn the neck of patience! It is one of the shortest Psalms to read but one of the longest to learn. It speaks of a young child, but it contains the experience of a man in Christ.

Lowliness and humility are here seen in connection with a sanctified heart, a will subdued to the mind of God, and a hope looking to the Lord alone. Happy is the man who can without falsehood use these words as his own; for he wears about him the likeness of his Lord, Who said, "I am meek and lowly in heart." C. H. S.

Vs. 1. *Lord, my heart is not haughty.* He begins with his heart, for that is the center of our nature, and if pride be there, it defiles everything; just as mire in the spring causes mud in all the streams. It is a grand thing for a man to know his own heart so as to be able to speak before the Lord about it. C. H. S.

*Nor mine eyes lofty.* Pride has its seat in the heart; but its principal expression is in the eye. The eye is the mirror of the soul; and from it mental and moral characteristics may be ascertained with no small degree of precision. What a world of meaning is sometimes concentrated in a single glance!

But of all the passions, pride is most clearly revealed in the eyes. There can scarcely be a mistake here. We are all familiar with a class of phrases, which run in pairs. We speak of sin and misery; holiness and happiness; peace and prosperity; war and desolation. Among these may be numbered, the proud heart and the haughty look. N. M'MICHAEL

*Neither do I exercise myself in great matters.* As a private man, he did not usurp the power of the king or devise plots against him; he minded his own business and left others to mind theirs. As a thoughtful man, he did not pry into things unrevealed; he was not speculative, self-conceited, or opinionated. As a secular person, he did not thrust himself into the priesthood as Saul had done before him and Uzziah did after him. It is well so to exercise ourselves unto godliness that we know our true sphere and diligently keep to it. C. H. S.

One cannot admire enough the prayer of Anselm, a profound divine of our own country, in the eleventh century. "I do not seek, O Lord, to penetrate Thy depths. I by no means think my intellect equal to them: but I long to understand in some degree Thy truth, which my heart believes and loves. For I do not seek to understand that I may believe; but I believe that I may understand." N. M'MICHAEL

Vs. 2. *Surely I have behaved and quieted myself.* Oh, how sapless and insipid doth the world grow to the soul that is making meet for heaven! There is no more relish in these gaudy things to my palate, than in the white of an egg; everything grows a burden to me, were it not my duty to follow my calling and be thankful for my enjoyments. OLIVER HEYWOOD

*As a child that is weaned of his mother.* It is not every child of God who arrives at this weanedness speedily. Some are sucklings when they ought to be fathers; others are hard to wean, and cry, and fight, and rage against their Heavenly Parent's discipline.

When we think ourselves safely through the weaning, we sadly discover that the old appetites are rather wounded than slain, and we begin crying again for the breasts which we had given up. It is easy to begin shouting before we are out of the wood, and no doubt hundreds have sung this Psalm long before they have understood it. C. H. S.

How patiently did Isaac permit himself to be bound and sacrificed by Abraham! (Gen. 22:9). And yet he was of age and strength sufficient to have struggled for his life, being twenty-five years old; but that holy young man abhorred the thought of striving with his father. And shall not we resign ourselves to our God and Father in Christ Jesus? JOHN SINGLETON

With such a simplicity of submission should we rest and depend upon God. Let us take heed of being overwise and provident for ourselves, but let us trust our Father which is in heaven and refer ourselves to His wise and holy government. THOMAS MANTON

There is such a thing as wearing out the affections. Solomon appears to have done this at one period of his life. "I have not a wish left," said a well-known sensualist of our own country, who had drunk as deeply as he could drink of the world's cup. "Were all the earth contains spread out before me, I do not know a thing I would take the trouble of putting out my hand to reach." C. H. S.

## PSALM 132

Title: "A Song of Degrees." A joyful song indeed: let all pilgrims to the New Jerusalem sing it often. The degrees, or ascents, are very visible; the theme ascends step by step from "afflictions" to a "crown," from "remember David," to "I will make the horn of David to bud." The latter half is like the overarching sky bending above "the fields of the wood" which are found in the resolves and prayers of the former portion. C. H. S.

Vs. 1. *Lord, remember David, and all his afflictions.* The request is that the Lord would remember, and this is a word full of meaning. We know that the Lord remembered Noah and assuaged the flood; He remembered Abraham and sent Lot out of Sodom; He remembered Rachel and Hannah and gave them children; He remembered His mercy to the house of Israel and delivered His people. No doubt innumerable blessings descend upon families and nations through the godly lives and patient sufferings of the saints. We cannot be saved by the merits of others, but beyond all question we are benefited by their virtues. C. H. S.

Vss. 1 and 2. If the Jew could rightly appeal to God to show mercy to His church and nation for the sake of that shepherd youth whom He had advanced to the kingdom, much more shall we justly plead our cause in the name of David's son (called David four times in the prophets). THEODORET AND CASSIODORUS

Vs. 2. *How he sware unto the Lord, and vowed unto the mighty God of Jacob.* We should be full of awe at the idea of making any promise to the mighty God: to dare to trifle with Him would be grievous indeed. C. H. S.

*He vowed unto the mighty God of Jacob.* He who is ready to vow on every occasion will break his vow on every occasion. It is a necessary rule that "we be as sparing in making our vows as may be"; there being many great inconveniences attending frequent and multiplied vows.

It is very observable that the Scripture mentioneth very few examples of vows compared with the many instances of very great and wonderful providences; as if it would give us some instances, that we might know what we have to do, and yet would give us but few, that we might know we are not to do it often. You read Jacob lived seven score and seven years (Gen. 47:28); but you read, I think, but of one vow that he made. HENRY HURST

The first holy votary that ever we read of was Jacob here mentioned in this text, who is therefore called the father of vows: and upon this account some think David mentions God here under the title of "the mighty God of Jacob" rather than any other, because of his vow. ABRAHAM WRIGHT

*The mighty God of Jacob.* Where the interpreters have translated, "the God of Jacob," it is in the Hebrew, "the mighty in Jacob." Which name is sometimes attributed unto the angels, and sometimes it is also applied to other things wherein are great strength and fortitude; as to a lion, an ox, and such like. But here it is a singular word of faith, signifying that God is the power and strength of His people; for only faith ascribeth this unto God.

Reason and the flesh do attribute more to riches and such other worldly helps as man seeth and knoweth. All such carnal helps are very idols, which deceive men and draw them to perdition; but this is the strength and fortitude of the people, to have God present with them. MARTIN LUTHER

Vs. 4. *I will not give sleep to mine eyes, or slumber to mine eyelids.* Oh, that many more were seized with sleeplessness because the house of the Lord lies waste! They can slumber fast enough, and not ever disturb themselves with a dream, though the cause of God should be brought to the lowest ebb by their covetousness. What is to become of those who have no care about divine things and never give a thought to the claims of their God? C. H. S.

Vs. 6. *We found it in the fields of the wood.* Alas that there should be no room for the Lord in the palaces of kings so that He must needs take to the woods. If Christ be in a wood, He will yet be found of those who seek for Him. He is as near in the rustic home, embowered among the trees, as in the open streets of the city; yea, He will answer prayer offered from the heart of the black forest where lone travelers seem out of all hope of hearing. C. H. S.

Christ has been found in the fields of the wood; in a low, mean, abject state, as this phrase signifies (Ezek. 16:5). The shepherds found Him rejected from being in the inn, there being no room for Him, and lying in a manger (Luke 2:7, 16); the angels found Him in the wilderness among the wild beasts of the field (Mark 1:13); nor had He the convenience even of foxes and birds of the air; he had no habitation or place where to lay His head (Matt. 8:20). And He is to be found in the field of the Scriptures, where the rich treasure and pearl of great price lies hid (Matt. 13:44). JOHN GILL

Vs. 7. *We will worship at His footstool.* It is well not only to go to the Lord's house, but to worship there: we do but profane His tabernacles if we enter them for any other purpose.

Before leaving this verse, let us note the ascent of this Psalm of degrees— "We heard . . . we found . . . we will go . . . we will worship." C. H. S.

Vs. 8. *Arise, O Lord, into Thy rest; Thou, and the ark of Thy strength.* Vain would it be for the ark to be settled if the Lord did not continue with it and perpetually shine forth from between the cherubim. Unless the Lord shall rest with us, there is no rest for us; unless the ark of His strength abide with us, we are ourselves without strength. C. H. S.

Vs. 9. *Let Thy priests be clothed with righteousness.* No garment is so resplendent as that of a holy character. In this glorious robe our great High-priest is evermore arrayed, and He would have all His people adorned in the same manner. Then only are priests fit to appear before the Lord and to minister for the profit of the people when their lives are dignified with goodness.

They must ever remember that they are God's priests and should therefore wear the livery of their Lord, which is holiness: they are not only to have righteousness, but to be clothed with it, so that upon every part of them righteousness shall be conspicuous. Whoever looks upon God's servants should see holiness if they see nothing else. C. H. S.

*And let Thy saints shout for joy.* Holiness and happiness go together; where the one is found, the other ought never to be far away. Holy persons have a right to great and demonstrative joy: they may shout because of it. Since they are saints, and Thy saints, and Thou hast come to dwell with them, O Lord, Thou hast made it their duty to rejoice and to let others know of their joy. The sentence, while it may read as a permit, is also a precept: saints are commanded to rejoice in the Lord. Happy religion which makes it a duty to be glad! Where righteousness is the clothing, joy may well be the occupation. C. H. S.

Vs. 10. *For Thy servant David's sake.* When Sennacherib's army lay around Jerusalem besieging it, God brought deliverance for Israel partly out of regard to the prayer of the devout Hezekiah, but partly also out of respect for the pious memory of David, the hero-king, the man after God's own heart.

The message sent through Isaiah to the king concluded thus: "For I will defend this city, to save it, for Mine own sake, and for My servant David's sake" (II Kings 19:32-34). What a respect is shown to David's name by its being thus put on a level with God! Mine own sake, and David's sake.
ALEXANDER BALMAIN BRUCE

Vs. 11. *The Lord hath sworn.* The most potent weapon with God is His own Word. AUGUSTUS F. THOLUCK

*He will not turn from it.* Jehovah is not a changeable Being. He never turns from His purpose, much less from His promise solemnly ratified by oath. He turneth never. What a rock they stand upon who have an immutable oath of God for their foundation! C. H. S.

Vs. 12. *Their children shall also sit upon Thy throne forevermore.* This verse shows us the need of family piety. Parents must see to it that their children know the fear of the Lord, and they must beg the Lord Himself to teach them His truth. We have no hereditary right to the divine favor: the Lord keeps up His friendship to families from generation to generation, for He is loth to leave the descendants of His servants and never does so except under grievous and long-continued provocation.

As believers, we are all in a measure under some such covenant as that of David: certain of us can look backward for four generations of saintly ancestors, and we are now glad to look forward and to see our children, and our children's children, walking in the truth.

Yet we know that grace does not run in the blood, and we are filled with holy fear lest in any of our seed there should be an evil heart of unbelief in departing from the living God. C. H. S.

The king was busy to build God's house; and see how God answers him, promising the building of the king's house! God requites a building with a building. There is very apt illusion in the Word, upon which the son of Syrach also plays, when He saith that children and the building of a city make a perpetual name; how much more if they be a royal offspring, that are destined to sit upon a throne? And God promiseth David sons for this honorable end — "to sit upon his throne." ARTHUR LAKE

*That I shall teach them.* Here is to be noted that he addeth, "which I will teach them"; for He will be the teacher and will be heard. He wills not that church councils should be heard, or such as teach that which He hath not taught . . . God giveth no authority unto man above the Word. So should He set man, that is to say, dust and dung, above Himself; for what is the Word, but God Himself?

This Word they that honor, obey, and keep, are the true church indeed, be they never so contemptible in the world; but they which do not are the church of Satan and accursed of God. And this is the cause why it is expressly set down in the text. C. H. S.

*The testimonies which I will teach them.* For so will God use the ministry of teachers and pastors in the church, that He notwithstanding will be their chief Pastor, and all other ministers and pastors whatsoever, yea, the church itself, shall be ruled and governed by the Word. MARTIN LUTHER

Vs. 15. *I will abundantly bless her provision.* Daily provision, royal provision, satisfying provision, overflowingly joyful provision the church shall receive; and the divine benediction shall cause us to receive it with faith, to feed upon it by experience, to grow upon it by sanctification, to be strengthened by it to labor, cheered by it to patience, and built up by it to perfection. C. H. S.

And beside all this, he hath the sweet and refreshing incomes of the Spirit, filling him with such true pleasure that he can easily spare the most sumptuous banquet, the noblest feast, and highest worldly delights, as infinitely short of one hour's treatment in his Friend's chamber. And, if this be his entertainment in the inn, what shall he have at the court? If this heavenly manna be his food in the wilderness, at what rate is he like to live when he comes into Canaan? If this be the provision of the way, what is that of the country? JOHN JANEWAY

*I will satisfy her poor with bread.* The breadth of earth is "the bread that perisheth," but the bread of God endureth to life eternal. In the church, where God rests His people shall not starve; the Lord would never rest if they did. He did not take rest for six days till He had prepared the world for the first man to live in; He would not stay His hand till all things were ready; therefore, we may be sure if the Lord rests it is because "it is finished," and the Lord hath prepared of His goodness for the poor. Where God finds His desire, His people shall find theirs; if He is satisfied, they shall be. C. H. S.

Christ is a satisfying good. A wooden loaf, a silver loaf, a golden loaf will not satisfy a hungry man; the man must have bread. The dainties and dignities of the world, the grandeur and glory of the world, the plenty and prosperity of the world, the puff and popularity of the world, will not satisfy a soul sailing by the gates of hell, and crying out of the depths; it must be a Christ. "Children, or I die," was the cry of the woman; a Christ, or I die — a Christ, or I am damned, is the doleful ditty and doleful dialect of a despairing or desponding soul. What of the world and in the world can give quietness, when Christ, the Sun of Righteousness, goes down upon the soul? RICHARD MAYHEW

Vs. 16. *I will also clothe her priests with salvation.* More is promised than was prayed for. See how the ninth verse asks for the priests to be clad in righteousness. God is wont to do exceeding abundantly above all that we ask or even think. Righteousness is but one feature of blessing; salvation is the whole of it. What cloth of gold is this! What more than regal array! Garments of salvation! We know Who has woven them, Who has dyed them and Who has given them to His people.

These are the best robes for priests and preachers, for princes and people; there is none like them; give them me. Not every priest shall be thus clothed, but only her priests, those who truly belong to Zion, by faith which is in Christ Jesus, Who hath made them priests unto God. These are clothed by the Lord Himself, and none can clothe as He does. If even the grass of the field is so clothed by the Creator as to outvie Solomon in all his glory, how must His own children be clad? Truly He shall be admired in His saints; the liveries of His servants shall be the wonder of heaven.

*And her saints shall shout aloud for joy.* Zion has no dumb saints. The sight of God at rest among His chosen is enough to make the most silent shout. If the morning stars sang together when the earth and heavens were made, much more will all the sons of God shout for joy when the new heavens and the new earth are finished, and the New Jerusalem comes down out of heaven from God, prepared as a bride for her husband. C. H. S.

It would astonish and amuse a European stranger to hear these natives sing. They have not the least idea either of harmony or melody; noise is what they best understand, and he that sings the loudest is considered to sing the best.

I have occasionally remonstrated with them on the subject; but the reply I once received silenced me forever after. "Sing softly, brother," I said to one of the principal members. "Sing softly!" he replied, "is it you, our father, who tells us to sing softly? Did you ever hear us sing the praises of our Hindoo gods? how we threw our heads backward and with all our might shouted out the praises of those who are no gods!

"And now do you tell us to whisper the praises of Jesus? No, sir, we cannot— we must express in loud tones our gratitude to 'Him who loved us, and died for us'!" And so they continued to sing with all their might and without further remonstrance. G. GOGERLY

Vs. 17. *Make the horn of David to bud.* In the beginning of the month of March, the common stag, or red deer, is lurking in the sequestered spots of his forest home, harmless as his mate and as timorous. Soon a pair of prominences make their appearance on his forehead, covered with a velvety skin. In a few days, these little prominences have attained some length and give the first indication of their true form.

Grasp one of these in the hand, and it will be found burning hot to the touch, for the blood runs fiercely through the velvety skin, depositing at every touch a minute portion of bony matter. More and more rapidly grow the horns, the carotid arteries enlarging in order to supply a sufficiency of nourishment, and in the short period of ten weeks the enormous mass of bony matter has been completed. Such a process is almost, if not entirely, without parallel in the history of the animal kingdom. J. G. WOOD

*I have ordained a lamp for mine anointed.* The great means of God's appointment for manifesting the glory of Christ to a lost world; He has provided "a lamp" for His Anointed. The use of a lamp is to give light to people in the darkness of the night; so the Word of God, particularly the Gospel, is a light shining in a dark place until the day of glory dawn, when the Lord God and the Lamb will be the light of the ransomed for endless evermore.

Vs. 18. *His enemies will I clothe with shame.* That is, shame shall so inseparably cover them that as wheresoever a man goeth, he carrieth his clothes with him; so wheresoever they go they shall carry their shame with them. THOMAS PLAYFERE

*But upon Himself shall His crown flourish.* Green shall be His laurels of victory. He shall win and wear the crown of honor, and His inherited diadem shall increase in splendor. Is it not so to this hour with Jesus? His kingdom cannot fail; His imperial glories cannot fade. It is Himself that we delight to honor; it is to Himself that the honor comes and upon Himself that it flourishes. If others snatch at His crown, their traitorous aims are defeated; but He, in His own person, reigns with ever growing splendor. C. H. S.

# PSALM 133

Title: "A Song of Degrees of David." We see no reason for depriving David of the authorship of this sparkling sonnet. He knew by experience the bitterness occasioned by divisions in families and was well prepared to celebrate in choicest Psalmody the blessing of unity for which he sighed. C. H. S.

Vs. 1. *Behold.* It is a wonder seldom seen; therefore behold it! It may be seen, for it is the characteristic of real saints — therefore fail not to inspect it! It is well worthy of admiration; pause and gaze upon it! It will charm you into imitation; therefore note it well! C. H. S.

*How good and how pleasant it is for brethren to dwell together in unity!* We can dispense with uniformity if we possess unity: oneness of life, truth, and way; oneness in Christ Jesus; oneness of object and spirit — these we must have or our assemblies will be synagogues of contention rather than churches of Christ. Christian unity is good in itself — good for ourselves, good for the brethren, good for our converts, good for the outside world; and for certain it is pleasant; for a loving heart must have pleasure and give pleasure in associating with others of like nature. A church united for years in earnest service of the Lord is a well of goodness and joy to all those who dwell round about it. C. H. S.

*Pleasant.* It is a pleasant thing for the saints and people of God to agree together; for the same word which is used here for "pleasant" is used also in the Hebrew for a harmony of music, such as when they rise to the highest strains of the viol, when the strings are all put in order to make up a harmony; so pleasant is it, such pleasantness is there in the saints' agreement.

The same word is used also in the Hebrew for the pleasantness of a corn field. When a field is clothed with corn, though it be cut down, yet it is very pleasant, oh, how pleasant is it; and such is the saints' agreement. The same word in the Psalmist is used also for the sweetness of honey and of sweet things in opposition to bitter things.

And thus you see the pleasantness of it, by its being compared to the harmony of music, to the corn field, to the sweetness of honey, to the precious ointment that ran down Aaron's beard, and to the dew that fell upon Hermon and the hills of Zion: and all this to discover the pleasantness, profitableness, and sweetness of the saints' agreement. It is a pleasant thing to behold the sun, but it is much more pleasant to behold the saints' agreement and unity among themselves. William Bridge

*Brethren.* Abraham made this name, "brethren," a mediator to keep peace between Lot and him: "Are we not brethren?" saith Abraham. As if he should say, Shall brethren fall out for trifles, like infidels? This was enough to pacify Lot, for Abraham to put him in mind that they were brethren; when he heard the name of brethren straight his heart yielded, and the strife was ended.

So this should be the lawyer to end quarrels between Christians, to call to mind that they are brethren. And they which have spent all at law have wished that they had taken this lawyer, to think, with Lot, whether it were meet for brethren to strive like enemies. Henry Smith

Vs. 2. *That went down to the skirts of his garments.* Is the man a believer in Christ? Then he is in the one body, and I must yield him an abiding love. Is he one of the poorest, one of the least spiritual, one of the least lovable? Then he is as the skirts of the garment, and my heart's love must fall even upon him.

Brotherly love comes from the head, but falls to the feet. Its way is downward. It "ran down," and it "went down": love for the brethren condescends to men of low estate, it is not puffed up, but is lowly and meek. This is no small part of its excellence: oil would not anoint if it did not flow down, neither would brotherly love diffuse its blessing if it did not descend. C. H. S.

The vessel was emptied on the High Priest's person, so that its contents flowed down from the head upon the beard and even to the skirts of the sacerdotal robes. In that very waste lay the point of the resemblance for David. It was a feature that was very likely to strike his mind, for he, too, was a wasteful man in his way.

He had loved God in a manner which exposed him to the charge of extravagance. He had danced before the Lord, for example, when the ark was brought up from the house of Obed-edom to Jerusalem, forgetful of his dignity, exceeding the bounds of decorum, and, as it might seem, without excuse, as a much less hearty demonstration would have served the purpose of a religious solemnity. Alexander Bruce

Vs. 3. *For there the Lord commanded the blessing, even life for evermore.* Oh, for more of this rare virtue! Not the love which comes and goes, but that which dwells; not that spirit which separates and secludes but that which dwells together; not that mind which is all for debate and difference, but that which dwells together in unity.

Never shall we know the full power of the anointing till we are of one heart and of one spirit; never will the sacred dew of the Spirit descend in all its fulness till we are perfectly joined together in the same mind; never will the covenanted and commanded blessing come forth from the Lord, our God, till once again we shall have "one Lord, one faith, one baptism." Lord, lead us into this most precious spiritual unity, for Thy Son's sake. Amen. C. H. S.

Men cannot enable others, or give them power to obey them; they may bid a lame man walk, or a blind man see; but they cannot enable them to talk or see: God with His Word giveth strength to do the thing commanded; as in the old, so in the new creation, "He spake, and it was done; He commanded; and it stood fast." George Swinnock

# PSALM 134

Title: "A Song of Degrees." We have now reached the last of the Gradual Psalms. The Pilgrims are going home and are singing the last song in their Psalter. They leave early in the morning, before the day has fully commenced, for the journey is long for many of them. While yet the night lingers, they are on the move. As soon as they are outside the gates, they see the guards upon the Temple wall, and the lamps shining from the windows of the chambers which surround the sanctuary; therefore, moved by the sight, they chant a farewell to the perpetual attendants upon the holy shrine.

Their parting exhortation arouses the priests to pronounce upon them a blessing out of the holy place: this benediction is contained in the third verse. The priests as good as say, "You have desired us to bless the Lord, and now we pray the Lord to bless you." C. H. S.

Whole Psalm: The Psalm before us was prepared for the priests who served the sacred place by night. They were in danger of slumbering; and they were in danger of idle reverie. Oh, how much time is wasted in mere reverie — in letting thought wander, and wander, and wander! The priests were in danger, we say, of slumbering, of idle reverie, of vain thoughts, of useless meditation, and of profitless talk: and therefore it is written, "Behold, bless ye the Lord, all ye servants of the Lord, which by night stand in the house of the Lord."

Is it your duty to spend the night in watching? Then spend the night in worship. Do not let the time of watching be idle, wasted time; but when others are slumbering and sleeping, and you are necessarily watchful, sustain the praises of God's house; let there be praise in Zion — still praise by night as well as by day! "Lift up your hands in the sanctuary and bless the Lord."
Samuel Martin

Vs. 1. *Which by night stand in the house of the Lord.* We can well understand how the holy pilgrims half envied those consecrated ones who guarded the Temple and attended to the necessary offices thereof through the hours of night. To the silence and solemnity of night there was added the awful glory of the place where Jehovah had ordained that His worship should be celebrated; blessed were the priests and Levites who were ordained to a service so sublime. That these should bless the Lord throughout their nightly vigils was most fitting: the people would have them mark this and never fail in the duty.

They were not to move about like so many machines, but to put their hearts into all their duties, and worship spiritually in the whole course of their duty. It would be well to watch, but better still to be "watching unto prayer" and praise.

When night settles down on a church, the Lord has His watchers and holy ones still guarding His truth, and these must not be discouraged, but must bless the Lord even when the darkest hours draw on. Be it ours to cheer them and lay upon them this charge — to bless the Lord at all times and let His praise be continually in their mouths. C. H. S.

# PSALM 135

The whole Psalm is a compound of many choice extracts, and yet it has all the continuity and freshness of an original poem. The Holy Spirit occasionally repeats Himself; not because He has any lack of thoughts, or words, but because it is expedient for us that we hear the same things in the same form. Yet, when our great Teacher uses repetition, it is usually with instructive variations, which deserve our careful attention. C. H. S.

Vs. 1. *Praise ye the Lord*, or "Hallelujah." Let those who are themselves full of holy praise labor to excite the like spirit in others. It is not enough for us to praise God ourselves; we are quite unequal to such a work; let us call in all our friends and neighbors, and if they have been slack in such service, let us stir them up to it with loving exhortations. C. H. S.

Hallelujah is the Hebrew word. It signifies, "Praise ye the Lord." By this the faithful do provoke one another to give thanks unto God, and they cheer up their hearts and tune their spirits to perform this duty in the best manner by making this preface as it were thereunto. True joy of the Holy Ghost will not endure to be kept and cooped up in any one man's breast and bosom, but it striveth to get companions both for the pouring out and imparting of itself unto them, that they may be filled and refreshed out of this spring of joy. THOMAS BRIGHTMAN

*Praise ye the name of the Lord.* Think of Him with love, admire Him with heartiness, and then extol Him with ardor. Do not only magnify the Lord because He is God; but study His character and His doings, and thus render intelligent, appreciative praise. C. H. S.

When we think of Him, we must raise our thoughts above all things else and think of Him as the Universal Being of the world, that gives essence and existence to all things in it: as Jehovah, holiness, purity, simplicity, greatness, majesty, eminency, super-eminency itself, infinitely exalted above all things else, existing in, and of Himself, and having all things else continually subsisting in Him: as Jehovah, mercy itself, pardoning and forgiving all the sins that mankind commit against Him, so soon as they repent and turn to Him. In a word, when we think of the Most High God, Father, Son, and Holy Ghost, we should think of Him as Jehovah, Unity in Trinity, Trinity in Unity, Three Persons, One Being, One Essence, One Lord, One Jehovah, blessed forever. This is that glorious, that Almighty Being, which the Psalmist here means when he saith, "Praise ye the name of the Lord." WILLIAM BEVERIDGE

*Praise Him, O ye servants of the Lord.* We do not praise enough; we cannot praise too much. We ought to be always at it; answering to the command here given — Praise, Praise, Praise. Let the Three-in-one have the praises of our spirit, soul, and body. For the past, the present, and the future, let us render threefold hallelujahs. C. H. S.

For ye will do nothing out of place by praising your Lord as servants. And if ye were to be forever only servants, ye ought to praise the Lord; how much more ought those servants to praise the Lord, who have obtained the privilege of sons? AUGUSTINE

Vss. 1, 2 and 3. As Gotthold was one day passing a tradesman's house, he heard the notes of a Psalm, with which the family were concluding their morning meal. He was deeply affected, and, with a full heart, said to himself: "O my God, how pleasing to my ears is the sound of Thy praise, and how comforting to my soul the thought that there are still a few who bless Thee for Thy goodness."

Alas, the great bulk of mankind have become brutalized and resemble the swine, which in harvest gather and fatten upon the acorns beneath the oak, but show to the tree, which bore them, no other thanks than rubbing off its bark and tearing up the sod around it.

Our soul ought to be like a flower, not merely receiving the gentle influence of heaven, but in its turn, and as if in gratitude, exhaling also a sweet and pleasant perfume. It should be our desire, as it once was that of a pious man, that our hearts should melt and dissolve like incense in the fire of love, and yield the sweet fragrance of praise: or we should be like the holy martyr who professed himself willing to be consumed, if from his ashes a little flower might spring and blossom to the glory of God. We should be ready to give our very blood to fertilize the garden of the church, and render it more productive of the fruit of praise.

Well, then, my God, I will praise and extol Thee with heart and mouth to the utmost of my power. Oh, that without the interruptions which eating, and drinking, and sleep require, I could apply myself to this heavenly calling! Every mouthful of air which I inhale is mixed with the goodness which preserves my life; let every breath which I exhale be mingled at least with a hearty desire for Thy honor and praise. CHRISTIAN SCRIVER

Vs. 3. *Praise the Lord; for the Lord is good.* He is so good that all good is found in Him, flows from Him, and is rewarded by Him. The word "God" is brief for good; and truly God is the essence of goodness. Should not His goodness be well spoken of?

*Sing praises unto His name; for it is pleasant.* The mind expands, the soul is lifted up, the heart warms, the whole being is filled with delight when we are engaged in singing the high praises of our Father, Redeemer, Comforter. When in any occupation goodness and pleasure unite, we do well to follow it up without stint: yet it is to be feared that few of us sing to the Lord at all in proportion as we talk to men.

Vs. 4. *For the Lord hath chosen Jacob unto Himself.* Election is one of the most forcible arguments for adoring love. Chosen! chosen unto Himself! Who can be grateful enough for being concerned in this privilege? "Jacob have I loved," said Jehovah, and He gave no reason for His love except that He chose to love. Jacob had then done neither good nor evil, yet thus the Lord determined and thus He spake.

If it be said that the choice was made upon foresight of Jacob's character, it is, perhaps, even more remarkable; for there was little enough about Jacob that could deserve special choice. By nature Jacob was by no means the most lovable of men. No, it was sovereign grace which dictated the choice. C. H. S.

*Jacob, Israel.* Oh! blessed be God that hath chosen me to be of the number of His peculiar people! Many have not the knowledge of God, and others live in the church but are carnal; and for me to be one of His peculiar people, a member of Christ's mystical body, oh, what a privilege is this! And then what moved Him to all this? Nothing but His own free grace. Therefore, praise the Lord. THOMAS MANTON

*His peculiar treasure.* Will not a man that is not defective in his prudentials secure his jewels? "They shall be Mine in that day when I make up My jewels, and I will spare them as a father his son that serveth him" (Mal. 3:17). If a house be on fire, the owner of it will first take care of his wife and children, then of his jewels, and last of all, of his lumber and rubbish. Christ secures first His people, for they are His jewels; the world is but lumber and rubbish. RICHARD MAYHEW

Vs. 5. *For I know that the Lord is great, and that our Lord is above all gods.* The greatness of God is as much a reason for adoration as His goodness, when we are once reconciled to Him. God is great positively, great comparatively, and great superlatively — "above all gods." Of this the Psalmist had an assured personal persuasion. He says positively, "I know." It is knowledge worth possessing. He knew by observation, inspiration, and realization; he was no agnostic, he was certain and clear upon the matter. C. H. S.

The word "I" is made emphatic in the original. Whatever may be the case with others, I have had personal and precious experience of the greatness of Jehovah's power, and of His infinite supremacy above all other gods. The author of the Psalm may either speak for all Israel as a unit or he may have framed his song so that every worshipper might say this for himself as his own testimony. HENRY COWLES

On what a firm foundation does the Psalmist plant his foot — "I know!" One loves to hear men of God speaking in this calm, undoubting, and assured confidence, whether it be of the Lord's goodness or of the Lord's greatness.

There is a knowledge that plays round the head, like lightning on a mountain's summit, that leaves no trace behind; and there is a knowledge that, like the fertilizing stream, penetrates into the recesses of the heart and issues forth in all the fruits of holiness, of love, and peace, and joy for evermore. BARTON BOUCHIER

Vs. 6. *Whatsoever the Lord pleased, that did He in heaven, and in earth, in the seas, and all deep places.* His will is carried out throughout all space. The king's warrant runs in every portion of the universe. The heathen divided the great domain; but Jupiter does not rule in heaven, nor Neptune on the sea, nor Pluto in the lower regions; Jehovah rules over all. His decree is not defeated, His purpose is not frustrated: in no one point is His good pleasure set aside. Jehovah works His will: He pleases to do, and He performs the deed. None can stay His hand. How different this from the gods whom the heathen fabled to be subject to all the disappointments, failures, and passions of men! How contrary even to those so-called Christian conceptions of God which subordinate Him to the will of man, and make His eternal purposes the football of human caprice.

Our theology teaches us no such degrading notions of the Eternal as that He can be baffled by man. "His purpose shall stand, and He will do all His pleasure." No region is too high, no abyss too deep, no land too distant, no sea too wide for His omnipotence: His divine pleasure travels post over all the realm of nature, and His behests are obeyed. C. H. S.

Upon the Arminian's plan (if absurdity can deserve the name of a plan) the glorious work of God's salvation, and the eternal redemption of Jesus Christ are not complete, unless a dying mortal lends his arm; that is, unless he, who of himself can do nothing, vouchsafe to begin and accomplish that which all the angels in heaven cannot do, namely, to convert the soul from Satan to God. How contrary is all this to the language of Scripture — how repugnant to the oracle of truth! "Whatsoever the Lord pleased, that did He in heaven and in earth." AMBROSE SERLE

His power is infinite. He can do what He will do everywhere; all places are there named but purgatory; perhaps He can do nothing there but leaves all that work for the pope. THOMAS ADAMS

Vs. 7. *He causeth the vapors to ascend from the ends of the earth.* Here we are taught the power of God in creation. The process of evaporation is passed by unnoticed by the many, because they see it going on all around them; the usual ceases to be wonderful to the thoughtless, but it remains a marvel to the instructed. It is the Lord Who causes them to rise, and not a mere law. What is law without a force at the back of it? C. H. S.

Dr. Halley made a number of experiments at St. Helena as to the quantity of water that is daily evaporated from the sea, and he found that ten square inches of the ocean's surface yielded one cubic inch of water in twelve hours—

a square mile, therefore, yields 401,448,960 cubic inches, or 6,914 tons of water.

From the surface of the Mediterranean Sea during a summer's day there would pass off in invisible vapor five thousand millions of tons of water. This being only for one day, the quantity evaporated in a year would be 365 times greater, and in two thousand years it would amount to four thousand billions of tons, which evaporation would in time empty the Mediterranean Sea; but we have good reason for believing that there is as much water there now as in the time of the Romans; therefore the balance is kept up by the downpour of rain, the influx of the rivers, and the currents from the Atlantic.

Now, let us consider the amount of power required for all this evaporation. Mr. Ioule, whose experiments have given to the world so much valuable information, says that if we had a pool of water one square mile and six inches in depth to be evaporated by artificial heat, it would require the combustion of 30,000 tons of coal to effect it; therefore to evaporate all the water that ascends from the earth it would take 6,000,000,000,000 (six trillion) tons, or more than all the coal that could be stowed away in half-a-dozen such worlds as this; and yet silent and surely has the process of evaporation been going on for millions of years. SAMUEL KINNS

*He maketh lightnings for the rain.* There is an intimate connection between lightning and rain. Lightning is not to be regarded as a lawless force, but as a part of that wonderful machinery by which the earth is kept in a fit condition: a force as much under the control of God as any other, a force most essential to our existence. The ever-changing waters, rains, winds, and electric currents circulate as if they were the life-blood and vital spirits of the universe. C. H. S.

All readily allow that God is the Author of rain, thunder, and wind, in so far as He originally established this order of things in nature; but the Psalmist goes farther than this, holding that when it rains, this is not effected by a blind instinct of nature, but is the consequence of the decree of God, Who is pleased at one time to darken the sky with clouds, and at another to brighten it again with sunshine. JOHN CALVIN

It is a great instance of the divine wisdom and goodness that lightning should be accompanied by rain to soften its rage and prevent its mischievous effects. Thus, in the midst of judgment, does God remember mercy. The threatenings in His Word against sinners are like lightning; they would blast and scorch us up were it not for His promises made in the same Word to penitents, which, as a gracious rain, turn aside their fury, refreshing and comforting our affrighted spirits. GEORGE HORNE

Vs. 8. *Who smote the firstborn of Egypt, both of man and beast.* Herein the Lord is to be praised; for this deadly smiting was an act of justice against Egypt; and of love to Israel. But what a blow it was! All the firstborn slain in a moment! How it must have horrified the nation and cowed the boldest enemies of Israel!

Beasts because of their relationship to man as domestic animals are in many ways made to suffer with him. The firstborn of beasts must die as well as the firstborn of their owners, for the blow was meant to astound and overwhelm, and it accomplished its purpose. The firstborn of God had been sorely smitten, and they were set free by the Lord's meting out to their oppressors the like treatment.

Is God unrighteous, then, that taketh vengeance? No; this is an act of retribution. The Egyptians had slain the children of the Israelites, casting their infants into the river. Now the affliction is turned upon themselves; the delight of their eyes is taken from them; all their firstborn are dead, from the firstborn of Pharaoh that sat upon his throne unto the firstborn of the captive that was in the dungeon. THOMAS MILLINGTON

Vs. 10. *Who smote great nations.* It is better that the wicked should be destroyed a hundred times over than that they should tempt those who are as yet innocent to join their company. Let us but think what might have been our fate, and the fate of every other nation under heaven at this hour, had the sword of the Israelites done its work more sparingly.

Even as it was, the small portions of the Canaanites who were left, and the nations around them, so tempted the Israelites by their idolatrous practices that we read continually of the whole people of God turning away from His service. But, had the heathen lived in the land in equal numbers, and, still more, had they intermarried largely with the Israelites, how was it possible, humanly speaking, that any sparks of the light of God's truth should have survived to the coming of Christ? Would not the Israelites have lost all their peculiar character; and if they had retained the name of Jehovah as of their God, would they not have formed as unworthy notions of His attributes and worshipped Him with a worship as abominable as that which the Moabites paid to Chemosh or the Philistines to Dagon?

But in these contests, on the fate of one of these nations of Palestine the happiness of the human race depended. The Israelites fought not for themselves only, but for us. It might follow that they should thus be accounted the enemies of all mankind; it might be that they were tempted by their very distinctness to despise other nations; still they did God's work; still they preserved unhurt the seed of eternal life, and were the ministers of blessing to all other nations, even though they themselves failed to enjoy it. THOMAS ARNOLD

Vs. 13. *Thy name, O Lord, endureth forever.* God's name is eternal and will never be changed. His character is immutable; His fame and honor also shall remain to all eternity. There shall always be life in the name of Jesus and sweetness and consolation. Those upon whom the Lord's name is named in verity and truth shall be preserved by it, and kept from all evil, world without end.

*And Thy memorial, O Lord, throughout all generations.* Men's memorials decay, but the memorial of the Lord abideth evermore. What a comfort to desponding minds, trembling for the ark of the Lord! No, precious Name, thou shalt never perish! Fame of the Eternal, thou shalt never grow dim! C. H. S.

Vs. 14. *He will repent Himself.* The original word "repent Himself" here has a very extensive signification, which cannot be expressed by any one English rendering. It implies taking compassion upon them with the intention of being comforted in their future, and of taking vengeance on their oppressors.

Such are the several meanings in which the word is used. Language fails to express the mind of God toward His faithful people. How dear ought His counsels to be to us and consideration of all His ways! This reflection was continually urged upon the nation of Israel, so liable as they were to fall away to idolatry. WILLIAM WILSON

Vs. 15. Now we come to the Psalmist's denunciation of idols, which follows most naturally upon his celebration of one only living and true God.

Vs. 15. *The idols of the heathen are silver and gold, the work of men's hands.* Their essential material is dead metal; their attributes are but the qualities of senseless substances; and what of form and fashion they exhibit, they derive from the skill and labor of those who worship them. It is the height of insanity to worship metallic manufactures.

One would think it less absurd to worship one's own hands than to adore that which those hands have made. Hands are better used in breaking than in making objects which can be put to such an idiotic use. Yet the heathen love their abominable deities better than silver and gold: it were well if we could say professed believers in the Lord had as much love for Him. C. H. S.

Herodotus telleth us that Amasis had a large laver of gold, wherein both he and his guests used to wash their feet. This vessel he brake and made a god of it, which the Egyptians devoutly worshipped. And the like idolomania is at this day found among Papists, what distinction soever they would fain make betwixt an idol and an image, which indeed (as they use them) are all one. JOHN TRAPP

Vss. 15, 16 and 17. The Rev. John Thomas, a missionary in India, was one day traveling alone through the country, when he saw a great number of people waiting near an idol temple. He went up to them, and as soon as the doors were opened, he walked into the temple.

Seeing an idol raised above the people, he walked boldly up to it, held up his hand, and asked for silence. He then put his fingers on its eyes, and said, "It has eyes, but it cannot see! It has ears, but it cannot hear! It has a nose, but it cannot smell! It has hands, but it cannot handle! It has a mouth, but it cannot speak! Neither is there any breath in it!"

Instead of doing injury to him for affronting their god and themselves, the natives were all surprised; and an old Brahmin was so convinced of his folly by what Mr. Thomas said, that he also cried out, "It has feet, but cannot run away!" The people raised a shout, and being ashamed of their stupidity, they left the temple and went to their homes. THE NEW CYCLOPAEDIA OF ILLUSTRATIVE ANECDOTE

Vs. 16. *They have mouths.* Jehovah speaks, and it is done; but these images utter never a word. Surely, if they could speak, they would rebuke their votaries. Is not their silence a still more powerful rebuke? When our philosophical teachers deny that God has made any verbal revelation of Himself they also confess that their god is dumb. C. H. S.

Vss. 16 and 17. *Mouths, but they speak not: ears, but they hear not.*

*A heated fancy or imagination*
*May be mistaken for an inspiration.*
*True; but is this conclusion fair to make —*
*That inspiration must be all mistake?*
*A pebble-stone is not a diamond: true;*
*But must a diamond be a pebble, too?*
*To own a God Who does not speak to men*
*Is first to own and then disown again;*
*Of all idolatry the total sum*
*Is having gods that are both deaf and dumb.*

JOHN BYROM

Vs. 17. *They have ears, but they hear not; neither is there any breath in their mouths.* It seems that these heathen gods are dumb, and blind, and deaf — a pretty bundle of infirmities to be found in a deity! They are dead; no sign of life is perceptible; and breathing, which is of the essence of animal life, they never knew. Shall a man waste his breath in crying to an idol which has no breath? Shall life offer up petitions to death? Verily, this is a turning of things upside down. C. H. S.

Vs. 18. *Like upon them.* A singular phenomenon, known as the Spectre of the Brocken, is seen on a certain mountain in Germany. The traveler who at dawn stands on the topmost ridge beholds a colossal shadowy spectre. But in fact it is only his own shadow projected upon the morning mists by the rising sun; and it imitates, of course, every movement of its creator.

So heathen nations have mistaken their own image for Deity. Their gods display human frailties and passions and scanty virtues, projected and magnified upon the heavens, just as the small figures on the slide of a magic-lantern are projected, magnified, and illuminated upon a white sheet. FROM ELAN FOSTER'S NEW CYCLOPAEDIA OF ILLUSTRATIONS

*So is every one that trusteth in them.* Others there are who believe in a baptismal regeneration which does not renew the nature, and they make members of Christ and children of God who have none of the spirit of Christ or the signs of adoption. May we be saved from such mimicry of divine work lest we also become like our idols. C. H. S.

Vs. 19. *Bless the Lord.* And not an idol (Isia. 63:3), as the Philistines did their Dagon, and as Papists still do their he-saints and she-saints. JOHN TRAPP

# PSALM 136

We know not by whom this Psalm was written, but we do know that it was sung in Solomon's Temple (II Chron. 7:3-6), and by the armies of Jehoshaphat when they sang themselves into victory in the wilderness of Tekoa. C. H. S.

Whole Psalm: When, in the time of the Emperor Constantius, S. Athanasius was assaulted by night in his church at Alexandria by Syrianus and his troops, and many were wounded and murdered, the bishop of Alexandria sat still in his chair, and ordered the deacon to begin this Psalm, and the people answered in prompt alternation, "For His mercy endureth forever." CHRISTOPHER WORDSWORTH

Vs. 1. *O give thanks unto the Lord.* We thank our parents; let us praise our heavenly Father; we are grateful to our benefactors, let us give thanks unto the Giver of all good. C. H. S.

*His mercy endureth forever.* This appears four times in Ps. 118:1-4. This sentence is the wonder of Moses, the sum of revelation, and the hope of man. JAMES G. MURPHY

Many sweet things are in the Word of God, but the name of mercy is the sweetest word in all the Scriptures, which made David harp upon it twenty-six times in this Psalm. HENRY SMITH

Mercy pleaseth Him. It is no trouble for Him to exercise mercy. It is His delight: we are never weary of receiving, therefore He cannot be of giving; for it is a more blessed thing to give than to receive! so God takes more content in the one than we in the other. ROBERT HARRIS

God's goodness is a fountain; it is never dry. As grace is from the world's beginning (Ps. 25:6), so it is to the world's end, from one generation to another. Salvation is no termer; grace ties not itself to times. Noah as well as Abel, Moses as well as Jacob, Jeremy as well as David, Paul as well as Simeon, hath part in this salvation.

God's gracious purpose the Flood drowned not, the smoke of Sinai smothered not, the Captivity ended not, the ends of the world (Saint Paul calls them so) determined not. For Christ, by Whom it is, was slain from the beginning—Saint John saith so. He was before Abraham; He Himself saith so. And Clemens Alexandrinus doth Marcion wrong, though otherwise an heretic, in blaming him for holding that Christ saved those also that believed in Him before His incarnation. The blood of the beasts under the law was a type of His. And the scars of His wounds appear yet still, and will forever, till He cometh to judgment. The Apostle shall end this: he is *heri* and *hodi* and *semper idem:* Christ is the same yesterday and today and forever. RICHARD CLERKE

Vs. 1 and 3. *O give thanks.*

*What! give God thanks for everything,*
*Whatever may befall—*
*Whatever the dark clouds may bring?*
*Yes, give God thanks for all;*
*For safe He leads thee, hand in hand,*
*To thy blessed Fatherland.*

*What! thank Him for the lonely way*
*He to me hath given—*

*For the path which, day by day,*
*Seems farther off from Heaven?*
*Yes, thank Him, for He holds thy hand*
*And leads thee to thy Fatherland.*

*Close, close He shields thee from all harm;*
*And if the road be steep,*
*Thou know'st His everlasting arm*
*In safety doth thee keep,*
*Although thou canst not understand*
*The windings to thy Fatherland.*

*What blessing, thinkest thou, will He,*
*Who knows the good and ill,*
*Keep back, if it is good for thee,*
*While climbing up the hill?*
*Then trust Him, and keep fast His hand,*
*He leads thee to thy Fatherland.*

THE CHRISTIAN TREASURY

Vs. 2. *O give thanks unto the God of gods.* If the heathen cultivate the worship of their gods with zeal, how much more intently should we seek the glory of the God of gods — the only true and real God! Foolish persons have gathered from this verse that the Israelites believed in the existence of many gods, at the same time believing that their Jehovah was the chief among them; but this is an absurd inference, since gods who have a God over them cannot possibly be gods themselves.

*For His mercy endureth forever.* Imagine supreme Godhead without everlasting mercy! It would then have been as fruitful a source of terror as it is now a fountain of thanksgiving. C. H. S.

Vs. 4. *To Him Who alone doeth great wonders.* What have the gods of the heathen done? If the question be settled by doings, Jehovah is indeed "alone." It is exceedingly wonderful that men should worship gods who can do nothing and forget the Lord Who alone doeth great wonders. C. H. S.

Does He "alone" do great wonders? That means, He does so by Himself, unaided, needing nothing from others, asking no help from His creatures.

As the Nile from Nubia to the Mediterranean rolls on one thousand three hundred miles in solitary grandeur, receiving not one tributary, but itself alone dispensing fertility and fatness wherever it comes; so our God "alone" does wonders. (See Deut. 32:12: Ps. 72:18, etc.) No prompter, no helper; spontaneously He goes forth to work, and all He works is worthy of God. Then we have no need of any other; we are independent of all others; all our springs are in Him. ANDREW A. BONAR

Christians should not be ashamed of the mysteries and miracles of their religion. Sometimes of late years there has been manifested a disposition to recede from the defence of the supernatural in religion. This is a great mistake. Give up all that is miraculous in true religion, and there is nothing left of power sufficient to move any heart to worship or adore; and without worship, there is no piety. WM. PLUMER

The longer I live, O my God, the more do I wonder at all the works of Thy hands. I see such admirable artifice in the very least and most despicable of all Thy creátures, as doth every day more and more astonish my observation.

I need not look so far as heaven for matter of marvel, though therein thou are infinitely glorious; while I have but a spider in my window, or a bee in my garden, or a worm under my foot: every one of these overcomes me with a just amazement: yet can I see no more than their very outsides; their inward form, which gives their being and operations, I cannot pierce into.

The less I can know, O Lord, the more let me wonder; and the less I can satisfy myself with marveling at Thy works, the more let me adore the Majesty and omnipotence of Thee, that wroughtest them. JOSEPH HALL

Vs. 5. *To Him that by wisdom made the heavens.* We find that God has built the heavens in wisdom, to declare His glory and to show forth His handiwork. There are no iron tracks with bars and bolts to hold the planets in their orbits. Freely in space they move, ever changing but never changed; poised and balancing; swaying and swayed; disturbing and disturbed, onward they fly, fulfilling with unerring certainty their mighty cycles.

The entire system forms one grand complicated piece of celestial machinery; circle within circle, wheel within wheel, cycle within cycle; revolutions so swift as to be completed in a few hours; movements so slow that their mighty periods are only counted by millions of years. THE ORBS OF HEAVEN

Vs. 6. *To Him that stretched out the earth above the waters.* Few even think of the divine wisdom and power which performed all this of old; yet, if a continent can be proved to have risen or fallen an inch within historic memory, the fact is recorded in the "transactions" of learned societies and discussed at every gathering of philosophers. C. H. S.

Vs. 7. *To Him that made great lights.* The Psalmist is making a song for common people, not for your critical savans — and so he sings of the sun and moon as they appear to us — the greatest of lights. C. H. S.

Vs. 8. *For His mercy endureth forever.* Day unto day uttereth speech concerning the mercy of the Lord; every sunbeam is a mercy, for it falls on undeserving sinners who else would sit in doleful darkness and find earth a hell. C. H. S.

Vs. 9. *The moon and stars to rule by night.* Hence, in all ages, a moonlight scene has been regarded by all ranks of men with feelings of joy and sentiments of admiration. The following description of Homer translated into English verse by Pope, has been esteemed one of the finest night-pieces in poetry:

*Behold the moon, refulgent lamp of night,*
*O'er Heaven's clear azure spreads her sacred light,*
*When not a breath disturbs the deep serene,*
*And not a cloud o'ercasts the solemn scene;*
*Around her throne the vivid planets roll,*
*And stars unnumbered gild the glowing pole;*
*O'er the dark trees a yellower verdure shed,*
*And tip with silver every mountain's head;*
*Then shine the vales; the rocks in prospect rise;*
*A flood of glory burst from all the skies;*
*The conscious swains, rejoicing in the sight,*
*Eye the blue vault and bless the useful light.*

THOMAS DICK

We enjoy all the advantages to which we have alluded as much as if the stars had been created solely for the use of our world, while, at the same time, they serve to diversify the nocturnal sky of other planets, and to diffuse their light and influence over ten thousands of other worlds with which they are more immediately connected, so that, in this respect, as well as in every other, the Almighty produces the most sublime and diversified effects by means the most simple and economical, and renders every part of the universe subservient to another, and to the good of the whole. THOMAS DICK

When the First Consul crossed the Mediterranean on his Egyptian expedition, he carried with him a cohort of Savans, who ultimately did good service in many ways. Among them, however, as might be expected at that era, were not a few philosophers of the Voltaire-Diderot school.

Napoleon, for his own instruction and amusement on shipboard, encouraged disputation among these gentlemen; and on one occasion they undertook to show, and, according to their own account, did demonstrate, by infallible logic and metaphysic, that there is no God.

Bonaparte, who hated all idealogists, abstract reasoners, and logical demonstrators, no matter what they were demonstrating, would not fence with these subtle dialecticians, but had them immediately on deck, and, pointing to the stars in the clear sky, replied, by way of counterargument, "Very good, messieurs! but Who made all these?" GEORGE WILSON

*For His mercy endureth forever.* The nightly guides and illuminators of men on land and sea are not for now and then but for all time.

They shone on Adam, and they shine on us. Thus they are tokens and pledges of undying grace to men. C. H. S.

Vs. 12. *For His mercy endureth forever.* If one plague will not set them free, there shall be ten; but free they shall all be at the appointed hour; not one Israelite shall remain under Pharaoh's power. God will not only use His hand but His arm — His extraordinary power shall be put to the work sooner than His purpose of mercy shall fail. C. H. S.

Vs. 13. *To Him which divided the Red sea into parts.* He made a road across the sea-bottom, causing the divided waters to stand like walls on either side. Men deny miracles; but, granted that there is a God, they become easy of belief. Since it requires me to be an atheist that I may logically reject miracles, I prefer the far smaller difficulty of believing in the infinite power of God.

He Who causes the waters of the sea ordinarily to remain as one mass can with equal readiness divide them. He Who can throw a stone in one direction can with the same force throw it another way; the Lord can do precisely what He wills, and He wills to do anything which is for the deliverance of His people. C. H. S.

Vs. 14. *For His mercy endureth forever.* Mercy cleared the road, Mercy cheered the host, Mercy led them down, and Mercy brought them up again. Even to the depth of the sea, Mercy reaches — there is no end to it, no obstacle in the way of it, no danger to believers in it, while Jehovah is all around. "Forward!" be our watchword as it was that of Israel of old, for mercy doth compass us about.

*Through the fire or through the sea*
*Still His mercy guardeth thee.*
C. H. S.

Vs. 15. *For His mercy endureth forever.* Sin is self-damnation. The sinner goes downward of his own choice, and if he finds out too late that he cannot return, is not his blood upon his own head? The finally impenitent, however terrible their doom, will not be witness against mercy; but rather this shall aggravate their misery, that they went on in defiance of mercy and would not yield themselves to Him Whose mercy endureth forever. C. H. S.

Vs. 16. *To Him which led His people through the wilderness.* God's dealings are mysterious, but they must be right, simply because they are His. What a multitude of mercies are comprehended in the conduct of such an enormous host through a region wherein there was no provision even for single travelers! C. H. S.

Vs. 18-20. The profane of our times may hence learn to take heed how they wrong the faithful. God is "wise in heart and mighty in strength" (Job.

9:4). Who ever waxed fierce against His people and hath prospered? For their sakes, He hath destroyed great kings and mighty.

*Sihon king of the Amorites . . . and Og the king of Bashan.* He can pluck off thy chariot wheels, strike thee in the hinder parts, cause thy heart to fail thee for fear, and in a moment fetch thy soul from thee: better were it for thee to have a millstone hanged about thy neck, and thou to be cast into the bottom of the sea, than to offend the least of these faithful ones; they are dear in His sight, tender to Him as the apple of His eye. JOHN BARLOW

Vs. 20. *And Og the king of Bashan.* He was of the race of the giants, but he was routed like a pigmy when he entered the lists with Israel's God. The Lord's people were called upon to fight against him, but it was God Who won the victory. C. H. S.

Vs. 20. When *Og the king of Bashan* took the field — a giant, a new and more terrific foe — he, too, fell. And the mercy that thus dealt with enemies so great, enemies so strong, one after another, "endureth forever."

When Antichrist raises up his hosts in the latter days, one after another — when the great, the famous, the mighty, the noble, the gigantic men, in succession assail the church, they shall perish: "For His mercy endureth forever." ANDREW A. BONAR

Vs. 23. *Who remembered us in our low estate.* For the Lord even to think of us is a wealth of mercy. Ours was a sorry estate — an estate of bankruptcy and mendicancy. Our estate was once so low as to be at hell's mouth; since then it has been low in poverty, bereavement, despondency, sickness, and heart-sorrow, and we fear, also, sinfully low in faith, and love and every other grace; and yet the Lord has not forgotten us as a dead thing out of mind; but He has tenderly remembered us still. We thought ourselves too small and too worthless for His memory to burden itself about us, yet He remembered us. C. H. S.

The word "remembered" is a pregnant word; it bears twins twice told, it is big of a sixfold sense, as so many degrees of mercy in it. To remember signifies to think upon, in opposition to forgetfulness. We may dwell in man's thoughts and not be the better for it, but we cannot be in God's remembering thoughts but we shall be the better for it.

*For His mercy endureth forever.* There is no reason to be given for grace but grace; there is no reason to be given for mercy but mercy: Who remembered us: "For His mercy endureth forever." RALPH VENNING

Vs. 24. *And hath redeemed us from our enemies.* Sin is our enemy, and we are redeemed from it by the atoning Blood; Satan is our enemy, and we are redeemed from him by the Redeemer's power; the world is our enemy, and we are redeemed from it by the Holy Spirit. We are ransomed; let us enjoy our liberty; Christ has wrought our redemption; let us praise His name. C. H. S.

Vs. 24. *And.* If the end of one mercy were not the beginning of another, we were undone. PHILIP HENRY

Vs. 25. *Who giveth food to all flesh.* Of Edward Taylor, better known as "Father Taylor," the Sailor Preacher of Boston, it is said that his prayers were more like the utterances of an Oriental, abounding in imagery, than a son of these colder Western climes.

The Sunday before he was to sail for Europe, he was entreating the Lord to care well for his church during his absence. All at once he stopped and ejaculated, "What have I done? Distrust the providence of heaven! A God that gives a whale a ton of herrings for a breakfast, will He not care for my children?" and then went on, closing his prayer in a more confiding strain. C. H. S.

# PSALM 137

This plaintive ode is one of the most charming compositions in the whole Book of Psalms, for its poetic power. If it were not inspired, it would nevertheless occupy a high place in poesy, expecially the former portion of it, which is tender and patriotic to the highest degree. Let those find fault with it who have never seen their temple burned, their city ruined, their wives ravished, and their children slain; they might not, perhaps, be quite so velvet-mouthed if they had suffered after this fashion. C. H. S.

Whole Psalm: The moaning of the captive, the wailing of the exile, and the sighing of the saints are heard in every line. W. ORMISTON

Vs. 1. *By the rivers of Babylon, there we sat down.* In little groups they sat down and made common lamentation, mingling their memories and their tears. The rivers were well enough, but, alas, they were the rivers of Babylon, and the ground whereon the sons of Israel sat was foreign soil, and therefore they wept. Those who came to interrupt their quiet were citizens of the destroying city, and their company was not desired. Everything reminded Israel of her banishment from the holy city, her servitude beneath the shadow of the temple of Bel, her helplessness under a cruel enemy; and therefore her sons and daughters sat down in sorrow. C. H. S.

*Yea, we wept, when we remembered Zion.* They did not weep when they remembered the cruelties of Babylon; the memory of fierce oppression dried their tears and made their hearts burn with wrath; but when the beloved city of their solemnities came into their minds, they could not refrain from floods of tears.

Even thus do true believers mourn when they see the church despoiled and find themselves unable to succor her: we could bear anything better than this. In these, our times, the Babylon of error ravages the city of God, and the hearts of the faithful are grievously wounded as they see truth fallen in the streets and unbelief rampant among the professed servants of the Lord. We bear our protests, but they appear to be in vain; the multitude are mad upon their idols. C. H. S.

A godly man lays to heart the miseries of the church. I have read of certain trees, whose leaves if cut or touched, the other leaves contract and shrink up themselves, and for a space hang down their heads: such a spiritual sympathy is there among Christians; when other parts of God's church suffer, they feel themselves, as it were, touched in their own persons. Ambrose reports, that when Theodosius was sick unto death, he was more troubled about the church of God than about his own sickness. THOMAS WATSON

What should we then do for our absence from another manner of Jerusalem? Theirs was an earthly, old, robbed, spoiled, burned, sacked Jerusalem; ours a heavenly, new one, into which no arrow can be shot, no noise of the drum heard, nor sound of the trumpet, nor calling unto battle: who would not then weep to be absent from thence? WALTER BALCANQUAL

Vs. 1-6. There are times when the world does not mock at the Christian. Often the Christian is filled with so strange a joy that the world wonders in silence. Often there is a meek and quiet spirit in the Christian, which disarms opposition. The soft answer turneth away wrath; and his very enemies are forced to be at peace with him.

But stop till the Christian's day of darkness comes — stop till sin and unbelief have brought him into captivity — stop till he is shut out from Zion, and carried afar off, and sits and weeps; then will the cruel world help forward the affliction — then will they ask for mirth and song; and when they see the bitter tear trickling down the cheek, they will ask with savage mockery, "Where is your Psalm singing now?" "Sing us one of the songs of Zion." Even Christ felt this bitterness when He hung upon the cross. Every true Christian loves praise — the holiest Christians love it most. But when the believer falls into sin and darkness, his harp is on the willows, and he cannot sing the Lord's song, for he is in a strange land.

He often finds, when he has fallen into sin and captivity, that he has fallen among wordly delights and worldly friends. A thousand pleasures tempt him to take up his rest here; but if he be a true child of Zion, he will never settle down in a strange land. He will look over all the pleasures of the world and the pleasures of sin, and say, "A day in Thy courts is better than a thousand" — "If I forget Thee, O Jerusalem, let my right hand forget her cunning." ROBERT MURRAY M'CHEYNE

Vs. 2. *We hanged our harps upon the willows in the midst thereof.* Music hath charms to give unquiet spirits rest; but when the heart is solely sad, it only mocks the grief which flies to it. Men put away their instruments of mirth when a heavy cloud darkens their souls. C. H. S.

*Willows.* It is a curious fact that during the Commonwealth of England, when Cromwell, like a wise politician, allowed them to settle in London and to have synagogues, the Jews came hither in sufficient numbers to celebrate the Feast of Tabernacles in booths, among the willows on the borders of the Thames.

The disturbance of their comfort from the innumerable spectators, chiefly London apprentices, called for some protection from the local magistrates. Not that any insult was offered to their persons, but a natural curiosity, excited by so new and extraordinary a spectacle, induced many to press too closely round their camp and perhaps intrude upon their privacy. MARIA CALLCOTT

Vs. 3. *Sing us one of the songs of Zion.* The insulting nature of the demand will become the more conspicuous, if we consider that the usual subjects of these songs were the omnipotence of Jehovah and His love towards His chosen people. WILLIAM KEATINGE CLAY

Fashion and frivolity and false philosophy have made a formidable combination against us; and the same truth, the same honesty, the same integrity of principle, which in any other cause would be esteemed as manly and respectable, is despised and laughed at when attached to the cause of the gospel and its sublime interests. THOMAS CHALMERS

Vs. 4. *How shall we sing the Lord's song in a strange land?* There are many things which the ungodly could do, and think nothing of the doing thereof, which gracious men cannot venture upon. The question, "How can I?" or "How shall we?" comes of a tender conscience and denotes an inability to sin which is greatly to be cultivated. C. H. S.

Again, the feelings of the present life are often adverse to praise. The exiles in Babylon could not sing because they were in heaviness. God's hand was heavy upon them. He had a controversy with them for their sins.

Now, the feelings of many of us are in like manner adverse to the Lord's song. Some of us are in great sorrow. We have lost a friend; we are in anxiety about one who is all to us; we know not which way to turn for tomorrow's bread or for this day's comfort. How can we sing the Lord's song?

And there is another kind of sorrow, still more fatal, if it be possible, to the lively exercise of adoration. And that is, a weight and burden of unforgiven sin. Songs may be heard from the prison-cell of Philippi; songs may be heard from the calm death-bed, or by the open grave; but songs cannot be drawn forth from the soul on which the load of God's displeasure, real or imagined, is lying, or which is still powerless to apprehend the grace and the life for sinners which is in Christ Jesus.

That, we imagine, was the difficulty which pressed upon the exile Israelite; that certainly is an impediment now, in many, to the outburst of Christian praise. And again, there is a land yet more strange and foreign to the Lord's song even than the land of unforgiven guilt—and that is the land of unforsaken sin. C. J. VAUGHAN

*The Lord's song.* There is no real sorrow in any circumstances into which God brings us, or where He leads and goes with us; but where sin is, and suffering is felt to be—not persecution, but—judgment, there is and can be no joy; the soul refuses to be comforted. Israel cannot sing beside the waters of Babylon. WILLIAM DEBURGH

Vs. 5. *If I forget thee, O Jerusalem.* Calvary, Mount of Olives, Siloam, how fragrant are ye with the name that is above every name! "If I forget thee, O Jerusalem!" Can I forget where He walked so often, where He spake such gracious words, where He died? Can I forget that His feet shall stand on that "Mount of Olives, which is before Jerusalem, on the east?" Can I forget that there stood the Upper Room, and there fell the showers of Pentecost? ANDREW A. BONAR

Vs. 6. *If I do not remember thee.* Either our beds are soft, or our hearts hard, that can rest when the church is at unrest, that feel not our brethren's hard cords through our soft beds. JOHN TRAPP

*If I prefer not Jerusalem above my chief joy.* If such the attachment of a banished Jew to his native land, how much more should we love the church of God, of which we are children and citizens! How jealous should we be of her honor, how zealous for her prosperity!

Never let us find jests in the words of Scripture, or make amusement out of holy things, lest we be guilty of forgetting the Lord and His cause. It is to be feared that many tongues have lost all power to charm the congregations of the saints because they have forgotten the Gospel and God has forgotten them. C. H. S.

Vs. 7. *Remember, O Lord, the children of Edom.* We are not to regard the imprecations of this Psalm in any other light than as prophetical. They are grounded on the many prophecies which had already gone forth on the subject of the destruction of Babylon, if, as we may admit, the Psalm before us was written after the desolation of Jerusalem. But these prophecies have not yet been fulfilled in every particular and remain to be accomplished in mystic Babylon, when the dominion of Antichrist shall be forever swept away and the true church introduced into the glorious liberty of the sons of God at the appearing of their Lord and Savior Jesus Christ in His own kingdom. WILLIAM WILSON

Edom's hatred was the hatred with which the carnal mind in its natural enmity against God always regards whatever is the elect object of His favor. Jerusalem was the city of God. "Raze it, raze it even to the ground," is the mischievous desire of every unregenerate mind against every building that rests on the elect Stone of Divine foundation.

God's election never pleases man until, through grace, his own heart has become an adoring receiver of that mercy which while in his ntaural state he angrily resented and refused to own in its effects on other men. From Cain to Antichrist, this solemn truth holds always good. ARTHUR PRIDHAM

# PSALM 138

This Psalm is wisely placed. Whoever edited and arranged these sacred poems, he had an eye to opposition and contrast; for if in Ps. CXXXVII, we see the need of silence before revilers, here we see the excellence of a brave confession. There is a time to be silent, lest we cast pearls before swine; and there is a time to speak openly lest we be found guilty of cowardly non-confession. The Psalm is evidently of a Davidic character, exhibiting all the fidelity, courage, and decision of that King of Israel and Prince of Psalmists.

Of course the critics have tried to rend the authorship from David on account of the mention of the Temple, though it so happens that in one of the Psalms which is allowed to be David's the same word occurs. Many modern critics are to the Word of God what blow-flies are to the food of men: they cannot do any good, and unless relentlessly driven away, they do great harm. C. H. S.

Vs. 1. *I will praise Thee with my whole heart.* His mind is so taken up with God that he does not mention His name: to him there is no other God, and Jehovah is so perfectly realized and so intimately known that the Psalmist, in addressing Him no more thinks of mentioning His name than we should do if we were speaking to a father or a friend. We need a broken heart to mourn our own sins, but a whole heart to praise the Lord's perfections. C. H. S.

*I will praise Thee.* Alas, for that capital crime of the Lord's people, barrenness in praises! Oh, how fully I am persuaded that a line of praises is worth a leaf of prayer, and an hour of praises is worth a day of fasting and mourning! JOHN LIVINGSTONE

*Before the gods will I sing praise unto Thee.* In these days when new religions are daily excogitated, and new gods are set up, it is well to know how to act. Bitterness is forbidden, and controversy is apt to advertize the heresy; the very best method is to go on personally worshipping the Lord with unvarying zeal, singing with heart and voice His royal praises.

Do they deny the Divinity of our Lord? Let us the more fervently adore Him. Do they despise the atonement? Let us the more constantly proclaim it. Had half the time spent in councils and controversies been given to praising the Lord, the church would have been far sounder and stronger than she is at this day. C. H. S.

Vs. 2. *I will worship toward Thy holy temple.* Even so, the true-hearted believer of these days must not fall into the will-worship of superstition, or the wild worship of skepticism, but reverently worship as the Lord Himself prescribes. C. H. S.

*And praise Thy name for Thy lovingkindness and for Thy truth.* The Person of Jesus is the temple of the Godhead, and therein we behold the glory of the Father, "full of grace and truth." It is upon these two points that the name of Jehovah is at this time assailed — His grace and His truth. He is said to be too stern, too terrible, and therefore "modern thought" displaces the God of Abraham, Isaac, and Jacob, and sets up an effeminate deity of its own making.

As for us, we firmly believe that God is love and that in the summing up of all things it will be seen that hell itself is not inconsistent with the beneficence of Jehovah, but is, indeed, a necessary part of His moral government, now that sin has intruded into the universe. True believers hear the thunders of His justice and yet they do not doubt His lovingkindness. But not only do men attack the loving kindness of God, but the truth of God is at this time assailed on all sides. The swine are trampling on the pearls at this time, and nothing restrains them; nevertheless, the pearls are pearls still, and shall yet shine about our Monarch's brow. C. H. S.

The mother may draw whole stores of comfort from a realization of the condescending thoughtfulness of God. He will be interested about her babe; if she commit it to Him, He Who made the universe will, with His infinite mind, think upon her cradle and the helpless creature that is rocked to sleep therein.

The sick man may draw whole stores of comfort from the same source, for he can believe the One by Whom the body was fearfully and wonderfully made will think over the sufferings of that body and alleviate them or give strength for the endurance of them if they must be borne. Condescension of thought marks all the dealings of God with His people. We read of great machines which are able to crush iron bars and yet they can touch so gently as not to break the shell of the smallest egg; as it is with them, so is it with the hand of the Most High; He can crush a world and yet bind up a wound. And great need have we of tenderness in our low estate; a little thing would crush us: we have such bruised and feeble souls that unless we had One Who would deal tenderly with us we must soon be destroyed. PHILIP BENNETT POWER

*Thou hast magnified Thy Word above all Thy name.* When God will, He can make more such worlds as this; but He cannot make another truth, and therefore He will not lose one jot thereof. Satan, knowing this, sets all his wits to work to deface this and disfigure it by unsound doctrine.

The Word is the glass in which we see God, and seeing Him are changed into His likeness by His Spirit. If this glass be cracked, then the conceptions we have of God will misrepresent Him unto us; whereas the Word, in its native clearness, sets Him out in all His glory unto our eye. WILLIAM GURNALL

God has sent His Word to us as a mirror, to reflect His glory, as a standard, to which everything may be referred. Of God's will we know nothing, but from the Word, as a fountain, from whence all His blessings emanate. Look over the face of the globe and see how many who were once under the unrestrained dominion of sin are now transformed into the image of their God. And then ascend to heaven and behold the myriads of the redeemed around the throne of God, uniting their hallelujahs to God and to the Lamb: to this state were they all brought by that blessed Word, which alone could ever prevail for so great a work.

Thus it is that God has magnified His Word; and thus it is that He will magnify it to the end of time; yea, through eternity will it be acknowledged as the one source of all blessings that shall ever be enjoyed. CHARLES SIMEON

We see this in nature. Here is a man so to be depended upon, so faithful to his word, that he will sacrifice anything sooner than depart from it: that man will give up his property, or life itself, rather than forfeit his word. So God has spoken of magnifying His Word above all His name. He would sooner allow all His other perfections to come to naught than for His faithfulness to fail. JOSEPH C. PHILPOT

God has a greater regard unto the words of His mouth than to the works of His hand: heaven and earth shall pass away, but one jot or tittle of what He hath spoken shall never fall to the ground. Some do understand this of Christ, the essential Word, in Whom He has set His name and Whom He has so highly exalted, that He has given Him "a Name above every name." EBENEZER ERSKINE

Vs. 3. *And strengthenedst me with strength in my soul.* This was a true answer to his prayer. If the burden was not removed, yet strength was given wherewith to bear it, and this is an equally effective method of help. It may not be best for us that the trial should come to an end; it may be far more to our advantage that by its pressure we should learn patience.

Sweet are the uses of adversity, and our prudent Father in heaven will not deprive us of those benefits. Strength imparted to the soul is an inestimable boon; it means courage, fortitude, assurance, heroism. By His Word and Spirit the Lord can make the trembler brave, the sick whole, the weary bright. C. H. S.

*Thou answeredst me, and strengthenedst me with strength in my soul.* He was now in a strait, and God comes in haste to him. Though we may keep a well friend waiting should he send for us, yet we will give a sick friend leave to call us up at midnight. In such extremities, we usually go with the messenger that comes for us: and so doth God with the prayer. We relieve the poor as their need increaseth; so Christ comforts His people as their troubles multiply. And now, Christian, tell me, doth not thy dear Lord deserve a ready spirit in thee to meet any suffering with, for, or from Him, Who gives His sweetest comforts where His people are put to bear their saddest sorrows? Well may the servant do his work cheerfully when his master is so careful of him as with his own hands to bring him his breakfast into the fields.

The Christian stays not till he comes to heaven for all his comfort. There indeed shall be the full supper, but there is a breakfast, Christian, of previous joys, more or less, which Christ brings to thee in the field, to be eaten on the place where thou endurest thy hardship. WILLIAM GURNALL

Vs. 4. *All the kings of the earth shall praise Thee, O Lord, when they hear the words of Thy mouth.* What an assembly! "All the kings of the earth!" What a purpose! Gathered to hear the words of Jehovah's mouth. What a preacher! David himself rehearses the words of Jehovah. What praise when they all in happy union lift up their songs unto the Lord! C. H. S.

Vs. 6. *The Lord hath respect unto the lowly.* This is a disposition that best serves God's great design of lifting up and glorifying His free grace. What think you, sirs, was God's design in election, in redemption, in the whole of the gospel dispensation, and in all the ordinances thereof?

His grand design in all was to rear up a glorious high throne from which He might display the riches of His free and sovereign grace; this is that which He will have magnified through eternity above all His other name.

Now, this lowliness and humility of spirit suits best unto God's design of exalting the freedom of His grace. It is not the legalist, or proud Pharisee, but the poor, humble publican, who is smiting on his breast and crying, "God be merciful to me, a sinner," that submits to the revelation of grace.
EBENEZER ERSKINE

*But the proud He knoweth afar off.* To a Cain's sacrifice, a Pharaoh's promise, a Rabshakeh's threat, and a Pharisee's prayer, the Lord has no respect. Nebuchadnezzar, when far off from God, cried, "Behold this great Babylon which I have builded"; but the Lord knew him and sent him grazing with cattle.

Proud men boast loudly of their culture and "the freedom of thought" and even dare to criticize their Maker: but He knows them from afar and will keep them at arm's length in this life and shut them up in hell in the next. C. H. S.

Vs. 7. *Though I walk in the midst of trouble, Thou wilt revive me.* If I am walking there now, or shall be doing so in years to come, I have no cause for fear; for God is with me and will give me new life. When we are somewhat in trouble, it is bad enough, but it is worse to penetrate into the center of that dark continent and traverse its midst: yet in such a case the believer makes progress, for he walks; he keeps to a quiet pace, for he does no more than walk; and he is not without the best of company, for His God is near to pour fresh life into him. If we receive reviving, we need not regret affliction. When God revives us, trouble will never harm us. C. H. S.

The wisdom of God is seen in helping in desperate cases. God loves to show His wisdom when human help and wisdom fail. Exquisite lawyers love to wrestle with niceties and difficulties in the law, to show their skill the more.

God's wisdom is never at a loss; but when providences are darkest, then the morning star of deliverance appears. Sometimes God melts away the spirits of His enemies (Josh. 2:24). Sometimes He finds them other work to do, and sounds a retreat to them, as He did to Saul when he was pursuing David. "The Philistines are in the land." "In the mount, God will be seen." When the church seems to be upon the altar, her peace and liberty ready to be sacrificed, then the angel comes. THOMAS WATSON

Vs. 8. *The Lord will perfect that which concerneth me.* I suppose that if the Mediaeval dream had ever come true, and an alchemist had ever turned a grain of lead into gold, he could have turned all the lead in the world, in time, and with crucibles and furnaces enough.

The first step is all the difficulty, and if you and I have been changed from enemies into sons, and had one spark of love to God kindled in our hearts, that is a mightier change than any that yet remains to be effected in order to make us perfect. One grain has been changed; the whole mass will be in due time. ALEXANDER MACLAREN

*Forsake not the works of Thine own hands.* All men love their own works; many dote upon them: shall we think God will forsake His? JOSEPH CARYL

Behold in me Thy work, not mine: for mine, if Thou seest, Thou condemnest; Thine, if Thou seest, Thou crownest. For whatever good works there be of mine, from Thee are they to me; and so they are more Thine than mine. For I hear from Thine apostle, "By grace are ye saved through faith; and that not of yourselves: it is the gift of God. Not of works, lest any man should boast. For we are His workmanship, created in Christ Jesus" (Eph. 2:8-10). AUGUSTINE

*Thine own hands.* His creating hands formed our souls at the beginning; His nail-pierced hands redeemed them on Calvary; His glorified hands will hold our souls fast and not let them go forever. Unto His hands let us commend our spirits, sure that even though the works of our hands have made void the works of His hands, yet His hands will again make perfect all that our hands have unmade. J. W. BURGON

# PSALM 139

One of the most notable of the sacred hymns. It sings the omniscience and omnipresence of God, inferring from these the overthrow of the powers of wickedness, since He Who sees and hears the abominable deeds and words of the rebellious will surely deal with them according to His justice.

The brightness of this Psalm is like unto a sapphire stone, or Ezekiel's "terrible crystal"; it flames out with such flashes of light as to turn night into day. Like a Pharos, this holy song casts a clear light even to the uttermost parts of the sea and warns us against that practical atheism which ignores the presence of God and so makes shipwreck of the soul.

Title: Of course the critics take this composition away from David, on account of certain Aramaic expressions in it. We believe that upon the principles of criticism now in vogue it would be extremely easy to prove that Milton did not write *Paradise Lost*. Knowing to what wild inferences the critics have run in other matters, we have lost nearly all faith in them and prefer to believe David to be the author of this Psalm, from internal evidences of style and matter, rather than to accept the determination of men whose modes of judgment are manifestly unreliable. C. H. S.

Whole Psalm: Aben Ezra observes that this is the most glorious and excellent Psalm in all the book: a very excellent one it is; but whether the most excellent, it is hard to say. JOHN GILL

There is one Psalm which it were well if Christians would do by it as Pythagoras by his Golden Precepts — every morning and evening repeat it. It is David's appeal of a good conscience unto God against the malicious suspicions and calumnies of men in Psalm 139. SAMUEL ANNESLEY

This Psalm is one of the sublimest compositions in the world. How came a shepherd boy to conceive so sublime a theme and to write in so sublime a strain? GEORGE ROGERS

"A Psalm of David." How any critic can assign this Psalm to other than David, I cannot understand. Every line, every thought, every turn of expression and transition, is his, and his only. As for the arguments drawn from the two Chaldaisms which occur, this is really nugatory. These Chaldaisms consist merely in the substitution of one letter for another, very like it in shape, and easily to be mistaken by a transcriber, particularly by one who had been used to the Chaldee idiom; but the moral arguments for David's authorship are so strong as to overwhelm any such verbal, or rather literal criticism, were even the objections more formidable than they actually are. JOHN JEBB

Vs. 1. *O Lord, Thou hast searched me, and known me.* How well it is for us to know the God Who knows us! There never was a time in which we were unknown to God, and there never will be a moment in which we shall be beyond His observation. Note how the Psalmist makes his doctrine personal: he saith not, "O God, Thou knowest all things"; but, "Thou hast known me." It is ever our wisdom to lay truth home to ourselves. How wonderful the contrast between the observer and the observed! Jehovah and me! Yet this most intimate connection exists, and therein lies our hope. Let the reader sit still a while and try to realize the two poles of this statement — the Lord and poor, puny man — and he will see much to admire and wonder at. C. H. S.

The godly may sometimes be so overclouded with calumnies and reproaches as not to be able to find a way to clear themselves before men, but must content and comfort themselves with the testimony of a good conscience and with God's approbation of their integrity, as here David doth. DAVID DICKSON

Divine truths look full as well when they are prayed over as when they are preached over: and much better than when they are disputed over. MATTHEW HENRY

*Searched.* The Hebrew word originally means to dig, and is applied to the search for precious metals (Job 28:3), but metaphorically to a moral inquisition into guilt. JOSEPH ADDISON ALEXANDER

Vss. 1 and 5. God knows everything perfectly, and He knows everything perfectly at once. This, to a human understanding, would breed confusion; but there can be no confusion in the divine understanding, because confusion arises from imperfection. Thus God, without confusion, beholds as distinctly the actions of every man, as if that man were the only created being, and the Godhead were solely employed in observing him. Let this thought fill your mind with awe and with remorse. HENRY KIRKE WHITE

Vs. 2. *Thou understandest my thought.* Before men, we stand as opaque beehives. They can see the thoughts go in and out of us, but what work they do inside of a man they cannot tell. Before God we are as glass beehives, and all that our thoughts are doing within us He perfectly sees and understands. HENRY WARD BEECHER

Vs. 2-4. Do not fancy that your demeanor, posture, dress, or deportment are not under God's providence. You deceive yourself. Do not think that your thoughts pass free from inspection. The Lord understand them afar off. Think not that your words are dissipated in the air before God can hear. Oh, no! He knows them even when still upon your tongue. Do not think that your ways are so private and concealed that there is none to know or censure them. You mistake. God knows all your ways. JOHANN DAVID FRISCH

Vs. 4. *For there is not a word in my tongue.* How needful it is to set a watch before the doors of our mouth, to hold that unruly member of ours, the tongue, as with bit and bridle. Some of you feel at times that you can scarcely say a word, and the less you say the better. Well, it may be as well; for great talkers are almost sure to make slips with their tongue.

It may be a good thing that you cannot speak much; for in the multitude of words there lacketh not sin. Wherever you go, what light, vain, and foolish conversations you hear! I am glad not to be thrown into circumstances where I can hear it.

But with you, it may be different. You may often repent of speaking; you will rarely repent of silence. How soon angry words are spoken! How soon foolish expressions drop from the mouth! The Lord knows it all, marks it all, and did you carry about with you a more solemn recollection of it you would be more watchful than you are. JOSEPH C. PHILPOT

"Where there is not a word in my tongue, O Lord, Thou knowest all"; so some read it; for thought are words to God. MATTHEW HENRY

Vs. 5. *Thou hast beset me behind and before.* Behind us there is God recording our sins or in grace blotting out the remembrance of them; and before us there is God foreknowing all our deeds and providing for all our wants. We cannot turn back and so escape Him, for He is behind; we cannot go forward and outmarch Him, for He is before. C. H. S.

What would you say if, wherever you turned, whatever you were doing, whatever thinking, whether in public or private, with a confidential friend telling your secrets, or alone planning them — if, I say, you saw an eye constantly fixed on you, from whose watching, though you strove ever so much, you could never escape . . . that could perceive your every thought? The supposition is awful enough. There is such an Eye. DEVERE

*And laid Thine hand upon me.* The prisoner marches along surrounded by a guard and gripped by an officer. God is very near; we are wholly in His power; and from that power there is no escape. It is not said that God will thus beset us and arrest us, but it is done — "Thou hast beset me." Shall we not alter the figure and say that our heavenly Father has folded His arms around us and caressed us with His hand? It is even so with those who are by faith the children of the Most High. C. H. S.

Vs. 6. *Such knowledge is too wonderful for me.* I cannot grasp it. I can hardly endure to think of it. The theme overwhelms me. I am amazed and astounded at it. Such knowledge not only surpasses my comprehension but even my imagination. C. H. S.

At this moment He is listening to the praises breathed by grateful hearts in distant worlds and reading every grovelling thought which passes through the polluted minds of the fallen race of Adam . . . At one view He surveys the past, the present, and the future. No inattention prevents Him from observing; no defect of memory or of judgment obscures His comprehension:

In His remembrance are stored not only the transactions of this world but of all the worlds in the universe; not only the events of the six thousand years which have passed since the earth was created but of a duration without beginning. Nay, things to come, extending to a duration without end, are also before Him. An eternity past and an eternity to come are, at the same moment, in His eye; and with that eternal eye He surveys infinity. How amazing! How inconceivable. HENRY DUNCAN

*It is high, I cannot attain unto it.* Mount as I may, this truth is too lofty for my mind. It seems to be always above me, even when I soar into the loftiest regions of spiritual thought. Is it not so with every attribute of God? Can we attain to any idea of His power, His wisdom, His holiness? Our mind has no line with which to measure the Infinite. Do we, therefore, question? Say, rather, that we therefore believe and adore.

We are not surprised that the most glorious God should in His knowledge be high above all the knowledge to which we can attain: it must of necessity be so, since we are such poor, limited beings; and when we stand a-tip-toe we cannot reach to the lowest step of the throne of the Eternal. C. H. S.

Vs. 7. *Whither shall I go from Thy Spirit?* Not that the Psalmist wished to go from God or to avoid the power of the divine life; but he asks this question to set forth the fact that no one can escape from the all-pervading Being and observation of the great, Invisible Spirit. C. H. S.

A heathen philosopher once asked, "Where is God?" The Christian answered, "Let me first ask you, 'Where is He not?'" JOHN ARROWSMITH

*Whither shall I flee?* Surely no whither: they that attempt it, do but as the fish which swimmeth to the length of the line, with a hook in the mouth. JOHN TRAPP

*Thy presence.* The presence of God's glory is in heaven; the presence of His power on earth; the presence of His justice in hell; and the presence of His grace with His people. If He deny us His powerful presence, we fall into nothing; if He deny us His gracious presence, we fall into sin; if He deny us His merciful presence, we fall into hell. JOHN MASON

The celebrated Linnaeus testified in his conversation, writings, and actions, the greatest sense of God's presence. So strongly indeed was he impressed with the idea, that he wrote over the door of his library: *innocue vivite, Numen adest*— "Live innocently: God is present." GEORGE SEATON BOWES

Vs. 7-11. You will never be neglected by the Deity, though you were so small as to sink into the depths of the earth, or so lofty as to fly up to heaven; but you will suffer from the gods the punishment due to you, whether you abide here, or depart to Hades, or are carried to a place still more wild than these. PLATO

Vs. 7-12. The Psalm was not written by a Pantheist. The Psalmist speaks of God as a person everywhere present in creation, yet distinct from creation. In these verses he says, "Thy spirit . . . Thy presence . . . Thou art there . . . Thy hand . . . Thy right hand . . . darkness hideth not from Thee." God is everywhere, but He is not everything. WILLIAM JONES

Vs. 9. *If I take the wings of the morning, and dwell in the uttermost parts of the sea.* Light flies with inconceivable rapidity, and it flashes far afield beyond all human ken; it illuminates the great and wide sea, and sets its waves gleaming afar; but its speed would utterly fail if employed in flying from the Lord. Were we to speed on the wings of the morning breeze, and break into oceans unknown to chart and map, yet there we should find the Lord already present. C. H. S.

Vs. 9-10. What! had Jonah offended the winds or the waters, that they bear him such enmity? The winds and the waters and all God's creatures are wont to take God's part against Jonah or any rebellious sinner. For though God in the beginning gave power to man over all creatures to rule them, yet when man sins, God giveth power and strength to His creatures to rule and bridle man. Therefore, even he that now was lord over the waters, now the waters are lord over him. HENRY SMITH

Vs. 10. *And Thy right hand shall hold me.* The exploring missionary in his lonely wanderings is led; in his solitary feebleness he is held. Both the hands of God are with His own servants to sustain them and against rebels to overthrow them; and in this respect it matters not to what realms they resort; the active energy of God is around them still. C. H. S.

Vs. 11. *If I say, Surely the darkness shall cover me.* The foulest enormities of human conduct have always striven to cover themselves with the shroud of night. The thief, the counterfeiter, the assassin, the robber, the murderer, and the seducer, feel comparatively safe in the midnight darkness, because no human eye can scrutinize their actions.

But what if it should turn out that sable night, to speak paradoxically, is an unerring photographist! What if wicked men, as they open their eyes from the sleep of death in another world, should find the universe hung round with faithful pictures of their earthly enormities, which they had supposed forever lost in the oblivion of night! What scenes for them to gaze at forever!

They may now, indeed, smile incredulously at such a suggestion; but the disclosures of chemistry may well make them tremble. Analogy does make it a scientific probability that every action of man, however deep the darkness in which it was performed, has imprinted its image on nature, and that there may be tests which shall draw it into daylight and make it permanent so long as materialism endures. EDWARD HITCHCOCK

Vs. 13. *Thou hast covered me in my mother's womb.* There I lay hidden — covered by Thee. Before I could know Thee, or aught else, Thou hadst a care for me, and didst hide me away as a treasure till Thou shouldst see fit to bring me to the light. Thus the Psalmist describes the intimacy which God had with him. In his most secret part — his reins, and in his most secret condition — yet unborn, he was under the control and guardianship of God. C. H. S.

The word here rendered "cover" means properly to interweave; to weave; to knit together, and the literal translation would be, "Thou hast woven me in my mother's womb," meaning that God had put his parts together, as one who weaves cloth, or who makes a basket. So it is rendered by De Wette and by Gesenius (Lex.). The original word has, however, also the idea of protecting, as in a booth or hut, woven or knit together—to-wit, of boughs and branches. ALBERT BARNES

Vs. 14. *I am fearfully and wonderfully made.* Instead of wondering at the number of premature deaths that are constantly witnessed, there is far greater reason to wonder that there are no more, and that any of us survive to seventy or eighty years of age.

*Our life contains a thousand springs,*
*And dies if one be gone:*
*Strange that a harp of thousand strings*
*Should keep in tune so long.*

Nor is this all. If we are "fearfully made" as to our animal frame, it will be found that we are much more so considered as moral and accountable beings. In what relates to our animal nature, we are in most instances constructed like other animals; but, in what relates to us as moral agents, we stand distinguished from all the lower creation.

We are made for eternity. The present life is only the introductory part of our existence. It is that, however, which stamps a character on all that follows. How fearful is our situation! What innumerable influences is the mind exposed to from the temptations which surround us! Not more dangerous to the body is the pestilence that walketh in darkness than these are to the soul.

Such is the construction of our nature that the very Word of life, if heard without regard, becomes a savor of death unto death. What consequences hang upon the small and apparently trifling beginnings of evil! A wicked thought may issue in a wicked purpose, this purpose in a wicked action, this action in a course of conduct, this course may draw into its vortex millions of our fellow-creatures, and terminate in perdition, both to ourselves and them.

The whole of this process was exemplified in the case of Jeroboam, the son of Nebat. When placed over the ten tribes, he first said in his heart, "If this people go up to sacrifice at Jerusalem, their hearts will turn to Rehoboam; and thus shall the kingdom return to the house of David" (I Kings 12:26-30). On this he took counsel and made the calves of Dan and Bethel. This engaged him in a course of wickedness from which no remonstrances could reclaim him.

Nor was it confined to himself; for he "made all Israel to sin." The issue was, not only their destruction as a nation, but, to all appearance, the eternal ruin of himself and great numbers of his followers. Such were the fruits of an evil thought! ANDREW FULLER

*I am wonderfully made.* Take notice of the curious frame of the body. David saith, "I am wonderfully made"; *acu pictus sum*, so the Vulgate rendereth it, "painted as with a needle," like a garment of needlework of divers colors, richly embroidered with nerves and veins.

What shall I speak of the eye, wherein there is such curious workmanship, that many upon the first sight of it have been driven to acknowledge God? Of the hand, made to open and shut, and to serve the labors and ministries of nature without wasting and decay for many years? If they should be of marble or iron, with such constant use, they would soon wear out; and yet now they are of flesh, they last so long as life lasteth.

But as yet we have spoken but of the casket wherein the jewel lieth. The soul, that divine spark and blast, how quick, nimble, various, and indefatigable in its motions! How comprehensive in its capacities! How it animateth the body, and is like God Himself, all in every part! Who can trace the flights of reason? What a value hath God set upon the soul! He made it after His image; He redeemed it with Christ's Blood. THOMAS MANTON

A chain or cable keeps a ship in its place; we lay the foundation of a building in the earth and the building endures. But what is it which unites soul and body? How do they touch? How do they keep together? How is it we do not wander to the stars or the depths of the sea, or to and fro as chance may carry us, while our body remains where it was on earth?

So far from its being wonderful that the body one day dies, how is it that it is made to live and move at all? How is it that it keeps from dying a single hour? Certainly it is as uncomprehensible as anything can be, how soul and body can make up one man; and, unless we had the instance before our eyes, we should seem in saying so to be using words without meaning.

For instance, would it not be extravagant and idle to speak of time as deep or high, or of space as quick or slow? Not less idle, surely, it perhaps seems to some races of spirits to say that thought and mind have a body, which in the case of man they have, according to God's marvelous will. JOHN HENRY NEWMAN

*Marvellous are Thy works.* We need not go to the ends of the earth for marvels, nor even across our own threshold; they abound in our own bodies. C. H. S.

Those who were skillful in Anatomy among the ancients, concluded, from the outward and inward make of a human body, that it was the work of a Being transcendently wise and powerful. Galen was converted by his dissections, and could not but own a Supreme Being upon a survey of this His handiwork. THE SPECTATOR

*And that my soul knoweth right well.* He was no agnostic — he knew; he was no doubter — his soul knew; he was no dupe — his soul knew right well. If we are marvelously wrought upon even before we are born, what shall we say of the Lord's dealings with us after we quit His secret workshop, and He directs our pathway through the pilgrimage of life? What shall we not say of that new birth which is even more mysterious than the first and exhibits even more the love and wisdom of the Lord? C. H. S.

Vs. 15. *My substance was not hid from Thee.* Should an artisan intend commencing a work in some dark cave where there was no light to assist him, how would he set his hand to it? In what way would he proceed? And what kind of workmanship would it prove? But God makes the most perfect work of all in the dark, for He fashions man in the mother's womb. JOHN CALVIN

*When I was made in secret.* Most chastely and beautifully is here described the formation of our being before the time of our birth. A great artist will often labor alone in his studio and not suffer his work to be seen until it is finished; even so did the Lord fashion us where no eye beheld us, and the veil was not lifted till every member was complete. C. H. S.

*And curiously wrought in the lowest parts of the earth.* "Embroidered with great skill" is an accurate poetical description of the creation of veins, sinews, muscles, nerves, etc. What tapestry can equal the human fabric? C. H. S.

Many locks and keys argue the value of the jewel that they keep, and many papers wrapping the token within them, the price of the token. The tables of the testament, first laid up in the ark, secondly, the ark bound about with pure gold; thirdly, overshadowed with cherubim's wings; fourthly, enclosed within the vail of the Tabernacle; fifthly, with the compass of the Tabernacle; sixthly, with a court above all; seventhly, with a treble covering of goats', rams', and badgers' skins above all; they must needs be precious tables.

So when the Almighty made man's head (the seat of the reasonable soul), and overlaid it with hair, skin, and flesh, like the threefold covering of the Tabernacle, and encompassed it with a skull and bones like boards of cedar, and afterwards with divers skins like silken curtains; and lastly, enclosed it with the yellow skin that covers the brain (like the purple veil), He would doubtless have us to know it was made for some great treasure to be put therein. How and when the reasonable soul is put into this curious cabinet philosophers dispute many things, but can affirm nothing of certainty. ABRAHAM WRIGHT

Vs. 15-16. "Which in continuance were fashioned" is wrong. The margin, though also wrong, indicates the right way: "My days were determined before one of them was." DAVID M'LAREN

Vs. 16. *Thine eyes did see my substance, yet being unperfect.* Many are shamed to be seen as God made them; few are ashamed to be seen what the devil hath made them. Many are troubled at small defects in the outward man; few are troubled at the greatest deformities of the inward man: many buy artificial beauty to supply the natural; few spiritual, to supply the defects of the supernatural beauty of the soul. ABRAHAM WRIGHT

*And in Thy book all my members were written, which in continuance were fashioned, when as yet there was none of them.* An architect draws his plans and makes out his specifications; even so did the great Maker of our frame write down all our members in the book of His purposes. That we have eyes, and ears, and hands, and feet, is all due to the wise and gracious purpose of heaven: it was so ordered in the secret decree by which all things are as they are.

The great truth expressed in these lines has by many been referred to the formation of the mystical body of our Lord Jesus. Of course, what is true of man, as man, is emphatically true of Him Who is the Representative Man. The great Lord knows who belong to Christ; His eye perceives the chosen members who shall yet be made one with the living person of the mystical Christ. Those of the elect who are as yet unborn, or unrenewed, are nevertheless written in the Lord's book. C. H. S.

Vs. 17. *How great is the sum of them!* What a contrast is all this to the notion of those who deny the existence of a personal, conscious God! Imagine a world without a thinking, personal God! Conceive of a grim providence of machinery — a fatherhood of law! Such philosophy is hard and cold. As well might a man pillow his head upon a razor edge as seek rest in such a fancy. But a God always thinking of us makes a happy world, a rich life, a heavenly hereafter. C. H. S.

Vss. 17-18. Behold David's love to God; sleeping and waking, his mind runs upon Him. There needs no arguments to bring those to our remembrance whom we love. We neglect ourselves to think upon them. A man in love wastes his spirits, vexes his mind neglects his meat, regards not his business; his mind still feeds on that he loves.

When men love that they should not, there is more need of a bridle to keep them from thinking of it than of spurs to keep them to it. Try thy love of God by this. If thou thinkest not often of God, thou lovest Him not. If thou canst not satisfy thyself with profits, pleasures, friends, and other worldly objects, but thou must turn other businesses aside, that thou mayest daily think of God, then thou lovest Him. FRANCIS TAYLOR

Vss. 17-18. Many little items make together a great sum. What is lighter than a grain of sand, yet what is heavier than the sand upon the seashore? As little sins (such as vain thoughts and idle words), because of their multitude, arise to a great guilt, and will bring in a long bill, a heavy reckoning at last; so, ordinary mercies, what they want in their size of some other great mercies, have compensated it in their number. Who will not say that a man shows greater kindness in maintaining one at his table with ordinary fare all the year than in entertaining him at a great feast twice or thrice in the same time? WILLIAM GURNALL

Vs. 18. *If I should count them, they are more in number than the sand.* The task of counting God's thoughts of love would be a never-ending one. If we should attempt the reckoning, we must necessarily fail, for the Infinite falls not within the line of our feeble intellect. C. H. S.

*When I awake, I am still with Thee.* Thy thoughts of love are so many that my mind never gets away from them; they surround me at all hours. I go to my bed, and God is my last thought; and when I awake, I find my mind still hovering about His palace-gates; God is ever with me, and I am ever with Him. This is life indeed. C. H. S.

It is no small advantage to the holy life to "begin the day with God." The saints are wont to leave their hearts with Him overnight, that they may find them with Him in the morning. Before earthly things break in upon us and we receive impressions from abroad, it is good to season the heart with thoughts of God and to consecrate the early and virgin operations of the mind before they are prostituted to baser objects.

When the world gets the start of religion in the morning, it can hardly overtake it all the day; and so the heart is habituated to vanity all the day long. But when we begin with God, we take Him along with us to all the business and comforts of the day; which, being seasoned with His love and fear, are the more sweet and savory to us. THOMAS CASE

Accustom yourself to a serious meditation every morning. Fresh airing our souls in heaven will engender in us a purer spirit and nobler thoughts. A morning seasoning will secure us for all the day. Though other necessary thoughts about our calling will and must come in, yet when we have dispatched them, let us attend to our morning theme as our chief companion.

As a man that is going with another about some considerable business, suppose to Westminster, though he meets with several friends on the way, and salutes some, and with others with whom he has some affairs he spends some little time, yet he quickly returns to his companion, and both together go to their intended stage.

Do thus in the present case. Our minds are active and will be doing something, though to little purpose; and if they be not fixed upon some noble object, they will, like madmen and fools, be mightily pleased in playing with straws. The thoughts of God were the first visitors David had in the morning. God and his heart met together as soon as he was awake and kept company all the day before. STEPHEN CHARNOCK

Vs. 19. *Surely Thou wilt slay the wicked, O God.* Crimes committed before the face of the Judge are not likely to go unpunished. God, Who sees all evil, will slay all evil. Such is His love of holiness and hatred of wrong that He will carry on war to the death with those whose hearts and lives are wicked. God will not always suffer His lovely creation to be defaced and defiled by the presence of wickedness: if anything is sure, this is sure, that He will ease Him of His adversaries. C. H. S.

*Depart from me therefore, ye bloody men.* He seems to say — If God will not let you live with Him, I will not have you live with me. Depart from me, for you depart from God. As we delight to have the holy God always near us, so would we eagerly desire to have wicked men removed as far as possible from us. We tremble in the society of the ungodly lest their doom should fall upon them suddenly and we should see them lie dead at our feet. We do not wish to have our place of intercourse turned into a gallows of execution; therefore let the condemned be removed out of our company. C. H. S.

Vs. 20. *And Thine enemies take Thy name in vain.* What a wonder of sin it is that men should rail against so good a Being as the Lord, our God! The impudence of those who talk wickedly is a singular fact, and it is the more singular when we reflect that the Lord against Whom they speak is all around them and lays to heart every dishonor which they render to His holy name. We ought not to wonder that men slander and deride us, for they do the same with the Most High God.

Vs. 21. *Do not I hate them, O Lord, that hate Thee?* He was a good hater, for he hated only those who hated good. Of this hatred, he is not ashamed, but he sets it forth as a virtue to which he would have the Lord bear testimony. To love all men with benevolence is our duty, but to love any wicked man with complacency would be a crime. To hate a man for his own sake, or for any evil done to us, would be wrong; but to hate a man because he is the foe of all goodness and the enemy of all righteousness, is nothing more nor less than an obligation. The more we love God, the more indignant shall we grow with those who refuse Him their affection. C. H. S.

Can he who thinks good faith the holiest thing in life, avoid being an enemy to that master who, as quaestor, dared to despoil, desert, and betray? Can he who wishes to pay due honors to the immortal gods, by any means avoid being an enemy to that man who has plundered all their temples? CICERO

*Am not I grieved?* It is said that Adam Smith disliked nothing more than that moral apathy — that obtuseness of moral perception — which prevents man from not only seeing clearly, but feeling strongly, the broad distinction between virtue and vice, and which, under the pretext of liberality, is all indulgent even to the blackest crimes.

At a party at Dalkeith Palace, where Mr............, in his mawkish way, was finding palliations for some villainous transactions, the doctor waited in patient silence until he was gone, then exclaimed: "Now I can breathe more freely. I cannot bear that man; he has no indignation in him."

Vs. 21-22. A faithful servant hath the same interests, the same friends, the same enemies, with his master, whose cause and honor he is, upon all occasions, in duty bound to support and maintain. A good man hates, as God Himself doth; he hates not the persons of men, but their sins; not what God made them, but what they have made themselves. We are neither to hate the men, on account of the vices they practice; nor to love the vices, for the sake of the men who practice them. He who observeth invariably this distinction, fulfilleth the perfect law of charity, and hath the love of God and of his neighbor abiding in him. GEORGE HORNE

Vs. 22. *I hate them with perfect hatred.* He does not leave it a matter of question. He does not occupy a neutral position. His hatred to bad, vicious, blasphemous men is intense, complete, energetic. He is as whole-hearted in his hate of wickedness as in his love of goodness.

*I count them mine enemies.* He makes a personal matter of it. They may have done him no ill, but if they are doing despite to God, to His laws, and to the great principles of truth and righteousness, David proclaims war against them. Wickedness passes men into favor with unrighteous spirits; but it excludes them from the communion of the just. We pull up the drawbridge and man the walls when a man of Belial goes by our castle. His character is a *casus belli;* we cannot do otherwise than contend with those who contend with God.

Vs. 23. *Search me, O God, and know my heart.* He had need be a true man who can put himself deliberately into such a crucible. Yet we may each one desire such searching; for it would be a terrible calamity to us for sin to remain in our hearts unknown and undiscovered. C. H. S.

*Try me, and know my thoughts.* What a mercy that there is one Being Who can know us to perfection! He is intimately at home with us. He is graciously inclined towards us, and is willing to bend His omniscience to serve the end of our sanctification. Let us pray as David did, and let us be as honest as he. We cannot hide our sin: salvation lies the other way, in a plain discovery of evil, and an effectual severance from it. C. H. S.

What fearful dilemma have we here? The Holiest changeth not, when He comes a visitant to a human heart. He is the same there that He is in the highest heaven.

He cannot look upon sin; and how can a human heart welcome Him into its secret chambers? How can the blazing fire welcome the quenching water? It is easy to commit to memory the seemly prayer of an ancient penitent.

The dead letters, worn smooth by frequent use, may drop freely from callous lips, leaving no sense of scalding on the conscience; and yet, truth of God though they are, they may be turned into a lie in the act of utterance. The prayer is not true, although it is borrowed from the Bible, if the suppliant invite the All-seeing in, and yet would give a thousand worlds, if he had them to keep Him out forever. The difference between an unconverted and a converted man is not that the one has sins, and the other has none; but that the one takes part with his cherished sins against a dreaded God and the other takes part with a reconciled God against his hated sins.

As long as God is my enemy, I am His. I have no more power to change that condition than the polished surface has to refrain from reflecting the sunshine that falls upon it. It is God's love, from the face of Jesus shining into my dark heart, that makes my heart open to Him and delight to be His dwelling-place. The eyes of the just Avenger I cannot endure to be in this place of sin; but the eye of the compassionate Physician, I shall gladly admit into this place of disease; for He comes from heaven to earth that He may heal such sin-sick souls as mine. WILLIAM ARNOT

Vs. 23-24. There are several things worthy of notice in the Psalmist's appeal, in the words before us. First, notice the Psalmist's intrepidity. Here is a man determined to explore the recesses of his own heart. Did Bonaparte, did Nelson, did Wellington, ever propose to do this? Were all the renowned heroes of antiquity present, I would ask them all if they ever had courage to enter into their own hearts.

David was a man of courage. When he slew a lion in the way, when he successfully encountered a bear, when he went out to meet the giant Goliath, he gave undoubted proofs of courage; but never did he display such signal intrepidity as when he determined to look into his own heart.

If you stood upon some eminence and saw all the ravenous and venomous creatures that ever lived collected before you, it would not require such courage to combat them as to combat with your own heart. Every sin is a devil, and each may say, "My name is Legion, for we are many." Who knows what it is to face himself? And yet, if we would be saved, this must be done. One of the attributes of sin is to hide man from himself, to conceal his deformity, to prevent him from forming a just conception of his true condition. It is a solemn fact that there is not an evil principle in the bosom of the devil himself which does not exist in ours, at the present moment, unless we are fully renewed by the power of the Holy Spirit. WILLIAM HOWELS

Vs. 23-24. Self-examination is not the simple thing which, at first sight, it might appear. No Christian who has ever really practiced it has found it easy. Is there any exercise of the soul which any one of us has found so unsatisfactory, so almost impossible, as self-examination?

To the child of God — the most intimate with Himself in all the earth — I do not hestitate to say — "There are sins latent at this moment in you, of which you have no idea; but it only requires a larger measure of spiritual illumination to impress and unfold them. You have no idea of the wickedness that is now in you."

But while I say this, let every Christian count well the cost before he ventures on the bold act of asking God to "search" him. For be sure of this, if you do really and earnestly ask God to "search" you, He will do it. And He will search you most searchingly; and if you ask Him to "try" you, He will try you — and the trial will be no light matter! JAMES VAUGHAN

But there is another kind of hypocrisy, which differs from both of these: I mean that hypocrisy by which a man does not only deceive the world but very often imposes on himself; that hypocrisy which conceals his own heart from him, and makes him believe he is more virtuous than he really is, and either not attend to his vices, or mistake even his vices for virtues. It is this fatal hypocrisy and self-deceit, which is taken notice of in these words, "Who can understand his errors? cleanse Thou me from secret faults." JOSEPH ADDISON

How beautiful is the humility of David! He cannot speak of the wicked but in terms of righteous indignation; he cannot but hate the haters of his God; yet, he seems immediately to recollect, and to check himself — "Try me, O Lord, and seek the ground of my heart." Precisely, in the same spirit of inward humility and self-recollection, Abraham, when pleading before God in prayer for guilty, depraved Sodom, fails not to speak of himself as being dust and ashes (Gen. 18:27). JAMES FORD

Pure gold fears neither the furnace nor the fire, neither the test nor the touchstone; nor is weighty gold afraid of the balance. He that is weight will be weight, how often soever he is weighed; he that is gold will be gold, how often soever he is tried, and the oftener he is tried, the purer gold he will be; what he is he will be, and he would be better than he is. JOSEPH CARYL

Vs. 24. *And see if there be any wicked way in me.* As I hate the wicked in their way, so would I hate every wicked way in myself. C. H. S.

This is a beautiful and impressive prayer for the commencement of every day. It is, also, a great sentiment to admonish us at the beginning of each day.

There is the way of unbelief within, to which we are very prone. There is the way of vanity and pride, to which we often accustom ourselves. There is the way of selfishness in which we frequently walk. There is the way of worldiness we often pursue— empty pleasures, shadowy honors, etc.

There is the way of sluggishness. What apathy in prayer, in the examination and application of God's Word, we manifest! There is the way of self-dependence, by which we often dishonor God and injure ourselves. There is, unhappily, the way of disobedience, in which we often walk. At any rate, our obedience is cold, reluctant, uncertain — not simple, entire, fervent.

How necessary is it, then, to go to God at once and earnestly to prefer the petition, "Lord, see if there be any wicked way in me" Let nothing that is wrong, that is opposed to Thy character, repugnant to Thy Word, or injurious and debasing to ourselves, remain or be harbored within us. T. WALLACE

I do not know how to define a higher point in religious attainment than supposing a man warranted in offering up the prayer of our text. I call upon you to be cautious in using this prayer. It is easy to mock God by asking Him to search you whilst you have made but little effort to search yourselves and perhaps still less to act upon the result of the scrutiny. HENRY MELVILL

*And lead me in the way everlasting.* By Thy providence, by Thy Word, by Thy grace, and by Thy Spirit, lead me evermore. C. H. S.

# PSALM 140

This Psalm is in its proper place and so fitly follows 139 that you might almost read right on and make no break between the two. Serious injury would follow to the whole Book of Psalms if the order should be interfered with, as certain wiseacres propose. It is the cry of a hunted soul, the supplication of a believer incessantly persecuted and beset by cunning enemies, who hungered for his destruction.

David was hunted like a partridge upon the mountains and seldom obtained a moment's rest. This is his pathetic appeal to Jehovah for protection, an appeal which gradually intensifies into a denunciation of his bitter foes. With this sacrifice of prayer, he offers the salt of faith; for in a very marked and emphatic manner, he expresses his personal confidence in the Lord as the Protector of the oppressed and as his own God and Defender. Few short Psalms are so rich in the jewelry of precious faith. C. H. S.

Vs. 1. *Deliver me, O Lord, from the evil man.* It reads like a clause of the Lord's prayer, "Deliver us from evil." David does not so much plead against an individual as against the species represented by him, namely, the being whose best description is—"the evil man." There are many such abroad; indeed we shall not find an unregenerate man who is not in some sense an evil man; and yet all are not alike evil. It is well for us that our enemies are evil: it would be a horrible thing to have the good against us. C. H. S.

*Preserve me from the violent man.* Evil in the heart simmers in malice and at last boils in passion. Evil is a raging thing when it getteth liberty to manifest itself; and so "the evil man" soon develops into "the violent man." What watchfulness, strength, or valor can preserve the child of God from deceit and violence? There is but one sure Preserver, and it is our wisdom to hide under the shadow of His wings.

It is a common thing for good men to be assailed by enemies: David was attacked by Saul, Doeg, Ahithophel, Shimei, and others; even Mordecai sitting humbly in the gate had his Haman; and our Lord, the Perfect One, was surrounded by those who thirsted for His Blood. We may not, therefore, hope to pass through the world without enemies, but we may hope to be delivered out of their hands, and preserved from their rage, so that no real harm shall come of their malignity. This blessing is to be sought by prayer and expected by faith. C. H. S.

Vs. 2. *Which imagine mischiefs in their heart.* They cannot be happy unless they are plotting and planning, conspiring and contriving. They seem to have but one heart, for they are completely agreed in their malice; and with all their heart and soul, they pursue their victim.

One piece of mischief is not enough for them; they work in the plural and prepare many arrows for their bow. What they cannot actually do, they nevertheless like to think over and to rehearse on the stage of their cruel fancy. It is an awful thing to have such a heart-disease as this. When the imagination gloats over doing harm to others, it is a sure sign that the entire nature is far gone in wickedness. C. H. S.

*Continually are they gathered together for war.* Literally, this clause reads, "who gather wars," and so some understand it. But it is well known that the prepositions are often omitted in the Hebrew, and no doubt he means that they stirred up general enmity by their false information which acted as a trumpet sounding to battle. JOHN CALVIN

Vs. 2-3. The wicked assault the righteous with three weapons: with the heart, by conspiracy; with the tongue, by lying; and with the hand, by violence. JOHN LORINUS

Vs. 3. *They have sharpened their tongues like a serpent.* The rapid motion of a viper's tongue gives you the idea of its sharpening it; even thus do the malicious move their tongues at such a rate that one might suppose them to be in the very act of wearing them to a point or rubbing them to a keen edge. The world's great poet puts it in "King Lear": "She struck me with her tongue, most serpent-like, upon the very heart."

To sharpen or whet the tongue imports the keenest and extremest kind of talkativeness, much more to sharpen the tongue "like a serpent." Naturalists tell us that no living creature stirs his tongue so swiftly as a serpent, and serpents are therefore said to have a treble tongue, because, moving their tongue so fast, they seem to have three tongues. The Pslamist means — the wicked speak thick and threefold, they sting and poison me with their tongues. JOSEPH CARYL

Is it not a fact that there are many men, the very existence of whom is a baneful poison, as it were? They dart their livid tongue like the tongue of a serpent; and the venom of their disposition corrodes every object upon which it concentrates itself; ever velifying and maligning, like the ill-omened bird of night. PLINY

*Adders' poison is under their lips.* It is sadly wonderful what hard things even good men will say when provoked; yea, even such as call themselves "perfect" in cool blood are not quite as gentle as doves when their claims to sinlessness are bluntly questioned.

This poison of evil-speaking would never fall from our lips, however much we might be provoked, if it were not there at other times; but by nature we have as great a store of venomous words as a cobra has of poison. O Lord, take the poison-bags away and cause our lips to drop nothing but honey. "Selah." This is heavy work. Go up, go up, my heart! Sink not too low. Fall not into the lowest key. Lift up thyself to God. C. H. S.

In St. James's day, as now, it would appear that there were idle men and idle women who went about from house to house dropping slander as they went, and yet you could not take up that slander and detect the falsehood there. You could not evaporate the truth in the slow process of the crucible and then show the residuum of falsehood glittering and visible. You could not fasten upon any word or sentence and say that it was calumny; for in order to constitute slander, it is not necessary that the word spoken should be false — half-truths are often more calumnious than whole falsehoods.

It is not even necessary that a word should be distinctly uttered; a dropped lip, an arched eyebrow, a shrugged shoulder, a significant look, an incredulous expression of countenance, nay, even an emphatic silence, may do the work; and when the light and trifling thing which has done the mischief has fluttered off, the venom is left behind, to work and rankle, to inflame hearts, to fever human existence, and to poison human society at the fountain springs of life.

Very emphatically was it said by one whose whole being had smarted under such affliction, "Adders' poison is under their lips." FREDERICK WM. ROBERTSON

Slander and calumny must always precede and accompany persecution, because malice itself cannot excite people against a good man, as such; to do this, he must first be represented as a bad man.

What can be said of those who are busied in this manner, but that they are a "generation of vipers," the brood of the old "Serpent," that grand accuser and calumniator of the brethren, having under their tongues a bag of "poison," conveying instant death to the reputation on which they fasten? Thus David was hunted as a rebel; Christ was crucified as a blasphemer; and the primitive Christians were tortured as guilty of incest and murder. GEORGE HORNE

Such is the nature of sin; enter where it will, it creeps from one member of the body to another, and from the body to the soul, till it has infected the whole man; and then from man to man, till a whole family; and stays not there, but runs like a wildfire, from family to family, till it has poisoned a whole town, and so a whole country, and a whole kingdom. WILLIAM CRASHAW

Vs. 4. *Keep me, O Lord, from the hands of the wicked.* No creature among the wild beasts of the wood is so terrible an enemy to man as man himself when guided by evil and impelled by violence. C. H. S.

From doing as they do, or as they would have me do, or as they promise themselves I will do. MATTHEW HENRY

Vs. 5. *They have set gins for me.* If a godly man can be cajoled, or bribed, or cowed, or made angry, the wicked will make the attempt. Ready are they to twist his words, misread his intentions, and misdirect his efforts; ready to fawn, and lie, and make themselves mean to the last degree so that they may accomplish their abominable purpose. "Selah." The harp needs tuning after such a strain, and the heart needs lifting up towards God. C. H. S.

Vs. 6. *The voice of my supplications.* The one safety for simple and unlearned people when assailed by the crafty arguments of heretics and infidels is not controversy, but prayer, a weapon their adversaries seldom use and cannot understand. BRUNO OF ASTE

Vs. 7. *O God the Lord, the strength of my salvation, Thou hast covered my head in the day of battle.* The shield of the Eternal is a better protection than a helmet of brass. When arrows fly thick and the battleaxe crashes right and left, there is no covering for the head like the power of the Almighty. C. H. S.

Vs. 9. *As for the head of those that compass me about, let the mischief of their own lips cover them.* The poet represents his adversaries as so united as to have but one head; for there is often a unanimity among evil spirits which makes them the more strong and terrible for their vile purposes. The *lex talionis*, or law of retaliation, often brings down upon violent men the evil which they planned and spoke of for others: their arrows fall upon themselves. When a man's lips vent curses, they will probably, like chickens, come home to roost. A stone hurled upward into the air is apt to fall upon the thrower's head.

David's words may be read in the future as a prophecy; but in this verse, at any rate, there is no need to do so in order to soften their tone. It is so just that the mischief which men plot and the slander which they speak should recoil upon themselves that every righteous man must desire it: he who does not desire it may wish to be considered humane and Christlike, but the chances are that he has a sneaking agreement with the wicked or is deficient in a manly sense of right and wrong.

When evil men fall into pits which they have digged for the innocent, we believe that even the angels are glad; certainly the most gentle and tender of philanthropists, however much they pity the sufferers, must also approve the justice which makes them suffer. We suspect that some of our excessively soft-spoken critics only need to be put into David's place, and they would become a vast deal more bitter than he ever was. C. H. S.

Vs. 10. *Let them be cast into the fire.* They have heated the furnace of slander seven times hotter than it was wont to be heated, and they shall be devoured therein. Who would have pitied Nebuchadnezzar if he had been thrown into his own burning, fiery furnace? C. H. S.

*Into deep pits, that they rise not up again.* When a righteous man falls, he rises again; but when the wicked man goes down, "he falls like Lucifer, never to hope again." C. H. S.

Vs. 11. *Let not an evil speaker be established in the earth.* Men of false and cruel tongues are of most use when they go to fatten the soil in which they rot as carcasses. All evil bears the element of decay within itself; for what is it but corruption? Hence the utmost powers of oratory are insufficient to settle upon a sure foundation the cause which bears a lie within it. C. H. S.

*Evil shall hunt the violent man to overthrow him.* Sin is its own punishment; a violent man will need no direr doom than to reap what he has sown. It is horrible for a huntsman to be devoured by his own hounds; yet this is the sure fate of the persecutor. C. H. S.

Vs. 13. *Surely the righteous shall give thanks unto Thy name.* On earth ere long, and in heaven forever, the pure in heart shall sing unto the Lord. How loud and sweet will be the songs of the redeemed in the millennial age, when the meek shall inherit the earth and delight themselves in the abundance of peace! C. H. S.

*The upright shall dwell in Thy presence.* How high have we climbed in this Psalm — from being hunted by the evil man to dwelling in the divine presence; so doth faith upraise the saint from the lowest depths to heights of peaceful repose. Well might the song be studded with Selahs, or uplifters. C. H. S.

# PSALM 141

Title: "A Psalm of David." Yes, David under suspicion, half afraid to speak lest he should speak unadvisedly while trying to clear himself; David, slandered and beset by enemies; David, censured even by saints, and taking it kindly; David, deploring the condition of the godly party of whom he was the acknowledged head; David, waiting upon God with confident expectation.

The Psalm is one of a group of four, and it bears a striking likeness to the other three. Its meaning lies so deep as to be in places exceedingly obscure, yet even upon its surface, it has dust of gold. In its commencement, the Psalm is lighted up with the evening glow as the incense rises to heaven; then comes a night of language whose meaning we cannot see; and this gives place to morning light, in which our eyes are unto the Lord. C. H. S.

Whole Psalm. Few Psalms in so small a compass crowd together so many gems of precious and holy truth. BARTON BOUCHIER

Vs. 1. *Lord, I cry unto Thee.* My prayer is painful and feeble and worthy only to be called a cry; but it is a cry unto Jehovah, and this ennobles it. C. H. S.

Misbelief doth seek many ways for delivery from trouble; but faith hath but one way—to go to God, to-wit, by prayer, for whatsoever is needful. DAVID DICKSON

No distress or danger, how great soever, shall stifle my faith or stop my mouth, but it shall make me more earnest, and my prayers, like strong streams in narrow straits, shall bear down all before them. JOHN TRAPP

*Unto Thee . . . unto me.* Our prayer and God's mercy are like two buckets in a well; while the one ascends, the other descends. EZEKIEL HOPKINS

*Let my prayer be set forth before Thee as incense.* As incense is carefully prepared, kindled with holy fire, and devoutly presented unto God, so let my prayer be. We are not to look upon prayer as easy work requiring no thought; it needs to be "set forth"; what is more, it must be set forth "before the Lord" by a sense of His presence and a holy reverence for His name. C. H. S.

*Set forth.* Prayer is knowing work, believing work, thinking work, searching work, humbling work, and nothing worth if heart and hand do not join in it. THOMAS ADAMS

*As the evening sacrifice.* This should be our daily service, as a lamb was offered up morning and evening for a sacrifice. But, alas! how dull and dead are our devotions! Lake Pharaoh's chariots, they drive on heavily. Some, like Balaam's ass, scarce ever open their mouths twice. THOMAS ADAMS

Vs. 3. *Set a watch, O Lord, before my mouth.* The tongue is the principal instrument in the cause of God; and it is the chief engine of the devil; give him this, and he asks no more — there is no mischief or misery he will not accomplish by it.

A man would never use this language without a conviction that he is in danger of transgression. And if David was conscious of a liableness to err, shall we ever presume on our safety? Our danger arises from the depravity of our nature. "The heart is deceitful above all things, and desperately wicked"; and who can bring a clean thing out of an unclean?

Our danger arises from the contagion of example. There is nothing in which mankind is more universally culpable than in the disorders of speech. Yet with these, we are constantly surrounded; and to these we have been accustomed from our impressible infancy.

We are in danger from the frequency of speech. "In the multitude of words there wanteth not sin." We must of necessity speak often; but we often speak without necessity. Duty calls us to intermingle much with our fellow-creatures; but we are too little in the closet and too much in the crowd — and when we are in company, we forget the admonition, "Let every man be swift to hear, and slow to speak."

A man would never use this language without a conviction of inability to preserve himself. The Bible teaches us this truth, not only doctrinally, but historically. The examples of good men, and men eminent in godliness, confirm it in the very article before us. Moses, the meekest man in the earth, "spake unadvisedly with his lips."

You have heard of the patience of Job, but he "cursed the day of his birth"; and Jeremiah, the prophet of the Lord, did the same. Peter said, "Though all men should be offended because of Thee, I will never be offended; though I should die with Thee, yet will I not deny Thee." But how did he use his tongue a few hours after? Then "began he to curse and to swear, saying, I know not the Man!" W. JAY'S SERMON ON "THE REGULATION OF THE TONGUE"

Nature, having made my lips to be a door to my words, let grace keep that door, that no word may be suffered to go out which may anyway tend to the dishonor of God or the hurt of others. MATTHEW HENRY

Let a seal for words not to be spoken lie on the tongue. A watch over words is better than over wealth. LUCIAN

Vs. 4. *My heart.* That man is like Esau, which had an inheritance, which had a heart, but now he hath not possession of his own; therefore, give God thy heart, that He may keep it; and not a piece of thy heart, not a room in thy heart, but thy heart. The heart divided, dieth.

God is not like the mother which would have the child divided, but like the natural mother, which said, rather than it should be divided, "let her take all." Let the devil have all, if He which gave it be not worthy of it. God hath no cope-mate; therefore He will have no parting of stakes, but all or none; and therefore He which asks here thy heart, in the sixth of Deuteronomy and the fifth verse, asketh "all thy heart, all thy soul, and all thy strength"; thrice He requireth all, lest we should keep a thought behind.

Yet it is thy heart, that is, a vain heart, a barren heart, a sinful heart, until thou give it unto God, and then it is the spouse of Christ, the temple of the Holy Ghost, and the image of God, so changed, and formed, and refined, that God calls it a new heart.

There is such strife for the heart as there was for Moses' body. "Give it me," saith the Lord; "give it me," saith the tempter; "give it me," saith the pope; "give it me," saith riches; "give it me," saith pleasure; as though thou must needs give it to someone. Now here is the choice, whether thou wilt give it to God or the devil; God's heart or the devil's heart; whose wilt thou be? HENRY SMITH

*To practice wicked works with men that work iniquity.* The way the heart inclines the life soon tends: evil things desired bring forth wicked things practiced. Unless the fountain of life is kept pure, the streams of life will soon be polluted. Alas, there is great power in company: even good men are apt to be swayed by association; hence the fear that we may practice wicked works when we are with wicked workers. We must endeavor not to be with them lest we sin with them.

It is bad when the heart goes the wrong way alone, worse when the life runs in the evil road alone; but it is apt to increase unto a high degree of ungodliness when the backslider runs the downward path with a whole horde of sinners around him. Good men are horrified at the thought of sinning as others do; the fear of it drives them to their knees. C. H. S.

*And let me not eat of their dainties.* The trap is baited with delicious meats that we may be captured and become meat for their malice. If we would not sin with men, we had better not sit with them, and if we would not share their wickedness, we must not share their wantonness. C. H. S.

Sin is not only meat, but sweet meat, not only bread, but pleasant bread to an evil heart. JOSEPH CARYL

Vs. 5. *Let the righteous smite me; it shall be a kindness.* He prefers the bitters of gracious company to the dainties of the ungodly. He would rather be smitten by the righteous than feasted by the wicked. He gives a permit to faithful admonition, he even invites it — "Let the righteous smite me." When the ungodly smile upon us their flattery is cruel; when the righteous smite us, their faithfulness is kind.

Sometimes godly men rap hard; they do not merely hint at evil, but hammer at it; and even then we are to receive the blows in love, and be thankful to the hand which smites so heavily. Fools resent reproof; wise men endeavor to profit by it. C. H. S.

Grace will teach a Christian to take those potions which are wholesome, though they be not toothsome. Faithful reproof is a token of love, and therefore may well be esteemed a kindness. It is a sign of a polluted nature for a man, like a serpent, if he be but touched, to gather poison, and vomit it up at the party. "Rebuke a wise man, and he will love thee." GEORGE SWINNOCK

Sincerity and serious repentance will be honorable in that person who is most careful to avoid sin, and most ready penitently to confess it when he hath been overcome, and truly thankful to those that call him to repentance; as being more desirous that God and His laws and religion should have the glory of their holiness, than that he himself should have the undue glory of innocency and escape the deserved shame of his sin.

It is one of the most dangerous diseases of professors and one of the greatest scandals of this age that persons taken for eminently religious are more impatient of plain, though just, reproof than many a drunkard, swearer, or fornicator; and when they have spent hours or days in the seeming earnest confession of their sin, and lament before God and man that they cannot do it with more grief and tears, yet they take it for a heinous injury in another that will say half so much against them, and take him for a malignant enemy of the godly who will call them as they call themselves. RICHARD BAXTER

The minister cannot be always preaching; two or three hours, maybe, in a week, he spends among his people in the pulpit, holding the glass of the gospel before their faces; but the lives of professors, these preach all the week long: if they were but holy and exemplary, they would be as a repetition of the preacher's sermon to their families and neighbors among whom they converse, and keep the sound of his doctrine continually ringing in their ears. "It behooves him," saith Tertullian, "that would counsel or reprove another, to guard his speech with the authority of his own conversation, lest, wanting that, what he says puts himself to the blush." We do not love one that hath a stinking breath to come very near us; such, therefore, had need have a sweet-scented life. WILLIAM GURNALL

*It shall be an excellent oil, which shall not break my head.* Some persons pride themselves on being blunt, or, as they call it, "honest"; but very blunt people do little good to others and get little love to themselves. The Scriptures recommend gentleness and kindness. Reproof should fall like the dew, and not like the rushing hail-storm. The "oil" insinuates itself; the stone wounds and then rebounds.

Christians should take heed of getting fond of the work of "rebuking." Such "spiritual constables" do a great deal of mischief without intending it. They are in a church what a very witty and sarcastic person is in society, or what a tell-tale is in a school; and approximate very closely to that class which the Apostle terms "busybodies in other men's matters." Our manner must be tender and winning. "The nail of reproof," says an old writer, "must be well oiled in kindness before it is driven home."

Meddling with the faults of others is like attempting to move a person afficted with the rheumatic gout: it must be done slowly and tenderly, nor must we be frightened by an outcry or two. The great thing is to show the person that you really love him; and if you manifest this in the sight of God, He will bless your efforts and give you favor in the sight of an erring brother. CHRISTIAN TREASURY

If David could say of his enemy that cursed him, "Let him alone, for God hath bidden him to curse"; much more safely mayest thou say of thy friend that reproves thee, "Let him alone, for God hath bidden him to smite." And as the Apostle saith of ministers, that God "doth entreat you by us"; so persuade yourselves that God doth reprove you by them. JOHN GORE

It was the saying of a heathen, though no heathenish saying, "That he who would be good, must either have a faithful friend to instruct him or a watchful enemy to correct him." Should we murder a physician because he comes to cure us; or like him worse, because he would make us better? The flaming sword of reprehension is but to keep us from the forbidden fruit of transgression. "Let the righteous smite me; it shall be a kindness: and let him reprove me; it shall be an excellent oil, which shall not break my head." Let him smite me as with a hammer, for so the word signifies. A Boanerges is as necessary as a Barnabas. WILLIAM SECKER

*For yet my prayer also shall be in their calamities.* Gracious men never grow wrathful with candid friends so as to harbor an ill-feeling against them; if so, when they saw them in affliction, they would turn around upon them and taunt them with their rebukes. So true is Christian brotherhood that we are with our friends in sickness or persecution, suffering their griefs; so that our heart's prayer is in their sorrows. When we can give good men nothing more, let us give them our prayers and let us do this doubly to those who have given us their rebukes. C. H. S.

Vs. 7. *Our bones are scattered at the grave's mouth.* David's case seemed hopeless: the cause of God in Israel was as a dead thing, even as a skeleton broken, and rotten, and shoveled out of the grave, to return as dust to its dust. C. H. S.

*As when one cutteth and cleaveth wood upon the earth.* How often have good men thought thus of the cause of God! Wherever they have looked, death, division, and destruction have stared them in the face. Cut and cloven, hopelessly sundered! Scattered, yea, scattered at the grave's mouth! Split up and split for the fire!

Such the cause of God and truth has seemed to be. "Upon the earth" the prospect was wretched; the field of the church was ploughed, harrowed, and scarified: it had become like a wood-chopper's yard, where everything was doomed to be broken up. We have seen churches in such a state and have been heart-broken. What a mercy that there is always a place above the earth to which we can look! C. H. S.

Vs. 8. *Mine eyes are unto Thee, O God the Lord.* If you would keep your mind fixed in prayer, keep your eye fixed. Much vanity comes in at the eye. When the eyes wander in prayer, the heart wanders. To think to keep the heart fixed in prayer, and yet let the eyes gaze abroad, is as if one should think to keep his house safe, yet let the windows be open. THOMAS WATSON

*Leave not my soul destitute.* To be destitute in circumstances is bad, but to be destitute in soul is far worse; to be left of friends is a calamity, but to be left of God would be destruction. Destitute of God is destitution with a vengeance. The comfort is that God hath said, "I will never leave thee nor forsake thee." C. H. S.

Vs. 9. *Keep me from the snares which they have laid for me.* He seems more in trouble about covert temptation than concerning open attacks. Brave men do not dread battle, but they hate secret plots. C. H. S.

Vs. 10. *Let the wicked fall into their own nets, whilst that I withal escape.* It may not be a Christian prayer, but it is a very just one, and it takes a great deal of grace to refrain from crying "Amen" to it; in fact, grace does not work towards making us wish otherwise concerning the enemies of holy men.

Do we not all wish the innocent to be delivered and the guilty to reap the result of their own malice? Of course we do, if we are just men. There can be no wrong in desiring that to happen in our own case which we wish for all good men. Yet is there a more excellent way. C. H. S.

# PSALM 142

Title: "Maschil of David." This "Maschil" is written for our instruction. It teaches us principally by example how to order our prayer in times of distress. Such instruction is among the most needful, practical, and effectual parts of our spiritual education. He who has learned how to pray has been taught the most useful of the arts and sciences. The disciples said unto the Son of David, "Lord, teach us to pray"; and here David gives us a valuable lesson by recording his own experience as to supplication from beneath a cloud. C. H. S.

Title: "The cave." Leaving our horses in charge of some Arabs, and taking one for our guide, we started for the cave now known as Mugharet Khureitun, which is believed to be the cave Adullam. After groping about as long as we had time to spare, we returned to the light of day, fully convinced that, with David and his lion-hearted followers inside, all the strength of Israel under Saul could not have forced an entrance — would not have even attempted it. WILLIAM M. THOMSON

Vs. 2. *I poured out my complaint before Him.* We may complain to God, but not of God. When we complain, it should not be before men, but before God alone. C. H. S.

*I showed before Him my trouble.* Note that we do not show our trouble before the Lord that He may see it, but that we may see Him. It is for our relief, and not for His information that we make plain statements concerning our woes: it does us much good to set out our sorrow in order, for much of it vanishes in the process like a ghost which will not abide the light of day; and the rest loses much of its terror because the veil of mystery is removed by a clear and deliberate stating of the trying facts.

Pour out your thoughts, and you will see what they are: show your trouble, and the extent of it will be known to you: let all be done before the Lord, for in comparison with His great majesty of love the trouble will seem to be as nothing. C. H. S.

The committing of our cause to God is at once our duty, our safety, and our ease. ABRAHAM WRIGHT

Vs. 3 *When my spirit was overwhelmed within me, then Thou knewest my path.* Truly it is well for us to know that God knows what we do not know. We lose our heads, but God never closes His eyes: our judgments lose their balance, but the eternal Mind is always clear. C. H. S.

The Lord is not withdrawn to a great distance, but His eye is upon you. He sees you not with the indifference of a mere spectator; but He observes with attention. He knows, He considers your path: yea, He appoints it, and every circumstance about it is under His direction.

Your trouble began at the hour He saw best — it could not come before; and He has marked the degree of it to a hair's breadth, and its duration to a minute. He knows likewise how your spirit is affected; and such supplies of grace and strength, and in such seasons as He sees needful, He will afford in due season. So that when things appear darkest, you shall still be able to say, "Though chastened, not killed." Therefore hope in God, for you shall yet praise Him. JOHN NEWTON

Although we as Christians possess the full solution of the problem of suffering, yet we frequently find ourselves in the position of Job, in regard to this or that particular affliction. There are sorrows so far reaching, so universal; there are losses so absolute and blows so terrible and inexplicable that it seems for a time as if we were wrapped in thickest gloom, and as if the secret of the Lord had not been revealed.

Why was this man stricken and that man spared? Why was such and such a being, in whom so many hopes centered, or who had already realized so many pleasant expectations, why was he withdrawn? Why was that other person left, a useless encumbrance to earth? Why was that voice, which found echo in so many hearts, suddenly silenced? Why have I been smitten? Why have I lost that which rendered my moral life beautiful and useful?

Oftentimes the soul seems lost for awhile in thoughts which overwhelm it; it loses its foothold, it tumbles about helplessly amid the deep waters of affliction. It seems as if all were over. Do not believe it. Remember Job; you cannot go to greater lengths of despair than he, and yet God had pity on him.

There is much comfort for you in this example of indescribable suffering, exasperated to the highest degree and yet pardoned and consoled. Cling to the memory of this blessed fact as to a cable of deliverance, a board or a plank amidst the shipwreck. And then remember that affliction forms part of God's plan, and that He also asks you to manifest ready and absolute confidence in Him. E. DE PRESSENSE, D.D.

*In the way wherein I walked have they privily laid a snare for me.* Wicked men must find some exercise for their malice and therefore when they dare not openly assail, they will privately ensnare. They watch the gracious man to see where his haunt is, and there they set their trap, but they do it with great caution, avoiding all observation lest their victim being forewarned should escape their toils. This is a great trial, but the Lord is greater still and makes us to walk safely in the midst of danger, for He knows us and our enemies, our way and the snare which is laid in it. Blessed be His name. C. H. S.

Snares on the right hand and snares on the left: snares on the right hand, worldly prosperity; snares on the left hand, worldly adversity; snares on the right hand, flattery; snares on the left hand, alarm. Do thou walk in the midst of the snares: Depart not from the way: let neither flattery ensnare thee, nor alarm drive thee off it. AUGUSTINE

Vs. 4. *I looked on my right hand, and beheld, but there was no man that would know me.* Strange to say, all were strange to David. He had known many, but none would know him. When a person is in ill odor, it is wonderful how weak the memories of his former friends become: they quite forget; they refuse to know. This is a dire calamity. It is better to be opposed by foes than to be forsaken by friends.

When friends look for us, they affect to have known us from our birth, but when we look for friends, it is wonderful how little we can make them remember: the fact is that in times of desertion it is not true that no man did know us, but no man would know us. Their ignorance is wilful. C. H. S.

*"Refuge failed . . . Thou art my Refuge."* Travelers tell us that they who are at the top of the Alps can see great showers of rain fall under them but not one drop of it falls on them. They who have God for their portion are in a high tower, and thereby safe from all troubles and showers. GEORGE SWINNOCK

Vs. 5. *I cried unto Thee, O Lord.* As man would not regard him, David was driven to Jehovah, his God. Was not this a gain made out of a loss? wealth gained by a failure? Anything which leads us to cry unto God is a blessing to us. C. H. S.

*I said, Thou art my refuge and my portion in the land of the living.* It is sometimes easier to believe in a portion in heaven than in a portion upon earth: we could die more easily than live, at least we think so. There is no living in the land of the living like living upon the living God.

Even in this one sentence we have two parts, the second rising far above the first. It is something to have Jehovah for our refuge, but it is everything to have Him for our portion. If David had not cried, he would not have said; and if the Lord had not been his refuge, he would never have been his portion. The lower step is as needful as the higher; but it is not necessary always to stop on the first round of the ladder. C. H. S.

Vs. 6. *Attend unto my cry.*

*Can I see another's woe,*
*And not be in sorrow, too?*
*Can I see another's grief,*
*And not seek for kind relief?*

*Can I see a falling tear*
*And not feel my sorrow's share?*
*Can a father see his child*
*Weep, nor be with sorrow filled?*

*Can a mother sit and hear*
*An infant groan, an infant fear?*
*No, no; never can it be!*
*Never, never can it be!*

*Think not thou canst sigh a sigh,*
*And thy Maker is not by;*
*Think not thou canst weep a tear,*
*And thy Maker is not near.*

*Oh! He gives to us His joy,*
*That our grief He may destroy:*
*Till our grief is fled and gone,*
*He doth sit by us and moan.*

William Blake

Vs. 7. *Bring my soul out of prison, that I may praise Thy name.* That God may be glorified is another notable plea for a suppliant. Escaped prisoners are sure to speak well of those who give them liberty. Soul-emancipation is the noblest form of liberation and calls for the loudest praise: he who is delivered from the dungeons of despair is sure to magnify the name of the Lord. C. H. S.

## PSALM 143

Title: "A Psalm of David." It is so much like other Davidic Psalms that we accept the title without a moment's hesitation. David's history illustrates it, and his spirit breathes in it. Why it has been set down as one of the seven Penitental Psalms we can hardly tell; for it is rather a vindication of his own integrity, and an indignant prayer against his slanderers than a confession of fault. It is true the second verse proves that he never dreamed of justifying himself before the Lord; but even in it there is scarcely the brokenness of penitence. It seems to us rather martial than penitential, rather a supplication for deliverance from trouble than a weeping acknowledgment of transgression. C. H. S.

Whole Psalm: At the making of this Psalm (as it plainly appeareth) David was cast into some desperate danger; whether by Saul when he was forced to flee into the cave, as in the former Psalm, or by Absalom his son, or by any other, it is uncertain. This worthy Psalm, then, containeth these three things: First, a confession of his sins. Secondly, a lamentation over his injuries. Thirdly, a supplication for temporal deliverance and spiritual graces. ARCHIBALD SYMSON

Vs. 1. *Hear my prayer, O Lord, give ear to my supplications.* Gracious men are so eager to be heard in prayer that they double their entreaties for that boon. The Psalmist desires to be heard and to be considered; hence he cries, "Hear," and then, "Give ear." C. H. S.

*Answer me and in Thy righteousness.* Forgiveness is not inconsistent with truth or righteousness, and the pardon which in mercy God bestows upon the sinner is bestowed in justice to the well-beloved Son, Who accepted and discharged the sinner's obligations. This is an infinitely precious truth, and the hearts of thousands in every age have been sustained and gladdened by it.

A good old Christian woman in humble life so fully realize this, that when a revered servant of God asked her, as she lay on her dying pillow, the ground of her hope for eternity, she replied, with great composure, "I rely on the justice of God"; adding, however, when the reply excited surprise, "Justice, not to me, but to my Substitute, in Whom I trust." ROBERT MACDONALD

Vs. 2. *And enter not into judgment with Thy servant.* Some years ago, I visited a poor young woman dying with consumption. She was a stranger in our town and had been there a few weeks before, sometime in her girlhood, and had attended my Sabbath-school class. What did I find was her only stay, and hope, and comfort in the view of the dark valley of the shadow of death, which was drawing down upon her? One verse of a Psalm, she had learned at the class, and never forgot. She repeated it with clasped hands, piercing eyes, and thin voice trembling from her white lips.

*Thy servant also bring Thou not*
*In judgment to be tried:*
*Because no living man can be*
*In Thy sight justified.*

No — no sinner can endure sight of Thee, O God, if he tries to be self-justified. JAMES COMPER GRAY

A young man once said to me: "I do not think I am a sinner." I asked him if he would be willing his mother or sister should know all he had done, or said, or thought — all his motions and all his desires.

After a moment he said: "No, indeed, I should not like to have them know; no, not for the world." "Then can you dare to say, in the presence of a holy God,

Who knows every thought of your heart, I do not commit sin?" JOHN B. GOUGH

*For in Thy sight shall no man living be justified.* This foolish age has produced specimens of a pride so rank that men have dared to claim perfection in the flesh; but these vain-glorious boasters are no exception to the rule here laid down: they are but men, and poor specimens of men. When their lives are examined they are frequently found to be more faulty than the humble penitents before whom they vaunt their superiority. C. H. S.

Vs. 3. *He hath smitten my life down to the ground.* Slander has a very depressing effect upon the spirits; it is a blow which overthrows the mind as though it were knocked down with the fist. C. H. S.

Vs. 5. *I remember the days of old.* When we see nothing new which can cheer us, let us think upon old things. We once had merry days, days of deliverance, and joy and thanksgiving; why not again? Jehovah rescued His people in the ages which lie back, centuries ago; why should He not do the like again?

We ourselves have a rich past to look back upon; we have sunny memories, sacred memories, satisfactory memories, and these are as flowers for the bees of faith to visit, from whence they may make honey for present use. C. H. S.

Vss. 5 and 6. *I meditate. I stretch forth my hands.* Meditation is prayer's handmaid to wait on it, both before and after the performance of supplication. It is as the plough before the sower, to prepare the heart for the duty of prayer; and as the harrow after the sower, to cover the seed when 'tis sown. As the hopper feeds the mill with grist, so does meditation supply the heart with matter for prayer. WILLIAM GURNALL

Vs. 6. *I stretch forth my hands unto Thee.* As a poor beggar for an alms. Beggary here is not the easiest and poorest trade, but the hardest and richest of all other. JOHN TRAPP

*My soul thirsteth after Thee, as a thirsty land.* As the soil cracks, and yawns, and thus opens its mouth in dumb pleadings, so did the Psalmist's soul break with longings. He was athirst for the Lord. If he could but feel the presence of his God, he would no longer be overwhelmed or dwell in darkness; nay, everything would turn to peace and joy. C. H. S.

*Selah.* It was time to pause, for the supplication had risen to agony point. Both harp-strings and heart-strings were strained and needed a little rest to get them right again for the second half of the song. C. H. S.

Vss. 7, 8, 10 and 11. *Quicken me, O Lord, for Thy name's sake.* Now this is exactly right: our prayers, as well as our other obedience, must be without partiality; nay, we should desire comfort for the sake of holiness, rather than holiness for the sake of comfort. JOHN FAWCETT

Vs. 8. *Cause me to hear Thy lovingkindness.* It is no marvel that such atheists and papists who altogether refuse the Word of God, live comfortless and die without comfort, because they refuse that instrument which should carry joy to them. Good reason they die athirst, since they reject that vessel, the Word of God, by which they might be refreshed. Therefore, since faith cometh by hearing of God's Word, and all our comfort cometh by it, let us pray God to bore our ears and our hearts that we may receive the glad tidings of reconciliation from God. C. H. S.

*Cause me to hear Thy lovingkindness in the morning.* But for afflictions to leave us, then we wish they had feet like hinds' feet, to run away from us, or we the wings of a dove to fly away from them and be at rest . . . What prisoner desires not to be presently set free, and that liberty's soft hand may loose his iron knots? What mariner wishes a long storm? What servant sighs not over his hard apprenticeship?

Yea, who is he, that if there were an appearance of an offering to take the cup of calamity from his mouth, saying, "Thou shalt drink no more," would answer, "This cup shall not yet pass from me, I delight to carouse and drink deeply of these bitter waters"? Yea, this desire extends so far that it comes to the Son of man, the blessed Seed of the woman, Who was so clad with human weakness that He earnestly prayed for speedy help from His heavy anguish; and that not once, but often—"Oh, my Father, if it be possible," etc.; and when His Father answers not, He cries like one ready to fall under the burden, "My God, my God, why hast Thou forsaken Me?"

The reason for Christ's thus complaining is to be fetched from thence, whence His flesh came — even from us. It was our human flesh, not His divine spirit, which was so weary of suffering; His spirit was willing, it was our flesh that was so weak. THOMAS CALVERT

Let it engage my thoughts and affections. It is well to have a subject like this to occupy our waking thoughts and to take hold of our first desires. If other thoughts get into our hearts in the morning, we may not be able to turn them out all the day. Prayer and praise, reading and meditation, will be sweet with such a subject occupying and influencing our minds. They will be exercises of cheerfulness, freedom, and blessedness. W. ABBOT

*Cause me to know the way wherein I should walk.* We are often brought to a stand, hedged up and hemmed in by the providence of God so that there seems no way out. A man is sometimes thrown into difficulties in which he sits down beginning to despair, and says to himself, "Well, this time it is all over with me"; like Sterne's starling, or worse, like Bunyan's man in the cage, he says, "I cannot get out." Then when God has drawn him from all self-confidence and self-resource, a door opens in the wall and he rises up, and walks at liberty, praising God. GEORGE BARRELL CHEEVER

Vs. 9. *I flee unto Thee to hide me.* Jesus has made Himself the refuge of His people: the sooner, and the more entirely we flee to Him the better for us. Beneath the crimson canopy of our Lord's atonement believers are completely hidden; let us abide there and be at rest. C. H. S.

Is David's valor come to this, that he is come now to be glad to fly? Had he not done better to have died valiantly than to fly basely? O my soul, to fly is not always a sign of baseness; it is not always a point of valor to stand to it; but then to fly when we feel our own weakness, and to Him to fly, in Whom is our strength —this is, if not valor, at least wisdom, but it is, to say true, both wisdom and true valor.

And now, O God, seeing I find my own weakness, and know Thy strength, what should I do but fly, and whither fly but only to Thee — to Thee, a strong fortress to all that build upon Thee; to Thee, a safe sanctuary to all that fly unto Thee. SIR RICHARD BAKER

This implies, 1. Danger: the Christian may be in danger from sin, self, foes. 2. Fear: his fears may be groundless, but they are often very painful. 3. Inability — to defend himself or overcome his opposers. 4. Foresight: he sees the storm in the distance and looks out for the covert. 5. Prudence: he hides before the storm, ere the enemy comes upon him. 6. A laudable concern for safety and comfort. The believer, if wise, will at all times flee to Jehovah. JAMES SMITH

Vs. 9-10. You must put away sin by repentance. Jesus Christ will not be a sanctuary for rebels; He will not protect evil-doers. Christ will never hide the devil nor any of his servants (Isa. 55:6-7): "Let the ungodly forsake his way," etc. David knew this; therefore he prays that God would teach him to do His will. RALPH ROBINSON

Vs. 10. *Teach me to do Thy will.* He saith not, "Teach me to know Thy will," but "to *do* Thy will." God teaches us in three ways: first, by His word; secondly, He illuminateth our minds by the Spirit; thirdly, He imprinteth it in our hearts and maketh us obedient to the same; for the servant who knoweth the will of his master, and doeth it not, shall be beaten with many stripes (Luke 12). ARCHIBALD SYMSON

Vs. 11. *Bring my soul out of trouble.* I can bring it in, but Thou only canst bring it out. JOHN TRAPP

Vs. 11-12. *Thy Name's sake . . . Thy righteousness' sake . . . And of Thy mercy.* Mark here, my soul, with what three cords David seeks to draw God to grant him his suits: for His Name's sake; for His righteousness' sake; and for His mercy's sake — three such motives, that it must be a very hard suit that God will deny, if either of them be used. But if the three motives be all of them so strong, being each of them single, how strong would they be if they were all united, and twisted, I may say, into one cord? SIR RICHARD BAKER

Vs. 12. *Of Thy mercy cut off mine enemies.* He desireth God to slay his enemies in His mercy, when rather their destruction was a work of His justice? I answer that the destruction of the wicked is a mercy to the church. As God showed great mercy and kindness to His church by the death of Pharaoh, Sennacherib, Herod, and other troublers thereof. ARCHIBALD SYMSON

# PSALM 144

It seems to us to be highly probable that the Psalmist, remembering that he had trodden some of the same ground before, felt his mind moved to fresh thought, and that the Holy Spirit used this mood for His own high purposes. To us the whole Psalm appears to be perfect as it stands, and to exhibit such unity throughout that it would be a literary vandalism as well as a spiritual crime to rend away one part from the other.

Title: It's title is "Of David," and its language is of David, if ever language can belong to any man. As surely as we could say of any poem, "This is of Tennyson," or "of Longfellow," we may say, "This is of David." Nothing but the disease which closes the eye to manifest fact and opens it to fancy could have led learned critics to ascribe this song to anybody but David. Alexander well says, "The Davidic origin of this Psalm is as marked as that of any in the Psalter." C. H. S.

Vs. 1. *Blessed be the Lord.* A prayer for further mercy is fitly begun with a thanksgiving for former mercy; and when we are waiting upon God to bless us, we should stir up ourselves to bless Him. MATTHEW HENRY

*The Lord my strength.* Agamemnon says to Achilles:

*If thou hast strength, 'twas heaven that strength bestowed;*
*For know, vain man! thy valor is from God.*

HOMER

*The Lord . . . teacheth:* and not as man teacheth. Thus he taught Samson by abstaining from strong drink and by suffering no razor to pass over his head. And so He taught the arms of the True David to fight when stretched on the cross: nailed, to human sight, to the tree of suffering, but, in reality, winning for themselves the crown of glory: helpless in the eyes of scribes and Pharisees; in those of archangels, laying hold of the two pillars, sin and death, whereon the house of Satan rested, and heaving them up from their foundation. AYGUAN

*The Lord my strength, which teacheth my hands to war.* There were three qualities of a valiant soldier found in Christ, the Captain of our salvation, in His war against Satan, which His followers are bound to emulate: boldness in attack, skill in defence, steadiness in conflict, all which He teaches by His example (Matt. 4:1, 4, 7, 10-11).

He was bold in attack, for He began the combat by going up into the wilderness to defy the enemy. So we, too, should be always beforehand with Satan, ought to fast, even if not tempted to gluttony, and be humble, though not assailed by pride, and so forth.

He was skillful in defence, parrying every attack with Holy Writ; where we, too, in the examples of the saints may find lessons for the combat. He was steadfast in conflict, for He persevered to the end, till the devil left Him and angels came and ministered unto Him.

And we, too, should not be content with repelling the first attack, but persevere in our resistance until evil thoughts are put to flight and heavenly resolutions take their place. NEALE AND LITTLEDALE

*Which teacheth my hands to war, and my fingers to fight.* A clergyman may be supposed to be taught of God, but people do not allow this to be true of weavers or workers in brass; yet these callings are specially mentioned in the Bible as having been taught to holy women and earnest men when the tabernacle was set up at the first. All wisdom and skill are from the Lord, and for them He deserves to be gratefully extolled. This teaching extends to the smallest members of our frame; the Lord teaches fingers as well as hands; indeed, it sometimes happens that if the finger is not well trained, the whole hand is incapable.

David was called to be a man of war, and he was eminently successful in his battles; he does not trace this to his good generalship or valor, but to his being taught and strengthened for the war and the fight. If the Lord deigns to have a hand in such unspiritual work as fighting, surely He will help us to proclaim the Gospel and win souls. C. H. S.

Vs. 2. *My goodness, and my fortress.* So is He Himself also our fortress and safe abode: in Him we dwell as behind impregnable ramparts and immovable bastions. We cannot be driven out, or starved out; for our fortress is prepared for a siege; it is stored with abundance of food, and a well of living water is within it. Kings usually think much of their fenced cities, but King David relies upon his God, Who is more to him than fortresses could have been. C. H. S.

The accumulation of terms, one upon another, which follows, may appear unnecessary, yet it tends greatly to strengthen faith. We know how unstable men's minds are, and especially how soon faith wavers, when they are assailed by some trial of more than usual severity. JOHN CALVIN

*My Shield.* The Hebrew word signifies, not the huge shield which was carried by an armor-bearer, but the handy target with which heroes entered into hand-to-hand conflicts. A warrior took it with him when he used his bow or his sword. It was often made of metal, but still was portable, and useful, and was made to serve as an ornament, being brightened or anointed with oil. David had made abundant use of the Lord, his God, from day to day, in battles many and murderous. C. H. S.

*Who subdueth my people under me.* Leaders in the Christian church cannot maintain their position except as the Lord preserves to them the mighty influence which ensures obedience and evokes enthusiastic loyalty. For every particle of influence for good which we may possess, let us magnify the Name of the Lord.

Thus has David blessed Jehovah for blessing him. How many times he has appropriated the Lord by that little word "My!" Each time he grasps the Lord, he adores and blesses Him; for the one word "Blessed" runs through all the passage, like a golden thread. C. H. S.

Vs. 3. *Lord, what is man, that Thou takest knowledge of him!* Infinite condescension can alone account for the Lord stooping to be the Friend of man. That He should make man the subject of election, the object of redemption, the child of eternal love, the darling of infallible providence, the next of kin to Deity, is indeed a matter requiring more than the two notes of exclamation found in this verse. C. H. S.

*Now, what is man when grace reveals*
*The virtues of a Savior's Blood?*
*Again a life divine he feels,*
*Despises earth, and walks with God.*

*And what in yonder realms above*
*Is ransomed man ordained to be?*
*With honor, holiness, and love,*
*No seraph more adorned than he.*

*Nearest the throne, and first in song.*
*Man shall His hallelujahs raise,*
*While wondering angels round Him throng,*
*And swell the chorus of His praise.*

JOHN NEWTON

*Lord, what is man?* Take him in his four elements, of earth, air, fire and water. In the earth, he is as fleeting dust; in the air, he is as a disappearing vapor; in the water, he is as a breaking bubble; and in the fire, he is as consuming smoke. WILLIAM SECKER

*Thou takest knowledge of him.* It is a great word. Alas! what knowledge do we take of the gnats that play in the sun; or the ants, or worms, that are crawling in our grounds? Yet the disproportion betwixt us and them is but finite; infinite betwixt God and us.

Thou, the great God of heaven, to take knowledge of such a thing as man. If a mighty prince shall vouchsafe to spy and single out a plain, homely swain in a throng, as the Great Sultan did lately a tankard-bearer; and take special notice of him, and call him but to a kiss of his hand and nearness to his person; he boasts of it as a great favor.

For Thee, then, O God, Who abasest Thyself to behold the things in heaven itself, to cast Thine eye upon so poor a worm as man, it must needs be a wonderful mercy. JOSEPH HALL

Vs. 3-4. Many a one besides David wonders at himself: one wonders at his own honor; and, though he will not say so, yet thinks, "What a great man am I! Is not this great Babel which I have built?" This is Nebuchadnezzar's wonder. Another wonders at his person, and finds, either a good face, or a fair eye, or an exquisite hand, or a well-shaped leg, or some gay fleece, to admire in himself: this was Absalom's wonder.

Another wonders at his wit and learning: "How came I by all this? *Turba haec!* This vulgar, that knows not the law, is accursed"; this was the Pharisee's wonder. Another wonders at his wealth "Soul, take thine ease"; as the epicure in the Gospel. David's wonder is as much above, as against all these: he wonders at his vileness: like as the chosen vessel would boast of nothing but his infirmities: "Lord, what is man?"

How well this hangs together! No sooner had he said, "Thou hast subdued my people under me," than he adds, "Lord, what is man?" Some vain heart would have been lifted up with a conceit of his own eminence: "Who am I? I am not as other men. I have people under me; and people of my own, and people subdued to me." This is to be more than a man. I know who hath said, "I said ye are gods." JOSEPH HALL

Vs. 4. *Man is like to vanity.* Adam is like to Abel. He is like that which is nothing at all. He is actually vain, and he resembles that unsubstantial empty thing which is nothing but a blown-up nothing — a puff, a bubble. Yet he is not vanity, but only like it. He is not so substantial as that unreal thing; he is only the likeness of it. Lord, what is a man? It is wonderful that God should think of such a pretentious insignificance. C. H. S.

The heathen historian could not but observe how Alexander the Great, when he had to carry on his great designs, summoned a parliament before him of the whole world, he was himself summoned by death to appear in the other world. The Dutch, therefore, very wittily to express the world's vanity, picture at Amsterdam a man with a full-blown bladder on his shoulders, and another standing by pricking the bladder with a pin, with this motto, *Quam Subito* — How soon is all blown down! GEORGE SWINNOCK

When Cain was born, there was much ado about his birth: "I have gotten a man-child from God," saith his mother: she looked upon him as a great possession, and therefore called his name Cain, which signifies "a possession." But the second man that was born unto the world bare the title of the world, "vanity"; his name was Abel, that is, "vanity." A premonition was given in the name of the second man what would or should be the condition of all men.

In Psalm 144:4, there is an allusion unto those two names. We translate it, "Man is like to vanity"; the Hebrew is, "Adam is as Abel"; Adam, you know, was the name of the first man, the name of Abel's father; but as Adam was the proper name of the first, so it is an appellative, or common to all men: now Adam, that is, man of all men, are Abel, vain, and walking in a vain show. JOSEPH CARYL

Vanity! in fact, all occupations and pursuits are worthy of no other epithet, if they are not preceded by, and connected with, a deep and paramount regard to the salvation of the soul, the honor of God, and the interests of eternity . . . Oh, then, what phantoms, what airy nothings are those things that wholly absorb the powers and occupy the days of the great mass of mankind around us! Their most substantial good perishes in the using, and their most enduring realities are but "the fashion of this world that passeth away." THOMAS RAFFLES

*His days are as a shadow that passeth away.* Observe that human life is not only as a shade but as a shade which is about to depart. It is a mere mirage, the image of a thing which is not, a phantasm which melts back into nothing. How is it that the Eternal should make so much of mortal man, who begins to die as soon as he begins to live? C. H. S.

The shadows of the mountains are constantly shifting their position during the day and ultimately disappear altogether on the approach of night: so is it with man, who is every day advancing to the moment of his final departure from this world. BELLARMINE

Vs. 5. *Bow Thy heavens, O Lord, and come down.* Earth cries to heaven to stoop; nay, the cry is to the Lord of heaven to bow the heavens and appear among the sons of earth. The Lord has often done this, and never more fully than when in Bethlehem the Word was made flesh and dwelt among us: now doth He know the way, and He never refuses to come down to defend His beloved ones. David would have the real presence of God to counterbalance the mocking appearance of boastful man: eternal verity could alone relieve him of human vanity. C. H. S.

This was never so remarkably fulfilled as in the incarnation of Jesus Christ, when heaven and earth were, as it were, brought together. Heaven itself was, as it were, made to bow that it might be united to the earth. God did, as it were, come down and bring heaven with Him. He not only came down to the earth, but He brought heaven down with Him to men and for men. It was a most strange and wonderful thing.

But this will be more remarkably fulfilled still by Christ's second coming, when He will indeed bring all heaven down with Him—viz., all the inhabitants of heaven. Heaven shall be left empty of its inhabitants to come down to the earth; and then the mountains shall smoke and shall indeed flow down at His presence, as in Isa. 64:1. JONATHAN EDWARDS

Vs. 7. *Rid me, and deliver me.* Away, you who theorize about suffering and can do no more than descant upon it, away! for in the time of weeping, we cannot endure your reasonings. If you have no means of delivering us, if you have nothing but sententious phrases to offer, put your hands on your mouths; enwrap yourselves in silence! It is enough to suffer; but to suffer and listen to you is more than we can bear. If Job's mouth was nigh unto blasphemy, the blame is yours, ye miserable comforters, who talked instead of weeping. If I must suffer, then I pray for suffering without fine talk! E. DE PRESSENSE

*From the hand of strange children.* Oh, to be rid of those infidel, blaspheming beings who pollute society with their false teachings and hard speeches! Oh, to be delivered from slanderous tongues, deceptive lips, and false hearts! No wonder these words are repeated, for they are the frequent cry of many a tried child of God. C. H. S.

Vs. 8. *And their right hand is a right hand of falsehood.* It is a dreadful thing when a man's expertness lies more in lies than in truth; when he can neither speak nor act without proving himself to be false. God, save us from lying mouths and hands of falsehood. C. H. S.

Vs. 9. *I will sing a new song unto Thee, O God.* Weary of the false, I will adore the true. Fired with fresh enthusiasm, my gratitude shall make a new channel for itself. I will sing as others have done; but it shall be a new song such as no others have sung. That song shall be all and altogether for my God: I will extol none but the Lord, from Whom my deliverance has come. C. H. S.

Vs. 12. *That our daughters may be as corner stones, polished after the similitude of a palace.* Home becomes a palace when the daughters are maids of honor and the sons are nobles in spirit; then the father is a king and the mother a queen, and royal residences are more than outdone. A city built up of such dwellings is a city of palaces, and a state composed of such cities is a republic of princes. C. H. S.

Vs. 15. *Happy is that people.* It is only a narrow and one-sided religion that can see anything out of place in this beatitude of plenty and peace. If we could rejoice with the Psalms fully and without misgiving, in the temporal blessings bestowed by heaven, we should the more readily and sincerely enter into the depths of their spiritual experience. And the secret of this lies in the full comprehension and contemplation of the beautiful and pleasant as the gift of God. A. S. AGLEN

*Yea, happy is that people, whose God is the Lord.* Admit the windows of the visible heaven were opened and all outward blessings poured down upon us; admit we did perfectly enjoy whatsoever the vastness of the earth contains in it; tell me, what will it profit to gain all and lose God? If the earth be bestowed upon us, and not heaven; or the material heaven be opened, and not the beatifical; or the whole world made ours, and God not ours; we do not arrive at happiness. All that is in the first proposition is nothing unless this be added, "Yea, happy are the people which have the Lord for their God." RICHARD HOLDSWORTH

The Syriac rendereth it question-wise, "Is not the people (happy) that is in such a case?" The answer is, "No," except they have God to boot (Ps. 146:5). Nothing can make that man truly miserable that hath God for his portion, and nothing can make that man truly happy that wants God for his portion.

God is the Author of all true happiness; He is the donor of all true happiness; He is the maintainer of all true happiness, and He is the center of all true happiness; and therefore, he that hath Him for his God and for his portion is the only happy man in the world. THOMAS BROOKS

# PSALM 145

This is one of the alphabetical Psalms, composed with much art, and, doubtless so arranged that the memory might be aided. The Holy Spirit condescends to use even the more artificial methods of the poet to secure attention and impress the heart.

Title: Certainly David's praise is the best of praise, for it is that of a man of experience, of sincerity, of calm deliberation, and of intense warmth of the heart.

It is not for any one of us to render David's praise, for David only could do that, but we may take David's Psalm as a model and aim at making our own personal adoration as much like it as possible: we shall be long before we equal our model. Let each Christian reader present his own praise unto the Lord and call it by his own name. What a wealth of varied praise will thus be presented through Christ Jesus! C. H. S.

Title: "The praise of David." Psalms are the praises of God accompanied with song; Psalms are songs containing the praise of God. If there be praise, but not of God, it is not a Psalm. If there be praise, and praise of God, if it is not sung, it is not a Psalm. To make a Psalm, there go these three: praise, God's praise, and song. AUGUSTINE

Vs. 1. *I will extol Thee, my God, O king.* David as God's king adores God as his King. It is well when the Lord's royalty arouses our loyalty, and our spirit is moved to magnify His majesty. The Psalmist has extolled his Lord many a time before; he is doing so still, and he will do so in the future: praise is for all tenses. C. H. S.

*King.* God is King in verity; others are called kings in vanity. MARTIN GEIER

Vs. 2. *Every day will I bless Thee.* Whatever the character of the day, or of my circumstances and conditions during that day, I will continue to glorify God. Were we well to consider the matter, we should see abundant cause in each day for rendering special blessing unto the Lord. All before the day, all in the day, all following the day should constrain us to magnify our God every day, all the year round. Our love to God is not a matter of holy days: every day is alike holy to holy men. C. H. S.

*Every day.* Then God is to be blessed and praised in dark as well as bright days. JOHANNES PAULUS PALANTERIUS

*I will bless Thee: I will praise Thy Name.* The repetition intimates the fervency of his affection to this work, the fixedness of his purpose to abound in it, and the frequency of his performances therein. MATTHEW HENRY

Vs. 4. *One generation shall praise Thy works to another.* While the church sits fainting under a juniper-tree in the wilderness, there shall fly prophets to feed her till the blessed resurrection of the witnesses. It's our high duty to study present work and prize present help and greatly rejoice when the Lord sends forth, as once He did, both Boanerges and Barnabas together.

Pray for the mantle, girdle, and blessing of Elijah, for the love of John, and the zeal of Paul, to twine hands together to draw souls to heaven; till the Beloved comes like a roe or a young hart upon the mountains of spices; till the shadows flee away; till the day dawn, and the Day-star arise in your hearts. SAMUEL LEE

Vs. 5. *I will speak of the glorious honor of Thy majesty.* Everything which has to do with the Great King is majestic, honorable, glorious. His least is greater than man's greatest; His lowest is higher than man's highest. There is nothing about the infinite Lord which is unworthy of His royalty; and, on the other hand, nothing is wanting to the splendor of His reign: His majesty is honorable, and His honor is glorious: He is altogether wonderful. C. H. S.

Vs. 6. *Thy greatness.* All men are enamored of greatness. Then they must seek it in God and get it from God. David did both. All history shows the creature aspiring after this glory. Ahasuerus, Astyages, Cyrus, Cambyses, Nebuchadnezzar, were all called "the great."

Alexander the Great, when he came to the Ganges, ordered his statue to be made of more than life size, that posterity might believe him to have been of nobler stature. In Christ alone does man attain the greatness his heart yearns for — the glory of perfect goodness. THOMAS LEBLANC

Vs. 7. *Abundantly utter the memory of God's great goodness.* God, then, is not praised at all if He be not greatly praised. Weak and dull praises are dispraises; for a person or thing is not honored or praised unless there be some proportion between the honor and praise and the worthiness of the person or thing honored and praise. HENRY JEANES

The Lord deliver us from the noise of fluent women; but it matters not how fluent men and women are if they will be fluent on the topic now before us. Open your mouths; let the praise pour forth; let it come, rivers of it. Stream away! Gush away, all that you possibly can.

Do not stop the joyful speakers; let them go on forever. They do not exaggerate; they cannot. You say they are enthusiastic, but they are not half up to the pitch yet; bid them become more excited and speak yet more fervently.

Go on, brother, go on; pile it up; say something greater, grander, and more fiery still! You cannot exceed the truth. You have come to a theme where your most fluent powers will fail in utterance. The text calls for a sacred fluency, and I would exhort you liberally to exercise it when you are speaking on the goodness of God. C. H. S.

Too many witnesses of God's goodness are silent witnesses. Men do not enough speak out the testimonies that they might bear in this matter. The reason that I love the Methodists — good ones — is, that they have a tongue to their piety. They fulfill the command of God — to be fervent in spirit. HENRY WARD BEECHER

*And shall sing of Thy righteousness.* Modern thinkers would fain expunge the idea of righteousness from their notion of God; but converted men would not. It is a sign of growth in sanctification when we rejoice in the justice, rectitude, and holiness of our God.

Even a rebel may rejoice in mercy, which he looks upon as laxity; but a loyal subject rejoices when he learns that God is so just that not even to save His own elect would He consent to violate the righteousness of His moral government. Few men will shout for joy at the righteousness of Jehovah, but those who do so are His chosen, in whom His soul delighteth. C. H. S.

*Thy righteousness.* It is easy to perceive God's righteousness declared in the punishment of sins; the Cross alone declares "His righteousness for the remission of sins." It magnifies justice in the way of pardoning sin, and mercy in the way of punishing it. JOHN M'LAURIN

Vs. 8. *And full of compassion.* If the Lord be full of compassion, there is no room in Him for forgetfulness, or harshness, and none should suspect Him thereof. What an ocean of compassion there must be since the infinite God is full of it! C. H. S.

*Slow to anger.* Even those who refuse His grace yet share in long-suffering. When men do not repent, but, on the contrary, go from bad to worse, He is still averse to let His wrath flame forth against them. Greatly patient and extremely anxious that the sinner may live, He "lets the lifted thunder drop" and still forbears. C. H. S.

Vs. 9. *The Lord is good to all.* Even the worst taste of God's mercy; such as fight against God's mercy taste of it; the wicked have some crumbs from Mercy's table. Sweet dewdrops are on the thistle as well as on the rose. The diocese where mercy visits is very large. Pharaoh's head was crowned though his heart was hardened. THOMAS WATSON

*And His tender mercies are over all His works.* Kindness is a law of God's universe: the world was planned for happiness; even now that sin has so sadly marred God's handiwork and introduced elements which were not from the beginning, the Lord has so arranged matters that the fall is broken, the curse is met by an antidote, and the inevitable pain is softened with mitigations.

Even in this sin-stricken world, under its disordered economy, there are abundant traces of a hand skilful to soothe distress and heal disease. That which makes life bearable is the tenderness of the great Father. This is seen in the creation of an insect as well as in the ruling of nations.

The Creator is never rough; the Provider is never forgetful; the Ruler is never cruel. Nothing is done to create disease; no organs are arranged to promote misery; the incoming of sickness and pain is not according to the original design but a result of our disordered state. Man's body as it left the Maker's hand was neither framed for disease, decay, nor death, neither was the purpose of it discomfort and anguish; far otherwise, it was framed for a joyful activity and a peaceful enjoyment of God.

Jehovah has in great consideration laid up in the world cures for our ailments and helps for our feebleness; and if many of these have been long in their discovery, it is because it was more for man's benefit to find them out himself than to have them labeled and placed in order before his eyes.

We may be sure of this, that Jehovah has never taken delight in the ills of His creatures but has sought their good and laid Himself out to alleviate the distresses into which they have guiltily plunged themselves. C. H. S.

True may he say, I have made myself, by sin, the vilest of all creatures; I am become worse than the beasts that perish; as vile as a worm, as loathsome as a toad, by reason of the venomous corruption that is in my heart, and my woeful contrariety to the nature of a holy God. But there is "mercy over all," even over such vile and loathsome creatures as these; there may be some over me, though wrath do now abide on me.

Oh, let that mercy, whose glory it is to stretch itself over all, reach my soul also! Oh, that the blessed and powerful influence thereof would beget faith in my heart! DAVID CLARKSON

Vs. 10. *All Thy works shall praise Thee, O Lord.* Ask of the countless tribes of plants and animals; and shall they not testify to the action of the great Source of Life? Yes, from every portion, from every department of nature, comes the same voice; everywhere we hear Thy name, O God! everywhere we see Thy love.

Creation, in all its length and breadth, in all its depth and height, is the manifestation of Thy Spirit, and without Thee the world were dark and dead. The universe is to us as the burning bush which the Hebrew leader saw: God is ever present in it, for it burns with His glory, and the ground on which we stand is always holy. "FRANCIS" (VISCOUNT DILLON)

*And Thy saints shall bless Thee.* None but blessed men will bless the Lord. Only saints, or holy ones, will bless the thrice holy God. If we praise Jehovah because of His works around us, we must go on to bless Him for His works within us. Let the two "shalls" of this verse be fulfilled, especially the latter one. C. H. S.

The lily lifts itself upon its slender stem and displays its golden petals and its glittering ivory leaves; and by its very existence, it praises God.

Yonder deep and booming sea rolls up in storm and tempest, sweeping everything before it; and every dash of its waves praises God. The birds in the morning, and some of them all through the night, can never cease from praising; uniting with the ten thousand other voices which make ceaseless concert before the throne.

But observe, neither the flower, nor the sea, nor the bird, praises with intent to praise. To them it is no exercise of intellect, for they do not know God and cannot understand His worthiness; nor do they even know that they are praising Him. They exhibit His skill and His goodness, and so forth, and in so doing they do much; but we must learn to do more.

When you and I praise God, there is the element of will, of intelligence, of desire, of intent; and in the saints of God, there is another element, namely that of love to Him, of reverent gratitude towards Him, and this turns the praise into blessing.

A man is an eminent painter, and you exclaim, "His pencil is instinct with life." Still, the man is no friend of yours; you pronounce no blessings on his name. It may be that your feeling towards him is that of deep regret that such abilities should be united with so ill a character. A certain person is exceedingly skilful in his profession, but he treats you unjustly, and, therefore, though you often praise him for his extraordinary performances; you cannot bless him, for you have no cause to do so.

I am afraid that there might be such a feeling as that of admiration of God for His great skill, His wonderful power, His extraordinary justness, and yet no warmth of love in the heart towards Him; but in the saints, the praise is sweetened with love and is full of blessing. C. H. S.

Vs. 11. *They shall speak of the glory of Thy kingdom.* No subject is more profitable for humility, obedience, hope, and joy than that of the reigning power of the Lord, our God. C. H. S.

*And talk of Thy power.* Who can calculate the reserve forces of the Infinite? How, then, can His kingdom fail? We hear talk of the five great powers, but what are they to the one great Power? The Lord is "the blessed and only Potentate." C. H. S.

Vs. 13. On the door of the old mosque in Damascus, which was once a Christian church, but for twelve centuries has ranked among the holiest of the Mahomedan sanctuaries, are inscribed these memorable words: "Thy kingdom, O Christ, is an everlasting kingdom, and Thy dominion endureth throughout all generations."

Though the name of Christ has been regularly blasphemed, and the disciples of Christ regularly cursed for twelve hundred years within it, the inscription has, nevertheless, remained unimpaired by time and undisturbed by man. It was unknown during the long reign of Mahomedan intolerance and oppression; but when religious liberty was partially restored, and the missionaries were enabled to establish a Christian church in that city, it was again brought to light, encouraging them in their work of faith and labor of love. JOHN BATE

Vs. 14. *The Lord upholdeth all that fall.* The fallen of our race, especially fallen women, are shunned by us, and it is peculiar tenderness on the Lord's part that such He looks upon, even those who are at once the chief of sinners and the least regarded of mankind. The falling ones among us are too apt to be pushed down by the strong: their timidity and dependence make them the victims of the proud and domineering. To them also the Lord gives His upholding help. The Lord loves to reverse things — He puts down the lofty and lifts up the lowly. C. H. S.

Vs. 15. *The eyes of all wait upon Thee.* Ah! shall the beasts in their own way cry to God, and wilt thou be silent? Hath the Lord elevated thee so far above these inferior creatures and fitted thee for the immediate acts of His worship and for a higher communion with Himself, and wilt thou not serve Him accordingly? Hath He given thee a heart and a spiritual soul as He hath given the brutes a sensitive appetite and natural desires, and shall they cry to God with the one and not thou with the other? ALEXANDER PITCAIRNE

*Eyes . . . wait upon Thee.* Many dumb beggars have been relieved at Christ's gate by making signs. WILLIAM SECKER

In agony, nature is no atheist; the mind which knows not where to fly, flies to God. HANNAH MORE

*Thou givest them their meat in due season.* Mr. Robertson told of a poor child who was accustomed to see unexpected provision for his mother's wants arrive in answer to prayer. The meal barrel in Scotland is everything to a hungry boy: so he said, "Mither, I think God aye hears when we're scraping the bottom o' the barrel." THE CHRISTIAN

Vs. 16. *Thou openest Thine hand.* God openeth His hand and satisfieth all creation, but He must purchase the church with His blood . . . In what a variety of ways are our wants supplied! The earth is fruitful; the air is full of life; the clouds empty themselves upon the earth; the sun pours forth its genial rays; but the operation of all these second causes is only the opening of His hand! Nay, further: look we to instruments as well as means? Parents feed us in our childhood and supply our youthful wants; ways are opened for our future subsistence; connections are formed, which prove sources of comfort; friends are kind in seasons of extremity; supplies are presented from quarters that we never expected. What are all these but the opening of His hand? If His hand were shut, what a world would this be! The heavens brass, the earth iron; famine, pestilence, and death must follow. ANDREW FULLER

Vs. 17. *The Lord is righteous in all His ways.* Nothing is more difficult in the time of trouble, when God has apparently forsaken us, or afflicts us without cause, than to restrain our corrupt feelings from breaking out against His judgments; as we are told of the Emperor Mauricius in a memorable passage of history, that seeing his sons murdered by the wicked and perfidious traitor Phocas, and being about to be carried out himself to death, he cried out "Thou art righteous, O God, and just are Thy judgments." JOHN CALVIN

*Holy in all His works.* God is good, the absolute and perfect; and from good nothing can come but good: and therefore all which God has made is good, as He is; and therefore if anything in the world seems to be bad, one of two things must be true of it: Either it is not bad, though it seems so to us; and God will bring good out of it in His good time, and justify Himself to men, and show us that He is holy in all His works, and righteous in all His ways. Or else, if the thing be really bad, then God did not make it. It must be a disease, a mistake, a failure of man's making or some person's making, but not of God's making. For all that He has made, He sees eternally; and behold, it is very good. CHARLES KINGSLEY

Vs. 18-19. *The Lord is nigh unto all them that call upon Him; He will fulfill their desire, He will hear their cry.* That God Who prepares His people's heart to pray, prepares also His own ear to hear; and He that promiseth to hear before we call, will never deny to hearken when we cry unto Him. As Calvin saith: "Oppressions and afflictions make man cry, and cries and supplications make God hear." F. E.

Vs. 19. *He will fulfill the desire of them that fear Him: He also will hear their cry, and will save them.* One said, "The greatest part of Christianity is to desire to be a Christian." And another said, "The total sum of a man's religion in this life consists in the true desires of saving grace." WILLIAM FENNER

God will not grant us every desire, that is our mercy; for some of them are sinful. David desired to be revenged on Nabal and his innocent family. Jonah desired Nineveh's ruin. What is the main desire of a seaman? That he may arrive at the haven. So saints will be brought to their desired haven. What of a pilgrim? (See Heb. 11:16). So all the desires of a Christian are summed up in this: That he may eternally enjoy God and be like Him. Doubtless there is great mystery in these things. However, I think it is certain that, when God raises a spiritual desire in a person, it is often, though not always, with an intention to bestow the object desired. ANDREW FULLER

God will fulfill the will of those who fear to disobey His will. SIMON DE MUIS

Vs. 21. *And let all flesh bless His holy name forever and ever.* Only holy hearts will praise the holy name or character of the Lord; oh, that all flesh were sanctified, then would the sanctity of God be the delight of all! Our hearts revel in the delight of praising Him. Our mouth, our mind, our lip, our life shall be our Lord's throughout this mortal existence, and when time shall be no more. C. H. S.

# PSALM 146

Division: We are now among the "Hallelujahs." The rest of our journey lies through the Delectable Mountains. All is praise to the close of the book. The key is high-pitched: the music is upon the high-sounding cymbals. Oh, for a heart full of joyful gratitude, that we may run, and leap, and glorify God, even as these Psalms do. C. H. S.

Whole Psalm: This Psalm gives in brief the Gospel of Confidence. It inculcates the elements of faith, hope, and thanksgiving. MARTIN GEIER

Vs. 1. *Praise ye the Lord.* The word here used is "Alleluia," and this is very proper to be constantly used by us who are dependent creatures and under such great obligations to the Father of mercies. We have often heard of prayer doing great wonders; but instances also are not wanting of praise being accompanied with signal events.

The ancient Britons, in the year 420, obtained a victory over the army of the Picts and Saxons, near Mold, in Flintshire. The Britons, unarmed, having Germanicus and Lupus at their head, when the Picts and Saxons came to the attack, the two commanders, Gideon-like, ordered their little army to shout "Alleluia" three times over, at the sound of which the enemy, being suddenly struck with terror, ran way in the greatest confusion and left the Britons masters of the field. A stone monument to perpetuate the remembrance of this "Alleluia victory," I believe, remains to this day, in a field near Mold. CHARLES BUCK

*Praise the Lord, O my soul.* Come, my whole being, my soul, my all, be all on flame with joyful adoration! Up, my brethren! Lift up the song! "Praise ye the Lord." But what am I at? How dare I call upon others and be negligent myself?

If ever man was under bonds to bless the Lord, I am that man; wherefore let me put my soul into the center of the choir and then let my better nature excite my whole manhood to the utmost height of loving praise. "Oh, for a well-tuned harp!" Nay, rather, oh, for a sanctified heart. Then if my voice should be of the poorer sort, and somewhat lacking in melody, yet my soul without my voice shall accomplish my resolve to magnify the Lord. C. H. S.

Vs. 2. *While I live will I praise the Lord.* I shall not live here forever. This mortal life will find a finis in death; but while it lasts, I will laud the Lord, my God. I cannot tell how long or short my life may be, but every hour of it shall be given to the praises of my God. While I live, I'll love; and while I breathe, I'll bless. It is but for a while, and I will not while that time away in idleness but consecrate it to that same service which shall occupy eternity. As our life is the gift of God's mercy, it should be used for His glory. C. H. S.

Mr. John Janeway, on his death-bed, cried out thus, "Come, help me with praises, yet all is too little. Come, help me, all ye mighty and glorious angels, who are so well skilled in the heavenly work of praise! Praise Him, all ye creatures upon earth; let everything that hath being help me to praise God. Hallelujah! Hallelujah! Hallelujah!

"Praise is now my work, and I shall be engaged in this sweet work now and forever. Bring the Bible; turn to David's Psalms, and let us sing a Psalm of praise. Come, let us lift up our voices in the praises of the Most High. I will sing with you as long as my breath doth last, and when I have none, I shall do it better."

George Carpenter, the Bavarian martyr, being desired by some godly brethren, that when he was burning in the fire he would give them some sign of his constancy, answered, "Let this be a sure sign unto you of my faith and perseverance in the truth, that so long as I am able to hold open my mouth, or to whisper, I will never cease to praise God, and to profess His truth"; the which also he did, saith mine author; and so did many other martyrs besides. JOHN TRAPP

*I will sing praises unto my God while I have any being.* I have no being apart from my God; therefore, I will not attempt to enjoy my being otherwise than by singing to His honor. Twice the Psalmist says, "I will"; here first thoughts and second thoughts are alike good. We cannot be too firm in the holy resolve to praise God, for it is the chief end of our living and being that we should glorify God and enjoy Him forever. C. H. S.

Vs. 3. *Put not your trust in princes.* Shakespeare puts this sentiment into Wolsey's mouth:

*O how wretched*
*Is that poor man that hangs on princes' favor!*
*There is, betwixt that smile we would aspire to,*
*That sweet aspect of princes, and their ruin,*
*More pangs and fears than wars and women have:*
*And when he falls, he falls like Lucifer,*
*Never to hope again.*

*Princes.* Earthly princes offer baubles to allure the soul from the pursuit of an eternal prize. Princes themselves have pronounced their principality to be their own greatest peril. Pope Pius V said, "When I was a monk, I had hope of my salvation; when I became Cardinal, I began to fear; when I was made Pope, I all but despaired of eternity." THOMAS LE BLANC

*Nor in the son of man, in whom there is no help.* There is none to be trusted, no, not one. Adam fell; therefore, lean not on his sons. Man is a helpless creature without God; therefore, look not for help in that direction. All men are like the few men who are made into princes — they are more in appearance than in reality, more in promising than in performing: more apt to help themselves than to help others.

How many have turned away heart-sick from men on whom they once relied! Never was this the case with a believer in the Lord. He is a very present help in time of trouble. In man there is no help in times of mental depression, in the day of sore bereavement, in the night of conviction of sin, or in the hour of death. What a horror when most in need of help to read those black words, "No Help!" C. H. S.

Vs. 4. *His breath* [*or spirit*] *goeth forth.* Strive, we must, to cast the world out of us; we may not cast ourselves out of the world. Saint Paul dareth not dissolve himself, though he could wish to be dissolved: God must part that which He joins; God giveth, and God taketh away; and if God say, as He doth to Lazarus, *Exi foras, "Come forth";* with faithful Stephen we must resign our spirit and all into His hands. When God biddeth us yoke, He is the wisest man that yieldeth his neck most willingly. When our great Captain recalls us, we must take the retreat in good part.

But it is heathenish to force out the soul; for when the misdeeming flesh, amidst our disasters, will not listen with patience for God's call, but rather shake off the thought of divine providence quite, then are we ready to curse God and die, and that is probably to leap *e fumo in flammam,* out of the sin of self-murder into hell. No, but God will have our spirits to pass forth upon good terms. *Spiritus* exit — "The spirit goeth forth." THOMAS WILLIAMSON

*In that very day his thoughts perish.* At death a man sees all those thoughts which were not spent upon God to be fruitless. All worldly, vain thoughts, in the day of death perish and come to nothing. What good will the whole globe of the world do at such a time? Those who have reveled out their thoughts in impertinences will but be the more disquieted; it will cut them to the heart to think how they have spun a fool's thread.

A Scythian captain having, for a draught of water, yielded up a city, cried out: "What have I lost? What have I betrayed?" So will it be with that man when he comes to die who hath spent all his meditations upon the world. He will say, "What have I lost? What have I betrayed? I have lost heaven, I have betrayed my soul." Should not the consideration of this fix our minds upon the thoughts of God and glory? All other meditations are fruitless; like a piece of ground which hath much cost laid out upon it, but it yields no crop.
THOMAS WATSON

*His thoughts.* To trust man is to lean not on a pillar but on a little heap of dust. The proudest element in man is his thought. In the thoughts of his heart, he is lifted up if nowhere else; but, behold, even his proudest thoughts, says the Psalmist, will be degraded and perish in that dust to which he will return. Poor, perishing pride! Who should trust it? JOHANNES PAULUS PALANTERIUS

Vs. 7. *Which executeth judgment for the oppressed.* Are we "evil entreated"? Are our rights denied us? Are we slandered? Let this console us, that He Who occupies the throne will not only think upon our case but bestir Himself to execute judgment on our behalf. C. H. S.

*Giveth food to the hungry.* We learn from this that He is not always so indulgent to His own as to load them with abundance but occasionally withdraws His blessing that He may succor them when reduced to hunger. Had the Psalmist said that God fed His people with abundance and pampered them, would not any of those under want or in famine have immediately desponded? The goodness of God is therefore properly extended farther to the feeding of the hungry.
JOHN CALVIN

*The Lord looseth the prisoners.* But then, 'tis further manifest, that those that were under any sore disease or lameness, etc., are said to be "bound by Satan" (Luke 13:16), and be "loosed" by Christ, when they were cured by Him. So saith Christ (verse 12), "Woman, thou are loosed from thine infirmity: and immediately she was made straight." Her being "made straight" was her being loosed out of her restraint, or bonds, or prison.

And in this latitude of the poetic or prophetic expression, the Lord's loosing the prisoners here will comprehend the walking of the lame, the lepers being cleansed, the hearing of the deaf, yea, and the raising up of the dead; for those of all others are fastest bound, and so when they were raised, the style is as proper as to Lazarus in respect of the grave-clothes, "Loose him, and let him go." HENRY HAMMOND

Vss. 7-8. It ought not to pass without remark that the name Jehovah is repeated here five times in five lines to intimate that it is an Almighty power, that of Jehovah, that is engaged and exerted for the relief of the oppressed; and that it is as much to the glory of God to succor them that are in misery as it is to ride on the heavens by His name Jah (Ps. 68:4). MATTHEW HENRY

Vs. 8. *The Lord openeth the eyes of the blind.* Jesus did this very frequently and hereby proved Himself to be Jehovah. He Who made the eye can open it, and when He does so, it is to His glory. How often is the mental eye closed in moral night! And who can remove this dreary effect of the fall but the Almighty God? C. H. S.

*The Blind.* The large number of blind persons to be seen feeling their way along the streets in Cairo and Alexandria has been noticed by Volney. "Walking in the streets of Cairo," he says, "out of a hundred persons whom I met, there were often twenty blind, eighteen one-eyed, and twenty others with eyes red, purulent, or spotted. Almost everyone wears bandages, indicating that they either have or are recovering from ophthalmia."

Ophthalmia is, in fact, one of the scourges of Egypt, as all physicians know. Its prevalence must be attributed in a great degree to the sand which the wind blows into the eyes; but one can understand how in Oriental countries in general the excessive heat of the sun must make blindness much commoner than it is with us.

It is not, therefore, surprising to anyone who knows the East to find the blind so often mentioned in the Gospel history and to meet in Scripture with so many allusions to this infirmity. Of the twelve maledictions of the Levites, there is one against him "who maketh the blind to go out of the way" (Deut. 27:18). "The Spirit of God hath anointed Me," said Jesus, quoting from Isaiah, "to preach the Gospel to the poor, and recovery of sight to the blind" (Luke 4:19). "The Lord," says David, "setteth at liberty them that are bound; the Lord giveth sight to the blind." FELIX BOVET

Vs. 9. *The way of the wicked He turneth upside down.* All the ten clauses preceding lift up the poor saint step by step, higher and higher. At one word suddenly, like Satan falling as lightning from heaven, the wicked are shown dashed down the whole way from the summit of pride to the depths of hell. JOHANNES PAULUS PALANTERIUS

A striking illustration of the folly of counting God out of one's plans for life is given in the course of William M. Tweed, whose death is recently announced. Here was a man who sought wealth and power and who for a time seemed successful in their pursuit.

Apparently he did not propose to obey God or to live for a life to come. What he wanted was worldly prosperity. He thought he had it. He went to Congress. He gathered his millions. He controlled the material interests of the metropolis of his country. He openly defied public sentiment and courts of justice in the prosecution of his plans. He was a brilliant and therefore a dangerous example of successful villainy. But the promise of prosperity for the life which now is, is only to the godly.

As William M. Tweed lay dying in a prison-house in the city he once ruled, his confession of bitter disappointment was, "My life has been a failure in everything. There is nothing I am proud of." If any young man wants to come to an end like this, the way to it is simple and plain. "The great God that formed all things both rewardeth the fool and rewardeth transgressors." "The way of the wicked, He turneth upside down." *American Sunday School Times*

Vs. 10. *Praise ye the Lord.* Again they said, "Hallelujah." Again the sweet perfume arose from the golden vials full of sweet odors. Are we not prepared for an outburst of holy song? Do not we also say, "Hallelujah"? Here endeth this gladsome Psalm. Here endeth not the praise of the Lord, which shall ascend forever and ever. Amen. C. H. S.

# PSALM 147

Subject: This is a specially remarkable song. In it the greatness and the condescending goodness of the Lord are celebrated. The God of Israel is set forth in His peculiarity of glory as caring for the sorrowing, the insignificant, and forgotten. The poet finds a singular joy in extolling One Who is so singularly gracious. It is a Psalm of the city and of the field, of the first and second creations, of the commonwealth and of the church. It is good and pleasant throughout. C. H. S.

Vs. 1. *Praise ye the Lord.* Or, Hallelujah. The flow of the broad river of the Book of Psalms ends in a cataract of praise. The present Psalm begins and ends with "Hallelujah." Jehovah and happy praise should ever be associated in the mind of a believer. Jove was dreaded, but Jehovah is beloved. C. H. S.

*It is good to sing praises unto our God.* The singing of men is in itself good and noble. The same God Who furnished the birds of heaven with the notes wherein they unconsciously praise their Creator gave to man the power to sing. We all know how highly Luther, for example, estimated the gift and the art of song. Let him to whom it is granted rejoice therein; let him who lacks it seek, if possible, to excite it; for it is a good gift of the Creator. RUDOLF STIER

*It is a good and pleasant thing.* There is no heaven, either in this world or the world to come for people who do not praise God. If you do not enter into the spirit and worship of heaven, how should the spirit and joy of heaven enter into you? Selfishness makes long prayers, but love makes short prayers, that it may continue longer in praise. JOHN PULSFORD

*Praise.* There is one other thing which is a serious embarrassment to praising through the song-service of the church, and that is, that we have so few hymns of praise. You will be surprised to hear me say so; but you will be more surprised if you take a real specimen of praising and search for hymns of praise.

You shall find any number of hymns that talk about praise and exhort you to praise. There is no lack of hymns that say that God ought to be praised. But of hymns that praise, and say nothing about it, there are very few indeed. And for what there are, we are almost wholly indebted to the old churches. Most of them came down to us from the Latin and Greek Churches . . . There is no place in human literature where you can find such praise as there is in the Psalms of David. HENRY WARD BEECHER

Vs. 2. *He gathereth together the outcasts of Israel.* Spiritually, we see the hand of God in the edification of the church and in the ingathering of sinners. What are men under conviction of sin but outcasts from God, from holiness, from heaven, and even from hope? Who could gather them from their dispersions and make citizens of them in Christ Jesus save the Lord, our God? This deed of love and power, He is constantly performing. Therefore, let the song begin at Jerusalem, our home, and let every living stone in the spiritual city echo the strain; for it is the Lord Who has brought again His banished ones and builded them together in Zion. C. H. S.

Vs. 3. *He healeth the broken in heart, and bindeth up their wounds.* The kings of the earth think to be great through their loftiness; but Jehovah becomes really so by His condescension. Behold, the Most High has to do with the sick and the sorry, with the wretched and the wounded! He walks the hospitals as the good Physician! His deep sympathy with mourners is a special mark of His goodness. The Lord is always healing and binding: this is no new work to

Him. He has done it of old; and it is not a thing of the past of which He is now weary, for He is still healing and still binding, as the original hath it. Come, broken hearts, come to the Physician Who never fails to heal: uncover your wounds to Him Who so tenderly binds them up! C. H. S.

As a man that hath a barbed arrow shot into his side, and the arrow is plucked out of the flesh, yet the wound is not presently healed; so sin may be plucked out of the heart, but the scar that was made with plucking it out is not yet cured. The wounds that are yet under cure are the plagues and troubles of conscience, the sighs and groans of a hungering soul after grace, the stinging poison that the serpent's fang hath left behind it; these are the wounds.

Now, the heart is broken three ways. First, by the law; as it breaks the heart of a thief to hear the sentence of the law, that he must be hanged for his robbery; so it breaks the heart of the soul, sensibly to understand the sentence of the law, "Thou shalt not sin; if thou do, thou shalt be damned."

If ever the heart come to be sensible of this sentence — "Thou art a damned man" — it is impossible to stand out under it, but it must break. "Is not My Word like a hammer, that breaketh the rock in pieces?" (Jer. 23:29). Can any rock-heart hold out and not be broken with the blows of it? Indeed, thus far a man may be broken, and yet be a reprobate; for they shall all be thus broken in hell, and therefore this breaking is not enough.

Secondly, by the gospel; for if ever the heart come to be sensible of the love of the gospel, it will break all to shatters. "Rend your heart; for the Lord is gracious," etc. (Joel 2:13). When all the shakes of God's mercy come, they all cry "Rend." Indeed, the heart cannot stand out against them, if it once feel them. Beat thy soul upon the gospel: if any way under heaven can break it, this is the way.

Thirdly, the heart is broken by the skill of the minister in the handling of these two, the law and the gospel: God furnisheth him with skill to press the law home and gives him understanding how to put the gospel, and by this means doth God break the heart: for, alas, though the law be never so good a hammer, and although the gospel be never so fit an anvil, yet if the minister lay not the soul upon it the heart will not break: he must fetch a full stroke with the law, and he must set the full power of the gospel at the back of the soul, or else the heart will not break.

Because Christ hath undertaken to do it. When a skillful physician hath undertaken a cure, he will surely do it: indeed, sometimes a good physician may fail, as Trajan's physician did, for he died under his hands; on whose tomb this was written, "Here lies Trajan, the emperor, that may thank his physician that he died." But if Christ undertakes it, thou mayest be sure of it; for He tells thee that art broken in heart that He hath undertaken it; He hath felt thy pulse already. Thou needest not fear, saying, "Will a man cure his enemies? I have been an enemy to God's glory, and will He yet cure me?" Yea, saith Christ, if thou be broken in heart, I will bind thee up. WILLIAM FENNER

To effect the healing of the broken heart, God has, moreover, appointed a Physician, Whose skill is infallible, Whose goodness and care are equal to His skill. That Physician is none other than the Son of God. In that character has He been made known to us. "They that be whole need not a physician, but they that be sick." The Prophet Isaiah introduces His advent in the most sublime language: "He hath sent me to bind up the broken-hearted, to proclaim liberty to the captives, and the opening of the prison to them that are bound." THOMAS BLACKLEY

Vs. 4. *He telleth the number of the stars.* Among the heathen every constellation represented some god. But the Scriptures show Jehovah, not as one of many starry gods, but as the one God of all the stars. He is, too, as He taught

His people by Abraham, the God of a firmament of nobler stars. His people are scattered and trodden as the sands of the seashore. But He turns dust and dirt to stars of glory. He will make of every saint a star, and Heaven is His people's sky, where broken-hearted sufferers of earth are glorified into glittering galaxies. HERMANN VENEMA

*He calleth them all by their names.* While Dr. Herschel was exploring the most crowded part of the milky way, in one quarter of an hour's time no less than 116,000 stars passed through the field of view of his telescope.

It has been computed that nearly one hundred millions of stars might be perceived by our most perfect instruments, if all the regions of the sky were thoroughly explored. But immeasurable regions of space lie beyond the utmost boundaries of human vision, even thus assisted, into which imagination itself can scarcely penetrate, but which are doubtless filled with operations of divine wisdom and divine omnipotence. THOMAS DICK

Vs. 6. *The Lord lifteth up the meek: He casteth the wicked down to the ground.* Proud men are, in their own esteem, high enough already; only those who are low will care to be lifted up, and only such will Jehovah upraise. C. H. S.

Vs. 9. *And to the young ravens which cry.* These wild creatures, which seem to be of no use to man; are they therefore worthless? By no means; they fill their place in the economy of nature. When they are mere fledgelings and can only clamor to the parent birds for food, the Lord does not suffer them to starve but supplies their needs.

Is it not wonderful how such numbers of little birds are fed! A bird in a cage under human care is in more danger of lacking seed and water than any one of the myriads that fly in the open heavens with no owner but their Creator and no provider but the Lord.

Greatness occupied with little things makes up a chief feature of this Psalm. Ought we not all to feel special joy in praising One Who is so specially remarkable for His care of the needy and the forgotten? Ought we not also to trust in the Lord, for He Who feeds the sons of the raven will surely nourish the sons of God! "Hallelujah" to Him Who both feeds the ravens and rules the stars! What a God art Thou, O Jehovah! C. H. S.

Vss. 10 and 11. *The Lord delighteth not in the strength of the horse: He taketh not pleasure in the legs of a man.* No man is favored by God because of his outward favor, because he hath a beautiful face, or strong, clean limbs; yea, not only hath the Lord no pleasure in any man's legs, but not in any man's brains, how reaching soever, nor in any man's wit how quick soever, nor in any man's judgment how deep soever, nor in any man's tongue, how eloquent or well spoken soever; but *The Lord taketh pleasure in them that fear Him, in those that hope in His mercy,* in those that walk humbly with Him, and call upon Him. JOSEPH CARYL

Vs. 11. *The Lord taketh pleasure in them that fear Him, in those that hope in His mercy.* It is a striking thought that God should not only be at peace with some kinds of men, but even find a solace and a joy in their company. Oh, the matchless condescension of the Lord, that His greatness should take pleasure in the insignificant creatures of His hand!

Who are these favored men in whom Jehovah takes pleasure? Some of them are the least in His family, who have never risen beyond hoping and fearing. Others of them are more fully developed, but still they exhibit a blended character composed of fear and hope: they fear God with holy awe and filial reverence, and they also hope for forgiveness and blessedness because of the divine mercy.

As a father takes pleasure in his own children, so doth the Lord solace Himself in His own beloved ones, whose marks of new birth are fear and hope. They fear, for they are sinners; they hope, for God is merciful. They fear Him, for He is great; they hope in Him, for He is good. Their fear sobers their hope; their hope brightens their fear: God takes pleasure in them both in their trembling and in their rejoicing. C. H. S.

Patience and fear are the fences of hope. There is a beautiful relation between hope and fear. The two are linked in this verse. They are like the cork in a fisherman's net, which keeps it from sinking, and the lead, which prevents it from floating. Hope without fear is in danger of being too sanguine; fear without hope would soon become desponding. GEORGE SEATON BOWES

Vs. 17. *He casteth forth His ice like morsels.* Or, shivers of bread. It is a worthy saying of one from this text — The ice is bread; the rain is drink; the snow is wool; the frost a fire to the earth, causing it inwardly to glow with heat, teaching us what to do for God's poor. JOHN TRAPP

"It is extremely severe," said his sister to Archbishop Leighton one day, speaking of the season. The good man only said in reply, "But Thou, O God, hast made summer and winter." J. N. PEARSON

Vs. 18. *He sendeth out His Word, and melteth them.* Israel, in the captivity, has been ice-bound, like ships of Arctic voyagers in the Polar Sea; but God sent forth the vernal breeze of His love, and the water flowed, the ice melted, and they were released. God turned their captivity, and, their icy chains being melted by the solar beams of God's mercy, they flowed in fresh and bouyant streams, like "rivers of the south," shining in the sun (see Ps. 126:4).

So it was on the Day of Pentecost. The winter of spiritual captivity was thawed and dissolved by the soft breath of the Holy Ghost, and the earth laughed and bloomed with spring-tide flowers of faith, love, and joy. CHRISTOPHER WORDSWORTH

Vss. 19 and 20. *He hath shewed His statutes unto Israel; He hath not dealt so with any nation.* What is the revelation of the gospel by the Son of God Himself? For although the law is obscured and defaced since the fall, yet there are some ingrafted notions of it in human nature; but there is not the least suspicion of the gospel.

The law discovers our misery, but the gospel alone shows the way to be delivered from it. If an advantage so great and so precious doth not touch our hearts; and, in possessing it with joy, if we are not sensible of the engagements the Father of mercies hath laid upon us; we shall be the ungratefulest wretches in the world. WILLIAM BATES

# PSALM 148

The song is one and indivisible. It seems almost impossible to expound it in detail, for a living poem is not to be dissected verse by verse. It is a song of nature and of grace. As a flash of lightning flames through space and enwraps both heaven and earth in one vestment of glory, so doth the adoration of the Lord in this Psalm light up all the universe and cause it to glow with a radiance of praise. The song begins in the heavens, sweeps downward to dragons and all deeps, and then ascends again, till the people near unto Jehovah take up the strain. For its exposition, the chief requisite is a heart on fire with reverent love to the Lord over all, Who is to be blessed forever. C. H. S.

Psalms 148-150. The last three Psalms are a triad of wondrous praise, ascending from praise to higher praise, until it becomes "joy unspeakable and full of glory" — exultation which knows no bounds. The joy overflows the soul and spreads throughout the universe; every creature is magnetized by it and drawn into the chorus. Heaven is full of praise, the earth is full of praise, praises rise from under the earth—"everything that hath breath" joins in the rapture. God is encompassed by a loving, praising creation.

Man, the last in creation, but the first in song, knows not how to contain himself. He dances; he sings; he commands all the heavens, with all their angels, to help him; "beasts and all cattle, creeping things and flying fowl" must do likewise; even "dragons" must not be silent; and "all deeps" must yield contributions. He presses even dead things into his service — timbrels, trumpets, harps, organs, cymbals, high-sounding cymbals, if by any means, and by all means, he may give utterance to his love and joy. JOHN PULSFORD

Whole Psalm. Milton, in his *Paradise Lost* (Book V., line 153, etc.), has elegantly imitated this Psalm and put it into the mouth of Adam and Eve as their morning hymn in a state of innocency. JAMES ANDERSON

Whole Psalm. This Psalm is neither more nor less than a glorious prophecy of that coming day when not only shall the knowledge of the Lord be spread over the whole earth as the waters cover the sea, but from every created object in heaven and in earth, animate and inanimate, from the highest archangel through every grade and phase of being, down to the tiniest atom — young men and maidens, old men and children, and all kings and princes, and judges of the earth shall unite in this millennial anthem to the Redeemer's praise. BARTON BOUCHIER

Vs. 1. *Praise ye the Lord from the heavens: praise Him in the heights.* Bernard, in his sermon on the death of his brother Gerard, relates that in the middle of his last night on earth, his brother, to the astonishment of all present, with a voice and countenance of exultation, broke forth in the words of the Psalmist. "Praise the Lord of heaven, praise Him in the heights!"

Vs. 3. *Praise ye Him, sun and moon: praise Him, all ye stars of light.* There is a perpetual adoration of the Lord in the skies: it varies with night and day, but it ever continues while sun and moon endure. There is ever a lamp burning before the high altar of the Lord. Light is song glittering before the eye instead of resounding in the ear. Stars without light would render no praise, and Christians without light rob the Lord of His glory. However small our beam, we must not hide it: if we cannot be sun or moon, we must aim to be one of the "stars of light," and our every twinkling must be to the honor of our Lord. C. H. S.

How does the sun specially praise Jehovah? 1. By its beauty. Jesus, son of Sirach, calls it the "globe of beauty." 2. By its fullness. Dion calls it "the image of the divine capacity." 3. By its exaltation. Pliny calls it *caeli rector,* "the ruler of heaven." 4. By its perfect brightness. Pliny adds that it is "the mind and soul of the whole universe." 5. By its velocity and constancy of motion. Martian calls it "the Guide of Nature." THOMAS LEBLANC

Vs. 4. *Praise Him, ye heavens of heavens, and ye waters that be above the heavens.* If we could climb as much above the heavens as the heavens are above the earth, we could still cry out to all around us, "Praise ye the Lord." There can be none so great and high as to be above praising Jehovah.

Let the clouds roll up volumes of adoration. Let the sea above roar, and the fullness thereof, at the presence of Jehovah, the God of Israel. There is something of mystery about these supposed reservoirs of water; but let them be what they may, and as they may, they shall give glory to the Lord, our God. Let the most unknown and perplexing phenomena take up their parts in the universal praise. C. H. S.

Vs. 5. *Let them praise the Name of the Lord: for He commandeth, and they were created.* The highest praise of God is to declare what He is. We can invent nothing which would magnify the Lord: we can never extol Him better than by repeating His name or describing His character. The Lord is to be extolled as creating all things that exist and as doing so by the simple agency of His Word. He created by a command; what a power is this!

Well may He expect those to praise Him who owe their being to Him. Evolution may be atheistic; but the doctrine of creation logically demands worship; and hence, as the tree is known by its fruit, it proves itself to be true. Those who were created by command are under command to adore their Creator. The voice which said, "Let them be," now saith, "Let them praise." C. H. S.

Vss. 5 and 6. This is the account of creation in a word—He spake; it was done. When Jesus came, He went everywhere showing His divinity by this evidence, that His word was omnipotent. These verses declare two miracles of God's Will and Word, viz., the creation and consolidation of the earth. Jehovah first produced matter, then He ordered and established it. JOHN LORINUS

Vss. 7 and 8. He calls to the deeps, fire, hail, snow, mountains and hills, to bear a part in this work of praise. Not that they are able to do it actively, but to show that man is to call in the whole creation to assist him passively and should have so much charity to all creatures as to receive what they offer and so much affection to God as to present to Him what he receives from Him.

Snow and hail cannot bless and praise God, but man ought to bless God for those things, wherein there is a mixture of trouble and inconvenience, something to molest our sense, as well as something that improves the earth for fruit. STEPHEN CHARNOCK

Vs. 8. *Snow.* As sure as every falling flake of winter's snow has a part in the great economy of nature, so surely has every Word of God which falls within the sanctuary its end to accomplish in the moral sphere. I have stood on a winter day and seen the tiny flakes in little clouds lose themselves one by one in the rushing river. They seemed to die to no purpose—to be swallowed up by an enemy which ignored both their power and their existence.

And so have I seen the Word of God fall upon human hearts. Sent of God from day to day and from year to year, I have seen it dropping apparently all resultless into the fierce current of unbelief — into the fiercer gulf-stream of worldliness which was sweeping through the minds and the lives of the hearers.

But as I stood upon the river's bank and looked upon what seemed to be the death of the little fluttering crystal, a second thought assured me that it was but death into life, and that every tiny flake which wept its life away in the rushing waters, became incorporate with the river's being.

So when I have seen the Word of God fall apparently fruitless upon the restless, seething, rushing current of human life, a recovered faith in the immutable declaration of God has assured me that what I looked upon was not a chance or idle death, but rather the falling of the soldier, after that he had wrought his life-force into the destiny of a nation and into the history of a world. And so it must ever be. The Word of God ever reaches unto its end. S. S. MITCHELL

Vs. 10. *Creeping things.* In public worship, all should join. The little strings go to make up a concert, as well as the great. THOMAS GOODWIN

Vs. 11. *Kings of the earth, and all people; princes.* The more intolerable is the wickedness of kings and princes who claim exemption from the common rule, when they ought rather to inculcate it upon others, and lead the way. He could have addressed his exhortation at once summarily to all men, as indeed he mentions people in general terms; but by thrice specifying princes, he suggests that they are slow to discharge the duty, and need to be urged to it. JOHN CALVIN

Vs. 12. *Old Men.* Your tongues are indeed inexcusable if they are silent in the praises of Him Whose glory is proclaimed by every object above or around them, and even by every member of their own bodies, and every faculty of their souls. But old men are doubly inexcusable if they are inattentive to those precious instructions which are given them by all the works of God which they had seen, or of which they have been informed, every day since the powers of their rational natures began to operate.

Consider how long you have lived. Is not every day of life, and even every hour, and every moment, an undeserved mercy? You might have been cut off from the breast and the womb, for you were conceived in iniquity and born in sin. How many of your race have been cut off before they could distinguish between their right hand and their left, before they could do good or evil.

Since you were moral agents, not a day has passed in which you were not chargeable with many sins. What riches of long-suffering is manifested in a life of sixty or seventy years! If you have lived in a state of sin all that time, have you not reason to be astonished that you are not already in a condition which would forever render it impossible for you to utter the voice of praise? Give glory, therefore, to that God Who has still preserved you alive. GEORGE LAWSON

Vs. 13. *The name of Jehovah.* Jehovah is a name of great power and efficacy, a name that hath in it five vowels, without which no language can be expressed; a name that hath in it also three syllables, to signify the Trinity of Persons, the eternity of God, One in Three, and Three in One; a name of such dread and reverence amongst the Jews that they tremble to name it, and therefore they use the name Adonai (Lord) in all their devotions.

And thus ought everyone to stand in awe and sin not by taking the name of God in vain; but to sing praises, to honor, to remember, to declare, to exalt, and bless it; for holy and reverend, only worthy and excellent, is His name. RAYMENT

Vs. 14. *Praise ye the Lord,* or, "Hallelujah." This should be the Alpha and Omega of a good man's life. Let us praise God to the end, world without end. The field of praise which lies before us in this Psalm is bounded at beginning and end by landmarks in the form of "Hallelujah's," and all that lieth between them is every word of it to the Lord's honor. Amen. C. H. S.

*A people near unto Him.* Jesus took our nature and became one with us; thus He is "near" unto us; He gives us His Holy Spirit, brings us into union with Himself, and thus we are near to Him. This is our highest honor, an unfailing source of happiness and peace.

We are near to Him when poor and when deeply tried; and if ever nearer at one time than another, we shall be nearest to Him in death. If we are near unto Him, He will sympathize with us in all our sorrows, assist us in all our trials, protect us in all our dangers, hold intercourse with us in all our lonely hours, provide for us in all seasons of necessity, and honorably introduce us to glory. Let us realize this fact daily — we are near and dear to our God. JAMES SMITH

# PSALM 149

We are almost at the last Psalm and still among the "Hallelujahs." This is "a new song," evidently intended for the new creation, and the men who are of new heart. It is such a song as may be sung at the coming of the Lord, when the new dispensation shall bring overthrow to the wicked and honor to all the saints. The tone is exceedingly jubilant and exultant. All through, one hears the beat of the feet of dancing maidens keeping time to the timbrel and harp. C. H. S.

Vs. 1. *Sing unto the Lord a new song.* Among our novelties there should be new songs: alas! men are fonder of making new complaints than new Psalms. Our new songs should be devised in Jehovah's honor; indeed, all our newest thoughts should run towards Him. C. H. S.

*A new song.* The old man hath an old song; the new man a new song. The Old Testament is an old song; the New Testament is a new song . . . Whoso loveth earthly things singeth an old song: let him that desireth to sing a new song love the things of eternity. Love itself is new and eternal; therefore, is it ever new, because it never groweth old. AUGUSTINE

Vs. 4. *For the Lord taketh pleasure in His people.* But why does the Lord "take pleasure" in them? Is there anything in them of their own which He can regard with complacency and delight? No: they know and feel that they have no pretensions of this kind. It is not for their sake, but for His own sake; for His name's, His truth's, and His mercy's sake, that He has now a favor unto them. The Lord "taketh pleasure in His people." because they are His people; those whom He has purchased by His Blood, renewed by His Spirit, and redeemed by His power. EDWARD COOPER

*He will beautify the meek with salvation.* They are humble, and feel their need of salvation; He is gracious, and bestows it upon them. They lament their deformity, and He puts a beauty upon them of the choicest sort. He saves them by sanctifying them, and thus they wear the beauty of holiness, and the beauty of a joy which springs out of full salvation. He makes His people meek and then makes the meek beautiful. Herein is grand argument for worshipping the Lord with the utmost exultation: He Who takes such a pleasure in us must be approached with every token of exceeding joy.

God taketh pleasure in all His children, as Jacob loved all his sons; but the meek are His Josephs, and upon these he puts the coat of many colors, beautifying them with peace, content, joy, holiness, and influence. A meek and quiet spirit is called "an ornament," and certainly it is "the beauty of holiness." When God Himself beautifies a man, he becomes beautiful indeed and beautiful forever. C. H. S.

Carry forward your thoughts to the morning of the resurrection, when this corruption shall have put on incorruption, this mortal immortality; when the body, raised in honor and glory, shall be clothed in its beauteous apparel and, being made like unto Christ's glorious body, shall shine as the sun in the firmament; when now, once more united to its kindred and sanctified spirit, it shall no longer be a weight, and a clog, and a hindrance, but become a furtherer of its joy, and a sharer and a helper in its spiritual happiness.

This is the meaning of the text; this is the beauty which He has designed for His people, and for which He is now preparing them. In the contemplation of these, with reason may it be said to them, "Praise ye the Lord." EDWARD COOPER

Vs. 5. Let the saints be joyful in glory: let them sing aloud upon their beds. When our bones are vexed, and our sleep departeth from us, we pray unto God to deal mercifully with us; but when our diseases are healed, we do not return to give thanks, being soon overtaken with heaviness and security. WILLIAM BLOYS

Vs. 5. *The saints in glory* shall rest from their labors, but not from their praises. ROBERT BELLARMINE

This verse has been fulfilled in solemn crises of saintly life. On beds of death, and at the scaffold and the stake, joy and glory have been kindled in the hearts of Christ's faithful witnesses. THOMAS LE BLANC

Vs. 6. *Let the high praises of God be in their mouth, and a two-edged sword in their hand.* The Word of God is all edge; whichever way we turn it, it strikes deadly blows at falsehood and wickness. If we do not praise, we shall grow sad in our confiict; and if we do not fight, we shall become presumptuous in our song. The verse indicates a happy blending of the chorister and the crusader.

Note how each thing in the believer is emphatic: if he sings, it is high praises, and praises deep down in his throat, as the original hath it; and if he fights, it is with the sword, and the sword is two-edged.

The living God imparts vigorous life to those who trust Him. They are not of a neutral tint: men both hear them and feel them. Quiet is their spirit, but in that very quietude abides the thunder of an irresistible force. When godly men give battle to the powers of evil, each conflict is high praise unto the God of goodness. Even the tumult of our holy war is a part of the music of our lives. C. H. S.

Cromwell's Ironsides were sneeringly called Psalmsingers; but God's Psalmsingers are always Ironsides. He who has a "new song in his mouth" is ever stronger, both to suffer and to labor than the man who has a dumb spirit and a hymnless heart. When he sings at his work, he will both do more and do it better than he would without his song. Hence, we need not be surprised that all through its history the church of God has traveled "along the line of music." WILLIAM TAYLOR

*The high praises of God.* I confess, consider men's highest praises of God, as they are man's performance, they are poor and inconsiderable things; but consider them as they are the testimonies and expressions of a believing heart, declaring and making known the unspeakable wisdom, faithfulness, bounty, and excellencies of God, exercised in His works; in this notion the Scripture declares the heart of God to be so taken with the desire of them that He is willing to give heaven, earth, Himself, and Son to poor men for the praises of their hearts, hands, and tongues; and accounts Himself abundantly satisfied. Therefore, when His people will speak good of His name, they speak of Him in the dialect of angels' notes, *the high praises of God.*

Vs. 8. *To bind their kings with chains.* Agrippa was captive to Paul. The Word had him in bands like a prisoner and made him confess against himself before Festus that he was "almost persuaded to be a Christian." Then it was verified which before was prophesied, "They shall bind kings in chains, and nobles in fetters of iron." Oh, the majesty and force of the Word! HENRY SMITH

It was once the saying of Pompey that with one stamp of his foot he could raise all Italy up in arms; and the mighty men of the world may have nations, kingdoms, and commonwealths at their command, but yet God is more powerful than they all. If He do but arise, they shall all of them fly before Him. If He once fall to fettering of princes, it shall be done so sure that no flesh shall be able to knock off their bolts again. STEPHEN GOSSON

Vs. 9. *To execute upon them the judgment written.* Israel as a nation had this to do, and did it, and then they rejoiced in the God Who gave success to their arms. We praise our God after another fashion; we are not executioners of justice but heralds of mercy. It would be a sad thing for anyone to misuse this text: lest any warlike believer should be led to do so, we would remind him that the execution must not go beyond the sentence and warrant; and we have received no warrant of execution against our fellowmen. C. H. S.

*This honor have all His saints.* Many are made converts by the godly ends of good men; as the centurion himself, who attended and ordered the crucifying of Christ, after His expiring, broke forth into that testimony of Him, "Verily, this was the Son of God." So, such as rail at, revile, curse, condemn, persecute, execute pious people, speak other language of them when such men have passed the purgation of death, and confess them faithful and sincere servants of God. **THOMAS FULLER**

# PSALM 150

We have now reached the last summit of the mountain chain of Psalms. It rises high into the clear azure, and its brow is bathed in the sunlight of the eternal world of worship. It is a rapture. The poet-prophet is full of inspiration and enthusiasm. He stays not to argue, to teach, to explain, but cries with burning words, "Praise Him, Praise Him, Praise ye the Lord." C. H. S.

Whole Psalm: The last Psalm ends with a chorus to the praise of God, in which the poet calls on all people, all instruments of sacred music, all the elements and all the stars to join. Sublime finale of that opera of sixty years sung by the shepherd, the hero, the king, and the old man!

In this closing Psalm we see the almost inarticulate enthusiasm of the lyric poet; so rapidly do the words press to his lips, floating upwards towards God, their source, like the smoke of a great fire of the soul waited by the tempest! Here we see David, or rather the human heart itself with all its God-given notes of grief, joy, tears, and adoration — poetry sanctified to its highest expression; a vase of perfume broken on the step of the Temple and shedding abroad its odors from the heart of David to the heart of all humanity! WILLIAM PLUMER

Whole Psalm: The first and last of the Psalms have both the same number of verses, are both short and very memorable; but the scope of them is very different; the first Psalm is an elaborate instruction in our duty, to prepare us for the comforts of our devotion; this is all rapture and transport, and perhaps was penned on purpose to be the conclusion of those sacred songs, to show what is the design of them all, and that is, to assist us in praising God. MATTHEW HENRY

Vs. 1. *Praise God in His sanctuary.* In this church below and in His courts above, Hallelujahs should be continually presented. In the person of Jesus, God finds a holy dwelling or sanctuary, and there He is greatly to be praised. C. H. S.

Vs. 2. *Praise Him according to His excellent greatness.* There is nothing little about God and there is nothing great apart from Him. If we were always careful to make our worship fit and appropriate for our great Lord, how much better should we sing! How much more reverently should we adore! Such excellent deeds should have excellent praise. C. H. S.

Vs. 4. *Praise Him with stringed instruments and organs.* Many men, many minds, and these as different as strings and pipes; but there is only one God, and that one God all should worship. The word translated "organs" signifies pipe — a simpler form of wind instrument than the more modern and more elaborate organ. Doubtless many a pious shepherd has poured out gracious pastorals from a reed or oaten pipe, and so has magnified his God. C. H. S.

Vss. 3, 4, 5. As St. Augustine says here, "No kind of faculty is here omitted. All are enlisted in praising God." The breath is employed in blowing the trumpet; the fingers are used in striking the strings of the psaltery and the harp; the whole hand is exerted in beating the timbrel; the feet move in the dance; there are stringed instruments (literally strings); there is the organ (the *ugab, syrinx*) composed of many pipes, implying combination, and the cymbals clang upon one another. C. WORDSWORTH

The plurality and variety (I say) of these instruments were fit to represent divers conditions of the spiritual man, and of the greatness of his joy to be found in God, and to teach what stirring up should be of the affections and powers of our soul, and of one another, unto God's worship; what harmony should be among the worshippers of God, what melody each should make in himself, singing to God with grace in his heart, and to show the excellency of God's praise, which no means nor instrument, nor any expression of the body joined thereunto, could sufficiently set forth in these exhortations to praise God with trumpet, psaltery, etc. DAVID DICKSON

Patrick has an interesting note on the many instruments of music in Psalm One Hundred Forty-nine, which we quote here: "The ancient inhabitants of Etruria used the trumpet; the Arcadians, the whistle; the Sicilians, the pectid; the Cretians, the harp; the Tracians, the cornet; the Lacedemonians, the pipe; the Egyptians, the drum; the Arabians, the cymbal (Clem. *Paedag.*, ii:4). May we not say that in this Psalm's enumeration of musical instruments, there is a reference to the variety which exists among men in the mode of expressing joy and exciting to feeling? ANDREW A. BONAR

Vs. 6. *Let everything that hath breath praise the Lord.* "Let all breath praise Him": that is to say, all living beings. He gave them breath; let them breathe His praise. His name is in the Hebrew composed rather of breathings than of letters, to show that all breath comes from Him: therefore, let it be used for Him. Join, all ye living things, in the eternal song. Be ye least or greatest, withhold not your praises. What a day will it when all things in all places unite to glorify the one only living and true God! This will be the final triumph of the church of God. C. H. S.

There is nothing in the Psalter more majestic or more beautiful than this brief but most significant finale, in which solemnity of tone predominates, without, however, in the least disturbing the exhilaration which the close of the Psalter seems intended to produce, as if in emblematical allusion to the triumph which awaits the church and all its members when, through much tribulation, they shall enter into rest. JOSEPH ADDISON ALEXANDER

*Praise ye the Lord.* Once more, "Hallelujah!" Thus is the Psalm rounded with the note of praise; and thus is the Book of Psalms ended by a glowing word of adoration. Reader, wilt not thou at this moment pause a while and worship the Lord, thy God? *HALLELUJAH!* C. H. S.

HALLELUJAH!

# INDEX

## OF AUTHORS QUOTED OR TO WHOM REFERENCE IS MADE

### A.



### B.

## C.

D.

G.

# INDEX

## H.

# INDEX

## I.



## J.



## K.



## L.

## M.

N.



O.



P.

## S.

## T.

## Y.